■ THE RESOURCE FOR THE INDEPENDENT TRAVELER

"The guides are aimed not only at young budget travelers but at the indepedent traveler; a sort of streetwise cookbook for traveling alone."

—The New York Times

"Unbeatable; good sight-seeing advice; up-to-date info on restaurants, hotels, and inns; a commitment to money-saving travel; and a wry style that brightens nearly every page."

—The Washington Post

"Lighthearted and sophisticated, informative and fun to read. [Let's Go] helps the novice traveler navigate like a knowledgeable old hand."

—Atlanta Journal-Constitution

"A world-wise traveling companion—always ready with friendly advice and helpful hints, all sprinkled with a bit of wit."

—The Philadelphia Inquirer

■ THE BEST TRAVEL BARGAINS IN YOUR PRICE RANGE

"All the dirt, dirt cheap."

—People

"Anything you need to know about budget traveling is detailed in this book."

—The Chicago Sun-Times

"Let's Go follows the creed that you don't have to toss your life's savings to the wind to travel—unless you want to."

—The Salt Lake Tribune

■ REAL ADVICE FOR REAL EXPERIENCES

"The writers seem to have experienced every rooster-packed bus and lunar-surfaced mattress about which they write."

—The New York Times

"Value-packed, unbeatable, accurate, and comprehensive."

—The Los Angeles Times

"[Let's Go's] devoted updaters really walk the walk (and thumb the ride, and trek the trail). Learn how to fish, haggle, find work—anywhere."

—Food & Wine

LET'S GO PUBLICATIONS

TRAVEL GUIDES

Australia 8th Edition
Austria & Switzerland 12th edition
Brazil 1st edition
Britain & Ireland 2005
California 10th edition
Central America 9th edition
Chile 2nd edition
China 5th edition
Costa Rica 2nd edition
Eastern Europe 2005
Ecuador 1st edition **NEW TITLE**
Egypt 2nd edition
Europe 2005
France 2005
Germany 12th Edition
Greece 2005
Hawaii 3rd edition
India & Nepal 8th edition
Ireland 2005
Israel 4th edition
Italy 2005
Japan 1st edition
Mexico 20th edition
Middle East 4th edition
Peru 1st edition **NEW TITLE**
Puerto Rico 1st edition
South Africa 5th edition
Southeast Asia 9th edition
Spain & Portugal 2005
Thailand 2nd edition
Turkey 5th edition
USA 2005
Vietnam 1st edition **NEW TITLE**
Western Europe 2005

ROADTRIP GUIDE

Roadtripping USA **NEW TITLE**

ADVENTURE GUIDES

Alaska 1st edition
New Zealand **NEW TITLE**
Pacific Northwest **NEW TITLE**
Southwest USA 3rd edition

CITY GUIDES

Amsterdam 3rd edition
Barcelona 3rd edition
Boston 4th edition
London 2005
New York City 15th Edition
Paris 13th Edition
Rome 12th edition
San Francisco 4th edition
Washington, D.C. 13th edition

POCKET CITY GUIDES

Amsterdam
Berlin
Boston
Chicago
London
New York City
Paris
San Francisco
Venice
Washington, D.C.

CENTRAL AMERICA

MANUELA S. ZONINSEIN EDITOR
JONATHAN BARDIN ASSOCIATE EDITOR
ANDREW CRESPO ASSOCIATE EDITOR

RESEARCHER-WRITERS
IAN CAMPBELL
LIZA COVINGTON
EDOARDO GALLO
EMILY MATCHAR
COREY RENNELL
MARIA LUISA ROMERO

STEF LEVNER MANAGING EDITOR
TALI MAZOR MAP EDITOR

ST. MARTIN'S PRESS ✠ NEW YORK

HELPING LET'S GO. If you want to share your discoveries, suggestions, or corrections, please drop us a line. We read every piece of correspondence, whether a postcard, a 10-page email, or a coconut. **Address mail to:**

> Let's Go: Central America
> 67 Mount Auburn Street
> Cambridge, MA 02138
> USA

Visit Let's Go at **http://www.letsgo.com,** or send email to:

> feedback@letsgo.com
> Subject: "Let's Go: Central America"

In addition to the invaluable travel advice our readers share with us, many are kind enough to offer their services as researchers or editors. Unfortunately, our charter enables us to employ only currently enrolled Harvard students.

Maps by David Lindroth copyright © 2005 by St. Martin's Press.

CONTENTS

HOW TO USE THIS BOOK

Central America continues to be both the backpacker's ultimate dream and challenge. Independence and motivatation will help, as the nascent infrastructure leaves the road wide open to interpretation. We encourage cross-country travel in order to explore both the eccentricities and universalities of the region.

COVERAGE LAYOUT. *Let's Go: Central America* was created to make the reliable information that you need easy to find. The region-wide introductory section includes the **Discover** chapter, which offers regional highlights, tips on when to travel, and itineraries (check out the new festivals guide). **History** glances at the past of this collection of countries. The **Essentials** chapter details the nitty-gritty of passports, transportation, money, communications, and more—everything you'll need to start your trip and stay safe on the road. **Alternatives to Tourism** advises on long-term stays: study abroad, volunteering, and work opportunities are just the beginning. Next come the seven individual **country chapters,** arranged alphabetically. Each begins with **Life and Times,** detailing history and culture, followed by Essentials, including important travel info specific to the country. Country-specific Alternatives to Tourism sections list organizations to start your alternative travel adventure. At the back of the book you'll find an expanded **Appendix** and **Glossary**— a crash course on sayings and popular words to get you through both the airports and the bars. Finally, our thoroughly updated **index** will make quick-reference a breeze. Check out the map index at the back, accompanied by a key. The black tabs on the side of each page separate chapters and help you navigate the book.

TRANSPORTATION. Both arrival and departure cities list information on transportation connections. Parentheticals usually provide the trip duration, followed by the frequency, then the price; unless otherwise noted, the price is for a one-way trip. Orientation sections in each country chapter describe how towns are organized, and how *Let's Go* lists directions and addresses. In general, 12/14 Av. Nte., 3/5 C. Pte. means the establishment is between *Avenidas* 12 and 14, and *Calles* 3 and 5 *Poniente.*

SCHOLARLY ARTICLES. Two experts tackle the issue for which Central America is most notorious—regional and domestic conflicts. Sarah Dix, Ph.D. takes on domestic peacekeeping initiatives (p. 52), while Richard Millett, Ph.D. considers regional relations from a military perspective (p. 310).

PRICE DIVERSITY. We list establishments in order of value, and our absolute favorites are denoted by the *Let's Go* thumbs-up (🔲). Since the best value does not always mean the cheapest price, we have incorporated a system of **price ranges** (❶❷❸❹❺) into our coverage of accommodations and restaurants (see p. xiv) for our **Price Diversity table**). At a glance, you can compare the cost of a night's stay in towns a mile apart or half-way across the region. The price ranges for each country can be found in the introductory section of the country chapters.

A NOTE TO OUR READERS. The information for this book was gathered by *Let's Go* researchers from May through August of 2004. Each listing is based on one researcher's opinion, formed during his or her visit at a particular time. Those traveling at other times may have different experiences since prices, dates, hours, and conditions are always subject to change. You are urged to check the facts presented in this book beforehand to avoid inconvenience and surprises.

RESEARCHER-WRITERS

Ian Campbell   *Belize and Northern Guatemala*

If ever there was a man destined to cover the beaches and islands of Belize with all the relaxed gusto of a manatee, it was Ian. While his brief foray into Guatemala gave him a new respect for the United States Postal Service, he kept his cool, returning impressive copy and insightful features. When not in Central America, Ian can be found wandering art galleries in France or guiding whitewater trips in his native Tennessee.

Liza Covington   *Guatemala*

Trekking through the ruralest of rural Guatemala, Liza sent back articulate prose full of cultural sensitivity and details on the nation's cheapest beers. She came to us prepared for anything, with the problem-solving skills of a seasoned bike mechanic. She dealt with multi-day strikes, sketchy rodeos, and the best (8000) corn tortillas Guatemala had to offer, returning to us content, with yet another destination on her list of conquered territories.

Edoardo Gallo   *El Salvador, Southern Honduras, Northern Nicaragua*

Born in Cuneo, Edo Gallo conducted his research "the Italian way." With "a wink and a smile," Edo charmed his way into the hearts of the Salvadoran people. With an eye for beauty and warm natives to guide him, Edo discovered all of El Salvador's natural and cultural splendors. That isn't to say that he didn't have to rough it—in fact, Edo was so accustomed to spartan accommodations that he spent his first night back home snuggled on the floor of a 24hr. ATM.

Emily Matchar   *Nicaragua*

When not writing fiction, preparing for med school, or costume designing, Miss Matchar likes to spar with fate. After enduring heat-waves and computer robbery while researching *Let's Go: Mexico 2004*, Emily thought Nicaragua would be smooth sailing. Averting disaster during nation wide political protests, shaking off poten-tially fatal mosquitoes, and surviving far-from-home sickness, Emily's fly-by energy and dry wit brought *Nica* daily *típica* to life.

Corey Rennell   *Honduras*

They haven't invented terrain rugged enough to stop Corey Rennell. Researcher *par excellence*, Corey's hard work transformed *Let's Go: Central America* into the best Honduras coverage on the mar-ket. Armed with years of travel experience and his trusty machete, this native Alaskan traversed wild jungles and even wilder cities. After a long summer on a strict rice-and-beans diet, a degree in eco-logical studies should be a piece of cake for our voracious vegan.

Maria Luisa Romero   *Panama*

World-traveler extraordinaire, Maria Luisa's return to native Pan-ama for *Let's Go* may have been her hardest tour yet. Rather than rely on her laurels, this Latin America specialist proved her dedica-tion to both the coverage and her *tierra* by tirelessly searching for the best deals, the newest trend, and the most beautiful island (we pity her). Braving endless cat calls, she returned copy bursting at the seams with detail and insider knowledge—enjoy.

CONTRIBUTING WRITERS

Rachel Nolan   *Southern Costa Rica, Osa Peninsula, Central Pacific*

Costa Rican ziplines and kayaks proved to be a cinch in comparison to resisting the advances of frat boys and hippies alike. She certainly won *our* hearts with crisp writing that betrayed her thorough research and sharp eye for detail.

Anna Pasternak   *Northwestern Costa Rica, Nicoya Peninsula*

Never one to define adventure in narrow terms, Anna braved the Costa Rican elements with grit and verve, coolly befriending entomologists, surfers, and mango vendors along the way. Her vibrant copy is infused with the same energy she devotes to daily life.

Stephen Zoegall   *Caribbean Lowlands, Northern Lowlands*

Also known as Esteban: RW on wheels, Steve always made sure he was traveling the country in style. Whether cruising on a scooter or barreling along in a bling-bling 4WD, Steve's flawless copy and laugh-out-loud marginalia was certainly consistent.

Sarah Thomas   *San José, Central Valley, Nicoya Peninsula*

A caffeine afficionado, Sarah was the perfect one to research Central Valley coffee plantations; as a self-proclaimed city girl, Sarah thrived in San José. She used her veteran skills to track down hidden deals and local lore, polishing her copy with unflagging wit.

Leslie Jamison   *Editor, Let's Go: Costa Rica*

Laura Martin   *Associate Editor, Let's Go: Costa Rica*

Sarah Dix is currently a lecturer in the Social Studies Department at Harvard University, and is involved in the instruction of courses on Latin America as well as Art and Society. She is researching judicial politics in Argentina.

Richard L. Millett is Professor Emeritus of History at Southern Illinois University at Edwardsville. After graduating with Honors from Harvard University, he went on to receive an MA and Ph.D. from the University of New Mexico. He has published widely on Latin America, in particular regarding international relations and the military's role.

ABOUT LET'S GO

GUIDES FOR THE INDEPENDENT TRAVELER

We believe that travel opens an immense world of opportunities—opportunities to learn from and be enriched by the places you visit, to grow and be challenged by ideas and ways of life different from your own, and to change yourself. In the same vein, we are unapologetically idealistic—we know that travel makes a difference in the lives of our writers and editors, and we believe it can make a difference in our readers and in the world as well. We also recognize that with those opportunities come responsibilities: the responsibility to try to dig deeper than the normal tourist experience, to share what you've learned during your travels, to give back to the communities you visit, and to protect them for future generations. We focus on budget travel not because we think of it as a last resort for the destitute, but because we believe it's the only way to travel. Traveling close to the ground almost always results in a more authentic experience and allows you to interact more directly with the places and people you've gone to see.

BEYOND THE TOURIST EXPERIENCE

To help our readers gain a deeper connection with the places they travel, our researchers give you the heads-up on both world-renowned and off-the-beaten-track attractions, sights, and destinations. They engage with the local culture, writing features on regional cuisine, local festivals, and hot political issues. We've also opened our pages to respected writers and scholars to hear their takes on the countries and regions we cover, and asked travelers who have worked, studied, or volunteered abroad to contribute first-person essays about their experiences. We've increased our coverage of responsible and sustainable travel and expanded and improved each guide's Alternatives to Tourism chapter to share with our readers more opportunities to experience the places they travel.

FORTY-FIVE YEARS OF WISDOM

Let's Go got its start in 1960, when a group of creative and well-traveled students compiled their experience into a 20-page mimeographed pamphlet, which they gave to travelers on charter flights to Europe. Four and a half decades later, we've expanded to cover six continents and all kinds of travel—while still retaining our founders' passionate, idealistic attitude toward the world. Our guides are researched and written entirely by students on shoestring budgets, adventurous and experienced travelers who know that train strikes, stolen luggage, food poisoning, and marriage proposals are all part of a day's work. This year, we're expanding our coverage of South America and Southeast Asia, with brand-new *Let's Go: Ecuador*, *Let's Go: Peru*, and *Let's Go: Vietnam*. Our adventure guide series is growing, too, with the addition of *Let's Go: Pacific Northwest Adventure* and *Let's Go: New Zealand Adventure*. And we're immensely excited about our new *Let's Go: Roadtripping USA*—two years, eight routes, and sixteen researchers and editors have put together a travel guide like none other.

A COMMUNITY OF TRAVELERS

We're a small company, and we stay that way because we believe that a close-knit staff that can lavish individual attention on every title we publish is the recipe for the best travel guides. We love it when our readers become part of the Let's Go community as well—please visit us online (www.letsgo.com), drop us a postcard (67 Mt. Auburn St., Cambridge, MA 02138, USA), or send us an e-mail (feedback@letsgo.com) to tell us about your adventures and discoveries.

ACKNOWLEDGMENTS

LET'S GO

TEAM CENTRAL AMERICA THANKS: Stef Levner, Laura Mot-Ahhn, Leslie Reiber, typist Kristin, The peace-loving people of CEAM, C-section bunny, The greater and lesser Bobs, the elusive quetzal, GI Noriega, Drudge Report, Seal, Jeremy, Teresa, Emma, hammock, Andy Dick. Oh, and my pimp hand is mighty.

MANUELA THANKS: Andrew and Jon, for keeping me sharp, and your patience. AC: like a rock; JB: music master. Tali, always cool under pressure. Stef, the queen bee, ready with a joke and gum. 7 Story St.: cigs, DC, dinner, tabloids, and the invasions. Alicia, Bess, Bets—my true loves. Felipe's and Tom, 7-11, my new pointe shoes. The family: Leo, Leni, and Jonas—keepin' it real, wherever they go.

JON THANKS: Andrew and Manuela: above all, two new friends. Tali=maptastic. IheartCORI. Liza, for your hard work and being so much fun, Ian, for working through frustration and making it good. Levna, for the car hookup. Kalilah, for on-site inspiration. 7 Roberts Rd., Dane St., Jack Bauer, The Wrap, Hung Kings, Colin Shepard's rubber legs. More than ever, my parents, brother, cousins, and Bubbe.

ANDREW THANKS: Noozle and Jon for a summer to remember and a book to be proud of. Corey and Edo for redefining "hardcore" and "suave" (respectively). Tali, snip snip snip. The Veritones, my family away from home. Mom and Dad for unending friendship, support, guidance and love. My lil' bro for being the best best friend a guy could ask for. And Abby for making me happier every day.

TALI THANKS: Manuela, Jon and Andrew for all their time and effort on these maps and, more importantly, for the hammock; my friends, who through their own insanity ensured I remained relatively sane this summer; and Mommy, Abba, Ofer and Yuval, for all their support and love.

Editor
Manuela S. Zoninsein
Associate Editors
Jonathan Bardin, Andrew Crespo
Managing Editor
Stef Levner
Map Editor
Tali Mazor
Typesetter
Melissa Rudolph

Publishing Director
Emma Nothmann
Editor-in-Chief
Teresa Elsey
Production Manager
Adam R. Perlman
Cartography Manager
Elizabeth Halbert Peterson
Design Manager
Amelia Aos Showalter
Editorial Managers
Briana Cummings, Charlotte Douglas, Ella M. Steim, Joel August Steinhaus, Lauren Truesdell, Christina Zaroulis
Financial Manager
R. Kirkie Maswoswe
Marketing and Publicity Managers
Stef Levner, Leigh Pascavage
Personnel Manager
Jeremy Todd
Low-Season Manager
Clay H. Kaminsky
Production Associate
Victoria Esquivel-Korsiak
IT Director
Matthew DePetro
Web Manager
Rob Dubbin
Associate Web Manager
Patrick Swieskowski
Web Content Manager
Tor Krever
Research and Development Consultant
Jennifer O'Brien
Office Coordinators
Stephanie Brown, Elizabeth Peterson

Director of Advertising Sales
Elizabeth S. Sabin
Senior Advertising Associates
Jesse R. Loffler, Francisco A. Robles, Zoe M. Savitsky
Advertising Graphic Designer
Christa Lee-Chuvala

President
Ryan M. Geraghty
General Manager
Robert B. Rombauer
Assistant General Manager
Anne E. Chisholm

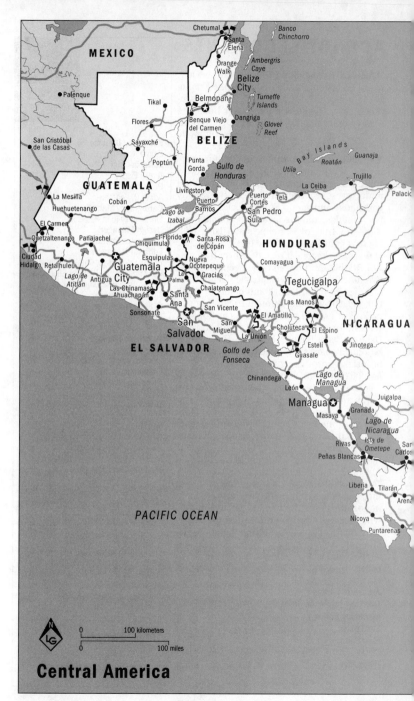

Central America

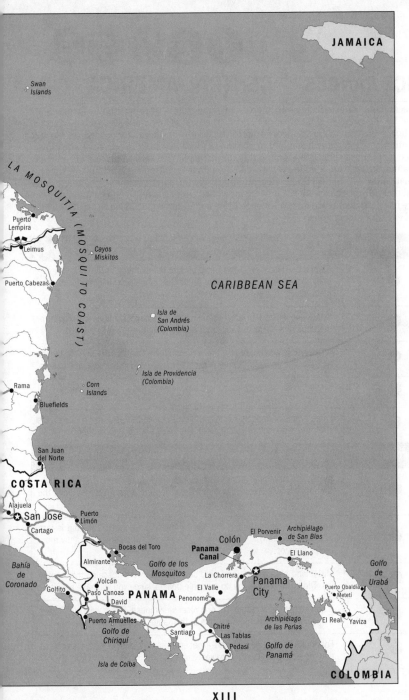

1 2 3 4 5

PRICE RANGES>>CENTRAL AMERICA

Our researchers list establishments in order of value from best to worst; our favorites are denoted by the Let's Go thumbs-up (🖑). Since the best value is not always the cheapest price, however, we have also incorporated a system of price ranges, based on a rough expectation of what you will spend. For **accommodations**, we base our range on the cheapest price for which a single traveler can stay for one night. For **restaurants** and other dining establishments, we estimate the average amount a traveler will spend. The table below tells you what you will *typically* find in Central America at the corresponding price range; keep in mind that no system can allow for every individual establishment's quirks, and that each country has particular price ranges for each price icon. Check the Essentials section at the start of each country chapter.

ACCOMMODATIONS	WHAT YOU'RE *LIKELY* TO FIND
❶	Camping; dorm rooms and basic budget hotels featuring running water, a bed, shared bath, and probably some insect friends. The lucky few may be blessed with hot water, TV, private bath, or a fan.
❷	Upper-end hostels or small hotels. You may have a private bathroom, or there may be a sink in your room and communal shower in the hall.
❸	A nicer room which probably has a private bath. Should have in-room amenities, such as phone or TV. Breakfast may be included in the price of the room.
❹	Similar to ❸, but may have more amenities or be in a more touristed area.
❺	Large hotels or upscale chains, often with an added perk, like a pool. If it's a ❺ and it doesn't have the amenities you want, you've paid too much.
FOOD	WHAT YOU'RE *LIKELY* TO FIND
❶	Mostly street-corner stands and cheap quick eats, often *comida típica*. Smoothie shacks and juice huts. Many dessert stops. You may have the option of sitting down or getting take-out.
❷	Sandwiches, appetizers at the bar, or low-priced entrees. Take-out is less frequent: generally a sit-down meal, sometimes with servers. Slightly more upscale decor.
❸	Mid-priced entrees, seafood, and some *carne*. More upscale ethnic eateries. The tip will bump you up a couple dollars, since you will have a waiter.
❹	A somewhat fancy restaurant or a nicer steakhouse. Either way, you'll have a special knife. Some restaurants in this range have a dress code.
❺	Food with foreign names and a decent wine list. Slacks and dress shirts may be expected. Don't slurp your *sopa*.

DISCOVER CENTRAL AMERICA

Central America is the backpacker's ultimate fantasy and ultimate challenge. The nascent tourist industry leaves room for exploring the road less traveled, and therein lies the catch—getting from place to place becomes an adventure in and of itself. Central America's seven countries are only a quarter of Mexico's size, but the diverse topography, culture, ecology, and activities coexist nowhere else in the world. Within the narrow isthmus, rainforest, volcanoes, coral reefs, and beaches await alongside Maya ruins. Largely marginalized and somewhat feared by travelers in past decades, Central American countries are finally emerging from years of violent political instability into a relatively peaceful period. All have democratic governments, and the wounds left by the once-prevalent civil wars are slowly healing. Once the destination only of bold (or foolhardy) adventurers, today's Central America—inexpensive and compact—is the budget traveler's new frontier.

WHEN TO GO

The most important climatic factor to consider when planning a trip to Central America is the **rainy season,** or *invierno* (winter), generally between May and November; the rest of the year is the **dry season,** or *verano* (summer). On the Pacific Coast and in the highlands, the seasons are distinct, while on the Caribbean Coast, some rain should be expected regardless of season. Temperature is determined by altitude rather than season; the highlands experience moderate highs and pleasantly cool nights while the coastal and jungle lowlands swelter. For a country-specific temperature chart, see the **Appendix** (p. 688).

Dry season is the tourist "high season," meaning larger crowds and larger prices. Budget travelers should consider a rainy season visit. Even then, the sun generally shines all day, excluding furious but fleeting afternoon rainstorms. Dry season travel is for those in search of a tan or access to areas where roads and trails can be washed out for weeks. The year's best parties are usually during **Semana Santa,** the week-long Easter holiday; for more celebration suggestions, check **Feasts and Fests** (p. 8). For more destination-specific info, see the country introductions.

THINGS TO SEE AND DO

THE WILD LIFE

Blessed with one of the most breathtaking and extensive park systems in the world, Central America is a nature-lover's paradise. The diversity of the region caters to every whim—whether you seek to stroll along well-maintained trails or machete your way through thousands of kilometers of jungle, the region provides.

In Belize, spelunk through **limestone caves** hollowed by underground rivers and dip into the subterranean waters (p. 102). Scramble to the top of **Cerro Las Minas** (p. 450), past gushing waterfalls and layers of cloudforest to the highest peak in Honduras. Or attempt to spot the impossible—an elusive quetzal—in El Salvador's largest national park, **El Imposible** (p. 280). In Nicaragua, ascend the charred slopes of **Volcán Masaya** (p. 558) and gaze into the still-smoking Santiago crater. In Costa

Rica's **Parque Nacional Manuel Antonio** (p. 201), hike along the powdery beach, stroll the forest paths, and lounge in the shade of a palm tree—all the while keeping an eye out for a resident anteater or sloth. Grab your binoculars and head for **Parque Nacional Soberanía** (p. 625), just an hour from Panama City and teeming with a mind-boggling 525 species of birds.

SEX ON THE BEACH

Tiny, quiet beach towns and great surf have made Central America the newest hot spot for the relaxed surfing community, and ocean-hungry travelers will find everything else they might desire: snorkeling, diving, and sunbathing. After all, where else are *two* oceans within such easy reach? **Bocas del Toro, Panama** (p. 670), is home to fine beaches, bountiful reefs, and impressive turtle-watching. In Costa Rica, **Playa Tamarindo** (p. 181) offers the perfect combination of gorgeous beach days and wild tropical nights, while **Jacó** (p. 195) is a partygoing surfer's paradise.

The world's second-largest barrier reef sits off the Caribbean coast of Belize and Honduras. Denizens of the deep flock to Belize's **Caye Caulker** (p. 74) and **Ambergris Caye** (p. 80), to swim with sting rays and sharks. If you're still not satisfied, Belize's Caribbean gems include the **Blue Hole,** an underwater cave 143m deep and twice as wide. The dreamy **Bay Islands** in Honduras (p. 494) boast silky white sand, elaborate coral formations, and the cheapest diving certification in the world.

El Salvador has some of the finest Pacific beaches in Central America, from the never-ending **La Costa del Sol** (p. 267) to the famed surfing at **La Libertad.** Offshore of Nicaragua's welcoming **San Juan del Sur** (p. 561), the deep-sea fishing is beyond comparison—you may hook into a wahoo or even a mighty sailfish.

DOWN THE ROAD TO RUINS

Over 2000 years ago, the inhabitants of Northern Guatemala began hauling huge slabs of limestone out of the ground and thrusting them skyward, constructing temples and palaces more than 70m high. The structures embody the mystery and grandeur of the great Maya cities, whose earliest remnants may date back more than 4000 years. The awesome temples, hieroglyphics, carvings, and statues that immortalize the ancients can be visited today at more than 30 sites in Guatemala, Belize, Honduras, and El Salvador. The most well-known is Guatemala's spectacular **Tikal** (p. 406), with more than 2000 structures and temples towering over the tropical rainforest. Equally impressive is **Copán,** Honduras (p. 456), home to intricate monuments and hieroglyphics. Less famous but still fascinating sites include **Uaxactún** (p. 410) and **Quiriguá** (p. 378) in Guatemala and **Lamanai** in Belize (p. 90).

Eventually, of course, the Spanish showed up in Central America, leaving behind an architectural legacy of their own. Ever-popular **Antigua,** Guatemala (p. 333), is a beautiful and well-preserved colonial city, with grand ruins and weathered cobblestone streets. Other fine examples of colonial architecture are scattered throughout the region, from the quiet towns of Honduras's **Western Highlands** (p. 437) to the cities of **León** (p. 544) and **Granada** (p. 552) in Nicaragua.

PEOPLE AND CULTURE

The warmth of Central America's people rivals the warmth of its beaches; nowhere else will you find such a diverse blend of Latin American, ancient Maya, and colonial European cultures.

While the region's ancient ruins have made it famous, few travelers realize that many of the ancient cultures have also passed the test of time. The **Western Highlands** of Guatemala (p. 333) are home to thousands of **Maya** who maintain many of their ancestral traditions. Visitors can interact with present-day Maya society first-hand at the famous handicrafts market in **Chichicastenango** (p. 350) and the traditional villages surrounding the gorgeous **Lago de Atitlán** (p. 342). In Panama, the **San Blas Archipelago** (p. 679) is a semi-autonomous Caribbean island chain inhabited entirely by the indigenous **Kuna.**

Travelers will feel the unmistakable mark of a colonial history in every town and building they visit, but the region's recent history is equally crucial to its present character. Central America's people have faced immense hardship during years of civil war and government unrest; many are eager to share their experiences, while others would rather leave the past behind. Small but poignant museums chronicle the horrors of the wars in **Perquín**, El Salvador (p. 304) and **Estelí**, Nicaragua (p. 574). These moving exhibits, in the heart of formerly war-torn towns, look back on a violent past as the region strives to move forward.

COME FOR A WEEK, STAY FOR A YEAR

It's not unheard of: unsuspecting travelers get tangled up in the web of Central America's allure, and, well, just can't leave. And who would want to? It's that one spot where the scene is just right—the people are friendly, scores of fascinating sites await exploration, and the food and culture make life a dream. Famous among such sites is the **Finca Ixobel** (p. 398), in the Petén region of Guatemala, where all-you-can eat dinners, tree-house accommodations, and exploration of the spectacular surroundings cast spells on wayward sojourners. Lazy afternoons and plenty of hammocks rope travelers in at Costa Rica's **Rancho Grande** (p. 197) where the black-sand **Playa Hermosa** earns its flattering name. If you don't want to spend your days twiddling your thumbs, there are numerous volunteer, work, and study options (see **Alternatives to Tourism,** p. 53).

▨ LET'S GO PICKS

BODACIOUS BEACHES: Where to begin? **Placencia**, Belize has miles of white-sand beach, as do **Tela**, Honduras, **Manzanillo**, Costa Rica, and **San Blas Archipelago**, Panama.

BEST DIVING AND SNORKELING: The **Bay Islands** of Honduras and **The Cayes** of Belize embrace the largest and most colorful reef in the western hemisphere.

BEST BIG ROCKS: Ruins at **Tikal**, Guatemala, are huge and impressive, but you'll avoid crowds at **Uaxactún**, Guatemala and **Caracol**, Belize. Don't miss the stunning intricacy of **Copán**, Honduras.

BEST HIDDEN SECRETS: Camp and cook in gorgeous Laguna de Lachuá near Chisec, Guatemala. Go wild in **La Mosquitia**, Honduras' untamed jungle. Stay on an isolated Caribbean island in the autonomous **Kuna region** of Panama.

BEST NATIONAL PARKS: Explore endless trails of unique flora, fauna and bird life in **Parque Internacional La Amistad**, which extends from Costa Rica into Panama. Mimic monkeys in **Parque Nacional Corcovado**, Costa Rica. Hike through virgin rainforest in **Parque Nacional Santa Barbara**, Honduras.

BEST PLACES TO GET STEAMROLLED BY PIPING HOT MAGMA: Climb **Cerro Chirripó**, Costa Rica's highest peak. If mere height isn't enough, **Volcán Arenál**, also in Costa Rica, froths lava nightly above the town of Fortuna.

BEST PLACE TO BUILD YOUR BATCAVE: At **Cavernas de Venado** in Costa Rica, spiders, bats, and rushing water are all that's keeping you from an underground waterworld. At Belize's **Tunich Hill Cave**, intact human skeletons are eager to greet visitors.

MOST CLICHÉD PHRASE IN THIS BOOK: "The %#*@ elusive quetzal."

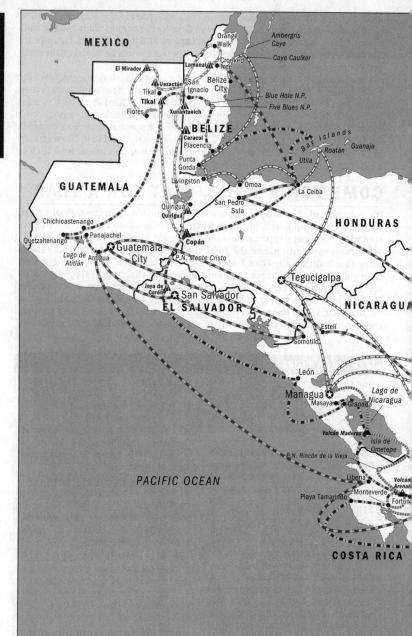

Central America: Suggested Itineraries

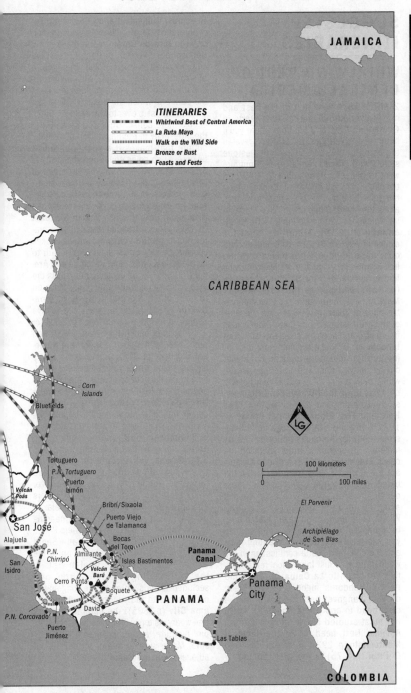

DISCOVER

SUGGESTED ITINERARIES

WHIRLWIND BEST OF CENTRAL AMERICA

2 MONTHS A selection of the best and most-talked-about tourist spots starts in **Guatemala City** (p. 323) from where you'll head west to **Antigua** (p. 333) and revel in the contrast between simple cobblestone streets and grand colonial ruins. Continue west to peaceful **Panajachel** (p. 342), on the shores of Lago de Atitlán. Cruise around the giant lake by ferry and stop in villages along the shore. Climb one of the encroaching volcanoes before heading to **Quetzaltenango** (p. 358), a starting point for exploring western Guatemala's endless outdoor opportunities. After hiking with the howler monkeys and the elusive quetzals, find a bus headed for **Chichicastenango** (p. 350), and peruse the world-famous Maya market. Jump north to the incomparable ruins of **Tikal** (p. 406) to see the work of their ancestors. From there, hop across into Belize and spend a couple days in **San Ignacio** (p. 97), the region's up-and-coming hub for adventure tourism; canoeing, caving, Maya ruins, and waterfalls are all within easy reach. Skip out of San Ignacio on a bus down the **Hummingbird Highway**, stopping along the way to explore **Blue Hole** and **Five Blues National Parks** (p. 107). Get a peek into Belize's eerie limestone underbelly—caves hollowed out by millennia of erosion. Farther south on the coast, **Placencia** (p. 112) provides a pleasant break from a busy itinerary. Sit on the beach and sip a fruit shake, or hire a boat out to one of the nearby cayes to snorkel along the world's second-longest coral reef. When you're ready to move on, grab a boat to **Honduras' Bay Islands** (p. 494), where you can take advantage of beautiful reefs and the cheapest scuba certification in the world. With your lust for tropical reefs satisfied, jet south to **La Ceiba** (p. 482) and party in Honduras' nightlife capital. Sleep off your hangover because you'll need a clear head to appreciate **Copán** (p. 456), the most studied Maya ruins in Central America. Next, head for **Parque Nacional Montecristo** (p. 293), where you can climb **El Pital** (p. 275), a mountain shared by

Honduras, Guatemala and El Salvador. For a different type of archaeological wonder, head to **Joya de Cerén** to see the Western Hemisphere's version of Pompeii: a Maya city preserved in volcanic ash. Then grab a bus south to **León** (p. 544), Nicaragua's liberal university city, where you can lounge in the park and watch the bustling young student life. Or, skip over to **Granada** (p. 552), León's more conservative counterpart and the oldest city in Nicaragua, for the eclectic culture that makes it a continual tourist favorite. Keep going south and shop 'til you drop at **Masaya** (p. 556), home to one of Nicaragua's most famous—and cheapest—craft markets. Push on to the **Isla de Ometepe** (p. 564), smack in the middle of Lake Nicaragua. Here the lush **Volcán Maderas** (p. 567) hides a tranquil lake within its crater. When all the volcano-climbing makes you hungry for some magma, roll south to Fortuna, Costa Rica, and watch **Volcán Arenal** (p. 164) belch fiery lava; don't miss the area's hot springs and waterfalls. Move on to cool off in the cloudforests of **Monteverde** (p. 166), then wander the Nicoya Peninsula to **Playa Tamarindo** (p. 181) for some serious beach time—surf, sleep, and party. Still farther south lies **Parque Nacional Chirripó** (p. 208), site of Costa Rica's highest point, where you can see the Atlantic and Pacific oceans at once. The last stop on the Costa Rica leg is uncrowded **Parque Nacional Corcovado**, where rainforest comes tumbling into the sea. Last, but certainly not least, head to Panama: stop first in **Boquete** (p. 660) and hike one of the area's many trails, including Panama's highest peak, **Volcán Barú** (p. 663), then try to spot those elusive quetzals you missed in Guatemala. **Bocas del Toro** (p. 670) promises pristine turquoise waters and spotless white-sand beaches. Relax in the Caribbean atmosphere before heading to **Las Tablas** (p. 646) on the Azuero Peninsula. If you arrive during Semana Santa (Easter Week), you'll get swept up in the wild *carnaval;* otherwise, revel in visits to the surrounding national parks and secluded islands. After all the roughing it, catch a bus to the very metropolitan **Panama City** (p. 605); the capital pampers trail-weary visitors with movie theaters, hoppin' nightlife, and great international cuisine. Make sure to sneak a peak at the adjacent **Panama Canal** (p. 623).

LA RUTA MAYA

3 WEEKS This tour loops out from **Flores, Guatemala** through some of the best Maya sites in the region, saving the power-hitters for the end. From Flores, your first stop is the secluded **El Mirador** (p. 411), perfect for the truly intrepid Maya enthusiast; swallowed by the forest, it's tough to reach and remains largely unexcavated and undisturbed. Continuing through the jungle, head to stately **Uaxactún** (p. 410), where ruins barely resist the encroaching trees. Next, cross the Belizean border to the northern ruins of **Lamanai** (p. 90), reached by a half-day river trip from the town of **Orange Walk** (p. 88). Stay in Belize and check out two more sites from **San Ignacio: Xunantunich** and **Caracol** (p. 103). From northern Belize take a leap south to the ruins of **Quiriguá** (p. 378) in eastern Guatemala. The stelae (pillar-like carved stones) are among the finest in the Maya world. Your tour rounds out with the two most impressive sites in the region. Researchers flock to the world-famous ruins of **Copán**, one of Central America's (and the world's) most impressive cultural treasures. Finish with a bang: **Tikal** (p. 406) is without a doubt the most outstanding Maya site of them all. Explore this ancient marvel from the town where the route started: Flores, Guatemala.

JUNGLE JAUNT

1 MONTH Beginning in the Nicaraguan capital, **Managua** (p. 535), an ecotourism jaunt through southern Central America begins with a stop at the **Isla de Ometepe** (p. 564) for the gorgeous twin volcanoes and the world's only freshwater sharks. Jump the border to Costa Rica and check out the piping hot lava of the active volcano at **Parque Nacional Rincón de la Vieja** (p. 174) just north of **Liberia** (p. 173). Continue south along the Interamerican Highway to **Monteverde** (p. 166), where you can coexist with the local fauna in biological reserves and an awe-inspiring cloudforest that sings with the sounds of living jungle. Before leaving town; stop off at **Volcán Arenal.** Bypass San José's urban confusion and head straight to **Parque Nacional Chirripó** (p. 208), accessible from **San Isidro** (p. 207), to capture a rare view of both the Atlantic and the Pacific from Costa Rica's highest point. Soak up some luxury at the nearby *aguas termales.* Tearing yourself away from the high, visit the coastal town of **Puerto Jiménez** (p. 218) and explore **Parque Nacional Corcovado** (p. 219) to witness untold varieties of birds, beasts, and botanical beauty. Journey south again to **Panama** and the town of **Cerro Punta** (p. 667) to hike Panama's highest peak through the haze of its cloudforest. From the nearby town of **David** (p. 654), hop a short flight to **Bocas del Toro** (p. 670) before cruising over to **Isla Bastimentos** (p. 674) for a glimpse of nesting turtles and other Atlantic wildlife. Lastly, fly to **Panama City** (p. 605) and Central America's only urban national park, **Parque Nacional Metropolitano** (p. 620).

BRONZE OR BUST: A CARIBBEAN COAST TOUR

1 MONTH Arriving in Belize City, take a boat to **Caye Caulker** (p. 74) and **Ambergris Caye** (p. 80) to scuba and snorkel the second largest barrier reef in the world. Fly or take the Hummingbird and Southern coastal highways to **Punta Gorda** (p. 116), Belize's sleepy southern gateway to the mountains and the country's largest Maya population. Take a ferry to **Livingston** (p. 383), home of Guatemala's vibrant Garífuna culture and rich *tapado* stew. Take another ferry to **Omoa** (p. 475), an idyllic Honduran fishing village with easy access to waterfalls, beaches, and transportation to Guatemala and inner Honduras. Use **La Ceiba** (p. 482) as your party port on the way to the **Bay Islands** (p. 494), the best white-sand beaches in Central America. Bus it to **Tegucigalpa** (p. 423) and catch a flight to **San José, Costa Rica** (p. 134). If you want to extend the itinerary, fly into **Managua, Nicaragua** (p. 535), and hop another flight to **Bluefields** (p. 585), a hip party town. From San José, fly to **Tortuguero** (p. 225), a small but increasingly popular seaside village accessible only by boat or plane. If your tan still isn't perfect, head to the ethnically diverse **Puerto Viejo de Talamanca** (p. 233) with numerous surfing beaches and a chill reggae vibe. Tear yourself away and journey on into **Panama** through the **Bribrí/Sixaola** (p. 678) border crossing. From **Almirante** (p. 676), take a water-taxi to **Archipelago de Bocas del**

Toro (p. 669), a grouping of islands ripe for hiking, diving, and fishing. If your pocket book still allows it, head by bus from Almirante to **David** (p. 654), then fly or take an express bus to **Panama City** (p. 605). From there, take a flight to **El Porvenir** (p. 681), the westernmost island of the **San Blas Archipelago** (p. 679), home of the **Kuna,** Central America's most independent traditional indigenous population. Take your time and explore the rich and diverse culture of the Kuna before heading home.

FEASTS AND FESTS. 4½ MONTHS Start this cultural party tour off right in **Crooked Tree, Belize** with the local **Cashew Festival** (first weekend in May). Enjoy the local cuisine, dance away the warm nights to the omnipresent *punta* music, and drink the delicious locally-made cashew wine, all in homage to the village's cash crop. Continue the festival tour with the **Carnaval** in **La Ceiba:** ask any Honduran and they'll tell you, "Tegucigalpa thinks, San Pedro Sula works, and La Ceiba parties." And Carnaval is the grand-daddy of them all (third week in May). **San Pedro Sula** takes a break from its work for **La Festival Juniana,** a cultural celebration whose entire month climaxes in the last week with street dancing, costumed parades and music by radio pop stars and the national symphonic orchestra (last week of June). Finish off the month at **Alajuela's** annual **Mango Festival,** in Costa Rica's Central Valley, where vendors, chefs, and farmers come together to celebrate their favorite produce in a region known informally as *la tierra de los mangos* (end of June-early July). From here, it's only a short commute to **Liberia,** where the **Expo-feria Ganadera Liberia** takes over in mid-July. This week-long party is the biggest *sabanero* (cowboy) rodeo in the country, bringing cattle ranchers together for bullfights, street games, and dancing (July 19-29). The town of **Antigua,** Guatemala, puts on a yearly local **Carnival.** The festive spirit of Antiguans comes out in full force with parades, calypso competitions, and, of course, all-night parties (July 25-Aug. 3). Just a short trip away, **Festival San Salvador** is the biggest party in El Salvador, with some 200,000 Salvadorans celebrating the capital city's patron saint with a circus, parade, and spectacular fireworks show (Aug. 3-6). Though not the blown-up experience of San Salvador, **Somotillo's** patron saint celebration for **San Lorenzo** is wellknown as an exceptional representation of the more local and simple celebrations of the region (Aug. 10). Head back up north as **Guatemala City** residents fill the streets with carpets for their saint and celebrate the crowning of their city as the nation's capital (Aug. 15). After the party, relax while listening to the best national musicians as they compete for recognition in two of the most traditional and region-specific music forms, in **Estelí** at the **Festival de Mariachis y Mazurcas** (third week in Aug.). At the end of August, the streets of **Limón** fill with parades and floats, dancing and music celebrating Costa Rica's Afro-Caribbean heritage. Look out for lectures, art displays, and beauty pageants. Conclude your festival extravaganza in good taste at the **Feria Internacional del Mar,** on **Isla Colón** in Panama, which serves up a variety of the amazing seafood the Caribbean waters have to offer (Sept. 15-19).

LIFE AND TIMES

THE LAND

GEOGRAPHY AND GEOLOGY

At 523,865 sq. km, Central America is one-fourth the size of Mexico, its neighbor to the north, and half the size of Colombia, its neighbor to the south. However, its geographic importance belies its tiny size. As the land bridge between two massive continents, Central America is an important barrier for ocean currents, separating the Pacific from the Caribbean and Atlantic. In geological years, Central America is a newborn babe. While the North and South American continents have existed as separate landmasses for nearly 140 million years, only five million years ago did the isthmus emerge heroically joining the two. A fractured piece of the North American continental crust formed the northern isthmus, and later volcanic activity and sedimentary deposits created southern Central America. Parts of Nicaragua and Panama were the last to form perhaps as recently as three million years ago. As it barred currents from circulating and then effectively warming the entire earth, the joining of the tectonic plates once led to an ice age.

The isthmus sits atop three tectonic plates—the Caribbean, North, and South American. The Cocos plate pushes into the Caribbean plate at a rate of 10m per century—a veritable geological sprint. As the South American subducts under, the Caribbean plate buckles, producing earthquakes and volcanoes. **Volcanic Highlands** run from Guatemala to Panama, comprised of 250 volcanoes. Although a quarter of these are extinct and half are dormant, this is still the most active volcanic belt in the Americas. Visitors can see the hot and steamy action live at volcanoes like Guatemala's **Pacaya** (p. 341) and Costa Rica's **Arenal** (p. 164) and Irazú (p. 152).

Besides the Volcanic Highlands, Central America has two other major mountainous regions. The non-volcanic **Crystalline Highlands,** or **Northern Sierra,** begin in Guatemala with the Sierra los Cuchumantes, stretch east through Honduras, and end with Cordillera Isabella in Northern Nicaragua. The inactive volcanoes of the **Cordillera de Talamanca,** or **Southern Sierra,** tower over Costa Rica and Panama.

The northernmost of the region's three major lowland regions is **El Petén,** a huge beast of a limestone shelf encompassing northern Guatemala, Belize, and Mexico's Yucatán. Formed by calcium secreted by marine life, the shelf is over 3000m thick and pockmarked with deep caves and depressions where the limestone has eroded. Farther east, the Caribbean Coast of Nicaragua and Honduras form **La Mosquitia** (Mosquito Coast), a sparsely populated lowland region of swamps and rivers comprising the largest forested region in Central America. The third major lowland is the **Nicaraguan Depression,** which cuts across the isthmus from the Gulf of Fonseca in western Nicaragua to the province of Limón in Costa Rica, including the Lago de Nicaragua and the Lago de Managua. With 2370km of Caribbean coast and 3280km of Pacific frontage, a sea is at most 200km away—at its narrowest point, in Panama's Darién, the isthmus is only 50km wide.

CLIMATE

Central America is essentially tropical, but due to variations in latitude, topography, and proximity to the sea, the climate can fluctuate substantially over short distances. The Caribbean coast is much wetter than the Pacific coast because of the typical easterly flow through the region: as it heads west, mountains trap humid air and force it to rise. Moist air is cooled past its dew point and falls as rain while warm dry air flows down the Pacific side, creating higher pressure on the Caribbean side and lower pressure on the Pacific side.

Altitude divides the isthmus into four distinct and creatively titled temperature zones. Lowlands below 900m are termed *tierra caliente* (hot land) with an annual average temperature of 72°F (22°C). The well-populated *tierra templada* (temperate land), at 1000-2000m, is a climate of eternal spring with an average temperature of 60-72°F (16-22°C). In the mountainous regions, 2000-3000m, the *tierra fría* (you guessed it—the cold land), chills below 46°F (8°C). The *tierra helada* (ice-land) exists only at the highest altitudes.

The seasons have little impact on temperature, but a huge impact on rainfall. Beginning in May, a low-pressure system, the Intertropical Convergence Zone, migrates north from its resting place in the central Pacific and sets itself squarely over Central America. This interrupts the otherwise constant trade winds and marks the beginning of the rainy season (*invierno;* winter) and lasting until December. The rainy season is marked by extremely powerful, but often brief, daily downpours, usually in the late afternoon. In December, the rains abate as the Convergence Zone moves back over the ocean; the trade winds resume their steady flow across the isthmus and bring the dry season (*verano;* summer) with them. Generally, the best time to visit is during dry season.

FLORA AND FAUNA

Central America's bio-diversity is due in part to its position between two continents. Both North and South American species dwell here, in addition to plants and animals unique to the region. With dry lowlands and humid rainforests, mountains, volcanoes and coral reefs, wildlife diversity shouldn't be surprising.

Tropical rainforest covers most of the eastern lowlands, while Belize and parts of Honduras are instead **pine or palm savanna.** Along the Pacific Coast and the inland valleys, lowland **dry forest** is most common; it grows on fertile land and has been almost entirely cut down for farming. At higher altitudes, lowland rainforest blends into **montane forest**—cool evergreen woods just below timberline. Pines predominate until the highest elevations, where only firs and yews remain. The steep coastal slopes around 1950m harbor **cloudforest** (in Costa Rica, Guatemala, Honduras, Panama, and Nicaragua), consisting of low moss-covered trees, permanently dripping with moisture and enshrouded in mist.

An equally diverse crew of animals make the isthmus their home. The **jaguar,** typically golden with black marks, once flourished in lowland forests; sadly, it is now endangered. Other big cats include **jaguarundis, ocelots,** and **pumas.** The **tapir,** a fantastical, pig-like creature is found in the rainforest, are joined by the such oddities as the **peccary** (a small, boar-like creature which can become aggressive if threatened), **anteater,** and a **tree sloth.** The call of the **howler monkey** resonates in the lowlands, while white-faced **capuchin monkeys** also cavort in the trees.

Caymans, crocodiles (*not* alligators), and **boas** all inhabit Central America's lowlands, originally arriving from South America. The bright red, blue, or green **poison dart frog** is omnipresent. Don't touch: the name isn't just for show. The **bushmaster snake** is the largest pit venom snake in the world; it tends to be nocturnal and lives in isolation. In higher altitudes, **rattlesnakes** and **kingsnakes** are common.

Birds—ranging from the **violet saberwing hummingbird** to the **monkey-eating harpy eagle**—inspire entire trips to the region. Most famous is the resplendent, albeit elusive, **quetzal,** endemic to Central America and found only in isolated cloudforests. The quetzal's long, brightly colored tail feathers were treasured by Maya kings. Other prized birds of the region include scarlet macaws, parrots, and toucans.

Pacific waters are colder, more turbulent, and more nutrient-rich than their Caribbean counterparts. **Plankton** thrive, as do open-water fish like **tuna, mackerel,** and **jacks,** and stationary filter-feeders like **oysters** and **sponges.** This environment is not conducive to coral growth, however, and in a few protected spots do reefs spring up (principally Panama and Costa Rica). By contrast, the Atlantic side is stable, warm, and shallow. **Coral reefs, seagrasses,** and **mangroves** form the foundation of the Caribbean ecosystem, supporting communities of animals, including sea urchins, lobsters, manatees, and porpoises. Five types of **sea turtles** visit Central America's beaches, coming ashore to nest in vast packs known as *arribadas.* The **green turtle** (see **Costa Rica's Parque Nacional Tortuguero,** p. 228), the **hawksbill,** and the rare **loggerhead** visit both coasts, while the **Olive Ridley** sticks to the Pacific.

Since Central America has been a historically impoverished region, with governments and citizens struggling to get by, the lure of a quick buck from environmental exploitation overrides the long-term benefits of preservation. A well-publicized solution to this problem is **ecotourism,** organized tourism of outdoor attractions and wildlife conducted in a way that protects the environment. For more info on how you can help out, see **Alternatives to Tourism,** p. 53.

HISTORY TO INDEPENDENCE

PRECOLONIAL HISTORY: THE MAYA

For over 2000 years, the Maya domain stretched from the Mexican Yucatán to Honduras. Geographic variation divided the area into three main regions: the Pacific plain and southern highlands; the central lowlands in Guatemala's Petén; and the northern lowlands in the Yucatán. Although they left a unified cultural legacy, the Maya were never politically cohesive; they lived in warring groups whose relative positions fluctuated. This did not impede the Maya's commercial interaction; trade flowed along long-distance routes, and the exchange of ideas followed the goods. Scholars use large-scale social change to divide Maya history into three periods: Pre-Classic, Classic, and Post-Classic.

THE PRE-CLASSIC: BUILD-IT-YOURSELF CITY-STATES (500 BC-AD 300). The appearance of highland cities near the Pacific Coast of the isthmus around 500 BC marked the beginning of the **Pre-Classic period.** Social stratification emerged soon after the establishment of these cities. Members of the highest socioeconomic class, the "elite," included priests, military rulers, or craftsmen and merchants. Political power was generally inherited A pyramidal division of labor allowed the elite to delegate responsibilities to their subordinates, who passed the buck to the laborers who harvested the maize, beans, and manioc. The elite encouraged intellectual development. Hieroglyphic writing was the fruit of this effort, but it is unknown whether the Maya created it themselves or were exposed to it through commerce with other cultures. To increase efficiency, the Maya developed new agricultural techniques, while chiefdoms vied for the best land.

By many accounts, the Maya were the most artistically and intellectually advanced of all the New World cultures. Foremost among the Maya's developments were their complex artistic and scientific practices, many of which were matched in Asia, and centuries later in Europe. They developed an **advanced mathematics** system involving zero, which did not evolved in Europe until later on. Arched and columned buildings in highland cities reflect precise geometrical calculations. The Maya developed the slash-and-burn farming method, allowing them up to 150 days off yearly from farming.

LIFE AND TIMES

The Maya were remarkable carvers, using flint, obsidian, and fire-hardened wood to carve hieroglyphics into blocks of stone. They transported enormous rocks across hundreds of kilometers of jungle. Given this technological sophistication, archaeologists were surprised to find no evidence of the wheel except in children's games. Moreover, although the Maya never domesticated animals, they developed advanced cultivation techniques such as terracing and irrigation.

The Maya developed a working **sidereal calendar** that measured years by gauging the earth's revolution relative not only to the sun, but also to the other stars, and resulted in an 365-day year. This extremely accurate method had practical uses, such as timing crop planting, and more abstract ones like astrological calculations. The **stelae** (tall marked altars, singular "stele") are inscribed with the date of their construction as calculated by this system. To write dates, the Maya established a fixed event as a chronological reference point and created the **Long Count** calendar. The Maya believed that at the end of every "great cycle" (about 5128 years) the world was created anew; the starting point of the Long Count may have been the beginning of the most recent great cycle, around 3114 BC. The dating unit was the day (rather than the year), making the numbers involved fairly large. A bar equaled five and a dot equaled one in this complex, base 20, mathematical system. This was often cumbersome, and **Short Count** used abbreviations reduced the number of glyphs necessary, thus leaving more room for other symbolic inscription.

THE CLASSIC: DYNASTIC ACCOMPLISHMENTS (AD 300-900). In the **Classic period**, scientific and cultural centers emerged in the hotter, more humid lands of Belize, northern Guatemala, the Atlantic coast of Honduras, and the Yucatán Peninsula—collectively known as the "lowlands." The highland mountain regions remained populated, ruled by Kaminaljuyú in southern Guatemala. By the end of this period, over 100 Maya cities existed; the largest at about 150,000 people.

The descent into the lowlands coincided with a solidification of existing social hierarchies, as chiefdoms became kingdoms. With strong **ahau** (kings), polities swelled in population, built grander architecture, and engaged in aggressive campaigns of conquest and expansion. The archetypal Classical period polity was **Tikal** (p. 406), located in the Petén region of present-day Guatemala. Tikal rose to prominence in the wake of nearby El Mirador's demise during the Early Classic period. Like other polities of the time, Tikal exhibited a state-level organization of dynastic rule. Nearby, less spectacular remains suggest that urban sprawl is hardly a new trend; extensive "suburban" networks and reams of paved highway connected thousands of inhabitants to the cities. Governed by its strong rulers, the city soon reached a population as large as 100,000. One target of Tikal's expansion was its northern neighbor Uaxactún (p. 410), a Maya center famed for the architecture of its ceremonial buildings aligned to function as an astronomical observatory. Under Smoking Frog, Tikal usurped Uaxactún in AD 378. In the late Classic period, however, other polities—such as Caracol (p. 103), led by Lord Water—used political alliances to compete with Tikal. In AD 682, when Ah Cacau ascended to the throne, Tikal experienced a brief revival. However, the city declined in the 9th century, and this time for good.

At about the time of Tikal's downfall, **Copán** (p. 456), in modern-day Honduras, had grown from its puny Pre-Classic size into the preeminent polis of the southeast lowlands. Records reveal that heavy construction occurred during the reign of Copán's 13th king, 18 Rabbit. The city's prosperity is thought to have resulted from sucking the life-blood out of its smaller neighbor Quiriguá (p. 378), in Guatemala. Apparently, 18 Rabbit stole Quiriguá's lunch money one too many times, and under the leadership of Cauac Sky, Quiriguá kidnapped 18 Rabbit and sacrificed him in AD 738. With Quiriguá's independence, Copán's power declined rapidly. Echoing Tikal, Copán briefly revived and then sank into permanent obscurity.

Copán is well-known for its **ballcourts.** Drawings found by archaeologists reveal that the Maya used these courts for a game in which players had to keep a hefty rubber ball aloft without using their hands or feet. Bouncing the ball from body to body, players attempted to pop it into one of the two circular stone goals mounted at either end of the enclosed court. According to hieroglyphic records, the captain of the winning team won a robe right off the back of each spectator in the audience, while the losing captain was ceremoniously beheaded.

THE POST-CLASSIC: MOVE OVER, MAYA (AD 900-1500). Of the numerous theories on why Maya civilization fragmented during the Classic period, natural disaster is among the most popular. Although there is evidence of an earthquake in Quiriguá and volcanic eruptions along the isthmus, epidemic disease is the most likely natural crisis. Skeletons found in Tikal and Copán show that malnutrition and possibly disease increased over time. Pottery records at Altar de Sacrificios and **Ceibal** (p. 400) show that outside forces overthrew the social order; the favored suspects are the Putun Maya, Chontal-speakers who lived on the Gulf Coast and may have monopolized trade routes. Most likely, a combination of these factors contributed to the ultimate demise of the Maya polities. Whatever happened, residents of great Classical cities migrated into the outlying jungle and Mexico, where they established cities of the **Post-Classic period.** The most important of these—Chichén Itzá, Mayapán, and Uxmal, (all in Mexico)—are popular among ruin-seeking travelers, but less so among archaeologists as the fruits of Classic Maya culture had been replaced by central Mexican influences.

NON-MAYA INDIGENOUS PEOPLES

Non-Maya indigenous groups inhabited more than half of Central America at the time of the Conquest. East and south of the Maya, the **Chibcha** inhabited Panama and Costa Rica after migrating from South America; the **Kuna** populated Panama; the **Pipil** and **Nicarao** groups lived in modern-day El Salvador and Nicaragua; and the **Miskito, Sumo,** and **Rama** tribes filled the Mosquito Coast of Honduras. These cultures were sedentary and agricultural like the Maya, but, for a variety of reasons, slower to organize. Chieftains—instead of building the massive pyramids, stelae, or temples that existed farther north—boosted their prestige with **ornamentation.** They used their wealth to import raw jadeite (a variety of a jade) from the Motagua Valley in Guatemala to fashion figurines and pendants. Around AD 600 they discovered metallurgy, and gold replaced jadeite and shells; the burial site **Sitio Conte,** near Penonomé in Panama, contained dozens of elaborate gold pieces. The gold trade, in addition to other markets, gained popularity in Costa Rican and Panamanian chiefdoms, which often served as middlemen between South American and Mayan empires. These southern groups stood up to the Spaniards, but the better-armed *conquistadores* subdued them without much difficulty.

CONQUEST AND COLONIES

When Columbus first stumbled upon the area in 1502, he was intrigued by the first few Maya inhabitants he saw—so he decided to take some back to Spain to "civilize" them. These were among the first of many losses levied against a native population which would later be robbed of millions of lives. Though a disputed number, modest estimates believe there to have been about 5.5 million people living in Central America. Within 200 years, the total population of Central America, including European settlers, was well below one million. The Spanish **Conquista** (Conquest) of the Americas, from Mexico to the Cape of Good Hope, was probably the most important in the history of these areas. The self-appointed task of conquering the New World and "evangelizing" its peoples took several centuries.

CONQUEST FROM THE NORTH (1520-1543). After **Hernán Cortés's** coup in Central Mexico, his forces proceeded southward under the command of Cortés's loyal henchman **Pedro de Alvarado,** notorious for his cruelty. Alvarado made his way through the jungle, finding Maya civilization in individual polities, vastly different from the imperial power structures that had been the fatal weakness of the Aztecs and Incas. These "city-states" were able to resist subjugation much longer than their counterparts. The Maya fought a jungle war, luring enemies into ambushes and eluding the Spanish in the mountains. After subduing the Pacific Coast, the Spaniards struggled for more than 175 years to control the northern jungles. The Guatemalan city of **Tayasal,** near modern-day Flores, fell to siege only in 1697, and the Lacandon people of Northern Guatemala and Southern Mexico resisted "assimilation," remaining wedded to subsistence lifestyles as late as the 1970s.

Nonetheless, many Maya polities, often weakened by smallpox, fell to Alvarado's onslaught. He continued southward, pushing into the western territories of modern-day El Salvador in 1524. The Pre-Classic Maya settlements of Tazumal and San Andrés had dissipated, but the indigenous **Pipil** remained to resist invasion. Alvarado later consolidated Cortés's control over Guatemala, Honduras, and El Salvador, founding the first Spanish capital of the region (on the old Cakchiquel site of Iximché) in July, 1524. After protracted squabbling with other *conquistadores* farther south, he became the uncontested governor of Guatemala. He died in 1541, and his widow, Beatriz de la Cueva, succeeded him as governor. Her rule was short, however; the capital city was squarely in the path of a volcano, and two days after her takeover a massive flood and mudslide destroyed the city, taking the new governor with it. A new capital was constructed in present-day Antigua.

CONQUEST IN THE SOUTH (1500-1563). While Cortés's other minions marauded in Guatemala, the Conquest moved forward in the rest of Central America. Spain, however, did not appoint qualified leaders—the selected governors of the region were themselves *conquistadores*, opportunists whose rivalries furthered violence among the Spaniards and hindered unification. After **Vasco de Balboa** crossed the Panamanian isthmus and "discovered" the Pacific Ocean, his title of governor and captain general of Darién (Panama) was handed over to **Pedrarías Dávila.** Balboa and Dávila feared and hated each other, ending in the latter's decapitating of the former. Dávila expanded his domain, breaching royal orders further by allowing brutal treatment of indigenous groups. The **Nicarao** of the Caribbean Coast, led by the famed **King Nicarao,** rebuffed Dávila's expansionist efforts. Yet Dávila, having encroached on the region's people and gold supply, set the stage for the pillage that would accompany later European immigration to Nicaragua.

In 1524, **Francisco Hernández de Córdoba** brought the first wave of successful colonists to settle in the eastern lowlands. They named the new country Nicaragua, after King Nicarao, and much later their descendents would call the local coin "córdoba," in honor of the king's European nemesis. Confrontation between the invaders and the invaded, while fierce in places, was brief and bloodless compared to the conquests of the Aztec and Maya empires. Nevertheless, the eradication of Nicaragua's indigenous people proceeded rapidly. Those whom Old World diseases did not kill right away were sold into slavery, and an indigenous population hundreds of thousands strong disappeared within 20 years. After establishing Granada and Managua, Córdoba tried to set up a kingdom independent of Panama. Dávila rewarded Córdoba's independent thinking with a beheading.

Costa Rica, meanwhile, was partially ignored by power- and wealth-hungry *conquistadores* because it had no large, rich indigenous empire and was thought poor in natural resources (read: gold). However, Costa Rica's few natives did suffer from the diseases brought by the Spanish, and were unable to resist the groups of settlers who colonized the area. Juan Vásquez de Coronado established the first permanent settlement at Cartago in 1563, and enjoyed a high degree of unofficial autonomy, since European monarchs were uneager to colonize a "poor" land so far from the region's colonial centers. As a result, Costa Rica developed much differently than other colonies—serfdom and debt-peonage were not implemented because the few natives did not provide the slave-labor force available elsewhere.

COLONIAL GOVERNMENT, OR HOW NOT TO RUN A CONTINENT (1500-1550). Much to the dismay of the *conquistadores*, colonizing efforts in Central America received little support from Spain. During the early 16th century, Spain ruled through scattered *ayuntamientos* (municipal councils). In 1530, Guatemala, Nicaragua, Honduras, Chiapas, and Panama all functioned under separate orders. The **Viceroyalty of New Spain** was established in Mexico City in 1535, comprised of Mexico, Guatemala, Honduras, El Salvador, Nicaragua, and Costa Rica—but its jurisdiction was unclear, thanks to a conflict with Panama over Nicaragua. In 1543, Spain managed to join the region from the Yucatán to Panama. Even after Central America was united as the Kingdom of Guatemala in 1548, the disorganization of governing bodies belied the monolithic title. Though the Spain failed to fully unify the isthmus, it did establish a collection of states: Mexico, Guatemala, Honduras, Nicaragua, El Salvador, and Costa Rica. The prosperous Panama, however, was not included in the Viceroyalty, disdaining its poorer brethren and remaining a loyal Spanish vassal until 1821, when it became a state within Colombia.

Belize, on the other hand, did not exist in 1535. The Spanish penetrated the area in the 1500s and 1600s and tried to convert the Maya to Christianity, with little success. British logwood cutters finally settled on the unfriendly coast in the mid-17th century. Spain, and later Guatemala, regarded the British as interlopers in their territory; in response, Britain took an unaggressive yet determined stance, referring to Belize as a "settlement," not a colony. Spain allowed the British to ply the logwood and mahogany trades, but only much later (1798) did Britain get Spain off its back, and finally in 1862, Belize was declared the colony of British Honduras.

THE NEW LAWS (1542-18TH CENTURY). The King's **New Laws** (*Nuevas Leyes*, 1542) were the work of **Bartolome de Las Casas**, the Bishop of Chiapas who insisted on abolishing the cruel *encomienda* system. *Encomenderos* were Spanish settlers who received parcels of land (*encomiendas*) and the (forced) labor of the indigenous inhabitants in return for "civilizing" and "christianizing" these inhabitants. The colonists, however, vigorously protested the New Laws as an unfair infringement on their "rights," and the King was forced to create the institution of the *repartimiento*, which basically allowed forced labor to continue under a different heading. The new system, however, changed indigenous life by allowing some measure of freedom for the Indians. They could live in their own villages, somewhat protected from former masters and more isolated from European influence. "Indian towns" developed in places like Quetzaltenango, Managua, and Masaya, and in some areas "closed, corporate communities" lived communally for protection and survival in the face of oppression. In some cases, these communities continued pre-conquest spiritual practices while paying lip service to Spanish missionaries. Despite this relative degree of freedom, however, the natives worked in conditions verging on slavery. Eventually, the *repartimiento* became the basis for the system of debt-peonage; a means for the Spanish to perpetuate the subjugation and manipulation of the indigenous population.

The number of Maya dwindled due to famine, disease, and overwork, and as a result, the Spanish lost their labor force. Although substantial indigenous groups remained in Guatemala, Honduras, and sections of El Salvador, parts farther south and west of the region suffered from depopulation. *Indígena* villages disbanded, and the Spanish had to eke out new trades. Regardless, the economy weakened, and the Kingdom of Guatemala was ill-equipped to deal with a series of earthquakes in 1717. The kingdom withdrew into a self-absorbed, feudal existence.

INDIGO, INDI-GONE (1760-1820). During the 18th century, Central America's economy stabilized. Immigrants from the world over (Europeans, black Carib slaves, German Mennonites, even Chinese) arrived, the resident Spanish population grew, and the native population rebounded. Spain encouraged mining in the area, but because mineral deposits were thin, agriculture was paramount. Cacao had been the principal 16th-century export, but indigo, needed as a dye in Peru's textile mills, soon replaced it. The indigo boom cemented the exploitative relationship which has marked nearly every political and economic conflict in Central America since. Displaced from their traditional subsistence farming locales, the indigenous populations became a landless and exploited labor force. Because indigo farms were in the hands of a few employers based in Guatemala City, the capital city became the center of a large monopoly. At the turn of the century, however, the indigo industry experienced the same shock as the cacao trade had decades earlier: outside competition usurped international trade. Although Central American indigo production decreased in importance, it remained the organizing element of life until the coffee-trade boom late in the 19th century.

The death of Charles II brought **Philip V** of the Bourbon family to the throne. Bourbon policy centralized authority and reasserted royal control, while bolstering the military and promoting agricultural export of cacao, tobacco, and indigo. As a result, the Guatemalan mercantile and bureaucratic establishment expanded. Provincial elites cultivated strong regionalist sentiments, while Creoles (European descendants born in the New World) resented favoritism for European-born leaders in royal policy. The **Cádiz Constitution** (1812) attempted to appease Creole frustration, granting elections for colonial offices and representation in Spanish parliament. This whetted the Creole appetite for independence. Local revolutions were quelled, and later, the Ferdinand VII annulled the 1812 constitution. After much protest, Spain restored Creole political participation in 1820.

THE PUSH FOR INDEPENDENCE (1820-1840). With the return of sanctioned Creole politics, the Liberal and Conservative parties, destined to dominate the scene for a century, emerged in embryonic form. The new political vitality, combined with a resentment of Spanish authority, yielded revolution. The members of the Viceroyalty declared independence in 1821. Internal instability allowed **Agustín de Iturbide** to seduce the republics into a brief affair with Mexico, but ended when Iturbide left office and the Mexican "empire" crumble. In 1823 Central America formed its own federal republic, the **United Provinces of Central America.**

The factionalism that had inspired independence also undermined the integrity of the federation. Each of the five autonomous states had its own president who ignored the federation's laws. Tension quickly arose between Conservatives and Liberals. The federation began during a Conservative regime under which only the upper classes could vote; slavery was abolished and the Roman Catholic church was preserved. In 1830, however, the elections favored Liberal **Francisco Morazán,** who undermined the Church and took measures to enhance trade. When tension mounted, he moved the capital from conservative Guatemala City to San Salvador. Unfazed, the Conservatives incited indigenous populations and started a revolution without him. **Rafael Carrera,** a *mestizo* rebel leader, seized Guatemala City in 1838, and the federation began to crumble. Two years later Carrera humiliated Morazán's on the battlefield. Morazán resigned, marking the end of the federation. Carrera and others tried unsuccessfully to reunite the states in the following years. The states went their separate ways and so did their histories; for the rest of the story, look to the **History Since Independence** section in each country's chapter.

PEOPLE AND CULTURE

About 66% Central America's population is of mixed race, or **mestizo** also called **ladinos**. About 5% are *mulatos*, of mixed European and African descent, and a small number are *zambos*, of indigenous and African descent. About 10% claim to be of pure European blood—the majority of these live in Costa Rica, which had a small native population to begin with. Recent estimates place the **indigenous** population at the time of the Conquest at around 5.5 million, with almost half concentrated around Maya civilization. The battles with conquerors and diseases decimated the population and even with the explosion of the last 50 years, *indígena* account for only four to five million of Central America's 29 million people—most are the Maya of Guatemala. Other native groups include the **Lenca** and **Chortí** in Honduras, the **Pipil** in El Salvador, the **Miskito, Pech, Sumu,** and **Rama** along the Mosquito Coast, and the relatively isolated **Kuna, Guaymí,** and **Emberá** in Panama.

In addition to the European and indigenous heritages, Central America also contains small **Chinese** and **East Indian** populations, descendants of indentured laborers brought to the area. Large **black** populations concentrate on the Caribbean Coast. These blacks are the descendants of African slaves who were either brought to Central America as laborers or escaped from the West Indies. One of these groups is the **Garífuna,** or Black Caribs, descendants of a group of mixed African and Carib Indian peoples who were deported to Honduras's Bay Islands in 1797. The Garífuna populate the coast from Belize to Nicaragua. For more specific information on people and culture, see the individual country chapters.

LANGUAGE

Spanish is the official language of six of the seven Central American countries and is the most common language on the isthmus. For those accustomed to Castillian Spanish, Central America may take some getting used to, as each country, or even each province, has its own cadence, speed, and vocabulary. On the other hand, the language tends to be crisp and clear, one reason Central America, and Guatemala in particular, is noted for its language schools. More isolated indigenous groups still speak traditional languages, sometimes exclusively. In parts of the Guatemalan highlands, along the Mosquito Coast, and in the San Blas territory of Panama, even a fluent Spanish speaker may be reduced to gestures. However, there is usually someone around who speaks Spanish, even if as a second language. The non-Spanish speaking nation is Belize, where English is the official language. English is also spoken in many Caribbean towns outside Belize; however, the Afro-Caribbean English at its extreme is barely intelligible to foreigners. The slang's catchy, though: you'll be greeting people with *"Allright, Goodnight"* long after you leave.

RELIGION

Roman Catholicism, the professed faith of over four-fifths of the population, is by far the dominant religion in Central America. In more urban areas where indigenous heritage has largely been effaced, European Catholicism is practiced. In more rural areas, the faith is highly syncretic, blending Catholic and indigenous beliefs and resulting in new strains of both. The polytheism of native religions often enabled indigenous integration of Catholic traditions. Other religious forces have recently begun to undermine the dynamic relationship. Nativistic movements are increasingly popular, advocating a rejection of the religious practices that arrived with the Conquest and a return to indigenous religions.

LIFE AND TIMES

LIFE AND TIMES

CUSTOMS AND ETIQUETTE

Etiquette throughout Central America is fairly universal. Time is somewhat arbitrary—no one is in a rush, and lateness is both tolerated and expected. Public displays of affection are acceptable. Between friends, it is customary to give a kiss on one cheek as greeting. Handshakes are acceptable greeting among men. *Machismo*, a cultural attitude subordinating women, still lingers; women don't usually go out unaccompanied, and men invariably pay for dinner. Women are advised to dress conservatively. Homosexuality is generally accepted, but not overtly displayed. Gifts should be accepted with great thanks. Always use the formal *usted* form of Spanish when addressing a stranger or authority figure. Address friends or more informal acquaintances with the *tú* form. Approach conversations about politics with care, as they may be sore subjects. Rules are more relaxed in cosmopolitan areas. For info on tipping and bargaining, see **Essentials** (p. 19).

ARTS AND CRAFTS

After the arrival of Spanish colonial rulers, Central America's art and culture were dominated by European ideals for several centuries. In the modern era, the region has begun to re-focus on pre-Colombian history and culture, and new excavations have given fuel to this process of rediscovery. The **folk art** of Central America is ubiquitous both in use and sale. Strong traditions of leatherwork, weaving, ceramics, embroidery, and woodcarving survive in many parts of Central America.

Vibrant traditional **music** flourishes on either end of Central America, in Guatemala and Panama, but is less prevalent in between. The *marimba* xylophone, is heard in plazas from Guatemala to Costa Rica; indigenous instruments are played in Maya churches; Afro-Carib music rocks the Caribbean coast; *Punta*, a percussion-based music and dance, is performed by Garifuna along the Honduran coast; Nicaragua's Bluefields has produced world-renowned reggae bands; and *música típica* combines European phrasing with African rhythms. Traditional, folk, and regional dancing is also vibrant; consider Panama's classic national folk dance, the *tamborito*, is performed in small towns in local permutations.

FURTHER RESOURCES

Central America: A Natural and Cultural History, edited by Anthony G. Coates (1997). An academically rigorous treatment of the history of Central America.

The Maya, Michael Coe (1993). Of the many introductions to the Maya, this is perhaps the most readable and engaging—and one of the shortest.

Scribes, Warriors, and Kings: The City of Copán and the Ancient Maya, William Fash (1993). An American archaeologist's account of the history of Copán.

Poesia Contemporánea en America Central, edited by Francisco Albizurez Palma (1995). A massive collection of Central American poetry in Spanish.

Incidents of Travel in Central America, Chiapas, and Yucatán, John Lloyd Stephens (1992 reprint). This classic account from the 1840s by the world-traveler Stephens was one of the pioneering works of Maya archaeology.

Volcán: Poems from Central America: A Bilingual Anthology, edited by Alejandro Murguia (1983). Published by City Lights, an excellent collection in Spanish and English.

And We Sold the Rain: Contemporary Fiction from Central America, edited by Rosario Santos (1996). A collection of short stories.

The Old Patagonian Express: By Train Through the Americas, Paul Theroux. Classic travel narrative with wry traveler's insights on 1970s Central America.

ESSENTIALS

PLANNING YOUR TRIP

ENTRANCE REQUIREMENTS
Passport (p. 19). Required of all visitors.
Visa (p. 20). See **Essentials** section for each country for specific information.
Letter of Invitation (p. 20). Not required.
Inoculations (p. 27). None required.
Work Permit. Required for all foreigners planning to work in Central America.

DOCUMENTS AND FORMALITIES

See individual country chapters for specific info on **Consular and Tourism** services.

PASSPORTS

REQUIREMENTS

Citizens of Australia, Canada, Ireland, New Zealand, the UK, and the US need valid passports to enter Central America and re-enter their home countries. Passports must be valid at least six months before date of entry, and at least 30 days after. Returning home with an expired passport is illegal, and may result in a fine.

NEW PASSPORTS

Citizens of Australia, Canada, Ireland, New Zealand, the UK, and the US can apply for a passport at any participating post office, a passport office, or court of law. Any new passport or renewal applications must be filed well in advance of the departure date, though most passport offices offer two week rush services for a very steep fee. Citizens living abroad who need a passport or renewal should contact the nearest passport office of their home country.

PASSPORT MAINTENANCE

Photocopy the page of your passport with your photo, as well as your visas, traveler's check serial numbers, and any other important documents. Carry one set of copies in a safe place, apart from the originals, and leave another set at home. Consulates recommend carrying an expired passport or an official copy of your birth certificate in your baggage separate from other documents. If you lose your passport, immediately notify the police and the embassy or consulate of your home government. To expedite its replacement, you must know all information previously recorded, show ID, and prove citizenship. In some cases, replacements take weeks to process, and may only be valid for a limited time. Any visas stamped in your old passport will be irretrievably lost. In an emergency, ask for temporary traveling papers from the embassy that will permit you to re-enter your home country.

VISAS AND WORK PERMITS

See specific country chapters for **visa** specific entrance information. US citizens can also consult http://travel.state.gov/foreignentryreqs.html. Admission as a visitor does not include the right to work, which is authorized only by a work permit. Entering Central America to study usually requires a special **work visa**. For more information, see **Alternatives to Tourism** (p. 53).

IDENTIFICATION

 Visa and work permit information is country-specific and can be found in individual chapters. For Belize, see p. 67; Costa Rica, see p. 133; El Salvador, see p. 247; Guatemala, see p. 321; Nicaragua, see p. 533; Panama, see p. 604.

When traveling carry at least two forms of identification on your person, including a photo ID; a passport and a driver's license or birth certificate is usually adequate. Never carry all of your IDs together; split them up in case of theft or loss, and keep photocopies of all of them in your luggage and at home.

STUDENT, TEACHER, AND YOUTH IDENTIFICATION

The **International Student Identity Card (ISIC),** the most widely accepted form of student ID, provides discounts on some Central American accommodations and laundromats; access to a 24hr. emergency helpline; and insurance benefits for US cardholders (see **Insurance,** p. 27). Applicants must be full-time secondary or post-secondary school students at least 12 years of old. Because of the proliferation of fake ISICs, some services (particularly airlines) require additional identity proof. The **International Teacher Identity Card (ITIC)** gives teachers the same insurance coverage as the ISIC and but fewer discounts. Travelers under 25, but not students can use the **International Youth Travel Card (IYTC),** with many of the same ISIC benefits.

Each of these identity cards costs US$22 or equivalent. ISIC and ITIC cards are valid through the issue calendar, unless issued after October in which case it will last for the rest of that year plus the following one. IYTC cards are valid for one year from issue date. Many student travel agencies issue the cards; for a list of issuing agencies or more information, see the **International Student Travel Confederation (ISTC)** website (www.istc.org).

CUSTOMS

Upon entering Central America, you must declare certain items from abroad and pay a duty on the value if it exceeds the allowance established by the country's customs service. Note that goods purchased at **duty-free** shops are not exempt from duty or sales tax; "duty-free" merely means that you need not pay a tax in the country of purchase. Upon returning home, you must declare all articles acquired abroad and pay a duty on the value in excess of your home country's allowance. In order to expedite your return, keep receipts for all goods acquired abroad.

MONEY

CURRENCY AND EXCHANGE

As a general rule, it's cheaper to convert money in Central America than at home. While currency exchange is available in international airports, it's wise to bring enough foreign currency to last for the first 24-72 hr. When changing money, try to go only to banks or change houses that have at most a 5% margin between their buy and sell prices. Since you lose money with every transaction, **convert large sums** (unless the currency is depreciating rapidly), **but no more than you'll need.**

If you use traveler's checks or cash, carry some in small denominations (the equivalent of US$50 or less) for times when you are forced to exchange at disadvantageous rates, but bring a range since charges may be levied per check. Store money in a variety of forms; ideally, at any given time you will have some cash, some traveler's checks, and an ATM and/or credit card. Travelers should carry some US dollars (about US$50 worth), which are often preferred by local tellers.

At land crossings, many Central American border guards will charge official or unofficial fees for both entry and exit. If the fee is of the off-the-books sort, it may be possible to get out of it by insisting upon a receipt. When flying out of Central America, you'll have to pay a very official departure tax of US$10-$30. For more details on border and departure fees, and currency exchange rates, see the **Essentials** sections of each country chapter.

TRAVELER'S CHECKS

Traveler's checks are the least troublesome means of carrying funds. American Express and Visa are the most recognized brands. Many banks and agencies sell them for a small commission, but require passport, proof of purchase, and often another picture ID with matching signatures and names. Check issuers provide refunds if the checks are lost or stolen, and many have additional services, such as toll-free refund hotlines abroad, emergency message services, and stolen credit card assistance. The checks are readily accepted in country capitals and other tourist-heavy areas. Ask about the location of refund centers when purchasing checks and always carry emergency cash. AmEx is most commonly accepted brand; they also offers a new travel card, the TravelFunds Card, which is basically a traveler's check in plastic. Unlike an ATM card, it's prepaid and if lost or stolen, funds are replaced within 24 hr.

> **American Express:** Checks available with commission at select banks, at all AmEx offices, and online (www.americanexpress.com; US residents only). AmEx cardholders can purchase checks by phone (☎800-721-9768). For purchase locations or more info call: Australia ☎800 68 80 22; New Zealand 0508 555 358; the UK 0800 587 6023; the Canada and US 800-721-9768; elsewhere, call the US collect 801-964-6665.

> **Visa:** Checks available (generally with commission) at banks worldwide. For office loca call: the UK ☎0800 89 50 78; US 800-227-6811; elsewhere, call the UK collect 44 173 331 8949. Available in Canadian, Japanese, European, British, and US currencies.

CREDIT, ATM, AND DEBIT CARDS

Where accepted, plastic has the best exchange rates—up to 5% better than bank retail rates. **Credit cards** may provide insurance or emergency help, and are sometimes required to reserve hotel rooms or rental cars. **Mastercard** and **Visa** are the cards of choice in Central America, but most establishments outside of the most touristed cities, are cash only. **ATMs** give the same wholesale exchange rate as credit cards and are increasingly available in Central America. Depending on your home bank's system, you can access personal accounts from abroad, but there is a limit on the amount you can withdraw per day (around US$500; US$1-$5 surcharge per withdrawal). **Debit cards** have the convenience of credit cards, yet the money is withdrawn directly from your checking account. Debit cards dual function as ATM cards and can be used wherever the associated credit company (usually Mastercard or Visa) is accepted. Major international networks are **Cirrus** (US ☎800-424-7787; www.mastercard.com) and **Visa/PLUS** (US ☎800-843-7587; www.visa.com).

GETTING MONEY FROM HOME

If you run out of money while traveling, the easiest and cheapest solution is to have someone back home make a deposit to the bank account linked to your credit or ATM card. Failing that, consider one of the following options. The online **International Money Transfer Consumer Guide** (http://international-money-transfer-consumer-guide.info) may also be of help.

ESSENTIALS

WIRING MONEY

It is possible to arrange a **bank money transfer**, which means asking a bank back home to wire money to a bank in Central America. This is the cheapest way to transfer cash, but it's also the slowest, usually taking several days. Note that some banks may only release your funds in local currency, potentially sticking you with a poor exchange. Money transfer services like **Western Union** are faster and more convenient, but also pricier. Western Union has locations worldwide; visit www.westernunion.com, or call in Australia ☎ 800 501 500, Canada 800-235-0000, the UK 0800 83 38 33, the US 800-325-6000.

US STATE DEPARTMENT (US CITIZENS ONLY)

In serious emergencies only, the US State Department will forward money within hours to the nearest consular office, which will then disburse it according to instructions for a US$30 fee. If you wish to use this service, you must contact the Overseas Citizens Service division of the US State Department (☎ 317-472-2328; nights, Sundays, and holidays 202-647-4000).

COSTS

In most respects, Central America is a great place for travel on the cheap. In the most inexpensive areas, the savvy budget traveler can survive on US$10 a day, although one may want to spend more for the sake of safety. Most penny-pinching voyagers should expect to spend US$20-45 a day, with Belize, Costa Rica, and Panama being pricier than the rest of the region. If you spend a lot of time in heavily touristed areas, or travel during peak season, you will spend more. The rainy season (May-Nov.) typically brings the best deals. Your single biggest expense will be a plane ticket (see **Transportation,** p. 32). Don't forget to factor in emergency reserve funds (at least US$200) when planning how much money to take. Before you go, spend some time calculating a reasonable daily budget.

TIPS FOR SAVING MONEY

Money can be conserved in many ways, including searching out free entertainment, splitting accommodations with trustworthy fellow travelers, and buying food in supermarkets rather. Do your **laundry** in the sink (unless you're explicitly prohibited from doing so). That said, don't go overboard—staying within your budget is important, but don't do so at the expense of your health or a great travel experience.

TIPPING AND BARGAINING

Tipping and especially bargaining in Central America are quite different and much more commonplace practices than you may be accustomed to; there are many unspoken rules to which tourists must adhere. In tourist and upscale restaurants, a 10% tip is common. In smaller restaurants frequented by locals, tipping is rare. Tour guides generally appreciate something extra, though taxi drivers do not expect to be tipped. At outdoor markets, handicraft markets, and some handicraft shops, bargaining is expected and essential. On the other hand, prices at supermarkets and most indoor stores are non negotiable. Bargaining for hotel rooms is often a good idea, particularly in the low season (or if the hotel simply isn't full.) For more on bargaining, see **The Art of the Deal** (below).

 THE ART OF THE DEAL. Bargaining in Central America is a given: no price is set in stone, and vendors and drivers will automatically quote you a price that is several times too high; it's up to you to get them down to a reasonable rate. With the following tips and some finesse, you might be able to impress even the most hardened hawkers:

1. **Bargaining needn't be a fierce struggle laced with barbs.** Quite the opposite: good-natured wrangling with a cheerful face may prove your best weapon.

2. **Use your poker face.** The less your face betrays your interest in the item the better. If you touch an item to inspect it, the vendor will be sure to "encourage" you to name a price or make a purchase. Coming back again and again to admire a trinket is a good way of ensuring that you pay a ridiculously high price. Never get too enthusiastic about the object in question; point out flaws in workmanship and design. Be cool.

3. **Know when to bargain.** In most cases, it's quite clear when it's appropriate to bargain. Most private transportation fares and things for sale in outdoor markets are all fair game. Don't bargain on prepared or pre-packaged foods on the street or in restaurants. In some stores, signs will indicate whether "fixed prices" prevail. When in doubt, ask tactfully, "Is that your lowest price?" or whether discounts are given.

4. **Never underestimate the power of peer pressure.** Try having a friend discourage you from your purchase—if you seem to be reluctant, the merchant will want to drop the price to interest you again.

5. **Know when to turn away.** Feel free to refuse any vendor or driver who bargains rudely, and don't hesitate to move on to another vendor if one will not be reasonable about the final offering price. However, to start bargaining without an intention to buy is a major *faux pas*. Agreeing on a price and declining it is also poor form. Turn away slowly with a smile and "thank you" upon hearing a ridiculous price—the price may plummet.

6. **Start low.** Never feel guilty offering a ridiculously low price. Your starting price should be no more than one-third to one-half the asking price.

7. **Know when to stop.** Despite the advice above, keep in mind that most Central American vendors barely survive on what they make. Just because you can bargain something down doesn't mean you should.

PACKING

Pack light. Lay out only what you absolutely need, then take half the clothes and twice the money. The Travelite FAQ (www.travelite.org) is a good resource for packing tips. The online **Universal Packing List** (http://upl.codeq.info) will customize a list of suggested items based on trip length, expected climate, and planned activities. If you plan to do a lot of hiking, see **Camping and the Outdoors,** p. 43.

LUGGAGE. In Central America most of your itinerary will be on-foot; a sturdy **frame backpack** is unbeatable (for the basics on buying a pack, see p. 46). In addition to your main piece of luggage, a **daypack** (a small backpack or courier bag) is useful.

CLOTHING. No matter when you're traveling, it's a good idea to bring a warm jacket or wool sweater, a rain jacket (Gore-Tex® is both waterproof and breathable), sturdy shoes or hiking boots, and thick socks. Flip-flops are must-haves for grubby hostel showers. You may also want one outfit for going out with a nicer pair of shoes. If you plan to visit religious or cultural sites you will need modest, respectful dress. Rain gear is particularly essential during the rainy season (May-Nov.). Take a sweater or fleece as he highlands get quite cold at night. Local men don't wear shorts; exceptions are beach towns and touristed locales. Not all local women dress conservatively but the female visitor is well advised to do so.

SLEEPSACK. Some hostels require that you either provide your own linen or rent sheets. Save cash by making your own sleepsack: fold a full-size sheet in half the long way, then sew it closed along the long side and one of the short sides.

TOILETRIES. Toothbrushes, towels, cold-water soap, deodorant, razors, tampons, and condoms are often available, but may be difficult to find. Contact lenses are likely to be expensive and scarce. Bring extra pairs, solution for your entire trip, glasses, and a copy of your prescription for emergency replacements.

FIRST-AID KIT. For a basic first-aid kit, pack bandages, a pain reliever, antibiotic cream, a thermometer, a pocket knife, tweezers, moleskin, decongestant, motion-sickness remedy, diarrhea or upset-stomach medication (Pepto Bismol or Imodium), an antihistamine, sunscreen, insect repellent, burn ointment, and perhaps a syringe for emergencies (get an explanatory letter from your doctor).

OTHER USEFUL ITEMS. For safety purposes, you should bring a **money belt** and small **padlock.** Basic **outdoors equipment** (plastic water bottle, compass, waterproof matches, pocketknife, sunglasses, sunscreen, and hat) may also prove useful. **Quick repairs** of torn garments can be done on the road with a needle and thread; also consider bringing duct tape for patching tears. If you want to do laundry by hand, bring detergent, a small rubber ball to stop up the sink, and string for a makeshift clothes line. **Film** is expensive in Central America, so consider bringing along enough film for your entire trip and developing it at home. Less serious photographers may want to bring a disposable camera. **Other things** you're liable to forget are an umbrella; sealable **plastic bags** (for damp clothes, soap, food, shampoo, and other spillables); an **alarm clock;** safety pins; rubber bands; a flashlight; earplugs; garbage bags; and a small **calculator.** A **cell phone** can be a lifesaver (literally) on the road; see p. 41 for info on acquiring one that will work at your destination.

IMPORTANT DOCUMENTS. Don't forget your passport, traveler's checks, ATM and/or credit cards, adequate ID, and photocopies of all of the aforementioned in case these documents are lost or stolen (see p. 20). Also check that you have any of the following that might apply to you: a driver's license (see p. 20); travel insurance forms; and/or an ISIC card (p. 20).

SAFETY AND HEALTH

GENERAL ADVICE

In any type of crisis situation, the most important thing to do is **stay calm.** Your country's embassy abroad (see individual country chapters) is usually your best resource when things go wrong; registering with that embassy upon arrival in the country is often a good idea. The government offices listed below in **Travel Advisories** provide information on emergency services for traveling citizens. In terms of the physical stability of your destination, much of Central America is either seismologically or volcanically active. See individual country chapters for more specific information on **natural disasters.**

LOCAL LAWS AND POLICE

Central American legal systems are renowned for being ineffective and police often succumb to bribery. These generalizations are less true in Belize and Costa Rica. Tourist police are present in tourist friendly cities and towns for peacekeeping and informational purposes. To learn which towns have tourist police, contact the tourism bureau in each country, listed in the respective chapters.

Because of Central America's turbulent relationship with narcotics, penalties are severe for **drug possession** and your home embassy will be of minimal assistance should you get into trouble. Remember that you are subject to the laws of the country in which you travel, not those of your home country; it is your responsibility to familiarize yourself with these laws before leaving. If you carry **prescription drugs** while you travel, have a copy of the prescriptions themselves and a note from your doctor. Avoid **public drunkenness;** in certain areas it is against the law, and can also jeopardize your safety and earn the disdain of locals.

TERRORISM

Terrorism is limited in Central America. However, there are occasionally political demonstrations in which tourists are taken hostage for short periods of time to bait the government, including a 2001 demonstration at Guatemala's Tikal. Such events are usually not physically dangerous to the tourist, as they are safely returned as soon as the conflict is over. The box on **travel advisories** lists offices to contact and webpages to visit to get the most updated list of your home country's government's advisories about travel.

TRAVEL ADVISORIES. The following government offices provide travel information and advisories by telephone, by fax, or via the web:

Australian Department of Foreign Affairs and Trade: ☎ 13 00 555135; www.dfat.gov.au.

Canadian Department of Foreign Affairs and International Trade (DFAIT): In Canada and the US call ☎ 800-267-8376, elsewhere call 1 613-944-4000; www.dfait-maeci.gc.ca. Call for their free booklet, *Bon Voyage...But.*

New Zealand Ministry of Foreign Affairs: ☎ 04 439 8000; www.mft.govt.nz/travel/index.html.

United Kingdom Foreign and Commonwealth Office: ☎ 020 7008 0232; www.fco.gov.uk.

US Department of State: ☎ 202-647-5225; http://travel.state.gov. For *A Safe Trip Abroad,* call ☎ 202-512-1800.

PERSONAL SAFETY

EXPLORING AND TRAVELING

To avoid unwanted attention, try to blend in as much as possible. Respecting local customs (in many cases, dressing more conservatively than you would at home) may placate would-be hecklers. Familiarize yourself with your surroundings before setting out, and carry yourself with confidence. Check maps in shops and restaurants rather than on the street. If you are traveling alone, be sure someone at home knows your itinerary, and never admit that you're by yourself. When walking at night, stick to busy, well-lit streets and avoid dark alleyways. If you ever feel uncomfortable, leave the area as quickly and directly as you can.

There is no sure-fire way to avoid all the threatening situations you might encounter while traveling, but a good **self-defense course** will give you concrete ways to react to unwanted advances. **Impact, Prepare, and Model Mugging** can refer you to local self-defense courses in the US (☎800-345-5425). Visit the website at www.impactsafety.org for a list of nearby chapters. Workshops (1½-3hr.) start at US$75; full courses (20-25hr.) run US$350-400.

If you are using a **car,** learn local driving signals and wear a seatbelt. Study route maps before you hit the road. If you plan on spending a lot of time driving, consider bringing spare parts. If your car breaks down, wait for the police to assist you. For long drives in desolate areas, invest in a cellular phone and a roadside assistance program (see p. 37). Always park in a well-traveled area. **Sleeping in your car** is very dangerous. For info on the perils of **hitchhiking,** see p. 37.

POSSESSIONS AND VALUABLES

Never leave your belongings unattended; crime occurs in even the most demure-looking hostel or hotel. Bring your own **padlock** for hostel lockers, and don't ever store valuables in any locker. Be particularly careful on **buses**; horror stories abound about thieves who wait for travelers to fall asleep. Carry your backpack in front of you where you can see it and keep important documents and other valuables on your person. When traveling with others, sleep in alternate shifts.

There are a few steps you can take to minimize the financial risk associated with traveling: **bring as little with you as possible**; buy a few combination **padlocks** to secure your belongings; and **carry as little cash as possible.** Keep traveler's checks, plane tickets, and ATM/credit cards in a **money belt** inside your clothes—not a "fanny pack"—along with your passport and ID. Store **a small cash reserve separate from your primary stash,** about US$50 (US dollars are easiest to change) in the depths of your pack, along with traveler's check numbers and document photocopies.

In large cities **con artists** often work in groups and may involve children. Beware of certain classics: sob stories that require money, rolls of bills "found" on the street, mustard spilled (or saliva spit) onto your shoulder as a distraction. **Never let your passport and your bags out of your sight.** Beware of **pickpockets** in city crowds and on **buses.** Be alert in public telephone booths; say your calling card number, quietly; if you punch it in, make sure no one can look over your shoulder.

If you will be traveling with electronic devices, such as a laptop computer or a PDA, check whether your homeowner's insurance covers loss, theft, or damage when you travel. If not, consider a separate insurance policy. **Safeware** (☎US 800-800-1492; www.safeware.com) specializes in computers and charges US$90 for 90-day comprehensive international travel coverage up to US$4000. It is strongly recommended that travelers to the region leave expensive electronics at home.

PRE-DEPARTURE HEALTH

In your **passport,** write the names of any people you wish to be contacted in case of a medical emergency, and list any allergies or medical conditions. Matching a prescription to a foreign equivalent is not always easy, safe, or possible. If you take prescription drugs, consider carrying up-to-date, legible prescriptions or a statement from your doctor with the medication's trade name, manufacturer, chemical name, and dosage. While traveling, be sure to keep all medication with you in your carry-on luggage. For tips on packing a basic **first-aid kit,** see p. 24.

IMMUNIZATIONS AND PRECAUTIONS

Travelers over two years old should make sure that the following vaccines are up to date: MMR (for measles, mumps, and rubella); DTaP or Td (for diphtheria, tetanus, and pertussis); IPV (for polio); Hib (for *haemophilus* influenza B); and HepB (for Hepatitis B). See **Inoculation Recommendations** below for details on vaccination. While yellow fever is not endemic to Central America, Belize, El Salvador, Honduras, and Nicaragua require a certificate of vaccination for travelers arriving from South America and sub-Saharan Africa. For recommendations on immunizations and prophylaxis, consult the CDC in the US or the equivalent in your home country, and check with a doctor for guidance.

INOCULATION RECOMMENDATIONS

There are a number of inoculations recommended for travel in Central America:

Hepatitis A, or immune globulin (IG), is a series of shots so consult your doctor a few weeks in advance.

Hepatitis B, particularly if you expect to be exposed to blood (e.g. health-care workers), have sexual contact, stay longer than 6 months, or undergo medical treatment. Hepatitis B vaccine is now recommended for all infants and for children age 12 years who did not receive the series as infants.

Rabies, for travel in rural areas or for people coming into contact with animals.

Typhoid, for travel in rural areas.

Yellow fever, for travelers to Panama who will be going outside urban areas.

As needed, booster doses for **tetanus-diphtheria** and **measles.**

Malaria pills, for travel in rural and malaria risk areas. These pills must be taken at least two weeks before and after your trip.

INSURANCE

Travel insurance covers four basic areas: medical problems, property loss, trip cancellation/interruption, and emergency evacuation. Regular insurance policies may extend to travel, but you may consider extra insurance if the cost of trip cancellation is greater than you can absorb. Full travel insurance runs about US$50 per week while trip cancellation/interruption may be purchased separately at a rate of US$3-5 per day depending on length of stay. **Medical insurance** (especially university policies) sometimes covers costs incurred abroad; **US Medicare** does not cover you abroad. **Canadian** provincial health insurance plans generally do not cover foreign travel; check with the provincial Ministry of Health or Health Plan Headquarters for details. **Homeowners' insurance** often covers theft during travel and loss of travel documents (passport, plane ticket, railpass, etc.) up to US$500. **ISIC** and **ITIC** (see p. 20) provide basic insurance benefits, including US$100 per day of in-hospital sickness for up to 60 days and US$5000 of accident-related medical reimbursement (see www.isicus.com for details). **AmEx** (US ☎ 800-528-4800) grants most cardholders automatic collision and theft car-rental insurance and ground travel accident coverage of US$100,000 on flight purchases made with the card.

INSURANCE PROVIDERS

STA (see p. 32) has a range of plans that can supplement basic coverage. Other private insurance providers in the US and Canada include: Access America (☎800-284-8300; www.accessamerica.com); Berkely Group (☎800-797-4514; www.ber-kely.com); Globalcare Travel Insurance (☎800-821-2488; www.globalcare-cocco.com); Travel Assistance International (☎800-821-2828; www.europ-assis-tance.com); and Travel Guard (☎800-826-4919; www.travelguard.com). For the UK Columbus Direct (☎020 7375 0011; www.columbusdirect.co.uk) provides insurance, while Australia has AFTA. (☎02 9264 3299; www.afta.com.au.)

USEFUL ORGANIZATIONS AND PUBLICATIONS

The US **Centers for Disease Control and Prevention** (**CDC;** ☎877-FYI-TRIP; www.cdc.gov/travel) maintains an international travelers' hotline and an informative website. The CDC's comprehensive booklet *Health Information for International Travel* (The Yellow Book), an annual rundown of disease, immunization, and general health advice, is free online or US$29-40 via the Public Health Foundation (☎877-252-1200; http://bookstore.phf.org). Consult the appropriate home government agency for consular info sheets on health, entry requirements, and other country-specific issues (see the listings in the box on **Travel Advisories,** p. 25). For quick information on health and other travel warnings, call the **Overseas Citizens Services** (☎888-407-4747 M-F 8am-8pm; after-hours ☎202-647-4000; from overseas 317-472-2328), or contact a passport agency, embassy, or consulate abroad. For information on medical evacuation services and travel insur-

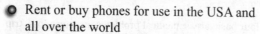

ance firms, visit the US government website at http://travel.state.gov/medical.html or the **British Foreign and Commonwealth Office** (www.fco.gov.uk). For general health info, contact the **American Red Cross** (☎ 800-564-1234; www.redcross.org).

STAYING HEALTHY

ONCE IN CENTRAL AMERICA

ENVIRONMENTAL HAZARDS

Heat exhaustion and dehydration: Avoid heat exhaustion by drinking plenty of fluids, eating salty foods (e.g. crackers), abstaining from dehydrating beverages (e.g. alcohol and caffeinated beverages), and wearing sunscreen. Continuous heat stress can lead to heatstroke, characterized by a rising temperature, severe headache, delirium, and cessation of sweating. Cool off victims with wet towels and see a doctor. Beach goers in should be careful of dehydration; symptoms include lightheadedness and vomiting.

Sunburn: Always wear sunscreen (at least SPF 30) outdoors. If you are planning on spending time near water you are at a higher risk of getting burned, even through clouds. If you get burned, drink fluids and apply an aloe-based lotion. Severe burns can lead to sun poisoning which affects the entire body, causing fever, chills, nausea, and vomiting. Sun poisoning should be treated by a doctor. Avoid falling asleep in the sun.

High Altitude: Allow your body a couple of days to adjust to less oxygen before exerting yourself. Note that alcohol is more potent and UV rays are stronger at high elevations.

INSECT-BORNE DISEASES

Many diseases are transmitted by insects—mainly mosquitoes, fleas, ticks, and lice. Be aware of insects in wet or forested areas, especially while hiking and camping; wear long pants and long sleeves, tuck your pants into your socks, and use a mosquito net. Use insect repellents such as DEET and spray your gear with permethrin (licensed in the US only for use on clothing). **Mosquitoes** (malaria, dengue fever, yellow fever, Japanese encephalitis, and others) can be particularly dangerous in wet, swampy, or wooded areas, namely the rain forests. **Ticks** (Lyme and other diseases) can be particularly dangerous in rural and forested regions.

Malaria: Transmitted by *Anopheles* mosquitoes that bite at night. The incubation period varies between 10 days and 4 weeks. Early symptoms include fever, chills, aches, and fatigue, followed by high fever and sweating, sometimes with vomiting and diarrhea. Make sure you see a doctor at least 4-6 weeks before a trip to a high-risk area to get up-to-date malaria prescriptions and recommendations. A doctor may prescribe oral prophylactics, like **mefloquine** or **doxycycline**; be aware that mefloquine can have very serious side effects, including paranoia, psychotic behavior, and nightmares.

Dengue fever: An "urban viral infection" transmitted by *Aedes* mosquitoes that bite during the day. The incubation period is 3-14 days, usually 4-7 days. Early symptoms include a high fever, severe headaches, swollen lymph nodes, and muscle aches. Patients also suffer from nausea, vomiting, and rash. See a doctor immediately, drink plenty of liquids, and take fever-reducing medication such as acetaminophen (Tylenol).

Other insect-borne diseases: Lymphatic filariasis is a roundworm transmitted by mosquitoes. Infection causes enlargement of extremities and has no vaccine. **Leishmaniasis,** a parasite transmitted by sand flies, usually occurs in rural Central America. Symptoms include fever, weakness, swelling of the spleen, and skin sores weeks to months after the bite. There is a treatment, but no vaccine. **CHAGAS disease (American trypanomiasis)** is a relatively common parasite transmitted by the cone nose and kissing bug, which infest mud, adobe, and thatch. Its symptoms are fever, heart disease, and, eventually, an enlarged intestine. There is no vaccine and limited treatment.

PERMETHRIN. Soak all your gear with Permethrin to keep the bugs away. Permethrin can be purchased in any gear shop.

FOOD- AND WATER-BORNE DISEASES

Prevention is the best cure when dealing with food and water: be sure that food is properly cooked and the drinking water is clean. Peel fruits and vegetables and avoid tap water (including ice cubes and anything washed in tap water, like salad). Beware of food from markets or street vendors that may have been cooked in unhygienic conditions. Other culprits are raw shellfish and unpasteurized milk. Buy bottled water, or purify your own water by bringing it to a rolling boil or treating it with **iodine tablets;** note, however, that some parasites such as *giardia* have exteriors that resist iodine treatment, so boiling is more reliable.

Traveler's diarrhea: Results from drinking fecally contaminated water or eating contaminated foods. Symptoms include nausea, bloating, and urgency. Eat quick-energy, non-sugary foods with protein and carbohydrates to keep strength up. Over-the-counter anti-diarrheals (e.g. Imodium) may counteract problems. The most dangerous side effect is dehydration. If you develop a fever or symptoms don't abate after 4-5 days, consult a doctor. Consult a doctor immediately for treatment of diarrhea in children.

Dysentery: Results from a serious intestinal infection caused by certain bacteria in contaminated food or water. The most common type is bacillary dysentery. Symptoms include bloody diarrhea (sometimes mixed with mucus), fever, and abdominal pain and tenderness. Dehydration can be a problem; bacillary dysentery generally only lasts a week, but it is highly contagious. Amoebic dysentery, which develops more slowly, is a more serious disease and may cause long-term damage if left untreated. A stool test can determine which kind you have; seek medical help immediately. Dysentery can be treated with the drugs norfloxacin or ciprofloxacin (commonly known as Cipro). If you are traveling in high-risk rural regions, obtain a prescription before you leave home.

Cholera: An intestinal disease caused by a bacteria found in contaminated food. Symptoms include severe diarrhea, dehydration, vomiting, and muscle cramps. See a doctor immediately; if left untreated, it may be deadly, even within a few hours. Antibiotics are available, but the most important treatment is rehydration.

Hepatitis A: A viral infection of the liver acquired primarily through contaminated water, including through shellfish. Symptoms include fatigue, fever, loss of appetite, nausea, dark urine, jaundice, vomiting, aches and pains, and light stools. The risk is highest in rural areas and the countryside, but it is also present in urban areas. There is a vaccine.

Giardiasis: Transmitted through parasites (microbes, tapeworms, etc.) and acquired via untreated water from streams or lakes. Symptoms include diarrhea, abdominal cramps, bloating, fatigue, weight loss, and nausea. If untreated it can lead to severe dehydration.

Typhoid fever: Caused by the salmonella bacteria; common in rural areas. While mostly transmitted through food and water, it can be acquired through personal contact. Symptoms include high fever, headaches, fatigue, loss of appetite, constipation, and sometimes a rash on the abdomen or chest. There is a vaccine and antibiotic treatment.

Leptospirosis: A bacterial disease caused by exposure to fresh water or soil contaminated by the urine of infected animals. Able to enter the human body through cut skin, mucus membranes, and ingestion, leptospirosis is most common in tropical climates. Symptoms include a high fever, chills, nausea, and vomiting. If not treated it can lead to liver failure and meningitis. There is no vaccine; consult a doctor for treatment.

OTHER INFECTIOUS DISEASES

Rabies: Transmitted through the saliva of infected animals (often dogs); fatal if untreated. By the time symptoms (thirst and muscle spasms) appear, the disease is in its terminal stage. Wash the wound, seek immediate medical care, and try to have the animal located. There is a vaccine, but is only semi-effective.

Hepatitis B: A viral infection of the liver transmitted via blood or other bodily fluids. Symptoms, which may not surface until years after infection, include jaundice, loss of appetite, fever, and joint pain. It can be transmitted through unprotected sex, contaminated needles, and unprotected health work. There is a vaccination; it must begin 6 months before traveling. Central America presents an intermediate risk for Hepatitis B.

Hepatitis C: Like Hepatitis B, but the mode of transmission differs. IV drug users, those with occupational exposure to blood, hemodialysis patients, and recipients of blood transfusions are at the highest risk. It can also be spread through sexual contact or sharing items like razors and toothbrushes that may have traces of blood on them. No symptoms are usually exhibited, but if any, they can include loss of appetite, abdominal pain, fatigue, nausea, and jaundice. If untreated, Hepatitis C can lead to liver failure.

OTHER HEALTH CONCERNS

MEDICAL CARE ON THE ROAD

In general, medical services in Central America are basic; only in the capital city of each country are you likely to find well-equipped facilities. Medical care is often available in emergency situations, but the quality of assistance varies widely by region. Be prepared to treat small problems yourself.

If you are concerned about obtaining medical assistance while traveling, you may wish to employ special support services. The *MedPass* from **GlobalCare, Inc.,** 6875 Shiloh Rd. East, Alpharetta, GA 30005, USA (☎800-860-1111; www.globalcare.net), provides 24hr. international medical assistance, support, and medical evacuation resources. The **International Association for Medical Assistance to Travelers (IAMAT;** Canada ☎519-836-0102; US 716-754-4883; www.cybermall.co.nz/NZ/IAMAT) has free membership, lists English-speaking doctors worldwide, and offers detailed info on immunization requirements. If your **insurance** policy does not cover travel abroad, you may wish to purchase additional coverage (see p. 27).

Those with medical conditions (diabetes, drug allergies, epilepsy, heart conditions, etc.) may want to obtain a **Medic Alert** membership (first year US$35, annually thereafter US$20), which includes a stainless steel ID tag, among other benefits, like a 24hr. collect-call number. Contact the Medic Alert Foundation, 2323 Colorado Ave, Turlock, CA 95382, USA (☎888-633-4298, outside US 209-668-3333; www.medicalert.org).

WOMEN'S HEALTH

Women traveling in unsanitary conditions are vulnerable to **urinary tract (including bladder and kidney) infections.** Over-the-counter medicines can sometimes alleviate symptoms, but if they persist, see a doctor. **Vaginal yeast infections** may flare up in hot and humid climates. Wearing loosely fitting trousers or a skirt and cotton underwear. Bring supplies from home if you are prone to infection, as they may be difficult to find on the road. **Tampons** and reliable **contraceptive devices** can be difficult to find. **Abortion** is legal throughout Central America, but generally only when the mother's life is threatened; penalties for illegal abortions are stiff.

GETTING TO CENTRAL AMERICA
BY PLANE

AIRFARES

Airfares to Central America peak between November and April; Easter and Christmas are also expensive. Midweek (M-Th morning) round-trip flights run US$40-50 cheaper than weekend flights. Not fixing a return date ("open-return") or arriving in and departing from different cities ("open-jaw") can be pricier than round-trip flights. Patching one-way flights together is the most expensive way to travel.

If Central America is only one stop on a more extensive globe-hop, consider a **round-the-world (RTW)** ticket. Tickets usually include at least 5 stops and are valid for about a year; prices range US$3400-5000. Try **Northwest Airlines/KLM** (US ☎800-447-4747; www.nwa.com) or **Star Alliance,** a consortium of 22 airlines including United Airlines (US ☎800-241-6522; www.star-alliance.com).

Roundtrip **fares** to Guatemala City, Guatemala; Belize City, Belize; Tegucigalpa and San Pedro Sula, Honduras; San Salvador, El Salvador; San José, Costa Rica; and Panama City, Panama from the US or Canada cost about US$600, US$350 in the off season (May-Oct.); from Australia AUS$2500; from Europe UD$750.

BUDGET AND STUDENT TRAVEL AGENCIES

While travel agents can make your life easy, they may not spend the time to find you the lowest possible fare—they get paid on commission. Travelers holding **ISIC** and **IYTC cards** (p. 20) qualify for discounts from student travel agencies.

CTS Travel, 30 Rathbone Pl., London W1T 1GQ, UK (☎0207 209 0630; www.ctstravel.co.uk). A British student travel agent with offices in 39 countries including the US, Empire State Building, 350 Fifth Ave., Suite 7813, New York, NY 10118 (☎877-287-6665; www.ctstravelusa.com).

STA Travel, 5900 Wilshire Blvd., Ste. 900, Los Angeles, CA 90036, USA (24hr. reservations and info ☎800-781-4040; www.sta-travel.com). A student and youth travel organization with over 150 offices worldwide (check the website for office listings), including US offices in Boston, Chicago, L.A., New York, San Francisco, Seattle, and Washington, D.C. Ticket booking, travel insurance, railpasses, and more. Walk-in offices also in Australia (☎03 9349 4344), New Zealand (09 309 9723), and the UK (0870 1 600 599).

Travel CUTS (Canadian Universities Travel Services Limited), 187 College St., Toronto, ON M5T 1P7 (☎416-979-2406; www.travelcuts.com). Offices across Canada and the US including Los Angeles, New York, Seattle, and San Francisco.

USIT, 19-21 Aston Quay, Dublin 2 (☎01 602 1777; www.usitworld.com), Ireland's leading student/budget travel agency has 22 offices throughout Northern Ireland and the Republic of Ireland. Offers programs to work in North America.

COMMERCIAL AIRLINES

The commercial airlines' lowest regular offer is the **APEX** (Advance Purchase Excursion) fare, which provides confirmed reservations and allows "open-jaw" tickets. Generally, reservations must be made 7-21 days ahead of departure, with 7-14 day minimum-stay and up to 90-day maximum-stay restrictions. These fares carry hefty cancellation and change penalties (fees rise in summer). Book peak-season APEX fares early. Use **Microsoft Expedia** (msn.expedia.com) or **Travelocity** (www.travelocity.com) to get an idea of the lowest published fares, then use the resources outlined here to try and beat those fares. Low-season fares should be appreciably cheaper than the **high-season** (Nov.-Apr.) ones listed here.

TRAVELING FROM NORTH AMERICA. Basic round-trip fares to Central America range from roughly US$250-600. Standard commercial carriers like American and United will probably offer the most convenient flights, but they may not be the cheapest, unless you find a promotion or catch the airlines in an airfare war.

TRAVELING FROM THE UK AND IRELAND. Flights from the UK and Ireland connect in major American gateway cities such as **Miami** and **Dallas.** Use the same airline for both legs of your trip as security delays can result while switching terminals. Fares range from US$400-800.

TRAVELING FROM AUSTRALIA. Qantas flies from Sydney to **San Jose, Costa Rica** via **Los Angeles.**

AIR COURIER FLIGHTS

Those who travel light should consider courier flights. Couriers help transport cargo on international flights by using their checked luggage space for freight. Generally, couriers must travel with carry-ons only and deal with complex flight restrictions. Most flights are round-trip only, with short fixed-length stays (usually one week) and a limit of a one ticket per issue. Courier flights generally depart and arrive in large cities and are not as viable in Central America as elsewhere in the world. However, good deals to the capital cities rarely surface.

TICKET CONSOLIDATORS

Ticket consolidators, or **"bucket shops,"** buy unsold tickets in bulk from commercial airlines and sell them at discounted rates. Look is in the Sunday travel section of any major newspaper (such as the *New York Times*), where many bucket shops place tiny ads. Call quickly, as availability is limited. Not all bucket shops are reliable; insist on a receipt with details of restrictions, refunds, and tickets, and pay by credit card (despite the 2-5% fee) so you can stop payment if necessary. For more info, see www.travel-library.com/air-travel/consolidators.html.

Travel Avenue (☎800-333-3335; www.travelavenue.com) searches for best available published fares and then uses several consolidators to attempt to beat that fare. **NOW Voyager,** 74 Varick St., Ste. 307, New York, NY 10013 (☎212-431-1616; fax 219-1793; www.nowvoyagertravel.com) arranges discounted flights. Other consolidators worth trying are **Interworld** (☎305-443-4929; fax 443-0351); **Pennsylvania Travel** (☎800-331-0947); **Cheap Tickets** (☎800-377-1000; www.cheaptickets.com); and **Travac** (☎800-872-8800; www.travac.com). Yet more consolidators on the web include: the **Internet Travel Network** (www.itn.com); **Travel Information Services** (www.tiss.com); **TravelHUB** (www.travelhub.com); and **The Travel Site** (www.the-travelsite.com). Keep in mind that these are just suggestions to get you started in your research; *Let's Go* does not endorse any of these agencies. As always, be cautious, and research companies before you hand over your credit card number.

CHARTER FLIGHTS

Charters are flights a tour operator contracts with an airline to fly extra loads of passengers during peak season. Charter flights fly less frequently than major airlines, make refunds particularly difficult, and are almost always fully booked. Schedules and itineraries may also change or be cancelled at the last moment (as late as 48 hr. before the trip, and without a full refund), and check-in, boarding, and baggage claim are often much slower. However, they can also be cheaper. **Discount clubs** and **fare brokers** offer members savings on last-minute charter and tour deals. Study contracts closely; you don't want to end up with an overnight layover.

BY BOAT AND BUS

There are no regularly scheduled boats from North America to Central America, but arrangements may be made on cargo ships or private yachts. When traveling from **Colombia** to Panama boats pass the Darién Gap (though you may be kidnapped and held against your will for some time) or travel by boat (see p. 684). Both of these routes are currently unsafe and not recommended.

BORDER CROSSINGS

Coming overland from North America means traveling via Mexico. Mexico has an extensive **bus** system that one can take from the US border to Guatemala or Belize. It's also possible to take your own **car,** but remember that Mexican insurance should be obtained at the border and preparation and planning is essential.

GETTING AROUND CENTRAL AMERICA

BY PLANE

Grupo Taca (www.groupotaca.com) is four of Central America's international airlines. Flying between capital cities avoids the long, arduous bus routes. **Domestic flights** are common throughout the region and are reasonably priced.

BY BUS

Everyone in Central America gets around by bus. Service varies from country to country, but the bus system is comprehensive overall. Direct, first-class trips are often available between cities; otherwise expect some harrowing adventures on what are called "chicken buses" in backpacker lingo. Worn shocks feel every bump in the rough roads, and drivers have few qualms about putting it into high

AIRCRAFT SAFETY. The airlines of developing world nations do not always meet safety standards. The *Official Airline Guide* (www.oag.com) can tell the type and age of aircraft on a particular route. This can be especially useful in Central America, where less reliable equipment is often used domestically. Grupo Taca flights are generally the standard of safety in Central America. The **International Airline Passengers Association** (US ☎800-821-4272, UK 020 8681 6555) provides region-specific info. The **Federal Aviation Administration** (www.faa.gov) reviews the airline authorities for countries whose airlines enter the US. **US State Department** advisories (☎202-647-5225; travel.state.gov/travel_warnings.html) sometimes involve foreign carriers, especially when bombings or hijackings may be a threat, though airline terrorism has not surfaced in Central America.

gear down hills. Snag a window seat (unless you're tall) to enjoy the view. Keep in mind that bus travel in much of Central America has become increasingly unsafe, especially with regards to petty crime. Traveling by bus at night can be particularly dangerous. Follow the safety instructions in the individual country chapters.

BY CAR

Roads outside of the capital cities are usually rough and unpaved and armed roadside banditry is not uncommon. Driving is possible, but not a good idea.

RENTING

Rental cars are readily available in Central America, but can be somewhat pricey, depending on the region. Cheaper cars tend to be less reliable and harder to handle on difficult terrain. Less expensive 4WD vehicles in particular tend to be more top heavy, and are more dangerous when navigating particularly bumpy roads.

RENTAL AGENCIES
In major Central American cities, national and international chains are easy to find. Well-known agencies and their local numbers are listed in the **Practical Information** sections of many cities and towns. You can generally make reservations from home by calling major international offices in your home country. To rent a car from most establishments, you need to be at least 21 years old, and most charge those aged 21-24 an additional insurance fee (about US$25 per day).

Thrifty Car Rental (☎800-847-4389, www.thrifty.com). Rents cars in Belize (US$330 per week), Costa Rica (US$102), El Salvador (US$144), Honduras (US$168), Nicaragua (US$120), and Panama (US$145). In El Salvador, Honduras, and Panama there is an additional daily surcharge of US$5 for drivers ages 21-24.

Dollar Rent-a-Car (☎800-800-3665, www.dollar.com). Rents cars in Costa Rica (US$94 per week), Guatemala (US$800), Nicaragua (US$118.20), and Panama (US$162). Additional daily fee of US$5-25 for drivers ages 21-24.

National Car Rental (☎800-227-7368, www.nationalcar.com). Rents cars in Costa Rica (US$132 per week), Honduras (US$200), and Panama (US$162). Additional daily fee of US$25 for drivers ages 21-24.

COSTS AND INSURANCE
Rates range from around US$40 per day in Costa Rica to US$140 in Guatemala, and also vary widely based on vehicle type. Expect to pay more for larger cars and for 4WD. Cars with **automatic transmission** can cost up to US$15 a day more than standard manual, and in some places, automatic transmission is unavailable.

Most rental packages in Central America offer unlimited kilometers. Return the car with a full tank of petrol to avoid high fuel charges at the end. Be sure to ask whether the price includes **insurance** against theft and collision. Remember that if you are driving a conventional vehicle on an **unpaved road** in a rental car, you are almost never covered by insurance. Cars rented on **American Express** or **Visa/Mastercard Gold or Platinum** credit cards in Central America might *not* carry the automatic insurance that they would in other countries. Insurance plans almost always come with an **excess** (or deductible) of around US$105 for conventional vehicles; deductibles increase for younger drivers and 4WD. This means you pay for all damages up to that sum, unless they are the fault of another vehicle. The excess you will be quoted applies to collisions with other vehicles; collisions with non-vehicles, such as trees, ("single-vehicle collisions") cost even more. The excess can often be reduced or waived entirely if you pay an additional charge. National chains often allow pick up in one city and drop off in another.

ON THE ROAD

Petrol (gasoline) prices vary, but average about US$1.50 per gallon in Central America. Unleaded gasoline is available in Guatemala, El Salvador, Honduras, and Costa Rica. If you must use leaded gasoline, always use the high grade/premium kind. Park your vehicle in garages or well-traveled areas, and keep valuables out of sight. When approaching a one-lane bridge, labeled *"puente angosto"* or *"solo carril,"* the first driver to flash headlights has the right of way.

DANGERS. The durability and security of your **car** are of incredible importance for successful travel in Central America. Be careful driving during the rainy season (May-Oct.), when roads are often in poor condition and landslides are common. In some areas the luxury of a 4WD vehicle may be well worth the extra rental cost. Most importantly, be sure to check with locals before venturing out on any road; carjacking and banditry has become increasingly common throughout the region.

CAR ASSISTANCE. Make sure your vehicle is ready for the road. Parts, gas, and service stations are hard to come by, so be prepared for every possible occurrence. Mechanically inclined drivers might want to order a "test" pipe from a specialty parts house to replace the converter so that the car can process regular fuel.

DRIVING PERMITS AND CAR INSURANCE

INTERNATIONAL DRIVING PERMIT (IDP). If you plan to drive a car while in Central America, you must be over 18 and have an **International Driving Permit (IDP)**, though certain countries (e.g. Costa Rica, Guatemala) allow travelers to drive with a valid American or Canadian license for a limited number of months. Info on the IDP is printed in ten languages, including Spanish. An application for an IDP usually requires two photos, a current local license, an additional form of identification, and a fee. The license is valid for one year, must be issued before you depart; contact the national or local branch of your country's automobile association.

CAR INSURANCE. Most credit cards cover standard insurance. If you rent or lease, you will need a **green card** (International Insurance Certificate) to certify you have liability insurance that applies abroad. Green cards can be obtained at rental agencies, car dealers (for leasing), some travel agents, and some border crossings.

BY THUMB

 Hitchhiking is dangerous and *Let's Go* never recommends it.

ESSENTIALS

Hitchhiking is common in most of Central America and may be the only way to get around in some places. *Let's Go* strongly urges you to consider the risks before you choose to hitchhike. Drivers expect compensation, but travelers usually pay after a ride—and rarely pay much more than bus fare. Rides are generally considered safest when offered to groups; women in particular should never hitchhike alone. Those who hitch should find out where the driver is going before getting in and think twice if he opens the door quickly and offers to drive anywhere. If you insist on hitching, don't get in without ensuring that you can get out. Letting a driver store luggage out of one's reach complicates matters should an escape be necessary—keep your luggage on your lap.

KEEPING IN TOUCH
BY MAIL

SENDING MAIL FROM CENTRAL AMERICA

Airmail is the best way to send mail home from Central America, though quality and timeliness of service varies within the region, from efficient (Belize, Costa Rica, El Salvador) to temperamental (Guatemala, Nicaragua). **Aerogrammes,** printed sheets that fold into envelopes and travel via airmail, are available at post offices. Write "airmail," "par avion," or "por avión" on the front. Most post offices will charge exorbitant fees or refuse to send aerogrammes with enclosures. **Surface mail** is by far the cheapest and slowest;—1 to 2 months to cross the Atlantic and 1 to 3 to cross the Pacific. This method is good for heavy items or non-necessities, such as souvenirs or other articles you've acquired along the way. Recognize that mail often gets delayed and time frames are inconsistent and unreliable.

In the best-case scenario, postcards and letters to the US and Canada generally take 8-10 days, though can take up to 2 weeks; to Europe and Australia the time frame is advertised as 10-14 days, though 3 weeks is not unlikely. Postcards cost anywhere between US$0.30-1, with letters a bit more expensive, around US$0.45-2. To Europe and Australia, expect to pay an average additional US$0.10. Express mail to Australia, Canada, Europe, and the US is officially 2-4 days; to Europe expect an additional 1-2 days. Postcards often get lost and have been known to delays up to 2 months. Package prices depend on weight, beginning at US$5, and experience similar delays to regular mail. If it's possible to register your mail (track or insure your packages) do so even if it costs a little more. Be prepared to have your parcel inspected. You may have problems sending post from remote areas, and many towns in the interior do not have a post office.

SENDING MAIL TO CENTRAL AMERICA

To ensure timely delivery, mark envelopes "airmail," "par avion," or "por avión." In addition to the standard postage system, **Federal Express** (www.fedex.com; Australia ☎ 13 26 10, Canada and US 800-463-3339, Ireland 1800 535 800, New Zealand 0800 733 339, UK 0800 123 800) handles most express mail services into Central America; for example, they can get a letter from New York to Central America in 4 days for US$48, and from London in 4 days for UK£45. Sending a postcard within Central America costs US$0.10, and domestic letters only slightly more expensive. The heavier the letter, the more expensive, though it will not exceed US$0.50.

It may be more reliable and efficient to send mail to a larger city. If you're sending anything remotely valuable, consider using a private carrier with offices also in Central America. See the **Essentials** section of each country chapter for more specific info on addressing mail to Central America. The delivery times below are more or less accurate for normal post, provided there are no customs delays.

Australia: www.auspost.com.au/pac. 7-8 days regular airmail. Postcard or letter up to 20g AUS$1; package up to 0.5kg AUS$10, up to 2kg AUS$65. 3-4 days EMS AUS$35.

Canada: www.canadapost.ca/personal/rates/default-e.asp. 2 weeks regular airmail. Postcard or letter up to 30g CDN$1.40; package surface mail up to 0.5kg CDN$35, up to 2kg CDN$37. 3-4 days Purolator International iCDN$145.

Ireland: www.letterpost.ie. 2 weeks regular airmail, but sometimes up to 15 weeks. Postcard or letter up to 25g €0.55; package up to 0.5kg starts at €4.50, up to 2kg starts at €11. Faster service: Swiftpost International, letter starts at €4.

New Zealand: www.nzpost.co.nz/nzpost/inrates. 1-2 weeks regular airmail. Postcard or letter up to 20g NZ$1.50-5; package up to 0.5kg starts at NZ$19, up to 2kg NZ$58. 2-5 day International Express NZ$41.

UK: www.royalmail.co.uk/calculator. 5 days regular airmail. Letter up to 20g UK£0.68; package up to 0.5kg UK£2.22, up to 2kg UK£9.50. For letters a day faster UK£4 extra.

US: http://ircalc.usps.gov. 4-7 days for regular airmail. Letter up to 1 oz. US$0.80; package up to 1 lb. US$9.25, up to 5 lb. US$22. 3-5days US Express Mail US$22.25.

RECEIVING MAIL IN CENTRAL AMERICA

There are several ways to arrange pick-up of letters sent to you by friends and relatives while you are abroad. Mail can be sent via **Poste Restante** (General Delivery in Belize; "*Lista de Correos*" in most of Central America, "*Entrega General*" in Panama) to almost any city or town with a post office. While the service is available in all seven countries, few continue to see this as a valuable and necessary system—accordingly, service suffers. If you intend to use Poste Restante, strongly consider using a main post office branch, usually in the largest or capital cities (especially since mail may be sent there regardless), and be sure it includes your name (with surname), followed by "Lista de Correos" (or "General Delivery in Belize), *Correo Central*, name of city and country. The mail will go to a special desk in the central post office. It is usually safer and quicker, though more expensive, to send mail express or registered. Bring your passport (or other photo ID) for pickup; there may be a small fee. If the clerks insist that there is nothing for you, have them check under your first name as well. *Let's Go* lists post offices in the **Practical Information** section for each city and most towns.

BY TELEPHONE

CALLING HOME FROM CENTRAL AMERICA

Central America's phone system is improving but still chock full of frustrations. National telephone offices are located in nearly every town, although in some cases better prices may be found at establishments or Internet cafes. A **pre-paid phone card** (see below) purchased there is probably your cheapest bet. Another option is a card from home; calls are billed collect or to your account. Collect call without a calling card by calling access number and following the instructions. To **obtain a card** from your national telecommunications service, contact one of the companies listed below. To **call home** with a calling card, contact the operator for your service provider in the current country in which you are traveling by dialing the appropriate toll-free access number (listed below in the second column).

COMPANY	TO OBTAIN A CARD, DIAL:
AT&T (US)	800-364-9292
Canada Direct	800-561-8868
MCI (US)	800-777-5000
Telstra Australia	13 22 00

You can usually also make **direct international calls** (see the below) from pay phones, but without a calling card, you will drop coins as quickly as words. Prepaid phone cards (see below) and occasionally major credit cards can be used for direct international calls. **MCI Worldcom** offers collect rates that are the same as calling from the US to Central America (US$0.29-.65) with a only a US$6 monthly fee for US customers. Some US carriers have surcharges if you are calling from a phone both as well.

 PLACING INTERNATIONAL CALLS. To call Central American countries from home or to call home from Central America, dial:

1. The **international dialing prefix.** To dial out of **Australia**, dial 0011; **Canada** or the **US**, 011; the **Republic of Ireland, New Zealand,** or the **UK**, 00; **South Africa**, 09; **Belize, Costa Rica, Honduras,** and **Nicaragua**, 00; **El Salvador**, 00 or 144 + 00; **Guatemala**, 00 or 130 + 00; **Panama**, 0.

2. The **country code** of the country you want to call. To call **Australia**, dial 61; **Canada** or the **US**, 1; the **Republic of Ireland**, 353; **New Zealand**, 64; **South Africa**, 27; the **UK**, 44; **Belize**, 501; **Costa Rica**, 506; **El Salvador**, 503; **Guatemala**, 502; **Honduras**, 504; **Nicaragua**, 505; **Panama**, 507.

3. The **local number.**

CALLING WITHIN CENTRAL AMERICA

The simplest way to call within the country is to use a card-based telephone, as coin-based phones are increasingly unavailable. **Prepaid phone cards,** available almost anywhere and consistently at newspaper kiosks, carry a certain amount of phone time depending on the card's denomination and rate. The computerized phone will tell you how much time, in units, you have left on your card. Another kind of prepaid telephone card comes with a Personal Identification Number (PIN) and a toll-free access number. Instead of inserting the card into the phone, you call the access number and follow the directions on the card. These cards can be used to make cheap **international calls** as well. Rates are typically highest in the morning, lower in the evening, and lowest late-night or Sunday. An new option is calling from Internet cafes which sometimes have the cheapest international rates, as they charge on a plan from a private line. From large cities, Internet phones (about US$0.20 per min. to the US; US$0.35 per min. to Europe) are becoming increasingly available. Calling card accounts such as MCI, AT&T, Bell South, and other prepaid international carriers are rarely accepted on public phones. Before settling on a calling card plan, be sure to research your options in order to pick the one that best fits both your needs and your destination.

CELLULAR PHONES

Cell phones are becoming increasingly popular and visible throughout Central America—however, in more rural areas it is still ostentatious to carry one. Ultimately, it depends on how much one expects to make phone calls. The international standard for cell phones is **GSM**, a system that began in Europe and has spread to much of the rest of the world. To make and receive calls in Central America you could use a **GSM-compatible phone** and a **SIM (subscriber identity module) card,** a country-specific, thumbnail-sized chip that gives you a local phone number and plugs you into the local network. Many SIM cards are **prepaid,** meaning that they come with calling time included and you don't need to sign up for a monthly service plan. Incoming calls are frequently free. When you use up the prepaid time, you can buy additional cards or vouchers to get more. Unfortunately, Central America is not itself hooked into the GSM system, so it will not be possible to purchase GSM equipment or accessories upon arrival. For more information on GSM phones, check out www.telestial.com, www.vodafone.com, www.orange.co.uk, www.roadpost.com, www.t-mobile.com, or www.planetomni.com. Another similar option, which is available for purchase in Central America, is a satellite phone, which you can rent before and upon arrival.

However, it is possible to rent cell phones in Central America, at the very least from airports. If the preference is to rent before arrival, various sites can be found on the internet: for example, www.rentcell.com or www.planetfone.com, www.phonerentalusa.com, or www.altel.com.ar.

 GSM PHONES. Just having a GSM phone doesn't mean you're necessarily good to go abroad. The majority of GSM phones sold in the US operate on a different frequency (1900) than international phones (900/1800) and will not work abroad. Tri-band phones work on all three frequencies (900/1800/1900) and function in most of the world. Additionally, some GSM phones are SIM-locked and will only accept SIM cards from a specific carrier. You'll need a SIM-unlocked phone to use a SIM card from a local carrier when you travel.

TIME DIFFERENCES

During the spring and summer, all of Central America is 6hr. behind **Greenwich Mean Time (GMT);** 2hr. behind New York; 1hr. ahead of Vancouver and San Francisco; 9hr. behind Johannesburg; 16hr. behind Sydney; and 18hr. behind Auckland. Panama, the lone exception, is only 5hr. behind GMT. During the winter, all of

Central America shifts forward to only 5hr. behind GMT (Panama is therefore 4hr. behind); 1hr. behind New York, 2hr. ahead of Vancouver and San Francisco; 8hr. behind Johannesburg; 17 hr. behind Sydney and 19hr. behind Auckland.

BY EMAIL AND INTERNET

Email and Internet access are becoming readily available throughout Central America. Every capital city has Internet cafes, as do many other major cities and tourist towns. In fact, Internet may be the fastest, cheapest, and most accessible mode of international communication in the region, even more so than telephone or "snail" mail. Though in some places it's possible to forge a remote link with your home server, in most cases this is a much slower (and thus more expensive) than taking advantage of free **web-based email accounts** (e.g., www.hotmail.com or www.yahoo.com). **Internet cafes** and the occasional free Internet terminal at a public library or university are listed in the **Practical Information** sections of cities and towns. For lists of additional cybercafes throughout Central America, check out www.cyber-star.com and www.planeta.com. Internet costs per hour vary significantly, increasing in cities, popular tourist locations, or difficulty of connection—on the average rates are between US$1-2.50 per hour. For information on insuring your laptop while traveling, see p. 26.

ACCOMMODATIONS

HOTELS AND HOSPEDAJES

WHAT TO EXPECT. Rooms in Central America can cost as little as US$3 per night, but usually range from US$5-10. Accommodations go by many different names; the differences between them are by no means consistent. *Hospedajes* or *casas de huéspedes* are usually the cheapest. However, there are also *hoteles*, *pensiones*, and *posadas*. Standards vary greatly, but generally speaking, for a basic room expect nothing more than a bed, a light bulb, and perhaps a fan; other amenities are a bonus. The very cheapest places may not provide towel, soap, or toilet paper. For a slight price jump you can get a room with private bath, and for a modest amount above that you might find a place with some character and charm.

 MOST IMPORTANT TIP EVER: Carry toilet paper with you. Everywhere.

AMENITIES TO LOOK FOR. In sea level areas, try to get a room with a fan (*ventilador*) or a window with a nice coastal breeze. In more upscale hotels, air conditioning will probably be available. Look for screens and mosquito netting near more tropical zones or the interior of the country. At higher elevations, hot shower and extra blankets are a must. Make safety an extra priority in urban areas; you can often get more comfort and security for only a couple extra dollars. In particular, check that doors remain locked except for keyholders; see that areas are well-lit; and consider whether the management maintains guest privacy. In isolated, non-touristed areas, accommodations will often be quite basic but friendly.

BATHROOMS. *Let's Go* quotes room prices with and without private bath. Note that "with bath" means a sink, toilet, and basic shower in the room, not an actual tub. Communal baths are typically the same sort of thing, just off the hall. Hot shower is a relative term in Central America, as "hot" can often be tepid at best. Quite frequently in rural areas and sometimes in cities, the water heating device will be electric coils in the shower head. Such devices work best at low water pressure. The electrical cord should be an easy reminder that water, electricity, and people do not mix well. Toilets in Central America often do not have seats and sewer systems cannot handle everything. As a rule, do not flush used toilet paper, tampons, or other waste products. Instead, use the receptacle (usually) provided.

GETTING A GOOD PRICE. Many countries have a hotel tax; double-check if this has been included in the rate. The prices we list are pre-tax values. Rooms shared with other travelers cost less per person. Often a hotel will first show you the most expensive room. Ask if there's anything cheaper (*¿Hay algo más barato?*). You can sometimes bargain for a lower rate at hotels, particularly during the low season or days when they are not full. A few places may also give student discounts.

BOOKING HOSTELS ONLINE. One of the easiest ways to ensure you've got a bed for the night is by reserving online. Click to the **Hostelworld** booking engine through **www.letsgo.com,** and you'll have access to bargain accommodations from Guatemala to Thailand with no added commission.

HOME EXCHANGES AND HOSPITALITY CLUBS

Home exchange offers the traveler various types of homes (houses, apartments, condominiums, villas), plus the opportunity to live like a native and to cut down on accommodation fees. For more information, contact HomeExchange.Com, P.O. Box 787, Hermosa Beach, CA 90254 USA (☎800-877-8723; www.homeexchange.com). **Hospitality clubs** link members with individuals or families abroad who are willing to host travelers for free or for a small fee to promote cultural exchange and general good karma. In exchange, members usually must be willing to host in their own homes; a small membership fee may also be required. **Global-Freeloaders.com** (www.globalfreeloaders.com) and **The Hospitality Club** (www.hospitalityclub.org) are good places to start. **Servas** (www.servas.org) is an established, more formal, peace-based organization, requiring a fee and an interview. An Internet search will find many similar organizations, some of which cater to specific travelers (e.g., women, gay and lesbian travelers, or members of certain professions.) As always, be sensitive to your new cultural environment, pay special attention to economic inequality that may exist between host and guest.

CAMPING AND THE OUTDOORS

EQUIPMENT. For lowland camping, a hammock and mosquito net are usually shelter enough—both can be easily purchased in Central America. If using a hammock, bring along a generous length of rope to reach a tree and a plastic tarp to keep you out of the rain. On the other hand, if you plan on camping at higher elevations, for example en route to a peak or volcano, a sleeping bag and other cold-weather gear will be essential. Because fuel supplies are inconsistent, camping stoves should be multi-fuel models. Camping supplies are usually available in big Central American cities, but it's better to purchase equipment before arrival.

Let's Go encourages travelers to follow the "Leave No Trace" ethic, minimizing their impact on natural environments and protecting them for future generations. Trekkers and wilderness enthusiasts should set up camp on durable surfaces, use cookstoves instead of campfires, bury human waste away from water supplies, bag trash and carry it out with them, and respect wildlife and natural objects. For more detailed information, contact the **Leave No Trace Center for Outdoor Ethics,** PO Box 997, Boulder, CO 80306, USA (☎800-332-4100 or 303-442-8222; www.lnt.org). Check out the listings below for more info on outdoor travel.

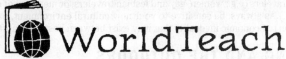

Sierra Club Books, 85 Second St., 2nd fl., San Francisco, CA 94105, USA (☎415-977-5500; www.sierraclub.org). Publishes general resource books on hiking and camping in Central America, including a guide with a particular focus on Belize.

The Mountaineers Books, 1001 SW Klickitat Way, Ste. 201, Seattle, WA 98134, USA (☎206-223-6303; www.mountaineersbooks.org). Boasts over 600 titles on hiking, biking, mountaineering, natural history, and conservation.

INTO THE WILD. Central America has hiking trails galore—from nature walks in national parks to rural paths used by locals—and provides ample opportunity for escaping all trappings of civilization. Any serious expedition requires much planning and research. However, even casual day-hikers will benefit from a few equipment basics. **Water bottles** are essential, as are **water-purification tablets** or a **filter. Raingear** in two pieces, a top and pants, is far superior to a poncho. **Synthetics,** like polypropylene tops, socks, and long underwear, retain warmth even when wet (unlike cotton). For anything beyond casual walks, good **boots** with strong ankle support are a necessity; to avoid blisters, be sure to break them in before your trip and wear layers of socks. No matter how short the hike, be sure to bring a first-aid kit, food, extra water, warm clothes, and a flashlight. For more information on **packing,** see p. 24.

ESSENTIALS

NATIONAL PARKS

The National Park systems across the isthmus vary in quality, upkeep, and regulations. Some National Parks have regulations they follow stringently, with a good ranger force and plenty of financial support to assure upkeep and protection. Others have less financial support and lack upkeep of paths and hiking trails, as well as maintenance of roads and entrances.

WILDERNESS SAFETY. Staying **warm, dry, and well-hydrated** is key to a happy and safe wilderness experience. Make sure prepare yourself for an emergency by packing a first-aid kit, a reflector, a whistle, high energy food, extra water, raingear, a hat, and mittens. For appropriate clothing

Check **weather forecasts** often and pay attention to the skies when hiking, as weather patterns can change suddenly. Always let someone—either a friend, your hostel, a park ranger, or a local hiking organization—know when and where you are going hiking. Know your physical limits and do not attempt a hike beyond your ability. See **Safety and Health,** p. 25, for information on outdoor ailments and medical concerns.

SHARKS—NOT YOUR AVERAGE JAWS. Sharks are becoming one of the main wildlife attractions in Central America, especially given the strong snorkeling and SCUBA pull of the area. Although there have been very few shark attacks in Central America and people fear them more than necessary, the following are a few tips to ensure safety. Stay our of the water at night, dusk or dawn; sharks are most active at night. Swim in a group, since sharks prefer to attack lone victims. Do not swim if you are bleeding, as sharks can detect small amounts of blood. Finally, keep close to the shore, since it will be easier for help to reach you in an emergency. In general, be careful on beaches, oftentimes there are strong undertows and rarely are beaches manned.

ORGANIZED ADVENTURE TRIPS. Organized adventure tours offer another way of exploring the wild. Activities include hiking, biking, skiing, canoeing, kayaking, rafting, climbing, photo safaris, and archaeological digs. Tourism bureaus often can suggest parks, trails, and outfitters. Make sure you hire a qualified guide who can advise you on (and help protect you from) the risks of poisonous snakes, scorpions and other dangerous insects and wildlife. Organizations that specialize in camping and outdoor equipment like REI and EMS (see above) also are good source for info. **Specialty Travel Index,** 305 San Anselmo Ave., Ste. 309, San Anselmo, CA 94960 (US ☎ 800-624-4030, elsewhere 415-455-1643; www.specialtytravel.com), is a good resource.

WHAT TO BUY

Sleeping Bag: Most sleeping bags are rated by season; "summer" means 30-40°F (around 0°C) at night; "four-season" or "winter" often means below 0°F (-17°C). Bags are made of **down** (warm and light, but expensive, and miserable when wet) or of **synthetic** material (heavy, durable, and warm when wet). Prices range US$50-$250 for a summer synthetic to US$200-$300 for a good down winter bag. Before buying a sleeping bag, look into the climate in the countries you will be traveling in. Four-season bags are a sound investment, but a summer bag will suffice for most of Central America. **Sleeping bag pads** include foam pads (US$10-$30), air mattresses (US$15-$50), and self-inflating mats (US$30-$120). Bring a **stuff sack** to store the bag and keep it dry.

Tent: The best tents are free-standing (with their own frames and suspension systems), set up quickly, and only require staking in high winds. Low-profile dome tents are the best all-around. Worthy 2-person tents start at US$100, 4-person at US$160. Make sure your tent has a rain fly and seal its seams with waterproofer. Other useful accessories include a **battery-operated lantern,** a plastic **groundcloth,** and a nylon **tarp.**

Backpacks: Internal-frame packs mold well to your back, keep a lower center of gravity, and flex adequately to allow you to hike difficult trails, while **external-frame packs** are more comfortable for long hikes over even terrain, as they carry weight higher and distribute it more evenly. Make sure your pack has a strong, padded hip-belt to transfer weight to your legs. There are models designed specifically for women. Any serious backpacking requires a pack of at least 4000 in^3 (16,000cc), plus 500 in^3 for sleeping bags in internal-frame packs. Sturdy backpacks cost anywhere from US$125 to 420—your pack is an area where it doesn't pay to economize. Either buy a **rain cover** (US$10-20) or store all of your belongings in plastic bags inside your pack.

Boots: Be sure to wear hiking boots with good ankle support. They should fit snugly and comfortably over 1-2 pairs of **wool socks** and a pair of thin **liner socks.** Break in boots over several weeks before you go to spare yourself blisters.

Other Necessities: Synthetic layers, like those made of polypropylene or polyester, and a pile jacket will keep you warm even when wet. A **space blanket** (US$5-15) will help you to retain body heat and doubles as a groundcloth. Plastic **water bottles** are vital; look for shatter- and leak-resistant models (such as those made by Nalgene). Carry **iodine tablets** for when you can't boil water. Although most campgrounds provide campfire sites, you may want to bring a small **metal grate** or **grill.** For those places that forbid fires or the gathering of firewood, you'll need a **camp stove** (the classic Coleman starts at US$50) and a propane-filled **fuel bottle** to operate it.

WHERE TO BUY IT

The list below includes both mail-order/online companies and local outlets which offer lower prices than many retail stores. A visit to a local camping or outdoors store will give you a good sense of the look and weight of certain items.

Campmor, 28 Parkway, P.O. Box 700, Upper Saddle River, NJ 07458, USA (US ☎ 800 525 4784; www.campmor.com).

Discount Camping, 880 Main North Rd., Pooraka, South Australia 5095, Australia (☎ 08 8262 3399; www.discountcamping.com.au).

Eastern Mountain Sports (EMS), 1 Vose Farm Rd., Peterborough, NH 03458, USA (☎ 888-463-6367; www.ems.com). Look for local branches.

L.L. Bean, Freeport, ME 04033 (US and Canada ☎800-441-5713, UK 0800 891 297; www.llbean.com).

Mountain Designs, 51 Bishop St., Kelvin Grove, Queensland 4059, Australia (☎07 3856 2344; www.mountaindesigns.com).

Recreational Equipment, Inc. (REI), Sumner, WA 98352, USA (US and Canada ☎800-426-4840, elsewhere 253-891-2500; www.rei.com). Look for local branches.

SPECIFIC CONCERNS

RESPONSIBLE TRAVEL

As the number of travelers on the road continues to rise, the detrimental effect on natural environments becomes an increasing concern. With this in mind, *Let's Go* promotes the philosophy of **sustainable travel.** Through a sensitivity to issues of ecology and sustainability, today's travelers can be a powerful force in preserving and restoring the places they visit. The choices you make during your trip can have potent effects on local communities—for better or for worse. Travelers who care about the destinations and environments they explore need to be aware of the social, cultural and political implications of their actions.

Ecotourism, a rising trend in sustainable travel, focuses on conserving natural habitats and using them to build up the economy without exploitation or overdevelopment. Travelers can make a difference by doing advance research and by supporting organizations and establishments that pay attention to their impact on their natural surroundings and strive to be environmentally-friendly.

Community-based tourism channels tourist money into the local economy by emphasizing programs run by members of the host community and often benefit disadvantaged groups. Community development and sustainable development through micro-level companies and cooperatives are an example of new activism in Central America. An excellent resource for general information on community-based travel is *The Good Alternative Travel Guide* (UK£10, plus postage), a project of **Tourism Concern** (☎020 7133 3330; www.tourismconcern.org.uk).

Environmental damage, cultural conflict, child sex tourism, and displacement are among the many issues currently facing Central American countries. In order to learn more about the problems facing the region, how your presence influences Central American people and environment, www.bigvolcano.com.au/ercentre/assoc.htm has links to relevant regional ecotourism sites; likewise, Planeta (www.planeta.com) and www.earthfoot.org are a good resources for parts of the Americas. Also see our **Alternatives to Tourism** section, p. 53.

TRAVELING ALONE

There are many benefits to traveling alone, including independence and greater interaction with locals. On the other hand, any solo traveler is a more vulnerable target of harassment and street theft. As a lone traveler, try not to stand out as a tourist, look confident, and be especially careful in deserted or very crowded areas. If questioned, never admit you are traveling alone. Maintain regular contact with someone at home who knows your itinerary. For more tips, pick up *Traveling Solo* by Eleanor Berman (Globe Pequot Press, US$15), visit www.travelaloneandloveit.com, or subscribe to **Connecting: Solo Travel Network,** 689 Park Rd., Unit 6, Gibsons, BC V0N 1V7, Canada (☎604-886-9099; www.cstn.org; membership US$28-$45).

ESSENTIALS

ESSENTIALS

WOMEN TRAVELERS

Women exploring on their own inevitably face some additional safety concerns, but it's easy to be adventurous without taking undue risks. Consider staying in hostels which offer single rooms that lock from the inside or in religious organizations with rooms for women only. Stick to centrally located accommodations and avoid solitary late-night treks or bus rides. The largest cities in Central America are known as being unsafe for solo women explorers—talk with locals about the specific concerns of this area.

Always carry extra money for a phone call, bus, or taxi. **Hitchhiking** is never safe for lone women, or even for two women traveling together. Look as if you know where you're going and approach older women or couples for directions if you're lost or uncomfortable. Generally, the less you look like a tourist, the better off you'll be. Dress conservatively, especially in rural areas. Try to dress as the women might dress in your country of travel. Wearing a conspicuous **wedding band** sometimes helps to prevent unwanted overtures.

Your best answer to verbal harassment is no answer at all; feigning deafness, sitting motionless, and staring straight ahead at nothing in particular will do a world of good that reactions usually don't achieve. The extremely persistent can sometimes be dissuaded by a firm, loud, and very public "Go away!" in the appropriate language. Don't hesitate to seek out a police officer, a store clerk, or a passerby if you are being harassed. Some countries have a **policía turística** specifically geared toward travelers. Memorize the local emergency numbers and consider carrying a whistle on your keychain. A self-defense course will prepare you for a potential attack and raise your awareness level of the surroundings (see **Self Defense**, p. 26). Also, pay attention to the health concerns facing female travelers (see p. 31).

GLBT TRAVELERS

Attitudes toward gay, lesbian, bisexual, and transgendered (GLBT) travelers are particular to each country. In **Belize** and **Nicaragua** homosexual activity is **illegal**, while the cities of San Jose, Manuel Antonio, and Quepos in **Costa Rica** are surprisingly tolerant. While Costa Rica has the most travel-friendly infrastructure for GLBT travelers, the other countries are becoming increasingly open and tolerant and gay bars are beginning to open in major cities and particularly touristy areas. However, this is a very recent development, and overwhelming intolerance cannot be understated—be careful about open association and realize that machismo and very strict gender role expectations are the norm. Keeping a low profile about your sexuality is probably your best bet. Homosociality (camaraderie between members of the same sex, particularly men) is much more common than you may be accustomed to; hand-holding between two men cannot be interpreted according to typical "Western" norms. To avoid hassles at airports and border crossings, transgendered travelers should make sure that all of their travel documents are consistent with respect to the gender that they report.

A number of contact organizations give advice and help gay travelers find existing organizations in the region. A good source is Richard Stern, at **Asociación Triángulo Rosa** in Costa Rica. (☎258 0214, English 234 2411; atritosa@sol.racsa.co.cr. Open M-F 8am-noon and 1-5pm.) **Out and About** (www.outandabout.com) offers a bi-weekly newsletter addressing travel concerns and keeps a continually updated newsbank of events in Central America. Listed below are organizations which offer materials addressing some specific concerns. The online newspaper **365gay.com** also has a travel section (www.365gay.com/travel/travelchannel.htm), though it does not focus on Central America. Guidemag (www.guidemag.com) and GuiaGay (www.guiagay.com) both cover GLBT travel experiences, largely through reader postings. The former site will unite travelers with similar interests.

Gay's the Word, 66 Marchmont St., London WC1N 1AB, UK (☎+44 20 7278 7654; www.gaystheword.co.uk). The largest gay and lesbian bookshop in the UK, with both fiction and non-fiction titles. Mail-order service available.

Giovanni's Room, 1145 Pine St., Philadelphia, PA 19107, USA (☎215-923-2960; www.queerbooks.com). An international lesbian/feminist and gay bookstore with mail-order service.

TRAVELERS WITH DISABILITIES

Traveling in Central America with disabilities can be very difficult, especially for travelers on a budget. Sidewalks are narrow and in disrepair; streets are busy and disorganized; safety is already a challenge for travelers without disability. Transportation is generally not wheelchair accessible, so planning with a tour group, though expensive, may be the best (or only) option. Those with disabilities should inform airlines and hotels of their disabilities when making reservations; some time may be needed to prepare special accommodations. Call ahead to restaurants, museums, and other facilities to find out if they are handicapped-accessible. **Guide dog owners** should inquire as to the quarantine policies of each destination country. The listings below are some organizations that can help plan your trip.

Accessible Journeys, 35 West Sellers Ave., Ridley Park, PA 19078, USA (☎800-846-4537; www.disabilitytravel.com). Designs tours for wheelchair users and slow walkers. The site has tips and forums for all travelers.

Getting Away, www.gettingaway.com, is a website with links to other sites, books, and resources for international travel, study, and work opportunities. In particular, Patricia Smither's book on planning travel for people with disabilities—*Access for Disabled Americans: A Guide for the Wheelchair Traveler* ($21) is a good resource.

Mobility International USA (MIUSA), PO Box 10767, Eugene, OR 97440, USA (☎541-343-1284; www.miusa.org). Provides a variety of books and other publications containing information for travelers with disabilities.

Society for Accessible Travel & Hospitality (SATH), 347 Fifth Ave., #610, New York, NY 10016, USA (☎212-447-7284; www.sath.org). An advocacy group that publishes free online travel information and the travel magazine *OPEN WORLD* (annual subscription US$13, free for members). Annual membership US$45, students and seniors US$30.

MINORITY TRAVELERS

More likely than not, if you are a tourist in Central America, you are the minority, especially if you are white. No matter what you may try to do to disguise it, Central Americans can spot a *"gringo"* from a mile away. This is not necessarily a bad thing; tourism is an important industry in many of the countries in the region and locals often go out of their way to cater to foreigners. However, tourists are at an especially high risk in some of the region's more dangerous areas. Anti-Western, and especially Anti-American sentiment may still be strong in some of the more war-torn countries, where the US funded and trained brutal military forces during the cold war. Travelers need to always be aware of the fact that they not only stick out, but are a prime target for Central America's less scrupulous residents.

DIETARY CONCERNS

Vegetarian cuisine is not hard to find in Central America's more touristed, cosmopolitan cities, but in more remote areas, beans and rice may become the only option. Many eateries in Central America do not consider pork or chicken to be "meat"; if you are concerned about the specific ingredients of dishes listed on the menu, be sure to ask very specific questions. For a brief lexicon of common foods, see the **Appendix** (p. 688). For travelers with specific religious or dietary concerns, living a vegetarian lifestyle while on the road might be a helpful, albeit compromised, alternative. Caution is advised in restaurants where many "vegetarian" dishes are cooked in a pork base.

The **North American Vegetarian Society,** P.O. Box 72, Dolgeville, NY 13329 (☎518-568-7970; www.navs-online.org), publishes information about vegetarian travel. The travel section of the The Vegetarian Resource Group's website, at www.vrg.org/travel, has a comprehensive list of organizations and websites that are geared toward helping vegetarians and vegans abroad. For more information, visit your local bookstore or health food store, and consult *The Vegetarian Traveler: Where to Stay if You're Vegetarian, Vegan, Environmentally Sensitive,* by Jed and Susan Civic (Larson Publications; US$13). Vegetarians will also find numerous resources on the web; try www.vegdining.com, www.happycow.net, and www.vegetariansabroad.com, for starters.

Travelers who keep kosher should contact synagogues in larger cities for information on kosher restaurants. Your own synagogue or college Hillel should have access to lists of Jewish institutions around the world. If you are strict in your observance, you may have to prepare your own food on the road. A good resource is the *Jewish Travel Guide,* edited by Michael Zaidner (Vallentine Mitchell; US$17). Travelers looking for halal restaurants may find www.zabihah.com a useful resource. According to http://shamash.org/kosher/, Panama is the only Central American country with kosher restaurants. More info on dietary concerns in Latin America can also be found through these resources:

The Vegetarian Traveler: Where to Stay if You're Vegetarian, Jed and Susan Civic. (Larson Publications; US$13). Covers only Costa Rica.

The Jewish Travel Guide, Jewish Chronicle staff (International Special Book Services; US$17). Lists synagogues, kosher restaurants, and Jewish institutions in Guatemala, Honduras, Costa Rica, and Panama.

Latin American Vegetarian Resources (www.vrg.org/travel/largupdate.htm) is a comprehensive resource of healthy regional stores and vegetarian restaurants as well as books pertaining to vegetarian issues.

OTHER RESOURCES

Let's Go tries to cover all aspects of budget travel, but we can't put *everything* in our guides. Listed below are books and websites that can serve as jumping-off points for your own research.

Hippocrene Books, Inc., 171 Madison Ave., New York, NY 10016, USA (☎718-454-2366; www.hippocrenebooks.com). Publishes foreign language dictionaries and language learning guides.

Hunter Publishing, PO Box 746 Walpole, MA 02081, USA (☎800-255-0343; www.hunterpublishing.com). Has an extensive catalog of travel guides and diving and adventure travel books.

Rand McNally, P.O. Box 7600, Chicago, IL 60680, USA (☎847-329-8100; www.randmcnally.com), publishes road atlases.

Alfatravelguide.com www.alfatravelguide.com focuses entirely on Central America and allows you to make reservations directly from the site.

BootsnAll.com: www.bootsnall.com. Numerous resources for independent travelers, from planning your trip to reporting on it when you get back.

How to See the World: www.artoftravel.com. A compendium of great travel tips, from cheap flights to self defense to interacting with local culture.

ESSENTIALS

Lycos: cityguide.lycos.com. General introductions to cities and regions throughout Central America, accompanied by links to applicable histories, news, and local tourism sites.

Travel Intelligence: www.travelintelligence.net. A large collection of travel writing by distinguished travel writers.

Travel Library: www.travel-library.com. A fantastic set of links for general information and personal travelogues.

World Hum: www.worldhum.com. An independently produced collection of "travel dispatches from a shrinking planet."

Atevo Travel: www.atevo.com/guides/destinations. Detailed introductions, travel tips, and suggested itineraries.

CIA World Factbook: www.odci.gov/cia/publications/factbook/index.html. Tons of vital statistics on the geography, government, economy, and people from countries in Central America.

Drive to Mexico, Pan American Highway, and Central America: www.drivemeloco.com.

PlanetRider: www.planetrider.com. A subjective list of links to the "best" websites covering the culture and tourist attractions of Belize, Costa Rica, El Salvador, Guatemala, Honduras, Nicaragua, and Panama.

Travel Documents and Visas: www.traveldocs.com. Lets you download visa applications for any country and will process the documents for you for a fee.

World Travel Guide: www.travel-guides.com has general overviews of all the countries in the region.

WWW.LETSGO.COM Our freshly redesigned website features extensive content from our guides; community forums where travelers can connect with each other and ask questions or advice—as well as share stories and tips; and expanded resources to help you plan your trip. Visit us soon to browse by destination, find information about ordering our titles, and sign up for our e-newsletter!

ESSENTIALS

A Joint Domestic and International Effort

Through the Organization of American States (OAS) and the United Nations (UN), foreign governments have played a key role in settling conflicts and building peace in Central America. Initially, the OAS was asked to investigate the Costa Rica/Nicaragua border disputes (1948-1979). In 1969, civilian OAS peacekeepers settled a conflict between Honduras and El Salvador. The UN became involved in peacekeeping in 1989, when the governments of Costa Rica, El Salvador, Guatemala, Honduras and Nicaragua requested assistance to implement a collective peace accord.

In **Nicaragua,** the OAS oversaw the 1990 elections with volunteers from across the Americas. After the Sandinista loss, the OAS was asked by Nicaragua and the US to monitor the transfer of power to the new government, and to assist in settling and rebuilding the country. In baseball fields across the country, contras lined up to hand over weapons to UN disarmament officers in exchange for OAS documentation, food rations, a physical, and onward transportation.

After the war ended and about 10,000 contras were demobilized, OAS peacekeepers played a dual role as relief and development workers, providing food rations, investigating human rights complaints, facilitating community development projects, and mediating armed conflicts. Funded by the US government, the OAS program tried to settle the contras. It was hard to achieve peace when serving only one part of the population, so the OAS turned to the European Union for funds to assist former Sandinistas.

As it turned out, the contras had kept almost as many weapons as they had handed over to the UN. So when the government failed ot improve their living conditions, they dug up their spare AK-47's from their backyards and formed various "recontra" groups. They set up roadblocks, took over municipalities, and grounded air traffic until the government agreed to concessions. They soon realized that their post-war situation was no different from that of Sandinista peasants, who—like them—had left their homes at a young age and did not know how to farm. Moreover, the rank and file members of the contras had enlisted not for ideology but for work, and often had relatives in the Sandinista army. So in the early 1990s, they joined forces to form a group popularly known as *los revueltos* (as in *huevos revueltos,* or scrambled eggs), and it took several years before peace-building was assumed by the Nicaraguan government and local organizations.

In **El Salvador,** after a decade of violent conflict, the government and Frente Farabundi Martí para la Liberación Nacional (FMLN) agreed to peace talks under UN arbitration, ending the war in 1992. The UN peacekeepers carried out military and civilian activities like those undertaken by the OAS and UN in Nicaragua. The OAS was not invited to do the same in El Salvador because the FMLN thought there may be bias from its previous work in Nicaragua. However, the UN had learned a few lessons: after the post-war presidential and legislative elections in 1994, the UN peacekeeping mission ended and they handed responsibilities to local organizations and police.

In the two years leading up to the 1996 peace agreement in **Guatemala,** UN human rights monitors, legal experts, indigenous specialists and police carried out verification and institution-building activities. In 1997, the UN added military and civilian observers to verify hostility cessation, separation and concentration of forces, and the disarmament and demobilization of almost 3000 former Unidad Revolucionaria Nacional Guatamalteca (URNG) combatants.

An important task was to settle land conflicts. As a result of the war, government presence in rural areas was limited to the military, who were accustomed to resolving conflicts through force. Land ownership tensions intensified with the return of refugees and those displaced during the war, since other peasants had occupied their land. Another important challenge for peacekeepers was to find new land for indigenous groups who had fled from the army. They formed communities in the mountains and wanted to be resettled with their fellow resisters. Although international peacekeeping in Guatemala had a positive impact, one shortcoming was that it publicized information in Spanish, not local languages. As a result, benefits didn't reach many indigenous communities.

Today, peace-building efforts are maintained by Central American citizens through non-profit organizations, governments, and local UN volunteers. Although in the long term sustaining peace in the region depends on locals, foreign observers continue to be present and needed. Volunteers with Peace Brigades International in Guatemala and Christians for Peace in El Salvador work with refugees, labor unions, indigenous and peasant groups, human rights organizations, and churches. In Nicaragua, Witness for Peace educates delegations of visitors on the impact of global economics, corporate practices, and US foreign, economic and military policies.

Sarah Dix received her BA and Ph.D from Yale University, after which she earned a Masters in Public Policy from Harvard. She was previously an OAS analyst in Nicaragua and Peru, and now lectures in the Social Studies Department at Harvard University, where she is currently studying judicial politics in Argentina.

ALTERNATIVES TO TOURISM

Traveling through a country or region for several weeks is an exciting and memorable experience. But if you are looking for a more rewarding way to see the world, you may want to consider more long-term opportunities. Working, volunteering, or studying can be an enriching way to explore and understand Central America. This chapter outlines some of the different opportunities available in the region. Numerous programs operate out of all seven nations and provide a wide variety of experiences, from helping disabled children in Honduras to studying ecology in Costa Rica and Belize. The complex issues facing Central American countries, include ecological preservation and growing economies. The rich and diverse cultures further enrich extended stays and give insight into unique communities. **Entrance requirements** and **visa information** are listed in the individual **Alternatives to Tourism** section at the beginning of each country chapter.

 ONLINE INFO. Start your search at ▓ **www.beyondtourism.com,** Let's Go's brand-new searchable database of Alternatives to Tourism, where you can find exciting feature articles and helpful program listings divided by country, continent, and program type.

STUDYING IN CENTRAL AMERICA

LANGUAGE SCHOOLS

Language schools are typically independently run organizations that do not offer college credit. While it is possible to study language at local universities (see below), language schools are a good alternative if you desire a less rigorous course load. Programs are especially popular in Guatemala, Costa Rica, and Nicaragua, but are also available in El Salvador, Honduras, and Panama. Most **language schools** include meals and a homestay with the instructor or an affiliated family. Packages generally costs US$100-140 per week, including five days of instruction. Choose a school based not only on relative quality but also on location; the social climate of urban centers and a sleepy villages are very different. Below are places to begin your search; the sites with the widest selection usually take a small commission or have booking fees:

123teachme (www.123teachme.com). A good international language school database. Browse by cost or quality of instruction. Over 700 programs listed.

Languageschoolsguide.com (www.languageschoolsguide.com). A wide base of options, including study abroad programs and job opportunities.

Amerispan (www.amerispan.com). A language school travel agent. US$100 fee.

Planeta (http://www.planeta.com/schoolist.html#CA). Planeta maintains a small but free list of direct links to Central American language schools.

STUDYING ABROAD

Study abroad programs take place in universities and range from basic language and culture courses to college-level classes. In order to choose a program that best fits your needs, you will want to find out what kind of students participate in the program and what sort of accommodations are provided. In programs that serve large groups of English-speaking students, you may feel more comfortable in the community, but you will not have the same opportunity to practice a foreign language or befriend other students. For accommodations, dorm life provides a better opportunity to mingle with fellow students, but there is less of a chance to experience the local scene and day-to-day life in that country.

Those relatively fluent in Spanish may find it cheaper to enroll directly in a university abroad, although getting college credit may be more difficult. Some American schools still require students to pay them for credits they obtain elsewhere. Most university-level study-abroad programs are meant as language and culture enrichment opportunities, and therefore are conducted in Spanish. Still, many programs do offer classes in English and beginner- and lower-level language courses. Try **www.study-abroad.com,** which has links to various semester abroad programs based on a variety of criteria, including desired location and focus of study.

VOLUNTEERING

Volunteering in Central America can be one of the most fulfilling and challenging experiences of your life. The few volunteer opportunities available in the region range from humanitarian aid to teaching to environmental work, with a preference for Spanish speakers. Many volunteer services charge you a fee to participate in the program and to do work. These fees can be surprisingly hefty, and while they likely cover most living expenses, they often do not include airfare. As with any trip, it is important to do research on a program before committing.

Most people choose to go through a parent organization that takes care of logistical details, and frequently provides a group environment and support system. There are two main types of organizations—religious (often Catholic) and non-sectarian—although there are rarely participatory restrictions for either. Each country chapter has a short list of its own volunteer programs, but the resources listed below will help you find programs that match your particular interests. As always, each country's Embassy may have networks of voluntary organizations to which they can direct you.

Most volunteer programs in Central America involve living conditions you may not be used to—talk to people who have previously participated and find out exactly what you're getting into, as living and working conditions can vary greatly by program. The more informed you are and the more realistic expectations you have, the more enjoyable the program will be.

ORGANIZATIONS

Habitat for Humanity International, 121 Habitat St., Americus, GA 31709, USA (☎229-924-6935 ext. 2551; www.habitat.org). Volunteers build houses in over 83 countries for varying length of time from 2 weeks to 3 years. Short-term program costs US$1200-4000.

Peace Corps, Office of Volunteer Recruitment and Selection, 1111 20th St., NW, Washington, D.C., 20526, USA (☎800-424-8580; www.peacecorps.gov). Operates across Central America.

United Nations Volunteers, Postfach 260 111, D-53153 Bonn, Germany (☎49 228 815 2000; www.unv.org). Created in 1970 to encourage development in regions needing assistance. The website has info about Central American opportunities as well as recruitment details.

ONLINE RESOURCES

Do-it.org (www.do-it.org.uk). A search engine based in the UK with an extensive international volunteering section, conveniently divided into student, environment, professional, and cultural foci.

Idealist.org (www.idealist.org). This search engine is geared toward organizations that provide opportunities for ecological, educational and humanitarian volunteering. Over 100 Central American listings. Type in your country of choice and go to town.

Transitions Abroad.com (www.transitionsabroad.com/listings/work/volunteer/index.shtml), offers a broad array of volunteer programs in Central America and across the world.

Volunteer Abroad.com (www.volunteerabroad.com). An online directory of overseas volunteer programs. Searching under "Latin America" yields over 225 volunteer options in Central America.

ALTERNATIVES TO TOURISM

ESSAY CONTEST WINNER!

beyondtourism.com

Last year's winner, Eleanor Glass, spent a summer volunteering with children on an island off the Yucatan Peninsula. Read the rest of her story and find your own once-in-a-lifetime experience at **www.beyondtourism.com!**

"... I was discovering elements of life in Mexico that I had never even dreamt of. I regularly had meals at my students' houses, as their fisherman fathers would instruct them to invite the nice gringa to lunch after a lucky day's catch. Downtown, tourists wandered the streets and spent too much on cheap necklaces, while I played with a friend's baby niece, or took my new kitten to the local vet for her shots, or picked up tortillas at the tortilleria, or vegetables in the mercado. ... I was lucky that I found a great place to volunteer and a community to adopt me. ... Just being there, listening to stories, hearing the young men talk of cousins who had crossed the border, I know I went beyond tourism." - Eleanor Glass, 2004

HYDROELECTRIC POWER: PROJECT BORUCA

Officials at the *Instituto Costaric-ense de Electricidad* (ICE), which is privately operated but government-owned, have pro-posed the placement of a new hydroelectric dam in the middle of the Boruca indigenous reserve. This plan, which would create a plant that could power most of Central America, has garnered massive amounts of controversy. Damming the Río Térraba would create an enormous lake, destroy-ing the habitat of thousands of species. It is also unclear what reparations would be made to the indigenous people whose land the dam would flood; they unhappily predict that they will simply be paid to relocate.

The government claims that the lake will promote tourism, pro-viding a location for new luxury hotels and resorts. But indige-nous poeple assert that their cul-ture is already a draw for travelers, and that after the erec-tion of the dam their skills will no longer be as marketable in a new location. Another obstacle to the project is that the lake would wash out part of the Interameri-can Highway. Options for recon-structing this section are limited, and the most convenient location to re-route the road is through the Parque Internacional La Amistatd, a move strongly opposed by con-servationists.

LITERATURE

Alternatives to the Peace Corps: A directory of third world and U.S. Volunteer Opportunities, by Joan Powell. Food First Books, 2000 (US$10).

How to Live Your Dream of Volunteering Overseas, by Collins, DeZerega, and Heckscher. Penguin Books, 2002 (US$17).

International Directory of Voluntary Work, by Pybus and Whet-ter. Peterson's Guides and Vacation Work, 2000 (US$16).

International Jobs, by Kocher and Segal. Perseus Books, 1999 (US$18).

Overseas Summer Jobs 2002, by Collier and Woodworth. Peterson's Guides and Vacation Work, 2002 (US$18).

Work Abroad: The Complete Guide to Finding a Job Overseas, by Hubbs, Griffith, and Nolting. Transitions Abroad Publish-ing, 2000 (US$16).

BIOLOGY/ECOLOGY PROGRAMS

Sustainable travel has become a central element of the Let's Go travel philosophy, parallel with the increasing number of environmental projects throughout the region. A rising trend in this form of travel is **ecotourism,** which focuses on the conserva-tion of natural habitats and the promotion of local economies without exploitation or over develop-ment. A plethora of ecological and environmental volunteer and work opportunities abound in Central America. Everything from spreading awareness in urban or more rural villages, to sustainable develop-ment and farming, to research, to outright work in the great outdoors--be it near water or rainforest--is available and is becoming an ever greater focus for these countries. Some of the most exciting opportu-nities include volunteer work preserving endangered turtle species in Costa Rica and Panama; sustainable coffee farming in Nicaragua; and environmental awareness education in Honduras.

Most programs make arrangements in weekly increments, and the majority stipulate a minimum stay period (since many of these programs necessi-tate volunteer training and some education in a spe-cific area). Though these opportunities often do not offer reimbursement, it may be possible to negotiate some support, for example room and/or board in exchange for English lessons. An excellent resource for ecological programs is **Rare** (☎703 522 5070; www.rarecenter.org), an international nonprofit that encourages sustainable and ecologically conscious tourist practices in Belize, Guatemala, El Salvador and Honduras.

WORKING

Some travelers want **long-term** jobs that enable them to get to know another part of the world while developing international connections (e.g. teaching English, working in the tourist industry). Other travelers seek out **short-term** jobs to finance their travel. They usually seek employment in the service sector, working for a few weeks at a time to finance the next leg of their journey. Most Central American countries do not need unskilled workers from abroad to perform the menial tasks that natives fight for a stab at. Bilingual speakers may find more opportunities in the cities, for example as secretaries. This section discusses both short-term and long-term opportunities for working in Central America. Each Central American country has slightly differing requirements for work visas—inquire with local consulates for more information and the appropriate paperwork. (see each country's **Alternatives to Tourism** section.) Finding a job in Central America will take a great amount of personal initiative. In general, employers seek college graduates with some proficiency in Spanish, but most importantly they expect dedication, responsibility, and respect for the job. Allow yourself enough time for gathering the necessary documents and for clearance, which often takes a few weeks.

LONG-TERM WORK

If you're planning on spending a substantial amount of time (more than three months) working in Central America, search for a job well in advance. International placement agencies are often the easiest way to find employment abroad, especially for teaching English. **Internships,** usually for college students, are a good way to segue into working abroad, although they are often unpaid or poorly paid (many say the experience, however, is well worth it). Be wary of advertisements or companies that claim the ability to get you a job abroad for a fee—often times the same listings are available online or in newspapers, or even out of date.

TEACHING ENGLISH

Teaching jobs abroad are rarely well-paid. Volunteering as a teacher in lieu of paying for room, board, and services is also a popular option, and even in those cases, teachers often get some sort of daily stipend to help with living expenses. Though salaries at private schools may be low compared to the US, a low cost of living makes it profitable. In almost all cases, you must have at least a bachelor's degree to be a full-fledged teacher, although often

THE LOCAL STORY

PEACE: A CHEESY IDEA

Marvin Rockwell was part of the original group of Quakers who came to Monteverde in 1951. Rockwell moved to Costa Rica with 43 other Quakers at the age of 28. Since then, he spent time in San José and Indiana, but has returned to Monteverde to run a few cabinas, a small restaurant, and a cheese factory.

On their cheese history: We wanted something for cash that wouldn't be too perishable. So we brought 50 white heifers up from Central Valley, built a little factory, and started making cheese...we were in correspondence with a couple who was organizing a milk-processing plant in Japan...that was the expertise we started with. The first week's production was 350 lb. and now the company makes 700 lb. per day...our cheese is sold all over Costa Rica and El Salvador, Panama, Honduras, Nicaragua.

On local tourism: Biologists and students started coming after the opening of the reserve in 1972. Monteverde became known as the "naturalist" place for people to come [laughs]. In 1977 there were only 3 places to stay, but everything's different now.

On the original group: There were 44 founders...of the original only 8 are still around. My sister is 97. The membership is currently around 70...we didn't want to form a little isolated community set down in Costa Rica, we wanted to become a part of the country, and I think we have.

times college undergraduates can get summer positions teaching or tutoring. There are an increasing number of international programs that arrange English-teaching positions in foreign schools.

Many schools require teachers to have a **Teaching English as a Foreign Language (TEFL)** certificate. This does not necessarily exclude you from finding a teaching job, but certification often yields higher pay. Native English speakers working in private schools are most often hired for English-immersion classrooms where no Spanish is spoken. Those volunteering or teaching in poorer public schools are more likely to be working in both English and Spanish. Placement agencies or university fellowship programs are the best resources for finding teaching jobs in Central America. The alternative is to make direct contact with schools or try your luck once you get there. If you are going to attempt the latter, the best time of the year is several weeks before the start of the school year. Two solid resources are **www.jobsabroad.com** and **World Teach, Inc.,** Center for International Development, 79 John F. Kennedy St., Cambridge MA 02138 (☎800-4-TEACH-0 or 617-495-5527; fax 617-495-1599; www.worldteach.org. Fees US$4000-$6000.)

SHORT-TERM WORK

Traveling for long periods of time can get expensive; many travelers try their hand at odd jobs on the road to make extra cash for another month or two of touring around. Another option is to work several hours a day at a hostel in exchange for free or discounted room and/or board. Most often, these short-term jobs are found by word of mouth or by talking to restaurant and hotel owners. However, it is often difficult to find short-term work due to lagging economies.

BELIZE

The least inhabited country in Central America, tiny, English-speaking Belize is graced with nearly untouched natural beauty and stable politics, leading to one of the most developed tourist infrastructures in the region. With a multi-racial population of 250,000 and a predominantly Caribbean atmosphere, Belize is also the only country in Central America where reggae is more common than *salsa*. Though a bit pricier than its neighbors, the country is extremely accessible: transportation is easy, and few other places in the world offer such mind-boggling biological and geographic diversity in such a small space (23,000 sq. km). In fact, ecotourism has bloomed into the nation's leading moneymaker; luckily, commercial development still remains modest. While Belize has its share of Maya ruins, they are less outstanding than their Guatemalan counterparts, and the nation's most popular destinations are its dozens of coastal cayes and national parks, nearly twenty of which have been set aside for conservation.

In one day, a enthusiastic traveler could snorkel the second-largest barrier reef in the Northern and Western hemispheres, scale Maya temples, and slide down waterfalls in a pine forest, stopping along the way at a jaguar or baboon preserve. And after savoring inexpensive lobster and sipping smooth Belikin beers on one of the country's many idyllic beaches, many find they never want to move again. Thousands of travelers come each year to explore the country's wonders and affirm the tourist bureau's slogan, "You better Belize it."

HIGHLIGHTS OF BELIZE

Colorful coral and fish in the **Belize Barrier Reef**, minutes from **Ambergris Caye**, Belize's most popular destination, and relaxed, budget-friendly **Caye Caulker** (p. 74).

The outdoor wonderland around **San Ignacio**, where Maya ruins, spectacular caves, pine-covered mountains, and jungle rivers are all ready to be explored (p. 97).

A dozen miles of perfect beach lead to the village of **Placencia**, in which sand, coconuts, reggae, and lobster burritos combine to create a piece of paradise (p. 112).

SUGGESTED ITINERARIES

1-2 WEEKS: NORTHERN BELIZE AND THE CAYES. This route has the best of all worlds: Maya ruins and nature preserves, and the brilliant blue ocean of the relaxing cayes. Beginning in Belize City, head north to **Orange Walk** (p. 88), a good base camp for daytrips to the impressive Maya ruins of **Lamanai** (p. 90) and **Cuello** (p. 90). Also near Orange Walk, a bird enthusiast's paradise, **Shipstern Nature Reserve** (p. 91) is home to over 22,000 species of feathered friends. From Orange Walk, catch a bus to **Corozal** (p. 92), a sleepy stepping stone for flights to **Ambergris Caye** (p. 80). This, along with **Caye Caulker** (p. 74), are the gems of Belize's Caribbean coast, offering world-famous scuba diving and snorkeling, and miles of clean beaches. Departures to **Belize City** (p. 68) via boat and plane leave from both cayes.

1 WEEK: THE CAYO DISTRICT. Leaving the beach to traverse Belize's highland region is a pleasant surprise. From Belize City, **Monkey Bay Wildlife Sanctuary** and **Guanacaste National Park** are both worth a visit on your way to **San Ignacio** (p. 97),

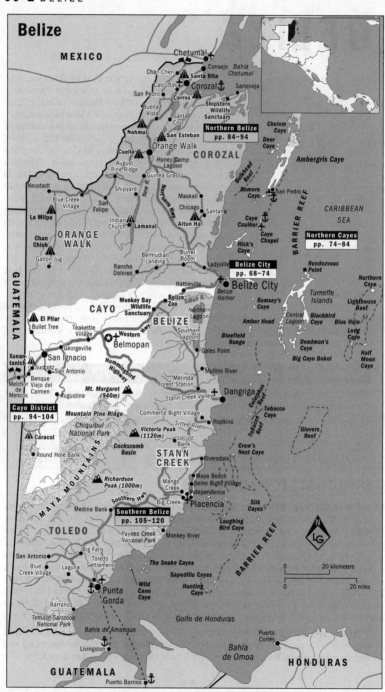

Belize

MEXICO

Chetumal

Chan Chen · Consejo · Bahía Chetumal
Santa Rita
Calcutta · **Corozal** ⚓
San Pedro
Buena · **Cerros**
Vista · Santa · **Shipstern**
Cruz · **Wildlife**
Sanctuary · Chelem Caye
Nohmul · **San Esteban** · Deer Caye
Orange Walk · Honey Camp
August · Lagoon · **COROZAL**
Cuello · Pine Ridge · Guinea Grass
Shipyard · New R. · Maskall · Bulkhead Reef · Ambergris Caye
Neustadt · Indian · Chicago · Santana · Romero
Blue Creek · Church · **Lamanai** · Caye · San Pedro · BARRIER REEF
Village · San · **Altun Ha** · Caye · CARIBBEAN SEA
La Milpa · Felipe · Caulker · **Northern Cayes**
ORANGE · Bermudian · Burrel · Caye · pp. 74-84
Chan · **WALK** · Landing · Room · Chapel
Chich · Rancho · Ladyville · Hick's · Rendezvous
Gallon Jug · Dolores · Hattieville · Caye · Point · Northern
Belize City · Caye
Monkey Bay · Belize · Sibun R. · pp. 68-74
CAYO · **Wildlife** · Zoo · **Belize City**
El Pilar · Sanctuary · Northern · Belize · Turneffe · Lighthouse
Bullet Tree · **BELIZE** · Lagoon · Harbor · Ramsey's · Islands · Reef
Teakettle · Western · Southern · Caye · Blue Hole
Georgeville · ★ · Hwy · Lagoon · Amber Head · Central · Blackbird · Long
Xunan- · **Belmopan** · Lagoon · Caye · Caye
tunich · **San Ignacio** · Hummingbird · Gales Point · Bluefield · Deadman's · Half
Succotz · San Antonio · Highway · Range · Caye · Moon
Melchor · Benque · Mullins River · Big Caye Bokel · Caye
de · Viejo del · Augustine · Melinda · **Dangriga**
Mencos · Carmen · **Mt. Margaret** · Forest Station · Columbus
(940m) · Stann Creek Valley · Tobacco · Reef
Cayo District · **Mountain Pine Ridge** · Commerce Bight Village · Hopkins · Caye
pp. 94-104 · Chiquibul · **Victoria Peak** · Sittee River · Glovers
National Park · **(1120m)** · Locust · Crow's · Reef
Cockscomb · Bank · Nest Caye
▲ **Caracol** · Basin · **STANN** · Riversdale
Round Hole Bank · **CREEK** · Maya Beach
Richardson · Seine Bight Village
Peak (1000m) · Mango · Independence · Silk
Southern Hwy · Creek · **Placencia** · Cayes
MAYA · Medina Bank · **Southern Belize** · Big Creek
MOUNTAINS · pp. 105-120 · Laughing
TOLEDO · Paynes Creek · Bird Caye
National Park · Monkey River · BARRIER REEF
Big Falls
San Antonio · Toledo · The Snake Cayes · N
Blue · Settlement · LG
Creek Village · Laguna · **Wild** · Sapodilla Cayes
Punta · **Cane** · Hunting · 0 · 20 kilometers
Gorda · **Caye** · Caye · 0 · 20 miles
Barranco
Temash-Sarstoon · Golfo de Honduras
National Park
Bahía de Amatique · Puerto · Bahía · Cortés
Livingston · de Omoa · HONDURAS
GUATEMALA · Puerto Barrios

GUATEMALA

BELIZE

the perfect town and base camp from which to explore the **Cayo District** (p. 94). Stop and take a peek into dark caves at **Actun Tunichil Muknal Cave** (p. 102), then hike the **Mountain Pine Ridge Reserve** (p. 102). One sight not to miss is **Caracol** (p. 103), Belize's largest and most impressive Maya ruin and a community that once rivaled Tikal in importance. From San Ignacio, it is easy to slide across the border into **Guatemala,** or head down the **Hummingbird Highway** (p. 105) to **Placencia,** a smooth, scenic delight with idyllic beaches and slow, warm nights.

LIFE AND TIMES

LAND, FLORA, AND FAUNA

Belize sits atop the immense limestone shelf that extends into Guatemala's Petén and Mexico's Yucatán Peninsula. The border with Guatemala is an escarpment from which the land falls east into the Caribbean. A slow, gradual slope covered by hardwood forests in the north, it becomes much steeper and somewhat tropical in the south, where the **Maya Mountains** of the Belizean Cayo District jut out of the limestone plain along the Guatemalan border. **Victoria Peak,** Belize's highest point (3681 ft.), lies in a spur of the Maya Mountains called the **Cockscomb Range.** The Cayo District is also distinguished by its many **cave** formations—water has eroded the soft limestone and shaped hundreds of tunnels. The coast itself is character- ized by inland lagoons and extensive swamp and mangrove systems. Offshore is one of Belize's foremost attractions: the **Belize Barrier Reef,** the second-largest coral reef in the world. Rising above the ocean surface are hundreds of tiny islands called the **Cayes,** including Ambergris and Caulker.

Flora have played an incredibly important role in the shaping of Belize's history, as logging once formed the basis of the economy. Today, however, only half of Bel- ize is second-growth forest. There are over 700 tree species including logwood, chicle, and mahogany, the national tree. Fruit trees abound: coconut, custard apple, mango, papaya, cashew, pineapple, and guava make Belize a rich source of produce. Belize has an estimated 4000 species of native flowering plants, including 250 species of orchids—the national flower is the black orchid. As more of the for- est becomes scientifically catalogued, some plants are being used for non-tradi- tional medicinal purposes (see **Curing Jungle Fever,** p. 100).

Since over 70% of Belize is covered by forest, it's not surprising that animal life flourishes. The revered jaguar has helped bring attention to the Cockscomb Basin Wildlife Sanctuary. There are also puma, jaguarundi, the endangered three-toed sloth, and "the mountain cow," or tapir, which is Belize's national animal. Over 200 species of migratory birds winter in Belize, including wood storks, herons, white ibis, and the black cat bird. The national bird is the keel-billed toucan.

Caribbean animal life off the coast of Belize is as rich as that of its land-bound neighbors. The endangered West Indian manatee makes its home in the reefs off the cayes, and grows up to 12 feet long and 1000 lbs. Three of the world's eight spe- cies of sea turtle, the Green, Loggerhead, and Hawksbill, nest in Belize; nesting season is June 1 to August 31. Groupers, jacks, swordfish, snapper, stingray, and nurse sharks swim the reefs and lagoons up and down the Caribbean coast.

HISTORY

Belize's unusual status within Central America stems partly from Spain's choice not to settle the area in the 16th century due to its lack of minerals and the Maya's initial resistance to Christianity. Shipwrecked English sailors settled the area and took large quantities of precious mahogany and logwood to finance buccaneering ventures. After the 1655 capture of Jamaica from Spain, British soldiers and their families joined the settlement because of its proximity.

BELIZE

By the early 18th century, white settlers were importing slaves from Jamaica and other English territories to log the forests. After 200 years of skirmishes with Spain, England won control over Belize at the **Battle of St. George's Caye** in 1798. By the time Belize was declared an official colony of **British Honduras** in 1862, the timber supply was waning. When the economy in decline, thousands of Creole workers, including slaves still indebted even after emancipation in 1838, were left in poverty. Subsistence farming became the chief economic activity in Belize.

Responding to the lack of democracy under British Colonial rule, unfair labor practices in the mahogany work camps, and the later economic hardships of the 1930's Great Depression, Belize's workers initiated a series of strikes calling for a Black Man's British Honduras. One consequence of this movement was the 1950s emergence of the **People's Unity Party (PUP)**, which blazed the path to independence. The party instituted a new constitution and self-government in 1964, achieving independence from Britain on September 21, 1981, and assuming the name Belize. Although land claim disputes with Guatemala still persist, Belize is officially recognized by both the United Nations and Guatemala.

The contemporary Belizean political scene has been dominated by the centrist PUP, headed until recently by the cautious liberal **George Price**. On June 30, 1993, in an early and close election called by the PUP, the **United Democratic Party (UDP)**, headed by **Manuél Esquivel**, broke PUP rule. Five years later, in 1998, the PUP regained leadership with **Said Musa**, who is still in power today.

TODAY

Belize has made headlines in the past years mainly for the severe weather: Hurricane Iris ripped through southern Belize in October 2001, killing 15 American tourists and destroying much of the nation's coastal development. While the hurricane shook up tourism, it was the September 11, 2001 terrorist attacks on New York City that hurt tourism most, causing tourism to drop by 22%. While much of the tourism industry is back up and running, the hurricane and drop in visitor numbers have left holes in parts of the nation's infrastructure.

Although once a subject of the Crown, Belize is inextricably tied to the US government; in an attempt to combat the Caribbean drug trade, the Belizean government negotiated a "hot pursuit" agreement with the US, opening its territorial waters to US Coast Guard vessels in pursuit of drug traffickers.

ECONOMY AND GOVERNMENT

Despite attempts at industrialization, Belize continues to rely on timber exports. The next largest and most rapidly expanding sector is tourism. Additionally, the illicit cultivation of cannabis for US export, concentrated especially in the areas northwest of the capital, is a large source of illegal revenue. Belize continues to struggle economically, trying to manage its resources while the US and Britain attempt to transform it into a prosperous, democratic country. Slash-and-burn farmers are starting to accept ecotourism as an efficient income source, but new restrictions on land use continue to frustrate. Nevertheless, national pride is strong. Belizeans cite their 53 cable channels as proof that the country isn't underdeveloped, and residents sport T-shirts with the resounding phrase *"Belize da fu we"* ("Belize, there for us!").

A member of the British Commonwealth, Belize's head of state is the British Monarch, and its government is structured according to the British parliamentary system. The political leader is the prime minister, currently Said Musa of the center-left PUP. Locally, there are city and town councils, while some traditional Maya villages are led by mayors, or *alcaldes*.

BELIZE

CULTURE AND ARTS

PEOPLE

Belize's diverse population stems largely from multi-ethnic immigration in the 19th century. Spanish-speaking *mestizos*, mostly of mixed Maya and European heritage, are Belize's largest ethnic group, comprising 40% of the population. Refugees from Guatemala, Nicaragua, Honduras, and El Salvador add to these numbers. The **Kekchi** and **Mopan-Mayan** speaking descendants of the Maya still dwell in Belize, their numbers augmented by refugees from the Yucatecan **Caste War** of 1847-48. A third of Belize's population is black Creole, descendants of African slaves and British Baymen, not to be confused with the **Garífuna,** Black Caribs of mixed Carib Indian and African descent who live in the country's southern districts. Most Garífuna speak their own Arawakan language. A few expatriate Americans, several thousand German **Mennonite** farmers, and descendants of South Asian and Chinese laborers who came seeking work in the 19th century round out the mix. Linguistic diversity is counterbalanced by the promotion of English as the official language, recalling the country's British roots. While the majority of Belizeans are Roman Catholic, nearly a third are Protestant, and evangelical and fundamentalist groups are small but growing.

FOOD AND DRINK

There are as many types of food in Belize as there are ethnic groups. The country's residents eat a lot of rice and beans, as well as beans and rice. (Yes, there is a difference: beans and rice consists of the two mixed and cooked together; rice and beans are separate.) Garífuna and Creole dishes combine seafood with fruits such as cassava, plantain, coconut, and green bananas, along with a dash of the ubiquitous Marie Sharpe's hot sauce. *Escabeche* is a potent Maya onion soup. A *garnache*, similar to a Mexican *tostada*, is a fried tortilla covered with beans, cheese, and vegetables; the more distinctive *salbute* is a fried puff-tortilla covered with chicken, fish, tomatoes, or cabbage; and a *panade* is a folded tortilla fried with fish (usually shark). For breakfast, fryjacks are similar to the sweet Mexican fried dough *sopapillas*; johnny cakes are closer to American pancakes. Lobster is available in season (June 15-Mar. 15), and "whole fresh fish" is available year round, but be prepared to dissect a fully intact specimen. Fruit juice competes with Belikin Beer as the most popular beverage in Belize; Belikin is light, smooth, and goes with just about everything. Lunch is the biggest meal of the day; dinner is sometimes referred to as "tea."

THE ARTS

The artistic tradition of Belize reflects the nation's unique blend of cultures and the daily lives and struggles of its people. A growing body of Belizean **literature** includes **Zee Edgell's** *In Times Like These*, which explores one woman's struggle for self-definition, and **Zoila Elli's** bright collection of short stories, *On Heroes, Lizards, and Passion*. Poetry also has a strong tradition in Belize. **James Martinez's** departure from English into free-flowing Creole poetry opened the way for folk literature and expression; **Hugh F. Fuller's** pieces elegantly depict the country's natural beauty; and **Evan X. Hyde's** works, such as *North Amerikkan Blues*, are laced with biting political criticism. Internationally renowned artist **Benjamin Nicholas** is at the fore of Belizean painting; his colorful depictions of daily life among the Creoles and Garífuna hang all over the country, particularly in Dangriga, where he lives. Additionally, **Yasser Musa,** son of Prime Minister Musa, has undertaken the role of Director of the **National Institute of Culture and History of Belize,** and has opened several theaters and museums, mostly in Belize City (see **Culture in the City,** p. 70).

POPULAR CULTURE

With a population blending such diverse backgrounds, it's no surprise that Belize has a flourishing **folk life**. In fact, *mestizos* are now the largest ethnic group in Belize, and their proverbs and old wives' tales are known throughout the country, particularly on the coast. They come in three parts: the Creole saying, the English translation, and the universal meaning. For example: *"Weh eyes nu seh, hart no grieve"* (what your eyes don't see your heart won't grieve), also known as "what you don't know can't hurt you." Belizean popular **music** is a combination of many elements, most notably Caribbean and Garífuna. A majority of the music in Belize, however, is not indigenous to the country, most notably American hip-hop and rock.

TELEVISION AND PERIODICALS

Belizeans proudly enjoy one of the best cable TV systems in the world, although it's unclear as to who is actually paying for it. International broadcasting is occasionally interrupted with reminders like, "Brought to you by Social Security." Four newspapers in Belize with online journals include *The Reporter* (www.belizereporter.com), *The Belize Times* (www.belizetimes.com), and *The Guardian*.

ESSENTIALS

PASSPORTS, VISAS, AND CUSTOMS.

Passport (p. 19): Required of all visitors. Must have at least 6 months left.

Visa: Not required for citizens of the US, UK, Ireland, Canada, South Africa, New Zealand, or Australia. Valid for 30 days. Extensions for up to 90 days granted by the Immigration Office in Belize City.

Onward ticket: Required of all visitors.

Proof of Funds: Visitors must show proof of sufficient funds: US$60 per person.

Inoculations and Medications (p. 27): None required.

Work Permit: Required of all foreigners planning to work in Belize. Must reside in Belize for at least 6 months prior to application. For more info contact the Immigration and Nationality Department (☎82 2611, 22 423).

Driving Permit (p. 37): Valid driver's license required.

Departure restrictions: Do not leave the country with fish, coral, or shells. Attempting to leave with certain marine species is punishable by jail time.

Departure Tax: BZ$27.50.

EMBASSIES AND CONSULATES

An updated list of Belizean embassies and consulates is available on the web at www.belize.gov.bz/diplomats.html.

Embassy of Belize, 2535 Massachusetts Ave., NW, Washington, D.C. 20008, US (☎202-332-9636; fax 332-6888). Open M-F 9am-5pm. For tourist info call ☎800-624-0686.

Consulate of Belize, 1110 Salzedo, Ste. 2F, Coral Gables, FL 33134, US (☎305-666-1121; bzconsulmi@aof.com). Open M-F 8am-noon. Belize has missions in Los Angeles, New York (☎ 212-599-0233), Chicago, San Francisco, Houston, Dallas, and other cities.

Consulate of Belize in Canada, c/o McMillan Binch Ste., 3800 South Tower, Royal Bay Plaza, Toronto, Ontario, Canada M5J 2JP (☎416-865-7000; fax 416-864-7048).

High Commission of Belize in Great Britain, 22 Harcourt House, 19 Cavendish Sq., London, England W1M 9AD (☎441 71 499 97 28; bzhc-lon@talk21.com). Open M-F 9am-5pm.

MONEY

CURRENCY	
US$1 = BZ$2.00	BZ$1 = US$0.50
CDN$1 = BZ$1.51	BZ$1 = CDN$0.66
UK£1 = BZ$3.65	BZ$1 = UK£0.27
AUS$1 = BZ$1.42	BZ$1 = AUS$0.70
EURO€ = BZ$2.45	BZ$1 = EURO.41

The rates above were accurate as of August 2004. The Belizean dollar (BZ$) is locked in to the US dollar at a rate of two to one. Dollars come in denominations of 100, 50, 20, 10, five, two, and one; there are coins of one dollar and 50, 25, 10, five, and one cents. The 25-cent piece is often referred to as a shilling. American paper currency is good nearly everywhere, but US coins are not. Prices are often quoted in both US and Belizean dollars; be sure to check.

Belizean banks typically change British pounds and US and Canadian dollars at slightly less than the two-to-one rate. Border money changers and local businesses may do better. **Barclay's Bank** changes **traveler's checks** and gives **cash advances** free of charge; it also accepts international **ATM** cards. **Credit cards** are widely accepted in Belize, but beware of extra fees. **Tips** of 10% on restaurant bills are customary. Taxi drivers are not tipped.

PRICE DIVERSITY

Belize is more expensive than most of its Central American neighbors; the same amenities you might receive in Guatemala or Nicaragua may cost you 2-3 times as much in Belize. Consider US$30 an estimated minimum daily budget. The following symbols are used throughout the book to describe establishments' prices.

SYMBOL	❶	❷	❸	❹	❺
ACCOMMODATIONS	BZ$0-20	BZ$21-30	BZ$31-45	BZ$46-60	BZ$61+
FOOD	BZ$0-5	BZ$6-10	BZ$11-15	BZ$16-30	BZ$31+

SAFETY

The non-medical hazards of Belize come in three flavors—the inebriated rowdy, the on-the-make male, and the eager-to-sell-drugs heavy. Particularly in English-speaking areas along the coast, expect hustlers and self-appointed "guides" to confront you. Firmly refuse their services and make it clear that you won't give them money, but don't be rude or the problem could escalate. Public drunkenness is common in Belize, and women should take more than usual precautions. Even the most careful may not be able to avoid being approached by a representative of the intense drug trade. Politely refuse and continue walking. Purchasing drugs is not only dangerous, but illegal. The nearest police station can be reached anywhere in Belize by dialing ☎911. For more info, see **Safety and Security,** p. 25.

HEALTH

Purified drinking water is available almost everywhere except for the Cayes. In cities and big towns, municipal water is generally chlorinated and safe for brushing teeth. In rural areas, use boiled water. For fruit and veggies, follow the Peace Corps rule: "Peel it, cook it, boil it, or vom-it." Though malaria is reported to be under control, precautions are advised. For general but vital info, see **Health,** p. 27.

BELIZE

BORDER CROSSINGS

MEXICO. Buses cross at **Chetumal,** Mexico from Belize City and Corozal.

GUATEMALA. There is a land crossing at **Melchor de Mencos.** For details coming from Flores, Guatemala, see p. 412; from Belize see p. 104. **Boats** go from **Punta Gorda** (p. 116) to **Puerto Barrios** (p. 382) and **Livingston, Guatemala** (p. 383).

HONDURAS. Weekly boats run between Placencia and **Puerto Cortés, Honduras** (p. 472) and between Dangriga-Mango Creek and Puerto Cortés.

KEEPING IN TOUCH

The **mail** system is fairly reliable. It costs BZ$0.60 to mail a letter from Belize to the US, BZ$0.30 for a postcard. To Europe, letters are BZ$0.75 and postcards are BZ$0.40. First-class airmail takes about 10 to 15 days to travel between the US and Belize. Pharmacies sell stamps and have mailboxes. You can have mail sent to you in Belize through **general delivery.**

> Ian CAMPBELL
> Poste Restante
> Orange Walk [city]
> BELIZE

Seven-digit **telephone** numbers including area codes are listed in this book. When calling from the US, dial the country code before the seven digit number. For US phone company access numbers, see this book's inside back cover. **Belize Telecommunications Limited (BTL)** currently owns all phone systems. You must buy a BTL phone card, sold in BZ$5 increments, to use any public pay phone. To use an international calling card, first dial 115. This reaches an operator, who will help you with your call. Calls to the US cost BZ$9.60 for the first three minutes and BZ$3.20 per minute thereafter. Calls to Europe are BZ$6 per minute. Collect calls are free.

COUNTRY CODE	501

TRANSPORTATION

The **international airport** is located 16km (10 mi.) northwest of Belize City, on the Northern Hwy. Try to share a cab to Belize City, as the fare has been set at BZ$35, but make all arrangements *before* approaching a driver; they strongly discourage the practice. Maya Island Air and Tropic Air have **domestic flights** from both Belize City international and Belize City **municipal airport** to points throughout Belize. **Buses** are cheap, efficient, and frequent, as are **boats** to and from the cayes.

ORIENTATION

Belize, forever the British oddball among its more Spanish neighbors, stands out for not having cities with a grid-like structure of *avenidas* and *calles.* There is, however, a preponderance of Main Streets, Front Streets, and Back Streets.

TRAVEL RESOURCES

Belize Tourist Board, 421 7th Ave., Ste. 1110, New York, NY 10001 US (☎800-624-0686 or 212-563-6011; fax 212-563-6033). Exhaustive info. In **Belize City,** P.O. Box 325, New Central Bank Building, 2nd level, at the end of Queen St. (☎02 31 913; fax 02 31 943; www.travelbelize.org).

Belize Audubon Society, 12 Fort St., Belize City (☎02 23 5004; base@btl.net; www.belizeaudubon.org). Info about all national parks, wildlife, and birds. Sells a guide on Belize's wildlife (BZ$8). Open M-F 8:30am-5pm.

Triton Tours, 812 Airline Park Blvd., Metairie, LA 70003, US (☎504-464-7964; fax 504-779-9015). Airfare and accommodations organized for diving and ecotourism.

HOLIDAYS

In addition to national holidays, which follow the British calendar, the Garífuna and the Maya communities have their own celebrations with traditional dancing and festivities. National holidays include: **January 1,** New Year's Day; **March 9,** Baron Bliss Day; **March/April,** Holy Week; **April 21,** the Queen's Birthday; **May 1,** Labor Day; **May 24,** Commonwealth Day; **September 10,** Belize National Day; **September 21,** Independence Day; **October 12,** Columbus Day; **November 19,** Garífuna Settlement Day; **December 25,** Christmas; **December 26,** Boxing Day.

ALTERNATIVES TO TOURISM

This section lists some of the organizations that offer opportunities outside the typical tourist experience. For more on Alternatives to Tourism and tools for finding programs on your own, see the chapter at the beginning of the book (p. 53).

VISA INFORMATION

All visitors are issued a 30-day visa upon arrival, which can be renewed at any immigration office for US$12.50 per month for up to six months. You must have resided legally in Belize for six months to obtain a **work permit.** Your prospective employer must then submit an **Application for Permission to Employ a Foreigner** to the Labor Department (☎822 204), along with three passport photos, US$10 in stamps, a valid passport, and proof that you are qualified for the job. They must also prove that all efforts to employ a native were exhausted, including a local advertisement of the job for at least three weeks with no qualified applicants. The work permit costs US$25-500, depending on the type of work. Another type of work permit is an **Application for Temporary Self-Employment.** You must legally reside in Belize with the proper visas and permits, but the six-month residence requirement is waived. Along with application, you must provide proof of sufficient funds for the venture and a reference from the appropriate Ministry. For more info on work permits, contact the **Immigration and Nationality Department** (Belmopan ☎822 611 or 822 423). **Student visas** are not required.

LANGUAGE SCHOOLS

If you wish to study Spanish during your time in Belize, hop over the border into **Guatemala** (p. 321). Popular cities include **Antigua** and **Quetzaltenango.**

VOLUNTEERING

BIOLOGY/ECOLOGY PROGRAMS

The Cornerstone Foundation, 90 Burns Av., San Ignacio, Cayo District, (☎824 2373, www.peacecorner.org), through the **Peace Initiative,** volunteers raise environmental awareness, enhance regional sustainability, and develop connections with numerous organizations. 3 month minimum for volunteers; US$1005.

Trekforce Expeditions, 34 Buckingham Palace Rd., London, England, SW1W 0RE (☎020 7828 2275; www.trekforce.org.uk), offers a pricey multi-month joint expedition and conservation program. 2 months US$6000, all inclusive.

EDUCATION

The Cornerstone Foundation, 90 Burns Av., San Ignacio, Cayo District (☎824 2373; www.peacecorner.org), enlists volunteers to teach 4-5 year olds from Spanish speaking villages the English they need to enroll in Belizean elementary school. 3 month minimum commitment; US$1005 contribution.

Pro World Service, P.O. Box 21121, Billings, MT, 59104, US (☎877-733-7378; www.proworldsc.org). A non-profit organization that provides teachers and teacher's assistants to Belizean schools. Possible roles include computer, English, or math teacher. 2 month program US$3500.

HUMANITARIAN

The NGO Connection, based in the Marine Terminal in Belize City, Brings together several non-governmental organizations and generates income for them by selling local handmade crafts in the Terminal. Volunteers can work in the kiosk or assist in other projects. Check in upon arrival in the Marine Terminal.

The Fajina Craft Center, in Punta Gorda, next to the post office. An organization of 21 Maya cheerleaders from southern villages who run a craft store open on market days. Volunteers needed for crafts and small business development.

Youth Enhancement Services (☎02 325 38; yes@btl.net). An alternative learning center in Belize City, for girls ages 12-17 who are not in school. Volunteers usually work on special projects (7-10 days), depending on skills. Volunteers should be flexible and pay their own expenses. No age requirement. Ask for Mrs. Karen Cain.

BELIZE CITY

Belize City is a city of unfortunate transitions. Once a graceful colonial town, the city (pop. 55,600) became both overcrowded and crime-ridden during the 20th-century, and was stripped of its capital status in 1971. Most visitors use "Belize" as an arrival point before escaping to the quieter, more spectacular parts of the country. Streams of sewage overflow the canals, buildings wobble on weak foundations, and traffic floods the crumbling narrow roads. Belize City does not have the beaches, wildlife, laid-back lifestyle, or Maya sites that draw tourists. However, some may appreciate its glimpse into the contemporary Belizean culture. Mestizos, Creoles, Garinaga, East Indians, and whites speak multiple languages and play many types of music, infusing the streets with a tangible sense of diversity. Belize City also has cultural facilities, museums, and colonial houses.

Belize City is by far the dirtiest and most dangerous place in Belize. Hustlers are in full force here; some will try to stop you and start a conversation, while more aggressive ones walk beside you, offering info, drugs, and prostitutes. If approached, be firm. In a bind, look for one of the khaki-shirted "tourist police."

✈ INTERCITY TRANSPORTATION

International Flights: Philip S.W. Goldson International Airport, in Ladyville, 10 mi. northwest of Belize City. Call airlines directly to make a reservation. Serves: **Continental,** 80 Regent St. (☎227 8309); **American Airlines,** (☎223 2522) intersection of New Rd. with Queen St.; and **Grupo Taca Airlines,** 41 Albert St. (☎227 7363).

Domestic Flights: Check with **Belize Air Travel Service,** Belize Municipal Airstrip, on the waterfront north of town. Serves **Tropic Air** (☎224 5671; www.tropicair.com) and **Maya Island Air** (☎223 1140; www.mayaislandair.com). Tropic Air flies to **Dangriga** (15min., every 1½hr. 8:30am-4:50pm, BZ$61); **Placencia** (45min., every 1½hr. 8:30am-4:50pm, BZ$118); **Punta Gorda** (1hr., every 1½hr. 8:30am-4:50pm, BZ$152); and

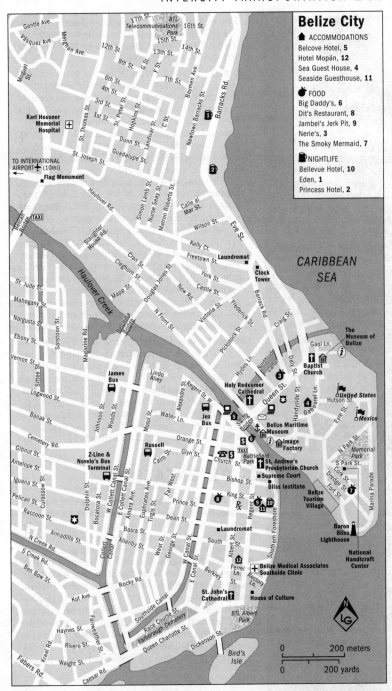

Belize City

♦ **ACCOMMODATIONS**
Belcove Hotel, 5
Hotel Mopán, 12
Sea Guest House, 4
Seaside Guesthouse, 11

🍴 **FOOD**
Big Daddy's, 6
Dit's Restaurant, 8
Jambel's Jerk Pit, 9
Nerie's, 3
The Smoky Mermaid, 7

📖 **NIGHTLIFE**
Bellevue Hotel, 10
Eden, 1
Princess Hotel, 2

BELIZE

THE LOCAL STORY

CULTURE IN THE CITY

Let's Go spoke with Yasser Musa, son of Belizean Prime Minister Said Musa and director of the National Institute of Culture and History of Belize, in his office at the Museum of Belize.

We have undergone a dramatic change in terms of our cultural landscape in Belize City. We built the Museum of Belize inside what was an aging prison. We opened the doors in February 2002, and since then we have seen over 40,000 visitors. We have various exhibits, right now including ones on Mayan culture, and the history of Belize. If you come to Belize, it's a must see.

The second great cultural change in Belize City is the construction of our new Bliss Center for the Performing Arts. Right now we are preparing two shows, every morning Monday through Friday at 11am and 1pm. One is a mythical show of traditional folkloric characters from the various cultures of Belize. You have music, drama, everything in a one-hour show. It's a Broadway-type musical using our own cultural folkloric characters. In the same facility is also our national collection of art, with a cafe and restaurant.

The House of Culture, right up the street from the Bliss, is in the government house where the colonial governors used to live. The grounds are landscaped with gardens, and there are displays on the building's colonial history.

San Pedro (15min., every hr. 7:40am-5:30pm, BZ$52). For visitors interested in **Tikal**, Maya Island offers a flight to **Flores, Guatemala** for BZ$176. A **taxi** from the airport costs BZ$40.

Buses: Be careful around the terminals at night; consider a taxi. Schedules change often, so check ahead. Buses have their destination written in the lower right corner of their front window. **Novelo's** now has a monopoly on the public market and owns both **Northern** and **Southern Transport,** with buses serving **Belmopan** (1¼hr., every hr. 5am-8:30pm, BZ$3.50), **Benque Viejo** (3hr., every hr. 5am-8:30pm, BZ$8), **Corozal** (2½ hr., every hr. 6am-3:30pm, BZ$9; express 2hr., 7 per day 6am-6pm, BZ$13), **Dangriga** (2-3hr., every hr. 8am-5pm, BZ$10), **Melchor** (3½ hr., every hr. 5am-8:30pm, BZ$9), **Orange Walk** (1½hr., every hr. 6am-3:30pm, BZ$5), **Placencia** (catch the bus to Dangriga), and **San Ignacio** (1hr., every hr. 5am-8:30pm, BZ$7). **Jex** runs only to **Crooked Tree** (1½hr.; 10:30am, 4:30, 5:30pm; BZ$4). **Russell** goes through Ladyville en route to **Bermudian Landing Baboon Sanctuary** (1½hr.; M-F noon, 4:30pm, and Sa noon, 12:15, 1, 4:30pm; BZ$3.50), and **James** offers the only direct route to Punta Gorda. Arrive at the station early, as buses leave ahead of schedule when they are full. Buses make frequent stops to pick up passengers along the route, and often arrive late to their destinations.

Boats: The most frequent departures to the Cayes are from **Belize Marine Terminal** on the northern end of the Swing Bridge, with trips to **Caye Caulker** (5min.; 8, 9, 10:30am, noon, 1:30, 3, 4:30, 5:30pm; BZ$15 one-way) and **San Pedro** (1½hr.; 8, 9, 10:30am, noon, 1:30, 3, 4:30pm; BZ$30 one-way, BZ$55 round-trip). **Triple J Water Taxi** offers less frequent departures, but you can haggle lower rates (Caye Caulker BZ$12 one-way, BZ$22 round-trip; **San Pedro** BZ$22 one-way, BZ$42 round-trip).

✦ ORIENTATION

UPON ARRIVAL. *Let's Go* **recommends that travelers take taxis from the airport to the city center.** However, it is possible to walk the 1km from the airport to the highway and catch a bus from there, as they run every 30min. (BZ$2). From the bus terminal, it's best to take a cab, especially at night. The bus terminals cluster around the **Collet Canal.** If you walk east, **Orange Street** leads to **Albert Street** and **Battlefield Park,** the center of town. Two blocks north lies the **Swing Bridge.** Most boats from the Cayes arrive at the **Marine Terminal** adjacent to the northern end of the Swing Bridge, or at the **Courthouse Wharf,** across the river from and slightly east of the Marine Terminal. Taxis offer direct service to the airport.

LAYOUT. The Caribbean Sea nearly surrounds the city. **Haulover Creek** runs southeast to the shore and splits the city into northern and southern parts. Most services are a short walk from **Swing Bridge**, which spans the creek mouth. South of Haulover Creek, most restaurants, hotels, and attractions are to the east of the **Southside Canal.** To the north of Haulover Creek, they are clustered along **Queen Street** and **Barracks Road.** The streets are not set out in any discernible pattern, but tourists have little reason to stray far from **Albert St.**

SAFETY. Belize City has declared the area east of Northside and Southside Canal as the official **tourism district.** The city has successfully secured the area by stationing khaki-uniformed police officers solely in the district. To avoid trouble, it is best to look as if you are heading to a specific destination. At night, walk in groups on main streets like Albert St., or take a taxi. The farther west one travels, the more dangerous and dilapidated the city becomes. Stay within the tourism district; if travel outside is necessary, travel in a group or take a taxi, especially at night.

▐ LOCAL TRANSPORTATION

Taxis: All have green license plates. Flag them down on any street or at the stand in **Battlefield Park**. Cabs in Belize City are now unionized and have the same set fares across companies. BZ$6 per stop within Belize City, plus BZ$1-2 for each extra person. Confirm fare before getting in, and never get into a car without a green plate. Take cabbies' claims that the hotel you ask for is "full" with a grain of salt. Drivers often collect a fee from hotel owners for bringing them business. Cabs from the airport to the city are expensive (BZ$40), but worth the safety and convenience. The cabs sometimes negotiate lower prices for longer trips outside the city.

Car Rental: Budget Car Rental, Western Hwy. (☎223 2435; www.budget-belize.com). **Hertz Car Rental,** 11 Cork St. (☎223 5395; safarihz@btl.net), across from the Radisson Fort George. Call 3-4 weeks in advance during high season. Remember that the companies require a large damage deposit and that gas is expensive (BZ$7 per gallon). AmEx/MC/V.

▟ PRACTICAL INFORMATION

TOURIST AND FINANCIAL SERVICES

Tourist Information: Belize Tourist Board, Gabourel Ln., New Central Bank Bldg., 2nd level (☎223 1913; www.travelbelize.org). Located behind the new Museum of Belize, in the huge bank building. Friendly staff offers free maps and brochures of Belize. Open M-Th 8am-noon and 1-5pm, F 8am-noon and 1-4:30pm.

Embassies and Consulates: The British High Commission (☎802 2146; brithicom@btl.net) is located in Belmopan. **Canada,** 80 Princess Margaret Dr. (☎223 1060). Open M-F 9am-1pm. **US,** 29 Gabourel Ln. (☎207 7161). From the Swing Bridge, take Queen St. northeast until it meets Gabourel and turn right—the string of white colonial houses on your left is the US compound. Entrance to the consulate is around the corner. Consular services open M-F 8am-noon and 1:30-4pm.

Banks: First Caribbean Bank, near Battlefield Park at 21 Albert St., offers Visa cash advances and currency exchange. Open M-Th 8am-2:30pm, F 8am-4:30pm. The 24hr. **ATM** accepts Visa. Foreign ATM cards work only inside the bank during business hours. **Belize Bank,** next to Battlefield Park on Albert St., also has a 24hr. **ATM** and similar services. Open M-Th 8am-3pm, F 8am-4:30pm. A **Western Union** is in the Marine Terminal. Many businesses accept, or even prefer, American dollars.

LOCAL SERVICES

Bookstores: Stock up here in Belize City; new books are hard to find in other parts of the country. **Brodie's** has cheap romance novels, current US magazines, and a great selection of titles on Belize. **Sunny's,** in the Marine Terminal, has US newspapers.

Supermarkets: Brodie's, on Albert St. off Battlefield Park, carries a wide selection of groceries. Open M-Th 8:30am-7pm, F 8:30am-8pm, Sa 8:30am-5pm, Su 8:30am-1pm.

Laundry: G's, on Dean St., between E. Canal St. and Albert St. BZ$9 per load. Open M-Sa 8am-6pm. **CA Coin Laundromat,** 114 Barrack Rd., across from Clock Tower. Open M-F 9am-9pm, Sa-Su 8am-9pm.

EMERGENCY AND COMMUNICATIONS

Emergency: Police ☎90, 911. **Fire** or **Medical:** ☎90.

Police: (☎227 2222). Located one block northeast of the Swing Bridge on Queen St. A 2nd station is at 9 Racoon St. Follow West Collet Canal St. south along Collet Canal from the bus station and turn right on Racoon St. Open 24hr.

Pharmacy: Brodie's Pharmacy (☎227 7070) is on the Regent St.end of Brodie's supermarket. Open M-Th 8:30am-7pm, F 8:30am-8pm, Sa 8:30am-5pm, Su 8:30am-1pm.

Hospital: Karl Heusner Memorial Hospital, (☎223 1548, 223 1564) on the way to the airport, along Princess Margaret Dr. Open 24hr. **Belize Medical Associates Southside Clinic** (☎227 0644, 227 0159), on Regent St. just past Hotel Mopan leading out of downtown. Open daily 8am-8pm. BZ$47 for non-residents. General practitioners only.

Telephones: Public phones are scattered around Queen and Albert St. Public phone at the Batty Station. **BTL,** 1 Church St. (☎227 7085), off Albert St, offers air-conditioned booths and sells phone cards. Open M-F 8am-6pm.

Internet: Ray Communications, 15 Regent St. West. BZ$4 per hr, BZ$2.50 per 30min. Open the iron gate, and the entrance is on your left. **KSG Internet** on the corner of Regent and King St. BZ$4 per hour. CD burning, photocopying, faxing available. Open daily 9am-7pm.

Post Office: Queen St., north of the Swing Bridge in the old colonial Paslow building. Open M-Th 8am-5pm, F 8am-4:30pm. Weekend Express Mail Services open Sa 8-10am and 1:30-5pm, Su 1:30-5pm.

ACCOMMODATIONS

Safety should be your first priority when choosing a hotel in Belize City. Beware of hotel curfews and carefully check the locks on all doors. Most hotels charge an extra 3-5% for credit card payments.

■ **Seaside Guest House,** 3 Prince St. (☎227 8339; seasidebelize@btl.net). Undoubtedly Belize City's most impressive hotel, combining tranquility, safety, helpful management, and affordability. A spectacular veranda has a water view. Pass through a gated garden area and three locks to rooms with fans and shared hot water showers. Homemade breakfasts BZ$4-8. Call ahead for reservations. Co-ed dorms BZ$24; singles BZ$42; doubles BZ$64; triples BZ$80; quads BZ$96. MC/V. ❸

Hotel Mopán, 55 Regent St. (☎227 7351), is a friendly, family-run hotel a block from St. John's Cathedral and near the waterfront. Rooms are spare but spacious. Mopán also operates a small bar with cable TV and a restaurant for breakfast and lunch. Has a nice 3rd-fl. balcony and roof access. All rooms include private hot bath, linens and fan. A/C extra BZ$20. Check-out 11am. Singles BZ$60; doubles BZ$80; triples BZ$100; quads BZ$110; 7% sales tax not included. ❹

BELIZE

Belcove Hotel, 9 Regent St. West (☎227 3054), is an elegant hotel with clean, spacious rooms. The spectacular balcony overlooks Belize City's motorboat trade and the Swing Bridge. Singles with fan BZ$33, with bath BZ$43; doubles BZ$43/BZ$54. Check-out 11am. MC/V. ❸

Sea Guesthouse, (☎200 0613 or 227 5678; www.seaguesthouse.com) on Gabourel Ln. near Handyside St., is well-locked with sparse rooms in the Fort George neighborhood. Singles with shared bath BZ$25; doubles BZ$30. ❷

🖸 FOOD

🖾 **Jambel's Jerk Pit,** on King St. a few meters west of the waterfront, serves up mouth-watering, spicy Jamaican and Belizean food in a clean, colorful setting. Reggae plays over the breezy, intimate outdoor patio. Specializes in seafood entrees (BZ$10-20). Try the Jamaica-mi-crazy shrimp (BZ$20) or the jerk fish filet (BZ$14) for a hotter taste. Open daily 11am-9pm. MC/V. ❸

Dit's Restaurant, 50 King St. This family-owned and operated restaurant serves up hearty dishes for breakfast, lunch, and dinner (BZ$5-8). Locals recommend the cakes and pastries. Open M-Sa 7am-8pm and Su 8am-4pm. ❷

Big Daddy's, in the hulking commercial center next to the mouth of Haulover Creek next to Battlefield Park. Serves dinner-style food fast and cheap, including hot dogs (BZ$1.75) and rice and beans (with chicken BZ$7). Large bay windows under cool fans provide a relaxing place to watch day tourists stampede to and from their cruise ships. Open daily 7am-4pm. ❶

Nerie's, on the corner of Queen St. and Handysine St., is the place to go in Belize City when you're hunkering for a gibnut (BZ$10), cowfoot soup (BZ$6.50), or the chance to frighten your vegetarian friends. Breakfast BZ$6.50-8.50. The bar upstairs is a local favorite and serves up various mixed drinks (BZ$4-12). ❷

The Smoky Mermaid, 13 Cork St., near the Radisson. This large bar/restaurant has real Caribbean flavor and atmosphere. Tropical frozen drinks (BZ$7-10) spill over the edge of their glasses. Shrimp or chicken pitas (BZ$10) are delicious, or try lobster in season (BZ$30-40). In the evening, the horseshoe bar fills with locals and tourists. Open daily 6:30am-10pm. AmEx/MC/V. ❹

🗗 SIGHTS

Many steps have been taken in recent months to improve cultural aspects of Belize's largest city, especially under the leadership of Yasser Musa, son of prime minister Said Musa. The tourist area east of the canals is small and easily walkable, with several interesting attractions along the way.

SWING BRIDGE. The center of the city is the Swing Bridge, an unusual, manually operated bridge that crosses the mouth of Haulover Creek. People cross back and forth constantly during the day, but take care on the narrow, unlit walkway at night.

HOUSE OF CULTURE. What was once the British Government House is now a hub for Belize City's revitalized high culture. There is a permanent exhibit on the house itself, along with two rotating visual arts exhibits. Next to the sea, the grounds are full of hibiscus and shade trees. Monthly Full Moon concerts in the open-air theater are a must-see. *(Across from St. John's Cathedral on Regent St.)*

ST. JOHN'S CATHEDRAL. The oldest Anglican cathedral in Central America was built in 1826 with bricks that were previously used as ballast on English ships. Today, the idyllic edifice stands out in an unhappily urban Belize City. Mrs. Elsie

BELIZE

Evans, the caretaker, sometimes sings spirituals and gives tours. *(At the southern end of Albert St., a 10min. walk south from the Swing Bridge. Open M-Sa 9am-noon and 2-7pm, Su 6am-noon and 6-7pm.)*

THE IMAGE FACTORY. Three doors down from the tourist office on North Front St., the Image Factory is a non-profit space devoted to Belizean art. Started by Yasser Musa, son of Said Musa, the current prime minister, this gallery rotates works of contemporary Belizean artists, natural history exhibits, and folkloric artifacts. *(Open M-F 8am-6pm, Sa 9am-noon. Free.)*

THE MUSEUM OF BELIZE. Opened in 2002, this worthwhile museum is housed in a fully restored edifice that formerly served as Her Majesty's Prison. There are plans to maintain rotating exhibits of Belizean interest. Currently features an exhibit on historical Belize City and another on Maya Masterpieces. *(On Gabourel Ln., next to the massive Central Bank Building. www.museumofbelize.org. Open Tu-F 10am-6pm, Sa 10am-3pm. BZ$10.)*

▣ NIGHTLIFE

It only takes one night on the town to be convinced of the musical and linguistic diversity of Belize City. The best nights to go out are Thursday, Friday, and Saturday. For *punta*, *soca*, and reggae dancing, locals swear by two places, **The Bellevue Hotel** and **Eden.** The Bellevue Hotel is the place to be Friday nights. Start the night upstairs with a little karaoke with the locals (5-10pm). After 11pm, venture downstairs to enjoy the hot live band music and to shake your booty on the intimate dance floor. Like the rest of Belize City, the party does not get jumpin' until midnight or later (dancing 10pm-2:30am). Eden is on Newtown Barrack Rd., at the first intersection past the large Fiesta Inn Belize on the left. Expect DJs and dancing. (Open Th-Sa 10pm-3am. Cover BZ$10.) The **Princess Hotel** has a casino, bowling alley, swimming pool, and the only movie theater in the country (BZ$15). To reach the hotel, go north on Queen St., turn left at the end, and follow the waterfront for 10min. Investing in a cab at night is a necessity.

NORTHERN CAYES

Few travelers overlook Belize's exquisite cayes (pronounced KEYS), strung along the second-largest barrier reef in the world. As Belize's number-one tourist destination, the cayes feature some of the best diving in the world. Although there are several hundred cayes off Belize's aquamarine coast, visitors primarily concern themselves with Ambergris Caye, with its top-end resorts and dive shops, and more rugged Caye Caulker, a budget traveler's haven. While the es are nice, it is the reef and its 400 species of fish that sets the Belizean Cayes apart.

CAYE CAULKER

This haven of tranquility, drawing more European tourists than American, is just a 45min. boat ride from grungy Belize City and the hustle and bustle of San Pedro. Caye Caulker (pop. 800) cools and calms the spirit. With no cars, no cabs, and hardly any bicycles, the relaxed atmosphere consists of people strolling the sandy streets, geckos sunning in the grass, and coconut trees swaying in the afternoon breeze. Even the most ambitious tend to sit back, nurse another rum punch, and forget what day it is. Of course, if you insist upon being active, snorkeling and scuba trips to the reef provide an escape from the heat, the mosquitoes, and the lethargy on the shore. For the majority of its history, Caye Caulker has made its living off lobster. Now tourism is prominent, but the annual **Lobster Fest,** held the first weekend in July,

BELIZE

Cayes

brings back the early memories. Though residents are very trusting, crime is rising; caution is advisable.

▣ TRANSPORTATION

The cheapest way to get to Caye Caulker is by boat.

Flights: Flights between **San Pedro** and **Belize City** will stop at **Caye Caulker;** mention it when buying your ticket. From the caye, call **Tropic Air** (☎226 0400), **Maya Island Air** (☎226 0012), or talk to one of the agents on Front St. for the return trip. Flights back to either city are on request.

Ferry: From the pier by the sandbox on Front St., boats head to the marine terminal in **Belize City** (45min.; 9 per day 6:30am-5pm; one-way BZ$15, open-ended round-trip BZ$25) and to **San Pedro** on **Ambergris Caye** (45min.; 8 per day 7am-5:15pm; one-way BZ$15, open ended round-trip BZ$25). Buy your tickets in advance from the water taxi office off the pier on Front St. Boats from the west pier go to San Pedro and the tourist village

Caye Caulker

ACCOMMODATIONS
Albert's Guesthouse, **9**
Mara's Place, **2**
Sandy Lane, **8**
Tina's Backpacker Hostel, **12**
Tree Tops Hotel, **21**

FOOD
Dave's Bar & Grill, **18**
Glenda's, **15**
Marin's, **19**
Syd's Rest. & Bar, **17**
Wish Willy, **10**

NIGHTLIFE
I&I Cafe & Bar, **20**
Lazy Lizard, **1**
Oceanside Bar, **6**
Sunset View Disco, **4**

DIVE/SNORKEL
Anwar Tours, **13**
Driftwood Snorkeling, **7**
Frenchie's Diving, **3**
Juni, **11**
Mario's Snorkeling, **16**
Paradise Down Diving, **5**
Ras Creek's Boat, **14**

in **Belize City.** A fun, leisurely way to spend a few hr. in San Pedro is to take a full-day snorkeling trip that stops for lunch in San Pedro (BZ$55-$70) and visits **Hol Chan Marine Reserve.** Most leave at 10:30am and reach San Pedro at 12:30pm.

✳ ⏻ ORIENTATION AND PRACTICAL INFORMATION

A creek called **"The Split"** divides Caye Caulker in half. The town stands at the northern tip of the southern portion, while the northern half remains largely uninhabited. The only street signs in Caye Caulker state the obvious: "Go slow." Three parallel dirt roads, known informally as **Front Street, Middle Street,** and **Back Street,** run north-south through town. **Water taxis** drop tourists off on the east side of the island. The first street parallel to the sea and in the center of town is Front St., lined with gift shops and eateries. Landmarks include the cream-colored **police station,** the **basketball court** just south of the station, and the two largest **piers** that jut out on the east and west sides of the island. The **airstrip** is at the southern end of Back St., within easy walking distance of town.

Tourist Information: Dolphin Bay Travel (☎226 2214; dolphinbay@btl.net), just up Front St. Ilna and Dianne are knowledgeable about all the island's offerings and are especially attuned to the needs of penny pinchers, as is Diane's sister **Tina,** proprietor of the Backpacker Hostel (see **Accommodations,** p. 77).

Banks: Atlantic Bank, on Middle St., parallel to the road connecting the 2 main piers. Cash advances on Visa (BZ$5) and traveler's check exchanges. Open M-F 8am-2pm, Sa 8:30am-noon. **Tropical Paradise Hotel,** at the southern tip of Front St., exchanges traveler's checks.

Bike Rental: Caye Caulker Gift Shop on Front St. rents bikes BZ$5 per hr., BZ$24 per day. Open daily 9am-9pm.

Book Exchange: Yoohoo, on Front St. next to the police office.

Supermarket: Chan's Minimarket, on the corner of Middle St. and the pier. Open daily 7am-9pm. Traveler's checks accepted. MC/V.

Police: (☎226 2120), in a green-and-cream house by the basketball court on Front St. Officer available 24hr.

Pharmacy: Jungle Roses (☎226 2231), on the south end of Front St., has both herbal and standard medicines.

Medical Services: Caye Caulker Health Center (☎226 2166), at the southern end of Front St. Open daily 8am-noon, 1-5pm. 24hr. emergency care.

Laundry: Coin Laundromat on the pier road between Front St. and Middle St. Wash and dry, BZ$4 each. Open daily 7am-9pm.

Telephones: BTL (☎226 0169), directly off the eastern pier on Front St. **Fax** service. Open M-F 8am-noon and 1-5pm. Many pay phones are on Front and Middle St.

Internet: Caye Caulker Cyber Cafe, on Front St. near the basketball court. 9 computers and A/C. Beverages half-price during happy hour (daily 3-6pm). BZ$7 per hr. Accepts traveler's checks. MC/V.

Post Office: Located at the southern end of Front St. in the same building as the health center. Open M-Th 8am-noon and 1-5pm, F 8am-noon and 1-4:30pm.

▞ ACCOMMODATIONS

Upon arrival, you will be greeted by locals asking if you need a room; do further research in your trusty guide book or at **Dolphin Bay Travel** (see **Orientation and Practical Information,** p. 76). In general, housing on Caulker is safe and secure. Look for a place on the Caribbean side where a steady ocean breeze will keep you cool and deter voracious mosquitoes and sand flies. Campers looking for sites can wander to the more isolated parts of the island. It is also worth inquiring at hotels to see if they allow camping. Accommodations often fill up quickly on Caye Caulker, so it is wise to call ahead, especially during the high season.

▨ **Tina's Backpacker Hostel** (dolphinbay@btl.net), on the beach just north of the water taxi terminal, is the best place to meet other travelers. It offers 5 small rooms, each with 4 bunk beds. Linens provided, but no towels. Communal kitchen with fridge, lounge with cable TV, radio, and a front beach legendary for its cricket and volleyball matches between guests. BZ$15 per person. ❶

Albert's Guesthouse (☎226 0277; arodriguez@btl.net), a few blocks north of the front pier on Front St. One of the best budget values on the island. Convenient oceanfront location, if a bit noisy at night. All rooms with fan, hammock, shared bathroom, shared balcony with chairs, and sea view. Singles BZ$21.50; doubles BZ$26.50. ❷

Sandy Lane (☎226 2217), located just south of the soccer field on Middle St. If you want the unbeatable price of a hostel, but the quiet and privacy of your own room, this is it. Some more expensive cabins in front. Rooms equipped with fan and shared bath. Singles BZ$20, with bath BZ$30; doubles BZ$25/$35. ❶

Mara's Place (☎206 2256), at the north end of Front St. just before the split. Overlooking Caulker's tiny beach, Mara's is a great value. *Cabañas* come with private bath, hot water, cable TV, and a porch with a hammock. Reservations recommended. Single or double *cabañas* BZ$60, BZ$10 per extra person. ❹

Tree Tops Hotel (☎226 0240; www.treetopsbelize.com). Friendly owners Doris and Terry make this well-decorated hotel a great value. Each themed room has beautiful artwork, cable TV, and an oceanfront view. Book exchange, purified drinking water, bike rental for guests (BZ$10 per day). 2-night stay required. Reservations recommended. Room BZ$75; with bath BZ$90; with A/C and private bath BZ$100. ❺

🔾 FOOD

Caye Caulker's restaurants are legendary for cheap seafood and laid-back service. For a quick and tasty breakfast, buy some **Creole bread** (BZ$1.50) from one of the many children and women on Front St. Stop by the pink **Light House,** just north of the basketball court, for excellent ice cream (BZ$1.50). Caye Caulker **does not have safe drinking water;** be sure to buy purified water and ice. The **Caye Caulker Bakery,** on the corner of Middle St. and the dock street, sells excellent fresh breads and pastries. (BZ$0.50-$2. Open M-Sa 7am-noon and 2-6pm.)

Glenda's, on Back St. Friendly family atmosphere with great food at great prices. Fresh orange juice (BZ$2); coffee, eggs, bacon, and warm cinnamon rolls (BZ$6); chicken burritos (BZ$2). Open M-F 7-10am and noon-1:30pm. ❶

Syd's Restaurant and Bar, on the corner of Middle St. and the back path by Glenda's. While not the most elegant dining environment, Syd's compensates by serving the tastiest lunch on the caye. Chicken *tostadas* BZ$1; trio of *garnaches* BZ$1; burritos BZ$2. Excellent fish (BZ$10) and lobster (BZ$20); island-renowned bbq Sa night (BZ$8). Open daily 10am-3pm and 6-9:30pm. Accepts traveler's checks. AmEx/MC/V. ❶

Marin's, at the south end of Middle St., west of I&I Cafe and Bar. Highly recommended by locals. Great veggie dinner BZ$9.50, simple garden salad BZ$3.50. Fried shrimp BZ$17, *tostadas* BZ$1. Open daily 8am-2pm and 5:30-10pm. ❷

Wish Willy, on North Front St. just before Albert's, hidden in a unique and bizarre plywood restaurant. Service is slow, but the good food and atmosphere make for long dinner conversations. If you're impatient, there's nothing that the free rum punch, served all day long, won't cure. Excellent lobster tail (BZ$13) and vegetable kebab (BZ$10). ❸

Dave's Bar & Grill, located on Middle St., 1 block west of Daisy's Hotel. Word on the street says this is the best place to munch on Caye Caulker's delicious fresh catch. Grilled whole lobster (BZ$25) and kebabs (BZ$12-18). ❹

🔾 NIGHTLIFE

After a short time on Caye Caulker, most travelers find themselves conforming to a cheap and relaxing nightlife pattern. Swim, fish, or simply bask in a beautiful Caribbean sunset at **The Split.**

The Lazy Lizard is a popular Split-side hangout for grizzled guides, locals, and sunburned tourists, especially during happy hour, daily 4-6pm. **Oceanside Bar,** a few blocks south of the Split, has 6-8pm daily drink specials, along with cable TV and pool tables and Caye Caulker's only live music. **I&I Cafe and Bar,** near the south end of Front St., about 50m west of Tropical Paradise, is a unique alternative. Walk up the rickety staircase to a treehouse theme and take a seat at one of the many swings, painted in bright colors. (Local beer BZ$3, Cuba Libre BZ$4.) If you need to escape the reggae, head to the roof and chat it up with the resident dreadlocked Rasta. **The Sunset View Disco,** at the northern end of Back St., is the perfect place to go after too many hours sitting on your bum for some alcohol-induced bumping and grinding. Blacklights and hip decor make this one of Belize's hippest dance scenes. Open Th-Sa until 2am. Entrance BZ$5.

🔾 WATERSPORTS

SNORKELING. Snorkeling off Caulker guarantees schools of multicolored fish and miles of coral that, despite rising costs, are still cheaper than those in San Pedros. Tours leave around 10am and 2pm. Walk-ins the day of the trip are welcome. All operators should be approved by the Tour Guide Association; ask to see a license.

Caye Caulker has fixed rates on snorkeling packages throughout the island. Half-day trips to the shallow coral reef near Caulker are typically the cheapest option. This usually includes three stops: one dazzling stop to swim and play with sting rays, one at the coral reef, and one at the shallow coral gardens (BZ$40). Full-day trips to gorgeous **Hol Chan Marine Park** and **Shark Ray Alley,** both off Ambergris Caye, run about BZ$70 and usually include a brief stop in **San Pedro.** Two reputable snorkeling companies are **Mario's Snorkeling** (☎226 0056), on the south end of Front St., and **Anwar Tours** (☎226 0327), across from the Sandbox Restaurant.

There are two excellent independent local guides whom travelers generally prefer to the one-size-fits-all tour companies. For the half-day tour, find **Ras Creek** (☎606 4299; rascreek@hotmail.com). His trip includes the three snorkeling stops, and an informational tour around the island. Ras usually leaves around 11am from the front pier in his colorful thatched-roof boat. (Tours BZ$30; snorkeling gear is not provided.) For a full-day snorkeling tour, **Juni** is praised for his knowledge and professionalism. He takes out his sailboat, "The Trinity," to the **Hol Chan Marine Park** at the cheapest rates (BZ$55). His office is located across from the police station. To explore Caye Caulker on your own, rent from any of the shops. Cheap rentals are at **Big Fish, Little Fish,** at the southern end of Front St. (BZ$5 per day).

SCUBA DIVING. Several dive companies offer similar services and prices in Caye Caulker. Four-day certification courses run BZ$500, two-tank dives are BZ$160; three dive trips to the world-famous **Ambergris Caye** (see **Ambergris Caye,** p. 83) and to Belize's other prized location, **Turneriffe Elbow** are about BZ$300. The two most reputable dive companies are **Frenchie's** (☎226 0234; frenchies@btl.net), on the dock close to the northern end of Front St., and **Paradise Down Scuba** (☎226 0437; www.paradisedown.com), in the Oceanside Bar.

OTHER WATERSPORTS. Caye Caulker delights with a variety of fun activities: canoeing, fishing, kayaking, sailing, windsurfing, and of course, swimming. **Canoes** are available at Toucan Canoe Rentals, located on Back St. next to the Sunset View Disco (BZ$10 per hr., 4 hrs BZ$30; 6 hrs BZ$45). **Fishing trips** are becoming increasingly popular; half-day trips through **Hummingbird Tours** run about BZ$300 for two to four people. Fishermen offer cheaper trips; just ask around the village. Travelers can rent fishing rods and buy bait at the store next to the Sandy Lane hotel office and cast off of the split. Prized catch includes red snapper, barracuda, and the blue marlin. **Kayaking** is a fun way to explore the shores of the island. Rentals are available at **Seaside Cabanas.** (1 person BZ$15 per hr., BZ$45 half-day; 2 people BZ$20/$60.) **Say L King** (☎226 0489; www.saylking.com) is a new sailboat rental store located in the back of Treasured Travels on North Front St. (rentals BZ$20 per hr.), and includes brief free lessons to beginners. Fred at the Seaview Hotel rents **windsurfing** equipment in high season. For **swimming,** the best spot is the Split.

◪ DAYTRIPS FROM CAYE CAULKER

Day and overnight trips to surrounding cayes and coral reefs are becoming increasingly popular, and include manatees and dolphin sightings. (Day trips BZ$75, 9:30am-5pm.) The centerpiece is the magnificent visit to the **manatee** community at nearby **Swallow Caye.** Afterwards, most guides take you to **Geoff's Caye** for a picture-perfect lunch. Situated on top of the reef, Geoff's has coconut trees, white sandy beaches, and great snorkeling. The last stop of the trip is **Sargent's Caye,** where **dolphins** abound. Nobody does this trip like **Chocolate** (☎226 2151), who has been protecting the endangered manatees for more than 20 years. He can be found near Chocolate's Gift Shop close to the north end of the island. A solid alternative is **Anwar Snorkel and Tours,** in the center of town on Front St. (☎226 0327. Trips BZ$75 include gear.)

BELIZE

AMBERGRIS CAYE

Ambergris Caye (am-BER-gris) sits offshore 36 mi. north of Belize City. Ambergris, once a major trading port, was home to at least 10,000 Maya. After they disappeared, the island fell out of favor and was purchased by James Howe Blake, a wealthy Creole landowner, for a paltry BZ$625. Ambergris Caye is the largest of Belize's 200 islands and spans some 25 mi., but the only real population center is the town of **San Pedro,** near the southern tip. Although fishing remains an important industry for many of the town's 5100 residents, tourists have become the island's most lucrative catch. Families, honeymooners, and even backpackers can't get enough of the island. During the day, the most popular area is the **Barrier Reef;** at night, sunburned tourists crowd the sandy streets.

Ambergris, usually referred to simply as San Pedro, is the most expensive area in Belize, though a few budget deals can be found. Known in Spanish as "La Isla Bonita," Ambergris Caye has a pleasant beach, and because the barrier reef is right next to the island's eastern shores, snorkeling and diving are more convenient, though pricier, than at Caye Caulker. Ambergris Caye rose to prominence in the US when American TV turned two of the island's luxury resorts into their "Temptation Island" to test the limits of reality shows.

▐ TRANSPORTATION

Flights: Reserve flights in advance during high season (Nov.-May). The **San Pedro airstrip** is at the southwest end of town and can be reached easily by foot or taxi (BZ$5). **Tropic Air** (☎266 2012) flies to: **Belize City Municipal** (20min., every hr. 7am-5pm, BZ$52); **Belize International** (20min., every hr. 7am-5pm, BZ$93); **Corozal** (35min., every 2hr. 7am-5pm, BZ$70).

Boats: Water Taxis depart for **Belize City** (1½hr.; 8 per day 7am-4:30pm; BZ$20, round-trip BZ$45 via **Caye Caulker**). Boats also leave for the same destinations at similar times from the **Coral Beach Dive Shop** pier near the center of town.

Taxis: They wait hungrily by the airport and the docks by day and near Elvi's Kitchen on Middle St., in the middle of town after 6pm. Local trips BZ$5, outside of town BZ$7.

▐ ▐ ORIENTATION AND PRACTICAL INFORMATION

The **airstrip** is south of the center of town. Boats from Belize City usually pull up to the **Texaco dock** or the **water taxi dock,** both on the eastern shore of the island. If coming from the east, the first sandy road you will hit is **Front Street,** officially **Barrier Reef Road.** The strip runs across the Caye from north to south, and is home to most accommodations, restaurants, and dive operations. Cheap restaurants and delis can be found on **Middle Street,** also referred to as **Pescador Drive,** which runs parallel to Front St. The center of town is on Front St. at the **Children's Park** and the Barrier Reef Hotel. Upscale resorts and homes sit south of San Pedro, while the vast stretch heading north of town is uninhabited save for a few secluded resorts.

Tourist Information: Ambergris Caye Information Center (☎206 2816), on Barrier Reef Dr. across from San Pedrano Hotel, has maps and info on more expensive options.

Banks: Atlantic Bank, just south of the town center on Front St., exchanges US dollars and traveler's checks. MC/V cash advances. BZ$10 fee. Open M-F 8am-2pm, Sa 8:30am-noon. **Castleberry Ltd.,** at the **Spindrift Hotel,** has a **Western Union.** Open M-F 8am-4pm, Sa 8am-noon, Su 10:30am-noon. **Belize Bank** on the north end of Front. St. has a 24hr. **ATM** and MC/V cash advances. Open M-Th 8am-3pm, F 8am-4:30pm.

Markets Rock's Store, on Middle St.,with fluorescent purple columns. Stocks everything from suntan lotion to fresh bread. Open daily 7am-10pm.

Laundry: Nellie's Laundry, on Middle St., 1 block south of Rock's Market, provides wash, dry, and fold service for BZ$11. Open M-Sa 7am-8pm, Su 8am-2pm.

Bike Rental: Joe's Bike Rentals (☎226 4371), located on Middle St., 1 block west of Fido's. BZ$5 per hr., BZ$18 per day.

Police: (☎90 or 226 2022), on Front St., just north of Atlantic Bank, next to the central park. Open 24hr.

Medical Services: San Pedro Health Center (☎226 3668), open M-F 8am-5pm; 24hr. for emergencies. **San Carlos Pharmacy** (☎226 2918), on the north end of Middle St. Open M-Sa 7:30am-9pm, Su 9am-noon and 6-9pm. 24hr. emergency service.

Telephones: Several public phones dot Front St. BTL (☎226 2199), at the north end of Middle St., past the loud generator. Open M-F 8am-noon and 1-4pm, Sa 8am-noon.

Internet: Coconet, on Front St., has a full bar inside to quench your thirst. BZ$5 per 15min., BZ$15 per hr. Free drink with Internet use. Open daily 8am-9pm.

San Pedro

▲ ACCOMMODATIONS
Caribbean Villas, **16**
The Conch Shell, **4**
Hotel San Pedrano, **5**
Hotel del Río, **2**
Ruby's Hotel, **1**
The Tides Hotel, **1**

🍴 FOOD
Caliente, **10**
Cocina Caramba, **8**
Micky's Place, **13**
Papi's Restaurant, **3**
The Reef Restaurant, **7**
Ruby's, **12**

🍸 NIGHTLIFE
Barefoot Iguana, **15**
Fido's, **6**
The Jaguar Temple Club, **9**
Shark's Bar, **11**

Post Office: on Front St. near the banks, in the pink building. Open M-Th 8am-noon and 1-4:30pm, F 8am-noon and 1-4pm.

ACCOMMODATIONS

Inexpensive rooms are more scarce here than on Caye Caulker, especially during high season. During low season many proprietors are willing to negotiate prices.

Ruby's Hotel (☎226 2063; rubys@btl.net), a 2min. walk from the airstrip on Front St.'s south end, is the best deal in town for budget travelers. Located right on the water, ample deck space makes for mingling and relaxing. Call to reserve. Singles BZ$35, with bath BZ$70; doubles with A/C BZ$100. Low-season discounts. ❸

Hotel San Pedrano (☎226 2054; fax 226 2274), about 2 blocks north of the park on Front St.; office is in the convenience store downstairs. Clean, spacious rooms have polished wooden floors. All have large, comfortable mattresses and private baths. Singles and doubles BZ$55. An extra BZ$5-$10 in high season. ❹

The Conch Shell (☎226 2062) is located just around the corner from Hotel San Pedrano. Clean breezy rooms have porches overlooking ocean. All rooms have private bath. Singles BZ$40; doubles BZ$50; high season prices increase. ❸

The Tides Hotel (☎226 2283; www.ambergriscaye.com/tides). Follow Middle St. north, turn right at the basketball court, and go north along the beach until you see a 3-story pink mansion. A great medium-range offering with a shaded yard area, and nice quiet location. Pristine swimming pool has an all-day bar nearby. Singles and doubles with fan BZ$90, BZ$120 in high season; singles and doubles with A/C BZ$100/BZ$150. ❺

Hotel del Río (☎226 2286; hodelrio@btl.net), just north of the Tides Hotel, has a quiet environment. Basic triples with bath BZ$60; 5-person *cabaña* BZ$150. MC/V. ❶

Caribbean Villas (☎226 2715; c-v-hotel@btl.net), about 1 mi. south of town, set in a garden right on the waterfront. Escape the hustle of San Pedro in this peaceful shaded retreat. All rooms include A/C, beautiful views, fan, bike rental, hot tub, small fridge, and access to the bird sanctuary on the grounds. Singles BZ$120; doubles BZ$130. High season prices increase. Also offers larger villas. ❺

▐ FOOD

Cheap restaurants are even more difficult to find than budget accommodations, especially at night. Delis on Middle St. usually provide the best values, though you have to eat standing up. The fast food shacks on Ambergris St. near the beach are a great lunch option. During daytime, the two **La Popular Bakeries** in town serve tasty fresh pastries and donuts (pastries BZ$1-$3; both open 7am-8pm). After 7pm carts offering Belizean dishes line Front St.

Micky's Place, at the intersection of Tarpen and Coconut Dr. just north of the airstrip, is an impeccably clean restaurant. Lunch doesn't get much better than this in San Pedro; try the fish burger or conch fritter (BZ$7) and fruit salad (BZ$8). Some breakfast items such as waffles (BZ$6) are also available. Dinner prices (BZ$20-$30) remind you that you're in a resort town. Open daily 6:30-10am, 11:30am-2pm, and 6-10pm. ❹

The Reef Restaurant, north of Rock's on Middle St. Festively decorated with sand floor and fishing decor. Large portions and classic meals make it a San Pedro staple. Open M-Sa 11am-2pm and 5-10pm. ❸

Papi's Restaurant, about 2min. south of the Hotel del Río. Owner Steve, known around the island as Papi, is perhaps the friendliest man in San Pedro and cooks up generous meals. Burgers (BZ$3.50); fried chicken (BZ$7); big banana or mango *licuados* are also tempting (BZ$3). Open daily 7-10am, 11am-2pm, and 6-10pm. ❷

Ruby's, next to the hotel of the same name on the south end of Front St., serves tasty banana bread, rum cake, and snacks like meat pies and burritos (BZ$2-$4). Get there before 7am for piping hot cinnamon rolls. For an authentic treat, try their Belizean johnnycake (BZ$1.50). Open M-Sa 5am-2pm and 4-7pm, Su 5am-11am. ❶

Caliente, located in the Spindrift Hotel on Front St., has the best atmosphere and Mexican food in town. Breezy dining overlooks the water. Savory chicken and seafood burritos (BZ$12-$20). Sadly, dinner prices increase, but the entrees are excellent (BZ$20-$45). Open 11am-6pm and 6-9pm. ❹

Cocina Caramba, located on Middle St. just before the Palace Casino, has the only all-you-can-eat buffet in San Pedro, including Belizean favorites (BZ$16). Menu items are a little pricier but good. Delicious fruit smoothies (BZ$3). Buffet served 11am-9pm. ❺

▐ NIGHTLIFE

For the best night out in San Pedro, stroll up or down Front St. and the beach and follow your ears—the party is at the live music venues. **Shark's Bar,** at the end of the water taxi pier on the southern side of town, is a good place to start a night. Mean margaritas on the rocks, tasty pizza, and Tu live music. Happy hour daily 4-5pm. Open M-Tu, Th-Su until midnight. **The Jaguar Temple Club,** right in the middle of town, on Front St., is where to party every Friday and Saturday night. **The Barefoot Iguana,** south of town, is renowned for its mud wrestling (F 9pm-midnight). Yes, guys, its true—women get naked in the mud and battle it out. Take their free shuttle. **Fido's** nightly live music tends to attract an older crowd, with its country-western vibe and guitar playing contests.

◪ WATERSPORTS

SNORKELING. Just off Ambergris, the **Hol Chan Marine Reserve** affords the opportunity to swim along the reef amid barracudas, moray eels, lobsters, yellowtail snappers, parrotfish, eagle rays, and the occasional (and usually benevolent) shark. **Shark-Ray Alley** almost guarantees a swim with the sharks: nurse sharks and sting rays flock as guides toss diced fish carcasses overboard. **Mexico Rocks** is a less trafficked site where it is possible to free dive through caves and canyon walls built from coral, and swim next to Nassau groupers, lobster, horse-eye jacks, and sand sharks.

Guided trips can be easily arranged. A half-day, two-stop snorkeling trip to Hol Chan and Shark-Ray Alley usually costs about BZ$50 per person (plus BZ$5-$10 for equipment and BZ$5 for Hol Chan entrance.) Trips to Mexico run about BZ$55, plus equipment rental. Two reputable operators are **SEArious Adventures** (☎ 226 4202; serious@btl.net), located behind Ruby's, and **SEAduced** (☎ 226 2254), located on the street running west from Ruby's. SEAduced trips are more relaxed than those of SEArious, which generally fits its namesake. Both companies offer a three-site trip with a stop at Caye Caulker (BZ$70) if you need to be dropped off. You don't even have to get wet on the *Southern Beauty*, a **glass-bottom boat** that leaves from the **Off Shore Express** dock. (☎ 322 2340. Daily 9am and 2pm for half-day excursions. BZ$45, snorkel gear BZ$8.) The **Rum Punch II**, a 38 ft. sailboat, will take you out on personal trips. (☎ 322 2340. BZ$100; delightful sunset cruises BZ$40.) Look for the sign on the beach south of the town center. For those unable to splurge, there is still hope. Most shops rent out fins and masks (BZ$5-$10) for you to explore the shores of Ambergris Caye on your own. However, **never attempt to swim out to the reef on your own**—always hire a guide.

SCUBA DIVING. It's possible to dive in the reefs right off the island. (US$35 for 1 tank, US$45 for 2.) The most famous nearby site is **Blue Hole.** The other worldwide renowned site is the **Turneffe Elbow.** The most highly recommended dive company is **Amigos del Mar** (☎ 226 2648; www.amigosdive.com), just south of Hotel Pedrano on a pier. An excellent alternative is the **Coral Beach Dive Shop** (☎ 226 2817), located a few blocks north of Ruby's on the end of a pier. **Hustler Tours,** on the pier before the Shark's Bar, has good rates and quality service. Other companies may offer lower rates; be sure to get second opinions on their quality. A great source of info on the dive companies is the **Blue Hole Dive Center** (☎ 226 2982; bluehole@btl.net). If you aren't scuba-certified but want to dive, the cheapest option is a **Discover Scuba** or resort **course,** which lets you make one or two dives with a dive-master after a morning of basic explanations. **Amigos del Mar** (p. 83) lists the course for BZ$350 and also a full menu of certification courses, including the **PADI openwater certification** for BZ$700.

OTHER AQUATIC ACTIVITIES. If being underwater doesn't suit you, or you just want to enjoy the view of the coastline, check out these options. **Sailsports Belize** gives **windsurfing** lessons and provides **boat rentals** and **sailing instruction**. (☎ 226 4488. Windsurfing BZ$90; boards BZ$50 per hr., boat rentals BZ$60; sailing instruction BZ$110.) For a semi-dry caye experience, you can get a guided **kayak tour** among the Mangrove Islands from **SEAduced** (☎ 226 2254) for BZ$100 per person, including lunch. **Innovations Watersports**, next to Ramon's Resort, rents kayaks. (☎ 226 3337. 1-person BZ$20 per hr.; 2-person BZ$30 per hr.) Many operators also have **charter fishing** trips (half-day BZ$300, full day BZ$400). **Parasailing**, at **Water Sports and Tour Headquarters,** across from Caliente on the dock, offers 12-15 min. trips, 200 ft. in the air. (1 person BZ$120, for 2 BZ$200, for 3 BZ$280.)

BELIZE

DEFENSIVE DIVING. The barrier reef along Belize and Honduras is the largest in the Western Hemisphere and second largest in the entire world. Many dive shops on the cayes offer travelers the chance to get certified for considerably less than in the US. Unfortunately, competition between shops has also caused some corner-cutting. Safety awareness and quality of instruction are sometimes sacrificed for mass-output certification. Shop around before settling on a dive center. Make sure the instructor is fully certified with NAUI or PADI, the biggest divers' organizations. If some ' deals seem too good to be true, they probably are. **Bad air or poor instruction can lead to decompression sickness and death,** so don't take chances. While preserving your safety, make an effort to protect the well being of the coral and sea life. Many dive operations in Belize have strict rules about not touching the coral or removing anything from the reef. Coral-heads that took eons to develop can be lost in a matter of seconds.

MAINLAND GETAWAYS. Those eager to dry off or escape the brunt of coastal tourism can hit a daytrip led by some of Ambergris' local outfits. **Blue Hole Dive Center** organizes excursions to the zoo (approximately a 2hr. trip) as well as to the ruins of **Lamanai** (BZ$250) and **AltunHa** (BZ$120). **SEArious** also takes people out to these ruins, though this is not the cheapest way to get there (☎ 226 4202).

NORTHERN BELIZE

Northern Belize is a low-lying area of pine savannas, swamps, jungles, and coastal lagoons. The region has much more of a Mexican feel than other parts of the country, and Spanish is prevalent in many areas. Given the long stretches of cane fields, smokestacks jutting up from refineries, and the abundance of cheap rum, it's easy to see that sugar is the basis of the northern economy. The Northern Highway turns inland after leaving Belize City and doesn't return to the coast until it reaches Corozal eight miles from the Mexican border, after reaching most of the region's landlocked Maya ruins and nature reserves. Highlights of the region include the impressive Maya site of Lamanai, accessible from mellow Orange Walk, as well as outstanding birding. Look for the rare Jaribu stork at Crooked Tree Wildlife Sanctuary, and explore the variety at the Shipstern Nature Reserve.

⬛ BERMUDIAN LANDING BABOON SANCTUARY

Russell's buses leave Belize City (M-F noon and 4:30pm, Sa 12:15, 1, 4, and 5pm; BZ$3.50) from the corner of Euphrates St. and Cairo St., opposite the basketball court. Return buses leave M-Sa 5:30, 6, and 6:30am, so plan to spend the night if you come by bus. Register before entering the sanctuary at the green building with the "museum" sign in Bermudian Landing (☎ 220 2181; www.howlermonkey.org). Speak to friendly Mrs. Jessie or Mrs. Joseph. A tour is included in the BZ$10 admission fee. Local guides usually ensure at least 1 sighting in each 1hr. tour. At the museum, which is also the sanctuary headquarters, you can arrange more extensive guided trips into the forest. (3½hr. canoe trip with guide BZ$50; night hikes BZ$20 per person; crocodile night tour BZ$100 per person; horseback riding BZ$50 per hr.)

For the true monkey lover, the sanctuary was founded in 1985 to protect the endangered black howler monkey, locally known as "baboon." Farmers in the tiny village of **Bermudian Landing**, an hour northwest of Belize City, and seven other communities voluntarily pledged to abide by conservation plans to protect the

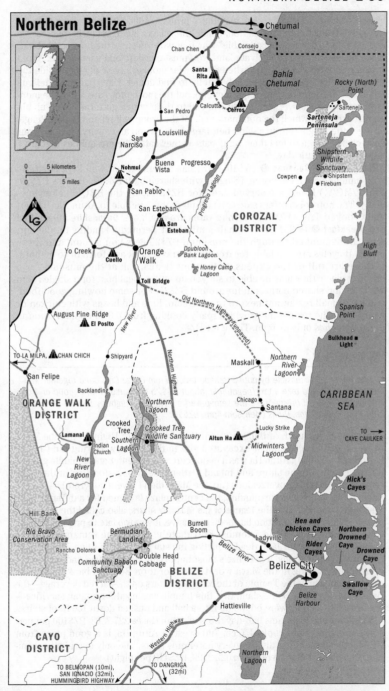

Northern Belize

howlers' habitat. The 20 sq. mi. sanctuary protects 1600 black howler monkeys. Instead of being treated as a national park, the villages share land with the reserve and attempt to live in a "sustainable" way that won't destroy the howlers' habitat. Since the sanctuary is on private land, you must check in and use a guide. Avoid trips after a heavy downpour, when the howler monkeys typically nap inside the trunks of palm trees, emerging only briefly to find dinner. Have patience and bug repellent—the monkeys are unpredictable, but the mosquitoes are not. If the monkeys are acting elusive, your guide will call to them with a guttural "uh-uh-uh-uh-uh-rarrrrrrrr!" to which the dominant male of the group will respond in challenge. At night the jungle tour is a good bet; large bats swoop and swerve around your head close enough to feel their wingbeats as they catch the mosquitoes that are a nuisance during the day.

Nature Resort Cabañas ❸ (☎610 1378) has several clean, well-kept *cabañas* with hammocks on the porch. (Singles with shared bath BZ$40; doubles BZ$80. AmEx/MC/V.) Meals are served daily for BZ$6-10; try the BBQ chicken specialty. The hotel also offers side trips for up to three people to Altun Ha (BZ$90) and Crooked Tree (BZ$120). Group rates are available. **Devonshire Village Bed and Breakfast** ❷ (☎221 2464) is half a mile past Bermudia Landing on the left, and can be booked through the museum. BZ$25 gets you a room and three meals. Bicycles are available for free use to travel back and forth or to explore. If these are full or too expensive for your tastes, ask at the museum for a cheaper place; they may be able to set you up with a local host for a single room with fan and shared bathroom for around BZ$25. For some howling good food, enter the small restaurant next to the museum. Rice and beans with chicken or beef BZ$8. The restaurant provides ready cooking from 6:30am-8pm. *Panadas* and *garnaches* only 8-10pm. Three for BZ$2.

◎ ALTUN HA

Altun Ha is not accessible by public transportation. From Belize City, band together with other travelers and take a taxi (negotiable, about US$25 per person with a group of 4 or 5) or rent a car. If driving, take the semi-paved old Northern Highway to mile 18.9 and then follow the signs. Ruins open 8am-4pm. BZ$10.

Thirty-one miles north of Belize City off the old Northern Highway are the Maya ruins of Altun Ha, the most excavated site in the country. During the Classic Period (AD 250-900), Altun Ha was a major ceremonial center and a middle ground for trade between the shore and inland settlements. The restoration of the main ruins has been a little overzealous (no, the Maya didn't invent concrete).

Each of the 13 temples surrounding the central plaza is named for a different god. The most famous is B-4, the **Temple of the Masonry Altars,** also called the sun god's temple. While the restoration has been extensive, it was too late to prevent bandits from ransacking 5 of the 7 tombs. Fortunately, one of the remaining tombs enclosed the beautiful Jade Head depicting the sun god, Kinick Ahua. Weighing in at nearly five kilograms, it is Belize's most important Maya artifact and the largest known jade carving in the Maya world. Look for it on Belizean banknotes. Also notice the image of the Temple of the Masonry Altars on the sacred beverage—the Belize Beliken Beer. Some claim that this temple was used for human sacrifice—the fortunate victims were bound up into a ball and pushed down 150 ft. of stairs.

S&L Travel and Tours runs half-day tours of Altun Ha. (☎227 7593. BZ$100 per person.) The village of Crooked Tree, 7mi. west of Altun Ha, is a good place from which to visit the ruins; almost every hotel runs tours. The only overnight accommodations are at **Maruba resort** (☎022 2199, BZ$119 per night).

CROOKED TREE WILDLIFE SANCTUARY

Adjacent to the village of the same name, **Crooked Tree Wildlife Sanctuary** is 33 mi. northwest of Belize City and 2½ mi. off the Northern Highway. The sanctuary was established in 1984 to protect the 300 different bird species that flock here by the thousands. The prized attraction is the rare **Jabiru Stork:** with a wingspan of up to 12 ft., it's one of the largest flying birds in the western hemisphere. The birds can be found nesting and feasting in the calm lagoons and waterways which stretch inland into the park's massive 16,400 acres. Joining the storks are boat-billed herons, kites, egrets, and ospreys. The sanctuary is best visited late February to early June when the Jabiru storks fill the park's lagoons. This is also the time when hotels are open and lagoon tours operate.

TRANSPORTATION. Crooked Tree is 2½ mi. off the Northern Highway, which connects Belize City and Orange Walk; take a **bus** between those two destinations. It is possible to get a direct bus from Belize City through **Jex** (M-Sa 10:55am from Regent St. West; 4:30 and 5:15pm from Pound Yard; return M-Sa 5, 6:30, 6:50am) or **Novelo's** (M-F 4pm, return M-F 6am). Otherwise, take any northbound bus from Belize or southbound bus from Orange Walk and ask to be let off at the Crooked Tree Junction. From there, arrange a ride to Crooked Tree or wait for the next passing vehicle. Locals are accustomed to giving lifts, although *Let's Go* does not recommend hitchhiking. Arrive 15min. beforehand, as buses fill up early. Don't be afraid to barge into an already packed bus, since chances are that another dozen or so passengers can be expected to create a sardine-can bus. Schedules change often; call the community phone for the latest update (☎209 7084). You can also walk to town (1hr.).

ORIENTATION. The park is accessible via tiny **Crooked Tree Village** (pop. 786). All visitors to the park must pay the BZ$8 admission fee at the **visitor center,** on the right as you enter the village (open daily 8am-4:30pm). In addition to helpful guides and maps of trails, the center has some interesting exhibits.

ACCOMMODATIONS AND FOOD. For a village of its size, Crooked Tree offers an extensive selection of rooming options, each of which is signposted at the junction just past the visitor center. The buses will take you close to each of the accommodations if you ask. **Rhaburn's Rooms ❶,** a 5min. walk from the visitor center, is the cheapest B&B in town. It has four rooms with fans and a clean communal bath. Turn left at the junction by the hotel signs, cut through the field just past the blue-green Church of the Nazarene, and look for the path at the far back corner of the field. As the path turns right, enter the gate on the left of Rhaburn's yellow wooden house. (☎225 7035. Meals BZ$6. Singles BZ$20; doubles BZ$30.) **Sam Tillet's Hotel ❹,** in the middle of the village, is a two-story *cabaña* in a yard filled with livestock. Follow signs from the visitor center (about 10min. on foot). Rooms are spacious, well swept, and bug free, with modern baths and A/C or fan. Suites provide the extra bonus of mosquito-netted beds and refrigerators. (☎220 7026. Singles BZ$55; doubles BZ$77; Jabiru Suite BZ$121.) Sam Tillet offers the only **Internet access** in Crooked Tree (BZ$10 per hr.), as well as numerous tours to surrounding sites in Belize.

Food options in town are limited. **Triple J Restaurant ❷,** to the right of the main junction, has good food at a low price. (Burger BZ$2.50, dinner entrees BZ$6-$9.) The best bet is usually to eat at your lodge.

ACTIVITIES AND GUIDED TOURS. The best way to sample Crooked Tree is with the visitor center's free trail map, bug repellent, boots, and a passion for bird-watching. Take the **Trogon Trail** out to the park's famous boardwalk, the largest in

Belize. The 3-4hr. venture is a great way to find the lagoon's many aquatic birds and other wildlife. The most recommended guide is **Sam Tillet** (☎201 2026). He runs excellent birding and boating tours on the lagoon. Call ahead, as the water level can sometimes be too low for boats and the Jabirus may be in Mexico. (Up to four people BZ$150.) **Bird's Eye View Lodge** (☎225 7027) and the **Paradise Inn** (☎225 7044) have the same tours for similar prices.

ORANGE WALK

Even though the town was named when European settlers planted a "walk" of orange trees outside the front door of the town church, it is sugar, not the orange, that reigns over Orange Walk today. The main road is filled with sugar cane, as are the trucks heading south to the refinery. Orange Walk (pop. 15,300) is a predominately Hispanic town, as its first settlers were Mestizos fleeing the Caste Wars of the Yucatan in the 1850s. Today, the town is ethnically diverse and includes people of Chinese, Maya, and Spanish descent, as well as uniformly-dressed Mennonites who periodically come into town to trade.

In the 1980s, as a result of depression in sugar prices, Orange Walk became notorious as the center of Belize's growing marijuana production. Today, with help from the US, the marijuana production has largely ceased, though an undercurrent is still noticeable. Despite being Belize's -largest city, Orange Walk's main attraction is not its bustling nightlife, but rather its proximity to the Maya ruins of Lamanai and Cuello. Most visitors use Orange Walk as a way station before embarking on a river tour to visit Lamanai.

█▌ TRANSPORTATION

Most **buses** leave from **Novelo's terminal,** located at the northern end of Orange Walk. Buses go to **Belize City** (2hr., every hr. 5am-8:30pm, BZ$5) and **Chetumal, Mexico** (2hr., every hr. 6am-9:30pm, BZ$7) via **Corozal** (1½hr., BZ$5). **Local buses** leave from Zeta's store for **Sarteneja**.

▓▌ ORIENTATION AND PRACTICAL INFORMATION

Buses from Belize City and Mexico drop off along the intersection between the principal north-south drag, which is called **Queen Victoria Road** north of the fire station, and **Belize-Corozal Road** south of the station. For quick orientation, remember that **Novelo's** bus terminal is at the very north end of town, and the **Town Hall** is in the center of town; both are on Belize-Corozal Road. Looking north from Town Hall, a lively **park** is across the street. **Main Street** also runs parallel to Queen Victoria Rd. another block east, close to **New River** on the edge of town. Don't ask locals where Main St. is, as they tend to direct tourists to Queen Victoria Rd instead. Orange Walk is not safe after dark, and women should be particularly cautious.

Banks: Belize Bank, on Main St., across from the People's Store. 24hr. **ATM** accepts foreign MC/V.

Car Rental: Melo's Auto Rental, 72 Belize-Corozal Rd. (☎322 2177). Head south on the Belize-Corozal Rd. to the yellow wooden house on the left, about a block past the juncture with Liberty Ave. There's no sign. BZ$50 per 12hr.

Market: The People's Store, 51 Main St. Open M-Th 8am-noon and 1:30-5pm, F-Sa 7am-9pm, Su 8am-noon. MC/V.

Police: (☎90 or 322 2022), 4 blocks north of the park on Belize-Corozal Rd. Open 24hr.

Pharmacy: Pharmacy Lucille (☎322 0346), half a block north of the Belize Bank on Main St. Open daily 8am-9pm.

Hospital: (☎322 2072), 1200 ft. north of the police office. Open 24hr.

Telephones: Public phones are located at various points along Belize-Corozal Rd. **BTL** (☎322 2196). Located next to the Belize Bank on Main St. **Fax** and telegram service. Open M-F 8am-noon and 1-4pm, Sa 8am-noon.

Internet Access: Cybernet Cafe, between the park and the Hotel Akihito on Queen Victoria Rd., has slow Internet at irregular hours (BZ$8 per hr.). Open daily 8am-noon, 2-5pm, and 7-9pm.

Post Office: 3 blocks north of the park on Belize-Corozal Rd., in the same building as the treasury. Open M-F 8am-4:30pm.

■ ACCOMMODATIONS

Akihito Hotel (☎322 3018; akihitolee@hotmail.com), on Queen Victoria Rd., kitty-corner from the Shell station. The best deal in the area. Clean rooms and a bar downstairs. Singles with fan and shared bath BZ$25, with A/C BZ$45; doubles BZ$35/BZ$55. ❷

St. Christopher's Hotel (☎302 1064; rowbze@btl.net), at the north end of Main St., before the bridge. Named for the patron saint of travelers, this hotel is a blessing for the weary. Large rooms are equipped with cable TV, ceiling fan, and hot bath. Doubles BZ$59, with A/C BZ$91; BZ$10 per additional person, new rooms with river views extra BZ$10. ❷

D'Victoria Hotel, 40 Belize-Corozal Rd. (☎322 2518), in the pink building at the south end of town, across the street from the Shell station. Spacious, tiled rooms with bath and cable TV. Extra perks include a pool and a bar downstairs. Check-out noon. Singles BZ$45, with A/C BZ$75; doubles BZ$60/BZ$86; triples BZ$85/BZ$107. MC/V. ❸

Mi Amor Hotel, 19 Belize-Corozal Rd. (☎322 2031), before the Shell station. Enter the office. On weekends, sleep is virtually impossible because of the booming disco downstairs. Rooms have cable TV, fans, and private hot baths. Check-out 1pm. Singles BZ$48, with A/C BZ$74; doubles BZ$59/BZ$86. Traveler's checks accepted. ❹

■ FOOD

Taco carts cluster around the park and offer some of the best and cheapest meals in town, including chicken sandwiches (3 for BZ$1), hot dogs (BZ$2), and drinks. Those with a sugar craving can grab pastries, cakes, and cookies for the road at **Pontificadora La Popular,** 1 Bethias St., north of the park. On Fridays and Saturdays, locals sell excellent bbq chicken (BZ$5 per plate) on Belize-Corozal Rd.

Juanita's, 8 Santa Ana St., north of the Shell station at the south end of town. This clean local favorite offers traditional Belizean fare in a town dominated by Chinese restaurants. Though the menu is not extensive, hungry travelers can fill up on bacon with eggs and beans (BZ$6), and beans with chicken (BZ$6). Those with adventurous palates might try the cow foot soup (BZ$8). Open M-Sa 6am-2pm and 6-9pm. ❶

Lee's Chinese Restaurant, 11 San Antonio Rd., 1 block west of the firehouse. The top among local Chinese restaurants. Go for the chicken curry (BZ$12) or the conch fried rice (BZ$10). Open M-Sa 10:30am-midnight, Su noon-midnight. ❸

■ SIGHTS

La Inmaculada Church, a 101-year-old Catholic church at the south end of Main St., is worth a look, and the **river bank** is a great picnic spot. Although the park in the center of town is cement rather than grass, it's good for resting and people-watching. A mile north of town is the **Godoy Orchid Farm.** Carlos is the expert for all the dirt on the orchids. If you're lucky, he'll be around to give a tour; call before you go

(☎ 322 2969). At night, if you're looking for a place with smaller crowds more conducive to a conversation, **Carl's** is a karaoke bar in the same building as D'Victoria (see **Accommodations**, p. 89). (Open Su, Tu-Sa 6pm.)

◢ DAYTRIPS: MAYA RUINS

LAMANAI

There is a BZ$10 entrance fee. Several area companies offer boat trips. In Orange Walk, try Jungle River Tours in Lover's Restaurant just east of the central plaza. The company is run by the knowledgeable Novelo brothers, who lead legendary treks through the ruins and also stop to discuss wildlife on the New River. (☎ 302 2293; lamanaimaya-tour@btl.net. Trips BZ$80 per person, 4-person min. Includes lunch and drinks.) Local hotels also arrange tours, but usually use the guides of Jungle River Tours. If a guided tour is beyond your budget, you may still get to Lamanai. Buses leave from beside the fire station in the village of Indian Church, 1 mi. from Lamanai. (Buses M, W, F 4pm, return 6am.) Call the Indian Creek community phone for current schedules. (☎ 309 2015.)

One of Belize's most impressive attractions, this site is believed to have been a vital agricultural and commercial center of the Maya world. Archaeologists think the structures here were first erected in 1500 BC and inhabited until the 17th century, when the community was ravaged by European diseases. Lamanai's claim to fame is that it is the only inhabited Maya site to be inhabited in all five archaeological eras: pre-Classic, Classic, post-Classic, Spanish, and English era.

While there is a gravel access road to the site, most visitors take the 33 mi. boat ride down the **New River Lagoon** from Orange Walk or the northern highway junction. Various water birds and the occasional crocodile line the riverbanks during the relaxing ride. At Lamanai itself, several short jungle paths reveal three well-excavated **temples** affording panoramic views of the area. In addition, loud **howler monkeys**, fruit trees, and other jungle foliage make for an enjoyable visit.

Boats arrive at a dock surrounded by souvenir stands. Up the hill and to the right lies a small but impressive display of pre-Classic Maya artifacts, which have been collected during excavation. Bear right at the fork and follow the trail for 5min. to the first and smallest pyramid, the Temple of the Mask. A 13 ft. tall face protrudes from the front side, surrounded by the gaping mouth of a jaguar. The mask itself was added during the reign of the powerful Lord Smoking Shell.

Five minutes farther along a windy path is the **High Temple**. At 30m, it is the third-largest building in the Maya world. The safest way to climb it is to go up the center steps, then take a left on the first platform and follow the path around the corner onto the 3 ft. wide steps that go the rest of the way. The top provides an impressive view of the jungle and the river that made Lamanai an important center of trade. Check out the finely detailed **Stela 9.** Located near the High Temple, this edifice commemorates Lord Smoking Shell's anniversary. Other attractions include the labyrinthine elite residences and the **Temple of the Jaguar,** complete with two imaginative jaguar friezes at the temple's bottom front corners. (Open daily 8:30am-5pm.)

CUELLO

Reach Cuello by walking west from Orange Walk (1hr.) or by taxi (BZ$10). Call ☎ 322 2141 for permission before visiting. Open daily 8am-noon and 1:30-6pm. Free.

Not nearly as impressive as Lamanai, but closer to Orange Walk, Cuello was once thought to be among the oldest Maya sites in Central America. Recent studies suggest, however, that this small, single temple, the Maya equivalent of a wine cellar, actually only dates back to 1000 BC. Nonetheless, excavations have uncovered more burials here than at any other Maya site. Some of the 200 skeletons had their skulls detached, suggesting that they may have been sacrifices for the new temple. Today Cuello retains a relatively untouristed tranquility.

SARTENEJA AND THE SHIPSTERN NATURE RESERVE

Situated across the Chetumal Bay from Mexico's Yucatán Peninsula, the **Sarteneja Peninsula** is endowed with a characteristically Yucatán climate. Much of the wildlife found in Sarteneja is unique to the area; this phenomenon led to the founding of the **Shipstern Nature Reserve,** which houses jaguars, pumas, and crocodiles, though the star attraction is the spectacular bird life: over 200 species can be found in the reserve's 22,000 acres. Three miles north is the colorful fishing village of Sarteneja, where the blue bay creates an idyllic spot for an afternoon swim and a beautiful sunrise. Sarteneja itself is a sleepy little town with two hotels, one small restaurant, two bars, and a few shops.

■ TRANSPORTATION. Located along the road from Orange Walk, the entrance to the Shipstern Nature Reserve is 3.1 mi. shy of Sarteneja village. You can ask the bus driver to let you off there. **Buses** make the bumpy 2hr. trip to Sarteneja from Orange Walk in the afternoons (3 buses between 2-5pm). All buses depart from outside **Zeta's Ice and Purified Water Store** on Main St., 1 block north of the **People's Store.** There is also a **boat** service that leaves Corozal at 3pm, and can stop in **Sarteneja** en route to **San Pedro.** Buses return from Sarteneja to Orange Walk en route to **Chetumal** or **Belize City** (M-Sa 4, 5, 5:30am) and depart from North Front St., next to **Fernando's Seaside Guesthouse.**

⚐ PRACTICAL INFORMATION. The **visitor center** is located at the entrance to the Shipstern Nature Reserve, 3 mi. south of Sarteneja Village. In the village, there are a few very small **grocery stores;** it is probably a better idea to stock up in Orange Walk, particularly with mosquito repellent. A pay phone is next to the basketball court in the center of town. The **police station** is on North Front Street.

⚑ ACCOMMODATIONS. If you are hiking the trails at Shipstern Nature Reserve, ask at the **visitor center ❶** for dorm rooms (BZ$20). Ranger Damien rents out a cabin next to the visitor center (BZ$80). There is no phone number, and reservations can be tough. Contact the Belize Audobon Society for more info. (☎223 5004; www.belizeaudobon.org.) In Sarteneja Village itself, there are spots with *cabañas* or rooms. **Fernando's Guesthouse ❹,** on North Front St., has four spacious double rooms. Each has two queen-size beds, hot bath, and fan. There is also a common room with TV and a porch overlooking the bay. Fernando's seafood is the best in town. Reserve ahead. (☎423 2085. Singles BZ$50; doubles BZ$60.)

🍴🎭 FOOD AND ENTERTAINMENT. There are limited dining options in Sarteneja. This is a bit surprising, since Sarteneja fishers deliver lobster all over Belize. **Lily's ❷** menu is three words long: rice, beans, chicken (BZ$8). Be sure to follow the restaurant rules written on the wall in red lipstick: "Eat with shirt on, do not spit on the floor, and pay for your food." **Fernando's Guest House Restaurant ❸** (see **Accommodations,** above) has incredible seafood.

Sarteneja also has two bars with the same menu—Belikin beer, a game of pool, rum, and loud music. **Noa Noa Bar** is a block north of **Richies** on North Front St. (open daily 8am-11pm).

◑⚘ SIGHTS AND ACTIVITIES. Established in 1981 for the conservation of hardwood forests, saline wetlands, and lagoon systems, the **Shipstern Reserve** is a birdwatcher's dream and a mosquito hater's nightmare. Its 22,000 acres support animals indigenous to the area and over 200 bird species, including many which are endangered or threatened. The forest is beautiful but young—all but three of the larger trees were lost to Hurricane Janet when it struck the peninsula in 1955. Today, most are less than 20m tall and many are just saplings.

Your first stop should be the **visitor center** at the reserve entrance. Knowledgeable rangers take guests through a display of animal skulls, tracks, and droppings. They also show off a peaceful butterfly house. This, and a guided 1hr. walk along the painstakingly labeled Chiclero Botanical Trail, are included in the BZ$10 admission. If you can tolerate the mosquitoes, the staff will guide you along a number of longer and more interesting trails through the forest (BZ$5 per hr.).

Between September and June, visitors can arrange a trip out to an island in the Shipstern Lagoon to see the rare **wood storks.** In the past, the birds' eggs and babies have fallen prey to villagers who consider them a delicacy. Now, a 24hr. staff protects the endangered birds. The trip to the island is BZ$30 for fuel, plus BZ$5 per hr. to hire a guide. For a bit more money, it's also possible for groups to hire a night or even an overnight boat tour. If crocodiles are your thing, ask to visit the 1000-acre Xo-Pol Parcel crocodile pond to see saltwater crocs.

Aside from the stunning sunsets over the bay, Sarteneja does not have much to see. If you're looking for more, contact **Fernando.** He runs excellent fishing trips, and trips to Bacalar Chico for snorkeling. (☎423 2085. See **Accommodations,** above. Fishing trips BZ$100 up to 4 people. Snorkeling BZ$200 up to 4 people.)

COROZAL

Touching the striking turquoise waters of the Chetumal Bay, Corozal (pop. 8900) is the northernmost town in Belize, just 8 mi. south of the Mexican border. A colorful **mural** by Belizean-Mexican painter Manuel Villamor in the town hall documents the history of this enchanting laid-back town. Children play games in the streets, and most people know each other by name, lending Corozal a hospitable, small-town atmosphere; it is a great place to spend a few relaxing days. Stroll through the town square, swim or picnic in the park-lined waterfront, visit several minor Maya sites, or delight in some of Belize's best food. Hurricane Janet ripped through in 1955 and wreaked such destruction that the people of Corozal had to rebuild from scratch. The town's well-ordered streets, paved roads, and recreational parks are the result.

▐ TRANSPORTATION. Flights from Corozal on **Maya Island Air** (☎422 2333) go to **San Pedro** on Ambergris Caye (20min.; 7:30am, 12:30, 5pm; BZ$70); **Tropic Air** (☎422 0356) does the same run. It is best to make reservations with the airlines directly, as some agencies charge commission. The airstrip is a 5min. taxi ride south of town (BZ$8). All **buses** leave from the **Northern Transport Terminal** at the intersection of 1st St. North and 7th Avenue, 2 blocks west of Central Park. Destinations include: **Belize City** (3hr.; every hr. 4am-noon, every 30min. noon-7:30pm; BZ$8); **Orange Walk** (1½hr., BZ$5); and **Chetumal, Mexico** (1½hr.; every 30min. 7:15-10:15am, every hr. 10:15am-2:15pm, express 11:20am; BZ$2.50.) **Thunderboat** sends out boats from the pier next to Corozal visitor center for **San Pedro** (☎422 2904; crivero@btl.net) and can stop in **Sarteneja**. (20min., daily 3pm, BZ$35.) **Hotel Maya** rents **cars** for around BZ$100 per day. Call **Hokol Kin** (see **Accommodations,** p. 93) in advance and they will have a **Budget** car waiting for you.

◼▐ ORIENTATION AND PRACTICAL INFORMATION. Despite the grid system, navigation in banana-shaped Corozal can be confusing. Major landmarks include the **Central Park** and **plaza** (home of the **town hall**) next to the **Catholic church** in the center of town. The **ocean** runs along the eastern side of the city. The avenues run parallel to the shore and are numbered consecutively starting at the bay. Streets run perpendicular to the bay and are numbered from the park. **First Street North** skirts the northern side of Central Park, and **First Street South** skirts the southern side. For quick orientation, remember that **Corozal Bay** is at the eastern edge and runs roughly north-south.

The new **Corozal Cultural and Visitor Center,** 2nd South St., houses a small **museum** that details Corozal's history. Head east to the sea from Central Park and turn right. It's the building with the bright orange roof. (☎422 3176; www.corozal.com. Open Tu-Sa 9am-noon and 1-4:30pm. Special exhibits BZ$3.) For money, **Belize Bank,** located at the north end of the park, has a 24hr. **ATM.** (Open M-Th 8am-1pm, F 8am-4:30pm. MC/V.) **U-Save Market** is at 4th Ave., 2nd St. South two blocks south of Central Park. (Open M-Th 7:30am-8pm, F 7:30am-9pm, Sa 7:30am-9:30pm, Su 7:30am-12:30pm.) **Police** are on the west side of the central park behind the post office. (☎422 2022, emergency 911. Open 24hr.) **J.B.'s Pharmacy,** 1st St., is just north of the park. Call for 24hr. service. (☎422 2982. Open daily 8am-10pm.) The **hospital** is located past the bus terminal about 200m up the Northern Hwy., on the left. (☎422 2076. Open 24hr.) **BTL,** 6th Ave between 2nd and 3rd St. South, has telephone and mail service. (Open M-F 8am-noon and 1-5pm, Sa 8am-noon.) **Public pay phones** are scattered on the street running along the park (☎422 2196). **ME Computer Systems,** on 3rd St., 3 blocks from the water, has **Internet.** (BZ$3 per 30min. Open 9am-8pm.) The **post office** is on the west side of Central Park, across from the taxi stand (open M-Th 8:30am-noon and 1-4:30pm, F 8:30am-noon and 1-4pm).

⚑ ACCOMMODATIONS. Few tourists come to this area. There is currently a dearth of true budget options, as several have gone out of business or, in the case of one, burned down. However, those with a higher pricetag are worth the extra money. **Marvirton Guest House & Lounge ❷,** at 16 2nd St. North, is the best budget option in Corozal. Basic rooms, clean bathrooms, and dry fountain area all come at the right price. (☎422 3365. Singles BZ$30; doubles BZ$45, with bath and TV BZ$58.) **Hotel Maya ❹,** in southern Corozal, on the shore road 1 Ave., is a comfortable abode offering the friendliest service in town. Tiled, well-kept baths have cute bars of soap. Restaurant serves breakfast; order lunch or dinner in advance. Laundry service is available. (☎422 2082. Singles with fan BZ$50, with TV BZ$60, with A/C BZ$85; doubles BZ$62/BZ$75/BZ$99. AmEx/MC/V.) **Hokol Kin ❹,** 4th Ave. 4 blocks south of the park on the water. This oceanfront treasure is the perfect choice for larger groups. Bright rooms with fans and 2 ultra-comfortable queen-size beds accommodate up to four. Modern bathrooms have hot water and the lounge has cable TV and refrigerator. Many rooms have a sliding door to a balcony complete with hammock and view of the bay. (☎422 3329. Singles BZ$60, with TV BZ$70; doubles BZ$85/BZ$95. Each additional person BZ$10.)

⚏ FOOD. Corozal has some of the tastiest, cheapest restaurants in all of Belize. **Le Café Kéla ❷,** 3 blocks north of the visitor center across the street from the coast, is hidden amidst lush gardens in a thatched *cabaña*. Specializing in Caribbean cuisine with a French twist, this restaurant is recommended by locals for a reason: it's unique, daring, and delicious. (Crepes BZ$4; pastas BZ$6. Fantastic ocean view. Open W-F 11:30am-2pm and 5:30-9pm, Sa 5-10pm.) **Jo-Mel-Inn ❷,** on 5th St., 1 block south of the west end of the park, was named after the manager's three children. This local standby is all you'll need; the blackboard outside details the special of the day. It's a bargain BZ$6-8 for a full meal and huge goblets of fresh fruit juice only BZ$2 (open M-F 6:30am-5pm, Sa 6:30am-2:30pm). **Cactus Plaza ❶,** on 6th St. South, 2 blocks from the waterfront, is the best deli in town and allows you to eat inside, outside, or on the roof. Serves sandwiches (BZ$2-4) and great milkshakes (BZ$2) inside one of the nicest discos around (open M-Sa 8am-midnight, Su

10am-2pm and 5pm-midnight). **Tony's Inn Y-Not Bar & Grill ❸**, the most romantic and luxurious setting in town, also serves excellent food. Located in a breezy *cabaña* on the southern beachfront with piers leading into the ocean, Tony's serves sizzling chicken fajitas (BZ$14); burgers (BZ$8); and Caribbean lobster (BZ$22). For breakfast, retreat indoors to the immaculate Vista Del Sol Restaurant. (Breakfast 7-11am, lunch and dinner 11am-7pm.)

◙ **SIGHTS. Santa Rita,** the "Ancient Corozal," inhabited from 900 BC-AD 1550, is a 20min. walk from Central Park. Take Rita Rd. (Northern Hwy.) north toward Chetumal, past the bus station. As the road splits in two, stay to the right, and proceed uphill. After about 100m, make the first left. Keep going until you see the ruins on your right. Archaeologists suspect that Santa Rita may have been the once-powerful Maya city of Chactemal. Only one main temple remains, partially excavated, after other buildings were pillaged for stone to use in Corozal's foundations. A small pyramid is the only worthwhile remaining structure. Mr. Wiltshire, the caretaker, sometimes gives tours. Entrance fee BZ$5.

▶ **NIGHTLIFE.** Corozal has abundant late-night options, ranging from relaxing beach bars to two very unique discos. **Butchie's Bar and Grill,** on 1st Ave., a block north of Hotel Maya overlooking the bay, is a great place to unwind and mingle or play pool with locals under the moonlight (open daily 11am-9pm, later on weekends). **The Cactus Plaza** (see **Food,** p. 93) is one of the best discos in Belize. Get your freak on on the dance floor with beautiful neon-lit Mexican paintings on the wall. Cactus has karaoke, DJs, and occasional live music (open weekends until 3am). **The Purple Toucan,** on 3rd St. North, 1 block from the coast, is the kind of place you immediately love or hate, as it is bright purple with a splash of neon yellow, and the small enclosed dance floor can be claustrophobic. The Toucan also offers food, pool tables, and lottery games. (Open daily, disco open F-Sa nights until 2am.)

CAYO DISTRICT

The Western Highway bisects Belize horizontally, cutting across the Cayo District and offering an avenue to rugged jungle adventure for those who have tired of the sandy beaches of the cayes. Far from the sea and the grassy savannas of northern Belize, and nestled within the lush greenery of the Maya Mountains, this area is Belize's only highland region. Along the Western Highway, Monkey Bay Wildlife Sanctuary and Guanacaste National Park tease travelers with hints of the tropical forests to come. From Mennonite farmland to the Maya village of San José Sucotz, this may be Belize's most culturally diverse district. Cayo is a mecca for outdoor adventure tourists. San Ignacio, the main town in Cayo District, makes a good base from which to explore the ruins, caves, and rivers of the region. Highlights include the Mountain Pine Ridge Reserve, with caves, waterfalls, and refreshingly cool temperatures, and Caracol, the largest Maya site in Belize.

FROM BELIZE CITY TO SAN IGNACIO

▨ THE BELIZE ZOO

To get to the zoo, take any non-express bus running to the Western border. On the way back, walk to the highway and flag down a bus going in the direction you want. ☎ 220 8004; www.belizezoo.org/zoo/zoo. Open daily 8:30am-5pm. Night tours BZ$20 per person, 5 person min.; guides can be hired during the day for BZ$50.

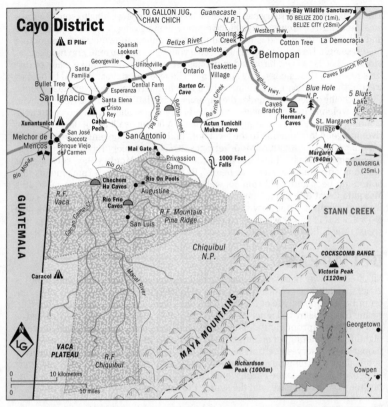

American naturalist Sharon Motola opened the Belize Zoo in 1983 after the filming of the documentary *Path of the Raingods* left seven semi-tame animals in the country. Thirty miles west of Belize City on the Western Highway, the zoo has expanded to house 35 species native to Belize and more than 100 animals total, including the jaguar, the beautiful toucan, the macaw, and the tapir. While not as ferocious as a jaguar or alligator, the tapir, Belize's national animal, has a ferocious bladder that surprises many tourists, much to the delight of the locals.

The zoo underwent massive renovation in 1991, is immaculately kept, and still refuses to capture from the wild. The animals arrive after injury and stay until they can be successfully released. The zoo is acclaimed for teaching the importance of wildlife conservation to Belizeans, and provides the only opportunity for many of them to see their nation's prized wildlife. The zoo is also a popular tourist spot, as many of its animals are difficult to spot in the wild. Check out the overpriced gift shop where the underfunded park ekes out its revenue; traveler's checks and Visa are accepted.

■ MONKEY BAY WILDLIFE SANCTUARY

Any bus running to the Western Border can drop you off. The research headquarters are about 100m down the gravel road. On the way back, flag down a bus on the highway. Research Station ☎ 820 3032; www.monkeybaybelize.org. Dorms BZ$15; camping BZ$10.

The Monkey Bay sanctuary has become a haven for those wishing to study Belize's environment. The area is rich in biodiversity, encompassing acres of tropical forest and the Sibun River, and is used mainly by students and professors conducting field research. Do not let the name deceive you; there are currently no monkeys at Monkey Bay. However, birds and mammals are abundant, and unlike many of Belize's reserves, this one is easily accessible. The **research station,** located two miles west of the Belize Zoo, was founded by a Dutch-American conservationist couple. Currently the sanctuary is under the supervision of Matthew and Marga Miller, who offer a welcoming place, meals, dorm beds (try to get one with a mosquito net), camping, and advice on visiting the sanctuary. A 30min. walk along the road to the river is a good introduction to the local flora and fauna; canoe rentals are available.

Four restaurants with outdoor terraces are near Monkey Bay along the highway. **Amigos Restaurant and Bar ❶,** on the left leaving Monkey Bay, serves great chicken with steamed rice and beans (BZ$5). Happy hour (5-7pm) means discounts on beer and local rum, as well as free homemade chips and salsa. **JB's Mosquito Coast Grill ❸** has the only TV in town along with free wireless or cable Internet, computer not provided. (Open 8:30am-10pm. MC/V.) **JB's Watering Hole ❸** (☎ 820 2071) is just west, plastered with mildly amusing bumper stickers and signs. (Meals BZ$10-15.)

BELMOPAN

Situated halfway between Belize City and San Ignacio, Belmopan (pop. 9200) is geographically and politically the center of Belize. However, the city is not the center of Belizean social life or the site of any significant tourist attractions. After Hurricane Hattie destroyed much of Belize City in 1961, Belmopan was constructed as a new disaster-proof capital. Far too small to support any significant culture or nightlife, it is waiting for an influx of Belizeans that has yet to come. For most, Belmopan merely serves as a transfer station for those heading west to San Ignacio or south along the Hummingbird Highway. Some visitors may appreciate a quick visit to Belize's Independence Plaza, which consists of the home to the National Assembly, the Foreign Ministry, and the stately Prime Minister's Office, among others.

▐ TRANSPORTATION. Buses leave from the Novelo's Bus Terminal, on Constitution Dr., to Belize City (1½hr., every 30min. 4am-7:15pm, BZ$4) and Benque Viejo (1¼hr., every hr. 6am-10pm, BZ$4). Buses to Dangriga (1½hr., every hr. 8:30am-5:30pm, BZ$6) follow the Hummingbird Hwy.

▐ ☷ ORIENTATION AND PRACTICAL INFORMATION. The Western and Hummingbird Hwy. junction, just west of town, is linked to Belmopan by **Constitution Drive,** forming the western portion of **Ring Rd. Independence Plaza,** the head of the national government, is the center of town. A pedestrian **walkway** cuts east to west through Independence Plaza, leading to almost all places of interest. For quick orientation, remember that **Novelo's Bus Terminal** is west and the **marketplace** is directly east of the terminal.

The **British** and **Mexican Embassies** are next to each other at the west end of North Ring Rd. (☎ 822 2611 or 822 2423. Open M-F 8am-4pm.) **Belize Bank,** just past Novelo's on Constitution Dr., has a 24hr. MC/V **ATM** (open M-Th 8am-3pm, F 8am-4:30pm). The **Angelus Press** on Constitution Dr., just before Belize Bank, contains a **Western Union,** and its bookstore boasts an excellent selection of Belizean titles (open M-F 8am-5pm). Look for the **hospital** at the northernmost extension of Constitution Dr. The office is around back. (Emergency ☎ 822 2623. Open M-F 8am-5pm.) The **police** are located northeast of the market in Independence Plaza. (☎ 822 2220, emergency 90. Open 24hr.) **The Techno Hub** in Novelo's bus terminal has **Inter-**

net. (BZ$6 per hr. Open M-F 8:30am-5:30pm, Sa 9am-2pm.) **Telephone** and **fax** are available at **BTL**, southeast of the market on Ring Rd. (☎822 2193. Open M-F 8am-noon and 1-5pm.) The **post office** is between the bus area and the police station (open M-Th 8am-4pm, F 8am-3:30pm).

⌐ ACCOMMODATIONS. Due to lack of tourist demand and inadequate competition, Belmopan's hotels are generally more expensive than they should be. **El Rey ❸**, 23 Moho, is Belmopan's only decent budget option, a 10min. hike (taxi BZ$5) from the market. Walk north past Caladium Restaurant and turn right onto Ring Rd., then left at the sign for El Rey. Take the second right onto Moho and you're there. Rooms have bath and ceiling fans. (☎822 3438; hibiscus@btl.net. Check-out 11am. Singles BZ$39; doubles BZ$49.) Belmopan sports two nicer options with significantly higher price tags. **The Bullfrog Inn ❺** is a 10min. walk from the market; walk north to North Ring Rd. and follow it to the east. The Inn is right around the bend on East Ring Rd. Spacious rooms have A/C, bath, and cable TV. (☎822 2111; Singles BZ$90-$120; doubles BZ$120-$150.) The oldest and most convenient option is the **Belmopan Hotel ❺**, across the street from Novelo's bus terminal. It has well-worn rooms with A/C, bath, cabana bar, cable TV, and pool. (☎822 2130; www.belmopanhotel.com. Singles BZ$96; doubles BZ$110.)

⌂⌐ FOOD AND ENTERTAINMENT. Burritos, *tamales* (BZ$3), and fresh fruit (BZ$1 per bag) are sold throughout the **market,** and several restaurants and stands cluster near the bus stop. A local favorite is speedy **Caladium ❶**, north of Novelo's. (French toast BZ$3.50, rice and beans with chicken BZ$6.75. Open M-F 7:15am-8pm, Sa 7:15am-7pm.) **Wade's Place ❸**, at the east end of North Ring Rd., next to the 99¢ supermarket, has an all-you-can-eat Belizean buffet. (Buffet begins at 11:30am, BZ$11. Open daily 8:30am-6pm.)

Many gather for drinks at the **Bullfrog Inn's** bar before heading out for karaoke and dancing at the **Roundabout,** close to the junction just outside of Belmopan (taxi BZ$6). Thursday night is the best time to party in Belmopan. The city comes alive when hosting popular live bands like *Griga Boyz* and *Punta Rebels.*

SAN IGNACIO

Known to many Belizeans as "Cayo" and conveniently situated on the bank of the Macal River, 10mi. from the Guatemalan border, San Ignacio (pop. 15,000) is the starting point for many outdoor adventures and offers so much that even the most eager traveler leaves wishing for more time. Canoe the Macal, hike a medicine trail, and visit the Maya ruins of Xunantunich. Guides lead expeditions to the Mountain Pine Ridge forest and the Five Sisters Falls; you can swim below the 1000ft. cascade. Cayo's limestone foundations yield some of Central America's most immense caves, many of which still hold relics of the Maya.

⌐ TRANSPORTATION

Buses: All buses and *colectivos* depart from the **Savannah Plaza,** next to the market. Almost anything along the Western Hwy. is easily accessible by bus from San Ignacio. Destinations include: **Belize City** (2½hr., every 30min. 4am-5pm, BZ$5) via **Belmopan** (45min., BZ$2); **Benque Viejo** (20min., every 30min. 3-11pm, BZ$1-1.50; or grab a bus to Melchor and ask to be let off at Benque); and **Melchor de Mencos** (25min., about every 30min. 7:30am-2:15pm, BZ$1.50).

Taxis and Colectivos: Taxis travel to: **Melchor** (BZ$25); **San Antonio** (BZ$50); **Bullet Tree** (BZ$12); and **Cahal Pech** (BZ$5). Colectivos look like taxis but take groups to and from the Guatemalan border crossing for BZ$5 per person. Ask the drivers to distinguish them, or have Bob at **Eva's** (see **Food,** p. 100) help you find one.

✈ 🛈 ORIENTATION AND PRACTICAL INFORMATION

Seventy-three miles west of Belize City and a smooth 20min. east of the Guatemalan border, San Ignacio is joined to its unremarkable sister city to the east, **Santa Elena,** by the **Hawkesworth Bridge**—Belize's only suspension bridge. Built in 1949, the single-lane bridge spans the **Macal River** and heads one-way, out of town. All buses and cars entering town from the northeast arrive over a small wooden bridge. Taking a left after the bridge, you'll pass the market area on the right and hit the heart of town. This five-way intersection is dangerous—there are no stop signs. **Burn's Avenue,** San Ignacio's main commercial strip, heads north. Be careful if driving; this place is made up entirely of one-way streets. The intersection of Burn's Ave. and **Waight's Avenue** is the town's center.

Tourist Information: Bob of **Eva's Restaurant** (see **Food,** p. 100) has served for years as San Ignacio's source of tourist info. Ask for anything from guides to canoes. Open Su-Th 6:45am-11pm, F-Sa 6:45am-midnight (see also **Guided Tours,** p. 101).

Banks: Belize Bank, on the corner of Burn's Ave and Hudson St., boasts the only 24hr. **ATM** that accepts foreign cards. Open M-Th 8am-3pm, F 8am-4:30pm, Su 9am-noon.

Laundry: Martha's Laundry, 10 West St., on the other side of Martha's Kitchen (see **Food,** p. 100). Open M-Sa 7am-5pm, closed Su except for pickup.

Police: (☎824 2022, emergency 90), just west of the bridge. Open 24hr.

Hospital: San Ignacio Hospital (☎824 2761, emergency 824 2066), on Waight's Ave. 24hr. emergency.

Pharmacy: 24 West St. (☎092 2510, emergency 092 3331). Open M-Sa 8am-noon, 1-5pm, and 7-9pm; Su 9am-noon.

Internet: Cayo Community Computer Center, on Hudson St., has the best rate in town. BZ$1.50 per 30 min. Open M-Sa 8am-9pm, Su 10am-6pm.

Telephones: BTL (☎824 2052), has several telephone booths with seats and A/C. Open M-F 8am-noon and 1-5pm. **Public phones** are on the corner of Eve St. and Church St. just past Novelo's bus terminal.

Post Office: On Hudston St., near the city center. Open M-Th 8am-noon and 1-4:30pm, F 8am-noon and 1-4pm.

⌂ ACCOMMODATIONS

San Ignacio boasts a high concentration of cheap, clean, backpacker-savvy hotels, and the jungle around San Ignacio hides retreats and lodges ranging from back-to-basics shacks to full-blown resorts.

▨ Pacz Hotel (☎824 4538; paczghouse@btl.net), on Far West St. Run by laid-back Diana, the Pacz features a nice lounge with cable TV, a book exchange, and five large, comfortable rooms with two clean bathrooms. The restaurant downstairs is excellent. Singles BZ$25; doubles BZ$40; triples BZ$50. AmEx/MC/V. ❷

Hi-Et (☎824 2828; thehiet@btl.net), up Waight Ave. across from Martha's, is not to be confused with the Hyatt. A perennial favorite with the backpacker crowd, it's the best budget hotel in San Ignacio. Four cubicle-sized rooms have private balconies and share hot-water bath. Relax downstairs on the veranda or in the living room with cable TV. Singles BZ$20; doubles BZ$25. ❶

Casa Blanca, 10 Burns Ave. (☎824 2080; casablanca@btl.net), a few blocks south of the Bank of Belize. Humphrey Bogart and Ingrid Bergman would be delighted to continue their passionate romance in this guest house. Pristine bedrooms with private

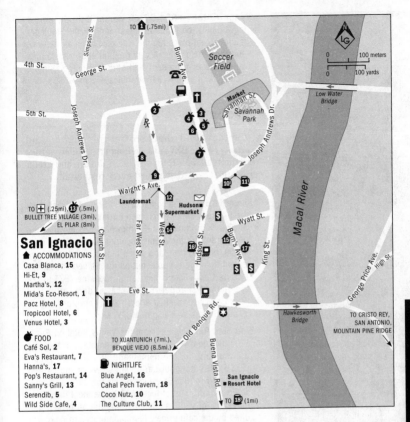

San Ignacio

🏠 ACCOMMODATIONS
Casa Blanca, **15**
Hi-Et, **9**
Martha's, **12**
Mida's Eco-Resort, **1**
Pacz Hotel, **8**
Tropicool Hotel, **6**
Venus Hotel, **3**

🍴 FOOD
Café Sol, **2**
Eva's Restaurant, **7**
Hanna's, **17**
Pop's Restaurant, **14**
Sanny's Grill, **13**
Serendib, **5**
Wild Side Cafe, **4**

🌙 NIGHTLIFE
Blue Angel, **16**
Cahal Pech Tavern, **18**
Coco Nutz, **10**
The Culture Club, **11**

baths and cable TV. The elegant upstairs common room has a kitchen and beautiful mahogany tables. Join fellow visitors on the balcony or roof. Singles BZ$42-80; doubles BZ$53.50. MC/V. ❸

Martha's (☎824 3647; www.marthasbelize.com), up Waight's Ave. above Martha's restaurant and laundromat. This guest house is truly your home away from home and most visitors feel like family with the gracious Martha as the host. A special ambience one only expects from luxury hotels—3 fl. of elegantly-decorated hallways, high wooden ceilings, balconies, artwork, and intimate lighting. Singles BZ$35; doubles BZ$45; 4-person penthouse suite BZ$147. MC/V. ❸

Mida's Eco-Resort (☎824 3172). Walk to the graveyard at the end of Burns Ave; make a right and then a left (15min. walk from the bus stop). Concrete, thatched-roof *cabañas* with private baths are set in a sparsely vegetated backyard. Fans and mosquito netting keep you cool and bug-free. A convenient respite from the hubbub of downtown, it also has nice **camping** facilities with toilet and shower (BZ$8.60 per person). Singles BZ$54; doubles BZ$70. Discounts in low season. ❹

Tropicool Hotel (☎824 3052), on Burns Ave., features a mini jungle-garden, low prices, and hot water in the shared bathrooms. Cleaner than most for the price. Bike rentals BZ$5 per hr. or BZ$20 per day. Singles BZ$22; doubles BZ$27; cabins BZ$55. ❷

BELIZE

URING JUNGLE FEVER

For Belizeans, the jungle is much more than a tourist attraction—it's a resource. Herbal teas are lauded by locals for their powers to cure various ailments. For those looking for a ready-made brew, such specialty teas can be found in a few local restaurants or markets. The selections below are a taste of what owner Jessica Matluck serves at the Wild Side Cafe in San Ignacio.

Cat's Claw: Made from small seeds with hooked barbs that resemble claws, this tea is said to strengthen the immune system and is used as a natural aphrodisiac.

Lime Leaf: Some believe this cures indigestion and gastritis, and use it as an after-dinner beverage.

Wild Basil: Said to detoxify the kidneys; has a strong, spicy flavor.

Black Ass Bitiers: As the name suggests, this horrible tasting brew is supposedly good for indigestion or cleaning parasites from the body.

Blood Tonic: Made from a combination of provision bark, wild yams, and china rot, some use it to treat anemia.

Lemongrass: Supposed to be stimulating and detoxifying and fights headaches.

Spice Vine: Has no caffeine but is drunk here in the mornings as an alternative to coffee.

Billyweb: A tea with a kick, and used to rejuvenate red blood cells. Also gives an energy boost.

Sorosi: This bitter brew is said to give strength to a weak body, and is what Belizean mothers give their children when they are ill.

Venus Hotel (☎ 824 3203; daniel@btl.net, emosfing@btl.net), on Burns Ave. just north of the Tropicool, is the largest place around with nice open-air hallways and large balconies. A very popular spot with tourists due to its ever-present billboard campaign. Singles BZ$30, with bath BZ$45; doubles BZ$34/BZ$53. ❷

🍴 FOOD

A few fast food shacks offer *gornachos* and *panades* (4 for BZ$1) as well as fresh juice across from the banks on Burn's Ave. US dollars and credit cards are accepted at almost every restaurant.

🦀 **Sanny's Grill,** on the corner of 23rd St. A short walk over the hill from Cahal Perch (see **Entertainment,** p. 101) or a quick taxi ride from downtown (BZ$5) provides the perfect setting for a quiet evening with superb food. Music, dim lighting, and green plants make for a nice retreat from the ever-present burrito. Grilled specialties include the delicious chicken in red wine (BZ$11) or the cilantro snapper (BZ$14). After dark, arrange a return taxi. Open M-Tu and Th-Sa 11am-2pm and 6-11pm, Su and W 6-11pm. MC/V. ❷

Wild Side Cafe, across from the Venus Hotel on Burns St. is the best vegetarian and vegan place in town. In the morning, try the homemade granola with yogurt (BZ$6). The coconut caribbean stews or the curried *chaya burrito* (BZ$6) are great bets for lunch or dinner. The wonderful herbal teas (BZ$2) are local medicinal remedies for various ailments, and are all picked and dried by the cafe owner, Jessica Matluck, an American expatriate from New York. Open daily 7am-9pm. ❶

Hanna's, on Burns Ave. across from Casa Blanca. A quality restaurant for traditional Belizean dishes (burritos BZ$6-7). Also offers numerous Indian curries and several vegetarian dishes (BZ$12-15). Open daily 6am-9pm. AmEx/MC/V. ❷

Café Sol, on West St. This vegetarian haven features a variety of healthy meals and coffees. Lunch and dinner menus change daily but always cater to herbivores (entrees BZ$10-15). The sunrise sandwich (BZ$5) is a great way to start the day. Open Tu-Sa 7am-9pm, Su 7am-2:30pm. ❸

Serendib, across from Tropicool on Burns Ave. Sri Lankan natives, the Pieris, serve up authentic Eastern favorites (BZ$10-16) that come highly recommended by the locals. Burgers BZ$3, yellow rice with chicken BZ$10. Open M-Th 10am-3pm and 6-10pm, F-Sa 11am-3pm and 6-10pm. ❷

Pop's Restaurant, on West St. This small, A/C diner serves breakfast all day (BZ$8). Provides friendly service and cheap meals while CNN keeps you informed. Hearty sub sandwiches (BZ$6) make for a great lunch. Open M-Sa 6:30am-2pm. ❷

Eva's Restaurant, 22 Burns Ave. The food is not the cheapest nor the best, but Eva's is the pulse of tourist life in San Ignacio—come for the lowdown on the local tour scene and meet guides and archaeologists. While investigating, try the behemoth chicken burrito (BZ$7.50) and the bigger-than-behemoth banana milkshake (BZ$3). Veggie options. Internet access. Open Su-Th 6:45am-11pm, F-Sa 6:45am-midnight. ❷

🎵 ENTERTAINMENT

After exploring Cayo's pristine forests and natural wonders, most travelers grab a beer with their guide before hitting the showers. Groups usually gather at **Eva's** and **Martha's** after dinner to chug some *Belikins* before heading over to their preferred hot spot. Recently, the **Cahal Pech Tavern,** perched on the hill and hoppin' with frequent live bands, has grown in popularity. The **Blue Angel** on Hudson St. offers loud music and good times for the hard-core partier. Cover charge on weekends for live bands varies (BZ$10-15), but it's always more for men than women. (Open Tu-Th 8pm-midnight, F-Sa 8pm-3am, Su 8pm-midnight.) **Coco Nutz** and **The Culture Club** are the premier hot spots downtown, located directly across from the bus station—if you get lost, just follow the music. The Culture Club offers a fun dance environment with live reggae. For less aerobic workout and more chilling out, Coco Nutz offers pool tables and a sitting area to enjoy your drink and good company (Th-Su). Another popular spot, especially on Friday, is happy hour at the **San Ignacio Hotel** (6-8pm).

🛈 GUIDED TOURS FROM SAN IGNACIO

In San Ignacio, anyone and everyone sells tours to any destination to which a naïve tourist is willing to go. There are several trips that require a guide (Actun Muknal Cave, Chechem Ha Cave, Barton Creek Cave, and Caracol). There are also several sites easily accessible by public transportation (Xunantunich, Cahal Pech, and the Macal and Mopan Rivers). Be wary of advice, as competition runs high in the San Ignacio tour industry, especially between local guides and foreign operators. The best and cheapest way to ensure a great trip is to go to directly to reputable guides. Head to **Dave "The Scotsman"** for info and guided tours. Also try **Bob** at Eva's, who organizes competitively-priced trips to popular sites on a commission-free basis. Eva's is also a great place for the solo traveler to join up with others for better deals.

🛈 OTHER ACTIVITIES AROUND SAN IGNACIO

Besides caves, waterfalls, and Maya sites, there are other exciting activities in Cayo. **Mountain biking** is quite popular; rent from the Tropicool Hotel in San Ignacio or Trek Stop (BZ$6 per hr., BZ$20 per day) on the Western Hwy. Avoid attempting the long trip into the Mtn. Pine Ridge from San Ignacio. Charlie Collins of **EasyRider** charges BZ$80 for a half-day of **horseback riding** (☎ 824 3743; easyrider@btl.net). Other options include saddling up at Clarissa Falls (BZ$75 per 3 hr. with guide) or Nabitunich (BZ$10 per hr.). Cayo is a mecca for **bird watching.** Excellent birding is offered on the beautiful grounds of Nabitunich (guided for BZ$10 per hr.), duPlooy's (free guide 6:30-7:30am), and Crystal Paradise.

🔲 DAYTRIPS FROM SAN IGNACIO

MACAL AND MOPAN RIVERS

For the Macal, trips start by the Hawkesworth bridge in town. Tony of Tony's River Tours takes trips down the Macal (8:30am-4pm; BZ$40.) The Mopan is a few miles outside of town, so it's best to arrange a daytrip with one of the guides listed below.

Canoers paddle and the languid drift in tubes down the mellow **Macal River** into peaceful jungle. Any place along the bank makes a refreshing swimming spot, and there are plenty of chances to see black vultures, iguanas, and even the deadly yellow-jaw snake. The best time to see animals is at night when they head to the river to drink. The **Mopan River** flows north to south with its source in the mountains of Guatemala. The river is quite picturesque, with some beautiful jungle stretches and minor white-water rapids. Be careful with the Mopan, especially when the water is extremely low. The Mopan is easily accessible from the hotels on its bank, all of which offer reasonable rental rates for canoes, kayaks, and water tubes. These include Trek Stop, Nabitunich, and Clarissa Falls.

Back in San Ignacio, you can rent a canoe on your own—**Mayawalk** or **Eva's** both charge BZ$25 per day—or arrange a guided paddle. For tubes, check with Bob at Eva's. Guides are not necessary but can be helpful. **Tony** of **Tony's River Tours** specializes in wildlife on the Macal and Mopan Rivers and works through Eva's. He takes trips on the Mopan from Xunantunich to Clarissa Falls (☎804 2267; evas@btl.net; BZ$25).

CAVES

Only 2 companies are allowed into Muknal (full-day tours BZ$160). Go for Carlos of Pacz (booked through Eva's, ☎804 2267; www.evasonline.com) or Renam of Mayawalk (☎824 3070; www.mayawalk.com) as your guide—both are highly knowledgeable and respected around town. For Barton Creek, book through Eva's (BZ$60 per person, minimum 2 people).

The hills south of San Ignacio provide some fascinating spelunking opportunities. The most impressive cave in Belize is ◼**Actun Tunichil Muknal Cave,** meaning "Cave of the Stone Sepulchre." Excavation, featured in *National Geographic* (Apr. 2000 and 2001), has just been completed, and thankfully the artifacts remain in their original locations. Trips involve hiking through the jungle and rivers (45min.), wading neck-deep through subterranean water, tiptoeing past ancient artifacts, and coming face-to-face with intact human skeletons. The tour is quite strenuous, so a spirit and physique fit for adventure are recommended.

Barton Creek Cave, only navigable by tube or canoe, is the most visited local cave due to its accessibility and lower price tag. The cave has an astonishingly high ceiling, intricate stalactite and stalagmite formations, and a few fascinating Maya artifacts.

MOUNTAIN PINE RIDGE RESERVE

The reserve is not accessible by public transportation. Follow Chiquibul Rd. out of town and turn right on Cristo Rey Rd. Stay to the left and watch for signs. A highly recommended tour guide for the Mountain Pine Ridge is Richard Zul (☎824 2545; richardzul126@hotmail.com), whose trips are inexpensive. An all-in-one alternative option is Angel Tours (☎824 3365 or 824 2267) through Eva's, which leads a trip to the Mountain Pine Ridge that includes 1000 Foot Falls, Big Rock Falls, Río Frío Cave, Río On Pools, and nature hiking for BZ$50, 5 person minimum. An excellent way to explore Cayo and its numerous attractions is by car, with 4WD recommended in the wet season. Roads are fairly well marked and directions are easy to obtain.

Mountain Pine Ridge, south of San Ignacio and parallel to the Guatemalan border, is a 230 sq. mi. reserve unique for its pine forest. It is graced by tall conifers, wide mountains, ancient caves, gorgeous waterfalls, clear streams, and exclusive jungle lodges. Much of the forest has died due to beetle infestation: you have to stomach a depressing drive to see what remains of this forest. The road into the reserve passes the Maya village of **San Antonio,** where the **García sisters** have a famous workshop and museum where they sell carved slate. The credit card machine seems out of place in the "traditional Maya home" and the slate is overpriced (donation BZ$10). At the entrance to the reserve, the guard at **Mai Gate** checks vehicles and provides info. The turn-off for **Hidden Valley Falls** is about 25min. driving past the reserve entrance. Ten miles off the main road, the **1000 Foot Falls** paradoxically plummet over 1500 ft. and reveal a panoramic view as far as Belmopan. Once back on the main road, it is about 1 mi. to the scenic **Big Rock Falls,** a wonderful place for a massage under the firmly pressing water. Several miles further, the main road crosses the **Río On Pools,** at a point where giant boulders form inviting swimming holes. Five miles beyond is the town of **Augustine,** with the only official **camping** in the park at the **Douglas D'Silva Forest Station.** A mile past Augustine is a series of caves surrounded by lush rainforest. The **Río Frío Cave** is actually a huge tunnel (65 ft. high) with impressive rock formations. Nearby is a small nature trail with *chicle*-producing sapodilla trees. On the return to San Ignacio, stop by the Five Sisters Lodge for a postcard-perfect view of the **Five Sisters Falls.** An over-the-top place to grab a beer (BZ$4) or an upscale meal is Francis Ford Coppola's **Blancaneaux Lodge ❹**, a few kilometers from **Mai Gate.**

CARACOL

Ruins accessible only by 4WD vehicles. For tours, hire guides at the entrance, or make arrangements in town. Rates run BZ$100 per person. Admission BZ$10. The cheapest option to explore Caracol is Everald's Caracol Shuttle, available through Eva's. (☎804 2267; evas@btl.net.) His trip to Caracol leaves around 7:30am, returns at 5pm, and stops at Río Frío and Río on Pools on the way home (BZ$100). Omar Kantun (☎824 4524) of Maya Mystic Tours is also recommended. Visiting Caracol is more difficult during rainy season. Few tours make the trip and the road is often closed by the government; it is best not to pre-pay a guide.

The largest Maya site in Belize is impressive: Caracol is a secluded yet expansive metropolis, empty and isolated in the midst of the thick jungle. Led by Lord Water, it was an active hub from about 300 BC to AD 700 and rivaled Tikal in importance. In fact, many archaeologists consider Caracol to be one of the greatest of all Maya sites. An altar found at Caracol depicts Caracol's victory over Tikal in 562. The population of Caracol is estimated to have been almost 150,000 distributed among 30,000 structures. The Belize Government and international funding are helping to position Caracol as the centerpiece of Belize's Mundo de Maya. Much of the site has been excavated and opened to tourists in the last couple of years. Not until 50 years after its discovery did archaeologists begin to understand Caracol's importance. Since 1985, archaeologists have discovered more than 4000 structures on the site's 88 acres, including a royal tomb, carved stone slabs depicting dwarves, and the 144 ft. **Canaa** ("Sky Palace"), which offers stunning views of the surrounding jungle-enshrouded hills.

XUNANTUNICH

The best way to get to Xunantunich is by colectivo, or Berque-based taxi that shuttles groups back and forth from San Ignacio (BZ$3 per person to the ruins). Otherwise, take any western-bound bus and ask to be let off at the ferry in San José Succotz (BZ$1.50). From Succotz take the small, cable-drawn ferry across the Mopan River to Xunantunich. Don't miss the last shuttle or you might get stranded. (M-F 7:30am-5:30pm, Sa-Su 7:30am-4:30pm. Free.) From the river it is a steep 2km to the ruins. Guides are available at the ruins (freelance, BZ$40 per group), but the visitor center next to the offices has enough info for you to guide yourself. Ruins open M-F 8am-5pm, Sa-Su 8am-4pm. BZ$10.

Xunantunich (Maiden of the Rock) was an important city in the Maya Late Classic period (AD 700-900) and is the most accessible Maya site in Belize. The aristocracy resided here while workers lived in the more fertile Mopan River valley. Like many of Belize's Maya ruins, Xunantunich is only partially excavated, but the main temple, **El Castillo** (130 ft. high), is easy to climb. From the temple's roof, see every village, mountain, cloud, and buzzard in the kingdom. People on the ground are larger than ants but smaller than cockroaches. Cahal Pech is visible in the distance, along with the neighboring cities of Benque Viejo del Carmen and Melchor de Mencos. God is rumored to visit the temple in the early mornings—just remember to bring along a good stone tablet. Leave the flip-flops and high heels at home, since the climb is steep and the staff has so far avoided the pesky guardrails found at Tikal. Climb the temple's lower portion to the first platform, where you'll see a fiberglass reproduction of the elaborate **stucco friezes** that stood on the temple's eastern and western sides. Examine the **stelae** in the **visitor center**. A great place to grab lunch or dinner is **La Plaza ❷**, right across from the ferry.

CAHAL PECH RUINS

From the police station, take Buena Vista St. out of town. You will pass the San Ignacio Resort Hotel on your left and after the road curves to the right the road sign for Cahal Pech appears shortly. Follow it and take a left onto a gravel road; continue to the top. Entry to the ruins on your left. Taxi BZ$5. The ruins are also accessible by Melchor/Benque bus; ask to get off by the ruins (BZ$1). Ruins open daily 6am-6pm. BZ$10.

A daytrip to visit Maya ruins couldn't be easier or better: a 30min. walk up a steep hill or a quick taxi (BZ$5) gets you to the site Mayans named the "Place of the Ticks." Although Cahal Pech was a medium-sized Maya center, it left some of the earliest evidence of occupation in the area (1000 BC to AD 900). Some restoration has been overly imaginative, especially the masks depicted on the temple and the main arch. The real attraction of Cahal Pech is at the rear of the plaza, where narrow paths visit the dark rooms of the royal chamber. These elite residential quarters are among the most extensive in the area. Caretakers sometimes give tours, but expect a tip.

WEST TO GUATEMALA

✗ BENQUE VIEJO AND THE BORDER WITH GUATEMALA

The border with Guatemala at **Melchor de Mencos** is about 1½mi. beyond the town of **Benque Viejo del Carmen.** All buses from Belize now stop here, which is a good walk or a quick cab ride to the border (BZ$5). The **immigration office** is open from 6am to 8pm. Leaving Belize, you must pay the environmental fee of BZ$7.50. Save your receipt if you'll be returning; if you aren't, you will also have to pay the Belize departure tax (BZ$20). Be aware that the Belizean dollar decreases in value from 10-15% across the border. Guatemalan immigration may try to charge unofficial fees, usually US$10. Some travelers have demanded a receipt and been excused from such fees. Entering Guatemala, buses leave from the market in **Melchor** (a 15min. walk over the bridge, up the hill, and to the right; taxi Q5) to **Santa Elena/Flores** (2hr., every 2hr. 7am-7pm, Q15). Entering Belize, buses depart from San Ignacio and Belize City. These leave from Benque Viejo, and not the border itself.

BELIZE

SOUTHERN BELIZE

Belize's southern frontier encompasses broad expanses of virgin rainforest, lush mountain jungles, miles of pristine beaches and mangroves, and small villages alive with Garífuna culture. The region is connected by a few rough dirt roads. Toledo, as the district is known, is largely uncharted and wildlife easily outnumbers people. Traveling here requires tenacity and a sense of adventure, but the few tourists who take advantage of the region's immense beauty and untouched wilds find their efforts richly rewarded. From beach villages entranced by the rhythms of Garífuna drums to the splendor of a living Maya culture, southern Belize holds many treasures between its impressive mountains and turquoise waters.

The 89km **Hummingbird Highway,** between Belmopan and Dangriga, is a lusciously green alternative to the bump-a-thon known as the Coastal Hwy. The Hummingbird cuts through citrus valleys and clear rivers, with the Maya Mountains loom in the background. The entire highway has recently been paved, and the smooth ride is a sign of increasing tourism to Placencia and Belize's sandy southern coasts.

HUMMINGBIRD HIGHWAY'S PARKS

⚠ BLUE HOLE NATIONAL PARK

To get to Blue Hole, hop on any Dangriga-bound bus from Belmopan (every hr. 7:30am-5:30pm, BZ$2) and ask to be let off at Blue Hole. For Caves Branch, ask to get off at Ian Anderson's Caves Branch Lodge, then walk 10min. down the unpaved turn-off. For more info, call the Belize Audobon Society (☎ 223 5004) and ask for Blue Hole. Open daily 8am-4pm. BZ$8; camping with toilets and bucket showers BZ$5 per person; flashlight BZ$5.

Blue Hole National Park, 11mi. south of Belmopan, consists of 575 acres of pristine forest, and is home to more than 300 species of birds. It is also home to the Blue Hole itself, an 8m deep limestone sinkhole. The Hole allows an underground tributary of the Sibun River to emerge briefly into a rocky pool before being swallowed up again by a cavern 50m away. Of the two entrances to the park, the main entry is the farthest west and includes excellent jungle trails to St. Herman's Cave, the observation tower, and the campsite. The breathtaking view from the top of the observation tower rewards those who brave the arduous climb from the visitors center; keep an eye out for orchids on the way. Spectacular **St. Herman's Cave** is about a 20min. hike along the trail from the visitor center. Explore on your own with a strong flashlight or hire a guard in San Ignacio for a better excursion.

Between Blue Hole and the park visitors center there is a small sign for **Caves Branch Jungle Lodge ❷,** mile 41.5 of the highway. Tiki torches light the pebble path to immaculate, comfortable rooms. The cozy bunkhouse and camping site have access to thatch-covered "jungle showers" and clean bathrooms with hot water. Each room comes with bottled water, mosquito netting, and a kerosene lamp. If your wallet allows, there are even nicer jungle *cabañas* and suites. Take advantage of the rope swing hanging over the crystal clear waters of the nearby Sibun River. The lodge also offers tasty, though expensive, buffet-style meals. Reserve in advance. Ian Anderson and his well-trained guides lead great caving and tubing trips. (☎/fax 822 2800; www.cavesbranch.com. Meals BZ$24-34. Bunks BZ$30; camping BZ$10; *cabañas* BZ$134; suites BZ$216. Trips BZ$150-$210 per person.)

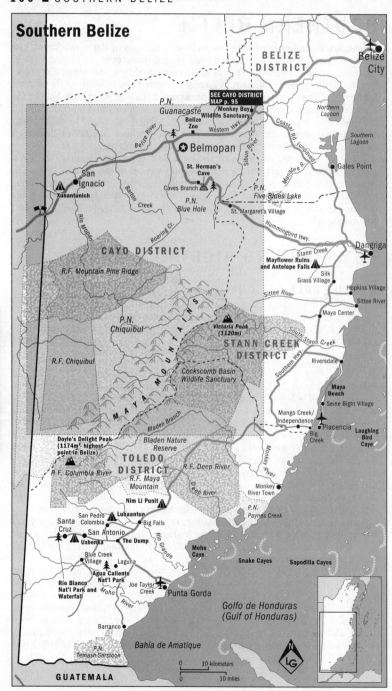

⚠ FIVE BLUES LAKE NATIONAL PARK

To get to the lake, take any Dangriga-bound bus from Belmopan and get off at St. Margaret's (every hr. 7:30am-5:30pm, BZ$3). Check in at the park office down the dirt road on your left. It is a 4 mi. hike to the heart of the park. If you're lucky, the park's only vehicle may be available to take you to the lake, a bumpy 20min. truck ride away (BZ$20 roundtrip). During the high season it is easy to thumb a ride; but Let's Go does not recommend hitchhiking. Otherwise, the walk into the heart of the park is an easy 2hr.

In the jungle-covered limestone foothills of the Maya Mountains 25 mi. southeast of Belmopan, Five Blues Lake National Park boasts 4200 acres of rugged, unspoiled wilderness centered around a crystal-clear 10-acre lake. The park depends upon entrance fees (BZ$8), donations, and grants for operation and independence from government control. Impromptu tours are provided by local village experts, usually youths who have as much fun as you do—if not more—exploring the park. Rugged hiking trails are plentiful, and bright orange markers point the way when branches and roots obscure paths. The saw-toothed caves and cliffs of Five Blues are quite unlike the smooth, slick underground caverns to the west: located mostly above ground, they form a fascinating, confusing labyrinth of rock stretching across hundreds of acres and towering into the sky.

Tread carefully if you wish to catch sight of the fleeting jungle leopard or gibnut. Spider monkeys, on the other hand, are surprisingly easy to find and leaf-cutting ants seem to follow you no matter where you go. The real gem of the park is the pristine lake, fed by collapsed river caves hundreds of meters below. When the sun is out, the lake fragments into brilliant shades of piercing blue. **Canoes** rent for about BZ$5, and **cave diving** is allowed if you bring the proper equipment.

DANGRIGA

Dangriga thrives today as the musical, artistic, and historical center of the Garífuna. Halfway down the coast between Belize City and Placencia, Dangriga (pop. 10,000) was founded as a trading post by Puritans from New Providence who farmed Tobacco Caye and the Coastal Belt. Today, most residents are Garífuna. While some travelers come to learn more about the Garífuna, most use it as a base to visit Tobacco Caye, Cockscomb Basin, or the deep South.

⧉ TRANSPORTATION

Flights: The **Airport** is a 20min. walk north of town or a BZ$5 taxi. **Tropic Air** (☎522 2129) flies to **Belize Municipal Airport** (20min., every 2hr. 7am-5pm, BZ$62) and **Punta Gorda** (45min., 5 per day 8:50am-5:20pm, BZ$112) via **Placencia. Maya Island Air** (☎522 2659) flies similar routes at similar prices.

Buses: Southern Transport (☎502 2160) serves **Belize City** (3hr., 10 per day 5:15am-5pm, BZ$10) usually via **Belmopan** (2hr., BZ$6); **Placencia** (2½hr., 12:15 and 5:15pm, BZ$10) via **Hopkins Village** (45min., BZ$4); and **Punta Gorda** (4½hr.; M-Sa 10:30am, noon, 3:30, 5:30pm; Su noon, 3:30, 5:30pm; BZ$13).

Boats: Captain Reyes (☎522 3227) heads to **Puerto Cortés, Honduras** (3hr., Sa 9am, US$50). Make arrangements at Catalina's or the Riverside Café a few hours early to allow time for exit stamps (BZ$7.50). Boats to **Tobacco Caye** (45min., BZ$30) leave irregularly from the Riverside Café on the south bank of Stann Creek. Ask around the docks on North Stann Creek to find a ride. Local Captain Buck makes the trip regularly.

■ 🛈 ORIENTATION AND PRACTICAL INFORMATION

The **Stann Creek River**, also called the Gumaragu River, flows east through town to the ocean. Running parallel to the coast, the main road has two names: **St. Vincent Street** south of the river and **Commerce Street** north of it. Hustlers congregate near the Stann Creek bridge and the Southern Transport Bus Station at the southern end of Dangriga. The center of town and the Stann Creek bridge are less than one-half mi. north of the bus station. Several blocks south of the bridge, **Mahogany Lane** connects St. Vincent St. to the sea and **Alijo Benji Park,** named after the Garífuna chief who led his people from Honduras to Dangriga. A large red-and-white sign for the Chaleanor Hotel marks the junction of St. Vincent St. and Mahogany Ln. Police warn that the "back-a-town" area by Havana bridge is unsafe at night.

Tourist Information: The **Belize Tourism Industry Association** (☎522 2277) has recently opened a tourist center in the Southern Transport Terminal, though it is not the best source of info. Louise at the **Bluefield Lodge** (☎522 2742) and Chadwick at **Chaleanor Hotel** (☎522 2587) know everything there is to know about Dangriga.

Banks: First Caribbean Bank, 3 blocks north of the bridge on the east side of Commerce St., gives credit card cash advances and changes traveler's checks and Canadian dollars. 24hr. **ATM** accepts Visa. Open M-Th 8am-2:30pm, F 8am-4:30pm. Change US traveler's checks at **Kuylen Hardware,** 30 ft. north of the main bridge. There is a **Western Union** in the building, but don't count on speedy service. Open M-Th 7:30am-noon and 1:30-5pm, Sa 7:30am-1pm.

Laundry Service: Val's Laundry and Internet, 1 Sharp St., with an entrance on Mahogany across from the post office. Wash BZ$5. Wash and dry BZ$2 per lb. **Internet** BZ$5 per hr. Open daily 7am-7pm.

Police: 107 Commerce St. (☎522 2022, emergency 90), north of the river, near First Caribbean Bank. Open 24hr.

Pharmacy: St. Vincent Drugstore (☎522 3124), at 12 St. and Vincent St. just south of the bridge. Open M-Sa 8am-9pm, Su 10-11am.

Hospital: (☎522 2078). Take the frontage road 2 blocks north and 2 blocks east of the bridge. Ambulance available. Open 24hr.

Clinic: Health Centre (☎522 2184), across from the hospital on the water. Open M-F 8am-5pm.

Telephones: BTL (☎522 2065; fax 522 2038), across the street from the police. No local charge on collect and credit card calls. **Fax** service. Open M-F 8am-noon and 1-5pm.

Post Office: 16 Caney St. on the 2nd fl. of the building across from Val's. Open M-Th 8am-noon and 1-5pm, F 8am-noon and 1-4:30pm.

🛈 ACCOMMODATIONS

🏨 **Bluefield Lodge** (☎522 2742; bluefield@btl.net), 1 block south and 2 blocks west of the bridge, is the stately swordfish of Dangrigan hotels. The friendly owner Louise Belisle maintains clean rooms with fans and firm mattresses in addition to being an encyclopedia of info on Dangriga. Lounge with cable TV and US magazines. Hot baths. Singles BZ$27; doubles BZ$37, with bath and TV BZ$48. ❷

Chaleanor Hotel 35 Magoon St. (☎522 2587). Nice 3-story hotel with balconies, roof access, and friendly owners. Economy rooms, with fan and shared bath, are a good value but share rather grim bathrooms. Free drinking water, coffee, and bananas in the morning. Singles BZ$18; doubles BZ$30. ❶

Pat's Guest House (☎522 2095), south of the bridge. The rooms right on the water are bright and airy, but cost more. Hot showers are small and cleanliness varies with price. Singles BZ$22, with bath BZ$38; doubles BZ$38.25/BZ$45; beach rooms BZ$10 extra per person. MC/V. ❷

Weyhoan Hotel (☎522 2398), on the west side of Commerce St. If the receptionist desk is closed, check the Asian convenience store downstairs. Basic singles with fan in a modern building with shared, clean, hot baths. BZ$10 key deposit; no smoking. Singles BZ$20; with bath and TV BZ$36; doubles with bath and TV BZ$68. ❶

Dangriga
▲ ACCOMMODATIONS
Bluefield Lodge, **8**
Chaleanor Hotel, **9**
Pat's Guest House, **10**
Weyhoan Hotel, **4**
🍴 FOOD
Kinburger Restaurant, **5**
Pelican Beach, **1**
Ritchie's Dinette, **3**
Riverside Café, **6**

🄵 FOOD

Dangriga's delicious fare is largely seafood based. Most options are near the Stann Creek bridge and easily accessible from the town center. Many restaurants are closed on Sunday so you may have to search around; grocery stores are usually open Sunday afternoons.

▨ **Riverside Café,** on the south bank of Stann Creek about ½ block east of the bridge. Situated right across from the boat docks, the cafe is a popular place to wait on a ride. The fried shrimp (BZ$17) is a hearty meal; in season, the lobster (BZ$18) is a real treat. Breakfast and lunch BZ$6-8. Open daily 7am-9pm. ❹

Ritchie's Dinette Creole and Spanish Food, 84 Commerce St., 2 blocks north of the bridge on the right. Ritchie offers up the typical Belizean breakfast, fry jacks, bacon, eggs (BZ$7), and fresh-squeezed OJ (BZ$1). For lunch, try a chicken burrito (BZ$3) or a fish filet (BZ$14). ❷

Kingburger Restaurant, 1 block north of the bridge. Burger King's dyslexic brother provides an old Western standby: all-beef burgers with fries BZ$6. The ice cream (BZ$2) is a favorite with locals; as is the extensive list of fresh juices (BZ$1.50). Open M-Sa 7am-3pm and 5-10pm, though hours are lax. ❶

Pelican Beach, ½ mi. north of the village on beautiful waterfront property next to the airport, is a 20min. walk or a short taxi ride (BZ$5), but well worth it. Prices are high but the dinners are delectable, especially the porterhouse steak (BZ$46). Breakfast 7-9am BZ$14-17. Dinner 6:30-9pm. ❺

🄟 NIGHTLIFE

For a town that is the birthplace of some of Belize's most popular bands, live music and exciting nightlife are surprisingly hard to find in Griga. Ask if the Griga Boyz or Punta Rebels are playing. Locals with beers on the street are probably headed for an evening of karaoke, hit-or-miss depending on who sings. Be aware that taxis don't run past 9pm. **Griga 2000,** on St. Vincent St., just south of the

BELIZE

THE LOCAL STORY

DRAWING CONCLUSIONS

Garífuna painter Benjamin Nicholas of Dangriga is one of Belize's most renowned artists. His colorful scenes of everyday life have garnered international fame, and he has been commissioned by the Queen of England and the Archbishop of Canterbury.

On his youth: In school I wouldn't be paying attention to the teacher, but rather observing the way the classroom, students, and professor looked. In the little village I grew up in, I was the only one doing these types of drawings, and the teachers soon had me helping their lessons by drawing illustrations on the board. Everyone talked about the little artist in Barranco.

On his artistic style: I do colorful portrayals of everyday Garífuna life: women making casava, men fishing, and people *punta* dancing and knocking their drums.

On his art's impact: Before I started painting, the world only knew the Garífuna people as savages. But now, I am so proud that have changed people's conception of them. People are now visiting the Garífuna because they have seen the paintings.

On Garífuna people today: Now Garífuna, Creole, Hispanics, and Indians are all mixing. It is hard to tell who is who just by looking. But the Garífuna are trying to guard against losing their culture by maintaining their lifestyle and cultural ties.

bridge, is the most popular nightclub. Karaoke (W and Su) draws a big crowd (open daily until midnight). The **Kennedy Club**, a few blocks north of the police station, is popular, jamming to *punta* and soul until 3am on Saturdays; music ends earlier on weekdays (11pm).

👁 📷 SIGHTS AND SHOPPING

The Garífuna, also known as Black Caribs, make up the majority of Southern Belize's population. **Garífuna Day,** November 19, commemorates the 1823 arrival of the Black Caribs into Belize with the biggest party of the year. Dangriga transforms itself completely, as usually placid and unassuming streets erupt into a frenzy of wild celebrations and exhaustive merry-making.

Dangriga is a great place to explore Garífuna culture. World-renowned artist **Benjamin Nicholas** welcomes visitors to his in-home workshop, just past the post office. Take a look at his numerous works-in-progress, typically colorful scenes of everyday Belizean life. To get there, turn left on Mahogany St., just past Ritchie's bus station south of the bridge. Mr. Nicholas asks that you call ahead and leave behind a BZ$20-30 "courtesy" for his time (☎ 522 2785).

Those with a musical bent should stop by the workshop of **Austin Rodríguez,** who handcrafts mahogany and cedar drums in traditional Garífuna style under the shelter of a thatched roof in his driveway. Rodríguez's daughters, Norielee and Deatha ("DAY-ta") have learned their father's craft and maybe willing to share their wealth of info about Garífuna culture. Look for the small shack at the southern end of Tubroose St. with wood shavings in the yard.

DAYTRIPS FROM DANGRIGA

TOBACCO CAYE

To reach the caye from Dangriga, ask boatmen near the bridge for a ride. Captain Buck is a reliable option. Most boats leave 9am-2pm at the dock by the Riverside Café; regular trips in high season, low season is more sporadic. (1hr., BZ$30 per person each way.) 9am daily return from the caye. Louise at Bluefield Lodge (☎ 522 2742) helps with travel plans, as do folks at Riverside Café (☎ 502 3499).

Squarely atop the reef, Tobacco Caye (pop. 20, yes, 20) is the ultimate easy-living hideaway, with hammocks out-numbering humans. Excellent swimming, snorkeling, and fishing are the chief attractions. The caye is a mere 4½ palm-tree-covered acres encircled by azure waters and a coral reef, the caye may not last forever as the ocean creeps up the shore a bit farther each year. Still, like everything else going on in Tobacco Caye, it's happening slowly. The reef is slowly recovering from Hurricane Mitch in 1998, and despite the distressing amount of damaged coral, snorkeling the reef yields an abundance of sea life.

The Caye's five hotels are solid competitors, as their room prices all include three meals a day. Make sure to have a reservation in high season. The best value is the aptly named **Tobacco Caye Paradise ❹**, owned by friendly Keith Hechavarria, brother of Louise of the Bluefield Lodge in Dangriga. The cook, Ezra, is famous in the area for her smile and delicious meals—the fried chicken might be the best in Belize. (☎ 520 5101. Snorkeling gear BZ$15. Singles with shared bath BZ$50; cabins with private bath BZ$70 per person.) **The Gaviota ❹**, in the center of the island, rents clean rooms with wood floors and three small but excellent meals per day. They occasionally make deals on snorkeling gear, canoes, and kayaks, especially in low season. (☎ 509 5032. Snorkeling gear and fishing poles BZ$10-$15 per day. Singles BZ$60; doubles BZ$100.) **Lana's Hotel ❹**, has basic rooms with shared bath and gourmet meals. Prices increase during high season. (☎ 509 5036. Singles BZ$60; doubles BZ$100.) Several hotels will permit **camping** on their beach; ask for permission in advance (BZ$10-20 per person); try **Larna's**, by the dock (BZ$20 per person). Find a sheltered spot for your tent, as winds are often very strong, especially on the ocean side of the island. Easy-going Kirk and Mark operate the island's primary hangout, a tiny **bar** near the northern dock where pop music jangles on the weekends. The going rate on the island for a Belikin is BZ$5, since everything is brought in by boat. Divemaster **Marla Jackson** has an office near Reef's End.

COCKSCOMB BASIN WILDLIFE SANCTUARY

The cheapest way to the site is by bus. Take any bus heading south from Dangriga in the morning (1hr., BZ$5) and ask to be let off at Maya Center. From here it is a 6mi. (2hr.) hike to the sanctuary. Buses back to Dangriga stop at 3pm, or hire a taxi from Maya Center (BZ$25 each way). A more expensive option is a tour from Dangriga. The best company is C&G Tours (☎ 522 3641), run by Godfrey Young, whose sanctuary trips return through Sittee River and Hopkins Village. (1-4 people BZ$360.)

About 32km south of Dangriga, the Cockscomb Basin Wildlife Sanctuary is the jewel of Belize's extensive list of nature reserves. It is bordered on three sides by the peaks and ridges of the Maya Mountains and covers over 120,000 acres. The sanctuary is generally referred to as the "World's First Jaguar Sanctuary." Stop at the village of **Maya Centre,** 6 mi. before the sanctuary on the Southern Hwy., to pay the BZ$10 entrance fee. There is also an extensive collection of carved slate, beaded jewelry and hand-woven baskets for sale. Head down the 7 mi. dirt road to the Visitors Center for maps (BZ$5) and info.

Night hikes offer the best shot at glimpsing one of the stealthy cats, but even the most persistent often see only tracks. Most visitors come to the park for its seclusion and the well-maintained trail system. Two of the trails are designed as guided educational hikes leaving from Maya Centre. Other trails include the spectacular Tiger Fern trail, a 2 mi. hike to a treeless hilltop followed by a dip in a refreshing waterfall. Hike to Ben's Bluff (2.5 mi.) for a lookout to Victoria Peak and another waterfall. These hikes can be quite strenuous, so make sure to leave ample time and take plenty of water. Another option is camping at designated sites in good locations along the trails. **Victoria Peak,** Belize's second-highest point (.7 mi.), is a National Monument within the sanctuary. The hike is a grueling 3-5 days, but the view from the top is majestic. Guides are required for the trek; **Emiliano Sho** (☎ 608 9127) is an excellent choice and has the cheapest rates (BZ$100 per day for a group).

Budget accommodations are available in Maya Centre and in the Sanctuary. **Nu'uk Che'il Cottages ❸**, is 200 yards past the Maya Centre turn-off. (☎520 3033. Bunk beds BZ$18; singles BZ$40; doubles BZ$50.) The **Visitor Center ❶** rents tents and beds as well. For reservations, contact the Belize Audobon Society. (☎223 5004; base@btl.net. Tent rental BZ$5-15. Camping BZ$10; rustic dorms BZ$16; newer dorms BZ$36; cabins BZ$74-100.) Julio Saqui, in the second building on the right from the turn-off, runs the only **bar**, an **Internet cafe** (BZ$8 per hr.), and **taxi** service to the shorter trails (BZ$100 per group). Remember that there is nothing more than a snack shop at the park visitor center, so bring food and drink along with you.

MAYFLOWER RUINS AND ANTELOPE FALLS

From Dangriga, take any bus going south and get off in Silk Grass Village (20min., BZ$4). There are no buses heading back to Dangriga from Silk Grass after 3pm. From Silk Grass, it is a 3 mi. hike to the park.

The **Mayflower** ruins and **Antelope Falls,** about 11 mi. from Dangriga, are currently under excavation and promise to be two of the most important Maya sites in Belize. There are two post-Classic Maya ruins: the Mayflower and T'au Witz, and the long wall of what was once a pyramid known as **Mainzunun,** probably built around AD 300. Recently, archaeologists at the Mayflower Archeological Reserve have uncovered what they suspect were viewing platforms for ball games. If you continue past Mainzunun and follow the narrow jungle trail (bear right at the fork), you'll reach the spectacular Antelope Falls. Along the way, you'll likely see hummingbirds, butterflies, and maybe an armadillo or two, but the jewel of the jungle is the 300 ft. falls, located just under 2 mi. from the pyramid. The last 650 ft. of the trail are steep and slippery, so bring sturdy shoes. Swimming here is great, but the water rushes fast and the rocks are slippery.

PLACENCIA

Perched at the end of a long peninsula slipping out into the warm Caribbean 45 mi. south of Dangriga, Placencia (pop. 800) is an inviting beach paradise. A fishing village until the lobster and conch populations began dwindling 20 years ago, Placencia retains a simple seaside charm despite emerging recently as one of Belize's most visited areas. The miles and miles of golden sandy beachfront, an impressive array of uninhabited islands just offshore, and undoubtedly some of the best seafood in the country make Placencia a worthwhile stop for any traveler.

▐ TRANSPORTATION

Flights: Placencia's airstrip is 1¾mi. from town. **Maya Island Air** (☎523 3475) flies to: **Dangriga** (20min., every 2½hr. 7am-4:30pm, BZ$68); **Belize City** (1hr., every 2½hr. 7am-4:30pm, BZ$118); and **Punta Gorda** (20min.; 8:50, 10:50am, 3:35, 5:35pm; BZ$59). **Tropic Air** (☎523 3410) runs a similar schedule at identical prices.

Buses: Buses leave for **Dangriga** from the gas dock (3hr.; M-Sa 5:30, 6am, 1:30pm; Su 7am, 1:30pm; BZ$8). From Punta Gorda, buses head to Independence, and then take a ferry to Placencia from there (see below). Buses from Mango Creek go to **Punta Gorda** (3hr., 11:30am and 5:30pm, BZ$10).

Ferries: Ferries leave from the **dock** for **Mango Creek/Independence** (25min., 10am and 4pm, BZ$10). Gulf Cruza makes weekly trips to **Puerto Cortés, Honduras** (5hr., F 9am, BZ$120 includes BZ$20 departure tax).

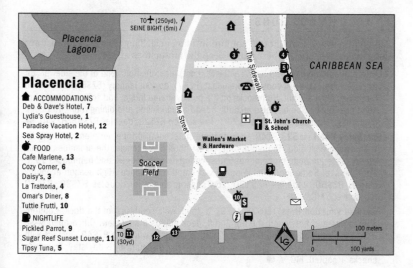

Placencia

■ ACCOMMODATIONS
Deb & Dave's Hotel, 7
Lydia's Guesthouse, 1
Paradise Vacation Hotel, 12
Sea Spray Hotel, 2

● FOOD
Cafe Marlene, 13
Cozy Corner, 6
Daisy's, 3
La Trattoria, 4
Omar's Diner, 8
Tuttie Frutti, 10

◗ NIGHTLIFE
Pickled Parrot, 9
Sugar Reef Sunset Lounge, 11
Tipsy Tuna, 5

❊🔁 ORIENTATION AND PRACTICAL INFORMATION

Boats and buses disembark near the gas dock at Placencia's southernmost point. Running north-south along the beach, a skinny sidewalk is the only artery through town. Just about every place in Placencia perches on the walkway or announces its proximity with signs and arrows. Walking leisurely through the entire village takes only 15 min. The road used by vehicles runs parallel to the walkway and is the only road that leaves Placencia to the north.

Tourist Information: Placencia Tourism Center (☎523 4045; www.placencia.com), is one of the best tourist offices in Belize, producing the *Placencia Breeze* magazine with transportation schedules, maps, and specials. Open M-F 9am-5pm, Sa 1-3pm.

Banks: Atlantic Bank, in the white building across from the bus stop, gives MC/V cash advances (BZ$10 charge). Open M-F 8am-2pm.

Markets: Wallen's Market, just north of the soccer field on the dirt road, is the best place for groceries. Changes US traveler's checks. Open M-Sa 8am-noon and 2-6pm.

Laundry: Cara's Laundry, in the same building as Omar's Diner (see **Food,** p. 114). BZ$8-$20 per load, depending on size. Closed Sa.

Police: (☎523 3129, emergency 90), to the right of the Purple Space Monkey near the end of the street. Open 24hr.

Clinic: The **health center** (☎523 3129) is behind the school, west of the walkway across from Omar's. Open M-F 8am-noon and 1-5pm.

Telephones: BTL (☎523 3109), near the center of the village on the path. Free collect calls, **fax** service. Open M-F 8am-12:30pm and 1:30-5pm.

Internet: The expensive **Placencia Office Supply** has the fastest connection in town. BZ$10 per hr. Open M-Sa 8:30am-noon and 1-7pm.

Post Office: Above the fishing co-op in the white building at the south end of the walkway, across from the dock. Open M-F 9-11am and 2-5pm.

ACCOMMODATIONS

The good news: budget hotels abound in Placencia. The great news: most are along the eastern shore where winds keep the mosquitoes at bay.

Lydia's Guesthouse (☎523 3117; lydias@btl.net), near the north end of the sidewalk on the west side. Lydia will cook you breakfast (BZ$7), do your laundry (BZ$8), and provide fans when it's really hot. Hammocks on the porch, shared fridge, and soft mattresses are additional perks. She has also recently added a full kitchen and dining room. Hot common baths. High season singles BZ$31, low season BZ$28; doubles BZ$46/BZ$40. ❸

Sea Spray Hotel (☎523 3148; www.seasprayhotel.com), on the north end of the sidewalk on the east side. Though it's the oldest hotel in Placencia, the amenities in this breezy place are quite modern: hot baths, coffee makers, fridges, and hammocks 10 ft. from the sea. Some rooms have better views and more space. High season economy singles BZ$50; *cabañas* BZ$120. Low season singles or doubles BZ$30, BZ$40 respectively. MC/V. ❹

Paradise Vacation Hotel (☎523 3179), a 3min. walk southwest of the dock. Comfortable rooms and hot water. The big 2nd-fl. deck affords a nice view. Office open M-Sa 9:30-11:30am and 1-8pm. Doubles BZ$30, downstairs with bath BZ$40, upstairs with bath BZ$50. BZ$10 extra per person. Low season discount for 3-day stay. Traveler's checks accepted. MC/V. ❶

Deb & Dave's Hotel (☎523 3207; debanddave@btl.net), has clean rooms with screened verandas and hammocks. Shared bath singles and doubles BZ$36. ❸

FOOD

Superb seafood defines dining in Placencia; some of the country's most mouth-watering restaurants are located along the beach.

Cafe Marlene, a 5min. walk west of the Tourism Center, directly on the water in the white building. Marlene cooks up a delicious meal each day of the week. Portions are huge, the food is mouth-watering, and Marlene is talkative. Breakfast of eggs, sausage, fruit, and coffee BZ$15. Open M-Sa 7am-2pm and 6-10pm. ❸

La Trattoria, on the water just before Sea Spray Hotel. This is the place for a romantic splurge. Authentic, intimate, romantic Italian atmosphere with delicious pastas (BZ$20) and vegetarian entrees (BZ$18). Open Tu and Th-Su 6:30-9pm. ❹

Daisy's, in the center of town west of the walkway, has a wide selection of options for the hungry traveler. Sandwiches and burgers (BZ$4-5). The seafood dinners (BZ$12-15) are delicious. Open M and W-Su 8am-10pm. ❸

Tuttie Frutti, north of the Tourism Center, has homemade ice cream that surpasses any parlor in the country. Heavenly banana and fresh fruit scoops, while the rum raisin is a true Caribbean treat. Daily flavor slushes are perfect for cooling-off afternoons. Two scoops BZ$3. Open M-Tu and Th-Su 9am-8pm. ❶

Cozy Corner, set on the beach behind the Advanced Diving Shack. This unassuming thatched-roof hut serves some of the best seafood around, and the continuous sea-breeze only adds to the ambience. You can't go wrong with the fish or conch dinner (both BZ$12). In season, conch fritters are an affordable addiction (BZ$2.50 per plate). Open Tu-Su 11am-10pm. ❸

Omar's Diner, in the maroon-and-white striped shack on the southern end of the walkway. Famous for its low prices and tasty seafood. The staff tends to take their time. Great burritos BZ$4.50-8. Combination of 2 seafoods with coconut rice and juice BZ$22. Tasty egg breakfasts with various sides BZ$5-$8. Fresh squeezed OJ. Open daily 7am-3pm and 6pm-9pm. ❷

🎵 🍷 ENTERTAINMENT AND NIGHTLIFE

Placencia is a sleepy town at night, and most bars don't stay open past midnight. Check to see if any new options have opened. In the early evening, crowds gather for happy hours at the **Pickled Parrot** (open M-Sa 10am-10pm, Su 5-10pm), located just before Wallen's on the dirt road, and **Tipsy Tuna**, a modern sports bar with pool tables. (Happy hour 7-8pm. Open M-F until midnight, Sa-Su until 2am.) Newly opened **Sugar Reef Sunset Lounge,** on the southwest tip of town, features a diverse activities list: Saturday bbqs, kayak, and canoe races. (Happy hour daily 6-7pm. Open until midnight.)

⚠️ 🛶 OUTDOOR ACTIVITIES AND WATERSPORTS

BEACHES. Seine Bight and nearby **Maya Beach** are perfect for a swim and the hotels are so incredible they alone make the visit worth it. You can rent a **bike** from **Deb & Dave's** or a kayak from **Sunset Reef.** *(Deb & Dave's ☎523 3207. BZ$5 per hr.; BZ$25 per day. Sunset Reef BZ$5 per hr.; BZ$30 per day.)*

CAYES. Deserted tropical getaways don't get much better than this. The water is steely blue, the sand is grainy, and the cayes are uninhabited. Boaters will ferry tourists to the picture-perfect islands around Placencia for fishing, snorkeling, diving, and camping. The best cayes are generally those farthest south and closest to the reef, where the mangroves, mosquitoes, and sand-flies are less abundant. Highly recommended are the **Silk Cayes,** a series of three gorgeous palm-covered islands bordered by gleaming white sand and fantastic coral, only 1hr. away by boat. **Laughing Bird Caye** is another perennial favorite. Trips to the cayes are best arranged through diving and snorkeling companies.

DIVING AND SNORKELING. Each company in Placencia offers similar services at comparable rates, most of which include lunch. Two reputable operators are **Ocean Motion Guide Service,** located on the sidewalk a couple minutes from the southern dock, and **Nite Wind,** just east of the southern dock. Prices may be discounted and negotiable in low season. You can also charter a boat. Companies also arrange camping trips to the cayes. **The Seahorse Dive Shop** is a quality operator located on the south dock by the info center and **Advanced Diving,** is on the sidewalk in front of the Cozy Corner. For a more extreme adventure, the incredible whale shark of the Caribbean, featured in *National Geographic,* draws both divers and snorkelers to Placencia. They are most abundant from April to June, especially during the full moon. Also popular is manatee watching in the lagoon near Placencia. Nite Wind, among others, runs trips for BZ$46. *(Ocean Motion Guide Service ☎523 3363; www.oceanmotion.com. Nite Wind ☎523 3487. Full day trips with both providers to Laughing Bird Caye and Silk Caye are BZ$80 and BZ$90, respectively. Half day snorkeling trips BZ$64. Seahorse Dive Shop www.belizescuba.com. Advanced Diving does whale shark snorkeling for BZ$108 per person; diving BZ$300. ☎523 4037.)*

KAYAKING. Kayak around the mangrove shores of the lagoon with a rental from the **Sunset Reef,** east from the dock along the beach in Dangriga. For serious kayaking, **Ali and Jimmy Westby** run camping tours for up to seven days to see the Silk Cayes and the Sapodillo Range, snorkeling and fishing along the way. One stop is at a 17th-century wreck in only 18 ft. of water. Meals are freshly caught seafood. *(Sunset Reef, kayaks BZ$5 per hr., minimum 2hr., BZ$30 for a full day. They also rent canoes. Ali and Jimmy Westhy ☎523 4073; pladejavu@btl.net. BZ$170 per day; 4-person minimum.)*

BELIZE

FISHING. The waters off the coast of Placencia are teeming with incredible marine life. **Nite Wind** and **Ocean Motion** run to the inner reef (BZ$430) or trips outside the reef (BZ$560-$600), and include gear and lunch. **Kingfisher Angler Adventure** is reputable and owner Charles has appeared on ESPN and the Discovery Channel for his fly-fishing prowess. **Earl and Kurt Godfrey** are also recommended. *(Kingfisher Angler Adventure, ☎/fax 523 3323. Earl and Kurt Godfrey, ☎ 523 3433.)*

PUNTA GORDA

In the far south of Belize, the Toledo District surrounding Punta Gorda has much to offer the adventurous traveler. Poorly maintained roads and long, bumpy bus rides have weeded out the weak, and Toledo's many natural wonders remain virtually untouched. Its mountains are home to the largest Maya population in Belize. The commercial center, Punta Gorda (pop. 4900), may be tiny, but it houses an amalgamation of Mopan and Kek'chi Maya, Garífuna, Creole, and East Indian communities, with some German Mennonites thrown in the mix. Wednesday and Saturday mornings are the best time to see this eclectic melting pot, as people from surrounding villages arrive by the bus load to buy and sell at the market on Front Street. Tourist infrastructure is lacking and poverty abounds, but the rich cultural appeal of Punta Gorda makes the visit time well spent.

▐ TRANSPORTATION

Flights: Tropic Air (☎ 722 2008) makes at least 5 daily flights to each of the following: **Belize City International** (1hr., BZ$187); **Belize City Municipal** (1hr., BZ$152); **Dangriga** (45min., BZ$68); and **Placencia** (20min., BZ$59). **Maya Island Air** (☎ 702 2072 or 722 2856) has similar rates and itineraries.

Buses: Southern Transport, on Back St. south of town, goes to **Belize City** (8hr.; 4, 5, 10am; BZ$22) via **Dangriga** (5hr., BZ$13) and **Independence** (for connections to **Placencia**). **James Buses** (☎ 702 2049) have more rapid service along the same route from King St., in the lot opposite the police station (7hr.; 6, 8, 11am, and noon; BZ$13). Buses leave near the clock tower in Central Park (11am-noon) to **Maya Villages** including: **Blue Creek, Laguna** (Agua Caliente National Park), **San Antonio, San Pedro Columbia** (Lubaantun), and **Santa Cruz** (Río Blanco National Park). The buses have their final destination on the windshield, ask the driver to be certain. As return service for all village buses leaves at 3-5am on M, W, F, Sa, it is not possible to use buses for day-trips.

Ferries: Several boats go back and forth to Guatemala from Punta Gorda. North of customs on Front St. is **Requena's Charter Service** (☎ 722 2070), which makes 1 trip daily to **Puerto Barrios, Guatemala** (50min., 9am, BZ$35). Go to the customs office by the wharf 30min. ahead of time to get your departure stamp and pay the BZ$7.50 conservation fee. The **Pichilingo,** a Guatemalan skiff, also heads to **Puerto Barrios** (1hr., M-Sa 4pm, BZ$35). Captain Rigoberto James goes to **Livingston** (Tu and F 10am, BZ$40). Boats to Puerto Barrios also stop in Livingston (5 person minimum, BZ$40). Alternatively, it's possible to get to Livingston by ferry from Puerto Barrios (BZ$10).

✦▐ ORIENTATION AND PRACTICAL INFORMATION

Punta Gorda hugs the coastline. For quick orientation, remember that the coastline runs roughly north-south, and the major roads parallel to the coast are **Front Street, Main Street,** and **Middle Street.** Most activity is concentrated on these streets. Far West St. traces the western boundary of "P.G.," as the city is most frequently called. Buses arrive at the south end of town. From the terminal make a right onto the road as you walk out (10min.) and look for the clock tower overhead. The tower is in the **central park**, and Main St. runs along it. The airstrip is northwest of town.

Punta Gorda

▲ ACCOMMODATIONS
Charlton's Inn, **2**
Nature's Way, **8**
The St. Charles, **5**

🍎 FOOD
Big Jer's Titanic, **9**
Earth Runnin's Café and
 Bukut Bar, **3**
Emery's, **4**
Gomier's Foods, **1**
The Ice Cream Parlor, **7**

Tourist Information: The **Belize Tourism Board** (☎722 2531) has an office on the waterfront, just south of the Customs Office (open Tu-Sa 8-noon and 1-5pm). Maps, brochures, bus schedules, and official advice. Inside, the **TEA office** plans trips to local Maya villages.

Banks: Belize Bank, on Main St., at the northeast corner of the park, changes US dollars and traveler's checks. MC/V cash advances (BZ$15 fee). The **ATM** accepts foreign cards. Open M-Th 8am-1pm, F 8am-4:30pm.

Supermarket: Vernon's Store, on Front St., south of customs, sells snacks and dry goods. Open M-W 8am-noon and 2-5pm except Th 8am-noon.

Police: (☎722 2022, emergency 90), next to the post office on Front St. Open 24hr.

Pharmacy: Rosalina's Pharmacy (☎722 2044), on the corner of Main and North St. Open daily 9am-noon and 2-5pm.

Medical Services: Punta Gorda Hospital (☎722 2026), at the end of Main St. near the bus station and the cemetery. Outpatient clinic and emergency room. Open daily 8am-noon and 1-5pm. Use the rear entrance for night emergencies. The **Hillside Health Care Center** (☎722 2312), located 6.5 km north of town, is American-run. Open M, W, F 8am-noon, Tu 4pm-7pm, or call for an appointment. The **Red Cross** is across from the hospital. Open M, W, F 9-11am.

Telephones: BTL (☎702 2048), on Main St., a block north of Central Park. **Fax** service. Open M-F 8am-noon and 1-5pm. Pay phones are located at the north end of Main St.

Internet Access: Carysha, on Main St., just southeast of the clock tower. BZ$3 per 15min. Open M-F 8am-noon and 1-5pm, Sa 8am-noon.

Post Office: Front St., across from the customs office. Open M-Th 8am-noon and 1-5pm, F 8-noon and 1-4:30pm.

🏠 ACCOMMODATIONS

Like much of the rest of Belize, Punta Gorda has not started catering to tourists. Rooms are adequate, but most guests stay for just a night.

THE HIDDEN DEAL

COMMUNITY LIVING, TOLEDO STYLE

f you're using this book, chances are you're interested in getting beyond superficial sightseeing. 'ou want to meet locals, eat tradiional foods, and live in the midst f the beauty and grandeur of the egion without being dominated y the day-to-day comforts of Western life. In short, you want to dissolve into another place, if only for a while.

The Toledo Ecotourism Association, or TEA, places travelers in ural Belizean villages as shorterm residents, and is set up so as to distribute tourism dollars evenly throughout those communities. The result is an equitable solution to tourism, in which all members of the community can ook forward to profits, making everyone's stay a better one. The association is comprised of nine ural villages in the Toledo district, each offering its own flavor of Belzean culture. The tourist possibiliies are endless, as the individual esponsibilities rotate: entertainers switch villages, families change from hosts to cooks. Every village also elects a TEA governing body every two years, instilling he value and efficacy of democratic decision-making.

Visit www.southernbelize.com/ ea. Sign in at the TEA office in Punta Gorda. Rooms are BZ$18.50 per night. Families alternate serving meals (BZ$7) at their homes, and will drop by to pick you up. Local ours are BZ$7 per hr.

Charlton's Inn, 9 Main St. (☎722 2197), at the north end of town. Big, modern accommodation within arm's reach of the sea. Rooms have a bath, desk, fan, TV. Singles BZ$25, with A/C BZ$50; doubles BZ$35/ BZ$60. MC/V. ❷

The St. Charles, 23 King St. (☎722 2149), left on the corner of King St., 1 block north of the clock tower. Simple, spacious rooms with multiple fans and TV. The office is in the bicycle shop downstairs. Singles with bath BZ$30; doubles BZ$30, with bath BZ$40, with A/ C BZ$60. ❷

Dem Dats Doin takes ecotourism to a new level. Take the San Pedro Columbia-bound bus (M, W, F, Sa noon; BZ$2.50) from the bank and ask to be let off at Dem Dats Doin, after the wooden bridge. Dats Doin is a self-sufficient "organic mini-biosphere" that runs on energy from photovoltaic cells and pig manure. 2hr. tour including butterfly ranch BZ$10. Breakfast included. Singles BZ$30; doubles BZ$40. ❷

Nature's Way Guest House and Restaurant (☎722 2119), at the south end of Front St. next to the large Catholic church. Excellent view of the sea, comfy hammocks, shiny common baths, and wooden floors. You may be awakened "nature's way" at 5am by roosters. Bring mosquito repellent. Ultra-cool owner "Chet" provides info on the jungle and Maya villages. Check-out 10am. Dorms BZ$22; singles BZ$32; doubles BZ$47. ❷

🍴 FOOD

Gomier's Foods. Head north about 3min. past the Texaco station until the fork where the 2 big roads meet. It's on the left, at the Plenty International Office. Gomier, a St. Lucian, prepares a veggie lunch special every weekday using local ingredients and soy milk. Tofu, okaru, or veggie burgers BZ$6-7. Thick soy shakes (BZ$4) are delicious. Curried or BBQ tofu entrees BZ$10. Open daily until 5pm. ❷

Earth Runnin's Cafe and Bukut Bar, at Middle St. and North St., is a vegetarian's dream come true. A unique atmosphere with low lighting, soft reggae music, Belizean crafts, and carved mahogany chairs. Most vegetables cooked are grown in owner Giovanni's backyard. Excellent steamed snapper with rice, beans, vegetables, and salad (BZ$12). Locals favor the vegetarian burrito (BZ$7). Try a drink at the Bukut Bar or surf the Internet before eating (BZ$12 per hr.). Serves lunch and dinner. Closed Tu. ❷

Emery's, on Main and North, down the street from the Texaco station. Quality fresh seafood entrees. Fish BZ$15, shrimp BZ$20. Open daily 10am-10pm. ❹

The Ice Cream Parlor, on the corner of Clement's St. and Main St. Nice quick small meals or snacks. Chicken soft taco BZ$2, burgers BZ$5-7. Open M-Sa 9am-2pm and 5-10pm, Su 5-10pm. ❶

Big Jer's Titanic, in the open-air 2nd fl. of the southernmost market building on Front St. The simple decor and seaside atmosphere are the big draws, second only to the price. Serves traditional Belizean entrees (BZ$9-16) as well as specialty Texas-style BBQ sandwiches (BZ$6-7). Service is very slow: if you lack patience, you'll learn it; if you have patience, you'll lose it. Open M-Sa 6:30am-8pm. ❸

⚑ DAYTRIPS FROM PUNTA GORDA

NIM LI PUNIT

Take any northbound bus from Punta Gorda along the Southern Hwy. and ask to be let out at Nim Li Punit. The last bus heading north from Punta Gorda is at noon, and the last bus heading south to Punta Gorda leaves Dangriga at 5:30pm. Follow the path to the visitors center. Open daily 8am-4:30pm. Entrance fee BZ$5.

A third of a mile from the Southern Hwy. 25 mi. north of Punta Gorda, the ruins of Nim Li Punit are an easy side trip between Punta Gorda and Dangriga. The site is a late-Classic Maya center which may have had a trading relationship with Copán in Honduras. In addition to temples, Nim Li Punit is best known for its array of impressive stelae with detailed interpretations of the hieroglyphs. **Stela 14,** in the modern **visitor center,** depicts a figure with a hat taller than he is, inspiring archaeologists to name the site Nim Li Punit (roughly, "large headdress").

Following the path from the visitor center, the first group of structures is the **E-group.** The raised platform may have functioned as an astronomical observatory. From here, it's easy to see the northernmost structure in this group, an immaculately reconstructed **ballcourt.** The original stones were used in the reconstruction, and though the mortar is new, it was made in Maya fashion, without concrete. North of the ball court is the **Plaza of Stelae** that provides an excellent view of the Toledo District. Just east up the small staircase are the tombs. The impressive **Tomb 1,** uncovered in 1986, held at least four members of the royal family, 37 ceramic vessels, and several jade items.

The visitor center provides details on several of the site's most impressive carved stelae, including the second largest stela in Central America. In addition, there is a small but extremely informative display providing some background about both ancient and contemporary Maya culture.

LUBAANTUN

You can reach the Lubaantun ruins by catching a bus between Dangriga and Punta Gorda on the Southern Hwy. destined for the Kekchí village of San Pedro Columbia. The bus drops you off at the dump, 3km from the village, but there are sometimes trucks waiting to take villagers to San Pedro from there. Direct buses run from Punta Gorda to San Pedro (M, W, F, Sa noon) but return the next day at 5am, making a walk back to the highway inevitable. There are no Su buses. From the village, the ruins are a well-labeled 20min. walk.

Probably the best known of the many Maya ruins near Punta Gorda, Lubaantun is 26km northwest in the village of San Pedro Columbia. Lubaantun ("Place of the Fallen Stones") is true to its name, consisting largely of what appear to be big piles of rubble. Thomas Gann found the ruins in 1903 and, in the manner of many "great archaeologists" of the day, blasted into them with dynamite—whether the stones had fallen before this explosive excavation isn't entirely clear. Like its somewhat more accessible neighbor Nim Li Punit, Lubaantun was recently reconstructed. The visitor center, surrounded by newly constructed paths, houses artifacts and pottery. Lubaantun's structures are generally a bit larger than those at Nim Li

BELIZE

Punit, and the site is more extensive—there are two ball courts, as well as a good-sized temple. Lubaantun's edifices, as well as the buildings in some nearby communities, differ from most Maya structures in their construction—instead of using mortar, blocks were carefully sculpted and seamlessly interlocked. If you need a place to stay, check out nearby **Dem Dats Doin** (see **Accommodations,** p. 117).

SANTA CRUZ, RÍO BLANCO NATIONAL PARK, AND UXBENKA

The Mopan Maya village of Santa Cruz is located 15km off the Southern Hwy. junction at the dump. The place to stay in Santa Cruz is with the Marcus Sho family. Though not TEA, the family is fun-loving and hospitable, and Marcus was a founding member of both TEA and Rio Blanco National Park. (BZ$30 per night includes meals, plus extra for any guided tours.) The bus driver will know the location.

Santa Cruz is still traditional, with an atmosphere that seems remarkably ancient. The village was devastated by Hurricane Iris in October 2001, but has rebounded with help from international aid organizations. **Río Blanco National Park** (BZ$5) is located a mile west of Santa Cruz on the only road. It has some of the area's most impressive waterfalls, including the signature **Río Blanco Falls**, with a natural 20 ft. high diving board. The waterfalls and overhanging cliffs create an inviting pool.

The unexcavated ruins of **Uxbenka** lie east of Santa Cruz and can be reached in a few minutes. Most of Uxbenka is comprised of a muddy mound of trees and shrubs hiding a minor Maya ceremonial site that contained some excellent examples of the Maya agricultural method of raised terraces.

LAGUNA AND AGUA CALIENTE NATIONAL PARK

Buses leave from Punta Gorda for Laguna Village (M, W, F, Sa noon; return M, W, F, Sa 5am; BZ$3.50). It might be possible to grab a ride with Pedro Chub (see below) if you can catch him ahead of time at the SAGE office.

About 45min. from Punta Gorda by bus, the village of **Laguna** is an extremely open and welcoming community, fully prepared to help visitors relax and enjoy its amazing setting, with access to hiking, canoeing, and caving. There are two accommodation options in Laguna, a **TEA Guesthouse ❶** or the almost-as-rustic **Friends of Lu-ha Guesthouse ❶** (☎ 702 2970). Both are BZ$18.50 per person, but Luha has more spacious rooms and bathrooms with running water.

In the vast wilderness area surrounding Laguna waits the **Agua Caliente National Park** and its 9 sq. mi. of wetland. An excellent 2-3hr. hiking trail starts from the info center—a 30min. hike from the village. During the dry season the trail is far more impressive. Between February and May, the trail leads farther into the park to a nesting site of jabiru storks, one of the largest flying birds in the western hemisphere. It's possible to arrange to meet a park official in Laguna if you contact the **SAGE** office (☎ 722 2721) in Punta Gorda on Far West St. beforehand. Ask anyone in the village for Pedro Chub, the super-helpful park coordinator. Pedro can also inform you about a hike up to a 500 ft. mountain ridge where spectacular views await. If you want to explore the nearby caves, rent flashlights (BZ$5-10) and hire a guide (BZ$7 per hr.). A guided canoe trip through the forest can cost as little as BZ$30 for five people.

COSTA RICA

When Christopher Columbus named this land "rich coast" in 1502, he certainly didn't anticipate the reasons people would eventually find to support his title. Bereft of gold and ruins, the country's initial wealth seemed to lie in its endless swarms of mosquitoes and its unforgiving jungles, neither of which appealed to colonial settlers. These days, however, most visitors to Costa Rica would probably attest that its name is pretty accurate. The well-oiled tourist industry is only too happy to recount the country's impressive statistics: though it covers only 0.03% of the world's territory, Costa Rica is home to six percent of the planet's plant and animal species. Meanwhile, the diverse terrain challenges visitors with overwhelming intrigue and possibility. Volcanoes, jungles, beaches, hot springs, coral reefs, hidden caves, lush deserted islands—all lie within a day's (or even an hour's) travel of one another. Sometimes it feels like the only thing this country *can't* offer is a corner that travelers haven't already found and conquered—leaving fusion bistros and high-tech canopy tours in their wake. But rustic spots never lie out of range, and Costa Rica's national character has remained surprisingly visible despite the trappings of its tourist infrastructure. Costa Rica might entice you with the convenience and flashy superlatives of its "paradise" reputation, but its more informal moments—a sudden jungle rainstorm or an unexpected roadside chat—are those that will probably capture your heart.

HIGHLIGHTS OF COSTA RICA

Monteverde Cloud Forest Reserve is one of Central America's most famous ecotourism destinations. Explore jungles full of monkeys, elusive quetzals, sloths, and jaguars.

Bask on the unspoiled black sand beaches of **Playa Hermosa**, where beachside cabañas and perfect waves promise idyllic days full of surf and relaxation.

Survey both oceans from the top of Costa Rica's highest mountain in **Parque Nacional Chirripó**, whose summit trails winds through a variety of distinct terrains.

Playa Tamarindo, on the Nicoya Peninsula, is one of the country's most famous surfing meccas. Travelers take to the waves by day and storm its lively clubs and bars by night.

Cahuita boasts the largest coral reef on Costa Rica's eastern coast, enchanting visitors with its stunning marine life and perfect turquoise waves.

SUGGESTED ITINERARIES

INTO THE WILD. Blessed with one of the most breathtaking and extensive park systems in the world, Costa Rica caters to every whim—whether you want to stroll along well-maintained trails or muscle your way through the underbrush armed with a machete and a healthy supply of optimism. Begin your tour at the **Monteverde Cloud Forest Reserve** (p. 166) which visitors can explore along an extensive network of trails, tree-top bridges, and ziplines. The slopes of nearby **Volcán Tenorio** (p. 172) are studded with hot springs, rugged craters, sparkling lakes, and surging waterfalls. Further north, **Parque Nacional Rincón de la Vieja** (p. 174) offers an even more elaborate geothermal variety show, complete with sulfuric lagoons and boil-

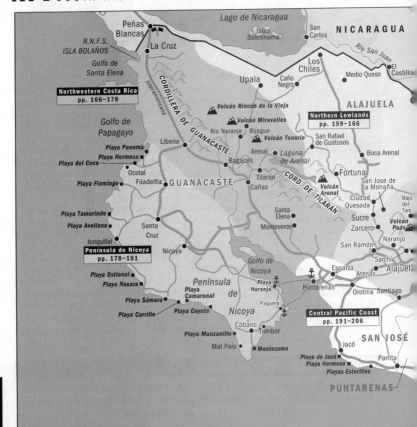

COSTA RICA

PACIFIC OCEAN

Costa Rica

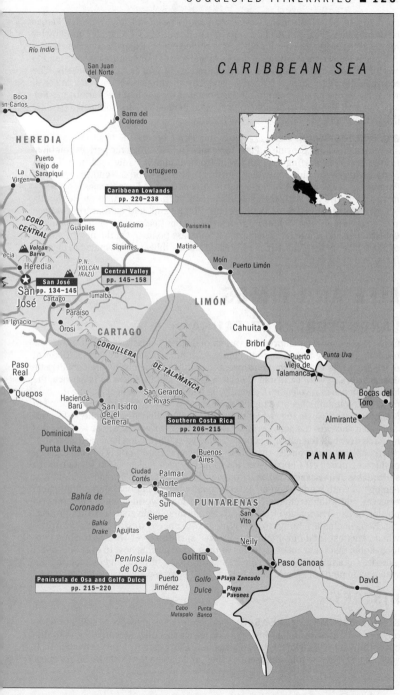

ing mud pits. Site of one of the Costa Rican army's best (and only) victories, **Parque Nacional Santa Rosa** (p. 175) now hosts an enchanting cast of spider and howler monkeys in forests that border miles of secluded beach. Enjoy famous hot springs and marvel at active lava flows at **Volcán Arenal** (p. 164), or venture underground to explore 10 stalactite "galleries" at the **Cavernas de Venado** (p. 164) nearby. The **Nicoya Peninsula** is a mecca for surfers and sun-worshippers on the western coast, while mangrove swamps and fossil-filled coral caves await at the Caribbean's **Refugio Nacional Gandoca-Manzanillo** (p. 236), and **Parque Nacional Tortuguero** (p. 228) draws thousands of nesting turtles each year.

BACK ON THE BEACH. No matter how you define beach-side bliss, Costa Rica's shores can probably provide it. **Playa Tamarindo** (p. 181) offers the perfect combination of gorgeous surfing days and wild tropical nights, while **Jacó** (p. 195) is a party-loving beach bum's paradise. Surfing is at its best on the endless waves of **Pavones** (p. 217), and avid surfers and sunbathers flock to **Playa Hermosa** (p. 197)—not to be confused with the upscale beach of the same name on Península Nicoya—for its relaxed atmosphere, hot black sand, and exhilarating waves. White-faced monkeys scamper through the coconut palms and smooth sands of **Cahuita** (p. 229), where horseback riding tours are popular. On the nearby shores of **Manzanillo** (p. 237), the pristine waters of the Caribbean are hemmed in by rainforest and coral reefs.

LIFE AND TIMES

LAND, FLORA, AND FAUNA

Costa Rica contains an impressive variety of distinct landscapes within its narrow borders, including four mountain chains with more than 60 volcanoes. Eight of these are active today. From northwest to southeast, the chains are **Cordillera de Guanacaste, Cordillera de Tilarán, Cordillera Central,** and **Cordillera de Talamanca,** the last of which is non-volcanic. Generally, as one proceeds southeast along the isthmus, the mountains become higher and the *cordilleras* broader, culminating in Mount Chirripó, Costa Rica's highest point (3820m). Between Cordilleras Central and Talamanca lies the high Central Valley, or Meseta Central, whose fertile soil is home to over half the nation's people. To the west, Pacific lowlands are narrower, drier, and four times longer than their Caribbean counterparts. The convergence of tectonic plates off Central America's Pacific coast makes Costa Rica prone to **earthquakes** and **volcanic eruptions.** Roughly 25% of Costa Rica's unique geology and ecology is contained within an extensive network of national parks, biological reserves, and wildlife refuges. No other country in the world defends a greater proportion of its territory, and Costa Rica's astonishing biodiversity is worth protecting. Ecosystems are home to everything from speedy *Jesu Christo* lizards—whose greatest (and only) miracles involve sprinting over water—to slow two-toed sloths that make up ecosystems of their own, playing host to over 900 insect parasites at a time. Costa Rica's parks and refuges surprise and delight visitors with a wide range of breathtaking habitats and impressively diverse inhabitants.

HISTORY

BEFORE COLUMBUS (PRE-1500). Long decried as an oasis of stability without an exciting or turbulent history, Costa Rica has only recently begun to discover the story of its own heritage. By the time European explorers arrived here, it was already home to four indigenous tribes, and though the Costa Rican conquest story is oft-narrated as a "settlement," this term is an unfortunate euphemism. In fact, the conquest was especially bloody, leaving few survivors, and today only 1% of Costa Rica's population descends from its original indigenous inhabitants.

THE COLONIAL PERIOD (1502-1821). Christopher Columbus discovered Costa Rica's eastern shores in 1502, on his fourth and final voyage west. Early settlement years were tumultuous, marked by ongoing conflicts between European colonizers and native residents as well as with British pirates along both coasts. Inferior bureaucrats and aristocracy ended up settling the questionably desirable territory of Costa Rica, due to its status as something of a remote outpost within the Spanish colonial kingdom. As a result, Costa Rica was unwittingly given the opportunity to develop under weaker colonial influence than its neighbors.

LIBERATION AND "EL GRANO DE ORO" (1821-1900). Although Central America officially gained independence from Spain on September 15, 1821, Costa Ricans didn't hear about it until a month later, when the news arrived by mule. Predictably, liberation brought internal conflict. While Costa Rica's four largest cities (San José, Cartago, Heredia, and Alajuela) all vied to govern the country from within, nearby nations (Guatemala, Mexico, and Nicaragua) aimed to govern it from beyond. Much of the country's development during the 19th century was defined by the growth of its coffee industry, a lucrative commodity that came to be known as its *grano de oro* (golden bean). The industry was urgently intentional: dictator **Braulio Carrillo** supported its growth in the 1830s because he could see that the country needed a cash crop, and coffee—rapidly gaining popularity in Europe—seemed like a good bet. Since most arable land had been divided on a small, equitable scale, increased income didn't lead to the stratified system of land-owning elites and working peasants that defined most of Central America.

INVASION AND DICTATORSHIP (1850-1890). The only serious external threat to Costa Rican national security during the late 19th century came from **William Walker,** a rogue gold miner from Tennessee who wanted to annex the country as a slave holding American state. Walker invaded Guanacaste in 1856, spurring a ragtag *tico* civilian army into action. They drove him back to Nicaragua, where a drummer-boy and precocious military strategist named **Juan Santamaría** set fire to Walker's troops' impromptu barracks, ending their deluded campaign and launching himself into the sparsely populated ranks of Costa Rican national heros.

General Tomás Guardia, one of Costa Rica's only dictators, seized power soon after in 1870. During Guardia's 12 years in power, his ambitious iron-fisted policies actually modernized the country in important ways, though they cost Costa Ricans their civil liberties and accrued a sizable trade deficit. After his dictatorship, the country saw a peaceful transition back to democracy. In 1890, Costa Rica conducted the first legitimate, large-scale elections in Central American history.

DOMESTIC DISCONTENT AND GLOBAL GROWTH (1900-PRESENT). Costa Rica underwent a rather ungraceful transition into the 20th century. These years were marked by border disputes with Panama and another dangerous flirtation with autocracy when **Alfredo González,** winner of the 1913 elections, was overthrown by the reactionary **General Federico Tinoco.** The dictatorship was unpopular and brief, however, and the decades to follow were smooth and prosperous. A powerful coffee elite continued to ensure that income taxes remained low (as they still are today), though social discontent grew among laborers and radicals.

A disaffected middle class rose up against **Rafael Angel Calderón Guardia's** progressive puppet regime during the **War of National Liberation** in 1948, under the leadership of **José Figueres Ferrer,** a wealthy coffee farmer and intellectual. Backed by

COSTA RICA

CIA forces looking to halt communism, Figueres defeated the government's machete-wielding forces in six weeks before inaugurating the **Founding Junta of the Second Republic** and instituting a wide range of important political reforms, including abolishing the Costa Rican military. Since dissolving its army in 1949, Costa Rica has enjoyed peace, political stability, and a relatively high degree of economic comfort, earning the nickname "the Switzerland of Central America," a dubious title that it nonetheless bears with pride. In 1987, former president **Oscar Arias Sánchez** earned the **Nobel Peace Prize** when he helped lay the groundwork for a unified Central American Parliament with the Plan de Paz Arias.

TODAY

Though one of the most prosperous countries in Latin America today, with a strong democracy and historical political stability, Costa Rica remains involved in the fate of its neighbors. Its tense border relations with Nicaragua have been aggravated by a continued influx of illegal *nica* immigrants, who have been met with extensive prejudice in the country's northern regions. Though often held up as an example of functional Central American politics, Costa Rica still struggles to balance national welfare and poverty with debt management.

Much of the economy relies on ecotourism, which remains a controversial industry. Supporters maintain that ecotourism benefits environment and travelers alike. While the government plans to steer tourism towards ecotourism in order to attract wealthier travelers seeking comfortable wilderness adventures, conservation groups are concerned that larger facilities will put a burden on ecosystems.

CULTURE AND ARTS

PEOPLE. Costa Rican Spanish uses the diminutive ending *tico* so often that *"ticos"* has come to refer to Costa Ricans in general. Out of over 4 million inhabitants, 94% of the population is of both European and *mestizo* descent. **Indígenas** comprise just over 1% of the population; the region's largest remaining indigenous groups are the **Bribrí** and **Cabécare,** who have a large presence in **Guanacaste.** Those of **African** descent make up 3% of the population and are concentrated on the Caribbean coast. Surprisingly, Chinese immigrants compose 1% of the population. Most *indígenas* in Costa Rica who maintain traditional lifestyles do so on one of the 21 reserves scattered throughout the country; however reserve boundaries are often disrespected, and indigenous lands are constantly threatened. Although times are changing, most people in the country are committed Catholics and their religious beliefs make sexual relations before marriage an ongoing taboo, especially among older generations.

Spanish is the country's official language, though Costa Ricans speak with a characteristic *tico* twist in accent and usage. Blacks along the Caribbean coast speak English, and indigenous groups like the Bribrí maintain their traditional languages. Costa Rica has more slang and country-specific vocabulary than many larger nations, speech generally known as *tiquismo*, much of which comes from adding "-ito" or "-ico" to many words in order to make them more "friendly." One of the country's most popular phrases is *pura vida* (cool, awesome), though you might be hard-pressed to discover on your own that *tuanis*, which has a similar meaning, was what became of the English phrase "too nice." When speaking Spanish in Costa Rica, you'll find an important distinction between *usted*, *vos*, and *tú*. Use *usted* when speaking to a stranger or someone older; it is more formal and respectful. However, Costa Ricans are distinct for using *usted* more broadly: with family, friends, children, and even pets. *Vos* is rarely used in the city anymore, but it is still common in the countryside

Costa Rica is a politically secular country with weak links between church and state. Practiced by about 90% of the population, Roman Catholicism is the official religion and only Catholic marriages receive state recognition—all others must be accompanied by a civil ceremony. Abortions are illegal and Catholic churches exist in nearly every town in the country, often at the center of local and cultural events. Holy Week, a national holiday which culminates in Easter Sunday, is a fervent balance of piety, pilgrimage, prayer, and party

FOOD AND DRINK. If it doesn't have rice and beans, it isn't *tico*. Rice and black beans are not just everyday staple foods; they have been appropriated as a no-frills national icon. In the same day, someone might enjoy them prepared for breakfast as *gallo pinto* (fried rice and beans cooked with spices; known as "spotted rooster" for all the predictable reasons), then take a *casado* for lunch and have a hearty bowl of black bean soup for dinner. The word *casado* literally means married man, and refers to the hearty combination plates that wives traditionally prepared for their husbands to take to work in the fields. These days, they're easy to find at any *soda*, one of the casual diners that serve flavorful, home-style cooking at inexpensive prices. Comida típica (native dishes) are less spicy than they are flavorful, though high levels of fat, salt, and carbohydrates have contributed to the country's stomach cancer rates, the highest in the Western world.

Though vegetables are not a large part of Costa Rican diet, fruits are popular snacks. Favorite varieties you may already know include pineapple, banana, melon, strawberries, and papaya, often blended into delicious *batidos* (fruit shakes). Perhaps because of the hot climate, a distinctive aspect of Costa Rican cuisine is its wide and tasty range of beverages. *Frescos* have taken the concept of "juice" to new levels of sweetness, combining fruits with sugar, with milk or water, though nothing can compete with the widespread appeal of Costa Rica's world-class coffee. Don't be surprised to see *ticos* of all ages enjoying a big mug of *café* (usually mixed with milk) more than once a day. Though coffee has captured the hearts of Costa Ricans, alcohol still puts up a fight for their livers. *Guaro*, made from sugar cane, is the national liquor. It mixes well with anything, though *coco loco* (with coconut juice) is popular. Anyone who's not a fan of Imperial, the national beer, is likely to get chased out of the country. Drinking is such a national pastime, however, that it's a national problem. Among the wide range of Central American superlatives that it claims, Costa Rica has secured the unfortunate distinction of having the region's highest alcoholism rate.

CUSTOMS AND ETIQUETTE. *Ticos* are family-oriented, and close extended families are common. This trend makes for fairly cohesive communities, particularly in rural areas. *Ticos* are known for their relaxed and helpful temperaments, as well as willingness to lend a hand, or even a home, in times of need. The phrase *quedar bien*, meaning "staying on good terms" is an essential tenet of Costa Rican lifestyle values. In general, *ticos* are affectionate and often physically expressive. Thankfulness is an admirable quality in house guests, and hospitality should be received with articulated gratitude—say "thank you," and say it often.

ARTS. Long before Columbus landed in 1502, Meso-American indigenous populations were creating records of near-forgotten sophistication and craftsmanship. Typical artifacts include **statues** in **gold, jade,** and **stone,** as well as heavy breast-plates featuring stylized jaguars, crocodiles, and hook-beaked birds.

LITERATURE. Before the 20th century, Costa Rican literature drew largely from European models, though it gained inspiration from folk tales and colloquial expression in a movement known as *costumbrismo*. The nation's working people were represented through *El Moto* and *Las Hijas del Campo* by **Joaquín García**

Monge. Despite the strength of this early movement, Costa Rican literature didn't find its most expressive voice until it began focusing on political and social criticism during the 20th century. **José Marín Cañas's** *Infierno Verde*, a depiction of the Chaco War between Paraguay and Bolivia, bolstered developing anti-imperialist sentiment. Playwrights **Alberto Cañas** and **Daniel Gallegos** accompanied the so-called "Circle of Costa Rican Poets" in an attempt to unite the nation's thinkers against agents of sociopolitical oppression. Spanish-language **newspapers** *La Nación* (www.nacion.co.cr) and *La República* (www.larepublica.net) represent alternative views of the two main political parties in Costa Rica. *La Nación* has slightly broader circulation, and is owned by the same company that puts out *Al Día*, a sensationalist paper devoted largely to sports and celebrity gossip.

POPULAR CULTURE. Much of Costa Rica's contemporary popular culture is imported from elsewhere, and often its "distinctive" cultural offerings remain frustratingly elusive to travelers hungry for authenticity. While the rule of thumb was once a simple American conditional (if it's *norteamericano*, it's cool), cultural tastes have grown more inclusive. US movies and singers like Britney Spears have substantial fan bases across the country, but people are also drawn to music and cinema from the rest of Latin America. Indeed, *discotecas* make no apologies for their juxtapositions: American pop hits from several years ago often serve as preludes to traditional Latin American beats. Reggae is popular throughout the Caribbean coast, where it's especially hard to escape sounds of "ragga" superstar Sean Paul, with a style and following all his own.

SPORTS AND RECREATION. Among Costa Ricans, there is no question as to which sport captures the country's full attention: *fútbol*. *Ticos* eat, drink, sleep and breathe *futbol*, known in the US as soccer. Indeed, these matches are one of the few events that everyone gets to on time. Costa Rica has one major national league with a season stretching August to May, but competition runs just as fierce on the local level as villages battle for territorial honor and unofficial crowns.

Costa Rica's outdoor adventures, while known for diversity and quality, charge higher prices than most other Central American countries. Many travelers come specifically to pursue these activities, that run the gamut from scenic to strenuous, including **sportfishing**, **surfing**, **scuba diving**, **snorkeling**, **kayaking**, **white-water rafting**, **mountain biking**, and **golf.** (Yes, golf: Costa Rica boasts the best 18-hole courses in Central America.) While tour groups and guides are more widespread than *típico* food, sheer numbers have forced them to offer competitive prices and conform to widely adopted, fairly stringent safety requirements.

Surfers come from round the globe to ride Pacific and Caribbean waves. Many of the best surfing beaches are within a four-hour drive from San José, where waves range from fast and hollow to consistent lefts and rights. Jacó, Playa Dominical, and Limón are among the best areas to begin lessons or hone skills; the best surfers head to Pavones and Playa Negra for the most challenging waves. Costa Rica hardly suffers from a lack of marine life, reefs, or guides; as such, **scuba diving** and **snorkeling** are extremely popular among travelers. Cahuita has large, beautiful reefs, as do Punta Gorda and Isla del Coco. Further inland, **white-water rafting** and **kayaking** are fun ways to see biodiversity first-hand. Costa Rica's rugged terrain, drainage network, and amount of runoff result in ideal conditions for paddling. Rapids range from Class II to Class V, ensuring prime conditions for adventurers with varying levels of technical skill. Some of the best sites are Quepos, Fortuna de San Carlos, Parque Nacional Santa Rosa, and Puerto Viejo de Sarapiquí.

HOLIDAYS. Like most of Central America, each town celebrates its patron saint, as does the entire country. National holidays include, but are not limited to, **March 24-25,** which are paid holidays celebrated with religious processions, especially in

Tres Ríos, Cartago and San Joaquín de Flores; **April 11,** Juan Santamaría Day commemorates the day Costa Rica's only national hero, Juan Santamaría, burned down the filibusters' fort and helped Costa Ricans win the Battle of Rivas (1856); **August 2,** Día de la Independencia; **November 2,** All Soul's Day; and of course Christmas, **December 25.**

ESSENTIALS

PASSPORTS, VISAS, AND CUSTOMS

Passport. (p. 19) Required of all visitors. Travelers for whom a visa is required must also hold passports valid for 6 months after date of entry.

Visa. Not required of citizens of Australia, Canada, Ireland, New Zealand, US, or members of the European Union.

Inoculations and Medications. None required.

Work Permit. (p. 133) Required of all foreigners planning to work in Costa Rica for more than one year.

Driving Permit. No special permit is needed—just a valid drivers license, registration, and car title.

Airport Tax: $26.

EMBASSIES AND CONSULATES

Embassies of Costa Rica: Canada, 325 Dalhouise St., Ste. 407, Ottawa, Ontario, K1N 7G2 (☎613-562-2855; fax: 562-2582). Open M-F 9am-5pm. **UK,** Flat 1, 14 Lancaster Gate, London W2 3LH (☎171 706 8844; fax 171 706 8655). Open M-Th 8am-noon and 12:30-4pm, F 8am-1pm. **US,** 2114 "S" St., NW, Washington, D.C. 20008 (☎202-234-2945; www.costarica-embassy.org). Open M-F 9am-5pm.

Consulates of Costa Rica: US, 80 Wall St., Ste. 718, NY, 10005, US (☎212-509-3066; fax 212-509-3068). Also in Boston, Los Angeles, and Miami.

MONEY

The currency chart below is based on August 2004 exchange rates. As a general rule, it's cheaper to convert money in Costa Rica than at home. The unit of currency in Costa Rica is the colón, which is divided into 100 céntimos, though these coins are becoming increasingly less useful as Costa Rican currency depreciates on the global market. Paper notes circulate in the following amounts: 50, 100, 500, 1000, 2000, 5000, and 10,000; you might hear them referred to by slang names rojo (1000) or tucán (5000).

CURRENCY (¢)		
AUS$1 = ¢310		¢100 = AUS$0.32
CDN$1 = ¢334		¢100 = CDN$0.30
EUR€1 = ¢535		¢100 = EUR€0.19
NZ$1 = ¢279		¢100 = NZ$0.36
UK£1 = ¢808		¢100 = UK£0.12
US$1 = ¢444		¢100 = US$0.23

Costa Rica's streets (particularly in San José) are full of money-vendors who will pass off counterfeit US dollars and colónes. Visitors should also be sensitive to the possibility of credit card fraud, which is widespread and one of the least appealing side effects of Costa Rica's blossoming tourism industry. Travelers

COSTA RICA

should take care to retain credit card receipts and check accounts regularly. Many of Costa Rica's touristed destinations (large nature reserves, the Nicoya Peninsula, much of the Central Valley) are full of establishments that prefer US dollars.

There is a 13% **sales tax** on all purchases in Costa Rica. In addition, restaurants add a 10% **service charge** on all bills. There is also a 3.39% **tourism tax** in addition to the sales tax on hotel rooms. Usually these charges will be included in the prices posted, but ask beforehand to be sure. Often Costa Rican restaurants will include two price columns: one with tax-inclusive prices and one without.

PRICE DIVERSITY

Trip cost will vary considerably, depending on where you go, how you travel, and where you stay. The rainy season (May-Nov.) typically brings the best deals. Transportation in remote areas can also be expensive. The most significant expenses will probably be your round-trip (return) airfare to Costa Rica. To give you a general idea, a bare-bones day in Costa Rica (camping or sleeping in hostels, buying food at supermarkets) would cost about US$15 (¢6500); a slightly more comfortable day (sleeping in hostels/guest houses and the occasional budget hotel, eating one meal per day at a restaurant, going out at night) would cost US$30 (¢13,000); and for a luxurious day, the sky's the limit. Don't forget to factor in emergency reserve funds (at least US$200) when planning how much money you'll need.

SYMBOL:	❶	❷	❸	❹	❺
ACCOMM.	¢440-¢5300	¢5300-¢11,000	¢11,000-¢28,500	¢28,500-¢43,900	¢43,900+
	US$1-$12	US$12-$25	US$25-$65	US$65-$100	US$100+
FOOD	¢440-¢1300	¢1300-¢2600	¢2600-¢3900	¢3900-¢5300	¢5300-¢6600
	US$1-3	US$3-6	US$6-9	US$9-12	US$12-15

SAFETY

LOCAL LAWS AND POLICE. Costa Rica is a democratic republic and maintains a strong emphasis on human rights and democracy. Costa Rican law requires that all foreigners carry their passports with them at all times and be able to demonstrate proof of legal entry. An aggressive program against sexual tourism exists in Costa Rica and any sexual activity with a minor is punishable by imprisonment. The only police force is domestic since there is no military. The **Practical Information** for each town lists the location and number of the local police station. In case of an emergency, dial ☎911, unless otherwise specified.

NATURAL DISASTERS. The rainy season in Costa Rica occurs between May and November, contributing to its average rainfall of 250cm per year; there are often **floods** during this time, especially near the Caribbean coast and areas surrounding major rivers. Costa Rica is located over two tectonic plates, which results in a significant number of **earthquakes.** Tremors are not unusual, but a large-scale earthquake hasn't occurred since 1991. If indoors during an earthquake, stand in a doorway or go under a desk. If driving, pull over to the side of the road.

HEALTH

Costa Rica carries the same health risks as other Central American countries. For descriptions of disease prevention, see **Safety and Health,** p. 25. The most serious health concerns for travelers are malaria and dengue fever.

BORDER CROSSINGS

NICARAGUA. There is one land crossing at **Peñas Blancas/Sapoa** (p. 178), 75km north of Liberia and near Rivas, Nicaragua.

PANAMA. There are three land crossings: **Paso Canoas** (p. 214) is 18km southeast of Ciudad Neily, Costa Rica, near David, Panama. **Sixaola/Guabito** (p. 238) is on the Caribbean coast 1½hr. from Puerto Viejo de Talamanca, near Changuinola, Panama. A third crossing at **Río Sereno**, east of San Vito, is rarely used.

KEEPING IN TOUCH

MAIL. To ensure timely delivery, mark envelopes *airmail, par avion*, or *correo aéreo*. There are several ways to arrange pick-up of letters sent to you by friends and relatives while abroad. Mail can be sent via **Poste Restante** (General Delivery; *Lista de Correos* in Spanish) to almost any city or town in Costa Rica with a post office. Address *Poste Restante* letters like so:

Laura MARTIN [first name, LAST NAME]

Lista de Correos

Alajuela [town/city name], Costa Rica

The mail will go to a special desk in the central post office, unless you specify a post office by street address or Postal Code. It's best to use the central post office, since mail may be sent there regardless.

PHONE CALLS. The simplest way to call within the country is to use a **coin-operated phone.** However, these are not as available as they once were, since most have been replaced by the more efficient prepaid phone card phones. **Prepaid phone cards** (available at newspaper kiosks, convenience stores, and bookstores), which carry a certain amount of phone time depending on the card's denomination, usually save time and money in the long run. The Instituto Costarricense de Electricidad (ICE) is the sole provider of **cell phone** service in Costa Rica. Most likely, your cell phone will not work with this system unless you make arrangements with ICE and your home carrier before arriving.

COUNTRY CODE	506

COSTA RICA

TRANSPORTATION

Domestic **air travel** is more expensive, but also more convenient than traveling by bus. Smaller, less regulated airlines do offer domestic flights, but it is recommended that you use the two larger airlines, **Sansa** and **NatureAir.** Sansa (☎221-9414; www.flysansa.com) and the pricier but more reliable NatureAir (☎220 3054 or 800-235-9272 in US or Canada; www.natureair.net), have flights connecting San José with destinations throughout Costa Rica (p. 135). Both have several years of experience and reach many destinations.

The **bus** system is thorough, cheap, and reliable; from San José, you can travel almost anywhere in the country for under US$6. However, it's not always immediately clear where the buses arrive, when they leave, or how much they cost. The bus system is labyrinthine; every destination is served by a different company, and each company is located in a different part of town. Keep in mind that a seemingly microscopic, direct distance between two points on a map often translates into hours on a bumpy, windy road. You can find the most accurate bus information, including detailed schedules and maps, at the **Instituto Costarricense de Turismo** (**ICT; ☎** 223 1733 or 800-343-6332 from the US), along Av. 2 in San José. You can also find ICT representatives at the base of the stairs just before you exit the airport.

If you're traveling by **car**, unlike in the rest of Central America, you'll have a good network of highways at your disposal. A seat belt must be worn by the driver and any passengers. Although the government has been working on paving and fixing roads, road conditions still vary and tend to be quite rough (by international standards) in some places. Random potholes and bumps might make it hard to relax while driving, and watch out for open manholes along side roads, especially after hard rains. In general, it is always key to be careful and drive defensively. Many places do require **4WD** vehicles, especially during the rainy season, so it's good to know where you're going and what roads are like before you rent your car. Car rental agencies should help with info on road conditions.

Boats are a fairly common mode of transportation along the Caribbean Lowlands—ranging from *panchas* or water taxis to larger ferries, they are just as reliable and more quaint than a bus ride. However, boats are almost always open to the elements, with little shelter from bad weather. Public boat transport is available daily out of Limón, but it might be easier to stick to prearranged packages set up by your hotel or by tour operators.

ORIENTATION

A word of advice: ask. Signs in Central America are very limited, so if you have any doubts, or carrying a map isn't helping, stop and ask; People will help. Landmarks are the way of the wise. If there is any organization, it will be in mid-range and larger towns: streets are in an orderly grid of *avenidas* (avenues) and *calles* (streets); the *avenidas* run east-west and the *calles* north-south. Usually odd-numbered *avenidas* increase in number to the north and even-numbered to the south, while odd-numbered *calles* lie to the east of the grid's center and even-numbered *calles* to the west. The grid generally centers around a *parque central* (central park), with Av. Central and C. Central as the axes. An address given as Av. 3/5, C. 2 means the building is between Avenidas 3 and 5, on C. 2. Locations are often specified by a certain number of *metros* from the *parque*, which refers to portions of city blocks, not actual meters. *100 metros al norte del parque central* indicates a building 1 block north of the *parque*.

CAMPING AND THE OUTDOORS

Costa Rica's extensive national park system provides good hiking and camping opportunities, but not all parks offer camping facilities. There are restrictions on how many people can be in a given park at the same time, and camping outside of official camping areas is usually not permitted. The **Ministerio del Ambiente y Energía** (Ministry of Atmosphere and Energy), commonly known as **MINAE**, is a government organization devoted to encouraging sustainable development in Costa Rica. MINAE has a strong presence in many of the natural sights of Costa Rica. In some cases it is required that you have a guide; inquire at the local MINAE office.

NATIONAL PARKS

The *parques nacionales* are the foundation of the ecotourism industry in Costa Rica. Twenty national parks spread across the country, drawing travelers and wildlife lovers from all over the world. While attracting large crowds every year, the national park system still manages to maintain conservation of each area, with only minimal human impact. Entrance fees vary by park, but are generally US$5-$10. The use of a guide also varies by park; in some, guides are required, while in others, the trails do not necessitate one. Not all parks are easily accessible by foot. MINAE has a fairly large presence in the national park system and often offers guides, maps, and trail advice in the more touristed parks.

ALTERNATIVES TO TOURISM

This section lists some of the organizations in Costa Rica that offer opportunities outside temporary tourism. Costa Rica's rich natural resources provide for promising volunteer work, especially in conservation and ecotourism; English teaching is also a popular opportunity. For more info on Alternatives to Tourism, tools for finding programs on your own, see the chapter at the beginning of the book (p. 53).

VISA INFORMATION

A work permit is required for all foreigners planning to work in Costa Rica for more than one year. Most short-term study, work, and volunteer programs do not require special visas and standard tourist visas will be valid. Foreign students registered in recognized public or private educational institutions planning to study in Costa Rica for more than six months may apply for temporary residence (US$100 deposit required, waived under special circumstances) at the embassy upon entering the country. Long-term programs requiring special entry documentation often process forms for participants. Double-check on entrance requirements at the nearest embassy or consulate for up-to-date info before departure. US citizens can consult www.pueblo.gsa.gov/cic_text/travel/foreign/foreignentryreqs.html.

LANGUAGE SCHOOLS

Costa Rican Language Academy, P.O. Box. 1966-2050, San José (US ☎ 866-230-6361 or 280 1685; www.spanishandmore.com). 1 week to 6 months of language and cultural study custom tailored for individual students. Homestays and weekend excursions, lessons in Latin dance, Costa Rican cooking, Spanish music, and conversation. 1 week starts at US$255.

Escuela Idiomas d'Amore, P.O. Box 67-6350, Quepos (☎777 1143, in the US 262-367-8598 or 310-435-9897; www.escueladamore.com). Spanish immersion classes for 2-6 weeks in a beach location, halfway between Quepos and Parque Nacional Manuel Antonio. Homestay available. 18+. Classes start at US$845 for 2 weeks.

Montaña Linda Spanish School (☎533 3640; www.montanalinda.com), set in the beautiful Orosi Valley about 1½hr. from San José. Some of the cheapest Spanish classes around. Includes dormitory-style accommodation in the charming Montaña Linda Hostel, 3hr. daily instruction in small classes or one-on-one, with the option of daily breakfast and dinner. Fees start at US$99.

VOLUNTEERING

Asociación ANAI (San Jose ☎224 3570, Talamanca 750 0020; www.anaicr.org). A small, non-profit organization which arranges wildlife conservation projects in the Talamanca region. Volunteers protect turtle eggs from poachers in the Gandoca-Manzanillo National Wildlife Refuge, track the seasonal migrations of birds within the Kékôldi Indian Reserve, and collect data for biomonitoring the wildlife in the rivers of Talamanca. Lodging US$7-$30 per night. Registration US$30-$160.

Asociación Salvemos Las Tortugas de Parismina (☎710 5183; www.costaricaturtles.com). Volunteers assist with turtle conservation efforts in Parismina. Help patrol the beach at night to watch for poachers, collect turtle eggs, re-locate them to the association's hatchery, and return hatchlings to the sea. Volunteers stay for anywhere from a few days to a few weeks. Ask anyone in town to direct you to Doña Vicky's house. Homestays for US$20 per day with 3 daily meals included. 18+.

ASVO, Asociación de Voluntario de Areas Protegias Silvestres, Apdo. 11384. San José (☎233 4989; info@asvocr.com). Links to virtually every national park in Costa Rica. Although some parks prefer that volunteers contact their conservation areas directly, you can always reach a specific park through this office. Live and work in the same conditions as the park rangers. 30-day minimum commitment.

▨ **Punta Mona Center** (☎614 5735; www.puntamona.org), located 5km south of Manzanillo, is an 85 acre organic farm and educational center dedicated to sustainable agriculture. Volunteers spend their days and nights picking (and eating!) 120+ varieties of tropical fruit, observing huge marine turtles nest on the beach, living in houses built completely of fallen trees, and using solar powered eco-friendly energy. Meals included. Email if interested internships. 1-month minimum commitment. US$200 per month.

Talamanca Dolphin Federation (TDF), 3150 Graf St. #8 Bozeman, MT 59715 USA. (US ☎406-586-5084, Manzanillo 795 5119; www.dolphinlink.org). A non-profit association of local naturalists, guides, business owners, and boat captains devoted to preserving the dolphins of coastal Talamanca. Volunteers assist visitors at the Dolphin Education Center and Dolphin Lodge, help out with the federation's organized tours, and teach local children about marine life.

WORKING

As with volunteering, work opportunities tend to fall into two categories. Some travelers want **long-term** jobs that allow them to get to know another part of the world as a member of the community, while other travelers seek out **short-term** jobs to finance the next leg of their travels. Costa Rica is generally reluctant to give jobs to traveling foreigners. It's not impossible, however, and making friends with locals can help expedite work permits or arrange work-for-lodging swaps. Costa Rica's **visa requirements** for working abroad are very stringent: in addition to passport photos, fingerprints, police and medical records, social security information, and academic and employment records, you must have a letter of employment from your Costa Rican employer and a labor contract. Verify for changes with the local consulate. If you're planning on spending a substantial amount of time (more than three months) working in Costa Rica, search for a job well in advance, as it takes three to six months to process a work visa. Note that many jobs require previous experience and/or some knowledge of Spanish. Short-term work in Costa Rica, however, is quite limited and not regularly offered. Travelers looking for jobs in Costa Rica usually ask around at local business if foreign help is needed and taking whatever positions are available. English-speakers are hugely in demand, so flaunt this skill. Popular types of employment include: tourist agencies/tour guides, Spanish-English translators, bartenders, and waiters.

SAN JOSÉ

San José is often a disappointing starting point for travelers beginning to explore the serenity and vibrant natural beauty of Costa Rica. The streets are clogged with honking cars, the air is full of diesel fumes, and *"Americana"* is scrawled with disdain across storefronts. However, those who stay a few days often find that San José has a more lively personality than first impressions suggest. While providing easy access to any amenity a traveler could want, San José provides a distinctly dressed-down *tico* flair. Surrounded by mountains and 1132m above sea level, San

José is the transportation and economic center of the country, home to two major universities and approximately 300,000 people, with over one million in the metropolitan area. Its nightlife and relatively temperate climate make it a worthy stopover between the coasts and not just a convenient way to pass between them.

⊠ INTERCITY TRANSPORTATION

FLIGHTS

Juan Santa María International Airport, about 15km northwest of San José in Alajuela, is most accessible by bus from San José to Alajuela (see **Buses,** p. 135). Taxis to and from San José charge US$10-$15. **Grayline Tours** (☎232 3681 or 220 2126) runs an airport shuttle from many mid-range and top-end hotels, US$6. Call for more info. International airlines include **American** (☎257 1266), **Continental** (☎800-044-0005), **Copa** (☎223 COPA/2672), **Delta** (☎800-056-2002), **Iberia** (☎441 2591), **Mexicana** (☎800-531-7921), **Taca** (☎296 9353), and **United** (☎220 4844). **Sansa** (☎221 9414; www.flysansa.com) flies to:

Barra del Colorado (30min., 6:45am, US$58); **Carillo** near **Sámara** (75min.; 8:10, 11:50am; US$71); **Golfito** (1hr.; 6, 10:30am, 2:15pm; US$71); **Liberia** (50min., 11:50am, US$71); **Nosara** (1hr.; 7:30, 11:50am; US$71); **Palmar Sur** (55min., 10:20am, US$71); **Puerto Jiménez** (55min.; 6, 9:30am, 2:05pm; US$71); **Punta Islita** (55min., 8:10am, US$71); **Quepos** (30min., 6 per day 7:45am-4:25pm, US$44); **Tamarindo** (50min., 7 per day 5:15am-3:50pm, US$71); **Tambor** (35min.; 10:25am, 4:25pm; US$58); **Tortuguero** (45min., 6am, US$58).

Tobías Bolaños Airport, in Pavas, serves **NatureAir** (☎220 3054, US 800-235-9272; www.natureair.net). More reliable than Sansa. Daily high season departures to4:

Barra del Colorado (30min., 6:15am, US$66); **Carillo** near **Sámara** (1¼hr., 1pm, US$80); **Golfito** (1hr., 6am, US$76); **Liberia** (50min., 8:30am, US$80); **Nosara** (1hr.; 8:30am, 1pm; US$80); **Palmar Sur** (55min.; 8:30, 9am; US$73); **Puerto Jiménez** (55min.; 6, 8:30, 11am, 2:30pm; US$84); **Punta Islita** (55min.; 8am, 1pm; US$80); **Quepos** (30min., 6 daily 7:30am-4:30pm, US$50); **Tamarindo** (50min.; 8:30, 11am, 4pm; US$80); **Tambor** (35min.; 8:30am, 1pm; US$66); **Tortuguero** (35min., 6:15am, US$66).

BUSES

Buses to almost every destination in the country arrive and depart from the city's many stops and terminals. Many cluster around **Terminal Coca-Cola,** Av. 1/3, C. 16/18. The schedule is available at the **ICT** at the Museo de Oro (see **Tourist Services,** p. 138).

Av. 1/3, C. 20: has buses to **Playa Panamá** (Tralapa ☎221 7202. 5hr., daily 3pm, ₡1855).

Av. 2, C. 1/3: departures to **Volcán Irazú** (2hr.; Sa, Su 8am; return 12:30pm; round-trip ₡1800).

Av. 2, C. 12/14: Alajuela-Airport (TUASA, ☎449 5141, 30min.; every 10min. 5am-midnight, 30min. after 10pm; ₡250); **Herredia** (Transportes Unidos 400 30min., every 10min. 5am-11pm, ₡770); and **Volcán Poás** (TUASA ☎222 5325. 2hr.; 8:30am; return 2:30pm; round-trip ₡2000).

Av. 3, C. 16 (Terminal Coca-Cola): Jacó (transportes Morales ☎223 1109. 2½hr.; 7:30, 10:30am, 1, 3:30, 6:30pm; return 5, 7:30, 11am, 3, 5pm; ₡1020); and **Quepos** and **Manuel Antonio** (Transportes Morales ☎223 5567. Direct 3½hr.; 6am, noon, 2pm; return 6, 9:30am, noon, 5pm; ₡1865. Indirect 5hr.; 7, 10am, 2, 4pm; return 5, 8am, 2, 4pm; ₡1455). Only direct buses continue to Manuel Antonio.

Av. 4, C. 9: Cartago (8:30pm-midnight, ₡225.)

Av. 5, C. 14/16: Golfito (Tracopa-Alfaro ☎222 2666; 7hr.; 7am, 3pm; return 5am, 1:30pm; ₡2750); **Playa Nosara and Garza** (Tracopa-Alfaro ☎222 2666; 6hr., 6am, ₡2600); **Playa Sámara** (Tracopa-Alfaro ☎222 2666; 5hr., 12:30pm, ₡2410); and **Playa Tamarindo** (Tracopa-Alfaro ☎222 2666; 5½hr.; 11am, 3:30pm; return 5:45am; ₡2205).

Av. 5/7, C. 24: Liberia (Pulmitan ☎256 9552. 4hr., every hour 6am-8pm; return 4am-8pm; ₡1735) and **Playas del Coco** (☎222 1650. 5hr.; 8am, 2, 4pm; return 4, 8am, 2pm; ₡2060).

Av. 6, C. 13: Turrialba (Transtusa ☎ 222 4464. 1¾hr.; every hour 5:15am-7pm; return 5am-5:30pm; ¢690).

Av. 7/9, C. 12 (Terminal Atlántico Norte): Fortuna (☎ 256 8914; 4½hr.; 6:15, 8:40, 11:30am; return 12:30, 2:30pm; ¢1255); and **Monteverde** (Autotransportes Tilarán ☎ 222 3854; 5hr.; 6:30am, 2:30pm; ¢1680).

Av. 12, C. 16: Puntarenas (Empresarios Unidos de Puntarenas ☎ 222 8231; 2hr.; every hr. 6am-7pm; return 4:15am-7pm; ¢890).

Av. 13, C. Central (Terminal Caribe): to **Cahuita** (☎ 257 8129. 4hr.; 6, 10am, 1:30, 3:30pm; return 7:30, 9:30, 11:30am, 4:30pm; ¢1020); **Cariari** (1¾hr.; 8 per day 6:30am-7pm; return 8 per day 5:30am-5:30pm); **Guápiles** via **Parque Nacional Braulio Carillo/Quebrada González:** (1½hr., every hr. 5:30am-10pm, ¢675); **Limón** (Caribeños ☎ 221 0610. 2½hr., every 45min. 5am-7pm, ¢1245); and **Siquirres** (1½hr., every hour 6:30am-7pm; return 5:30am-7pm; ¢750).

Av. 18/20, C. 5: Cartago (SACSA ☎ 233 5350. 50 min., every 10min. 5am-midnight).

Private Buses: Grayline Tours (☎ 232 3681 or 220 2126) has buses to and from destinations all over Costa Rica, US$21-$25 one-way. 1-2 daily buses between **Arenal, Jacó, Manuel Antonio, Playa Hermosa, Playa Tamarindo, Puerto Viejo de Talamanca,** and **San José.** Most leave daily 7-8:30am. Call for reservations.

International Buses: El Salvador: TicaBus, Av. 2/4, C. 9 (☎ 221 8954). 48hr. with 1 night in Managua (6, 7:30am, noon; ¢19,400). **Guatemala: TicaBus,** Av. 2/4, C. 9 (☎ 221 8954). 60hr. with 1 night in Nicaragua and 1 night in El Salvador (6, 7:30am; ¢24,000). **Honduras: TicaBus.** 48hr. with 1 night in Managua (6, 7:30am; ¢18,000). **Managua: TicaBus** (11hr.; 6, 7:30am; ¢6000). **Panaline,** Av. 3/5 C. 16 (☎ 256 8121. 11hr., 4:30am, ¢6000). **Panamá City: TicaBus** (19hr., 10pm, ¢10,000); **Panaline** (19hr., 1pm, ¢10,000).

📍 ORIENTATION

San José's design follows a typical Costa Rican grid, with *avenidas* running east-west and *calles* running north-south. **Avenida Central** (called **Paseo Colón** north of C. 22) is the main drag, with a pedestrian area between C. 2 and 5. The **Mercado Central** is west of the city center, bordered by Av. Central/1 and C. 6/8. **Barrio Amón** is northeast of Av. 5 and C. 1, and **Barrio Otoya** is slightly east of Amón. West of downtown past C. 42, **La Sabana** is home to the Parque Metropolitano La Sabana. Five kilometers west is the quiet, hilly suburb of **Escazú.** Upscale **Los Yoses** lies east of downtown, while nearby **San Pedro** is home to the University of Costa Rica and some of the city's best entertainment.

Although San José is a relatively safe Central American city, theft, prostitution, and drugs still make some areas a bit risky. Problem spots include: Terminal Coca-Cola, south of Av. 8 between C. 2 and 12, Av. 4 to 6 between C. 4 and 12, and north of the *mercado central*. Generally, areas beyond a couple of blocks from San José center pose a threat after dark. After dark, the safest way to get around is by taxi, especially for women traveling alone.

🚌 LOCAL TRANSPORTATION

Bus: Local buses run every 5-10min. 5am-10pm and go all over San José, including suburbs and the airport. No official printed schedules; timing is generally approximate. Ask locals and drivers for info; most bus stops are marked with their destination. Local destinations run no more than ¢200; carry small change. Major bus stops include: **Escazú** (Av. 1/Central and C. 16); **Guadalupe** and **Moravia** (Av. 3, C. 5/7); and **San Pedro** (Av. 2, C. 11/13 and Av. Central, C. 9/11).

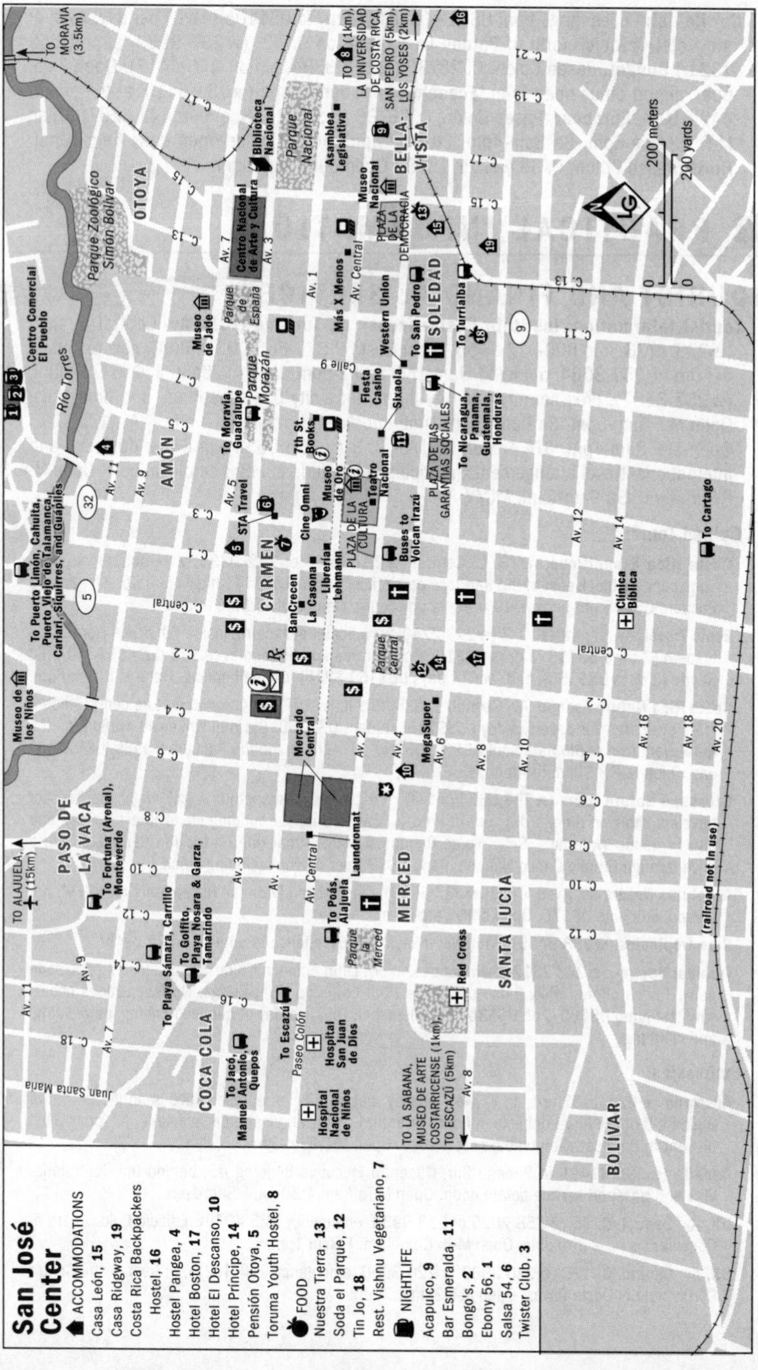

San José Center
ACCOMMODATIONS
Casa León, 15
Casa Ridgway, 19
Costa Rica Backpackers Hostel, 16
Hostel Pangea, 4
Hotel Boston, 17
Hotel El Descanso, 10
Hotel Príncipe, 14
Pensión Otoya, 5
Toruma Youth Hostel, 8
FOOD
Nuestra Tierra, 13
Soda el Parque, 12
Tin Jo, 18
Rest. Vishnu Vegetariano, 7
NIGHTLIFE
Acapulco, 9
Bar Esmeralda, 11
Bongo's, 2
Ebony 56, 1
Salsa 54, 6
Twister Club, 3
TO ALAJUELA (15km)
TO MORAVIA (3.5km)
TO 8 (1km), LA UNIVERSIDAD DE COSTA RICA, SAN PEDRO (5km), LOS YOSES (2km)
TO LA SABANA, MUSEO DE ARTE COSTARRICENSE (1km), TO ESCAZÚ (5km)
PASO DE LA VACA
OTOYA
AMÓN
CARMEN
MERCED
SOLEDAD
BELLA-VISTA
SANTA LUCIA
COCA COLA
BOLÍVAR
Parque Zoológico Simón Bolívar
Río Torres
Centro Comercial El Pueblo
Museo de los Niños
Museo de Jade
Biblioteca Nacional
Parque Nacional
Centro Nacional de Arte y Cultura
Parque de España
Parque Morazán
Asamblea Legislativa
Museo Nacional
PLAZA DE LA DEMOCRACIA
Más X Menos
Western Union
Fiesta Casino
Sixaola
7th St. Books
Cine Omni
Museo de Oro
Teatro Nacional
PLAZA DE LA CULTURA
PLAZA DE LAS GARANTÍAS SOCIALES
Librería Lehmann
La Casona
BanCrecen
STA Travel
Mercado Central
Laundromat
Parque Central
MegaSuper
Parque la Merced
Red Cross
Clínica Bíblica
Hospital San Juan de Dios
Hospital Nacional de Niños
Paseo Colón
Juan Santa María
To Puerto Limón, Cahuita, Puerto Viejo de Talamanca, Cariari, Siquirres, and Guápiles
To Fortuna (Arenal), Monteverde
To Playa Sámara, Carrillo
To Golfito, Playa Nosara & Garza, Tamarindo
To Jacó, Manuel Antonio, Quepos
To Escazú
To Poás, Alajuela
To Moravia, Guadalupe
Buses to Volcan Irazú
To San Pedro
To Turrialba
To Nicaragua, Panama, Guatemala, Honduras
To Cartago
(railroad not in use)
200 meters
200 yards
Av. Central
C. Central
Calle 9

COSTA RICA

Car Rental: Prices range from US$19 (small sedan) to US$105 (4WD) per day. **Avis,** at the Hotel Corobicí north of Parque La Sabana on C. 42. (☎232 9922, airport 552 1321.) **Budget,** Paseo Colón, C. 28/30 (☎223 3284, airport 440 4412). Open 7am-6pm; airport office open 24hr. **Economy,** in Sabana Norte (☎231 5410, at the airport 442 8100). **Europcar,** Paseo Colón, C. 36/38 (☎257 1158, airport 442 5257). Open M-F 7:30am-6pm, Sa 8am-4pm, Su 8am-3pm; airport office open daily 6am-10pm. **Hertz,** Paseo Colón, C. 38 (☎221 1818). Open daily 7am-6pm.

🛂 PRACTICAL INFORMATION

TOURIST AND FINANCIAL SERVICES

Tourist Information: Instituto Costarricense de Turismo (ICT), Av. Central/2, C. 5 (☎223 1733, info 800-012-3456, US or Costa Rica 1-866-COSTARICA), next to Museo del Oro (☎257 8064; open M-F 9am-1pm and 2-5pm), and Av. Central, C. 5/7, 2nd fl. (☎257 3857). Free country and city maps, intra-city bus schedules, and brochures. Open M-F 8am-5pm, Sa 8am-noon. Another office inside the post office, Av. 1/3, C. 2. Open M-F 8am-4pm. **STA Travel,** Av.1/3, C. 3 (☎256 0633), provides domestic and international travel arrangements, particularly for students. ISIC card available. Open M-F 8am-6pm, Sa 9am-1pm. MC/V.

Guided Tours:

Costa Rica Expeditions, Av. 3, C. Central (☎257 0766 or 222 0333; www.costaricaexpeditions.com), 1 block east of the San José post office. Class III and IV whitewater rafting on the Río Pacuare US$95 per person. 10% student discount. Open daily 5:30am-9pm.

Ecole Travel, Av. Central/1, C. 7 (☎223 2240; www.ecoletravel.com), inside 7th Street Books. Tortuguero (2 days US$95, 3 days US$125); Volcán Arenal and Monteverde (4 days US$260); Río Sierpe (3 days US$155); and Jacó (4 days US$169-$215). Online booking. Open M-F 9am-6pm.

Costa Rica Nature Escape, Av. Central/1, C. 5, 2nd fl. (☎257 8064; www.crnature.com). Student rates available. Tortuguero 3 days US$186, student US$160. Class III whitewater rafting on the Río Reventazón or Río Sarapiquí US$69/US$60. Class IV on the Río Pacuare US$85/US$70 per day. Open M-F 8:30am-5:30pm.

Ecoscape Nature Tours (☎297 0664 or 240 5106; www.ecoscapetours.com). Highlights Tour for travelers short on time: 1-day tour of Volcan Poás and its surrounding cloud forest, La Paz and San Fernando Waterfalls, Selva Verde Rainforest Lodge, boat ride on the Río Sarapiquí, and a drive through Braulio Carillo National Park, US$79 per person including lunch.

Aventuras Naturales, Av. 5, C. 33 (☎225 3939). Class III and IV on the Río Pacuare for US$95 per person, students US$75. Open daily 7am-8pm.

Ríos Tropicales (☎233 6455). Whitewater kayaking. Experience required. US$25 per hr.

Tropical Bungee (☎248 2212; www.bungee.co.cr), Latin America's oldest and safest bungee company. Jumps offered daily 9am-4pm at the 80m Colorado River Bridge. No reservations necessary. 1st jump US$60, 2nd US$30. Full Adrenaline Tour is a day of bungee jumping, paragliding, and climbing.

Embassies:

Australia (☎224 1152, ext. 111). No embassy, but an official representative is on the 2nd fl. of Building B of the Plaza del Este in front of Centro Comercial. Visa forms available. All forms must be sent to the Australian embassy in Mexico. Open M-F 8am-5pm.

Canada (☎296 4149), in Sabana Sur, Oficentro Ejecutivo building #5, behind the Contraloría. Visa and passport service before noon. Open M-Th 8am-4:30pm, F 8am-1pm.

UK, Av. Central, C. 35 (☎258 2025 or 233 9938, emergency 225 4049), Edificio Colón, 11th fl. Consular services available. Open M-Th 8am-4pm, F 8am-1pm.

US, Av. Central, C. 120 (☎220 3939 or 220 3050, emergency 220 3127), in front of the Centro Comercial del Oeste Pavas. Open M-F 9am-4:30pm.

Immigration: Dirección de Migración (☎220 0355), on the Autopista General Cañas Hwy., the road to the airport. Take the red bus to Alajuela from Av. 2, C. 12/14 or C. 10/12, and get off at La Oficina de Migración.

Banks: Dozens of banks all over San José; nearly all of them have Cirrus/Plus/V **24hr. ATMs.** Most cash traveler's checks. **Banco Central,** Av. Central/1, C. 2 (☎243 3333; open M-F 8:30am-3:30pm); **Banco de Costa Rica,** Av. 3, C. Central (☎211 1177; open M-F 8:30am-6pm); **Banco Nacional,** Av. 1/3, C. 4 (☎255 0620; open M-F 8:30am-3:45pm); **Banco de San José,** Av. 3/5, C, Central (☎295 9595; open M-F 8am-7pm).

American Express: Av. 3/5, C. Central (☎257 1792), across from Banco de San José. Lost or stolen hotline ☎800-011-0271 or 800-012-3211. Open M-F 8am-4:15pm.

Western Union: Av. 2/4, C. 9 (US ☎800-777-7777). Open M-F 8:30am-5pm, Sa 9am-12:30pm.

LOCAL SERVICES

English-Language Bookstores: 7th Street Books, Av. Central/1, C. 7 (☎256 8251). Foreign newspapers. New and used books. Open M-Sa 9am-6pm, Su 10am-5pm. AmEx/MC/V. **Librería Lehmann,** Av. Central, C. 1/3 (☎223 1212). Small book selection and stationary supplies. Open M-F 8am-6:30pm, Sa 9am-5pm. The **Internet and laundry** facility on Av. 2, C. 1, 1 story below street level in the small strip mall on the northwest corner, exchanges books. Bring 3 books, get 2 free; bring 2, get 1 free. Buy used books starting at US$2.

Gay-Lesbian Organizations: Triángulo Rosa (☎234 2411).

Supermarkets: Más X Menos, Av. Central, C. 11/13. Open M-Sa 7am-midnight, Su 8am-9pm. The larger, more modern **MegaSuper** is at Av. 4/6, C. 2, across from Soda el Parque. Open M-Sa 7am-9pm, Su 8am-6pm.

Laundry: Lavandería, Av. Central/1, C. 8, next to Gran Hotel Imperial. ¢2000 per load. Open M-F 8am-6pm, Sa 8am-5pm. **Sixaola,** Av. 2, C. 7/9. Same-day service if in by 10am. ¢1000 per kg. Open M-F 8am-6pm, Sa 8am-1pm. **Lavandería,** Av. 2, C. 1, 1 story below street level in the small strip mall on the northwest corner. Wash ¢1100, dry ¢700. Open daily 7am-11pm.

EMERGENCY AND COMMUNICATIONS

Police: Emergency ☎911. To report a theft, contact the **Organismo de Investigación Judicial (OIJ),** Av. 6/8, C. 17/19 (☎295 3000). During business hours, contact the **Crime Victims Assistance Office** (☎295 3271 or 295 3565; victimadelito@poder-judicial.go.cr). Open M-F 7:30am-noon and 1-4:30pm, on the 1st fl. of OIJ.

Pharmacy: Farmacia Fischel, Av. 3, C. 2 (☎295 7600). Pharmacy and beauty products. Open M-Sa 7am-7pm, Su 9am-5pm. AmEx/MC/V.

Hospitals: Hospital San Juan de Dios, on Paseo Colón, C. 14/18 (☎257 6282). Large white building where Av. Central turns into Paseo Colón, after C. 14. 24hr. emergency. **Clínica Bíblica,** Av. 14/16, C. 1 (☎257 5252). 24hr. emergency and pharmacy. English spoken.

Telephones: Card and coin phones are all over town; most take ¢5 and ¢10 coins. Buy a card from Más X Menos (see **Supermarkets,** p. 139). **Radiográphica,** Av. 5, C. 1 (☎287 0489). Collect calls US$3. AT&T, MCI, and Sprint service. International calls only. Open daily 7:30am-9pm. **Directory assistance** ☎113. **Instituto Costarricense de Electricidad (ICE),** Av. 2, C. 3 (☎257 7743). Open M-F 7:30am-7pm, Sa 8am-7pm.

Internet Access: Café Internet, Av. Central, C. 13/15, down the street from Más X Menos. ¢250 per 30min., ¢350 per hr. Open M-Sa 9am-9pm, Su 9am-4pm. **Café Digital,** Av. Central, C. 5/7, 2nd fl. (☎223 6051). ¢500 per hr. Scanner, printing, and copies available. Open M-Sa 7am-midnight, Su 8:30am-10pm. **Netopia,** Av. 1, C. 9/11 (☎233 6320). Free coffee. ₡500 per hr. Open daily 9am-10:30pm. The **Internet/ Laundry** facilities (see **English-Language Bookstores,** p. 139) has cheaper rates during off-hours: all day Su and M-Sa 7-11pm ₡300 per hr., ₡500 per 2hr.; normal business hours ₡300 per 30min., ₡500 per hr.

Post Office: Av. 1/3, C. 2, in the large green building. San José has no street mailboxes, so all mail must be sent from here. Open M-F 7:30am-6pm, Sa 7:30am-noon. **Postal Code:** 1000.

▐ ACCOMMODATIONS

San José has hundreds of accommodations for every budget. That said, it's best to steer clear of the cheapest lodgings; paying the relatively "pricey" US$10 for dorms is worth it for clean, comfortable lodgings. The accommodations **east** of the *parque central* are highly recommended. Hotels **south** of the *parque central* are generally reasonably priced, but often louder and uglier. Though they are often the cheapest options, try to avoid places **north** and **west** of the *parque*; these tend to be the least safe areas.

EAST OF THE PARQUE CENTRAL

▨ **Hostel Pangea,** Av. 11, C. 3/5 (☎221 1992 or 396 0364; www.hostelpangea.com). Hostel Pangea is a backpacker's paradise. Bright dorms and tons of amenities: free 10min. phone call to Canada or the US each day's stay, laundry (US$6), kitchen, unlimited coffee, and free Internet. Bar loft, bean bag lounge, and big screen TV room. English spoken. Breakfast included. Lockers US$1. 24hr. airport transport US$12. Reception open 24hr. Dorms US$9; private rooms US$12-$15. ❶

▨ **Costa Rica Backpackers Hostel,** Av. 6, C. 21/23 (☎221 6191; www.costaricabackpackers.com). This backpacker magnet feels like a luxurious college dorm. Shared hot baths, night guard, free Internet, kitchen, TV room, tourist info, and swimming pool. 24hr. reception. Free baggage storage, and lockers in all rooms. Laundry US$6. Check-out 11am. No phone reservations. Dorms ₡3870; private doubles US$20. ❶

▨ **Casa Ridgway,** Av. 6/8, C. 15 (☎222 1400; fax 233 6168; friends@racsa.co.cr), in the short, dead-end street running parallel to Av. 6/8. This active Quaker peace center is popular with backpackers and volunteer groups. Communal kitchen, dining area, meeting room, and library. Hot baths. Public phone, laundry (US$5), and storage. Quiet hours 10pm-7am. Dorms US$10; singles US$12; doubles US$24. ❶

▨ **Casa León,** Av. 6, C. 13/15 (☎222 9725). Turn right onto C. 13 from Av. 2 and take the sharp left to follow the train tracks. Casa León is on your left. Laundry (₡2000), kitchen, and private hot baths help make it popular with students. Dorms US$10; singles US$15; doubles US$30, low season US$25. ❶

SOUTH OF THE PARQUE CENTRAL

Hotel Príncipe, Av. 6, C. Central/2 (☎222 7983), 1 block north of Hotel Boston. Noise from nearby bars might prove a bit bothersome. Worn, spacious rooms have bright sheets, comfy beds, and hot baths; rooms on the upper floors afford impressive views. Bar and small lobby with cable TV. Safe deposit box available M-F 8:30am-8pm. 24hr. reception. Quiet hours after 10pm. Singles ₡5000; doubles ₡6000; triples ₡7000. ❷

Hotel Boston, Av. 8, C. Central/2 (☎257 4499, 221 0563). Spacious rooms have TV, and clean private bath, most with hot water. Phone available. 24hr reception. Singles ₡3500; doubles ₡5000; triples ₡6000; quads ₡8000. AmEx/MC/V. ❶

OTHER NEIGHBORHOODS

■ **Toruma Youth Hostel (HI),** Av. Central, C. 29/31 (☎/fax 224 4085; reca-jhi@racsa.co.cr). Take the San Pedro bus (¢105) from Av. Central, C. 9/11, and get off at Kentucky Fried Chicken; Toruma is the yellow building across the street. Over 80 beds. Shared hot baths. Bright lobby has sofas and cable TV. English spoken. Free Internet and luggage storage. Breakfast included. Reception daily 7am-10pm. 24hr. guard. Reservations recommended. Dorms US$10, with HI card US$8; singles US$20/$16; doubles US$40/US$32. MC/V. ❷

Pensión Otoya, Av. 3/5, C. 1 (☎221 3925). Spacious rooms with wall-to-wall (albeit industrial) carpet. Pleasant sitting area popular with backpackers. Free baggage storage. Laundry ¢1000. 24hr. reception. Singles ¢3000, with bath ¢3700; doubles ¢5300/¢6600; triples ¢7500; quads ¢10,000. ❸

Hotel El Descanso, Av. 4, C. 6 (☎221 9941), entrance on C. 6. Safe, classy lodgings with comfy, plaid-clad beds, private hot baths, and TV. 24hr. reception. Check-out noon. Singles US$10; doubles US$20. ❶

◘ FOOD

Black beans, white rice, and fried chicken are San José's staples, though American culture has left its mark, and fast-food joints abound. Vegetarian and international cuisines are also popular, offering respite from the monotony of chain-dining. *Tico* fare like *casados* and *gallo pinto* can be found at hundreds of *sodas* across the city. Most have cheap lunch and dinner specials (¢600-¢1200 for a complete meal).

SAN JOSÉ

The **mercado central** sells cheap meals and produce. Most of the higher-quality and more pleasant *sodas* and restaurants are in the vicinity of Av. Central.

■ **Tin Jo,** Av. 6/8, C. 11, is the place to splurge. Exotic Asian fusion cuisine hits the spot when you tire of rice and beans. Indoor fountain and tapestries on the walls make the place feel decidedly dynastic. Veggie-friendly menu. Sushi ¢1800-¢3000, curries ¢2800-¢4500, noodles ¢2000-¢3000. Open M-Th 11:30am-3pm and 5:30-10:30pm, F-Sa 11:30am-3pm and 5:30-11pm, Su 11:30am-10pm. AmEx/MC/V. ❸

■ **Restaurant Vishnu Vegetariano,** Av. 1, C. 1/3 (☎256 6063). Locals and tourists praise the yummy food and quick service. Whatever they put in the lasagna (¢1250) is so delicious you'll plead for the recipe. Don't leave without trying the *morir soñando* ("die dreaming;" ¢650). Veggie hamburgers ¢750, *plato del día* ¢1525. Open M-Sa 8am-9:30pm, Su 9am-7:30pm. AmEx/MC/V. ❶

Nuestra Tierra, Av. 2, C. 15 (☎258 6500). Burlap sacks, candle-lit tables, *vaquero*-uniformed waiters, and meals served on palm leaves remind you of rustic cooking from rural Costa Rica. English menus. *Plato del día* ¢750. Open 24hr. ❶

Soda el Parque, Av. 4/6, C. 2 (☎222 4890). Suit-clad businessmen at lunch and late-night revelers just before dawn eat cheap and tasty *comida típica* in the spacious seating area. Breakfast ¢650-¢1400. *Casados* ¢1175. Open 24hr. AmEx/MC/V. ❶

SAN PEDRO

Restaurante Il Pomodoro, 100m north of JFK Park on Av. Central (☎224 0966). Garlic aromas entice passers-by into this authentic Italian eatery. Generous portions of crispy thin-crust pizza (¢1500-3500) and pasta (¢1700-¢2000). Beer ¢630. Open M and W-Th 11:30am-11pm, F-Sa 11:30am-midnight. AmEx/MC/V. ❷

Restaurante Vegetariano, 200m north of JFK Park on Av. Central. Animal murals and hanging mobiles may remind you of pre-school. Excellent food: veggie burger ¢725, burrito ¢900, falafel ¢1300. Open M-F 10am-6pm. ❶

Jazz Café, 150m east of C. 3 on Av. Central. Live performances almost every night; Tu and Th jazz. Salads ¢1400-¢2100. Cocktails (¢1000-¢2000) attract large late-night crowds. Open daily 6pm-2am. AmEx/MC/V. ❷

◉ SIGHTS

TEATRO NACIONAL. Back in 1897, the construction of this National Theater was inspired (and funded) by Costa Rican citizens clamoring for more cultural venues. The extravagant theater is graced with sculpted banisters overlaid in 22.5-carat gold, marble floors, and high-ceiling frescoes. The lobby also features Costa Rica's most famous **mural,** a beautiful collage of the crops that brought the country its turn-of-the-century prosperity, bananas and coffee. Performances include opera, dance, drama, and music. *(Av. 2, C. 3/5, off the Plaza de la Cultura. ☎ 221 1329. Open M-F 9am-4pm, Sa 9am-noon and 1-5pm. Tours US$3. Tickets ¢2000-¢5000.)*

MUSEO NACIONAL. During the past 50 years, this museum transformed from a military headquarters (the Cuarto Bellarista) into a collection of artifacts. Though the front is still riddled with bullet-marks from the 1948 Revolution, the interior is full of pre-Columbian art, along with exhibits on Costa Rican history, colonial life, archaeology, and geology. Don't miss the view from the museum's gazebo. *(Av. Central/2, C. 17. ☎ 257-1433. Open Tu-Su 8:30am-4:30pm. ¢1750, students ¢900.)*

MUSEO DE JADE. The 11th floor of Costa Rica's Social Security building is an unlikely location for this stunning collection of artifacts, reportedly the world's largest collection of American jade (pronounced *ha-day* in Spanish). The emerald-colored mineral was of particular importance to Costa Rica's indigenous groups, and displays here contain a number of tools, pots, jewelry, religious figures, and weapons dating back to pre-Columbian and Mayan times. Don't miss the spectacular, panoramic ◨bird's-eye view of San José. *(11th fl. of INS Building, Av. 7, C. 9/1. ☎ 287 6034. Open M-F 8:30am-3pm. US$2, Costa Rican nationals ¢500.)*

MUSEO DE ORO. Established in 1950 to preserve Costa Rican cultural heritage, the Museo de Oro houses a three-part exploration of Costa Rican culture. Located underneath the Plaza de Cultura, the museum has a permanent exhibition of gold and pre-Columbian items dating to 500 AD; other exhibits house bills, coins, and *boletos de café* (coffee tokens) from the 16th century, as well as a range of rotating fine arts and archaeological exhibits. *(Av. Central, C. 5. ☎ 243 4202. Open daily 10am-4:30pm. US$5, students and ages 7-12 ¢300.)*

CENTRO NACIONAL DE ARTE Y CULTURA. This impressive walled fortress of the arts offers a calendar of artistic and cultural events in some of Costa Rica's oldest edifices—buildings that have survived earthquakes and civil unrest. Stop by to see if a performance is running. *(Av. 3, C. 15/17. ☎ 257 7202, press office 221 2154. Open Tu-Sa 10am-5pm. ¢600, students ¢300. Tickets average ¢2500.)*

♫ ENTERTAINMENT

A number of 24hr. casinos have opened up in San José, many in hotels clustering on Av. 1 near C. 5. **Fiesta Casino,** Av. Central, C. 7/9, has a good mix of tables and slots if you want to try your luck. You must be 18+ to gamble. Several movie theaters throughout San José show recent US releases with Spanish subtitles. In the center of downtown is **Cine Omni,** Av. Central/1, C. 3 (☎ 221 7903), in the Edificio

Omni (¢1100). **Sala Garbo** (☎223 1960) and **Teatro Laurence Olivier** (☎222 1034), on Av. 2, C. 28, show a selection of older films from Latin American countries and North America (¢1000). **Multicines San Pedro** (☎280 9585), in San Pedro Mall, has 10 modern theaters with digital sound (¢1500, W ¢750). For fun on wheels, try out your roller skates at **Salón de Patines Music,** 200m west of the JFK park in San Pedro. (Open M-F 7-10pm; Sa, Su, holidays 1-3:30pm, 4-6:30pm, and 7-10pm.)

▓ NIGHTLIFE

San Pedro pulses at night: scenes range from karaoke bars full of *ticos* to American sports bars packed with tourists. **C. de la Amargura** has the casual atmosphere for meeting young *ticos;* **El Pueblo** is the best dance scene; **San José center** caters to a slightly older crowd. Most bars and clubs charge ¢1000 for cover, sometimes higher for men, though it typically includes a few drinks. Dress is usually casual; jeans and sandals are fine in **San Pedro** bars, but you'll want dressier threads for El Pueblo or San José clubs. Bouncers demand good ID (18+).

CENTRO COMERCIAL EL PUEBLO

Ebony 56 (☎223 2195), in the main parking lot. Attracts a mix of travelers and locals to its silver stage and space-age couches. Music from reggae and rave to salsa and pop. Beer ¢700, cocktails ¢1500. Th ladies' night. Open daily 6pm-6am.

Twister Club (☎222 5746), toward the back and on the left of El Pueblo, attracts a late-20s crowd that dresses to impress. Crowds form early. Beer ¢700, cocktails ¢1000-¢1500. Open daily 6:30pm until the crowd dies out.

Bongo's (☎222 5746). Around the corner at Twister's sister club, a mixed-age crowd gathers above a backdrop of thumping house music. TVs and foosball, but less dancing than Twister. Beer ¢700, cocktails ¢2000. M ladies' night, W men's. Open 5pm-4am.

NEAR THE CITY CENTER

Acapulco, Av. Central, C. 17/19 (☎221 2586), 1 block east of the northeast corner of the Museo Nacional. A strong local following gathers early for drinks. Flashing lights and thumping music inspire a varied crowd to show off their *salsa* skills. Beer ¢450, sandwiches ¢500-¢600. Open M-Sa 11am-1am.

Salsa 54, Av. 1/3, C. 3, 2nd fl. (☎223 3814), features a mix of love songs, 60s hits, and *salsa.* Many of the dancers are experts, but don't let that stop you. Beer ¢500. Cocktails ¢800-¢1200. Cover Th-Su ¢1000. Tu and W pool and karaoke. Open Tu-Su 7pm-2am.

Bar Esmeralda, Av. 2, C. 5/7 (☎221 0530), caters to an older crowd. Live Mariachi music offers a soothing alternative to pop. Open daily 24hr., music starts around 10pm.

SAN PEDRO

Though the enormous bar scene near the University of Costa Rica is student-oriented, it's diverse enough to accommodate almost any party seeker. People and music overflow into the streets, so the area is relatively safe, though partiers should still take precautions. C. 3, north of Av. Central, known as **C. de la Amargura,** is the heart of this scene. Relatively few tourists come. **Caccio's** has a breezy but loud outdoor patio (beer ¢600; open M-Sa 11:30am-1am); **Mosaiko's** is laid-back, although dark and rather loud (M hip hop, Tu reggae, W electronic, Th-Sa rock, pop, alternative; beer ¢500; cover ¢1000; free tequila for girls Sa 8-10pm; open 11am-2am); and **Bar Tavarúa,** a surf and skate bar, opens a back room for dancing on crowded nights (beer ¢450; cover ¢1000, ladies free Th; open M-Sa 11am-2am). All on C. de la Amargura close earlier on weeknights depending on turnout.

COSTA RICA

Bars near San José center tend to be populated by older men and their girl-friends or female escorts. **Raíces,** Av. 2, C. 45, across from the Mall San Pedro and around the corner from All Stars Bar, is a *tico* favorite. This reggae bar draws an alternative student crowd. (Beer ¢500; ¢1000 cover includes 2 drinks. Open W-Sa 7pm until the crowds leave.) **El Cuartel de la Boca del Monte,** Av. 1, C. 21/23, in between San José and San Pedro, showcases live local Latin bands on Mondays and no cover for ladies. (VIP area and lots of seating. Cover ¢1500 for music. Beer ¢800, cocktails ¢1500. Th Spanish rock, Sa 80s. Open daily 6pm-2am.) **La Avispa,** Av. 8/10, C. 1, is a gay hub featuring three dance floors, a courtyard, and pool tables (¢500 per hr.) as well as an indoor waterfall and music video projection on the walls. (☎223 5343. Cover ¢1000. Beer ¢600, cocktails ¢1500. Open Tu and Th-Su 8pm-2:30am. Ladies' night last W of the month, no men admitted).

▶ DAYTRIP FROM SAN JOSÉ: TRAM

Though the tram is only 20km from Guápiles, most people visit from San José. Take a bus to Guápiles from Terminal Caribe, Av. 13, C. Central. (50min., every 30min. 5am-9pm, ¢670.) A free shuttle takes visitors the 1.5km from the entrance of the park to the tram platform. Tours from San José can be arranged through the tram office on Av. 7, C. 7. (☎257 5961; www.rainforest.co.cr; US$80 per person, students US$40;) tours include transportation to and from your hotel, guided trips on the tram line, a 45min. nature trail hike, and breakfast or lunch. Reservation only for the guided tour and nature trail hike US$50 per person, students US$25. The office offers late-night rides. As elsewhere in Costa Rica, venomous ants and snakes abound; pants, sturdy footwear and bug repellent are recommended, as are reservations. Tram open M 9am-4pm, Tu-Su 7am-4pm.

Located at the edge of the Braulio Carillo National Park, the Rainforest Aerial Tram was designed by naturalist Don Perry and completed in 1994. After spending years exploring the rainforest canopy on ropes suspended high atop the trees, Perry designed a simple pulley system with 22 ski-lift-like tram cars suspended along an almost 2km aerial track.

The tram ride takes 45min. each way, affording a one-of-a-kind experience in rainforest life. Mating calls from thousands of cicadas are a constant sound track to the journey. The first half of the ride takes you beneath the canopy, which receives only 10% of the area's total sunlight. Keep an eye out for the *labios ardientes,* or "hot lips"—named for its curled red protective sheaths as well as the supposedly aphrodisiacal fruits inside. Halfway through the tour, the tram stops at a lookout for an excellent view of Carillo Park and the mountains of Tortuguero. The return trip brings you high above the canopy, where toucans, honey creepers, wrens, and tanagers can often be seen flying together in the same flock—a phenomenon unique to the rainforest, much to nature photographers' delight.

Since life here is quite removed from human bustle and the roar of cars, the resulting quiet means wildlife sightings will be much more likely—even more so early in the morning. However, visitors should remember that vegetation is dense and most animals are nocturnal, so many will be identifiable only by their unique calls. The 475-hectare reserve area around the tram has a few nature trails open to visitors. Ten cabins with private hot shower and balconies are available just outside the reserve; reserve with the tram office.

ESCAZÚ

It's only a short bus ride from San José, but the tranquil suburb of Escazú feels like another world. Though the town center has only a few shops and services, the lush green hills on the outskirts hide some relaxing and luxurious B&Bs, and some of San José's classiest restaurants are scattered along the road to San Rafael de

Escazú, 1km northeast. From San José, buses to Escazú leave from the stop at Av. Central/1, C. 16 (about every 15min., ¢135) and drop passengers off on Av. Central at the north side of the *parque central*. The road to **San Rafael de Escazú** starts at C. 5, 3 blocks east of the *parque*, and continues 1km northeast. Many restaurants are along this stretch of road. Local services include: **Banco de Costa Rica,** at the northeast corner of the *parque* (24hr. **ATM**); **Banco Nacional,** at the southwest corner of the *parque* (open M-F 8:30am-3:45pm); **Palí** supermarket, 100m north and 50m west of the bank (open M-Th 8am-7pm, F-Sa 8am-8pm, Su 8am-1pm); and the **post office,** 1 block north of Banco de Costa Rica (open M-F 8am-5pm, Sa 7:30am-noon). **Postal Code:** 1250.

Many in Escazú's growing expat community maintain relaxing B&Bs just outside the town center. Most guests find that cars make commuting to nearby restaurants and San José easier, but public transportation and walking are feasible. ■**Costa Verde Inn ❸** is outside of the town center. Follow Av. Central west out of town until you reach the cemetery; turn left and follow the signs. This country inn has a hot tub, private baths, a sun deck, and living room with fireplace. The hotel offers airport pickup, gourmet breakfast in the tropical gardens, and tour service. (☎228 4080; www.costaverdeinn.com. Internet US$0.15 per min. Laundry US$0.30 per piece. Reception open 7am-10pm. Singles US$45; doubles US$55. Apartments with kitchen US$75 per day.) Escazú boasts some of the country's most elegant dining options. ■**Parillada Argentina El Che ❸,** at the end of the road to San Rafael de Escazú, is a favorite with local businessmen and foreign residents. An array of meats are grilled to perfection and flavored with Costa Rican and Argentine flavors. (☎228 1598. Salads ¢1300-¢1500. Most entrees ¢4000-¢8000. Open daily 11am-2am, kitchen noon-10pm. AmEx/MC/V.) On the road to San Rafael de Escazú, ■**Chango ❸** is recommended by Escazú natives. The dining area looks like a country club, the perfect atmosphere to dine on exquisitely prepared steak, ribs, and Mediterranean entrees. (☎228 1173. Fried calamari ¢2300, capellini ¢2700, shish kebobs ¢3500-¢4800, tenderloin ¢5300, baklava ¢1500. Open daily 11:30am-2am.)

CENTRAL VALLEY

The Central Valley, or Meseta Central, truly makes up the heart of Costa Rica, as both its demographic and geographic center. Cordoned off by the two great volcanic ranges that divide the country, it is home to almost two-thirds of the entire *tico* population, and four of Costa Rica's five largest cities. Two of the region's towering volcanoes (Irazú and Poás) are still active. Residual volcanic ash has also blessed these temperate plains with enough fertile soil to cultivate crops and rich coffee for several nations. Many travelers skip over the landlocked Central Valley and rush to better-touristed vacation spots on either coast, just a half-day's journey away in either direction. Travelers will not regret exploring the Central Valley—it provides a taste of urban convenience, while massive volcanoes, peaceful butterfly gardens, and the country's wildest rafting rivers are just a daytrip away.

ALAJUELA

Alajuela, 3km from the country's international airport and 17km northwest of San José, serves as a convenient base for excursions to the Butterfly Farm, Zoo-Ave, Volcán Poás, and Sarchí. Except for the colorful central market, which takes up an entire block, the west side of the town goes downhill, literally and figuratively. In all other directions, however, Alajuela—perhaps the safest and cleanest of the Central Valley cities—maintains a sunny character with friendly people.

Central Valley

COSTA RICA

Parque Nacional
Volcán Poás ▲

Volcán Barva ▲

CORDILLERA CENTRAL

Parque Nacional
Volcán Irazú

Volcán Irazú ▲

Mirador de Cartago ■

Parque Monte de la Cruz ■
El Castillo Country Club ■

Tobías Bolaños
Airport ✈

Juan Santamaría
International Airport ✈

Reserva Forestral
Pico Blanco

Naranjo · Sarchí Norte · Sarchí Sur · Grecia · San Pedro de Poás · San Antonio · San Rafael · ALAJUELA · Río Segundo · Tambor Desamparados · Concepción · San Juan de Tibás · San Francisco · San Isidro · San Joseíto · San Joseíto · Concepción · San Rafael · San Pedro · San Joaquín · San Rafael · Santa Bárbara · Birrí · HEREDIA

Atenas · Concepción · Turrúcares · San Antonio de Belén · Santa Ana · San Rafael · Escazú · San Antonio · Salitral · Piedades · Colón · Guayabo · Tabarcia · Palmichal · San Ignacio de Acosta · Santiago de Puriscal

SAN JOSÉ · Hatillo · Alajuelita · San Josecito · Aserrí · San Rafael Arriba · San Miguel · Tabarca · Desamparados

San Vicente de Guadalupe · Moravia · San Pedro · Zapote · Curridabat · Tres Ríos · San Isidro de Coronado · Rancho Redondo · Llano Grande · Tierra Blanca · San Rafael

CARTAGO · Tejar · San Rafael de Oreamuno · Dulce Nombre · Paraíso · Orosi · Cot · Cipreses · Santa Rosa · Pacayas · Santa Cruz · Santa Rosa · Turrialba · Juan Viñas · Jardín Lancester

Tobosi · Corralillo · San Cristóbal Norte · San Cristóbal Sur · Tabarca

6 miles
6 kilometers

120 · 125 · 130 · 146 · 13 · 15 · 11 · 137 · 3 · 32 · 7 · 4 · 222 · 2 · 235 · 10 · 227 · 8 · 230 · 2

TRANSPORTATION. From the TUASA station, Av. Central/1, C. 8 (☎442 6900), 350m west of the southwest corner of the *parque central,* **buses** go to **San José** (45min., every 5min. 4am-10pm, ¢250) and **Volcán Poás** (1½hr.; M-Sa 9:15am, return 2:30pm; ¢1650 round-trip). Buses to **Sarchí** depart from 100m west of the station (1¼hr.; M-Sa every 25-30min. 5am-10pm, Su every 25min. 6:10am-10pm; ¢310). **Taxis** to or from the airport should cost no more than US$3.

ORIENTATION AND PRACTICAL INFORMATION. Arriving at the TUASA bus station, Av. Central/1, C. 8, take a right to the end of the block, then walk to the right for 3 blocks until you reach the *parque central,* boxed in by Av. Central/1 and C. Central/2. Look for the white **cathedral** on the far end and a white dome-like shelter over a stage. The streets of Alajuela form the standard Costa Rican grid, but street signs are rare and often point in the wrong direction, so it's best to count the blocks in your head or use landmarks, as locals do. To complicate things, both Av. 9 and C. 12 are called **Calle Ancha.**

There are several **banks** in Alajuela. **Banco Nacional,** Av. Central/1, C. 2 (open M-F 8:30am-3:45pm) and **Scotiabank,** Av. 1/3, C. 2 (☎441 1131; open M-F 8am-5pm, Sa 8am-4pm) both have MC/V 24hr. **ATMs.** Scotiabank changes Visa traveler's checks. **Banco San José,** Av. 3, C. Central/1, changes AmEx traveler's checks for a

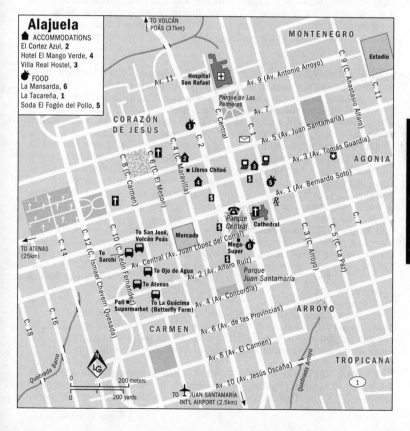

Alajuela

♠ ACCOMMODATIONS
El Cortez Azul, **2**
Hotel El Mango Verde, **4**
Villa Real Hostel, **3**

🍴 FOOD
La Mansarda, **6**
La Tacareña, **1**
Soda El Fogón del Pollo, **5**

COSTA RICA

US$1 fee (☎443 4380; open M-F 8am-7pm, Sa 9am-1pm), and there is a BCAC/Bancrédito 24hr. **ATM** on Av. Central/2, C. 2. **Western Union** is inside Palí. (☎442 6392. Open M-Th 10:30am-1:30pm and 3:30-8pm, F-Sa 10am-2pm and 4-8pm, Su 9am-noon and 2-6pm). **Libros Chiloé,** Av. 5, C. 2/4, across from Hotel Cortez Azul, buys and sells used books. (☎442 7419. Open M-Sa 8:30am-6pm.) The largest **supermarket** is **Palí,** 4 blocks west and 1 block south of the southwest corner of the *parque.* (☎442 6392. Open M-F 8:30am-8pm, Sa 7:30am-8pm, Su 8:30am-6pm.) **MegaSuper,** on the south side of the *parque* at Av. Central, C. Central/2, is smaller, but closer to the town center. (☎441 1384. Open daily 8am-9pm.) The **mercado central,** 2 blocks west of the *parque,* is a crowded collection of meat, cheese, fruit, and vegetable stands (open M-F 7am-6pm, Sa 6am-6pm). The **police** station is 1 block north and 3 blocks east of the *parque's* northeast corner, around the corner from the fire station. (☎443 4511 or 911. Limited English. Open 9am-5pm. Emergency 24hr.) Medicines and toiletries are available at **Farmacia Fischel,** at the corner of Av. 1, C. 1. (☎443 7626. Open M-Sa 8am-10pm, Su 10am-10pm. AmEx/MC/V.) The **hospital,** Av. 9, C. Central/1, is 5 blocks north of the northeast corner of the *parque,* facing Parque de las Palmeras. (☎443 4042, emergency 440 1333. Open 24hr.) Both coin- and card-operated **phones** are available at the *parque.* **Internet** cafes are scattered across the city. Try **Mani's Club Café,** Av. 3, C. 1. (☎430 7436. ¢300 per hr. including free coffee or tea. Open M-Sa 9am-10pm.) For better rates but fewer computers, head to **Café Interactivo,** across the street from Banco San José at Av. 3, C. Central/1. (¢150 per 30min., ¢250 per hr. Open M-Sa 9am-8pm. AmEx/MC/V.) The **post office,** Av. 5, C. 1, is 2 blocks north and 1 block east of the northeast corner of the *parque.* (Open M-F 8am-5:30pm, Sa 7:30am-noon.) **Postal Code:** 4050.

▮▮ ACCOMMODATIONS AND FOOD. Like its fruity moniker, the inside is the best part of **Hotel El Mango Verde ❶,** Av. 3, C. 2/4. with a garden courtyard, three open-air sitting areas with cable TV and video games, patio, and a kitchen. (☎441 7116 or 441 6330; mirafloresbb@hotmail.com. Reservations recommended. Singles US$10, with bath US$15; doubles US$20/$25.) In the common area of **El Cortez Azul ❷,** Av. 5, C. 2/4, a dramatic wooden sculpture carved by the manager greets you. Visitors have kitchen access, two sitting areas, and cable TV. Tour services available. (☎443 6145; cortezazul@latinmail.com. Singles with shared bath US$10; rooms of varying sizes with private baths US$12-$15.) **Villa Real Hostel ❷,** Av. 3, C. 1, is 1 block north and 1 block east of the northeast corner of the *parque.* Coffee is always brewing in the common room. Two common baths serve all. The kitchen is available to guests. (☎441 4022; villareal@hotmail.com. Rooms US$12; shared quads US$40. AmEx/MC/V.)

   La Mansarda Bar and Restaurant ❷ is a second-floor restaurant 25m south of the southeast corner of the *parque.* Fresh fish is beautifully presented, with zesty shrimp *ceviche* (¢1800) and a steamy *sopa de mariscos* (seafood soup; ¢1800). Try the house speciality: sea bass with mushroom sauce. (☎441 4390. Open daily 11:30am-11:30pm, F-Sa open until midnight. AmEx/MC/V.) **La Tacareña Bar and Restaurant ❶,** Av. 7, C. 2, is a low-lit, cozy refuge, with quick service and tasty food. Burgers and sandwiches (¢700) are served beneath posters of volcanoes and rock bands. (☎442 1662. Entrees ¢900-¢3000. Open daily 10:30am-11pm. V.) **Soda El Fogón del Pollo ❶,** Av. 1/3, C. 4, is owned by an Argentinian who knows his chicken, as you may be able to tell from the decor and the menu. (☎443 1362; luvihe@yahoo.com. Chicken *casados* ¢1100. Open M-F 7am-7:30pm.)

◣ PARQUE NACIONAL VOLCÁN POÁS. Located 55 km northwest of San José, this is one of the most popular protected areas in the country, largely because of its proximity to San José. Its appeal isn't simply one of convenience—the park's highlight is a crater at the top of active Volcán Poás (2574m). Inside the massive crater (1320m across and 300m deep) is a turquoise acid pool and *fumaroles* (vents in the earth's crust) that audibly release bursts of volcanic steam. The cone itself looks like a rainbow carved into the terrain, with vibrantly colored layers of gray, white, and red earth that trace the history of the volcano's eruptions.

The most direct route to the crater is a 10min. walk up a gentle, paved path from the visitor center. A 15min. walk beyond the crater is **Laguna Botos,** the collapsed cone of another volcano filled with rain water but still too acidic to sustain life. Look for the paved trail marked "Laguna Botos," just before the crater viewing area. Poás is most enjoyable in the morning, especially from May to November, as clouds and rain obscure the view by noon. Try to avoid visiting on Sundays, when the park is usually packed. *(Buses depart daily from San José's TUASA station at 8:30am. ₡2000 round-trip. Return bus 2:30pm. Open daily Dec.-Apr. 8am-4:30pm, May-Nov. 8am-3:30pm. US$7.)*

◪ ZOO-AVE. The biggest bird reproduction center in Central America, Zoo-Ave breeds and rehabilitates birds, reptiles, and mammals before reintroducing them to nature. Visitors can see 100 bird species, like the elusive quetzal, falcons, and owls, along with monkeys and crocodiles. *(In Alajuela, buses leave from the lot south of Av. Central/2, C. 8. ☎ 433 8989. Open daily 9am-5pm. ₡3000, ages 2-10 ₡500.)*

◪ SARCHÍ. Those who charge Costa Rica with the decay of its own national culture might want to pause at this town. Sarchí, the nation's biggest crafts center, keeps old traditions alive in the form of brilliantly decorated *carretas* (wooden oxcarts). Although these days oxcarts have become a slightly kitschy symbol for the entire country, and cheaper, miniature knock-off carts appear throughout Central America, the originals are worth the visit. Nearby natural wonders include Bajos del Toro Amarillo and Parque Nacional Juan Castro Blanco. *(Buses to Alajuela, Grecia, and Naranjo pass by the west side of the parque in Sarchí Norte and by the stop in front of the Plaza de Artesanía in Sarchí Sur every 25min. from 6am-11pm.)*

PARQUE NACIONAL BRAULIO CARRILLO

About 25km northeast of Heredia, these 45,900 hectares of land are named after Costa Rica's third chief of state. When Rte. 32 was constructed from San José to Puerto Limón in 1978, the park was born from conservationist efforts to save the area's biodiversity—over 6000 species of plants (roughly half the total in Costa Rica) and 500 species of animals. Despite improved access to the forest from the highway, this national park remains largely unexplored and untouristed.

⬛ TRANSPORTATION. Access the park from **Heredia,** or from the San José-Puerto Limón Hwy. (Rte. 32). From Heredia, take a **bus** to **Paso Llano** via **San José de la Montaña,** departing from Av. 6/8, C. 4, on the west side of the *mercado municipal* (1hr.; M-F 6:25am, 12:15, 4pm, Sa 6:25, 11:15am, 4pm; Su 6:45, 11am, 4pm; ₡220). Try catching an early bus—the temperature will be much more bearable for the long hike ahead. If you miss the three daily buses, hourly buses are an option, but prepare for an additional 7km hike up a steep, unshaded road. The bus drops you off across from Champo's Bar in Paso Llano from where buses return to Heredia (M-F 7:50am, 1:30, 5:15pm; Sa 7:50am, 12:30, 5:15pm; Su 8am, 1, 5:15pm). To access the **Quebrada Ranger Station** near the Rainforest Aerial Tram from Heredia, catch a bus to **San José,** and another to **Guápiles** (1½hr., every 30min-1hr., 6am-9pm). Ask the driver to let you off near the ranger station. No buses make regular stops at the ranger station, but they pass by every 30min.

■ ◼ **ORIENTATION AND PRACTICAL INFORMATION.** Combining forces with the 4.5m of rain that the park sees annually, Braulio Carrillo's varied terrain lends itself to hundreds of rushing waterfalls and river canyons. The park is comprised of two dormant volcanoes, **Volcán Cacho Negro** and **Volcán Barva.** Apart from Volcán Barva, the trails near the northeast corner of the park are the only areas of the forest that can be easily hiked, although rangers say car theft and armed robberies on the trails are not uncommon. It's best to go in a group. *Let's Go* does not recommend hiking these trails alone or after dark.

About 25m back from the bus stop in Paso Llano is a paved road marked with signs to Volcán Barva. This road climbs 4km to the tiny village of **Sacramento.** From Sacramento, it's another 4km uphill to the ranger station and park entrance. One kilometer out of town the road turns rough and rocky and it is difficult to find a cab willing to make this trip. The park entrance and ranger station are at the end of the road. Since the volcano is 2.9km above sea level, cold rain and wind should be anticipated. (☎283 5906. Open Tu-Su 7am-4pm. US$7, students US$1.) Call 1 week ahead; camping or 4-person cabin US$2 per person.) Ask the ranger where to camp and notify him when you leave. The facilities have space for 10 tents, potable water, and toilets, although campers should bring drinking water in March and April. **Camping** is allowed only near the ranger station at Volcán Barva.

◖◗ **FOOD AND ACCOMMODATIONS.** Even though Heredia is the base for exploring the park, it doesn't see many tourists. However, it still maintains some good and inexpensive accommodations. Even places outside the city center are relatively loud. **Hotel Las Flores ❷,** Av. 12, C. 12/14, is a gem in budget accommodations. Marble floors, pleasant owners, bright rooms, and private hot showers make the 10min. walk from the *parque* worth it. (☎261 8147. 24hr. reception. Singles US$12; doubles US$18; triples US$25.) **Hotel Colonial ❶,** Av. 4, C. 4/6, has a familial atmosphere, complete with a pet dog and sitting room. Owners live in the building. Shared hot baths, and mid-sized rooms appeal to young backpackers. (☎237 5258. 24hr. reception. Singles ¢2500; doubles ¢4500.)

Sodas line every street, and some nicer cafes surround the *parque central*. A handful of American fast food joints are just south of the Universidad near Av. 2, C. 9. **Vishnu Vegetarian/Mango Verde ❶,** Av. Central/1, C. 7, is a vegetarian chain that offers a break from greasy *soda* fare. The *plato del día* is a steal at ¢1450. Wash down healthy veggie burgers (¢775) and pita sandwiches (¢1050) with a *refresco natural*. (☎223 4683 or 237 2526. Open M-F 9am-7pm, Sa 9am-6pm. AmEx/MC/V.) **Fresas ❷,** Av. 1, C. 7, does wonders for fresh fruit salads (¢400-¢700), fruit drinks (¢475-¢1100), and fruit desserts. (☎262 5555. Open daily 8am-midnight. AmEx/MC/V.) Located on the ground floor of Hotel America, and most often visited by guests of the hotel, **Restaurante América ❷,** Av. 2/4, C. Central, is a good find for any traveler. Its mix of *típica* and *criolla* cuisine is tasty but slightly greasy. (☎260 9292. Open daily 6am-9pm. AmEx/MC/V.)

◤ **HIKES.** The main trail is a 2km, 45min. uphill hike to three lagoons at the volcano's summit. About 300m down the trail, **Sendero Álvaro,** a 1.8km path, veers off to the right. Another 300m leads to a 900m turnoff for **Mirador La Vara Blanca,** from which—if it's clear—you can see the Caribbean. About 35min. up the trail, bear left at the sign to ascend the remaining 200m to the edge of **Laguna Barva,** an acidic pool cupped by an extinct volcano (70m across, 8.5m deep, with an average temperature of 11°C.) A second trail—which is muddy and difficult in the rainy season—leads 2km up to **Laguna Copy** (40m across). The third lagoon, **Laguna Danta** (500m across), is inaccessible by foot. To see the view from the volcano rim, fork right at the sign and turn left when the trail ends.

From start to finish, the hike from Paso Llano to the summit and back takes about 5½hr. If you take the 6:30am bus from Heredia, you should have time to climb to the top, see both lagoons, and descend the volcano to catch the 1:30pm bus. It is not advisable to stray from the trails.

CARTAGO

Cartago (pop. 30,000) had its time in the limelight when it served as the nation's capital from 1563 until 1823, before the seat of power shifted 22km northwest to San José. Its size, power, and remarkable colonial architecture have since suffered from earthquakes and volcanic eruptions, reducing the once busy urban center to a quiet town. However, a few overpriced hotels provide an easy base for visiting nearby Volcán Irazú or Parque Nacional Tapantí.

▣ TRANSPORTATION. Bus departure points are scattered around town. There is no printed schedule, but bus and taxi drivers are a good source of info for departure times and locations. Buses from Av. 1/3, C. 6 depart to **Orosi** (40min.; about every 30min. M-Sa 5:30am-10:30pm, Su 7am-10pm; ¢240); from Av. 3/5, C. 6 to **Paraíso** for Lankester Botanical Gardens (15min., every 10min. 5am-10pm, ¢105); from Av. 4, C. 2/4 to **San José** (SACSA ☎551 0232 or 233 5350. 40min.; every 10min. M-Sa 4:45am-11pm, Su 5-11pm; ¢225); from Av. 6/8, C. 4 to **Tierra Blanca** (30min.; every hr. M-Sa 5:30am-10pm, Su 7am-10pm; ¢195); and from Av. 3, C. 8/10 to **Turrialba** (1½hr.; daily every hr. 6am-10pm, ¢415, ¢600 direct). To get to **Volcán Irazú,** see p. 152. **Taxis** line the west side of the *parque* on Av. 1/2, C. 4.

▣▣ ORIENTATION AND PRACTICAL INFORMATION. Unlike most Costa Rican towns, Cartago is anchored by Av. and C. 1, which form the southern and western edges of the *parque central*. East of the *parque* are **Las Ruinas,** the ruins of a cathedral destroyed by an earthquake, while the stately **La Basílica de Nuestra Señora de los Ángeles** is at the east end of town. The *mercado central*, between Av. 4/6 and C. 1/3, is northwest of the *parque*. **Volcán Irazú** soars 32km northeast of town, and the **Jardín Botánico Lankester** is about 8km southeast. Though the city is relatively safe, don't wander too far north or west of the *mercado central*, and take taxis whenever possible at night.

Banco Popular, Av. 1, C. 2/4 (open M-F 8:15am-3:45pm, Sa 8:15-11:30am), and **Banco Nacional,** Av. 4, C. 5 (open M-F 8:30am-3:45pm), change traveler's checks and cash, give cash advances, and have 24hr. **ATMs. Palí Supermarket** is located on Av. 4, C. 6. (Open M-Th 8:30am-7:30pm, F-Sa 8:30am-8pm, Su 8:30am-6pm.) **Laundry** service is available at **Lavandería Fabimar,** Av. 2, C. 11. (¢475 per kg. Open M-F 8am-noon and 1-6pm, Sa 9am-3pm.) In an **emergency,** dial ☎911. The **police** (☎551-0455) are in the yellow building on Av. 6, C. 2/4. The **Red Cross** is on Av. 5, C. 1/3 (☎551 0421), while **Farmacia Central** is south of Las Ruinas on Av. 1, C. 2 (☎551 0698; open M-Sa 8am-8pm); **medical services** are available at **Hospital Dr. Max Peralta Jiménez,** Av. 5/9, C. 1/3 (☎550 1999). For **Internet,** try **Cafe Internet,** on Av. 4, C. 6/8 (¢300 per 30min., ¢500 per hr.; open daily 10am-10pm), or **Ah. Quí Internet,** on Av. 2, C. 11. (¢350 per hr. Open M-Sa 9am-10pm, Su 2-7pm.) The **post office** is on Av. 2, C. 15/17 (open M-F 7:30am-5:30pm, Sa 7:30am-noon). **Postal Code:** 7050.

▣▣ ACCOMMODATIONS AND FOOD. Cartago's lack of safe accommodations make San José and Orosi better places to stay, although Cartago has some quality lodgings. **Los Ángeles Lodge ❷,** Av. 4, C. 14/16, is a bit expensive, but it has a scenic location overlooking the Basílica. (☎551 0957. Breakfast included 7:30-9am. Private baths. Reception 24hr. Singles US$20; doubles US$35; triples US$50; quads

ON THE MENU

FROM CROP TO CUP

n Costa Rica, coffee is not just a beverage, it's a way of life. Ever since the crop came to Costa Rica at the end of the 18th century, it has defined the nation's culture, economy, and diet.

At first, the plant was just a ocal crop. In the 18th century, he government began distributing coffee plants and land plots, cutting taxes for *tico* farmers willng to grow export-grade coffee. Since then, it has become the country's single greatest source of evenue and is exported all over he world.

Costa Rica enjoys several geographic advantages for coffee growing. Coffee grown at higher altitudes makes a better roast, because the beans mature more slowly in the cold and are less ikely to break during the roasting process. Costa Rica's volcanic anges also influence coffee crops n surprisingly productive ways: volcanic ash in the soil leaves mineral deposits that enrich the bean's flavor.

By law, *tico* farmers can only grow Arabica coffee, which is sweeter and less caffeinated than robusta (the world's other drinkable crop). Costa Ricans see this as a choice of quality over quanity, as Arabica tends to produce smaller harvests. Costa Rican coffee is harvested by hand, though most of the harvest laborers come rom Nicaragua, as upper- and middle-class *tico* culture moves away from agriculture.

US$70; quints US$80. MC/V.) **Hotel Dinastía ❸**, Av. 6/8, C. 3, just north of the *mercado central*, has uninspiring rooms that tend to vary in quality. The lobby has a comfy sitting area with TV and sofas. (☎551 7057. 24hr. reception and guard. Singles and doubles with fan and shared bath ¢5000, with TV and hot shower ¢6500; triples with hot shower ¢7500.) **La Puerta del Sol ❷**, next door to Los Ángeles Lodge, serves good standard food in a large dining area with elegant pillars and archways. (☎ 551 0615. *Gallo pinto* with eggs ¢1150, sandwiches ¢550-¢1050, *platos fuertes* ¢1950-¢2350. Open daily 8:30am-11pm.) **Soda y Restaurante Friendly's ❶**, Av. 1/3, C. 4, is a tasty and inexpensive option. (☎591 2723. Burgers ¢350-¢1000, *gallo pinto* ¢650, sub sandwiches ¢550-¢800. Open daily 7am-10pm.)

◙ SIGHTS. La Basílica de Nuestra Señora de los Ángeles, Costa Rica's most famous place of worship, stands at the eastern edge of town. Thousands of *ticos* make an annual pilgrimage to this cathedral on August 2 for El Día de la Virgen to worship the statue of **La Negrita,** an indigenous image of the Virgin said to have great healing powers. La Negrita was declared the patron saint in 1824, about 100 years before the Basílica was destroyed by an earthquake and later rebuilt in the beautiful Byzantine style visible today. The church's real treasures lie just to the left of the altar, hidden in a small room crammed full of offerings to the Virgin. Glass cases line the wall, displaying hundreds of miniature metal body parts offered to the Virgin in gratitude for the magical blessings that her supplicants believe helped cure their maladies. A shelf at the front of the room is filled with medals, miniature house models, and even graded school exams, testament to *ticos'* widespread faith in La Negrita's powers. From this room, stairs lead down to the **Cripta de la Piedra** (Crypt of the Stone), which contains the boulder where La Negrita is said to have been first sighted. (Open daily 5:30am-8pm. Free.)

▣ DAYTRIP FROM CARTAGO: VOLCÁN IRAZU. With an elevation of 3432m, **Volcán Irazú** is Costa Rica's tallest active volcano. The name commemorates an indigenous village that once perched daringly on these capricious slopes. Though sulfurous fumaroles continue to roll off a few of the volcano's five craters, Irazú is relatively inactive and is one of the few volcanoes that can be observed up close. If you're lucky—mornings in the dry season are best— you can see the Atlantic Ocean, Pacific Ocean, and Lago de Nicaragua from the summit. For the best view, follow the paved road from the ticket office to the top and turn left on the small path that turns off to the right before the parking lot. Past the lot is the cement path that leads to Irazú's three main craters. The expansive **Cráter Playa Hermosa** is the first crater on the left. To the right is the **Cráter Diego de la Haya** (690m wide, 100m deep). Straight ahead is the **Cráter Principal** (1050m wide, 300m deep), the only active crater, which boasts an enormous cauldron. Both Diego de la Haya and Principal cradle sulfurous iguana-green lakes; the color comes from chemicals produced by volcanic gases emitted into the water. Be sure to bring rain gear and a few extra layers of warm clothes. A small cafeteria, next to the main parking lot and the entrance to the craters, serves overpriced snacks, hot drinks, and souvenirs. There is no camping or lodging. (Coming during the week is difficult without private transportation. A bus leaves Cartago at 8:30am, 100m south of the southeast corner of the ruins, across the street from Iglesia Los Capuchines (round-trip from Cartago¢900). During the week, take a taxi from Cartago or Tierra Blanca. ¢7000 one-way, ¢15,000-¢20,000 to have the taxi wait and drive you back. Buses leave from the Tierra Blanca, stop in Cartago for San Juan de Chicua, 6km from the peak. ☎219 7187; call ahead for confirmation. 1hr., M and Th 11am, ¢400. Open daily 8am-3:30pm. US$7.)

OROSI

Regretfully overlooked by most travelers scurrying away to the more touristed coasts, small Orosi (pop. 8000) has a great deal to offer beyond its apparent quiet. The true gems here are the nearby nature reserves, hot springs, coffee farms, and raging rivers. Orosi's seclusion, natural beauty, and small-town charm make it well worth the complicated trip from San José.

▣ TRANSPORTATION. Buses to Orosi leave Cartago from Av. 1/3, C. 6 (40min.; about every 30 min. M-Sa 5:30am-10pm, Su 7am-10pm; ¢240) and return to Cartago from the northeast corner of the soccer field on the main road (40min.; every 30min. M-Sa 4:45am-9:10pm, Su 5:45am-7:15pm; ¢240). **Taxis** also leave from the northeast corner of the soccer field (☎533 3343, 841 4665, or 533 3276).

▣▨ ORIENTATION AND PRACTICAL INFORMATION. Despite the lack of street names, Orosi is easily navigable by landmarks. Buses and taxis arrive on the main drag, which runs north to south through town; you'll be traveling south along this road past the soccer field. **La Iglesia de San José Orosi** is on the west side of the field. **Parque Nacional Tapantí** is about

During the harvest, the red coffee fruit is plucked off the tree and placed into large water tanks. The ripe fruit is heavier and sinks, while unripe fruit, twigs, and leaves float to the top and are removed. The ripe berries are peeled and the two seeds (the beans) are removed. These seeds are cleaned and put in the sun to dry on large patios.

The roasting process mostly takes place at larger coffee companies like Café Britt in Heredia. The dry green beans are heated to 400°F to release flavor and carmelize sugars. The longer the beans roast, the darker and more flavorful they become. Once the coffee is roasted, it must be protected from air, sunlight, and water, and is usually stored in vaccuum-packed bags. Sometimes you'll still see coffee prepared traditionally, in muslin sacks called chorreadores that hold the ground coffee as hot water is poured through and the bitter liquid strains out.

Coffee is a point of pride for ticos and many believe it is good for one's health. They often drink their coffee black, unwilling to tamper with its natural flavors. Even black coffee often comes already sugared, however, and a few higher-end coffee shops offer espresso drinks and frozen coffee concoctions. But don't expect to see Starbucks showing up anytime soon; there are no foreign brands of coffee sold in Costa Rica.

10km east of town on the main drag. A **tourist office** at Orosi Lodge arranges horseback rides and tours, and rents mountain bikes. (☎533 3578. Bikes US$10 per day, horses US$7 per hr.) The newly opened **Orosi Tourist Info and Adventure Center,** 300m south of the southwest corner of the soccer field, has tourist info, as well as the only **mailbox** in Orosi (☎533 1113). Many accommodations in town also arrange tours and rent bikes (see **Accommodations,** p. 154). **Groceries, fax, bike rental** (US$1-$2 per hr.), and **photocopy service** are available at **Super Anita #2,** 250m south of the southeast corner of the soccer field, where they might change US dollars if you buy something. (Open daily 7am-8pm. MC/V.) The **police** station is directly north of the soccer field (☎533 3082), and the **medical clinic** is next to the police. (☎533 3052. Open M-F 8:30am-4pm.) In emergencies, call the **Red Cross** in Paraíso (☎574 6066). **Internet** access at **PC Orosi,** 100m south of Super Anita #2 (¢200 per 30min., ¢300 per hr.; open M-Sa 8am-8pm) and **Vallenet Internet,** 100m south of the southwest corner of the soccer field (¢200 per 30min., ¢300 per hr.; open M-Th 10am-9pm, F-Su 10am-10pm). There are no banks in Orosi, but some MC/V cards work in the **ATM** next to Super Anita #2 (open 5am-10pm).

ACCOMMODATIONS. Montaña Linda ❶/B&B ❷, 200m south and 200m west of the southwest corner of the soccer field, feels like a tree house with its ladder-access rooms. Backpackers love the shared kitchen (US$1) and hot baths, breakfasts and dinners (US$2.50/$4.50) and Spanish classes (US$99-$285). If you seek the luxury of private baths and killer mountainside views, try their B&B up the street. (☎533 3640, B&B 533 2153; info@montanalinda.com. Laundry US$5. Dorms US$6.50; singles US$10.50; doubles US$17; B&B rooms US$25-$35; camping US$3 per person, with tent US$4.) The **Orosi Lodge** ❸ is 400m south and 100m west of the southwest corner of the soccer field. Rooms are equipped with fridges, coffee makers, fans, and private hot baths. Private balconies afford views of the nearby volcanoes and the hotel's interior jungle garden. A small cafe is attached. (☎533 3578; www.orosilodge.com. Internet ¢750 per 30min. Reception 24hr. Cafe open daily 7am-7pm; breakfast US$5. Doubles US$45, low-season US$38; triples US$55/$48. AmEx/MC/V.)

FOOD, NIGHTLIFE, AND ENTERTAINMENT. Bar Restaurante Coto ❷, at the northeast corner of the soccer field, serves up some of the town's best *típico* in an elegant palm-filled terrace. Don't miss the steak in mushroom sauce (¢2100). Sandwiches (¢600-¢900), soups, and salads (¢1200) are also tasty. (☎533 3032. Beer ¢550, cocktails ¢1000. Open daily 8am-midnight.) Soda Luz ❶, 100m north of the northwest corner of the soccer field, serves cheap, tasty, and generous portions. (Burgers ¢400; spaghetti ¢800; *casados* ¢800-¢1000. Open M-Th 7am-4pm, F-Su 7am-8pm.)

Orosi offers a few solid options for a fun night out. **Bar Restaurante El Nido,** 200m north of the northeast corner of the soccer field, is a favorite among locals and travelers. El Nido provides the best in bar basics—simple decor with plastic tables and chairs with ample space and music variety. (☎533 3793. Beer ¢500, cocktails ¢1000. Open daily 11am-1am.) **Bar Zepelin,** 200m east of the southeast corner of the soccer field, is popular among locals. Zepelin features a small dancing platform complete with strobe light. Four TVs broadcast music videos from the 80s to the present; ask to see the list and you can make a request. (Beer ¢500, cocktails ¢1000, snacks ¢300-¢500. Open daily 2pm-2:30am.) **Orosi Tourist Info and Adventure Center** (☎533 1113), 300m south of the southwest corner of the soccer field, offers an alternative to the bar scene in Orosi. Recently opened to serve as a cultural exchange for locals and visitors, the Center has Spanish school classrooms, a kitchen, pool tables, restaurant, TV, poetry nights, and concerts.

◙ **SIGHTS.** Built in 1743, **La Iglesia de San José Orosi** is remarkable because it is one of the country's oldest operational churches, and because of its impressive architectural fortitude—it has survived earthquakes that wiped out entire nearby villages. Defying tradition, the church is reputed to be Costa Rica's only eastward-facing church. Adjoining the church, the **Museo Franciscano** houses a collection of Christian relics from the early 18th century. (West of the soccer field. Open Tu-Sa 1-5pm, Su 9am-noon and 1-5pm. Su mass 10am, 6:30pm. ₡300, children ₡150.)

Balneario Termal Orosi, the more accessible of Orosi's two hot mineral baths, has four simple pools at 35°C, a drastic drop from the scalding 60°C water at the source. Basic showers and a reasonably priced restaurant are available. (☎533 2156. 300m south and 100m west of the southwest corner of the soccer field, next to Orosi Lodge. Open Su-M and W-Sa 7:30am-4pm. ₡700.) Slightly farther and more scenic than Balneario Termal Orosi, **Balenario de Aguas Termales Los Patios** has six warm mineral pools (41°C) and two cold pools in a country-club-like atmosphere. (☎553 3009. 2km south out of town along Orosi's main road. Open Tu-Su 8am-4pm. ₡800.)

La Casa del Soñador, an old-fashioned, intricately designed "Dreamer's House," is the masterpiece of late Costa Rican sculptor Macedonio Quesada, who built the bamboo and wooden *casita* in 1989. Now maintained by Quesada's sons Hermes and Miguel, as well as the handful of assistants who seem to be constantly working away downstairs, the house is filled with nativity scenes and *campesino* figures exhibiting a mix of Latin American, indigenous, and East Asian influences. Everything in the house, from the doors to the window shutters, is carefully chiseled from variously sized sticks of bamboo. (11km from Orosi on the road to the town of Cachí. From Orosi, walk east along the main road past the Balneario Los Patios until you see a sign for Hotel Río Palomo. Turn left and walk another 15min. to the hotel; make another left and continue 4.5km past the hotel to La Casa del Soñador. Most Cartago-Orosi buses will go as far as the town of Palomo. From there it's a 4.5km walk. A taxi from Orosi costs ₡2500-₡3000.)

Las Ruinas de Ujarrás draw a constant flow of tourists, despite the village's abandonment after being virtually destroyed by a flood in 1833. Set in a well-kept park and surrounded by coffee plantations, the 17th-century church is said to have been built when an Indian found a wooden box in a river, which he brought to Ujarrás. Upon opening it, the Indian found a statue of the Virgin and was no longer able to move it from Ujarrás. The statue, known as La Virgen de Candelaria, has actually been moved to the town of Paraíso in the years since, along with the rest of Ujarrás's residents. Locals continue to celebrate their sacred Virgen with an annual parade from Paraíso to Ujarrás in late March or early April. (Catch a bus to Paraíso from the northeast corner of the soccer field. 20min., every 30min. 4:45am-9:15pm, ₡140.) From Paraíso, buses leave every 20-30min. for La Represa de Cachí. From there it's a 1km walk; ask the driver to point you in the right direction. To return to Orosi, confirm with the driver for a bus that can pick you up from the drop-off point at Cachí. Open daily dawn to dusk. Free.)

◙ **GUIDED TOURS.** Many Orosi hotels and the tourist office arrange tours of the nearby attractions and provide equipment for you to fully enjoy the views. The **Montaña Linda** hotel (see **Accommodations,** p. 154) offers whitewater rafting and guided tours of Orosi Valley, Volcán Irazú, and Monumento Nacional Guayabo. (Rafting US$70; Orosi tour US$5; Irazú US$12, not including park fee. Monumento Nacional Guayabo US$25, including park fee, minimum 2 people.) Montaña Linda gives out hiking directions to a swimming hole, natural hot springs, waterfall, and other scenic walks. The **Orosi Lodge** leads combined tours of Volcán Irazú, Mirador Orosi, and La Basílica de Nuestra Señora de los Ángeles (US$40); Parque Nacional Tapantí (US$45); and Orosi Valley, a sugar cane mill, La Casa del Soñador, and the Lankester Botanical Gardens (US$40).

COSTA RICA

▲! PARQUE NACIONAL TAPANTÍ. Wildlife-refuge-turned-national park, Tapantí is famous for the highest average annual rainfall (7m per year) in Costa Rica. The resulting 150+ rivers and streams criss-cross 61 square km of pristine rainforest inhabited by an enormous diversity of wildlife: 45 species of mammals, 260 of birds, 32 of reptiles and amphibians—including three types of vipers—and an average 80-160 species of trees per hectare. The huge amount of rainfall that Tapantí receives is used to generate hydroelectric power for most of San José's population. From the main road, Camino Principal (1.6km) leads to the ranger station, where the park's three trails begin—the Oropéndola (1.2km), La Pava (400m), and the Árboles Caídos (2km), in increasing order of difficulty. The last trail has some steep inclines but can be finished in 1-1½hr. Oropéndola leads to a pool in the Río Grande de Orosi, where swimming is possible. An extension to the La Pava trail, called La Catarata, leads to a waterfall and a panoramic view of the Orosi valley. Although camping is not permitted, the park offers very basic rooms in a 15-person capacity cabin. (¢1000 per person. Call ☎551 2970 in advance to secure a bed.) The communal showers have warm water. Bring a sleeping bag and food to cook in the kitchen. Spanish and English language maps (¢200) are available at the ranger station. *(From Orosi to Parque Nacional Tapantí is a 12km hike. Head south along the main road from Orosi; the first half of the hike is fairly flat, but the road gets steeper and rockier near the park. If you're short on time or energy, you can take a cab (one-way ¢3000), and walk back down or arrange for the cab to pick you up. ☎771 5116, 771 3155, 551 2970, or 771 4836. Open daily 7am-5pm. US$7.)*

TURRIALBA

Often bypassed by travelers uninterested in adventure tours or on budgets too limited to afford them, suburban Turrialba generally stays off the tourist radar. Its proximity to the Ríos Reventazón and Pacuare, however, has brought the town international recognition; both rivers are packed with Class III-V rapids and some of the world's best river runs. Whitewater rafters and kayakers of all abilities splash through during the low season while other travelers stay here on the way to Costa Rica's most significant archaeological site, Monumento Nacional Guayabo.

▐ TRANSPORTATION. Turrialba has two main **bus stations.** From the bus station 100m west of the southwest corner of the *parque* (☎556 0159), **buses** leave for **San José** (direct 1¾hr., every hr. 5am-4pm, 5:30pm; indirect 2¼hr., every 1½hr. 5am-9pm; ¢690) via **Cartago** (1½hr., ¢415), and **Siquirres** (2hr.; Tu-Th every 2hr. 6am-6:15pm, Sa-M every hr. 6am-7pm; ¢580) via **CATIE** (10min., ¢100). Free private bus shuttles passengers to and from CATIE; pick it up at the stop opposite the Red Cross. On weekends and in the high season, you might have to buy tickets to San José in advance to ensure a seat. From the other station, 100m south and 50m west of the southwest corner of the *parque*, buses leave for **Monumento Nacional Guayabo** (1hr.; M-Sa 11am, 3:15, 5:15pm; return M-Sa 12:30pm; Su 9am; 12:30; 4pm; ¢175). **Taxis** are also available (☎556-7070).

▐ ORIENTATION AND PRACTICAL INFORMATION. Turrialba, 62km east of San José, is arranged in a fashion similar to most Costa Rican cities. Most streets have names, but no one uses them. With the *parque central* as a reference point, things aren't too tough to find. As you exit the bus station (coming from San José or Cartago), the *parque* is on the next block to your left (east), and the **church** is just south of the *parque*. There is no official **tourist office**, but Doña Blanca or Luis at **Hotel Interamericano** (see **Accommodations,** p. 157), will provide info about the town and nearby sights. **Banco de Costa Rica,** 200m south and 100m east of the southeast corner of the *parque*, spits US dollars from its **ATM.** (☎556 0472. Open M-F 8:30am-3pm.) **Banco Nacional** is just a few meters west of Banco de Costa Rica.

(☎556 1211. Open M-F 8:30am-3:45pm.) **Banco Popular** is 50m east of the southeast corner of the *parque*, next to Popo's. (☎556 6098. Open M-F 9am-4:30pm, Sa 8:15-11:30am.) **Western Union** is 100m south and 50m east of the southwest corner of the *parque*. (☎556 0439. Open M-Sa 8am-6:30pm.) Diagonally across from the post office, 120m north of the northwest corner of the *parque*, the **bookstore** sells a wide selection of second-hand classics and best-sellers (¢1000-¢2000) in English, Spanish, French, German, and Portuguese. (☎556 1697. Open M-F 8:30-11am and 2:30-5:30pm.) **Supermercado Compromás** is at the northwest corner of the *parque* (open M-Sa 8am-8pm). The **police** station (☎556 0030) is just outside of the town center, up the hill and to your right, heading west on Av. 4. In an **emergency**, dial ☎911. For medical services, the **Red Cross** is 100m west and 50m south of the northwest corner of the *parque* (☎556 0191; open daily 7am-10pm), **Farmacia San Buenaventura** is 100m south of the southeast corner of the *parque* (☎556 0379; open M-Sa 8am-8pm, Su 8am-6pm; AmEx/MC/V), and the **hospital** (☎556 1133) is 100m south and 600m west of the southwest corner of the *parque*. **Internet** access is available at **Turrialba.net Cafe Internet,** in the Centro Comercial Yee, 100m west and 50m south of the southwest corner of the *parque*. (¢250 per 30min., ¢400 per hr. Open M-Sa 9am-9pm, Su 1-7pm.) The **post office** is 200m north of the northwest corner of the *parque* (open M-F 8am-noon and 1-5:30pm). **Postal Code:** 7150.

⌐ ACCOMMODATIONS. Although most of Turrialba's hotels are pricier, they usually offer much-missed comforts like hot water and soft beds. ◪**Hotel Interamericano ❶,** the yellow building 200m south of the southwest corner of the *parque*, has tons of info on sights, guides, and restaurants. Amenities include hot showers, breakfast (entrees US$3), luggage storage, laundry (¢1000 per kg), a large sitting area with English-language books and magazines, Internet, cable TV, and 24hr. reception. (☎556 0142; www.hotelinteramericano.com. Singles US$10, with bath US$20; doubles US$20/$30; triples US$30/$45; quads US$40/$60.) **Hotel Wagelia ❸,** 150m west of the southwest corner of the *parque*, is one of Turrialba's upscale hotels, boasting 18 comfortable rooms with private hot bath, cable TV, phone, and safe deposit box. Some rooms have A/C. A restaurant and bar is attached. Laundry and tour services are available. Breakfast is included. (☎556 1566; www.wagelia.com. Singles US$55; doubles US$69; triples US$76. Traveler's checks accepted. AmEx/MC/V.) **Costa Rica Rios Bed and Breakfast ❸** recently opened to house those on the week-long tour with Costa Rica Rios (see **Outdoor Activities and Guided Tours,** p. 158), but all guests are welcome. Ten airy rooms with private baths, parking, high-speed Internet, and 24hr. reception. Dinner and breakfast included. (☎556 9617 or 556 8482; www.costaricarios.com. Singles US$45; doubles US$60.)

◖ FOOD. Food in Turrialba is much less exciting than the town's raging rivers. It lacks exotic options, but has some excellent restaurants and basic *sodas*. **Restaurante Don Porfi ❷,** 4km outside of town on the road to Volcán Turrialba, is well worth the ¢1000 cab ride. Generous portions of gourmet-quality fare are served by candlelight. Excellent dishes include mixed seafood platters (¢2000-¢2500), beef tenderloin (6 varieties; ¢2800), and chicken in garlic sauce. (☎556 9797. Open M-Tu, Th-Su 11am-11pm. Reservations recommended. MC/V.) **La Feria ❶,** 200m east of the southeast corner of the *parque*, past Hotel Wagelia, has a charming setting—local artists' work decorates the walls, and soothing jazz plays in the background. Feria serves excellent *casados* (¢1000), club sandwiches (¢1450), and hamburgers. (☎556 0386. Open M and W-Su 11am-10pm, Tu 11am-2pm. AmEx/MC/V.) **Restaurante and Bar Garza ❷,** across from Supermercado Compromás at the northwest corner of the *parque*, serves *comida típica* that's far better than the average *sodas*. (*Casados* ¢1595, meat dishes ¢1000-¢3000, spaghetti ¢1650. Open daily 11am-11pm. AmEx/MC/V.)

COSTA RICA

⚠️📋 OUTDOOR ACTIVITIES AND GUIDED TOURS. Capitalizing on Turrialba's legendary rafting and kayaking opportunities, several tour operators offer adventure trips for all abilities. A day on the raging rapids is expensive, but the experience is unforgettable. If you have your own equipment or rent from one of the tour companies, Hotel Interamericano (see **Accommodations**, p. 157) will help arrange truck transport to nearby rivers. The hotel will also set you up with information about the nearby **serpent farm** (Serpentario Viborana; 10km away; ☎538 1510), **Volcán Turrialba,** and the **Aquiares waterfall. Costa Rica Rios,** 150m north of the northeast corner of the *parque*, is the most reputable rafting and kayaking operator. Although they specialize in pre-booked multi-day adventure and kayak trips, and all-inclusive week-long tours, several full-day and half-day options are available (kayaking US$80-$100, canyoning US$38-$105, rafting US$63-$150). Their newly opened B&B houses week-long tours. (☎556 9617 or 556 8482; www.costaricarios.com. AmEx/MC/V.) **Loco's** (☎556 6035 or 396 8079; riolocos@racsa.co.cr) prefers small groups, but will accommodate groups up to 36 with advance notice. These self-proclaimed Río Pacuare specialists offer rafting trips, horseback rides and boat tours. (Class III-IV rafting on the Pacuare and Reventazón half-day US$55, full day US$75-$100; full-day horseback tours along a jungle train line, US$55; Volcán Turrialba on horseback US$85; trip to Monumento Nacional Guayabo US$40.) **Tico's River Adventures** (☎556 1231 or 394 4479; www.ticoriver.com), a small local company, has years of experience. Specializing in rafting trips, Tico arranges daytrips to the Pacuare (Class IV), and Reventazón. 1-day trips US$75-$90, lunch included. Multi-day, all-inclusive trips also available.

◨ MONUMENTO NACIONAL GUAYABO. Located 19km northeast of Turrialba, the monument is Costa Rica's most important archaeological site and the country's only declared National Monument. The park covers 218 hectares, although the archaeological site is just 20 hectares, only four of which have been excavated. Much remains unknown about the civilization that built and eventually abandoned the site, though current estimates suggest that approximately 10,000 people lived here from 1500 BC to AD 1400. Some scientists say that the Guayabo people migrated to Colombia, and, in fact, many indigenous Colombians claim to have northern ancestors of similar traditions. The remnants of their cities, seen at the end of an easy 1.5km trail through rainforest are the focal point of the site, though you will pass a monolith, coffin graves, and several intricate petroglyphs on the way. Another 1km trail from the park entrance leads to a rushing stream with potable water. Both trails, especially the shorter one, are muddy in rainy season: be sure to bring boots and rain gear. As there are no official guided tours, it's worth asking the rangers for a quick briefing, or shelling out ¢100 for a pamphlet. The ruins are interesting, but there's not much else to see. Fast hikers who take the 11am bus from Turrialba and only hike the 1.5km trail may be able to make it back to the entrance in time to catch the 12:30pm bus back. There's a **campsite** at the monument (US$2 per person) that has a toilet, a cold-water shower, and barbecue pits. (Buses to the park entrance station leave from the local bus terminal in Turrialba at Av. 2, C. Central/2. 1¼hr.; M-Sa 11am, 3:15, 5:15pm, Su 9am; ¢175). There is one snag: buses return from Guayabo at 5:30, 6:30am, and 12:30pm only, so a same-day trip requires either a very quick visit to the ruins or a 4km walk downhill to the main paved road where buses pass more frequently (7am, noon, 1:30, 4pm). Alternatively, you can hire a cab to the monument (¢4000-¢4500) and take the 12:30pm bus back. Getting there is easier on Sunday and there is an extra return bus at 4pm. ☎559 1220. Open daily 8am-3:30pm. US$4, under 12 US$1.)

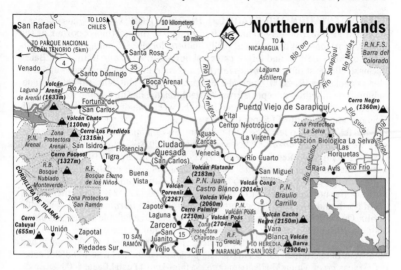

NORTHERN LOWLANDS

Visitors to Costa Rica's northern region are exposed to a wealth of natural attractions. Territories that were once dense tropical forests are now pasture land, and the abundance of *natilla* and *queso* signs testify to the fact that this is Costa Rica's cow country. Yet the region is the focus of some of the government's most ambitious conservation and reforestation efforts. Thrill-seekers will also find their interests well-accommodated among several extreme-sports meccas. Close to Nicaragua in geography and culture, the ranchers, fruit farmers, and country-style *sodas* of the northern lowlands continue to charm travelers away from the coasts.

CIUDAD QUESADA (SAN CARLOS)

Hovering amid the Cordillera Central's sloping green hills, Ciudad Quesada (more commonly and informally known as San Carlos) marks the fusion of the *campo tico* with everyday small city life. The agriculture and ranching center of the north, Ciudad Quesada pumps out much of the country's beef and milk. Northwest of San José (110km), the city is also a transportation hub within the Alajuela province.

⌨ TRANSPORTATION. The city's bus station (☎ 460 5064), referred to as *parada nueva* by locals, is 500m north of town. A shuttle bus leaves from the *mercado*, 100m north of the northeast corner of the *parque*, to the terminal (¢85)—a bus schedule is on the *mercado* wall directly across from the pickup zone. Here, catch **buses** to **La Fortuna** (1½hr., 12 per day 6am-8pm, ¢420); **Los Chiles** (3hr., 16 per day 4:30am-7:15pm, ¢955); **Pital** (1hr., 19 per day 5:30am-10:30pm, ¢275); **Puerto Viejo de Sarapiquí** (3hr.; 4:50, 6, 10am, 3, 5:30pm; ¢520); **San José** (3hr.; 12 per day M-Sa 5am-7:15pm, Su 6, 9:15, 10am, 4, 5, 5:30pm; ¢855); and **San Miguel** (1½hr.; 9:15am, 12:30, 1:30, 5:15, 8pm; ¢330). **Taxis** line up on the north side of the *parque*. **Adobe Rent-A-Car** is 275m north of the northeast corner of the *parque*. (☎ 460 0650. Open M-Sa 8am-8pm, Su 9am-noon.)

█▪ 🛈 ORIENTATION AND PRACTICAL INFORMATION. Ciudad Quesada has a standard grid layout—Av. 0 and C. 0 intersect at the northeast corner of the *parque central*—but none of that really matters; locals go by units of 100m (*cuadras*) up, down, right, and left. A **cathedral** borders the *parque* to the east. **Banco Nacional,** 50m east of the *parque*'s northeast corner, exchanges currency and traveler's checks. (☎461 2000. Open M-F 8:30am-3:45pm.) The 24hr. **ATM** at Cocique, behind the cathedral, accepts Cirrus. **Western Union,** sharing a complex with Restaurant Coca Loca and another bank, is on the west side of the *parque*. (Open M-F 8am-noon and 1-5pm.) **Super Granada** is opposite the northeast corner of the *parque* (☎760 0703; open M-Sa 7am-midnight, Su 7am-5pm) and several more markets are north of the *parque*. The **police station** (☎460 0375, emergency 911) is 1km east of the *parque*. **Red Cross** (☎460 0101) is 150m north and 100m west of the northwest corner of the *parque*. **Farmacia Lizano** is 200m north of the northeast corner of the *parque*. (☎460 2554. Open daily 8am-10pm.) The **hospital** is 3km north of the northeast corner of the *parque*. (☎460 1176. 24hr.) **Internet Café** is 100m north and 50m east of the northeast corner of the *parque*. (☎460 7454. ¢400 per hr. Open M-Sa 9am-8:30pm, Su 3-8pm.) Fax is also available at the **post office,** 300m north and 150m west of the northwest corner of the *parque* (open M-F 7:30am-6pm, Sa 7:30am-noon); **UPS** service is available at **Aeronort,** 300m north and 50m west of the northeast corner of the *parque*. (☎460 3711 or 460 3636; ecoservi@racsa.co.cr. Open M-F 8:30am-6pm, Sa 9am-1pm.) **Postal Code:** 4400.

🛏🍴 ACCOMMODATIONS AND FOOD. Costa Rica Treehouses Hotel ④ is a 45min. bus ride north of the town center toward Fortuna; ask the driver to let you off 100m north of Cementerio de Santa Clara. Three treehouses with two double beds, A/C, hot baths, and balconies with a 360 degree view are perched in 78 acres of forest canopy. Breakfast is included. (☎461 8451, cell 352 2044, US 239-278-5598; www.treehouseshotelcostarica.com. Treehouse US$50. MC/V.) **Hotel del Norte ❶,** 100m east and 150m north of the northeast corner of the *parque*, features rooms with fans and cable TV. (☎460 1959 or 460 1758. Singles ¢3000, with bath ¢4500; doubles with bath ¢6500. MC/V.) **Hotel Central & Casino ❷,** on the west side of the *parque*, hosts many businesspeople. Reserve rooms (with cable TV, fan, phone, and private bath) one to two weeks in advance in the high season. (☎460 0301; hcentral@racsa.co.cr. Singles ¢6000; doubles ¢10,000.) *Lomito* is what's for dinner in Ciudad Quesada. Even the humblest *soda* serves high-quality beef, and most of the restaurants around the *parque* can marinate a steak to perfection. **La Terraza ❷,** 250m north of the northeast corner of the *parque*, serves what is considered the best steak in town. Its terrace with a vista of cloud-enshrouded mountains will go well with your *corvina tartará* (sea bass tartar; ¢1700) or fettuccine alfredo. (☎460 5287. Open daily 11am-midnight. MC/V.) **Restaurant Coca Loca ❸** faces the west side of the *parque*. Its swinging saloon doors set you up for a thick filet mignon (¢2800) or T-bone steak. (☎460 3208. Open daily 11am-11pm. MC/V.) When nostalgia for cheap fast-food calls, head to **Charlie's Burger ❶,** next to Restaurante Cristal. (☎460 2454. Delivery available. Open daily 7:30am-11pm.)

🖽 SIGHTS. El Zoológico la Marina is an impressive zoo and park where jaguars, elastic-nosed tapirs, toucans, crocodiles, and spider monkeys are rehabilitated. La Marina is low-key and frequented mainly by locals, although Mr. Rojas welcomes volunteers. Take any bus (35min., ¢130) heading north from the terminal toward Puerto Viejo, Pital, Venecia, or Río Frío and ask to be let out at the Zoológico La Marina. (☎474 2100. Open daily 8am-4pm. US$5, children US$3.)

COSTA RICA

The volcanic activity in the area around Ciudad Quesada has created several natural hot-water thermal pools. **El Tucano Resort and Thermal Spa**, 2km south of La Marina, offers the most luxurious experience. For ¢5000 you can access the resort's pool, sauna, and three thermal-water jacuzzis, with a ¢2500 credit toward the hotel's restaurant. (☎ 460 6000. Open daily 8am-6pm.) Near El Tucano is **El Tucanito**, a roadside *soda* with the cheapest access to the hottest pool in the area. (☎ 366 3038. *Soda* open 8am-11pm. Pool open 8am-4pm; ¢800, children ¢300.)

PUERTO VIEJO DE SARAPIQUÍ

Though most travelers pass through Puerto Viejo de Sarapiquí en route to Volcán Arenal, an increasing number of nature enthusiasts are lingering to take advantage of some of Costa Rica's most densely concentrated wildlife diversity.

TRANSPORTATION. All **buses** leave from the station opposite the northwest corner of the soccer field. A schedule is posted inside at the ticket counter. Buses go to: **Ciudad Quesada (San Carlos)** (2½hr.; 5:30, 9:15am, 12:15, 2, 3:30pm); **Guápiles** (1hr.; 5:30, 7:10, 9:10am, 12:10, 2:30, 4:10, 6:40pm; ¢485); **Río Frío** (1hr.; 6:45, 9, 11am, 1, 3, 5, 6pm; ¢295); **San José** via **El Tunel Zurquí** (2hr.; 5:30, 7, 8, 11am, 1:30, 3, 5:30, 6:40pm; ¢1020); **San José** via **Vara Blanca** (50min.; 5, 7:30, 11:30am, 4:30pm; ¢1020); **San Julian** (1½hr.; 10:30am, 12:30, 4:30, 6:30pm; ¢390) via **Oropel** (75min., ¢330); and **San La Colonía** (1hr.; 8:30, 10am, 12:45, 2:30, 4:30, 6:30pm; ¢270). Buses also stop at **Bajo de Chillamate** and **La Virgen**. **Taxis** line up along the main street just north of the soccer field. A taxi to La Virgen costs about ¢2700.

ORIENTATION AND PRACTICAL INFORMATION. Puerto Viejo extends along one main street. A **soccer field** marks the town center. The **bus station** is opposite a **church** on the soccer field's northwest side. Less than 1km west of town, the main road forks south toward Guápiles and the entrance to Estación Biológica La Selva and southwest toward the entrances of the Centro Neotrópico Sarapiquí and the Serpentario. Another 100m down the main road, a second small road to the right leads to a few hostels and the **port** along the Río Sarapiquí.

For the most comprehensive **tourist information,** talk to Alex Martínez, owner of **Andrea Cristina B&B** (see **Accommodations,** p. 161). Alex can tell you everything you need to know about regional ecological issues and activities. Closer to town, Luis Alberto offers info and tours at **Souvenirs Río Sarapiquí,** 100m east of the soccer field. (☎ 766 6727. Rafting US$45, river tours US$15 per hr. Open M-F 8:15am-6pm, Sa-Su 8:15am-6pm.) Exchange traveler's checks and US dollars at **Banco Nacional,** at the intersection of the main road and the road to the port. (☎ 766 6012. 24hr. ATM. Open M-F 8:30am-3:45pm.) The **police** station (☎ 766 6575, emergencies 911) is down the first small road off the main road, next to the post office. The **hospital** (☎ 766 6212) is 250m west of the soccer field on the left, and **Farmacia Alfa** is 1 block east of the soccer field on the left. (☎ 766 6348. Open M-Sa 7am-8pm.) **Sarapiquí Internet** is 300m west of the soccer field, just past the hospital. (¢300 per 30min., ¢500 per hr. Open daily 8am-10pm.) The **post office** is across from Banco Nacional at the port turn-off (open M-F 7:30am-6pm). **Postal Code:** 3069.

ACCOMMODATIONS AND FOOD. Many travelers who come through Puerto Viejo stay at upscale nature lodges a few kilometers outside the village, but the town center offers a relatively good selection of budget options. **Mi Lindo Sarapiquí ❷,** west of the soccer field and opposite the bus station, has cabin-like rooms with hot baths, fans, and TV. Laundry is available. (☎/fax 766 6074. Singles ¢5800; doubles ¢9000; triples ¢10,000. MC/V.) **Andrea Cristina B&B ❸** is 1km west of the town center. Walk west for 500m until you reach the fork, turn right, and walk another 0.5km; the B&B is to your right. Six cabins with hot showers and fans. Breakfast is included. (☎766 6265; www.andreacristina.com. Singles US$20/¢8700; doubles $US40. Camping US$5 per person. AmEx/V.) Puerto Viejo doesn't offer much in terms of dining variety; *sodas* line the main and side-streets. **Restaurante La Terraza ❶**, 100m east of the soccer field, is a two-story *soda* with big *casados* and low prices (¢1000-¢1500); after 9pm on weekends its blaring speakers lure locals for drinks. (Open 8am-11pm. MC/V.) **Restaurante Mi Lindo Sarapiquí ❸**, attached to the hotel of the same name, provides an upscale menu that includes rice dishes (¢1150-¢1500), pastas (¢1600-¢2400), and seafood. (Open daily 9am-10pm. MC/V.)

▶ **DAYTRIPS FROM PUERTO VIEJO.** Founded in 2000 by Wisconsin-based Tirimbina Rainforest Center, the non-profit ■**Centro Neotrópico Sarapiquí** is a preserve dedicated to cultural, biological, and ecological awareness. Unlike other Costa Rican national parks, it is accessible to visitors of all ages and abilities. The gem of the center is the 350-hectare **Tirimbina Rainforest Preserve.** A number of easy trails wind through beautiful forests laced with suspension bridges. **El Puente Colgante,** the largest pedestrian suspension bridge in Costa Rica, stretches 262m across the rushing Río Sarapiquí, while the smaller **El Puente Del Dosel** hovers above the dense rainforest canopy. A spiral staircase descending from El Puente Colgante leads to a small island formed by Río Sarapiquí. A few trails cross the island and clear natural pools on the island's edge are ideal for swimming. Otters and kingfishers are often spotted on the riverbanks. Both day and night tours are available; morning tours are better for bird-watching, while night tours often include bat, armadillo, and kinkajou sightings.

The on-site **ecolodge,** restaurant, and bar overlook the reserve and follow the *palenque* architectural style of indigenous peoples. The center runs an extensive **education program** for over 2000 local children with hundreds of foreign volunteers, teachers, and ecologists. Student and volunteer lodgings are also provided on the center grounds. **Volunteer opportunities** are most frequently offered to groups of students, but individual opportunities can be arranged. All profits are reinvested in conservation efforts, education, and scientific research. (☎ *761 1004; www.sarapiquis.org. Open daily 7am-5pm. Take a bus to La Virgen; ask the driver to let you off at the entrance to Centro Neotrópico Sarapiquí or take a taxi ¢2700. Tours 8am, 2, 7:30pm. US$15 per person; minimum 5 people. Students US$10, ages 6-16 US$6. Reservations for tours strongly recommended. Self-guided tours US$10, students and children US$8. No entry fee for the botanical garden.)*

The **Río Sarapiquí,** flowing calmly alongside Puerto Viejo's eastern boundary, continues north for 40km before meeting the Río San Juan, which forms the border between Costa Rica and Nicaragua. Flanked on one side by dense forest and on the other by banana plantations, the "river with two personalities" highlights an ongoing battle between the conservationists who want to protect the rainforest and the farmers who need to use the land commercially. Most tours of the Sarapiquí consist of 2-3hr. rides in slow-moving boats. Guides stop periodically to observe the diverse river-dwelling wildlife; frequent sightings include alligators, crocodiles, turtles, howler monkeys, and a vast range of birds. Catch an early morning tour for the best chance to see wildlife. Boatmen also offer day and overnight trips up to and along the Río San Juan (which is technically Nicaraguan territory), as well as to Oro Verde, Tortuguero, Barra del Colorado, and other locations along the river. Ask the boatmen at the port for more information or inquire at any of the tour providers mentioned above. Guided tours offered by Alex Martínez (☎766 6265; 2-6 people US$150 per day), Souvenirs Río Sarapiquí, and Oasis Tours. See **Practical Information,** p. 161).

LA FORTUNA

La Fortuna is a gateway to Volcán Arenal, which awoke from its 450-year dormancy in 1968 and has been spewing lava and boulders since, gradually growing above the small town of La Fortuna. The area offers diverse wilderness exploration options including hot springs at the base, rainforest, and waterfalls.

TRANSPORTATION. The main street into La Fortuna runs east-west; along its north side is the *parque central.* The church sits on the field's west side. La Fortuna doesn't have a **bus** terminal, but departure times are posted on a billboard on the north side of the *parque;* on the south side, buses pick up passengers and head to: **Ciudad Quesada** and **San Carlos** (1½hr., 10 per day 5am-5:30pm, ¢420); **San José** (4½hr.; 12:45, 2:45pm; ¢1120); and **Tilarán** (3hr.; 8am, 5:30pm; ¢1050) via **Arenal** (2hr., ¢870). On the north side of the field, buses depart for **San Ramón** (2½hr.; 5:30, 9am, 1, 4pm; ¢495), to transfer to a direct bus to San José (45min., ¢220). **Taxis** line up on the east side of the *parque.* Two **car rental** companies offer similar services, vehicles and rates. **Alamo** is behind the church on the main drag (☎/fax 479 9090; open daily 7:30am-6pm); **Poas Rent-A-Car** is 1 block north. (☎479 8027; www.carentals.com. Open daily 6am-10pm.)

PRACTICAL INFORMATION. Banco Popular, on the main drag 2 blocks east of the *parque,* has currency exchange and a 24hr. **ATM.** (☎479 9422. Open M-F 8:30am-3:30pm, Sa 8:15-11:45am.) **Banco Nacional** is 1 block east of the northeast corner of the *parque.* (☎479 9355. Open M-F 8:30am-3:45pm.) **Western Union** is at **Grupo Coocique,** 100m east and 75m south of the southeast corner of the *parque.* (☎479 9121. Open M-Sa 7am-5pm, Su 8am-noon.) The **Super Christian** supermarket is across from the southeast corner of the *parque* (open M-Sa 7am-10pm, Su 8am-noon). The **police** station is 1½ blocks east of the *parque.* (☎479 9689, emergency 911. Open 24hr.) **Farmacia Catedral** is 25m east of the southeast corner of the field. (☎479 9518. Open M-Sa 8am-9pm, Su 8am-7pm.) The **medical clinic** is 100m east and 50m north of the northeast corner of the *parque.* (☎479 9142. Open M-F 7am-4pm, 4-10pm for emergencies; Sa-Su and holidays 8am-8pm.) You can make international **phone calls** at **Sunset Tours** and **Pura Vida Tours,** both on the southeast corner of the *parque* (open daily 7:30am-10pm). Get fast **Internet** at **Expediciones Fortuna,** on the southeast corner of the *parque.* (☎479 9101. ¢600 per hr. Open daily 8am-9pm.) The **post office** is opposite the north side of the church. (Fax available. Open M-F 8am-noon and 1-4:30pm, Sa 8am-noon.) **Postal Code:** 4417.

ACCOMMODATIONS AND FOOD. The most expensive resorts lie a few kilometers west of La Fortuna. In the town center, fierce competition ensures a wide selection of reasonably priced lodgings. Though most feel that the town is safe, women traveling alone should bear in mind that certain sections along the river are poorly lit at night. **Cabinas Sissy ❷,** 100m south and 200m west of the southwest corner of the *parque,* facing the Río Burío, has six rooms with hot bath, free laundry, kitchen, and volcano view. (☎479 9256. Singles US$12; doubles US$12-$20. Camping in backyard US$3.) **La Posada Inn ❶,** 300m east of the *parque* on the main street, is a backpacker magnet. Rooms come with communal hot showers, fans, and a kitchen. The front porch is open for lounging. (☎479 9793. Internet ¢500 per hr. Rooms US$5/¢2175 per person. Camping ¢800 per person.) **Soda la Casa de Ara ❶,** 100m south and 150m east of the southeast corner of the *parque,* delights locals and tourists with delicious *comida típica* and value buffet. (Buffet ¢150-¢700 per item. Open daily 6am-10pm.) **Java Jungle ❶,** 50m south of the southwest corner of the *parque,* serves a breakfast popular among backpackers. (☎479 8142. Open M-Sa 7am-9 or 10pm, Su 7am-noon.) **Lava Rocks ❷,** on the southwest corner of the *parque*, is also good for breakfast (fruit pancakes ¢890) and delicious fish plates like grilled Chilean sea bass, come dinner time. (☎479 8039. Open daily 7am-10pm. MC/V.)

⚑ OUTDOOR ACTIVITIES. Tour operators in La Fortuna offer a bewildering variety of activities including hiking, kayaking, bird-watching, rappeling, ziplining, canoeing, spelunking, windsurfing, horseback, and more. Everyone offers basically the same set of options with small, confusing variations. Whatever you choose to do, avoid individuals who approach you on the street. Reputable operators include: **Jacamar Tours** (☎479 9767 or 479 9768; www.arenaltours.com); **Sunset Tours** (☎479 9800; www.sunsettourcr.com); **Aventuras Arenal** (☎479 9133; www.arenaladventures.com); **Eagle Tours;** and **Pura Vida Tours** (☎479 9045; www.puravidatrips.com).

◪ DAYTRIPS FROM LA FORTUNA

Created in 1994, **Parque Nacional Volcán Arenal** covers 12,016 hectares, including the towns of Tilarán, San Carlos, and San Ramón. The **Ranger Station** is 17km west of La Fortuna. Just beyond the station is a lava and volcano **lookout point.** The park has three short, pleasant trails. Since the 1968 eruption, plants have sprung up along **Sendero Las Heliconias** (1km). **Sendero Las Coladas** (2.8km) crosses the 1993 lava flow trail. **Sendero Los Tucanes** (1km) runs through thick primary forest and delivers a stellar view of the volcano, Cerro Chato, and the Arenal Dam. Hikers are forbidden to stray from the trail. The road west of La Fortuna has good but distant views of the volcano; one of the best is from **Montaña del Fuego Inn,** 9km from town (round-trip taxi ¢3000). Be warned that climbing the volcano is dangerous and strongly discouraged. *(The station is accessible by bike, car, or taxi (US$6-$7), but it's easier to take one of the guided tours: Sunset Tours, US$27. 2½hr. walking tour through lava trails and secondary forest leaves La Fortuna at 8am and 3pm. Station open daily 8am-4pm. Park admission US$6.)*

Just 5.5km outside of the town center, **Río Fortuna** tumbles down through 70m of rainforest canopy, forming **La Catarata Fortuna.** After a 20min. walk down the rocky trail, you come across the waterfall basin and a separate runoff area that's safe for bathing. The sign advising against swimming may seem mild, but bathing in the waterfall basin is extremely dangerous: the outward-flowing surface waters conceal a powerful undertow that is impossible to swim against, and there are no lifeguards. Guided **horseback tours** are also available through Pura Vida Tours (US$25). From the parking lot, there is a trail to **Cerro Chato,** the dormant sidekick of Volcán Arenal that has an impressive crater lake at the top. The climb takes about 2½hr. one-way. *(Head south from the west side of the church. After 1km, a dirt road branches off to the right. After a 1½-2hr. uphill walk, you hit the waterfall parking lot. Taxis go as far as the parking lot, ¢2000. Follow the trail to the falls. US$6.)*

The famous **hot springs** of **Tabacón,** 12km west of La Fortuna, actually come from a single river of hot water. The **Tabacón Resort** has 10 hot and cool swimming pools, including one with a swim-up bar, a pricey restaurant, great views of the volcano, and a man-made waterfall cascading over rocks. **Las Fuentes Termales,** diagonally across from Tabacón, is a slightly cheaper extension of the resort's hot springs, with a larger local clientele. There are also several unattended springs along the road. Continue past the resort for a few hundred meters and look for the trails—there are no signs. Hot springs at **Baldi Termae,** 4km west of town, are closer and, like Tabacón, feature a swim-up bar in the middle of one pool. *(Buses to Tilarán from La Fortuna 8am and 5pm. Alternatively, bike or take a taxi, ¢2500 each way. Tabacón Resort*

☎ 256 1500; www.tabacon.com. Open daily 10am-10pm. US$29. Las Fuentes Termales ☎ 460 8050. Open M-F 10am-9pm, Sa-Su 8am-9pm. US$9. Baldi Termae ☎ 479 9652. US$12 with dinner US$17. Open daily 10am-10pm.)

In the *cantón* of San Carlos de Guatuso, in a *pueblo* named La Tigre, are the relatively unknown but spectacular **Venado Caves.** The caves were discovered in 1942 by two hunters chasing a *tepescuintle* (pig-like animal). Guides take you in to discover 10 galleries full of stalactites, stalagmites, *columnas* (called papayas for their resemblance to the fruit), waterways, and fossils. If you visit during the summer, gallery Boca de la Serpiente receives a magical stream of light from 11am to 1pm, but beware of bats. During the rainy season, an 18m waterfall from Río de La Muerte awaits you halfway through the 1½hr. tour. These caves are not ideal for claustrophobes, nor for those who have just eaten lunch—the passageways get very narrow. You'll be wading waist-deep through bat guano, so bring a change of clothing to slip into after your cold shower by the parking lot. Try also to avoid wearing glasses, which fog up underground and could be damaged. A waterproof camera is best for pictures. *(Buses leave Ciudad Quesada and San Carlos at 7am and 2:25pm, 3hr., ¢550. Caves are 2.5km from the bus drop-off. Alternatively, set up a tour with an operator in La Fortuna. For more info contact cave manager Yoleni Cuero, pager ☎ 296 2626 #900566. Spanish tour ¢3000. Fee includes equipment and on-site showers.)*

REFUGIO NACIONAL CAÑO NEGRO

Where there's water, there's life, and Refugio Caño Negro has plenty of both. The refuge gets 3.5m of rain every year, and 85% of its land (100 sq. km) is flooded from May to December. The Laguna Caño Negro refills every May when the banks of the Río Frío and Río Caño Negro overflow. This swampy labyrinth harbors one of the most important wildlife shelters in the country, with over 315 types of birds and 160 species of mammals. For most of the year guided boat tours are the only way to visit the refuge, but between February and April you can hike in over the dried-up lake, although there are no official trails. (Park open daily 7am-4pm. US$6.)

E TRANSPORTATION. By **car,** the shortest route to Caño Negro from **San José** is to head north on the road toward Los Chiles. The entrance to the Refugio is 1km after the Tanques Gas Zeta (19km before Los Chiles), followed by 12km of bumpy unpaved roads (approximately 4hr.). Despite the poor road condition, public **buses** do pass by Caño Negro on a circuit between Upala and Los Chiles; always ask and make sure you're on the right bus. Buses go from **Los Chiles** to **Upala** via **Caño Negro** (1½hr.; daily 5am, 2pm, extra departure M 10am; ¢500) and from Upala to Los Chiles via Caño Negro (2hr.; 5am, 4pm; ¢600). Wait for the bus on the northwest side of the *parque* or in front of the hotels on the town's main entrance road.

▟◪ ORIENTATION AND PRACTICAL INFORMATION. The bus stops at the northwest corner of the *parque.* There you'll find a **mini-super** (☎ 461 8466; open M-Sa 7am-8pm, Su 7am-noon) next to the church. The **refuge entrance,** under the RAMSAR sign, is on the southeast corner of the *parque.* The **MINAE** office, 200m west of the mini-super, provides **tourist information.** (☎/fax 471 1309. Open M-F 8am-4pm, Sa-Su 8am-9am.) Another info booth is in front of Albergue Caño Negro, 200m north of the northwest corner of the *parque* (open daily). There is no bank and the nearest medical facility is the **Red Cross** in Los Chiles (☎ 471 1061). A **health center** is on the northwest side of the *parque.* (☎ 471 1531. Open daily 7am-4pm.) The **police station** is on the southeast side of the *parque,* and can be reached by radio in an emergency, with the help of local businesses, MINAE, or the tourist info booth. The town has several **public telephones** at the mini-super, across from the information booth, and 100m west of the church. (☎ 461 8442. ¢10 per min.)

◢◖ ACCOMMODATIONS AND FOOD. Albergue Caño Negro ❶, 200m north of the northwest corner of the *parque*, sits on a field that directly borders the Laguna Caño Negro, with charming cabins on stilts. Cabins have fans and outdoor grills. (☎/fax 471 1438. US$7per person; camping US$5 per person.) **Cabinas Martín Pescador ❷** is 100m past the MINAE office in the field at the end of the road. Check in at reception 100m north and 50m east of the park's northwest corner. Rooms have fans and covered porches. (☎471 1369; ☎/fax 471 1116. US$10 per person.) It is possible to **camp ❶** on the grounds of the Caño Negro MINAE office, with access to cold showers (¢300 per person). There are not many places to eat in Caño Negro, but **Sodita la Palmera ❶**, on the southeast corner of the *parque*, will satisfy almost any appetite. (☎471 1045. *Gallo pinto* ¢600; entrees ¢800-¢1000. Open daily 7am-8pm.) **Salón, Bar, and Restaurante Danubio Azul ❷**, on the southeast side of the *parque*, has a breezy eating area that turns into a discotheque from Monday to Wednesday. The house specialty is guapote fish (¢1500-¢2000). Meals start at ¢400. (☎471 1295. Open daily 10am-2:30am.)

◤ VISITING THE REFUGE. The park is best seen by boat, though it is possible to hike. If hiking in the Refugio, bring sunblock and insect repellent; wear pants and rubber boots or sturdy waterproof hiking shoes—biting ants await, along with 10 of Costa Rica's 17 species of venomous snakes. **Colibrí Tours,** run by Dolores and Julia, organizes trips to the refuge. (☎471 1501. 2½hr. tours for 5 people US$45; US$40 for individuals or smaller groups.) Antonio at **Cabinas Martín Pescador** takes people out on his canopied *lancha*. (2hr., 1-4 people US$40. US$10 per extra person.) Jesús at **Albergue Caño Negro** also leads tours. (2hr., 1-2 people US$40; 3 or more US$50; combined canoeing and hiking tours can also be arranged.) Both Jesús and Colibrí Tours offer **fishing** tours (8hr.; 1-3 people; US$120 per person). Serious fishermen should bring their own gear. Other hotels, including **Cabinas Martín Pescador** (3hr., US$20 per hr.) and **Natural Lodge Caño Negro** (2½hr., US$30 per person; horses US$10 per hr.), also offer tour services. Larger tour operations run out of La Fortuna and Los Chiles.

Prices for wildlife and fishing trips do not include park entrance (US$6) or fishing license (US$30). You can pay the fee to the ranger in the kiosk at the refuge entrance, on the southeast corner of the *parque*. Fishing is prohibited April through August. Call the Area de Conservación Huetar Norte in Upala with any questions (☎471 1309).

NORTHWESTERN COSTA RICA

The two mountain chains that stretch across northwestern Costa Rica guard some of the country's most famous attractions. The world-renowned Monteverde Reserve protects what remains of the cloud forests that once covered all of the Cordillera de Tilarán, while the Cordillera de Guanacaste holds three spectacular national parks further north. Volcán Arenal, Central America's most active volcano, bubbles magma at a cratered peak nestled between these two majestic ranges. Though the arid lowlands of Guanacaste cannot offer comparable natural splendor, they have a *sabanero* (cowboy) charm all their own.

MONTEVERDE AND SANTA ELENA

The Monteverde region, located 184km northwest of San José and due north of Puntarenas, is the main reason that many travelers come to Costa Rica in the first place. Private reserves in the area, including the famous Monteverde Cloud Forest **Reserve,** protect some of the country's last remaining primary cloud forest, provid-

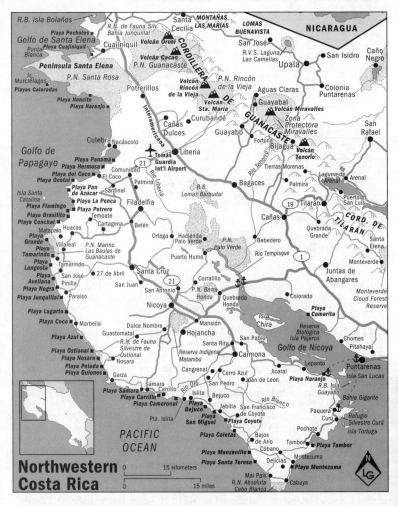

Northwestern Costa Rica

R.B. Isla Bolaños
R.N. de Fauna Silv.
Bahía Junquillal
Golfo de Santa Elena
Playa Pochotes
Punta Blanca
Playa Cuajiniquil
Cuajiniquil
Santa Cecilia
MONTAÑAS LAS MARÍAS
LOMAS BUENAVISTA
San José
NICARAGUA
Volcán Orosí
Peninsula Santa Elena
Volcán Cacao
P.N. Guanacaste
CORDILLERA
R.V.S. Laguna Las Camelias
Upala
San Isidro
Caño Negro
Is. Murciélagos
Playas Coloradas
P.N. Santa Rosa
Potrerillos
Volcán Rincón de la Vieja
P.N. Rincón de la Vieja
Aguas Claras
Colonia Puntarenas
Playa Nancite
Playa Naranjo
Curubandé
Volcán Sta. María
Volcán Miravalles
Guayabal
San Rafael
Cañas Dulces
Guayabo
Zona Protectora Miravalles
Golfo de Papagayo
Culebra
Nacáscolo
Liberia
Fortuna
Bijagua
Volcán Tenorio
Playa Panamá
Playa Hermosa
Playa del Coco
Playa Ocotal
Comunidad
El Coco
Tomás Guardia Int'l Airport
21
Palmira
Río Tenorio
Tierras Morenas
Isla Santa Catalina
Playa Pan de Azúcar
Sardinal
Palmira
Bagaces
Playa La Penca
Playa Potrero
Filadelfia
Tempate
R.B. Lomas Barbudal
Palmira
Laguna de Arenal
Arenal
Playa Flamingo
Playa Brasilito
Playa Conchal
Cartagena
Belén
Cañas
19
Tilarán
Puerto San Luis
CORD. DE TILARÁN
Matapalo
Huacas
Ortega
Hacienda Palo Verde
P.N. Palo Verde
Quebrada Grande
Santa Elena
Playa Grande
Villareal
P.N. Marino Las Baulas de Guanacaste
Puerto Humo
Río Tempisque
Monteverde
Playa Tamarindo
Tamarindo
Santa Cruz
21
Corralillo
1
Juntas de Abangares
Playa Langosta
San José
27 de Abril
Pinilla
San Juan
San Antonio
Quebrada Honda
P.N. Barra Honda
Colorado
Monteverde Cloud Forest Reserve
Playa Avellana
Playa Negra
Paraiso
Nicoya
Isla Chira
Playa Camarita
Playa Junquillal
Playa Lagarto
Playa Coco
Marbella
Dulce Nombre
Guastomatal
Mansión
Hojancha
San Pablo
Santa Rita
Reserva Biológica Isla Pájaros
Golfo de Nicoya
Chomes
Pitahaya
Playa Azul
R.N. de Fauna Silvestre de Ostional
Nosara
Reserva Indígena Matambú
Carmona
Puntarenas
Playa Ostional
Playa Nosara
Cangrenal
Cerro Azul
Jicaral
Juan de Leon
Playa Naranjo
Isla San Lucas
Playa Pelada
Playa Gulones
Garza
Sámara
Carrillo
San Pedro
Bejuco
Río Blanco
R.B. Isla Guayabo
Bahía Gigante
Playa Sámara
Playa Carrillo
Playa Camaronal
Islita
Jabilla
San Francisco de Coyote
Paquera
Curú
Refugio Silvestre Curú
Isla Tortuga
Pta. Islita
Playa Bejuco
Playa San Miguel
Playa Coyote
Playa Caletas
Bajos de Ario
Cóbano
Pochote
Tambor
Playa Tambor
PACIFIC OCEAN
Playa Manzanillo
Playa Santa Teresa
Delicias
Montezuma
Playa Montezuma
Mal País
R.N. Absoluta Cabo Blanco
Cabuya

0   15 kilometers
0   15 miles

ing refuge for elusive quetzals in the trees, foraging coatis on the ground, and a host of other creatures in-between. The town of Monteverde was founded in 1951 when a group of US Quakers moved to the region and used existent oxcart trails to bring in cows and start up a successful cheese business. Santa Elena, a nearby town full of tourist facilities and practical amenities, is connected to Monteverde by a dirt road.

TRANSPORTATION. Direct **buses** to **Santa Elena** and **Monteverde** run from **Puntarenas, San José,** and **Tilarán.** From **Liberia,** you can take a San José-bound bus as far as **Lagarto,** and take a bus to Monteverde from there (9:30am, 3, 5pm; ₡1750). All buses make a stop in Santa Elena and many continue along the road through Monteverde until the cheese factory, 2.5km from the reserve. Leaving Monteverde, buses head to: Puntarenas (3½hr., 6am, ₡880); San José (4½hr.; 6:30am, 2:30pm;

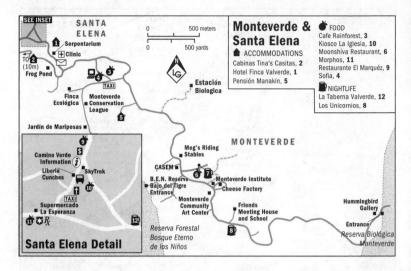

Monteverde & Santa Elena

🔥 FOOD
Cafe Rainforest, **3**
Kiosco La Iglesia, **10**
Moonshiva Restaurant, **6**
Morphos, **11**
Restaurante El Marquéz, **9**
Sofia, **4**

🏠 ACCOMMODATIONS
Cabinas Tina's Casitas, **2**
Hotel Finca Valverde, **1**
Pensión Manakín, **5**

🍸 NIGHTLIFE
La Taberna Valverde, **12**
Los Unicornios, **8**

¢1675); **Tilarán** (3hr., 7am, ¢620). Purchase tickets on the bus. Buy return tickets from Monteverde in advance at the Marza Transport ticket office half a block south of Banco Nacional in Santa Elena. (☎645 5159. Open daily 5:30am-5pm.)

■★🛈 ORIENTATION AND PRACTICAL INFORMATION. Arriving buses stop in the town of Santa Elena, which has most of the affordable local services, hotels, and restaurants. From here, an unpaved road heads 6km southeast to the Monteverde Reserve. The actual settlement of **Monteverde** is strung along this road, with more expensive restaurants and hotels. Unless otherwise noted, the following services are in Santa Elena: **Camino Verde Information Center** (☎645 5916 or 645 6296) is across from the bus stop. **Camara de Turismo** (☎645 6565) is at the end of street across from Supermercado la Esperanza. Both book reservations to the Santa Elena reserve, nearby canopy tours, ATV rides, and more (open daily 6am-9pm). Those searching for tour companies will find no shortage along the main street, though it's worth shopping around because commissions vary widely. **Banco Nacional,** northwest of the bus stop, changes traveler's checks and US dollars and gives Visa cash advances (open M-F 8:30am-3:45pm). The **Western Union** is next to the post office and **Supermercado La Esperanza** is on the corner at the south end of the road from Banco Nacional (☎645 5331; open daily 6am-8pm). **Librería Chunches,** a half block southwest from Banco Nacional, sells US newspapers and magazines, books, and music, a great source of local info and coffee. (☎645 5147. Open M-Sa 8am-7pm, Su noon-6pm.) Most hotels offer laundry services, and even more options line the main road. Available at **Librería Chunches,** ¢2000 per load. Call the **Red Cross** for emergencies (☎128 or 645 6128). The **police** are at the south end of the road from Banco Nacional. (☎645 5127, emergency 117. Open 24hr.) **Vitosi Pharmacy** is next to the police station. (☎645 5004. Open daily 8am-8pm.) **Clínica Monteverde** is 50m west and 150m south of the sports field. (☎645 5076. Open M-F 7am-4pm, Sa-Su 7am-7pm.) **Internet** access is available at **Pura Vida Internet** across the street from Banco Nacional (US$3.20 per hr.), or for a cheaper price at a place next to La Taberna (¢600 per hr.). The **post office** is up the first hill on the way to Monteverde, beyond the Serpentarium. (¢100 per page. Fax available. Open M-F 8am-noon and 1-4:30pm, Sa 7:30am-noon.) **Postal Code:** 5655.

⚑ ACCOMMODATIONS. Pricey hotels line the road to Monteverde, while most budget places are in or near Santa Elena. **◪Cabinas Tina's Casitas ❶** is located down the hill from the police station, with charming bungalows that feature beds made of branches. Laundry services can be arranged (¢1500) and an outdoor kitchen is available for guest use. (☎ 645 6321; tinas_casitas@hotmail.com. Singles US$7, with bath US$10.) **◪Pensión Manakín ❶**, about 1km from Santa Elena toward the Monteverde Reserve, is owned by locals Mario and Yolanda who provide town gossip and healthful veggie meals; breakfast is included. (☎ 645 5080; www.manakinlodge.com. Rooms US$12 per person, with bath US$15; cabin with kitchen and refrigerator US$50 per person. AmEx/MC/V.) **Hotel Finca Valverde ❹** is just down the road from Santa Elena's center, but it's quiet enough to hear the birds sing. Take a small bridge over the creek to this oasis, where spacious rooms offer views of a nearby coffee plantation. (☎ 645 5157; info@monteverde.co.cr. Singles US$35, high season US$46; doubles US$52/$64; triples US$64/$75.)

⬚ FOOD. In Santa Elena, check out **◪Kiosco La Iglesia ❶**, next to the church on the main street, where the menu is simple and includes classics like *casados* (¢1350). Portions are generous and come cheaper than anything else in town. (Open daily 6am to around 8pm.) **Restaurante El Marquéz ❷**, located near the info center, serves specials like heart-of-palm fish (¢2200) in an interior decorated with fishing nets and ocean murals. (☎ 645-5918. Open daily noon-11pm. MC/V.) **Morphos ❷**, across the street from the supermarket in Santa Elena, is popular with tourists indulging in subs and burgers (¢1600) to get away from rice and beans. (Open daily 11:00am-9:30pm. MC/V.)

Monteverde's dining options are generally more expensive, and cater to tourist tastes. **◪Sofia ❸** is a classy restaurant serving elaborate *nuevo latina* concoctions like plantain-encrusted sea bass (US$7.50) and chicken with guava compote. (☎ 645 7017. Open daily 11:30am-9:30pm. MC/V.) **MoonShiva Restaurant ❸** is a mellow jungle enclave dishing out international dishes like falafel (¢1850) in a secluded forest locale. The tables are moved aside for dancing and movie nights. (☎ 645 6270; moonshiva@racsa.co.cr. Open M-Sa 10am-10pm.) **Cafe Rainforest ❶** is a funky eatery that serves Monteverde coffee (¢500) and banana bread with coconut frosting (¢300) under a roof made from coffee bags. (Open daily 6am-8pm.)

⬚ NIGHTLIFE. Monteverde's greatest assets aren't nocturnal, and its nightlife scene is fairly minimal. A few small-scale clubs host modest crowds where *ticos* and American tourists engage in awkward courtship rituals. **La Taberna Valverde**, located 300m from Banco Nacional on the road to the Reserve, is a small club that displays artfully disarrayed party debris—broken bottles, credit cards—and a sign on the wall reads: "Don't enter the heart of a woman like a tourist." (☎ 645 5825. Open daily 11am-1am.) **MoonShiva Restaurant** is a hybrid restaurant, bar, cinema, and hippie den. Movies are shown at 8pm on Monday and Wednesday nights; selections range from Latin American melodrama to American kitsch. Friday nights bring DJs from San José and Saturdays feature live music for a laid-back crowd decked out in sandals with *mojitos* in hand (¢1100). People usually show up around 8pm. **Los Unicornios** is on the road towards the Santa Elena Reserve and across the street from the local school. This simple one-room bar hosts a fairly local crowd. (Guaro shots ¢500. Open daily noon-midnight.)

⬚ THE RESERVES. Positioned directly on the continental divide, **Reserva Biológica Monteverde** encompasses 10,500 hectares of land, protecting 2500 plant types and over 400 animal species. The wildlife population includes jaguars, mountain lions, peccaries, and the elusive quetzal. Though visitors frequently see coatis and white-faced monkeys, spotting inhabitants of this dense forest can prove difficult, and many visitors find that guides can be quite helpful as nature-translators or human binoculars. Guides are able to hear monkey calls from the ground or pick out creatures hidden in the trees. Trail highlights include **La Ventana lookout** (along the continental divide) and a long **suspension bridge.** *(The reserve is 6km uphill from Santa Elena. Walk, take a taxi, or a 45min. public bus that leaves Santa Elena Monday through Saturday at 6:25am and 1:15pm and returns from the reserve at 1:15pm and 4pm. Visitor center ☎ 645 5122 or 645 5112; www.cct.or.cr. Guided tours 7:30, 8am, and 1pm, US$15; call the night before. Open daily 7am-4pm. US$12, students and those under 12 US$6. Night hikes start at 7:15pm, US$15; transportation is included. The Visitor Center has dorms with bunks, communal showers, and 3 meals, US$26. Inside the reserve are 3 shelters with cooking areas, water, and showers. Reserve in advance. Bring a sleeping bag and food. US$4-$5.)*

Though tourists often overlook **Santa Elena Reserve,** established in 1992 to diffuse Monteverde's tourism burden, it offers similar flora and fauna on more sparsely populated trails, where howler monkeys make a raucous in the *liana* vines that dangle from the trees. The peaks within the reserve are the highest in the region (some over 1700m). There are four main **trails,** all short enough (1-5km) to be done as day hikes. Morning hikes make for better weather, views, and animal watching. **Guided tours** can be arranged a day in advance. *(Walk on the road north from Banco Nacional, take a taxi, ¢3500, or catch the reserve's minibus in front of Banco Nacional at 6:45, 11am, and 2pm, ¢700. The bus returns at 10:30am, noon, and 3pm for ¢500. Make reservations for buses after 6:45am. ☎ 645 5390; rbnctpse@racsa.co.cr. Day tours 7:30 and 11:30am, US$15 per person not including entrance fee; night tour 6:30pm, US$15 per person including entrance fee. US$9, with student ID or ages 10-12 US$5, under 10 free.)*

Under-appreciated **Bosque Eterno de los Niños (Children's Eternal Rain Forest)** is the nation's largest private reserve. The lower-elevation Bosque Eterno covers 22,000 hectares, and its sparse foliage makes for better bird-watching than Monteverde. The **Bajo del Tigre** entrance is 3.5km southeast of Santa Elena. True to its name, this place has a youthful bent, focused on educational exploration. One of its trails is designed for children. Farther away, two **field stations, San Gerardo** and **Poco Sol,** have accommodations available, but you must arrange with the league two weeks in advance. *(Monteverde Conservation League. ☎ 645 5003; acmmcl@sol.racsa.co.cr. Bajo del Tigre entrance open daily 8am-5pm. US$4, students US$2. Lodging US$20 per person, US$40 with meals. Student and group discounts.)*

⧉ ⚠ SIGHTS AND OUTDOOR ACTIVITIES. Four companies offer **zipline tours,** while the **Sky Walk** takes visitors along a network of bouncing suspension bridges nestled in the canopy of the Santa Elena Reserve. **Selvatura, Sky Trek, Aventura,** and the original **Canopy Tour** all offer similar packages (US$15-$45, students US$12-$35, children US$6-$25) with harrowing zip lines, though each company has its own style. (Aventura ☎ 645 6901; www.aventuracanopy.com. Canopy Tour ☎ 645 5243; www.canopytour.com. Sky Trek ☎ 645 5238; info@skywalk.co.cr. Selvatura ☎ 645 5929; www.selvatura.com. SkyWalk ☎ 645 5238. Natural Wonders Tram ☎ 645 5960; www.naturalwonderstram.com.)

The banana and coffee plantations that once operated on the **Finca Ecológica de Monteverde** have been transformed into private reserves. Food is sometimes put out for the animals, so they are more likely to be hanging around than at some of the larger reserves. Printed guides are available at the visitor center. The night tour frequently features porcupines, sloths, and kinkajous. (The well-marked turn-off from the Monteverde road is between Pizzeria Johnny and Paradise Café, almost 1km from Santa Elena. ☎ 645 5554; fincaecologica@racsa.co.cr. Open daily 7am-5pm. Guides recommended. Call a day ahead. Guides US$15 per 2½hr. tour. Night tour 5:30-7:30pm, US$14 including entrance fee, arrive around 5pm. US$7; students and Costa Rican nationals US$5; ages 6-12 US$3.)

Founded in 1982 to provide economic support for local women, **Casa de Arte-sanos de Santa Elena de Monteverde (CASEM)** has 93 artisans selling their handicrafts. Embroidered belts ¢4000, jewelry ¢6500. (3.25km from Santa Elena on the road to Monteverde. ☎645 5190. Open M-Sa 8am-5pm, Su 10am-4pm.) The **Monteverde Community Art Center** offers classes with local artists specializing in crafts ranging from stained glass to hammock-making. Kids under 12 play with clay for free. Reservations for workshops must be made in advance. (Across the road and over the bridge from the cheese factory. ☎645 6121. Shop open daily 9am-5pm; class times flexible. Prices depend on class, US$30-$50 per day.)

The **Jardín de Mariposas (Butterfly Garden)** focuses on the study of all sorts of insects, from the elegant to the nasty. Special cameras zoom in on their ambitious small-scale endeavors. (Turn off the Monteverde road about 1km from Santa Elena; signs will direct you. ☎645 5512; www.best.com/~mariposa. Open daily 9:30am-4pm. US$7, children or student ID US$5. Call about volunteer opportunities. Guided tours included in entrance fee.)

There are many opportunities for **horseback riding. Meg's Stables,** 2.5km from Santa Elena, is next to Stella's. (☎645 5419. Call ahead for reservations. 2hr. ride US$23, 5hr. ride to San Luis and 80 ft. waterfall US$45.) Caballeriza El Rodeo (☎645 5764) and El Refuge (☎645 6803) offer sunset and local tours.

TILARÁN

About the only travelers who don't breeze in and right out of this gusty little town are windsurfers setting sail on **Laguna de Arenal,** 5km away, a man-made lake that provides 60% of the country's energy as well as spectacular views of Volcán Arenal. The church is east of the *parque central* at the center of town. **Buses** leave half a block west from the *parque's* northwest corner (☎695 5611) to: **Arenal** (1½hr., 5 per day 5am-4:30pm, ¢280); **Cañas** (1hr., 8 per day 5am-5pm, ¢200); **Ciudad Quesada** (4½hr.; 7am, 12:30pm; ¢700) via **Fortuna** and **Arenal; Guatuso** (3½hr., noon, ¢500); **Monteverde/Santa Elena** (3hr., 12:30pm, ¢800); **Puntarenas** (2½hr., 6am and 1pm, ¢700); and **San José** (4hr., 5 per day 5am-4:55pm, ¢1200). All of these buses stop at **Laguna de Arenal** as well.

For **tourist information** in English, visit **La Carreta** hotel and restaurant or **Hotel Mary** (see **Accommodations** below). **Banco Nacional** lies across from the southwest corner of the *parque.* (Open M-F 8:30am-3:45pm.) The **police** station is half a block west of the bus station. (☎695 5001. Open 24hr.) The **Red Cross** (☎695 5256) is 100m east of the *parque's* northeast corner, and the **hospital** (☎695 5093) is 200m west of the *parque's* southwest corner. **Cafe Internet** lies across from the bus terminal. (¢500 per hr. Open M-F 9:15am-9pm, Sa-Su 10am-9pm.) Walk northeast of the *parque,* and you'll see the **post office.** (Open M-F 8am-noon and 1-5:30pm.)

Hotel Tilawa ❹, 10km north of Tilarán, feels like an amusement park built in homage to ancient Cretan palaces. Features an on-site tennis courts and pool, along with kayaks (US$10 per hr.), a windsurfing center, and a skateboard park overlooking the lake. (☎695 5050; www.hotel-tilawa.com. Singles US$58; doubles US$68; triples US$78; suites US$108; US$10 discount in low season.) **Hotel Mary** ❶, on the south side of the *parque,* has homey rooms with private baths and TVs. Some rooms with bunk beds. (☎/fax 695 5479. Singles ¢3000; singles and doubles with bath ¢4000.)

At the **Indoor Market** next to the bus station, stalls sell inexpensive *comida típica* along with fresh produce and baked snacks. **El Nilo** ❷, 100m north and 100m east of the *parque,* is a cheerful *soda* serving *leche durmida* ("sloppy milk" made with cinnamon) as a specialty. (☎695-8270. Open 7am-9pm.) **Taqueria Las Leñitas** ❶, north of the park, squeezes five benches into a small room filled with the smells of Mexican-inspired entrees like ginger-pineapple chicken. (Open M-F 11am-9pm, Sa 2-9pm, Su 5-9pm.)

Laguna de Arenal is one of the world's premier **windsurfing** spots, with a high season from December to May that peaks in April. The **Hotel Tilawa** rents boards and offers classes. (☎695 5050. Boards half day US$35, full day US$45. 3-4 classes US$55). The windsurfing center is on the lake shore; call or drop by daily. (☎695 5710. Open daily 8am-5pm.) Hotel Tilawa also has information on other activities: kite boarding (US$65 per hr.), boat trips to Volcán Arenal and hot springs (US$200 minimum 6, maximum 10 people); fishing (boat with equipment; 3hr. US$150); trips to *Cataratas de Viento Fresco* (Fresh Wind Waterfalls); and tours to see the petroglyphs by Corobici Indians at Finca Archeologica Las Lomas.

VOLCÁN TENORIO

Although this area was decreed a *parque nacional* in 1995, the infrastructure necessary to make this grand volcano accessible to tourists and biologists was not developed until 1997. Tenorio, rising up 1916m and extending 12 sq. km, is now accessible thanks to the growth of nearby **Bijagua,** as well as the construction of two beautiful mountain hotels. MINAE has been working hard at its new posts in **Río Naranjo** and at **El Pilón,** researching the local flora and fauna of the volcano. This unpopulated area is rich with under-explored wonders, including bridges through the rainforest, hot and cold springs under the thick canopy, and the impressive sapphire-blue **Río Celeste** as well as its majestic waterfall.

The best way to get to Volcán Tenorio is to rent a car. You can also take the **bus** from **Upala** to **Bijagua.** (☎669 0216. 45min., 7 per day, ¢300.) If you are coming from San José, take the bus heading toward Upala through **Cañas,** which makes a stop in Bijagua. To get to *El Pilón* (also called *Casona de San Miguel*), the entrance and visitor center from which hikers can depart for various sights, you will need to seek out one of the two local **taxis** from Bijagua (¢10,000 round-trip). The less popular entrance to Tenorio is the community of **La Paz,** where farm owner Pedro Elbarado (look for his signs around La Paz) can guide you to Río Celeste. In Bijagua, there is a small **Banco Nacional** 10m north of the pizzeria on the main road, at the corner of the unpaved street heading to Albergue Helconia. (☎466 8555. Open M-F 8:30am-noon and 1-3:30pm.) **Super Paika** is in front of Bar Tropical. (☎466 8011. Open M-Sa 7am-8pm, Su 7:30am-noon.) The **Centro Commerical El Pueblo** is next door. (☎466 8021. Open M-Sa 7am-8pm, Su 7:30-11:30am.) To the right of Banco Nacional is a **police station.** (Open 24hr.) Though there is a small clinic to the right of Soda El Kiosco, the closest **hospital** is in Upala. For **medical assistance,** direct yourself to the **MINAE** office in Río Naranjo, 5km south of Bijagua. Three **public phones** are at your service along the main street; **Internet** is available to the left of Super Paika. (Open M-Sa 9am-noon and 1-7pm.)

There are two *cabinas* in the town of Bijagua, which are an expensive taxi or car ride away from the most appealing natural sights. **Cabinas Samora ❶** offers two spacious rooms that sleep three. (☎466 8896. ¢3500.) **Cabinas Bijagua ❶,** on the main road in front of Distribuidora Bijagua, has five clean rooms with private baths. (☎466 8050. ¢1500 per person.) A more remote lodging option is the spectacular ▓**Carolina Lodge ❸,** 10km up a windy dirt road on the right, going 3km from Bijagua towards Upala in **Areno.** This beautifully decorated eco-resort has great food but no electricity, providing a few well-chosen luxuries that make it ideal for nature-lovers who don't want to rough it completely. (☎380 1656; info@lacarolinalodge.com. Package US$45.)

From El Pilón you can explore the bright blue Río Celeste waterfall and swimming hole beneath it. The **Misteriosos del Tenorio** are hot and cold springs that lie a bit farther along the trail, surrounded by enormous rocks. The hot springs are cooler near the river, and boiling close to the trail. (3½hr. hike; US$6.) If visitors want to hike to the volcano crater, they must request special permission from the information center at El Pilón.

PARQUE NACIONAL PALO VERDE

Parque Nacional Palo Verde is one of Central America's most dynamic wetland areas, and is an important sight for conservation. Known primarily for its aviary life, the *parque* has 278 species in residence, including jabirus, egrets, ibis, and a rare colony of scarlet macaws. Its array of habitats—including mangroves, riparian forest, and flood-plain marsh—is home to at least 1400 other species.

▐ TRANSPORTATION. The *parque* entrance is 30km southwest of the town of **Bagaces**, off the Interamericana Hwy., where **buses** running between **Cañas** and **Liberia** will drop you off. There is no public transportation between Bagaces and the *parque*, but you can get a **taxi** (₡8000 one-way). When school is in session (early Feb.-Dec. except the first 2 weeks of July) there is a **student bus** that runs from Bagaces, outside the medical clinic, to **Bagatzi,** near the *parque* entrance. (M-F 3pm, return at 5:15am—spend the night or call a taxi to return. ₡500.)

▓▐ ORIENTATION AND PRACTICAL INFORMATION. Parque Nacional Palo Verde lies on the northwest corner of the Gulf of Nicoya, about 30km west of Cañas. From the entrance, the main road traverses the *parque's* length. After 6km, a road branches left from the main road, leading 5km down to **La Bocana**, a lake popular with birds, and 9km down to **Catalina,** the park's first ranger station. From there, a 2.5km trail ascends to lookouts on **Cerro Pelón.**

Back on the main road, 1km past the fork, a trail leads to **Mirador La Roca.** This 570m trail offers views of much of the park. Four hundred meters farther up sits the **biological station,** an independent research facility run by the renowned **Organization of Tropical Studies (OTS).** Palo Verde, the second ranger station, lies 1.5km beyond the biological station. The regional MINAE office overseeing Parque Nacional Palo Verde is on the west side of the gas station on the Interamerican Hwy. They have information and can contact ranger guides. The park is open daily 6am-6pm. Boat tours show off the birds in the gulf and take visitors around nearby islands (2½-3hr., US$20). Call **Tempisque Conservation Area** (☎/fax 671 1290) or the **MINAE** office in Bagaces in advance. (☎671 1062. Open M-F 8am-4pm.)

▐ ▛ ACCOMMODATIONS AND CAMPING. Six kilometers from the entrance, the road branches left from the main road, leading 9km to **Catalina,** a **ranger station** with water and camping facilities. **Puesto Palo Verde,** the second ranger station, lies 1.5km beyond the biological station and has potable water and bathrooms. The station also offers dorm rooms with fans (US$13; low-season US$10).

▐ HIKING. A 30min. hike from the Palo Verde station leads to **Mirador Guayacán,** the best viewpoint in the park. Crocodiles laze along the banks, and nearby **La Isla de Pájaros** is the most important breeding ground for water birds in Central America. At the end of the main road, 2km beyond the ranger station, is **Puerto Chamorro,** a dock along the banks of Río Tempisque. From the Catalina station, a 2.5km trail ascends to lookouts on **Cerro Pelón.** The rangers arrange **boat tours,** which are the best way to see many of the park's bird species; contact them in advance.

LIBERIA

The commercial center of Guanacaste and the cultural heart of this cowboy region, Liberia (pop. 70,000) is more visibly entrenched in history than many other Costa Rican towns: *sabaneros* strut by colonial houses while a flag rustles in the breeze above the *parque*. Apart from seasonal festivities like the annual celebration of **Guanacaste Day,** there's not much to see in Liberia, though it works as a base for visits to national parks Rincón de la Vieja, Santa Rosa, and Palo Verde.

COSTA RICA

Liberia is a major transport hub for Northwestern Costa Rica, and makes a convenient stopover en route to Nicaragua or Pacific beaches. Flights run from San José through **Sansa** ☎ 442 8088 (50min.; high-season 5:15, 11:50am; return 6:20am, 12:50pm; low-season 11:35am; return 12:25pm, US$66) and **NatureAir** (50min.; high season 6, 8:30, 11:30am; return 7:30, 9:55am, 3:05pm, low-season 5:30, 8, 11am; return 7:05, 9:35am, 12:35pm; US$73). Flights arrive at the airport 12km west of Liberia, accessible by taxi or any Nicoya bus.

Bus schedules often change, so check in advance. Unless otherwise noted, buses leave across the street from the market to: **Cañas** via **Bagaces** (1hr., 11 per day 5am-5pm, ¢500); **Managua, Nicaragua** (from Hotel Guanacaste; 5hr., 5 per day 8am-12:30pm, US$12.50); **Nicaraguan border** at **Peñas Blancas** via **La Cruz** (1hr., 10 per day 5:30am-8pm, ¢600); **Nicoya** via **Santa Cruz** and **Filadelfia** (2hr., every 30min. 4:30am-8:20pm, ¢530); **Playa del Coco** (1hr., 7 per day 5:30am-8:20pm, ¢500); **Playa Hermosa** and **Playa Panamá** (1hr., 6 per day 5am-5:30pm, ¢300); **Playa Tamarindo and Flamingo** (2hr., 10 per day 3:50am-8:20pm, ¢400); **Puntarenas** via **Cañas** (3hr., 7 per day 5am-3:20pm, ¢1060); and **San José** (4½hr., 6 per day 5:30am-5pm, ¢1700; from the Pulmitán terminal south of the main terminal, every hr. 4-10am and every 2hr. 10am-8pm, ¢1410). **Taxis** line up at the north side of the *parque*. (**Taxi Liberia** ☎ 666 1778.)

Visitors making an extended trip to the park often stay at nearby Liberia (25km). Many rates increase during the high season. **Hotel-Lodge La Casona ❶** is 3 blocks south of the *parque's* southeast corner, with pleasant common baths and cable TV in the lounge. Laundry service available. (☎ 666 2971. Singles US$7; doubles with private bath US$12; triples US$21; quads US$25.) **La Posada del Tope ❶**, 1½ blocks south of the *parque*, keeps their charming rooms peacefully neat and bright, hidden away from the main road. (☎/fax 666 3876. ¢2000 per person.) **Hotel Liberia ❶** is a ½ block south of the *parque's* southeast corner. Simple rooms are separated from the street by the hotel's nicest feature: a tiled patio with hammocks and TV. (☎ 666 0161; www.hotelliberia.com. Offers tours and rides to local sights. 24hr. reception. Parking available. US$5, with private bath US$7.50-$9. MC/V.) Always ask if restaurants are serving good traditional drinks, made from **coyol** or flower seeds called *chan*.

Los Comales ❶ is 2½ blocks north of the northeast corner of the *parque*, with a second location 3 blocks west of the *parque*. Twenty-five women run the place, serving hearty Guanacaste *típico* to all the locals. (☎ 665 0105. *Arroz de maíz* ¢650; *tamales* in banana leaves ¢300; *arroz con leche* ¢400. Open daily 6:30am-9pm.) **El Cafe Liberia ❶** (☎ 665 1660) opened recently near the southwest corner of the *parque*, roasting home-brewed coffee to serve alongside delicacies like Pesto and goat cheese sandwiches (¢2000) that won't spoil your appetite for their tempting array of desserts (open M-F 10am-6pm). **La Toscana ❷** recently opened near the park. With sparkling wooden floors and an imposing stone oven, it's the most elegant place to eat in Liberia. Homemade specialities like ravioli with vodka sauce (¢2200) fill the elegant leather-bound menus. (☎ 665 0653. Open M-Th noon-11pm, F-Sa noon-midnight, Su noon-10:30pm. MC/V.)

PARQUE NACIONAL RINCÓN LA VIEJA

While the rest of Costa Rica parties to the *tico* groove amidst ocean breezes, restless travelers head north from Liberia to seek seclusion and peace in a park full of waterfalls, raging rivers, and endless forests. The colorful blooms and wafting sulfur vapors make it an enthralling experience in (and for) every sense. Though its gigantic active volcano is the park's highlight, hikers also enjoy exploring the sulfuric lagoons, boiling mud pits, and thermal waters that dot its slopes.

⊞▣ TRANSPORTATION AND ORIENTATION. The park has two entrances, **Las Pailas** and **Santa María,** each with a ranger station (☎ 661 8139). Las Pailas, with trails leading past waterfalls and up the volcano, is visited more frequently. The nearby river is perfect for dry-season swimming. The park is open daily 7am-4pm. Entry costs US$6, with an extra US$2 for camping per person per night. The park is 25km northeast of Liberia, but public transportation covers only some of this distance. By car, a dirt road leads from Liberia's Barrio La Victoria to the Santa María entrance. Another dirt road starts 5km north of Liberia on the Interamericana and heads 10km east to the town of Curabanda; from there it is another 10km east to the Las Pailas entrance (¢700 to drive on the private road). Buses go only as far as Curabanda. From there, some catch a ride with occasional traffic, although *Let's Go* does not recommend hitchhiking. More reliable tourist shuttles from Liberia are offered by various hotels in Liberia.

⌐ ACCOMMODATIONS. Both ranger stations have campgrounds with showers and pit toilets. (US$2 per person.) Near Las Pailas there are a number of lodges that offer meals and activities for those seeking refuge from Liberia's urban congestion. **Rincón de la Vieja Lodge ❸** is 2.5km before the entrance, with quiet woodsy cabins—some with bunk beds—and hammocks on porches. The property is a 400-hectare working *finca* with a canopy tour and horses. (☎/fax 661 8198; www.rincondelaviejalodge.com. Canopy tour US$50; 3hr. horseback tour to hot springs US$30. Mountain bike rental US$5 per hr. Breakfast 6-7:30am US$6.50, lunch 12:30-1:30pm US$10, dinner 6:30-7:30pm US$10. Singles US$47, with bath US$58; doubles US$47/$58; triples US$57/$70. The **Hacienda Lodge Guachipelín ❸**, 5km before the entrance, is a 19th-century cattle ranch-turned-hotel. Activities include a 10-platform canopy tour and horseback tours of the park. Walking tours in the park US$15-$45. Transportation from Liberia round-trip US$50 or US$10 to the park. (☎ 666 8075; www.guachipelin.com. Restaurant buffet: breakfast 7-9am US$7 for non-guests; lunch noon-3pm US$12; dinner 7-9pm US$12. Breakfast included. Singles US$42, with all meals US$66; doubles US$60/$110; triples US$76/$150.)

▨ HIKES. East of Las Pailas ranger station is a 3km loop trail **Sendero Las Pailas,** which passes turn-offs to a sulfuric lagoon, a *volcancito,* boiling mud pits, and a picturesque waterfall that flows during the rainy season. At the halfway point, a well-marked branch leads another 6km east to the **Santa María station.** A trail to the west of the Las Pailas leads 5km to the park's biggest waterfalls: **Cataratas Escondidas** and the awesome **Catarata La Cangreja.** If you only have time for one hike, visit Catarata La Cangreja and the blue lagoon beside it. For a swim without the 2hr. hike, there's a crystal-clear **swimming hole** just 600m down the trail toward the waterfalls. It's 8km to the **crater** of Rincón de la Vieja; allow a day for the round-trip journey (about 7-8hr.) and register at the park office. Solo hikers must be accompanied by a guide. Access to the crater trail and the waterfalls closes after 11am, as the area is prone to floods. From the Santa María station, a 3km trail leads west through thick forests to the **aguas termales** (hot springs), 6km east of Las Pailas, which can get undesirably crowded during high season.

PARQUE NACIONAL SANTA ROSA

Established in 1971 as one of the first national parks in Costa Rica, Santa Rosa preserves the largest remaining tropical dry forest in Central America and is a UNESCO World Heritage Site. The park stretches over most of the Península Santa Rosa, at Costa Rica's northwest corner, and has managed to keep its beaches relatively untouristed, though they're famous for surfing and turtle-watching. The park is part of the **Area de Conservación Guanacaste (ACG),** one of 11 con-

COSTA RICA

THE LOCAL STORY

LA CARRETA SIN BUEYES

Given the prominence of the *carreta* in the Costa Rican imagination, it's not surprising that the oxcart has its own spooky tale. The *carreta* has been a familiar object in Costa Rican life since the 19th century, when it served as the primary mode of transportation in rural areas. Wives recognized the disctinctive "music" of their husbands' carts, and all knew the sound of their neighbors' *carretas*, even from a kilometer away. Many *campesinos* were so skilled at the art of listening that the minute a stranger's cart approached, they knew it was a *carreta desconocida* (unknown cart), and would look out the window to see who was coming.

Legend has it that in the small mountain *pueblos*, in the deepest dark just before dawn, the sound of an unfamiliar oxcart would fill the air. When the *campesinos* looked to see who was driving, they saw no one; the oxcart seemed to be driving itself, without oxen or a *boyero*. The *carreta sin bueyes* (cart without oxen), as it came to be known, simply drove by, ominously and mysteriously.

Parents warned children not to stay out too late, or else they might encounter the haunted cart in person. Children took the story to heart, and upon hearing any cart at night, would run inside. The *carreta sin bueyes*, though a mystery, was a great help to overprotective parents (or perhaps...it was even their invention).

servation areas in Costa Rica, and comprises almost 200,000 hectares of land and sea. The unique flora includes the Guanacaste tree, Pochote, Naked Indian, and Caoba, as well as 115 species of mammals (lots of deer and monkeys), 250 species of birds, and more than 30,000 species of insects.

The park also houses a famous historical site, **Hacienda Santa Rosa (La Casona)**. On March 20, 1856, a ragtag Costa Rican army defeated invading troops sent from Nicaragua by American imperialist William Walker. The region's penchant for stunted military intrigue persisted: invasions were also prevented here in 1919 and 1955. Sadly, La Casona did not withstand its most recent invasion, on May 20, 2001, when two vindictive deer hunters snuck into the park and set fire to the site, burning over half the fort to ash. The arsonists, apparently angered by recent hunting restrictions, were eventually caught and convicted. Costa Ricans raised ¢200,350,000 to rebuild the fort, and La Casona now stands restored, with roof tiles from 1886 and (appropriately) a state-of-the-art fire alarm system. Out front, you can watch cattle going through immersion baths in preparation for their truck journey from the *embarcadero* to the *corrales de piedra*.

TRANSPORTATION. Buses traveling along the Interamericana Hwy. (like the Liberia-Peñas Blancas bus leaving Liberia every 2hr. 5:30am-7pm) drop off at the entrance station (La Casetilla). About 12 buses per day pass in each direction. No buses run the 7km to the administration center or along the dirt road to the beach, so those without wheels walk or hitch, though *Let's Go* does not recommend hitchhiking. Hotel Guanacaste and Hotel Liberia arrange transportation, but it is often cheaper to find your own taxi. (Park open daily 8am-4:30pm. US$6, US$2 extra for camping.) Park information is available at the administration center. (☎666 5051, ext. 219; www.acguanacaste.ac.cr. Open daily 7:30am-4pm.)

ORIENTATION. The national park's entrance station is 35km north of Liberia and 24km south of La Cruz, on the west side of the Interamerican Hwy. From here, a dirt road leads 7km to the park's administration center, with **MINAE** offices and an info center. A bit farther to the left is the campground, and to the right, past the cabins, is the *comedor* (cafeteria). Beyond the administration center is a 4WD road (often closed to traffic during the low season) leading to the coast, 12km away. The road forks after

7km; the left branch leads 4km to **Playa Naranjo,** a popular campsite and famed surfing beach, and the right heads 8km to the turtle-hatching beach of **Playa Nancite,** a trip that requires special permission.

The park's **Sector Murciélago,** encompassing the isolated northern coastline of Península Santa Rosa, isn't accessible from the rest of the park; visits require starting from Cuajuniquil, a town 8km off the Interamerican Hwy. and reachable by bus from La Cruz or Liberia, then a 9km walk on a dirt road to the sector's ranger station. On the coast, you can swim at **Bahía El Hachal, Bahía Danta, Coquito, Santa Elena,** and **Playa Blanca,** or hike the 600m trail **(Poza del General).** You can also **camp** in the area with sufficient notice and a passport.

ACCOMMODATIONS AND FOOD. The park offers **lodging** in small houses near the main offices (US$15, students US$10) and decent meals (¢800-¢1300) in the *comedor.* Reserve lodging at least one to two weeks before (☎666 5051) and give a few hours' notice for food, which is always served at noon. An on-site snack bar is open to all. A campground near the administration center has drinking water, flush toilets, and cold-water showers. The campground at Playa Naranjo has toilets and non-potable water. Ask about overnight **camping** options.

SIGHTS AND HIKING. La Casona, near the administration center (follow signs past the administration center to the left), is the main building of the historic **Hacienda Santa Rosa** where the battle of 1856 was fought. (Open daily 8am-4pm.) The **Monument to the Heroes of 1856 and 1955** lies beside La Casona, with a windy view of nearby volcanos Orosi, Cacao, and Rincón de la Vieja. The lookouts **Mirador Tierras Emergidas,** and **Mirador Yalle Naranjo** are about halfway to the administration center from the entrance on the way to the coast, and offer stellar views. All **trails** and points of interest are marked on a useful map available at the entrance (US$2). The short (800m) **Sendero Indio Desnudo** (a.k.a. *Gringo Pelado,* or "Peeled Gringo") begins near La Casona and displays an impressive selection of regional plants. **Sendero Los Patos,** 5km beyond the administration center on the road to the coast, is one of the best trails for wildlife viewing. The 2km **Sendero Palo Seco** lies near Playa Naranjo, as does the 4km **Sendero Carbonal** that leads to **Laguna el Lirubo,** a crocodile hangout. Right next to Laguna el Lirubo is the **Estacion Experimental Forestal Horizontes** (Experimental Forest Horizons Station), an investigation center which is part of the ACG project. (Accessible only from the Interamerican Hwy. 12km south of the park's main entrance, 23km north of Liberia.)

BEACHES. The famous fast waves of **Piedra Bruja** (Witch's Rock) break onto the 80-million-year-old stone off **Playa Naranjo.** Though there are great waves all along the shoreline, the particularly prime sandbars where the estuary meets the ocean at Piedra Bruja are best December to April. Bring a mosquito net if you plan to use the campground at Playa Naranjo, and beware of nasty biting *chitras* on the beach at dawn and dusk. **Playa Nancite** hosts the country's 2nd-largest arrival of **olive ridley sea turtles.** The nesting season is July-December and is best October-November, during the eight days of the crescent moon, when 1000-6000 turtles arrive along 800m of beach each night around 9pm. Access to Playa Nancite is restricted, and you need permission at the administration center. (No charge; maximum 30 people per day. Call administration center, ☎666 5051 ext. 233, 20 days ahead to reserve camping near the beach; US$10 for up to 20 people.) If you arrive by car, it is forbidden to drive to Nancite. Drop the vehicle at Playa Naranjo: a guard will watch it for you.

COSTA RICA

✕ PEÑAS BLANCAS: BORDER WITH NICARAGUA

Liberia is only 1hr. away from the border at Peñas Blancas, which is more frontier than town: just a few houses (and a whole lot of police) are scattered along the tree-lined road to Nicaragua. Buses run frequently from Liberia to the border. (1½hr., 10 daily 5:30am-7pm, ¢600.) To reach Peñas Blancas from **San José,** catch a **bus** between Av. 3 and 5, and C. 14. (6hr.; M-F 6 per day 5am-4:10pm, Sa-Su more frequent; ¢1860.) To get to Peñas Blancas from **La Cruz,** catch the bus from Liberia (¢200) or take a **taxi.** (¢500 per person if in a group.)

Both Nicaraguan and Costa Rican immigration offices are "open" 8am-8pm, but get there well before closing time because bureaucracy and transit from one to the other can take a long time: up to 6hr., though 1-3hr. is a more likely estimate. The Costa Rica immigration office (☎ 677 0230 or 677 0053) has two lines of people: one for those entering Costa Rica (US$2) and the other for those exiting Costa Rica (US$8). If you're leaving Costa Rica, buy an exit stamp from any *cambista* outside, or from the booth. Once you get your passport stamped, you can have a snack (hamburger or *casado*) at **Restaurante de Frontera** inside, or change your money in long lines at tiny **Banco Credito Agricole. Money changers** abound on both sides of the border, but rates are better on the Nicaraguan side. Hotel Guanacaste in Liberia will also change money. **Buses** from the Nicaraguan border run to **Rivas** (1hr., every 30min. 4am-7pm, ¢10), and continue to **Managua.** For **San Juan del Sur,** take the Rivas bus, get off at La Virgen (30min., ¢4), and change there for San Juan (30min., every 30min. 5am-6pm, ¢4).

NICOYA PENINSULA

While the roads can be difficult, the gorgeous beaches and world-class waves of the Nicoya Peninsula are worth the trek for most travelers. Surfers come from all over the world for Tamarindo's waters, while the reef at El Coco draws novices and experienced divers alike.

PLAYA HERMOSA

Playa Hermosa is known across the country as a prime swimming and diving beach because of its calm waters and diverse marine life: eels, octopi, and sea horses are frequently seen offshore. That said, tourism levels have not yet overwhelmed the town; travelers can still find some measure of shore-side peace.

⎀ TRANSPORTATION. Buses to **Hermosa** depart from San José on Av. 5/7, C. 12, 1 block north of the Atlántica Norte Terminal (4½hr., 3:30pm, ¢1700) and from Liberia (1hr., 6 per day 5am-5:30pm, ¢300). **Taxis** are available from El Coco to Playa Hermosa (15min., ¢2000). Out of Playa Hermosa, buses leave from **Playa Panamá** and pass the second entrance to Playa Hermosa. Buses run to **San José** (4½hr., 5am, ¢2600) and Liberia (1hr., 7 per day 8am-7pm, ¢300) via **Sardinal.**

■✿ ORIENTATION AND PRACTICAL INFORMATION. The town of Playa Hermosa runs north-south; the beach is to the west. **Playa Panamá** is about 3km farther along the main road to the north. The **Aqua Sports MiniSuper** is 500m west and 25m south of the second entrance to the beach. (☎ 672 1100. Open daily 6am-9pm. ¢300 to shower.) There are **public showers** and **toilets** at **Pescado Loco Bar y Restaurant** (see **Accommodations,** below). A **telephone** can be found 150m east of the beach at the second entrance. Public **Internet** access is available at the Villa Acacia resort, 350m east of the beach. (¢1000 per 30min., ¢1500 per hr. Open daily 6am-9pm.)

ACCOMMODATIONS, FOOD, AND ENTERTAINMENT. The town's budget selection is surprisingly appealing—scarcity is more than compensated for by quality. **Ecotel ❷**, the most unique place to stay in town, is set amongst trees right on the sand. Walk 500m down the road from the second beach entrance, and turn left at the last road before the beach. The owner is a long-time conservationist who offers bunk rooms and indoor lofts. (☎672 0175. Use of snorkel, canoe, and Internet are all included. Bunks US$10-15; shared lofts US$10. Camping US$10 per tent. Rustic cabins US$20.) **Hotel Playa Hermosa Bosque del Mar ❸** keeps breezy cabins that serve as the best beachfront deals in town. (☎/fax 672 0046 or 672 0019; www.hotelplayahermosa.com. Singles US$25-$35; doubles US$35-$45. MC/V.)

Restaurants are geared almost exclusively toward tourists and generally come attached to local hotels. Budget deals are rare, and *comida típica* (for once) is not the norm. **Ginger ❸** features an Asian-Mediterranean-*tico* fusion menu with specials like mango *dorado* (₡2400). The desserts take Costa Rica's three largest exports—pineapple, banana, and coffee—and subject them to various delicious innovations. (☎672 0041. Open daily 5-10pm. MC/V.) **Pescado Loco Bar y Restaurant ❷**, 500m toward the beach from the second entrance and 50m to the right, fills up its bar stools with local men drinking beer. (*Casado* ₡1100; squid in its own ink ₡1800. Open daily 8am-midnight.) **Monkey Bar and Pizzeria ❶**, set back between the two beach entrances, feels a bit like a treehouse bar. (Large pizzas ₡4000. Open M-Sa noon-11pm, Su 10am-2pm.) **Restaurant Vallejos ❸** is the only true beachside restaurant in Hermosa, and accordingly maintains a relaxed atmosphere right on the sand. ("Devil style" jumbo shrimp ₡5800. Open daily 10am-9pm.)

WATERSPORTS. Hermosa's calm, clear water is ideal for **snorkeling, kayaking**, or **waterskiing.** Following the signs from the second entrance to the beach, **Aqua Sport** runs waterskiing (US$60 per hr.), windsurfing (US$15 per hr.), not-to-be-missed banana-boat rides (₡7500), kayak rentals, and snorkeling tours (US$26 per person). (☎672 0050. Boat trips 5-person max. per boat. Open daily 6:30am-8pm.) Another option for diving and snorkeling is **Diving Safaris**, 300m from the Villa Acacia complex. (☎672 0012; www.costaricadiving.net. Morning dives daily from 8:30am-1pm. Several levels of training available. Two-tank dives US$80 including equipment. Snorkeling US$30. Beginner instruction and dive US$115. PADI certification course also available. Open daily 7am-4pm.) The owner of Ecotel (see **Accommodations,** p. 179) offers a variety of guided tours including Rincón de la Vieja (US$75), leatherback turtle nesting in Playa Grande (US$65), Santa Rosa, and the Caño Negra Wildlife Refuge. (☎672 0175. 2-person minimum.) If you're up for a canopy tour but don't want to travel far from the beach, **Witch's Rock Canopy Tour** (☎666 7546; witchsrockcanopytour@hotmail.com) has just opened up off Golfo de Papagayo, with 23 platforms, four hanging bridges, and a sound tunnel in the tropical dry forest.

PLAYA DEL COCO

The dark and dingy Coco shores give no indication of the treasures that lie beyond them, but many say that Coco has the best diving in Costa Rica. A plaque in the town's park commemorates the woman who first brought tourism to Playa del Coco in the 1970s, and it's an appropriate testimony to her lasting legacy—the public culture of the town revolves around the hordes of tourists who come to enjoy the local snorkel and scuba.

TRANSPORTATION. Buses head to **San José** (5hr.; 4, 8am, 2pm; ₡2000) and **Liberia** (1hr., 8 per day 5:30am-6pm, ₡300) via **Sardinal** (5min., ₡120). Hermosa to the north and Ocotal to the south can only be reached by **taxi**. Getting to beaches

COSTA RICA

near **Flamingo** and **Tamarindo** can take up to 4hr.; catch the bus for Liberia and get off at the main highway (at a stop called La Comunidad); from there you'll need to get another bus to Belen, and then connect to your beach of choice.

▄ 🖪 ORIENTATION AND PRACTICAL INFORMATION. The main road runs from the highway to the beach, where you will find an unassuming *parque central* with public phones at its center. Buses stop on the *parque*'s south side. When facing the beach, the **soccer field** is about a block to the left. **Banco Nacional,** 750m inland from the beach on the main road, provides Visa cash advances and exchanges US dollars or traveler's checks (open M-F 8:30am-3:45pm). You can also exchange currency at **Supermercado Luperón** to the right of Banco Nacional. (☎670 0950. Open M-Sa 7am-8pm, Su 8am-2pm.) **Police** (☎670 0258) are across from the bus stop, though unfortunately the nearest **Red Cross** (☎697 0471) is in Sardinal. To reach **Medical Clinic Ebais,** walk 150m east on the road north of Lizard Lounge, turn right after the bridge and left after Hotel la Puerta del Sol. (☎670 0987. Open M-Th 7am-4pm, F 7am-3pm.) **Farmacia Cocos** is next to Rich Coast Diving. (☎670 1186. Open M-Sa 8:30am-8pm, Su 9am-1pm.) **Internet Juice Bar,** offers Internet access for ¢800 per hr., in addition to bike rentals and ¢800 *batidos.* (☎670 0261. Bike rental US$7 per day. Open M-Sa 8am-8pm.) **Internet Leslie** is another option. (☎670 0168. ¢800 per hr. Photocopy ¢15 per page. Lamination ¢500 per page. US$8 bike rental per day. Laundry, ¢500 per kilo. Open M-Sa 8am-9pm, Su 2pm-9pm.) The **post office** is in the same building as the police. Open M-F 8am-noon and 1-5:30pm. **Postal Code:** 5019.

▌ ACCOMMODATIONS. **Cabinas Coco Azul ❶** is 100m west and 50m south of the soccer field. Arched doorways, airy tiled bathrooms, and bright colors give this place more flair than other cheap deals. (☎670 0431. US$10-$15 per person.) **Laura's House B&B ❷,** northeast on the road next to Lizard Lounge, is a cute house run by its namesake, an energetic young woman who also keeps a small bar in back. A simple breakfast is included. (☎670 0751; casalauracr@yahoo.com. Singles US$15-$25; doubles US$25-$35. Each additional person US$10. MC/V.) **Cabinas Arrecife ❶** has lovely wood-paneled rooms with comfortable beds, balconies and large, clean shared bathrooms. (☎843 8635. Rooms US$6-$10.)

🖪🖫 FOOD AND NIGHTLIFE. Local options are surprisingly eclectic. 🏮**Chile Dulce ❷,** on the main road heading away from the beach, serves some of the best salads in Costa Rica. Their tropical concoction of pineapple, shrimp, and toasted coconut is delicious and you might not be able to stop yourself from ordering chicken-stuffed plantains (¢1200) as well. (☎670 0465. Open M and W-Su 12:30-10:30pm.) **Restaurante El Sol y La Luna ❸** is a place where Coco Italians bring their native flavors to the candlelit table. Finish off dinner with decadent tiramisu (¢1500) or a shot of amaretto. (☎670 0195. Open M and W-Su 6-10pm.) **Marisquería La Guajira ❷** serves a shellfish soup (¢2450) that members of the national soccer team are said to purchase by the liter before each game. (☎670 6107. Open daily 10am-10pm.) **Lizard Lounge,** 150m south of the parque, is mellow until the weekend, when the floor livens up with a mixed crowd of *ticos* and tourists. ("Lizard shot" of tequila and green mint ¢1200. Open M-Sa 5pm-3am.) The same crowd spends some of their time at **Banana Surf Bar and Restaurant,** on the same road as the Lizard Lounge. A small disco ball speckles light onto thatched tables. (Beer ¢600. Open daily 6pm-2:30am.)

🖎 WATERSPORTS. Prime dive season is April-September. The best scuba and snorkeling sites, as well as turtle, shark, and octopus grounds on the nearby **Catalinas** and **Bat Islands,** are reached by boat. The warm water and abundance of fish make up for mediocre visibility. **Rich Coast Diving,** 300m south of the *parque,* offers diving excursions, including a multi-day trip to the Bat Islands (US$495), training for a variety of levels, and equipment rentals. (☎/fax 670 0176, in North America 1-800-4-DIVING; dive@richcoastdiving.com. Open daily 8am-5pm.) **Deep Blue Diving Adventures,** run out of the Hotel Coco Verde, has the best rates on snorkeling and scuba trips and equipment. They also offer PADI certification courses. (☎670 1004; www.scuba-diving-in-costa-rica.com. 2-tank morning dive US$35. Open water certification US$235. Open daily 8am-5pm.) **Roca Bruja Surf Operation** takes surfers to some of the best sights in Costa Rica, at **Ollie's Point** and **Witch's Rock,** as well as lesser-known **Laberinto** and **Palmares.** (☎670 1020; www.costaricasurftrips.com. US$180 per boat to Witch's Rock. Open daily 6am-6pm.)

PLAYA TAMARINDO

Though its long white shores have some rocky patches, Tamarindo is perhaps Costa Rica's most cosmopolitan beach. Here you'll find more resort-hoppers than backpackers, more signs in English than in Spanish, and more international restaurants than *sodas*. Socialites can find plenty of people to schmooze with when they get tired of surfing, diving, and beach lounging, while surfers are happy to amuse themselves around town when they get struck by the low-tide blues.

◧ **TRANSPORTATION. Flights** from San José are run by Sansa (50min.; 7 daily 5:15am-3:50pm, return 7 daily 6:20am-4:55pm; US$70) and NatureAir (50min.; 3 daily 8:30am-4:50pm; return 3 daily 6am-12pm; US$70), arriving at the airstrip 3km north of town. **Buses** from Tamarindo to **San José** leave from the Alfaro office in the Tamarindo Resort driveway, 200m east down the road and 200m north of the semicircle (6hr.; M-Sa 3:30, 5:45am, Su 5:45am, 12:30pm; ¢2200). Reserve tickets at least 1 day in advance. From the semi-circle, buses go to **Santa Cruz** (1½hr., 6 per day 6am-10pm, ¢350) and **Liberia** (9am, 4:45pm, ¢500); they can also be flagged from anywhere along the main road. Coming to Tamarindo from **Nicoya,** take the bus to Santa Cruz (45min., 14 buses 3:50am-6:15pm, ¢125), then walk to the *mercado* bus station, 300m south and 300m west of where the bus drops you off. Buses leave from there to Tamarindo (1½hr., 5 per day 4:30am-3:30pm, ¢250).

For **car rentals,** try **Elegante Rent A Car**, in the Hotel Pueblo Dorado north of the Best Western. (☎653 0015. Open daily 8am-5pm. US$1000 deposit; 25+.) Or try **Budget** in the Best Western. (☎653 0829. Rents to under 21. Open daily 9am-6pm.) **Pura Mar** south of the Best Western on the main road, has **bike rentals.** (☎653 1355. Half-day US$5, full-day US$10. Open daily from around 9am-4pm.)

◪◪ **ORIENTATION AND PRACTICAL INFORMATION.** The main road in Tamarindo extends 2.4km, from Parque Nacional Las Baulas at the northeastern end of town to the main bus stop, ending in a semi-circle of shops and restaurants on the southwest edge. There are two main beach entrances—one off the semi-circle, and another in the middle of the strip. Everything along the main street is geared to travelers' needs. **Centro Comercial Aster** is a strip of shops 200m north of the circle.

For **tourist information,** see **CR Paradise,** next to Banco Nacional (open daily 7:30am-6pm). There are several options for **Tours and Surfing Equipment. Witch's Rock** is a hotel and surf school across from Rodamar Restaurant on the main road. (☎653 1238. Surf lessons US$35 for 1½hr. class. Reservations recommended. Open daily 6am-10pm.) **Iguana Surf Tours** has two locations, one 800m north of the circle, and the other up the street immediately south of the Centro Comercial Aster and to the right. (☎653 0148 or 653 0613; iguanasurf@aol.com. 2hr. group surf lessons US$30. Surfboard rentals US$3-$4 per hr. Open daily 8am-6pm, until 8pm at location south of Aster.) **Tamarindo Adventures and Surf School**, up the street south of Centro Comercial Aster and below Hightide Surfshop, features an impressive selection of old and new boards. (☎653 0108. Surf lessons US$25. Open M-Sa 8am-7am, Su 9-6pm.) **Banco Nacional,** 375m north of the circle, changes traveler's checks and gives Visa cash advances. Lines are long, so get there early (open M-F 8:30am-3:45pm). **Supermercado Tamarindo** is south of the bank (☎653 1072; open M-Sa 7:30am-9pm, Su 9am-8:30pm), and **Supermarket 2001** is across from the police station. (☎653 0935. Open daily 7am-10pm.) For **laundry** services, **Punto Limpio Lavandería** is before Lazy Wave food company. (☎653 0870. ¢600 per kg. Open M-Sa 7am-10pm.) **Police** (☎653 0238, emergency ☎911) are 200m east on the road and 200m north of the circle, in a bungalow in the Tamarindo Resort driveway. Tamarindo lacks a proper hospital or clinic, but **Emergencias Tamarindo** is across from Cabinas Pozo Azul, north of the Best Western. **Internet access** is available at **Inter-Link,** on the circle. (¢1050 per 30min., ¢2100 per hr.; open daily 9am-10pm) as well as on the second floor of **Maresía's Surf Shop,** 375m north of the circle. (¢500 per 30min. Open M-F 9am-7pm, Sa 9am-6pm.)

▐▊▐▌ ACCOMMODATIONS AND FOOD. ▨**Arco Iris ❸** is hidden up the hill behind Pachanga, about 500m south of the Centro Comercial Aster. Cabins have wildly decorated rooms, cozy hammocks, porches, and private baths. (☎653 0330; www.hotelarcoiris.com. Doubles US$46, low-season US$21; 2-room apartment with kitchen US$46. US$10-$15 per additional person.) **Hostel Botella de Leche ❷,** past Tamarindo Adventures, is the best place to meet other travelers. Surfers lounge on bean bags and couches. (☎653 0944; www.labotelladeleche.com. Laundry ¢2000 per load. Shared room and bath US$12. HI discount.) **Cabinas Marielos ❸,** next to Iguana Surf, is worth the splurge because of its beachside location and striking decor—hand-painted designs are by a local artist. Some rooms have balconies. (☎/fax 653 0141. Singles US$20-$30; doubles US$30-$48, with A/C US$35-$45. AmEx/MC/V.) There are no amazing deals in Tamarindo, though it's a good place to splurge at inventive fusion restaurants. ▨**The Lazy Wave Food Company ❸** is on the road south of the Centro Comercial Aster, across from the mini-super. The menu changes nightly to ensure the freshest ingredients. Chill out in the courtyard—a "swinging" lounge with wooden swings. (Entrees US$10-$15. Open M-Sa 6pm-10pm. MC/V.) **El Pescador ❷,** is located on the beach 100m south of the circle; turn right (west) on the road beyond Iguana Surf. Glass tables showcase shells and coins from around the world. Lobster and prawn flambé is prepared at the table for ¢8000. (☎653 0786. Open daily 6am-10pm. Fast food and bar open until 2am.) **Pachanga ❸** is 400m east on the same road as the Lazy Wave. Try the marinated tuna over puffed pastry and tomatoes. (☎653 0404. Entree, appetizer, and dessert, ¢8200. Open M-Sa 6-10pm.) **Panadería de Paris ❶,** across from Hotel Pueblo Dorado, just north of the Best Western, sells pastries, cookies, and other baked treats. Chocolate croissants (¢350) sell out early. Crocodiles hang out in the lagoon out back. (☎653 0255. Open daily 6am-7pm.)

▧ NIGHTLIFE. Although high-season nightlife gets thumpin', the low-season scene generally consists of folks relaxing at beachside bars with a beer and some music. **Cantina Las Olas** is next to Iguana Surf, east of the main drag. Walk up the street next to the Centro Comercial Aster, take your first right, and follow the beat. (W ladies' night. M free pool and margaritas. Open M-Sa 6pm-2:30am.) **Mambo Bar,** on the circle, has unpredictable crowds, though many partiers come here once other scenes have died out for the night. Courtship rituals take place over pool and techno music. (Guaro-ginger-fresca ¢500. Open M and W-Su 7pm-1:30am.) **Hotel Kalifornia Lounge,** across the street from Tamarindo Adventures, is an eclectic cultural hodge-podge decorated with fuzzy chairs and beaded curtains. An older crowd enjoys "bloody Barbie" shots with secret ingredients (¢500) and sushi nights on Tuesdays (open M-Sa 9pm-2am).

⚠️ 📷 OUTDOOR ACTIVITIES AND GUIDED TOURS. Those looking for secluded surfing have a number of options nearby: 10km south is **Playa Avellana,** home of the right reef-break "Little Hawaii;" 15km south is **Playa Negra**; finally **Playa Langosta,** with left and right breaks at the river mouth. **Playa Grande,** farther north, is another good beach break and home to the spot "La Casita." Playa Grande is one of the most consistent beach breaks in Costa Rica; the waves are almost always bigger and less crowded than Tamarindo if you avoid the main peaks. Nature-seekers can also head to Playa Grande, now part of the 420-hectare **Parque Nacional Las Baulas,** on the northeast end of the village. From mid-October to mid-February, the park is a nesting site for the *baula*, the Leatherback turtle. Sportfishing is another great option; contact any tourist office or surf store offering trips. **Agua Rica Diving Center,** by the bank, is the most professionally equipped when it comes to diving. (☎ 653 0094. Certification available; half-day with 2 dives US$85, US$8 snorkel equipment rental. Open M-Sa 9:30am-6:30pm, Su 3-6:30pm.)

NICOYA

Nicoya, 78km south of Liberia, is the main settlement on the peninsula. Although it is considered a city, horses have remained a common form of transportation and cows still graze on small pastures "downtown." Though an unexciting destination in its own right, Nicoya features more tourist services than nearby towns, and is a crucial transportation hub for navigating the peninsula.

📧 TRANSPORTATION. From the main bus stop 200m east and 200m south of the *parque*, **buses** leave for: **Nosara** (3½hr.; 5, 10am, noon, 3pm; ¢560); **Playa Sámara** (1¼hr., 5 per day 5am-9:45pm, ¢400); **San José** (4½hr.) via **Liberia** (5 per day 5am-2:30pm; ¢2115). You must first take a **ferry** (7 per day 3am-5:20pm; 5-5½hr.) Buy all tickets at the window in advance (open daily 7am-5pm). From another stop, 100m north and 150m east of the *parque*, buses run to **Liberia** (2hr.; M-Sa 26 per day 3:50am-10pm, Su and holidays 12 per day 5am-7pm; ¢450) via **Santa Cruz** (45min., ¢140) or **Filadelfia** (1¼hr., additional bus Su and holidays 10pm, ¢300). Nicoya's **taxis** don't have meters; the standard fare is ¢265 per km.

📋 📷 ORIENTATION AND PRACTICAL INFORMATION. The two landmarks in the city center are the *parque central* and the main road, **Calle 3,** which runs north-south 1 block east of the *parque*. The bus drops you off at various locations, so your best bet is to ask for the *parque*. Once in the *parque*, Hotel Venecia is north, the *municipalidad* is south, Banco de Costa Rica is west, and Soda el Parque is east. The **Banco de Costa Rica,** on the west side of the *parque* with V/Plus **ATM,** cashes traveler's checks and gives Visa cash advances. (☎ 685 5010. Open M-F 8:30am-3pm.) There's also an **ATM** next door to **Western Union** that accepts Cirrus. **Libreria Ayales,** next to Soda Yadira, offers photocopy services and paper supplies. (☎ 685 5187. Open M-Sa 8am-6pm.) **Country House,** across the street from Verdulería Samy, sells sundries and produce in charming wooden boxes. (☎ 686 4800. Open M-Sa 8am-7pm, Su 8am-5pm.) The **police** (☎ 685 5516, emergency ☎ 117) are 150m south of the bus station, next to the airport; the **Red Cross** (☎ 685 5458, emergency 128) is 500m north and 50m west of the *parque*. **Farmacia** and **Clínica Médica Nicoyana** is 100m east and 10m south of the northeast corner of the *parque*. (☎ 685 5138. Farmacia open M-F 8am-7:30pm, Sa 8am-6pm. Clínica open M-F 8:30am-12:30pm and 2-5:30pm, Su 8am-noon.) **Hospital de la Anexión** (☎ 685 5066) is 100m east and 600m north of the *parque*. Phones for international calls can be found at the **Instituto Costarricense de Electricidad (ICE)** office, 125m north of northeast corner of the *parque* (open M-F 7:30am-5pm, Sa 8am-noon). **Nicoy@ Netc@fe,** next to Western Union, offers **Internet** access. (Open M-Sa 8am-9pm, Su 1-9pm. ¢400 per hr.) The **post office** is across from the southwest corner of the *parque*. (☎685 5088; fax 685 5004. Open M-F 8am-5:30pm, Sa 7:30am-noon.) **Postal Code:** 5200.

ACCOMMODATIONS AND FOOD. Hotel Elegancia ❶, next to Hotel Venecia on the north side of the *parque*, has bright spacious rooms. (☎685 5159. Dorms ¢1500; singles with bath ¢3000; doubles ¢4000; triples ¢5100.) **Hotel Chorotega ❶,** 150m south of the post office, keeps clean, old rooms with private baths, some with TVs. (☎685 5245. Singles ¢1500, with bath ¢3000; doubles ¢6000; triples ¢7500.) **Che Cafeteria and Pizzeria ❷,** across the street from the gas station, serves enormous *patacones* the size of pancakes (with beans and cheese; ¢1000), and pizzas on foccacia. (Open daily 8am-11pm.) **Café Daniela ❶,** 100m east and 50m south of the northeast corner of the *parque*, offers the biggest selection of *comida típica* in town. (*Casados* ¢900. Open M-Sa 7am-9:30pm, Su 5-9:30pm.) **Verdulería Samy ❶** sells fresh produce on the *parque*.

DAYTRIP FROM NICOYA. Located 22km northeast of Nicoya, **Parque Nacional Barra Honda** features a series of limestone caves that date back 70 million years. Before they were fully explored in the 1960s, people thought they were volcanoes because of the noise the bats made (and the mysterious fumes of their guano). Only 14 of the 42 caves have been mapped, and only one, **Terciopelo,** is open to the public. With three guides, harnesses, and rappeling gear, you can descend 62m underground to an amazing stalactite and stalagmite forest. In several distinct caverns, you'll have the chance to make music on long, hollow spikes of calcium and wander amongst waterways and columns, as well as a variety of formations that have managed to inspire even more creative names: popcorn, flowers, shark teeth, and fried eggs. The caves are all about a 1½hr. hike from the park entrance—the first half is a bit of a climb, but then it levels out.

Buses leave for **Santa Ana** from the main bus stop in Nicoya, 200m east and 200m south of the *parque*, and drop you off 1km from the park entrance (M-Sa 12:30pm and 4:30pm). To visit as a daytrip, you can hire a **taxi** (30min., ¢4200). Buses returning to Nicoya stop at the sign 1km from the entrance at 6am. To ensure that there will be enough **guides** (one speaks English), call the MINAE office in Nicoya (on the northeast corner of the *parque*), or drop by the day before.

If you use public transportation, you'll have to spend the night. There are two options: you can **camp** in a small grassy area (¢500 per person with toilets and showers nearby), or stay in dusty cabins. (1 bath for 8 people; US$5 per person.) Basic meals are available through MINAE if you call ahead (breakfast US$2, lunch and dinner US$4). *(Barra Honda office ☎659 1551. MINAE ☎685 5667. Open M-F 8am-4pm. Park ranger station open 24hr. Park entrance open daily 7am-4pm. If going into the cave, you must begin by 1pm; US$6. Trail guides and cave guides US$22. Spelunking equipment US$12.)*

OSTIONAL

This gritty strip of black-sand beach is Costa Rica's most important breeding ground for Olive Ridley Turtles, and at the start of a new quarter moon (usually at the end of the month), females flock here by the thousands to lay their eggs. During that time, the tiny town of Ostional comes to life: two modest hotels fill to the brim and the fires at the two *sodas* never die down. The arrival of the turtles is termed *arribada* and on these special days, most turtles arrive between 3 and 8pm, though a trickle continues through most of the night. The hordes travel in from as far away as Peru and Baja California to give their progeny a chance to begin life in the same place they themselves were born. During the process, the sand is barely visible under the hundreds (sometimes thousands) of turtles digging up other eggs to find cozy holes for their own. Sometimes the beach gets so full that turtles overflow onto the town's roads. To make sure you don't miss this event, contact biologist Rodrigo Morera (☎/fax 682 0470; adioturt@sal.racsa.co.cr) at La Asociación de Desarollo Integral de Ostional, 100m north of Soda La Plaza (see below), or check in with the tourist agencies in Nosara or Sámara. If you do miss the *arribada*, just wait a few weeks to see the baby turtles make their way to the water. Surfing is prohibited during the *arribada*.

The trip between Nosara and Ostional (8km) makes for a pleasant 1½hr. bike ride over dirt roads lined with cow pastures. Or, hop on one of the many **buses** from the bigger hotels in the surrounding towns. One bus makes the bumpy 3hr. ride between Santa Cruz and Ostional. (Cabinas Guacamayas in Ostional 5am, Santa Cruz noon.) Contact **Clemente** at Cabinas Agnnel for a **taxi**. (☎ 682 0058 or 682 0142. 20min., ¢3500-¢4000.) **Cabinas Ostional ❶**, across from Soda La Plaza, has simple triples and quads with private baths and nice balconies. (☎ 682 0428. ¢2500 per person.) **Hospedaje Guacamayas ❶**, 125m left of Soda La Plaza if you're facing the beach, keeps basic rooms with whimsical bird murals. (☎ 682 0430. ¢1500 per person.) The central **Soda La Plaza ❶** has a mini-market stocking snacks and a menu of all the *típico* basics for bargain prices. This is the only place to eat near the beach. (*Casados* ¢1100. Open daily 7am-9pm.) **Camping** is allowed next to the beach behind Soda. (Portable toilet. US$3 per person, 3 meals per day ¢3500.)

PLAYA SÁMARA

Not too long ago, Sámara was a tiny fishing and farming community where the soccer field was the center of activity and development was limited to a few *cabinas* and *sodas*. But with one of Costa Rica's prettiest and most swimmable beaches, this little village was fated for discovery. *Ticos* and tourists alike now flock in droves to its powdery white sands and pristine blue waters.

◪ TRANSPORTATION. Since the roads along the southwestern Nicoya Peninsula are in such poor shape, getting to Sámara via public transportation from places like Montezuma and Mal País in the southern Nicoya Peninsula involves going back to Paquera, catching the ferry to Puntarenas, taking a bus to the town of Nicoya, and then taking a final bus to Sámara. You'll be better off arranging for private transportation to Sámara in a **4WD** vehicle or coming via bus from San José (6hr.; M-Sa 12:30pm, return 4am; Su 1pm), Liberia, or other points in northwestern Costa Rica. A complete **bus** schedule is posted in **Super Sol y Mar,** on the main drag. Buses leave from in front of Hotel Giada to: **Carrillo** (25min.; 11am, 1, 4:30, 6:30pm; return 11:20am, 1:30, 5pm; ¢200); **Nicoya** (1hr.; M-Sa 6 per day 5:30am-4:30pm, Su 7am, 12:45, 4:30pm; return M-Sa 7 per day 6am-5pm, Su 8am, 3pm; ¢400); and **San José** (5½hr.; M and F-Sa 4:30, 8:45am, Tu and Th 4:30am, Su 8:30am, 1pm; ¢1780). Purchase San José tickets in advance from Super Sol y Mar. Buses leave for San José more frequently from Nicoya (5hr., 6 per day 5am-5pm, ¢1680). Buses to **Nósara** leave from La Bomba, a gas station 5km from the town center (1hr., 1 per day 10:30-11am, ¢365). There are no local **taxis**, but call Super Sámara (☎ 656 0256) and ask Rafael; ride to **La Bomba** ¢600, to **Carrillo** ¢1500.

◪◪ ORIENTATION AND PRACTICAL INFORMATION. Playa Sámara is on the west coast of the southern Nicoya Peninsula, 8km east of Playa Carrillo and 35km southwest of Nicoya. The main drag runs south into town and ends just before the beach; orient yourself by remembering that the beach is south. The closest banks are in Nicoya, so stock up on colónes beforehand.

Koss Art Gallery, a 500m walk east along the beach, keeps a few English-language paperbacks for exchange (usually open M-Sa 9am-5pm). **Super Sámara,** 200m east down the side-road closest to the beach, has **Internet.** (Open M-Sa 8am-8pm, Su 8am-6pm.) The **police** (☎656 0436) are at the far south end of the main drag, on the beach. There is also a pharmacy in town, **Farmacia Sámara.** (☎565 0123. Open M-Sa 8am-8pm, also Su during high season. AmEx/MC/V.) For medical emergencies, go directly to the hospital in Nicoya. **Clínica Ebais** (☎656 0166), 1km west of Sámara in Congrejal, can help with minor injuries and illness. Hotel Giada has a credit card **phone** for calls to North America. The **post office** is next to the police station (open M-F 8am-noon and 1-5pm, but hours change often). **Postal Code:** 5235.

█ ACCOMMODATIONS. Because of its popularity with all kinds of travelers, Sámara has accommodations suiting every budget. Anyone looking for tranquil accommodations should check out **Casa Valeria ❶,** 50m east of Super Sámara on the side-street closest to the beach. Even the simpler rooms are cozy—with pink walls, ceiling fans, shell decorations, patios, and hot baths. (☎656 0317. Singles US$15, high-season US$20; doubles US$35/$50; triples US$25/$35; *casitas* US$40/$60.) **Hotel Giada ❸,** 300m north of the beach on the main drag, is one of Sámara's nicer options and is often full of international students enrolled in nearby language schools. Breakfast is included. (☎656 0132; www.hotelgiada.net. Singles US$38; doubles US$45; triples US$55. AmEx/MC/V.) **Camping los Cocos ❶,** 300m west of the main drag on the beach, is the best campsite, with large, shady palms and sandy floors, and plenty of showers, sinks, and bathrooms. (☎656 0496. Electricity until 10pm. ¢1000 per person.)

❒❒ FOOD AND NIGHTLIFE. Sámara's increasing population of foreign residents means that you'll find as many Italian and French restaurants as simple *típico sodas.* Not surprisingly, everything is a bit pricier, but generally worth it. **Soda Sheriff Rustic ❶** delights with its tree stump tables. (*Gallo pinto* ¢700-¢800. *Batidos* ¢400. Open daily 7am-8pm.) **Terra Nostra ❷,** off the main drag heading west, feels like Little Italy. The owner oversees his perfected seafood menu. (Fish ravioli ¢3500. Open M-Sa 6pm-10pm. AmEx/MC/V.) **El Sandel ❶,** on the highway before the main drag, is the only bakery in town, selling fresh baguettes (¢250) and apple strudel (¢330) earlier than most people wake up (open daily 6:30am-7pm).

Sámara's nightlife is lively and crowded in the high season and during school holidays, when youngsters pack the beachfront bars and discos. **Bar El Lagarto,** about 250m west of the main drag on the beach, is a good place to start. (Beer ¢400. Open daily 7pm until the crowds leave.) **La Góndola,** 175m north of the beach on the main road, is a prime spot for games and revelry of all sorts. Ping pong, pool, darts, and a mix of reggae and Latin music delight all kinds of cats. (Pool ¢1500 per hr. Darts or ping pong ¢600. Beer ¢400. W 2-for-1 drinks. Open daily 8pm-2:30am.) **Tutti-Frutti Disco,** on the beach, is dark and loud, generally drawing a younger *tico* crowd. Come after 11pm for the peak dancing. (Beer ¢600. Cover ¢500 in high season. Open daily 8pm-2:30am; low season F-Su 8pm-2:30am.)

█▌ OUTDOOR ACTIVITIES AND GUIDED TOURS. If you somehow tire of the beach, several hotels and tour operators have trips to suit every interest. Most are geared toward the water, as there are excellent **fishing, snorkeling,** and **surfing** spots nearby. **Dolphin-watching** is also popular. **Hotel Giada** (see **Accommodations,** p. 186) offers dolphin-watching tours kayaking, diving, and Ostional turtle pilgrimages. **Alexis y Marco Boat Tours** (☎656 0468; boattours@samarabeach.com) is 500m west of the main drag on the beach. (Dolphin and snorkel trips US$120 per 4hr., US$200 per 8hr. Fishing trips US$120 per 4hr., US$200 per 8hr. 4-person max. per trip.) **Jesse's Gym and Surf** (☎656 0055), 500m east of the main drag next to Koss Art Gallery on the beach, rents a small gym and surf equipment. (Gym US$3 per day. Surfboards US$6 per hr., US$20 per day. Surf instruction US$35 per hr. Open M-Sa 9am-6pm.) **Flying Crocodile** (☎383 0471; www.flying-crocodile.com) is 4km northeast of town. One of Flying Crocodile's licensed and trained commercial pilots will fly you in an ultra-light glider and if you'd like, he'll teach you how to fly the ultra-light yourself. (Ultra-light tours US$60; ultra-light charters US$70; ultra-light instruction US$100 per hr. Traveler's checks accepted. V.)

MAL PAÍS AND SANTA TERESA

Don't be fooled by the literal translation of this remote surfing village near the southern tip of the Peninsula; with long, empty beaches, stunning rock formations, and scenic coves, Mal País could hardly be called "bad country." Only committed peace-worshippers and wave-riders trek all the way out here, but those who come often stay, enchanted by the easy-going atmosphere and top-notch waves.

F TRANSPORTATION. Most travelers take the **ferry** from Puntarenas to **Paquera** and either **drive** directly to Mal País or head first to Montezuma and then take a **bus** to Mal País. From Montezuma, take the bus to **Cóbano** (15min., 6 per day 5:30am-4pm, ¢200) and catch a connecting bus from the same stop to **Santa Teresa** via **Mal País** (1hr.; 10:30am, 2:30pm; ¢500). Return buses start in Santa Teresa and pick passengers up at the main crossroad by Frank's Place before heading back to Cóbano (7, 11:30am). Almost no **taxis** drive around town, but the service in Cóbano can send a **4WD car** to shuttle you to Mal País. (☎819 9021 or 640 0261. ¢5000.) Bad roads and infrequent public transportation make leaving Mal País complicated, so transfer services may prove well worth the cost. **Montezuma Expeditions** (☎642 0919 or 440 8078) and **Collective Taxi Transfer Service** (☎642 0084) arrange private transportation to just about anywhere in the country (4 people, US$120-$150), and **Bernadino Samora** (☎640 0151) can take you on his boat to **Cabo Blanco, Montezuma, Sámara,** or **Tortuga** (US$25 per hr.).

⚫⚫ ORIENTATION AND PRACTICAL INFORMATION. The area that most surfers and locals refer to as Mal País is actually three separate beaches stretching along 6km of shoreline on the southwest corner of the Nicoya Peninsula, 11km southwest of Cóbano. Buses from Cóbano stop first at the crossroad, which marks the center of the bumpy dirt road that spans the length of the area. All accommodations and services are off this main drag. From the crossroad, **Mal País** stretches 3km south (to the left facing the beach), and **Santa Teresa** stretches 3km north (to the right). **Playa Carmen** is 100m west down a gravel road directly in front of the bus stop. **Tropical Tours** functions as a **tourist information** center, offering private transportation, **Internet** access (¢1400 per hr.), and organized tours. (☎640 0384; tropicaltours@caboblancopark.com. Open daily 8am-8pm.) **Buena Luna** offers info along with falafel. (☎640 0452; www.buenaluna.santereza.net. Open daily 9am-10pm.) The nearest **bank** is the **Banco Nacional** in Cóbano (open M-F 8:30am-3:45pm), but **Super Ronny's** (☎640 0127), 350m down the road to Santa Teresa, cash traveler's checks with a purchase of ¢4000 or more (open M-Sa 8am-8pm, Su 8am-noon and 5-8pm). In addition to Super Ronny's, **Super Tierra Mar** is 100m down the road to Santa Teresa. (Open M-Sa 7:30am-8pm, Su 7:30am-5pm.) **Bambú**, 1km down the road to Mal País, has English-language newspapers and book exchange (open daily 8am-1pm). "Honey" organizes an organic produce **market** every Sa near the main beach entrance. For quick **laundry service,** drop by the house marked by the *lavandería* sign 150m down the road to Santa Teresa (¢800 per kilo). **Karla** (☎640 0225), in front of Cabinas Las Tres Pinedras, charges similar prices. To reach **police**, dial ☎117.

ACCOMMODATIONS AND CAMPING. A few **camping areas** provide sandy grounds for the bare-bones traveler: **Zeneida's Cabinas y Camping ❶** is the best, with a prime beachfront location 3km down the road to Santa Teresa (☎640 0118. ¢1000 per person). **Hotel the Place ❸**, 150m down the road to Mal País, proves that elegance and style don't have to come at prohibitive prices. "The place," features a sandbox in the yard, hammocks all over the bamboo gardens, and a pool with a miniature waterfall. (☎640 0001; www.hoteltheplace.com. Bungalows US$60-$70, low-season US$40-$50.) **Mal País Surf School and Resort ❶** is 500m down the road to Mal País. This "surf camp" caters to young surfers with a diverse price range of accommodations and, weirdly, a mechanical bull for night-time revelries. (☎640 0061; www.malpaissurfcamp.com. Open-air dorms US$10; *cabinas* US$35; surfer package with 3 meals, board rental, and basic room US$50 per day. AmEx/MC/V.)

FOOD AND NIGHTLIFE. The long road running through Mal País and Santa Teresa is sprinkled with good cafes, restaurants, and *sodas*, but many keep unpredictable hours despite their "official" schedules. **Soda Piedra Mar ❶**, 2km down the road to Mal País and then 200m down a dirt path toward the beach, is a quiet little *soda* nestled between towering rocks and crashing waves. The standard *típico* entrees are delicious, and the views are truly amazing. (*Gallo pinto* ¢600. Open M-Sa 7am-8:30pm.) **Mary's ❷**, 3km down the road to Mal País, gathers huge crowds of surfers enjoying fish tacos and spicy shrimp pizzas. (Dishes ¢1800-¢3100. Open daily 5:30-10pm.) **Jungle Juice ❶** puts just about anything on pita bread, but the lentil-veggie burger (¢1800) is their speciality (open Tu-Th 10am-4pm and 6-9pm). **Bar Tabu**, right off the beach, hosts full moon parties with fire dancers, trapeze artists, and trippy techno music (open M and W-Su 4pm-2am). The only other bar in town is **Bar El Secreto**, past Cabinas Charlie, open four nights a week. Ladies' night on Thursday offers free girly drinks (shots that taste like bubble gum) while Sundays feature Latin music (open Tu and Th-Su 5pm-2am).

BEACHES AND SURFING. The Mal País area is known as a world-class surf spot, not because the waves are extraordinary, but rather because the swells are consistent and the crowds faithful. Its location between the Central Pacific and Guanacaste lends it big southern swells in the rainy season and good offshore breaks in the dry season. The currents are strong, however, so swimming is dangerous. There are actually several isolated surf spots along the coast with slightly different conditions. South of the crossroads, **Playa Mal País** is a poor spot for surfing and is better for tide pool exploration. **Playa El Carmen**, directly ahead of the crossroad, has a long right wall and a shorter left breaking on a soft sandy bottom. The best spot on **Playa Santa Teresa** is 3km north of the crossroad behind Cabinas Santa Teresa. It's a more powerful, consistent break than El Carmen, and holds a better wave at low tide. **Playa Hermosa**, the next beach north of Santa Teresa, has almost no crowds and fast peaks rise along the beach. Four kilometers north of the crossroads is **Playa de Los Suecos**. It needs a stronger swell to break, but it's a good place to head when Carmen and Teresa are gnarly. Several surf shops in Mal País and Santa Teresa rent boards and provide instruction. **Corduroy to the Horizon**, 100m west of the crossroad down the path to Playa El Carmen, offers the best selection around. (Surf lessons, as well as board design, rental, and repair. Open M-Sa 7:30am-7pm, but hours vary.) **Santa Teresa Surf Camp**, 2.2km down the road to Santa Teresa, is one the most comprehensive and well-run surf shops around, with a juice bar and video rentals. (☎640 0049, reservations 381 2035. Laundry service US$6 per load. Surf board rental US$10 per half day, US$15 per day. 2-3hr. surf lessons plus half-day board rental US$45. Open M-F 9am-5pm.) **La Cavana de Surf,**

200m down the road to Santa Teresa, buys, sells, and trades surf boards. (Board or bike rental US$8 per 5hr., US$10 per day. Also sells hammocks and a small selection of beach wear. Open daily 7am-6pm.)

OUTDOOR ACTIVITIES AND GUIDED TOURS. Mal País offers plenty of diversions beyond the beach. Those weary of the waves need only walk 6.5km to the **Reserva Natural Absoluta Cabo Blanco;** call ahead to make sure these gates will be open. Otherwise, rent a snorkel and explore the **tide pools** just behind Sunset Reef Hotel. To get there, walk 2.5km down the road to Mal País, turn right at the fork, and continue another 500m until you see the hotel at the end of the road. Those with more cash can take one of the package tours offered by many around town. Check out a wide range of options at **Tropical Tours** or **Buena Luna. Pacific Divers,** 1km down the road to Mal País, offers beginner "Discover SCUBA" courses US$35 (4hr.), open-water certification US$300 (4-6 days). Specialty dives, equipment rental, and underwater photography are also available. Call at least 24hr. in advance. (☎640 0242 or 640 0187; www.pacificdivers-costarica.com. Traveler's checks accepted. V.) **Horse Tours** (☎640 0007; www.costaricabyhorse.com), is 30m down the road to Santa Teresa, in a house set back from the road on the left.

MONTEZUMA

Montezuma is a tiny beach haven stuck in a slightly larger time warp: flocks of batik-clad flower girls and starry-eyed, dread-locked rasta boys flit through this 1960s Neverland. Its dirt roads and endless beaches lead to some of the peninsula's most spectacular waves, while nearby hills are full of waterfalls and wildlife.

TRANSPORTATION. If you're coming from other towns on the north or northwest peninsula, backtracking to Puntarenas and taking the ferry to Paquera is the fastest way to reach Montezuma, even though other routes look shorter on a map. **Buses** go to: **Paquera** (1½hr.; 5 per day 5:30am-4pm, return 6 per day 6:15am-6:15pm; ¢700) and **Cabo Blanco** (30min.; 8, 10am, 2:05, 4:30, 7:10pm; return 7, 9am, 1, 4pm; ¢400) via **Cabuya** (25min., ¢380). To go to **Santa Teresa** via **Mal País,** take the 10am or 2pm bus to **Cóbano,** where the Mal País bus to Santa Teresa will be waiting (1½hr.; 10:30am, 2:30pm; return 6:45, 11am; ¢500). Buses run from Mal País to **Cóbano** at 7 and 11:30am, where you can connect with buses to **Montezuma.**

   Montezuma Eco-Tours (☎642 0467) arranges vehicles with A/C for up to 4 people to: **Arenal** (US$180); **Manuel Antonio** (US$130); **Monteverde** (US$160); **Sámara** (US$120); **San José** (US$130); **Tamarindo** (US$140). Make reservations one day in advance, as transports leave in the morning.

ORIENTATION AND PRACTICAL INFORMATION. Near the southern tip of the Nicoya Peninsula, Montezuma is 41km southwest of Paquera and 8km south of Cóbano. Most services are in Cóbano. Montezuma consists almost entirely of accommodations, restaurants, and souvenir shops. **Chico's Bar,** where the bus stops, is on the main drag and functions as the center of town. All directions here are given in terms of right and left as you stand with your back to Chico's and the ocean. The road intersecting the main drag at Chico's points directly west and leads to a fork 100m up the road. Turning right at the fork heads to Cóbano. Turning left leads to a number of restaurants, accommodations, and Reserva Natural Absoluta Cabo Blanco, 11km away.

   The tourist center at **Aventuras en Montezuma,** near Soda Monte del Sol, will exchange traveler's checks and US dollars with 2% commission. (Open M-Sa 8am-8pm, Su 9am-8pm in high season; in low season 8am-2pm and 4-8pm.) The closest **Western Union** is in Cóbano. **Montezuma Eco-Tours** rents equipment. (☎642 0467.

Mountain bikes US$15 per day; ATVs half-day US$45, full-day US$60). **Librería Topsy** (☎642 0576), 100m to the right of Chico's, carries a huge selection of fiction and travel books in several languages. (Book rental ¢500 for 2 weeks, ¢4000 deposit. Open M-F 8am-4pm, Sa-Su 8am-noon.) **Public phones** are in between Chico's and the supermarket. The tourist services office at Aventuras en Montezuma allows **international calls**. (US$1 per min. to Central America; US$1.50 per min. to rest of America; US$2 per min. to the rest of the world.) Cheapest **Internet** rates are at the **Pizza Net**, next to Chico's. (¢20 per min., ¢1000 per hr. Minimum 10min. Open daily 9am-9pm.) Librería Topsy (see above) sells stamps, mails letters.

⚑⚑ ACCOMMODATIONS AND CAMPING. Catering to the young and budget-oriented crowd that makes up the bulk of its visitors, Montezuma is packed with good inexpensive rooms. **Camping** on the beach is free, relatively safe, and popular, especially in high season. A relative splurge, **Amor de Mar ❷** is a 10min. walk down the road to Cabo Blanco, where a river runs through an ocean-bordered lawn strewn with hammocks. (☎/fax 642 0262. Killer Su brunch ¢3000. High-season US$35-$80; low-season US$25-$65.) **Hotel La Cascada ❷**, just before the river on the road to Cabo Blanco, is a getaway whose spacious balcony hosts a lively social crowd as they enjoy delicious crepes (¢800) and the sounds of a nearby waterfall. (☎642 0057. Singles and doubles US$35, low-season US$20; extra person US$15.) **Luna Loca Hostel ❶**, 100m up the hill on the road out of town, is the one true backpackers' hostel in Montezuma, with satellite TV, bean bags, and a garden lit by funky lanterns and candles. (☎642 0390 or 813 5079. Kitchen available. Breakfast included. Safe deposit box. Three private rooms available. Dorms US$10.)

◨ ▣ FOOD AND NIGHTLIFE. ▨La Playa de los Artistas ❸ is on the beach 400m down the road to Cabo Blanco. Moon-lit waves reflect the light of dim lanterns hanging from the dried palm leaf roof. The authentic Mediterranean menu changes constantly. (☎642 0920. Entrees US$8-$15. Open M-Sa 10am-10pm.) **Bakery Cafe ❶**, 100m down the road to the right of Chico's, does breakfast better than anywhere else in town. (☎642 0458. *Gallo pinto* with guacamole ¢1050, banana and chocolate pancakes ¢1100. Open daily 6am-4pm.) **El Sano Banano ❷**, 50m up the road leading west from Chico's, serves coffee concoctions with its nightly English movies. (☎642 0638. Most entrees ¢1500-¢3000. Open daily 7am-10pm. AmEx/MC/V.) Masses of tourists congregate at the **Tucán Movie House** in El Sano Banano to take in English-language movies. (Movies daily 7:30pm. Free with minimum ¢2000 food or drink order.) From there, everyone moves on to either **Chico's Bar** (beer ¢450; open daily 11am-2:30am) or **Bar Moctezuma** (beer ¢450, cocktails ¢1000; open daily 8am-2:30am.) At both, music ranges from reggae to *salsa* to old US rap, and there are as many stray dogs on the dance floor as hip-shaking *merengue* experts.

◪ BEACHES. The main beach at Montezuma has striking rock formations and a strong **riptide**; take precautions when swimming. Tide pools teeming with fish and aquatic plants lie farther south; rent snorkel gear from any tour agency. Beaches north of Montezuma, the largest of them **Playa Grande**, tend to be less crowded. **Playa Cedros**, 2km south along the road to Cabo Blanco, is popular for sunbathing.

⚑▣ OUTDOOR ACTIVITIES AND GUIDED TOURS. Hike to one of several **waterfalls** near town. The best one is also the closest, about 7min. walking along the road to Cabo Blanco; a sign just past Hotel La Cascada marks the entrance. From there, take the short woods trail to the river and hike about 20min., climbing over rocks or treading through water until you see the 80 ft. waterfall to your left. Past this waterfall, another trail climbs through steep and loose banking to a flatter trail, eventually leading to a smaller waterfall; you can jump off the edge and swim in a large natural pool. It takes at least 1hr. to reach these falls. **Do not jump off the first large waterfall**—the pool is small, and many people have died trying. Wear sturdy, waterproof footwear and be careful climbing the slippery river rocks.

Several tour agencies in Montezuma offer organized packages to nearby sights and activities. **Montezuma Eco-Tours,** across from Chico's Bar, offers trips to Isla Tortuga, including breakfast, snorkeling and a barbecue, kayak tours with snorkeling gear, fishing tours, scuba diving, and horseback tours. (☎642 0467; ecotoursmontezuma@hotmail.com. Isla Tortuga US$35; kayak tours US$25; fishing US$170 per 3½hr.; 2 scuba dives US$75; horseback tours to waterfalls US$25-$30. Open daily 8am-8pm, hours shortened during low season.) **El Sano Banano** (see **Food,** p. 190) provides similar tours, and **Aventuras en Montezuma** has comparable prices. (Bird-watching tour US$15, whitewater rafting US$95. ☎642 0050. Open high season M-Sa 8am-9pm, Su 9am-8pm; low season M-Sa 8am-noon and 4-8pm.)

⚑ RESERVA NATURAL ABSOLUTA CABO BLANCO. A bumpy dirt road runs the 8km from Montezuma to the Reserva Natural Absoluta Cabo Blanco, Costa Rica's first protected tract of land and the cornerstone of the country's reserve system. Cabo Blanco is home to the Nicoya Peninsula's most important population of pelicans and Central America's largest concentration of brown booby bird nests in the reserve's trees. The bus from Montezuma will drop you off at the **Ranger Station** where you can view a small exhibit, purchase a map and plant guide (¢200), and fill up on potable water. Two trails begin at the station. The 4.5km **Sendero Danés** (Danish Loop) is hilly and tiring, but the trails are well-maintained, there is wildlife aplenty, and the views are fantastic. A second trail, the **Sendero Sueco** (Swedish Loop), begins about 800m from the ranger station, makes a 1km loop that crosses the Danish Loop and several streams. The trip to the beach and back should take about 4hr. at a moderate pace. *(From Montezuma, take the Cabuya/Cabo Blanco minibus from outside Chico's Bar 30min.; 8, 10am, 2:05, 4:30, 7:10pm; return 7, 9am, 1, 4pm; ¢400. Park ranger station ☎642 0093. Open Su and W-Sa 8am-4pm. US$8.)*

CENTRAL PACIFIC COAST

The Central Pacific shore is Costa Rica's poster child: snapshots of its rocky sunsets are a familiar sight from travel brochure covers, and travelers range from vacationing *tico* families to resort-hopping honeymooners. Popularity brings inevitable drawbacks, and major beach towns like Jacó and Quepos are invariably more crowded and expensive than Costa Rica's more remote Caribbean side. Plenty of beaches, however, have maintained their seclusion along the coast.

PUNTARENAS

Though Puntarenas once seemed to have a promising future as a resort town, modern developments have not been kind to this city. Puntarenas is now a shadow of its former self, with vacant lots and rising crime rates, though its former glory remains visible in its towering church and cobblestone *parque*. Some *ticos* still loyally vacation here, especially during *fiesta* season, but most tourists only pass through to catch a ferry to the beautiful beaches of the Nicoya Peninsula.

▆ TRANSPORTATION. Puntarenas is primarily known as a transportation hub connecting Nicoya to the rest of the country. From Av. 1, C. Central/1, just past the Farmacia Puntarenas, **buses** run to: the Barrio Carmen **ferry terminal** (10min., every 10min. 6am-9:30pm, ¢65); **Orotina** (1hr., 8 per day 6am-8pm, ¢345); **El Roble** (25min., every 15min. 5:30am-8pm, ¢2000). From the stop on Av. 1/3, C. 2, just south of the

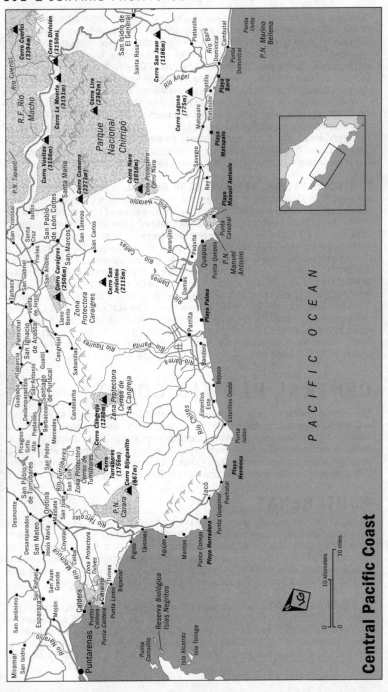

Central Pacific Coast

mercado central and in front of Importadora Elizabeth, buses leave for **Caldera** (40min., every 2hr.
7:30am-5:30pm, ¢190). The main **intercity terminal** is at
the corner of C. 2 and Paseo de los Turistas. From
inside the terminal, buses leave for **San José**, dropping passengers at the **Alajuela airport** en route (2hr.,
about every 30min. 4am-9pm, ¢1026). From the covered stop just across the street from the terminal,
buses run to: **Filadelfia, Nicoya,** and **Santa Cruz** (3hr.;
6am, 4pm; ¢720); **Las Juntas** via **Monteverde** and **Santa
Elena** (3hr.; 1:15, 2:15pm; ¢940); **Miramar** (45min.,
about every 30min. 6am-9:40pm, ¢180); **Quepos** via
the entrance to **Jacó** (3hr.; 6:10am, 12:30, 4:30pm;
¢1050); **Tilarán/Cañas** via **Arenal** (2½hr.; 11:45am,
4:30pm; ¢680); and **Libreria** (5hr.; 4:40, 5:30, 7, 8:30,
9:30, 11am, 12:20, 3pm; ¢900).

Ferries leave from the Contramar Terminal near Av.
3, C. 31/33 on the far northwest side of the peninsula
to **Paquera** (☎ 641 0515 or 661 2084; 1½hr.; every 2hr.
4:30am-8:30pm, ¢710, cars ¢4450). From Paquera,
buses connect with ferries to **Montezuma** via **Tambor,
Pochote,** and **Cóbano.** Ferries (☎ 661 1069 or 661 1069;
www.coonatramar.com) also leave for **Puerto Naranjo**
(1hr.; 6, 10am, 2:20, 7pm; return 7:30am, 12:30, 5,
9pm; ¢650, children 3-12 ¢300, cars ¢4400). From
Puerto Naranjo, buses connect to **Nicoya. Taxis** (☎ 663
5050 or 663 2020) are also available.

⊞ 🔧 ORIENTATION AND PRACTICAL INFORMATION.
Puntarenas is a long, skinny peninsula 110km west
of San José. Nearly 60 *calles* stretch northwest
across the town's entire 1km width, while only five
east-west *avenidas* span its length. The center of
town is marked by the *parque central,* bordered by
Av. Central to the south, Av. 1 to the north, and C. 7
and 3 to the west and east. The main **bus terminal** is
on the southeast edge of town on C. 2, and ferries
arrive and depart from the **dock** at the northwest end
of town near Av. 3, C. 31/33. Along the peninsula's
southern border runs Av. 4, more commonly
referred to as **Paseo de los Turistas.** Travelers should
note that no part of Puntarenas is safe past dark,
especially around the *mercado central.* If you must
go somewhere at night, it's best to take a cab. The
main **tourist office** is just opposite the main ferry terminal, with currency exchange, Internet service,
and a post office. (☎ 661 9011. Internet ¢300 per
30min., ¢600 per hr. Open daily 7am-7pm.) The peninsula's banks cluster along Av. 3 between C. 1 and
Central, with branches on the eastern end of the
Paseo. **BCAC** (open M-F 10:30am-12:30pm and 1:30-
7pm, Sa 10am-12:30pm and 1:30-6pm), **Banco Nacional** (open M-F 8:30am-3:45pm), and **Banco de Costa**

THE LOCAL STORY

VIRGIN OF THE SEA

In some ways, religious fervor has
never been stronger. Puntarenas's
largest spectacle dates back to
the 1920s, when a boatful of
divers was caught in an enormous
thunderstorm. Facing the pros-
pect of almost certain shipwreck,
they prayed to the Virgin of Carmen, patron saint of fishermen,
swearing to venerate her image in
an annual festival if she saved
their lives. The clouds cleared and
they made it safely back to shore.
True to their word, the divers had
a small celebration the following
year, which they called the "Fiesta
del Virgin Del Mar."

From this humble ceremony,
an annual tradition has grown:
every year Puntarenas fills with
parties and parades on the weekend closest to July 16th. The festivities open with the construction
of a large carnival ground, complete with rides, moonwalks, cotton candy, *chincharon* vendors,
fruit hawkers, and sarong sales-
men. Sunday's parade is the
main event, when local men carry
the image of the Virgin through
the streets on their shoulders,
depositing her in a decorated fishing boat. The boat is chosen by
lottery each year, as multiple vessels vie for the honor of transporting the scupture. A fleet of more
than fifty "bishop-blessed" boats,
decorated with stars and papier
maché swans, escort the image
up the coast. When it's over, local
fishermen make speeches of gratitude and ask the Virgin to ensure
their safety for the following year.

Rica (open M-F 8:30am-3pm) have 24hr. **ATMs. Lavandería Millenium** is on the bottom floor of the Internet cafe. (☎661 4759. Loads ¢850 wash, ¢850 dry. Open M-Sa 8:30am-6pm.) The **police station** (☎661 0640, emergency 911) is on the northeast edge of town behind Banco Nacional. 24hr. **Red Cross** (☎661 0184) is located 250m west of the northwest corner of the *parque*. **Farmacia Puntarenas** is next door to Palí supermarket. (☎661 3074. Open M-Sa 8am-8pm.) **Hospital Monseñor Sanabria** (☎663 0033) is 8km east of town; take any bus for Esparza, Miramar, Barranca, El Roble, or Caldera. **Millenium Cyberc@fe** is on Paseo de los Turistas at C. 17. (¢600 per hr. Coffee ¢150. Open daily 10am-10pm.) **Internet Café Puntarenas** is east of the church in the *parque*. (☎/fax 661 2156. ¢400 per 30min., ¢800 per hr. Open daily 9:30am-9:30pm.) The **post office** is across from the BCAC. (☎661 2156. Open M-F 8am-5:30pm, Sa 7:30am-noon.) **Postal Code:** 5400.

⚓☕ ACCOMMODATIONS AND FOOD. Camping on the beach is unsafe and unsanitary, but plenty of good budget accommodations are available. **Hotel Cabezas ❶**, Av. 1, C. 2/4, has friendly owners, small rooms, and communal cold baths. (☎661 1045. ¢3000.) **Hotel Ledezma ❶**, on the eastern edge of the *parque*, feels like a grandmother's house—complete with upholstery and lace—though the rooms are pretty basic. (☎661 1919. ¢2500.) **Hotel Chorotega ❷**, Av. 3, C. 1, diagonally across from Banco Nacional, offers privacy and comfort. (☎661 0998. Singles ¢3500, with bath ¢6500; doubles ¢5500; triples ¢8500.) Decent restaurants serving seafood and *típico* fare line Paseo de los Turistas. **Restaurante Kahite Blanco ❷**, Av. 1, C. 15/17, 100m northwest of the stadium, has the best seafood place in town. (Rice and shrimp ¢2450, *ceviche* ¢1400. Open daily 10am-11pm.) **Pizzería Italiana la Terraza ❷**, on Av. 1, C. 3, has a variety of pizzas and pastas (¢1550-¢2200) prepared with authentic methods imported by the Italian owner. (Delivery ☎661 5556. Open M-F noon-9pm, Sa 5-9pm. AmEx/MC/V.)

PARQUE NACIONAL CARARA

Although it only encompasses 5242 hectares, Parque Nacional Carara protects a unique transitional zone between the southern jungles and the drier northern forests. Its ecosystems are home to great anteaters, spider monkeys, American crocodiles, and poison arrow frogs. Carara's newest addition, **Acceso Universal,** is the first and only **wheelchair-accessible** trail in any national park in Central America.

🚌 TRANSPORTATION. Buses traveling along the Costanera Hwy. pass by the reserve regularly. From **Jacó** or **Playa Hermosa,** take any Puntarenas-, Orotina-, or San José-bound bus (see **Transportation** sections) and ask the driver to let you off at the entrance. To return, you'll have to rely on the buses that pass along the highway from San José or Puntarenas to Jacó or Quepos. If you're en route to San José or Puntarenas from Jacó, you can take an early morning bus to the park, have the ranger watch your bags while you're hiking, and then flag down a bus.

📋🔢 ORIENTATION AND PRACTICAL INFORMATION. Located 17km northeast of Jacó and 60km west of San José, the park was originally created to facilitate scientific studies and investigations. Its three easily traversed trails are evenly sloped and well-shaded. (Park open daily 7am-4pm high season; 8am-4pm low season. US$8, ages 7-12 US$1, including a handy trail map.)

🥾 HIKING. Acceso Universal is a flat 2.7km path that takes about 1hr. one-way, leading from the ranger station through primary rainforest to two other trails which form a figure eight. **Las Aráceas,** the first loop (1.2km), takes about 1hr. **Que-**

brada **Bonita,** the second loop (1.5km), takes about 1½hr. and involves a shallow river crossing. These trails pass through similar primary forest, but you're more likely to see wildlife on the Bonita trail. A less trodden fourth trail, **Laguna Meándrica,** is 4km each way and takes about 2½hr. to complete. The trail's lagoon lookout is a good place to spot birds, water plants, and crocodiles. All visitors to the park must register at the ranger's office before beginning this hike.

◙ **SIGHTS.** Hidden under Carara's thick foliage are 15 pre-Colombian archaeological sights, dating back as far as AD 300. Though these are currently inaccessible to the public, the most extensively studied is **Lomas de Entierro,** an ancient village with housing and funeral remains at the top of the hill facing the Río Grande de Tárcoles. About 2km north of Parque Nacional Carara's ranger station, on the highway to Puntarenas and San José, is the **Río Tárcoles Bridge,** also known as the **Crocodile Bridge.** Guides claim that the crocs living below it prey on farm animals that roam the surrounding pastures, and there have been at least a few reports of people being eaten alive or having limbs chewed off. If you happen to want a closer look, call **Jungle Crocodile Safari** for a 2hr. tour down the Río Tárcoles, complete with a bilingual guide that will do some daring crocodile tricks (☎236 6473 or 637 0338. US$25).

JACÓ

Swimmers may be intimidated by the waves that beat against Jacó's cinnamon-colored sands, but surfers flock here in droves. All this activity comes with a price—restaurants charge more, budget accommodations aren't as cheap, the streets are littered with tour agencies, the beaches are far from pristine, and crime and prostitution become more common each year. However, travelers can find peace on the black sands of Playa Hermosa, a few kilometers south.

▛ **TRANSPORTATION.** Except for those coming from San José, **buses** drop off passengers along the main road toward the center of town. Otherwise, buses passing near Jacó along the Costanera Sur Hwy. will drop off at the far south end of town. It is a 1km walk or a ¢500 taxi ride to Jacó center. Buses to **San José** (3hr.; 5, 7:30, 11am, 3, 5pm; 6am M only; ¢1020) arrive and depart from Plaza Jacó, opposite the Best Western, 1km north of town on the main drag. Buses go to: **Orotina** (1½hr.; 7, 9, 10am, 12:30, 2, 4, 5pm; ¢350); **Puntarenas** (1½hr.; 9am, noon, 4:30pm; ¢500); **Quepos** (1½hr.; noon, 4, 6pm; ¢500). **Taxis** line up in front of Más X Menos. (☎663 5050 or 663 2020. Playa Herradura ¢1500-¢2000, Playa Hermosa ¢1000.)

▟▛ **ORIENTATION AND PRACTICAL INFORMATION.** Jacó center stretches about 1km along its main road, which runs northwest to southwest parallel to the beach. For simplicity's sake, it will be described here as north-south, with the far north end of town marked by the **Best Western.** Jacó has no official tourist office, but many tour operators and shop owners speak English. A few particularly helpful folks are Eric of **Mexican Joe's Internet Cafe** (see below), and Bobby of **Coast 2 Costa Rica** (see **Guided Tours,** p. 196). **Banco Nacional** is in the center of town (open M-F 8:30am-3:45pm). **Banco Popular** is 100m south of Banco Nacional (open M-F 10:45am-5pm, Sa 8am-noon). Both have 24hr. **ATMs. Western Union** is on the north side of town near La Hacienda, inside Happy Video. (☎643 1102. Open daily 7:30am-5pm.) **National Rent-a-Car** is 100m south of Banco Nacional, between Banco Popular and Guacamole. (☎643 1752. 21+. US$24 per day, US$230 per week. AmEx/MC/V.) **Más X Menos** is just south of Banco Nacional. (Open M-Th 8am-9pm, F-Sa 8am-10pm, Su 8am-8pm. AmEx/MC/V.) **Puro Blanco Laundry** is on the side-street across from Más X Menos. (¢3500 per 5kg, min. 2kg. ¢2000. Ironing ¢200 per item. Open daily 8am-6pm.) **Aquamatic Lavandería** is 50m south of Banco Nacional. (Self-service wash ¢950, dry ¢950; pick up ¢1100. Open M-Sa 7am-12:30pm and 1:30-5pm. AmEx/MC/V.) **Emergency:** ☎ 117. To reach the **police** (☎ 643 3011), walk south along the main road for about 500m past Banco Nacional, and turn right when the road forks. A 24hr. **Red Cross** (☎ 643 3090), is 50m south of Banco Popular. **Farmacia Fischel** is in the same complex as Tsunami Sushi. (☎ 643 2709 or 643 2686. Open M-Sa 8am-10:30pm, Su 8am-10pm.) **Clínica de Jacó** is a 5min. walk south of town along the main road, on the same street as the post office. (☎ 643 1767. English spoken. Open daily 6am-5pm.) Both Internet cafes offer international calls anywhere in the world (US$1 for the first 5min., then US$0.20 per min.). **JacóCafé.com**, in the Centro Comercial El Paso, about 150m north of Banco Nacional (¢700 per hr.). **Mexican Joe's Internet Café** is about 125m south of Banco Nacional. (¢700 per hr. Open daily 9am-10pm.) The **post office** is on the south side of town, near Hotel Jacó Fiesta (open M-F 7:30am-6pm, Sa 7:30am-noon). **Postal Code:** 4023.

⌂ ACCOMMODATIONS AND CAMPING. Jacó's main drag and the surrounding side-streets are lined with small *cabinas*, the majority with clean and reliable budget or mid-range rooms. Rooms can fill up quickly during weekends or the high season; it's not a bad idea to reserve a few days in advance. **Chuck's Rooms and Boards ❶**, 700m north of the bridge, displays surf-slang bumper stickers from the hundreds of surfers who have crashed here. (☎ 643 3328. Dorms ¢3300; doubles with cold bath ¢8000; cabin with A/C, full kitchen, hot bath, and TV US$50.) **Cabinas Sol Marena ❶**, right next door to Chuck's, is a more private option, with tile rooms and private baths. (☎ 643 1124. Rooms for 3 US$15-$30.) **Camping El Hicaco ❶**, on the side-street 100m south of Banco Nacional, sports a shady yard with showers, toilets, laundry basins, and grills. (☎ 643 3070. ¢1500 per person.)

▢ FOOD. Though the diverse food options will give you the chance to take a break from rice and beans, you might not want to; locals claim that Jacó's *sodas* are some of the best in the country, especially for fresh fish. **Pasta Italiana Mónica ❶**, 50m down the second side-street south of the bridge, serves delicious food made by native Italians. Lasagna night draws a crowd on Friday. (Classic Italian pastas US$6-$7. Open M-Sa noon-2pm and 6-9pm.) **Tsunami Sushi ❷** is in the same complex as the pharmacy, 100m north of Banco Nacional. (California rolls US$5, dragon rolls US$11. Open daily 5-11pm.) **Soda la Flor ❶**, across from Zuma Rent-a-Car, is one of the best places to get cheap *tico* food in town. (*Casados* ¢800; rice with squid ¢1850. Open M-Th 7am-9pm, F-Su 7am-10pm.)

⚄ OUTDOOR ACTIVITIES AND GUIDED TOURS. Intense Sunset Tours, next to Banco Nacional, has multilingual guides offering horseback riding (US$35), canopy tours (US$45), and Class IV rafting (US$80). (☎ 643 1555; fax 643 1222. Open daily 7am-11pm. V.) **Green Tours,** 50m south of Restaurante Colonial, has an extensive selection of tours and services. (☎ 643 2773, 24hr. 643 1936. Trips to Manuel Antonio, Volcán Poás, Arenal, and Monteverde US$65-$110. Canopy tours US$50, and snorkeling trips to Turtle Island US$70. Open daily 7am-8pm.) **King Tours,** 150m north of Banco Nacional, arranges well-organized tours that satisfy all manner of adventure cravings. (☎ 643 2441, 24hr. 388 7810. National park tours US$49-$59, snorkeling by kayak US$55, rafting US$89. Scooters US$25 per day, motorbikes US$50 per day. Open daily 8am-8pm. V.) **Coast 2 Costa Rica** is based out of **JacóCafé.com.** (☎ 643 2601; www.coast2costarica.com. 2-3hr. surf lessons US$40. Trips to Manuel Antonio US$65, "Tres Piscinas" US$25. Open daily 8am-9pm.) **Jacó**

COSTA RICA

Equestrian Center, 325m north of Banco Nacional, provides horseback tours of their mountain farm. (☎643 1569. Morning and afternoon tours US$55-$65, or design your own. AmEx/MC/V.) **Ricaventura** is just north of Banco Nacional. (☎/fax 643 1981. Scooters US$30 per day, motorbikes US$50 per day. Dirt bike tours US$80. Rates tend to fluctuate by season. Open daily 10am-6pm. V.)

█ **NIGHTLIFE.** Jacó's high-season nightlife is serious business, with locals and foreigners packing the clubs and bars from dusk until dawn all week. Most of the town's hotspots empty out during the low season. Be aware that Jacó's drug problems are on the rise, and prostitutes linger in many bars. **Club Ole,** across the street from La Hacienda Bar, draws in skilled *tico* dancers along with hapless tourists. If you fit into the second category, never fear—you can always have a go on the mechanical bull in the middle of the club. (Beer ¢550. Cover ¢110. Open F-Sa 6:30pm-4am.) The bar at **Hotel Oz,** down a side-street across from Más X Menos, is a popular hangout with an assortment of party toys: TVs, pinball machines, and nightly live Latin and rock music. (Open daily 12:30pm-2am.) **Discotheque la Central,** 100m south of Banco Nacional and 100m down the side-street, attracts crowds after 11pm. (☎643 3076. Cover Th-Su ¢800. Open daily 9pm-5am.)

◤ **BEACHES AND SURFING.** One of Costa Rica's most famous surf spots, the waters around Jacó have some of the country's most consistently diverse waves. Jacó's main beach has gentler waves that break on dark sand—ideal conditions for beginners and intermediates. Experts craving more challenging surf head to **La Roca Loca,** a rocky point about 1.5km south of Jacó, with good rights that break over submerged rocks. Just 5km away, **Playa Hermosa** (p. 197) has a challenging beach break also popular with advanced surfers. North of Jacó is **Boca Barranca.** Most of these have good, isolated surf spots where you won't have to wait behind loads of others to catch a wave. Buy, sell, or rent boards at **Chuck's Chosita del Surf,** a few stores down from his *cabinas* (☎643 1308; open M-Sa 8am-8pm, Su 8am-5pm), or **Walter Surf Shop,** in the center of town. (☎643 4080. Open daily 8am-8pm.) Surfboard virgins eager to ride a wave can take a brief introductory **lesson** from one of many private or group instructors in Jacó. Most lessons include board rental, land and water practice, and a guarantee that you'll stand up at least once on your first day out. Recommended instructors are **Chuck** from Chuck's Chosita del Surf, and **Gustavo Castillo,** who spent four years on the national surf team (☎643 3574).

PLAYA HERMOSA

Veteran surfers at Hermosa will tell you to skip Jacó and head directly to this idyllic surf community. A stark contrast to the upscale beach with the same name on the Nicoya Peninsula, Hermosa is a paradise for those seeking long days in hammocks or near-perfect waves that roll onto the long, black-sand beach.

▐ **TRANSPORTATION.** Any Quepos-bound **bus** from San José, Puntarenas, Orotina, or Jacó will drop you off in town. You can also rent a **bike** in Jacó to make the trip (a hilly 30min. ride). Follow the main road to the south end of Jacó and turn right in front of the *municipalidad.* Keep straight for 1km until you reach a fork in the road, where you will turn right. At the next fork shortly after that, turn right, away from the gas station. The road will lead you directly there. A slightly more expensive option is to take a **taxi** from Jacó. (☎643 2000, cell 367 9363. ¢1300.) Arrange a return time or ask a hotel to call a taxi when you're ready. From Hermosa, buses depart from the seats in front of the MiniSuper for: **Puntarenas** (2½hr.;

6am, noon, 4:30pm; ¢740); **Quepos** (2hr.; 6:30, 8, 9:30am, 1, 4:30, 5, 6, 7pm; ¢600); and **San José** (3hr.; 6:30, 8, 9:30am, 3:30, 5pm; ¢800). Allow 20min. in both directions on all bus departures, and check with locals and hotels for the most up-to-date times, as schedules change frequently.

▣▐ ORIENTATION AND PRACTICAL INFORMATION. Playa Hermosa is 5km

south of Jacó and 85km north of Quepos, stretching about 1km along the **Costanera Sur Hwy.** The main road actually runs northeast-southwest, but all directions here are simplified to north and south. From Jacó, you will ride south into town, passing Hotel La Terraza del Pacífico and Rancho Grande (at the north end of town). **The Backyard Bar** marks the southern end of town, and the **supermarket** MiniSuper Pochotal is near the town center. (Open daily 7am-9pm.) On the northern end of town, Goola Café, next to Jungle Surf Café, offers **Internet** (¢800 per hr.) with their huge fruit shakes (¢600) and baked goodies. (Open daily 9am-4pm.)

▐▯ ACCOMMODATIONS AND FOOD. All accommodations face the beach to

take full advantage of spectacular views. Generally catering to surfers who stay for several weeks, most of Hermosa's hotels and *cabinas* are pricier than their counterparts in other small towns. ▨**Cabinas Rancho Grande ❶** is decorated like a tree house. Bamboo-walled rooms have hot baths, and many guests spend their time shooting pool on the patio or playing with the owners' energetic children. (☎ 643 3529. Communal kitchen available. US$10 per person.) **Cabinas Las Olas ❸,** near the center of town, is a great group value. Wooden ladders grant access to second-floor private bungalows; three smaller cabins have patios and A-frame upstairs lofts. (☎ 643 3687. Singles US$25; doubles US$40; triples US$60; 6 people US$110. Discounts for low season and long stays.) Like Jacó, most food at Playa Hermosa is geared toward American visitors. Though this can feel a bit touristy, it also ensures an eclectic variety of options. **Costanera ❷,** two doors north of Cabinas Las Olas in the Costanera B&B, has a limited menu of tasty pastas and creative bruscetta appetizers cooked with imported Italian ingredients. (Pastas US$5-$6. Open daily 6:45am-9pm.) **Jungle Surf Café ❷** is on the north end of town. A rotating menu offers fantastic fresh fish. Tuna steak with garlic teriyaki sauce, wasabi, mashed potatoes and veggies (¢3000) is a favorite. (Open daily 7:30am-10pm.)

▣▨ SIGHTS AND GUIDED TOURS. Budget travelers won't have to break the

bank to hike the steep **Monkey Trail,** which begins on the dirt road across from Bar Palmarenos and sees steady traffic from monkeys and sloths. If you're around anytime between July and December, you'll have a good chance of seeing the 3000-4000 **Olive Ridley turtles** that emerge from the water to lay their eggs. **Hotel La Terraza del Pacífico,** 300m north of town, has a variety of activities for those with a bit more cash to spend, including a zipline canopy tour (US$78), ski lift tree ride, (US$50), snorkeling tours of Isla Tortuga (US$90-$100), and surf lessons (US$45) with a Costa Rican national champ. (☎ 643 3222. AmEx/MC/V.)

▰ SURFING. Intermediate and expert surfers swear by Hermosa's perfectly cas-

cading waves, which regularly reach heights of 8-13 ft. before breaking onto its endless black-sand beaches. High tide translates into dozens of skilled surfers in and out of the white foam, but except for a few busy weeks in high season, you won't have to dodge boards to catch a wave. For a memorable moon-lit ride, inquire at Hotel La Terraza about when they plan to flood-light the waves after dark. True experts flock to Hermosa for the annual **surf competition** held by Hotel La Terraza, usually from the first week to the end of May. Those still learning can sign up for extended programs at **Loma del Mar Surf Camp** (☎ 643 1423 or 643 3908).

QUEPOS

Located just 3½hr. south of San José, the city of Quepos is one of the Central Pacific's most well-trodden destinations. The town's appeal lies more in its proximity to tourist-magnet Parque Nacional Manuel Antonio than in its urban hustle or unremarkable beach. Quepos serves as a base for dozens of tour operators who run trips through the raging rivers and wild mountain terrain just outside town.

⊏ TRANSPORTATION. Sansa (☎777 1170) has **flights** to San José (25min; high season 7 per day 8:30am-5pm, return 6 per day 8:30am-5:10pm; low season 4 per day 8:30am-2pm, return 4 per day 8:20am-1:40pm; US$47.50). NatureAir (☎777 2548 or 800-235-9272; www.natureair.com) also flies to San José (high season 4 per day 7:35am-5:05pm, return 4 per day 7am-4:30pm; low season 4 per day 7:35am-2:05pm, return 4 per day 7am-1:30pm). Flights arrive at the airstrip 5km northwest of town.

From **San José, buses** depart from Av. 1/3, C. 16 (direct 3½hr., 6am, noon, 6, 7:30pm; indirect 5hr., 5 per day M-F 7am-5pm; ¢1230). From the main bus station in Quepos, buses go to **Manuel Antonio** (25min., approx. every 30min. 6am-10pm, ¢100); **Parrita** (45min., 7 per day 5am-4pm, ¢155); **Puntarenas** (4hr.; 4:30, 7:30, 10:30am, 3pm; ¢800) via **Jacó** (2hr.; 4:30, 10:30am, 3pm; ¢660); **San Isidro** (2hr.; 5am, 1:30pm; ¢700); **Uvita** (1½hr.; 10am, 7pm; ¢600); **San José** (3½hr.; 6:15, 9:30am, noon, 5pm, extra Su bus at 3pm; ¢1665; indirect stops in **Jacó** en route; 3½hr.; 5, 8am, 2, 4pm; ¢1300). **Taxis** (☎777 1207) line up across the street from the bus station. A taxi to Manuel Antonio should cost no more than about ¢1500.

▓ ⊡ ORIENTATION AND PRACTICAL INFORMATION. Quepos is 144km southeast of San José, 65km south of Jacó, and 7km north of **Parque Nacional Manuel Antonio.** The bus station marks the center of town; the beach is on your right (west) when you face the supermarket with your back to the terminal, and the soccer field and road to Manuel Antonio are 2 and 3 blocks to your left, respectively.

Banco Popular, 1 block south and toward the beach from the bus terminal, changes traveler's checks and has a Plus/V **ATM.** (Open M-F 8:15am-3:30pm, Sa 8:15-11:30am.) **Lynch Travel,** west of the bus station, exchanges US dollars and traveler's checks. (☎777 1170. Open daily 7am-6pm.) **La Buena Nota** is an English-language bookstore in Manuel Antonio that also changes traveler's checks, 750m northeast of Restaurante Mar y Sombra near Cabinas Piscis. (☎777 1002; buenanota@sol.racsa.co.cr. Open daily 9am-6pm. MC/V.) **Super Más** is across from the bus station. (☎777 1162. Open M-Sa 7:30am-8pm, Su 8am-noon. AmEx/MC/V.) **Lavandería Aquamatic,** on a curving road southwest of the soccer field, has self-service (¢2100) and full-service (¢2500) wash and dry. (☎777 0972. Open M-Sa 8am-noon and 1-5pm. AmEx/MC/V.) In an **emergency,** dial ☎911. Contact the **police** at the **Organización de Investigación Judicial (OIJ),** 100m behind the bus station. (☎777 0511. Open 24hr.) The **Red Cross** is 25m east of the bus station. (☎777 0116 or 777 2128, emergency 128. Open 24hr.) **Farmacia Catedral** is located across from the bus station. (☎777 0527. Open M-Sa 7am-11pm, Su 8am-8pm. AmEx/MC/V.) The **hospital** (☎777 0922), 5km northeast of town on the Costanera Sur Hwy., is reachable by bus to Silencio and Londres. (5-10min., M-F 5am-10pm, ¢100. Taxi ¢1000.) **Internet** prices are fairly consistent throughout town; **Quepos Diner,** 1 block toward the beach from the bus terminal, is conveniently located. (¢300 per 20min., ¢600 per hr. Open daily 10am-10pm.) **Internet Café,** 50m west and 50m north of the southwest corner of the bus station, across from Hotel Pueblo, has similar prices. (¢10 per min., ¢600 per hr. Open M-Sa 9am-11pm.) The **post office** faces the soccer field on the north side. (☎777 1471. Fax available. Open M-F 8am-noon and 1-4:30pm, Sa 7:30am-noon.) **Postal Code:** 0057.

C O S T A   R I C A

ÆÐ ACCOMMODATIONS AND FOOD. Budget accommodations are more plentiful and less touristy in Quepos than in Manuel Antonio, making it a cheaper albeit less scenic, base for visits to the park and beaches. Places are split between the bar-filled town center and quieter outskirts. **Mar y Luna ❶** has a cozy common area with TV. With your back to the bus station, walk to the end of the block, turn right, and then left at the next corner. (☎777 0394. Laundry ¢700 per kilo. Singles US$7; doubles US$12; triples US$24.) **Hotel Ramu's ❶** is a few doors down from Mar y Luna. Clean bedrooms each have two fans. (☎777 0245. ¢3000 per person.) **Hotel Malinche ❶,** across from Mar y Luna, has well-furnished rooms with cold communal baths, fans, and TV. (☎777 0093. US$10 per person, with A/C and hot bath US$30; fully-equipped cabin with 3 double beds US$75.) The restaurants in Quepos cater to *gringos* with American-style breakfasts, Tex-Mex, and seafood that are all pricier than standard *típico* fare. You can find cheaper meals at the *sodas* near the bus station. ▓**Escalofrío ❶,** 1 block toward the beach from the bus station, is an open-front Italian restaurant. Three types of bruschetta (¢2000-¢2500) will whet your appetite for large brick-oven pizzas (¢1500-¢3500). Save room for the creamy *gelato* dessert (¢400) or a "sweet pizza." (☎/fax 777 0833. Open Tu-Su 2:30-10:30pm.) **Tropical Sushi ❸** is a brightly painted hut across from El Banco Bar, serving California rolls (¢1500) and sashimi. (☎777 0395. Open M and W-Su 5pm-1am. AmEx/MC/V.) Travelers and fishermen gather at **Gran Escape ❸,** on the beachfront road. The fish is fantastic and the burgers are creative ("killer raptor" burger, ¢3200) and filling. (☎777 0395; granescape@racsa.co.cr. Kitchen open 7am-11pm, bar until midnight. AmEx/MC/V.)

▓ NIGHTLIFE. For a fairly small city, Quepos has quite a few bars and clubs that are packed during the high season, but mellow in the rainy months. Sports fans flock to big-screen TVs in **El Banco Bar,** 100m west of the bus station. The owners will cook your catch for ¢2000. Local bands perform most weekends during high season. (☎777 0478. High-season open daily 11am-2am; low-season M-Tu and Th-Su 4pm-2am.) *Salsa, merengue,* and reggae beats get bodies moving at fortress-like **Discotheque Arco Iris,** 1 block after the bridge out of Quepos heading north-west. (Beer ¢450. Cover F ¢300, Sa ¢500. Open W-Su 10pm-2:30am.) **El Tiburón,** marked by a shark sign on the street just west of the bus station, is the perfect place to enjoy a nutella crepe (¢600) or the popular blue margarita (open daily 6pm-1am). **Tío Fernando,** between Hotels Ramu's and Mar y Luna, is a local bar popular with local men. (Beer ¢350. Open M-Sa 11am-midnight, Su 3pm-midnight.)

▞▚ OUTDOOR ACTIVITIES AND GUIDED TOURS. Most tourists find themselves in Quepos ready for an outing—the surrounding environs offer a variety of tempting options, including rafting, canopy tours, mangrove exploration, and some of Costa Rica's best sportfishing. **Iguana Tours,** at the southeast corner of the soccer field, arranges hiking and horseback tours to nearby parks, (US$44-$85), mangrove boat trips to Damas Island (US$60), and water rafting trips. (☎777 1262 or 777 2183; www.iguanatours.com. Open daily 7am-7pm.) **High Tec Sportfishing and Tours** is one street north of the main road, across from the soccer field. (☎777 3465, 24hr. 388 6617. Half-day, in-shore fishing high-season US$296, low-season US$250; half-day, off-shore fishing US$345/$300. Student and senior discounts. AmEx/MC/V.) **H₂0 Adventures,** across from the *lavandería* in the red building, offers the lowest prices for whitewater rafting on the Río Savegre (full-day US$95), or half-day trips on Río Naranjo, US$65 (☎777 4092; www.aventurah2o.com). **Fourtrax Adventure,** near the southeast corner of the soccer field, 50m past the lavandería, offers exhilarating full-day ATV tours (US$95) to the town of Londres. (☎777 1829. Open daily 7am-9pm.) **Rainmaker Conservation Project** features a series of five **canopy bridges,** one of which is Central America's highest (250 ft.) and longest (270 ft.), and can only be visited on an organized tour (4½hr., US$65 per person). (☎777 3565 or 777 3566; www.rainmakercostarica.com). The Quepos office is located between Tío Fernando's and Hotel Ramu's.

PARQUE NACIONAL MANUEL ANTONIO

Parque Nacional Manuel Antonio offers a popular combination of Costa Rica's most scenic terrains; jade-green waves lapping at the roots of a tropical forest. Despite government efforts to regulate local development, this once pristine park is beginning to show the effects of heavy tourist traffic—litter, crowds, and car exhaust. An encounter with the park's most outgoing and fearless inhabitants, white-faced monkeys, is almost guaranteed.

■ ▐ ORIENTATION AND TRANSPORTATION. Parque Nacional Manuel Antonio is located 7km south of Quepos and is surrounded by the small tourist town that bears its name. From Quepos, the **bus** will drop you off at a T intersection (25min., every 30min. 5:30am-9:30pm, ¢100). From here, you'll see a small street winding uphill and inland, marked by the Restaurante Marlin on the left; many budget and mid-range accommodations line this road. The direct buses from **San José** to Quepos also continue to Manuel Antonio (3½hr.; 6am, noon, 7:30pm). A **taxi** from Quepos shouldn't cost more than ¢1500.

▐ PRACTICAL INFORMATION. The **park entrance** and **ranger station** are located on the beach past the loop in the road. To get to the station you must cross an estuary, which is wadeable at low tide, but becomes a small river at high tide. Small boats are available to paddle you across for ¢100. (Park open Tu-Su 7am-4pm. US$7. Maps ¢1000.) English-speaking **guides** are available (2hr., US$20). In an emergency, call the **police** (☎911 or 777 0196). **Internet** is available for the same price at both Costa Linda or Los Almendros Steak House (¢500 per 30min.).

▐ ▌ ACCOMMODATIONS AND FOOD. Staying in Quepos may be cheaper than options in the small and touristy town of Manuel Antonio itself, though it's not as convenient or scenic. **Camping** is only allowed on public beaches, some in the park itself. **Albergue y Travotel Costa Linda ❶,** 300m up the inland road, is an inviting backpacker crash-pad. (☎777 0304. Laundry ¢200 per item. Single-sex dorms US$7; singles US$9; doubles US$14; triples US$18; quads US$20; large double suite with bath US$25.) **Cabinas Ramírez ❶,** a short walk towards Quepos just 80m from the beach, keeps three basic rooms with cold baths. (☎777 5044. Singles US$20; doubles US$24, low-season US$16-$20.) **Casa Buena Vista B&B ❷** is a charming B&B with gorgeous ocean views. Call ahead for reservations. (☎777 1002; www.casabuenavista.net. Rooms US$35, low season US$25.)

■**Restaurante Mar y Sombra ❶,** where the road from Quepos meets the beach, is one of the few places you can eat in Manuel Antonio without breaking the bank. Leafy almond trees shade diners enjoying the T-bone steak (¢3200). If the crowd is big enough, the restaurant moves the tables and pumps out techno and *salsa* at night. (☎777 0003. Open daily 7:30am-11pm, until 2am on dance nights.) At **Bar and Restaurante Balu ❶,** just beyond Mar y Sombra, the "floor" is nothing but sand, and the place is so close to the coast that sea foam sometimes moistens customers' toes. (☎777 0437. Pizza with palm hearts ¢2000. Open daily 7am-10pm.) **Los Almendros Steak House ❶,** 50m down the road, is a classier joint where you can dine on breaded steak (¢2000) over a game of chess while enjoying live local music. (Internet ¢500 per 30min. Open daily 7am-10pm.)

⚑🏊 BEACHES AND HIKING. Although it is the smallest of Costa Rica's national parks with 683 terrestrial and 550 marine hectares, Manuel Antonio receives more national and international tourism than any of its counterparts. **Playa Espadilla** is a large public beach that runs parallel to the town's main drag. Flanked by mangroves and estuaries, this scenic shore is often crowded because it is free. The waters are nice for wading, although the strong **riptide** makes deep swimming risky. **Playa Espadilla Sur,** popular with visitors and monkeys, stretches from the north limit of the park to the **Punta Catedral Peninsula** and is accessible immediately after the entrance. A short path along the base of the peninsula connects the south end of Playa Espadilla Sur to **Playa Manuel Antonio,** also known as **Playa Tres.** Picnic areas, bathrooms, showers, and a refreshment stand are all available here. Set in a rocky cove, Playa Manuel Antonio has calm surf, narrow shores and clear water that's perfect for bathing, swimming, and snorkeling. The next big stop along the main trail leads to less-visited **Playa Escondida** (1.5km), only accessible during certain times of the year. **Puerto Escondido Trail** circles Punta Catedral, once a large island that has become linked to the land by sediment build-up. The path, full of red crabs, leads to **Playa Gemelas,** then returns to the south tip of Playa Espadilla Sur and leads to Playa Manuel Antonio. The **Sloth Trail (Sendero Perezoso)** is a 1.3km hike originating at the same place as the Puerto Escondido trail and leads to the spectacular **mirador,** by way of a 30min. hike through butterflies, hanging vines, and the slow tree-dwellers for whom it was named. **Sendero Cataratas** breaks off the Sloth Trail's gravel road and leads to a **waterfall.** Walk 15min. up to a sign (before the cement bridge), which marks the Sendero Cataratas. This trail winds 700m through the forest and over a stream to a small waterfall.

DOMINICAL

With rocky chocolate-brown beaches and reliable waves year-round, tiny Dominical (pop. 300) is a surfer's paradise, 50km south of San Isidro on the Pacific coast. This three-road town is also a close-knit community of people who came on vacation and never left; the overwhelming American influence might make Dominical a less-than-ideal destination for those seeking *tico* culture.

🚌 TRANSPORTATION. The official **bus** station is a covered bench across the street from San Clemente, in the north part of town, but you can catch a bus anywhere along the main road. Schedules are unpredictable; come 30min. early. Buses head to: **Ciudad Neily** via **Cortés** (3hr.; 9:15, 10am; ¢450); **Quepos** (2½hr.; 5:25, 8:15am, 1:40, 2:45pm; ¢400); **San Isidro** (1½hr.; 6:35, 7am, 2:40, 3:30pm; ¢500); **San José** (6hr.; 5:25am, 1:40pm; ¢1500); and **Uvita** (45min.; 5:15, 9, 10, 11:30am; ¢300). The only **taxi** service available is **TAXI Dominical** (☎814 4444).

🏛🛈 ORIENTATION AND PRACTICAL INFORMATION. The north end of the main road hits the **Costanera Sur Hwy.** A side-street forks off the main drag, forming a well-trodden shortcut to the parallel beach road. The **San Clemente Bar & Grill** will exchange dollars and traveler's checks. Come to Dominical with cash—prices are high, and the nearest **ATM** is in San Isidro. The cheapest laundry service in town is **Lavandería Las Olas,** in the town center. (☎787 0105. ¢750 per kg. Open 7am-9pm.) In an **emergency,** dial ☎911. **Police** are on the main road, south of the side-street. **Farmacia Dominical** is in the large complex on the north end of the main drag. (☎787 0197. Open daily 8am-8pm.) **Clínica de Primeros Auxilios** (☎787 0310 or 787 0024) is next to Diu Wok. You can make **international calls** with your own phone card at **Diu Wok** (¢350 per call). **Internet Río** is in the complex at the north end of town. (☎787 0159. ¢400 per 15min., ¢1400 per hr. Fax available. Open M-Sa 9am-7pm, Su noon-8pm.) **San Clemente Bar & Grille** sends and receive mail. They also sell envelopes, postcards, and stamps.

⌐ ACCOMMODATIONS. The logistics of staying in Dominical vary quite a bit by season, though its accommodations will suit all budgets. Prices rise substantially during the high season, when reservations are necessary. Generally, you won't get as much luxury for your buck in less touristed towns. **Camping** on the beach is possible, although belongings and equipment should never be left unattended. Check with the police for up-to-date security information. **Cabinas San Clemente ❷**, toward the north end of the beach road, is partially obscured by a jungle-like garden; spacious rooms feature tiled floors and luxurious designs. (☎787 0026. Laundry ¢800 per kg. Doubles with fans and cold baths US$30, low-season US$20; with hot baths and A/C US$50/$40.) **Dominical Backpackers' Hostel ❶**, with check-in at Cabinas San Clemente next door, has bamboo furniture, an upstairs balcony, hot baths, a communal TV, and kitchen. (☎787 0026. US$10.) At **Camping Antorchas ❶**, guests stay in cheerful rooms and have access to communal kitchen and bath. Other amenities include: basketball court, hammocks, and river tubes. (☎787 0307. US$5, low season $4, with tent US$6/$5; Dorms US$8/$6.)

⌐ FOOD. New restaurants come and go here; it's hard to count on anything staying around for too long. Get groceries from **Diu Wok,** where the side-street splits off the main road (☎787 0087; open daily 5am-10pm) or the *abastecedor* across from Cabinas San Clemente. (Open daily 8am-6pm.) **Restaurante El Rincon ❷**, set back from the north end of the main road, is a charming spot raised on stilts over an estuary. (☎787 0416. Open daily 11:30am-10pm.) **San Clemente Bar & Grille ❷** is a local hangout serving TexMex and beer in the center of town. The high ceiling is hung with broken surfboards, though a flaming Elvis shrine might also command your attention. Taco Tuesday features ¢500 tacos and ¢900 margaritas. (Restaurant closes at 10pm. Breakfast 7-11:30am.) **Jazzy's River House ❸**, behind the Fishline store next to the *abastecedor,* serves full-course veggie meals (¢1800-¢2000; dessert ¢700) before their live shows. Reservations required. (☎787 0310. Kitchen closes when shows begin at 7pm on W, 8pm on Sa).

⌐ NIGHTLIFE. Hordes of *ticos*, surfers, and other tourists tend to pack into the same spots, which vary in popularity depending on the day of the week. **San Clemente Bar & Grille** brings in a DJ on Friday nights to mix *salsa, merengue*, pop, and funk (open daily 10pm-2am, bar until 11pm). **Roca Verde**, 1km south of Dominical along the highway, draws even the surfers who can't afford to stay here. (Cover ¢600. Sa 10pm-3am. Other nights the bar usually closes by midnight.) **Jazzy's River House** hosts live music ranging from Irish folk to rock or classical, and serves cinnamon rolls (¢400) to accompany the Saturday night music. Frat party vibes fill **Tortilla Flats**, where Thursday hours (open till 1am) draw crowds. (☎787 0033. Other nights closes at 11pm.)

⌐ OUTDOOR ACTIVITIES. Going swimming in untouristed **Dominicalito** is a relaxing change of pace from *gringo* Dominical. There are two options: the mild waves on an all-but-deserted beach, or *La Poza Azul* farther inland (literally, "the blue pond"), with a small waterfall, natural swimming hole, and rope swing. To get to either destination, travel south on the highway 4km by car (5min.); on a bus headed to Uvita (5min.; 5:15, 9, 10, 11:30am; ¢75); by bike (10min.); or by foot (20min.). Across the highway from the beach, a soccer field marks the center of town. To get to the pond, follow the main road inland past the soccer field and church and take a right at the top of the hill. Check out **Don Lolu's Nauyaca Waterfalls,** next door to **Restaurante Su Raza,** for tours that include horseback rides to the waterfalls. (☎787 0105 or 787 0148; www.ecotourism.co.cr/navyacawaterfalls/index.html; tours US$40.) **Posada del Sol** rents **horses** (¢2500 per hr.). The **Surf Shack,** next to San Clemente, rents boards and bikes and offers surf lessons. (Surfboards US$7-$15 per day; boogie boards US$5; surf lessons 1-2hr. US$35; bikes US$15 per day, more than 2 days US$10. Open daily 7am-2pm.) **Tortilla Flats** will take you on a mountain bike tour through nearby terrain. (Full-day tours US$45 with lunch, half-day US$30 with snack. Board rentals US$10 per day; bikes US$10 per day.) For those bored of ecotourism, Kim at Jazzy's River House offers lessons in everything from basket-weaving to yoga (see **Food,** p. 203).

At the **Dominical Visitor Center** (☎787 0096), the English-speaking staff makes reservations all over the country. **Diamond Tours** runs hikes to gargantuan private waterfalls, topped by caves outfitted with beds and toilets. (Overnight US$100 per person, daytrip US$60 per person. Meals included. Open daily 8:30am-6:30pm.) For more watery adventures, **CR Nature Explorers** offer full- (US$80-$90) or half-day (US$40-$70) whitewater rafting on Ríos General, Guavo, and Terraba. Their popular ocean kayak trips explore caves along the Parque Nacional Marina Ballena's coast (US$45 per person). Office located above San Clemente's Bar & Grille. (☎787 0304 or 813 9420. Open daily 8:30am-5:30pm.)

🔁 **DAYTRIP FROM DOMINICAL.** Jack and Diane Ewing moved onto **Hacienda Barú** in 1972, but their original plan to farm on it was eclipsed by their delight at finding endangered animals using the trees as migration corridors. These days, Hacienda Barú offers uncrowded jungle trails which casual visitors can hike as a daytrip. The **Strangler Trail** (1km) features primeval terrain full of strangler figs and sloths. It connects to the 1.5km **Pizote Trail,** an excellent bird-watching trail that crosses through wetlands full of sunbathing caimans. The 2.5km **Lookout Trail** is the steepest hike here, but is well worth it for the chance to spot white-faced capuchin monkeys. The entrance fee includes a tour of the **butterfly garden,** which features some of Costa Rica's most colorful species—no small feat, considering that there are more types of butterflies in this small country than in the entire continent of Africa. Six **cabins** are available for overnight stays. (5-person cabins US$34 for 1 person, US$10 per additional person.) Tour options include a **tree climb** 25m into the rainforest canopy (US$35), and a zipline **canopy tour** (US$100). Call ahead to stay or arrange tours. *(Take a left on the Costanera Sur and cross the bridge; walk 3km past the road to San Isidro, and take the first left after the gas station. From Dominical or San Isidro, any Quepos-bound bus will drop you off at the gas station. A taxi ride costs ¢2500, and buses returning to Dominical or Uvita pass by at 7am and 3:30pm.* ☎787 0003; www.haciendabaru.com. US$6.)*

UVITA

The little-used highway from Dominical to Uvita has recently been paved, and the coastal village's previous isolation is still evident. The pebble and sand beach is more frequently visited by vacationing Costa Ricans than tourists. A sign on the beach indicates the northern boundary of **Parque National Marino Ballena,** whose unspoiled beaches mark the edge of waters full of tortoises and coral reefs.

📧 **TRANSPORTATION. Buses** go to **San José** (7hr.; 5am, 1pm; ¢1700); **San Isidro** (2½hr.; 5, 6, 9am, 1, 2pm; ¢650) via **Dominical** (45min., ¢300); and **Ciudad Cortés** (1½hr.; 5, 11am, 3pm; ¢450). In Ciudad Cortés you can connect with buses to **Neily.** All buses leave from the fork of the main road in Bahía.

⊞ ⁊ ORIENTAT!JN AND PRACTICAL INFORMATION. Uvita is 1km west of Bahía along the highway (past Río Uvita), on a strip of road heading north. Uvita is split into two distinct sections: the village up on the highway, called **Uvita,** and Playa Bahía Uvita, or **Bahía,** 2.5km to the northeast on the national park border. Most buses to Uvita continue into Bahía; all others will let you off at the start of the main gravel road.

The biggest **supermarket** in the Uvita area is **Supermercado Don Israel,** located along the highway toward Dominical, at a rest stop 200m up the gravel road to Bahía. (☎743 8038. Open daily 6:30am-8pm. AmEx/MC/V.) Closer to the beach is **Abastecedor Tatiana;** follow the sign for the *supermercado* off the gravel road 600m before the fork in Bahía. (☎743 8078. Open daily 7am-8pm.) Local businesses have radio contact with the **police station,** 3km from Bahía (emergencies ☎911). **Internet** access is available at the same rest stop as Supermercado Don Israel. (☎743 8103. Open M-F 8am-5pm; ¢300 per 15min.)

⁊⁊ ACCOMMODATIONS AND FOOD. Uvita is full of a slew of charming budget *cabinas* that are remarkably similar bargains. ▧**Villa Hegalva ❶** occupies an acre of grassy land 25m before the fork on the right. Rooms are cheery, while separate huts have thatched roofs, outdoor toilets, and showers. A *soda* is attached. (☎743 8016. *Soda* open daily 7am-8pm. Huts ¢1500-¢2000 per person; rooms ¢3000-¢4000. Camping ¢800.) **Cabinas Las Gemelas ❶** offers three separate buildings with private baths in a family's backyard. (☎743 8009. Laundry ¢2000 per load. Triples ¢12,000; low-season ¢9000.) **Cabinas Punta Uvita ❶,** past the fork on the left, has rooms with bamboo doors overlooking a private garden. The owner sells earrings (¢1000) and necklaces (¢1500) made from fish bones. (☎743 8015. Singles ¢2500; doubles ¢3500, with bath ¢4000.) It's not hard to find basic food in Uvita; typical *sodas* are everywhere. **Restaurante and Bar La Pachanga ❶** is conveniently located facing the entrance to the park. The painting of a four-armed god might look out of place next to Latin MTV, but the satisfying *comida típica* is well worth the distracting decor. (☎743 8082. Fried fish ¢1800. Open daily 10am-10pm.) **Restaurante Marino Ballena ❶** is a trek from the beach, next to the Internet store on the highway, but it has the largest menu around. This open-air eatery is the most upscale (read: touristy) dining experience in Uvita. Entrees include chicken in pineapple sauce. (☎743 8104. Open daily 6:30am-9pm. AmEx/MC/V.)

⧉ GUIDED TOURS. Villa Hegalva will set you up with Saúl, who runs a 7hr. **horseback ride** into the mountains inland of Bahía. Saúl can take you into the national park to go snorkeling off Isla Ballena and Tres Hermanas. (☎743 8016. Horseback tour US$25 per person, including lunch. Snorkeling 2hr., US$30 per person including equipment.) Next door, **Delfín Tour** offers a 2hr. tour of the marine park by land and motorboat for a minimum of two people. (☎ 743 8169 or 825 4031. US$25 per person.) Jonathan Dunam of **Ballena Adventure,** on the left after the fork, offers snorkeling, fishing, and boat tours. (☎370 9482; ballenavent@hotmail.com. AmEx/MC/V.)

⁊ DAYTRIP FROM UVITA: PARQUE NACIONAL MARINO BALLENA. Parque Nacional Marino Ballena was founded in 1989 as the first (and only) national aquatic park in Costa Rica. If you enter past one of the four **ranger offices,** they will request a ¢400 donation. In general, the park is loosely run, with flexible hours and stray chickens wandering the grounds. The park consists of 115 terrestrial hectares and 5375 marine hectares, with an extensive reef containing five types of coral. The light brown beaches are shaded with coconut palms and almond trees. **Snorkeling** is possible off Punta Uvita when the tide is right (check the tide chart at the ranger office or ask at Villa Hegalva), or from a boat off the rock islands of **Piedra Ballena** and **Tres Her-**

manas. (See **Guided Tours,** above.) If you need gear, ask at Villa Hegalva (see **Accommodations,** p. 205). From January to March, you may spot whales migrating from Southern California with their newborns. From September to November, whales return from the south through the park. Baby tortoises hatch in a sand pit next to the ranger station from June to September. It is possible to camp in the park with permission from the rangers. Vacationers usually camp on a beach south of Punta Uvita. *(Ranger offices are located at all 4 of the major entrance points to the park. North to south these are: Punta Uvita in Bahía, Playa Colonia, Playa Ballena, and Playa Pinuela. Because of its proximity to accommodations, Punta Uvita is most frequented. To get to any of the others, take a bus heading to Cuidad Cortés and ask the driver to stop.* ☎/fax 743 8236 or 743 8236.)

SOUTHERN COSTA RICA

With the notable exception of Parque Nacional Chirripó, this relatively isolated area doesn't really cater to tourists. Travelers principally value these southern towns as gateways into the secluded wilderness beyond—and those who choose to explore more remote areas are richly rewarded. Parque Nacional Chirripó offers lush cloud forests and unique ridge views of both coasts, while the area's diversity of cultural outposts—from the artistry of indigenous reserves to the Italian heritage of San Vito—keep its small-town life uniquely vibrant.

Southern Costa Rica

SAN ISIDRO

San Isidro's location makes it a convenient springboard for trips into southern Costa Rica, whose rustic splendor contrasts sharply with the city's noisy bustle. Though its urban streets are kept immaculate enough for locals to walk barefoot, some might quickly find themselves impatient to explore the world beyond its asphalt terrain, and most remember it primarily as a transportation hub.

TRANSPORTATION. Though the city is small enough to keep everything within walking distance, finding the right **bus** out of San Isidro may seem a bit overwhelming at first—there are six different bus companies. TUASUR (☎771 0418) has service to **San José** (3½hr.; 6:30, 9:30am, 12:30, 2:30, 3:30pm; ¢1700). MUSOC (☎771 0414) buses leave for **San José** from the terminal next to Vargas Rojas on the Interamerican Hwy. between C. 2 and 4 (5am, every 1-2hr. 5:30am-4:30pm; ¢1700). Transportes Blancos (☎771 2550) is located on the curve between Av. 2 and 4 on the east side of town the ticket office is open daily 6:15-10am and 12:30-4pm. Buses head to: **Dominical** (1½hr.; 7, 9am, 1:30, 4pm; ¢550); **Puerto Jiménez** (6hr.; 6:30am, noon, 3pm; ¢1330); **Quepos** (3hr.; 7am, 1:30pm; ¢655); **Uvita** (2½hr.; 9am, 4pm; ¢505) via **Playa Hermosa** (2hr., ¢480). TRACOPA on the corner of the Interamerican Hwy. and C. 3 (☎771 0468); offices are open M-Sa 4:30am-7:30pm, Su. 4:30am-3pm. Buses go to: **Golfito** (4½hr.; 10am, 6 pm; ¢1450); the **Panamanian border** at Paso Canoas (4½hrs.; 8:30, 10:30am, 2, 4, 7:30, 9 pm; ¢1500); and **San Vito** (3½hr.; 5:30am, 2pm; ¢1450). GAFESO (☎771 1523) is located next to Transportes Blancos; buses leave for **Buenos Aires** (1¼hr.; M-Sa 11 per day 5:15am-5pm; ¢400). From the west side of the *parque* across from Restaurante Delji, buses run to **San Gerardo de Rivas** (1½hr., 5:30am, ¢500). Another bus to San Gerardo leaves at 2pm from the main terminal, located on the south side of the *mercado*. **Taxis** line the *parque central*. (To San Gerardo ¢7000.)

ORIENTATION AND PRACTICAL INFORMATION. Some streets are marked, but most addresses in San Isidro, as in most of Costa Rica, do not include street names. **Avenida Central** and **Calle Central** meet at the northwest corner of the **parque central**. **Ciprotur** on Av. 1/3, C. 4, provides information on outdoor activities. (☎771 6096; www.ecotourism.co.cr. Open M-F 7:30am-5pm.) **Selva Mar,** 50m south of the southwest corner of the *parque* on Av. 2/4 C. Central, can set you up with tours on both coasts. (☎771 7878; www.exploringcostarica.com. Open M-F 8am-noon and 1:30-5pm, Sa 8am-noon. AmEx/MC/V.) **Ministerio de Ambiente y Energía (MINAE),** on Av. 2/4, C. 2, has info on national parks and reservations. (☎771 4836 or 771 3155. Open M-F 8am-4pm.)

    Banco Nacional de Costa Rica, on the northeast corner of the *parque* at Av. Central, C. 1, changes traveler's checks, gives cash advances on Visa, and has a V/Plus 24hr. **ATM.** (☎785 1000. Open M-F 8:30am-3:45pm.) **Western Union** is on Av. 2, C. 0/2. (☎ 771 8535 or 771 3534. Open M-F 7am-5pm, Sa 7am-12pm.) **Laundry** service is available at Av. Central/2, C. 4, next to Planet Hollywood. (☎771 4042. ¢450 per kilo. Open M-F 8am-5:30pm, Sa 8am-4pm.) **Supermercado La Corona** is on Av. 2 between C. 3 and the highway. (☎771-5252. Open M-Sa 7:30am-8pm, Su 8am-4pm. AmEx/MC/V.) The **police** station (☎117) is 5km from San Isidro's center, just after a small bridge over Río San Isidro. **Red Cross** provides emergency service (emergency ☎911, toll-free 128, ambulance service 771 0481), and **Farmacia San Isidro,** on Av. Central across from the *parque*, sells medical supplies. (☎771 1567. Open M-Sa 7am-8:30pm, Su 8am-1pm. AmEx/MC/V.) **Hospital Escalante Pradilla** (☎771 0318 or 771 0874), is 5 blocks south of the cathedral on C. 1, facing the stadium. **Internet** access is readily available. **PC@Web,** on Av. 1/3 C., has the cheapest rates in town. (☎770 6444; www.pcwebinternet.com. ¢400 per hr., students ¢300 per hr. Color copies ¢150, regular ¢60. Open M-Th 8am-10pm, F, Su 8am-5pm.) **Brunca Café Internet,** on Av. Central on the north side of the *parque*, a few stores east of Hotel Astoria, sells a limited selection of books. (☎771 3235. ¢150 per 15min. Scanning ¢100 per image. Fax US$2.35 per min. M-Sa 8am-8pm, Su and holidays 9am-5pm.) The **post office,** C. 1, Av. 6/8, on the way to the hospital, offers fax service. Open M-F 8am-5:30pm, Sa 7am-noon. **Postal Code:** 8000.

▐▌ ACCOMMODATIONS AND FOOD. Hotel Astoria ❶ keeps sparse rooms facing the *parque*, with fans to help block out noise from Av. Central. (☎771 0914. Singles ¢1500, with bath ¢2500; doubles ¢2800/¢4000.) **Hotel Chirripó ❶** is on the south side of the *parque*, at Av. 2, C. Central/1. Free parking until 10pm, fans, and TV make this a good deal for bigger groups. (☎771 0529. Singles ¢2000, with bath ¢3500; doubles ¢3500/¢5000; triples ¢7000; quads ¢8500.) **Soda Chirripó ❶** is on Av. 2, C. 1 at the southeast corner of the *parque*. Catering mostly to locals watching sports on its small TV, this is the biggest *soda* in town. It serves heaping plates of *casados* (¢500-¢1200) and *sopa negra* (¢850), and has a cheap fast-food menu. (☎771 8287. Open M-Sa 6:30am-6pm, Tu until 7pm. AmEx/V.)

CHIRRIPÓ AND SAN GERARDO DE RIVAS

A popular destination for nature enthusiasts, Parque Nacional Chirripó is home to the tallest peak in Costa Rica (3820m). The well-marked route ascends through vast pastures dotted with livestock before winding into cloud forests curving around the side of the mountain. If the weather cooperates, you can see both the Atlantic and Pacific Oceans from the rocky peak. The 20km trip up is an accesible climb for the average fit traveler, though it can take up to three days. Fitness extremists and foolhardy masochists flock to the annual Chirripó marathon on March 25th, when hundreds of daring runners from around the world come to challenge the mountain. San Gerardo, the gateway to Parque Nacional Chirripó, is geared towards accommodating the sore legs and hungry bellies of visiting hikers, with its natural hot springs, tasty local food, and abundant hospitality.

▐ TRANSPORTATION. The 5:30am bus from San Isidro will drop you off at the edge of town in front of the ranger station (2km from the trail), and the 2pm bus will drop you uphill at the town center. Catch the return bus at the ranger station (1½hr.; 7am, 4pm; ¢1000) or in front of the church 15min. earlier.

▐▌ ORIENTATION AND PRACTICAL INFORMATION. San Gerardo stretches for 1.5km along an uphill section of road. The town center consists of a large white church and a school with a soccer field across from the small **pulpería** (open daily 6:30am-8pm). Some travelers get dropped off at the station, check in, and then find a nearby hotel. Most prefer to find a hotel closer to the trail (i.e., in town), stash their gear, and then walk down to check in at the ranger's. Reservations are recommended for those planning to stay at hotels closer to the trail during the high season (Dec.-Apr.); call the town phone (☎771 1866). Best bets for food are the restaurants and *sodas* attached to numerous accommodations. Your first stop in the area should be the ranger station in San Gerardo, where the buses drop you off. (☎200 5348. Open daily 6:30am-4pm.) Rangers can give you updates on the latest conditions and advice for the trail. Park admission US$10 per person, with additional charges for camping (US$5) or hostel lodging (US$10).

▐ ACCOMMODATIONS. Albergue Urán ❶ appeals to hikers because of its convenient location only 100m downhill from the trail entrance as well as its standing offer to pick up visitors from the ranger station for free. (☎388 2333; www.hoteluran.com. US$7 per person; triple with bath US$24.) **Albergue Vista a El Cerro ❶**, the second-closest hotel to the trail (1km from Urán), is marked by a large blue sign. Ask for the *cama de roca*, a bed perched atop a set of stone stairs. Owner Eneida offers free parking, shared hot baths, and great vegetarian food for low prices. (☎373 3885 or 305 3885. US$7 per person.)

Hikers almost always stay at Base Crestones on their way to the summit. Reservations are required, but cancellations are frequent and you may be able to nab a spot from the San Gerardo rangers. It's usually easy to find space in the rainy season, though reservations can be made up to a month in advance from the MINAE office in San Isidro. (☎771 4836 or 771 3155. Open 8am-4pm.) You might be required to pay by wire transfer to secure a reservation.

⚑ OUTDOOR ACTIVITIES. The hike up **Parque Nacional Chirripó** leaves from San Gerardo de Rivas. Signs to the trailhead start at the ranger station 2km below, and the trail is easy to follow the whole way up. The hike begins as a rocky path across mountainous farmlands and turning into moist reddish clay as it snakes through the cloud forest, where the ground is littered with red flowers and trees are hung with aptly named "old men's beards." The final stretch passes through a unique *páramo* ecosystem, where the tallest trees barely reach 4ft. Reaching the summit, which is marked by a Costa Rican flag, is especially satisfying on clear days, when the views will take your breath away.

For most hikers, it isn't possible to climb Chirripó in a day. It's a difficult 14.5km uphill climb to a rugged but well-equipped **hostel** at the base of the peak; this could take anywhere from 7-16hr., depending on your fitness level. Rangers recommend beginning the hike early in the morning (5-5:30am), because in high season the heat can become unbearable by mid-afternoon on the first part of the trail (it's called "the thermometer" for this reason); in low season, heavy rains begin around 1pm. While hiking during low season, pack clothes in plastic bags to keep them dry. The hostel, officially named Centro Ambientalista el Páramo but more commonly known as **Base Crestones,** is a top-of-the-line facility run by knowledgeable and friendly rangers, 500m vertical below the summit. It has beds with mattresses, a phone, limited solar power, and showers. One thing it doesn't have is heat—the temperature at the base can drop to 7°C at night from May to December and as low as 6°C from January to April—so plan accordingly. (☎770 8040. Sleeping bags ¢700 per night, stoves ¢500, blankets ¢300, shirts ¢3000, drinks ¢500.) From Base Crestones it is another 5.5km of steep vertical climb to the summit—allow at least 2hr. even if you're fit. The fastest way to climb Chirripó is to hike to Base Crestones, stay overnight, climb to the peak and then return the second day. This option is fairly strenuous, however, and rangers encourage travelers to take two nights at Base Crestones so that they can climb the peak at a more leisurely pace.

Though everyone comes here to trek up the mountain, the area offers other diversion that nicely complement the climb. Soothing **aguas termales** tucked into a nearby forest are worth a steep uphill walk and perilous bridge-crossing. Take the path to the left of the white bridge 50m uphill from the ranger station. Proceed uphill about 800m, and follow the right-hand trail marked with a yellow-bordered sign. Cross the suspension bridge and follow the red marks uphill for 10-15min. (Baths ¢900 or US$2 per day; pay at the *soda* on top of the hill. Open 7am-6pm.) **Francisco Elizondo** of Cabinas El Descanso (see **Accommodations,** p. 208) and his family offer guided **treks** in English through their **Finca El Mirador,** with views of the entire valley and a lesson on **coffee harvesting** and production (4hr., US$5). Francisco will take you on a trout fishing tour to catch your own dinner or guide Chirripó hikes for small groups (US$30). Marcos Romero Valverde, of Albergue Urán, will take you on **horseback** to nearby **waterfalls** (¢3500 per person). You can rent horses from Marcos or Cabinas El Descanso.

COSTA RICA

🔊 **AN ALTERNATE ROUTE.** Serious hikers have recently begun exploring a three-day hike along the *Cordillera Talamanca*, the highest mountain range in the country (Chirripó is one of its peaks). This range divides the Atlantic and Pacific sides of the country, and 80% of the trail (about two days) consists of a ridge path that offers stunning views of both coasts. Some say that **Cerro Urán**, a distinctive two-peaked mountain, provides an even more beautiful view of the country than Chirripó. The trail, **Urán Chirripó**, originates in a neighboring village called Herradura, located 3km uphill from the San Gerardo ranger station. The rangers require that hikers take a guide from Herradura with them, and they will help you contact Rodulfo Elizondo, an extremely kind man who will help you camp out at designated spots along the way (☎ 771 1199 or 770 8040; 10 people or less, US$30; 10-16 people, US$50).

BUENOS AIRES

Hemmed in on all sides by lucrative pineapple plantations, Buenos Aires remains a small and sleepy town. In contrast to cooler San Isidro, which lies 64km northwest, the town has few attractions, though tourists often find it a necessary layover on southern-bound bus routes.

Two **bus** companies operate in town. GAFESO (☎ 771 1523, 730 0215 or 771 0419) is on the left bottom corner of the market. Buses leave for **San Isidro** (1¼ hr.; M-Sa 6, 7:30, 10am, 12:15, 5pm; Su 6, 10am, 5pm; ¢475). TRACOPA buses are inside the market; they leave for: **Cortes** (2hr.; 1:15, 7:15pm; ¢850); **Neily** (2½ hr.; 6, 8:45am, 1:45, 4:15pm; ¢1325) **San Isidro** (1¼ hr. every hr. 6am-7pm, ¢570); **San José** (5 hr; M-Sa 6:15, 9:15am, 4:30pm; Su. 9:15am, 1:15, 4:30pm; ¢1700); and **San Vito** (2½ hr.; 6:45am, 3:15pm; ¢1115). Hail a **taxi** from the park (☎ 730 0700 or 730 0800).

Facing uphill, the city center from left to right consists of a central marketplace, the *parque central*, and a white church. The **Banco Poplular** is next to the left corner of the market (open M-F 8:30am-3:15pm, Sa 8:15-11:30am). For quick cash, the attached 24hr. **ATM** takes Visa. Groceries and basic toiletries are available at the **Mega Super** (☎ 730 0938), 1 block downhill from the market (open M-F 7am-8pm, Sa 7pm-8pm, Su 8am-6pm). **Public toilets** are available in the market (¢50 for men; ¢100 for women.) The **police** station, open 24hr., is 50m uphill from the front of the church. The **Red Cross** (☎730 0068 or 412) faces the TRACOPA terminal in the market. The **hospital** (☎730 0116) is about 2km out of town walking uphill from the police station. **Public phones** are located on the downhill left corner of the *parque central*. The **post office** is next door to the bank. (Open M-F 8am-12pm and 1pm-5:30pm). **Postal Code** 8100.

Most tourists don't stay longer than is necessary to make their bus connections, so options are limited. **Cabinas Fabi** ❶ (☎730 1110, or call the owner's cell ☎828-1763) is conveniently located next to the GAFESO bus terminal. Rooms boast private baths and TVs. (Doubles ¢5000; triples ¢6000; quads ¢7000. Prices negotiable on weekends or with groups.) **Rancho Azteca** ❷ is only reachable by taxi (¢300), but it is the center of the town's entertainment with a large thatch hut restaurant and roller skating rink (¢500) with a built-in bar that pumps American techno and disco. (☎730 0162 or 730 0212. *Comida típica* ¢600-¢1000, seafood ¢1200-¢1400.) **Soda El Dorado** ❶ faces the GAFESCO terminal on the downhill side of the market. Locals gather here for morning coffee served in homey mismatched mugs and filling *comida típica*. (*Casados* ¢800. Open M-Sa 6am-5pm.) The town's best seafood is at **Marisquería Felipe** ❶, downhill from the GAFESO bus terminal, where local families gather to enjoy fish fillets (¢1000) while watching Spanish cartoons. (☎730 1050. Open daily 10am-10pm.)

❷ DAYTRIP FROM BUENOS AIRES. The **Reserva Indígena Boruca** is a vibrant and welcoming community of indigenous people 20km south of Buenos Aires. Although the Boruca have adopted modern dress and the Spanish language, many traditional customs persist. The primary occupations of the village are agriculture and *artesanía*, vocational crafts that span from woven goods to paintings and carvings. Approximately 90% of the community are artists, and they preserve a sense of heritage in many of their crafts; for example, the women use natural dyes and pre-Columbian backstrap looms to weave cotton textiles, and male artisans craft balsa wood carvings and masks for the famous *Fiesta de los Diablitos* (Festival of the Little Devils).

A one-room museum called the **Museo de la Comunidad Indígena** is located in a *rancho* downhill from the *pulpería* and is open for perusal at any time. If the staff is given prior notice, they can set up crafts for purchase and display, including handmade cotton belts, bags, money purses, small blankets, and tablecloths. The Boruca people are eager to share their artwork with tourists, though they also value the relative isolation of their village. Many of these extremely hospitable people have extra beds in their houses and will invite you to stay with them. When staying with a family, it is expected that guests leave about ¢2000. Villagers ask that tourists in groups call at least two days ahead to the village's phone so that they may prepare the museum and the *cabinas*. *(Buses leave Buenos Aires from the TRA-COPA station, 2hr., 11:30am and 3:30pm, ¢400. Schedules are subject to change, ask the "bus-stop" fruit stand for information. ☎ 730 1673. Open daily 7am-5pm. Rooms ¢2000 per person.)*

SAN VITO

Hilly San Vito stands 980m above sea level, offering respite from the humid southern heat with its cool days and crisp nights. When Italian settlers arrived in the 1950s, they carved this town out of thick woods and established the coffee plantations that still comprise most of its economy. These days, San Vito makes a convenient base for exploring the Wilson Gardens or Parque Internacional La Amistad.

▐ TRANSPORTATION. Buses to **San José** via **San Isidro** (8hr.; 7:30, 10am, 3pm; ¢2615) or go direct (4hr., 5am, ¢2615), from the TRACOPA terminal (☎ 773 3410) located 300m north of the *parque* on the main street. Additional buses to San Isidro run at 6:45am and 1:30pm. (2½hr., ¢1460.) To reach **Neily,** take a bus (2hr.; 5:30, 7, 7:30, 9, 11am, noon, 2, 5pm; ¢450) from the **Santa Elena and Cepul** terminal (☎ 773 3848). Find the terminal by walking down the main street from the *parque*, taking your first left, and continuing up the hill 250m. **Taxis** line the edge of the park furthest uphill.

▟▐ ORIENTATION AND PRACTICAL INFORMATION. The **Centro Cultural** faces the park and is located on the main street, **Calle Dante Alighieri,** which leads uphill to the Wilson Botanical Gardens and Neily. Downhill, the main street leads to the TRACOPA bus station and post office. **Banco Nacional** has two **ATMs** and will exchange traveler's checks. (☎ 773 3601. Open M-F 8:30am-3:45pm.) **Banco de Costa Rica** offers similar services. (☎ 773 4203. Open M-F 8:30am-3pm.) **Supermarket Automarket BM** is tucked between the intersection of the main street and the bus terminal. (☎ 773 3525. Open daily 7am-8pm.) The **police station** (☎ 773 3225, emergencies 911) is on the main street, and the **Red Cross** (☎ 773 3191) is just past the Cepul bus station. The **Coto Brus pharmacy** has a decent selection. (☎ 773 3076. Open M-Sa 7:30am-6:30pm, Su 8am-11am.) The **hospital** (☎ 773 4125 or 773 4203) is 1.5km from the park past the Banco de Costa Rica. **Internet** access is available at

NeuroTec. (☎ 773 3521. ¢500 per hr. Open M-F 8am-noon and 1-8pm, Sa 8am-noon and 1-5pm.) The **post office** is on the main street near the police. (☎ 773 3130. Open M-F 8am-5:30pm, Sa 7:30am-noon.) **Postal Code:** 8257.

[] [; **ACCOMMODATIONS AND FOOD.** The genially managed **Hotel Rino ❷**, 200m north of the park, has spacious rooms arranged around a second-floor balcony. Well worth the extra colónes, rooms come with carved bed frames, cable TV, tiled hot baths, and complimentary breakfast at the attached *soda*. (☎ 773 4030 or 773 3071. Singles ¢4200; doubles ¢4384. AmEx/MC/V.) **Cabinas Neily ❶**, 500m downhill from the Cepul terminal, offers basic comfortable rooms with private baths and a small communal TV lounge. (☎ 773 4735. ¢2000 per person; singles, doubles, triples available.) **Hotel El Ceibo ❸**, tucked away down a quiet dead-end street, has 40 luxurious rooms with TV, private hot baths, and fans. Rooms on the second floor have balconies over the landscaped front yard. (☎ 773 3025. Singles ¢7000; doubles ¢11,650. V.) Though San Vito's Italian restaurants are charming, they are not as numerous as one might suspect. **Pizzería Liliana ❶**, past the taxi lines with lanterns around its sign, was the town's first Italian restaurant and remains the local favorite. (Pizzas ¢1200-¢3000. Open daily 10am-10pm. V.) For swanky service and excellent salads (with tuna ¢1300), try the restaurant in **Hotel El Ceibo ❷**, located down a driveway to the left of the main street with your back to the park. (☎ 773 3025. Open daily 6:30am-9:30pm.) **Restaurante Jimar ❶** serves fast food amid funky decor next to the ICE office on the right edge of the park. A collection of model cars threaten to distract patrons from hamburgers (☎ 773 4050. Burgers ¢500. Open daily 10am-11pm.)

◙ SIGHTS. The **Centro Cultural Dante Alighieri** is a small museum dedicated to the town's Italian heritage. Housed in a beautiful wooden building with decorative window grates, black-and-white photographs document the arrival and beginnings of early settlers. (☎ 773 3570. Open M-F 1-7pm.) **Finca Cántaros**, 2km outside town, features 10 hectares of trails surrounding a lagoon full of birds. The lodge has a children's library and a craftwork store selling indigenous *artesanía* from the Boruca and Guaymi (another nearby tribe) as well as pieces by Panamanian artists. The *finca* is accessible by taxi (¢500), by foot (uphill about 30min.), or by any bus headed to the Wilson Botanical Gardens. (☎ 773 3570. ¢350. Open daily 8am-4pm. If the lodge door is shut, just knock.)

◪ DAYTRIPS FROM SAN VITO. Founded in 1963, the **Wilson Botanical Gardens'** 25 acres overflow with a mind-boggling variety of plants and birds. There are over 700 species of palms alone, the second-largest collection worldwide. The **Natural History Trail** is a 2hr. highlight tour featuring violet-colored bananas, colossal bamboo shoots, and the entertaining "marimba palm." Rub a stick along its spines to watch it dance. Follow trails like the **Palm Tour** (the park's most famous), the **Orchid Tour**, the **Hummingbird Tour**, or the **Anthurium Trail**, designed by famous Brazilian landscaper Roberto Burle Marx, a Pablo Picasso disciple. Call in advance to arrange a guided tour (in English or Spanish) with a resident biologist. (☎ 773 4004. US$10.) Maps of the hikes are included with entrance fee. Reserve a spot before 10am if you want to eat in the garden's dining room with resident scientists and students. Comfortable *cabinas* available for those who want to explore at greater length. *(Singles US$70; doubles US$175; meals included. The gardens are a 6km, 10min. bus ride from San Vito. Only buses headed to Neily via Agua Buena drive by the gardens; tell the driver where you are going. Buses leave from San Vito's Cepul terminal at 7, 9am, 2, and 5pm; ¢150. Outside the park entrance, 10 buses per day head back to San Vito 6:30am-5:15pm. Some people walk or take a taxi for ¢1000. ☎ 773 4004, reservations 240 6696; www.ots.ac.cr. Open daily 8am-4pm. US$6, with Costa Rican residency US$2.)*

CIUDAD NEILY

Although this town is a major center for the African palm-oil industry and an important transportation hub, it doesn't boast many tourist attractions. If you find yourself staying here for more than one night, ask the English-speaking pharmacy owner for directions to the mysterious caves 2km from town.

⊟ TRANSPORTATION. All **buses** leave from one main terminal uphill from the center of town: **Golfito** (1½-2hr., 13 buses per day 6am-7:30pm, ₡350); **Zancudo** (3hr.; 9:30am, 12:15pm; ₡500); **Paso Canoas** (45min., 23 buses per day 6am-7:30pm, ₡175). Tracopa (☎783 3227) runs to **San José** (7-8hr.; 4:30, 5, 8:30, 11:30am, 3:30pm; ₡2750). CEPUL runs buses to **San Vito** (2hr., 7 per day 6am-5:30pm, ₡500). Térraba (☎783 4293) goes to: **Ciudad Cortés** (30min., 9 buses per day 5am-4:15pm, ₡345); **Dominical** (5 hr., 6am, ₡1150); **Palmar Norte** (1hr., 9 buses per day 5:20am-4:30pm, ₡330); and **Puerto Jiménez** (4½hr.; 7am, 2pm; ₡1140). **Taxis** line up on the diagonal street at the bottom right corner of the *parque* (☎783 3183).

▉▉ ORIENTATION AND PRACTICAL INFORMATION. The town's commercial center lies between the *parque* and the Interamerican Hwy. The main drag starts 1 block to the right of the big gas station, facing north. The **Banco de Costa Rica,** across from the gas station, has two 24hr. Visa **ATMs.** (Open M-F 8:30-3pm.) The ATMs at **Banco Nacional** accept all other cards. Farther north, the **Banco Popular** has another ATM. (☎783 3300. Open M-F 9am-4:30pm, Sa 8:15am-11:30am.) **MegaSuper** offers basics for cheap prices. (☎783 3015 or 783 4044. Open daily 8am-9pm.) The Banco Popular has free **public toilets.** The **Red Cross** and **police** are located at the north end of town; call the same number for both. (☎783 4066; both open 24hr.) For emergencies call ☎911. The **Santa Lucía pharmacy** at the center of town is well-stocked. (☎783 3600. Open M-Sa 8am-8pm.) The **hospital** (☎773 4111) is 2km from town along the Interamericana Hwy. **Public phones** are in the *parque central*, and **Internet** access is available at air-conditioned **NeuroTec,** next door to Hotel Andrea. (☎783 4455. Open M-F 8am-noon and 1-8pm, Sa 8am-noon and 1-7pm. ₡500 per hr. AmEx/MC/V.) The **post office** is next door to the police. (☎783 3500. Open M-Sa 8am-noon and 1-4:30pm, Su 7:30am-noon.) **Postal Code:** 8250.

▉▉ ACCOMMODATIONS AND FOOD. The city is full of affordable places to sleep, most of which are clustered around the gas station. At **Cabinas Elvira's ❶,** rooms are grouped around a private courtyard full of plants. Guests share a common room with cable TV; rooms have fans and tiled baths. (☎783 3057. Singles ₡2000; doubles ₡3000.) **Cabinas El Rancho ❷** has rooms at every price level. Turquoise *cabinas* with tiled floors and private baths are spread across a rocky lot. (☎783 3063. Singles ₡3000; doubles ₡400; more for TV and fan. *Cabina* for 6, ₡8000.) Every street in Neily is strewn with small, dirt-cheap *sodas*. For a wider menu selection, try **Restaurante Moderno ❶,** where *ticos* gather to feast on generously portioned pizzas (₡1500-₡2500) and soups (₡600-₡950) in a large wooden dining room. (☎783 3097. Open daily 6am-10pm. AmEx/MC/V.)

PARQUE INTERNACIONAL LA AMISTAD

Because of its remote location and lack of publicity, Parque Internacional La Amistad remains one of the best-kept secrets of Costa Rican ecotourism. Recently designated a UNESCO World Heritage Site, Amistad offers gorgeous vistas of the southern edge of the Cordillera de Talamanca, a range that stretches well into Panama. The easiest place to begin exploring La Amistad is the **Estación Altamira** entrance point. Altimira is most readily accessible from Buenos Aires via Las Tablas, though the trip is also possible from San Vito. The park is not really a feasible daytrip, so plan on staying overnight.

⌷ TRANSPORTATION. To get to **Altamira**, you must travel through **Las Tablas.** Departing from **San Vito**, head to the TRACOPA station and take the Autotransportes Saenz 10am bus to **San José**, getting off at **Las Tablas** (45min., ₡500). Another option is to take the GAFESO bus from San Isidro to **Buenos Aires** and then switch to a bus for Las Tablas. There is a direct bus to Las Tablas from the TRACOPA station in San Isidro (1 per day, 5:30am). From Las Tablas, buses run directly to **Altamira** (45mins.; 12:30am, 5pm, return 5am, 3pm).

⌷ CAMPING. Estación Altamira ❶ is well-equipped for camping, with bathing facilities, potable water, electric outlets, and a picnic area. There is also an exhibition room, an amphitheater, and a biodiversity lab. Bring your own food and camping equipment, and restock in the nearby town of Altamira, 2km down the hill. Even in high season, reservations are not generally necessary, though visitors should call ahead to the MINAE office in Buenos Aires. (☎730 0846. Open M-F 8am-4pm. Camping US$2 per person.)

⌷ HIKING FROM ESTACIÓN ALTAMIRA. Though the views from the station itself are gorgeous, several trails might entice you to explore further. Guides (₡5000 per day) are advisable and often required. Arrange for a guide in advance through the ranger station or MINAE office.

The **Sendero Gigantes del Bosque,** named for its towering 40m trees, is a 3-4hr., 3km hike through well-marked secondary and primary forest. There is a birdwatching observatory at the border of the primary forest along the trail. Wear long pants; the grass is hip-deep on the second half of the route, but can be avoided by turning around at the abandoned house.

The 20hr. round-trip journey through the lyrically titled **Sendero Valle del Silencio** (Valley of Silence) is the best known and the most highly recommended trail in La Amistad. Hikers attest to the trail's eerie tranquility, claiming even nearby rivers are silent. The hike extends more than 20km each way through cloud forest.

Sendero Altamura-Sabanas Esperanzas takes you to natural savannas 1808m above sea level, leading past an indigenous cemetery to yield dizzying views of the small towns below. Keep an eye out for elusive quetzals in the trees. To reach this trail, take a left instead of a right at the fork in the road next to the church in Altamira. This dirt road will lead to the town of Biolley, where a small ranger station can give you directions to the trailhead.

⌷ PASO CANOAS: BORDER WITH PANAMA

Take a bus to Ciudad Neily and transfer onto 1 of the buses that run regularly to Paso Canoas (45min., 23 buses per day 6am-7:30pm, ₡175). They will drop you at the main intersection. Taxis travel between the towns for ₡2000/US$5. Paso Canoas is 50km from the Panamanian town David, with LaFron buses running between them every 10min. (☎727 6511. ₡800, US$2). Bus terminals are located 100m from the border on the Panamanian side. On either side, TRACOPA (☎732 2119 or 727 6581), 100m west and east of the intersection, sells tickets to David (7-8hr.; 4, 8am, 3pm; ₡2545, US$7) and San José (8hr.; 4, 8, 9am, 3pm; ₡2890/US$7).

Sprawling out from the immigration offices at the Panama-Costa Rica border, Paso Canoas is hardly scenic. The fairly painless passport and tourist card process is necessary for those advancing further into either country.The main street, **Calle Central,** runs north-south, cutting perpendicularly across two main *avenidas* running along the border (Panama on the east, Costa Rica on the west). All establishments take US dollars, and most Panamanian stores accept colónes. The **Interamerican Highway** from Neily and San José cuts straight through town toward David and Panama City. Though the immigration process doesn't usually take more than 45min., the wait is completely dependent on lines. To cross the border, go to the Costa Rican **General de Migración**, 175m west of the main intersection, and get your passport stamped. (☎732 2150. Open daily 7am-10pm.) **Customs** is next door. (☎732 2801. Open M-Sa 6am-10pm, Su 6-11am, 1-5pm, 6-10pm.) Entering Panama, travelers need a passport, a 30-day tourist card (available at the border checkpoint; US$5), and a return ticket. Entering Costa Rica has the same requirements. Tourist cards are sold at **Instituto Panameño de Turismo** on both sides. (Open daily 6-11am and 1-5pm, though schedules vary.) Both sides have additional checkpoints 1km down the Interamericana, so keep your passport handy. **Money changers** abound. On the Costa Rican side, **Super Ahorro** sells all the basics. (☎732 2086. Open daily 6am-9pm.) The **police** are 50m from both borders. (Costa Rica ☎732 3402, Panama 727 6521, emergencies 911.) Buses drop off in front of the **post office** in Costa Rica (☎732 2029. Open M-F 8am-noon and 1-5:30pm), and there is another **post office** in Panama (open M-F 8-11am and 2-5pm, Sa 8am-noon). Though it might lack interesting sights, Paso Canoas certainly won't leave you hungry, and its hotels offer respite to travelers who get their feet stuck in bureaucratic mud. **Cabinas Bar and Restaurante Interamericana ❷**, 200km east of the Interamericana, keeps its cheap rooms immaculate. (☎732 2041 or 732 2478. Rooms US$5/₡2000 per person; ₡500 less for groups. V.) Expect the same fast food from either side of the border: everything will be plentiful and fried. The **Restaurante Tracopa ❶** has a menu of *tico* favorites painted next to its seascape mural. (Meals under ₡1000. Open daily 6am-7pm.)

PENÍNSULA DE OSA AND GOLFO DULCE

The Peninsula de Osa provides seclusion and splendor without parallel, described by the National Geographic Society as "the most biologically intense place on earth." Bounded by long, empty beaches, the untouched wilderness seems endless. Puerto Jiménez, the only sizeable city on the peninsula, is a convenient base for exploring Corcovado, though visitors looking to escape other travelers might want to try the virgin nature reserves around Golfito. Visitors test their surfing skills on one of the world's longest lefts in Pavones, and snorkel among rainbow fish and dolphins off the coast of Reserva Biológica Isla de Caño. While visitors might feel immersed in nature, every town has banks, police, and Internet cafes.

SIERPE AND BAHÍA DRAKE

There are several beach towns on and around the *península* that attract surfers and loungers alike. **Sierpe,** founded 60 years ago, was originally a community of banana plantation farmers, though the 10km gravel road leading to this serene rural community is now lined with palm tree farms and cattle ranches. Residents of Sierpe are friendly to travelers and eager to show them around. **Bahía Drake** is named after Sir Francis Drake, though none of the Spanish currency he supposedly buried here has ever been found. Though Bahía Drake is not conducive to budget traveling, few who travel to this coastal beach regret the expense.

To get to Sierpe or Bahía Drake from anywhere in Costa Rica, you must first travel to **Palmar Norte. Buses** run from there to Sierpe (45 min.; 8, 9, 9:30am, noon, 2:30, 5:30pm; ₡175). Buses leaving Sierpe to Palmar depart across the street from El Fenix (every 2-3hr., 5:30am-8pm, ₡300). **Taxis** leave from the same spot (US$10).

If you do spend the night here, **Hotel Margarita ❶** in Sierpe offers the best rates in the area. (☎786 7574. US$5. Doubles with warm baths US$12.) For a bite to eat, Sierpe's riverfront ▧**Bar and Restaurante Las Vegas ❶** is *the* place to be during the crowded tourist months of the dry season.

Península de Osa and Golfo Dulce

GOLFITO

Golfito (pop. 18,000), former home of the United Fruit Company headquarters, sits on the northeast coast of the Golfo Dulce. Officials tried to jump-start the economy in 1984 by establishing a duty-free zone in the northern end of the city. This now-famous shopping area draws *ticos* year-round, while water taxis ferry tourists to more exciting locales like Pavones, Zancudo, or Puerto Jiménez.

Flights run daily from San José through **Sansa** (☎ 775 0303. 1hr.; 7, 11:25am, 3:10pm; US$74.50) and **NatureAir** (1hr.; high season 6, 8:30am, 2:30pm; return 7:20, 10am; low season 6, 8:30am; return 7:30, 10am; US$76) to the **airport** 4km north of Golfito. The Sansa office is 100m north of the docks, across from hotel and restaurant Uno. **Buses** depart from the **TRACOPA** bus terminal (☎ 789 9037 or 789 9013) to **San Isidro** (4hr.; 5am, 1:30pm; ¢1870) and **San José** (6½hr., 5am, ¢2750; indirect 8½hr., 1:30pm, ¢2750). From the *muellecito* a **ferry** runs to **Puerto Jiménez** (1-2hr., 11:30am, ¢1000). Nearby, a **water taxi** service run by Froilan Lopez (☎ 775 2166) heads to **Playa Zancudo** (¢10,000) and other destinations like **Cacao, Casa Orquídeas, Pavones**, and **Playa Azul.**

Golfito runs along a 4km north-south stretch of beach road, with the gulf to the west. The city is physically and economically divided in two; the shopping zone is to the north. **Police** (☎ 775 1022, emergency 117) are located in the duty-free zone. The major pharmacy in town is **Farmacía Golfito**. (☎ 775 2442. Open M-Sa 8-noon and 1-7pm.) The **Hospital** (☎ 775 1001) is 1km north of the *muellecito*. **Internet** access is under Hotel Golfito. (☎ 775 2424. ¢300 per 15-20min., ¢500 per hr.)

There are cheap, simple accommodations in and around *Pueblo Civil*. **Hotel Golfito Bay** ❶ is a breezy blue and white building overlooking the water, full of traditional Costa Rican oxcarts and wooden fish mobiles. (☎ 775 0006; telefax 775 2189. Singles ¢2000-¢3000; triples ¢7000.) You can grab a meal anywhere along the road between the Banco Nacional and the *muellecito*, which is crowded with *sodas*. **Restaurante La Cubana** ❶ offers tasty *tico* food with more style and less grease than surrounding *sodas*. (☎ 775 2153. Open daily 10am-10pm.)

Though **Playa de Cacao** is easily accessible from Golfito, its lush jungles and smooth sand bars are rarely crowded. Cacao is known locally as **Captain Tom's**, named for the sailor who intentionally shipwrecked his boat here 50 years ago so that he could gain the right to stay in Costa Rica without proper immigration papers. (6km north around the bay from Golfito; a 1½hr. walk. Taxi about ¢3000. Taxis from the *muelle bananero* are a cheaper, more enjoyable option. ¢1000.)

Poorly publicized **Refugio Nacional de Fauna Silvestre Golfito** protects the steep hills above Golfito, encompassing a variety of distinct terrains that are home to 125 species of trees. Walk past the landing strip to the marked beginning of the trail. A wide path intersects the river and splits into two trails. **Cataracta 1** is a 5min. hike to a waterfall. **Cataracta 2** is a longer trail on muddier terrain to an equally beautiful, slightly smaller waterfall. (☎ 789 9092; rioclaro@ns.minae.go.cr. Open M-F 8am-4pm.)

PAVONES

Home to some of the second longest left-hand waves in the world, Pavones is known across the country for its **surfing.** Bronzed international surfers tend to stay for months, and a vibrant community of farmers has called this place home for years. Vast expanses of sand with fewer surfers can be found at **Punta Banco,** 5km southeast. The center of town is right on the beach. All **buses** pick up and drop off on this dirt road, at the entrance to the beach throughway. Two buses per day run from Pavones to **Golfito** (2½hr.; 5:30am, 12:30pm; return 10am, 3pm; ¢600 including a ferry ride en route). The Golfito bus stops in **Comte,** where a bus on its way from

Neily to **Playa Zancudo** waits for people to make the connection from Golfito (noon, 4:30pm; ¢300). During the high season, an afternoon bus runs between Pavones and Zancudo but in low season the only way to make the trip is by bus connection or by forking over US$40 for a **water taxi**.

The gravel road to the beach is lined with *cabinas* perfect for a variety of budgets. Oceanside **Cabinas Esquina del Mar ❶** in Pavones is a true surfer hangout with a popular *cantina*. (☎383 6737. ¢2000-¢3000 per person, negotiable for students and longer stays.) Fresh thin-crust pizza and pasta made by resident Italians can be had at ▣**Aleri ❶**, just up the street from Esquina La Plaza. (Pasta ¢1500-¢2000; 2- to 3-person pizza ¢3000-¢4000. Restaurant open daily at 6pm.)

ZANCUDO

With 5km of black sand beaches, top-notch ocean swimming, and world-record **sportfishing,** Zancudo should probably be full of tourists and outrageously high prices to match, but it's not. Its seclusion is only interrupted during major Costa Rican holidays (the weeks around Christmas and Easter) when the town swells under an influx of hundreds of *tico* families camping on the beach. From Golfito, **taxi boats** are the easiest but most expensive option (5-person boat US$40). The easiest way to arrive by **bus** is through **Pavones** (2½ hr.; 10am, 3pm; ¢600), and **Comte,** where a bus from Neily heading to Zancudo waits for people to make the connection. (Noon, 4:30pm; ¢300.) During the high season only, an afternoon bus runs between Golfito and Zancudo.

The town runs along a 3km beach road with the gulf to the west and the estuary to the east. The southern end of the beach is choppy enough for some gentle surfing, while the northern end mainly attracts sunbathers. The **police station** (☎911 or 776 0166) is 100m from the deck, past the school on the road bearing left. **Telephones** are numerous, but they only work with Costa Rican calling cards. **Coloso del Mar,** 2km south of the docks, offers the only **Internet** service in town. (☎776 0050. ¢1700 per hr.)

PUERTO JIMÉNEZ

Puerto Jiménez has become known as the backpacker alternative to Bahía Drake, offering far lower prices along with more options for collective transportation and tours into the nearby Parque Nacional Corcovado. The town is undeniably convenient, but the high concentration of passing tourists has all but stripped it of its individual character. However, Jiménez is not without its charms: parrots feeding in the almond trees along the soccer field demonstrate the spectacular wildlife that draws so many travelers here in the first place.

▣ **TRANSPORTATION. Flights** are available to Jiménez through both **Sansa** and **NatureAir.** Sansa (☎735 5017) is 3 blocks down from the soccer field on C. Comercial to the right, and NatureAir (☎735 5062; fax 735 5093) is another block beyond Sansa. Both fly daily to and from **San José**: Sansa (55min.; depart 7:05am, 2pm; return 6am, 1pm; US$75); NatureAir (55min.; depart 7, 9:50am, noon; return 6, 8:30, 11am). Reservations are always necessary, and tickets sell out quickly during the high season. **Buses,** operating out of a terminal 1 block right of the soccer field facing inland, go to **San José** (8hr., 5am, ¢2575) via **San Isidro** (5hr., ¢1765); another bus stops in San Isidro (5hr., 1pm, ¢1765); two buses depart daily for **Neily** (3hr.; 5:30am, 2pm; ¢1150). Getting to Golfito is easiest by **ferry,** but it's possible to take a Neily bus and transfer at Río Claro (1hr; 6am; ¢1000 high season, ¢800 low season).

▣ ⑦ ORIENTATION AND PRACTICAL INFORMATION. The **Calle Comercial** (main road) runs from the **soccer field** in the north to a **gas station** in the south. Buses arrive 1 block to the right of the soccer field. The beach road runs just north of the soccer field and heads east to the ferry pier and airstrip.

CafeNet El Sol (☎735 5718), 1 block south of the soccer field on C. Comercial, is not a formal **tourist office,** but it connects visitors to general info about area adventuress. The **police** station (☎735 5114, emergency 911) is a few steps south of the soccer field on the main street. The **post office** is on the west side of the soccer field. (☎735 5045. Open M-F 8am-noon, 1-5:30pm.) **Postal Code:** 8203.

▛ ACCOMMODATIONS AND FOOD. Cabinas Thompson ❶, behind Soda Marilys, 1 block behind and to the right of the soccer field, has plain rooms with fans and private baths. (☎735 5142. ¢2000 per person, students ¢1500.) Although the town has a wealth of tourist offerings, there are surprisingly few dining options. **Juanita's ❶,** next to CafeNet El Sol, features semi-authentic Mexican food. (☎735 5626. Happy hour 4-6pm. Beer ¢400. Open daily 10am-11pm)

▤ GUIDED TOURS. Puerto Jiménez serves as a launching point for the Osa Peninsula, and a number of tour operators have sprung up to satisfy this demand, providing access to places that would be difficult to reach on your own. **▨Escondidos Trex,** inside Restaurante Carolina 1½ blocks south of the soccer field on C. Comercial, is the oldest and widest-ranging operation. Trips are led by English-speaking naturalists, and include sunset dolphin-watching (US$35), kayaking (US$35), waterfall-rappeling (US$75), rainforest day treks (US$45), and multi-day hikes through Corcovado. (☎735 5210; www.escondidotrex.com. Open daily 8am-8pm.)

PARQUE NACIONAL CORCOVADO

Though the Osa Peninsula comprises only 4% of the Costa Rican land mass, it hosts 50% of its biodiversity, including sloths, jaguars, monkeys, tapirs, anteaters, and almost 400 bird species. Corcovado still awaits full exploration; countless species within its boundaries remain undiscovered.

▣ ORIENTATION. There are four **ranger stations** inside the park; each has water, bathrooms, dining facilities, and campgrounds. Three of these form a triangle connected by trails—**Sirena** on the southwest tip, **La Leona** on the southeast tip, and **Los Patos** to the north. Sirena and La Leona are the only stations with beds (see **Accommodations,** below). **San Pedrillo,** on the northwest tip of the park, is accessible along the beach from Sirena from December 1 to April 31. Seldom used by through-hikers, **El Tigre** is another station located outside park boundaries. **Los Patos** and **La Leona** are best reached from Puerto Jiménez; San Pedrillo is accessible from Bahía Drake.

▣ TRANSPORTATION. Puerto Jiménez (p. 218) is the largest town on the peninsula and offers the most affordable and accessible transportation into the thickets of the national park. Most independent hikers choose this town as their base. To get to the ranger station at **La Leona,** take the *colectivo* truck or a **minibus** from Puerto Jiménez to **Carate** (2½hr.; M-Sa 6am, 1:30pm; return 8am, 4pm; US$6, with Costa Rican residency US$2), which leaves from Soda Thompson, 1 block right of the soccer field facing inland. From Carate, turn right onto the beach and walk about an hour to the park entrance at La Leona. To get from Puerto Jiménez to **Los Patos** (1hr., 6 per day 5am-3pm, ¢500), take a bus from the front of Soda Thompson and ask to be dropped at **La Palma.** From there, hike 2km to **Guadalupe.**

71 PRACTICAL INFORMATION. The park has a US$8 per day entrance fee; make reservations one to two weeks in advance. Getting into the park shouldn't be a problem, especially during the low season, but beds in the lodges are usually in high demand. You can reserve these lodgings through **MINAE** or **Osa Natural** for US$2. If you plan on walking along the coast, pick up a **tide chart** from the ranger station, Osa Natural, or MINAE, because water levels are often too high to cross. The heaviest rain falls March-August, with daily rain lasting until December. Stop at MINAE and ask for a helpful printout with safety info.

ACCOMMODATIONS AND CAMPING. Most overnight trekkers spend three days in the park: the first to hike to Sirena; the second to explore, using Sirena as a base (the route to Los Patos is most popular); and the third to hike out. Rangers arrange lodging and meals. (Breakfast US$8. Lunch and dinner US$11. Dorms US$8; bring sheets and mosquito net. Camping US$4 per person; only allowed inside the station.) La Leona is the only *tico*-run station, and the main ranger cooks phenomenal meals that are well worth the price. **La Leona Lodge Camping ②** has 13 tents with small air mattresses, sheets, towels, and boogie boards at no extra cost. (☎ 735 5705 or 735 5704; www.laleonalodge.com. Lodging singles US$20; doubles US$15 per person. Children under 3 free, ages 3-8 US$8. With lodging, trail use, and three meals: singles US$65; doubles US$120.)

HIKING. In addition to a tide chart, guides are recommended for attempting the three long-distance hikes in the park. The first trail goes from **La Leona** to **Sirena** (19.5km; 6-7hr.) along a sandy beach with several parallel, well-marked forest trails. Two sections (Salsipuedes and Punta La Chancha) are impassable at high tide. The second hike, from **Los Patos** to **Sirena** (20km; 6-8hr.), is especially difficult during the low season, particularly the crossing of the Río Pavo. This trail passes through the heart of the rainforest near a swampy lagoon, and is the best place to find consistently visible wildlife. The third trail, from **Sirena** to **San Pedrillo**—is only open December 1-May 1—hugs the beach and ends in the forest (25.5km; 8-10hr.). The last 7.5km is considered to be the most majestic ecological terrain in Central America, with gargantuan trees rising up to 75m.

CARIBBEAN LOWLANDS

The boggy coastal lowlands along Costa Rica's Caribbean shore offer a drastic contrast to the terrain and culture of the Pacific seaboard. Coconut palms, unbroken beaches, and inland tidal marshes—all kept unfathomably muggy by constant precipitation—line the relatively deserted and remote Caribbean coast. With fewer upscale resort hotels and a laid-back traveling culture, the southern Caribbean is a particularly popular alternative for young backpackers, while less-accessible northern areas draw turtle conservation volunteers and nature enthusiasts. The Caribbean Lowlands have a reputation for theft and casual drug use, so travelers may feel less than comfortable here. Travelers willing to follow safety guidelines, however, will find much to enjoy on this slow-paced, reggae-loving coast.

PUERTO LIMÓN

Limón boasts a cultural diversity found nowhere else in Costa Rica, and is also a convenient launching point for excursions to Tortuguero, Playa Bonita, and other Caribbean towns. At night, taxis are advisable; the city has a reputation for crime. The annual October 12 carnival celebrating Día de la Raza (Columbus Day), now officially named Día de las Culturas, demands attention, as music, dancing, and drinking spill out into the streets for almost a week.

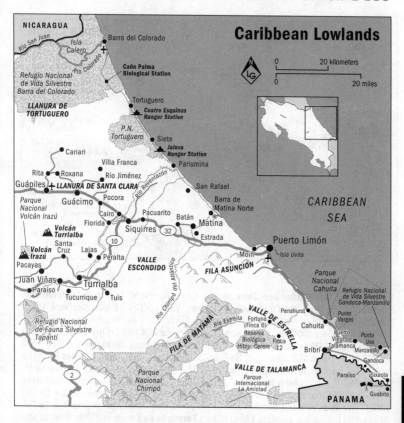

Caribbean Lowlands

█ TRANSPORTATION. NatureAir (☎ 232 7883) and Sansa (☎ 666 0306) run **flights** to and from **San José.** The airstrip is 4km south of town. Auto Transport Caribeños and Prosersa **buses** (in San José ☎ 222 0610, in Limón 758 0385 or 758 2575) leave from **Gran Terminal del Caribe,** Av. 1/2, C. 7, and go to: **Guápiles** (1½hr., every hr. 6am-6pm, ¢905); **Moín** (1½hr., every hr. 6am-7pm, ¢100); **San José** (2½-3hr.; 16 per day 6am-7pm, Su 8pm; ¢1250); and **Siquirres** (1hr., every hr. 6am-7pm, ¢365). The smaller **Coope Limón** (☎ 798 0825), across the street from the Gran Terminal, sends buses to **San José** (2½-3hr., 10 per day 5:30am-4pm, ¢950). Buses depart from the **MEPE station** (☎ 758 1572 or 758 3522) on the corner, 1 block north of the northeast side of the market, to **Manzanillo** (2½hr.; 6, 10:30am, 3, 6pm; ¢750); **Puerto Viejo de Talamanca** (1½hr., 12 per day 7am-6pm, ¢600) via **Cahuita** (45min., ¢410); and the **Panamanian border at Sixaola** (3hr., 14 per day 5am-6pm, ¢620). **Taxis** line Av. 2 and pick up all over the city. A taxi to **Moín** costs US$3.

█ █ ORIENTATION AND PRACTICAL INFORMATION. Like most major Costa Rican cities, Puerto Limón is laid out in a grid of north-south *calles* and east-west *avenidas*, but finding street signs is nearly impossible. Orient yourself by the **mercado municipal,** Av. 2/3, C. 3/4, where buses drop passengers. All hotels and restaurants are within a few blocks of the *mercado.*

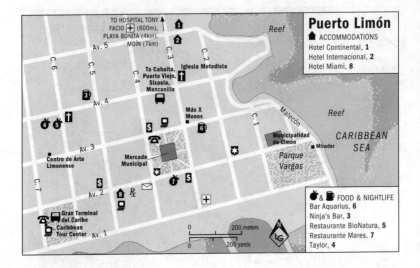

Caribbean Tour Center and Store, in the Gran Terminal, has **tourist information.** (☎798 0816 or 798 1792. Open daily 8am-6pm. AmEx/MC/V.) **Banco Nacional,** at the southeast corner of the market, exchanges US dollars and traveler's checks (2% commission) and offers Visa cash advances. (☎758 0094. Open M-F 8:30am-3:45pm.) The **ATM** at **Banco San José** is on the north side of the market. (☎798 0155 or 798 0167. Open M-F 8am-5pm, Sa 7am-1pm. Cirrus/MC/V.) **Más X Menos** is on the northeast corner of the market. (☎798 1792. Open M-Sa 8am-9pm, Su 8am-8pm. AmEx/MC/V.) In an **emergency,** dial ☎ 911. One police branch is at the southwest corner of the market, and another is 100m east of the northeast corner (☎758 0365). The **Red Cross** is 1 block south of the southeast corner of the market. (☎758 0125 or 911. English spoken. Open 24hr.) **Farmacia de Limón** is 250m west of the southwest corner of the market. (☎758 5450. Open M-Sa 7am-9pm, Su 8am-5pm.) **Hospital Tony Facio** (☎758 2222) is 300m north along the boardwalk. **Telephones** are everywhere, including the north side of the *mercado municipal.* **Cyber Cafe Interurbano,** on the 2nd fl. across from the north side of the market, has 24hr. **Internet** access (US$1 per hr.). Also try the **Instituto de Computación** on the 2nd fl. of the Gran Terminal. (☎798 0128. US$1 per hr., includes free coffee. Open daily 8am-9pm.) The **post office** is southwest of the market (open M-F 8am-5:30pm, Sa 8am-noon). **Postal Code:** 7300.

⚓ ACCOMMODATIONS. Be cautious of ultra-cheap places: they usually don't have strong locks. Most hotels have electronic locks, so you may have to wait to be buzzed in. **Hotel Continental ❷** and **Hotel Internacional ❷** are both 2 blocks north of the northeast corner of the *mercado,* 25m from the beach, and share the same owner and prices. Basic rooms have fans and baths. (Continental ☎798 0532, Internacional 758 0434. Singles ₡3500, with A/C ₡4000; doubles ₡4000/₡4800; triples without A/C ₡5000.) **Hotel Miami ❷,** half a block west of the southwest corner of the market, has large rooms with fans, hot baths, and lots of light. More expensive rooms come with A/C, telephone, and TV. (☎758 0490 or 758 4888. Singles ₡5500-₡8250; doubles ₡7150-₡10,870; triples ₡9500-₡13,200. AmEx/MC/V.)

◻◻ **FOOD AND NIGHTLIFE.** Limón's usual grub combines standard *soda* fare with a Caribbean twist. Curb-side eateries dishing out stews and sandwiches are scattered along the periphery of the *mercado*. Women traveling alone should take taxis after dark. ◪**Restaurante BioNatura** ❶, facing the west side of the cathedral, is Limón's first macrobiotic restaurant, serving up healthy, authentic Caribbean fare with imagination and flair. BioNatura uses the freshest local organic produce, oils, breads, and pastas in its innovative entrees. Savor *patacones* (mashed green plantains with beans and soy cheese; ¢950) and fruit and soy milk *batidos*. (☎ 798 2020. Sandwiches ¢400-¢700; entrees ¢950. Open daily 8am-8pm.) **Caribbean Food Center "Taylor"** ❶, Av. 4, C. 6/7, 50m west of the cathedral, is popular with locals and tucked away from the bustle of the *mercado*. Taylor serves a handful of traditional Afro-Caribbean staples like johnny cakes (¢200), *bisteck de bochinche* (spicy beef with pasta and salad; ¢1000), and *sopa de mondongo* (open M-Sa 8am-9pm). **Restaurante Mares** ❸, across the street from the south side of the *mercado*, has cushioned wicker chairs, an overcrowded fish tank, and a ship's wheel. The posh atmosphere caters to foreigners, though it feels somewhat out of place in low-key Limón. The seafood is great, but a bit pricey. (☎ 758 1347. Open daily 9am-2am. MC/V.) **Ninja's Bar,** on the north side of the cathedral, overwhelms guests with a greenhouse entrance, 3 bars, 7 TVs, pulsing house beats, and more flashing lights than Times Square. (☎ 758 2833. Beer with *bocadillo* ¢600. Open M-Sa 11am-late.) **Bar Aquarius,** a club in the Hotel Acón, across from Más X Menos, pounds reggae and *salsa* into the night. (☎ 758 1010. Th-Sa cover ¢700, women free; 2-for-1 drinks Sa 8pm-midnight. Open daily 7pm-late.)

◙ **SIGHTS.** The most spectacular sight in Limón is the brand-new **Catholic cathedral** being built on the site of the old Vicariato Apostólico. Construction began in November 2001, but has since stalled due to a lack of funding. Even half-finished, the cathedral still awes with its towering spire and ultra-modern, angular design. **Parque Vargas,** in the southeast corner of town, is a gorgeous refuge from the town's bustling center. Waves pound against the seawall nearby, and you might even see a sloth or two bumbling in the treetops. Be sure to check out the impressive **seaside mural** of Limón's rich and tangled history.

A young crowd looking for waves and rays usually heads over to **Playa Bonita,** 4km northwest of Limón. On one side, the water is calm and perfect for wading; on the other, broad, powerful waves give surfers all the lift they need. To get to Playa Bonita, take the Moín bus from the Gran Terminal del Caribe (every hr. 6am-7pm, ¢70), and get off at one of the first stops (ask the driver); or take a taxi (¢1000).

PARISMINA

The tiny hamlet of Parismina (pop. 500) is sandwiched between the Río Parismina and the Caribbean. Most travelers cruise right by the 150 sq. km island in boats from Moín on their way to Tortuguero, 50km north. Though Parismina's ecotourism industry is less developed than Tortuguero's, it has many advantages over its northerly neighbor. Parismina is less touristed, less pricey, and less remote than Tortuguero, while providing similar turtle watching and conservation programs.

◻ **TRANSPORTATION.** Parismina has no roads and is accessible only by **boat.** The most inexpensive way to arrive from San José is to take a **bus** from Terminal Caribe at Av. 13, C. Central, to **Siquirres** (1½hr., every 2 hr. 6:30am-6pm). From the Gran Terminal Siquirres, where the bus drops off, walk to the old bus station on the north side of the soccer field and catch a bus to **Caño Blanco** (2hr.; M-F 4am, 1pm, Sa-Su 6am, 2pm; ¢300). From Caño Blanco, a **public boat** shuttles passengers to Parismina (8min., ¢750). You can also hire a **private boat** from the Caño Blanco dock to Parismina (US$25 for a shared boat). Be sure to arrive at Caño Blanco at least 30min. before 6pm as boats leave the dock early and there are no overnight facilities. Travelers continuing to **Tortuguero** can park their cars in Caño Blanco and hire a boat (US$30-$50). From farther south in the Caribbean, jump on a boat from Moín to Tortuguero and tell the captain you only need to go to Parismina. The ride should cost no more than US$20.

From Parismina, it's possible to continue to Tortuguero on one of the boats passing by the docks from Moín on the way to the national park. It's often difficult to flag a boat, so try arranging in advance to be picked up with one of the captains in Moín; call or drop by the **Asociación Salvemos Las Tortugas de Parismina** kiosk. **Modesto Watson** (☎226 0986) is a good captain to call. To return to **Siquirres**, take the boat to Caño Blanco (M-F 5:30am, 2:30pm, Sa-Su 8:30am, 4:30pm; ¢750) and catch the bus back to Siquirres (M-F 6am, 3pm, Sa-Su 10am, 5pm).

■🔁 **ORIENTATION AND PRACTICAL INFORMATION.** It shouldn't take you much time to find your way around tiny Parismina. From the main dock, a dirt path leads 200m to the town center, meters away from the church and soccer field. There are few services here, so take care of essentials beforehand. The Asociación kiosk in town and María Ester at the **Cariblanco Lodge** are the best sources of info on the town and turtle-watching activities. Pick up basic supplies and snacks at the **pulpería,** about 350m up from the docks. A doctor visits twice a week, usually on Tuesdays and Fridays; check with locals. **Telephones** are available at the dock and opposite Soda Eduardo. (Local calls ¢20 per min. Calls to US ¢800 per min. Open daily 6am-8pm.) **Internet** access is available at the Asociación kiosk.

🔒 **ACCOMMODATIONS.** Budget accommodations are slowly expanding in Parismina. Sport fishermen with more cash to spend usually stay at one of the sportfishing lodges just outside the village. These lodges require private boat transportation from the village. **The Thorny Rose Inn** ❶ is a short walk from the dock; walk 200m up the dirt path and take the first right. The Thorny Rose, known as La Rosa Espinosa, is on your left. Eight breezy rooms have fans and hot baths, complemented by a charming attached restaurant, and a pleasant balcony. (☎711 0974, cell 390 9963. ¢3500 per person, with meals ¢8000.) To reach the **Cariblanco Lodge** ❷, walk toward the dock about 400m to the end of the main path, turn right for 100m, then turn right again for another 100m; the lodge will be on your right. It often serves as the summertime locus for high school students on ecological study abroad programs. The resort-like *cabinas* have tile floors, fans, and private hot baths. (☎710 1161. US$20.)

◖🔲 **FOOD AND NIGHTLIFE.** Although accommodations in Parismina are gradually expanding, the food and nightlife have stayed pretty basic. Don't expect much variety. **Soda Eduardo** ❶, about 250m up the main path from the docks, is one of the friendliest places to eat in town. Dine on *empanadas* (¢200), fried chicken (¢700), and *casados*. (Open daily 8am-8pm.) **Restaurante Cariblanco** ❷, in the Cariblanco Lodge, offers fancier meals with Caribbean influences, including combinations of rice and beans, *casados*, *gallo pinto*, and creative seafood dishes. (Most entrees ¢1200-¢2500. Open for breakfast, lunch, and dinner, but no set hours.) Bar and disco **Salon Naomi,** in the center of town, has the monopoly on Parismina nightlife. It usually picks up on Saturday nights with loud *salsa, merengue*, reggae, and rock music. A good crowd of locals and visitors dance and mingle the night away. (Beer ¢500. Open daily 11am-2am.)

⚠ OUTDOOR ACTIVITIES. Parismina has recently taken an active interest in protecting its turtle population. Green turtles primarily nest between June and October, leatherbacks from February to June, and hawksbills sporadically throughout the year. Visitors can explore the canals around Parismina village that teem with wildlife, or go white-water rafting, hiking, fishing, and horseback riding. **La Asociación Salvemos Las Tortugas de Parismina,** Parismina's own turtle conservation association, organizes turtle-watching tours, volunteer activities, homestays, and dance and Spanish lessons. Fee includes meals, laundry, turtle-watching expeditions, and participation in local conservation efforts. Proceeds benefit the families of Parismina and the Asociación. (☎ 710 5183; www.costarica-turtles.com. US$20 per day. 5-day min. stay preferred. One or two day advance notice for homestay reservations requested. Guided tour US$12. Spanish and merengue lessons US$5 per hr.) **La Asociación de Boteros de Parismina,** a small private group of boat captains, offers tours of the river canals from Caño Blanco. Several captains are bilingual. Look for the boat captains at the Caño Blanco docks; be sure to get there at least 30min. before 6pm. Prices range from US$5 per person for the short ride to Parismina to US$150 for a round-trip ride to Tortuguero. **Rainforest World** (☎ 556 2678; www.rforestw.com) runs 2-3 day all-inclusive tours that include visits to Jalova ranger station, crocodile tours, a visit to an animal rehab station, sea kayaking, fishing, and more. (2-day, 1-night packages start at US$165; white-water rafting US$65 per day.)

TORTUGUERO VILLAGE

The tiny village of Tortuguero is the gateway to the entrance of Parque Nacional Tortuguero at the Cuatro Esquinas Ranger Station. Despite thousands of visitors every year, however, touristed Tortuguero (pop. 700) retains a surprisingly unspoiled small-town flavor. The slender strip of land on which this village lies is drenched by an average yearly rainfall of 5-6m and is accessible only by boat.

🚍 TRANSPORTATION. **Flying** from **San José** (see **San José: Flights,** p. 135) to the airstrip, a few kilometers north of Tortuguero, is faster and more convenient than a lengthy bus-boat combo. Sansa departs from Juan Santa María International Airport in Alajuela (☎ 221 9414; www.flysansa.com. 35min., 6am, US$62); NatureAir departs from Tobías Bolaños Airport in Pavas. (☎ 220 3054, reservations in US 888-535-8832; www.natureair.com. 35min., 6:15am, US$65.)

The best-known route along the Southern Caribbean coast via the port town of **Moín** is the most scenic, but not the cheapest. Some backpackers prefer this route despite its cost because it practically guarantees crocodile, bird, and monkey sightings. From **San José,** take a **bus** from Terminal Caribe to **Limón** (2½hr., every hr. 5:30am-7pm, ¢1005) and from Limón, catch a bus to **Moín** (30min., every 30min. 6am-6pm, ¢95). *Lanchas* depart early in the morning for Tortuguero from Moín's small dock behind Restaurante Papa Manuel (8-10am; try to arrive no later than 8:30am—the last bus from San José that will get you to Moín in time to catch a shared water taxi leaves at 6:30am). The *lancha* trip is 3-5hr. through canals bursting with wildlife (US$30; round-trip US$50). Large groups make for cheaper rides; if you're traveling alone, a tour guide might request up to US$180 for the trip. Captains Willis Rankin (☎ 798 1556), Alexis Soto (☎ 758 4297), and Sebastian Torres (☎ 798 6059) are all experienced and reliable guides. They all offer reasonable rates and are open to negotiation for group package deals. If you need help arranging transportation, call Daryl Loth or Bárbara Tinamon in Tortuguero (see **Orientation and Practical Information,** p. 226). A more formal option is **Tortuguero Odysseys Tours** (☎ 758 0824, cell 369 8907), which sells day packages with *lancha* trips and lunch (US$50); or longer 2-day trips with food and lodging (US$75-$85).

A much cheaper route from **San José** to Tortuguero is through **El Caribe Bus Terminal** (☎221 2596), with direct **buses** to **Cariari** (2hr.; 6:30, 9am; ¢720). The cheapest route from Cariari is by bus to **Pavona** (1½hr., noon, ¢1000), departing from the old bus station. From Pavona, Captain Juan Castro runs a **boat** to **Tortuguero** (45min.; 9am, 1:30pm; US$7). The more traditional route from Cariari is to catch the bus to La Geest-Casa Verde (noon, ¢500), staying on until the end of the line in La Geest. A *lancha* to Tortuguero meets the bus at the river's edge at 1:30pm; most locals pay ¢1500, though tourists are charged US$10 for the 1hr. trip. Rubén Bananero makes the trip from La Geest to Tortuguero (☎382 6941 or 833 1076; www.tortuguero-costarica.com) twice daily from the main docks in La Geest (1½hr; 7, 11am; call for prices). Juan Castro's boat leaves daily for **Pavona** (45min.; 6, 11:30am; US$7/¢3045). Make reservations for all traveling arrangements the day before, at Restaurante El Muellecito opposite the dock. The connecting **bus** leaves for **Cariari** from La Geest at 9:30am (1½hr., ¢600, ask for hours from Pavona), and buses to **San José** leave Cariari at 11am and 1pm. There are a few days every year when water levels are too high or too low to make the journey. To confirm times or check on info, call Daryl Loth (☎833 0827 or 709 8094; safari@racsa.co.cr) or Bárbara Tinamon (☎pager 223 3030, #3761; tinamon@racsa.co.cr), both of whom are guides in Tortuguero.

⚡🔀 ORIENTATION AND PRACTICAL INFORMATION. The village of Tortuguero is only 500m long, with sandy gravel paths winding their way through the scattered buildings. The **airstrip** is a few kilometers north of town and is accessible only by boat. Most travelers arrive at the *lancha* dock in the center of town. From the docks, with your back to the water, north is to your left and south is to your right. The **main path** runs from the Caribbean Conservation Center at the far north end of the village to the **ranger station** at the park entrance on the southern end of town. Frequent blackouts in the rainy season make a flashlight highly advisable.

The **kiosk** north of the soccer field has information on park activities and the history of turtles. Information guru **Daryl Loth** (☎833 0827 or 709 8094; http://tortuguero_s.tripod.com) runs 🐢**Tortuguero Safaris Information Center,** 100m north of the docks opposite the church. If the Center is not open, knock on the yellow house next door—the site of his new bed and breakfast. From the **Sansa Ticket Office** at the center, manager Victor Barrantes can arrange plane, bus, and boat reservations, as well as rafting, hiking, and turtle-watching excursions. (☎709 8055; tortuguero@flysansa.com. Open daily 8am-noon and 1pm-5pm.) **Barbara Tinamon,** a multi-lingual biologist in the purple house 100m past Cabinas Tortuguero, is a great guide and source of information. At **The Jungle Shop** (☎391 3483), 100m north of the docks across from Tortuguero Safaris, Antoinette Gutiérrez and Elvin sell souvenirs and give advice (open daily 9am-6pm). There are no banks or ATMs in Tortuguero, so stock up on colónes before you arrive. **Souvenirs Paraíso Tropical,** 200m north of the docks, exchanges traveler's checks if they have the cash. **Souvenirs Pura Vida,** 30m north of the main docks, exchanges US dollars for colónes for a ¢5 per-dollar commission. Both are open daily 8am-9pm. **Super Morpho** is directly opposite the docks (open daily 7am-10pm). **La Riveriana** is 200m north of the docks (open daily 6am-8pm). **Police** are in the blue building 75m north of the dock (emergency ☎117). A **doctor** can be reached at the south end of town in the central headquarters of the park service (Administración de Tortuguero). For a serious **medical emergency,** The Jungle Shop (☎391 3483) can call a doctor in Limón. **Telephones** can be found at the Super Morpho in front of the docks; behind Souvenirs Paraíso Tropical; and next to Cabinas Aracari. (Local calls ¢20 per min. International calls with calling card only. ¢200 flat rate for connection. Dial ☎113 for information.)

The Sansa ticketing office at the Tortuguero Safaris Information Center provides **Internet** access (US$4 per hr. Open daily 8am-noon and 1pm-5pm.) Souvenirs Pura Vida provides **post office services.** (Open daily 8am-9pm.)

▐ ACCOMMODATIONS. All the ritzy expensive hotels that cater mostly to organized tours are located across the canal and are accessible almost exclusively by boat. In Tortuguero Village, lodgings tend to be strictly budget and just minutes from the park entrance, beach, and restaurants. Camping is not allowed on the beach, but backpackers can pitch tents for US$2 per night (plus a one-time US$7 park entrance fee) at the ranger station at the southern end of town.

In **Tortuguero Village, Cabinas Aracari ❶** has a hospitable *dueña* who keeps rooms with window screens, private hot showers, fans, and porches. From the docks, head south on the main path and turn left on the path just past the Centro Turístico La Culebra; Aracari is the last house 150m down the path. (☎709 8006. Singles US$7; doubles US$14; triples US$21.) **Casa Marbella ❸** is the yellow house next door to Daryl's place, with four comfortable cabins and solar-powered hot water. Breakfast is included. (☎392 3201. Singles US$25; doubles US$35.) On the canals, **El Manatí ❸** is the most affordable of the lodges. Eight simple *cabinas* have fans and private hot baths. The hotel often fills up with tourists on Ecole Tours package trips; call ahead and make sure there's room. (☎383 0330 or 534 7256. Singles US$30; doubles US$40; triples US$50.)

▐▐ FOOD AND NIGHTLIFE. For such a small village, Tortuguero has a number of good restaurants, *sodas*, and cafes. Though most places are pretty affordable, prices tend to be a bit higher than they might be elsewhere because of the difficulties of shipping food here. One look at ▩**Cabinas y Restaurante La Casona ❷**, on the soccer field, with its tree stump patterned floor and thatched roof, and you won't want to eat anywhere else. Don't miss delicious banana pancakes (¢1300), heart of palm lasagna (¢1800), or garlic-and-butter grilled shrimp with rice (¢3000). Its guest book is signed by visitors from all over the world. (Open daily 6am-10pm.) At ▩**Miss Junie's ❷**, 200m north of the docks, the results are always a bit different but they're uniformly delicious. She'll cook whatever is caught or bought that day with her special flavorful Caribbean touch. Tell her in the morning or the day before what you'd like to eat. (Breakfast ¢1200; lunch and dinner ¢2700. Open daily 7am-9pm.) **Punto del Incontro,** 50m south of Super Morpho, has a long U-shaped bar pointing toward the biggest flat-screen TV in Tortuguero. Punto is quiet on weekdays, but packs in a lively mix of locals and tourists with comedy and disco on Friday and Saturday nights. (☎826 6246 or 709 8108. Unspectacular entrees ¢1000-¢2000. Beer US$2-$3/¢600-¢800; mixed drinks US$2-$3/¢800-¢1000. Open M-F noon-1am, Sa 2pm-2am, Su noon-2am.)

◨ SIGHTS. Before going to see the turtles, check out the non-profit **Caribbean Conservation Corporation Natural History Visitor Center (CCC)** at the north end of town. Follow the dirt path that runs along the beach, toward the right, for about 1km past the docks. The Center is a must-see for anyone wishing to learn about the plight of the endangered marine turtles. In the past 50 years, the CCC has tagged over 50,000 turtles, making it the world's largest green turtle tagging program of its kind. Visitors can "adopt" a turtle with a US$25 donation and, in turn, receive an adoption certificate, photograph, turtle <fact sheet, and information about the tagged turtle when it is found. The admission fee is used to further the efforts of the CCC. (☎709 8091; www.cccturtle.org. Open M-Sa 10am-noon and 2-5:30pm, Su 2-5:30pm. ¢400. MC/V.)

PARQUE NACIONAL TORTUGUERO

Sheltering the most important nesting site for marine turtles in the entire Western Hemisphere, Parque Nacional Tortuguero encompasses 261 sq. km of coastal territory and 501 sq. km of marine territory 84km north of Limón. It is almost exclusively accessible and navigable by boat. Its 35km of beach, where thousands of turtles return each year to lay their eggs, has brought the park international fame and thousands of visitors. Not content to surrender the show, howler monkeys echo in the treetops, rainbow-beaked toucans coast overhead, and leathery caimans glide stealthily through the canals that flow into the park's swampy regions.

The most famous turtles are the *tortugas verdes*, which nest from the end of June through September. Three endangered species also nest in the park: Leatherbacks (Mar.-July), Hawksbills (May-Sept.), and Loggerheads (June-Oct.). Today researchers tag turtles and use satellite tracking to determine travel tendencies, a practice that has revealed amazing information about their migratory habits: one turtle tagged near Tortuguero was found just one month later on the coast of Senegal, and several reports show that female turtles, after visiting beaches all around the world, return to their birthplace to nest 30 years later.

AT A GLANCE

AREA: 9261 sq. km of coastal territory; 501 sq. km of marine territory.

CLIMATE: 26°C (79°F)

HIGHLIGHTS: Turtle nesting site.

GATEWAYS: Tortuguero (p.225)

CAMPING: US$2 per person at Cuatro Esquinas Ranger Station.

FEES AND RESERVATIONS: US$7

TRANSPORTATION AND ORIENTATION. Tortuguero is the gateway town for Parque Nacional Tortuguero. See **Transportation,** p.225, for details to and from Tortuguero. Park headquarters are at the Cuatro Esquinas Ranger Station, at the north end. To reach the station from Tortuguero, follow the main path to the south, walking through locals' yards and over a makeshift bridge. The less-frequented Jalova Ranger Station is at the park's south end.

PRACTICAL INFORMATION. There are two ranger stations in the park. Cuatro Esquinas Ranger Station is to the north of the park, and is accessible from Tortuguero village. The Jalova Ranger Station on the south end of the park is less frequented. The ranger station has maps (¢200), info on the park's wildlife and vegetation, and preserved turtles and turtle eggs on display. Park entrances open daily 6am-6pm. Combination 4-day ticket for Tortuguero and Barra del Colorado US$10.

HIKING. Starting from the **Cuatro Esquinas Ranger Station, Sendero El Gavilán** (1hr., 2km) is not a difficult hike, although it can be muddy and buggy. The trail winds through the forest and ends on the beach; take a left and walk back to town. Another pleasant trail, although it's tricky to reach, is **Sendero Tucán** (1.5km), which runs alongside the Caño Negro Waterway. The trail starts at the **Jalova Ranger Station,** about 15min. from Parismina by motor boat. Parismina itself is 1hr. away by canal. You will have to hire a guide to take you there (see **Guided Tours**, below), but most guides and locals say that the price of the boat ride is not worth the dearth of activities at Jalova. Quiet hikers may spot monkeys, toucans, and red poison dart frogs along the trails. The frogs make venom in their sweat, so don't lick them. Two mini-trails (600m) are also enjoyable. **La Ranita Roja** makes a semicircle around Caño Harol, while **Tragón** follows a straight path.

■ **TURTLE WATCHING.** The park's feature presentation is the nightly *deshove*, when turtles come to lay their eggs. The female turtle emerges from the sea, makes her way up the sand, constantly pausing to check for danger, until she finds the perfect spot, where she uses her flippers to dig a body pit one-foot deep. She finally lays her eggs, carefully burying them in the sand, and leaves them, never seeing the final product. The intriguing process takes about two hours.

Visitors must be with a guide certified by the national park. (Ask to see a license.) Don't try to watch the *deshove* unguided; the beaches are dangerous at night due to unexpected waves and vast quantities of driftwood. Turtle tours leave nightly at 8 and 10pm (US$10). Talk to any of the guides mentioned below to set up a tour or show up (daily 5-6pm) at the Cuatro Esquinas Ranger Station, where local guides await, to obtain the necessary permission slips. Wear good walking shoes and dark clothing. Don't bring a flashlight or camera—bright lights blind the turtles and hinder their return to the sea. Official park rules state that once a tour group has seen the egg-laying process, they must leave, regardless of whether or not the two hours have elapsed.

■ **GUIDED TOURS.** Entirely enveloped by water, Tortuguero is best explored by kayak, canoe, or motorboat. Although it's possible to go alone, hiring a guide is much more fun. Keep in mind, however, that guides abound in Tortuguero and the competition is cutthroat. Many guides harass people on the street. If you want a particular guide, stick with him, even if competitors try to mislead you. Daryl from **Tortuguero Safaris Information Center** is a fantastic guide, and his boat has an electric motor that is ecologically friendly and quiet (US$5 per hr.; design your own tour). **Bárbara Tinamon** (842 6561; www.tinamontours.de), in the purple house 100m past Cabinas Tortuguero, owns **Tinamon Tours** and leads canoe, hiking, and village tours in English, Spanish, French, or German. She prefers small groups of 4-5 people (US$5 per hr.).

CAHUITA

Reggae, sea-spray, and coral reefs lure travelers to charming Cahuita. On the southeast side of the village is Parque Nacional Cahuita, home to sloths, howler monkeys, white-sand, and the largest coral reef on Costa Rica's Caribbean coast. To the northwest, sun-worshippers bask on the black sands of Playa Negra. Some warn that not all of Cahuita is idyllic, so take precautions, especially at night.

■ **TRANSPORTATION. Buses:** The MEPE **bus** company (San José ☎257 8129, Limón 758 1572) has buses departing from the front of the park to: **Limón** (1hr., 15 per day 6:15am-6:45pm; ¢450); **Manzanillo** (1½hr.; 7, 11:30am, 4, 7pm; ¢340) via **Puerto Viejo** (30min., 8 per day 6am-7pm; ¢180); and **San José** (3½hr.; 7:30, 9:30, 11:30am, 4:30pm; ¢2150). Taxi drivers include Wayne (☎755 0078), Enrique (☎755 0017), and René (☎755 0243).

■ **ORIENTATION AND PRACTICAL INFORMATION.** A road branching off the Limón-Puerto Viejo Hwy. extends for 1km before intersecting with Cahuita's main road in the middle of town, in front of a small municipal park. The main road, **Avenida Alfredo González Flores,** goes from northwest to southeast. Facing the bus stop (with the park in front of you), northwest is to your left and southeast is to your right. **Playa Negra** is on the northwest end of town; **Playa Blanca** lies in Cahuita National Park over the bridge to the southeast. **Mr. Big J,** 1 block southeast of the bus stop, is the most comprehensive source of info and tours in town. (☎755 0328. Open daily 9am-noon and 3-6pm.) The **MINAE** office (☎755 0060; fax 755 0455), 2 blocks northwest of the bus stop, can answer questions about parks. If you're hit-

COSTA RICA

THE LOCAL STORY

BOMBS OVER BARRA?

Guests at the Río Colorado Lodge in Barra del Sur are occasionally puzzled to find a tall, misshapen metal pole preventing easy entry to the outdoor jacuzzi. Though it may be a momentary annoyance, the pole is also the only remaining evidence of the crucial role this sleepy fishing village played in the Nicaraguan civil wars of the 1980s. It was once the support mast for a radio that facilitated two-way communication between the CIA and one of the most infamous residents of Barra del Sur: the Nicaraguan contra leader Edén Pastora, better known by his *nom de guerre* Comandante Cero Commander Zero).

Pastora had been a hero of the Sandinsta revolution of 1978 but quickly became disenchanted with the regime. He settled in Barra del Sur to form a paramilitary group that began to recieve funding from the CIA in 1981. Although support was officially cut off when it was discovered that Pastora's rebels were also running drugs to raise money, cash and communiqués continued to flow. Though many believed the location was perfect because the Sandinistas would never dare to launch an invasion into Costa Rica, long-time residents claim they remember one night when the area was strafed by the Sandinsta Air Force in the mid-1980s. The attack was careless, however, and Comandante Cero lived to fight another day.

ting the beach for the day, store your valuables in a steel case at Mr. Big J (¢1000 per day). The closest banks are in Limón and Bribrí. **Cabinas Safari** exchanges traveler's checks (3% commission) and over a dozen currencies with a 3.2% commission. (Open daily 7am-4pm.) **Western Union** is inside Cahuita Tours, 2½ blocks northwest of the bus stop. **Mr. Big J** also does **laundry**, and will wash, dry, and fold clothes. (¢2500 per load. 2½hr. Open M-F 8am-4pm.) In an **emergency** dial ☎911. **Police** are located at the northwest end of the main road, 3 blocks from the bus stop right next to the post office. (☎755 0217. Open 24hr.) To reach the **Red Cross**, call ☎758 0125. (English spoken. Open 24hr.) For a **pharmacy**, walk 10min. out of town on the main road, or hop on a bus headed for Puerto Viejo and ask to get off at the clinic on the right. Call ahead if possible. (☎750 0136 or 750 0003. Open M-F 7am-4pm.) **Clínica Cahuita** offers basic medical services. Walk 500m south of the bus stop toward the main highway; it will be on your right. (☎755 0466. Open M, W, Th 7am-4pm, F 7am-noon.) **Telephones** are everywhere: next to the bus stop, at **Cahuita Tours**, in Hotel Cahuita, 2 blocks northwest of the bus stop, and in front of the police station. Fax service is available at Cahuita Tours and Cabina Vaz (about ¢100 per page). **Willie's Tours**, 1 block north of the bus stop on the left, has **Internet** access. (¢1000 per hr. Open 8am-noon and 2-9pm.) The **post office** is at the northwest end of the main road, 3 blocks from the bus stop. (☎755 0096. Open M-F 8am-noon and 1-5:30pm.) **Postal Code:** 7302.

📍 **ACCOMMODATIONS.** *Cabinas* far outnumber other options in Cahuita, and it is only easy to get cheap rooms in groups. Most *cabinas* are clean and comfortable, and several have lovely ocean views. The seaside location of **Spencer Sea-Side Lodge ❷** cannot be beat; walk 2 blocks down the crossroads from the bus stop and turn right at the beach. Large rooms with iguana murals have private hot showers. (☎755 0027. Daily reef tours US$15 per person. Internet access ¢1000 per hr. Rooms US$10 per person; doubles with fridge and hot water US$25, each extra person US$5. Accepts traveler's checks.) **Kelly Creek Hotel-Restaurant ❸**, to the right of the park entrance, has enormous rooms with hand-woven (and somehow elegant) mosquito nets, ceiling fans, private hot baths, and closets. (☎755 0077; www.hotelkellycreek.com. Doubles US$40/¢17,400.) **Backpackers ❶**, half a block southeast of Edith's, caters to budget travelers with its basic rooms, ceiling fans, and a communal cold shower. The owner prepares banana pancake breakfasts, ¢400. (☎755 0174. Singles US$8; doubles US$10; triples US$15.)

◖ **FOOD.** Catering primarily to tourists, most restaurants in town serve gourmet food at gourmet prices. There are a few unremarkable *sodas* by the intersection of the main road and the road leading back to the highway. No visit to Cahuita would be complete without a taste of the exquisite homemade *paella* that has earned ▩**Kelly Creek Hotel-Restaurant ❸** and its chef local fame. Located to the right of the park entrance, it also serves other Spanish mainstays like *gazpacho* and *jamón serrano*. (☎ 755 0077. at least 4hr. notice requested for *paella;* ¢4000 for 2 people. Seafood entrees ¢2400-¢7500. MC/V.) Legendary Caribbean food is served at a Caribbean pace at ▩**Miss Edith's ❸,** 3 blocks northwest of the bus stop; turn right at the end of the side road past the police. Prices are high, but locals swear by her cooking. Feast on incredible vegetable soup (¢1500), fish with coconut, curry, and yucca (¢2500), or lobster. (Open daily 8am-10pm.)

◪◩ **SIGHTS AND GUIDED TOURS. Cahuita Butterfly Farm** merits the hike from town with an unprecedented 20 varieties of butterfly in 2 distinct habitats. Walk 1km back to the main highway, make a right and continue for a few minutes until you see the sign. A sheltered perimeter and seating area permit a lovely view of the elusive, sought-after deep-blue *Morpho peleides*. (☎ 755 0361. US$7. Discounts for groups. Open daily 9am-4pm.) **Mr. Big J** (see **Practical Information,** p. 229) is run by Mañuela and the amiable Mr. Big J himself. They arrange an endless repertoire of services, including snorkeling trips in the park (gear rental US$6, 3hr. guided trips US$20), horseback tours on the beach or through waterfalls (beach 3hr., US$30; waterfalls 5hr., US$40 with lunch), and fishing trips (US$45). **Roberto Tours,** 1 block southeast of the bus stop, guarantees fresh catch on his fishing trips. (4hr. daytrip US$50; deep-sea fishing night-trips US$100; equipment included.) Cook your own catch at Roberto's Caribbean-style seafood restaurant next door. He also offers early-morning dolphin tours and snorkeling trips. (☎/fax 755 0117. Bike rental ¢350 per hr., ¢2000 per day. Open daily 7am-8pm, in low season M-F 7am-3pm. AmEx/MC/V.) **Willie's Tours,** 1 block north of the bus stop on the left, has guided fishing trips (6hr., US$40/¢17,400), canopy tours (4hr., US$40/¢17,400), and treks through the Gandoca Refuge. Most excursions include lunch. (☎ 843 4700; williestours@hotmail.com. Internet access. Open daily 8am-noon and 2-9pm.)

PARQUE NACIONAL CAHUITA

Parque Nacional Cahuita's claim to fame is its spectacular 600 hectare coral reef. Though 22,400 hectares of the park are marine, the accessible coastal rainforest is worth exploring as well. **Playa Blanca** (named for its warm white sand) is south of the station, where less active park visitors laze and take dips in the surf.

AT A GLANCE	
AREA: 23,000 hectares of ocean, 1067 hectares of land.	**GATEWAYS:** Cahuita (p. 229).
CLIMATE: Hot and humid. Average 29°C/84°F.	**CAMPING:** Permitted near the Puerto Viejo side. 50 sites available with facilities at the ranger station.
FEATURES: Punta Vargas on the 600 hectare coral reef, Playa Blanca, hiking the rainforest trails, surfing, snorkeling.	**FEES AND RESERVATIONS:** US$8 park entrance fee if you enter from the Puerto Viejo station. There is no fee at the Kelly Creek station; donations are welcome.

🔳🔳 TRANSPORTATION AND ORIENTATION. Parque Nacional Cahuita lies on the south end of the Atlantic Coast in the province of Limón. Cahuita is the gateway town for Parque Nacional Cahuita. See **Transportation,** (p. 229) for info on how to get to and from Cahuita. The park has two ranger stations, both accessible from Cahuita. The **Kelly Creek Ranger Station** is 3 blocks southeast of the bus stop just over the small bridge at the edge of town. **Puerto Vargas,** the second station, is off the main highway between Puerto Viejo and Limón. To enter the park through the Puerto Vargas ranger station, take the Puerto Viejo de Talamanca bus in Cahuita and ask to be dropped at the Puerto Vargas *entrada* (entrance).

🔳 PRACTICAL INFORMATION. If you enter through the **Kelly Creek Ranger Station** you must register in their logbook before entering. They accept donations at the park entrance (open daily 6am-5pm). A standard US$8 national park admission fee is required if you enter from the Puerto Vargas Station. (☎ 755 0302 or 755 0060; aclac@ns.minae.go.cr. Open M-F 8am-4:30pm, Sa-Su 7am-5pm.) **Camping** is permitted near the Puerto Vargas side of the park (US$2). The 50 camping sites are set back from the hiking path and include ocean views and access to showers, sinks, and toilets at the ranger station. Swimming is only allowed in designated areas. Surfing, volleyball, and soccer, are allowed in certain areas.

🔳 RAINFOREST TRAIL. An easy 9km (2½hr.) trail leads from the Kelly Creek Station in Cahuita for 4km to Punta Cahuita, and continues 3km until it reaches Puerto Vargas. The hike finishes 2km past the station. The trail seems more like a narrow road than a path, with bikers and local mothers pushing babies in carriages. Sometimes the tide is so high that the road floods, soaking hikers and bikers alike. A little farther on the path is the Río Suarez which, during high tide, can reach 1m in depth. On one side the rolling waves of the Caribbean drum against the white-sand **Playa Vargas;** on the other, is swampy forest with brush and towering coconut palms. The treetops of Cahuita are among the best in the country for spotting howler and white-faced monkeys; at sunrise and sunset, the reclusive primates sometimes come down to meander near the shoreline.

🔳 THE CORAL REEF. Fish of all shapes, sizes, and colors populate Cahuita's 600 hectare coral reef; elkhorn, brain, and other coral species line the ocean floor. In the past few years, the reef has shrunk, due in part to the accumulation of eroded soil from banana plantations. Earthquakes have also heaved the coral upwards towards the sun; now there's too much dead coral floating around for snorkelers to find good sites on their own. It's better to check with the rangers or go on a guided tour (see **Cahuita: Guided Tours,** p. 231); the most popular spot to visit is **Punta Vargas.** It's also a bad idea to go out the day after a heavy night storm has stirred up debris and dead coral in the water.

🔳 HIKES. Sendero Catarata begins at the station with a 10min. jungle path that eventually intersects the Río Cerere. Build a cairn, or small pile of stones, to help you recognize the jungle exit when returning. The rest of the trip is not a trail, but rather an effort to follow the river. Depending on recent rainfall, you could end up crossing the river 7-15 times to reach drier, more manageable paths. Follow the river for 2km until you reach the first waterfall. The trail isn't marked but it is nearly impossible to get lost. The waterfall at the end provides luxurious bathing. A second waterfall, 1km farther, is off-limits without a guide. **Sendero Tepezcuintle** (1km, 45min.) loops through the woods near the ranger station offers the best views of Hitoy-Cerere flora and fauna. It is light, safe, and well-marked, but watch out for the poisonous tiny bright red frogs.

△. ▨RESERVA BIOLÓGICA HITOY-CERERE. The Reserva Biológica Hitoy-Cerere is cradled between the Talamanca Mountain Range and the Estrella Valley, as well as by the three major indigenous reservations of Tayni, Telire, and Talamanca. It receives approximately 3500mm of rainfall every year. This area is full of undiscovered beauty. Tourists rarely visit; biologists stay for years. One famous resident here is the **luminous blue butterfly.** It is not customary to be guided by a ranger, but they will gladly help to arrange a local guide. These guides are generally cheaper (¢8000-¢10,000 per day) than any arranged in Cahuita or Limón, and have lifelong experience in the area. Except for the two well-described trails, rangers request that visitors travel with a guide. *(This reserve is most easily accessible from Cahuita. Take any bus north and ask to be let off in Penhurst (20min., ¢170). From the gas station buses to Finca 6 leave hourly. Ask to be let off at Finca 12 (30min., ¢220). Walk 1.5km uphill along the only dirt road in the area. The ranger station has sheet-less beds (US$7), outdoor and indoor bathrooms, and a friendly staff (open daily 8am-4pm). Camping not permitted. Catch a ride back with the rangers who descend daily. Guided tours of Hitoy-Cerere are available through agencies in Cahuita and Puerto Viejo (p. 231, p. 233). Private taxis from Cahuita cost US$55. Admission US$8.)*

PUERTO VIEJO DE TALAMANCA

A visit to Puerto Viejo, 61km southeast of Puerto Limón, is all about unwinding for a little while—or even longer, as the growing population of resident Europeans and *gringos* can attest. These recent immigrants have diversified the already eclectic mix of Afro-Caribbean, Spanish, and indigenous influences that define its cultural climate. The pace of life here is slow, anything beyond catching the perfect wave or the perfect tan is considered excessively ambitious.

▤ TRANSPORTATION. Buses leave for: the **Panamanian border at Bribrí/Sixaola** (Bribrí 30min., ¢200; Sixaola 1½hr., 12 per day 6:30am-7:30pm, ¢590); **Limón** (1½hr., 12 per day 5:30am-5:30pm, ¢605) via **Cahuita** (45min., ¢170); **Manzanillo** (45min.; 7:30am, noon, 4:30pm; ¢220) via Punta Uva (30min., ¢170); and **San José** (4½hr.; daily 7, 9, 11am, 4pm, also 1:30pm F and Su; ¢2545). Though most of Puerto Viejo's attractions are within easy walking or biking distance and bus service is fairly extensive, **taxis** are available. Walk ½ block west of ATEC and you'll see a sign on the south side-street for Charlie's Taxi Service. Everyone knows Charlie as "Bull" (☎ 750 0112, cell 836 8219). If Bull's red minivan isn't there, ask for him at ATEC. Also try Poposa (☎ 844 9913), Juan (☎ 844 5446), Junior (☎ 824 4671), or Wilfred (☎ 378 6896).

▤◪ ORIENTATION AND PRACTICAL INFORMATION. The main road comes in from the west, crosses the bridge, and cuts through town before heading east to Manzanillo. To get to the center of town from the bus stop, head south away from the beach 1 block, and turn left. The ATEC office is 1½ blocks east.

Many **tour offices** overstress the necessity of a guide; a more neutral source may be your hotel owner. You can also take your questions to the **Talamanca Association for Ecotourism and Conservation (ATEC)** in the center of town. The organization was founded to promote local tourism while preserving the region's heritage and ecology, and offers tours of Yorkín, Shiroles, and Kékôldi reserves with native guides (half-day tours start at US$25), **Internet access** (¢15 per min. or ¢900 per hr.), and photocopy services. (☎ 750 0398; atecmail@racsa.co.cr. Open daily 8am-9pm; occasionally closes for lunch.) **Puerto Viejo Tours** (☎ 750 0411; fax 755 0082), across from the bus stop, also gives tour advice. Around the block from ATEC, **Los Almendros** exchanges US dollars (1% commission) and cashes traveler's checks and money orders. Cash advances are available on AmEx/MC/V with a passport for

11% commission. (☎750 0235. Open daily 7am-6pm.) **Pulpería Manuel León,** on the beach half a block west and 2 blocks north of ATEC, offers similar services at similar rates. "El Chino," the owner, can help with directions. (☎750 0422; fax 750 0246. Open M-Sa 7am-6pm, Su 7:30am-2pm.) **Banco Nacional** (☎751 0068), the nearest bank, is 30min. away in Bribrí. **Super Buen Precio,** the grocery store opposite the bus stop, faces the beach. Accepts payment in US dollars and gives colónes at a decent rate. (☎750 0060. Open M-Th 6:30am-8pm, F-Su 8:30am-8:30pm. AmEx/MC/V.) For **laundry,** head 20m south of the post office. (☎750 0360. Wash US$3, dry US$3. Delivery service included. Locals or extended-stay tourists often negotiate special rates. Open M-Sa 7am-7pm, Su 10am-2pm.) **Police** are half a block east and 1½ blocks north of ATEC facing the beach. (☎750 0230, emergencies 911. Open 24hr.) The **Red Cross** is located in Limón. (☎758 0125 or 911. English spoken. Open 24hr.) **Farmacía Amiga** is next to the post office. (☎750 0698. Open M-F 9am-6pm, Sa 9am-2pm.) For **medical services,** Dr. Rodríguez and Dr. Ríos have a small office half a block west and 1 block north of ATEC. (☎750 0303, emergencies 750 7500. Open M-F 4:30-8pm, Sa 8am-noon.) The **dentist** is next door (☎750 0820). **Video Mundo,** next to ATEC, has international phone service and fast **Internet** (☎750 0651. Calls ¢350-¢400 per min., Internet ¢20 per min. or ¢850 per hr. Open daily 7am-9pm.) The **post office** is half a block west and 25m south of ATEC. (☎750 0404. Open M-F 8am-noon and 1-5:30pm.)

⌂⌂ ACCOMMODATIONS AND CAMPING. An influx of long- and short-term European and North American tourists has inflated prices in Puerto Viejo. However, most of the hotels and *cabinas* are well-maintained, and several offer gorgeous grounds. ◪**Cabinas Casa Verde ❸** is the perfect place to kick back. From ATEC, continue half a block east on the main road and turn right, then turn left at the first street; look for the green signs. Well-kept rooms have fans, mosquito nets, and private porches. Exquisite grounds include a pool and extensive tropical garden. Prices vary by season and method of payment. (☎750 0015; www.cabinascasaverde.com. Singles US$22-$34; doubles US$24-$45; triples US$30-$60; quads US$36-$72. AmEx/MC/V.) The quirky, creatively designed ◪**Jacaranda Cabinas ❸** are half a block west and 2 blocks south of ATEC. Rooms have mosquito nets, fans, and hot baths. Guests are allowed to use the kitchen. Massages are given in the on-site pagoda. (☎750 0069. Singles US$20, with bath and porch US$25; doubles US$25-$30; triples and quads US$35. MC/V.)

⌂ FOOD. Food in Puerto Viejo is often not authentically Caribbean and aims to please (and overcharge) tourists. However, the places listed below are owned by locals and feature high-quality cuisine. ◪**El Loco Natural ❸,** 2 blocks west of ATEC, offers Afro-Caribbean fusion cuisine in a candle-lit ambience. Savor the marlin with Malaysian guayaba green curry (¢3000) or the tuna with Indo-Caribbean tropical madras curry (¢3000). Music, artwork and pottery are all creations of the multi-talented staff. (☎750 0263. Vegan options. Calypso and reggae Th and Sa. Reservations recommended. MC/V.) **Soda Isma ❷,** 1 block west of ATEC on the main road, is famous for its *rondon,* a local dish made with fish in coconut sauce that must be ordered a day in advance (4 hr. notice for 1 or 2 people; ¢3500). Spur-of-the-moment types feast on tasty *gallo pinto* (¢750), tiny sandwiches (¢650), *casados* (¢1200-¢3500) or delicious coconut bread. (Open daily 8am-9pm.)

◪ SIGHTS. The majority of Costa Rica's indigenous population resides on reservations throughout this region. The most accessible to outsiders is the **Reserva Indígena Cocles/Kéköldi,** 4km west of Puerto Viejo. Established in 1977, it is home to approximately 40 Bribrí and Cabécar families. To tour the reservation, you must have an authorized guide, available through ATEC, Puerto Viejo Tours, and

Terraventuras. (1-day trips US$25-$45.) The ATEC guides, Alex and Mauricio, are members of the reservation. Tours include a hike on ancient trails through old cacao plantations, secondary forests, and farms. Many stop for lunch at an impressive waterfall in the center of the reservation (US$3). Tours concentrate more on nature than culture in order to create a relationship of privacy and respect between the community and the tourist. Located at the entrance to the reservation is the **Iguana Farm,** a project begun by two Bribrí women to bolster the reservation's declining iguana population. A guide is not necessary to visit the farm—a series of cages and pens house thousands of reptiles. Take the bus to Bribrí and ask the driver to let you off at the "Abastecedor El Cruce" 4km from Puerto Viejo. 15min., ¢150. To get back, catch one of the buses that pass the Abastecedor hourly. ¢450.

◪ NIGHTLIFE. Though laid-back by day, Puerto Viejo's hot spots pack in locals and tourists alike night after night. Every Monday and Friday, the bar dance club **◪Bambú,** 300m east of ATEC on the main road on the beach, busts out roots and reggae for its dancing, drinking, and smoking revelers until 2am (most beers ¢650). Make a cameo at cocktail hour from 4-7pm, or eat anytime from 8am-7pm (Caribbean *casado* ¢1100-¢2300). For a more mellow scene, groove at **◪Discoteca Stanford** next door (2 beers ¢750). On Monday and Friday the two open-air floors of dancing tourists pour out onto the beach. **Jhonny's Place,** half a block west of ATEC and 2 blocks north along the beach, is the place to be on Saturday nights, when it becomes a pulsing, disco-blasting rock, *salsa*, reggae, and techno. (Beers ¢500-¢600.) **EZ Times Bar and Grill,** 1 block west and half a block north of ATEC, is a good place for a beer after a long day in the sun. (Beers ¢500. Guacamole with chips ¢1400; pizzas ¢2300-¢6000. Pizza delivery ¢500. Open 11am-2am.)

◪◪ OUTDOOR ACTIVITIES AND GUIDED TOURS. Most **surfers** head straight over to **La Salsa Brava,** an extraordinary surf-hole east of the village, where waves break over a coral reef. However, if you're less experienced with a board, and getting drilled into the coral doesn't sound like fun, **Beach Break** is a 15min. walk east along the beach, where comparable waves break on soft sand. **Aventuras Bravas** (☎849 7600), in front of Stanford's (see **Nightlife,** p. 235), rents surf and boogie boards, ocean kayaks (US$5 per hr., US$10 per half-day, US$15 per day), and bikes (¢2000 per day). John Wheatley of Aventuras offers surfing lessons (US$35) and massages (¢100 per minute). Just 2km south is another surf-worthy beach, **Playa Chiquita;** 2km southeast of Puerto Viejo, **Playa Cocles** offers what many claim is the best surfing on the Caribbean.

Terraventuras, half a block west of ATEC and 2 blocks north, rents snorkeling gear (US$5 per day), offers guided snorkeling in Parque Nacional Cahuita, a hiking tour of Gandoca-Manzanillo Wildlife Refuge, walking and canopy tours of the Kékôldi and Talamanca Bribrí Indian reserves (US$35-$40), as well as trips to Tortuguero. (☎750 0750 or 750 0426. Open M-Sa 8am-6:30pm. AmEx/MC/V.) **Reef Runner Divers,** half a block west of ATEC and 2 blocks north, specializes in scuba diving and offers PADI certification courses and diving excursions (open water certification US$280/¢121,800. 2hr. excursions offered for US$60/¢26,100.) All dives include full equipment, guide, and boat. (☎/fax 750 0480. Open daily 8am-6pm. AmEx/MC/V with 8% surcharge.) **Puerto Viejo Tours,** across from the bus stop, offers informal tours similar to Terraventuras', along with surfing lessons and gear rental. (☎/fax 750 0411. Surf boards US$10/¢4350 per day.) **Sucurucu Rental,** across the street from the bus stop, rents scooters and offers ATV tours. All prices include safety helmet and basic insurance. (☎841 5578. Scooters US$15 for 3hr., US$24 for 8hr., US$30 per day. ATV tour of Sucurucu Vista Mountain US$60 per person, US$75 per couple. Open M-F 8am-6pm, Sa-Su 9am-5pm.)

GANDOCA

Twenty years ago, this isolated town would have been completely overlooked by tourists. Now it is one of the most popular destinations of the Southern Caribbean coast for nature-conscious travelers. A dearth of basic amenities hardly dissuades legions of volunteers (over 300 during turtle season) from spending a week to six months participating in a project to save an endangered population of leatherback turtles. Others are attracted by extensive coral reefs with 37 algae species and 34 kinds of mollusks. If marine-life vigils aren't your thing, check out the **Refugio Nacional de Vida Silvestre Gandoca-Manzanillo,** which extends to the Panama border.

Depending on the weather, Gandoca can be reached by two equally difficult routes. To hike the route from Manzanillo, follow the trail between Restaurant Maxi and the beach for a few hundred meters past a soccer field until you reach a lagoon. From there, cross a small stream, and you'll see the trail begin amid a forest of coconut-laden palms. Wear sturdy shoes, use insect repellent, and bring bottled water. It's a bad idea to try this hike shortly after rainfall, as it is easy to lose the trail in the undergrowth and fallen leaves. After about 10min., the trail climbs uphill and reaches an excellent lookout. The trail continues another 8km to **Punta Mona,** named for its resident population of persistently vocal howler monkeys.

Another option is to take a **bus** heading toward or coming from Sixaola, and ask to be dropped at the entrance to Gandoca or "Finca 96" (12km from the border along the highway). From Finca 96, it is a 10km walk to the beach along a small unpaved road. Hitchhiking is possible, though cars infrequently enter this road and *Let's Go* does not recommend hitchhiking. **Taxis** can be hired in Sixaola, but charge between US$25-$30. Whichever route you take, you must hire an ANAI-certified guide to hike in the Refuge.

Gandoca runs along a road connecting the beach and ranger station, continuing inland to Finca 96. On either side of the road are wetlands and forest. No trails extend from Gandoca, but locals know how to navigate the nearby area. There is a single **police officer** in the town, usually posted at the ranger station. Next door to the police station is **Centro de Salud,** visited by a doctor every eight days. There are two unlabeled *pulperías* in town; ask around to get one opened for you.

Volunteers are assigned accommodations with a local family. (US$16 for a room, bathroom access, and 3 meals.) For those on guided tours, the only option is **Cabinas Restaurante Las Orquideas ❷,** labeled by a wooden sign 100m from the shore. Rooms are slightly musty. (US$25 per person includes 3 meals. Laundry ¢100 per item.) The **Ranger Station** has beds and cooking facilities, but permission to stay must be obtained in advance from a MINAE office in Cahuita or Limón. **Camping** for volunteers is available behind the ANAI station (US$8); facilities have convenient locations and shower access. Camping on the beach is prohibited.

Volunteering for the ANAI sea turtle project is demanding but rewarding (see **Alternatives to Tourism,** p. 133). Other ways to get to know the area include hiring a local guide to explore the refuge. Monkeys are everywhere and crocodiles lurk in the nearby lagoon, which can be explored by canoe. The region is home to the last surviving red mangroves in Costa Rica. The lagoon, often frequented by manatees looking for food, begins 200m from the ranger station and spills into the ocean. Guides, boats, and directions can be obtained through **MANT** guides and MINAE rangers (see **Manzanillo,** p. 237). **Aquamor** in Manzanillo also organizes half-day hiking and kayaking excursions with certified guides to the Gandoca Lagoon. (☎759 9012; aquamor1@racsa.co.cr. US$65.)

MANZANILLO

Six kilometers southeast of Punta Uva, Manzanillo is bounded by waves and jungle. The main reason to come to Manzanillo is to visit the breathtaking **Refugio Nacional Gandoca-Manzanillo.** A dense jungle trail stretches from the village through the refuge all the way to Panama. Founded in 1985 to protect endangered flora and fauna, the refuge includes 5013 hectares of private and public land—65% of which is tropical rainforest—and 4436 hectares of ocean. The refuge is a perennial favorite of nature-lovers because of its unmatched density and diversity of animal, marine, and plant life. The wetlands teem with crocodiles, alligators, sloths, pumas, and monkeys, while sandy beaches and fossil-lined coral caves offer gorgeous previews of the beauty beneath the water. Five different types of coral make this reef a particularly rewarding spot for underwater exploration. A red mangrove tree swamp sits beside the **Gandoca Lagoon** protecting the only natural population of mangrove oysters on the coast. The lagoon is also home to the nearly extinct manatee. The waters off rocky **Punta Mona** are frequented by tucuxi, bottlenose, and Atlantic spotted dolphins. Trails are not well-marked, and heavy rains year-round make them very poorly maintained. However, your mandatory guide will have the equipment and know-how to get you through almost any impasse.

Buses run daily from Puerto Viejo (7:30am, noon, 4:30, 7:30pm; returns 5am, 8:30pm; ¢220), passing through **Punta Uva** and the other beaches. You can also take a taxi (¢4500) or walk (3hr.) from Puerto Viejo. The walk along the beach, though lengthy, is gorgeous and peaceful. **MANT** (☎759 9064), located in the green and yellow building on main street, is a coalition of MIAE-certified native guides who give various tours, including hikes, turtle watching, night walks, horseback rides, snorkeling, fishing, and just about any other adventure a traveler might want to tackle in the Refuge. (Most tours US$15-$20. 2-day, 1-night tours of the refuge US$50.) A little farther down the road on the right, facing the beach, is the bright-green MINAE office. (☎759 9000; fax 759 9001. Open M-F 8am-4pm.) A map and history of the refuge are available with donation and volunteers can use beds for free. The **police station** is next to the MANT office. **Phones** are located in front of Restaurant Maxi. **La Lavendería Caribeña** (☎759 9043) is 50m behind Manzanillo Restaurant in a residential house labeled "Local Guide."

The cheapest place to stay in town is **Cabinas Maxi ❶,** behind Restaurant Maxi at the end of the town road. It has basic digs with private baths, no mosquito netting, stiff mattresses, and large windows that open onto the beach. (☎759 9061. ¢6000 per room with single and double bed; ¢4500 for the solo traveler.) Another option is the colorful **Pangea Bed and Breakfast ❸;** look 100m down from Aquamor for a sign pointing inland on a side-street between the MINAE office and Maxi's. A vibrant garden leads to two artfully decorated double rooms with ceiling fans and hot baths. The owner, a well-traveled gourmet chef, will prepare discounted dinners. (☎759 9204; pangaecr@racsa.co.cr. US$35 per room. AmEx/MC/V.)

Restaurant Maxi ❸, at the end of the town's main street, serves fresh seafood from an upstairs porch (catch of the day ¢2500-¢2850, veggie dish ¢1200) and is the the town's social center with a full-page drink menu. Maxi's lobster (¢4200) is famous throughout the region. (Open daily 11am-10pm.) The cheapest food in town is 50m down the street from Aquamor at **Soda Rinconcito Alegre ❷,** where generous portions of pancakes and fruit (¢600) or *ceviche* (¢1500) attract tourists and locals. (☎759 0640. Open daily 7am-7pm.)

If you want to explore the park from the water, check with the watersports shop **Aquamor,** the last right off the main road before Maxis. They rent kayaks and snorkeling gear and offer diving trips and dolphin observation excursions. (☎759 9012;

COSTA RICA

aquamor1@racsa.co.cr. Kayaks US$6 per hr., with guide US$15 per hr. Snorkel gear US$3, with guide US$24 per 2hr. Dives US$30-$37. Dolphin tours US$35 per person. Open daily 7am-6pm.) Aquamor helped start the **Talamanca Dolphin Foundation,** an organization that researches and protects the region's dolphins and their ecosystem. Get in touch with Aquamor for information on how to volunteer for the TDF or contact them directly (☎ 759 9118 or 759 9115; www.dolphinlink.org).

☎ **BORDER WITH PANAMA.** The Panamanian side of the border in **Guabito** is open daily 8am-6pm. The Costa Rican side, in **Sixaola,** is open daily 7am-5pm; the time zone difference assures the two coincide (☎754 2044). Both close for lunch (noon-12:30pm). A tourist card is necessary (US$5/¢2175). Officials reserve the right to ask for proof of economic independence (about US$200 will suffice). For all practical purposes Panama uses US dollars.

EL SALVADOR

The smallest country in Central America, El Salvador (pop. 6,587,541) is also the most densely populated. Memories of a long and bloody civil war in the 1980s and 90s tend to keep tourists at bay; however, now that peace has been restored, the country is safer and wide open for discovery. Mountain towns, black-sand beaches, and picturesque volcanoes eagerly await ecotourists. Perhaps more inviting than the landscape are the people. Salvadorans will spend endless hours helping you find hidden hotels, discussing the state of US-Salvadoran relations, or just shooting the breeze. These conversations are perhaps the most rewarding part of any visit, allowing you to see first-hand a nation on the road to recovery.

HIGHLIGHTS OF EL SALVADOR

San Vicente's scenic highlands, colonial church and dense market are watched over by the massive Volcán Chichontepec (p. 296).

Remote **Parque Nacional El Imposible** is alive with quetzals, agoutis, and anteaters, and laced with orchids and bromeliads (p. 280).

The beach town of **La Libertad,** boasting some of the best waves on the Pacific, is a great place to kick back and hang ten (p. 263).

Santa Ana, currently undergoing a renaissance, is exploding anew with impressive cultural and artistic sights (p. 285).

SUGGESTED ITINERARY

2-3 WEEKS: NATURE HIGHLIGHTS. In between the size of Northern Ireland and the state of New Jersey, El Salvador is small enough to be explored however you like. Park yourself in **San Salvador** (p. 249) and start planning daytrips. Head to the incredible ruins of **Joya de Cerén** (p. 261), known as the "Pompeii of the Americas," to see an ancient town perfectly preserved in ash. When you're back in San Salvador, get a permit from **Salva Natura** (p. 254) for **Parque Nacional El Imposible** (p. 280). Take some time to hike the park, and then head to **Santa Ana,** a great base for a number of natural sights like **Cerro Verde** (p. 288) and **Volcán Izalco,** the country's oldest and youngest volcanoes respectively. If you can't get enough of Maya ruins, check out **Tazumal** (p. 290), a ceremonial center that is less impressive than Tikal, but still interesting. Last but not least, take a dip in the gorgeous **Lago de Coatepeque** (p. 290), home to fancy weekend homes, splurge hotels, and excellent swimming. For an extended itinerary, head north of Santa Ana to **Metapán** (p. 291), a pleasant, isolated ranching village. From there head to the cloudforest reserve of **Parque Nacional Montecristo** (p. 293) where you can skip from El Salvador to Honduras to Guatemala in a smaller circle than you'd need for ring-a-round-a-rosy.

LIFE AND TIMES
LAND, FLORA, AND FAUNA

El Salvador's landscape is dominated by a chain of active volcanoes that runs west to east down its center. The **Crystalline Highlands,** spreading north into Honduras and Guatemala, slope on either side toward fertile plains and highlands. Due to a

EL SALVADOR

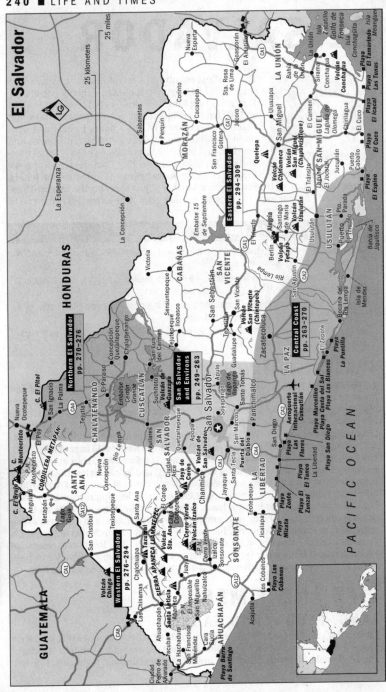

historically high level of over-cultivation in addition the government's past disregard for the environment, El Salvador is the most ecologically damaged country in the Americas. A mere 1.5% of the original forest remains, many of the country's watersheds are polluted, and the supply of potable water is running out. Though these ecological woes are substantial, a conscientious effort on the part of the Salvadoran government, foreign businesses, and tourists could make a big difference.

Plant and wildlife have understandably suffered under El Salvador's extended lack of eco-awareness. The country's varying climate allows for a high degree of plant diversity; however, deforestation and cash crops make native species harder to find. That said, some areas have remnants of oak and pine forests, mahogany, laurel, and balsa wood trees, as well as the *maquilishuat*, the national tree. The tree population pales in comparison to the over 200 species of orchid that make their home here; the national flower is the izote. Unfortunately, larger animals, such as jaguars and crested eagles, have either fled El Salvador's hills in search of hospitable conditions or been eradicated altogether. That said, El Salvador must have hosted a wealth of wildlife in the past, as over 400 species of birds, including a whopping 17 different types of hummingbird continue to nest here.

HISTORY

Around the year 1800, resentment of colonial favoritism for Guatemala in the indigo market generated the first stirrings for independence in El Salvador's planter elite. El Salvador rejected their Spanish status along with the rest of Central America in 1821. After 15 years as part of the United Provinces of Central America, Salvadorans achieved independent status in 1838.

EL SALVADOR ON ITS OWN (1838-1960). Political and commercial instability marked the nation's first year of independence. When the government forced El Salvador's indigenous population to relinquish its last remaining territory to large landowners, coffee capital cemented the link between land ownership and political power. An extremely small and powerful elite, the "Fourteen Families," organized an effective stranglehold on the country's land and money. Though their power peaked from 1913-1927, their influence survives to this day.

During the 1930s El Salvador's plutocracy degenerated as coffee profits plummeted worldwide. The oligarchy's demise opened the door for dictatorship. Struggling under pressures of the Great Depression, coffee plantation workers instigated a brief revolt—neither the country's first nor last, but certainly its bloodiest. Under the direction of **Augustín Farabundo Martí,** the founder of El Salvador's Communist Party, thousands of farm workers rebelled in 1932. In response, President **General Maximiliano Hernández Martínez** orchestrated the crushing massacre known as *la matanza*, executing over 10,000 Salvadoran civilians suspected of involvement in the uprising. In total, 30,000 people were killed before Martínez felt the rebels had learned their lesson. Martínez, who sought to emulate the better-known fascists of the time, stayed in power until a coup deposed him in 1948. Following the massacre, a series of dictators took the helm through the 70s, though each simply enacted the will of the paranoid landed elite. During this time, the last of the indigenous peoples were forcibly assimilated into *mestizo* culture.

THE RISE OF THE RIGHT (1964-1979). By the mid-60s, El Salvador had achieved relative economic stability and several reform programs resulted in new levels of economic diversity and international exchange. Despite increased economic security, most laborers continued to live in poverty. An emerging middle class began to support labor rights and welfare measures, promoted by **José Napoleón Duarte,** leader of the Christian Democratic Party (PDC) and mayor of San Salvador. Given the development of more liberal ideals among some Salvadorans, in 1961 the conservative landowners responded by covertly organizing a large, right-wing paramilitary force named ORDEN ("order"), which played a silent yet prominent role in the ongoing repression of the Salvadoran left.

Internal strife was replaced by international confrontation during the **Guerra de Fútbol** ("Soccer War"), when nationalist tensions with neighboring Honduras erupted over a sporting match in 1969. ORDEN troops seized the opportunity to place one of their own in power during the 1972 presidential elections. Despite obvious, nearly overwhelming support for Duarte, **Colonel Arturo Molina,** the more conservative, actively anti-Communist candidate favored by the ORDEN troops, was declared the winner. Following the election, the **Roman Catholic Church** joined the struggle against the conservative federal government and shifted the focus of its Salvadoran mission to Liberation Theology, fueling the fires of mass movements already responsible for many public protests and strikes. The ruling regime responded as they had in 1932, quelling dissent via brutal oppression. Violence reached an extreme in 1975, when ORDEN troops gunned down students protesting government corruption surrounding the Miss Universe pageant.

THE CIVIL WAR (1979-1991). A military coup in 1979 marked the official beginning of the nation's infamous civil war. Officers running the ruling junta initially allowed for members of more leftist groups to have seats on their governing committee, but political assassinations and civil oppression soon drove non-military members away. When things seemed most dire, the PDC formed an alliance with the military, creating a new civil junta. Duarte, in Venezuelan exile since his presidential "defeat" in 1972, returned to a hero's welcome to lead the new government. Unfortunately, the stability was short-lived. In the wake of political shifts toward the left, the elite aligned with the middle class and urban centers in order to ensure their economic, social, and political survival. Roberto d'Aubuisson organized the Alianza Republicana Nacionalista, or **ARENA,** to apply leverage against the extreme left wing. With the weight of the military on its side, ARENA managed to squeeze Duarte into an impossible position between the conservative officer-corps and leftist guerilla groups.

The lines of division were drawn: ARENA, the military, Duarte's government, and the middle class on one side—the guerillas (supported by the Catholic Church and country laborers) on the other. Although Duarte was not interested in annihilating the rebels, he was little more than a figurehead for the military by this point. The ensuing struggle resulted in over a decade of conflict resulting in 100,000 deaths, 750,000 refugees, and numerous child disappearances. Investigations continue into these cases, spearheaded by the Association to Support the Search for Children established in 1995.

Despite Duarte's opposition to the continued warfare, he was powerless to halt the flow of public funds to the right-wing "death squads" or into overt campaigns against the guerrillas. Furthermore, El Salvador had been singled out by the US as an example of how the military might of the West could be used to suppress "Communist insurgencies." The US government donated over US$4 billion worth of military aid to the right during the war, funding ORDEN and the death squads.

FMLN: UNITE AND CONQUER (1980-1992). In 1980, as ARENA was first marshaling its forces, the various guerrilla groups unified into the **FMLN** (Farabundo Martí para la Liberación Nacional) and declared war on the government. FMLN was able to maintain its guerilla sabotage tactics despite concentrated efforts to divide and conquer its small forces. Much of their success came from attacks on national infrastructure and actual military targets, causing an estimated US$2 billion in damage and many military deaths. Fighting was most intense in the mountainous northeast, which was subsequently leveled by random relentless bombings of peasant villages in the army's attempts to find the elusive rebels. Tens of thousands of innocent civilians were killed during the war, many of them by US weapons wielded by soldiers trained at the School of the Americas in Georgia.

One of FMLN's heroes, **Archbishop Oscar Romero,** was assassinated while giving mass in March 1980; later that year, the army raped and murdered three American nuns who had been working on missions of mercy in FMLN-controlled territories.

In the late 80s, citizens grew unhappy with Duarte's moderate, limping government and the shattered economy. With allegations of rampant corruption in Duarte's administration, the public overlooked Duarte in the 1989 presidential elections and elected **Alfredo Cristiani,** ARENA's charismatic candidate. Cristiani punished public sedition and rebel support more openly than his allies had, but at the same time was able to maneuver with enough freedom to consider seriously the FMLN's demands for social justice. In 1992, under UN supervision, an accord was reached between the two warring factions. The FMLN forces and much of the government army were disbanded, replaced by a new civilian police force that included former members of both forces. The peace faced its first true test in 1997 when president **Armando Calderón Sol** of the right-wing ARENA party faced a legislature composed of the newly social-democratic FMLN. Interestingly, it was the religious left that mediated between the two, preserving the fledgling peace.

TODAY

Active political involvement during the war allowed FMLN to carve out a legitimate niche for itself in the post-war government; however, all of El Salvador's post-war presidents have been from the ARENA party. On March 2, 2004, El Salvador elected its most recent ARENA President, **Antonio Saca.**

The new millennium brought with it natural forces as devastating as the nation's former political woes. On January 13th and February 13th, 2001, earthquakes rocked the country. San Vicente, Santiago de María, and most of the department of La Paz were hardest hit. Summer of 2001 followed up with a drought which slashed coffee profits and rural incomes. Hurricane Mitch and El Niño damage reduced the coffee yield substantially and delivered a harsh blow to the economy.

ECONOMY

Since the end of the civil war, El Salvador's recovering economy has been plagued by high unemployment. The economy remains predominantly agricultural; however, El Salvador imports most of its food because cash crops for export occupy most of the fertile land. The industrialization wave that ended at the beginning of the war is regaining momentum, but in the face of extreme environmental destruction, there is pressure to regulate industry in favor of a non-toxic environment.

CULTURE

PEOPLE. El Salvador is the most demographically homogeneous country in Central America, with most of the population representing a mix of indigenous and European backgrounds. The indigenous **Pipil** Indians were aggressively driven off their lands during the last few centuries, culminating in the mid-1800s, when they were forced into labor on the booming coffee plantations. Today they represent a scant 1% of the population, in comparison to 43% in neighboring Guatemala.

FOOD AND DRINK. The cuisine of El Salvador is similar to that of other Latin American nations. Tortillas are featured in every meal and beans are never far behind. Breakfast, served early in the morning, typically consists of eggs, plantains, cheese or cream, beans, and, of course, tortillas. For plain eggs, ask for *solo huevos;* otherwise, expect a plate of eggs with tomatoes and onions to land on the table. For lunch and dinner, replace eggs and cheese with meat and *arroz* (yellow

ON THE MENU

BODACIOUS BREWS

Remember how each fraternity at your school was obsessed with their signature brand of beer? Well Central America is just like those frats, minus the Mud-wrestling Mondays.

El Salvador's ales are all blondes, but local connoisseurs will stringently protest if you claim they are all the same. Ironically, the beers are all produced by the same company. Industrias la Constancia doesn't just have a monopoly on domestic beers; they lead a strong lobby that bars many foreign imports as well. Like them or not, Industria's beers are the ones you'll probably be drinking, so here's a quick rundown:

Pilsener: If you pass through El Salvador without having one, then you haven't really been here. The classic Salvadoran beer is tastier than a Corona and the aroma lasts longer.

Bahía: Recently launched, Bahía has already become the new fashion among young people. It has a very distinctive flavor. Give it a try—you'll either love it or hate it.

Suprema, Premium, Regia: Honestly, none of these are too different from Pilsener. Suprema has more of a lime flavor and the aroma melts quickly in your mouth. Premium is the only one sold internationally, and Regia is popular for its big, brown bottles.

Golden Light: Light beers=water. Counting carbs=silly.

fried rice). The meat is usually *pollo dorado* (roast "golden" chicken), *carne asada* (roasted meat), or *encebollado* (stewed with veggies and lots of onions and either chicken or beef). *Pupusas* (tortillas filled with cheese or beans) are everywhere. As for drinks, Salvadorans prefer fruity ones. Fruit-shake *licuados* and sweet coconut-juice concoctions are rivaled only by Kolashanpan, an ultra-sweet local soda whose taste defies description. The most popular brands of beer are Pilsener and Suprema. For ultimate intoxication, mix Coke with Tic-Tack, a ferocious rum-like concoction distilled from sugar cane.

THE ARTS. El Salvador's early literature focuses not on pressing social issues but on depicting human emotion. Early romantic poets include **José Batres Montúfar** (1809-1844) and **Arturo Ambrogi** (1874-1936), who is also known for his short stories. **Carlos Bustamante's** *Mi Caso* reflects on the most intimate human feelings, as did the works of the first acclaimed Salvadoran woman poet, **Claudia Lars** (1899-1974), whose books such as *Tierra de Infancia* (1959) expressed a refreshing feminine perspective. In the early days of the century, **Alberto Masferrer** (1868-1932) contributed important essays and poetry to this tradition.

More recent literature strives to catalyze change by evoking optimistic impressions of what might one day be, rather than harping on the recent war. Artists like **Dorian Díaz** and **Gilberto Arriaza** tap into common experience to evoke images of harmony and peace. Díaz's *El Pescado* and Arriaza's *La Luna* are among the colorful works which have recently arrived on the national art scene.

POPULAR CULTURE. US pop and top 40 artists are well known in El Salvador. In rural areas and small towns, tastes are more traditional, but there are few strictly Salvadoran musical groups. *La Prensa Gráfica* (www.laprensa.com.sv) and *Diario de Hoy* (www.elsalvador.com) are the best Salvadoran daily newspapers. In San Salvador, the *El Salvador News Gazette* gives bilingual tips and news. Six TV stations deliver the usual soap operas, news programs, and soccer games.

HOLIDAYS. Each town has its own patron saint and a designated day of celebration. The country has a day of unity in celebration of El Salvador's patron saint. National holidays include: **March/April,** Semana Santa, Thursday, Friday and Saturday before Easter; **May 1,** Labor Day; **August 3 to 6,** Festival de El Salvador del Mundo; **September 15,** Independence Day; **October 12,** *Día de la Raza*; **November 2,** All Souls Day; **November 5,** the First Cry of Independence.

ESSENTIALS

PASSPORTS, VISAS, AND CUSTOMS
Passport (p. 19): Required of all visitors.

Visas and Tourist cards (p. 247): US citizens can get a free visa from a Salvadoran Consulate on US territory, or pay US$10 for a 60-day tourist card. Canadians can get a visa for CDN$30 or can get a tourist card for US$10. Prearranged visas are required for visitors from New Zealand and Australia; travelers from the UK do not need prearranged visas.

Inoculations and Medications (p. 27): None required; see **Health**, p. 246.

Work Permit: Required for all foreigners planning to work in El Salvador.

Driver's Permit: Drivers entering El Salvador need car registration, driver's license, and proof of insurance. Visitors can drive with their US license for up to 30 days. Permits are required for longer stays and can be purchased from the National Police (US$10). Rental car drivers enjoy a 90-day grace period. For more information, consult the **Auto Club of El Salvador** (☎221 0557).

Airport Exit Fee: US$27.15.

EMBASSIES AND CONSULATES

The following are Salvadoran embassies located outside of the country; for embassies located in El Salvador, see the **Practical Information** section of **San Salvador** (p. 254). **Canada,** 209 Kent St., Ottawa, Ontario K2P 1Z8 (☎613-238-2939; embajada@elsalvador.ca.org; open M-F 9am-5pm). **UK,** Mayfair House, 3rd fl., 39 Great Portland St., Sr. London W1N 7JZ (☎44 20 7436 8282; embajadalondres@rree.gob.sv; open M-F 10am-5pm). **US,** 2308 California St. N.W., Washington, D.C. 20008 (☎202-265-9671, 265-9672, or 265-9675; www.elsalvador.org; open M-F 9:30am-5:30m). Salvadoran **consulates** are in a number of foreign cities: **Canada,** 151 Bloor Street West Suite, 320, Toronto, Ontario M5S 1S4 (☎416-975-0812); **US,** 46 Park Avenue, New York, NY 10016 (☎212-889-3608); 1724 20th St., N.W., Washington, D.C. 20009 (☎202-331-4032).

MONEY

US DOLLARS		
AUS$1= US$0.72	US$1 =AUS$1.39	
CDN$1= US$0.76	US$1 =CDN$1.31	
EURO€1 = US$1.24	US$1 =EURO€0.81	
NZ$1 = US$0.67	US$1 = NZ$1.50	
UK£1= US$1.84	US$1 =UK£0.54	

Exchanges listed above are accurate as of August 2004. The **US dollar** is official legal tender in El Salvador and has replaced the colón as the country's official currency. Traveler's checks are difficult to cash; your best bet is at **Banco Cuscutlan** and **Banco Salvadoreño** where you can also get cash advances on credit cards. Some **ATMs** accept only Visa, but travelers should not have trouble finding machines that accept AmEx/Cirrus/MC/V as well.

A 5-10% **tip** is appropriate for the majority of restaurants. Expect to pay more for lodgings and food in El Salvador than elsewhere in Central America, with reasonably priced rooms costing US$7-$15 per night and meals costing US$5-$15.

US DOLLARS	❶	❷	❸	❹	❺
ACCOMMODATIONS	US$1-5.50	US$5.50-9	US$9-12	US$12-16.50	US$16.50+
FOOD	US$1-3	US$3-5.50	US$5.50-7	US$7-11	US$11+

EL SALVADOR

SAFETY

Although demonstrations and sit-ins were common occurrences in 2002, El Salvador has recently become much more stable. Travelers should always be vigilant and cautious while conducting financial exchanges either inside the bank or at ATMs, even though the country is not the bandits' den it once was. The **tourist police,** mostly found in national parks, will accompany travelers to volcanoes and mountain peaks for free. In some cases a formal letter may need to be written to request a police guide. In these cases the letter should be typed with the name of the destination, date, and number of people and addressed to the *Jefe Delegación de* (name of the city). The **emergency phone number** throughout the country was recently changed to ☎911; the **Red Cross** number is ☎222 5155, and the San Salvador **fire department** is ☎271 1244. For other safety tips, see **Personal Safety,** p. 26.

HEALTH

El Salvador carries the same health risks as other Central American countries. The most serious health concerns for travellers are **malaria** and **dengue fever.** The Center for Disease Control recommends chloroquine as the most effective anti-malarial medicine. Avoid tap water to avoid an upset stomach and overly frequent trips to the bathroom. For descriptions of disease prevention, see **Health,** p. 25. Nearly every Salvadoran town has a host of pharmacies; hours usually span from 8am to 6pm. Throughout El Salvador, it is best to avoid tap water, uncooked vegetables, and peeled fruit.

BORDER CROSSINGS

GUATEMALA. There are four land crossings. The northernmost is **La Hachadura/ Ciudad Pedro de Alvarado,** on the Pacific Coast 66km west of Sonsonate. Farther south is **Las Chinamas/Valle Nuevo,** 25km west of Ahuachapán (p. 283). Below that, **San Cristóbal,** 30km from Santa Ana, sends buses to Guatemala City. The southernmost land crossing is **Anguiatú,** 12km north of Metapán, near Esquipulas.

HONDURAS. There are three land crossings. **El Poy,** in the northern highlands, is closest to Nueva Ocotepeque, Honduras (p. 454). **El Amatillo,** in the east, is 15km east of Santa Rosa de Lima, and near Choluteca, Honduras (p. 304). Last is **Sabanetas,** near Perquín north of San Miguel; see San Miguel for buses (p. 299). There are irregular **ferry** departures from **La Unión** to ports in Honduras and **Nicaragua** in the Gulf of Fonseca (p. 307).

KEEPING IN TOUCH

Mail sent to the US or Europe from El Salvador is relatively reliable; air mail letters take one to two weeks. Sending a letter to North America costs US$0.45, to Europe, Australia, and New Zealand $0.75; post cards costs US$0.29/US$0.72; packages to North America cost US$1.43 per 1kg. Express mail services in San Salvador, such as **DHL,** tap into the US Postal Service. For example, they can get a letter from New York to El Salvador in two to three days for US$22.25. **Federal Express** (www.fedex.com; Australia ☎13 2610, Canada and US 800-247-4747; New Zealand 0800 73 3339; UK 0800 12 3800) can get a letter from El Salvador to London in two to three days for UK£37. Letters sent to San Salvador's main post office should be addressed to "Centro de Gobierno, San Salvador."

> Edoardo GALLO [First Name, LAST NAME]
> Lista de Correos
> Santa Ana [CITY]
> República de El Salvador

Salvadoran **phone** numbers have seven digits and require no area code. **Telecom** is the most common private company. Calls to the US or Europe are expensive, so it's better to use a calling card. US access numbers for El Salvador: AT&T ☎ 800-1785, MCI 800-1767, and Sprint 800-1776.

COUNTRY CODE	503

TRANSPORTATION

Cars and **buses** are the easiest ways to get around El Salvador. **Driving** in El Salvador requires significant defensive skills. The roads are poorly maintained, and traffic laws are not strictly enforced. Drive with your doors locked and windows raised, and avoid travel outside metropolitan areas after dark. Banditry, carjackings, and kidnappings occur on unpaved roads. There are many local and inter-city bus systems: every bus route has a number and the dispatcher at every bus station has the most recent schedules. Buses labeled *ordinario* will be slower than ones labeled *directo*. Radio-dispatched **taxis** are the safest way to travel if you don't have a car. **Pickups** have become a semi-formal mode of transport in some areas with regular schedules and fixed fares, but always be sure the vehicle is safe and that your destination and fare are agreed upon before leaving.

ORIENTATION

El Salvador's larger towns, like those of Nicaragua, Honduras, and Guatemala, have streets gridded with north-south *avenidas* and east-west *calles*—the opposite of Costa Rica. Most cities have a central *avenida* and a central *calle*. Even-numbered streets and avenues are on one side of each main drag, odd numbers on the other. In most cities (including San Salvador), odd-numbered *avenidas* and *calles* increase in number to the west and north of the center, respectively; likewise, even-numbered *avenidas* and *calles* increase toward the east and south. An address given as "3/5 Av., 2 C.," is on Calle 2 between Av. 3 and 5.

NATIONAL PARKS

El Salvador contains a number of national parks *(parques nacionales)* that have put the country on the fast track to becoming a big ecotourist destination. The largest and most impressive is **El Imposible** (p. 280). The regulations for visitors vary for each park: for example, El Imposible requires a permit from Salva Natura in San Salvador. Other parks may require you to hire a guide, while some have no restrictions. Be sure to check the descriptions of each park listed by *Let's Go* before planning a trip. For more information visit: www.nps.gov/centralamerica/honduras www.honduras.com/travel/parks.

ALTERNATIVES TO TOURISM

This section lists some of the organizations in El Salvador that offer opportunities outside the typical tourist experience. For more information on Alternatives to Tourism as well as tools for finding programs on your own, see the chapter at the beginning of the book (p. 53).

VISA INFORMATION

To apply for a **work permit** in El Salvador, you must legally be in El Salvador with the proper visas and permits, and then submit the following to the Ministry of the Interior: a residency request form, an original birth certificate, a good conduct certificate issued by the Salvadoran consulate in your home country and from the Ministry of Foreign Relations, two recent passport-sized photos, results of an HIV test, a health certificate, a work contract stating the terms of the contract (salary, job duties, working hours, and location of the job), a notarized letter requesting residency, a personal data form, and authenticated photocopies of everything previously stated. Student visas are not normally required, but check with the Salvadoran consulate of your home country to be sure.

LANGUAGE SCHOOLS

Escuela Cuzcatlan, 1 Av. Norte, Pasaje Vienna #10, Barrio San Miguelito, San Salvador (☎869 6185; http://salvaspan.homestead.com), offers small class sizes. Instruction is available by the hour (US$8) with an average week-long program including 20 hrs. Classes are geared toward beginners.

Escuela Mélida Anaya Montes, Blvd. Universitario #4, Colonia el Roble, San Salvador (☎226 2623; www.cis-elsalvador.org/spanish_school.htm), aims beyond language instruction toward true cultural exchange. As part of the Centro de Intercambio y Solidaridad (Exchange and Solidarity Center), this school teaches Spanish in political, social, and cultural contexts. The weekly fee of US$208 includes classes, a political-cultural program, meals, and a homestay. Classes start every M. Apply online (US$25).

International Partners for Study Abroad (IPSA), 3646 W. Brown St., Suite A, Phoenix, AZ 85051, US (fax 602-942-6734; www.studyabroadinternational.com), offers Spanish programs in La Libertad, Santa Ana, and San Salvador. IPSA offers a number of services including weekly classes (US$150 per week), personal lessons (US$10 per hr.), and homestays (US$90 per week). IPSA also offers semester long Spanish classes that are accepted for credit at certain universities.

VOLUNTEERING

BIOLOGY/ECOLOGY

Volunteers for Peace, 1034 Tiffany Rd., Belmont, VT 05730, US (☎802-259-2759, www.vfp.org), has a wide array of volunteer opportunities. The environmental programs include environmental education, wildlife surveying, park maintenance, and organic farming. Participants live in groups of 8-12. Open to US and Canadian citizens. Accommodations and food included (US$200).

EDUCATION/HUMANITARIAN

CRISPAZ, 122 DeWitt Drive, Boston, MA 02120, US (☎617-445-5115; www.crispaz.org), stands for "Christians for Peace" and is an organization focusing on 4 main areas: high-risk youth, economic development, rural community development, and north-south solidarity. CRISPAZ offers 2 volunteer options: summer immersion (US$1450) and long-term (US$4000-$6000) with a 15 month minimum commitment.

HELP International, 363 N. University Ave. Ste., #110, Provo, UT 84601, US (☎801-374-0556, www.help-international.org), provides the unique opportunity for volunteers to design their own project. HELP's 3 main areas of focus are economic development, health and nutrition, and English education. Some previous projects included microbusiness training, garden planning, English classes, and orphanage volunteering. The program fee (US$2750) covers lodging, food, and transportation and remains the same regardless of program length (6 weeks to 4 months).

SAN SALVADOR

If arriving in San Salvador from more relaxed rural areas, travelers may be a bit shell-shocked by this bustling metropolis. Like many Central American cities, San Salvador is really two cities in one: the shopping malls, nightclubs, and wealthy homes in the city's Zona Rosa are a world apart from the crime, pollution, and noise of the city center. Still, San Salvador's many parks and trees work to diminish the concrete-jungle feeling that plagues other big cities. All the modern conveniences and luxuries not available elsewhere make the capital an excellent base from which to explore the country. Conveniently located at the center of the country, San Salvador is only a short bus ride away from every other town in El Salvador, making it the beating heart of this small Central American republic.

✈ INTERCITY TRANSPORTATION

Flights: The **San Salvador Comalapa International Airport,** 44km south of the city, is serviced by **Taca** (☎267 8222); **American** (☎298 0777; open M-F 8am-6pm); **Air France** (☎263 8101); **Continental** (☎260 3263; open M-F 8am-6pm); **Mexicana** (☎271 5936); and **United** (☎298 5462; open M-F 8am-7pm). To get there, **Acaya taxis,** 19th Av., 3 C. (☎271 4937), next door to Puerto Bus, runs a microbus to the airport (6, 7, 10am, 2pm; US$3). Alternatively, the #400 minibus departs from the south side of Plaza Barrios (1hr., every 15min. 5am-5pm, US$1), and the #138 departs from Terminal del Sur. (1hr., every 5min., US$0.50). Taxi to the airport with **Acaya** US$16.

Domestic Buses: There are 3 primary terminals in town that serve as departure points for west-bound, east-bound, and south-bound buses.

Terminal Occidente: On Blvd. Venezuela near 49 Av., can be reached by bus #34 from the center of town, or bus #44 from Metrocentro, exit on Blvd. Venezuela. Buses run to: **Ahuachapán** (#202 or 204, 2hr., every 18min. 4am-7:30pm, US$0.70); **Santa Ana** (#201, 2hr., every 10min. 4am-5:30pm, US$0.65); and **Sonsonate** (#205, 1½hr., every 25min. 4:45am-7:45pm, US$0.35).

Terminal Oriente: Down Alameda Juan Pablo II in the far eastern portion of the city, accessible by bus #29 from Metrocentro and east-bound bus #34. Buses to: **Chalatenango** (#125, 2hr., every 10min. 4am-6:30pm, US$1.25); **Cojutepeque** (#113, 1hr., every 5min. 4am-9pm, US$0.50); **Ilobasco** (#111, 1½hr., every 10min. 5am-7:30pm, US$2); **La Palma** (#119, 4hr., every 30min. 4am-4pm, US$1.50); **La Union** (#304, 4hr., every 30min. 3:45am-7pm, US$2; direct 7 and 8am, US$4); **San Miguel** (#301, 3hr., every 10min. 3:30am-5pm, US$2; direct 7 and 8am, US$2.25); **Santa Rosa de Lima** (#306, 5hr., every 40min. 3:45am-3:45pm, US$2. Bus continues to **El Amatillo**); **San Vicente** (#116, 1¾hr., every 10min. 4:40am-9pm, US$0.65); **Suchitoto** (#129, 1½hr, every 15min. 5am-7pm, US$0.50; after 6pm, US$0.35).

Terminal del Sur: Take bus #26 from the National University or town center all the way to its last stop in San Marcos. Buses to: **Costa del Sol** (#495, 1hr., every 30min., US$0.85); **Puerto El Triunfo** (#185, 1½hr., every 30min. 9am-5:30pm, US$1.45); **Usulután** (#302, 2hr., every 10min. 4am-5pm, US$1); **Zacatecoluca** (#133, 1½hr., every 10min. 4am-8pm, US$0.35).

Buses leave independently to **La Libertad** from 6 C. Pte., between 13 Av. and 15 Av., south of Parque Bolívar (#102, 45min., every 10min. 5am-7:30pm, US$0.60) and to **Panchimalco** from Av. 29 de Agosto and 12 C. Pte. (#12; every 20min. 5:30am-7:20pm; US$0.35).

International Buses:

King Quality: ☎271 1361, shares its offices with Puerto Bus (below). Destinations include: **Guatemala City, GTM** (US$23); **Managua, NIC** (5:30am, US$30); **San Pedro Sula, HND** (6:30am, 12:30pm; US$23); and **Tegucigalpa, HND** (6:30, 10:30am, 1:30pm; US$25).

Puerto Bus: ☎222 2158, has two offices, one located in the strip-mall: at 19 Av., Alameda Juan Pablo II, across the street from the Federal Reserve Bank building, and another on Blvd. del Hipodrómo #4115 next to the Zona Rosa. Buses run to: **Guatemala City, GTM** (every hr. 4am-4:30pm, US$7; luxury bus US$10).

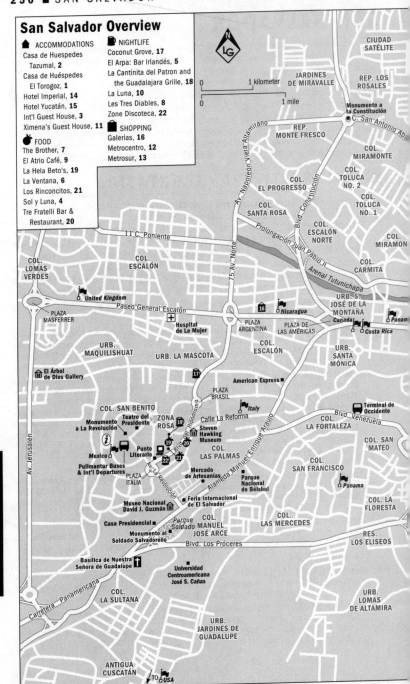

San Salvador Overview

▲ ACCOMMODATIONS
Casa de Huespedes
  Tazumal, 2
Casa de Huéspedes
  El Torogoz, 1
Hotel Imperial, 14
Hotel Yucatán, 15
Int'l Guest House, 3
Ximena's Guest House, 11

🍎 FOOD
The Brother, 7
El Atrio Café, 9
La Hela Beto's, 19
La Ventana, 6
Los Rinconcitos, 21
Sol y Luna, 4
Tre Fratelli Bar &
  Restaurant, 20

📷 NIGHTLIFE
Coconut Grove, 17
El Arpa: Bar Irlandés, 5
La Cantinita del Patron and
  the Guadalajara Grille, 18
La Luna, 10
Les Tres Diables, 8
Zone Discoteca, 22

🛍 SHOPPING
Galerías, 16
Metrocentro, 12
Metrosur, 13

EL SALVADOR

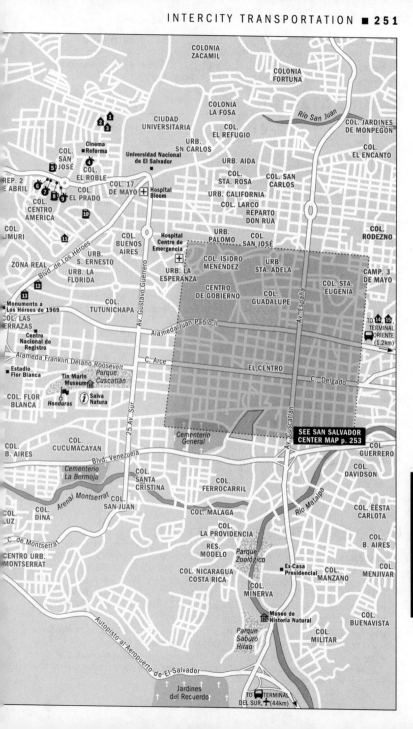

Pullmantur: ☎ 243 1300, departs from the San Salvador Marriott, Av. de la Revolución and runs a bus to **Guatemala City** (7am, 3pm; US$25).

Tica Bus: 10 Av. Nte., C. Concepción (☎ 222 4808), has daily buses leaving to: **Managua** (11hr., 5am, US$25); **San José** (1½days, 5am, US$35); **Panama City** (5am, US$60).

✈ ORIENTATION

UPON ARRIVAL. The **airport** is 44km south of the capital. The safest way to get to the capital after dark, is to take a **taxi**. **Taxis Acaya** (☎ 271 4937) run for US$16 while mini-vans split the total cost (US$14) among more people. Another option is to take microbuses, which leave from the intersection, 100m along the main road in front of the airport. The **#400** microbus goes to the city center, dropping you off in front of the **Cathedral** (1hr., every 15min. 5am-5pm, US$1), while the **#138** will take you to the **Terminal del Sur**, on the southern edge of the city (45min., every 5min., US$0.50), where you will have to take the **#26** to the **city center** (30min., US$0.20). Though infrequent, the most reliable option may be the shuttle run by **Taxis Acaya** which brings you through the *centro* to their station at **19th Av., 3 Calle** (9am, 1, 5:30pm. US$3). For bus information see **Local Transportation** below.

LAYOUT. San Salvador employs the standard grid system in the older *el centro* (see map p. 247). However, outside of the city center it is easiest to navigate by major streets and landmarks because the streets conform to the terrain. *Avenidas* run north-south, and *calles* run east-west. **El centro histórico,** usually called just "*el centro,*" is the city's old colonial district, located on the eastern side of town around the **cathedral**. Many of the main streets confusingly change names in this area. The main *calle* runs along the church's northern side and is called **Calle Delgado** to the east and **Calle Arce** to the west. The principal north-south *avenida* is called **Av. Cuscatlán** south of the cathedral and **Av. España** north of the cathedral. Running east-west, **2 Calle Oriente** changes into **Calle Rubén Darío** before becoming **Alameda Franklin Delano Roosevelt,** and then **Paseo General Escalón** before terminating at the **Plaza Masferrer** at the western border of the city.

The **Zona Rosa** covers the southwest portion of San Salvador, where embassies, luxury hotels, and raging clubs all combine to create a sophisticated atmosphere. Smack in the middle of town between Zona Rosa and El Centro is the area called **Metrocentro,** named after the ever-popular malls **Metrocentro** and **Metrosur.** Metrocentro is the juncture for all the highways through San Salvador, including **Blvd. de los Héroes** which jets north of the malls and is a haven for fast-food chains and drive-thrus. The Boulevard continues to the **University** and toward **Calle San Antonio,** which has a lively international scene.

⌐ LOCAL TRANSPORTATION

Local Buses: Buses cruise to destinations throughout the city from 6am-9pm, depending on the route. The fare is US$0.20 no matter where you go. Buses stop only at designated stops, which are clearly marked with route numbers. There are also microbuses (US$0.34) that run the same routes and use the same route numbers. Buses do not necessarily return via the same path. It is easiest and fastest to ask locals for help finding the bus to take to your destination. The main lines are:

#34: Main east-west line, runs from the Plaza Italia in the west to the **Terminal de Occidente** through the *centro* by the Mercado Central. Ends at the **Terminal de Oriente.**

#30b: Main bus for the Blvd. de los Héroes area. Runs from the **Universidad Nacional,** along Blvd. de los Héroes to **Metrosur,** then on to **Plaza Las Américas** along Paseo General Escalón, and finally to the **Zona Rosa** and **Plaza Italia.**

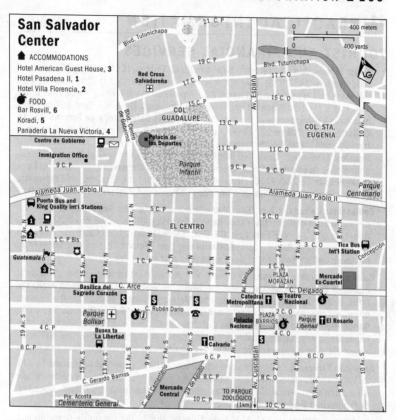

San Salvador Center

ACCOMMODATIONS
Hotel American Guest House, **3**
Hotel Pasadena II, **1**
Hotel Villa Florencia, **2**

FOOD
Bar Rosvill, **6**
Koradi, **5**
Panadería La Nueva Victoria, **4**

#30: Useful north-south route from **Universidad Nacional** through **Metrocentro/Metrosur,** and then to the *centro* on C. Rubén Darío until **Parque Libertad.** Return bus on 1 C. Poniente.

#44: Runs from the **Metrocentro** passing close to **Terminal de Occidente** before reaching the **Autopista del Sur** and **Antiguo Cuscatlán.** Microbuses reach the US Embassy in Antiguo Cuscatlán.

#52: Runs from **Terminal de Oriente** via JPII, past Metrocentro, to Plaza Las Américas, and on to **Plaza Masferrer.** Returns along same route.

#24: Runs from **Metrocentro** to **Terminal de Oriente.**

#26: Runs from **Plaza Barrios** on the cathedral's west side to **Terminal del Sur.**

#101: Runs from **Plaza Barrios,** past Metrosur, down Alameda Araujo and beyond the Feria Internacional, returning along roughly the same route. This is the bus to get to the US embassy. Heads to **Santa Tecla** southwest of the city. Also connects **El Centro** to **Plaza Italia. 101D** goes west to Plaza Masferrer before heading south.

Taxis: Taxi Acaya, 19th Av., 3 C. (☎271 4937).

Car Rental: Budget, Condominio Balam Quitze, Paseo Gral. Escalón, Local 3-A (☎263 5583); **Dollar,** Prolongación C. Arce 2226, Col. Flor Blanca (☎260 2424); **Avis,** Colonia Flor Blanca, 43 Av. Sur #137 (☎260 7157). 25+ except Dollar 21+. Credit card required for deposit and insurance; AmEx/MC/V. US$50-$120 per day. Call in advance for cheaper rates.

EL SALVADOR

🛈 PRACTICAL INFORMATION

TOURIST AND FINANCIAL SERVICES

Tourist Information: Corporación Salvadoreña de Turismo (CORSATUR), 508 Blvd. del Hipódromo (☎243 7835). Take bus #30b or #34 to Plaza Italia in Zona Rosa. Go past the plaza onto Hipódromo and follow it all the way up the hill. Though a little out of the way, this is the best place for free maps and brochures. Open M-F 8am-5:30pm. They also have a branch office at the airport. The **Instituto Salvadoreño de Turismo (ISTU),** C. Rubén Darío 619 (☎222 8000), located between 9 Av. Sur and 11 Av. Sur, has a friendly staff useful for any traveling need and information on 14 different national reserves. Free maps. Open M-F 8am-4pm. If you happen to stay at Ximena's Guesthouse (see **Accommodations,** below), a convenient source of information is **Lena Johannessen** (☎260 7475), the regional manager for the Guatemalan English-language magazine *Revue.* Pick up a free copy at Ximena's for info on events in the city.

Embassies: Canada, 63 Av. Sur, Alameda Roosevelt (☎279 4659). Open M-F 8am-noon and 1:30-4:30pm. **UK,** Paseo General Escalón #4830 (☎263 6520). Open M-Th 8am-1pm and 2-4pm, F 8am-1pm. **US,** Blvd. Santa Elena, Antiguo Coscatlán, bus route #101A. Open M-F 8am-4:30pm. **Australia** and **New Zealand** have no embassies here; the **tourist office** has a list of more embassies and consulates.

Banks: Big banks and *casas de cambio* will change most currencies into US dollars; traveler's checks are accepted less frequently. Hotels charge the steepest exchange rates. **Banco Cuscatlán,** downstairs in the Metrocentro mall, across from the Telecom office, will change traveler's checks and US dollars. Open M-F 9am-6pm, Sa 9am-2pm. **Banco Hipotecario** is located on Av. Cuscatlán, 4 C. Open M-F 9am-4:30pm, Sa 9am-noon. Major gas stations, malls, and many banks throughout the city have **ATMs**; all accept MC/V and some accept Cirrus/Plus. Metrocentro mall has numerous machines.

American Express: C. la Mascota and Interamerican Hwy., Comercial la Mascota (☎279 3844, travelers checks help 964 6665). Take bus #101 from the city center or bus #30b from Metrocentro. This is the best place to exchange traveler's checks. Open M-F 8am-noon and 2-5pm, Sa 9am-noon.

Immigration Office: (☎221 2111), on 15th Av. Nte. in the Centro de Gobierno just north of Alameda Juan Pablo II. Extends visas and tourist cards. Open M-F 8am-4pm.

Special Permits: Salva Natura, 33 Ave. Sur #640 in Colonia Flor Blanca (☎279 1515; fax 279 0220). Head south to 16 Décima C. from Av. Roosevelt. Gives permits for **Parque Nacional El Imposible.** You will need to bring or fax a letter with the dates you plan to visit and the names of everyone going. Permits US$5 per person, include a guide who will meet you at the park. Office open M-F 8am-12:30pm and 2-5:30pm. **Ministerio de Agricultura,** Servicio de Parques Nacionales (☎294 0566; fax 294 0575), on Canton and C. El Matezano in the eastern suburb of Soyapango, take bus #33a from the northern edge of Parque Libertad. Grants permits for **Parque Nacional Montecristo.** Letter or fax with names and dates must be submitted a week in advance of visit. The **ISTU** office (p. 254) can also help arrange park permits.

LOCAL SERVICES

English Bookstores: Punto Literario, on the North side of the Plaza Italia, near the Zona Rosa, is the best place in town for English books. Take bus #30b from Metrocentro or #34 from *el centro* to Plaza Italia. Open daily 10am-7pm. AmEx/MC/V. **Eutopia,** in the Galerías, has a smaller selection. Most luxury hotels have American magazines and newspapers at their newsstands (US$0.50-$0.75).

Markets and Malls: The **Mercado Central** is technically located between C. de Cementero and Av. 29 de Agosto, but branches out through most of *el centro*. Everything—from used clothes to cell phones—is on sale. The frantic pace can be invigorating, but take care not to get lost; street signs are hard to see behind vendors' booths. Open daily 7am-5pm. The **Mercado Ex-Cuartel**, 8 Av. and C. Delgado, to the east of Plaza Barrios, features *artesanía* and handicrafts. Open daily 8am-5pm. Two large malls offer all modern conveniences and extensive shopping options. **Metrocentro** sits on Blvd. de los Héroes and is home to a supermarket, movie theater, and countless ATMs. The more ritzy **Galerías** is on Paseo Escalón between Plaza las Americas and Plaza Beethoven.

EMERGENCY AND COMMUNICATIONS

Police: ☎911 on 15 Av. Nte., 1 C. Pte.

Red Cross: ☎ 222 5155, in the Centro de Gobierno.

Pharmacy: Farmacia Internacional, 49 Av., Blvd. de los Héroes and Alameda Juan Pablo II, in the mini-mall just south of Metrosur. Open 24hr.

Telephones: Telecom, 5 Av., C. Rubén Darío, just southwest of Plaza Barrios. Open M-F 8am-6pm, Sa-Su 8am-noon. US$3-$5 phone cards available. Smaller branch downstairs in the Metrocentro, across from the Banco de Cuscatlán. To US US$0.60 per min., to Europe US$2 per min. Open M-Sa 9am-6pm.

Internet Access: Ciber Café Hot, on the corner of 3 C. Pte. and 17 Av. Nte. in the centro has more than 20 high-speed computers (US$0.50 per hr.), and offers photocopying, scanning, and CD burning. **Infocentros,** on Blvd. del Hipódromo before Plaza Italia, is the best place for Internet access. US$2.25 per hr., students US$1 per hr. Open M-Sa 8am-8pm, Su 9am-6pm. Other internet cafes line the city streets, particularly on C. San Antonio and in the Northwest area of *el centro*. Most charge about US$1 per hr.

Post Office: on Blvd. Centro Gobierno, a couple blocks north of Alameda Juan Pablo II. Internet access is also available. Open M-F 8am-4pm, Sa 8am-noon. Another **branch** in Metrocentro. Open M-F 8am-7pm, Sa 8am-noon.

▐ ACCOMMODATIONS

San Salvador's budget accommodations involve a little give and take. Consider spending a bit more, as cheap rooms are often in unsafe neighborhoods. A good compromise are dorm-style accommodations; cheap beds in secure neighborhoods make it easy to meet other travelers. The best places to stay in terms of safety, amenities, and prices cluster between **Los Héroes** and the **University. El Centro** has a few nice options, while the area around **Terminal de Oriente** is more unsafe.

BETWEEN LOS HÉROES AND THE UNIVERSITY

The guest houses between Blvd. de los Héroes and the National University are safe, moderately cheap, and located in a relatively tranquil and smog-free area. The Metrocentro mall, to the south on Blvd. de los Héroes, promises to fulfill your every material need, while C. San Antonio Abad to the north is lined with university-influenced bars satisfying cravings for live music and good beer.

▨ **Casa de Huéspedes El Torogoz** (☎235 4172), on 35 Av. Nte. north of Blvd. Universitario. Recently expanded to include a swimming pool, common kitchen, Internet, and laundry. Spanish lessons offered. Rooms are clean and spacious with cable TV, fan, and phone. One hot bath for every two rooms. Ask about the special *Let's Go* discount. Breakfast included. English spoken. Singles US$22; doubles US$30. AmEx/MC/V. ❺

▨ **Ximena's Guest House,** 202 C. San Salvador (☎260 2481; www.ximensguest-house.com). From Blvd. de los Héroes, turn west onto C. Gabriela Mistral; take your first left and then first right. Homey rooms and friendly staff make this place very popular.

Organic breakfast and lunch menu available (US$2-$5). Common room has cable TV. English spoken. Laundry service and safe deposit box available. The **Spanish School Cihuatán,** located on the premises, offers one-to-one lessons with certified teachers (US$4.60 per hr.). Ask manager Lena about organized tours. Dorms US$5-$7; singles with bath and TV US$18, with fan US$22; doubles US$22/$27. ❷

International Guest House (☎ 226 7343), on 35 Av. Nte., is a Salvadoran version of a bed and breakfast. Breakfast included. Ask to stay in the International Student Residence if you are staying more than one week (US$60 per week). Singles US$15, with bath US$18; doubles US$25/$30. Reserve a day or two in advance. AmEx/MC/V. ❹

Casa de Huespedes Tazumal (☎ 235 0156), on 35 Av. Norte opposite the International Guest House. Clean rooms have TV, some have fan and bath. Breakfast and unlimited Internet included. Singles US$15-$25; doubles US$35-$45. AmEx/MC/V. ❹

EL CENTRO

Staying in San Salvador's *centro histórico*, also called *el centro*, will put you in the middle of the action. Buses running to all parts of the city pass through constantly and the frenetic rush of street vendors and markets wail outside your door. It is not a safe area to walk around after 8pm when the streets empty and everything shuts down; nightlife options are limited.

▨ **Hotel Pasadena II,** 3 C. Pte., 17/19 Av. Nte. 1037 (☎ 221 2782, 221 4786), has a friendly staff and plenty of amenities at unbeatable prices. The cafeteria serves breakfast and lunch. Clean rooms have fan and private bath. Singles US$10, with cable US$11; doubles US$11/$16. ❸

Hotel Villa Florencia, 3 C. Pte., 17/19 Av. Nte. 1023 (☎ 221 1706). All rooms have TV, fan, and private bath. Singles US$11; doubles US$16; triples US$19. ❸

Hotel American Guest House, 17 Av. Norte, between C. Arce and 1 C. Pte. (☎ 222 8789; fax 222-2597). Breakfast not included, but available at the cafeteria. All rooms have TV and fan. Singles US$10, with bath US$16; doubles US$10/$20. ❸

NEAR THE TERMINAL DE ORIENTE

The hotels around the Terminal de Oriente are convenient. However, the area is dirty and dangerous; walking around at night is risky. For those wishing to simply pass through the city, there are several relatively safe hotels about a five minute walk from the terminal on C. Concepción. To get there, head west from the terminal, bearing right onto Alameda Juan Pablo II where the highway splits. After a few blocks, turn right on C. Concepción before the Esso station. You may find it worth the money to take a taxi (US$4-$5) to Los Héroes.

Hotel Imperial (☎ 222 4920), 2 blocks north of the Esso station on C. Concepción, has an air of faded grandeur and large, basic rooms. US$4, with bath US$7. ❶

Hotel Yucatán, north of the Imperial. Concrete rooms are dark and dusty, but the beds are thick and comfy. Singles US$3.50, with bath US$7; doubles US$6/$10. ❶

◖ FOOD

San Salvador cooks up a wide variety of culinary options, from cheap and tasty pupuserías to sophisticated international cuisine. Restaurants are often open past midnight. Small *pupusa* stands are ubiquitous, even in some of the quieter residential neighborhoods. The cheapest places to eat are the *comedores* and *pupuserías* in **El Centro.** Metrocentro and surrounding areas on Blvd. Los Héroes are home to several US fast-food chains. Pricier, higher-quality restaurants line Blvd.

Hipódromo in the **Zona Rosa** and the **Paseo de Escalón** to the north. An international collection of bars and restaurants on **Calle San Antonio Abad** covers a broad range of price options.

EL CENTRO

▨ **Panadería La Nueva Victoria** (☎222 0947), on the corner of 6 Av. Sur and C. Delgado. The cozy ambience contrasts with the chaos of *el centro* by replicating a relaxing European square. Meals are inexpensive (US$1.50-$5) and include vegetarian options. Try the freshly baked bread. Open daily 6am-8pm. ❶

Koradi, 11 Av. Nte., C. Rubén Darío. A small *cafetería* and health-food store, Koradi serves veggie food at decent prices, including fresh salad (US$1), rice (US$0.80), and hearty rolls in a typical *comedor* setting. Open M-F 8am-5:45pm, Sa 8am-3:45pm. ❶

Bar Rosvill, (☎222 5319) near the corner of Av. España and C. Delgado. Ideal for coffee and a pastry (US$0.40-$3). Wide selection. Open daily 7:30am-6:45pm. ❶

CALLE SAN ANTONIO ABAD

▨ **El Atrio Café**, C. San Antonio Abad 2257 (☎257 9685; www.elatrio.com.sv). The artsy entrance promises an entertaining evening, and it doesn't disappoint. M-Tu are movie nights (8pm, mostly European films); Th is dedicated to dance performances; F-Sa feature theater performances (8-10pm) and live concerts (10pm-midnight). Sandwiches, pasta, and salads US$4-$5. Open 11am-2am. AmEx/MC/V. ❷

▨ **La Ventana** (☎235 1492; ventana@integra.com.sv), C. San Antonio Abad, in front of Centro Comercial San Luis. This ultra-hip, ultra-trendy, ultra-popular restaurant boasts fancy food plus a great wine and liquor selection. Meals US$4-$8, desserts US$2-$4. Open M 5pm-1am, Tu-Sa 8am-1am, Su 10am-1am. AmEx/MC/V. ❷

The Brother (☎235 1492), C. San Antonio Abad, close to Centro Comercial San Luis. This is the place for an inexpensive meal before a night on the town. Excellent, large portions of meat are grilled in front of you on the front deck. Scrumptious garlic bread accompanies your meal. Full dinners US$4-$6. Open daily 6am-3am. ❶

Sol y Luna, on Blvd. Universitario. A nice vegetarian restaurant that serves *típico* minus the meat. Soy hamburger US$2. Open M-Sa 8am-9pm. ❶

ZONA ROSA

▨ **La Héla Beto's** Blvd. del Hipódromo 230 (☎223 6865). The bustle of the city fades away as you soak in the atmosphere of this restaurant that is part upscale dining, part traditional village. Their specialty is *mariscos*

IN RECENT NEWS

¿IRAQ? NO, ¡EL CENTRO!

In July 2004, a San Salvadoran comic strip depicted a boy dressed up in combat fatigues talking with his mother in the kitchen. The mother asked, "Where are you going dressed up like that? Iraq?"

"No," the son answered, "downtown!"

The cartoon refers to an episode from the day before when police stormed *el centro* to dislodge unlicensed market vendors. Fearful of losing their only source of livelihood, vendors defended their stands—forcefully. Street fights ensued, sending a few vendors to the hospital.

This episode is representative of a daily problem in San Salvador and many country towns. Mindful of the tourism industry, authorities want to clean up town centers that are swallowed up by temporary tents and plagued by poor hygiene. Impromptu markets often damage historic buildings and create environments that encourage pickpocketing—both consequences that discourage tourists. Yet it is hard to forget that the people coming into town are poor *campesinos* who need to sell their wares in the overcrowded markets in order to eat. As El Salvador continues trying to develop its urban tourism, it will have to figure out how to do so without pushing its most marginalized citizens further into poverty.

(US$6-$17) and all dishes are an original combination of traditional and international cuisine. Bar has a wide selection. Billiards and Internet available. Open M-Sa 11am-2am; Su 11am-midnight. AmEx/MC/V. ❹

Los Rinconcitos, Blvd. del Hipódromo, close to La Héla Betos, serves up gourmet meals in a cosmopolitan setting. At night, it fills with a well-dressed crowd heading to nearby *discotecas*. Meals US$5-$10. Open daily 4pm-3am. AmEx/MC/V. ❸

Tre Fratelli Bar and Restaurant, Blvd. del Hipódromo 307 (☎230 838 3940; www.tre-fratelli.com). Italian charm blends with chic Zona Rosa style. Specialty dish is *frutti di mare* (US$11.30). Open M-Th noon-11pm; F-Su 7am-11pm. AmEx/MC/V. ❹

◙ SIGHTS

Most of the historical sights in San Salvador are downtown in the *el centro*. All major sights are easily accessible by local buses. Access may be limited by ongoing restorations from 2001 earthquake damage. Check out "Planeta Alternativo" for music and theater listings throughout the country every Thursday in *La Prensa Graphica*. The **Teatro Nacional** (☎222 5731, on the west side of the plaza) and the **Palacio Nacional** (on the corner of Av. Cuscatlán and C. Rubén Darío) are two impressive sights that were unfortunately closed for restoration at the time of publishing. Call to inquire about their current status or check at the tourism office.

CATEDRAL METROPOLITANA. Looming over the north side of Plaza Barrios, the colorful, tiled dome of the Cathedral is one of San Salvador's central landmarks. Built in 1808, it was severely damaged by earthquakes in 1873 and 1986, and by fire in 1951. Eight paintings hang over the altar alongside two empty frames, a reminder that the road to restoration is slow going. *(Main entrance on 2 C., on the cathedral's south side. Open daily 6am-6pm; Sa noon-6pm. Free.)*

IGLESIA EL ROSARIO AND PARQUE LIBERTAD. Strikingly simple in its modernity, the church of El Rosario is composed of two arcs 30m apart. This graffiti-covered church depicts religious scenes through modern sculptures made of steel rebars and other scraps. The lights in the interior blend with the sculptures to create an atmosphere of mystic intensity. Across the street, performers and locals make Parque Libertad a calm and enjoyable people-watching spot. *(Open daily during daylight hours. Free.)*

MERCADO NACIONAL DE ARTESANÍAS. This market, on the site of the international fairgrounds, sells *artesanía* from all over the country. Prices tend to be quite a bit higher than in the towns where the pieces originate, but the selection is unbeatable. *(C. Manuel Enrique Araujo. Accessible by bus #30b. Open daily until 6pm.)*

MONUMENTO A LA REVOLUCIÓN. Built to commemorate the Revolution of 1948, this soaring, modernist mosaic depicts a figure breaking free of his shackles and reaching for the sky as he surveys the entire eastern side of San Salvador. Ironically, this monument to the downtrodden people of Central America is situated in the center of San Salvador's most exclusive neighborhood. *(Straight uphill from the Plaza Italia. Accessible by bus #34 or #30b.)*

EL ÁRBOL DE DIOS GALLERY. Fernando Llort, the man famous for simple, brightly colored wooden *artesanía*, displays more complex and interesting work here in his city gallery. *(Av. Jerusalem at C. Mascota, 4 blocks south of the Plaza de Masferrer, or take #101D leaving from Metrocentro. Open M-Sa 9am-6pm.)*

PARQUE ZOOLÓGICO. Impressively large and considered one of the most modern in Central America, this zoo boasts an outstanding variety of amusing monkeys and bright tropical birds. (☎270 0828. 1.5km south of downtown. Take bus #2 from the west side of the cathedral heading south. Open W-Su 8am-5pm. US$0.60.)

BOTANICAL GARDENS. If you prefer flora over fauna, the Botanical Gardens provide a relaxing retreat where you can walk trails lined with thousands of indigenous and foreign plant species. The gardens sit at the base of a dormant volcanic crater, which was a lagoon until an 18th-century eruption. (☎243 2012. #101C bus from 3 Av. Sur and C. Rubén Darío; get off in Antiguo Cuzcatlan and follow the signs. The #44 minibus from Blvd. de los Héroes also stops here. Open Tu-Su 9am-5pm. US$0.45.)

🏛 MUSEUMS

🏛 **MUSEO NACIONAL DAVID GUZMÁN.** Built in 1883, this museum's recent renovation makes it the best in the country. The museum houses fine Maya artifacts, including the intricate **Stela of Tazumal** from El Salvador's most famous Maya site. Repairs are ongoing. (☎243 3750. On Av. Revolución, just up the crossroad with Alameda Manuel Enrique Araujo; accessible by bus #34 and 30b. Open Tu-Sun 9-noon, 2-5pm. US$1.50)

STEPHEN HAWKING MUSEUM. This hands-on museum will give you the chance to learn about the country's geography and natural disasters while having fun with 3-D demonstrations and distorting mirrors. An awesome satellite photo of El Salvador is worth checking out, either before or after you head out to conquer the peaks and enjoy the lakes. (☎223 3027. C. Reforma in Zona Rosa, 3 blocks south of Blvd. Hipódromo. Open M-Sa 10am-4pm. US$1.20.)

🎭 🎵 NIGHTLIFE AND ENTERTAINMENT

Zona Rosa and the area around **Calle San Antonio Abad** are the prime areas to have fun in San Salvador. Zona Rosa is where the rich and the beautiful come to shake their stuff until sunrise—you haven't been to San Salvador until you've seen this. Some clubs have dress codes, but they are generally pretty lax. C. San Antonio Abad is the exact opposite: instead of trying to be cooler than everyone else, party goers in this bohemian area try to outdo each other in degrees of laid-backness.

BLVD. DE LOS HÉROES AND CALLE SAN ANTONIO

🌙 **La Luna,** 228 C. Berlin (☎260 2921; info@lalunacasayarte.com). The anchor of San Salvador's bohemian scene and one of the city's only concert venues. Live music W-Sa at 9pm (Jazz on W). Screenings of art-house films M 6:30pm. Beer US$1; mixed drinks US$1.50-$3; meals starting from US$5. Pick up a schedule at Ximena's or at the restaurant; reservations recommended for some events. Open M-Sa 10am-12pm; 4pm-1am. US$3, free before 9pm.

Les Tres Diables, C. San Antonio Abad, Av. Izalco 2241 (☎225 5609). Don't let the French name fool you; this bar is unpretentious and draws a fun, young crowd. Midweek specials lure the local tough guys (M US$1 Pilsener draft, W 2-for-1, Th US$1 tequila shot). No cover. Beer US$1.50-$2; cocktails US$1.50-$3. Open daily 3pm-midnight. AmEx/MC/V.

El Arpa: Bar Irlandés, Av. A off C. San Antonio Abad, behind Nash. The only thing Irish about this bar is its name, but it has an unpretentious menu (hamburgers US$4) and a wide selection of Salvadoran beer. Open M-Sa 3:30pm-midnight. AmEx/MC/V.

THE ZONA ROSA

▨ **Coconut Grove,** on the corner of 79 Av. Sur and C. La Mascota (☎264 2914, 264 2915). The place to be on weekends if you want to chill with the Salvadoran elite. F karaoke night. Try the tropical drinks at the terrace-bar, or stargaze on the patio. Also has a restaurant with Mexican cuisine and seafood. Open M-Sa 11-2am. AmEx/MC/V.

La Cantinita del Patron and the Guadalajara Grille. Around the block from Rinconcitos (see **Food,** p. 243). With non-stop partying, this bar's rowdy groups and neon beer signs will remind you of your college days, especially if you forget the whole night the next morning. La Cantinita hosts a steamy disco. W ladies night with open bar for women W 10-11:30pm. Bar open 7pm-3am, disco 10pm-2am, later on weekends.

Zone Discoteca, close to Rinconcitos. This disco has all the staples, from loud bass to strobe lighting and lots of bodies heating up the dance floor. As far as discos go, it's fairly relaxed. F-Sa US$4 cover. Open Th-Sa 9pm until late.

MOVIES

The capital is a great place to catch a movie. Theaters typically show subtitled Hollywood movies. (Admission US$3-$3.50; most theaters are half-price W. Last showing 9pm.) **Cinemark,** the gigantic red monster looming over Microcentro, has eight screens showing the newest flicks in town. (☎261 2001. 2nd branch in Galerías.)

▶ DAYTRIPS FROM SAN SALVADOR

Just kilometers from the capital city are a variety of outdoor activities to suit all moods. La Puerta del Diablo is a popular trip, though many incredible sites and activities in the area remain undiscovered. For relatively unique adventure, head to Volcán San Salvador, or to get even more off the beaten path, talk to Lena at Ximena's Guesthouse. She can help you to explore an organic farm, a newly discovered site of prehistoric fossils, or the most recently uncovered Maya ruins.

LAGO DE ILOPANGO

To the Turicentro: Take bus #15 from the bus stop in front of the Palacio Nacional. (55min., every 15min. until 7pm, US$0.35.) From the Terminal de Oriente or Blvd. de los Héroes, an easier and faster option is to take the #29 bus to the town of Ilopango (tell the driver where you're going), where you can catch the #15 to Apulo (6am-8pm, US$0.35.). Turicentro open daily 8am-5pm. Boat trips US$5 per 30min. for up to 6 people; tubing US$1 per 30min.; water-skiing US$10 per 30 min. Admission US$0.80.

Lago de Ilopango, just 16km east of the capital, is the largest and deepest crater lake in El Salvador. Steep lush hillsides drop rapidly to the shores of the lake, and several uninhabited islands poke up through the placid surface of the deep-blue water. The easily accessible **Turicentro ❶**, at Apulo on the north shore of the lake, is the accommodation of choice for weekenders looking for a little waterfront relaxation; on weekdays you'll have the place to yourself. Two clean pools, picnic areas, showers, changing rooms, and several restaurants line the lake shore, and small bungalows on the edge of the beach can be rented for the day. (Bungalows US$4, US$2 key deposit. Meals US$1-$3.) Watersports and boat trips are popular. *Lanchas* are plentiful and their owners are willing to take you for a spin.

For the best views of the lake, the crater, and the volcanoes to the east, take the bus a few kilometers uphill back towards San Salvador to **Restaurante Mirador 70 ❸**, where you can have a drink or a relaxing meal on the terrace overlooking the lake. The restaurant is right on the highway; ask the driver to let you off. (☎295 4768. Meals US$8-$14. Open daily noon-7pm.)

VOLCÁN SAN SALVADOR

El Boquerón is both the name of the town near the volcano and the volcano's crater. Take San Salvador bus #101 from Plaza Barrios to Santa Tecla (25min.) or #101D, which stops in front of Metrosur. Bus #103 heads to the town of Boquerón from 4 Av. Nte. and C. Daniel Hernández, near the church (45min., every 45min. 6am-5pm, US$0.35). To arrange a pickup for the day, talk to the taxi drivers at the parque central, who can help you contact a driver and find a guide. José Misrael Nerios, whose house is 5min. from the bus stop in Boquerón, on the right past the first bend in the road, is an effective body-guard (necessary for safety reasons; US$6) or will guide you down the trail to the bottom of the crater (US$12, includes bodyguard fee).

Volcán San Salvador, situated northwest of the capital, 11km north of Santa Tecla, stuns travelers with its breathtaking views. The most enjoyable part of the trip is gazing down 540m into the gaping crater known as **El Boquerón** ("Big Mouth"). Thickly forested cliffs tumble down to the crater floor. A perfect 50m high cone, the result of a 1917 eruption, rises out from the crater. A path winds its way down to the bottom of the crater (about 2hr.), and another leaves from the right of the viewpoint and follows the rim of the crater all the way around (2-3hr.).

The volcano is not all pretty views and symmetrical cones. The 30min. walk from the bus stop in Boquerón to the park entrance is dangerous for foreigners and should under no circumstances be done alone. Physical assaults by thieves are not uncommon. In light of this, the safest way to see the volcano is to hire a **taxi** or **pickup truck** for the day. Don't descend into the crater without a local guide; the cone traps tourists trying to run from muggers.

JOYA DE CERÉN

Take bus #108 going to the town of Opico from Terminal Occidente (40min., every 10min., US$0.50). Get off immediately after crossing the bridge over the Río Sucio, at the sign for the entrance to the site. If you feel adventurous, you can find guides at San Andrés who will take you here on horseback. Site and museum open Tu-Su 9am-4pm.

Forget about Tikal or Copán, this is something completely different. Central America's most well-preserved archaeological site is a full time-warp. Similar to Italy's Pompeii, this site gives a glimpse into the life of a small village frozen under 3m of ash from nearby Ilopango Volcano. While not exactly impressive in scale or grandeur, the well-preserved remains of this 1400-year-old village were declared a UNESCO World Heritage Site in 1993, and offer an opportunity to observe and study the daily life of common Maya people. The town's extended slumber ended abruptly when bulldozers accidentally unearthed it in 1976. Full-scale excavations began in 1989, yielding the discovery of 18 structures, ranging from adobe houses to a steam bath to the office of the local shaman. The inhabitants apparently had enough time to flee (no human remains have been found at the site), but not to do the dishes or put away food after their evening meal; corn, beans, and a variety of other fruits and vegetables were preserved in the volcanic ash. Cerén's findings have helped to fill in the details of the daily existence, commerce, and familial relations of the ancient Maya. The small but comprehensive on-site **museum** contains good examples of ceramics, utensils, and foodstuffs from the period. The information in the museum is in Spanish, but **CORSATUR** in San Salvador gives English explanations. Knowledgeable Spanish-speaking **guides** can take you around the three main excavation sites.

SAN ANDRÉS

Take bus #201 from Terminal Occidente heading to Santa Ana (US$0.50) and get off at the sign for San Andrés, then walk about 200m down the dirt road to the ruins. From Joya de Ceren, hop back on the #108 and ride to the junction with the highway to Santa Ana

(10min., US$0.20) to catch a westbound #201 to San Andrés (10min., US$0.20). From the highway, head down the dirt road, pay at the entrance booth, and continue to the visitors center. Open Tu-Su 9am-4pm. US$3, includes tour. Visitor center has a cafeteria.

Veterans of Tikal or Copán might be underwhelmed by the San Andrés archaeological site, though the ruins are the second largest in El Salvador behind Tazumal. The site consists of two ceremonial plazas (North and South), ringed by mounds and pyramids. Occupied by Maya and Pipil, San Andrés was constructed from AD 600 to 900 and originally consisted of nearly 200 structures. Little is known about the decline of San Andrés, which flourished in the heyday of Maya glory along with Tikal, Palenque and Copán.

Enter the site on the South Plaza, near the **Acropolis,** a large mound partially reconstructed with concrete. The other mounds ringing this plaza have been partially restored with concrete as well, leading to a rather disappointing aesthetic appearance and an unfortunate loss of cultural history. North of the Acropolis, most of the structures have not been excavated and therefore remain unspoiled. The most interesting part of the ruins, the base of **structure 5,** is under a thatched roof in this section.

The sprawling **visitors center** and **museum** complex, before the entrance to the ruins, is perhaps more interesting than the site itself. The museum gives a very informative and extensive overview of Maya culture in the area, and San Andrés in particular. You can also see interesting exhibits covering El Salvador's colonial past, including a display on **El Obraje,** the best preserved indigo factory in the world. When exiting the center to the north, El Obraje is to the right and the ruins are to the left. **Guides** wait at the museums' entrance and exit.

LOS PLANES DE RENDEROS

Bus #12 leaves from Av. 29 de Agosto and 12 C. Pte. on the southeastern edge of the mercado central in front of the government building and goes to: Parque Balboa (30min., open 24hr., free); Parque de la Familia (30 min., open Tu-Su 8am-8pm, US$1); and La Puerta del Diablo (45min., every 10min. 5am-6pm). From the same departure point, Bus # 17 takes you to Panchimalco (45min.); the 2 routes cross at el triangulo, a crossroad just down Parque Balboa.

A great half-day trip from the capital, Los Planes de Renderos area boasts a number of great attractions all close together. To make touring easier, local boys will gladly show you around and entertain with stories in exchange for a lunch and a few dollars. Try to get to **La Puerta del Diablo** in the early morning to enjoy one of the most impressive views in El Salvador. On your way back, **Pupusería Toñita,** conveniently located at the entrance of **Parque Balboa,** is the place to stop for delicious traditional *pupusas* (small US$0.50, large US$0.80). Parque Balboa is ideal for a relaxing stroll or a post-lunch workout on the soccer and basketball fields. In addition, Parque La Familia hosts a variety of performances on weekends. Not far away from the tourist parks is **Panchimalco** and its native traditions.

PUERTA DEL DIABLO

A few kilometers from the tourist parks, two gigantic rocks and a smaller one in between frame an awe-inspiring view of the valleys below. Originally named when a villager thought he saw the devil standing between the rocks, the site unfortunately lived up to its diabolical name—during the revolution countless executions were conducted here. Looking toward the valley, the biggest rock is the one on the left, but the other has a better view and is an easier climb.

The site along the highway has a carnival feel on the weekends, attracting young and old. Couples, rebellious teens, and a serious rock-climber or two will likely be your company during the week. Serious climbers can contact the Club 9/a de Escalada or **Alligatours** (☎ 211 0967; www.alligatour.com) for information about the 35 rapelling routes set up at La Puerta del Diablo.

PANCHIMALCO

Twenty minutes past *el triangulo*, Panchimalco is a village of cobblestone streets and workshops inhabited by the Pancho Indians, some of whom still wear the traditional dress of their ancestors. The local church, Santa Cruz, has an octagonal dome with eight saints blessing the town from each side. At kilometer 12 on the road to Panchimalco, the lookout on los Planes de Renderos offers impressive views for those not inclined to climb to Puerta del Diablo.

THE CENTRAL COAST

El Salvador's most popular beaches hug the Central Coast south of the capital. Just 34km from San Salvador, La Libertad draws surfers from around the world. The town of Zacatecoluca is a gateway to the seemingly endless palm-fringed coastline of the Costa del Sol, the country's premier resort area. Farther east is the mangrove-lined Bahía de Jiquilisco.

LA LIBERTAD

La Libertad

⌂ ACCOMMODATIONS
Hotel La Hacienda
  de Don Rodrigo, **6**
Hotel Rick, **4**
La Posada de Don Lito, **7**
La Posada Familiar, **1**

🍴 FOOD
Mango's Lounge, **2**
Restaurante Punta Roca, **5**
Restaurante Sandra, **3**

Reputed to have the best surfing in Central America, the stars have aligned to bless La Libertad (pop. 40,000) with a rare combination of wind, current, and shore that yields constant swells of at least 1.5m. Surf culture has definitely overtaken the town; even local fishermen rush to "The Point" after work to catch a few breaks. Serious surfers rise with the sun to ride the best waves off of the famed Punta Roca. When the ocean's flat, the most interesting sight (and smell) is the bustling fish market on the pier—if it lives in the sea and can be eaten, it's for sale here. But the town is not all flip-flops and bleached hair; drugs and crime are all too common and tourists are frequent targets. Nonetheless, the variety of beaches and seafood grants both the surfer and sunbather a pristine playground with the benefits of the sea and the beauty of the tropical coast.

🚍 TRANSPORTATION. Buses depart from several points on the east side of town, although many of them cruise 2 C. and C. Calvario before leaving. The primary departure point is around the corner of C. Barrios and 4 Av. The bus to **San Salvador** leaves from this corner (#102, 1¼hr., every 8min. 4:20am-6:20pm, US$0.60). From 4 Av. Norte and 1 C., on the northeast corner of town, buses head to: **Zacatecoluca** (#540, 1¾hr., 8 per day 5:30-4:30pm, US$0.60); **Sonsonate** (#287, 3hr., 6am and 1:45pm, US$0.70); **La Perla** (#192; 1hr., every 40min. 7am-5:20pm, US$0.45) via **Playas El Tunco, Zunzal, El Palmercito**, and **El Zonte; Comalapa** (#187, 1hr., every 20min., US$0.35), from where you can connect to an **airport-bound bus** in San Luis Talpa. To get to **La Costa del Sol**, take #540 and get off at **La Flecha**, where you can catch the #193 or #495 to Costa del Sol. You can also get to **Sonsonate** by taking the #261 from La Perla. Local bus #80 heads west to **Zunzal** (every 10min. 6am-6pm, US$0.20), and east to **Playa San Diego** (every 20min. 6am-6pm, US$0.20); ask the driver to make sure you're going the right way, since they all face the same direction.

■■**🛈** **ORIENTATION AND PRACTICAL INFORMATION.** The small downtown grid of this port town slopes gently toward the bay and continues to the **pier,** which is an extension of 4 Av. The slightly hidden **church** sits at the north end of the *parque central* and the main intersection is on the *parque's* northwest corner. The main *avenida* is called **Avenida Bolívar** to the north and **Avenida Luz** to the south; the central *calle* is **Calle Barrios** to the east and **Calle Calvario** to the west. Two blocks south of C. Barrios, **4 Calle** runs along the beach and meets 5 Av. on the town's west side before heading to **La Punta Roca** on the west side of the bay.

In a mini-mall next to the main bus stop, **Banco Hipotecario,** 4 Av., 1 C., has **Western Union** service, cashes traveler's checks, and exchanges US dollars (open M-F 8:30am-4:30pm, Sa 8:30am-noon). ATMs in La Libertad do not take international cards. The **mercado municipal** is bordered by 2/4 Av. and Calles Barrios/1. The El Salvador **Spanish School** (☎449 0331) also operates in La Libertad, and offers daily lessons and homestays. The **police** (☎335 3121) are on 1/3 Av. and C. Calvario and open 24hr. **Dr. Stanley Moises Mendoza Jiménez** is available on C. Barrios, east of 4 Av. on the south side of the street, 24hr. for emergencies. (☎335 3531, emergency 335 3154. Open daily 9am-6pm.) **Farmacia Jerusalem** is on Av. 1/Bolívar, C. Calvario. (☎335 3508. Open M-Sa 7am-6pm.) **Telecom,** at the corner of 2 Av. and 2 C., also offers **Internet** service. (US$1.50 per 30min. Open daily 8am-6pm.) **Internet** at **Infocentros,** in the mini-mall on 4 Av. north of C. Barrios, has the best rates. (US$1.15 per hr. Open M-Sa 8am-5pm, Su 8am-noon.) The **post office,** 2/4 Av. Sur, 2 C. Ote. is open M-F 8am-5pm, Sa 8am-noon.

🛏 ACCOMMODATIONS. The all-important combination of safety, quality, and affordability in lodgings is hard to come by, but there are a few reasonable options. With a gate, patio and laid-back cafeteria, **La Posada Familiar ❷,** half a block up from the beach on 3 Av. provides an evening hang-out spot. Simple rooms have great beds and most share clean baths. (☎335 3252. Singles US$6, with bath US$9.) The recently renovated **Hotel Rick ❺,** on 5 Av., 4 C., has impeccable rooms and dainty toilet covers, all with new double beds and A/C. A pool table, TV, and VCR are at your disposal. (☎335 3033. US$20-$25. AmEx/MC/V.) **Hotel La Hacienda de Don Rodrigo ❺** and **Hotel La Posada de Don Lito ❺,** just off Punta Roca on 5 Av. Sur at Playa La Paz, are pricier options. Rooms are very comfortable with A/C, private bath, and TV. (☎335 3166. Doubles US$55; triples US$62. AmEx/MC/V.) The cheapest and certainly most appealing way to take in the coast is to stay at either **Ver Mar ❶,** in El Palmercito, or **Surf Camp Horizonte,** at Playa Zonte (see **Beaches Near La Libertad,** p. 266).

🍴 FOOD. Cheap seafood shacks crowd the pier area; regular *comedores* and *pupuserías* huddle around the market and *parque.* Fancier restaurants have cropped up in the upscale hotels east of town on the road called *La Curva,* and above Playa las Flores (take bus #80 to San Diego). *Mariscada,* a creamy seafood chowder chock-full of every sea creature imaginable, makes for a delicious meal.

You can't beat the views from **🖼Restaurante Punta Roca ❸,** across from Hotel Rick at 5 Av. and 4 C. The owner, Bob Rotherhan, is a Miami native who serves the best food in town including several dishes that you can find only here. (☎335 3261; www.puntaroca.com.sv. Meals US$6-$9; seafood specials US$12-$15). To absorb a little local surf culture over good, simple food and tasty *licuados,* head to **Mango's Lounge ❷** on 5 Av. at C. Calvario. Try the shrimp with potatoes (US$2.25); other seafood dishes (US$4-$7). The small place is chill, though full at night, and is a prime place to meet travelers or get surfing tips. (☎335 3782. Happy Hour 5-6pm. Breakfast US$1.50-2. Open Tu-F noon-10pm, Sa-Su 10am-10pm.) Just opposite Mango's is **Restaurante Sandra ❸,** with a varied menu of seafood and meats. (☎335-3280. Meals US$5-$9. Open M-Tu and Th-Su 9am-9pm.)

⛰ SURFING. Standing on the pier looking back at the shore, **Playa el Malecón** is on the right side, while **Punta Roca** extends off the end of **Playa la Paz** to the left. The best and biggest waves in the area break off Punta Roca, with 1.2-4.6m swells. Surfing the point is only for experts. The smaller, inconsistent waves that come into Playa la Paz are good for beginners, but the beach is rather rocky and polluted, making **Playa Zunzal** to the west is a more attractive option altogether. Prime surfing months are April to October. For non-surfers, the beaches are sandiest and the waves smallest in December.

To rent boards, head to **Mango's Lounge,** which rents good **surf and boogie boards** with multi-day discounts (US$5 per 2hr., US$12 per day). You can also rent **bikes** (US$2 per 2hr. US$6 per day), **fishing gear,** and **snorkeling gear** there. Slightly more beaten-up rental boards are available at the **Hospital de Tablas,** located just north of the Posada Familiar on 3 Av. (US$2 per hr., US$7 per day) For lessons, **Punta Mango Tours,** located at Mango's Lounge, can arrange an instructor for US$16-$18 per hr. or group lessons for a bit less per person. They also offer complete surf-and-stay packages in addition trips around La Libertad and nearby beaches.

BEACHES NEAR LA LIBERTAD

Bus #80, leaving from 4 Av. south of C. Barrios in La Libertad, runs east to Playa San Diego (every 20min. 6am-6pm, US$0.20) and west to Playas Conchalio, Majahual, El Tunco, and El Zunzal (every 10min. 6am-6pm, US$0.20). Bus #192, leaving for La Perla from 4 Av. and 1 C., passes the same eastern beaches but goes farther to Playa El Palmercito and Playa Zonte (35min., every 40min. 5am-5:20pm, US$0.30). Minibuses to Playa las Flores cruise 2 Av. (US$0.30).

If you're not a surfer, the rocky, polluted waters of the bay of La Libertad hold less appeal. Have no fear: cleaner, sandier beaches dot the coast on both sides of town. However, if hanging ten is how you chill your chakra, Punta Roca, just a few hundreds meters away from La Libertad, has the best waves around. If you're looking for stretches of sand and good swimming, head east. Dining options vary at each beach. Crowds vanish come Monday.

PLAYA EL TUNCO. A fun beach with a young crowd of Salvadoran teens in town for the weekend, Playa El Tunco is good for swimming and for surfing. A 20min. bus ride from La Libertad, the beach is about 800m from the town of El Tunco, so make sure to tell the bus driver to let you off at the *playa* El Tunco. It is marked by a "Pilsener" sign and signs for **El Tubo** surf lodge. From there, a dirt road runs down to the beach at the mouth of Río Tunco. Just left of the river mouth is the break **La Bocana,** a favorite among local surfers. To the right, striking rock formations stretch all the way to Punta Zunzal (see below).

A small **surf village** has sprung up along the river at Playa el Tunco. Marked just "Hotel," the folks at **Tienda Erika ❶,** along the road close to the beach, rent decent rooms with common baths. (☎827 5349. US$5.25 per person). Along the road 1 block from the beach are two laid-back surf lodges. First is **El Tubo ❶** (☎826 6084, 826 7610), where doubles with fan and shared bath cost US$8-$10. Here there is a complete surf shop where you can also collect surf information and maybe rent a board from the local surf hero **Papaya.** Just past El Tubo down a driveway is the attractive new lodge **La Tortuga Surf Lounge ❹,** with nice rooms and private beach. (☎298 2986; rob.gal@vianet.com.sv. Singles US$12, with bath US$16.) **Restaurante La Bocana ❷,** on the beach at the Río Tunco, has meals ranging US$3-$11, and doubles as weekend night spot. (Beer US$0.80. Open daily 7am-8pm.)

PLAYA ZUNZAL. West of El Tunco, this wide beach is less rocky, with consistent waves far from shore. Recommended for beginning surfers, Zunzal is also one of the best options for swimming and tanning. Walk west on the beach from Río

Tunco until you reach **Punta Zunzal**. If coming by bus, get off at **Café Zunzal ❹**, located at km 43.5 on the coastal highway, one of the best restaurants around with a great view of the beach and amazing seafood (☎328 0132 or 328 0098. Specials US$12.50. Open Tu-Su 11am-5pm.)

PLAYA EL PALMERCITO. Less crowded, this soft curve of a beach seems to be a bit of a secret. A 400m walk down a cobblestone road from the sign "Puente El Palmar," the calm water is great for swimming and the sand is nice and toasty. **Hotel Ver Mar ❶**, a 2min. walk from the beach along the road from the highway, offers clean, cheap rooms ideal for backpackers. Ask **Mario** about special group rates, surf trips, or lessons. (☎867 8845. Hammocks US$3; dorms US$5; 1-6 person rooms US$20, with A/C and private bath US$30. Camping US$2 per person.) **Restaurante Las Palmeras ❷** is a relaxed place where you can bunk up with the family in a cramped room upstairs. (Shrimp plates US$4-$6, soup US$1-$2. Rooms US$18.) East on Playa Palmar, the idyllic oasis **Atami ❺** is perched on a cliff. You can enjoy the crisply manicured resort with its great beach access, three pools, deck chairs, bathrooms, showers, and requisite waterslide for only US$7, though spending the night is expensive. (☎274 6206 or 886 2260; shangrila@pro.com.sv. Rooms US$70-$80.)

PLAYA ZONTE. A slightly isolated, smaller beach, Zonte draws surfers and a small, local crowd despite the rocky shore and dark sand. Stunning trees and cliffs make up for the drab shacks along the beach. Only 15min. beyond Zunzal, buses deposit you on an unmarked road which brings you to the beach (stay to the right). The newly opened ▓**Surf Camp Horizonte ❷**, run by friendly surfer Saburo, features the best prices in the area and provides an extremely comfortable (if not immaculate) environment for enjoying the beach. Guests may use the pool and kitchen, and board rental (US$9 per day) includes an hour of free instruction. The rooms are set around a bar with great views of the beach and cliff. (Dorms US$7; singles US$9; doubles US$10. Camping US$2.) Other accommodations can be found by asking locals about spare rooms; prices and quality vary.

BEACHES EAST OF LA LIBERTAD. East of La Libertad are two beaches, each large enough to make finding a peaceful spot easy. **Playa las Flores,** below the section of road known as La Cerra, a few kilometers east of La Libertad, has parts that are relatively clean. About 15 min. farther on bus #80 brings you to **Playa San Diego,** a long gray beach lined with homes and public beach access paths every 100m. The beach is wide and more or less clean; at the farthest point (where the bus stops to turn around) is an estuary, a cluster of beach shacks, and *comedores*. To enjoy the sand, hop off the bus along the road to San Diego (7km after it leaves the highway) at any of the many little groups of stores or small restaurants, and take an access path to the shore. **Restaurante Carlos Mar ❷** is one of the nicer options available along the beach road (fish US$3-$6, chicken US$3).

ZACATECOLUCA

Informally known to locals as Zacate (pop. 75,000), this town was one of the biggest cities in the country before the war, however years of street violence have stripped it of its former grandeur. The town itself doesn't have too much to offer, but step into one of the shops if you get a chance—Zacate's jewelers are well-renowned. Above all, Zacate is a good place to stay if you want to explore la Costa del Sol while avoiding expensive coastal prices.

▐ **TRANSPORTATION.** From the terminal at 5/7 Calles and Av. Villacorta/Delgado, **buses** go to: **San Salvador** (#133, 1½hr., every 8min. 3:30am-6:10pm, US$0.57); **La Costa del Sol** and **La Puntilla** (#193, 1½hr., every 30min. 4:30am-4:10pm, US$1.50);

La Libertad (#540, 1¾hr., every 3hr 4:30am-3:40pm, US$1.15*)*; and **La Herradura** (#153, 1½hr., every 30min., 4:30am-4:30pm; US$0.57). Bus #177 to **San Vicente** leaves on the corner of 1 C. and Av. Villacorta (1hr., every 15 min. 5am-6pm, US$0.57). Bus #302 to **Usulatán** via **Jiquilisco** from hwy. 1 block north of Av. Villacorta (1hr., every 8 min. 4:30am-4:30pm, US$1.50).

⚡️ 🔼 ORIENTATION AND PRACTICAL INFORMATION. Zacate uses the usual Salvadoran grid with its center at the intersection of **Av. José Matías Delgado/José Simeon Cañas** and **Calle General Rafael Osorio/Nicola Peña**, just 1 block south of the southwest corner of the *parque*. What would be 1 Av. is instead named **Av. Vicente Villacorta/José Manuel Rodríguez.** Most buses turn north from the carretera at the Shell station and run up Av. Villacorta to the *parque central*, passing the bus terminal at 5/7 Calles on the way.

Banco de Comercio, on the southwest corner of the *parque*, changes traveler's checks and has an **ATM** (open M-F 8am-4pm, Sa 8am-noon). The 24hr. **Hospital** (☎334 0190) is 10 blocks down Av. Rodríguez from the *parque*. **Farmacia Santa Lucia** is in front of the *parque*. (☎334 2002. Open M-Th 8am-6pm, F 8am-1pm.) The 24hr. **police** station (☎334 1690) is on Av. Delgado between 5 and 7 C. facing the bus station. **Telecom** (☎334 1475) has an office on the *parque*. (Open M-Sa 8am-6pm, Su 8am-noon. AmEx/MC/V.) **Internet access** is available at **Ciber C@fé**, on the corner of 1 Av. Ote. and 1 Av. Sur. (US$0.75 per hr. ☎334 2988.) The **post office** is on 3 Av. Sur between 1 and 3 C. (☎334 4544. Open M-F 8am-5pm, Sa 8am-noon).

🔳🔳 ACCOMMODATIONS AND FOOD. The **Hotel Primavera ❷**, on Av. Villacorta across from the bus terminal, has a wide variety of amenities: jacuzzi, small swimming pool, and recreation center with aerobics equipment, foosball, football court, and ping-pong. Fifteen big rooms have fans, private baths, and TVs. (☎334 1346. Singles and doubles US$8, with A/C US$15.) Half a block away, on 7 C., just east of Av. Villacorta, the **Hotel Brolyn ❷** has clean basic rooms with baths, fans, and TVs. (US$7 per person, with A/C US$9.15.)

Comedores selling *comida a la vista* line the streets around the *parque*. **El Ranchito del Sabor ❶**, on 1 C. Ote. between Av. Delgado and Villacorta, has the best *comida a la vista* (buffet-style) in town (US$1.50), served in a cool environment with wooden tables. (☎334 4751. Open 8am-5pm daily. Cash only.) **Comedor El Viajero ❶**, on 3 C. Ote between 1 and 3 Av. Sur, offers a simple ambiance with nicely chosen tablecloths. (☎334 1061. *Sopa de res* US$2, *pollo dorado* US$2. Open Su-F 7am-7pm.) **Restaurante y Bar Karaoke Bolero ❷**, in front of the *parque*, is one of the most popular local hang-outs, with karaoke on the weekends (open daily noon-2am). If you're more into dancing, head to **Sky Discotek**, on the corner of Av. Monterrey and 1 C. (☎334 4046. Open F and Su 2pm-3am, Sa 6pm-3am.)

LA COSTA DEL SOL

La Costa del Sol, the most popular beach getaway of the Salvadoran elite, is an endless peninsula of whitish-gray sand. The ocean stays shallow for some distance off shore, so there are plenty of opportunities for a great swim. Hotels and restaurants are quite developed, so if you come here mid-week you will be able to enjoy all the amenities while having the beach almost to yourself. Keep in mind that prices go up during high-season (end of July through mid-August). For the adventurous, there are boat trips to desert islands or through the mangroves at the estuary of the Río Lempa.

🔲 TRANSPORTATION. Buses depart from La Puntilla and run up the peninsula road before heading to **San Salvador** (#495, 2½hr., every 30min. 4:30am-6pm, US$1.20); **San Vicente** (#193-D; 2¼hr.; 8:20, 8:40am; US$1.20); and **Zacatecoluca**

EL SALVADOR

(#193; 1½hr.; every 30min. 6:30-9am and 3:25-5pm, departures also at 12:15 and 2:05pm; US$1.05). If you miss the Zacatecoluca or San Vicente departures, take the #495 and get off at the junction of **La Flecha,** where east-bound buses pass frequently (US$0.40 from La Costa).

⊞*I* ORIENTATION AND PRACTICAL INFORMATION. The beaches lie on the Pacific side of the peninsula, which is bordered by the estuaries of the Río Jiboa and Lempa. Bus routes follow the Carretera Costa del Sol, which bisects the peninsula, and pass the town of **Las Isletas,** where most services are located. The main beaches, in increasing distance from Las Isletas, are Playa Marcelino, Costa del Sol, Los Blancos, and Puntilla at the tip of the peninsula.

Main services are in Las Isletas. When arriving, the bus from San Salvador or Zacatecoluca will leave you at a crossing of three dirt roads; the one on the right takes you to the center of town while the one on the left is the continuation of the bus route to the beaches. **Supermercado Costa del Sol,** at Km 57.5 on Carretera Costa del Sol, has everything you need from food to beach supplies. (☎338 2589. Open daily 9am-6pm.) There is no bank or Internet service in the area. A 24hr. **police** station (☎354 4340) is 20m up the road to the centre, and the 24hr. **Farmacia San Ernesto** is 1 block up the same road. (☎354 4010. Open M-Sa 8am-8pm.) To reach **Hospital Unidad de Salud Canton Las Isletas,** walk 1 block up from the pharmacy then 2 blocks left and half a block right. (☎354 4045. Open 24hr for emergencies, M-F 7:30am-4pm.) There are pay phones in the **Telecom** in front of the church, 300m from the pharmacy. (☎354 4011. Open daily 7am-7pm.)

⊠ ⊠ PLAYA LOS BLANCOS. This is the best beach on Costa del Sol. If you are looking to tan and swim, this is where you should be. Aside from the five-star hotels, the smartest vacation package is staying the night at an inexpensive hotel and spending the day at the turicentro (see above), or, better yet, at a private recreation center. The best option is ⊠**Mini-Hotel y Restaurante Mila ❹** on la Carretera about 1km after the turicentro, with a clean swimming pool and a nicely-arranged dining area. The restaurant serves typical dishes. (☎338 2074. Rooms US$14, with bath US$17, with TV US$20, with A/C US$28; quads US$36. Special *Let's Go* discount. English spoken. Breakfast US$1.50-$3, *mariscada* US$3-$8.50, sandwiches US$1-$2. Restaurant open daily 8am-9pm.) For higher prices, head to nearby **Hotel Haydee Mar ❺.** Rooms have baths, fans, and TVs, though some of the facilities are literally falling apart. (☎338 2046. Singles US$20, with A/C US$25; doubles US$35; triples US$40. Restaurant open daily 8am-7pm.) The best recreation center in the area is **Kilo 14 - Centro Recreativo,** just before Haydee Mar on the *carretera,* which has a big space with palm trees and *cabañas,* several swimming pools, a restaurant, and plenty of *vigilantes* to watch over your belongings. The restaurant serves a good selection of *mariscadas* (US$3.50), *pescado* (US$3-$5) and classic *pupusas.* (☎338 2069. Open daily 7am-5pm. Entrance US$3, US$2 for 5-12 years old, under 5 free.)

⊠ PLAYA SAN MARCELINO. This beach is home to some of the best restaurants on la Costa del Sol. ⊠**Hotel y Restaurante Brisas Marina ❸,** at Km 58 on la Carretera Costa del Sol, is a calm and relaxing place to stay, complete with palm trees and a well-maintained swimming pool. Rooms have A/C, bath, and TV. A *fútbol* field is on the premises. (☎338 2642. Doubles US$20; rooms for up to five people US$35.) The hotel restaurant sells a broad selection of dishes (*mariscos* US$6-$15, soups US$8-$9, sandwiches US$1.75-$3.50) under a big *cabaña* near the swimming pool. (Open 7:30am-7pm.) Another great beach-front spot is **KennyMar ❹,** on Km 60 of la Carretera, which has earned local renown for its phenomenal seafood, especially the chowder casserole (US$9). (☎338 2578. AmEx/MC/V.)

TURICENTRO AND PLAYA COSTA DEL SOL. The expansive turicentro is a cheap way to spend one day on the beach. For the low prices, you'll have plenty to do: swimming pools for children and adults, football field, basketball court, and a secure place to store your belongings when you go for a swim. (Entrance US$0.80, *cabañas* US$3. Open daily 7am-4pm.)

LA PUNTILLA. As the name suggests, this is the tip of the peninsula. The beaches are less clean and inviting then at Los Blancos, but it's still a good hub for exploring the surrounding *islas*. **Turicentro Rancho Los Titos ❶**, the concrete structure with faded signs, offers bare rooms with thin mattresses. Spotty running water and no electricity will have you outside enjoying the deck and two small pools. (☎225 3670. Doubles US$8.) On the north side, *lanchas* head to the **Isla Tasajera**. Boats go to the **Isla de los Pájaros** (US$25), a mangrove island swarming with birds, and also to the mouth (*bocana*) of the **Río Lempa** (US$50), where the freshwater river makes for some great swimming. The captains can accommodate different trips based on your interests.

ISLA TASAJERA. For a more intense escape, **Isla Tasajera** is just off La Puntilla, where 250 families live and fish with plenty of beach at their fingertips. *Lanchas* to the island pass through the estuary and land at the island's north side at a point known as **La Palmera**, named for the rare coconut palm tree that splits three ways near its top. The cost of the trip is about US$120, no matter how many passengers there are—as long as everyone can fit in the boat (maximum 10-12). From the two food-and-drink stands at La Palmera, it's a 10min. walk across to the isolated Pacific beach that stretches to the end of the island. There are no street names here, but the island is so small that you can see it all in a few hours.

   Hotel y Restaurante Oasis de Tasajera ❺ is truly an oasis, with a nicely decorated courtyard and pleasant lodgings. Rooms feature fans, hammocks, and private baths. However, you will need to hire a *lancha* to get there, making your stay pricier. (☎888 0526. Singles US$18; doubles US$25; quads US$34.)

PUERTO EL TRIUNFO AND BAHÍA DE JIQUILISCO

The small fishing hamlet of Puerto El Triunfo (pop. 15,900) sits on the Bahía de Jiquilisco, 15km south of the Carretera Litoral. The pleasant port town and its buzzing marina afford a thorough look at the local fishing industry, ranging from family-run teams who drag nets behind dugout canoes to 45 ft. trawlers with sonar fish finders. Puerto El Triunfo is also the most convenient launching point for day-trips into the Bahía de Jiquilisco, a beautiful bay dotted with mangrove islands.

TRANSPORTATION. Coming to Puerto El Triunfo, any **bus** driving the *carretera* between Zacatecoluca and Usulután can drop you off near the town of Jiquilisco, where you can catch #363 to the port. From the northwest corner of the *parque,* buses leave Puerto El Triunfo bound for: **Usulután** (#363; 40min., every 10min. 4am-5:30pm, US$0.50), passing through **Jiquilisco** near the *carretera* (20min., US$0.30); **San Miguel** (#377; 2½hr., every 40min. 3:50am-2:50pm, US$1.30); and **San Salvador** (#185; 1½hr., every 30min. 4-7am and 3pm; US$1.30), via **Zacatecoluca** (1¼hr., US$0.70). It is easier to take the #363 to the highway or to Usulután and make connections from there rather than waiting around in Puerto El Triunfo.

EL SALVADOR

■ ■ ORIENTATION AND PRACTICAL INFORMATION. Though the streets here have names, the town is small enough to allow you to orient yourself in terms of the *parque central*. Buses pass by the church that faces the *parque* before arriving a block after the *parque* and 2 blocks north of the marina.

Change traveler's checks at **Banco Agrícola** in front of the *parque central* in Jiquilisco (open M-F 8am-5pm, Sa 8am-noon). The 24 hr. **police** branch (☎ 663 6300) is just before the marina on the left in the same building as the port's customs office. **Farmacia** faces the *parque central*. (Open daily 6:30am-8pm.) **Telecom** is 1 block north and 1 block east of the *parque*. (☎ 663 6011. Open daily 7am-7pm.) The **post office** is 2 blocks north and 1½ blocks east of the *parque* on the north side of the street (open M-F 8am-noon and 2-5pm, Sa 8am-noon).

■ ■ ACCOMMODATIONS AND FOOD. The only hotel in town is the **Hotel El Jardín ❷**, half a block north of the *parque* on the southbound *avenida*. It features basic but remarkably clean rooms with fan and private bath. (☎ 663 6047. Singles US$8.) The **Restaurante El Jardín ❸** has amazing seafood (US$6-$12), and locals claim the *camarones a la plancha* (US$9) are the best you can get on the coast.

The **terminal turístico** is a Canadian-funded project designed to promote the area of La Marina, on a dock on the shore. It is composed of half a dozen seafood places (US$3-$6) and a dozen or so typical Salvadoran *comedores* (US$0.30-$3). The fish is brought in every day by boats arriving at the dock.

■ THE MARINA. The marina area jumps all day with fishermen bringing in catch, women selling fish, families returning to the bay's islands, and the big fishing boats docking at the main marina. Decaying steel-hulled trawlers at the end of the main pier are remainders from the collapse of the local fishing industry in the mid-1980s, after the FMLN bombed nearby bridges and effectively cut off the port from San Salvador. The well-kept *malecón* (sea wall) is a nice touch.

■ EXCURSIONS INTO BAHÍA DE JIQUILISCO. The best thing you can do here is to hire a *lancha* for the day and visit some of the many islands in the bay: **Islas La Parilla, Coral de Mula, and de Menéndez** are all a boat ride away. The only regular boat service is to Isla Coral de Mula (US$0.80, every hour or so). Lancha prices vary depending on boat quality and destination, so bargain hard (US$20-$50 is a good range). Before leaving, buy food, drinks, and your own hammock, since you will find no facilities on the islands. **La Península de Coral de Mulas** protects the entire bay from the Pacific. **Isla Menéndez**, on the peninsula's western end, has a sea turtle nursery. In town you'll have the chance to buy refreshments, and a 30min. walk brings you to the isolated Pacific beaches. There's not much to see most of the year, except mid-August through September when the 1500 eggs hatch. On the eastern end of the peninsula is the small community of **Coral de Mulas**, from where you can cross the peninsula to another deserted Pacific beach. It is a hot 30min. walk, but the scenery is wonderful. On Isla El Jobal, there is a **Cooperativa de Cocos**, a coconut farm that decided to make money not just by selling coconuts, but also by showing off how to use them for unconventional purposes. A note of caution: watch out for falling coconuts. (☎ 632 1802; info@barillasmarina.com; boat to the island is about US$30).

NORTHERN EL SALVADOR

North of the capital, pastures yield to remote mountains that hide treasures for those tourists willing to cross the poorly maintained roads. Suchitoto's fine architecture, beautiful scenery, and traditional lifestyle attract travelers drawn by El

Salvador's cultural history. Local *artesanía* thrives in several areas, including La Palma and Ilobasco, towns known for pottery and hammocks. Nature lovers enjoy Lago Suchitlán's 14 species of fish and more than 200 types of birds, while more restless travelers heed the call of El Pital, El Salvador's highest peak.

SUCHITOTO

With narrow cobblestone streets and fine architecture, Suchitoto (pop. 52,000) is the best-preserved colonial town in El Salvador, every building a testament to its fascinating history. Once the biggest producer of indigo in the country, this town of renowned filmmakers and painters is now known for its thriving arts scene. In addition to rich cultural festivals—including the **Grand November Fair** (2nd Su. in Nov.) and **Virgen de Santa Lucía** (Dec. 6-13)—the area is great for birdwatching and cave exploration.

☲ TRANSPORTATION. Buses run from San Salvador's Terminal Oriente to Suchitoto (#129; 1½hr., every 20min. 4:30am-7:45pm, US$0.45), and drop you off on the corner of 2 Av. and C. Morazán. From the road along the market, you can take the #129 back to San Salvador (every 25min. 3:45am-5:45pm, US$0.45). Leaving 1 block west of the *parque*'s southwest corner, the #163 bus goes to Aguilares (1¼hr., every 45min. 4:45am-5:30pm, US$0.50).

▨▨ ORIENTATION AND PRACTICAL INFORMATION. Calle San Marcos/ Morazán intersects **Av. 5 de Noviembre/15 de Septiembre** on the corner of the *parque central*. C. San Marcos runs along the right side of the **cathedral** and becomes C. Morazán after the intersection; Av. 15 de Septiembre runs along the length of the *parque* and becomes Av. 5 de Noviembre after the intersection. **Parque San Martin** starts on the corner of 4 Av. Norte and 4 C. Poniente. The **market** is between C. Morazán and 4 C. Poniente, and 2 and 4 Av. Norte.

Stop by the brand new **tourist office** on the corner of 2 Av. and Calle Morazán for **tourist info,** bike rentals, and horse rides to nearby waterfalls. (☎ 335 1782. Bikes US$1 per hr., US$10 per day. Open daily 8am-5pm.) Another precious source of information is the ◪**Centro Artex Café,** on C. San Marcos in front of the *parque*, an NGO focusing on the preservation of local art. DSL **Internet** service (US$0.75 per hr.), free maps, coffee, and snacks are all available here. (☎ 335 1440; www.suchitoturismo.com; English and Japanese spoken.) There is **no bank** in Suchitoto. **Farmacia Santa Lucía** is on C. Morazán between 2 Av. and Av. 15 de Septiembre. (☎ 335 1063. Open daily 6.30am-noon, 1:30-8pm, on-call 24hr.) **Hospital Nacional de Suchitoto** (☎ 335 1062), on the corner of 4 Av. Sur and 5 C. Pte., has 24hr. ambulance service. The **police** (☎ 335 1141) are on 2 C. Pte. between 2 Av. Nte. and Av. 15 de Septiembre. **Telecom,** on C. Morazán, allows collect calls and international phone cards. (☎ 335 1020. Open M-Sa 8am-noon, 2-6pm.) **Internet** at **Infocentros** is on the *parque*'s southwest corner. (US$1 per hr. Open M-F 8am-7pm; Sa-Su 8:30am-4pm.) The **post office** is on the corner of C. Morazán and 2 Av. Sur (open M-F 8am-5pm, Sa 8am-noon).

▨ ACCOMMODATIONS. Suchitoto is a budget traveler's dream with plenty of exceptional accommodation options at reasonable prices. Most hotels double as restaurants. ▨ **Restaurante Villa Balanza ❸,** in front of Parque San Martin on the corner of 6 Av. Norte and 6 C. Pte., looks like a colonial convent and has an open-air museum full of local art and culture. Clean rooms with fans look out on a dreamy lake vista. (☎ 335 1408. US$10 per person.) A pricier option is ◪**El Tejado ❺,** on Av. 15 de Septiembre about 3 blocks away from the *parque*, which has a swimming pool alongside an amazing view of the lake. Rooms are spacious and clean with fan, private bath, and TV. Breakfast is included. (☎ 335 1769. US$45 per room; triples US$55-$60. Pool US$3 for non-guests.) Housed in a colonial-style building that fits right in with Suchitoto's architecture, **Hotel Posada Altavista ❹** is on Av. 15 de Septiembre #8. Rooms come with a fan and TV, some with bath. (☎335 1645 or 335 1648; www.hotelaltavista.com.sv. Singles US$15; doubles US$25; triples US$35. Laundry available.) For lower rates, **Obraje ❸**, on 2 C. Ote. to the side of the cathedral, has clean rooms, fans, and hot water. (☎335 1173. Singles US$10; doubles US$15. Restaurant open Tu-Su 8am-9pm.)

◖ FOOD. Dining in Suchitoto is a truly enjoyable experience. Many establishments share space with the hotels listed above. ◨**Restaurante Villa Balanza ❷** offers a variety of local and international dishes (meals US$3-$6); the table under the bell-tower may well be the most romantic dining setting in the country (open Tu-Su 10am-8pm). ◨ **El Tejado ❹** serves an extensive selection of international dishes, while **2 Gardenias Hostal Zuka Fé y Bar ❷** serves Caribbean and Mexican dishes (US$3-$5). **La Fonda El Mirador ❷** is the place for traditional dishes (seafood US$5) complemented by an amazing view of the lake. (☎335 1126. Open daily 10am-6pm.) For good *pupusas* and a popular Sunday lunch, try **Pupusería Vista al Lago ❶**, close to La Fonda El Mirador. (US$0.20-0.40. Open F-Su 5:30-8pm.)

◙ SIGHTS. Suchitoto's colonial charm infuses all of its attractions. With impressive Corinthian columns, **Catedral de Santa Lucía** has a white facade and a well-preserved wood altar in the interior (open during daylight hours). The **Parque San Martín** (see **Orientation,** p. 271) has views of Lago de Suchitlán and an open-air art gallery; the town's artists have transformed the small park using sculptures incorporating "war garbage." Close to **Obraje,** a few women practice the art of cigar-rolling, filling the street with the aroma of their work. **Lago de Suchitlán** is only a 30min. walk away from town. Take 3 Av. Norte north until the three-way fork. Continuing straight ahead, you will be rewarded with views of the lake before a descent to the shore. Trucks run from the bottom of the hill for US$3 per person, but cost less for a group ride. Bearing right makes for a longer but more gradual walk to the shore. Some travelers thumb for rides back to town, since either route back is a 45min. uphill hike, but *Let's Go* does not recommend hitchhiking.

A national celebrity and flamboyant character, Alejandro Coto recently moved his **Casa de Alejandro** to town, showing off an impressive and eclectic art collection. Another of the area's well-known artists, **Víctor Manuel Sanabria,** nicknamed "Shanay," has a studio and gallery on 3 Av. Norte between 2 and 4 C. Oriente. There are no hours; knock any time during the day and he'll be happy to show you around. To discover more about Suchitoto's troubled past, explore **Cerro Guazapa,** a civil war battleground just outside of town. The **tourist office** can find you a guide.

◪◩ OUTDOOR ACTIVITIES AND GUIDED TOURS. The **tourist office** organizes horse rides to **Los Tercios,** a 25m high waterfall with strange cubic-rock formations (US$20-$25 per person, discounts for groups). **2 Gardenias Hostal Zuka Fé y Bar** also organizes tours to various sites. The unmapped **Chinnapa Caves** are a few minutes away from town. Local folklore says that a hidden treasure is buried in the caves and remains undiscovered because a magnetic force field distorts compass readings. Ferries making the short trip to **Isla de los Pájaros** and **Isla Ermilaño** leave from the docks at the end of Av. 15 de Septiembre.

CHALATENANGO

Situated between the La Peña mountains to the north and the Lago de Suchitlán to the south resides the bustling commercial center of Chalatenango (pop. 15,900), capital of the department of the same name. "Chalate" proudly exhibits the longest arched walkways in Central America, in addition to one of the most imposing military garrisons in the country. Town life centers on the frenetic market, where you can buy anything from socks to US pop music tapes.

Buses coming in from San Salvador stop at the corner of 6 C. and Av. 1 (2hr., every 10min. 3:30am-5:40pm, US$1.25). From the north, get off at Amayo, a junction on the highway from El Poy, and hop on the #125 (35min., every 15 min. 5:15am-8:15pm, US$0.30). Buses to **Concepción Quezaltepeque** leave from the same area 2 blocks south of the church (#300B; 30min., every 30min. 6:30am-5pm, US$0.30). An erratic **ferry** leaves from nearby San Luis del Carmen and crosses the Lago de Suchitlán, landing in Suchitoto on the southern side of the lake.

Facing the front of the **cathedral,** the first street on your right is C. San Martin, which becomes C. Morazán 1 block away from the central square. Standing at this crossroad with your back to the cathedral, Av. Libertad is to your right and Av. Fajardo to your left.

Banco de Comercio, on the corner of 1 C. and 1 Av., has an **ATM,** changes traveler's checks and US dollars, and gives cash advances on MC/V (open M-F 8am-4pm, Sa 8am-noon). The **market** spreads out around the main crossroad in town and a **supermarket** is on C. S. Martin between 1 Av. and Av. Fajardo. **National Hospital** is 4 blocks past the Banco de Comercio; when you reach the church turn right and go 2 blocks. (☎301 0905. Open 24hr.) The **police** (☎335 2422 or 309 9806) are located in a large building 1 block past the church on the left. **Telecom** has an office on C. S. Martin; walk across the *parque* away from the cathedral for 2 blocks (open daily 8am-6pm). **Infocentros,** across from the cathedral, is the town's Internet hookup. (US$1 per hr. Open M-F 8am-6pm, Sa 8am-noon.) The **post office** is on the corner of Av. Fajardo and 3 C. (open M-F 7am-5pm, Sa 7am-noon.)

The best accommodation option is **Hotel la Ceiba ❹,** located in a bright, sparkling, modern building on 1 C. Head away from the cathedral past the military garrison. Rooms have A/C, phone, private bath, and TV. (☎301 1080. Singles US$15; doubles US$20; triples US$25. AmEx/MC/V.) **Hotelito San José ❷,** Av. Fajardo/2 Av., 3 C., is more economical. (☎301 0148. Single US$7; double US$10.) Further away, **Hotel Posada del Jefe ❸,** 1 block down C. Morazán after the main crossroad, has big rooms with fan, phone, bath, and TV. (☎335 2450. Singles US$11.50; doubles US$17.)

Restaurante El Rinconcito Chalateco ❸, on C. Placido Peña, just past the military garrison, combines a panoramic view with a rich menu. (☎335 2268. Most dishes US$5-$7, Surf and Turf US$12. Karaoke Th, live music F.) Another option is **Restaurante Sunpul ❷,** located on 4 C. Oriente in Barrio S. Antonio, with its clean and spacious dining area (open M-Sa 10am-midnight). For a cheaper and quicker meal try **El Carboncito ❶,** 3 Av. Sur # 33 (US$0.35-$1.35). **Pupusa stands** cluster on 1 Av. between C. San Martin and 1 C.

Chalate has few sights, but the spacious interior of **Catedral de Chalatenango de San Juan Bautista** stands as a beautiful example of a colonial-style church. You can't miss the huge **military garrison,** just on the side of the cathedral, a constant reminder of when the FMLN was fighting in the streets of Chalate.

DAYTRIPS FROM CHALATENAGO

◪ **CONCEPCIÓN QUEZALTEPQUE.** Renowned for its hammock industry, Concepción Quezaltepeque is only 12km northwest of Chalatenango. Multi-colored hammocks woven in small workshops around town are sold at the **Empresa Asociativa de Artesanías Hamacas,** a cooperative of local artisans located 1½ blocks south of the *parque central* along the road the bus stops on. (Hammock US$8-$30.) You can also look into **Artesanía Quezaltecas,** at the top of the hill just before the *parque central* on the right. Ask friendly, Spanish-speaking owner Miguel for a free hammock-making lesson. *(#300B, 30min., leaves Chalatenango every 30min., 6:30am-5pm, US$0.30; return buses run 6am-3:20pm. Trucks waiting at the bus stop run until 4 or 5pm, US$0.30.)*

◙ **PARQUE ARQUEOLÓGICO CIHUATÁN.** Easily accessible from the nearby town of Aguilares, the **Parque Arqueológico Cihuatán** reigns as the largest ancient site of indigenous civilization in El Salvador. Dating back to the early postclassic period (AD900-1200), the remains are of unclear origin. The site consists primarily of a ceremonial center surrounded by a large wall. As you enter, the first structure you encounter is the **West Ballcourt.** From the largely unexcavated pyramid, you can't miss the silhouette of a woman formed by the peaks of nearby Volcán Guazapa. To the left is the **North Ballcourt** with its oddly outward-slanting walls.

The town of Aguilares is located at the intersection of the Troncal del Norte highway and the east-west *carretera* joining Santa Ana and Suchitoto. Aguilares itself is a busy commercial junction with a large daily market. If you get stuck in Aguilares, **Hospedaje Crucero del Amor ❷** has reliable, basic rooms with bath (1-3 people US$7). Food options are slim, but **Mr. Pan ❶**, off the *parque central*, sells pizza. *(Bus #117 heads to San Salvador from the parque central. 1 hr., every 10min. 3:45am-7pm, US$0.40. Bus #163 heads to Suchitoto every 45min. daily 4am-5:45pm, US$0.60. To get to the park, take a bus for US$0.17 heading north from Aguilares, leaving from the Texaco station 2 blocks north of the parque. There is no entrance fee.)*

LA PALMA

Just 12km south of the Honduran border, in the shadow of El Pital, the quiet town of La Palma rests amid dazzling flowers and mighty rivers. Enjoying the town's relaxed pace, villagers create brightly painted wooden and ceramic *artesanía*. The tradition began in the 1970s, when Salvadoran artist Fernando Llort moved to La Palma and started teaching locals how to paint simple images of Christ and mountain villages. His lessons took hold: an impressive 75% of the town's 3100 people are artisans.

◪ **TRANSPORTATION. Buses** pass directly in front of the *parque central* heading north to the Honduran border at El Poy (40min., every 30min. 6am-6pm, US$0.45) and south to San Salvador (4hr., every 30min. 6am-6pm, US$0.90).

◪ **PRACTICAL INFORMATION. Banco de Cuscatlán,** at the northwest corner of the *parque*, changes traveler's checks (open M-F 8:30am-noon and 1-4pm, Sa 8:30am-noon). The **police station** is 1 block down the hill on the opposite side of the *parque* from the bank. (☎335 9184. Open 24hr.) **Farmacia Elizabeth,** a block up the hill behind the church, (☎335 9017, open daily 7:30am-1pm and 2-8pm) stands next-door to **Laboratorio Clínica La Palma** (open daily 8am-4pm). **Telecom** is just up the hill from the *parque*, off the main road from the front of the church. (☎335 9011. Open M-Sa 8am-7pm, Su 8am-5pm.) For **Internet** service, head to **Dinosaurias Cibernéticos,** next to Cooprativo Semilla de Dios (US$2 per hr.). Next to the Casa de la Cultura is the **post office** (open M-F 8am-noon and 2-4pm, Sa 8am-noon).

▮◪ **ACCOMMODATIONS AND FOOD.** None of La Palma's accommodations fall in the low budget range. The best, albeit priciest, option is **Hotel Posada Real ❺**, where the service is great and rooms all have fans, hot bath, and TV. (☎335 9002. Singles US$28; doubles/triples US$35. Meals US$2.) A cheaper option is **Hotel La Palma ❺,** 2 blocks up the hill from the front of the church, with large log-cabin rooms that have hot water. (☎335 9012. US$18 per person.) An even cheaper choice is the town of San Ignacio, which is better situated for enjoying nearby sights. **La Posada de San Ignacio ❶** is located right along the north side of the *parque* (US$5 per person).

Restaurante La Estancia ❶, 1 block up the hill in front of the church on the main road, boasts the great combination of a varied menu, decent prices, hearty portions, and local artwork decor. (Chicken and beef dishes start at US$3. Open 8am-7pm. AmEx/MC/V.) The **Pupusería El Buen Gusto ❶**, next to the *parque* in San Ignacio, keeps it simple and delicious (*pupusas* US$0.30).

◙ ⌂ SIGHTS AND CRAFTS. Homes producing *artesanía* cluster down the hill from the church in Barrio San Antonio. Of the town's artists, local painter **Alfredo Linares** is particularly well known. His gallery, half a block south of the *parque* along the western road, showcases rural scenes and modern art, all in a rich variety of colors. The gallery also sells paintings by other local artists like Alfredo's brother Oscar. (Postcards US$1, reprints US$13, originals US$10-$600. Open 9am-noon and 1-5pm. AmEx/MC/V.) Local artisans show off their trade at the **Asociación Cooperativa La Semilla de Dios,** 1 block down the hill from the front of the church and then left for 2 more blocks.

▟ EL PITAL AND RÍO CHIQUITO

Bus #509 leaves from the street 2 blocks north of San Ignacio's parque central to Río Chiquito (1hr., every 2hr. 7:30am-4:30pm, US$0.80). Ask the driver to let you off at El Pital. The peak is a 1½hr. hike from Río Chiquito. Entrance US$1.

If the sight of the mountains surrounding La Palma leaves you restless, climbing **El Pital,** the highest mountain in El Salvador (2730m), is just what you need. The jaw-dropping views of Honduras to the north and the cones of El Salvador's volcanoes to the south make this hike a worthwhile daytrip. It is best to leave as early as possible in the morning to beat the rain that tends to fall in the afternoon. Tiny Río Chiquito, the departure point for the ascent, lies near other hikes and the neighboring town of Las Pilas. Definitely take the bus to Río Chiquito. Though the town is only 10km from San Ignacio (or 10min. north of La Palma on the road to the border) the steep and bumpy uphill road will feel longer.

Once the bus lets you off at Río Chiquito, much of the hard work has already been done for you as the top of the peak is less than a 1½hr. hike from town. From the main road in Río Chiquito, turn left on the dirt road (where the town's few houses are), and continue along a steep 4WD road until you reach the peak, bearing right at any forks along the way. You'll pass three barbed-wire gates. During the rainy season, this road can become quite muddy. At the top, a US$1 entrance fee is required. There is a camping area with a toilet (US$2 per person including admission). Bring your own gear and come prepared for chilly temperatures.

From Río Chiquito, a couple other trails lead to interesting destinations. A rewarding hike with impressive views heads up to **Miramundo.** Just past the bus-drop-off at Río Chiquito, the road begins to dip; bear right at the fork instead of heading down to Las Pilas and continue on for about 45min. to reach the peak. **Hostal Miramundo ❶**, with a restaurant, bar, and rooms with a view that sleep up to six people (US$30), boasts the best views from the top. Ask and they'll gladly let you walk around their picnic area and soak up the vistas of El Salvador, Honduras, and El Pital itself.

A short trip to **Las Pilas,** 6km down the main road, will allow you to sample a wide selection of international produce. Walk or take the same bus from San Ignacio (#509, 30min., every 2hr. 7am-5pm, US$0.15). The town lets you see the agricultural economy and culture of northern El Salvador up close. The market in town is also the best place around to find fresh fruits and veggies; in fact, you may even be able to pick the fruit yourself. There is a nice hike from Las Pilas to the **Río Sumpul,** a river that forms the border with Honduras and originates at El Pital. Turn right in the center of town, and make the 20min. walk to the river, where you can find pleasant bathing pools.

The summit's owner, **Arturo,** who lives just outside of town toward Las Pilas, is around every day in the dry season, but only on weekends during the rainy season. If you'd like him to arrange a guide (US$2-$3) to take you to some of the surrounding woods, be sure to ask for him in Río Chiquito before heading up the mountain. One favorite tour is to La Piedra Rajada, a gigantic rock formation 30min. from El Pital. The trail crosses several streams, and you must cross a log bridge over a 20m precipice to reach the rock; going with a guide is advisable. A new addition to the park is **El Pital Highland ☉,** a restaurant and hotel set among exotic flowers and a small deer farm. The *cabañas* sleep four (US$104) and nine (US$125). Reserve at least eight days in advance. Though the restaurant is only open on weekends, call in advance for a hot meal whenever you're passing by. (☎222 2009. Hot dog and fries US$3; spaghetti US$4.60.)

✖ EL POY: BORDER WITH HONDURAS

The border is 11km from El Poy and 5km from San Ignacio. Immigration open 6am-10pm. Bus 119 leaves from a lot down the street from the gate, running regularly to La Palma (30min., every 30min. 4am-4pm, US$0.60), continuing on to San Salvador (3hr., US$1.70). King Quality buses also go to San Salvador (2hr., 10:30am and 5pm, US$8).

Travelers en route to the Maya ruins at Copán often pass through El Poy. **Money changers** on both sides of the border will change any Central American currency. Banks at the border are of little use, and those in Nueva Ocotepeque and La Palma will only change US dollars into the local currency at about 1-2% below the actual rate. Cars have to make an additional stop at the customs house.

WESTERN EL SALVADOR

Hilly terrain covered by national parks, lakes, volcanoes, and coffee plantations make the west one El Salvador's most captivating regions. Santa Ana, the country's most pleasant city, boasts a newly renovated theater and impressive cathedral, while the small towns of Apaneca, Juayua, and Nahuizalco offer an idyllic mountain escape. Traces of the region's history are visible at the archaeological site of Tazumal. For a more extreme escape, head into the cloud forest of Parque Nacional Montecristo, near Metapán in the north, or visit El Salvador's last untouched wildlife reserve at Parque Nacional El Imposible.

SONSONATE

In contrast to its surroundings, Sonsonate (pop. 57,400) buzzes with energy, chokes on diesel fumes, and swelters under the pressure of rapid modernization. The city is most important to travelers as a transport hub; many pass through en route to the Pacific Coast, La Ruta de las Flores, Parque Nacional El Imposible, or the Guatemalan border at La Hachadura. This is not El Salvador's safest city; be especially careful at night.

⎐ TRANSPORTATION. Buses leave from the well-organized modern terminal on Paseo 15 de Septiembre, 8 blocks east of the parque between 14 and 16 Av., to: **La Libertad** (#281/287, 2½hr.; 6:15am, 3:45pm, or transfer in San Salvador; US$0.70);

Santa Ana via **Cerro Verde** (#209A; 1½hr., every 30min. 5am-5pm, US$0.55); **Santa Ana** via **Los Naranjos** (#216, 1¾ min., every 20min. 3:30am-6:30pm, US$0.60); and **San Salvador** (#205, 1½hr., every 5min. 3:30am-6:30pm, US$0.85). Buses also leave from half a block south of Av. 15 de Septiembre on 10 Av. going to **Los Cobanos** (#257, 40min., every 30min. 5am-6pm, US$0.40) and the **Guatemalan border** at **La Hachadura** (#259, 1¾hr., every 10min. 4am-7:30pm, US$0.55), via **Cara Sucia** (1hr., US$0.50). The bus to Ahuachapán and La Ruta de los Flores picks up on the street along the north side of the parque (#249; 1hr. 40min., every 35min. 4:30am-6pm, US$0.65). Local bus #53F will take you all the way to la Nueva Terminal, one half kilometer down Av. 15 de Septiembre.

Local buses travel between the parque and the terminal (#53F; every 5min., US$0.50), to **Nahuizalco** (#53D; every 10min.) and to **Izalco** (#53A; every 5min.). However, to go to Nahuizalco you are better off taking the #249 from the terminal. Because of one-way streets, buses return to the parque along 1 Av. A few routes of #53 also pass Metrocentro and are clearly marked. Bright yellow **taxis** line up all around the *parque* and outside the bus terminal, and charge US$2 for travel between the two points.

■ ⁊ **ORIENTATION AND PRACTICAL INFORMATION.** The focal point of the town's grid is the intersection of C. Obispo Marroquin/Paseo 15 de Septiembre and Av. Rafael Campos/Morazán; facing the **Cathedral of the Holy Spirit**, this intersection is on your right. Streets parallel to Av. Morazan are *avenidas*: Sur to your right, Norte to your left, odd-numbered behind you, even-numbered in front of you. Streets parallel to C. Marroquin are *calles*: odd-numbered to your left, even-numbered to your right, Oriente in front of you, Poniente behind you.

Banco de Comercio, on 2 Av. Nte. between C. Marroquin and 1 C. Pte.–changes traveler's checks and has an **ATM** that accepts major cards (open M-F 8:30am-5pm, Sa 8:30am-noon). The **municipal market** is on C. Marroquín between 6/8 Av. In an emergency, the **Police** (☎ 451 1099, emergency 121), located on the corner of 12 Av. Nte. and 1 C. Oriente and **Hospital Municipal** (☎ 451 0200), between 3 and 5 Av. Nte. and 1 and 3 C. Pte., has a doctor on call 24hr. The **Farmacia Fernández** (☎ 451 0465), on C. San Antonio is open M-Sa 8am-6pm, Su 8am-noon. **Telecom** is on the corner of Av. Campos and 2 C. (Internet US$2 per hr. Open daily 7:30am-7:30pm.) Another **internet** option is **Infocentros**, 3 C. between Av. Morazán and 1 Av. Nte. (US$1 per hr. Open M-F 8am-6pm, Sa 8am-noon.) The **post office** is on the corner of 1 Av. Nte. and 5 C. Pte. (open M-F 7am-5pm, Sa 7am-noon).

⁊ ◨ **ACCOMMODATIONS AND FOOD.** Hotels and *hospedajes* near the bus terminal tend to be rough and dirty, while those near the *parque central* are better and only a 10min. walk from the bus station. The best place to stay is **Hotel Orbe ❷**, on the corner of 2 Av. Sur and 4 C. Ote. Rooms are clean with private bath (☎ 451 1517; fax 451 1416. Singles US$9, with fan US$12, with TV US$18; doubles US$15/$17/$22.) For something more upscale, try **Hotel Agape ❺**, a 10min. bus ride east of town on the road to San Salvador. Rooms have A/C, phone, private baths, and TV. (☎ 451 1456, 451 2626; ramon@intradec.com. Singles US$16; doubles US$22; 5 person suite US$40. AmEx/MC/V.) **Hotel Sagitario ❷**, on Paseo 15 de Sept. between 16 and 18 Av., is as cheap as you can get. Basic rooms all have private bath. (☎ 451 1174. Singles US$6; doubles US$12.) If you feel like treating yourself, then **Hotel Plaza ❺**, on the corner of 8 Av. Nte. and 7 C. Ote. is probably the nicest option in town with a pool, laundry service, a bar, and a restaurant. Rooms all have A/C, bath, TV, and telephone. (☎ 451 6626 or 451 3610. Singles US$25; doubles US$36. AmEx/MC/V.)

For the best seafood in the area, check out **Restaurante Acajutla ❺,** a 10min. bus ride east of town on the road to San Salvador. The lobster stuffed with shrimp (US$12.50) is a real treat. (☎451 2322. Open 8:30am-10:30pm.) Food carts and *pupuserías* line the *parque* and the many *pastelerías* around town, are a nice option for breakfast or a quick snack. (Two are on 8 Av. Nte. between C. Marroquín and 1 C. Ote. Pastries US$0.40-1. Open 8am-6pm.) The fast food row can be found at the intersection of 12 Av. and C. Marroquín, near the bus terminal. **Restaurante La Terraza ❶,** on the corner of 10 Av. Nte. and 7 C. Ote., serves good-sized meals at decent prices. Try the house special surf and turf for US$8.75. (Meat or chocolate crepes US$1.75. Open until 9:30pm. AmEx/MC/V.)

🎥 📷 **SIGHTS AND ACTIVITIES.** The most interesting sight in town is the **Iglesia del Pilar,** on the corner of 3 Av. Nte. and 5 C. Pte. Its 18th-century white facade and interior artwork combines indigenous and traditional styles. A small town north of Sonsonate, **Izalco** is home to the two oldest churches in El Salvador. The **Iglesia de la Anunción,** the first church on your right as you proceed along the town's main road, dates back to 1580. **Iglesia de los Dolores,** at the top of the road, is 10 years older. **Turicentro Atecozol** has two pools, waterslide trails, basketball courts, and *comedores.* Bus #53A departs from the *parque central* in Sonsonate and brings you to the entrance of the Turicentro before returning. (Pool open daily 7am-4:30pm. Buses 20min., US$0.17; last bus back leaves Turicentro at 5:30pm. Entrance fee US$1, car fee US$0.80.)

🏃 **DAYTRIP FROM SONSONATE: PLAYA LOS CÓBANOS**

Buses leave from C. Marroquín and Av. Quiñonez (12 Av.) in Sonsonate (#257, 45min., every 30min. from 6am, US$0.10). The last return bus leaves the beach at 6pm.

Just 25km south of Sonsonate, Playa Los Cóbanos is popular with locals for its gently curving beach. Soft, seashell-strewn sand and bits of coral yield to large black rocks at the water's edge, creating a stunning contrast. When the tide is out, you can walk hundreds of meters out from shore. The main beach sits between two rocky peninsulas. **Punta Remedios** is on the west side, and, at low tide, you can walk west to the more soothing **Playa Los Remedios** where several other tranquil beaches lined with private houses await. Some of the best **scuba-diving** in the country lies offshore from Los Cóbanos, in El Salvador's largest coral reef. Conditions are good only in the summer (Nov.-May, Dec. and Jan. are best). During that time you can arrange dives with several dive shops based in San Salvador. **El Salvador Divers** organizes full-day trips that include two dives, lunch, equipment, and transportation. (☎264 0961. US$40 per person.) **Oceánico Diving School** does similar trips. (☎263 6931. US$50 per person, minimum four people; reserve guide two days in advance.)

 Beware: high tide will block your way back to Los Cóbanos.

Hotel Mar de Plata ❺, attached to the restaurant of the same name, rents dark cabañas with porches. Shared bathrooms are a walk away. (US$9 for day only, US$18 with night.) The last hotel to the right is **Hotel Solimar ❸,** which rents cabañas on the beach. They also have public showers (US$0.40), toilet facilities, and daytime cabins where you can sleep if you bring your own mattress. (Beach cabins single bed US$12.50; queen bed with fan and bath US$18. Daytime cabins US$6.)

LA RUTA DE LAS FLORES

High in the mountains of the Cordillera Apaneca-Ilamatepec, between Ahuachapán and Sonsonate, the towns of **Juayua, Nahuizalco,** and **Apaneca** makeup "La Ruta de Las Flores." These villages provide access to one of the most majestic mountain ranges in the country, filled with rivers, crater lakes, coffee plantations, and, yes, a wide array of flowers. Each town each retains a certain colonial charm as well as a rich cultural history, evident in local traditions and *artesanía*.

The towns are connected by **bus #249,** which runs frequently between Ahuachapán and Sonsonate (every 15min., daily 5am-7pm). Nahuizalco is also accessible by bus #53D from Sonsonate's *parque central*.

NAUHUIZALCO

About 10km north of Sonsonate, Nahuizalco is known for its wicker baskets and carpentry. With 90% of the population involved in one of the two trades nearly every home and workshop around town is devoted to handicrafts. Wicker and woodworking shops line the street that heads out to Sonsonate, selling everything from full living room sets to wicker toilet paper holders. An incredible sight to behold is the unique *mercado nocturno*, where the marketplace, fed by numerous stands cooking up an array of *platos típicos*, continues to bustle by candlelight (open nightly 7-10pm). Guides can be found at the **Casa de la Cultura** (☎453 0129), on the corner of 3 C. and 1 Av., or at the **Alcaldía;** they charge only US$0.50 to show you the many workshops around town. The only food option is **Restaurante Tío Alex ❷**, where you can get a US$1.70 breakfast in a family-like setting.

JUAYUA

The largest of the towns (pop. 35,000), Juayua (why-YOU-ah) is about 16km from Sonsonate. The most famous sight is the **Templo del Señor de Juayua,** on 3 Av. between 2 and 4 C. Built in 1957, the building has an impressive nave and black marble columns that frame the main attraction: the statue of **El Cristo Negro** behind the altar. Carved by Quiro Cataño, the sculptor of the world famous Cristo Negro in Esquipulas (p. 376), this statue displays the same artistic expertise minus the huge crowds (open daily during daylight hours). Increasingly popular is the food festival and fair, **La Feria Gastronómica,** that occurs every weekend and includes music, art, and over 50 different *platos típicos*. Once a month, the festival showcases a specific country's food, music, and culture. (*Platos* US$1-$4. Open Sa-Su 10am-5pm.) Close by Juayua, you'll find various lakes and a number of rivers and waterfalls. The local tourism committee erected a **Caseta de Información** on the *parque*, where guides will show you around town; if you come on a weekday, ask for **Jaime Salgado.** The most popular tour is the **Ruta de las Cinco Cascadas,** a dayhike to a number of waterfalls, including Salto Papalunate (80m), and ending at Los Chorros with its lovely swimming holes. (☎452 2916. Guides US$2-$8, call the day before. Open Sa-Su.)

Banco de Comercio, 1 block west of the church on the road out of town, will change traveler's checks and give Visa cash advances (open M-F 8:30am-4:30pm). **Hostal de Doña Mercedes ❹**, on the corner of 2 Av. and 2 C., is a reasonably priced option; double rooms have TV, fan, and bath (☎452 2207. Singles US$15; doubles US$20.) Two blocks behind the left-hand side of the church sits **Hotel El Mirador ❹**. Though there is no sign, the hotel furnishes clean simple rooms with private baths. (☎452 2432. 1-4 people, US$13 per person.) **Pollo Rico ❶**, on the corner of 2 Av. and C. Mercedes, is the most reasonably priced restaurant in town (chicken US$0.60/

piece; meals US$2-$3). Salvadoran and international dishes are served at **Restaurante La Colina ❸**, located at the entrance of town coming from Salcoatitán. (☎452-2916. Open daily noon-2:30pm and 6-9pm.)

⬛ APANECA

The smallest and most charming of the villages on La Ruta de las Flores, Apaneca is a 40min. drive south of Ahuachapán on the road to Sonsonate. The bus drops you off along the highway and you have to walk about 5 blocks up the hill to get to the town center. The town, surrounded by forests and coffee plantations, gets pleasantly cool at night. Founded in 1525, the coffee industry has supported Apaneca for over 400 years, currently employing 80% of the population. Buses from Ahuachapán drop off facing north; those from Sonsonate drop off facing south.

Information on local arts and crafts, as well as hikes and horseback riding, is available at **Casa de la Cultura,** on the corner of Av. 15 de Abril and C. Menendez. (☎433 0163. Open M-F 8am-4pm.) Two hikes into the volcanic region leave from points just outside of town, but the trip isn't safe to make alone. Fortunately, the local **police** (☎433 0037), located 2 blocks west of the *parque*, are happy to guide and protect travelers. A 7km walk from Apaneca leads to **Laguna Verde,** a beautiful and popular crater lake surrounded by pine slopes. From the highway at the edge of town, take the dirt road to the right of the Jardín de Flores garden center; this road winds up and around the mountain and passes some viewpoints of Ahuachapán (3hr.). The smaller **Laguna Las Ninfas,** a 45min. walk from town, has good bird-watching. It can be reached by heading straight from the garden center and then, after about 20min., bearing right onto a dried-out creek bed. The *laguna* area has nice views but dries up in times of low rainfall. It's easy to get lost—arrange a guide at Casa de la Cultura.

Hostal Rural Las Orquídeas ❷ is a lovely bed and breakfast. Follow the yellow signs, go 2 blocks south from the church, turn left, and walk half a block. There's a sitting room, courtyard, and hot showers. (☎433 0061. Singles US$9; doubles US$12.) **Hotel Las Ninfas ❷,** on the corner of 1 Av. Norte and 9 C. Pte., offers a family style environment where you can learn about local culture and folklore. Rooms come with private bath and fan (☎433 0059 or 433 0089. Singles US$6; doubles US$10.) The most well-known "attraction" in town is without a doubt ⬛**La Cocina de Mi Abuela ❺,** the yellow restaurant 2 blocks north of the park on 1 Av. People from all over the country come to enjoy a gourmet meal at one of the wooden tables, and admire the antique photographs, plates, and railings. Live music and beautiful gardens accompany the exquisite *típico*. (Meals US$12-$15. Reservations required. Open Sa-Su 11am-7pm.) **Comedor Carmela ❶,** 2 blocks east of the church, has good, cheap *comida típica* and helpful maps detailing tourist sights in town. (*Pupusas* US$0.30. Open daily 7am-7pm.) **Complejo de Ventas de Comidas ❶,** near the bus stop, is a series of local eateries that offer inexpensive meats, soups, and the usual *pupusas* (US$0.30-1).

PARQUE NACIONAL EL IMPOSIBLE

Dubbed *el último refugio* (the last refuge), Parque Nacional El Imposible is El Salvador's largest and most impressive national park, home to a biodiversity that's the last of its kind. Deep green mountains and ridges covered with dense primary-growth tropical forest protect the delicate ecosystems that have been obliterated just about everywhere else the country. The park's 3600 hectares are home to nearly 400 different species of trees, 500 species of butterflies, two plant species unique to the park, and several endangered animals, including the *tigrillo* and puma. Impressively managed by the non-governmental agency Salva Natura, the park protects three zones of vegetation and the sources of eight rivers. The park's name derives from its pre-refuge days, when local coffee growers had to traverse a precarious mountain pass to get their coffee to market; "El Imposible" was a wide gap in the cliff trail that often sent *burros*, coffee, and men falling 100m to their deaths. In 1968, however, the government built a permanent bridge over the pass and erected a sign reading: "In 1968, it ceased to be impossible."

There are two ways to plan your trip: an official **Salva Natura** guide or an unofficial guide from **Tacuba** (p. 282). The latter is certainly easier and more rewarding. Tacuba, a town on the northeastern edge of the *parque*, has all the amenities of a small town and very knowledgeable local guides, most of whom have lived in the area their entire lives. The Salva Natura alternative requires securing a permit (US$8) in advance from the office in San Salvador and making a long journey around to San Miguelito, a small town with no amenities, to meet the guide.

▐ TRANSPORTATION. Getting to El Imposible can be tricky. The first step is to get to **Cara Sucia,** the nearest major town. From the terminal in **Sonsonate,** buses leave for Cara Sucia every 10min., also stopping at 10 Av. just south of C. Marroquín on their way out of town (#25, 1hr., 5:30am-6pm, US$0.50). About 10min. east of Cara Sucia on the *carretera,* a large park sign marks a dirt road that heads north into the hills for 13.5km to the park's **San Benito** entrance. Two daily pickups (11am and 2pm) travel from Cara Sucia to the park entrance at **San Miguelito,** the tiny village at the San Benito entrance to the park (1¼hr.). Alternatively, you can walk to **El Refugio,** a small town 3km downhill from San Miguelito (1hr.). **Buses** run from Cara Sucia to El Refugio (1hr., daily 10am and 3:20pm, US$0.45). Both the bus and the pickup leave from across the street from the bus stop in Cara Sucia, in front of Bazar Hernandez. Pickups fill up early (30min. prior).

Returns are all early in the day. A pickup from San Miguelito descends to Cara Sucia at 5:30am and a bus leaves at 7am. Buses from El Refugio return to Cara Sucia at 7am and 12:30pm. Farmers occasionally take pickups from San Miguelito to Cara Sucia, and some travelers hitch a ride to the highway, where buses for Sonsonate pass by though *Let's Go* does not recommend hitchhiking.

▐▐ ACCOMMODATIONS AND FOOD IN SAN MIGUELITO. Half the fun of any trip to El Imposible is spending a little time in the tranquil village of **San Miguelito,** where the people are friendly and the coffee is outstanding. The village has no electricity and the sporadic running water is still something of a novelty.

Don Rafael and **Doña Hilda ❶,** in the last house on the right before the park entrance, marked by the painted stones forming an arrow, will cheerfully fix you up with a bed or hammock in a rustic, candlelit room (US$3). Doña Hilda's typical Salvadoran kitchen, also known as **❚Comedor La Montaña ❶,** prepares delicious and authentic *típico* food. **Tienda El Tucán,** down the road across the street, stocks a limited selection of water, sodas, snacks, and staples like rice, oil, and candles. Depending on the length of your stay, it may be a good idea to bring your own food, water, and iodine tablets, since the store sometimes closes in the middle of the day.

▐ INSIDE THE PARK. A few minutes up the hill from the entrance gate is the **Visitors Center,** or **Casco,** with bathrooms, showers, and an ecological education center with maps of the park. Just beyond the visitors center the road splits, with the right fork heading down to the only two permissible **camping areas ❶** (free with your permit from Salva Natura). Sites have bathrooms with running water, firepits, and tables.

Three moderately strenuous, well-maintained trails run through the park. At the juncture beyond the visitors center, the path heading to the right becomes **El Sendero de Mulo,** a pleasant 1km forest stroll including 10 informative stations that describe the various plants and animals along the way. A few steps up the right fork lies a *mirador* with spectacular views north and east of territory within the *parque* and the cultivated lands beyond it. In the distance, you can just make out the waterfall at a point known as **Los Enganchos.** The trail to **Los Enganchos** breaks off to the right and heads steeply downhill to a crystal-clear river and small waterfall. Swimming here is a very pleasant cooldown before the difficult ascent back (1½-2hr.). The second trail brings you to the **Piedra Sellada,** one of the nine archaeological sites in the park where symbolic carvings cover a large rock. It is believed that the site was of religious importance to the indigenous societies of the region (1hr. each way). **Cerro León** is the park's third circuit. From the Sendero de Mulo, the trail branches left and winds up and down through the mountains and incredibly verdant primary and secondary forests. After 45min., a trail forks off to the right, leading to the ruins of an old church near **Tacuba** on the north side of the park. Special permission from Salva Natura is required for this 3hr. hike. The panoramic views from the **summit** of Cerro León, at 1100m above sea level, stretch from the Cordillera de Apaneca to the north, to the mountains of Guatemala in the distance to the west, and to the Pacific Ocean as far as Acajutla port to the south.

As you descend the Cerro, the trail that gave the park its name appears to the east as a faint cut-line in the forest skirting the top of cliffs that drop hundreds of meters to the valley floor. After retracing the trail you came up, the loop continues along another trail to the right. You will pass the small, pure **Río Ixcanal,** one of the eight rivers that originate in the park. The *río* also has a nice swimming spot. The trail heads back up and brings you home to the Visitors Center (3-4hr. trip).

TACUBA

A charming town (pop. 5000) on the northeastern edge of El Imposible, Tacuba's refreshing climate makes an ideal place to rest from the heat of the coast or big cities. With some of the best scenery in El Salvador and rich traditions in folkloric music, dances, arts, and crafts, Tacuba is a fun addition to your trip to El Imposible.

Bus transportation from Ahuachapán is fast and reliable. (#267, 1hr., every 30min. 3:30am-7pm, US$0.30.) The bus will drop you in the center of town at the *parque municipal,* in front of the ruins de la Iglesia Colonial. Facing the Iglesia Colonial, the street to your right is Av. España Nte. Tourist information and free maps are available at **Casa de la Cultura,** (☎417 4453), on the corner of Av. Cuscatlán Sur and 2 C. Pte. The **police** (☎417 4303) are on 8 C. Pte. between 1 and 3 Av. Sur and the **Red Cross** is on Av. España Nte. between 1 and 3 C. Pte. **Telecom,** (☎417 4300) is on the corner of 1 C. Pte. and 2 Av. Nte. (open M-F 8am-6pm, Sa-Su 8am-noon, 1-5pm). **Internet service** can be found close to Hotel Las Cabañas on 1 C. Pte (open M-Sa 8am-5pm). The **Post office** on Av. España Nte. between C. San Juan and 1 C. Pte. (open M-F 8am-4.30pm, Sa 8am-noon).

The best place to stay in town is ▨**Manolo's House ❶,** on the corner of Av. Cuscatlán and 10 C. Pte. Manolo will pick you up anywhere in Tacuba or even in Ahuachapán. His place has three very clean rooms and home cooked meals (US$2). Manolo also has a host of CDs and DVDs you can use, in addition to mountain bikes for rent. (☎417 4268. US$10 per person, discounts for large groups.) A pricier option is **Hotel la Cabaña Tacuba ❺,** on 1 C. Pte. between 1 and 5 Av. Sur, with its spacious garden and swimming pool. Sparkling rooms come with fan, bath, and TV. (☎417 4332. Breakfast included. Singles US$40; doubles US$50. AmEx/MC/V.)

One of the best restaurants in town is **Restaurante Miraflores ❷** (☎417 4746), on 2 Av. Nte. in front of the parque, which serves traditional food. (US$4-$5. Open daily 7am-8pm.) An even more inexpensive option is **Puma Express ❶**, on Av. España Nte. between 7 and 9 C., with a very clean environment and local dishes (☎417 4755. Meals US$1-$1.50 with free soda. Open daily 7am-6pm.) When you are in town, don't forget to go and see **Las Ruinas de la Iglesia Colonial.** Originally built in 1603, it was toppled twice—in 1773 and then again by an earthquake in 1984. It is one of the oldest constructions in El Salvador, and in the 17th century it was the biggest church in the country.

AHUACHAPÁN

Capital of its department, Ahuachapán, 35km from Santa Ana (pop. 100,000), is the most densely populated and one of the oldest cities in the country. Founded by the Pok'onáme Indians in the fifth century, it was conquered by the Pipil at the end of the 1400s, but the original culture endured in many respects, including the city's name which is Pok'onáme for "City of Oak Houses." The modern city is a natural hub for people crossing the border to Guatemala, and it is a convenient stop to explore La Ruta de las Flores or the isolated southern beaches.

⬛ TRANSPORTATION. From the terminal at 10 C. and Av. Menéndez, 1 block north of Parque Menéndez, **buses** head to: **Santa Ana** (#210, 1¼hr., every 10min. 4:30am-7pm, US$0.70), via **Chalchuapa** (40min., US$0.17); **San Salvador** (#202, 2½hr., every 10min. 3am-5:30pm, US$1); **Sonsonate** (#249, 2hr., every 12min. 4:30am-6pm, US$0.60) via **Apaneca** (40min., US$0.25), **Juayua** (1hr., US$0.55 regular), and **Nahuizalco** (1½hr., US$0.45); and **Tacuba** (#267, 1hr., every 30min. 3:30am-7pm, US$0.30). Buses and micro-buses to the **Guatemalan border** at **Las Chinamas** leave from 8 C. and 2 Av., on the northwest corner of Parque Menéndez (#263 and #11, 30min., every 8min. 4:50am-7:30pm, US$0.45). Be sure to get on the bus bound for the *frontera* (ask the driver); some go only as far as the town of Las Chinamas, a few kilometers short.

⬛ ORIENTATION AND PRACTICAL INFORMATION. Arriving from San Salvador, buses will drop you in the market on **Av. Menéndez,** just above 10 C. **Parque Menéndez,** bounded by 6/8 Calles and Av. 2/Menéndez, the more northern of the town's two parks, is marked by the trees towering over the market stalls. Arriving from the border at Las Chinamas, the bus will drop you on 2 Av. on the west side of Parque Menéndez, next to **Iglesia El Calvario.** Streets are laid out in a grid: Av. Menéndez is the main north-south artery and **Calle Barrios,** 3 blocks south of Parque Menéndez, is the primary east-west thoroughfare. Odd-numbered *avenidas* and *calles* increase to the east and south, respectively, while their even-numbered counterparts increase to the north and west. The other *parque,* **La Concordia,** is 5 blocks south of Parque Menéndez and bounded to the east by the church **Nuestra Señora de la Asunción.**

Tourist information is at **Casa de la Cultura,** 2 Av. Nte., 2 C. and C. Barrios. Banks and ATMs are now over-abundant; most cluster around 1 Av. Nte, C. Barrios, and 2 C. **Banco Cuscutlan** has an **ATM** that takes all major cards and cashes traveler's checks (open M-F 9am-5pm, Sa 9am-noon). **De Todo Supermarket,** on the northeastern corner of Parque Menéndez is open daily 7:30am-7pm. The **police station** (☎441 0911) on 2 C. closer to 10 Av. Nte. has 24hr. emergency service. **Farmacia Central,** is on Av. 2, 2 C. and C. Barrios. (☎443 0158. Open daily 8am-7pm, call 24hr.) Next door, the **Centro de Emergencias** has 24hr. medical emergency response. You can also call **Clínica Rodezno** (☎852 7697). The **hospital** (☎443 0039 or 443 0046) is on 16 Av. Pte., C. Zacamil. **Telecom** is on 3 C., 2 Av. in front of the *parque.* Log on to the

EL SALVADOR

Internet at **Infocentros,** located on 3 C. Ote. and 1 Av. Sur along the north side of La Asunción Church. (US$1 per hr. Open M-F 7:30am-7pm, Sa-Su 8am-5pm.) The **post office,** on the corner of 10 C. Oriente and 1 Av. Sur., has three day Express Mail to Europe and US. (Open M-F 8am-5pm, Sa 8am-noon. **Postal code:** 2101.)

ACCOMMODATIONS AND FOOD. The best option in town, ⬛**Restaurante Brisas de Santa Monica ❹,** at km100 on Carretera a las Chinamas, is a hotel, a restaurant, and the only disco in town all rolled into one. The view over the lake is perfect for relaxing and enjoying the rich traditional menu of seafood (US$6-$10) and international cuisine (pasta US$5). Safety is not an issue for guests, as they run a shuttle that will pick you up wherever you are in town. Ask friendly manager Mauricio Castaneda about boat rides on the lake (US$2; US$5 non-guest) and tour packages to Tazumal. (☎443 0774 or 443 0775. Doubles US$25. Disco US$4 cover for non-guests. Restaurant open 10am-8pm. English spoken. AmEx/MC/V.) **Hotel San José ❷,** on 6 C. between 2 Av. and Av. Comercial, on the south side of Parque Menéndez, has comfortable rooms with clean sheets, fans, and baths. (☎413 1908. Singles US$9; doubles US$15.) For affordable luxury, try **Hotel Casa Blanca ❹,** 2 Av., C. Barrios. Spotless rooms set around a courtyard have ceiling fans, gorgeous hot-water baths, TV (US$2.50 per day), and telephones. (☎443 1505; fax 443 1503. Singles US$16, with A/C US$23; doubles US$26/32. AmEx/MC/V.)

Visit one of the town's ancient homes, the "Villa Carmen," for a meal at **Restaurante La Estancia ❷,** on 1 Av., 1 C. and C. Barrios. (☎443 1559. US$3-$4. Open M-Sa 8am-6pm.) **Mixta's ❶,** half a block north of Parque Concordia on 2 Av., 1/3 Calles, has the best *licuados* in town (US$1). Try a *mixta* (US$1.50), pita bread stuffed with meat and a secret sauce (open daily 9am-8pm). Next door to Casa Grande, **Restaurante Casa Grande ❷,** serves inexpensive meals (US$3-$9). Another tasty snack is a *tostada* (US$0.30), your choice of guacamole, beans, cheese, and salsa on a crispy tortilla, made on Sunday afternoons in Parque La Concordia.

SIGHTS. The **Parroquia de Nuestra Señora de La Asunción,** in front of Parque La Concordia, dominates the southern part of the town with its huge dome. The facade of this 18th-century church was recently redone, with an exquisite stained-glass window that complements the marble altar and traditional tiled floor. (Open daily 6am-6pm. Free.) **Iglesia El Calvario,** on the west side of Parque Menéndez, is a rather plain church built in the 1950s, notable for the beautifully carved image of Christ on the altar. Damaged by the 2001 earthquakes, it is undergoing renovations which may limit tourist access.

Follow 8 C. from the northern side of Parque Menéndez 1.5km west to Las Chinamas, to see the still intact gate to the 16th-century Spanish town. About 4km outside of town in the same direction are the **ausoles,** geysers of steam and boiling mud. The nine wells are from 800-2000m deep and eject steam which is captured to generate electricity.

LAS CHINAMAS: BORDER WITH GUATEMALA

Buses and minibuses head to Ahuachapán (#263 and #11; 30min., every 15min. 5:20am-8pm, US$0.50-0.60). For San Salvador change in Ahuachapán or try to get on one of the international Pullmans. Across the border in Guatemala, buses leave for Guatemala City (3hr., every hr. 4am-6pm, Q30 or US$6).

A 30min. bus ride north of Ahuachapán, Las Chinamas is the busiest of El Salvador's borders with Guatemala. Called Valle Nuevo on the Guatemalan side, this is the most direct route between San Salvador and Guatemala City. The post is open 24hr. At the border, you can find **comedores,** a **Telecom** office (open daily 7am-7pm), and a last-resort *hospedaje* in the yellow house up the hill (US$5). **Money changers** abound on both sides and will change any Central American currency.

SANTA ANA

Santa Ana (pop. 169,900), El Salvador's second largest city, modestly calls itself the "Queen of the West," and rightly so given its rich culture. The neo-gothic cathedral, luxurious theater, colonial-style town hall, and many churches make the architecture of Santa Ana the best in the country. The fertile volcanic soil is ideal for agriculture and the plethora of coffee plantations have made this area one of the richest in the nation. Wide, clean streets sharply contrast to the chaotic and dirty San Salvador. A number of easily reachable interesting sites include Parque Nacional Cerro Verde, Volcanos Izalco and Santa Ana, the ruins of Tazumal, and Lago de Coatepeque.

⊏ TRANSPORTATION

Intercity Buses:

Main terminal is close to the *mercado*, between 10 and 14 Av. Sur and 13 and 15 C. Pte. Mind that buses drop off on 14 Av. Sur, but departures are on 10 Av. Sur. Buses run to: **Ahuachapán** (#210, 1hr., every 15min. 4am-7pm, US$0.65); **Metapán** (#235, 1½hr., every 15min. 4am-6:20pm, US$0.65); **San Cristóbal** (#236, 1hr., every 15min. 5:30am-7:30pm, US$0.35); **San Lorenzo** (#277, 2hr., every 15min. 6:25am-6pm, US$0.50); **San Salvador** (#201, 2hr., every 10min. 4am-6pm; US$0.75; luxury route 1hr., US$1); and **Sonsonate** (#216, 1½hr., every 15min. 5am-6pm, US$0.65).

Santa Ana

🏠 ACCOMMODATIONS
Hotel El Viajero, **1**
Hotel Livingston, **9**
Motel La Casita, **2**
Motel La Libertad, **3**

🍴 FOOD
Café Fiesta, **8**
El Molino, **12**
Los Horcones, **5**
Lover's Steak House, **13**
Pastelería Ban Ban, **6, 7**
Pip's Carymar, **11**
Restaurante Ky'Jau, **4**
Tiffany Pastelería, **10**

EL SALVADOR

Transportes La Vencedora runs buses from its terminal at 11 C. Pte. and Av. Fray Felipe, a block west of Parque Colón. Buses run to: Cerro Verde (#248, 1¾hr., M-Th 5 per day 8:40am-3:30pm, US$0.74; F-Su 7:40pm US$0.79); El Congo (#201 or #209 connect with #248 to Cerro Verde); and Guatemala City (About every hr. 5am-5:15pm, US$7; last bus US$10).

Local Buses: Slow but useful local route will take you outside the center. The #51 is the main north-south route, although it does a lot of east-west travel as well, passing a block south of the cathedral and eventually heading to the Metrocentro on the southern edge of town. The #55 is the main east-west route, passing 1 block south of the cathedral and then to the hospital on the city's eastern edge. Both routes have various sub-routes, marked by letters which only increase the confusion. Most indicate their main stops on the front. Both buses pass near the bus terminal and run 6am-8pm daily. Fare US$0.17.

Taxis: ☎441 1661. Cabs are clustered on the north side of Parque Libertad as well as behind the Alcaldía. US$2-$3 around town. If you are outside the centro at night you'll have to call one.

ORIENTATION AND PRACTICAL INFORMATION

Santa Ana's grid makes the city easy to navigate. The intersection of **Avenida Independencia** and **Calle Libertad** marks the grid's center. *Avenidas* west of C. Libertad are labeled *poniente* and east of C. Libertad are labeled *oriente*. South of Av. Independencia *calles* are odd-numbered and named *sur*; north of Av. Independencia they are even-numbered and named *norte*.

Tourist Information: City maps are sold at the teatro's (p. 288) lobby office (US$1.75). Open M-F 8am-noon and 2-5pm, Sa 8am-noon.

Banks: Banco Comercio, on C. Libertad at 2 Av., has an ATM and will change traveler's checks (AmEx/MC/V). Open M-F 9am-5pm, Sa 9am-noon. Branch at Av. Delgado, 5/7 Calles. Open M-F 9am-5pm.

Market: One market is between 1 and 3 C. Pte. and 4 and 8 Avenida Sur. Another is between 13/15 C. Pte., and 12/14Av. Sur. Both are open during daylight hours.

Mall: Super-modern Metrocentro, at the end of Av. Independencia, is accessible by taxi and bus #51. Multiple ATMs accept AmEx/Cirrus/Plus. Movie theater in mall (US$3), Super Selectos grocery store, Cyber Cafe, and food court.

Supermarket: Super Selectos has a location just behind the Alcaldía, 2 Av. and 2 C. Ote, as well as a larger store on Av. Frey Felipe and 11 C. Ote. Open M-Sa 8am-9:30pm, Su 8am-8pm. AmEx/MC/V.

Hospital: 13 Av. Sur, 3 C. Oriente (☎447 4124). Open 24hr. for emergency.

Pharmacy: Farmacia Moderna (☎447 2126, 441 3468), 3 C. Pte. and Av. Independencia. Open M-Sa 8am-7pm, Su 8am-noon.

Telephones: Telecom, on C. Libertad Ote. between 7/9 Av. Open daily 7am-7pm. Optica Cosmos (☎441 0939), C. Libertad just before Telecom Office, is the only place in town where you can send international faxes. Open M-F 8am-noon, 2pm-6pm; Sa 8am-noon, 2pm-4pm.

Internet: Ciber Café (☎/fax 441 2035), on the corner of 2 Av. Sur and 2 C. Pte. US$0.50 per 30min. Another Internet cafe is on C. Libertad between 3 and 5 Av. US$0.75 per hr.

Post Office: (☎441 0084), on Av. Independencia between 7 and 9 C. Express mail services available. Open M-F 7am-5pm, Sa 8am-noon. DHL (☎441 0686), Av. Independencia, 3/5 Calles. Open M-Sa 8am-12:30pm and 1:30-6pm.

ACCOMMODATIONS

In Santa Ana there are many motels that offer comfortable budget accommodations, as long as you don't mind "working girls" occasionally checking in with their clients for a couple of hours. If you don't want to listen to your neighbor and his "friend," you'll have to pay a little extra for nicer hotels.

Hotel Livingston, 10 Av., 7/9 C. (☎441 1801). Very clean and secure, many doctors and other professionals stay here when in town for meetings. Rooms with fan, private bath, and TV. *Let's Go* discount: singles US$14; doubles US$18. English spoken. AmEx/MC/V. ❹

Motel La Casita, 3/5 Av. Nte., 4 C. Ote. (☎441 1039). Cozy rooms with fan, private baths, and TV vary in size. Singles US$12; doubles US$15. English spoken. ❸

Motel La Libertad, 1/3 Av. Nte., 4Calle Ote. (☎441 2358). Though perhaps in need of some renovation, the rooms here are big with fan, private bath, and TV. Singles US$12; doubles US$20; triples US$24. ❹

Hotel Posada Real (☎440 4767), Urb. Loma Linda #43, in a residential area near the city's new southern commercial zone. Rooms with A/C, private bath, and TV; laundry and parking available. Singles US$23; doubles US$46. ❺

Hotel El Viajero (☎441 1090), 4 blocks north of the Alcaldía on 10 C. Pte. between Av. 4 and Av. 6. Has spacious, clean rooms with cable TV. 1-2 people US$12. ❸

FOOD

Many cafes and bakeries line C. Libertad between Parque Libertad and Parque Menéndez, as well as Av. Independencia south of Parque Libertad. The nicest restaurants cluster in the new neighborhoods and on the outskirts of the city. As usual, pupuserias and street vendors are not hard to find.

Lover's Steak House, 4 Av. Sur, 17 C. Pte. (☎440 5717). The cozy, rustic ambiance is ideal for romantic or family dinners. A wide selection includes meats (steaks US$8-$12), seafood, Chinese, Italian, and traditional food. An appetizer comes with every beer you order. Open M-Th 11:30am-10pm, F-Sa 11:30am-11:30pm, Su 11:30am-9pm. AmEx/MC/V. ❹

El Molino (☎447 0204) on Carretera Antigua, at the end of 25 Av. Sur., accessible by taxi or bus #51. The locals' favorite place for a drink before a night out, this restaurant is a laid-back alternative to the weekend clubbing scene. Nice atmosphere with impeccable service. Meals US$6-$18. Live music on F. The dance floor is full F-Sa. Open Tu-Su 10am-midnight, F-Sa 10am-2am. AmEx/MC/V. ❹

Pastelería Ban Ban (☎447 1865) has several locations around the city, including one near the *parque* on the corner of Av. Independencia and C. Libertad; and another on Av. Independencia between C. Libertad and 1 C. Ote. Ideal for breakfast, it has the best coffee in town (US$1.25) and a selection of sumptuous pastries (US$0.33-0.80). The soda-pastry-sandwich combo (US$2.45-2.75) can't be beat for a quick lunch. Open daily 8am-7pm. ❶

Los Horcones (☎447 2038), on the east side of Parque Libertad, close to the cathedral. The upstairs dining area offers views of the cathedral's facade. Meats US$2-$10 and seafood US$10. Open daily 10:30am-10pm. AmEx/MC/V. ❸

Pip's Carymar, Av. Independencia, 7/9 C. (☎441 3935 or 448 0506), is a happening place with a large menu. Known for making typical Salvadoran food just right, the place has great service too. *Pupusas* of all types US$0.88, pastries US$0.33-1. Open daily 8am-9pm. ❶

Tiffany Pastelería, Av. Independencia, 7/9 C. (☎441 2852), serves a wide selection of pastries and inexpensive lunches with traditional food (chicken US$2). Open daily 9am-7pm. ❶

Café Fiesta, (☎441 1871) 1 C. Oriente, Av. Independencia and 1 Av. Sur, is one of the many cafes available in town with a simple and spacious setting. Meals US$1.50, *pupusas* US$0.30. Open M-Sa 7am-10pm, Su 2pm-10pm. ❶

Restaurante Ky'Jau, 4/6 Av. Sur, C. Libertad. Locals flock here for good Chinese food and cheap lunch combos (US$2-$3). Breakfast menu has a selection of *típico* items to mix-and-match. Open daily 9am-9pm. ❶

👁 SIGHTS

CATHEDRAL. Located directly on Parque Libertad, this is one of the most impressive neo-Gothic cathedrals in the area. Built in 1905, it is a testament to the once-great aspirations of local coffee magnates. The church's design sought to unite Gothic elegance and Byzantine strength: the imposing interior holds statues dating from the 16th century. *(Open daily 6am-6pm. Free.)*

TEATRO NACIONAL DE SANTA ANA. The impressive renaissance-style theater on the north side of the *parque* was begun in 1902. In an attempt to reverse the deterioration caused during its stint as a movie theater from 1933 to 1986, the long restoration project is now close to its completion. See "Planeta Alternativa" in the Thursday edition of the *Prensa Gráfica* or the free English magazine *Revue* for event listings. *(☎447 6268 or 448 1094. Open M-F 8-noon and 2-6pm, Sa 8am-noon.)*

PALACIO MUNICIPAL. The city government building is another example of the grandiose architecture popular here in the early 20th century. The courtyard in the middle centers on a nice fountain. *(On the west side of Parque Libertad. Open M-F 8am-noon and 2-5pm, Sa 8am-noon. Free.)*

MUSEO REGIONAL DEL OCCIDENTE. Upstairs, exhibits dedicated to aspects of indigenous pre-Hispanic cultures change every few months. Downstairs in the old bank vault, the history of Salvadoran money is on permanent display—from the the Spanish real, through the various editions of the *colón*. *(Located in the old Federal Reserve Bank. Open Tu-Sa 9am-noon and 1:30-5pm, US$0.35.)*

IGLESIA EL CARMEN. Two palm trees frame the one-bell tower that looks like it's straight out of a Hollywood movie. The church itself is small, but sparkling bright and perfect for pictures. *(On 7 C. Oriente between Av. Independencia and 3 Av. Sur. Open during daylight hours and religious celebrations. Free.)*

CASINO SANTA ANA. This beautifully maintained structure with shiny wooden floors operates as an elite social and business club. *(On the corner across from the theater and the Palacio Municipal. Closed to the public, but check at the office for upcoming events. Peek in the window for a free glimpse.)*

🏔 OUTDOOR ACTIVITIES

PARQUE NACIONAL CERRO VERDE AND AROUND

Buses leave Santa Ana for Cerro Verde daily (#248, 1¾hr., 8:40am-3:30pm, US$0.70), dropping off at a small building where you have to pay US$1 to continue walking up to Cerro Verde. In Santa Ana, the #248 bus leaves from La Vencedora terminal. Info on the park is available at the San Salvador ISTU office (☎222 8000). The park has recently re-opened and is now very well organized for tourists. Written explanations in English describe the attractions and numerous guides lead visitors to the different sites (unaccompanied walks to any site are forbidden). Trips to the Santa Ana and Izalco volcanoes leave at 11am. The park information desk is open daily 8am-5pm (☎873 3594).

EL SALVADOR

From the El Congo junction, 15km southeast of Santa Ana, a road heads to Cerro Verde, a long-extinct 2030m volcano that has recently been transformed into a national park. The road that reaches all the way to the crater makes the park one of the most accessible in the country.

There are three main trails within Cerro Verde. **Una Ventana a la Naturaleza** ("A Window on Nature") is a 45min. walk looping around the Cerro Verde crater. Two lookout platforms present impressive views of Volcán Santa Ana and Lago Coatepeque respectively. Several signs in both Spanish and English explain different aspects of the forest life. **El Orquediario** ("The Orchid Path") is a 30min. trail among 37 different orchid species; the best times for this hike are December to January and April to May when most of the flowers are blossoming. **Caminata a l'Hotel** ("Walk to the Hotel") is a 15min. walk to the Hotel de Montana, which offers an outstanding view of Volcán Izalco.

Nearby, Volcán Santa Ana and Volcán Izalco are still active. The three volcanoes in such close proximity to one another provide a fascinating lesson in volcanic development and aging. Rich vegetation covers Cerro Verde, the oldest, while Izalco, the youngest, remains almost entirely composed of rough volcanic rock. Santa Ana lies in the middle, with both plant life and volcanic stone. Hiking the three volcanoes affords three very different and exhilarating experiences.

⚑ VOLCÁN SANTA ANA. With its last eruption in 1904, Volcán Santa Ana (2365m) is a young though not very active volcano. The clearly marked trail departs from the Ventana a la Naturaleza trail about 100m after the *mirador* toward the volcano. It heads 200m down to a farm, behind which a narrow path leads up to the volcano. The trail is a creek bed so you will have to navigate among the rocks. As you reach the top, an enormous abyss unfolds: 500m deep and 1km in diameter, the crater is filled with grayish water and spews out clouds of sulfuric vapor. The highest point of the volcano is on the opposite side. Circling around, views of Volcán Izalco, the coast, Apaneca, Santa Ana, Lago, and finally Cerro Verde open in front of you. This volcano, while forested at its base, is mostly bare rock and volcanic sediment by the time you reach the top. The ascent is mildly strenuous (about 3hr. round trip from Cerro Verde, plus another 1½hr. if you want to walk around the rim).

⚑ VOLCÁN IZALCO. The trail to Volcán Izalco is just a few meters above the bus drop-off from Santa Ana. For an idea of what the other volcanoes looked like in their infancy, and to complete a three-stage

tour of volcanic evolution, head to Volcán Izalco, one of the youngest volcanoes in the world. Legend says it formed on Feb. 23, 1770 and kept erupting without interruption for 183 years, giving it the name of "The Lighthouse of the Pacific." The hike is the most dramatic and intense in the park, with barren cone rising up to the southwest of Cerro Verde. A marked path leads off the road just before the Cerro Verde parking lot, starting off on a 1km descent through the forest to the base of Izalco. The ascent begins from there, and involves strenuous rock climbing at times. For other stretches you struggle for footing among the loose, tumbling rocks. The view of the coast and the contrast between barren lava and lush forests make the trip more than worth it. Steam and sulfuric gas force their way up through holes in the rock. The descent is terrifying at first, but can be fun if you learn the technique and let yourself go: dig in your heels with toes up, lean back and slide. The entire trek to and from Cerro Verde requires 4hr. and sturdy shoes.

▶ DAYTRIPS FROM SANTA ANA

CHALCHUAPA AND TAZUMAL

Chalchuapa and Tazumal can be reached by the bus running between Santa Ana and Ahuachapán (#210; 20min. from Santa Ana, 40min. from Ahuachapán; every 15min. 4am-7pm; US$0.20). There is also a bus running from Santa Ana to Chalchuapa; catch it at Parque Colón (#218, 20min., every 10min. 5am-6pm, US$0.20). The bus leaves you at the cemetery on the southern edge of Chalchuapa. Walk straight toward the gas station about 500m, turn left at the welcome sign and walk 2min. to the entry gate. Site open Tu-Su 9am-4:30pm. US$3, guides US$3-$4.

The Maya ruins of Tazumal are 13km west of Santa Ana, on the outskirts of the town of Chalchuapa. Tazumal is just one of a series of sites in the larger area, which marks the southeastern border of the ancient Maya civilization. Though the most important ruins in El Salvador, they don't compare to their counterparts in neighboring countries in size or in quality of restoration. The buildings preserved at Tazumal were the ceremonial center of a settlement that once covered more than 10 sq. km. The design of the imposing 24m **step-pyramid** has been linked to the step-pyramids of Teotihuacan in Mexico. Midway up the pyramid is a reconstructed altar. On the far side of the pyramid is the **ballcourt,** and to the right of the ballcourt is **Structure 2,** a temple dedicated to the god Quetzalcoatl. The **museum,** on the left as you enter the site, displays an impressive collection of pottery from the site as well as reconstructions of the original city. The most important discovery here, the **Stela de Tazumal,** is in the Museo Nacional in San Salvador. It portrays a human figure believed to represent the Tlaloc's wife, the goddess of water.

The town of **Chalchuapa** supports active commerce and agriculture but has retained a certain charm. Strolling through the residential side streets you'll see some old cobblestone streets plus examples of Spanish architecture adorned by bushes and flowering trees. The **Iglesia Santiago Apostal,** located 7 blocks west of the small park on the main road, merits a stop.

LAGO DE COATEPEQUE

Bus #220 leaves from the terminal in Santa Ana and heads for the lake (45min., every 25min., US$0.30). Coming from San Salvador, catch the #201 toward Santa Ana and get off in El Congo, where you can catch the #220 for the 5km down to the lakeshore. After descending to the level of the lakeshore, buses make a sharp left turn and follow a dirt road along the northeast shore of the lake past private estates, a few hotels and restaurants, and a few public beach access points before turning around and heading back. All the lakeside spots on this strip are within walking distance of each other. The often-full last bus to Santa Ana leaves at 5:25pm.

Roughly 16km from Santa Ana and 5km from El Congo, Lago de Coatepeque, formed by an ancient volcanic crater and surrounded by lush slopes, is easily accessible. The lake attracts San Salvadoran weekend visitors, who justifiably claim that it is among the most beautiful lakes in Central America. Although much of the prime real estate here is occupied, there are still places where you can stop and soak up the scenery. Public beaches are generally smaller and dirtier than beaches at the hotels, where non-guests can usually get in for a small fee or by buying a meal or a drink. The lake is great for swimming, and boats and jet-skis are available for rent.

The **Amacuilco Guesthouse ❷**, a 10min. ride from where the buses turn on to the lake road, has accommodations and a restaurant, as well as canoe rental and trips to nearby volcanoes. The beach section is narrow but adequate, and there is also a small pool. Both are open to non-guests for US$1 or the purchase of a meal at the restaurant. (☎441 0608. Dorms US$6; private rooms US$15.) **Hotel Torremolinos ❹**, a well-kept hotel, has two pools, a beach, boat rental, and a restaurant. (☎447 9515. Beach and pool access free with purchase of meal or drink. Su live music 2-5pm, US$1. 30min. boat rides, US$1 per person up to 10. Restaurant open daily 8am-8pm. Rooms US$15.) There are two *comedores* on the lake road beyond Hotel Torremolinos. Restaurant **El Mirador ❶** provides tables with an extraordinary view of the lake as you descend into the crater (beer US$1.30).

METAPÁN

Metapán (pop.18,100), 45km north of Santa Ana, sits in splendid isolation in the mountains of northwest El Salvador. Treacherous mountain passes didn't save the town from the worst of the civil war, but Metapán survived largely due to its fiercely independent spirit. Ranching is the main livelihood, and older *vaqueros* still mosey into town on horseback. Serenely lording over the town below is the cloud-ensconced Cerro de Montecristo. At the top of this hill, the borders of El Salvador, Honduras, and Guatemala converge in the midst of a cloud forest known as El Trifinio, part of Parque Nacional de Montecristo.

▐ TRANSPORTATION. Buses leave from the terminal on the main highway, between C. El Tamarindo and 2 C. Oriente, and head to: **Citalá**, a hop, skip, and a jump from the Honduran border at **El Poy** (#463; 3½hr.; 5am at the terminal; noon, 2:30pm from 2 C., 2 blocks west of the terminal); the Guatemalan border at **Anguiatú** (#211A, 30min., every 30min. 5am-4:30pm, US$0.30); **Santa Ana** (#235, 1½hr., every 15min. 4am-6:15pm, US$0.60); and **San Salvador** (#201A, 5 per day 4am-12:25pm, US$1).

▐▐ ▐ ORIENTATION AND PRACTICAL INFORMATION. The road to Metapán comes in from the south and passes the eastern border of the town before heading north to the Guatemalan border. The bulk of the town is on **Calle 15 de Septiembre** and **2 Calle**, which run parallel to each other, perpendicular to the highway, and lead downhill 5 blocks to the *parque central*. If you have just crossed the border and need to change money, head to **Intercambio**, on C. 15 de Septiembre. (☎442 0048. Open M-F 8am-noon and 2-5pm, Sa 8am-noon.) **Banco Comercio**, 4 blocks west from the terminal down C. 15 de Septiembre on 2 Av., gives cash advances on Visa and has an **ATM** (open M-F 8am-4:30pm, Sa 8am-noon). Seven blocks from the bus terminal down C. 15 de Septiembre and half a block north on Av. Benjamín E. Valiente you'll find the **municipal police station**. (☎442 0013. Open 24hr.) The **hospital** is on the highway heading south to Santa Ana. (☎442 0184. Open 24hr. for emergencies.) A number of **markets** are across from the bus station and **Supermarket De Todo** is next to Hotel San José on the highway (open daily 7:30am-7pm). **Farmacia**

San Pedro, 1½ blocks toward the highway from the park opposite the town hall, is available in emergencies. (☎442 0251. Open daily 7am-6pm, call 24hr.) **Telecom** is on 2 C., a block toward the terminal from the post office, and **Internet** is available at **Infocentros,** behind the city hall off the *parque central* (open daily 8am-6pm, US$1 per hr.). The **post office** is on 2 C., 3½ blocks west of the terminal (open M-F 8am-noon and 2-5pm, Sa 8am-noon).

ACCOMMODATIONS AND FOOD. Hotel California ❷ has plenty of room, a green patio, and pristine rooms with bath and fan. To get there, walk out from the bus terminal; facing the town, turn right on the highway and walk about 500m; the hotel is on the left just before the ESSO station. (☎442 0561. Singles US$7; doubles US$9.) **Hospedaje El Paso** ❷, 1½ blocks south of 2 C. and a block west of the bus terminal, has spacious rooms near the center of town. The shared baths are immaculate, and there's a small roof-deck with impressive views of the surrounding mountains. (☎402 1781. Singles US$7; doubles US$9.) A slightly more upscale option is **Hotel Christina** ❸, located between Calles 2 and 15 de Septiembre on 6 Av., 2 blocks west of the terminal. All rooms in this friendly hotel have fans, hot bath, and telephones. The top-floor rooms center around a roof terrace with chaise longues. (☎442 0044. US$11.50 per person.)

There are many *comedores* and *pupuserías* around 2 and 4 Av., all serving cheap, tasty breakfast and lunch for US$1-$3. **Chickenbell** ❶, located 1½ blocks west on 2 C., might have a fast-food feel, but the service is typical Salvadoran. (Chicken piece, 2 for US$1.30; pancakes US$0.40. Open daily 7am-9pm.) A standout for quality and price is **Tropy Jugos** ❶, on 2 C., 4 blocks west of the highway. Huge, super-fresh fruit drinks (US$0.80-$1); try a sandwich or burger with a small side dish for US$1.50-2. (Open daily 7:30am-8pm.)

SIGHTS. Metapán's **church,** la Iglesia de San Pedro, located in front of the park between 1 and 3 C. Poniente, dates to 1743. Restored in 1963, the church has a vaulted ceiling, elaborate golden side altars, and **catacombs,** one of which is easily accessible via a wooden trap door in the tiled floor of the center aisle. To tour the catacombs, stop by after 9am during the week and ask for Carlos, the caretaker, who can show you around by candlelight as he explains the church's history in Spanish. During the last week of June, the church is decorated with flowers for the nine-day **Festival de San Pedro,** celebrating the town's patron saint. The days of processions, music, carnival, and an acclaimed rodeo conclude joyously with a closing parade, complete with fireworks and marching bands.

LAGO DE GÜIJA. To the south of Metapán, the tranquil **Lago de Güija** sits on the border between El Salvador and Guatemala. While not as scenic as some of El Salvador's other lakes, Güija is much less crowded; the only people you're likely to see are local men and women fishing while their children play in the shallows. The lake's principal attractions are **Las Figuras,** a series of faded pre-Columbian rock carvings on the boulders lining the lake's small peninsula. Though the most impressive and well-preserved carvings now sit in museums, there are still many interesting carvings of snails, men, and indecipherable designs. Like an archaeologist, you can view the carvings up close and personal, touching the ancient art and hunting for new designs. Don't be fooled by the clever forgeries: the peace sign carved into one of the rocks is probably not pre-Columbian. If you look closely, you may notice some obsidian fragments, pieces of tools, or pottery along the shore. The walk out to the point along Cerro de las Figuras' west shore is a pleasant 30min. stroll encompassing all of the major carvings, as well as views across the lake to Guatemala. *Lanchas* are usually available for lake tours. A couple of houses advertise rentals, but gouge you at US$15 per hr. Try local fishermen, who should take you around for about US$5-$7 per hr. The last bus passes Desagüe around 6pm. *(Take bus #235 south toward Santa Ana and ask to get off at Desagüe, an unmarked but well-known village about 20min. south of Metapán, US$0.30. Walk about 100m along a dirt road, bearing right at the fork. Follow the railroad tracks across the bridge on the left and then leave the tracks and continue on the trail as it slopes to the right. You will pass through a small village before coming to the lake.)*

PARQUE NACIONAL MONTECRISTO

The cloudforest reserve Parque Nacional Montecristo covers the northwestern corner of El Salvador and sprawls across the border into Honduras and Guatemala. The three countries converge at **Trifinio**, which is on **Montecristo**, the park's highest peak. The park protects an amazing variety of wildlife—quetzals, guans, agoutis, porcupines, and anteaters, to name a few. The 2hr. hike to the spectacular uppermost part of the park gives you the opportunity to hop from El Salvador to Guatemala to Honduras without having to pay off border guards. During breeding season, from May to October, the higher areas of the park are closed. Hiking through the cloudforest rewards travelers with glimpses of sprawling forests and diverse wildlife. Get a permit in San Salvador if you plan on camping.

☐ TRANSPORTATION. Getting to the park is a more difficult task than the hiking once you get there. Vehicles are a necessity, but the park does not provide them. **Pickup trucks** leave Metapán around 7am, but go only as far as the Casco Colonial Visitors Center, 3km past the *caseta* entrance gate (US$0.40). The Los Planes area of the park is 12km farther up the road, and is accessible only by vehicle. The best way to cover the rocky road is to hire a pickup. Hang out at the corner next to the Hotel San José in the morning and ask around. A round-trip, including waiting while you hike, should cost no more than US$40-$45. Next-day pick up should cost about US$70-$80. Be prepared to bargain. As always, use common sense and follow your instincts when choosing a ride.

▦ ▟ ORIENTATION AND PRACTICAL INFORMATION. From Metapán, a painfully treacherous dirt road climbs 20km to the main tourist area of the park at **Los Planes.** Beginning in Metapán, the road to the park branches right from the highway at Hotel San José and continues 4km along a dirt road to the park's entrance at the **Caseta de Información.** Visitors need to pay the US$5 fee plus US$1 per vehicle. From the Caseta, the road winds 3.5km to the **visitor center,** known as the **Casco Colonial.** At the foot of Trifinio, 12km past the Casco Colonial, the **Los Planes** visitors area has campgrounds, picnic areas, and bathrooms. A number of well-maintained trails depart from the two visitor areas, heading to waterfalls, viewpoints, and rivers. The **Caseta de Información** is staffed 24hr., but entry hours are generally 7am to 3pm; if you want to camp for the night, you must arrive before 3pm. Camping is allowed only in the Los Planes campgrounds, and permits are required if you plan to spend the night. A **permit** must be obtained at the Ministerio de Agricultura, Servicio de Parques Nacionales in San Salvador (see **San Salvador: Special Permits,** p. 247). If you plan to visit just for the day and arrive without a permit, the guards will let you pay the entrance fee and continue on. You will have to pay the entrance fee for your driver as well. Officials at the *caseta* will radio ahead and arrange for a guide to meet you at the Casco Colonial or Los Planes (free, but tips are appreciated). Guides are required for hiking in these areas, but they only speak Spanish.

▟ CAMPING. Los Planes is the only location within the park where camping is allowed. Camping expenses are included in the entrance fee. The three campgrounds at Los Planes are well equipped with bathrooms and running water, as well as plenty of trails through secondary pine and cypress forest. Camping areas

#2 and 3 are smaller and more tranquil. Warm clothes are essential to fight off nighttime cold. There are a couple of small **stores** run by locals where you can restock on camping supplies. Each day in the park is US$5.

🖼 🚶 **CASCO COLONIAL VISITORS CENTER.** The well-preserved *hacienda* Casco Colonial is surrounded by beautiful flowers and lined with cobblestone streets. The interpretative center in the back explains the history of the park, gives the cultural background of its inhabitants, and provides information on animal specimens found within the park. From the visitors center there are also two short trails: the first, **Sendero de Curiosidades de la Naturaleza,** is a 20min. stroll that begins in front of the buildings; the other, **Sendero de los Pioneros,** is a slightly more interesting 35min. hike through secondary forest that leads to a 15m high lookout tower and the remains of a 1992 plane crash. To reach the second trail, go over the footbridge near the visitors center and continue a few minutes on the dirt road until you see signs for the *sendero.* Smaller paths wind behind the center around the stream trickling by. *(Open daily 8am-3pm. US$0.70.)*

🚶 **TRAILS FROM THE MAIN ROAD.** Along the road up to Los Planes, ask your guide to direct the driver to nearby sights that you can get out and explore. At km 12 a road forks off and continues 1km to a 17m high *mirador* known as **Desvío de la Torre,** which provides impressive views of the surrounding jungle. The tower is manned by a *vigilante* keeping his eyes peeled for forest fires. There is another **mirador** at km 13, with views of a beautiful waterfall, and one at km 15 looking over Metapán and the Lago de Güija. Around km 19, there is a dirt road which forks left and continues 7km up to **Trifinio.** This trail is a rewarding and intense hike, but the trail leading to Trifinio from Los Planes is a more convenient starting point.

🚶 **TRAILS FROM LOS PLANES.** Twenty kilometers along the main road (after 1½hr. of driving) you will come to Los Planes. Once there, find **El Jardín de Cien Años,** with trails winding through a well-kept garden of orchids and tall ferns. There is an educational center where each of the 74 species of orchids is labeled.

Several winding trails leave from Los Planes. **Sendero Maravillas y Procesos de la Madre Naturaleza,** a 45min. loop leaving from the soccer field at the campgrounds, passes a striking *mirador.* Another trail, **Sendero El Río Hondurano,** starting from camping area #2, continues for 1hr. before it ends outside the park at a pleasant swimming area on a river. While none of these hikes are spectacular, if you head out around dusk and stay quiet you're bound to come across plenty of animals. The trail heading up to Trifinio leaves from the road next to the *jardín.* The trail climbs from 1850m above sea level to 2418m over the course of 7km and should take under 2hr. Guides should accompany you.

EASTERN EL SALVADOR

The region most severely devastated by the civil war, Eastern El Salvador is still recovering from its days as the FMLN stronghold. Economic recovery is well on its way, even though the government still tends to favor the less rebellious West. San Miguel, with its long and rich history, is the biggest city in the "Wild East" and an ideal transportation hub to most sites. Perquín's Museo de la Revolución Salvadoreña and La Ruta de la Paz shock and humble visitors through stark and powerful civil war testaments. The eastern beaches west of the Golfo de Fonseca are rather underdeveloped in terms of tourist facilities, but some of them, especially El Espino, are among the most beautiful in Central America. Finally, do not forget to stop by Ilobasco on your way east; their ceramics are internationally renowned.

ILOBASCO

This world-famous ceramics center (pop. 80,000) is a must-see. Visitors watch artisans craft beautiful (and cheap) pieces before their eyes. The town's spacious cobblestone streets and gorgeous *parque central* are ideal for peaceful strolls.

█ TRANSPORTATION. Buses officially depart 2 blocks north of the *parque*, on 7 C., 2/4 Av., but it's easiest to wait at marked bus stops along Av. Bonilla. Bus #111 departs for **San Salvador** (1½hr., every 10min. 3:45am-6pm, US$1) via **Cojutepeque** (30min., US$0.40), and bus #530 goes to **San Vicente** (50min.; 5:45, 7, 9am, noon, 2, 4pm; US$0.60). The #111 or a **pickup** will give you a lift to the Interamerican Hwy. (20min., US$0.30) where you can catch eastbound buses to **San Miguel.**

█ █ ORIENTATION AND PRACTICAL INFORMATION. The usual Salvadoran grid centers on the intersection of **Av. Carlos Bonilla/Calle de la Cerámica** and **Calle Bernardo Perdomo/Enrique Hoyos,** 1 block east and 1 block south of the *parque central.* Buses enter towns from the south passing through C. de la Cerámica. El Triangulo, where El Monumento del Alfarero is located, is on C. de la Cerámica 2 blocks down the main intersection.
   Banco Salvadoreño (☎332 2321), on C. Perdomo between 1 and 3 Av. Nte., changes traveler's checks (open M-F 8am-4.30pm, Sat 8am-noon); it also has an **ATM** for international cards. A **Western Union** is located in the International Courier (see below). There is **Supermercado de Todo** (☎332 2574), on the corner of 2 Av. Nte. and 1 C. (open daily 7am-7pm). The 24 hr. **Hospital** (☎384 3209, 24hr.) is on 4 C., 9 blocks from C. de la Cerámica. **Farmacia El Aguila** (☎332 2032, 24hr.), on 2 Av. Nte. in front of the *parque*, is open daily 7am-6pm. **Telecom** (☎332 2345), opposite Supermercado de Todo, is open M-Sa 8am-6pm. Access the **Internet** at **Internet Colomba's Café** (☎384 4203. US$1 per hr. Open M-F, Su 8am-6pm.) The **post office** (☎384 3077), on 2 Av. Nte. close to the *farmacia,* is open M-F 8am-noon, 2-5pm; Sa 8am-noon. **Postal code:** 1402. For urgent service go to **Urgente Express International Courier** (☎332 2581), on Av. Bonilla between 2 C. Pte. and Av. Perdomo. (Open 7:30am-5pm, US$23 for express service to the US.)

█ █ ACCOMMODATIONS AND FOOD. Ilobasco's best, and only, option for accommodations is the well-maintained and friendly **Hotel Ilobasco ❶**, on 4 C. Ote. between 5 and 7 Av. Sur. Fifteen spacious rooms are clean with baths, big TVs, and fans. Laundry service available. (☎332 2563. Singles US$6, with bath US$12; doubles US$11/$20; triples US$18.) **Ricky's Restaurant ❷**, (☎384 4860), Av. Bonilla, 2/4 Calles, has New York Yankees memorabilia on the walls that matches well with the rustic, cool ambience. The menu includes *carne asada* for US$3.75 and *lomito de res* for US$4 (open Tu-Su noon-3pm and 6-8:30pm).

█ █ SIGHTS AND CRAFTS. Ilobasco's ceramics are internationally renowned and represent the town's main economic activity. However, the tradition is not so old: it started in the 1940s when a few families started making painted small figures out of clay. Most artisan shops are concentrated on **█Calle de la Cerámica.** Window-shop around and try to bargain before buying anything; you will get an idea of what the fair price for each item is (and if you multiply by three you will get the price in San Salvador). Typical prices include: 50cm tall figures US$8-$10, 25cm figures US$4, small houses to hang on the wall US$6-$10, big vases US$10-$14, and tiny animals US$0.50. Look out for the famous *sorpresas* (US$0.80-$1), egg-shaped containers that open up to show a small figure carved in the finest details. They are of two types: *profesionales* representing various professions, and *picas* depicting kama sutra-like erotic scenes. Most shops are open daily 8am-

5pm. The ■**Casa Artesanal** of the **Association Moje** (☎/fax: 384 4770; jota22002@yahoo.com), on the intersection of 4 C. with C. de la Cerámica, deserves particular mention because all crafts are made by troubled youth who benefit from the education and supportive environment provided by the organization. The **Monumento del Alfarero**, at El Triangulo, further reaffirms the importance of ceramics for Ilobasco; it pictures a pair of hands embracing a globe with the following words inscribed: "Dios fue el primero alfarero y el hombre primer cacharro" ("God was the first artisan, and man the first craft").

Take a break in the grassy *parque central*, blanketed with flowers and shaded by trees. The **Catedral de San Miguel**, on the east side of the *parque*, dates from the 1730s and doesn't hide its age; renovations are progressing slowly (open Tu-Su 6am-6pm). **La Iglesia de los Desamparados**, 3 blocks east of the cathedral, is home to the famous statue of the **Virgen de los Desamparados**, an icon jealously venerated by locals but visible to tourists on weekends (open daily 6am-5pm).

SAN VICENTE

Located in one of the most beautiful valleys in the country, the Torre Vicentina, the coffee plantations on the surrounding hills and the double peak of Volcán Chichontepec make up the stunning panorama that is San Vicente (pop. 80,000). The relaxing town makes a pleasant stop on the way east, with many traditional restaurants. Hikers will definitely enjoy the view from atop Volcán Chichontepec.

▐ TRANSPORTATION. The **bus station** is on the corner of 15 Av. and 6 C., but you can wait for all outgoing buses on 2 Av. in front of the *parque* and get off from all incoming on Av. Cornejo in front of the *parque*. Buses go to: **Ilobasco** (#530; 50min.; 6, 7, 9, 11:30am, 2, 4:30pm; US$0.50); **San Salvador** (#116, 1½hr., every 10min. 4:30am-7pm, US$0.70); **Santa Clara** and **Laguna de Apastepeque** (#156A, 1½hr., every 30min., 6am-5pm, US$0.60); and **Zacatecoluca** (#177; 50min., every 15min. 4:30am-6:15pm, US$0.50). Any bus and a regular pickup service will whisk you up the *desvio* where the buses to **San Miguel** (#301) and other points east and west pass regularly. Buses to **Tepetitán** (#191; 30min., every 30min. 5:45am-6:30pm, US$0.30) leave from C. Osorio at 9 Av., 5 blocks west of the *parque*.

▐▐ ORIENTATION AND PRACTICAL INFORMATION. The usual Salvadoran grid radiates from the intersection of Av. Miranda/Cornejo with C. Alvaro Quiñonez/1 de Julio 1823, 1 block south of the southwest corner of the *parque*. Standing at this crossing, facing the direction of the *parque:* increasing odd-numbered *avenidas* are to the left, increasing even-numbered to the right, *sur* behind, *norte* in front; increasing even-numbered calles are behind you, increasing odd-numbered in front, *oriente* to the left, *poniente* to the right.

Banco Salvadoreño, on 1 C. Ote. between 1 and 3 Av. Sur, changes traveler's checks (open M-F 8:30am-1pm, 1.45-5pm; Sa 8:30am-noon). **Banco del Hipotecario,** on Av. Cornejo just off the *parque*, also has a **Western Union** (open M-F 8:30am-4:30pm, Sa 8:30am-noon). There is no ATM for non-national cards in town. On 1 Av. Nte. just off 1 C. Ote., is a **Supermercado De Todo** (open daily 7am-7pm). The 24hr. **Hospital Santa Gertrudis** (☎ 393 0267, open 24hr.) is on 2 Av. Sur between 4 and 6 C. Ote. **Farmacia Santa Clara** (☎ 393 0025), in front of the *parque*, is open daily 6am-6pm. A 24hr. The **police** station (☎ 399 3800) is on the corner of 1 Av. Nte. and 3 C. Ote. Facing Supermercado de Todo is a **Telecom.** (☎ 393 5228. Open M-F 8am-6pm, Sa 8am-noon.) **Internet Cafes** line 4 C. Ote. between 1 Av. Sur and Av. Miranda; **Cyber World** (☎ 393 6194; open M-Sa 8:30am-9pm; US$0.75 per hr.) and **Cyber Space** (open daily 8am-10pm; US$1 per hr.) are two options. The **Post Office** is in a *casita* on C. 1 de Julio between 2 Av. Sur and Av. Cornejo. (☎ 393 2413. Open M-F 8am-5pm, Sat 8am-noon.) **Postal Code:** 1701.

▐▌ ACCOMMODATIONS AND FOOD. Hotel y Restaurante Central Park ❷, facing the *parque*, has clean rooms and a terrace with beautiful views of the *parque*. Amenities include: fan, phone, private bath, and TV. Restaurant offers *comida a la vista* (☎393 0383. Breakfast US$0.35, served daily from 6:30am-9pm. Singles US$10, with A/C US$12; doubles US$12/$18; triples US$20/$30.) **Casa de Huéspedes El Turista ❶**, 1/3 A. Sur, 4 C., has a bare concrete courtyard but spacious rooms with bath, fans, hammocks, and TV. (☎393 0323. Singles US$8, with bath US$10; doubles/triples US$15. English spoken.)

No fancy restaurants here, but many nice and inexpensive options. The best *comida a la vista* in town is at **▨Comedor Rivoly ❶**, on 1 Av. Sur between 2 and 4 C. Pte., which offers cheap meals (US$1-$2) and *licuados* (US$1) in a spacious and well-kept dining area surrounded by a garden setting. (☎393 0492. Open daily 7am-4pm.) **Restaurant "Casa Blanca" ❸**, on 2 C. between 2 and 4 Av. Sur, has hanging plants all over that make it look like a jungle and a fake mini-facade of a house at the entrance. Typical Salvadoran cuisine (*carnes* US$5-$7, fish US$4-$8). Nearby swimming pool is US$1/person. The bar plays music in the evening. (☎393 0549. Open daily 11am-8:30pm.) **Restaurante y Pastelería Betania ❶**, 3 Av. Sur, 1/3 C. Ote., with colorful tablecloths is ideal for breakfast (US$1.50), or a quick lunch (*pollo/carne/pescado* US$1.75, burrito, taco, soda combo US$3). (☎393 0712. Open M-Sa 5:30am-8:30pm.)

▟ VOLCÁN CHICHONTEPEC. Nahuat for "mountain of two breasts," the name obviously comes from the two peaks, one cone-shaped and the other flat, rising 2,200m to form the volcano. To get there, walk for about 2hr. along the stone road that begins 2 blocks north of the *parque*. You will pass the **Finca Camón**, one of the best plantations in the country, owned by former President Cristiani, signer of the 1992 Peace Accords. Where the stone road begins to descend, a dirt road branches uphill. Because of an earthquake, the final stretch of this road is rocky and uneven. One hour more will bring you at last to the military helicopter deck, where the army staff will happily let you recover as you soak in the panorama that encompasses the Pacific Coast, San Salvador, and the Honduran border. The whole trip takes 7-8hr., so start early—afternoons often bring rain. Large groups should have no safety problems; groups of less than three should contact the police in San Vicente in advance to arrange for a guide. One of the most interesting parts of the hike, however, doesn't require going up to the top: *los infernillos*, the hot springs, surrounded by sulfuric smoke, make you doubt that the volcano is as dead as people claim. (*The "easiest" approach begins in Tepetitán at the base of the volcano reachable by bus #191 from C. Osorio at 9 Av. 30min., every 30min., 5:45am-6:30pm, US$0.30.*)

▟ LAGUNA DE APASTEPEQUE. About 10km northeast of San Vicente, on the other side of the Interamerican Hwy., is Laguna de Apastepeque, a small, quiet lake with corn and sugarcane fields descending to its shore. Take a swim, watch the locals fish, or stroll around the lake enjoying the view of Volcán Chichontepec. **Turicentro Apastepeque** is on the other side of the lake from the bus stop. To get there, walk along the lake shore for about 10min. This is the smallest turicentro in the country, but one of the cleanest and most pleasant. The lake is 100m deep in the center and there are no life guards; beware if you decide to take a swim. The on-site restaurant overlooking the water serves burgers (US$1.15), chicken (US$2.30), and beers (US$0.68). **Restaurant Casa Blanca ❶** has nice gardens and plenty of hammocks for *siestas*. (*Take the bus heading for Santa Clara from the east side of the parque central, stops at the laguna. #156A or #156; 30min., every 20min. 6am-5pm, US$0.30. You'll see the laguna and a yellow sign for the Turicentro Apastepeque on the left. Descend to the level of the lake and take the road along the lake shore for a more scenic walk. The last bus back passes at 5pm. Turicentro open daily 8am-5pm. US$1/person; cabaña US$5.*)

EL SALVADOR

SANTIAGO DE MARÍA

Resting in the saddle between two mountains and enveloped in thick, moist clouds, Santiago de María (pop. 25,000) is a coffee town with easy access to spectacular hikes. The Laguna de Alegriá, an emerald-green volcanic circular lake with the village of Alegriá on its shores, is quickly becoming one of the main tourist attractions in the East. Cerro El Tigre and Cerro Oromontique are just two of many hiking options around Santiago; you can basically walk in any direction outside of town and there will be a hike waiting for you.

■ TRANSPORTATION. From the bus terminal, **buses** leave for **San Salvador** (#302; 2hr.; 4, 4:30, 5am, 1:10, 2:45pm; US$1) and **San Miguel** (#323; 3hr., every hr. 5am-3:30pm, US$1). It is easier to head to **Villa El Triunfo**, at the intersection of the *Interamericana* and the road to Santiago, and catch one of the frequent **#301** buses running between San Salvador and San Miguel. To get to Villa El Triunfo, wait at the intersection of Av. M Gonzalez (extension of Av. 15 de Septiembre) and 2 C. for bus #349 to **Usulutan** or #359 (20min., every 15min. 4:30am-5:30pm, US$0.30). Bus **#348** goes to the nearby towns of **Alegría** (15min., $0.30) and **Berlín** (30min., US$0.45) and leaves every 30min. from the bus terminal (6am-4pm daily).

■ ■ ORIENTATION AND PRACTICAL INFORMATION. The intersection of Av. Mariscal Gonzalez/15 de Septiembre and C. Mansferrer/Bolivar for the center of the grid, 1 block west of the *parque's* northwest corner. The **church** is on the east side of the *parque*, and **Cerro El Tigre** looms behind it farther to the east. The town's makeshift **bus terminal** is at the triangular *parque* south of 4 C. between 3 Av. and Av. 15 de Septiembre, a block south and a block west of the main square.

Banco Salvadoreño, on the south end of the square, cashes traveler's checks and does Visa cash advances. (Open M-F 8:30am-5pm, Sa 8:30am-noon.) The 24hr. **police** (☎ 663 0063), at their office on 6 Av., 2/4 C., should be contacted in advance for hikes to El Cerro. **Telecom** (☎ 663 4378) is in front of the *parque*, open M-Sa 7:30am-7:30pm, Sun 8am-noon). **Internet access** is available at **Infocentros**, Av. 15 de Septiembre, 2/4 C. (US$1.15 per hr. Open M-Sa 8am-6pm, Su 9am-5pm.) The **post office** is at 4 C. Pte., 5 Av. Sur. (Open M-F 8am-4pm, Sa 8am-noon.)

■ ■ ACCOMMODATIONS AND FOOD. Hotel de Montaña Posada Marques ❸, 1 Av. Nte., 3 C. Pte., is your best option with a nice courtyard and free parking. Rooms have bath, fan, and TV. (☎ 663 1682; laposadadelMarqués@hotmail.com. Singles US$10; doubles US$18.) A less expensive option is **Hotel Villahermosa** ❷, on 3 Av. Nte. between C. Mansferrer and 1 C. Pte., with a big courtyard full of plants and couches. Rooms with fan and private bath. Parking available. Restaurant is open 7:30am-6pm. (☎ 660 0146. Singles US$8; doubles US$15.)

Comedores and *pupuserías* abound near the *parque*. A surprisingly cool place with excellent food, **Buffalo's** ❷, 1 block from the *parque* on Av. 15 de Septiembre, grills up various tasty meats (US$3-$6) in a relaxed outdoor setting with a bar and pool. **Restaurant La Cumbre** ❶, 2 Av. Nte., C. Mansferrer, serves delicious dishes at affordable prices (breakfast US$1.75, lunch/dinner US$2.50-$3.50).

■ SIGHTS. Just east of town, **Cerro El Tigre** first affords views of the town, nearby volcanoes, and the Río Lempa. Head east on 4 C. at the southeastern corner of town and follow a stone path over a small hill. You will pass through the gate of Finca El Tigre on the way up (1½-2hr.). Contact the police for safety information; often, they will send an officer with you. An easier hike is to **Cerro Oromontique**, less than 1km south of town; the flat top is ideal for picnics (3-4 hr.).

ALEGRIÁ AND THE LAGUNA

Make your way to the bus terminal at 3 Av. and 4 C. where bus #348 heads to Alegría (15min., every 30min. 6am-4pm, US$0.30). Just shy of Alegría are a few signs marking the cobblestone turnoff to the left that leads up to the Laguna de Alegría, a 35-45min. hike away through coffee fincas and impressive views. Open daily 8am-5pm. US$0.40.

A rewarding daytrip from Santiago leads to the Volcán de Tecapa, the deep green Laguna de Alegría that sits inside it, and the tiny village of Alegría. The green lagoon sits in a beautiful crater beneath the ridge of the Volcán. If you want the place all to yourself, stick around and **camp** for US$5 per person. Tell the caretaker when you arrive that you want to camp and he'll show you the latrine, fire pit, and best areas to pitch your tent. Swimming in the lagoon is not recommended, as it's quite shallow, and a surprising number of locals have drowned. Some attribute their deaths to a mermaid who lies in wait for handsome young men, others to glue-like sulfurwood lining the bottom—either way, park yourself on the sand. For a bird's-eye view of the *laguna* and a view of surrounding volcanoes and valleys, head up the ridge of the volcano. Just return to the *laguna* entrance and follow the road up to the ridge; a 1½hr. hike will bring you to the top.

The nearby village of **Alegría** is becoming a tourist mecca in the east of the country because of its traditional atmosphere and the amazing views. The **tourist office,** in front of the *parque central,* has plenty of info about the village and surrounding sites. (www.alegria.gob.sv. Open daily 8am-5pm.) Coming from the *laguna,* keep left on the way down the trail; once you hit the road, take a left onto it, and the town is just 5min. away. Alternatively, if you don't go to the *laguna,* the bus from Santiago will drop you off right at the *parque.* **La Fonda de Alegría Restaurant and Plant Nursery ❷**, on Av. Gólgota in Barrio El Calvario, hosts a very well-kept plant nursery and serves delicious typical food at affordable prices. (☎628 1010; fondadealegria@hotmail.com. Meals US$3-$7.) **Vivero & Restaurante Cartagena ❸**, on Final Barrio El Calvario, has an amazing panoramic view that you can enjoy in the midst of orchids and exotic plants. Inexpensive typical cuisine will certainly satisfy your appetite. (☎628 1131 or 789 7625. Dishes US$4-$6.)

You can climb the volcano from Alegriá, leaving from the southwest edge of town. It can be difficult to follow, however, so you may want to head to the **Centro de Desarrollo Cultural** (☎628 1038), next to the church, where **Narciso Marroquín** runs a guided service to the volcano, the *laguna,* and hikes to flower nurseries in the area (US$8-$15 per day depending on the hike).

SAN MIGUEL

With the self-ascribed nickname "Pearl of the East," it's pretty clear that San Miguel (pop. 300,000) yearns to match the "Queen of the West," Santa Ana, in prestige. While perhaps not as grand as Santa Ana, San Miguel is a city with a rich and troubled history, making it an interesting site to explore. After years as the epicenter of civil war, the city has undergone a remarkable economic boom, rebounding into a bustling commercial center. Just by walking through the frenetic central market you will see the resilience of this formerly war-torn city. In addition, nearby sights—such as **Volcán Chaparrastique,** the bird-filled **Laguna El Jocotal,** and the largely unexcavated Lenca site of **Quelepa**—combine with prime location to make San Miguel perfect for exploring the eastern part of the country.

▐ TRANSPORTATION

Buses: The most tourist-friendly **bus terminal** in El Salvador is on 6 C., 8/10 Av. Destinations include: the **Honduran Border at El Amatillo** (#330 continuing from Santa Rosa de Lima, 1½hr., 7:10am-5:30pm, US$1.50); **Jucuapa** (#338, 30min., every

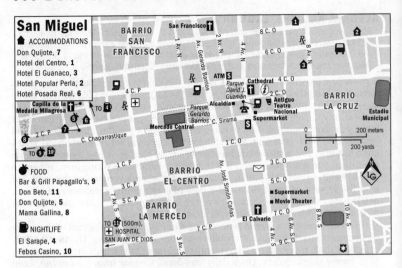

San Miguel

⌂ ACCOMMODATIONS
Don Quijote, **7**
Hotel del Centro, **1**
Hotel El Guanaco, **3**
Hotel Popular Perla, **2**
Hotel Posada Real, **6**

🍴 FOOD
Bar & Grill Papagallo's, **9**
Don Beto, **11**
Don Quijote, **5**
Mama Gallina, **8**

NIGHTLIFE
El Sarape, **4**
Febos Casino, **10**

15min., 5:40am-6:15pm, US$0.50); **Perquín** (#332 A/E via Torola, 2hr., every 1¼hr. 6:20am-3:20pm, US$2); **Playa El Cuco** (#320; 1½hr., every 30min. 5:25am-7pm, US$0.90); **Playa El Tamarindo** (#385, 2½hr., every 20min. 5am-5pm, US$1.50); **San Francisco Gotera** (#328, 1½hr., every 30min. 4:30am-6:10pm, US$0.60); **San Salvador** (#301, 3hr., every 15min. 3am-4:15pm, US$2.50; direct 2½hr.; 7, 8am, 3pm; US$3.50. Super 2½hr; every hr. 5-8am; US$5 with A/C, toilet, and TV); **Santa Rosa de Lima** (#330, 1hr., every 10min. 4:30am-6pm, US$1); **Torola** (#332 A/E, 3½ hr., every 1¼hr 6:20am-3:20pm, US$2); **La Unión** (#324, 1½hr., every 10min. 4:30am-6pm, US$1); and **Usulutan** (#373, 1½hr., every 10min. 4am-5:30pm, US$1).

Local Buses: City buses run 6am-7pm; fare US$0.17. Most buses stop at **Parque Guzmán**. The **#90f** is the most useful north-south route, running from the **University** to the **Metrocentro**, up to **Parque Guzmán**, then over to Av. Roosevelt and **El Triángulo**. In the city center, it runs south on 4 Av. and north on 2 Av. Bus **#88**, the most useful east-west route, passes close to the bus terminal, heading west on 4 C. past **Parque Guzmán** out to Av. Roosevelt, and then farther west to the **hospital**. The eastbound #88 runs along 2 C. before going to the **bus terminal** on 6 C. Both **#90b** and **#13** will get you from the city center down to the **Metrocentro** and back. **#94** leaves from the north side of Parque Guzmán and passes the **Turicentro** at **Altos de la Cueva**. **#90g** goes to **Quelepa**. Bus **#91** travels 3 Av. from Av. Roosevelt to the bus terminal.

Taxis: At **Metrocentro** on Av. Roosevelt, the west side of **Parque Guzmán**, El Triángulo, and near the **bus terminal** at 6 C. and 8 Av. Cabs run late. Within the city US$2-$4.

◢🛈 ORIENTATION AND PRACTICAL INFORMATION

The downtown area of San Miguel is bounded on the south and west by the **Interamerican Hwy.**, called **Av. Roosevelt** after it intersects with C. Chaparrastique, which enters from the south. It meets the **Ruta Militar** at the northwest corner of the city at a spot known as "**El Triángulo**" (Av. Roosevelt at 1 C.). The **city center** is in front of **Parque Gerardo Barrios** where **Calle Chaparrastique/Sirama** meets **Av. Gerardo Barrios/Cañas**. Av. Barrios goes north while Av. Cañas runs south; C. Sirama heads east while C. Chaparrastique goes west. **Metrocentro** is the name of the mall about 2km south of **Parque Guzmán**. Cabs are recommended after dark.

Casa de la Cultura, 2 C. Ote. # 200, has general **tourism info.** Traveler's checks and US dollars can be changed at **Banco de Comercio,** 2 Av., 4 C. Ote., on the northwest corner of Parque Guzmán, which also gives cash advances on Visa, and has an **ATM.** (☎660 2968. Open M-F 9am-5pm, Sa 9am-noon.) **Metrocentro** mall has ATMs and a Credomatic that changes traveler's checks. The **mercado central** starts at 1 Av., C. Chaparrastique and spreads out in many directions, swallowing up everything on the way. **Uno Rent-a-Car,** on Av. Roosevelt near 7 C. Pte., rents cars starting at US$50 per day. (☎211 2111. 25+. AmEx/MC/V.) The **Policía Nacional Civil,** 10 Av. Sur at 11 C. (☎661 2033), is in the Centro de Gobierno complex and the **Red Cross,** 10 C. Pte., #404 (☎661 1771) is available for medical assistance. **Farmacia Brasil** has one location on the corner of 4 C. Pte. and 5 Av. Nte. and a second on the corner of 6 C. Ote. and 8 Av. Nte. (☎661 6872 or 661 6280. Open M-Sa 7:30am-6pm. Second location open M-Sa 7am-10pm, Su 8am-noon.) **Hospital San Juan de Dios** (☎661 1425 or 661 1211), on the west end of town at 11 C. Pte., has 24 hr. emergency service. Take bus #88 from the center. Closer to the center of town is **Hospital Clínica San Francisco,** 4 C. Pte., 5 Av. Nte. (☎661 1991. Open 24hr.) **Telecom,** 4 Av., 2 C. (☎661 0814), by the southeast corner of Parque Guzmán, is open M-Sa 8am-6pm and Su 8am-noon. **Internet service** is at one of two **Infocentros,** 4 C., Av. 1/ Barrios and at 4 C. Pte. between 5 and 7 Av. Nte. (Open M-Sa 8am-6pm, Su 9am-5pm. US$1.15 per hr.) The **Post Office,** 4 Av., 3 C. (☎661 3709), is open M-F 7:30am-5pm, Sa 8am-noon.

🏠 ACCOMMODATIONS

While several upscale hotels line Av. Roosevelt to the west and south of the city, most of the more affordable and convenient options are within a few blocks of the bus terminal. For security reasons, you'll generally want to be in your hotel after dark, so it makes sense to choose a place where you won't mind spending a few hours. Be sure to pick a spot with a night watchman and a locking gate. *Let's Go* advises travelers to avoid the hotels lining 10 Av. and 4 Calles near the bus station.

📖 **Hotel Posada Real** (☎661 7174 or 661 7175), on the corner of 2 C. Pte. and 7 Av. Nte., is a solid option in a safe neighborhood. Impeccable service and cleanliness. Modern, comfortable rooms have A/C, phone, private bath, and TV. Parking and laundry service available. Singles US$24; doubles US$31; triples US$45. AmEx/MC/V. ❺

THE LOCAL STORY

SAN MIGUEL DE LA FRONTERA

Mauricio Herrera is a prominent figure in San Miguel. He explains the cultural differences between Eastern and Western El Salvador.

LG: What are the cultural origins of Eastern El Salvador?
A: We are descendants of the Lenca. They had no connection with the Maya and the Pipi, who occupied the regions that are now Central and Western El Salvador. Ethnically speaking, we should be *Hondureños* or *Nicaragüenses,* not *Salvadoreños.*
LG: What is being done to preserve this cultural difference?
A: Nothing. Even the people here don't know about it. At Casa de la Cultura in San Miguel there is now an exhibit about Joya de Cerén, a Maya site that has nothing to do with our region. At the same time, prominent Lenca archaeological sites are left unexcavated.
LG: Do you think this is a planned governmental policy?
A: Yes. They are afraid of a separatist movement, and therefore they have undermined the development of the education sector here to avoid the formation of a broad intellectual community.
LG: What is your dream for the future?
A: An autonomous state, under the sovereignty of El Salvador, named, as it once was, San Miguel de la Frontera. Nobody wants another war just the recognition of our cultural identity.

■ **Hotel El Guanaco** (☎ 661 8026), on 8 Av. Nte. between 4 and 6 C., is a welcoming colonial style building with spacious rooms. Restaurant open 7am-11pm. Rooms include A/C, fan, bath, and TV. Singles US$20; doubles US$30; triples US$40. ❺

Restaurante Don Quijote (see below) recently opened a guest house with a family-like environment. Special *Let's Go* discounts. A/C and TV. Breakfast included. English spoken. Knowledgeable Mauricio Herrera runs tours. Singles US$9; doubles US$14. ❸

Hotel del Centro (☎ 661 6913 or 661 5473), on 8 C. Ote. and 8 Av. Nte. Very clean and secure with big courtyard. 35 rooms with A/C, phone, private bath, and TV. Parking and laundry available. Singles US$12; doubles US$15; triples US$18. AmEx/MC/V. ❹

Hotel Popular Perla, 10 Av., 6 C. Ote. (☎ 661 4113). One of the friendliest hotels in town with cable TV, a deck, a lounge, and a restaurant. Front gate locks at 9:30pm. Single with fan and private bath US$11, with A/C US$15. ❸

🍴 FOOD

San Miguel boasts a variety of dining options ranging from international cuisine to typical Salvadoran food. Most, but not all, restaurants are on Av. Roosevelt. The *comedores* in the city center cluster around the Parque Guzmán and bus terminal, and fast food joints are highly visible downtown and in the Metrocentro mall.

■ **Restaurante Don Quijote,** 2 C. Pte., 7/9 Av. Nte. (☎ 661 2718), serves authentic Spanish cuisine and dishes that you won't find elsewhere in town. Decorated with a tasteful international flair. Breakfast US$2, sandwiches US$1.50-4, meals US$3-$12. Try the famous *jamón serrano* and the wide selection of international beers. The bar hosts upscale clientele. Open Tu-Su 7-10am, 11am-3pm, 5:30pm-midnight. ❸

■ **Restaurante Mama Gallina,** Av. Roosevelt, 2 C. Pte. (☎ 661 2021; mamagallina@elsalvador.com). Take bus #88 from the city center. Friendly and spacious filled with loyal customers on the weekends. The *licuados* are the best in the city (US$2), and the menu presents a variety of international dishes. Try the *gallina india* (US$4) and the *mariscos* dishes (US$10-$12). Open daily 11am-10pm. AmEx/MC/V. ❷

Restaurante Don Beto (☎ 661 6729), on Av. Roosevelt at 11 C. Take bus #88 from the city center. This Mexican-themed restaurant serves every imaginable dish in a tasteful decor. Tacos US$2.50-$3, burritos US$2.50-$3.50, *camarones* US$11-$12. Open daily 11am-10:30pm, F-Sa until 11pm. AmEx/MC/V. ❸

Bar and Grill Papagallo's (☎/fax 661 0400; papagallo@elsalvador.com), at Centro Comercial Plaza Chaparrastique #5 on Av. Roosevelt Sur. Spacious bar with billiards and a young weekend crowd. Menu has a huge selection of Mexican dishes (US$2-$5), meats (US$7-$11), and seafood (US$11-$15). Try the rib-eye (US$16). Live music W, mariachi Th, karaoke Tu-Th, disco Th-Sa. Open Tu-Su 11am-2am. AmEx/MC/V. ❹

🎲🎵 NIGHTLIFE AND ENTERTAINMENT

■ **El Sarape** (☎ 669 5904), on Av. Roosevelt Nte. in front of gas station at El Triangulo, is a prime spot for good music. If you're more into history than hotties, you'll be interested to know that FMLN and ARENA signed an important agreement here during the civil war. Karaoke W-Th and Su; F-Sa live international music. US$5 cover F-Sa.

Febos Casino (☎ 661 8274), on Plaza Chaparrastique # 4 on Av. Roosevelt Sur, is a good option on weekdays when discos are closed. Classic casino games in a fancy but friendly environment. Open 1pm-4am daily. AmEx/MC/V.

👁 🏔 SIGHTS AND OUTDOOR ACTIVITIES

Dominating San Miguel's center are the **Alcaldía,** on the south side of Parque Guzmán, and the **Catedral de Nuestra Señora de la Paz** on the *parque's* east side, whose domes are visible from nearly everywhere in the downtown area. The mock-colonial-style Alcaldía dates from 1935 and gives excellent rooftop views of the cathedral, volcano, and entire downtown area. Tourists are not allowed inside, but many sneak in or sweet-talk the guard. The Catedral de Nuestra Señora de la Paz has an 18th-century beige and white facade topped by a statue of Jesus spreading his arms out to the plaza below. Beautiful stained glass remains today in the ancient church. The statue of the Virgin Mary is claimed to have saved San Miguel from destruction by lava at the beginning of the century. A block east of the cathedral, on 2 C. at 6 Av., the **Teatro Nacional Francisco Gavidia,** built in 1903, is one of the most historic buildings in town, but the show schedule is often interrupted by renovations. Check at the office for show times. (☎ 661 9026. Open M-F 8am-noon and 2-5pm, Sa 8am-noon.) The **Capilla de la Medalla Milagrosa,** 7 Av., 4 C., is known throughout the country because the church formerly housed a hospital where miraculous healings were thought to come from a medal of the Virgin Mary. The entrance to the church is framed by a cobblestone path.

To escape the heat of the city, head out on bus #94 (from the north side of Parque Guzmán) to the *turicentro* at **Altos de la Cueva,** where you can cool off in four clean pools and join local kids on the waterslide. (Open daily 7am-5pm. US$1.) The most obvious challenge around town is the **Volcán Chaparrastique,** the 2100m volcano that looms over San Miguel from the southwest. You must first type a polite letter of request with your name and date of trip addressed to "Señor Jefe de la Delegación PNC San Miguel" and bring it to the Centro de Gobierno at least two days prior to departure. With this letter you can get a free guide. To get there, take bus #90D from 7 Av. and C. Chaparrastique to **Las Placitas,** where a road leads to the southern edge of town. It is about a 4hr. hike through coffee farms to the summit, from where you can continue into the crater.

🏃 DAYTRIPS FROM SAN MIGUEL

QUELEPA

From San Miguel, bus #90g heads to Quelepa from the west side of Parque Guzmán (20min., every 30min. 5am-6pm, US$0.30) and will drop you off right in front of the Casa de la Cultura on the south side of Quelepa's parque central. From there, the site is a 30min. walk (about 2km) northeast of town. If you can't get someone at the Casa de la Cultura to accompany you, head to the northeast corner of the parque (a block north of the Casa de la Cultura), turn right on 4 C., and follow it until you come to the Río San Esteban. Hop across the river on the rocks and stop to ask for directions at one of the houses on the right after you cross. The ruins are about a 15min. walk east through the fields, at the base of Cerro Tamboral, the largest of the mountains looming to the north.

A daytrip to the Lenca ruins at Quelepa is like a foreign-language film: you enjoy yourself, but most of the details go right over your head. Since most of the site has been left unexcavated, much of this large Lenca settlement is unfortunately still hidden from view. You'll need an active imagination or a Ph.D. to truly understand the ruins' significance, but you can still appreciate the relaxing walk through cow pastures and fields that now cover much of the original ceremonial center.

Dating back to about 400 BC, Quelepa was a flourishing Lenca settlement, peaking from the 7th to the 10th centuries. The pottery, sculpture, and other artifacts found on site indicate strong trade links to Maya settlements in Mexico and Honduras. Among the nearly 40 structures identified, the main ones are a paved road, several pyramids, and a buried ballcourt. The small village of Quelepa, about 2km southwest of the ruins, is pleasant and quiet, and the **Casa de la Cultura** in the town has a helpful and knowledgeable staff and guides at your disposal (open M-F 8am-noon and 2-5pm, Sa 8am-1pm).

LAGUNA EL JOCOTAL

From San Miguel, catch bus #373 to Usulután; tell the driver to let you off at the turnoff for the Cantón Borabollón at km132 (40min., every 10min. 4am-5:30pm, US$0.45). The lake is a safe 10min. walk through town to the left of the highway.

This lake is a "hub" for avian migratory routes, with over 250 bird species stopping here between November and April. To really appreciate the site you have to take a boat with a local fisherman (1 hr., US$4). If you have more time, visit one of the four islands in the laguna; La Monca is the best for bird-watching.

✈ EL AMATILLO: BORDER WITH HONDURAS

Along the Río Goascorán, the Honduran border at El Amatillo is crowded, dirty, and full of **money changers** who provide the only decent opportunity for exchanging currency. This border crossing can be time-consuming given the crowds, so it is advisable to travel on a luxury bus like TICA or TRANSNICA. From the Honduran side, **buses** depart to **Tegucigalpa** (4hr., every 30min. 4:30am-4:30pm, L30) and **Choluteca** (2¼hr., every 45min. 3:30am-5:45pm, L20). **Immigration** is open daily 6am-10pm. Buses leave Santa Rosa de Lima every 10 min. for the border. The **Telefónica** office has a **Western Union** (open daily 8am-5pm). On the Salvadoran side there is a **Telecom** office (open daily 7:30am-5pm), several *comedores*, and two hotels.

Motel Antony D'May ❺ practically has a monopoly on the town, which accounts for the high prices. (Doubles with A/C, bath, and TV $25.) **Motelito Dos Hermanos** ❸, can give you a good bed in case you get stuck here. (Doubles with fan $12.) Both hotels are up the hill from the border to the left. **Hotel Los Arcos** ❶, on the Honduran side, is a reasonable place to stay if for some reason you end up literally at the border for the night. (Singles L40; doubles L70.)

PERQUÍN

A tiny mountain town, Perquín (pop. 6000) uniquely combines an educational experience with a truly emotional one. Located in the northern region of Morazán (2½hr. from San Miguel) the peaceful village has a unique concern with preserving its tragic history for present and future generations. Perquín served as FMLN headquarters during the war, and the mountains surrounding the town saw some of the fiercest fighting, including the massacre of **El Mozote**. Every year on December 9th, the town comes together to remember the 1000 people killed by 800 US-trained Salvadoran troops. When the war ended, the town resolved to never forget its past, erecting the powerful **Museo de la Revolución Salvadoreña** and the monument at El Mozote. Perquín is one of six towns throughout the department in **La Ruta de la Paz,** which was created to celebrate local culture and the dawn of peace.

🚍 TRANSPORTATION. Buses and **pickups** arrive from the south and can drop you off at either of the lodging options south of town or at the *parque central*. Throughout the morning, bus #332-A/E departs San Miguel for **Torola,** passing through Perquín on the way. (2hr., every 1¼hr. 6:20am-3:20pm, US$1.) The easiest way to get there is to take a bus to **San Francisco Gotera** from San Miguel (#328, 1½hr., every 30min. 4:30am-6:10pm, US$0.60) and then from the *desvío* (detour) after the town, catch a pickup to Perquín. Coordinated by a collective, the pickup service is reliable. (1hr., every 30min. 5am-6pm, US$0.60.)

🔧🔢 ORIENTATION AND PRACTICAL INFORMATION. The following town services cluster around the *parque central*. The **church** sits up the hill on the eastern side of the *parque* with the **museum** 2 blocks uphill to the left. There is a **tourist office** next door to the **Casa de Cultura** that has plenty of information on hikes and excursions in the area. Special permits to El Río Sapo are issued here. (☎680 4086. Open M-Sa 8am-4:30pm.) The **police** are located near the northeast exit of town, a block north and a block east of the *parque*. (☎680 4040. Open 24hr.) **Farmacia Fuente de Vida** is right off the *parque* (☎680 4082. Open M-F, Su 6am-6pm.) The **Hospital Unidad de Salud** is below the cemetery down the hill along the highway. (☎680 4082. Open 24hr.) **Telecom** offers its standard service. (☎680 4111. Open M-F 8am-noon, 2-5pm; Sa 8am-noon, 2-4pm.) The **post office** is next door to La Casa de Cultura. (☎680 4019. Open M-Tu and Th-F 8am-noon and 1-4pm.)

🔣🔤 ACCOMMODATIONS AND FOOD. 🏨 **Perquín Lenca Hotel de Montaña ❺**, on the main road from San Miguel about 1km before town, cheers visitors with pastel colored cabañas. Breakfast is included at the restaurant, which also serves up a variety of local and international cuisine. Laundry service available. (☎680 4046; www.perkinlenca.com. Singles US$30; doubles US$37.50; triples US$47. Special 25% discount with *Let's Go;* group discounts.) A cheaper option is just 100m up the road at **Casa de Huespedes El Gigante ❷**. Spacious rooms come with a fan. The restaurant serves meals daily for US$5-$6. (☎680 4037. Doubles US$12.)

A variety of comedores can be found in town, especially around the *parque*. **Comedor Las Colinas ❶** (☎680 4044), in front of the *parque*, serves meals for an incredibly affordable US$2-$4. On the road to the museo, **Restaurante Palmeras ❶** has tasty local coffee. (☎680 4006. Chicken plate US$2. Open daily 6:30am-8pm.)

🔲 SIGHTS. The 🏛 **Museo de la Revolución Salvadoreña** vividly tells El Salvador's tragic military history. Events are told from the FMLN perspective, explaining their take on the causes of the war and the main struggles. Though information is only in Spanish, the language of the photos, weapons, and paraphernalia is universal. A visit will give every hill and village in the area new meaning as you learn of the guerrillas who died fighting here. For a fuller understanding of events, ask for Carlos, a former FMLN radio operator who is willing to give his first-hand account of the war. (US$1-$2 tip expected.)

The **Monumento El Mozote** is a permanent lesson from the past to the future. A metal sculpture silhouetting the members of a family—father, mother, daughter and son holding hands—is accompanied by the inscription "They did not die. They are with us, with you, and with all humanity." To walk to El Mozote from Perquín, follow the signs heading first to Alameda (20 min.), and then follow the main road for about an hour. If you prefer going by bus, catch the only ride at 8am from the junction about 1-2km down from Hotel Perquín Lenca (see above). A better option is to arrange a tour a day in advance at the tourist office in Perquín.

The areas around Perquín were once the epicenter of the country's 12 year civil war and it is fitting that they now form the **Ruta de la Paz**. In honor of the tranquillity of recent years, the pueblos of Perquín, Arambaia, Villa del Rosario, Joateca, Cacaopera, Corinto, and Guatajiagua invite tourists to come and see first-hand an area whose wounds are still too fresh to be called "history." Locals share their personal war stories in an attempt to keep the memories of lost loved ones alive, creating a uniquely raw, honest, and emotional cultural interaction. Public transportation from San Francisco Gotera or Perquín is quite irregular; go to the tourist office in Perquín to arrange a tour.

EL SALVADOR

◆ **HIKES.** Before heading to El Río Sapo, visitors need to stop at the **tourist office** (see above) for a special permit and a mandatory guide (US$15 per day). The two main hikes are **Secretos de la Naturaleza** (45min.) and **Manquilha del Bosque** (30min.) Camping facilities have shower, toilets and kitchens (US$5 per person). Adventurous enjoy the reserve's extreme sports.

▶ **DAYTRIPS FROM PERQUÍN.** Descendants of the Lenca and Ulua tribes, the inhabitants of **Cacaopera** proudly preserve their artistic, cultural, and folkloric traditions. The town is renowned for handmade cotton and hennequin hammocks, pottery, and sugarcane sweets. The **Museum Winakirika** highlights the artistic achievements of the town. (☎651 0251. Open Sa afternoon and all day Su.) A 1hr. walk from town leads to colorful hieroglyphics in **Cueva Unamá.** Find a guide and info at the tourist office in front of the *parque* (open M-Sa 8am-4:30pm). **Buses** leave San Francisco Gotera every 30min. until 4:30pm (US$0.50).

Guatajiagua is a small bean- and coffee-producing village once inhabited by the Lencas and Potonas. It is known for the manufacture of a unique style of black pottery colored with nacascol, a dye extracted from a special type of shell. Corinto, on the road to Cacaopera and just 11km east of Perquín, draws tourists to La Gruta del Espíritu Santo, a cave with petroglyphs that have been dated to the year 1000 BC. (Open Tu-Su 10am-4pm. Entrance US$1. Guides at tourist office in Perquín.)

EASTERN BEACHES

Along the southern edges of the departments of San Miguel and La Unión, the waves of the Pacific crash into wide-open white sand beaches. Travelers will have large areas of beach all to themselves, especially on weekdays. However, the lack of tourist traffic comes at a cost—accommodations are scarce and restaurants cater to local appetites. The best deserted beaches are hard to reach without a car, but you will definitely be rewarded if you make the trek.

Uninhabited by people, **Playa El Espino** is populated instead by swaying palm trees. One of the best beaches in Central America, getting here is quite a challenge. Any bus between San Miguel and Usulután drops off at the *desvío* to El Espino. (#351, 2hr., 7 per day 6am-2:40pm, US$0.60.) Get off at the highway juncture (1hr., US$0.35) where the road splits with **Arcos Del Espino** to the right and **Playa El Espino** to the left. Both have similar beaches but Arcos is more deserted. Playa El Espino has two *comedores* (lunch US$0.30-0.50).

Playa el Cuco is another gem on the eastern coast, with a gorgeous view of Volcán Chaparrastique and a wide beach that stretches on for kilometers. Unfortunately, the secret of Playa el Cuco is out, and on weekends it is almost impossible to find an empty plot of sand. On the up side, there are plenty of facilities and during the week it's not too crowded. **Buses** conveniently run from San Miguel (#320, 1½hr., every 30min. 5:25am-7pm, US$0.90) to the center of town, from where you can walk along any of the shop-lined roads to the beach. Small restaurants, all specializing in shellfish, cluster near the town.

The dreary town has a **police** station (☎619 0911), a **post office** (☎619 7645), and a **Telecom** office (☎619 6435) all located close to the central square. Better than the options off to the east, **El Rancho Escondido ❸,** on the western side of town along the ocean (follow signs), has spacious and clean rooms, a nice restaurant, a bar, and a great chunk of cliff-enclosed Pacific shoreline. (☎619 9017. Singles US$9; doubles US$12.) Two upscale options, **Hotel Leones Marinos ❹** (☎619 9015) and **Hotel Viña del Mar ❹** (☎619 9017), are 150m outside of town along the road parallel to the beach up from Palmeras. Both have large rooms with fan, hammock, and private bath. (Doubles US$29, with A/C US$40. Use of facilities US$2.)

One of the safest beaches for swimming, **Playa Icacal** stays shallow a good way out from shore. The beach is 8-10km from El Cuco to La Unión. Buses conveniently run from San Miguel (#385; 2½hr., every 20min. 5am-5pm, US$1.50). Travelers typically get off at the turnoff from the coastal highway and catch a ride to the beach, but *Let's Go* does not recommend hitchhiking. A few comedores dot the sand (lunch US$0.30-0.50).

The fishing village of **Playa Tamarindo** and its tranquil, often-deserted beach occupy the gently curving tip of the country's southeastern peninsula. The sheltered, calm waters are ideal for swimming. On the horizon, the mountainous islands in the **Golfo de Fonseca** stand silhouetted against the sun. Buses depart from the center of town, pass the length of the beach, **Playas Negras**, and **Playa Las Tunas** before connecting with the *carretera* and heading to **San Miguel** (#385; 2½hr., every 20min. 5am-5pm, US$1.50) and **La Unión** (#383; 1½hr., every hr. 4:30am-5pm, US$0.60). The town has a **post office** (☎ 649 1529) and a **Telecom** office (☎ 649 1129) located on the road along the coast. The **police** (☎ 649 0911) are stationed just south of town on the beach side. The **beach** is accessible from any hotel. Alternatively, walk down the right fork when the main road splits.

Tamarindo is not the cheapest place to stay. Try **Hotel Tropitamarindo** ❺, 2km along Tamarindo beach before town; follow the bus route. Big, white-tiled rooms with A/C, bath, and cable TV sleep up to four. The pool, picnic area, baths, and beach are US$8 for non-guests and the restaurant serves lunch and dinner (US$5-$15) in a slightly nicer atmosphere than its downtown competitors. (☎ 649 5082. Rooms US$65. MC/V.)

LA UNIÓN AND GOLFO DE FONSECA

The Golfo de Fonseca, with more than 30 islands, is bordered by the shores of Honduras, El Salvador, and Nicaragua. In accordance with a 1992 decision by the International Court of Justice, all three countries share control of the gulf. Once the most important seaport in El Salvador, La Unión (pop. 65,000) fell on hard times when the war forced the port to close. Recently, however, there has been a resurgence of activity and optimism. La Unión remains the best base from which to explore the beautiful eastern beaches or the many islands of the gulf.

TRANSPORTATION. There are two bus terminals. **Buses** leaving from the terminal on 3 C., Av. 4/6, go to: San Miguel (#324, 1½hr., every 10min. 4:15am-6pm, US$1); Santa Rosa de Lima (#342, 1½hr., every 30min. 4am-5:45pm, US$1); and San Salvador (#304, 4hr., every 30min. 3am-2:30pm, US$3). Two blocks south on C. San Carlos, Av. 4/6, you'll find a bus to Playa El Tamarindo (#383, 1½hr., every 20min. 4:30am-6:30pm, US$0.60), and Playitas (#418, 25min., every hr. 6am-5:30pm, US$0.20). **Boats** leave from the waterfront at 1/3 Av. to the islands of the gulf and to Potosí in Nicaragua (2-3hr.; very irregular schedule, check with immigration; US$10-$12 per person). It's a long wait unless you pay big bucks for a private trip (up to US$200-$250 to Nicaragua per boat).

ORIENTATION AND PRACTICAL INFORMATION. The bay borders the northern edge of town, and most streets run downhill to the north. Incoming **buses** enter from the west on 1 C. and pass by the *parque central*, largely hidden by the market. The church is east of the *parque*, and the main intersection, where C. General Menéndez/San Carlos meets Av. General Cabanas, is on its southwest corner. The standard *norte/sur* and *poniente/oriente* divisions, as well as the odd and even numbering system, hold true in La Unión.

SALVADORAN SNACKS

So you've been in El Salvador for a month and there's one question you can't get out of your head: "How am I ever going to justify spending more than $0.50 on a meal again?" If cheap eats have you hooked, you'll need to know how to cook these famous Salvadoran goodies—just in case your home town doesn't have a "Freddy's Fritura" on the corner.

Totopostes:

Ingredients: 4 cups of corn massa, 6 oz. of butter, 1 cup of cheese (corriente y quesillo).

Mix the cheeses until you have a uniform and soft mix. Mold the massa, butter, and cheese and mix together with your hands. Once you get a uniform mix, make balls and wrap them in aluminum foil. Bake at high temperatures for 10-15 min. until golden.

Horchata:

Ingredients: 4 teaspoons of rice, 2/3 of a glass of milk, sugar, nutmeg, cinnamon.

Cook the rice in a pan until golden. Be careful not to burn it. Grind the rice into powder and put it into a glass filled 2/3 with milk and 1/3 with water. Season to taste with nutmeg, cinnamon and sugar; your personal taste rules here. Serve with ice.

The **immigration office,** on Av. Cabañas at 5 C., knows the boat schedules. Get an exit stamp here if you're heading to Nicaragua (open daily 6am-8pm). **Banco Salvadoreño,** on Av. Cabañas at 3 C., changes traveler's checks, gives cash advances on Visa, has **Western Union** service, and an **ATM** (open M-F 8:30am-1pm, 1:45-4.30pm; Sa 8:30am-noon). The **mercado** branches off from the southeast corner of the *parque* and the **Despensa Familiar supermarket** is on the east side of the *parque* (open daily 7am-7pm). Round-the-clock emergency assistance is a short phone call away at the **police station** (☎604 0911), on 1 Av. Nte. between 3 and 5 C. Pte., and the **hospital** (☎604 4104), on 4 Av. Nte. close to the intersection with 1 C. Ote. **Telecom phone,** (☎604 2842) on 1 C. Ote., 5 Av. Nte is open daily 8am-7pm, Su 8am-noon, but you need to go to **Infocentros,** on 1 C. Ote. between 2 and 4 Av. Nte., has **Internet** service. (☎604 1950. US$1.15 per hr. Open M-F 8am-6pm, Sa 8am-noon.) The **post office** on Av. Cabañas, 3/5 Calles, occupies a basement office. (☎604 4002. Open M-F 7:30am-5:30pm, Sa 7:30am-noon.)

⚑ ACCOMMODATIONS. Some of the cheaper *hospedajes* rent rooms by the hour; opt for a nicer place instead. The best option in town is **Hotel Portobello ❶,** on the corner of 1 C. Pte. and 4 Av. Nte., which has a cool roof-top deck. Rooms come with fan, hammock, and TV. (☎604 4113. Doubles US$9, with A/C and bath US$20. Parking available.) Another good find is the spotless **Hotel San Francisco ❷,** on C. Menéndez, 9/11 Av. Spacious rooms with high ceilings have bath, fan, and hammock. Laundry service is available. (☎604 4159. Doubles US$12, with TV US$15, with A/C US$25; Triples US$18/$20/$35. English spoken.) **Hotel Centroamericano ❺,** on 4 C. Ote. between 1 and 3 Av. Sur, looks like a military garrison from the outside, but the security makes up for its lack of aesthetic appeal. (☎604 4029. Singles with A/C, bath, and TV US$19; doubles US$29; triples US$43.) Bargain-hunters head **Boarding House Night and Day ❶,** 11 Av. Sur, 2 C. Ote. (☎604 3006. Singles with bath, fan, and hammock US$5; doubles US$6.)

🍴 FOOD. 🖫Captain John's Seafood ❸, on the corner of 3 Av. Sur and 4 C. Ote., can't be missed. The delicious food is reasonably priced. (☎604 3013. Fish US$3-$8, Shrimp US$5-$15. Open daily 8am-midnight. AmEx/MC/V.) If you're in the mood for some Mexican food, try **Cafeteria y Comida a la Vista Restaurante Guadalajara ❶,** on the corner of 1 C. Ote. and 2 Av. Nte. (Nachos, tacos, burritos US$2.30. Open daily 6am-6pm.) With a view of the bay and a real safari setting, **Restaurante Miramar ❸,** on Final C. Ote. and the waterfront, has meals for US$5-$9. **El Marinero ❸**, on the corner of Av. Cabañas and 3 C., serves excellent seafood (☎604 4254. Meals US$3-$12, *mariscada* US$12. Open daily 6am-7pm.) For breakfast or a quick snack in a crisp A/C setting, head to **Pastelería Yoly ❶**, on 3 Av. Nte. close to 1 C. Pte, or a second location on 1 C. Ote. (☎604 1853; cakesyoly@navegante.com.sv. Open 7am-6pm.)

PLAYITAS. Immerse yourself in the bay and soak up the scenery at this little beach 25min. south of the city. Buses, 2 blocks south on C. San Carlos, Av. 4/6, regularly make the bumpy trip to the row of *comedores* (US$0.30-0.40) that line this gentle bend of sandy beach. (#418, 25min., every hr. 6am-5:30pm, US$0.20.)

🖪 **ISLANDS OF THE GULF.** The gulf islands **Isla Zacatillo, Isla Martia Pérez, Isla Conchagüita,** and **Isla Meanguerita** have deserted beaches and are accessible by **ferry** from La Unión. Most *lanchas* travel to and from the islands before 10am, with an afternoon trip to Zacatillo. **Comedor Montecristo** on the harbor has plenty of *lancha* information. A daytrip to any of the islands departs around 6am and returns around 3pm (US$80 per person, discounts for big groups; prices negotiable). Martia Pérez and Meanguerra are the most highly recommended beaches, and **El Mirador** (☎648 8072) on Meanguerita provides the option to stay the night.

Central America's Tortured Regional Relations

A cursory glance at Central America's history might lead one to view Central America's nations as mere replicas of one another: "banana republics" with similar economies, societies, and predatory political systems. In reality, diversity is a stronger theme: Panama was historically attached to Colombia and economically tied to the United States and world commerce; Belize is an Afro-Caribbean nation with a British Parliamentary system; Guatemala's Maya population is still strong; Honduras has a heritage of domination by its neighbors; and Nicaragua has suffered heavy internal conflict in addition to a series of US interventions stretching back to the mid-19th century.

All this contributes to a series of complicated love/hate relationships, reflecting both fears and inter-dependencies which the region's nations continue to grapple with. Following independence, the region, excluding Panama and Belize, was a single nation. However, soon after, local rivalries and foreign intrigues broke this up. Central Americans have tried to resurrect the union multiple times, creating a series of regional institutions, including a Common Market, a bank, a court and even a Parliament. However, they have fought over twice as many wars among themselves as have all of Latin America's other nations. Until the last decade, they constantly interfered in each other's politics, often supporting exile invasions. For example, Honduras has been a principal victim in conflicts as Guatemala, El Salvador, and Nicaragua strove for regional dominance.

Domestic politics in Guatemala, El Salvador, Nicaragua and, to a lesser extent, Honduras, have been violent and polarized. Militaries, originally armed partisans of political factions, became the ultimate arbiters of politics as they professionalized, ultimately benefiting their officers as the rest of their countrymen became increasingly poor. Fear of potential indigenous population political power led to even bloodier repression, notably in Guatemala and El Salvador.

As internal conflicts intensified, leaders often preferred foreign intervention rather than defeat at the hands of domestic opponents. At first the British, as well as the Americans, were candidates for this role, but by the 20th century the US was clearly dominant. The United and Standard Fruit Companies often played as important a role as the US government in determining the results of domestic and international conflicts. US interventions dominated the history of Nicaragua and Panama and a 1954 CIA-sponsored exile invasion of Guatemala shaped its conflicts for the rest of the century. Central American elites both blamed the US for many of their problems and looked to Washington for support and solutions. The attitude was summed up by an anonymous citizen who, following one US intervention, scrawled on a wall "Yankee go home and take me with you." Today it can be seen in both a fear of economic dominance and frantic efforts to conclude free trade agreements with Washington.

Organized gang control, often linked to counterparts in the United States, have become the dominant security issue. Their membership is estimated at well over 100,000 and they continue to grow. Even Salvadoran immigrants in the US say visits to their country today are more dangerous then they were at the height of the civil conflict in the 1980s. The winning candidate in the last Honduran presidential election gained much of his credibility because his son had been a victim of criminal violence, indicating that his fellow citizens strongly identify with this issue.

Central America has been transformed by its recent conflicts. On the positive side they destroyed the myth that violence was the path to progress and that interfering in a neighboring country could produce beneficial results. They gave Central America a network of international contacts and the immense resources of foreign remittances. Negative results include damage to economic infrastructures, problems of justice and reconciliation, weapons and land mines left behind, and a pattern of social decomposition that shows few signs of healing. The hate side of the love/hate relations between the nations has diminished, but internal politics remain polarized, especially in Guatemala, El Salvador, and Nicaragua. The love/hate relationship with the US is, if anything, even stronger today than it was in the past.

Richard Millett has published over 100 items, largely focusing on Latin America, in such professional journals as Foreign Policy, The New Republic, *and* The Wilson Quarterly, *and is the author of* Beyond Praetorianism: The Latin American Military in Transition. *He has also appeared on every major national television network. In 1993, Dr. Millett was Chair of Military Affairs at the U.S. Marine Corps University.*

GUATEMALA

In a region famous for startling contrasts, Guatemala contains both Central America's most diverse landscape and the most clear class division. Crisp mountain peaks, towering volcanic ridges, thick rainforest, and mellow Caribbean ports all coexist within Guatemala's borders. While possessing the strongest modern Maya presence in Central America (around 46% of the population), Guatemala is also highly urbanized, with over 40% of the population living in cities. Nevertheless, a two hour bus ride from the frenzy of Guatemala City transports you to the rolling western highlands where Maya women in colorful traditional garb weave *huipiles* on the volcanic shores of Lake Atitlán. In many highland villages, travelers will find that Spanish can take them only so far—each of Guatemala's 23 Maya groups has its own language. Take it from the swarms of returning travelers: Guatemala is *the* place for culturally adventurous budget travel in Latin America.

HIGHLIGHTS OF GUATEMALA

The pyramids of **Tikal,** one of the most awesome ancient sites in the world (p. 406).

Cobblestoned **Antigua,** one of Central America's beautiful Colonial towns (p. 333).

Sunday and Thursday markets in **Chichicastenango,** a lush cacophony of color, incense, and sound, with an unparalleled selection of indigenous artwork (p. 350).

The **Lago de Atitlán's** volcanoes and many indigenous villages, ranging from tourist meccas to the very traditional (p. 342).

A boat ride through the spectacular gorges of the **Río Dulce** (p. 387).

The remote mountain villages of **Nebaj** and **Todos Santos Cuchumatán,** where Maya tradition is strong and the scenery superb (p. 354 and p. 367).

SUGGESTED ITINERARIES

1 WEEK: LA RUTA GRINGA. Starting in **Guatemala City** (p. 323), catch a frequent bus to **Antigua** (p. 333), the colonial city known for its cobblestone streets, elegant ruins, ubiquity of English, and language schools. Nearby fun climbs await at **Volcán Agua** (p. 341) and **Volcán Pacaya** (p. 341). A hop, skip, and a 2½ hour jump away is the mythically important and unbelievably beautiful **Lago de Atitlán** (p. 342). Base yourself in convenient (if commercial) **Panajachel** (p. 342), and allot enough time to visit the other towns via boat—some people take years. If you yearn for the hustle of a market and the blood rush of a successful bargain, head to **Chichicastenango** (p. 350) for its world-renowned Thursday and Sunday market.

2-3 WEEKS: VERAPAZ HIGHLANDS, PETÉN, AND EASTERN GUATEMALA. Head first to **Cobán** (p. 389), a cosmopolitan center smack dab in a wilderness paradise. Using Cobán as your base camp, visit some of the nearby *fincas*, parks, and hiking trails, including the many sites accesible from **Chisec** (p. 395). Traversing north, head to **Sayaché** (p. 399) in the **Petén** region. Like Cobán, Sayaché is a great home base from which you can explore nearby **Ceibal** (p. 400), Maya ruins that are accessible by boat or pickup, and the ruins around **Lake Petexbatún** (p. 400). From Say-

Guatemala

GUATEMALA

Petén
pp. 398–412

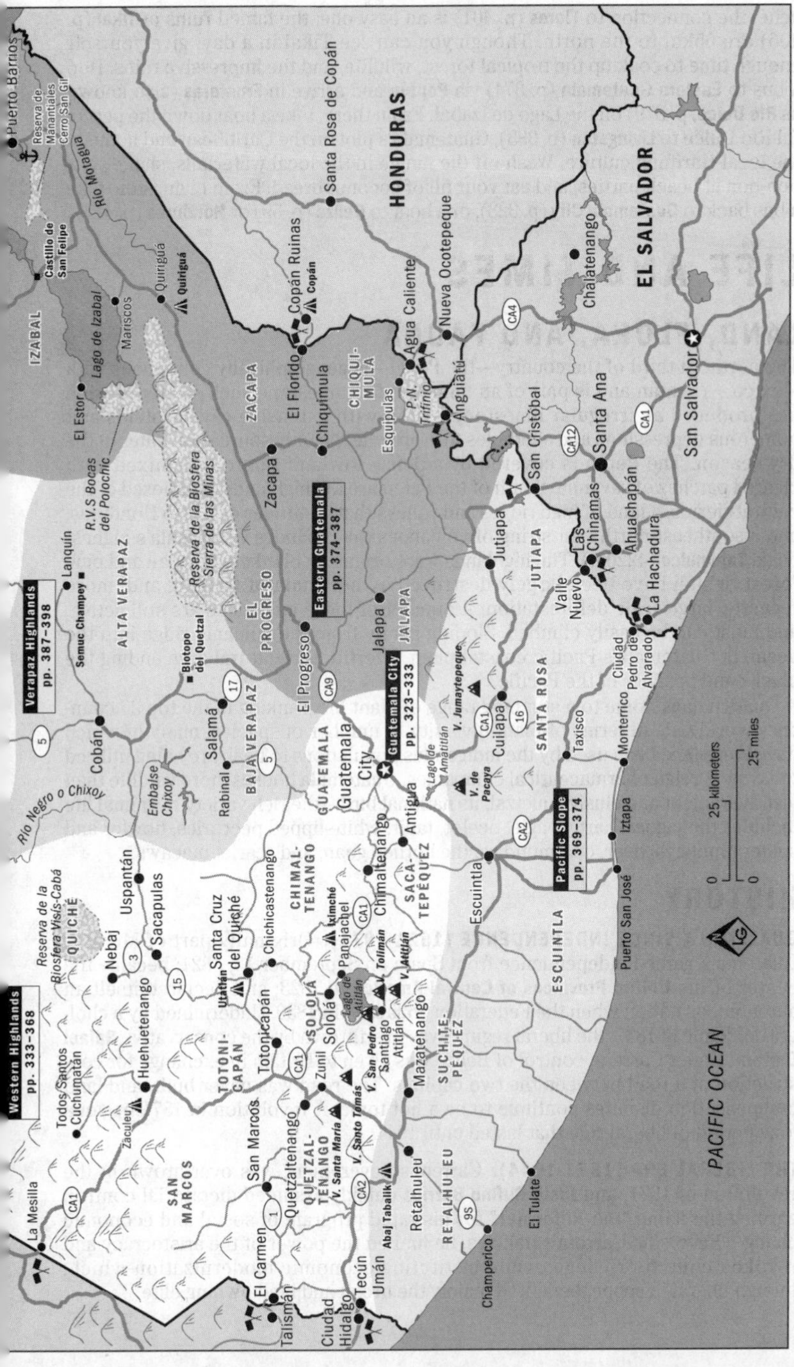
Western Highlands
pp. 333–368
Verapaz Highlands
pp. 387–398
Eastern Guatemala
pp. 374–387
Guatemala City
pp. 323–333
Pacific Slope
pp. 369–374
HONDURAS
EL SALVADOR
PACIFIC OCEAN
QUICHÉ
ALTA VERAPAZ
BAJA VERAPAZ
IZABAL
ZACAPA
EL PROGRESO
CHIQUI-MULA
JALAPA
JUTIAPA
SANTA ROSA
ESCUINTLA
GUATEMALA
CHIMAL-TENANGO
SACA-TEPÉQUEZ
SOLOLÁ
TOTONI-CAPÁN
QUETZAL-TENANGO
SAN MARCOS
RETALHULEU
SUCHITE-PÉQUEZ
Puerto Barrios
Reserva de Manantiales Cerro San Gil
Castillo de San Felipe
Río Motagua
Quiriguá
Mariscos
Lago de Izabal
El Estor
R.V.S Bocas del Polochic
Reserva de la Biosfera Sierra de las Minas
Lanquín
Semuc Champey
Biotopo del Quetzal
Cobán
Salamá
Rabinal
Embalse Chixoy
Río Negro o Chixoy
Reserva de la Biosfera Visís-Cabá
Uspantán
Sacapulas
Nebaj
Santa Cruz del Quiché
Chichicastenango
Utatlán
Iximché
Huehuetenango
Todos Santos Cuchumatán
Zaculeu
La Mesilla
Totonicapán
Quetzaltenango
San Marcos
El Carmen
Talismán
Ciudad Hidalgo
Tecún Umán
Abaj Takalik
Retalhuleu
Champerico
El Tulate
Zunil
V. Santa María
V. Santo Tomás
V. San Pedro
Santiago Atitlán
Lago de Atitlán
V. Tolimán
V. Atitlán
Sololá
Panajachel
Chimaltenango
Antigua
Mazatenango
Escuintla
Puerto San José
Iztapa
Monterrico
Taxisco
Guatemala City
Lago de Amatitlán
V. de Pacaya
Cuilapa
V. Jumaytepeque
El Progreso
Jalapa
Jutiapa
Zacapa
Chiquimula
El Florido
Copán Ruinas
Copán
Santa Rosa de Copán
Nueva Ocotepeque
Agua Caliente
Esquipulas
P.N. Trifinio
Anguiatú
San Cristóbal
Santa Ana
Chalatenango
San Salvador
Las Chinamas
Ahuachapán
La Hachadura
Valle Nuevo
Ciudad Pedro de Alvarado
CA1
CA2
CA4
CA9
CA12
25 kilometers
25 miles

aché, the connection to **Flores** (p. 401) is an easy one; the famed ruins of **Tikal** (p. 406) are 65km to the north. Though you can see Tikal in a day, give yourself enough time to soak up the tropical forest, wildlife, and the impressive ruins. Hop a bus to **Eastern Guatemala** (p. 374) via **Poptún** and arrive in **Fronteras** (also known as **Río Dulce**, p. 379) on the Lago de Izabal. From there, take a boat down the peaceful Río Dulce to **Livingston** (p. 383), Guatemala's plot on the Caribbean and home to the local Garífuna culture. Wash off the jungle in the local waterfalls, shake your bon-bon at beach parties, and eat your fill of coconut bread. From Livingston, take a bus back to **Guatemala City** (p. 323), or a boat to **Belize** (p. 59) or **Honduras** (p. 413).

LIFE AND TIMES

LAND, FLORA, AND FAUNA

The northern third of the country—the Petén—is geographically contiguous with Mexico's Yucatán and is part of an immense flat limestone shelf. Water erosion has produced an irregular limestone region with extensive cave systems and numerous depressions and sinkholes that provide the only sources of water in the dry season. The Petén is covered by a dense lowland rainforest, mixed with cleared patches of savanna. South of the Petén are the highlands, composed of the central sierras, a land of high ridges and valleys that continues east into Honduras, and a southeast-northwest string of volcanoes that includes Guatemala's highest peak, **Tajumulco** (4220m). The highlands were originally blanketed by oak and pine forest, which have been largely destroyed by millennia of farming and, more recently, large-scale deforestation. A number of these volcanoes are still active, and most can be easily climbed. Sloping gently from the volcanic ridge into the ocean is Guatemala's Pacific coastal plain, a fertile agricultural area ending the black-sand beaches of the Pacific.

Guatemala is home to a stunning range of plant life, ranking in the top 25 countries worldwide in terms of plant diversity. A number of species, many of which have long since been used by the indigenous populations to heal, are being utilized today by foreign pharmaceutical companies. Guatemala houses more wildlife than just the radiant and elusive quetzal, its national bird—the rich variety of animal life includes the jaguar, harpy eagle, ocelot, tapir, white-lipped peccaries, howler and spider monkeys, deer, coatmundies, the horned guan, and scarlet macaws.

HISTORY

GUATEMALA SINCE INDEPENDENCE (1821-1871). Originally part of Mexico, Guatemala gained independence from Spain on September 15, 1821; became the center of the **United Provinces of Central America** in 1823; and declared itself an autonomous nation when the Federation collapsed in 1839. Undermined by a cholera epidemic in 1837, the liberal regime was overthrown by the conservative **Rafael Carrera.** Under Carrera, control of Belize was given to Britain in exchange for construction of a road between the two capitals. The road was never built, and land compensation disputes continue to be a hot topic. A revolution in 1871 began a long period of liberal rule that lasted until 1944.

THE LIBERAL ERA (1871-1944). Carrera's government was overthrown in the revolution of 1871, and **Justo Rufino Barrios** quickly assumed dictatorial control, earning the name "the Reformer" for his rapid program of social and economic change. Reversing Carrera's policies, he limited the power of the aristocracy and revoked church privilege, while instituting economic modernization which, though liberal in scope, benefited mainly the urban and land-owning elite.

In 1898, **Manuel Estrada Cabrera** continued Barrios' policies of economic modernization, making large land deals with the American-owned **United Fruit Company**. Deposed in 1920, Cabrera's successor **Jorge Ubico** streamlined the Guatemalan Liberal State and worked to strengthen economic relations with the United States at the expense of domestic democratic politics and labor organization. Not until he suspended freedom of speech and press in 1944 did a group of dissidents called the **"October Revolutionaries"** take action, leading a general strike and flinging him from power.

LAND REFORM (1945-1954). The revolutionary process, culminating in the October Revolution, led to the 1945 democratic election of **Juan José Arévalo**. Drawing much of his support from communist-led organized labor, he enacted a labor code, established a social security system, allowed extensive freedoms of speech and press, and pursued a reconciliation with the indigenous population. Successor colonel **Jacobo Arbenz** pursued Arévalo's radical program of social change, including legalizing the communist **Guatemalan Labor Party** in 1952. Focusing on agrarian reform, Arbenz and the National Congress expropriated and redistributed idle lands that had been given to the United Fruit Company and other land-holding elites. United Fruit had powerful allies in the US government, and Washington quickly responded; in 1954, an army covertly trained by the US invaded and forced Arbenz to resign, ending agrarian reform before it had begun.

LA VIOLENCIA (1954-1996). The military junta that took power after the invasion reversed previously instituted social reforms and crushed any opposition through a campaign of violence, all in the interest of American big business. The military government's oppression incited increasingly violent resistance, and many workers joined oppositional guerrilla groups demanding land reform and democracy. The violence that began in the early 60s engulfed Guatemala for the next 35 years in a nearly genocidal clash over rights to land and liberty. The term **La Violencia** describes the period from the late 70s through the 80s, when the conflict extended into the most remote corners of Guatemala. A series of rigged elections and puppet presidents controlled by the military continued through the 1960s. At the same time, right-wing vigilantes formed the **Secret Anti-Communist Army (ESA)** and the **White Hand** to go after students, professionals, and peasants they suspected of leftist activity. The reign of **Carlos Arana Osorio** introduced "death squads," who eliminated opposition, to the Guatemalan political landscape. The squads focused on the guerrilla forces but affected peaceful opposition as well. Meanwhile, foreign-owned business expanded, instigating social tensions. The death toll from political violence rose to the tens of thousands as conflict polarized the nation.

As the civil war continued into the 1980s, the government—headed by 1982 coup-leader **General Efrain Rios Montt**—pursued "scorched earth" tactics against the guerrillas. Several guerrilla organizations organized in 1982 into the **Unidad Revolucionario Nacional Guatemalteco (URNG)**. Though Montt was quickly replaced, the army razed hundreds of Maya villages, torturing and killing indiscriminately with the dual purpose of eliminating possible rebels and discouraging those left from joining the insurgency. Many were forced to relocate into camps known euphemistically as "model villages." Others sought refuge in Mexico or Honduras, or wandered through the highlands in a desperate attempt to avoid the army's violence. Recently declassified Guatemalan documents state that roughly 650,000 citizens—10% of the population—were marked for death.

Under increasing financial pressure from the international community, peace negotiations finally began in the 1990s. **Alvaro Arzú Irigoyen** was elected president in 1996, and in March of that year, he signed a temporary cease-fire. Peace accords followed on December 29, 1996, ending the four decades of civil war with a death toll of 200,000, a displaced population of upwards of one million, and tens of thousands of *desaparecidos* (abducted dissidents) that were never found.

TODAY

Demobilization of the guerrillas proceeds slowly, and many of the ex-rebels and soldiers have turned their guns to the profitable enterprise of highway robbery. Recently-discovered mass graves contain hundreds of bodies, and hundreds more mass burial sites are believed to exist. In one of the most horrifying acts since the cease-fire, **Bishop Juan Gerardi Conedera** was beaten to death on April 26, 1998, two days after he presented a long-awaited report on human rights violations during *La Violencia*. The report, *Never Again in Guatemala*, based upon 6000 interviews with survivors, attributed 85% of the violations to the Guatemalan Army.

In February 1999, the Guatemalan Truth Commission released a report of the atrocities of the civil war which stated that the Guatemalan military and its agents committed acts of genocide against the Maya. In spring 1999, President Clinton surprised the world by acknowledging and apologizing for the US role in the atrocities. While Guatemala is slowly building a democracy, substantial social and economic inequalities continue to threaten peace. Then-president **Alfonso Antonio Portillo Cabrera,** of the rightist **Guatemalan Republican Front (FRG),** has pledged to seek justice for those affected by *La Violencia*, and in 2001 he asked President Bush to back legislation making it easier for Guatemalan refugees to obtain US citizenship. Justice for Bishop Conedera was served June 20, 2001, when three military officers were found guilty of his murder. Mob violence is unfortunately not uncommon. Some Guatemalans see vigilante justice as their only means of peacekeeping, often at the expense of more sanctioned means.

Recently elected in 2004, President Oscar Berger has joined forces with human rights groups to push forward the Commission for the Investigation of Illegal Bodies and Clandestine Security Apparatus. The Commission involves both the UN and the OAS (Organization of American States) and is viewed worldwide as a positive step towards the dismantling of harmful entities within Guatemala. The United States' recent decision to remove Guatemala from its list of drug war allies, however, reminds one how far the nation still has to go.

ECONOMY AND GOVERNMENT

Guatemala's economy is still mostly agricultural, divided between the subsistence, small-scale agriculture of the highlands, where corn and squash are the main crops, and the larger, commercial farming of the Pacific slope, where coffee, bananas, and sugar are produced for export. Industry, mostly centered around Guatemala City, is growing now that IMF stabilization plans have curtailed the slump of the 1980s. Growth, however, has not resulted in equitable income distribution or the alleviation of poverty. Recently, the service sector, especially tourism, has been the fastest growing sector of the economy.

The strength of democracy is growing. Officially, the nation is a republic, and power is divided between three branches: legislative, executive, and judicial. The entire republic is divided into 22 *departamentos*, each of which is headed by a governor. Guatemalan political parties create a constantly changing landscape. Besides the FRG, other currently visible parties include the National Advancement Party (PAN), the Revolutionary Party (PR), the centrist Guatemalan Christian Democratic party (DCG), and the right-wing National Liberation Movement (MLN). The army also continues to make its presence felt.

In 2003, Guatemala signed the CAFTA Agreement (Central American Free Trade Agreement). The agreement removed many tariffs on products moving between Central and North America, including agricultural goods. The agreement also loosened regulations and augmented protections for US investment in the region.

CULTURE AND ARTS

PEOPLE

Guatemala is home to the majority of the region's indigenous population (7 of every 8 Central American indigenous people live in Guatemala) and is characterized by a sharp distinction between the six million *indígenas* and *ladinos* (of European ancestry) or assimilated *indígenas*. The indigenous population, concentrated in the central and western highlands, is almost uniformly Maya. Yet the Maya of Guatemala themselves consist of a number of different ethnic groups and speak 23 different languages. The largest of these groups are the **Quiché** (K'iche'), who live around Lake Atitlán; the **Mam**, who live west of the K'iche' near the Mexican border; the **Cakchiquel,** who live just west of Guatemala City; and the **Kekchi** (Q'eqchi), who live in a large area in the central and northern sierras. *Ladinos* (Spanish-speakers) live mostly in the urban centers, along the Pacific slope, and in the Petén, where they are relative newcomers.

Guatemalans consistently characterize themselves as Roman Catholic, though Protestant sects have been growing in popularity among the urban poor in the last few decades. Most Maya practice what may be the most impressive syncretistic mixture of Catholicism and native religious customs found in Central America.

FOOD AND DRINK

Chicken rules supreme in Guatemalan *típico* fare; sometimes the bird is served with the feet still attached. But while the meat's the treat, meals are filled out with rice, beans, eggs, and thick tortillas. There is good reason why tortillas in Guatemala are made from corn—according to the Popol Vuh and traditional Quiché myths, humans came from corn, and the grain is the human essence. Along the coasts, seafood is common, usually spiced with Caribbean Creole flare. Don't miss the famous *tapado* on the Caribbean coast. Despite the fruit's thorny exterior, the juicy, pulpy white core of the *guanábana* (soursop) deserves a try. Nearly every town has a tent-strewn market, stocked with fruits, vegetables, and other tasty items at a nominal cost. Coffee is the *bebida preferida* throughout Guatemala; locally grown beans are export quality and make a good gift. Fruit juice *licuados* are also favorites. Local beers include Gallo, Moza, and Dorado.

LITERATURE

Guatemalan writers have continuously tried to bridge the gap between indigenous myth and European literary forms; magic recurs in Guatemalan literature, coloring even the most modern writing with traces of indigenous beliefs. The country has produced few well-known playwrights, though **Vicenta Laparra de la Cerda** (1834-1905) movingly portrayed the plight of women in *Angel caído* (*Fallen Angel*, 1880) and *Hija maldita* (*Accursed Daughter*, 1895). Modern poet **Rafael Arévalo** Martínez (1884-1975) is said to have led the way toward magical realism through short stories such as *El hombre que parecía un caballo* (*The Man Who Resembled a Horse*, 1915). Another father of magical realism is **Miguel Angel Asturias** (1899-1974), the poet, novelist, and ambassador who in 1967 won the Nobel Prize in Literature, and whose novels examine the deep political realities of this century. Most notable among his writings is *Viento fuerte* (*Strong Wind*, 1950), which was mentioned in his Nobel Prize citation. Guatemala's other Nobel Prize winner

GUATEMALA

is the internationally known social activist **Rigoberta Menchú,** who won the Peace Prize in 1992 for her efforts to gain recognition of the plight of the country's indigenous peoples. Her world renowned testimonial *Me llamo Rigoberta y así nació la conciencia* (1983, translated *I, Rigoberta* in 1984) highlights her family's involvement in revolutionary action against the government's civil rights abuses.

POPULAR CULTURE

In both circulation and sheer mass, *Prensa Libre* (www.prensalibre.com) is the biggest Guatemalan daily newspaper, followed by *Siglo XXI* (www.sigloxxi.com) and *La Hora* (www.lahora.com.gt). *Diario de Centroamerica* is the government publication. The biweekly journal *Crónica* provides analyses of national and international events. The monthly *Crítica* is a forum for Guatemalan intellectuals.

CRAFTS

The beautiful Maya **weavings** found in villages throughout the country are meaningful for those who make and wear the textiles. However, in places, their role as a tourist commodity may be eclipsing their traditional importance.

ESSENTIALS

PASSPORTS, VISAS, AND CUSTOMS

Passport (p. 19): Required for all visitors. Stamps usually valid for 30 days, but extra time may be granted upon request at entry. Extensions also can be granted at an immigration office.

Visa: Not required for citizens of the US, Canada, UK, Ireland, or New Zealand. Visitors from Australia need a visa.

Inoculations and Medications (p. 27): None required.

Work Permit: Required for all foreigners planning to work in Guatemala.

Driving Permit (p. 37): No special permit is necessary; permit valid for 30-90 days issued upon arrival with valid US license. US Drivers must carry valid driver's license, title, and registration to drive across the border.

Departure Tax: US$20-25 if leaving by air, Q5-10 by land.

EMBASSIES AND CONSULATES

Embassies of Guatemala: US, 2220 R St. NW, Washington, D.C. 20008 (☎202-745-4952; www.mdngt.org/agremilusa/embassy.html). Open M-F 9am-5:00pm. **Canada,** 130 Albert St., Suite 1010, Ottawa, Ontario KIT 5Z4 (☎613-233-7188; fax 233-0135). **UK,** 13 Fawcett St., London, SW 10 9HN (☎ 441 7351 3042; fax 376 5708).

Consular Services of Guatemala: 57 Park Ave., New York, NY 10016, US (☎212-686-3837; fax 447-6947). Open M-F 9am-2pm for document processing. Guatemala also has consulates in Washington, Los Angeles, San Francisco, Miami, and Chicago.

MONEY

The above exchange rates were accurate as of August 2004. Be advised, however, that rates change frequently. The Guatemalan unit of currency is the **quetzal,** named for the elusive bird and abbreviated with a "Q." The quetzal is divided into 100 centavos, and there are coins of 25, 10, 5, and 1 centavos. Bills come as 50 centavos and 1, 5, 10, 20, 50, and 100 quetzals. Torn notes are not always accepted.

QUETZALES		
US$1 = Q7.91		Q1 = US$0.13
EURO€ = Q9.78		Q1 = EURO€0.10
CDN$1 = Q6.05		Q1 = CDN$0.17
UK£1 = Q14.57		Q1 = UK£0.07
AUS$1 = Q5.68		Q1 = AUS$0.18
NZ$1 = Q5.27		Q1 = NZ$0.19

US dollars are the only foreign currency to have, though the BanQuetzal branch at the Guatemala City airport may accept others. Exchanging dollars for quetzals is straightforward enough at most banks; there's also a black market, though rates are little better than the official ones. **Traveler's checks** are widely accepted in Guatemala. For **credit card** advances or **ATM** withdrawals, Visa (accepted at most Banco Industrials) is easy. **Tipping** is not customary in *comedores*, but if a restaurant has a menu, it's generally a good idea to leave a 10% tip; sometimes it will be included. **Bargaining** is the norm in Guatemala's many markets and handcraft shops, but not in urban shopping centers.

PRICE DIVERSITY

Guatemala is a budget traveler's dream. The attentive traveler might come across beds for as little as US$3-4 per person, and basic eateries offer meals for US$2 or less, though you may want to treat yourself to more than this—and you'll have to in popular tourist areas like Antigua and Panajachel. Even so, the very frugal traveler could get by on about US$100 a week, twice that for rooms with private bath and more upscale meals. Taxis, tourist shuttles, guided tours, and tourist bars can quickly add to these figures. The number icons below describe establishments' prices throughout the chapter.

QUETZAL	❶	❷	❸	❹	❺
ACCOMMODATIONS	Q1-30	Q31-45	Q46-60	Q61-80	Q80+
FOOD	Q1-10	Q11-20	Q21-35	Q36-45	Q46+

SAFETY

Although Guatemala is the safest it's been in 30 years, travel between cities after dark is still considered unsafe. **Armed bandits** have stopped city buses and tour buses along highways at night, and bus drivers are sometimes in on the job. Decrease risk by restricting travel to the daytime and, in particular, to roads the tourism industry considers safe. Local buses, moreover, are rarely subject to attacks—tour buses are more frequently targets. **Pickpockets** and purse snatchers constitute a perennial hazard in Guatemala City and elsewhere, especially in the central markets. Climbing **volcanoes** in Guatemala can be risky, as tourists have been assaulted in the recent past. It is very important to check on the safety of an area before venturing out. US citizens, particularly those staying for an extended period of time, may want to register with the Consular Section of the US Embassy in Guatemala City. An application, two photos, and proof of citizenship are required. One can register informally by mail or fax; include a local address and telephone number, itinerary, emergency contact in the US, and length of stay. Do *not* carry drugs in Guatemala. Under a 1992 anti-narcotics law, anyone caught in the possession of even small amounts of drugs can spend several months in jail before their case is decided. Those convicted face very stiff sentences. For more info see **Personal Safety**, p. 26.

GUATEMALA

HEALTH

The most serious health concerns for travellers are **malaria** and **dengue fever,** and the greatest danger exists on the coast and in the Petén. The Center for Disease Control recommends **Chloroquine** as the most effective anti-malarial medicine for travelers to Guatemala. Stay away from tap water to avoid an upset stomach and overly frequent trips to the bathroom. For more information, see **Health,** p. 25.

BORDER CROSSINGS

MEXICO. There are three land crossings. In the highlands, **La Mesilla,** 90km west of Huehuetenango, has buses to San Cristóbal de las Casas, Mexico. Buses from Huehue, Guatemala City, and other towns go to La Mesilla. **El Carmen/Talismán** is west of Quetzaltenango and Retalhuleu, near Tapachula, Mexico. **Tecun Umán/ Ciudad Hidalgo** on the Pacific coast, is 75km west of Retalhuleu. Buses head there from Quetzaltenango, Retalhuleu, and Tapachula, Mexico. There are several **land/ river crossings** from Flores toward **Palenque, Mexico** (p. 369).

EL SALVADOR. There are three land crossings, listed from south to north. **Valle Nuevo/Las Chinamas** serves from Area 1 in Zona 4 of Guatemala City (see p. 327); **San Cristóbal** has buses from Guatemala City and Santa Ana, El Salvador. Buses run to **Anguiatú** from Esquipulas and Metapán, El Salvador.

HONDURAS. There are three land crossings. **El Florido** is along a dirt road between Chiquimula and Copán Ruinas, Honduras. Buses run on the Guatemalan side (p. 374), and pickups run on the Honduran side. **Agua Caliente** is 10km east of Esquipulas, near Nueva Ocotepeque, Honduras (p. 378). **Corinto,** near Puerto Barrios, has connections to Omoa, Honduras (p. 475).

BELIZE. There is one land crossing at **Melchor de Mencos/Benque Viejo de Carmen** (p. 412). **Boats** run between Puerto Barrios and **Punta Gorda,** Belize (p. 116) and between Livingston and Punta Gorda (p. 383).

KEEPING IN TOUCH

Guatemala's **postal service** has improved in the last few years, after being purchased by a Canadian company. A letter costs Q0.40 within Guatemala. If necessary, packages can be sent to the US using private mail carriers such as **DHL** (about US$30 per lb.). **First-class air mail** ought to take 10 to 14 days to reach the US, but it's not uncommon for a letter to take several months. You can receive mail general delivery at most post offices through the *lista de correos*.

> Liza COVINGTON [first name] [LAST NAME]
> Poste Restante
> Guatemala City [city]
> GUATEMALA

Guatemalan phone numbers have seven digits and require no area codes. For US phone company access codes, see this book's inside back cover. **Telephones** are handled by **Telgua,** the national communications network. Phoning can be difficult, so try the more expensive hotels when placing international or domestic calls. All calls within the country made from Telgua offices cost the same: Q3.50 for the first three minutes and Q0.35 for each additional minute. Pay phones in Guatemala City and some other cities have been replaced with electronic, pre-paid calling cards available at many shops—look for the sign in the window.

TRANSPORTATION

Taca Inter offers **flights** between Guatemala City and a number of domestic destinations. Several airlines fly between Guatemala City and Flores (near Tikal). Common **buses**, cursed by some as "mobile chicken coops," are converted school buses that sit three to a bench. Some travelers have reported being charged a higher "gringo rate." Inquire about the price ahead of time and try to pay in exact change. **Driving** your own vehicle in Guatemala can be a hazardous experience. Some road conditions are poor. Those involved in accidents can be put in jail regardless of who is at fault, and armed car robberies are common enough that the US State Department warns against highway travel. The safest strategy if cornered by armed bandits on the road is to surrender your car without resistance.

ORIENTATION

Directions favor landmarks over addresses. Nevertheless, most Guatemalan cities, like their Honduran, Salvadoran, and Nicaraguan brethren, label streets in a grid of numbered north-south *avenidas* (avenues) and east-west *calles* (streets). Generally, *avenidas* increase in number to the west, and *calles* increase to the south. "6 Av. 25" refers to #25 on 6th Avenue. You will also see "6a Av. 25," which means the same thing ("6a" short for *sexta*). A building at 6 Av., 1/2 C., is on 6 Av. between 1 and 2 C. Guatemala's larger cities are divided into *zonas* (zones); *Let's Go* designates the zone after the address (e.g. 6 Av. 25, Zona 1).

TRAVEL RESOURCES

Instituto Guatemalteco de Turismo (INGUAT), 7 Av. 1-17, Zona 4 (☎331 1333, US toll free 888-INGUAT1, Guatemala toll free 801 INGUAT1; www.guatemala.travel.com.gt, www.travel-guatemala.org.gt) in the Centro Cívico just south of the Zona 1 border in Guatemala City. Some of the staff speak English, and tourist brochures are available. There are other INGUAT offices in Antigua, Quetzaltenango, Panajachel, and Flores; see specific cities for local INGUAT listings.

The Revue, an English-language publication, has information about goings-on throughout Guatemala, concentrating on Antigua.

HOLIDAYS

Guatemalans are serious about festivals: patron saints' days include firecrackers, costumed dancers, and religious processions ranging from solemn to frenzied. There is, quite literally, a festival going on somewhere every day of the year. National holidays include: **January 1,** New Year's Day; **March/April,** *Semana Santa;* **May 1,** Labor Day; **June 30,** Army Day; **August 15,** Guatemala City Day; **September 15,** Independence Day; **October 20,** Revolution Day; **November 1,** All Saints Day; **December 24-25,** Christmas Eve/Christmas; **December 31,** New Year's Eve.

ALTERNATIVES TO TOURISM

This section lists some of the organizations in Guatemala that offer opportunities outside the typical tourist experience. For more information on Alternatives to Tourism as well as tools for finding programs on your own, see the chapter at the beginning of the book (p. 53).

VISA INFORMATION

A **work permit** in Guatemala is valid for one year and can be extended if necessary. Your employer must apply to the Ministry of Labor and Security with the following materials from you: an authorization of your temporary or permanent residency in

Guatemala; a police record citing a lack of criminal activity in your home country during the previous six months; a notarized letter in which the employer takes full responsibility for your conduct; a certification of the number of Guatemalan and foreign employees working for the company and the wage statistics; a notarized photocopy of the letter of hire; a sworn statement of your Spanish proficiency; and documents that prove your qualifications for the job (such as high school or college diploma). All documents that come from your home country must be authenticated by the nearest Guatemalan consulate.

LANGUAGE SCHOOLS

Academia de Español Guatemala, 7 C. Oriente #15, Antigua, (☎/fax 832 5057; http://acad.conexion.com/). Language program highly acclaimed by participants. Daily activities include latin dance classes, roundtable discussions, and community outings. Q1500 per week covers tuition, homestay, and organized recreation.

Instituto Central America (ICA), 19 Av. 1-47, Zona 1, Quetzaltenango (☎/fax 502 763 1871, US 402-439-2943; www.guatemalaspanish.com). This fully accredited language school takes a "total immersion approach." US$140 per week Sept.-May, US$150 per week June-Aug. includes homestay, meals, and 5 hours a day of one-on-one language instruction. Those willing to volunteer for a minimum of 3 weeks and 4-5 hr. a day at ICA can pay Q225 per week to live with a family, or Q24 per week to live at the school; intermediate Spanish required.

Proyecto Lingüístico de Español/Mam "Todos Santos," main street, Todos Santos Cuchumatán, at the entrance to town. Instruction in Spanish and indigenous Mam. US$115 for a seven-day homestay in a traditional Mam household with meals and 25hr. of language instruction. Also includes village-wide evening meal with marimba music. Traveler's checks accepted.

VOLUNTEERING
BIOLOGY/ECOLOGY PROGRAMS

Volunteer Petén, in the **Parque Ecológico Nueva Juventud,** San Andrés, Petén, (☎711 0040; www.volunteerpeten.com), aids development by training international volunteers to participate in designing and constructing sustainable infrastructure. Areas of focus include organic farming and sustainable building, but the organization is willing to accept volunteers with a wide range of goals and skills. (US$350 for 4 weeks, US$650 for 8 weeks, US$950 for 12 weeks.) Also, after volunteering for 12 weeks, volunteers are eligible to rent houses for US$50 a week.

Involvement Volunteers (www.volunteering.org.au/animals.html#guatmala), lists several programs, 2-8 weeks, that concentrate on animal rescue and rehabilitation. US$100 per week includes meals and accommodations.

EDUCATION

Global Vision International, Nomansland, Wheathampstead, St Albans AL4 8EJ, England, UK (☎440 870 608 8898; www.gvi.co.uk), brings internationals to **Antigua** to volunteer as teachers for impoverished indigenous children. Subjects include English and art. Fee from US$1535.

i-to-i, 190 East 9th Ave., Suite 320, Denver, CO 80203, US or Woodside House, 261 Low Lane, Leeds, LS18 5NY, UK (US ☎1-800-985-4864 or UK 870 333 2332; www.i-to-i.com), is an established international program that offers orientation, language training, airport pickup, and insurance (room and board an additional US$11 per day). Volunteers will teach English in villages on the outskirts of Guatemala City. Programs range 4-12 weeks, US$1500-2095.

HUMANITARIAN

Quetzaltrekkers, Casa Argentina, 12 Diagonal, 8-37, Quetzaltenango, (☎761 5865; www.quetzaltrekkers.com). A project in **Quetzaltenango** designed to aid impoverished children. All funds stem from guided hiking trips that Quetzaltrekkers runs for tourists. Cooperatively run by Guatemalan school teachers and international volunteers.

Habitat for Humanity Guatemala, Av. Las Americas 9-50, Zona 3, Supercom Delco, Office 324, Quetzaltenango (☎763 5608; www.habitatguate.org), is the Guatemalan branch of the gigantic international humanitarian organization. Volunteers assist with basic building projects. Minimum 2 day participation; no maximum. Offices are in Quetzaltenango, but projects take place all over Guatemala.

GUATEMALA CITY

Guatemala City, or Guate (GUAH-te), is the largest urban area in Central America. Smog-belching buses and countless sidewalk vendors, together with the sheer number of people, the volume of noise, and the endless expanse of concrete, render the city center claustrophobic. Add to this a general concern for safety and it's easy to understand why many visitors flee the capital for the surrounding highlands. However, poking around Guate for a day or two does have its rewards. Some fine architecture dating back to the 1700s and several worthwhile museums make for an engaging stay, and after camping in the countryside and hiking through jungles, the city's modern conveniences and hot showers can be quite welcoming. While travelers may find comfort in Guate, many residents do not. Poverty is laid bare here, standing in harsh contrast to the antiseptic shopping malls and guarded, fortress-like mansions in the wealthiest neighborhoods. This disparity is particularly evident in Guatemala's large refugee population, mainly Mayans who fled the civil violence in their home villages.

Guatemala City was named the country's capital in 1775 after an earthquake in Antigua left the government scrambling for a safer center, though powerful tremors shook the new capital in 1917, 1918, and 1976. Despite the whims of Mother Nature, the city and its three million inhabitants persevere, expanding ceaselessly into the surrounding valleys.

■ INTERCITY TRANSPORTATION

Flights: La Aurora International Airport (☎331 8392), about 7km south of Zona 1 in Zona 13, serves all the flights listed below. Airlines with outbound flights from Aurora include: Grupo Taca (☎470 8222, www.taca.com); American (☎337 1177); Continental (☎366 9985); Delta (☎337 0642); United (☎332 1994); Mexicana (☎333 6001); Iberia (☎332 0911); KLM (☎366 9480).

Flights to Flores: The most common domestic flight and the one budget travelers usually consider is from Guate to Flores, near Tikal. Four airlines serve this route: **Grupo Taca** (☎470 8222; www.taca.com), **Tikal Jets** (☎332 5070), **Aereo Ruta Maya** (339 0502), and **Rasca** (☎361 5703). Taca has the most service and the largest aircraft, followed by Tikal Jets. Specials are often available on this route; it's worth checking with a travel agent, but expect to pay Q700-950 round-trip.

Other Domestic Flights: During peak season, Grupo Taca offers spotty domestic service via its regional affiliate, **Inter.** It's a pricey way to go, but destinations include **Huehuetenango, Puerto Barrios, Quetzaltenango,** and **Río Dulce.** Rasca can arrange charter flights, but these also tend to be very expensive.

Domestic Buses: The **bus terminal** is located in the southwest corner of Zona 4, framed by Av. 4, Av. de Ferrocarril, and C. 8. Many 2nd-class services depart from here; ask around to find an exact departure point. Departures are scattered throughout the blocks surrounding the main terminal. Domestic buses that do not depart from the Zona 4 Terminal depart from various locations around Zona 1. See **Orientation** () for information on how to decipher addresses in Guate. Be advised that none of these bus "stations" have ticket offices; brace yourself for chaos. You pay for the trip on the road, but get money ready before you step on—you don't want to fumble with your wallet on a crowded bus.

Antigua: Many leave from the crowded parking lot at 18 C., between 4 and 5 Av, in Zona 1. (1hr., every 15min. 7am-8pm, Q4.50.)

Belizean border: Fuentes del Norte, see Flores (13hr.; 2:30, 5, 9pm; Q75.)

Biotopo del Quetzal: Take any Cobán bus. (3½hr., every hr., Q20.)

Chichicastenango: Veloz Quichelense, Zona 4 Terminal; any Santa Cruz del Quiché bus runs here, too. (3½hr., every hr. 5am-6pm, Q12.)

Cobán: Escobar y Monja Blanca, 8 Av. C. 15/16. (☎238 1409. 4½hr., every hr. 4am-5pm, Q30.)

Esquipulas: Rutas Orientales, C. 19, 8-18, Zona 1. (☎253-7282. 4½hr., every 30min. 4:30am-6:30pm, Q30.)

Flores: Fuentes del Norte, C. 17, 8-46, Zona 1. (☎238 3894. 9-10hrs., every hr., Q80.) **Línea Dorada,** 16 C. 10-55, Zona 1. (☎232 9658. Departures at 10am, 9, 10, 10:30pm; Q240.)

Huehuetenango: Velásquez, C. 20 1-37, Zona 1. (☎221-1084. 5hr., every hr. 8-11am, Q20.) Also **Los Halcones,** 7 Av. 15-27. (☎238 1929. 5hr.; 4:30, 7am, 2, 5pm; Q30.)

Iztapa: Zona 4 Terminal. (1¾hr., every 20 min. 5am-6pm, Q11.)

Mexican border at Tecún Umán: Fortaleza, 19 C. 8-70. (☎230 3390. 5hr., every 15min. 12:15am-12:30pm, Q35.) Some continue to the border at Talismán (6hr., Q40). Also try **Rapidos del Sur** at 20 C. 8-55 (☎251 6678), and **Chinita,** 9 Av. 18-38 (☎251 9144).

Mexican border at La Mesilla: Velásquez buses to Huehuetenango continue here (8hr., 8am-5pm, Q37.50).

Monterrico: Cubanita, Zona 4 Terminal. (Direct 3½hr.; 10:30am, 12:30, 2:20pm; Q15.) Alternatively, take a bus to Taxisco (from the **Pullman El Condor,** Zona 4 Terminal; 2hrs.; 6, 11am, 1:30pm; Q15) and transfer there to **La Avellana** (30min., every hr. 7am-2:30pm, Q3).

Panajachel: Rebulli, 21 C. 1-34, Zona 1. (☎230 2748. 3hr.; every hr. 5:30am-3:30pm; direct at 6, 9, 10am, 3, 4pm; Q12.) Or, from the Zona 4 Terminal, take any western highlands bus and change at Los Encuentros junction.

Puerto Barrios: Litegua, 15 C. 10-42. (☎253 8169. 5hr., every hr. 4:45am-3pm, Q40.)

Quetzaltenango: First-class service on **Líneas Americas,** 2 Av. 18-74, Zona 1. (☎232 1432. 3hr.; 5, 9:15, 11:30am, 3:15, 4:30, and 7:30pm; Q30). Second-class service on the less desirable **Galgos,** 7 Av. 19-44 (☎253 4868). 9 buses leave daily between 7am-4:15pm.

Rabinal: Dulce María, 9 Av., 19 C., Zona 1. (☎250 0082. 4½hr., every hr. 5am-5pm.)

Retalhuleu: All buses running to the Mexican border at Tecún Umán stop here. (4hr., Q30.)

Río Dulce: Take any Flores-bound bus. (5hr., Q40-90.)

Salamá: Take a Rabinal bus. (3½hr.)

Tecpán: Veloz Poaquileña, C. 20 and Av. Simón Bolívar, Zona 1. (2hr., every 15min. 5am-7pm, Q7.)

International Buses: Buses to **San Salvador, El Salvador** leave on King Quality and Comfort Line (☎369 0404) from 18 Av. 1-96 in Zona 15 (5hr.; 6:30, 8am, 2, 3pm; Q150). Tica Bus, 11 C. 2-72, Zona 9 (☎331 4279), leaves at 12:30pm for **Panama City,** traveling through **San Salvador, Tegucigalpa, Managua,** and **San José.** The entire trip takes 4 days. For **Tapachula, Mexico,** Galgos (☎253 4868) runs 3 buses daily; Tica Bus departs at noon. Border-bound buses: see information under **Domestic Buses.**

✦ ORIENTATION

UPON ARRIVAL. Both international and domestic flights arrive at **La Aurora International Airport,** in Zona 13. The posh hotels of Zona 10 are close, but the budget spots in Zona 1 require a bit more of a trek. Bus #83 departs from outside the terminal and runs to Zona 1; watch your luggage carefully. Though more expensive, a taxi (Q50) is an easier and safer way of getting to your hotel.

Guatemala City

🏠 ACCOMMODATIONS
Dos Lunas Guesthouse, 14
Hotel Mayastic, 4
Las Torres, 7
Los Próceres, 13

🍴 FOOD
Danny's Pancakes, 6
Del Tingo Al Tango, 5
San Martín and Co., 8

🍸 NIGHTLIFE
Kahlua, 12
Xtreme, 9

🏛 MUSEUMS
Museo de los Niños, 11
Museo Ixchel, 2
Museo Nacional de
   Arqueología, 10
Popul Vuh Museum, 3

PLAZA MAYOR
Parque del Centenario
PL. DE LA CONSTITUCIÓN

ZONA 2

ZONA 1

15-Av. (Av.-de-los-Árboles)

MIGUEL ÁNGEL ASTURIAS CULTURAL CENTER

SEE GUATEMALA CITY CENTER MAP p. 327

INGUAT

Teatro IGA

ZONA 8
ZONA 4

Market
Bus Terminal

Yurrita

ZONA 5

C.-de-los-Cipreses

TO ANTIGUA (45km)

Jardín Botánico

Campo de Marte
C. Mariscal Cruz

Parque Centroamérica

United States

Museo 2 🏛🏛 3

ZONA 15

Blvd.-de-Vista-Hermosa

Río Negro

Av.-de-la-Reforma

ZONA 13
Parque La Aurora

PL. ESPAÑA

Canada

C.-Real-de-la-Villa-de-Guadalupe

Blvd.-Liberación

Av.-la-Castellana

0   400 meters
0   400 yards

Museo 10
Zoo
Mercado de Artesanías
La Aurora Int'l Airport

ZONA 9

UK

Japan, Holland

Centro Comercial Los Próceres

℞

TO Israel (50m)

TO (1km)

SEE GUATEMALA CITY CENTER MAP p. 327

GUATEMALA

If arriving by **bus,** prepare for some confusion. Many second-class services arrive in the Zona 4 market area, referred to as the main bus terminal. Taxis are plentiful here; if you want to take a bus to Zona 1, walk to the corner of 2 C. and 4 Av. Other second-class buses arrive at scattered locations throughout the city. Most of these are in Zona 1, within walking distance or a short taxi ride from downtown hotels. Terminal addresses are listed under **Transportation** (p. 323). Avoid arriving by bus at night; if you do, take a taxi from the terminal.

LAYOUT. Although Guate is overwhelmingly large, sights and services are concentrated in Zonas 1, 4, 9, 10, and 13. The major thoroughfare is 6 Av., beginning at the Plaza Mayor in the north and continuing south through Zonas 4 and 9. **Zona 1,** the city's oldest section and the true city center, houses budget hotels and restaurants. **Zona 4** lies immediately south of Zona 1. An industrial area, Zona 4 houses the INGUAT office, the second-class bus terminal, and the market area. **Zonas 9** and **10** house the boutiques, embassies, fancy restaurants, and five-star hotels. The two zones are divided by the north-south **Av. de la Reforma:** Zona 9 is to the west, and Zona 10 is to the east. *Avenidas* run parallel to Av. de la Reforma and the street numbers increase eastward. *Calles* run east-west and increase southward. The southern portion of Zona 10 is the **Zona Viva** (Lively Zone), home to the bulk of the city's most happening clubs. **Zona 13** is south of Zona 9. Its two notable features are the international airport and the **Parque La Aurora,** which contains museums, a market, and a zoo. Some possible causes for confusion: 1a Av. of Zona 1 is different from the 1a Av. of Zona 5. Also, some streets are nameless for a block, and some calles in Zona 1 have secondary names. Note that many streets—especially in Zona 1—do not have street signs, so it's best to ask for directions.

> **STREET-SMART** Despite the apparent disorganization, Guate's addresses are logically arranged. For example, look for "8 Av. 12-65, Zona 1" at no. 65 on Avenida 8, located above 12 C. (between 12 and 13 C.), in Zona 1.

SAFETY. Personal safety is a definite concern in Guatemala City. Exploring the city on your own during the day is generally not a problem; be aware of your surroundings and carry yourself as if you always know where you are going, even if completely lost. Don't be afraid to step into an establishment if in need of help. Wandering alone at night is strongly discouraged by locals. The streets of Zona 1 are not safe after dark. If you must, travel by taxi and never alone. Nighttime bar and restaurant hopping in Zona 10 is reasonably safe, provided you stick with the crowds and have a companion. Pickpockets are ubiquitous, especially in Zona 1 and the Zona 4 bus terminal area. Always keep your money and valuables close to your body and distribute bills among multiple pockets so that you don't lose everything if you are robbed. Thigh or waist money belts are recommended. Female travelers should expect cat calls and whistles all over the city. The best response is to remain quiet and move on.

LOCAL TRANSPORTATION

Local Buses: Guate's city bus system is extensive and relatively efficient, but it takes a while to get the hang of it. The nicer and slightly more expensive buses are called *preferenciales,* which are large and red (Q1, Su Q1.25), while the 2nd-class option is to ride the *corrientes* (Q1). Buses run from 7am until about 8pm, though you'll find the occasional bus running later. Buses have destinations clearly marked on the front, and the best places to catch them in Zona 1 are 4 Av. or 10 Av. The latter is the place to go for the more useful buses headed towards the airport. Bus **#82** travels from the city

Guatemala City Center

🛏 ACCOMMODATIONS

Hotel Ajau, **8**
Hotel Colonial, **7**
Hotel Monte Carlo, **9**
Hotel Spring, **5**

🍴 FOOD
Delicadezas San
  Hamburgo, **1**
Restaurante Altuna, **4**
Restaurante y Cafetería
  Cantón, **6**
Tao Restaurant, **2**

🍷 NIGHTLIFE
La Bodeguita del Centro, **3**

center to Zona 4 and down Av. la Reforma between Zonas 9 and 10. Returning, it goes north on Av. de la Reforma, through Zona 4, and up 9 Av. in Zona 1. Bus **#83** runs from 10 Av. in Zona 1 to the airport and the Zona 13 sights and returns to 9 Av. in Zona 1. Bus **#101** runs from Av. de Los Proceres in Zona 10 past the INGUAT office in Zona 4.

Car Rental: The most inexpensive places, like **Tally**, rent for 2 days or more with prices beginning at Q700, including tax and insurance. At the big chains, these prices may jump to Q1200 per day: **Tally,** 7 Av. 14-60 (☎232 0421), Zona 1 and at the airport (☎332 6063); **Avis,** 6a Av. 7-64 (☎332 6209), Zona 9 and at the airport (☎331 0017); **Hertz,** 7 Av. 14-76(☎470 3800), Zona 9, and at the airport (☎470 3838). The cheapest means of securing private transportation in the city may be the hiring of a taxi for a certain period of time; be sure to agree upon the price beforehand.

🛈 PRACTICAL INFORMATION

TOURIST AND FINANCIAL SERVICES

Tourist Information: Instituto Guatemalteco de Turismo (INGUAT), 7 Av. 1-17 (☎331 1333, toll-free 801 INGUAT, or in the US 888-INGUAT; www.guatemala.travel.com.gt) Zona 4, in the Centro Cívico south of the Zona 1 border. Some of the staff speak basic

English and tourist brochures are available. If you're interested in volcano climbs or adventure travel, ask the front desk to direct you to the "Sillón de Guías" in the same building. Open M-F 8am-4pm, Sa 8am-1pm. There is also a branch in the **post office** in Zona 1.

Embassies and Consulates: Belize: Av. de la Reforma 1-50 #803 (☎334 5531) Zona 9, Edificio El Reformador. Open 9am-1pm and 2-5pm. **Canada:** Embassy, 13 C. 8-44 (☎333 6102) Zona 10, Edyma Plaza Niv. 8. Open M-F 8am-4:30pm. Consulate, 6th fl. of the same building (☎333 6140). Open M, Th, F 9am-4:30pm. **US:** Embassy, Av. de la Reforma 7-01 (☎331 1541, emergency 332 3347) Zona 10. Open M-F 8am-5pm. **UK:** Av. de la Reforma 16-00 (☎367 5425) Zona 10, Torre Internacional, 11th fl. Open M-F 9am-noon and 2pm-4pm. Citizens of **Australia** and **New Zealand** can report lost passports here as well as any other concern.

Immigration Office: 41 C. 17-36, Zona 8. Catch bus #71 from 10 Av. Open M-F 8am-3pm. A smaller, more convenient office is on the 2nd fl. of the INGAUT office.

Banks: Generally, smaller bank branches exchange only paper money, especially in Zona 1; head to the larger branches for cashing traveler's checks. AmEx is by far the most commonly accepted form of traveler's check; head to any branch of **Ban Café** to exchange them. **Banco Continental,** framed by 5 Av. and 9 C. in Zona 9, will exchange MC/V checks. **ATMs** *(cajeros)* are fairly common, as long as you have Visa access. You'll usually find them beside banks or in shopping centers. All banks are closed Su, with the exception of **BanQuetzal** at the airport, which also exchanges some European currencies. Open M-F 6am-8pm, Sa-Su 6am-6pm. Banks cluster on and around the *parque central* in Zona 1 and around La Zona Viva in Zona 10.

American Express: Diag. 6 10-01 (☎470 4848) Zona 10, Centro Gerencial. Las Margaritas Torre II 7th fl. Open M-F 8:30am-noon and 2-5pm.

LOCAL SERVICES

English Bookstore: VRISA Bookshop, 15 Av. 3-64 (☎761 3237) Zona 1. Small shop with a wide range of genres in both Spanish and English. Open M-Sa 9am-7pm.

Supermarkets: Paiz and **Super del Ahorro,** across from each other on 7 Av., 17 and 18 C., Zona 1. Both open daily 8am-9pm.

Laundromats: El Siglo, 9 Av. 13-09, Zona 1, or 7 Av. 3-50, Zona 4. In Zona 10 try **USA,** Av. La Reforma 8-15, Zona 10.

Crafts Market: Central Market, 8 and 9 Av., 6 and 8 C., Zona 1, in an underground garage. Home to the best deals on textiles. Open M-Sa 6am-6pm, Su 8am-noon.

EMERGENCY AND COMMUNICATIONS

Police: 6 Av. 13-71 (☎110 or 120) Zona 1. English-speaking staff available.

Ambulance: ☎128.

Fire: ☎122 or 123.

Red Cross: 3 C. 8-40 (☎125 or 232 2026) Zona 1. 24hr. emergency service. Also located at 4 Av. 9-38 (☎362 5237) Zona 10.

Pharmacy: Farmacia El Ejecutivo, 7 Av. 15-01 (☎230 3734) Zona 1. **Farmacia Osco,** 4 Av., 16 C. (☎337 1566) Zona 10. Both open 24hr.

Telephones: Telgua, main office at 7 Av., C. 12/13 (☎238 1098). Next to the post office. **Fax** service. Cash or collect calls only. Can be oppressively crowded, so it is often better to simply ask an operator (☎147 120) for help with small problems. Open M-F 8am-6pm, Sa 8am-1pm. To use domestic or international calling cards call from public phones on the street or from hotels. Many travelers report problems using MCI and Sprint prepaid phone cards, so be prepared to call the card's office collect; Telgua offices, stores, and pharmacies sell Telgua phone cards for use in phone booths.

Internet:

Café Carambola, 14 C. 7-39 (☎220 8080) Zona 1, has super-fast connections. Q10 per 30min. Open daily 8:30am-8:30pm.

@com, in the Centre comercial Los Proceres, 3rd fl., is packed in the afternoon with wandering shoppers and students. Q20 per hr., open daily 10am-7pm.

Cafe Virtual, (332 8027), in the Centre Comercial Los Proceres, ground fl. Grab a beer or a latte while you type or take a break on the outdoor patio. Q20 per hr. Open daily 9am-8pm.

Post Office: Central Post Office, (☎801 CORREOS) 7 Av. 11-66, Zona 1, in the huge orange building. Open M-F 8:30am-5:30pm, Sa 9am-1pm. United Parcel Service, 12 C. 5-53, Zona 10. Open M-Sa 8am-8pm. DHL, 12 C. 5-50. Open M-F 8am-7:30pm, Sa 8am-1pm.

🛏 ACCOMMODATIONS

Almost all of Guate's budget hotels are located in Zona 1, the city's aging downtown area. Because robberies do occur here, prioritize safety when choosing a hotel: windows should be barred, balconies secure, locks functional, and management conscientious. Given nighttime safety concerns, a reservation or an early arrival might be a good idea. Female travelers or those traveling alone may feel more comfortable paying slightly more for the safer surroundings in Zona 9 or 10. All listed hotels have hot water showers, but these can be unreliable. If none of these options pan out, inquire at the **tourist office** (p. 327) for other recommendations. Again, make safety a top priority in your choice.

ZONA 1

🏅 **Hotel Spring**, 8 Av. 12-65 (☎230 2858). Set in a well-maintained colonial home complete with open air courtyard, the roomy and well-lit accommodations provide an excellent escape from the noise and grime of the city. Call ahead for reservations. Singles Q96, with bath Q136; doubles Q136/175. MC/V. ❺

Hotel Colonial, 7 Av. 14-19 (☎232 6722). Gorgeous mahogany furniture and huge rooms. Very helpful staff. Pricey, but if you're looking for elegance for under Q200, look no further. Singles Q99, with bath Q139. ❺

Hotel Monte Carlo, 9 Av. 16-20 (☎238 0735). No race cars or royalty; instead the well-kept rooms with mosaic floors and cable TV make you feel at home. Singles Q60, Doubles Q120. ❸

Hotel Fenix, 7Av. 15-81 (☎251 6625). Perhaps the cheapest hotel in the city, Hotel Fenix also has character like no other. A warped wooden house with well-furnished rooms and many international travelers. Singles Q43, doubles Q50. ❷

Hotel Posada Oslo, 8Av. 14-60 (232-4556). Small and family-oriented. The rooms are decorated with European and Guatemalan travel scenes. Singles Q80, with bath Q100; doubles Q90/120. ❹

Hotel Ajau, 8 Av. 15-62 (☎232 0488). Small, slightly claustrophobic windowless rooms come with all the handy conveniences: safety boxes and a *Telefónica* phone. Internet access right in the lobby. Singles Q64, with bath Q100; doubles Q75/Q115. ❹

OTHER ZONAS

Las Torres, 13 C. 0-43 (☎334 2747; www.lastorres.com) Zona 10. Intended for long-term stays, Las Torres is a plush, English-friendly apartment complex filled with vibrant colors and artwork. A little pricey, but well worth it if you can get a room for just a couple of days. Call in advance. Singles Q250. MC/V. ❺

GUATEMALA

STICKS AND STONES

Upon arriving at La Aurora Airport in the evening, I was informed that the whole city was on strike because of a recent tax increase. Almost all services were closed, and those in operation were attacked with rocks, sticks, and fire. Being the newby to the country, I predictably fled to touristy Antigua. The strike was news, but it was also part of the daily grind of life in the strife-ridden capitol. Guatemala City remained shut down for three days while people gathered with banners and horns in front of the Palacio National begging President Berger for help.

As it turns out, this multi-day *huelga* has become a nearly annual occurance. One local Antiguan told me that August is now know as *agosto negro* for the sheer number of strikes and deaths experienced. The violence varies: sometimes there are deaths, sometimes only noise. However, the reason is almost always the same: taxes on living necessities like food, water, gas and electricity continue to rise, while wages invariably fall.

This strike was the first for president Oscar Berger, but it won't be the last. Since the end of the 37-year civil war in 1996, the government has faced pressure to pay off debt and promote economic growth. Unfortunately, debt payment continues to be a priority, while the domestic economy remains stagnant, leaving most citizens hungry for more.

—*Liza Covington*

Hotel y Restaurante Los Próceres, 16 C. 2-40 (☎363 0746) Zona 10. Safe and convenient, Los Próceres is splurge-worthy for these two reasons alone. The mirrored reception area doubles as Internet cafe with daily papers. Rooms are well-furnished and clean; ask for a room away from the street. Singles Q290. AmEx/MC/V. ❺

Hotel Mayastic, 5 Av. 11-23, (☎331 0824) Zona 9. 14 large, foam-green rooms with private bath and cable TV within a five minute walk from Zona 10 nightlife. 3rd fl. deck gives a nice view of the city. Singles Q153; doubles Q177. ❺

Dos Lunas Guesthouse, 21 C. 10-92, (☎/fax 334-5264; lorena@pronet.net.gt) Zona 13, Aurora II. A welcoming guest house with clean rooms and a friendly, English-speaking Guatemalan owner. Cable TV in the living room, Internet downstairs. Free rides to and from the airport; call upon arrival. Call ahead for reservations, particularly if arriving in the evening. Q90 per person. ❺

▣ FOOD

Sidewalk vendors offer the cheapest grub during the lunch hours, but make sure to avoid veggies. The friendly neighborhood *comedor* is usually inexpensive, offering daily *típico* menus for Q10-20. There's also no dearth of American fast food joints.

Restaurante Altuna, 5 Av. 12-31 (☎232 0669) Zona 1. In a beautifully restored colonial home, old-fashioned, upscale Altuna has a long-standing reputation as the nicest restaurant in downtown Guate. Excellent Spanish food, and some of the dishes aren't quite as pricey as the atmosphere might suggest. Paella Q47, desserts Q15-25. Open Tu-Sa noon-10pm, Su noon-4pm. Reservations recommended. AmEx/MC/V. ❺

Restaurante y Cafetería Cantón, 6 Av. 14-29, Zona 1. Unlike many Chinese restaurants in Guate, Cantón looks and tastes authentic. Sizeable portions, friendly service, and great Chinese art on the wall. The chicken with chile sauce is without equal (Q41). Open daily 9am-10pm. AmEx/MC/V. ❹

Delicadezas San Hamburgo, 5 C. 5-34, Zona 1. Part floral cafe, part 50s diner, this downtown restaurant offers good *típico* fare. Chicken with curry sauce Q42, burger with fries Q34. Open daily 6:30am-9:30pm. ❹

San Martín and Company, 2 Av. and C. 13, Zona 10. When strolling along the posh boulevard of the Zona Viva in the late evening or early morning, stop in here for a touch of Europe while watching the upper crust of Guatemalan society. Don't miss the heavenly ice-cream pastry *totito San Martín* (Q15). ❷

Tao Restaurant, 5 C. 9-70, Zona 1. A real-deal vegetarian eatery amid a flourishing garden. Daily lunch menu (Q40) is the only thing served, so check it out before sitting down. ❹

Del Tingo Al Tango, 12 C. 4-05, Zona 9. Take the #83 bus from any Parque Aurora sight toward the airport. In case you didn't get your fill of animals at the nearby Aurora Zoo, this Argentine steakhouse will take care of it. Sink your teeth into a Delmonico (Q105) or team up with a buddy and polish off an *Asado de Tira* for 2 (Q155). Vegetarian salad bar Q30, fettuccine with tomato sauce and mushrooms Q56. Open daily noon-10pm. AmEx/MC/V. ❺

Danny's Pancakes, 12 C. 5-10, Zona 9. The perfect dinner spot after a long night the Zona Viva. The purple interior keeps up the festive spirit. Banana pancakes (Q20) and a chocolate milkshake (Q18) will fix any cravings. Open 24hr., except Su closes at 9pm, reopens M at 6:30am. MC/V. ❷

◉ SIGHTS

ZONA 1

PLAZA MAYOR. Surrounded by some of the finest architecture in the city, the Plaza Mayor has been stripped to its basic elements: a slab of concrete and a large fountain. Formerly known as "the center of all Guatemala," the space is now mostly filled with pigeons, shoeshines, and men playing card games. The exception to this rule comes on Sunday, when the plaza is flooded with indígenas selling textiles, families out for a stroll, and political protesters. (Bounded on the west and east by 6 and 7 Av. and on the north and south by 6 and 8 C.)

CATEDRAL METROPOLITANA. The stately Catedral Metropolitana, reconstructed after the 1917 earthquake, rises dramatically against the Plaza. Inside the neoclassical structure are the usual saints and religious images—it is on the outer pillars where the magic lies. Etched into the twelve front columns are the names of all those who disappeared during the recent civil war, making the trip to the Catedral a pilgrimage for many families. It is perhaps the quietest spot in the city. *(East of the Plaza. Open M-F 7am-12:15pm and 3-7pm, Sa 7am-12:30pm and 3-6:30pm, Su 6:30am-7:30pm. Sunday services 8, 10am, noon, 1, 4, 6pm. Other services M-Sa 7:30am and 12:15pm.)*

PALACIO NACIONAL. This grand *palacio* was built between 1928 and 1943 under the orders of President Jorge Ubico. Currently, the public is allowed to see only a few of the imposing palace's 350 rooms, but even the corridors are magnificent. La Sala de Recepción awes visitors with its massive Bohemian crystal chandelier, replete with graceful brass and gold quetzals. The Presidential Balcony offers commanding views of the plaza and the surrounding highlands. The second floor houses a fairly complete collection of modern Guatemalan art, including rotating exhibitions of the most renowned Guatemalan artists. In 1980, a car bomb shattered the stained glass windows of the central corridor which had depicted the 10 virtues of a good nation, and some have yet to be reconstructed. *(North of the Plaza. Open daily 9am-11:45pm and 2-4:45pm. Free; tip expected for guided tours.)*

MIGUEL ANGEL ASTURIAS CULTURAL CENTER. Located at the south end of Zona 1 across 7 Av. from the INGAUT offices, the cultural center is home to the **Teatro Nacional** (National Theater), along with both chamber and open-air theaters. Completed in 1978, the main building is said to represent a jaguar in the jungle. There's also a small military museum (Q5) and art gallery. *(24 C. 3-81. ☎232 4041. Free tours last anywhere from 30min. to 3hr., depending on your level of interest—an hour is probably sufficient. Tip expected for guides. Open M-Sa 8am-4pm, military museum open M-Sa 7am-4pm.)*

CASA MIMA. A renovated 19th-century home, the Casa MIMA is a quirky look into the former glory of Guatemala. The house includes a fully furnished chapel and 1920s era kitchen. *(8 Av. 14-12. Open M-F 9am-12:30pm and 2pm-6pm; Sa 9am-12:30pm and 2pm-5pm. Q20, students Q15.)*

ZONA 4

IGLESIA YURRITA. Decked out in vermilion, this outlandish neo-Gothic curiosity was built in 1929. The color scheme inside the church, including an unusual window painted like the daytime sky, is nearly as blinding as the exterior. *(Ruta 6 and Vía 8. Open Tu-Su 7am-noon and 4-6pm.)*

TORRE DEL REFORMADOR. Check out this smaller (and considerably less polished) take on the Eiffel Tower, named in honor of forward-looking President Justo Rufino Barrios, who held office between 1871 and 1885. *(7 Av., 2 C.)*

ZONA 10

MUSEO IXCHEL DEL TRAJE INDÍGENA. A must see for any travelers interested in buying Guatemalan textiles. A detailed step-by-step of the traditional jaspee dye process and its use in indigenous garb informs those interested in purchasing items. The museum is on the campus of the Universidad Francisco Marroquín in a valley with well-landscaped picnic areas. The tranquil atmosphere here makes it a nice escape from the congested city center and an especially fine place to bring lunch. *(Take 6 C. Final east off Av. de la Reforma; the museum is located at the bottom of a large hill. ☎ 331 3622. Open M-F 9am-5pm, Sa 9am-12:50pm. Q25, students Q8. MC/V.)*

JARDÍN BOTÁNICO. Over 700 species of plants labeled in Spanish and Latin. Perfect for a quiet picnic. *(1 C. off Av. de la Reforma. ☎ 333 0904. Open M-F 8am-3pm. Q5.)*

POPOL VUH MUSEUM. Named after the sacred Maya text, the museum has a first rate collection of pre-Columbian Maya pottery, as well as exhibits on colonial art and indigenous folklore. *(Next to the Museo Ixchel del Traje Indígena at the university; follow directions above. ☎ 361 2301. Open M-F 9am-5pm, Sa 9am-1pm. Q25, students Q10.)*

ZONA 13

The sights of Zona 13 are clustered within the vast **Parque La Aurora**, near the airport. Several government-run museums reside here. The area can be reached by bus #83.

MUSEO DE LOS NIÑOS. This museum features colonial architecture—of a lunar colony, that is. The space-age pyramids house a myriad of entertaining exhibits, which teach children about peace and morality through playing (they're also a whole lot of fun for adults). Bounce around the moon simulator, play a giant game of Operation, and ride a bicycle as a skeleton mirrors your motions. The huge R2D2 Lego model is not to be missed. Note: the static electricity generator, the centrifugal force cycle, and the earthquake room might not be approved for use in other, more safety-conscious children's museums. *(Open Tu-Th 8am-noon and 1-5pm, F 8am-noon and 2-6pm, Sa-Su 10am-1:30pm and 2:30-5pm. Q35, students Q20. MC/V.)*

MUSEO NACIONAL DE ARQUEOLOGÍA Y ETNOLOGÍA. This museum traces eons of Maya history with hundreds of Maya artifacts and an excellent scale model of Tikal. The exhibits are strikingly similar to those of the Popol Vuh. *(Located in the park at the corner of 7 Av., 5 and 6 C., Edificio #5. ☎ 472 0489. Open Tu-F 9am-4pm, Sa-Su 9am-noon and 1:30-4pm. Q30.)*

MERCADO DE ARTESANÍAS. La Aurora also holds an INGUAT-sponsored craft market. The traditional textiles, ceramics, and jewelry may make good gifts, but bargaining is off-limits. *(Open daily 9am-6pm.)*

🎵 🎭 ENTERTAINMENT AND NIGHTLIFE

Although the city's frenetic pace tends to die down after dark, there are several options for evening entertainment. The capital is a good place to catch an American flick. Two convenient Zona 1 theaters are the **Capitol,** 6 Av., 12 C., and **Palace,** across the street. **La Cúpula,** 7 Av 13-01, Zona 9, is a theater convenient to Zona 9 and 10 hotels. Theater and opera performances (all in Spanish) are staged at **Teatro IGA,** Ruta 1 4-05 (☎ 331 0022) Zona 4, and in the **Teatro Nacional** (p. 331) on Friday and Saturday nights. For a listing of cultural events, check *La Prensa Libre* or any local newspaper.

The best places to shake your booty are in Zona Viva (Zona 10). The pace picks up around 10pm and winds down around 2am. The hottest club is currently **Kahlua,** 1 Av. 15-06, Zona 10, which comes complete with two dance floors, a chill-out room, and a dance/Latin pop music blend. (No cover.) **Sambuka,** 10 C. and 2 Av., and **Xtreme,** 3 Av. and 13 C., in the Zona Viva are also popular clubs playing Latin/dance music. If you're looking for a bar with incredible live music and room to dance, visit local haunt **Bodeguita del Centro,** 12 C. 3-55, Zona 1.

WESTERN HIGHLANDS

For most travelers, the Western Highlands are the reason they come to Guatemala. A vast expanse of rolling farm land rises up to dense jungle volcanoes and twisting roadways lead to stunning miradores. Meanwhile, the majority of Central America's indigenous population is packed into the region's untouched tiny hillside villages. Dialects of Mam, Ixil, and Cakchiquel echo in the vibrant markets, and men stand outside churches swinging coffee-can censers filled with smoldering resin while chanting the cycles of the Maya calendar.

The graceful colonial splendor of Antigua serves as a gateway to the *altiplano*. The unsurpassed beauty of Lago de Atitlán is ringed by traditional Maya villages, while the colorful Maya market of Chichicastenango is one of the country's most famous sights. Quetzaltenango, Guatemala's 2nd-largest city, has increasingly popular language schools and easy access to hot springs and Mayan markets. Two beautiful mountain towns offer a more serene highlands atmosphere: traditional Todos Santos, in the Cuchumatanes, and Nebaj, situated in northern Quiché.

ANTIGUA

Antigua is Guatemala's most popular tourist destination, and it's easy to see why. Picture-perfect cobblestone streets lead to grand colonial ruins, and the supremely civilized central plaza stands in striking contrast to the rugged green mountains nearby. Antigua (pop. 34,200) was the third colonial capital of Guatemala and served as such from 1541 until 1773, when massive earthquakes prompted the government to relocate to Guatemala City. More recently, the colonial legacy and appealing locale have attracted new residents—and many travelers. Restaurants and hotels catering to tourists have cropped up everywhere, lending the city a wealthy and cosmopolitan air. However, the foundation of Antigua's romantic facade is the breadth and diversity of its indigenous communities. As the main gateway to the western highlands, or *altiplano*, Antigua bears witness to the interplay between mestizo and *indígena* lifestyles, particularly on market days when truckloads of calla lilies and *indígenas* compete with colonial ruins. Enjoy the creature comforts that the city has to offer, but remember that Antigua is merely the first step in exploring a country whose beauty goes beyond the rows of tourist restaurants and *gringo*-filled bars.

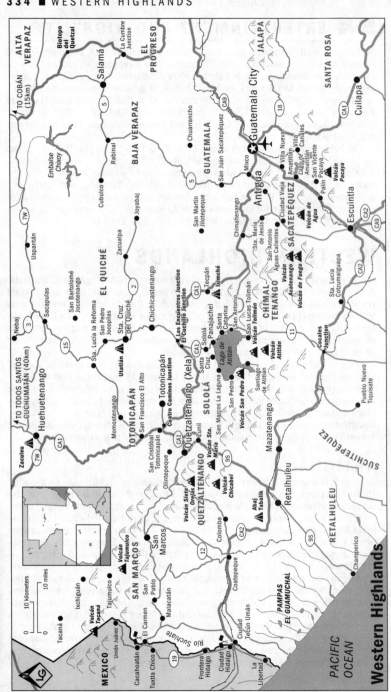

▐ TRANSPORTATION

Buses: All services except the direct bus to Panajachel leave from the main terminal on the southern half of the main market. Departures to: **Chimaltenango** (50min., every hr. 6am-4pm, Q3); **Escuintla** (1½ hr., every hr. 6:45am-4pm, Q5); **Guatemala City** (1hr., every 15min. 5:30am-6:30pm, Q5); **Panajachel** from the Texaco gas station on 4 C. Pte. (2½hr., one first-class daily 7am, Q30), or change buses in **Chimaltenango** (1½hr., Q10); **San Antonio Aguas Calientes** (25min. every 30min. 6am-8pm, more frequent on M, Th, and Sa, Q2). For other Western Highland towns such as **Quetzaltenango** (3hr., Q22) and **Chichicastenango** (2hr., Q13), change buses in **Chimaltenango.**

Tourist Shuttles: Virtually any travel agent will arrange a shuttle. (For a list of recommended agencies, see **Practical Information,** below.) The shuttles are quicker, more comfortable, and more expensive than the public buses. Frequent service to the **airport** and **Guatemala City** (Q55-80), **Panajachel** (Q80), and, on Th, Sa, and Su, **Chichicastenango** (Q94). You can also arrange trips to more far-flung destinations including Río Dulce, Tikal, Monterrico, and Copán, Honduras. Most will pick you up at your hotel.

Car Rental: Ahorrent Car Rental, 5 C. Ote. No. 113 (☎832 0968). Open daily 7am-7pm. Required deposit Q770, plus copy of passport. Cars Q250 per day. **Tabarini,** 5 Av. Nte. 15 (☎832 1017). Variety of sedans, SUVs, and vans offered, new models only. 25+. Q320-1080 per day. Open M-Sa 9am-6:30pm.

Motorcycle Rental: La Ceiba, 6 C. Pte. 15 (☎832 0077). Q300 per day.

▐ ORIENTATION AND PRACTICAL INFORMATION

Antigua's streets are laid out according to the standard grid system (p. 321). Its centerpiece is the *parque central*, bounded by 4/5 C. on the north and south and by 4/5 Av. on the east and west. From the northeast corner of the *parque*, all *avenidas* to the north are designated **Norte** (Nte.), and all to the south are designated **Sur.** All *calles* to the east are dubbed **Oriente** (Ote.), and all to the west **Poniente** (Pte.). Segments of some of the streets have been confusingly reverted to their colonial names, although most businesses and residents still refer to the numbered *calle* or *avenida.* Many streets are also unmarked, so don't be too shy to ask for directions. The **bus terminal** is located at the *mercado*, three lengthy blocks west of the *parque central.* To reach the *parque* from the bus terminal, cross the tree-lined street, Alameda Santa Lucía, and continue straight. **Volcán de Agua** looms over the city to the south. Although INGUAT-authorized "guides" roam the bus terminal, do not follow them to a hotel or anywhere else. While they are authorized as guides, many take tourists to travel agencies or hotels that are not.

TOURIST AND FINANCIAL SERVICES

Tourist Information: INGUAT (☎/fax 832 0763), on the southeast corner of the *parque*, near the cathedral. Bilingual staff. Open M-F 8am-5pm, Sa-Su 9am-5pm. Sometimes closed noon-1pm.

Travel Agencies and Guided Tours: Local travel agents are useful for booking flights, shuttles, package deals, and (generally pricey) tours, but not all agencies in Antigua offer high-quality service. High quality package deals to Tikal run around Q1200. Always verify that the agency is INGUAT approved and check with other travelers' experiences. The following are recommended: **Turansa** (☎832 2928, info@turansa.com) in the Radisson Hotel at 9 C. south of town; **Vision,** 3 Av. Nte. 3 (☎832 3293, vision@guatemalainfo.com); and **Rainbow Travel Center,** 7 Av. Sur 8 (☎832 0478; myers@gua.gbm.net).

Antigua

ACCOMMODATIONS
Hotel Cristal, **1**
Hotel la Casa de Don
  Ismael, **13**
International Mochilleros
  Guesthouse, **4**
La Sin Ventura, **25**
La Tatuana, **23**
Posada Asjemenou, **6**
Posada Ruíz #2, **8**
The Yellow House, **2**

FOOD
Café Condesa, **18**
Café Flor, **19**
Café La Escudilla, **10**
Casa de las Mixtas, **12**
Doña Luisa's, **16**
The Dish, **22**

NIGHTLIFE
Casa El Escudo, **15**
La Casbah, **5**
La Chimenea, **9**
Mono Loco, **24**
Reilly's, **7**

MUSEUMS
Casa del Tejido Antiguo, **3**
Casa K'ojom, **11**
Casa Popenoe, **21**
Museo de Arte Colonial, **20**
Museo de Santiago, **17**
Museo del Libro Antiguo, **14**

Banks: Banks near the *parque* have 24hr. **ATMs. BanQuetzal,** on the north side of the *parque,* exchanges traveler's checks. Open M-F 8:30am-7pm, Sa-Su 9am-1pm. **Currency exchange** closes 1hr. before the bank closes. Note that every other Sa is payday; lines of check-cashing locals can wind around the block.

LOCAL SERVICES

English Bookstores: Trading bookstores abound and many hostels have collections. The largest and most organized is **The Rainbow Reading Room,** 7 Av. Sur 8, with books for sale and rent. Trade in books and earn credit for new ones. Also has a pleasant cafe with several vegetarian options (Q28 each). Buyers receive 25min. of free Internet for every book purchased. Open daily 8am-10pm; cafe open M-F noon-2pm. **Hamlin and White,** 4 C. Oriente, #12-A, inside Jades S.A., carries many current English magazines, as well as some bestsellers and used books. Open daily 9am-6:30pm.

Markets: main market, on Alameda de Santa Lucía next to the bus terminal, extends from 1 C. Pte. to 4 C. Pte. Open daily 7am-6pm. **Mercado de Artesanías,** across the street, winds along 4 C. Pte. up to the *parque central.* US dollars accepted. Open daily 8am-5:30pm. Th and Su are the largest market days.

Supermarket: La Bodegona, 4 C. Pte. 27, half a block from the bus terminal. Enter through the gas station; check bags upon entry. Open M-F 7:30am-8:30pm, Sa 8am-8pm, Su 8am-7:30pm.

Laundry: **Central Laundry,** 5 C. Pte. 7-B. Open M-Sa 8am-7pm. Q5 per lb., students Q4 per lb.; one machine load (9lbs.) Q31.

EMERGENCY AND COMMUNICATION

Fire and Medical: Los Bomberos Voluntarios (☎832 0234), on the north side of the bus station. 24hr. ambulance service.

Police: Policía Nacional (☎832 0251, 832 2264, or 832 2266, emergency 122 or 123), on the south side of the *parque central* in the Palacio de los Capitanes Generales. 24hr. emergency service. **Tourist Police,** 4 Av. Nte. (☎832 7290), half a block north of the *parque's* northeast corner. Open 24hr. English spoken. The tourist police will be happy to provide directions. They also offer security for the **Cerro de la Cruz** (p. 340) at 10am and 3pm daily. Contact the Policía Nacional in an emergency.

Pharmacy: Farmacia Ivori, 4 C. Pte. 33 (☎832 4087). Open 24hr.

Hospital: Centro Médico Antigua, C. del Manchén No. 7 (☎832 0884). Office open M-F 8am-5pm, Sa 8am-noon. Emergency service 24hr.

Telephones: The often crowded Telgua, on 5 Av. Sur 2 (☎832 0498), is just south of the southwest corner of the *parque.* Open M-F 8am-5:45pm, Sa 9am-5pm, Su 10am-3pm.

Internet: Cyber cafes are all over town. **Conexión,** 4a C. Oriente, #14, in La Fuente, has basic service (Q5 per 30min., Q2.50 per additional 15min.), as well as premium service with larger monitors (Q8 per 30min.). Open daily 8:30am-7pm. **Funky Monkey,** 5 Av. Sur 6, inside the small complex of shops known as the Mono Loco, makes going cyber cool (Q3 per 15min.). Internet access, Brazilian jazz, and electronica. Owner speaks English. Open daily 8am-10pm.

Post Office: On the corner of Alameda de Santa Lucía and 4 C. Pte. Open M-F 8am-6pm, Sa 9am-noon. **DHL** on the corner of 6 Av. Sur, 16 C. Pte. (☎832 3718). Open M-F 8am-6pm, Sa 8am-noon.

▌ ACCOMMODATIONS

From every crack in Antigua's cobblestones sprouts a budget hotel. Many families also provide homestays (usually for language school students) for about Q470 per week. For more info, contact INGUAT (p. 335).

▨ **La Tatuana,** 7 Av. Sur 3 (☎832 1223). Huge bedrooms, spotless bathrooms, cyprus doors and signature celeste furniture make this hotel one of the best picks of Antigua. Knock on the door for service. Singles Q112, doubles Q194. ❺

Hotel Cristal, Av. El Desengaño Nte. 25 (☎832 4177). A small, friendly hotel that's a long walk from the *parque central,* but only 1½ blocks from the quiet and gringo-free Plaza San Sebastián. Though it's not the cheapest option, you get what you pay for—gorgeous courtyards, spotless rooms, and free luggage storage. Reservations recommended. Singles Q75, with bath Q85; doubles Q90/Q110. ❹

La Sin Ventura, 5 Av. 8 (☎832 0581). Hang up the boots, throw on the flip-flops and give those aching feet a rest; from this 2nd-fl. hotel, nothing is more than a 30 second walk. Half a block from the *parque,* right above a movie theater (see **Cinema Bistro** p. 340) and a hot bar (see **Mono Loco** p. 341). The rooms are huge, the bathrooms pristine, with laundry and Internet access available. Reservations recommended. Singles Q200; doubles Q305. 25% discount with ISIC. ❺

The Yellow House, 1 C. Pte. 24 (☎832 6646). Across from Mochilleros. Look no further for dorm-style rooms gone deluxe: double beds, hot water, kitchen facilities, free Internet and *panqueque* breakfast included. There is also a reliable travel agent in the front of the house. Fills fast so arrive early. Q50 per person. ❸

SAY WHAT?

With more than half the nation's population claiming Maya descent, many Guatemalans have little need to know Spanish. The four largest language groups (Mam, K'iche', Kaqchikel, Q'eqchi') can be heard all over the country, and it is helpful to know a few universal basics when entering villages:

—The letter C is always a hard sound like K.
—The letter U makes a "wa" sound at the beginning of a word, and a "oo" sound if in the middle or end of a word.
—The letter X always sounds like "sh" (ie: ixil= isheel).

Maya languages are difficult to get your tongue around, but locals will be impressed if an attempt is made. The Q'eqchi' language, the most prevalent of the four, is used by more than 371,000 people and spans a huge area of Guatemala and into Belize. Here is a headstart on some important Q'eqchi' words:

Goodbye= Incuan
Thank you= B'anyox or Bantiox
Water= Ha' (pronounced ah)
Chocolate= Kakaw (like the Spanish cacao)
Coffee= Cape
One= Jun
Two= Ca'ib
Three= Oxib
Four= Caib
Five= O'ob

Posada Asjemenou, 5 Ave. Nte. 31 (☎832 2670). Right below the Arco de Santa Catalina and next to some of the hottest bars in Antigua (p. 340), the Asjemenou has a festive air. Colored lights in each big room and the blooming courtyard. Fabulous banana pancake breakfast included. Single Q135, with bath Q175; doubles Q155/Q200. ❺

Posada Ruíz #2, 2 C. Pte. 25. Look for the rocky arched doorway. Bare-bones rooms are cheap and popular. Despite the communal bath and lack of colonial charm, this social *posada* is a great place to meet fellow travelers. Laundry machine available. Singles Q25; doubles Q35; triples Q50; quads Q60. ❶

Hotel La Casa de Don Ismael, 3 C. Pte. 5, (☎832 1932, hdonismael@hotmail.com). Set back from the street in the 2nd small alley on your right if walking from Alameda Santa Lucía. This hotel encloses a lush patio with an open terrace and a 2nd fl. sun room. Friendly staff. Free purified water and coffee. Singles Q60; doubles Q80. ❸

International Mochilleros Guesthouse, 1 C. Pte. 33 (☎832 0520). Clean rooms around a shady garden. No private baths, but a good bargain. Q45 per person. ❷

🍴 FOOD

Dining in Antigua runs the gamut from the experimental, cosmopolitan gourmet to cheap *comedores* cuisine. No matter what your taste is, good food is easy to find.

The Dish, 4 Av. Sur 4 across the street from Café Flor. Owned by Greg the Brit, The Dish has great cheap food in a posh atmosphere decorated with local art and plush couches. Taco Tuesdays Q19. Daily full five-course menu Q19. Open M-Sa 8am-10pm. ❷

Cactus, 7 Av. Nte. 2. The essentials of Mexican food are crammed into this tiny five-table restaurant. Incredible guacamole and tasty salsa made right in front of you. Veggie quesadilla Q25. Open daily noon-10pm. ❸

Café Flor, 4 Av. Sur 1, ½ block south of the southeast corner of the *parque*. Highly recommended by locals for its outstanding Asian food, suave ambience, huge portions, and great service. Vietnamese spring rolls Q25. *Gadu Gadu* with tofu Q35. Open M-Sa noon-10pm. ❸

Café Condesa, on the west side of the plaza, through the Casa de Conde Libreria. Ask the management to tell you the vaguely creepy stories behind the names of the dishes. Try the "Count" (beef on wheat, Q41), or the "Countess" (emmenthal and gouda on wheat with avocado dressing, Q42). Don't miss the "Butler's Revenge" (brownie with ice cream, chocolate sauce, whipped cream, and almonds, Q29). Brunch Su noon-2pm (Q50). Open daily 8am-10pm. ❸

IT'S AS EASY AS

one, two, three

uno, dos, tres

un, deux, trois

один, два, три

일 , 이 , 삼

Immerse yourself in a language.

Rosetta Stone® software is hands-down the fastest, easiest way to learn a new language — and that goes for any of the 27 we offer. The reason is our award-winning Dynamic Immersion™ method. Thousands of real-life images and the voices of native speakers teach you faster than you ever thought possible. And you'll amaze yourself at how effortlessly you learn.

Don't force-feed yourself endless grammar exercises and agonizing memory drills. Learn your next language the way you learned your first — the natural way. Order the language of your choice and get free overnight shipping in the United States!

Available for learning:
Arabic • Chinese • Danish • Dutch • English
French • German • Hebrew • Hindi • Indonesian
Italian • Japanese • Korean • Latin • Pashto
Polish • Portuguese • Russian • Swahili • Swedish
Spanish • Thai • Turkish • Vietnamese • Welsh

The guaranteed way to learn.

Rosetta Stone will teach you a language faster and easier than other language-learning methods. We guarantee it. If you are not satisfied for any reason, simply return the program within six months for a full refund!

Learn what NASA, the Peace Corps, thousands of schools, and millions around the world already know: Rosetta Stone is the most effective way to learn a new language!

FREE OVERNIGHT SHIPPING
In the United States
(Use promotion code lge005s)
1-800-788-0822
www.RosettaStone.com/lge005s

Personal Edition. Solutions for Organizations also available.

Casa de las Mixtas, 3 C. Pte. and 7 Av. Norte. Tucked into the 1st alley off 3 C. on the right, (coming from C. Santa Lucía) this small, sunny *comedor* offers excellent food and generous portions. Breakfast and lunch under Q20; try the pancake combo with eggs, toast, and coffee or tea (Q12). Open M-Sa 9am-7pm. ❷

Doña Luisa's, 4 C. Ote. 12, on 2nd fl. of a 17th-century house. The basic menu is well executed. *Huevos rancheros* Q15. Sandwiches Q20. Great homebaked desserts Q4. Offers the best whole wheat bread in Antigua (Q9.50). Open daily 7am-9:30pm. Accepts traveler's checks. AmEx/MC/V. ❷

Café La Escudilla, 4 Av. Nte. 4, in the Casa El Escudo (see **Nightlife**, p. 340), a beautiful colonial house ½ block north of the northeast corner of the *parque*. Popular and cheap, the setting is leisurely with fast service. Fruit salad Q5, rich pastas Q30. Open daily 7am-midnight. Bar open M-Sa until 1am, Su until 8pm. ❸

👁 SIGHTS

Although all of the following are worth visiting, it is the combined effect of colonial ruins, multicolored buildings, rambling cobblestone streets, and the ever present shadow of Volcán Agua that has made Antigua famous.

THE PARQUE CENTRAL AREA

PARQUE CENTRAL. The *parque*, one of the finest in the Americas, is centered around a 250-year-old fountain, **La Llamada de las Sirenas (The Sirens' Call),** whose stony babes enthrall visitors with their leaky breasts. By day locals, students, and tourists dot the *parque's* benches as *indígenas* sell their handicrafts and wares. The evening belongs to couples publicly displaying affection.

CATEDRAL SAN JOSÉ. Standing to the east of the *parque*, the cathedral is a mere shadow of its colonial self. The once spectacular edifice was leveled by an earthquake in 1773. The two restored chapels along with the ruins are collectively known as the **Church of San José.** The interior is unimpressive but holds a carving of Christ by Quirio Cataño, carver of the famed Cristo Negro of Esquipulas. The ruins of the rest of the cathedral can be entered from 5 C. Ote. *(Ruins open daily 9am-5pm. Q3. Church open daily 9am-noon and 3-6pm. Free.)*

PALACIO DEL NOBLE AYUNTAMIENTO. The *palacio's* meter-thick walls, built in 1743 on the north side of the *parque*, were some of the few to survive the earthquakes of 1773 and 1776. Once a jail, the building now houses two museums. The small **Museo de Santiago** exhibits pottery, Maya and Spanish weapons, and colonial paintings. The **Museo del Libro Antiguo** (Old Book Museum) displays a reproduction of the first printing press in Central America, an 18th-century lexicon of Guatemala's indigenous languages, a 1615 copy of *Don Quixote*, and a gigantic manuscript of Gregorian music. *(Both open Tu-F 9am-4pm, Sa-Su 9am-noon and 2-4pm. Q10 each; Museo del Libro Antiguo free Su.)*

NORTH OF THE PARQUE

🔲 CONVENTO DE LAS CAPUCHINAS. The impressive and very well-preserved ruins of the convent of Las Capuchinas are definitely worth a visit. Founded in 1726 by the Capuchín nuns, the remains paint a picture of the sisters' difficult 18th-century lifestyles. Two of the residential cells have been restored; visitors can tour the underground cellar and cloister areas. *(Northeast of the main plaza, at the corner of 2 C. Ote. and 2 Av. Nte. Open daily 9am-5pm. Q20, students Q15.)*

IGLESIA LA MERCED. One of Antigua's most memorable churches, La Merced was originally built in 1548 and survived the 1760 earthquake only to collapse in another quake 13 years later. The wonderfully restored yellow facade offers the best example of Antigua's Baroque architecture. Left of the entrance is the doorway to the ruined cloisters and gardens. Don't miss the view of the city and surrounding volcanoes from the upper cloister. Evening services feature lively marimba music. *(Ruins open daily 9am-6pm; Q3. Church open 7am-noon and 3-8pm; services M-Sa 5, 8am, 5, 6, 7pm; Su 5, 9, 11am, 7pm.; free.)*

CERRO DE LA CRUZ. A 15min. walk northeast of town, this hill has a fine view of the valley and a respite from the tourists in the *parque central*. Muggings have been common here, though the presence of the tourist police has improved matters; they offer walking protection at 10am and 3pm beginning at the tourist police office (p. 337).

SOUTHEAST OF THE PARQUE

MUSEO DE ARTE COLONIAL. The museum building, former home of the University of San Carlos, founded in 1676 as the 3rd university in all of Latin America, is among the finest of colonial Antigua's architectural survivors. Cast your eyes heavenward to see the graceful *mudéjar* arches of the central patio or the colonial ceilings of its large gallery. *(½ block east of the parque on 5 C. Ote. Open Tu-F 9am-4pm, Sa-Su 9am-noon and 2-4pm. Q25.)*

CASA POPENOE. This beautifully restored colonial mansion gives an excellent sense of the lives of the wealthy during Antigua's glory days. Although it's only open two hours a day the *casa's* beautiful gardens and nice rooftop views are worth a visit. *(Corner of 5 C. Ote. and 1 Av. Sur. Open M-Sa 2-4pm. Q10.)*

SANTA CLARA AND SAN FRANCISCO CHURCHES. At the end of a palm-lined plaza stand the church and convent of **Santa Clara.** The original building on the site was destroyed in 1717, but the 1773 surviving version is fairly well preserved with an elaborate facade. Nearby is **San Francisco,** one of Antigua's oldest churches, built in 1579 and still in use today. The ruins of the monastery next door, which include a plaza and multiple arched doorways amongst rolling hills, are a pleasant haven. *(Santa Clara at 6 C. Ote. and 2 Av. Sur. San Francisco at 1 Av. Sur and 7 C. Ote. Church open daily 9am-5pm. Ruins open daily 9am-5pm. Q3.)*

WEST OF THE PARQUE

LA RECOLECCIÓN. One of Antigua's most impressive ruins, this church—once among Antigua's finest—was built between 1701 and 1708 and opened in 1717. It suffered considerable damage in an earthquake soon thereafter, and the 1773 quake was the nail in the coffin for this grand structure. Tourist police maintain information on recent muggings. *(C. de la Recolección. Open daily 9am-5pm. Q30.)*

MAYA MUSEUMS. Two museums west of the Plaza are tributes to the great Maya culture that thrived in Guatemala before the Spanish showed up. **Casa K'ojom** is a wonderful museum dedicated to the traditions of *indígena* music and dance. *(About a 20min. walk from the parque central, just past the outskirts of town. Check with the tourist office for directions and a map.)* The **Casa del Tejido Antiguo,** on the northern edge of the market, is small but contains some nice examples of Maya weavings from the early 20th century. *(1 C. Pte. 51, ½ block past San Jerónimo on the left. Open M-F 9am-5pm, Sa 9am-4pm, Su noon-5pm. Q5 gets you a bilingual guide in full Maya dress.)*

▣♫ NIGHTLIFE AND ENTERTAINMENT

The tourists that roam the streets during the day also dominate the Antigua nightlife. Running into other travelers is not a problem. Bars in Antigua close at 1am due to a law that forbids the sale of alcohol after that hour.

▨ **Casa El Escudo,** 4 Av. Nte. 4, is Antigua's most popular nightspot, always packed with language school students, travelers, and locals. Besides a restaurant (p. 339), there are 3 bars: the lively, jazz-filled **Riki's Bar,** the low-key **Paris,** and the Greek **Helas.** Riki's happy hour 7-10pm with pitchers of Gallo Q23.

La Casbah, 5 Av. Nte. 30. Step through the Arabic double doors into a smoky, candle-lit club with a subterranean feel. The place oozes mystery and intrigue. Th is ladies night. Beers and screwdrivers Q15. Cover W-Th Q20; F-Sa Q30, includes 1 drink. Open W-Sa 7pm-1am.

Mono Loco, 5 Av. Sur 6, #5, inside the small complex of shops. The place to watch *gringo* boys try to pick up *gringa* girls. The crowd gathers on the ground fl., but don't miss the upstairs terrace where you can take in some moon rays. You can also watch sports on TV or play darts. Burgers Q25-35. Beer Q12-16.

La Chimenea, 7a Av. Nte. 18. A lively Latin *discoteca*. Cover Q20.

Reilly's, 5 Av. Nte. 31, for all those craving something a little heavier than Gallo, this is your spot. Guiness is Q30 a bottle, but it may be the only one available in Guatemala. Happy hour 2-7pm.

Local cinemas are popular; they're mostly rooms with big-screen TVs (Q10). Check schedules at Doña Luisa or El Escudo, as shows are sporadic. Try **Cinemaya,** the Ground Zero Café, 6 C. Pte. 7 (Dinner and movie Q32); **Cinema Bistro,** 5 Av. Sur 14 (☎ 832 5530); and **Maya Moon,** 6 Av. Nte. 1A. All show international flicks.

◪ OUTDOOR ACTIVITIES

Rolando Pérez (☎ 832 7988) offers **horse rentals** with trail rides through the mountains and a 3hr. tour of four pueblos accompanied by a guide (Q260). **La Ronda** (☎ 832 0857), recommended by INGUAT, also offers horse rentals. **Mayan Bike Tours,** 1 Av. Sur 15 (☎/fax 832 3383), is run by Beat, a skilled pro who gives guided **bike tours** (2½hr., Q118). You can also **rent a bike** for solo spins. (Q12 per hr. Open daily 8:30am-7:30pm.)

▸ DAYTRIPS FROM ANTIGUA

SANTA MARÍA DE JESÚS AND VOLCÁN DE AGUA

The lovely *indígena* town of Santa María de Jesús, 30min. by bus from Antigua, has a beautiful view over the valley. The trail to Volcán de Agua, by far the easiest of Guatemala's big volcanoes to climb, begins in town (4hr. up, 3hr. down). To reach the trailhead from the plaza in Santa María, follow the street opposite the church and walk uphill for three or four blocks. Before the next church (at the end of the hill) go right and then your 1st left. No guides are available at the base of the volcano; it is best to arrange a guide in Antigua.

There are several **buses** per day between Antigua and **Santa María de Jesús,** with more frequent service on Antigua market days; to be on the safe side, catch a bus back no later than 5pm.

VOLCÁN PACAYA

Visitors to Volcán Pacaya (2552m) come face to face with one of the world's most active volcanoes. The sulfurous fumes, pockets of hot lava, and barren plains are otherworldly, and on the way up the vistas are magnificent. The glowing lava of Pacaya is most spectacular at night and when it's more active.

G U A T E M A L A

Pacaya is closer to Guatemala City than Antigua—and if you want to travel there independently there are good buses from Guate. However, most people visit on a guided tour from Antigua, since it's easier. Crime against tourists on the mountain has been a problem, but due to police patrols incidents are now relatively rare. The trail can be challenging, so get a guide.

▐ TRANSPORTATION. Guided **tours** from Antigua typically leave around 1pm and return at 10pm. Security officers and guides are supplied, but bring your own water, snacks, warm clothes, and a flashlight. (Q40-120 per person. Q45 entrance fee to national park.) Two good companies are Eco-Tour Chejos and Gran Jaguar Tours. (For contact information see **Antigua Practical Information,** p. 335.) Eco-Tour Chejos sells two different packages for Q40 and Q80. Although they claim to provide more security and a more flexible time schedule for the extra money, there is little noticeable difference.

From Guatemala City take a **bus** from the Zona 4 terminal to **San Vicente de Pacaya** (7am and 3:30pm), and then walk to **San Francisco** (1½hr.), the starting point for the trail. For safety, walk in groups. You can arrange for guides in either town, but your best bet is to ask for a guide in San Francisco. The hike begins at an office at the entrance to the national park. It is possible to find a place for the night by asking around; check before starting out.

▨ THE TRAIL TO PACAYA. From San Francisco, the trail winds through fields and forests, and views quickly improve. About 30min. into the climb, you'll arrive at a gorgeous lookout with views of Guatemala City. After 1½hr., the trail emerges onto a windy ridge of volcanic rock. A few feet away, at the edge of a massive bowl of cooling lava, Pacaya's starkly beautiful cone looms above. The trail continues around the rim of the crater, and then it's a challenging 30min. scramble to the summit over loose volcanic rocks. The trek back down is equally exhilarating, as you jump and slide down the steep slope back to the base.

LAGO DE ATITLÁN

According to Quiché legend, Lago de Atitlán was one of the four lakes that marked the corners of the world. Today, the majestic lake is indeed one of the most beautiful in the world. Encircled by green hills and three large volcanoes, Atitlán's waters change color constantly, from emerald to azure. Surrounding it are three traditional villages peopled by Maya of Cakchiquel and Tzutuhil descent, blending the cultural and natural beauty into a stupendous mosaic.

The tourist mecca of **Panajachel** is the first stop for almost every visitor. Several of the towns that ring Atitlán—bustling **Santiago Atitlán,** isolated **Tzununá,** and, on the eastern shore, **San Antonio Palopó**—are among the few in all of Guatemala in which the men wear traditional dress. **San Pedro de la Laguna** has the most established budget traveler scene on the lake, while **San Marcos, Santa Cruz,** and **Jaibalito** are home to beautiful lakeside hotels. **Sololá** is a traditional town above the lake.

PANAJACHEL

Although it is not the largest or most traditional lakeside town, Panajachel (pop. 11,900) has long been a tourist magnet. Back in the 1960s and 70s, it became a permanent hippie hangout. Today, the old-time peace-lovers sell goods and grub, alongside traditional Mayans, to the bus loads of daytrippers from Antigua. "Pana," as it is affectionately called (or less affectionately, "Gringotenango") is one of the most touristed towns in Guatemala. Although more developed than other stops in the region, Pana has its own unique culture and provides an important and fascinating look at what Guatemala means to foreigners and *indígenas* alike. For a smaller version of gringo culture in Guatemala, visit nearby **San Pedro.**

Lago de Atitlán

TRANSPORTATION

Buses: Leaving C. Principal, buses head to: **Antigua** (Rebulli direct pullman 2½hr., M-Sa 10:45am, Q35), or take any bus heading to Guatemala City and change in Chimalt-enango; **Chichicastenango** (1½hr., every hr. 7am-3pm, Q10; pullman direct 6:45am, Q15); **Guatemala City** (3hr., 10 per day 5am-3pm, Q20; pullman direct 6, 11am, 2pm; Q30). Connect to most western highlands destinations from **Los Encuentros** (1hr., frequent service, Q5); **Quetzaltenango** (2½hr.; 6 per day 5:30am-2pm, Q12); **Sololá** (20min., every 30min. 5am-6pm, Q2); **Tecún Uman, El Carmen,** and the **Pacific Coastal Highway** change in **Cocales** (2½hr., 8 per day 6am-3:30pm, Q10).

Boats: There are two docks in Panajachel. The first, by the **Hotel Barceló del Lago,** at the end of C. del Rancho, serves Santiago Atitlán, the eastern shore, and lake tours (every 90min. 7am-4:30pm). The second, at the end of **Calle del Embarcadero,** serves San Pedro la Laguna, Santa Cruz and all towns in between (every 30min. 7am-5pm.) Some boats on this route start at Barceló del Lago pier, but they'll stop at the Embarcadero. You can also hire a private *lancha* at the dock. **Lake tours** are offered by the ferry companies. (To San Pedro, Santiago, and San Antonio Palopó; 7hr., 8:30am, Q50.)

✦🔼 ORIENTATION PRACTICAL INFORMATION

Panajachel is small enough that addresses and street names are not used often, and signs point to accommodations off the main street. Buses pull into Pana along **Calle Principal** and stop at or near the town's main intersection, where it meets **Calle Santander.** Santander runs to the shore and has many budget establishments. **Avenida Los Árboles** is home to a cluster of restaurants, bars and discos.

TOURIST AND FINANCIAL SERVICES

Tourist Information: INGUAT (☎ 762 1106), new office on C. Santander near the main junction. Limited English. Open daily 9am-5pm.

Travel Agencies: Agencies will arrange tours to just about any destination. They also offer package deals to popular sites such as Tikal, Río Dulce, and Chichicastenango. Two reliable agencies are **Atitrans** (☎ 762 0146), in Centro Comercial Rincón Sai on the left side of C. Santander facing the lake (open daily 7am-7pm) and **Servicios Turísticos Atitlán** (☎ 762 2075, turisticosatitlan@yahoo.com), farther down Santander toward the lake.

Banks: Banco Inmobilario, on the corner of C. Principal and C. Santander. Open M-F 9:30am-5pm, Sa 9am-1pm. **Banco Industrial,** near Mario's Rooms, on the right side of C. Santander facing the lake. 24hr. Visa-friendly **ATM.** Open M-F 9am-4pm, Sa 9am-1pm. **Banca Red,** at the end of Av. de los Árboles, also has an ATM.

LOCAL SERVICES

Bike and Motorcycle Rental: Motos Emanuel (☎ 762 2790), on C. 14 de Febrero next to Hospedaje García. Motos (gas included) Q70 per hr., Q350 per 8hr. day. Deposit Q300. Bikes Q5 per hr., Q35 per day. M-F 8am-6pm; Sa 8am-1pm.

Market: The town market is at the north end of C. Principal. From the bus stop, continue straight past the church on your left. Textiles, carvings, and other tourist goods are sold in stands all along C. Santander.

Laundromat: Lavandería El Viajero, C. Santander before the intersection with C. Principal, above Atitrans travel agency. Drop-off service Q4 per lb. Open daily 8am-7pm.

EMERGENCY AND COMMUNICATIONS

Police: (☎ 762 1120), at the end of C. Principal away from the lake, across from the church and to the left of the municipalidad. Limited English. The **tourist police office** is located below INGUAT on the beach.

Pharmacy: Farmacia Santander (☎ 762 2657), across from the Banco Inmobilario, at the intersection of C. Principal and C. Santander. Open daily 8am-11pm, closed occasionally for lunch.

Medical Services: There is a **hospital** located on the road between Pana and Sololá. **Centro de Salud** provides free basic medical care.

Telephones: Telgua, halfway down C. Santander, on the 2nd fl. across from Banco Industrial. Open M-F 8am-5:30pm, Sa 9am-1pm.

Internet: There are a few Internet cafes on C. Santander. In the new Plaza Atitlán is **Atitlán Cafe Internet** with super fast connections for good prices, in addition to cheap international call rates (Q2 per 15 min, international rates Q3 per min.) Open daily 9am-8pm. **Mayanet,** across from the school, is similarly priced (Q2 per 15min.). Open M-Sa 8am-10pm, Su 2:30-8pm.

Post Office: C. Santander, 200m from lake. Open M-F 8:30am-5:30pm, Sa 9am-1pm. **DHL:** (☎ 762 2333) next to Atitrans travel agency. Open M-F 8am-noon and 2-6pm; Sa 9am-1pm.

ACCOMMODATIONS

Mario's Rooms, (☎762 2370) at C. Santandar and C. El Chali. Recently renovated rooms are clean and nicely furnished with colorful curtains and basic dressers. Pleasant courtyard with sun terrace. Good location and attached restaurant. Singles Q40, with bath Q70; doubles Q75/Q100. Prices slightly higher in July and Aug. ❷

Hospedaje Del Lago, C. El Viajero (☎762 0131). ½ block away from the lake off C. Santander, look for the small dirt path on the left. New, spacious rooms with big windows and basic furnishings. Communal baths have reliable hot water. Singles Q50; doubles Q80. ❸

Hospedaje García, C. El Chali (☎762 2187), left off C. Santander when walking toward the lake. Removed from the bustle of the main street, the García family keeps the rooms clean and the atmosphere relaxed. Rooms are small but affordable. Q35 per person. ❷

Hotel Fonda del Sol (☎762 1162), near the bus station on C. Principal, is a good deal for a more upscale accommodation. Rooms on the far side of the yard are nicest and priciest. Bus station makes some rooms noisy. Singles Q40, with bath Q95; doubles Q80/Q180. ❷

Hospedaje Sánchez, C. El Chali (☎762 2224). The best view of the lake in any budget hotel. Simple, cheap, and quiet, with a friendly owner and spacious rooms. Singles Q30; doubles Q40; triples Q45. ❶

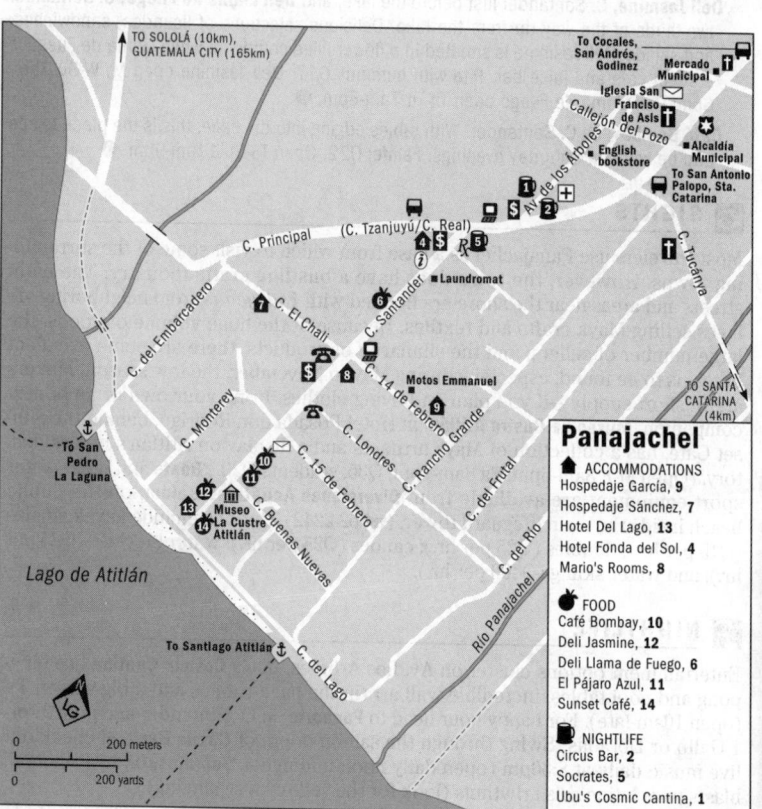

Panajachel

🏠 **ACCOMMODATIONS**
Hospedaje García, **9**
Hospedaje Sánchez, **7**
Hotel Del Lago, **13**
Hotel Fonda del Sol, **4**
Mario's Rooms, **8**

🍴 **FOOD**
Café Bombay, **10**
Deli Jasmine, **12**
Deli Llama de Fuego, **6**
El Pájaro Azul, **11**
Sunset Café, **14**

🍸 **NIGHTLIFE**
Circus Bar, **2**
Socrates, **5**
Ubu's Cosmic Cantina, **1**

GUATEMALA

FOOD

Covering everything from Chinese cuisine to homemade apple pie, the tourist industry has shaped Pana's restaurant business. Most restaurants cater to a healthy, all-natural clientele, signified by the abundance of whole wheat bread in the town's establishments.

Sunset Café, at the end of C. Santander facing the beach. A little pricey, but worth it for the great lake-side view and local music performance at 7:30pm. The sizzling *fajitas* (chicken Q35, shrimp Q41) come highly recommended. Great *chile relleno*, Q35. Open M-F 11am-midnight, Sa-Su 7am-11pm. ❹

Guajimbo's, on C. Santander. A jam-packed, street-side Uruguayan grill. They guarantee you won't leave hungry, serving up huge portions of steak, potatoes, and veggies. The house specialties are the *Chivitas Hernandarias*, a combination of tenderloin, melted mozzarella, and green olives (Q42) and the *chorizo al plato* (Q33). Basic veggie options like spaghetti with marinara sauce (Q28). Open daily 11am-9pm. ❸

El Pájaro Azul, next to the post office on C. Santander. This chic cafe offers delectable vegetarian options and mouth-watering crepes. Try the "Jamaican" (banana, brown sugar, and vanilla ice cream; Q19). Open daily 10am-10pm. ❷

Deli Jasmine, C. Santander just before the lake, and **Deli Llama de Fuego,** C. Santander two-thirds of the way up from the lake. Delicious selections of licuados, sandwiches, and salads. Deli Jasmine is situated in a flower-filled courtyard, while Llama de Fuego is a street cafe and juice bar. Pita with hummus Q17. Deli Jasmine open M, W-Su 7am-6pm; Deli Llama de Fuego open Th-Tu 7am-6pm. ❷

Café Bombay, on C. Santander. With tables edging into the *calle*, this is the place to see and be seen on Saturday evenings. Falafel Q22. Open Tu-Su 11am-9pm. ❸

SIGHTS

Most travelers use Panajachel as a base from which to visit some of the surrounding towns. However, the town does have a bustling crafts industry. The main streets and areas near the shore are flooded with *indígenas* from neighboring villages selling Maya crafts and textiles. Because of the huge volume of goods, the large number of sellers, and the similarity of products, there are some excellent bargains to be found, especially during May to November, the low season. Mirrors are in short supply—if you plan on buying clothes, bring your own or an honest companion. **Museo La Custre Atitlán,** in Hotel Posada don Rodrigo, behind the Sunset Café, has a collection of Maya artifacts and a display on Atitlán's natural history. (Open M-F 8am-6pm, Sa 8am-7pm; Q35, students Q20.) **Boats** and other water sport equipment are available from **Diversiones Acuáticas Balam,** on the public beach inside the main lifeguard tower. (☎762 2242). Options include kayak singles (Q15 per hr.), doubles (Q25 per hr.); canoes (Q25 per hr.); water bicycles (Q25 per hr.); and water skiing (Q400 per hr.).

NIGHTLIFE

Entertainment options cluster on Av. Los Árboles. **Ubu's Cosmic Cantina** has ping-pong and pool tables, incredible wall art (in the back room), and a big-screen TV (open 10am-late). For happy hour head to **Panaarte** on C. Santander and grab 2-for-1 Gallo or Doradas. Swing through the saloon doors of **Circus Bar** and check out live music daily at 8:30pm (open daily noon-midnight). **Socrates,** on C. Principal, blasts pure latino salsa rhythms (look for the yellow overhanging).

SAN PEDRO

Surrounded by the San Pedro Volcano Reserve and pristine lakeside cliffs, San Pedro (pop. 9600) is an ideal base for climbing, exploring the lake, or simply relaxing. Although nothing could interfere with the mellowness of some of the town's visitors, the center erupts during its festival week, the third week of June.

TRANSPORTATION. *Lanchas* leave **Panajachel** (30min., every 30min. 7am-5pm, Q15). Ferries between **Santiago** and **San Pedro** (40min.; every hr. 8am-1pm, 3:30, 5pm; Q10). Two early buses run to **Quetzaltenango** (3½hr., 4:30 and 5:30am).

ORIENTATION AND PRACTICAL INFORMATION. There are two main docks in San Pedro. Boats to and from Santiago arrive at a dock on the south side of town, while the eastern dock serves Panajachel and all other lakeside towns. The two docks are within walking distance along a curvy **lakeside road** that runs through the lower village. The walk takes 20min., and it is best to ask for directions as you wind through the fields. From either dock, a walk straight uphill on the paved road will take you to the **town center,** where there's a **Banco Rural** that exchanges traveler's checks and has a **24hr. ATM.** (Open M-F 8:30am-5pm, Sa 9am-1pm.) **Telgua** is about halfway up the paved road from the Santiago dock. (Open daily 7am-noon and 1-6pm.) Internet can be found in many hostels as well as at **Planet Outreach** halfway up the road from the Santiago dock. (Open M-Sa 8am-8pm, Q10 per hr.) The **post office** is behind the massive gray stone church. Try not to walk between the two docks at night; a few muggings have been recently reported.

ACCOMMODATIONS. Close to the lakeside near the Pana dock, **Hospedaje Casa Elena ❶** offers large rooms, hot water, and a patio with views of the lake (Q25 per person). Also close to the Pana dock with Internet and hot water is **Hotel Mansión del Lago ❷** (☎721 8041. Q40 per person). **Hotel Ti'Kaaj ❶,** on the lakeside road close to the Santiago dock, is simple and super cheap. Offering basic cement rooms and a leafy courtyard with hammocks, this is a popular place for young backpackers. (Singles Q12; doubles Q22; triples Q32.)

FOOD AND ENTERTAINMENT. When the munchies strike, head for **Nick's Place ❸,** at the Pana dock. It serves huge breakfasts for low prices (Q12) and has tasty pizzas (Q30-35) as well as a big-screen TV which regularly shows soccer and the occasional movie. (Open daily 7:30am-10pm.) For even classier cuisine, enjoy a baguette with mozzarella and beef (Q20) and evening drinks and movies upstairs at **D'Noz ❷.** (Open 9:30am-late.) Across the street, **Restaurant El Fondeadero ❷** has nice views and a patio. Chicken sandwich with fries Q10. (Open daily 6am-9pm.) On the uphill road from the Santiago dock is **Café de Arte ❷,** operated by well-known local artist Pedro Rafael González Chavajay, who showcases his work on the walls. The food is good and cheap, and Pedro may even sit down to chat. (Open daily 7am-11pm.)

SIGHTS AND OUTDOOR ACTIVITIES. If admiring the lake isn't activity enough, you can rent **canoes** or **horses** through **Bigfoot Guides** (☎721 8203; Q20 per hr.) on the path by the lake close to the Pana dock. The 4-5hr. climb up **Volcán San Pedro** (3020m) is rewarding but not without risks. Robberies occur and the trail is notoriously hard to follow; it's a good idea to go with a guide. Check around the Pana dock with Bigfoot (around Q50), or arrange with a tourist office in Pana. You can vegetate in hot water at **thermal waters** or at the competing **solar pools,** both located along the lakeshore between the docks.

SANTA CATARINA AND SAN ANTONIO

An outing to **Santa Catarina Palopó** (pop. 10,400) and **San Antonio Palopó** (pop. 3600) from Panajachel, is an easy way to escape the bustle of Pana. The residents of Santa Catarina Palopó make beautiful weavings and wear an aqua and purple costume (a design dating back only to the 1970's). Foot-operated looms are in nearly every home along the main road offering visitors a look into the costumes' creation. Larger San Antonio is often included on the three-town tour of the lake offered by the launch companies. Residents are accustomed to peddling their wares to visitors, but a sense of tradition and isolation still remains.

If you'd like to stay in Santa Catarina or San Antonio, options are limited. In Santa Catarina, try the **Hospedaje 5-Apuj ❶.** Really just a couple of rooms rented out by a local family, there are great views of the lake and plenty of local kids to show you all the hidden gems of the village. (☎762 2981. Q30 per person.) In San Antonio, **Hotel Terraza del Lago ❺,** to the right 400m along the road past the dock, has nine spacious, wood-panelled rooms with excellent views and private hot-water baths. The adjacent *comedor* serves traditional breakfast and dinners. (☎/fax 762 0157. Singles Q170; doubles Q240.)

SANTIAGO DE ATITLÁN

The largest of the lakeside *pueblos* with over 30,000 inhabitants, Santiago de Atitlán is nestled between the San Pedro and Tolimán volcanoes. The Tzutuhil people who live here were Pedro de Alvarado's allies in subduing the Cakchiquel of Panajachel. Santiago dominated Atitlán until Panajachel eventually regained control. Although it has a busy, commercial feel, Santiago remains a traditional place. You might see the striking women's *xocopes*—extraordinary, 10m long red straps worn around the head. The famed Santiago *xocop* is depicted on the 25-centavo coin. On July 25 (the festival of Santiago) and during *Semana Santa*, the village is awash in traditional colors.

Ferries between Panajachel and Santiago run regularly (1hr.; 8 per day 5:45am-4:30pm, 7 returns per day 7am-4:30pm; Q10). **Buses** depart the plaza for Guatemala City (4hr.; 11:30am, noon, 2pm; Q20). Also near the plaza are the **Banco G&T** (Open M-F 9am-5pm, Sa 9am-1pm) and **post office** (open M, Th 2-4:30pm, Sa 9am-1pm).

To find the modest **Chi Nim Ya ❶** hotel from the docks, walk up the hill and take your first left. (☎721 7131. Singles Q30, with bath Q50; doubles Q60; triples with bath Q90.) **Hotel Tzutuhil ❶** (☎721 7174) offers the same rates and excellent lake views. It's very close to the main town plaza; if you're facing the church, walk right and then take the first street on the right. The entrance is half a block downhill on the second floor.

From the dock, head up the hill into the village. After the initial climb, turn left and head toward the **Church of Santiago Apostle** in the town's main plaza. The church, with its wide, colorful nave, was founded in 1547. As Santiago was one of the villages most affected by the violence of the civil war, the church is a memorial to those killed, including the parish priest in 1981. There isn't much else to see in Santiago, though **Maximón's Shrine** is worth a visit. **Parque Nacional Atitlán,** 5km north of Santiago, was created to protect the now-extinct Atitlán grebe, but the remaining bird life is interesting. You can get there by canoe (ask at the docks) or by foot on the road to San Lucas Tolimán (30min.).

SAN MARCOS LA LAGUNA

San Marcos' (pop. 2400) big selling point is appealing accommodations—including a respected yoga and meditation retreat—hidden in a lakeside canopy. There isn't much to do, which is exactly why most people come. The **hiking** along the nearby shore is particularly rewarding; try the 3hr. walk to Santa Cruz with a buddy.

Ferry captains running between San Pedro and Pana will stop in San Marcos upon request (and can be flagged down once you're here). If you're already in one of these smaller towns, flag a boat down or ask a hotel to call one. There's also a new road from San Pedro (truck ride Q3). There are two docks at San Marcos. The first is a five minute walk to the left (facing away from the lake). The second is right in front of the path leading to all the hotels.

The best value in town is the **Hotel Quetzal ❶.** To reach it, take a left just before Paco Real, and follow the trail as it snakes to the right. Quetzal has comfortable private accommodations and dorms in a modest, 2-story house with meals and hot water. (☎306 5039. Dorms Q25; private rooms Q30 per person.) A few steps down the path from the dock lies the **Posada Schumann ❺.** The rambling garden accompanies slightly pricey but beautiful rooms and bungalows with kitchens and hot water. Schumann also offers a year-round restaurant (☎202 2216). Up the path on the left is **Las Pirámides Meditation Center.** The grounds are suitably inviting and peaceful, and there's a very good vegetarian restaurant. They also offer spiritual healing sessions and excellent **massages.** (☎/fax 205 7151. Q70-90 per day includes lodging, courses, and use of facilities; sessions coincide with the lunar cycle.)

TZUNUNA AND EL JAIBALITO

These two lakeside villages are notable for their lack of traffic. **Tzununa** (zoo-NOO-nah), especially, has a feeling of isolation and tradition. The women wear beautiful multicolored *huipiles.* Cakchiquel is the language of choice; visitors must be creative with their communication, as many residents speak no Spanish or English.

Pana-San Pedro *lanchas* stop here upon request (as will some ferries). If you're already in one of these smaller towns, flag a boat down or ask a hotel to call one.

There's little in **El Jaibalito,** but the fabulous **◼La Casa del Mundo ❺** is reason enough to come. From the town dock, walk to the right along the lake for five minutes. Owned and operated by an Alaskan and Guatemalan family, the house clings to a steep hillside above the water, and the view is the best on the lake. Each cozy room has water vistas, hand-made furniture, and a private balcony. For your own jacuzzi, ask for room #12. Bill and Rosa serve delicious, family-style meals and have evening fires on the main porch. Bill also rents out top-of-the-line river and sea **kayaks** for exploring the lake (Q25-50 per hour). Bill and Rosa prefer guests to visit from the town dock as opposed to their private dock in order to cut down on local pollution. (☎218 5332. Doubles Q175, with bath Q280. Dinners Q65.)

SANTA CRUZ

Santa Cruz (pop. 1400), a modest town above the lake, is home to a lovely 16th-century church. Most visitors, however, care only about the collection of hotels that line the shore below. Like other towns along the shore, Santa Cruz is a fantastic setting in which to relax, read, and meet fellow travelers. **La Iguana Perdida** (below) offers **scuba diving** in the lake; PADI certification costs only Q1400. Although it's only a short hop by boat back to Panajachel, the path along the lake is impossible to follow. A better **hike** is from Santa Cruz to Sololá (about 3½hr., take a bus back to Pana). Pana-San Pedro *lanchas* stop here upon request (as will some ferries). If you're in one of these smaller towns, flag a boat down or ask a hotel to call one.

All of the accommodations listed here serve food, so you won't need to move very far from your hammock or easy chair. Note that there's no electricity or hot water. **La Iguana Perdida ❸,** right by the dock, is a backpacker's haven with an assortment of glorified bamboo huts—and even a treehouse—among the green trails of its backyard. Bring lots of repellent and a mosquito net if you want to sleep in this exposed building. The atmosphere is extremely friendly; family-style dinners are served for Q42. (Dorms Q25; in the tree Q22; singles Q48; doubles Q70.) The **Arca De Noé ❸,** next to the dock, run by friendly German owner Anna, tries to compensate for the lack of modern conveniences with daytime solar-heated water and a few hours of solar-powered lighting at night. Comfortable, stone bungalows are set around well-landscaped grounds. Multiple-course dinners prepared by Anna (Q65, reservations required for non-guests) are excellent. (☎306 4352; thearca@yahoo.com. Singles Q60; doubles Q90; double bungalows with bath Q240.)

SOLOLÁ

One of the largest Maya towns in Guatemala, Sololá (pop. 32,000) sits beautifully in the hills and offers a gorgeous view of the lake below. Tradition is strong here and the impressive **Friday market** (starts in the early morning) attracts *indígenas* from surrounding villages. There's a smaller market on Tuesdays and weekends. The well-priced **El Pasaje ❶**, 5/6 Av., 9 C., two blocks from the *parque central*, has a pleasant courtyard and clean rooms with hot-water communal baths that are rough but passable. (Singles Q25; doubles Q35.) Sololá, along the road between Panajachel and Los Encuentros junction, is easily accessible by bus. It's an inevitable stopover on your way from Guate to Panajachel.

CHICHICASTENANGO

Chichicastenango's famous Thursday and Sunday markets bring people from across Guatemala and the world to what is considered by many to be the country's greatest attraction. Tour groups flood in from Antigua and Panajachel. The foreign invasion has brought with it the bad and the good: both cheap knock-offs of traditional textiles and the most beautiful products the Guatemalan countryside has to offer are available in the packed stalls. Nevertheless, "Chichi," with its nearly 50,000 inhabitants, is still very much an *indígena* town, as the soot from charcoal cookfires, the lilt of spoken Quiché, and the haze of devotional incense all attest.

Like the town's bustling markets, its history is tumultuous. Chichi was built by the Spanish in the 16th century as a home for refugees from Utatlán, the Quiché capital the Spaniards had brutally leveled. During the 19th century, the Guatemalan government used forced-labor laws written during the colonial era to pull Quiché workers from the mountains to work on coffee plantations. Tensions rose again in the late 1970s and early 80s, when guerrilla activity disturbed the area. In 1993, it was the site of the assassination of the Jorge Carpio, cousin of then-president Ramiro de León Carpio, a symbol of the firm hand of landowners held over the region. Despite periods of persecution, the region's combination of indigenous and Catholic religious tradition continues to thrive today.

▐ TRANSPORTATION

Buses: Buses pass by the corner of 5 Av. and 5 C. On Thursday and Sunday market days, plenty of **tourist shuttles** run back and forth from **Panajachel and Antigua.**
Guatemala City (3hr., every 10min. 3am-5pm, Q15); **Santa Cruz del Quiché** (30min., every 30min. 3am-5pm, Q3); **Quetzaltenango** (2½hr., 5 per day 5am-3pm, Q11); and **Panajachel** (1½hr.; 9, 11am, 2pm; Q11). Any Guatemala City bus will drop you off at **Los Encuentros** and **Chimaltenango** for transfers to other towns. Check with the tourist office for updated information and possible bus transfers.

▚ ▐ ORIENTATION AND PRACTICAL INFORMATION

Chichi is centered on the *parque central.* The *parque* is bordered by 4/5 Av. on the west and east, and 7/8 C. on the north and south, but it is hardly discernible most of time when streets are covered by market stands. **5 Av.**, the street with most tourist services, passes in front of the church on the east side of the *parque* and runs north. There are many tourist services on 6 C.

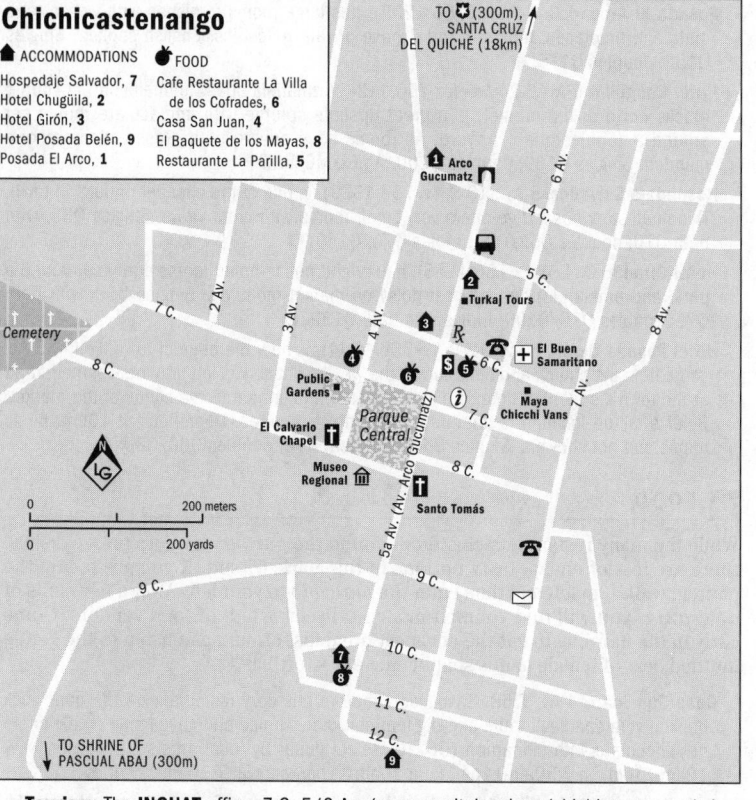

Chichicastenango

ACCOMMODATIONS
Hospedaje Salvador, **7**
Hotel Chugüila, **2**
Hotel Girón, **3**
Hotel Posada Belén, **9**
Posada El Arco, **1**

FOOD
Cafe Restaurante La Villa
de los Cofrades, **6**
Casa San Juan, **4**
El Baquete de los Mayas, **8**
Restaurante La Parilla, **5**

TO (300m),
SANTA CRUZ
DEL QUICHÉ (18km)

Arco
Gucumatz

Turkaj Tours

El Buen
Samaritano

Public
Gardens

Parque
Central

El Calvario
Chapel

Maya
Chicchi Vans

Museo
Regional

Santo Tomás

Cemetery

0 ———— 200 meters
0 ———— 200 yards

TO SHRINE OF
PASCUAL ABAJ (300m)

Tourism: The **INGUAT** office, 7 C. 5/6 Av. (www.comitelocal.org/chichicastenango), has maps, bus schedules, and recommendations on local travel agencies.

Travel Agencies: Chichi Turkaj Tours (☎913 9874) on 5 Av. 5-24 offers information and extensive tourist shuttle service to most of the country; English spoken.

Banks: Banks line 6 C. A good option is **Bancafé**, 5 Av., half a block from the *parque* toward the arch. Exchanges US dollars and traveler's checks and gives Visa cash advances up to Q2000. Open Su-F 9am-5pm, Sa 9am-1pm.

Pharmacy: Farmacia Girón is on 5 Av., 5-70. Open M-W 7am-12:30pm and 2-9pm, Th 7am-9pm, F-Su 7am-12:30pm and 2-9pm.

Police: The Station is a 10min. walk down the hill 4 blocks past the arch, next to the school.

Hospital: El Buen Samaritano, 6 C. 3-60 (☎756 1163), offers 24hr. emergency service. For more extensive services go to the hospital in **Santa Cruz del Quiché** (p. 353).

Telephone: Telgua, 6 C. 5-70 (☎756 1399), has telephone service and 15 min. of free Internet. Open M-F 8am-6pm, Sa 9am-1pm.

Post Office: 7 Av. 8-47, open M-F 8:30am-5:30pm, Sa 9am-1pm.

◤ ACCOMMODATIONS

Hotels can fill up weeks in advance for Thursday and Sunday market days; if you plan on staying one of these nights, call ahead for a reservation.

GUATEMALA

Posada El Arco, 4 C. 4-36 (☎756 1255), has large rooms furnished with woven reed mats and fireplaces; rooms 6 and 7 have private balconies. English spoken. Singles Q152; doubles Q175. ❺

Hotel Chugüila, 5 Av. 5-24 (☎/fax 756 1134; luzmarielarodas@hotmail.com), a couple blocks north of the market, is a great upscale splurge with immaculate rooms set around a cobblestone courtyard. All rooms have private bath. Reservations recommended. Singles Q160; doubles Q200. AmEx/MC/V. ❺

Hospedaje Salvador, 5 Av., 10 C. (☎756 1329), is one of the cheaper options in town. This multi-story *hospedaje* offers very small rooms with great views. Singles Q35, with bath Q70; doubles Q52/Q75; triples Q75/Q150. ❷

Hotel Girón, 6 C. 4-52 (☎756 1156), has bright, oak-trimmed rooms arranged around a patio and parking lot, but can get noisy on market mornings. Singles Q50, with bath Q75; doubles Q70/Q100; triples with bath Q130. ❸

Hotel Posada Belén, 6 Av., 12 C. (☎756 1244), is near the edge of town. Follow 5 Av. south from the church and continue all the way until it curves left into the last main road at the town's edge; the hotel is 1 block farther. In contrast to the chaos of the market, Belén's hilltop location is tranquil with countryside views. Doors lock at 10pm. Basic rooms and hot showers. Singles Q50, with bath Q70; doubles Q60/Q80. ❸

▐ FOOD

While the many restaurants clustered around the *parque* serve up pricey dishes, there are lots of cheap, tasty options in the market itself. If you are facing the church, walk 10m left and then enter the *mercado* to your left. After a few stalls of *artesanía*, you will find yourself in a colorful labyrinth of food vendors. Come early in the morning to eat the cheapest breakfast around and listen to the gentle muffled beat of female hands shaping the day's tortillas.

Casa San Juan, 4 Av. 6-58. Savor tasty food in this cozy restaurant off the park. Kick back at your candle-lit table and dig into chicken with rice and guacamole (Q30) or sip hot chocolate with cinnamon (Q6). Classical guitar by local artists F-Sa. Open M-W 10am-11pm, Th 7:30am-11pm, F-Sa 10am-11pm, and Su 7:30am-11pm. ❸

Cafe Restaurante La Villa de los Cofrades, on the corner of 5 Av. in the two-story building. Try the biggest house special breakfast in Guatemala: cornflakes, two eggs, steak, beans, cheese, fruit, and coffee (Q28). Open daily 7am-10pm. ❸

Restaurante La Parilla, 6 C. 5-37. Surrounding a tiny, fountain-graced courtyard and tucked away from the street, La Parilla serves ample portions with good service for a low price. *Pollo a la parilla* Q25, veggie plate Q25. Open daily 7am-9pm. AmEx/MC/V. ❸

El Banquete de los Mayas, 5Av. 10-09, right below the Hospedaje Salvador. The *el banquete*—tenderloin, steak, and lamb—is a deal at Q44. Open M-W 10am-5pm, Th 10am-8pm, F-Sa 10am-5pm, and Su 10am-8pm. ❹

◉ ▐ SIGHTS AND CRAFTS

▧ **MARKET.** Although a few stands remain open all week, the scheduled Thursday and Sunday markets are well worth extra planning (Sunday is larger). On these days, the otherwise calm, peaceful streets of Chichi undergo a drastic transformation, as every inch of space is blanketed with vendors hawking their crafts and handiwork. The main vegetable market is inside the Centro Comercial on the north side of the *parque*. If you're shopping for *artesanía*, remember that bargaining is expected (aim for 30% off the asking price). While the prices in Chichi certainly aren't the lowest in the country, you can find some good deals. Asking prices for wooden masks (Q20-100), hammocks (Q80-300), and big blankets (Q80-150) vary greatly depending on quality. Shop around before making a purchase; bargain later in the afternoon when the market people are packing up their goods.

■ **IGLESIA DE SANTO TOMÁS.** Looming over the central market park, the church provides a fascinating glimpse into the converted Catholicism of the Quiché Maya. An incense fire is kept burning at the base of the church's steps and, on market days, brightly dressed *indígena* women cover the stairs with hibiscus, lilies, roses, and gladiolas, selling the blooms to churchgoers as offerings. The church is built on an ancient Quiché Maya holy site and is therefore sacred to local indigenous communities. *Indígenas* make an elaborate ritual of ascending the steps and repeatedly kneeling. Inside are altars surrounded by candles and petals dedicated to both Catholic saints and Quiché ancestors. Dress modestly. *(Use the side entrance, to the right, as the front entrance is reserved for senior church officials and cofradías, or is blocked by fire and ceremonies. No photography allowed. Free small donations appreciated.)*

SHRINE OF PASCUAL ABAJ. A lovely 20min. walk from town through pine forest leads to the shrine of Pascual Abaj, a ceremonial rock surrounded on three sides by a low stone wall. There's usually a small fire burning in front, as well as a profusion of flowers, liquor, and candles. The best time to go is Sunday mornings, when gatherings are larger and more frequent. Ask before taking photographs. *(Walk downhill 1 block from the Santo Tomás church on 5 Av. Turn right on 9 C. and follow it as it curves downhill and to the left. When the road veers to the right, continue straight, following the large sign. Pass through a courtyard and a small museum of ceremonial masks and enter a forested area. The trail zigzags up the hillside until flattening out in a small meadow dotted with pines. About 30m on the right is the shrine. Exercise caution as robberies have occurred.)*

OTHER SITES. The chapel of **El Calvario,** on the opposite side of the *parque* from Santo Tomás, is smaller than its counterpart, but still worth a quick look. Next to it are some pleasant **public gardens.** Between the two churches, the **Museo Regional** has a collection of pre- and post-Classical Maya bowls and figurines. There is also a series of jade arrowheads and necklaces, along with a detailed history of the region. *(Open Tu-W, Th 8am-4pm; F-Sa 8am-noon and 2-4pm; Su 8am-2pm. Admission Q5.)*

SANTA CRUZ DEL QUICHÉ

Located about 18km north of Chichicastenango and 40km northeast of Quetzaltenango, Santa Cruz del Quiché (pop. 22,100) is the departmental capital and an important transportation hub for those heading to more remote parts of the highlands, but is neither particularly attractive nor exciting. The nearby Quiché Maya ruins of Utatlán are perfect for a brief escape from the city.

TRANSPORTATION. Buses arrive at and leave from 1 Av., 10 C., Zona 5. To reach the *parque central* from there, turn right on 1 Av. (with your back to the buses), and walk four blocks; turn left and walk another three blocks. Buses head to **Guatemala City** (3½hr.; every 30min. 2-10am and noon-4:30pm, 2 6am buses leave from the west side of the *parque*; Q16) via **Chichicastenango** (30min., Q3). Hop off at **Los Encuentros** for connections to **Quetzaltenango** or **Panajachel** (1hr, Q6); hop off at **Chimaltenango** to make the connection for **Antigua** (2hr., Q12). There are also a few early direct buses to Quetzaltenango (3hr.; 5, 6, 7am). Service to **Nebaj** (3hr.; 5am, noon, 6pm; Q10) goes through **Sacapulas** (1½hr., Q7). Heading to **Cobán**, take a Nebaj-bound bus to **Uspantán** and then grab a pickup truck there.

PRACTICAL INFORMATION. Banco Reformador Construbanco is on the northern edge of the parque on 3 C. (Open M-F 9am-7pm, Sa 9am-1pm.) **BanCafé**, next door, has a 24hr. **ATM.** One street over, **Banco Industrial** gives Visa cash advances.

(Open M-F 9am-5:30pm, Sa 9am-1pm.) The **police** are on 0 Av., 4 C., Zona 1 (☎755 1106, open 24hr.); you can reach the **Bomberos Voluntarios** on 2 C. 0-11, Zona 1, for **emergencies** (☎755 1122). The **pharmacy** is on 3 C./2 Av. (Open Su-F 8am-1pm and 2-8pm; Sa 8am-noon.) A good-sized **market** lies just south of the *parque*. **Internet, phone,** and **fax** are at **Megatel**, on la Av./3 C., Zona 5, in the blue Edificio Plata Azul Las Américas. (Internet Q10 per hr.; free calls to Sprint. Open M-Sa 7am-7pm, Su 7am-1pm.) The **post office**, 0/1 Av., 3 C., is around the corner from police headquarters. (Open M-F 8:30am-5:30pm, Sa 9am-1pm.)

▌▐ ACCOMMODATIONS AND FOOD. ▧Hotel Maya Quiché ❷, on 3 Av. 4-19, a block off the *parque*, has spotless rooms in an inviting atrium. Those with private bath have cable TV, and there's a restaurant on the premises. (☎755 1667. Q40 per person, with bath Q60.) At **Hotel San Pascual ❷**, 7 C., 1-43, Zona 1, the clean, bright rooms are set around a courtyard. Hot water runs from 6:30-7:30am. (☎755 1107. Singles Q36, with bath Q60, with cable TV Q72; doubles Q60/Q96/Q120.) The nicest restaurant is the carnivore's heaven **El Torito ❸**, on 4 C., 3/2 Av., half a block from the *parque*. Though better cuts of meat are pricey, less expensive choices exist. (Filet mignon Q45. *Pollo en salsa blanca* Q28. Open daily 7:30am-9pm.) Friendly **La Toscana ❷**, on 1 Av. 1-06, serves small portions of lasagna and garlic bread for Q17, as well as pizza slices for Q7.50. (Open daily 10am-9pm.)

NEAR SANTA CRUZ DEL QUICHÉ

UTATLÁN

To get to the ruins of Utatlán, follow 10 C. out of town (begin at the bus terminal), eventually walking past La Colonia. At the sign for the SCEP, take a right up the hill to the park entrance. The walk is about 30min.—it's only 3km, but there are no directional signs. Traffic is light. For Q55-65 you can hire a taxi at the bus terminal to take you there, wait, and bring you back. Museum open daily 8am-4pm; gates close a little later. The only facilities are the museum's outside toilets. Admission Q10. Free camping in the parking lot.

Near Quiché lies Utatlán, the Spanish name for K'umarkaaj, capital of the Quiché Kingdom during the post-classic period of Maya civilization (AD 1250-1523). Under the rule of Q'uk'ab, the Quiché domain extended from the Pacific almost to the Atlantic, encompassing nine different nations including the Tzutuhil and Cakchiquel, two major indigenous groups around Lago de Atitlán today. The official archaeological site of K'umarkaaj—"Houses of Old Reeds"—covers an area of eight sq. km but the few discernible structures are located around a single *parque*. To reach it, follow the path right from the Visitors Center. Perhaps most interesting is a small cave 100m along an indicated trail to the right and then down from the *parque* (follow the sign saying "La dirección de la Cueva"), where religious healing ceremonies have taken place for the last 500 years. If you are lucky, you may stumble across a religious ceremony in process. You need a flashlight to see more than a few meters into the cave; bring your own, as there is only a slight chance the museum may have one to rent (Q2). Continue down the path to reach two secondary caves and a tiny museum.

NEBAJ

Though a mere 40km north of Santa Cruz del Quiché, winding dirt roads and imposing mountain passes lend Nebaj (pop. 19,600) a tangible sense of isolation. Situated in a fertile, stream-fed valley high in the Cuchumatanes, Nebaj marks the southwest point of the Ixil Triangle—the region that the Ixil (ee-SHEEL) Maya call home, defined by Chajul to the north and Cotzal to the east. Nebaj is a beautiful, traditional town, and the local clothing is striking; women dress in deep-red *cortes* and adorn themselves with elegant, forest-green shoulder drapes with sewn golden birds and matching head wraps. Nebaj celebrates the Fiesta de Santa María Agosto August 12-15 with religious ceremonies, artwork displays, and sporting events. Nebaj's beauty, however, belies a scarred past: much of the surrounding farm land is just beginning to recover from burns and land mines suffered during Guatemala's civil war in the late 70s and early 80s.

▐ TRANSPORTATION

Bus service can be erratic in this remote region, so it's a good idea to check the schedules at the station. The **bus terminal** is half a block north of the market, and three blocks down from the very western edge of the church. Buses run out of Nebaj to **Santa Cruz del Quiché** (3hr., 9 per day 12:30am-11:30pm, Q12) via **Sacapulas.** Early and less reliably, buses head to **Cotzal** and **Chajul;** check at the terminal.

✴▐ ORIENTATION AND PRACTICAL INFORMATION

The **church** towers over the east side of the *parque central.* Nebaj's three main streets run east-west, all more or less parallel. The road passing the *parque* on the south heads to **Sacapulas,** and the road on the north side is the road to **Chajul.** One block farther north, a daily market on the **market street** sells mostly fruits and vegetables and is huge on Sundays.

Bank: BanCafé, on the market street, has a 24hr. **ATM,** exchanges currency and traveler's checks, and gives cash advances on MC/V until noon. Open M-F 9am-4pm, Sa 9am-1pm.

Farmacia Xelaju, half a block north of the *parque* on Batzbacá. Open daily 8am-8pm.

Police: On the west side of the *parque.* Open 24hr.

Internet: Tulvi.com, on the south side of the *parque,* has the fastest, most reliable service. Q8 per hr. Open daily 8am-8pm.

Post Office: 4 Av. 4-27, a block west of the *parque,* across from the communications tower. Open M-F 8:30am-1pm and 2-5:30pm, Sa 9am-1pm.

▐ ACCOMMODATIONS

Many establishments are poorly marked—you may want to let one of the young guides at the bus station lead you to your destination for a couple of quetzals.

▨ Hotel Ilebal Tenam, a couple of long blocks west of the *parque* on the road to Chajul and just past Comedor Sarita on the left. An excellent value with space for more than 80 people and an inviting backyard garden. Call ahead for reservations on weekends. Singles Q22, with bath Q45; doubles Q45/Q95; triples Q70/Q105. ❶

Anexo del Hotel Ixil (☎ 756 0036), on the market street 2 blocks east of the *parque,* is a more modern hotel run by the same owners of Hotel Ixil (look for the white house with a black gate on the corner). Comfortable rooms with ultra-soft beds; private bath with hot water. Q50 per person. ❸

Hostal Ixil Don Juan (☎ 570 5206). Walking away from the *parque* on the road to Chajul, take a left at the Quetzal gas station and follow the road as it forks to the right. Look for the small black sign and the large wooden bench out front. The well-preserved colonial home has a couple of private rooms and a shared bath for Q20 per person. The house has a sauna as well (Q15). ❶

Hotel Ixil, 10 C., 6 Av., Zona 4 (☎ 800 7309), 4 blocks east of the *parque.* Clean rooms with common baths around a courtyard. Q20 per person. ❶

FOOD

▓ **Restaurante Asados Pasabién,** on the road to Sacapulas by the bus terminal, is a dark hangout with low prices and hefty portions. Tasty *churrasco* with crispy roast potatoes, salad, and tortillas Q25. Open daily 12:30-4pm and 6:30-10pm. ❸

El Descanso, on the market street down from the bank. A touristy cafe with a varied menu, English books to read and exchange, and comfy couches. Pick up their copy of *Filosofía para Principiantes* as you contemplate a veggie burrito (Q22) or pasta with mushrooms (Q20). Also home to hiking guides **Ixil Tours** (see **Sights and Guided Tours** below) and a decent Internet cafe (Q10 per hr.). Open daily 11:30am-11pm. ❷

Cafe and Comedor Elsim, the yellow storefront next to the police department. Another good choice for basic eats. The breakfast is particularly good (Q12). ❷

Pizza Cesar's, across from the BanCafé on the market street. Surprisingly good pizza for a traditional mountain village. The ham-and-mozzarella cheese by the slice (Q5.50) and a Gallo (Q10) make for a good lunch or afternoon snack. Open daily 7:30am-9pm. ❶

Comedor Lupita, on the Chajul road a block east of the *parque*. Friendly service and home style atmosphere. *Pollo asado* and a drink Q12. Open daily 7am-9pm. ❷

SIGHTS AND GUIDED TOURS

There isn't much to do in Nebaj proper beyond enjoying the scenery, which is enough for most. For a chuckle, check out the **Nebajenese Santa Claus**—an escaped garden gnome known as "Enanito"—on the fountain in front of the church. You can also head over to the bustling fruit and vegetable **market** (especially Su). The colorful market sells everything from coffee beans to mangos and chili peppers. For **guided tours, hikes,** and **horseback riding,** head to **Pablo's Tours,** at 3 C. before 6 Av. Zona 1, diagonally across from Hospedaje La Esperanza. Pablo's leads hikes to San Juan Acul (6hr., Q150) and trips to Chajul and Cotzal. **Ixil Tours,** inside El Descanso (p. 356), also guides a wide range of hikes and tourist services. The hike to the airfield (Q50) with a guide includes a stop-over at a local home for lunch and a brief history of the armed conflict in the area.

HIKES FROM NEBAJ

ACUL. A challenging road hike leads to the village of Acul and the cheese farm **Hacienda San Antonio.** From the police station on the *parque*, head north past Comedor Irene and down the hill. After 15min., continue straight over a small concrete bridge on a rougher and wider road. About 30-45min. after the bridge, turn right, leaving the smaller, straight path. About an hour into the hike, the path flattens out and runs past a long, thin field. At the end of the field, take the well-worn path to the right (the left path will get you there, too; it's just longer). After 10-15min., you'll go around a bend and the village of Acul will come into sight. Follow the road through Acul with the fields on the left and the village on the right. About 10min. up the same road on the left is the **Hacienda San Antonio.**

Set in a picturesque pasture with a forested hillside rising behind it, the *finca* seems more like something out of the Swiss Alps. The farmers inside will show you a room filled with circular blocks of fine Swiss cheese produced on the premises (Q30 per lb.). The surrounding valley is perfect for a picnic. Small *tiendas* in the village sell drinks and snacks. Allow 3-5hr. for the whole trip and set out early in the morning when the air is cool and the skies are clear.

LA PISTA DE ATZUMAL. A hike to the old military airfield in the tiny town of Atzumal provides a first-hand glance at the effects of the area's violent history. Atzumal was built partly by foreign volunteers in the 80s and used to house displaced Ixil families after their homes were razed during the war. The fresh new homes contrast the traditional lifestyle of their inhabitants. At the top of town is the old military airfield, a barren and silent strip of ground surrounded by a minefield to ward off guerrillas. The minefield has been detonated, leaving the landscape awkwardly uneven. Watch out for **barbed wire.**

From the church in town, follow the road to Chajul until you reach the Quetzal gas station, where you should take the left fork. When this paved road ends, take a quick left, and then immediately turn right onto the dirt road heading down the hill. After following this for about 30-45min., you'll come to the only junction (at the tall *Feliz Viaje* sign); take the right fork down the slope. After passing a couple of houses and *tiendas*, make a left onto the path just past a blue-painted *papelería*. At the end of the path, turn right, then left. You should now see *la pista* in front of you.

LAS CASCADAS DE PLATA. Las Cascadas de Plata is a less rigorous hike. The largest *cascada*, 1-1½hr. from Nebaj, is a jagged rock face carved out of a tree-lined hillside. The water here divides into many small cascades, making a truly beautiful display. The walk to the falls is a leisurely stroll through the pastures and valleys surrounding Nebaj. From the church in town, follow the road west to Chajul until you reach the first bridge. Take the road that veers left just before the bridge and stay on it for the rest of the walk. About 10min. from the bridge, the valley narrows and the hillsides grow steeper. Less than 1hr. from the *parque* there's a small waterfall on the left and some small waterfalls on the right. Continuing on, the road soon curves sharply to the left and drops steeply downhill to the largest fall. Allow at least 2½hr. for the entire trip.

COCOP. Another half-day hike leads to the remote, newly rebuilt village of Cocop. Like Atzumal and Acul, the village saw more than its share of activity during the war years. Particularly harrowing were the massacres during which 98 villagers were brutally slaughtered by the army. The few who were out in the fields working returned to find the village smoldering without a single survivor. After that, many left the village to avoid the 'poisonous' spirits lurking in the hills. Only recently have inhabitants begun to return.

To get to Cocop, start at the BanCafé on the market street in Nebaj and head east. At the end of the street, take a right, then a left down the hill. Cross over the small stream and continue on the well-worn path to a collection of wooden houses in the village of Xemamatzé. Take a left and follow the rutted road uphill for 2hr. There is one shop in town and the owners there will put you up in a room at the school for the night (Q15 per person). Otherwise, take the path towards Río Azul down the valley. Río Azul is on the road to Coatzal and from there you can walk the couple of hours back to Nebaj. The total trip is 4-5hr.

▶ DAYTRIP FROM NEBAJ

CHAJUL AND SAN JUAN COTZAL

Chajul's market days are Tu and F; Cotzal's are W and Sa. On these days, buses leave the Nebaj station around 6am; pickups and trucks are also frequent until around 10am. Those who catch a pickup follow the road to Chajul to the gas station and wait there, though Let's Go does not recommend hitchhiking. About 20-30min. into the trip, the road branches right to Cotzal and left to Chajul. Buses return daily to Nebaj from Cotzal at 11am, and daily from Chajul at 12:30 and 2:30pm. Trucks usually leaves Chajul for Cotzal at 11am on market days. Transportation is subject to change, so check in Nebaj first. On non-market days, buses run from Nebaj to Cotzal (30min., 6 and 10:15am).

Chajul and San Juan Cotzal, the towns that join Nebaj to create the Ixil Triangle, are set on the stunning rolling hills of the Cuchumatanes. Though well off the standard tourist path, the strong sense of tradition and natural beauty may exceed even Nebaj's and make it worth a visit. An unpaved road and a few winding trails between the two villages make for a lovely 2-3hr. walk. Ask around for directions.

CHAJUL. Chajul is the least bilingual and most remote of the three towns. It is composed mostly of smoke-filled, picturesque adobe homes in front of which women weave their fantastic *trajes*. In the plaza, the colonial **church**, Iglesia de San Gaspar, is relatively bare inside, except for two notable elements: the trough of fire in the aisle, devoted to the assassinated Father José María Gran, and the gold-plated altar of *Christ of the Golgotha*, to whom pilgrimage is made on the second Friday of Lent. Two angels stand guard on either side of the altar wearing the traditional Nebaj male dress. Many of the other religious figurines inside the church are also colorfully dressed in traditional Ixil garb, and the artfully carved wood at the main entrance displays fine Maya designs.

Market days are also a sight to be seen, with people from all three villages overflowing the market area and filling the plaza. Occasionally men will wear their white pants and blue sash *trajes* and women always wear their colorful blue *huipiles* and pom-pom head wraps.

At **Hostal Ixil-Chajul ❶,** the Ortega family rents out two basic rooms, speaks Spanish, and serves the very traditional *boxbolito* lunch. To get there, face the church from the plaza and take a right on the road that runs in front of the church. Follow this road 200m downhill to the Tienda Hernandez, make a left, and walk about 500m. The unmarked white house will be on your right-hand side. (☎ 765 6071. Q20 per person. Sauna Q20. Meal Q10-15; call a day in advance for lunch.)

SAN JUAN COTZAL. Along the road that branches away from the route to Chajul sits **San Juan Cotzal,** larger, more developed, and closer to Nebaj. It remains a tranquil town in a rolling green valley from which various excursions into the hills are possible. If you have to spend the night, you can check out the **Hotel Maguey ❶,** across from the police station and up from the left side of the church, which has clean, basic rooms (Q25 per person). A better option, however, is to inquire about some of the town's homestays; ask around town or at **Cantina Las Dalias,** in the Barrio Xecuruz, for more information. To find the Cantina, walk up the main street away from the church. Follow it all the way up the hill and, near the photocopy shop, hang a left and walk down about 2 blocks. It will be on your left. For a quick bite to eat, head for the **Comedor Ixtil ❷** on the main plaza. The flies are plentiful, but so are the tortillas (lunch Q12). San Juan celebrates its patron saint with a festival the week of June 24, featuring religious ceremonies and costumed dances in the afternoon; ask around for schedules.

QUETZALTENANGO

Quetzaltenango (pop. 125,000) is more commonly known as Xela (SHAY-lah), meaning "under the 10" in reference to the 10 mountain gods believed to inhabit the peaks surrounding the city. Xela is the largest and most important city in Guatemala's Western Highlands, lying at the intersection of major roads from the capital, the Pacific coast, and Mexico. Aside from the often bitter-cold evenings, it's a pleasant place, with polite locals, Neoclassical architecture, and an increasingly cosmopolitan nightlife. There isn't a whole lot to see in town beyond the well-maintained *parque central*, but daytrips into the surrounding countryside promise hot springs, rugged volcanic peaks, and colorful markets.

SAN ANTONIO Quetzaltenango Overview

Map labels:
Terminal Minerva
CIUDAD MINERVA
Mexico
Hipódromo Municipal
7 C.
19 Av.
17 Av.
15 Av.
14 Av.
13 Av.
12 Av.
Parque Zoológico
Mercado Municipal
Brigada Militar
ZONA 3
EL ROSARIO
Templo de Minerva
Calzada Revolución
4 C.
Transportes Alamo
Hospital Privado de Quetzaltenango
Estadio Tecún Umán
Centro Universitario
25 Av.
23 Av.
21 Av.
Parque Benito Juárez
Estadio Mario Camposeco
ZONA 2
Mall Mont Blanc/Paiz Supermercado
1 C.
Mercado La Democrocia
Gimnasio Municipal
TO GUATEMALA CITY (206km)
Canal
C. Rodolfo Robles
Av. Jesús Castillo
La Rotonda
Líneas Américas
ZONA 5
Galgos
Cda. Sinforoso Aguilar
ZONA 1
6 Av.
Cda. Independencia (7 Av.)
Diagonal 2
Cementerio General
Parque Calvario
Palacio Municipal
Cathedral
TO PARQUE NACIONAL CERRO EL BAUL (100m)
Diagonal 11
Diagonal 12
SEE QUETZALTENANGO CENTER MAP p. 360
Av. Central
ZONA 4
0 400 meters
0 400 yards
TO ZUNIL (10km), RETALHULEU (67km)
Zone Divisions

TRANSPORTATION

Intercity Buses: There are 2 terminals.

Terminal Minerva: at the end of Zona 3, sends buses to: **Chichicastenango** (2½hr., 8 per day 5am-3:30pm, Q8); **Guatemala City** (4½hr., every 30min. 5am-4pm, Q16); **Huehuetenango** (2½hr., every 30min. 5am-5:30pm, Q10); **Mazatenango** (1½hr., every 30min., Q8); **Mexican border at La Mesilla** (Union Froteriza y Aguas Calientes, 4hr., 6 per day 5am-2pm, Q12); **Mexican border at Tecún Umán** (4hr., every hr. 5am-2pm, Q12); **Momostenango** (2½hr., every 2hr., Q4); **Panajachel** (2½hr., 6 per day 5am-3pm, Q12); **Retalhuleu** (1½hr., every 30min. 5am-6pm, Q8); **San Andrés Xecul** (1hr., every 2hr., Q2); **San Marcos** (1hr., every 30min. 6am-5pm, Q6); and **Totonicapán** (45 min., every 20 min., Q2.50).

Zona 2 Terminal: Jesús Castillo, 1/3 Av., Zona 2 (near La Rotonda). Buses to **Guatemala City** (Líneas Américas ☎ 761 2063, 5 per day 5:15am-2pm), **Salcaja** (15min., about every 30min., Q1.50), **San Francisco El Alto** (1hr., every hr., Q4).

Local Buses: Routes run 6:30am-7pm and are constantly changing; check with the driver (Q0.85). As of August 2004, only minibuses were allowed to pass by the *parque central;* ask the driver to drop you off as close as possible.

ORIENTATION AND PRACTICAL INFORMATION

Quetzaltenango follows the mighty Guatemalan Grid. The **Parque Centroamérica,** the *parque central,* at the center of town in Zona 1, is bordered by 11 Av. on the east, 12 Av. on the west, 4 C. to the north, and 7 C. to the south. Walk a few blocks east or west of the *parque* and you'll find "diagonals" thrown into the mix. Most hotels, restaurants and services can be found in Zona 1 near the *parque.*

GUATEMALA

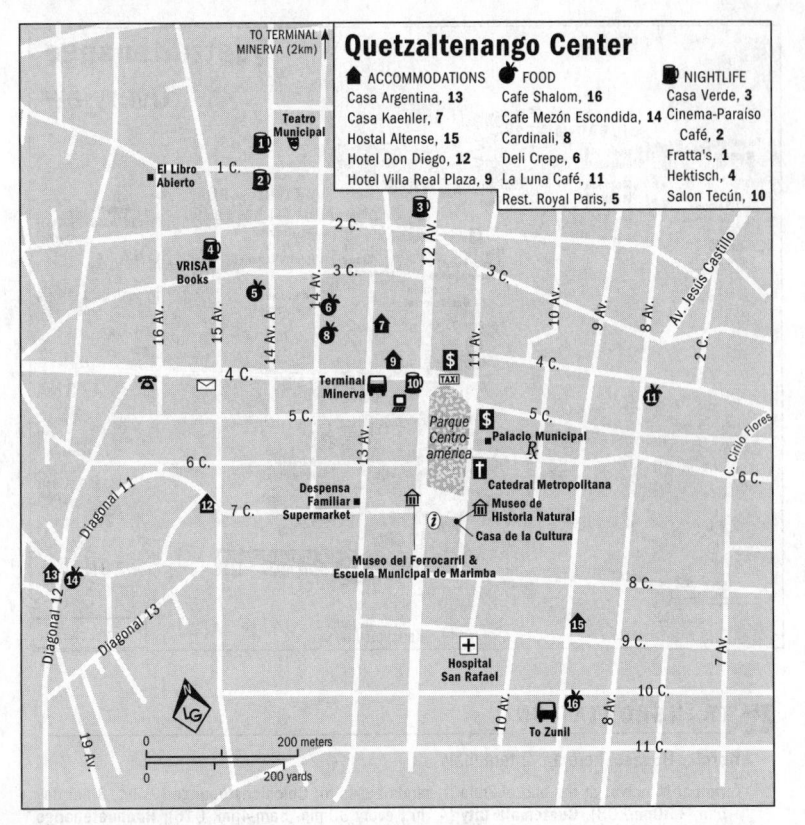

Quetzaltenango Center

🏠 ACCOMMODATIONS

Casa Argentina, **13**
Casa Kaehler, **7**
Hostal Altense, **15**
Hotel Don Diego, **12**
Hotel Villa Real Plaza, **9**

🍴 FOOD

Cafe Shalom, **16**
Cafe Mezón Escondida, **14**
Cardinali, **8**
Deli Crepe, **6**
La Luna Café, **11**
Rest. Royal Paris, **5**

🍸 NIGHTLIFE

Casa Verde, **3**
Cinema-Paraíso
Café, **2**
Fratta's, **1**
Hektisch, **4**
Salon Tecún, **10**

Terminal Minerva, the second-class **bus station,** is in Zona 3, northwest of the city center. If you arrive here, walk straight through the bustling market and then across an empty lot to the street on the other side. Any of the city buses heading to the left will take you to the *parque central.* (Q1; buses marked *"parque."*) Taxis usually wait by the buses (Q20 to Zona 1). If you arrive on a first-class Pullman bus, ask for directions at the bus office, as each company has its own terminal. Taxis also congregate at the north and south ends of the *parque central.*

TOURIST AND FINANCIAL SERVICES

Tourist Information: INGUAT, 7 C. 11-35, 12 Av. (☎761 4931), on the south side of the *parque.* Free city maps and list of authorized Spanish language schools. Bus schedules. Limited English. Open M-F 9am-5pm, Sa 9am-1pm.

Tours: The highly regarded ▧**Quetzaltrekkers,** Diagonal 12 8-37, Zona 1 (☎761 5865; www.quetzaltrekkers.com), located inside Casa Argentina (see **Accommodations,** p. 361), leads several multi-day trips, including treks to Volcán Tajumulco (the highest peak in Central America at 4211m) and Lake Atitlán. Trips usually run on the weekends (Q305-460), and price includes warm clothes, boats, tent, sleeping bags, transport, and meals. Guides are skilled, friendly, and English-speaking. Profits go to a local charity, for which donations of equipment or school supplies are warmly accepted. Volunteer guides are always needed and require a 3-month minimum commitment. **Adrenaline,** located next to Salon Tecún on the west side of the *parque,* organizes trips to Volcán Santa María and hikes throughout the region.

Banks: Banco Occidente, 4 C. 11-38, on the north side of the *parque.* Cash and traveler's checks exchanged, and credit card advances. Open M-F 9am-7pm, Sa 8:30am-1:30pm. Similar services and Visa **ATM** at **Banco Industrial,** on the east side of the *parque.* Open M-F 9:30am-7:30pm, Sa 9:30am-1:30pm.

LOCAL SERVICES

Market: Next to Terminal Minerva in Zona 3. There is a **flower market** near Casa Argentina, 8 C., Diagonal 12. Both open daily, but the largest day is Sa.

Bookstore: VRISA Bookshop, 15 Av. 3-64, Zona 1. Has an active book trade. Huge selection of used English books. Open M-Sa 9am-7pm. Also try **El Libro Abierto,** 15 Av. "A" 1-56, Zona 1. Open M-Sa 9:30am-6:30pm.

Laundry: Laundry Tikal, Diagonal 13 8-07, Zona 1. Q12 per load.

Supermarket: Despensa Familiar, 13 Av. 6-94, Zona 1, 1 block from the southwest corner of the *parque.* Open M-Sa 8am-7pm, Su 8am-6pm.

Mall: Centro Comercial Mont Blanc, 18/19 Av. and 3/4 C., in Zona 3.

Car Rental: Tabarini, 9 C. 9-21 (☎ 763 0418). Q460 per day. 25+. Bring a copy of your passport. Open M-Sa 8am-noon and 2-6pm. AmEx/MC/V.

EMERGENCY AND COMMUNICATIONS

Police: ☎ 110, 761 4991, 761 2589, or 761 5805 for the municipal police; emergency 120, on 14 Av. in the Hospital Antiguo, Zona 1. Open 24hr. Limited English.

Fire: Bomberos Voluntarios (☎ 761 2002 or 121). Open 24hr.

Red Cross: ☎ 761 2746, emergency 125. Open 24hr.

Pharmacy: Farmacia Nueva, corner of 6 C., 10 Av., 1 block from the *parque.* Open M-Sa 8am-8pm. Every pharmacy posts the *farmacia de turno,* open 24hr. for that day.

Medical Services: Hospital Privado de Quetzaltenango, 5 C. 12-44, Zona 3 (☎ 763 5421 or 763 5391), is widely regarded as the best hospital in the city. **Hospital San Rafael,** 9 C. 10-41, Zona 1 (☎ 761 2956), is the closest to downtown. Clinic open daily 7am-7:30pm. Emergency service 24hr. AmEx/MC/V.

Internet: Upstairs at **Salón Tecún** (see **Entertainment**) is popular and cheap. Q5 per hr. Open daily 8am-11pm. **La Cafetería,** 15 Av., 8 C., Zona 1, is less crowded and has a nice, breezy cafe. Q6 per hr. Open daily 7:30am-9:30pm.

Telephones: Telgua, 15 Av. "A," 4 C. (☎ 763 2050). Open M-F 8am-6pm, Sa 9am-1pm. Try **Salón Tecún** for cheap international phone calls (Q3.50 per min. to US).

Post Office: 4 C. 15-07, Zona 1. Open M-F 8am-5pm, Sa 8am-noon. **DHL** at 12 Av., 1 C. Open M-F 8am-5pm, Sa 8am-noon. AmEx/MC/V.

▐ ACCOMMODATIONS

Budget hotels in Xela have cropped up around the city center, catering to the increasing number of students and travelers passing through. Most are quite reasonable and are located within a few blocks of the *parque.* Weekends tend to be busiest, when crowds of new Spanish language students wait for homestay assignments. Xela can be quite cool and damp at night; ask about hot water and extra blankets. All hotels are in Zona 1.

▩ **Casa Argentina,** Diagonal 12 8-37 (☎ 761 2470). Though hard to find, this is the most popular budget hotel in town. Look for the small sign diagonally across from Helados Danni's, near the end of Diagonal II. It's easy to feel at home: you can cook your own food, wash your own clothes, and make plenty of friends. Many guests stay months at a time. The communal baths are clean and have hot water. Dorms Q20 per person; tiny private rooms Q25 per person (depending on availability); Q600 per month. ❶

Hotel Don Diego, 7 C. 15-20, (☎761 6497) has small, dark rooms that are balanced out by the spacious, lush courtyard. Breakfast and 30 min. of Internet use included. Q35 per person; Q500 per month. ❷

Casa Kaehler, 13 Av. 3-33 (☎761 2091). Bright yellow rooms with private bath on the 2nd fl. balcony of a refurbished, colonial-style house. Front door is always locked for safety. Singles Q75; doubles Q100. ❹

Hostal Altense, 9 C. 8-48 (☎761 2811). A bit removed from the touristy *parque central*, this hostal has basic rooms with private bath set around a flowery courtyard. Singles Q50; doubles Q100; triples Q150-180. ❹

Hotel Villa Real Plaza, 4 C. 12-22, (761 4045), half a block west of the *parque*. If you're looking for class, this is the place. A spiral staircase leads up to elegant verandas overlooking an indoor courtyard and the *parque central*. Enormous rooms have spotless baths. Singles Q265; doubles Q310; triples Q380. AmEx/MC/V. ❺

🔲 FOOD

Xela has plenty of affordable *típico* cuisine, augmented by fast-food joints and a thriving cafe and bar scene that caters to the entire community. Unless otherwise noted, listed restaurants are in Zona 1.

🔲 La Luna Café, 8 Av., 4 C. Each of Cafe Luna's theme rooms is decorated with unique Guatemalan antiques and newspaper clippings about the city from the 1800s. Succulent desserts and a warm atmosphere make this the perfect place to relax after dinner. *Californiano* (pure hot chocolate with vanilla and chocolate ice cream) Q10. Open M-F 9:30am-10pm, Sa-Su 4-9pm. ❷

Restaurant Royal Paris, 14 Av. "A" 3-06. The menu of this elegant yet laid-back French restaurant quickly reveals its sophistication; try the *camembert* (Q43) or the house special *trout a la Florentine* (Q95). Service is slow; order a bottle of wine, grab one of the many card games littering the tables, and make an evening of it. Open M 6-11pm, Tu-F noon-3pm and 6-11pm, Sa noon-11pm, Su noon-10pm. AmEx/MC/V. ❺

Cafe Shalom, 9 Av., 10 C. Feast on a tofu burger or chickpea curry dish while relaxing to 1930s American tunes in this intimate vegetarian restaurant. The food is scrumptious and cheap. Entrees Q12-20, *lassi* Q7. Open Th-Tu 11am-9:30pm. ❷

Cafe Mezón Escondida, 12 Diag. 8-07. Menu reflects tourist influence. Delicious breakfasts. Whole wheat waffle with juice and fruit Q18. Soy latté Q7. M-Sa 7am-6pm. ❷

Cardinali, 14 Av. 3-25, attempts to create authentic Italian food surrounded by walls covered in wine bottles and Italian flags. Diverse pizza toppings, including mozzarella, walnuts and asparagus. Small pizzas Q25-40, large Q50-75. AmEx/MC/V. ❸

Deli Crepe, 14 Av., 3/4 C. and 8 C. 11-29. Popular enough to have 2 locations, Deli Crepe's filling breakfasts, dinner burritos, and sweet crepes earn many a repeat customer. *Desayuno típico* Q10, burritos Q4, banana crepe with chocolate sauce Q13. Open daily 8:00am-9pm. ❷

🔵 SIGHTS

PARQUE CENTROAMÉRICA. On the east side of the *parque* presides the **Municipalidad,** a stately structure built in 1897. There's a courtyard inside the main entrance. The first Sunday of each month explodes with the commotion of traditional clothing, outdoor concerts and impromptu street performances.

MUSEO DEL FERROCARRIL. Near the south end of the *parque*, this museum rec-reates the brief life of an electric railway that connected Xela and Retalhuleu. The novel 1930 train lasted only three years before being catastrophically damaged during a winter storm. *(7 C., 12/13 Av. Open M-F 8am-noon and 2-5pm. Q6.)*

MUSEO DE HISTORIA NATURAL. Located in the **Casa de la Cultura**, the collection includes a few Maya artifacts, ceramics, and a collection of soda bottles from throughout the ages. Don't miss the traditional funeral urn: legend says that a small donation to the urn can bring good luck. Though not the most polished museum around, the place has charm. *(On the southern side of the parque. Open M-F 8am-noon and 2-6pm. Q6, students with ISIC free.)*

TEATRO MUNICIPAL. This beautiful Neoclassical structure hosts sporadic perfor-mances of traditional music and dance; call ahead or consult the tourist office for show schedule. *(4 Av. "A," 1 C., Zona 1. ☎ 761 2181.)*

NIGHTLIFE

Salon Tecún, Pasaje Enríquez, west side of the *parque*, Zona 1. With a central location and a big screen TV showing sports all day, it's no surprise it gets a bit rowdy. Popular hangout for *gringos* and locals alike. Open mic on M. Meter of beer (13 Gallos) Q110. Open daily 8am-1am.

Cinema-Paraíso Café, 14 Av. "A," 1 C., Zona 1 (☎ 795 6867; www.cinema-paraiso@go.com). Watch a wide selection of well-regarded international movies, docu-mentaries, and the occasional Hollywood blockbuster while sipping excellent tea. English-language library, art exhibitions. Live music M. Tea Q3, nachos Q10. Admission Q10, students Q8. Open daily 4pm-midnight.

Hektisch, 15 Av 3-64, Zona 1. Late-night hip-hop club. Look for the flaming torches over the door. Open Tu-Sa 8pm-late.

Casa Verde, 12 Av. 1-40, Zona 1. This airy joint sometimes hosts poetry readings and dance classes. Th *salsa* and *merengue* nights are packed. W disco night and F live music. Open daily 9am-12:30am.

Fratta's, 14 Av. "A" and 1 C., Zona 1. In front of the *teatro municipal*. Wildly popular for W night *salsa* with language students and locals. Free lessons 8-9pm. Rum and coke Q15. Open M-Sa 8pm-2am.

DAYTRIPS FROM QUETZALTENANGO

ZUNIL AND FUENTES GEORGINAS

Buses run to Zunil from 9 Av., 10 C., Zona 1 in Xela (20min., every 30min. until 6:30pm, Q2). To get to Fuentes Georginas from Zunil, hire one of the pickups that wait in the parque *across from the church (20min., Q25-40 for up to 8 people). The walk uphill is lengthy and unsafe. If you must, proceed uphill to the main highway and turn right. Soon on the left you'll see a sign pointing to Fuentes Georginas; from there, it's an 8km uphill climb. Fuentes (hot springs) open M-Sa 8am-5pm, Su 8am-4pm. Cooperative open M-Sa 8:30am-5pm, Su 2-5pm. Q20.*

For a great daytrip from Xela, strike out to the picturesque town of Zunil, tucked in a lush river valley about 8km southeast of the city, then go on to the nearby **hot springs** of Fuentes Georginas. Zunil's immense white **church** is delicately crafted both inside and out. The town is also noted for its idol **Maximón**, also known as San Simón. The saint lives on through a life-sized dummy who moves from house to house. His outfits are changed by the townspeople every two days—one of the trendiest includes a cowboy hat, red bandana, and sunglasses. The **Cooperative**

Tejedoras Santa Ana, half a block down the steep hill to your left as you face the church, was founded in 1970 and employs more than 500 women of Quiché Maya descent as seamstresses.

A 15min. ride into the verdant hills overlooking Zunil brings you to the utopian **Fuentes Georginas.** Often shrouded in mist, the hot springs sit in a steep and narrow gorge with hanging tropical vegetation. Relax in one of five steaming pools, and the largest features a pool-side restaurant and bar. It's possible to stay overnight in one of the worn, musty *cabañas* (singles Q90; doubles Q120).

The 30min. trek up to the steam vents in the hills above the pools makes an interesting side-trip before or after your bath. The climb takes you through lush green vegetation and at the top you can see huge vats of sulfur steaming up from the mountainside. The hike starts from the main road leading to the Fuentes, about 20m shy of the entrance on the left. The trail is unmarked, so it's best to ask one of the guards to show you where the hike begins. Rain gear is highly recommended, and robberies have occurred in the area; take a guide along for the hike.

VOLCÁN SANTA MARÍA

To get to the start of the climb, take a bus from Xela's Minerva terminal to Llanos del Pinal (about every hr. 5:30am-5:30pm, last bus back 6:30pm). 5-7hr. round-trip hike.

Visible from downtown Quetzaltenango on a clear day, the inactive Volcán Santa María (3772m) forms a perfect cone 10km southwest of the city. The climb to the top is rigorous and sweaty, but well worth it for the view of the whole valley. Since the trail is unmarked and a bit confusing, and robberies have occurred, *Let's Go* does not recommend hiking here alone. **Adrenaline** (p. 360) leads trips regularly on the weekends and **Quetzaltrekkers** (p. 360) does a full moon hike every month (both Q100). It is possible to do it as a long daytrip from Xela, but watching the sun rise is well worth hauling along some camping gear. The weather tends to be quite cold and wet; arm yourself with lots of water, warm clothes, and rain gear.

SAN FRANCISCO EL ALTO

Buses for San Francisco leave Xela from the Zona 2 terminal on Av. Jesús Castillo (45min., about every hr., Q4). Return buses leave from 1 C. and 1 Av.

On a hill overlooking Xela, 17km away, San Francisco El Alto comes alive every Friday with one of the largest markets in the country, selling everything from parrots to denim. Wednesday and Thursday market days lead up to the Friday bonanza. **Hotel Vista Hermosa ❶,** on 3 Av. 2-22, Zona 1, has views true to its name. (☎ 738 4010. Singles Q25, with bath Q50; doubles Q50/Q100; triples Q75/Q150.)

TOTONICAPAN

Buses for Totonicapan leave Xela from Terminal Minerva (45 min., every 20min., Q2.50). Return buses leave from the Toto bus terminal at the end of 3 C.

Totonicapan, or "Toto" for short, is a small district capital at the heart of one of the most heavily populated areas of the highlands. Famous for its insurgent rebellions, the most recent in August 2001 over a VAT increase, the town has been otherwise peaceful and quiet since. Today it is the heart of commercial weaving, producing much of the jasped clothing seen in traditional dress. Many workshops are scattered throughout town and open to the public, making it an excellent place to view weaving. Guides (Q50-100) and maps (Q5) are obtainable at the **Casa de Cultura** near the bus terminal (☎/fax 766 1517).

After dark, the streets of Toto are deserted, but if you're looking for a place to stay **Hospedaje San Miguel ❶,** 8 Av. 2 C., has homey windowed rooms and hot water for good prices. (☎ 766 1434. Singles Q30, with bath Q60; doubles Q60/ Q120.) For a decent bite to eat, try **Restaurante La Hacienda ❷,** on 8 Av. 4 C., which offers spicy *pinchos* for Q20.

MOMOSTENANGO

Buses for Momo leave from the Zona 2 Terminal in Xela (2hr., about every 2hr., Q4) and travel via Cuatro Caminos and San Francisco El Alto. The last direct bus back leaves mid-afternoon, though it is possible to change at Cuatro Caminos.

An hour north of Xela, in the heart of Guatemala's wool-growing region, Momostenango's popular Sunday market sells—you guessed it—inexpensive woolen goods (blankets Q70-110, hooded pullovers Q80). Momostenango makes a pleasant daytrip on non-market days. The town is also famed for its naturally occurring open-air **riscos,** clay formations that usually only occur in underground caves. A 20min. walk on the road to the left as you face the church will take you to the **Baños de Payexú,** where boiling water literally bursts out of the river. Follow the road and take a left at the bridge. The views are far more impressive than the actual baths, which reek of sulfur. The nicest place to stay is **Hotel Estiver ❶,** 1 C. 4-15, Zona 4, 3min. from the plaza. Rooms are clean and comfortable, and the upper floors boast a prime view. (☎ 736 5036. Singles Q25, with bath Q30.)

OTHER EXCURSIONS

Zunil buses to El Recreo depart from 9 Av., 10 C., Zona 1 (10min., about every 30min. until 6pm, Q1.25), and there's also service from Minerva terminal. Take note: the baths stay open late, but the last return bus leaves around 7pm. Buses to Salcajá leave Xela from the Zona 2 terminal (15min., about every 30min., Q1.50). Buses for San Andrés leave Xela's Minerva terminal (45min., about every 2hr., Q2).

Another trip from Xela is a visit to **El Recreo,** the best of a number of bath houses near the town of **Almolonga** that take advantage of a natural volcanic water heater. **Salcajá,** 9km from Xela on the way to **Cuatro Caminos,** is known for its embroidered textiles and is home to one of the oldest churches in Guatemala. On a side route off the main road to Cuatro Caminos and surrounded by cornfields is the *indígena* village of **San Andrés Xecul.** The village's canary-yellow church, complete with a technicolor collage of angels, icons, and adornments, contrasts sharply with the town's mud-brick houses. Hike uphill 15min. to a chapel with views of the whole town and surrounding farmland.

HUEHUETENANGO

With fewer than 30,000 inhabitants, Huehue (WAY-way) has an inviting small-city feel and much-welcomed creature comforts like ice cream cones and real milk. Though there's not much to do, it's a nice stop-over on the way to or from the Mexican border at La Mesilla or nearby Todos Santos Cuchumatán. Huehue began as a suburb of Zaculeu, the nearby Mam capital now in ruins; nearly every hill in the area hides some memory of the Mam. Since the Spanish conquest, the area has witnessed a couple of minor silver rushes and a region-wide coffee boom. The mineral has since petered out, but *café* still holds its own.

▐ TRANSPORTATION. The easiest way to get to Huehue from the Highlands is to take a **bus** to the Cuatro Caminos junction, then switch to a Huehue-bound bus (2hr.). Buses leave Huehue to **Antigua** (4hr., take a capital-bound bus and change at Chimaltenango); **Chichicastenango** and **Panajachel** (3hr., take a capital-bound bus and change at Los Encuentros); and **Guatemala City** (5hr., every hr. 1am-9pm, Q25). Alternatively, **Transportes Sosa Lopez** (☎ 764 2251) offers direct Pullman service to **Guate** from its 7 Av., 3-62 terminal (4:30, 7am, 2pm; Q29); **La Mesilla** border with **Mexico** (2hr., every 15min. 3am-6pm, Q8); **Nebaj** via Sacapulas on **Rutas García** (3hr.; 8:45, 11:30am; Q10); and **Todos Santos Cuchumatán** (2½hr., 8 per day 3am-2pm, Q9).

Buses to **Zaculeu** leave from 7 Av., 2 C. (every hr. 6am-6pm, Q1); buses leave to **Chiantla** from 1 C., in front of El Calvario (every 20min. 6am-6pm, Q1). **Local buses** run within town and to the terminal daily 6am-7pm (Q1).

■ ▪ **ORIENTATION AND PRACTICAL INFORMATION.** Huehue adheres to Guatemala's typical grid system (see map p. 321). The *parque central* is in **Zona 1**, bounded by **2/3 Calles** on the north and south sides and by **4/5 Avenues** on the east and west. Most services, hotels, and restaurants are located within a few blocks of the *parque central*. Buses pull into the well-organized **terminal** about 2km outside of town. City buses head into Huehue from the terminal about every 15min. (Q1); to find them, walk through the building with the bus company offices (the one with an archway in the middle) and cross the lot. Alternatively, take a taxi (Q20).

The **tourist office,** at 2 C. past 4 Av., provides up-to-date local information. (☎539 1984. Open daily 8am-noon and 1-5pm). For money services, there are two good options. **Banco G & T,** 2 C. 4-66, on the *parque,* changes traveler's checks, and has an **ATM** and a **Western Union** office (open M-F 9am-8pm, Sa 9am-1pm). **Banco Industrial,** on 6 Av., 1 C., has a 24hr. ATM and gives Visa cash advances.

If you want to make your own meals, there is a huge **Paiz** in **Centro Comercial El Triángulo** (open daily 8am-9pm). Car rentals are possible at **Tierra Alta Renta Auto,** (☎764 9356, ext. 71) at Hotel Chachumatanes in Zona 7 (open daily 7:30am-10pm). There is an **open-air market** between 1/2 Av. and 3/4 C., near the *parque.* Thursday and Sunday are market days. A smaller daily market is next to the bus terminal. The **Policía Nacional Civil** is at 3 Av., 3 C. (☎764 1465 or 704 0986. 24hr. emergency.) The only pharmacy in town is **Farmacia Del Cid,** 5 Av., 4 C. (☎764 1366. Open daily 8am-1pm and 2-7:30pm.) **Hospital de Especialidades,** 5 Av., 6/7 C., provides basic medical services and 24hr. emergency care (☎764 1414). **Telgua,** 2 C. 3/4 Av., has its usual telephone services (open M-F 8am-6pm). **Ciberplanet,** in Centro Comercial El Triángulo, offers fast **Internet** service. From Zona 1, take a bus from 6 Av., 2 C. (Q10 per hr. Open daily 8:15am-9pm.) The **post office** is at 2 C. 3-51 (open M-F 8:30am-5:30pm, Sa 9am-1pm).

▪ **ACCOMMODATIONS.** A plethora of budget hotels await in Huehue. The cheapest are those around the bus terminal, but Zona 1 choices tend to be safer and nicer, if slightly pricier. Unless otherwise noted, all listings are in Zona 1. ▪**Todos Santos Inn ❷,** 2 C. 6-64, 1½ blocks from the *parque.* Comfortable beds, plants, and hot water make this the best budget place in town. Some rooms have cable TV. (☎764 1241. Singles Q35, with bath Q45; doubles Q60/Q80.) **Hotel Zaculeu ❺,** 5a Av. 1-14, is a more upscale option with large rooms around a jungle of a courtyard. Bath, cable TV, and hot water in every room. The newer rooms towards the back are a bit nicer. (☎764 1086. Singles Q115; doubles Q170.) **Hotel Mary ❸,** 2 C. 3-52, across from the post office, boasts a central location. The modern, pink stucco rooms surround a multi-story atrium. Extremely hot water is available 6-9am and 6-9pm. (☎764 1618. Singles Q60; doubles Q90.) **Hotel San Luis de la Sierra ❺,** 2 C. 7-00, is right in front of the bus stop and is a modern hotel with modern conveniences. Views of the Cuchumantes are unmatched. (☎764 9217. Singles Q153; doubles Q214. AmEx/MC/V.) **Casa Blanca Hotel ❺,** 7 Av. 3-41, is the luxury choice for downtown accommodations. Spacious rooms all have cable TV and private bath. The regal courtyard has a large fountain and attendants waiting on your every need. (☎769 0777. Singles Q180; doubles Q228. AmEx/MC/V.) **Hotel Vásquez ❷,** 2 C. 6-67, has bare-minimum rooms that are offset by an inviting communal area and spotless hot shared baths. Good deals for two or more. (☎764 1338. Singles Q43, with bath Q73; doubles Q55/Q73; triples Q92.)

📑 FOOD AND NIGHTLIFE. Food in Huehue doesn't stray far from *platos típicos* for breakfast, lunch, and dinner. ▓**Jardín Café Restaurante ❷**, 6 Av., 3 C., serves ¼lb. burgers and a massive *menu del día*, making Jardín popular with locals during the lunchtime rush. (Chicken, soup, salad, rice, tortillas, and drink Q28; hamburgers Q12. Open daily 6am-10pm.) **Restaurante Bouganvilias ❷**, on the *parque* across from the church, is surely one of the country's only 4-story *comedores*. It serves up both fine views and tasty *típico* dishes. (Lunch Q20 includes drink. Open daily 6:30am-10pm.) **Mi Tierra ❸**, 4 C. 6-46, is a great spot for a light dinner and a couple of cold ones after a long day; popular with locals and Spanish students. (Fully-loaded nachos Q18, sizzling fajitas Q26. Open daily 7am-9pm.) **La Cabaña Del Café ❶**, 2 C. next to Todos Santos Inn, serves up cappuccinos (Q6) and Dunkin' Donuts all the way from the capital (Open daily 7am-9pm). There's not a whole lot going on in Huehuetenango by night, but try the *discoteca* **Cactus** (4 Ca., 6 Av.), and **Bob's Bar** (2 Ca. and 3 Av.).

🔁 ZACULEU. Buses to Zaculeu ruins (not Zaculeu center) leave Huehue from the small plaza at 7 Av., 2 C. (10min., every 30min. 6am-6pm, Q1). To walk there, head west out of town on 2 C. and look for signs pointing to the ruins. Any local will also be able to direct you. Allow 30-45min. for the walk. The last bus returns at 5pm. About 3km west of Huehuetenango lies the ancient Maya site of Zaculeu, which served as the center of the Mam. Long ruled by the Quiché, the Mam managed to free themselves just as the Spanish arrived in the 15th century. When an army led by Gonzalo de Alvarado met the Mam on the battlefield, the Mam took one look at the fearsome Iberians, riding animals they had never seen, and retreated to their base. Though Zaculeu was a study in defense—the temples, plaza, and ball court on the present site were fortified on three sides and the fourth side was protected by a jungle ravine—the modern Spanish weapons proved to be too much, and after a few months the Mam were forced to surrender for lack of food.

In 1946, the United Fruit Company sponsored an overzealous restoration of Zaculeu. As a result, Zaculeu is not what you'd expect from ancient ruins: the original stones are slathered in stucco, no jungle vines envelop the area, and the temples are free of rubble.

▓ TODOS SANTOS CUCHUMATÁN

In a high mountain valley amid the frigid Cuchumatanes, Todos Santos (pop. 3000) is a spectacular 40km uphill ride from Huehuetenango. Ascending more than 1000m, the road snakes around sharp ravines before flattening out on a harsh stretch. Just when the land seems most desolate, the road dives into the scenic river valley, revealing the glorious town of Todos Santos. Tradition remains strong: among the Mam-speaking inhabitants, the men (unlike most men in Guatemala) still wear traditional clothing, sporting red and white striped pants and cowboy hats, and the women dress in intricately woven *huipiles* and dark blue *cortes*. The pueblo's determination to maintain tradition has persisted despite brutal military repression that forced many locals to flee their homes for Mexico in the 1980s. Todos Santos is also known for its partial observance of the traditional Maya calendar, though its most famous festival, All Saints Day, is Catholic. The celebration lasts October 31 to November 5, and its highlight is a unique horse race on November 1.

📧 TRANSPORTATION. Most **buses** pull into the central plaza. Buses back to Huehue leave early (2½hr., 5 per day 4:45-6:30am, Q10), though two pass around midday (11:30am and around 2pm). Buses are crowded so arrive early. Some pickup trucks let tourists hop in for a fee, but *Let's Go* does not recommend hitchhiking.

GUATEMALA

⚡ PRACTICAL INFORMATION. On the edge of the plaza, **Banrural** exchanges dollars and traveler's checks (open M-F 8:30am-5pm, Sa 9am-1pm). Three co-operative **language schools** make their home in Todos Santos, creating a small but visible *gringo* scene. **Nuevo Amanecer** (escuela_linguistica@yahoo.com), located toward the beginning of the main street, down the hill from the church, runs a **book exchange** and sells a small stock of textiles. The **Spanish and Mam Academy Hispanomaya** is a block up the hill from the *parque*, to the left near the **Hotelito Todos Santos** (see below). Both also serve as impromptu tourist offices, leading hikes, arranging homestays, and hosting dinners. Down the alley before the *parque* is **Rebecca's Place**, a small English-language bookstore open daily 9am-9pm. There are **pharmacies** up and down the main street. The **police station** (open 24hr.) is right next door to the **bank** on the main street, and the **post office** is at the head of the plaza (open M-F 8:30am-1pm and 2:30-5:30pm, Sa 9am-1pm).

🏠🍴 ACCOMMODATIONS AND FOOD. The town's best rooms are at **Hospedaje Casa Familiar ❶**, 30m uphill from the *parque*. Small, cozy rooms have clean communal baths. Perks include a terrace with great views, fresh banana bread (Q10), and a place to meet fellow travelers. (Dorms Q25; rooms Q30 per person.) **Hotelito Todos Santos ❷** is another fine place to lay your head. To reach the Hotelito, head uphill from the *parque* and take your first left at a sign directing you to Todos Santos. The communal baths are new and have reliable hot water. (Q35 per person.) **Hotel El Viajero ❶**, run by a friendly family, offers rooms as well as kitchen access. (Short-term homestays are available through the language schools for Q25 per person, Q33 including meals.)

🍴 Rebecca's Place ❸ serves up tourist-oriented specialties; the ginger vegetable stirfry is particularly good (Q25). Some of the best meals in town are the fabulous vegetarian home-cooked ones at the **language schools ❷** (Q20 for all-you-can-eat dinner; Th and F only). If you're in the mood for *típico*, stop in at the **Comedor Martita ❷** across from the Hotelito Todos Santos. Walk through the dark and warm kitchen and into the back room, where social dining tables, a great view, and cheap, delicious food await (lunch Q13). **Café Cuchamatlán ❷**, a bar and restaurant with erratic hours and next door to Proyecto Lingüístico, serves up pizza and delicious vegetable chow mein (Q20). **Comedor Katy ❷**, uphill from the *parque*, is also a good place for traditional grub. (Meals Q20. Open daily 6am-9pm.)

📷 SIGHTS AND ACTIVITIES. The normally tranquil town gets busy for the **Saturday market**, though you can shop for textiles in the *tiendas* along the main street. Inquire at the language schools for info about **dance classes** (up to Q20 per hr.), **weaving classes** (Q10 per hr.), visits to a **sauna** (Q12 per person), daily hikes (Q15), and movies (Q5). In the upper reaches of town is the small, unexcavated Maya site of **Tojcunanchén**. This secluded place boasts great views of the valley, perfect for a nap, and is 10 min. up the hill from the *parque* (past Casa Familiar).

There are several other day hikes. A resident Swiss named Roman has begun leading guided trips in the area, including multi-day treks to Nebaj; more info available at Casa Familiar. One such hike is **🏃 Caminata a Tzunul**, a 4hr. roundtrip to Tzunul. Go down the steep paved road and cross the river, follow the path until it meets the main road on the other side of the valley, then take the road down the valley (3km.) to Tzunul, where families weave in their homes and welcome interested visitors. To find the houses, turn left at the soccer field. Returning, take the small path in front of the first house after the soccer field. At the fork, go left downhill and follow the zigzagging path. When the path runs into a road, follow it downhill. Cross three streams in as many hills; the path eventually leads back to Todos Santos.

PACIFIC SLOPE

Guatemala's Pacific Slope is a sweltering plain that contrasts sharply with the mountain vistas of the highland region. Here, on rich fertile land divided into vast *fincas* (plantations), bountiful crops like sugarcane, bananas, and rubber make a vital contribution to the nation's economy. The Pacific Slope does not, however, usually make the tourist's hit list. The dusty inland trade towns tend to be busy but unappealing, and the black-sand coast is too often marred by trash and debris. There are exceptions: along the busy coastal highway between the Mexican border and Guatemala City, **Retalhuleu** is a pleasant town with the interesting Maya ruins of Abaj Takalik and a few beaches nearby. Farther east, as the coast makes its way toward the border, laid-back **Monterrico** captivates visitors with hammock-lined stretches of fine beach and verdant nature reserve.

▓ THE BORDER WITH MEXICO

There are two places in the Pacific slope region bordering Mexico: **Ciudad Tecún Umán** and **Talismán/El Carmen**. Tecún Umán, closer to the Pacific coast, and with slightly better service to Guatemala City, is more crowded. Both, however, stay open 24hr. and are equidistant from Tapachula on the Mexican side. The nearest Mexican consulates are in Tecún Umán and Malacatán (near El Carmen).

CIUDAD TECÚN UMÁN. From the bus terminal, take a bicycle taxi to the border (Q10) and then another across the 1km bridge from the Guatemalan to Mexican immigration posts (Q6). Foreigners entering Mexico are required to pay a Q5 entrance fee; entering Guatemala is free. In Guatemala, buses from Tecún Umán head to **Guatemala City** (5-6hr., every 30min. 1am-8pm, Q35) via **Retalhuleu** (1½hr.) and **Escuintla** (4hr.); a few are direct and faster. If you get stuck for the night, try the respectable **Maxcel ❸**, 3 Av., 4 Guillón 82, Zona 2, a few blocks from the *parque*. (Singles Q60, with A/C Q125; doubles Q90/Q175.) Or try tidy **Lourdes ❸**, 1 Av. A, Zona 1. (Singles and doubles Q50; triples Q60; all with private bath.)

TALISMÁN. It's 200m between the Guatemalan and Mexican border posts. Money changers are on both sides. The nearest town is **Malacatán;** frequent minibuses connect this with the border (30min., Q2). In Malacatán, you can spend the night at **Pensión Santa Lucía ❷**, 5 C. 5-25 (singles Q45; doublesQ90). There are six buses daily to **Guatemala City** (5½hr.); if you miss those, connect through Malacatán. Talismán is connected to the western highlands by way of **San Marcos** (1½hr. away).

RETALHULEU

Reu (RAY-oo), as Retalhuleu (pop. 36,400) is concisely nicknamed, is the most pleasant town on the Pacific slope. Buildings surrounding the *parque central* testify to colonial pretensions, from a stately neoclassical city hall to a snow-white church flanked by royal palms. Laid-back Reu is a logical stopover on the way to or from the Mexican border. Visit the Maya ruins of Abaj Tabalik, slide down fake ruins at the Xocomil water park, or take a trip to nearby Pacific beaches.

▐ TRANSPORTATION. Because Reu is just 5km southwest of El Zarco junction, where the coastal highway (CA2) meets the road to Quetzaltenango, there are plenty of **buses** heading toward the Mexican border and the highlands. Retalhuleu's main **bus terminal, La Galera,** is marked by food stands between 7/8 Av. on 10 C. A second bus terminal a few blocks west of the *parque* serves Champerico and the coast. Grab a bus along 8 Av. and ask to be dropped off at the terminal (Q1) or get a taxi (Q10 from the main bus terminal). Walking from the park, follow 5 Av. until it runs into 2 C., turn left onto 6a av., then right, and walk until you see

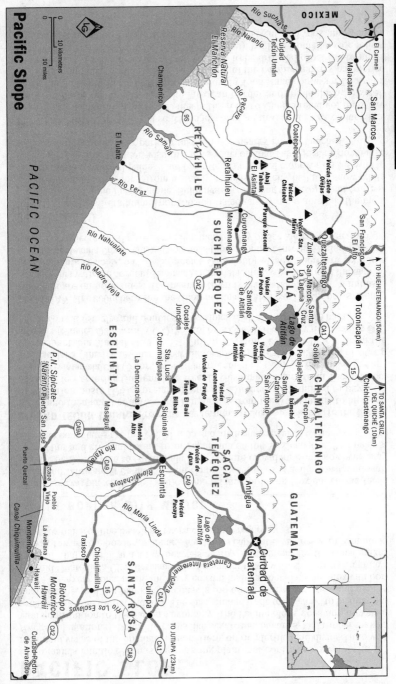

Pacific Slope

GUATEMALA

PACIFIC OCEAN

parked buses. They run to the Mexican border at **Tecún Umán** (1½hr., every 30min. 4am-6pm, Q10); most continue to the Mexican border at **El Carmen** (2½hr., Q15). Buses also run to **Quetzaltenango** (1½hr., every hr. 5:30am-6pm, Q7) and **Guatemala City** (3½hr., every 30min. 2:30am-9:30pm, Q20-25) via **Escuintla** (2½hr.).

⊞ ☷ ORIENTATION AND PRACTICAL INFORMATION. To reach the **parque central,** turn left on 7 Av., walk four blocks to 6 C., then turn right and go straight one block. The *parque* is bordered by 6/5 Av. and 5/6 C. Most services are near the *parque* or on 7 Av. between the bus stop and the center of town. Exchange currency at **Banco Agrícola Mercantil,** on 5 Av. (Open M-F 8:30am-7pm, Sa 9am-1pm.) **Banca Red,** behind the G&T Continental Bank across from the church, has a Visa **ATM,** as does **Banco Industrial,** behind the church. The following services are on the *parque* unless otherwise noted: **Farmacia Las Palmas II** (open M-Sa 8am-1:30pm and 2:30-7pm); **police** (☎771 0120; open 24hr.); **Telgua,** 5 C. 4 Av., a block away from the *parque* (open M-F 8am-6pm, Sa-Su 8am-noon); and **Internet** at **Cafe Internet Antigua,** on the corner of 6 Av. and 5 C. (M-Sa Q10 per hr, Su Q8 per hr; open daily 8:30am-10pm), or at **Asys Computación,** on 6 Av. 9-16 (☎771 5272; Q10 per hr.). Next to the Museo (see **Sights,** below) is the **post office** (open M-F 8:30am-5:30pm, Sa 9am-1pm).

⌐▢ ACCOMMODATIONS AND FOOD. Hospedaje San Francisco ❶, 6 C. 8-30 Zona 1, has mediocre rooms. (Singles Q20, with fan Q30, with bath Q50; doubles Q35/Q45/Q70.) **Hotel Modelo ❹,** 5 C. 4-53, half a block from the *parque*, is run by an amiable older couple who provide spacious rooms with ceiling fans and cold-water private baths. (☎771 0256. Singles Q65; doubles Q85.) Across the street is upscale **Hotel Astor ❺,** a splurge-worthy indulgence. Large rooms with A/C, a pool and jacuzzi, and a cabinet of Maya relics. (☎771 6475. Singles Q130; doubles Q215.)

For cheap eats, head to the popular, clean **Cafetería La Luna ❷,** on the *parque* at the corner of 5 Av., 5 C. (*Almuerzo del día* Q20. Open daily 7:30am-10pm.) Or try **Restaurante El Patio ❷,** 5 C. across from Telgua. Listen to your favorite Iglesias ballad on the jukebox while enjoying the *almuerzo del día* for Q12. (Hamburgers, filled tortillas, and sandwiches Q8. Open daily 7am-9:30pm.)

◪ SIGHTS. The **Museo de Arqueología y Etnología,** on the parque in the municipal building, has a good collection of Maya artifacts from the pre- to post-classical periods, and a rotating gallery with everything from photographs of Reu's early history, to model aircraft. (*Open Tu-Sa 8:30am-5:30pm, Su 9am-12:30pm, Q10.*)

▣ DAYTRIPS FROM RETALHULEU

ABAJ TAKALIK

From Reu, take a bus to El Asintal (1 hr., Q1.50). Ride it to the end of the line, which leaves you at the parque central. From there, it's a 4km walk continuing up the road you were traveling, which will take you through a coffee plantation and to the ruins. Between 6am and 5pm there are pickups for hire near the parque that will take you to the site. Admission Q25, including guide.

Though only partially open and excavated, Abaj Takalik is one of the more interesting Maya sites outside of Petén. The settlement, probably occupied between 800 BC and AD 900, once covered 9 sq. km. Today you can see several temple platforms and a series of carved sculptures and stelae, including frogs and an alligator.

PARQUE XOCOMIL

The park is 15min. outside Reu; hop on a Xela-bound bus and ask the driver to drop you off. (☎771 2673 from Guatemala City. Open daily 9am-5pm. Adults Q75, kids Q50.)

Sure, Abaj Takalik sounds kind of cool, but why bother with *real* ruins when you can dive into a "Maya-inspired" wave pool or speed slide? Parque Xocomil (pronounced SHOW-koh-meal) is a well-maintained, modern water park with many theme slides and raft rides, food service, and locker rooms.

THE COASTAL HIGHWAY

East of Retalhuleu, the highway passes **Cuyotenango**, where a side road runs 45km south to the nondescript beach of **El Tulate**. Further east on the highway are the towns of **Mazatenango** and **Cocales**. Buses from here run north to Santiago Atitlán and Panajachel. After another 23km, the coastal highway reaches **Santa Lucía Cotzumalguapa**, famous for its archaeological sites. Next up on the highway is rundown **Siquinalá**. A branch road serviced by bus heads to the coast by way of **La Democracia**. The site of Monte Alto is east of La Democracia, but the town plaza is home to its highlight: massive stone heads that may be as many as 4000 years old. Before winding its way to Guatemala City, the coastal highway from Retalhuleu runs though **Escuintla**, a transportation hub. From here, one road goes to **Taxisco**, a town en route to **Monterrico** (p. 372) and the southernmost border with El Salvador. Another road runs to the large, scruffy beach "resort" of **Puerto San José** and the tiny beach town of **Iztapa.**

MONTERRICO

If you have time to visit just one spot along the Pacific coast, this is the place to go. Separated from the mainland by the Chiquimulilla canal and encircled by a mangrove swamp, Monterrico (pop. 1000) lives by the motto "puravida": friendly and relaxed. Its narrow stretch of black-sand beach and powerful surf are some of Guatemala's finest, drawing both traditional fisherman and visiting students. A sand shelf protects Monterrico from the rain, ensuring sunny and cloudless days, but allows visitors to watch the frequent lightning storms a few kilometers offshore. Grab a hammock and let the crashing waves of the Pacific lull you to sleep.

■ TRANSPORTATION

Buses: To get to **Monterrico**, first take a bus from the Zona 4 terminal either direct to **La Avellana**, with Transport Cubanita (3½hr.; 10:30am, 12:30, 2:20pm; Q15) or first to **Taxisco** on a chicken bus or the **Pullman El Condor** (2hr.; 6, 11am, 1:30pm; Q15); change there for a bus to La Avellana (30min., every hr. 7am-2:30pm, Q3.50), to meet the ferry. Buses leave from La Avellana for Taxisco every hr. 6am-3pm. To **Guatemala City**, take the Taxisco bus and transfer.

Ferry: From **La Avenalla** to **Monterrico** (30min., leaves when full, usually about every hr., Q4). *Lanchas* from **Iztapa** to **Puerto Viejo** (5min., Q2.50), where you can take a bus to Monterrico (1hr.; 8am, noon, 2, 4, 6pm; Q15). A ferry leaves **Monterrico** for **La Avellana** 30min. before each bus to Taxisco.

Microbus: Travel agencies in **Antigua** offer express round-trip service to La Avenalla. This is the easiest way to get to Monterrico. Try Don Quijote Travel (☎/fax 832 7513, Q50).

ⓘ ✳ ORIENTATION AND PRACTICAL INFORMATION

Monterrico has one main road, which begins at the *lancha* dock and ends at the beach. All of the hotels and restaurants are either on this street, along the beach, or set back one block from the beach. There are **no banks or police** in Monterrico, so bring cash and be careful. Although Monterrico is considered one of the safest towns in Guatemala, female travelers should be especially cautious after dark. Walking toward the ocean on the main street, there is a **pharmacy** 50m to the left (open daily 7am-7pm) next to the Catholic Church. with an unreliable **post office** nearby on the main street. (Open M-F 8am-5:30pm, Sa 9am-1:30pm.) The best source of local **tourist information** is the fabulous Frenchman Henry, owner of the bar **El Animal Desconocido** (see below). Also try Geovani at the Proyecto Linguistico, a language school half way towards the beach on the main road. There is an **internet cafe** on the main road, **The Donde Walfer** (Open M-Su 8am-9pm, Q6 per 1/2 hr.). The unreliable **post office** is on the main street near the **pharmacy**.

🏠 ACCOMMODATIONS

Hotels tend to jack up their prices on weekends, during high tourist season in July and August, and during Guatemalan holidays, especially Semana Santa (March/April). Make sure to get a room equipped with mosquito netting or bring your own.

Hotel El Mangle Eco Resort (☎ 514 6517). From the beach at the end of the main road, head to the left a few hundred meters. The only thing truly "eco" about this "resort" is its proximity to the nature reserve and the overpriced wood carvings scattered around the central courtyard. Rooms come with mosquito nets, fans, and more wood-carved decor. Q70 per person, negotiable with larger groups (3 or more people). ❹

Hotel El Delfin (☎ 702-6701). Facing the ocean on the main road, on the right next to the Animal Desconocido (p. 373). Popular with the Guatemalans and backpackers. Simple accommodations are spruced up by an abundance of hammocks, a well-behaved dog, and a large, well-kept swimming pool. Also has a good *comedor*. Q35 per person, Q50 on weekends. ❷

Kaiman Inn (☎ 599-0058), on the beach about 200m to your left when facing the ocean at the end of the main road. A decent place with quiet surroundings. Wood-fired pizza is featured in the restaurant (Q60). Q40 per person, Q75 on weekends. ❷

The Guesthouse, off the beach. Walking toward the beach, turn left at the post office and walk a few hundred meters. The 4 double rooms come with fans and mosquito netting; shared bath, kitchen, and laundry facilities. Q35 per person. ❷

👁 🎵 FOOD AND ENTERTAINMENT

The beachfront restaurant of the **Hotel Pez de Oro** ❹ is the best bet for a nice meal, offering fresh fish (Q60-75) and banana flambé (Q20). The **Taberno el Pelicano** ❸ features vegetarian meals (Q35) with a side of entertainment from a live pet pelican. Take a left at the end of the main road at to the nature reserve. There are several *comedores* along the main road. Near the beach, smoky **Divino Maestro** ❷ specializes in shark steak (Q35). Across from the soccer field on the main road is a new Chinese restaurant, **The Mangrove** ❸ is run by an American expat. Huge portions of orange chicken await (Q25).

On the weekends, there are several options for night owls. **El Animal Desconocido,** 100m to the right after the end of the main road, is a good bet. Henry, the bar's owner, speaks English, French, and Spanish, and will give you directions or other local tourist info. Try his specialty, *El Animal Desconocido* (Q15), a mix of Malibu, milk, and cacao. (Open daily 5pm-late, happy hour 8-10pm.) **El CaraCol,** 100m to the left at the end of the main road, is the main competition and also offers surf rentals. (Happy hour daily noon-1pm and 5-7pm and F-Sa 9-11pm, closed Wed.)

👁 🏞 SIGHTS AND OUTDOORS

BIOTOPO MONTERRICO-HAWAII. Established to protect three species of nesting sea turtles, Biotopo Monterrico-Hawaii also preserves one of Guatemala's last remaining mangrove swamps and is home to thousands of birds. The Biotopo encompasses 2800 hectares, including Monterrico and several smaller towns. Pole-pushed sunrise boat tours offer a chance to catch the animals in their natural habitat as well as a spectacular view of **Volcán Tecuamburro.** *(Ask Iguanatours, off the main street and down the road across from the soccer field, to arrange a tour for you. Q35-40 for 2hr.)*

OTHER NEARBY SIGHTS. Reserva Natural de Monterrico (CECON) offers an up close and personal view of iguanas, baby turtles, and caimans. Not ones to miss out on the fun, the volunteers at the Reserva organize their own version of happy hour: turtle races to the sea every Saturday morning during the hatching season (September-November). The lucky winner gets a free dinner for two at the local restaurant of their choice. *(Next to the Hotel Baule Beach. Open 8am-noon and 2-5pm. Q3 for nationals, Q8 all others.)*

▓ BORDER WITH EL SALVADOR

Chiquimulilla and Taxisco are the best places to catch a ride to the border (45min., every hr. 5am-5pm, Q10). If you're entering Guatemala at this border crossing, buses head toward Guatemala City via Chiquimulilla and Taxisco. Pullman buses run (4hr., every 30min. 9am-4pm, Q30) as do 2nd-class buses (4½hr., every hr. 6am-3:30pm, Q15). Taxisco is the transfer point for Monterrico. On the El Salvador side, frequent buses run to Sonsonate. Immigration offices open daily 6am-10pm.

The bustling crossroad of **Ciudad Pedro de Alvarado** sits at Guatemala's southern-most border crossing with El Salvador, dominated by long-distance truckers on the Interamerican Highway and government officers. **La Hachadura** on the Salvadoran side provides easy access to Sonsonate, though it's not the most convenient way to reach San Salvador. Americans and Canadians must buy a US$10 tourist visa in El Salvador. At the border, street exchangers will change US dollars, quetzals, and Salvadoran colones. Keep a close eye on their calculations, as they are prone to dropping a zero here and there. (Open daily 6am-9pm.)

EASTERN GUATEMALA

Guatemala's short Caribbean coastline, squeezed into the right angle between Belize and Honduras, is a world away from the jungles and highlands of the rest of the country. Populated mainly by people of African descent, the towns along the coast boast delicious seafood, numerous boating and hiking opportunities, and a distinct local culture. The region's two main attractions are laid-back Livingston, a well-known and tourist-friendly town, and the Río Dulce, which begins at the northeastern end of Lago Izabal and flows into Livingston.

There are two ways to get to the Caribbean coast. The first is to take the Atlantic Hwy. to its end in Puerto Barrios, where boats leave for Livingston. The highway passes numerous historically significant sites: the ruins of Quiriguá, home to some of the best preserved Maya stelae; a branch road to Esquipulas, one of the most important pilgrimage sites in all Central America; and Chiquimula, a gateway to the Maya ruins of Copán in Honduras. The second option is to head to Fronteras, at the beginning of the Río Dulce on the Lago de Izabal, and boat down the river.

CHIQUIMULA

Thirty-two kilometers south of the Atlantic Hwy., hot and bustling Chiquimula (pop. 39,400) is primarily a transport hub for those coming to and from the Honduran Copán ruins.

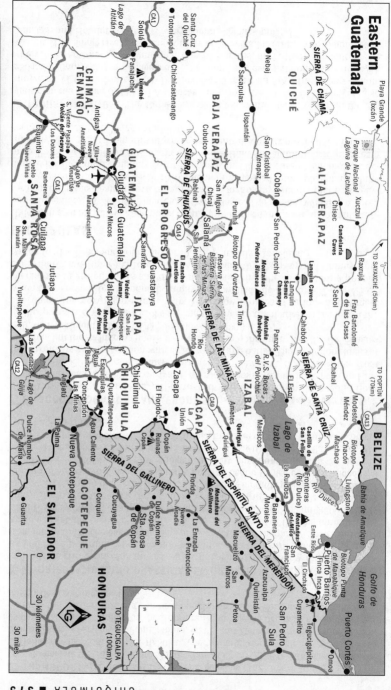

📠 TRANSPORTATION. Buses leave for: **Esquipulas** (1hr., every 10min. 5am-7pm, Q8); **Guatemala City** (3½hr., every 30min. 2am-3:30pm, Q20); the **Honduran border** at **El Florido** (2½hr.; 6:30, 7, 9:30, 10:30am, every 30min. noon-4:30pm; Q8-15); **Puerto Barrios** (4hr., every hr. 4:30am-2:45pm, Q20); and **Zacapa** (30min., every 30min. 4:30am-5:30pm, Q4): **trucks** on the Honduran side head to **Copán** (it's best to set out early as the border crossing can be a lengthy process). For more information on the border crossing, see p. 456.

▦ 🛈 ORIENTATION AND PRACTICAL INFORMATION. Hilltop Chiquimula is laid out in a grid. *Avenidas* run across the hill, while *calles* follow the slope down. As you head downhill, *avenida* numbers increase, and *calle* numbers increase from left to right. The **bus station** is at 10 Av., 1/2 C., and the *parque central* is at 7 Av., 3 C. **BanCafé**, on the corner of 8 Av., 4 C. and in front of the bus terminal, has a 24hr. Visa **ATM** and changes traveler's checks (open M-F 8:30am-4:30pm, Sa 1-5pm). There are **markets** at the terminal and the *parque*, and a **Paiz** supermarket on 7 Av., 3 C. (open daily 8am-9pm). Other services include: **police** (☎942 0356), at the end of 8 Av. across from the station; **Hospital Centro Clínico de Especialidades**, 9 Av., 4 C. (☎942 2053; open 24hr.); **Telgua**, on 7 Av. just downhill from the *parque* (open M-F 8am-6pm); **Internet** at **Enet Cafe** on 3 C., 9/10 Av. (open 9am-9pm; Q10 per hr.); and the **post office** in the alley across from the bus stop (open M-F 8:30am-5pm, Sa 9am-1pm).

🛏 🍴 ACCOMMODATIONS AND FOOD. By the terminal, **Posada Doña Eva ❸**, 2 C. 9-71, rents out a couple of well-furnished, breezy rooms on the second floor around an orange-tree-filled courtyard. All rooms come with private bath and TV. (☎942 4956. Q50 per person). **Hotel Hernández ❷**, 7/8 Av., 3 C., down the street from the *parque*, is a decent option with clean rooms and baths. The front door locks at 10:30pm, but the swimming pool stays open late into the night. (☎942 0708. Singles Q40, with bath and cable TV Q60; doubles Q50/Q90.)

Cheap *comedores* line 8 Av., 3/4 C., and the ones in the market to the left of the church off the *parque* are dirt cheap. You know a place is serious about meat when they serve it by the pound. Family-run **Parrillada de Calero ❹**, 7 Av., 4/5 C., specializes in grilled meats and offers no vegetarian dishes. (Q170 for 4 people. Open daily 9am-10pm.) **El Tesoro ❸**, 7Av. between 4/5 C., has good Chinese and *típico* food. (Sweet and sour chicken Q27. Open daily 11am-9pm.)

ESQUIPULAS

Hidden in a small valley, Esquipulas (pop. 19,500) hosts the most important Catholic shrine in all of Central America, **El Cristo Negro.** The shrine, which is revered for its miraculous healing powers, consists of a mahogany crucifix that was delivered by Spanish missionaries in 1595, and is now housed in the gleaming, white-domed Basílica de Esquipulas. Most famously, in 1737, it cured bishop of Guatemala Pardo de Figueroa of his ailments. More than one million visitors stream through every year (a majority of whom are Central Americans), and the bustling, seedy town makes its living catering to them.

📠 TRANSPORTATION. The Rutas Orientales bus station is across from the gas station on the corner of 11 C., 1 Av. **Buses** leave from the stretch of Doble Vía (also known as 11 C.) in front of the Basílica for: **Guatemala City** (4hr., every 30min. 2:30am-4:30pm, Q24) and **Chiquimula** (1hr., minivans every 10min. 5am-6pm, Q8), where connections go to Quiriguá, Puerto Barrios, and other stops along the Atlantic Hwy. **Minibuses** run to the borders of El Salvador (1hr., every 30min. 6am-3pm, Q8) and Honduras (20min., every 30min. 4:30am-5pm, Q10).

⊞⚡ ORIENTATION AND PRACTICAL INFORMATION. Buses drop pilgrims on **Doble Vía**, also called 11 C., the main east-west drag crossing in front of the *basílica* and the *parque central*. The main avenue used to be the highway and has a handful of names. It is **3 Avenida**, but you may hear **Camino Real** or **Quirio Octaño**. It heads north and downhill from Doble Vía at the *basílica*. With your back to the church, *avenidas* increase in number left to right; *calles* increase as they near the *parque*. **BanCafé**, 4 blocks down 3 Av. from the *basílica*, changes money, accepts traveler's checks, and has a 24hr. **ATM** (open M-F 8:30am-7pm, Sa 9am-1pm). Other services include the **Despensa Familiar Supermarket**, 3 Av., 3 blocks south of the Basílica (open M-Sa 7am-7pm, Su 7am-6pm); **police**, at the end of 6a Av., across from the post office (☎943 1207; open 24hr.); **Farmacia San Rafael**, at the beginning of 3a Av., across from the *basílica* (☎943 1216; open 7am- 8pm); **Telgua** office, 5 Av., 9 C., Zona 1 (open M-F 8am-6pm; after hours, use the phones outside); and **Internet** at **Glob@l**, 3 Av. 8-87 (Q10 per hr.; open daily 9am-9:30pm). The **post office** is between 2/3 C. at the northern end of 6 Av. (open M-F 8:30am-5:30pm, Sa 9am-1pm).

⚡ ACCOMMODATIONS. Esquipulas treats its wealthier pilgrims well with several high-class hotels. Unfortunately, many cheaper places are not as attractive or friendly. Prices double on weekends and during festivals when crowds descend on the town, though prices are never fixed and bargaining is a possibility at most places. Reservations are a must around the feast of El Cristo Negro de Esquipulas (Jan. 15) and during Lent. **Hotel La Favorita ❷**, 2 Av. and 10 C., is a popular mid-range choice due to the especially clean communal baths and tasty attached *comedor*. (Singles Q40; doubles Q60. Rooms with private bath Q75 per person.) **Hotel Monte Cristo ❸**, 3 Av., 9-12, is one of the nicest mid-range hotels around. Rooms are large and sparkling clean. (☎943 1453. Singles Q55, with private bath Q100; doubles Q110/Q150.) **Hotel Villa Edelmira ❸**, 3 Av. and 8 C., is in the mint green building. Popular with younger visitors, the Villa has simple rooms and a balcony overlooking the busy street below. (☎942 9431. Q50 per person.) **Pensión San Antonio ❶**, 3 Av. 9-19, has tiny, fairly clean rooms. Communal baths are slightly above average. Second floor is nicer than the first floor. (Q25 per person.)

◗ FOOD. Cheap restaurants line 3 Av., and snack carts cluster on 11 C. Prices are more reasonable farther away from the *basílica*. **La Hacienda Steakhouse ❺**, 2 Av. and 10 C., is a high class option for a good piece of meat and some live *mariachi* music. Try the full steak dinner with salad and a drink, Q75. (Open daily 7am-10pm. MC/V.) Another high quality dining option, complete with proper table cloths and napkins, is **Restaurante Las Fronteras ❸**, on Doble Vía across from the *basílica*, serving mostly Guatemalan food with some international options. (Cheese ravioli Q35, flan Q6. Open M-F 7am-10pm, Sa-Su 6:30am-11pm. AmEx/MC/V.) **Restaurant El Angel ❹**, 11 C. and 2 Av., also below the *basílica*, has not-so-authentic but nonetheless tasty Chinese food in a clean setting. (Duck with vegetables Q42. Open daily 11am-9pm.)

◎ SIGHTS. The **Basílica de Esquipulas** and its **Cristo Negro** are the city's main attractions. The entrance is outside to the left of the *basílica*. Once inside you will be surrounded by praying visitors and the soft light of burning candles. El Cristo Negro is behind the altar protected by glass. Walls in the hallway are lined with small metal plaques of thanks and images of body parts that the Cristo has healed. On Sunday and religious holidays, you may wait hours for a twenty-second glimpse of the statue. Remember to exit backwards down the ramp or pilgrims will think you're turning your back on the Lord. Benedictine monks bless lines of people with holy water to the right of the *basílica*.

GUATEMALA

If you are lucky, you may catch a religious ceremony at the **Cueva de las Minas**. Although there is significant evidence that Spanish sculptor Quirio Octaño fashioned the Cristo Negro, many still believe it was discovered in this cave. To get there, follow the street to the right of the *basílica* until you reach the highway, then take a left. The ticket booth is 50m up the road on the right, past the Texaco station (Q5). Walking the entire 15min. path leaves you at a well-maintained park, with a refreshment stand, playground, small zoo, and a cave shrouded in religious myth. Watch your head when walking through the tunnel and don't touch the walls lest you wish to emerge black with soot. For a panoramic view of Esquipulas, climb up to the **Franciscan convent** on the opposite end of town. Follow 3 Av. north to its base where it becomes a dirt road; turn left, and after two blocks it will deadend. Walk 1km up the rocky road on the right. Just uphill, the **Cruz del Perdón** (Cross of Pardon), is surrounded by hundreds of plastic bags filled with small rocks and hanging from tree branches. Maya pilgrims bring the rocks with them as a penance for their sins and leave them at the cross to gain forgiveness.

✈ AGUA CALIENTE: BORDER WITH HONDURAS

From the center of Esquipulas, *colectivo* drivers can take you to **Agua Caliente**, the site of the border crossing (20min., every 30min. 4:30am-5pm, Q10). Another *colectivo* will whisk you the 2km from Guatemalan to Honduran immigration (Q2). Though there are also money exchangers in Esquipulas, better rates can be found at the border; ask around for the best value. US dollars and American Express traveler's cheques can be changed at **Banco de Occidente** on the Honduran side (open M-Sa 8am-3pm, Su 8am-2pm). The **immigration office** is open 24hr. If you're driving across the border, go to the *tránsito* office around the corner from immigration. The forms that you have to fill out and how much you pay depend on your plans. Standard entrance tax is L17. Guatemalan immigration officials may try to ask for an unofficial exit fee, usually of about Q10. Refuse, saying *"la salida no cuesta nada"* (the exit doesn't cost anything). If they insist, which they likely will not, ask for a receipt with the officer's name on it so you can hold him responsible for overcharging you. Once in Honduras, **buses** go to: San Pedro Sula (5hr., every hr. 4am-midnight, L100); Tegucigalpa (8hr.; 4, 6am, 4pm, L135); and Ocotepeque (every 30min. 4am-7:15pm, L10). The San Pedro Sula and Tegucigalpa buses crawl sluggishly over the misty hills and stop at Santa Rosa de Copán (2-3hr., L55) and La Entrada (3-3½hr., L70), where you can catch buses to Copán Ruinas.

QUIRIGUÁ

While Quiriguá, a recently minted UNESCO World Heritage Site, is smaller than other sites on La Ruta Maya, it contains some of the grandest and best-preserved stelae, *altares*, and zoomorphs (sculptings with images of both humans and animals). Quiriguá's beginnings have been traced back to AD 300. The city remained subservient to the empire of Copán for several centuries and was probably valued for its strategic position on the River Motagua. Under the leadership of K'ak Tiliw, "Two-Legged Sky," Quiriguá defeated Copán by AD 737 and became an independent power. During the Cauac Sky Dynasty Quiriguá's power continued to grow. Among the monuments erected were the spectacular stelae, many of which bear Cauac Sky's now-crumbling visage.

▐ TRANSPORTATION. To get to town from the ruins, take a bus down to the highway (Q1) and walk. Alternatively, take any bus traveling the Atlantic Hwy. and ask to be let off at Quiriguá. For the ruins, a regular bus zips visitors 4km from the highway drop-off through a Del Monte banana plantation to the site (10 min., every

30min. 7:30am-5:30pm, Q2); the road is well traveled and many passing trucks will let you hop in the back for Q1 or nothing at all, though *Let's Go* does not recommend hitchhiking. Back at the highway turnoff from the main road, **buses** leave for **Chiquimula** (2hr., every 30min. 6am-6pm, Q12); **Guatemala City** (4hr., every 45min. 3am-5pm, Q35); and **Puerto Barrios** (2hr., every 30min. 5am-9pm, Q15). Nearby Los Amates is a stop-off for **minibuses** heading all over the area, including "El Cruce," where connections can be made south and north to **Petén**. A minibus to **Mariscos** on Lago Izabal leaves every 30min. (Q7).

For the ruins, walk or catch the shuttle to the highway (0.75km, Q1), turn right on Atlantic Hwy. or take any bus heading toward the turn-off to the ruins (1.5km, Q1, sometimes free). Then catch a bus to the ruins (4km, Q1). The combined trips take about 30min.

▚ ▙ ACCOMMODATIONS AND FOOD. Pickings are slim for food and hotels; the ruins are best as a stop en route to somewhere else along the Atlantic Hwy. The most reasonable place to stay in the village is **Hotel Royal ❶,** where simple rooms are large and clean, providing a fine place to rest your inscription-filled head. (Singles Q30, with bath Q50; doubles Q60/Q90; six-person suites Q120.) The **restaurant ❶** in front serves standard Guatemalan fare. (Q15-Q35; vegetarian meals available.)

◙ THE RUINS. Thatched roofs protect the monuments from the elements and a paved walking path protects visitors from fire ants. The stelae and zoomorphs (designated with letters of the alphabet) stand like sentinels in the site's *plaza central*. The plaza is an open field, making sunscreen and mosquito repellent a necessity. **Stela E,** a towering 12m, is the tallest in Central America and is on the Guatemalan 10-centavo coin. **Stela D** contains some of the most fantastically designed and best-preserved artwork in the region. Look for the **ballcourt** at the southwest end of the plaza (near the mango tree) and the **Acropolis,** the residence of the elite, to the south of the plaza. A bilingual history of the site is available at the entrance kiosk (Q10). There is also a fabulous free museum at the entrance which has photos and histories of the site and a helpful museum guide. (Spanish only. Ruins open daily 7:30am-5pm. Q25.)

LAGO DE IZABAL

Lago de Izabal, northwest of the Atlantic Hwy., is an expansive lake gradually developing into a tourist draw. The largest lake in Guatemala, it's a great place to enjoy water activities. The town of Fronteras (Río Dulce), along the Atlantic Hwy., is the launching point for excursions to the Spanish fortress El Castillo de San Felipe and the swimming holes and waterfalls of Finca El Paraíso, as well as the worthwhile river trip to Livingston. Other lake towns with accommodations are El Estor (connected by a slow bus to Cobán) and Mariscos.

FRONTERAS (RÍO DULCE)

More commonly called Río Dulce, Fronteras lies at the foot of Lago de Izabal. The town is rundown but is an important transportation hub and is pleasant for a night.

▐ TRANSPORTATION. The bus station and the main *lancha* dock, jutting off of Restaurante Río Bravo on the northeast side of the bridge, are on the northwest side of the bridge. **Buses** to **El Estor** depart from 2 long blocks from the north side of the bridge and to the left down the first cross street. (1hr., every hr. 7am-3pm, Q10); **Guatemala City** on Litegua buses (5hr.; 3, 5:45, 7:45, 11:45am; Q40); **Puerto Bar-**

A NEW FEATHER

After years of promoting recycling and proper trash disposal with little success, it seems that the Guatemalan government has finally found the answer in the form of the baby chick. In small villages, an aluminum recycling program has recently launched: one pound of soda cans warrants one chick in exchange. Eventually, the chick may end up on the table next to the very Coke can it was traded for.

While other recycling centers struggle to collect cans in exchange for money (Q2 per lb), the *aldeas* surrounding Lago Izabal have flourished under the chick incentive.' The process requires very little: once every two months, pickups loaded with cardboard boxes of birds head out with a megaphone and a kickin' stereo system blasting *salsa* music. Kids pour into the street dancing while ladies hurriedly gather up crates of cans. In Juarez alone, 50 lbs of cans have been collected in under 10 min, distributing 50 chicks. While the chicks are only worth Q1 a piece, and the cans are valued at Q3 per lb., the convenience of the system offsets lost money.

Although this exchange is concentrated in poorer areas, the possibilities are huge. Guatemala City's dump could benefit from this program as much as remote mountain towns. In a country that is notable for its litter, a little chick can go a long way.

rios (3hr., every 1½hr. 7am-5pm, Q12); and **Flores** (6hr.; 7 daily 7am-5pm; Q50, Q70 with a reserved seat) via **Poptún** (Q30). Inquire at **Tijax Express** near the dock for more regular departures to Guatemala City (every hr. 10:30am-2:30am) and Flores (roughly every hr. from 9am-3am). If you need *lancha* transport in the evening, the information booth 50m before the bridge on the turn-off toward the dock will call one for you until 8pm.

🛈 PRACTICAL INFORMATION. All places of interest are located on the north side of the bridge. The **INGUAT** office is 200m from the bridge (open M-Sa 9am-5pm). The **Tijax Express** tourist office is also well informed; English spoken. **Bancafé** and **Banrural,** 300m from the bridge, exchange traveler's checks and both have 24 hr. **ATMs** (open M-F 9am-5pm, Sa 9am-1pm). **Internet** is available at **Captain Nemo's Communications** in Bruno's Hotel complex right before the bridge (Q20 per hr., open M-Sa 8am-8pm.) or at Hotel Backpackers (see below; Q15 per hr., open daily 8am-noon and 4-10pm), and the **post office** is a few blocks past the banks away from the bridge (open M-F 9am-5pm).

🛏🍴 ACCOMMODATIONS AND FOOD. Hotel Backpackers ❶, on the waterfront at the end of the less-populated south side of the bridge, has everything going for it except its remote location. Run by the center for troubled youth, Casa Guatemala, it offers a communal kitchen, dorm rooms, private rooms, and space for hammocks. The outdoor **restaurant ❸,** though a little pricey, has a beautiful view and excellent lasagna for Q30. (☎930 5169. Restaurant open daily 7am-9:30pm. Laundry Q20 per load. Bunks Q25; simple rooms Q60 per person, with bath Q75.) A more upscale place to stay is the **Hotel Tijax ❸.** Located on a working rubber plantation across the water, it provides a free ferry (ask at the info box near the dock), or you can walk in if you get off a bus at the sign 2.4km before town. Tijax offers horseback riding, sailing, hiking, and a nice swimming pool. The **restaurant ❸** is expensive but delicious (fusilli with pesto Q34), and popular with an older crowd. Camping available, as are half-day walking tours of the plantation. (☎930 5505; www.tijax.com. Restaurant open daily 7:30am-9pm. Singles Q60; cabin with bath Q200; doubles Q96/Q288. Tours Q80 per person. AmEx/MC/V.) For options on the more populated side of the bridge, **Hospedaje Don Paco ❷** is down the street from the El Estor bus stop. Small rooms with cement floors, fans, and shared baths surround a courtyard. (☎930 5123. Singles Q40; doubles Q60; triples Q90.)

🔢 EL CASTILLO DE SAN FELIPE. El Castillo de San Felipe is 3km past the bridge at Fronteras. The original Spanish fortress was built in 1651 to stave off plundering pirates intent on looting warehouses on Lake Izabal. The reconstructed version rests on the original foundations. The charming village of **San Felipe** is a 5min. walk north from the castle. **Hotel and Restaurant Don Humberto ❷** is a peaceful place to plop down for the night. Humberto's small cement rooms have plush beds and private baths, and are a good budget value. Rooms are Q36 per person. *(San Felipe and the castle are a 45min. walk from Fronteras. Heading away from the bridge, take the first left at Pollito Tienda; bear left at the fork. Boats coming from Livingston will drop you off in San Felipe if you ask, and Río Dulce boat tours often include a stop here. Direct lancha from Río Dulce Q37. Open daily 8am-5pm. Grounds open daily 7am-6pm. Q10; Q5 to use the pool.)*

🔢 🏴 FINCA EL PARAÍSO. Along the north side of the lake between San Felipe and El Estor, the beautiful **Finca el Paraíso** is a working ranch 10min. walking distance from a fascinating and beautiful hot waterfall that cascades into clear, cold pools perfect for swimming, and a sauna. Caves are nearby (bring a flashlight), and horse and rowboat rentals are available (horses Q50 per hr., boats Q25 per 30min.) along with **camping** (Q25; hammock rentals Q25). A bit farther down the road to El Estor is **El Boquerón**. A 500m hike down a dirt path from the bus drop-off leads to an outhouse and a small collection of unmanned canoes. One of the guys around will paddle you up into the dramatic limestone canyon about 15 min. until a series of impassable river rapids and a rocky beach appear (Q20); or you can rent a canoe and paddle yourself (Q15). Across from the rapids is a series of stalactites hanging over the water and a large cave used for Maya rituals. To get back, jump into the lime green waters and float down the lazy river. *(The Finca is occasionally included on Río Dulce boat tours. It's also reachable on any bus traveling between Fronteras and El Estor. From Fronteras, you can get to Finca el Paraíso and Boquerón by hopping on a bus to El Estor and asking to be let off at either one for Q7. Otherwise, from El Estor grab a bus to Fronteras and tell the driver where you want to get off (Q2-Q4). From either city, it's no problem to see both the canyon and the waterfalls in one day. Buses drop passengers at 6 Av. on 3 C., the main drag, in El Estor. Last bus back to Fronteras passes the Finca at 4:30pm. Admission Q10.)*

🔢 🏴 BOCAS DEL POLOCHIN AND EL ESTOR. Smushed between the Bocas del Polochin wetlands and the Sierra de Las Minas reserve, the research station run by **Defensores de la Naturaleza** is the spot to see elusive wildlife in Guatemala. The wetlands are home to the largest population of manatees in Guatemala as well as over 250 species of birds, ocelots, and jaguars. Part of this is due to its prime position in the Mesoamerican Migration Corridor and the new and well-maintained walking trails surrounding the station. Because of this unique locale and the unmatched wildlife reserves surrounding it, the site is, unfortunately, difficult to reach. The community boat may be the cheapest way, but package deals offered by Defensores de la Naturaleza are cheaper for multi-day trips since they include food and accommodation. For more details on packages, or to customize your own, contact the non-profit ahead of time (☎ 949 7237; rbocas@defensores.org.gt).

It is also possible to see the wetlands on a 4hr. boat trip from El Estor. Oscar Paz, owner of the **Hotel Vista al Lago ❹**, 6 Av. 1-13, can arrange a tour. His hotel is a good place to crash for the night: clean, spacious rooms with bath have lake views. (☎ 336 3752. Tours Q250 for two people. Singles Q79; doubles Q142. AmEx/MC/V.) Good vegetarian and *típico* eats can be found 2 blocks down along the water at **Chaabil ❶**. Oscar can also arrange for a basic but cheap room. Vegetarian meals start at Q20. Rooms are Q25. *(Buses go to El Estor from Río Dulce, 1½ hr., every hr. 6am-4pm, Q10. To access the Reserva de Vida Silvestre Bocas del Polochin, boats leave on M, W, and Sa at noon from the main dock. The price depends on the passengers and gas prices.)*

PUERTO BARRIOS

United Fruit Company exports once made Puerto Barrios (pop. 51,500), at the end of the highway from Guatemala City to the Caribbean, the nation's most crucial port. Commerce has since shifted to Pacific ports and the city's significance has faded; today the dusty, palm tree-lined streets of the city boast many pharmacies, but little of interest to the healthy traveler. Puerto Barrios is more of a passageway to Livingston, Belize, or Honduras. **Walking the streets at night is not recommended.**

TRANSPORTATION. Buses wait by the railroad tracks where 9 C. and 6 Av. intersect, 4 blocks up and 3 blocks over from the dock. Look down the line to find the bus with your destination printed on the window. Litegua buses (☎948 1172) go to **Guatemala City** (5-6hr.; every 30min. 1am-4pm; regular Q30, *especial* Q40). There's also service to **Chiquimula** (4hr., every hr. 5am-5pm, Q20) and **Río Dulce** (1hr.; 6, 9, 11:30am, 1pm; Q10). Take a Guatemala City bus to La Ruidosa for connections to Río Dulce and the **Petén**; Río Hondo for connections south to **Esquipulas** and **El Salvador**; or El Rancho for connections to **Cobán** and the **Verapaces**.

The **boat** dock is at the end of 12 C. A ferry heads to **Livingston** (1½-2hr.; 10:30am, 5pm; Q10). *Lanchas* also make the trip (30min., 6:30am-5pm, Q25) and head to **Punta Gorda, Belize** (50min.; M, W-Th, Sa-Su 10am, Tu and F 8am; Q70). Paco's ferry heads to Punta Gorda (10am, BZ$25). Before departing for Belize, go to the immigration office for an exit stamp. Head down 12 C. 1 block to the small red building on the corner of 3 Av. (open daily 7am-7pm).

ORIENTATION AND PRACTICAL INFORMATION. The **municipal boat dock** serves as a busy stepping-stone to Livingston, Honduras, and Belize. The dock is at the end of 12 C. *Avenidas* run north-south, increasing in number away from the water; *calles* run east-west, increasing in number from north to south. The **immigration office** is a block from the dock on the corner of 3 Av. and 12 C. **Banco Industrial,** 7 Av., 7 C., changes currency and has a 24hr. **ATM** (open M-F 8:30am-5pm, Sa 9am-1pm). **Banco Internacional,** at 6 Av., 8 C., has **Western Union** services (open M-F 9am-6pm, Sa 9am-1pm). The **market** is at 9 C., 6 Av. **Farmacia La Fé** is on 5/6 Av., 9 C., next to the Litegua office at the bus terminal. (☎948 0796. Open M-F 7am-9pm, Sa 7am-8pm, Su 7am-noon). In an **emergency,** call **Los Bomberos** at 5 Av., 5/6 C. (☎122. Open 24hr.) The privately-owned **Clínica Médica** is on 7 C., 6/7 Av. (open M-F 7am-noon and 2-7pm; Sa 7am-noon). The **police station** is at 6 Av., 5 C. (☎120 or 385. Open 24hr.) **Phones** and **fax** are available at **Telgua,** 10 C., 8 Av. (☎948 2198. Open M-F 8am-6pm.) **Internet** can be used at **Café Internet** across from Texaco on 6 Av and 13 C. (Q10 per hr. Open daily 8am-10pm.) The **post office** is at 6 Av., 6 C. (open M-F 8:30am-5:30pm).

ACCOMMODATIONS AND FOOD. Hotel Miami ❷, 3 Av. 11/12 C., offers simple rooms with private baths close to the dock and a bit of sea breeze. (Singles Q45; double Q90.) Next door to Hotel Miami is **Hotel Europa 2 ❸,** 3 Av. 11/12 C. The rooms are slightly nicer and cleaner than next door and the breeze is refreshing. All rooms come with private bath and fan. (☎948 1292. Q50 per person.) Upscale **Caribbean Hotel Calypso ❹,** 7 C., 6/7 Av., near the terminal, has A/C and cable TV. (☎948 1121. Singles Q72, with A/C Q94; doubles Q107/Q136; triples Q143/Q164.) North of Hotel Miami and 1 block from the water, the **Hotel La Caribeña ❸,** 4 Av., 10/11 C., has parking lot views. (☎948 0860. Singles Q55, with A/C Q120; doubles Q80/Q180; triples Q100; quads Q135.) There is an attached **restaurant ❷** (lunch and dinner Q13; open daily 6am-11pm). **Pizza Luigi ❸,** on 5 Av. and 13 C., is famous for its pies. (Small Q35. Open Tu-Su 10am-1pm and 4-9pm.) **Parrillada Fogón Porteño ❸,** 6 Av.and 9 C., across the street from the Litegua bus station, is a funky old wooden house with a breezy balcony. (½lb. sirloin Q25. Open M-Sa 8am-11pm.) **Maxim ❸**, 6 Av., 8 C., is a good Chinese and Guatemalan eatery. The colorful restaurant is a clean retreat from the dirty streets. (Chicken with curry Q32. Open daily 10:30am-midnight.) **Café Vistalmar ❷** on 1 Av., as it approaches 9 C., serves great *tapado* (Q70) and *menú del día* for Q13 (open daily 7am-1am).

◈ BORDER WITH HONDURAS

Minibuses run from Puerto Barrios, across from the Despensa Familiar on 8 C. and 6 Av., to the Honduran border (30min., about every 20min., Q10). The minibus from Puerto Barrios drops you off across the border in no-man's land. From there, Honduran pickup trucks (L5) shuttle you 3km to their **immigration office** in Corinto, where money changers swarm outside. From Corinto, buses leave for Omoa and Puerto Cortés, Honduras on the Caribbean coast (every hr. at about 20 past the hour). The trip from Puerto Barrios to Omoa takes about 4hr. in decent weather; rains sometimes close the road on the Honduran side. The "jungle trail" and boat crossings to Honduras are no longer used.

LIVINGSTON

Life is sweet in Livingston (pop. 11,300), where the Río Dulce tickles the waves of the Atlantic and the Belizean Cayes are minutes away. Guatemala's largest Garífuna population, the descendants of African farm slaves and Carib Indians, dominates the town with their unique language and culture, providing taste of the laid-back Belizean lifestyle that waits just across the border. The Garífuna have a wandering history, being constantly shuttled from island to island by Spanish and English invaders to be put to work in floundering farming economies. Cut down by disease, they finally stopped permanently in southern Belize at the beginning of the 19th century. Today's 6000 Guatemalan Garífuna identify more with New York culture than with their highland compatriots. Basketball is the chosen sport and reggae, rap, and traditional *punta* drumming music are more common than *salsa* or *merengue*.

Once the largest ports in Central America, Livingston now spends its days partying and transporting tourists to an array of beautiful sites nearby, including the cascades of the Seven Altars and the effervescent *aguas calientes* (hot springs). The greatest tourist attraction is the beautiful Río Dulce boat ride, which starts in Livingston and heads to Lago de Izabal. In town, steady infusions of coconut bread, fresh fish, and reggae jams redefine *tranquilo*. Don't let the town's relaxed nature lull you into *too* peaceful a slumber; some crime (mainly drug-related) has found its way here. The appearance of tourist police has lowered the crime rate.

◧ TRANSPORTATION

Livingston is accessible only by water; most visitors arrive by ferry from Puerto Barrios or by boat along the Río Dulce.

Ferries: Leaving, ferries head to **Puerto Barrios** (1½hr., 5am and 2pm, Q10). Private *lanchas* leave from the same dock as soon as 12-16 people gather (30min., Q25 per person). The one departure you can count on is the first of the day—6:30am. The trip up the Río Dulce will bring you to **Fronteras**, where you can get buses to **Flores, Tíkal**, or **Guatemala City**. Other *lanchas* go to: **Punta Gorda, Belize** (1hr., 6-8 person min., Q100 each); **Omoa, Honduras** (6-person min., Q277 each); and **Puerto Cortés, Honduras** (8-person min., Q277-Q360 each). **Happy Fish** (see **Food**, p. 385) has daily shuttles to **Omoa** (Q200) and **Copán** (Q238). **Exotic Travel** sends a boat to **Omoa** (2hr., Tu and F 7am, Q277). Don't forget to have your passport stamped (see **Immigration Office**, below).

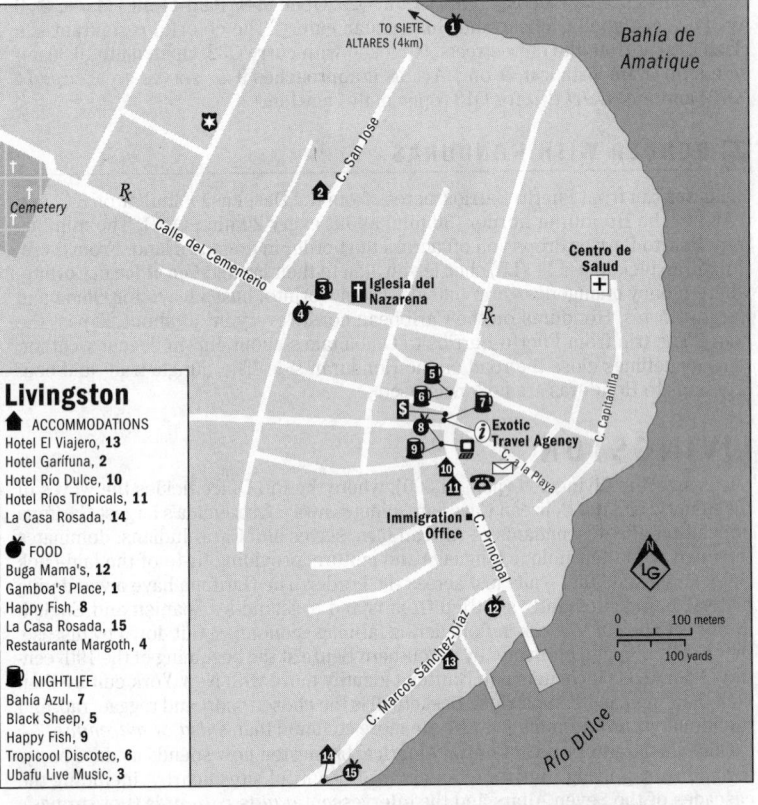

TO SIETE
ALTARES (4km)

*Bahía de
Amatique*

C. San José

Cemetery

Calle del Cementerio

Centro de
Salud

Iglesia del
Nazarena

C. Capitanilla

Exotic
Travel Agency

la Playa

Immigration
Office

C. Principal

Livingston

🏠 ACCOMMODATIONS
Hotel El Viajero, 13
Hotel Garífuna, 2
Hotel Río Dulce, 10
Hotel Ríos Tropicals, 11
La Casa Rosada, 14

🍖 FOOD
Buga Mama's, 12
Gamboa's Place, 1
Happy Fish, 8
La Casa Rosada, 15
Restaurante Margoth, 4

🍸 NIGHTLIFE
Bahía Azul, 7
Black Sheep, 5
Happy Fish, 9
Tropicool Discotec, 6
Ubafu Live Music, 3

C. Marcos Sánchez-Díaz

Río Dulce

0   100 meters
0   100 yards

✈🛈 ORIENTATION AND PRACTICAL INFORMATION

It's almost impossible to get lost in Livingston. The town's main street—**Calle Principal**—leads directly up a hill from the main dock and hooks to the left at the public school painted with big blue Pepsi signs. Most of the action occurs along C. Principal and continues after the left onto what is sometimes called **Calle del Cementerio. Calle Marcos Sánchez-Díaz** runs parallel to the Río Dulce. Coming from the dock, take the first left at the playground. C. Marcos Sánchez-Díaz has a number of good budget hotels and restaurants. The other roads are dirt walking paths meandering towards the beach.

Tourist Information: Exotic Travel Agency (☎947 0151) has a small office in Bahía Azul restaurant, halfway up C. Principal. Free maps and advice on border crossings, tours, and transportation. Little English spoken. Open daily 7am-midnight.

Immigration Office: Get your exit stamp at the **Immigration Office** across from the Hotel Villa Caribe on C. Principal. Open daily 7:30am-6pm.

Banks: Bancafé, just above Bahía Azul on C. Principal, changes traveler's checks and gives cash advances on MC/V. There is a 24hr. **ATM,** but it is frequently out of order due to vandalism. Beware of high transaction fees at many establishments on the main drag (upwards of 7% per charge). Open M-F 9am-5pm, Sa 9am-1pm.

Police: (☎948 0120). Down C. del Cementerio, then turn right and walk 100m. Knock if the door is closed. Open 24hr.

Pharmacy: Livingston, on the right side of the main street about 50m after the split with C. del Cemeterio. Open daily 8am-9pm, sometimes until 10pm, but will open at any hour if you knock. **Farmacia Sucey,** 350m down C. del Cementerio, has a larger stock of goods. Open daily 8am-9pm.

Hospital: Centro de Salud, uphill on C. Principal, right after the Restaurant Tiburón to the end of C. a Capitanía. Look for the large yellow building on the left. Open 24hr.

Telephones: Coming from the dock, the **Telgua** office is on the side street on the right, just past and opposite the Hotel Villa Caribe. **Fax** service available at various establishments along the main street, among them Happy Fish.

Internet: Happy Fish Restaurant, up the hill about 100m from the clock, on the left. Q20 per hr., or Q12 per hr. with a meal. **Telgua** gives 20min. of free access.

Post Office: Coming from the dock on C. Principal, make a right after the Hotel Villa Caribe. It's on the left, next to Telgua. Open M-F 8:30am-12:30pm and 3:30-5:30pm.

ACCOMMODATIONS

Budget rooms are around every corner, but the crush of visitors during the high season leaves only the nicest rooms available. Book in advance.

Hotel Ríos Tropicales, (☎566 2707), on top of the hill on C. Principal in the center of town. New and colorful, there is a general beach theme in the warped wooden house. Hammocks, coral, and conch shells are strewn about the common patio. Rooms are large and come with fans. Q40 per person, Q75 with bath. ❷

Hotel Garífuna (☎947 0183), 100m to the right after the sign on C. del Cemeterio. Hidden from the crowds of tourists downtown and in the heart of the Garífuna Barrio San José. Immaculate rooms with fan and private bath. The brick building is secured with a wrought-iron gate at night. Fax and international phone service available. Singles Q45; doubles Q60. MC/V. ❷

La Casa Rosada (☎947 0303), left on C. Marcos Sánchez-Díaz from C. Principal, a few houses after the small bridge, on the left. Exotic furniture, hammocks, a patio, and ocean views make even guests of other hotels stick around. Bungalows are artfully simple, with mosquito netting, fans, and hand-painted furnishings. Clean shared hot baths. Excellent food and tours; English spoken. Beds on the open balcony are an overpriced Q50, while the annex across the street is bare-bones. Laundry Q2.50 per piece. 2-person bungalows Q150; dorms Q50; annex Q40. MC/V. ❸

Hotel El Viajero, a couple minutes down C. Marcos Sánchez-Díaz, is the cheapest place in town. Basic rooms with fans surround a safe, quiet courtyard. Towels and soap provided. The restaurant out back overlooks the river and provides a welcome afternoon breeze. In the evening, the owner grills up a mean chicken or steak upon request (Q10). Singles Q21; doubles Q32, with bath Q42. ❶

Hotel Río Dulce (☎947 0764), next to Hotel Ríos Tropicales. A two-story wooden house run by an older Italian gentleman. Rooms are clean and airy. Popular because of the central locale. Q45 per person. ❷

FOOD

Tapado, a local seafood and plantain favorite drenched in a spicy coconut broth, surprises by fitting an insane number of critters into a single bowl (watch out for fish heads). Far superior to inland beans and rice, Caribbean rice and beans ("rays an bins") are stir-fried in coconut milk. For dessert, the *pan de coco* and *pie de piña* will leave you wobbling back to your hammock, woozy with ecstasy. For a quick, heaping plateful of savory local food (Q10), join the *lancha* drivers at the cart by the dock (open daily 10am-5pm).

■ **La Casa Rosada** (see **Accommodations,** above), has some of the most mouth-watering dinners in town (if not in Guatemala). All meals include a healthy salad and delicious desserts. Enjoy outdoor dining while local chefs mix up the menu every night, though a veggie special can always be counted on. Prices range from Q35 for vegetarian pasta to Q110 for a pound of lobster. *Tapado* is offered every night (Q65). Open for breakfast and lunch 6:30am-5pm; dinner is served at 7:30 pm with orders placed by 6pm, though the staff sometimes accepts later orders. ❺

Gamboa's Place, beyond Playa Ocho on the beach. Serves traditional Garífuna eats and the cheapest *tapado* in town (Q50). Open daily 9am-3am. ❺

Happy Fish, just up the hill on C. Principal on the left. Snazzy outdoor lighting makes for stylish dining under a thatched roof. Huge portions and great bread. Dip in *tapado* for a real treat (Q60). Most meals Q30-Q40. Occasional live music at 8pm. Open daily 7am-9pm. ❸

Buga Mama's, on the corner of C. Principal and C. Marcos Sanchéz Díaz next to the playground. A bit of everything is served here to a mix of 90s music. Granola and milk Q15, pizzas starting at Q35, *tapado* Q70. Open daily 7am-9pm. MC/V. ❸

Restaurant Margoth, on the cemetery leg of the C. Principal, across from the Iglesia del Nazarena. Good, simple food served on brightly covered tables. Very coconuty rice and beans. Fish filet Q35. Open daily 8am-9pm. ❸

■ NIGHTLIFE

A mellow village by day, Livingston apparently conserves its energy for nighttime partying. Most establishments are open until 3am but people stay out until dawn. Things are wild during the **Garífuna festival** November 20-27. The cemetery has a happening party November 1 and 2 (All Saints Day and All Souls Day respectively).

The Garífuna music scene and dance party begins and ends with **Ubafu Live Music,** 50m down the C. del Cementerio leg of the C. Principal. The live music here never disappoints. (*Coco loco* Q20. Open daily until 3am.) The **Black Sheep** and **Tropicool Discotec,** attached to the Bahía Azul restaurant, show movies daily at 5:30pm (Q15); happy hour 8-9pm and the music lasts until dawn (closed during low season, June and July). The **Bahía Azul** and **Happy Fish** (see **Food,** p. 385) have excellent live music by local drumming groups (donations appreciated) starting 8pm daily with a party ensuing (*Mojito* Q20). Locals head to the beach for late-night dancing to recorded *punta* music (read: intense booty shakin') at Playa Ocho (1 L Sol Q15; open daily 10pm-3am).

■ DAYTRIPS FROM LIVINGSTON

SIETE ALTARES

A 1½hr. walk down the narrow spit of beach. There have been some reports of robberies. The arrival of tourist police along the walk has helped, but always use common sense: travel in groups and leave valuables behind. Head out early, both to avoid intense heat and to ensure an early return; around 5pm a rising tide makes travel difficult. At the end of C. Principal, make a left onto the beach. After about 40min. you'll reach the Quehueche River. Cross the bridge and keep walking until you reach the end of the beach. Continue up the hillside trail 5min. until you see the Balthazar family entrance stand and the cascades on your left. Entrance is Q8. With your back to the sea, the trail on the right side of the pools leads to more cascades. You can also go by lancha colectiva (9am, Q25) or hire a guide. Exotic Travel Agency's trip includes a mountain hike, canoeing, and lunch (Q50 per person). Happy Fish Restaurant offers similar trips, guides, and prices. (Most leave at 9am. Sign up a day in advance as they only go if they have 6 or more.)

On the Caribbean side of Livingston cascade the **Siete Altares** waterfalls. Catching the waterfalls at their peak is a matter of delicate balance: if it hasn't rained in a while, there won't be much to see; if it's been pouring, access to the upper falls can be difficult and dangerous. Assuming reasonable conditions, the trip is well worth it, as the crisp, clear pools glittering with sunlight are light-years better than Livingston's sub-par beaches. The falls' big attraction is swimming; the water only crashes down a few feet. The upper falls, although a slippery 10min. walk upriver, are well worth the extra effort. A cool place to stop on the way back is **Larubella,** a Garífuna bar about 10min. before town. They assault patrons with *guífiti* (bitters): *aguardiente* (strong liquor, literally translated "fire water") passed through herbs and sticks and valued as a purgative and an aphrodisiac (Q5 per flask).

UP THE RÍO DULCE

Visits may be arranged in either Livingston or Fronteras/Río Dulce. Head to the docks to arrange a trip with any of the boaters, or book at almost any of the hotels in Livingston or Río Dulce for about the same price. (2 hr; 9:30am and 1pm guaranteed departures; Q75, round-trip Q120.) La Casa Rosada in Livingston offers a thorough and enjoyable tour leaving Livingston at 9am.

A boat ride along the Río Dulce reveals lush green cliff faces, calm, wide stretches of water, and varied wildlife. The stretch nearest to Livingston, where the river narrows and the cliffs loom over 100 ft. high, is probably the most breathtaking. Most *lanchas* stop at the sulfur **aguas calientes,** where scalding water surfaces along the rocky bank and mingles with the cool-flowing fresh water. They also pass by **Isla de los Pajaros,** a tiny island swarming with *garzas* (storks).

Another 15-20min. up the river is the **Biotopo Chocón Machacas,** a manatee sanctuary. The shy sea cows, however, are often elusive. Giant tree ferns and butterflies are more abundant, but the highlight of the park may be the small and eclectic museum. The *biotopo* includes several scenic lagoons good for swimming and a **camping** area with bathroom and kitchen facilities. Ask the pilot before you leave the dock to stop here. (Open daily 7am-4pm. Q40; includes camping.)

If you would like to stay on the Río Dulce, the **Finca Tatín** is a backpacker's jungle paradise hidden deep in the swamps. The *finca* offers an on-site Spanish school, kayak rentals, and is swimming distance of the *biotopo*. To get there call them and ask for a pick-up or get a *lancha* driver to drop you off. (☎902 0831, www.fincatatin.centroamerica.com. Dorm beds Q35; bungalows Q75 per person.)

VERAPAZ HIGHLANDS

No great geographic divide separates the Verapaces from the Western Highlands, though travelers will immediately sense the difference between Baja Verapaz's unique combination of near-desert and tropical forests and the densely-forested green hills of Alta Verapaz. Cobán, the capital of Alta Verapaz and the region's transportation hub, is a convenient base from which to explore the surrounding highlands, including Chisec, which is itself a wonderful jumping off point for numerous outdoor wonders.

The cloud-covered Alta Verapaz exists in sharp contrast with the high-pines of the highlands. It consists of limestone pockmarked with sinkholes, humid tropical forest, and mammoth caves. When oil was discovered here, the region's first road—the Transversal del Norte—was built, and K'ekchi' from the war-torn highlands settled the area. Today, it remains a sparsely populated agricultural frontier criss-crossed by a baffling web of routes built by the oil and cardamon industry. If you're looking for an off-the-beaten-path adventure, a trip through the region is worth the hassle. Its magnificent natural sites, the Candelaria Caves

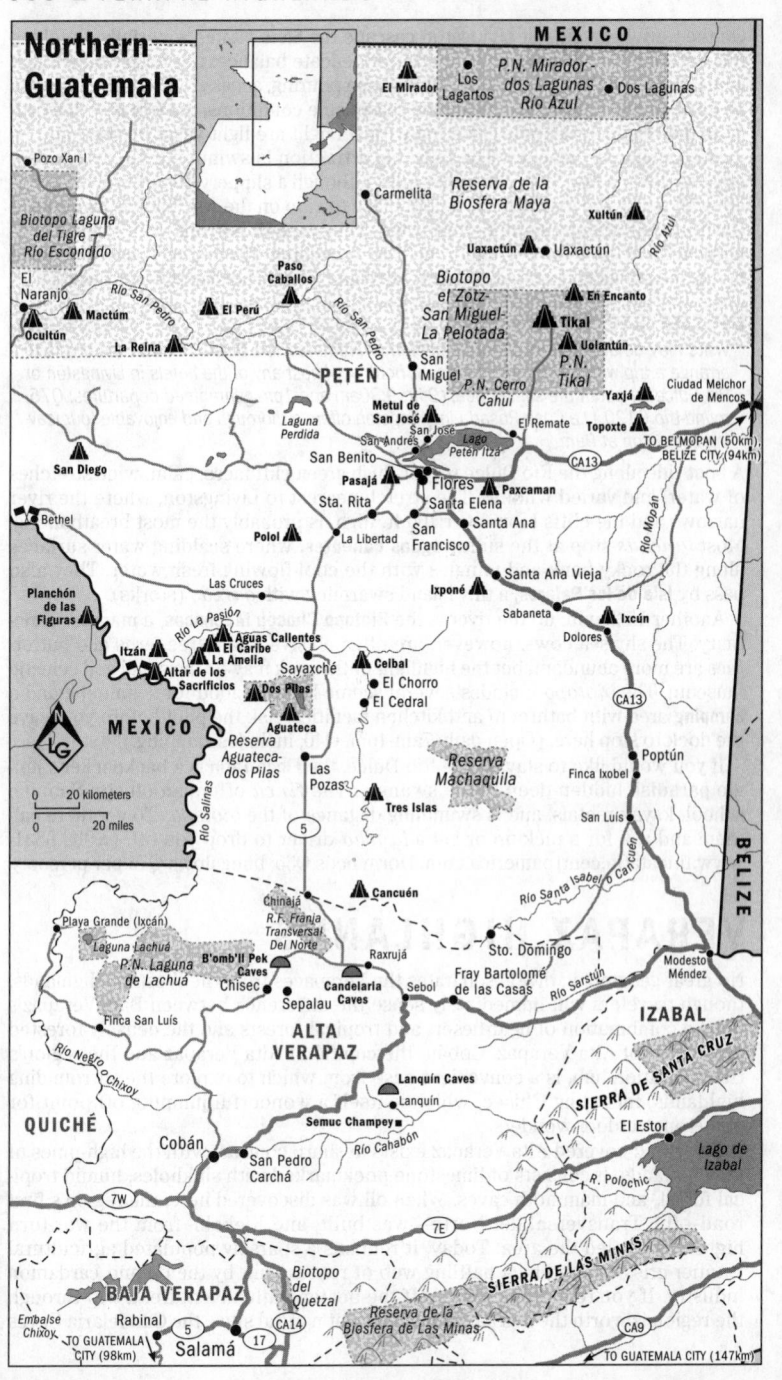

Northern Guatemala

MEXICO

Pozo Xan I

P.N. Mirador-dos Lagunas
Río Azul

El Mirador
Los Lagartos
Dos Lagunas

Carmelita

Reserva de la Biosfera Maya

Xultún

Biotopo Laguna del Tigre Río Escondido

Río San Pedro
Paso Caballos

El Naranjo
Mactún
Ocultún
La Reina

El Perú

Río San Pedro

Uaxactún   Uaxactún

En Encanto

Biotopo el Zotz-San Miguel-La Pelotada

Tikal
Uolantún

P.N. Tikal

PETÉN

San Diego

Laguna Perdida

Metul de San José
San José
San Andrés
San Benito

Pasajá
Sta. Rita

Lago Petén Itzá

Flores
Santa Elena

El Remate

Yaxjá
Topoxte

Ciudad Melchor de Mencos

CA13
TO BELMOPAN (50km),
BELIZE CITY (94km)

P.N. Cerro Cahuí

San Miguel

Paxcaman

Bethel

Polol
La Libertad

San Francisco

Santa Ana

Río Mopán

Santa Ana Vieja

Ixponé

Sabaneta

Ixcún

Planchón de las Figuras

Las Cruces

Dolores

Itzán
El Caribe
Aguas Calientes
La Amelia
Altar de los Sacrificios

Río La Pasión

Sayaxché

Ceibal
El Chorro
El Cedral

Dos Pilas

Aguateca

Reserva Aguateca-dos Pilas

Las Pozas

Tres Islas

Reserva Machaquila

Poptún

Finca Ixobel

San Luís

CA13

MEXICO

Río Salinas

Cancuén

Río Santa Isabel o Canchén

Chinajá

R.F. Franja Transversal Del Norte

Raxrujá

Sto. Domingo

Fray Bartolomé de las Casas

Río Sarstún

Modesto Méndez

Playa Grande (Ixcán)
Laguna Lachuá
P.N. Laguna de Lachuá

B'omb'il Pek Caves

Candelaria Caves

Sebol

IZABAL

Chisec
Sepalau

Finca San Luís

ALTA VERAPAZ

Lanquín Caves
Lanquín

El Estor

Lago de Izabal

SIERRA DE SANTA CRUZ

Río Negro o Chixoy

QUICHÉ

Cobán
San Pedro Carchá

Semuc Champey
Río Cahabón

R. Polochic

SIERRA DE LAS MINAS

7W

7E

Embalse Chixoy

Rabinal

BAJA VERAPAZ

Biotopo del Quetzal

Salamá

5
17

CA14

Reserva de la Biosfera de Las Minas

CA9

TO GUATEMALA CITY (98km)

TO GUATEMALA CITY (147km)

0   20 kilometers
0   20 miles

GUATEMALA

BELIZE

and Parque Nacional Laguna de Lachuá, remain little touristed. Its reconstructed towns ring with K'ekchi' and are scented with *caldo de chunto*, and although the region may not boast the vibrant colors of the highlands, the Maya here remain undisturbed in their traditional lifestyle. The festive towns of Salamá and Rabinal are in Baja Verapaz, near the highway from Guatemala City to Cobán.

It was the area's long, successful resistance to the Spanish conquest that gave it the name Tuzuntohil, or "Land of War." Thanks to Fray Bartolomé de las Casas and the Franciscan friars, however, the region has earned its present Spanish name, Verapaz, or "True Peace." When the Fray organized a campaign in defense of the *indígenas*, the Spanish empire halted its military conquest and granted him five years for the "humane" conversion of the local people. The chiefs, assured that the friars were not interested in their gold and land, accepted them, and a peaceful conversion followed. By the end of the 19th century, however, the Guatemalan coffee boom had established large *fincas* in Verapaz, which strained available land and labor and disrupted many indigenous villages. Despite these tensions, the *indígena* presence in the region remains strong. Much of the native population speaks K'ekchi' and Pokomchí; a small population in the south of the region speaks Quiché. On a practical note, it takes a while to navigate this area. Transportation is like the quetzal: elusive, and most active in the early morning.

COBÁN

Though touristed enough to be home to plenty of cosmopolitan pleasures, Cobán (pop. 51,100) gives the distinct impression that nature is never too far away. The lush green heart of the Alta Verapaz appears within arm's reach as the city's edges quickly fade into country terrain. Even though rain is common, the sun does show most days, and tourists use Cobán as an attractive base for exploring the natural wonders nearby, including the Biotopo del Quetzal, Rey Marcos, Semuc Champey, and the Grutas de Lanquín. When you need a break from the outdoors, Cobán is happy to oblige: sip a cup of the famous local coffee in a cafe and rest your head at one of several charming hotels.

▐ TRANSPORTATION

Buses: Unless otherwise noted, buses leave from the **main terminal** at 1/3 Av., 2/3 C. in Zona 4. Coming into town, some buses stop conveniently to the west of the *parque*, on 1 C. near the Telgua offices. Buses heading south also depart from this location. Make sure to get to the terminal at least 30min. early, especially for destinations toward Alta Verapaz and the Petén. Ask ahead for the latest info—services change frequently. Buses depart to:

Biotopo del Quetzal: Board any Guatemala City bound bus. (1hr., Q6.)

Fray Bartolomé de las Casas: (7hr., 5am-9pm, Q20.) Microbuses only.

Grutas del Rey Marcos: From 5 C., 5 Av. in Zona 3. Take the bus to Chamelco (20min., Q3), where you can change buses and head to Chamil, which passes by the Grutas.

Guatemala City: Transportes Escobar y Monja Blanca, on 2 C. 3-77, Zona 4, offers 1st-class service (4-5hr., every 30min. 2-4pm, Q26). "Special direct" buses play movies (5 per day 4:30am-2pm). Chicken buses leave from the main terminal (4½-5hr., 5 per day 4am-1pm, Q17).

Lanquín: Leaves from the main bus terminal (3 hr.; 5:30, 11:30am, 1:30, and 3pm; Q15).

Playa Grande: Buses, microbuses, and pickups leave from the terminal on 1 Av. (5hr.; every hr. 5am-2pm; Q25, microbus Q40.) They leave more frequently if there are enough passengers. Drop-off near **Parque Nacional Laguna de Lachuá**; walk to the entrance.

Raxrujá: (5hr., 4 and 6am, Q20.) An additional bus leaves at noon from San Pedro Carchá. Some pickups also go to Raxrujá in the morning from Sebol; take the bus headed to **Chisec** and transfer at Sebol (about 2hr.).

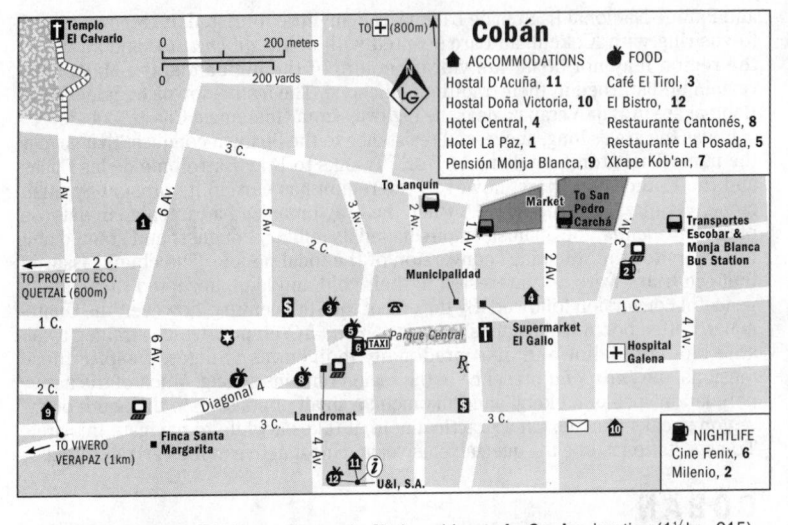

Salamá and Rabinal: Take any Guatemala City-bound bus to **La Cumbre** junction (1½hr., Q15). Minibuses leave frequently for **Salamá** (10min., Q3).

San Pedro Carchá: From the corner of 2 C. and 3 Av. (15min., every 10-15min. 6am-7pm, Q1.)

Sayaxché and the **Petén:** Either take the bus to **Raxrujá** or a pickup to **Cruce del Pato** via **Chisec** and then hop on a bus or pickup to Sayaxché. Direct buses can be caught heading south down 1 Av. in front of Ban Rural or BanCafé. (6 and 11am; Q90.)

Tactic: Any Guatemala City-bound bus. (30min., Q3.)

Uspantán: From Uspantán, buses leave for any Western Highland locale, including **Santa Cruz del Quiché** via **Sacapulas** (where you can grab a bus to **Nebaj**). Leave from in front of Telgua offices on 1 C. (5hr., 10, 11am noon, Q15.)

Taxis: Around the *parque central*, at the western tip and northern side of the cathedral.

■ 🛈 ORIENTATION AND PRACTICAL INFORMATION

The two main streets in Cobán, **1 Avenida** and **1 Calle**, adhere to the standard grid (see map above). They divide the city into **quadrants:** northwest Zona 1, southwest Zona 2, southeast Zona 3, and northeast Zona 4. The city's **cathedral** towers at 1 Av., 1 C. The neighboring *parque central* is directly west in Zona 2. The cathedral and *parque* rest atop a hill that encompasses Cobán. Numbered *avenidas* and *calles* continue through different *zonas*. Addresses on 1 Av. and 1 C. may be in any of the *zonas* they run through, depending which side of the street they lie on.

Tourist Information: There is no INGUAT office, but **Hostal D'Acuña,** 4 C. 3-11, Zona 2, is a great information source, and providing maps and bus schedules.

Guided Tours: At the **Hostal de Acuña, U&I, S.A.** (☎ 951 0482; uisa@amigo.net.gt) runs guided tours throughout the Verapazes, including Lanquín, Semuc Champey, and the Parque Nacional Laguna de Lachuá, as well as up to Flores (daytrips Q280). **Proyecto Eco-Quetzal,** 2 C. 14-36, Zona 1 (☎ 952 1047), works to protect the cloud forest of the Sierra de Caquipec and organizes trips to learn about the life of Kekchí families. Guides show you the forest, its medicinal uses and agriculture, and familiarize you with the Kekchí. Proceeds benefit environmental protection. 2-days, 1-night homestays Q210 per person; 3-day, 2-night Q320 per person. Guide included.

Banks: BanCafé, 1 Av. 2-66, Zona 2, accepts most types of traveler's checks, advances cash on credit cards, and has a 24hr. Visa **ATM.** Open M-F 9am-7pm, Sa 9am-1pm. **Banco Continental,** across from Hotel La Posada on 1 C., changes all traveler's checks and has a Mastercard ATM. Open M-F 8:30am-7pm, Sa 10am-2pm.

Supermarket: El Gallo, on 1 C. Open M-Sa 9am-8pm, Su 9am-6pm.

Laundromat: Lavandería La Providencia, Diagonal 4 2-43, Zona 2, near the movie theater. Q25.75 per load. Open M-Sa 8am-noon and 2-5pm.

Car Rental: Tabarini, 8 Av. 2-27, Zona 2 (☎951 0661). Open daily 8am-noon, 2-6pm.

Police: 1 C. 5-12, Zona 2 (☎952 1225), past Hotel la Posada. Open 24hr.

Pharmacy: Farmacia Central, 1 Av., 2 C., Zona 2, on the *parque.* Open M-Sa 7am-7pm, Su 7am-noon.

Medical Emergency: Los Bomberos, 3 Av., 3 C., Zona 4 (☎952 1212). Open 24hr.

Red Cross: 3 C. 2-13, Zona 3 (☎952 1459).

Hospital: Poliolínica Galeno, 3 Av. 1-47, Zona 3 (☎951 3175). This well-equipped private clinic has emergency service, though not always 24hr. Walk-in hours M-Sa 10am-noon and 4-8pm. Public **Hospital Nacional de Cobán** 8 C. 1-24, Zona 4 (☎952 1315). Open 24hr.

Telephones: Telgua near 3 Av., 1 C., Zona 1 (☎951 3098), in the large, unmarked white building on the *parque.* Public phones in front. Open M-F 8am-5pm.

Internet: Cybernet, next to Cine Fenix. Fastest connection in town and lots of computers. Q6 per 30min. Open daily 8am-8pm. **Infocom,** 2 C. 6-03, Zona 2, has quality machines. Q10 per hr. Open M-Sa 8am-9pm.

Post Office: 2 Av., 3 C., in Zona 3. Open M-F 8:30am-5:30pm, Sa 9am-1pm.

ACCOMMODATIONS

Hostal D'Acuña, 4 C. 3-11, Zona 2 (☎951 0484). With a colorful, inviting atmosphere, this is the best budget option and the center of tourist activity in Cobán. Bunkbeds are arranged in homey rooms for 2 or 4 people. The small courtyard garden rings with Ella Fitzgerald and Louis Armstrong, and the restaurant is delicious (though not cheap). Hot water and dressers with padlocks. Dorms Q50 per person. AmEx/MC/V. ❸

Pensión Monja Blanca, 2 C. 6-30, Zona 2 (☎952 1712). A dignified place with friendly service and a courtyard. Elegant rooms with cable TV, free *agua pura,* and hot bath. Those with shared bath are comfortable but basic. Also on the premises is a good *comedor.* Singles Q50, with bath Q100; doubles Q100/Q200. ❸

IN RECENT NEWS

LAND DISPUTES

Central America's history is marred by wars and political coups over land rights, and Guatemala is no exception. Since the peak of the Maya empire, survival has been closely tied to land ownership and the basic supplies, such as maize, that the land provides. As the population expands and more food becomes necessary, the disputes for land are once again at the forefront of daily Guatemalan life.

The Altaverapaz is where much of Guatemala's primary rainforest survives and, despite its officially protected status, loggers, firewood cutters, and furniture makers enter the forest to cut huge swaths without penalty. Moreover, the rapid rate of deforestation by slash-and-burn techniques is destroying treasured lands.

In an attempt to placate landless *campesinos* and protect the remaining forest, the government has begun (and is actually following through on) a redistribution plan. The new plan gives property to Maya families already working the land in exchange for the promise to protect the forest near their plots. The plots distributed surround the most vulnerable protected areas, serving as a buffer zone between future loggers and the forest, and providing proof of harmony among people, land, and national politics.

Hostal Doña Victoria, 3 C. 2-38, Zona 3 (☎951 4213). A musty colonial home with plush beds and hand-carved wooden furniture. 4-person dorms are a good deal. Dorms Q40; singles Q110; doubles Q150. AmEx/MC/V. ❷

Hotel La Paz, 6 Av. 2-19, Zona 1 (☎952 1358). Large, clean rooms, some with wooden furniture. Singles Q30, with private bath Q44; doubles Q61/Q74. ❶

Hotel Central, 1 C. 1-79, Zona 4 (☎952 1442). Clean rooms with hot-water private baths and a courtyard. More pricey rooms are spacious, well-lit, and come with cable TV. Singles Q62, with TV Q83; doubles Q112/Q132; triples Q161/Q182. ❹

⬛ FOOD

El Bistro, at Hostal D'Acuña, offers Euro-style candlelit dining, good service, delicious home-cooked food, and plenty of *música tranquila.* Grab a table by the fire and enjoy a crepe with chicken and light parsley cream sauce (Q60), vegetarian cannelloni (Q40), or a piece of chocolate cake (Q10). Open daily 6:30am-10pm. ❹

Xkape Kob'an, Diag. 4 5-13, Zona 2, is a new touristy cafe-cum-Q'eqchi' cultural center in a rebuilt colonial home. Legends and a Q'eqchi' dictionary are included on the menu as well as a wide array of Q'eqchi' books scattered on the wooden tables. Dishes out traditional duck soup called *Kaq-ik* (Q40) and a milky cinnamon drink called *horchata* (Q6). Wide cappuccino selection starts at Q7. Open daily 6am-7pm. ❹

Restaurante Cantonés, Diagonal 4 4-24, Zona 2. Authentic Chinese food served in a typical Cobán house. Some dishes are pricey; others are a good value for their generous portions. General Tsao's chicken Q56. Open daily 11am-10pm. MC/V. ❺

Café El Tirol, 1 C. 3-13, Zona 1. Even hardened caffeine junkies will be impressed by the endless selection of coffees and teas at this relaxing cafe. Sandwiches and light meals are also served. Basic cup o' joe Q6; *café krupnik*—a vodka-based concoction—Q15. Open M-Sa 7:30am-9pm. ❷

Restaurante La Posada, 1 C. 4-12, Zona 2, at the pointed part of the *parque.* A high-class Spanish-decor restaurant with *típico* dishes and an international menu. *Chili rellenos* with beef Q56. Open M-Th 7am-9pm, F-Sa 7am-10pm. ❺

⬛ SIGHTS

For a bird's eye view of Cobán, head out to **Templo El Calvario.** The hillside church dates back to 1559, but it's the expansive view from the church, reached by climbing 135 steps, that really makes the visit worthwhile. Follow 7 Av. north until you reach the stairway.

Vívero Verapaz is an orchid farm showcasing thousands of different species, including the *monja blanca* (white nun), the national flower of Guatemala. Follow the diagonal road (Diagonal 4) that begins at the end of the *parque* (left of Hotel la Posada). At the bottom of the hill turn left and continue for 15min. (Open M-Sa 9am-noon and 2-5pm. Q5.)

Cobán's passion for **coffee** spills outside the town's cafes and into the surrounding *fincas,* many of which were once owned by wealthy Germans. For insight into the coffee culture, check out **Finca Santa Margarita,** 3 C. 4-12, Zona 2. Guided tours of the plantation explain the *finca's* history and give a detailed look at modern coffee production; some provide coffee samples (the same stuff they send to Starbucks) for visitors to savor and compare. Spanish and English-speaking guides are available. (☎/fax 951 3067. Tour 45min., Q20 per person. Open M-F 8am-12:30pm and 1:30-5pm, Sa 8am-noon.)

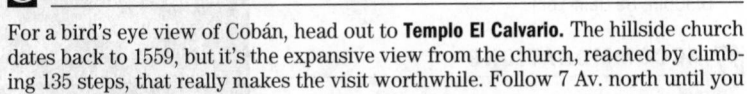

GUATEMALA

NIGHTLIFE

If you're looking for nightlife, your best bet is **Milenio**, on 3 Av., half a block north of 1 C. in Zona 4. The front bar has a more upscale feel, but the atmosphere stays pretty laid back, with *fútbol* on the widescreen TV and a dance floor in back. There are two main lounges and *salsa* is the music of choice (open daily until 1am). Catch a movie at **Cine Fenix** at the pointed end of the *parque* inside Imperial Pizza, daily at 5 and 8pm (Q5).

DAYTRIPS FROM COBÁN

BIOTOPO DEL QUETZAL

Buses on the route between Cobán and Guatemala City pass the biotopo. Buses also leave the biotopo to Guatemala City (3hr., every 30min. 3-7am, every hr. 7am-5pm) and Cobán (1hr., every hr. 7am-8pm, Q6). Open daily 7am-5:30pm; last entrance 4pm.

About 30km southeast of Cobán is the Biotopo Mario Dary Rivera, commonly known as the Biotopo del Quetzal (Quetzal Reserve), an expanse of rugged cloud forest home to Guatemala's national bird, the elusive quetzal, which cannot survive in captivity. Two trails twist their way through the park: **Sendero los Helechos** (1hr., 1.8km) is the shorter trail, while **Sendero los Musgos** (2hr., 3.5km) takes you deep into the dense forest. The longer route provides better vistas while the shorter leads to a waterfall, but both give excellent tours of the forest and an equally good chance of spotting the elusive quetzal. The road at the entrance to the reserve is actually one of the best places to catch a glimpse of the beautiful birds; they're seen most often in April and September in the early morning. Look in the large leaves of the **aguacatillo**; its small green fruit is a favorite treat for elusive quetzals. But even if the bird eludes you (and odds are, it will), the beautiful forest canopy and a swim in the waterfalls are still worth a visit.

You can stay the night at **Hospedaje Los Ranchitos ❶**, just down the road toward Cobán from the entrance to the reserve. It offers rustic accommodations and is a good place to look for the elusive quetzal. The *hospedaje* has its own patch of forest, complete with a private trail and a basic *comedor*. (Breakfast Q15-20, lunch or dinner Q18-25. Singles Q30, with bath Q50; doubles Q60/Q80; triples Q90/Q100.) **Camping** is also available inside the reserve for Q10 per person.

GRUTAS DEL REY MARCOS/BALNEARIO CECILINDA

To reach the Grutas from Cobán, take a bus to Chamelco from 5 Av., 5 C. in Zona 3 (20min., Q2), where you can find morning buses or pickups to Chamil. Ask to be dropped off at the road to Rey Marcos/Balneario Cecilinda, then walk about 500m to the entrance; follow the sign. Coming back, pickups to Chamelco are less frequent in the afternoon but still pass by. The last bus to Cobán departs in the late afternoon.

For adventure seekers who enjoy crawling and climbing through unlit caves, the Grutas del Rey Marcos are not to be missed. Listen to the roar of a sacred, underground Maya river, and splash around under gorgeous natural waterfalls. Discovered in May 1998 and open to the public since January 1999, the caves are believed to be the site of religious ceremonies that took place in pre-Columbian times; the Maya still hold the site sacred and ceremonies continue even today. The inner sanctuary of the cave is rumored to be the source of a large, mystic energy field, and Iván, the owner and occasional tour guide, warns that everyone who enters will leave carrying a blessing or a curse. Mysticism aside, a tour of Rey Marcos is an exhilarating experience and makes for a worthwhile daytrip from Cobán. After getting muddy exploring, cool off in the **Balneario Cecilinda**, the natural swimming area set into the mountainside below the caves. (Open daily 8am-5pm. Admission including guided tour, rubber boots, helmet, and flashlight Q25.) And for those adventurers who just can't get enough of the Grutas, a pleasant farm and hostel has opened not 500m from the entrance. **Don Jeronimo's ❺** (☎308 2255), run by an American, is an all-inclusive resort. For Q200 per day (Q360 for a couple), three full vegetarian meals and a pleasant *cabaña* next to a gurgling river are available.

LANQUÍN AND ENVIRONS

About 40km northeast of Cobán rests the village of Lanquín and two nearby natural wonders, the beautiful pools of **Semuc Champey** and the cave network known as the **Grutas de Lanquín.** Guided tours from Cobán are convenient and often a good deal for one or two travelers; the guides are excellent and will point out the sights' hidden marvels. **Hostal D'Acuña** (see **Accommodations,** p. 391) offers a "Semuc Special," which includes transportation, breakfast, lunch, and guides. (Q260 per person, 4 person minimum) Also, both **Hostal D'Acuña** and **Hostal Doña Victoria,** 3 C. 2-38, Zona 3 (☎952 2213), organize 4WD transport to **Semuc Champey** (US$25 per person, 4 person minimum; discounts for larger groups).

Many travelers make daytrips to Lanquín, catching the 6am bus from Cobán and returning on the 2:30pm bus. Buses from Cobán (2½hr., 6 per day 6am-3pm, Q10) and return buses from Lanquín (2½hr.; 6 per day 3:30am-2:30pm; Q10, minibus Q15) make several trips per day. Pickups can also be found in the mornings heading from Lanquín to Pujal, and then on to Cobán. Go early and be prepared to wait. Should you want to stay the night, there are a few good options. Travelers rave about the English and Guatemalan owned ▧ **El Retiro ❶,** a budget complex on the Lanquin River 10min. east of town. The laid-back style, beautiful setting, and terrific vegetarian food seduces travelers for weeks at a time. Arrive early as dorms fill quickly. Free pickup is available at the bus stop. (☎983 0009. Dorms Q25; private bungalows Q50 per person; with bath Q80 per person. Dinners Q38.) About 100m downhill from the town entrance, **Hotel el Recreo ❶** rents spacious rooms with private bath. The hotel also has decent budget bungalows with clean communal bath in forested grounds. (☎983 0056. Bungalows Q25 per person, singles Q144; doubles Q190. MC/V.) Uphill and to the right of the town entrance is **Hospedaje La Divina Providencia ❶,** with plain clapboard rooms, hot water, and an attached *comedor* and pharmacy. (☎983 0041. Q20 per person.)

GRUTAS DE LANQUÍN

Visitors to Grutas can explore the well-lit cave network, which extends more than 3km through five large "rooms." The Grutas de Lanquín are about 1.5km along the road toward Cobán and down a short drive that veers to the right off the main road. The path tends to be slippery, so sneakers are necessary. Some of the larger stalactites are named after famous people and animals like "La Virgen" and "El Sapo." The caves' thousands of bats pour out into the night sky around dusk and are well worth the wait; since the park will be closed, this can only be done from outside the entrance. If you do stick around, bring a flashlight to find your way back to Lanquín, and wear other clothes and shoes you don't mind getting dirty—especially if you venture out past the walkway. (Open daily 8am-5pm. Q20.)

▧ SEMUC CHAMPEY

The 300m natural limestone bridge of Semuc Champey creates quite a show, with the mighty Cahabón River thundering into the depths below. The top of the bridge, by contrast, is pure tranquility. A descending series of clean pools, perfect for swimming, flow above the river. Framed by steep forested hillsides, the waters turn marvelous shades of blue and green as the sun moves across the sky. Upon arriving at the Semuc parking lot, follow the trail past the small *tienda*. Alongside the pools is a covered *rancho* for camping and picnicking that has bathrooms. To reach the departure point for the Cahabón River, start with the parking lot at your back and follow the trail that crosses over to the right side of the pools and continues past the picnic tables. Follow the slippery rocks carefully, and don't get too close to the waterfalls. The trail which branches to the right before the changing rooms continues steeply uphill for 30-45min. to the photo-op location overlooking the whole series of pools. (Open daily 8am-5pm. Q20, collected in the parking lot.)

Semuc Champey is best reached by **pickup,** but you can do the 3hr. (8km) hot uphill hike by following the gravel road heading away from the river. Bring water. Pickups (Q10) pass by Café Semuc, most frequently on market days (M, Th), but the best bet is to take a round-trip pickup from El Retiro (Daily 9am, Q30).

If you don't want to bother with transportation and want to spend several days at the pools, the new **Posada Las Marias ❶** is the place to hang. Popular with travelers, the full service Las Marias is only 1km away from the Semuc Champey parking lot. The hostel has both dorm rooms and loft space. It can be a bit buggy, so bring a mosquito net or a strong bottle of DEET. Although it is isolated, Las Marias offers tasty *típico* grub so travel back and forth to Lanquín is not necessary. Minibus drivers from Cobán are more than happy to drop you off for a few extra quetzals; another option is to flag down a pickup in Lanquín. (Dinner Q25. 4-bed dorms Q25 per person; lofts Q20 per person.)

CHISEC

Long a traveler-forbidden frontier territory, new roads have made Chisec (pop. 13,500) and its natural beauty accessible to all. Dominated by the K'ekchi' Maya, the area remained virtually unpopulated until 40 years ago when refugees entered en mass to avoid the war. Unfortunately, the war found them. The town itself was burned and bulldozed twice during the 80's and is still recovering. Very little Spanish is spoken and creative hand motions are a necessity. The main attractions are the turquoise rivers and limestone cave systems that dot the region, though they are well off the beaten track.

Minibuses drop off and depart from the southeast corner of the *parque* on the main road for: Cobán (2 hr., every 15 min. 5am-4pm, Q20), Raxrujá (45 min., every 30 min. 5am-6pm, Q10); for Flores take a Raxrujá bus and ask to be dropped at El Cruce (30min., Q5). **Buses** to Sepalau leave from the Banrural. (30 min., Q2).

THE HIDDEN DEA[L]

SOUL FOOD

Amongst the rows of *comedores* and market vendors in Chise[c] hides a gem of a restaurant. O[n] the sign they claim to be revolu[-]tionizing both *comida típica* and Guatemala one customer at a time. A mix of American classics, fresh veggies, and *típico* chicke[n] dishes, the food is savory and refreshing. Picnic-style pasta salads are served alongside tama[-]les. The food, however, is where the international aspect stops.

La Huella's focus is on raising money to invest in women's development projects and schol[-]arships for the small Chisec com[-]munity. Projects include buying a foot-loom to make traditional tex[-]tiles for struggling war-widows and scholarships to prepare girls for the tourism industry, either as guides or as trip planners. The restaurant itself demonstrates this dual purpose, as all the man[-]agers and employees are women making it one of few establish[-]ments in all of Guatemala tha[t] can make that claim.

The righteous goals go dow[n] smooth for travelers because o[f] the reasonable prices. Hug[e] pieces of fresh carrot cake wit[h] raisins are a paltry Q6, an[d] strong, organic, locally-grown co[f]fee is Q3.

To get to La Huella, walk downhil[l] on the main road 100m from the central park. It is on the right. Ope[n] daily 7am-9pm. For more info o[n] affiliated Guatemala NGOs visi[t] www.deeproots.org.

Finding your way around Chisec is fairly simple, and Pedro at La Huella Digital (see below) knows the area well and can provide any **tourist info**. The **Banrural** on the *parque* exchanges travelers checks and currency (open M-F 8:30am-5pm, Sa 9am-1pm). The **police** can be found on the east side of the *parque* and are open 24hr. There is a **Centro de Salud** 2 blocks to the right (when facing uphill) from the bus stop. (Open M-F 8am-4pm, emergency service 24 hr.) **Farmacia Sarai**, next to Hotel Nopales, is open M-Sa 8am-7pm. **Internet and international calls** are available at **La Huella Digital**. They have a fast satellite connection and new computers. There is also a small **library** with English and Spanish books.

Hotel La Estancia ❸, on the main road on the north side of town, is the most comfortable option in town. Large, spotless room with tile floors help travelers feel at home. Hammocks, a pool and caged toucans are in the main courtyard. Soap and towels are provided. All rooms have bath and an overhead fan. (☎514 0800. Q50 per person.) **Hotel Los Nopales ❷**, is across the *parque central* from the bus stop. The clean, basic rooms are arranged around a dingy rain-water filled pool. All rooms with bath and fan. (☎514 0624. Q35 per person.) **◗Cafetería La Huella ❷** is just north of the *parque* on the main street. Huella is the center of *gringo* activity and a local hangout; a card game or board game is almost always being played. The fixed up wooden house has been painted in bright, cheery colors and the walls are decorated with local art; all profits go to support local women's groups. Peace Corps volunteers have introduced a wide array of Americanized food in addition to the *típico* plates. (*Pollo frito* Q12, chocolate cake Q6. Open daily 7am-9pm.)

▷ **DAYTRIPS FROM CHISEC.** The beautiful and remote **Candelaria Caves**, located halfway between Chisec and Raxrujá, are part of an underground system more than 30km long and widely considered the largest and most awe-inspiring in Central America. French spelunker Daniel Dreux discovered the caves in 1974, following a six-year search that began when he read about a sacred underground river in the *Popol Vuh*, the Quiché Maya holy book. The area encompassing the caves was declared a national park and has been opened from two different sides.

The more impressive entry of the two is at the community of Candelaria Camposanto. There are two enormous dry caves and a 15 min. tube ride on the subterranean Río Candelaria. The Ventana de Seguridad cave (accesible either by tube or land) is a cathedral-sized vault with a large opening in the roof, collapsed from a 1976 earthquake, which lets in a filtered column of light from the jungle above. Deeper in the cave are a series of unmarred stalactite, crystalline formations. Part of the caves are not open to tourists as they are still thought to be a sight sacred to the K'ekchi'. The community runs 2 hr. tours lead by knowledgeable students from the local school. Ask at the marked thatched-roof hut. Dry tour Q30, tube tour Q35. *(From Chisec, take any bus to Raxrujá and ask to be let dropped at Candelaria Camposanto. Bring a flashlight.)*

Surrounded by wild primary jungle and towering limestone rocks, the turquoise **Lagunas de Sepalau** make a nice retreat from the heat of the region. There are actually four lakes, but only two have the turquoise color which comes from mineral-laden underground springs. One of the lakes is sacred (and also supplies drinking water to the community) and swimming in that lake is off limits. Long ago, legend has it, the sacred lake had quite a temper, turning violent and churning when approached by humans. Now the lakes have become accustomed to frequent visitors and have returned to their tranquil, lazy state perfect for an afternoon of swimming and sunning. *(To get to the lagunas, take a bus or catch a pick up to Sepalau village, 30 min., Q2. Otherwise it is a hot 7km walk to the village. Follow the road in front of the Chisec municipality out of town onto the dirt road and continue straight. Stop off in the office in town to pay the entrance fee and get a guide to show you through the 40min. long jungle trail to the lakes. The 2nd of the 2 is for swimming. Q25 per person includes guide and canoe ride.)*

Just 2km from Chisec on the road towards Raxrujá, the **B'omb'il Pek Caves** ("painted rock") are home to the first Maya cave paintings discovered in Guatemala. But viewing the paintings and colorful rock flow formations requires a little technical assistance. To enter the passage, descend the steep rope ladder or for a little extra rush rappel into the darkened caves (don't forget the head lamp!). The 2km walk through the forest to the cave entrance is through lush, jungle habitat and fields of flowering cardamon, the spicy local crop. If rapelling wasn't enough excitement, a 15 min. float down fast flowing rapids of the **San Simón River** (good put-in is next to the reception area for the caves) may create a little adrenaline. *(Tubes are available for rent at the reception area for Q20. A complete tour of the cave takes about 3 hrs., longer if tubing. Entrance Q30 includes guide and rapelling equipment.)*

Laguna de Lachuá, one of the least-visited national parks in Central America, is a hidden gem. A new road from Cobán to Playa Grande has made accessing Lachuá much easier. Eons ago, a giant meteor landed on this remote stretch of rainforest, creating a clear, deep, limestone-ringed lagoon. A single river feeds the lagoon, and two drain it. The park was established in 1975 to protect the area's humid tropical forest and the animals that live in it. Speedy lizards and colorful butterflies abound on the 4.2km trail leading to the lagoon and bathing/camping area. Other less visible fauna include jaguars, tapirs, wild boars, and hundreds of bird species, including parrots and toucans. The only **trail** in the 14 sq. km park is the one leading from the entrance to a tranquil lagoon. Bathe with fish and wonder how on earth this slice of the Caribbean became trapped in the wilderness. A building by the shore has rustic cooking facilities (bring your own food and water), solar-powered lighting, and bunk beds with mosquito netting (Q30). Latrines and a covered *rancho* for **camping** (Q25) are nearby. (Open daily 7am-4pm. Park admission Q20.)

Staying in nearby **Playa Grande,** which is neither a *playa* nor *grande,* is a more accommodating but less scenic option. Alternatively dusty and muddy, Playa Grande was constructed as a model village, a settlement for war refugees, and has all the grace and charm one would expect from the work of a military architect. If you stay the night, **Hotel Torrevisión ❶** is past the Municipalidad on the first road heading to the left, down the street from where the bus drops off. (Singles Q30, with private bath Q75; doubles Q60/Q100.) **Cafetería Long Beach ❷,** down the street, is clean and cheap. Across the way, **Guatemex ❸** has classier dishes (lobster Q70; steak Q22). *(Microbuses or trucks from Cobán will drop you off in San Luis, a small settlement 5km from the park entrance—tell the driver you want to go to Lachuá. In San Luis, you might find a pickup heading east toward the park. From the park entrance it is 4.2km to the base camp. Returning to Cobán, walk the fairly straightforward 5km back to the Playa Grande-Cobán road and wait—departures are fairly frequent in the morning.The not-so-well-traveled road in front of the park runs east; a single bus passes by around 3:30am before taking the long road to Cobán via Chisec. To get to the Candalaria Caves, the bus will drop you off at a crossing where a pickup can take you farther.)*

BAJA VERAPAZ

The road to the Verapaz highlands branches off from the Atlantic Highway at El Rancho junction. Up the road, at La Cumbre junction, is the turnoff to **Salamá,** the pleasant regional capital, and the smaller **Rabinal,** both of which are best visited during their annual fiestas (weeks of Sept 17 and Jan 25, respectively). The main road continues past the Biotopo del Quetzal before making its way to Cobán.

RABINAL AND SURROUNDINGS

Rabinal lies about 1hr. west of Salamá, in the area's next large valley. Rabinal (pop. 10,000) is famous for its impressive *artesanía* and the local dances showcased during the town's annual *fiesta* from January 19-25. If you can't make it to the *fiesta*, a jaunt over to the Thursday and Sunday markets to look at the renowned carvings and pottery is worthwhile. For area **tourist information,** see the energetic Raul Fernández (☎940 1780) at the ESSO gas station in Salamá.

Rabinal suffered a great deal during the war—hidden graves are still being uncovered—and a few sights in town memorialize the tragedy. By the altar of the *parque*'s colonial church hang two striking murals, painted in 1998. One is of the town's troubled past, with fires in the woods (the army destroyed vast areas of forest in their campaign against the insurgents) and tormented faces. The other, featuring among other things a marimba and a computer, depicts Rabinal's rich culture and anticipates a bright future. There is also a small **community museum** on 2 C. 4 Av., Zona 3, with exhibits ranging from drawings of an indigenous anti-hyperthyroidism dance to over 300 photographs of local war victims.

Buses from Guatemala City head to **Rabinal** via **Salamá** (4½hr., about every hour). Most buses heading from Salamá to Rabinal continue west to **Cobulco.** The best place to stay in Rabinal is ☒**Posada San Pablo ❶**, 3 Av. 1-50, Zona 1. The clean rooms are equipped with top-of-the-line mattresses, and the communal baths are fair. An on-site *comedor* serves three meals per day. (Singles Q16, with bath Q25; doubles Q32/Q42.)

PETÉN

Guatemala's northernmost region once boasted one of the world's most advanced civilizations, but ever since the Maya mysteriously abandoned their power center at Tikal, humans have more or less avoided this foreboding area. The thick forest and thin soil kept the Spanish settlers away, and today the Petén region contains a third of Guatemala's land mass but less than 3% of its population. Even so, nature's dominance is being threatened by new residents, slash-and-burn agriculture, and ranching. Conservation efforts have helped slow the destruction, most notably the establishment of the Maya Biosphere Reserve in 1940. With roads rolling over cleared grasslands dotted with banana trees, jaguars prowling, and stone pyramids hidden behind hanging jungle vines, Petén feels cinematic and surreal.

The region's great attraction is Tikal, arguably the most beautiful of all Maya sites. Flores and its sister city, Santa Elena, have the most visitor services in Petén and serve as pleasant bases. El Remate, between Flores and Tikal, is a quiet lakeside village, increasingly popular with visitors to the ruins. Sayaxché provides river access to smaller Maya sites, and the famous traveler's hangout of Finca Ixobel lies along the coastal highway to Guatemala City. North of Tikal are some isolated Maya ruins, including Uaxactún and spectacular El Mirador.

Unfortunately, in recent times political and social instability have overshadowed these magnificent sights. Petén was a constant battleground during the civil war, and shocks from the conflict continue to reverberate. In the 1980s and early 90s paramilitaries would frequently stop buses along the highway and rob them at gunpoint. Such incidents decreased in number after the signing of the 1996 Peace Accords; however, the signing failed to address the issues of the paramilitaries (Patrulleros de la Autodefensa Civil, or PAC) scattered across the country. In June 2002 over 20,000 ex-PAC paralyzed Petén, blocking roads, the Tikal International Airport, and seizing an oil refinery. They demanded Q20,000 each for services rendered during the war, and ended their blockade of the region only after the government promised some form of compensation to be paid for by a national tax.

FINCA IXOBEL

All buses on the Guatemala City-Flores route pass by the turn-off to the finca (from which it is a 15min. walk to the property). Microbuses from Flores will drop you right at the entrance. Departures to Guatemala City (7-10hr.; every hr. 9:30am-1:30pm, 3:30, 10:30,

11:30pm; Q55-190) via Río Dulce (2hr., Q30). Going to Flores, buses leave every hr. and there is a night bus (2hr., 8:30am-6:30pm and 10pm, Q20-40). Buses heading to Flores after 10:30am are coming from Guatemala City. Finca Ixobel can also arrange minibuses, a cheaper option for large groups.

Finca Ixobel has become notorious for the spell it casts on travelers, who come with plans for only a day and end up staying for weeks or months. Run by American Carole DeVine, the 400-acre *finca* set in pine-covered hills is a peaceful spot, though travelers frustrated by hordes of backpackers might be disappointed. The homemade all-you-can-eat buffet dinners (Q50) are nothing short of delicious. The staff offers a range of excursions into the surrounding wilderness. (Horse treks 2hr., Q75; 1 day Q150; 2 days with camping Q400. Jungle treks, 2-4 days, Q200 per day. Inner-tubing trips, 1 day Q100. A popular river cave trip, full day, Q70.) Dinner is served at large benches where travelers tell stories before heading over to the secluded bar, open until the last guest stops drinking. There are a few short-term volunteer opportunities (see **Alternatives to Tourism**, p. 321). Relaxing accommodations vary from sheltered camping and dorms to simple rooms with private bath. (☎410 4307; www.fincaixobel.com. Camping Q22 per person; blanket or hammock rental Q3. Dorms Q30; simple rooms Q60, with bath Q115; doubles Q90/Q175. Treehouse singles Q75; doubles Q100.)

SAYAXCHÉ

Sleepy Sayaxché (pop. 7800) sits on the Río de La Pasión about 50km southwest of Flores. Although there's little to do here, the town makes a great launching point for trips to El Ceibal, Aguateca and other ruins in the southwest Petén. Sayaxché is also a good place to stop over before heading south toward Tikal or Cobán and the Verapaz Highlands. During the rainy season, however, the river often floods its banks, making travel through the area exciting but dangerous.

⬛ TRANSPORTATION. South-bound **buses** depart from the town *parque* for: **Cobán** via **Raxrujá** (2½hr.; 4, 5am; Q20; departing near the *parque*, on the main side of town. Frequent minibuses also depart until 5pm; Q20.); **Flores** (1½hr.; 6, 8am, 1pm; Q10. Frequent **minibuses** also depart until 6pm; Q10); and **Guatemala City** (12-15hr.; 4:30 and 5pm via **Flores**).

🞧 PRACTICAL INFORMATION. Tourist Info can be obtained at the **INGUAT** office, 1½ blocks up from the waterfront and a block to the left (open M-F 9am-5pm.). Exchange currency or traveler's checks at **Banoro**, 1 block from the waterfront dock on the left (open M-F 9am-4pm, Sa 9am-1pm) or at **Banrural** on the northern corner of the parque, 2 blocks up from the river and 1 block left. They also have a 24hr. Visa **ATM** (open M-F 8:30am-5:30pm, Sa 9am-1pm). **Farmacia Arteaga** is 2 blocks from the waterfront on the right (open daily 6:30am-8:30pm). With your back to the dock, the **post office** is 5 blocks to the left and 4 blocks to the right, in a small office next to the large "Fondo de Tierras" building (open M-F 8am-4:30pm).

🞧🞧 ACCOMMODATIONS AND FOOD. Hotel Petexbatún ❺, 1 block up from the river and 2 blocks to the right, is a bit far from the action, though it is the cleanest hotel in town and the best value. Large comfortable rooms with bath, fan, TV, and wooden furniture. (☎928 6166. Singles Q105; doubles Q115.) **Hotel Guayacán ❷,** by the dock, is a bit pricey, but has clean, comfortable rooms with private bath. (☎/fax 928 6111. With fan Q150, with A/C Q175.) An annex across the street has more basic rooms with shared bath. (Singles Q40; doubles Q70; triples Q100.) **Hotel Mayapan ❶,** half a block from the waterfront and another half-block to the left, has a variety of rooms. The cheapest of them is as hot as a steam bath. The clean doubles with fan are much nicer and a better value. (☎560 9049. Singles Q30; doubles Q40; triples Q50; room with private bath Q60.)

El Bontanero ❸ is 2 blocks up from the river and to the left. It's all about the attitude at this eatery and disco. The decor is "log-cabin-disco" complete with stools carved from tree trunks and a dance floor with swirling lights. (*Pollo a la plancha* Q34. Open M-Sa 8am-3am, Sa 9am-7:30pm.) Another good place to eat is **Comedor Esmeralda ❷**, 1 block up from the waterfront and 1 block to the right, on the left side. Friendly owner Doña Rita and her 12 children love making friends, and the food is delicious. (Eggs, beans and tortilla Q15.)

SAYAXCHÉ DAYTRIPS: RUINS

🎯 CEIBAL

The best way to reach Ceibal from Sayaxché is a1hr. boat journey along the Río de la Pasión through pastures, hamlets, and the Parque Nacional Ceibal. The best service is provided by Don Pedro. His office is to the right on the water. He also has a large collection of photos from his 25 years of operating lanchas which charts the transformation of the ruins and of Sayaxché. The short but steep trail from the landing climbs through thick forest before flattening out near the ruins; head straight until reaching the informal center. (☎928 6109. Round-trip including a few hours at the ruins Q250-Q300 for 1-5 people.) A slightly cheaper and faster way is to hire a direct pickup truck (45min., Q150 roundtrip) although this may be possible only in the dry season. The cheapest option is to take a collective pickup from the bus terminal across the river to Aldea Paraíso (10min., every 30 min., Q3) and then walk the dirt road veering left to the ruins. It's a hot, 8km walk (1½-2½hr.), so start early in the day. Ruins open daily 7am-3pm. Q25.

The grandest of the Maya ruins near Sayaxché is Ceibal, 15km east of town. With only 3% of the ruins restored, the site is small but still impressive. The main attractions are the wonderfully preserved **stelae** with both original and reconstructions on the site. Unlike the limestone stelae of Tikal, these were carved out of hard stone found only in the small area surround the site; the monkey-faced 'stelae 2' is particularly unique. Ceibal reached its peak around AD 900 with more than 10,000 residents and seems to have been strongly influenced by the Toltec dynasties of Mexico. Most of the site surrounds several plazas off to one side of the guard's quarters. A path heading in the opposite direction from the information center leads to the only other restored structure, the **pirámide circular,** a Toltec-influenced platform used for astronomy. Free **camping** is permitted, but bring tent, mosquito netting, water, and enough food to share with the guards (no joke). For tours of the ruins, hire a guide at the entrance.

👁 🏔 LAKE PETEXBATÚN

Aguateca is 1½hr. by boat from Sayaxché. Getting to the path to Dos Pilas takes 45min., but you must walk from there. Servicio de Lanchas Don Pedro and Viajes Turísticas La Montaña also arrange trips to Aguateca and Dos Pilas. During the dry season (Jan.-May), a 4WD pickup sometimes runs to Dos Pilas, leaving Sayaxché at 7am.

From Sayaxché, a 30min. ride down the southern branch of the Río de la Pasión leads to the secluded Lake Petexbatún (Peh-tesh-bah-TOON), surrounded by forest and teeming with wildlife. The area was once an important trading center for the Maya, and the ruins of **Aguateca** overlook the southern edges of the lake. Occupied until about AD 790, the site has plazas, unexcavated temples, well-preserved stelae, and the only known Maya bridge. The ruins are undergoing restorations, scheduled for completion in 2004. The guards will show you around and let you camp if you bring food and equipment. Raingear, mosquito netting, and lots of bug repellent are advisable. Nearby is the **Petexbatún Lodge ❺**, a well-kept hotel on the shores of the lake. (☎331 7561 or 926 0501. Dorms US$10 per person. Singles with bath US$35; doubles with bath US$36.) A second Maya site, **Dos Pilas,** is a 13km hike west of the lake. Find guides (Q300) at the Finca el Caribe. Built in a unique east-west linear pattern, these ruins include stelae and hieroglyphic stairways.

⊙ AGUATECA

Accessible only by a 1¼hr boat ride up the Río Pasión (between Q300-Q350 for roundtrip and a few hours at the site including entrance and tour guide; guides appreciate a small tip), Aguateca is one of the shortest-lived Maya sites in the Petén region and has recently become one of the more heavily excavated and studied sites in the area. Occupied between early AD 700 and AD 790, the city was thought to be closely aligned with nearby Dos Pilas. There have even been similar stelae found at both sites chronicling the defeat of El Ceibal. It is one of the more interesting sites geologically as it is set high on a limestone platform, protected on three sides by a large rock wall and gorge. There is a slippery two-hour walk around the edge of the site that goes down into the gorge and deep into the surrounding jungle full of monkeys, snakes, mosquitoes, and sloths. The city came to its surprising end during construction of the palace dedicated to the fifth governor when enemy attack forced them to flee and never return, and the massive pile of rocks waiting to be erected still sits in the center of the main plaza. It is a three-hour walk on a game path from Aguateca to Dos Pilas.

FLORES

Surrounded by the tranquil Lake Petén Itzá, the relaxed island city of Flores (pop. 17,100) serves as a welcoming base for visitors to the Petén. Flores began life as the Itzá capital of Tayasal, the last independent Maya city, holding off Spanish conquest until 1697. The colorful homes and cobblestone streets contrast nicely with the typical Petén town. While Flores may be the departmental capital, most of the down and dirty business gets done across the man-made causeway in down and dirty Santa Elena (pop. 30,000), home to buses, banks, and planes.

▣ TRANSPORTATION

Flights: Tikal International Airport is 2km east of Santa Elena on the highway to Tikal. Minibuses to the airport generally leave from 4 C. in Santa Elena (2min., Q10). Town **buses** leave from near the causeway in Flores (every 10-15min. 6am-7pm, Q1), and pass by 4 C. in Santa Elena. Grupo Taca (☎926 0451; 7:35am and 4:10pm, Q680) goes to Cancún, Mexico (1½hr., Q1160) and Guatemala City (30min.), Tikal Jets (☎926 0386; 4:30pm, Q600) and Rasca (☎926 0596; Q440) also go to Guate. Maya Island Air (☎926 3386) and Tropic Air (☎926 0348; 9:30am and 3:30pm) go to Belize City.

Buses: Fuentes del Norte is located along 4 C. in Santa Elena; 1st and 2nd class buses depart from there. The other major company is **Pinita,** which departs from the San Juan Hotel in Santa Elena.

Belizean Border at **Melchor de Mencos:** Pinita bus. (2hr.; 5am, 8am, 10am, 1, 4, 6pm; Q20.)

Bethel: Pinita bus. (5hr., 5am, 10am, 1pm, Q30.)

Cobán: There are 2 options: the longer but more comfortable is to take a Guate-bound bus as far as El Rancho (6hr., about Q70) and catch a Cobán bus there (2hr., Q25). A bumpier, shorter route is via Sayaxché (2hr., Q20) and then Raxrujá or Chisec and on to Cobán (4hr., Q40).

El Remate: Tikal-bound buses will drop you here. (45min., noon, 3, 4pm, Q5.)

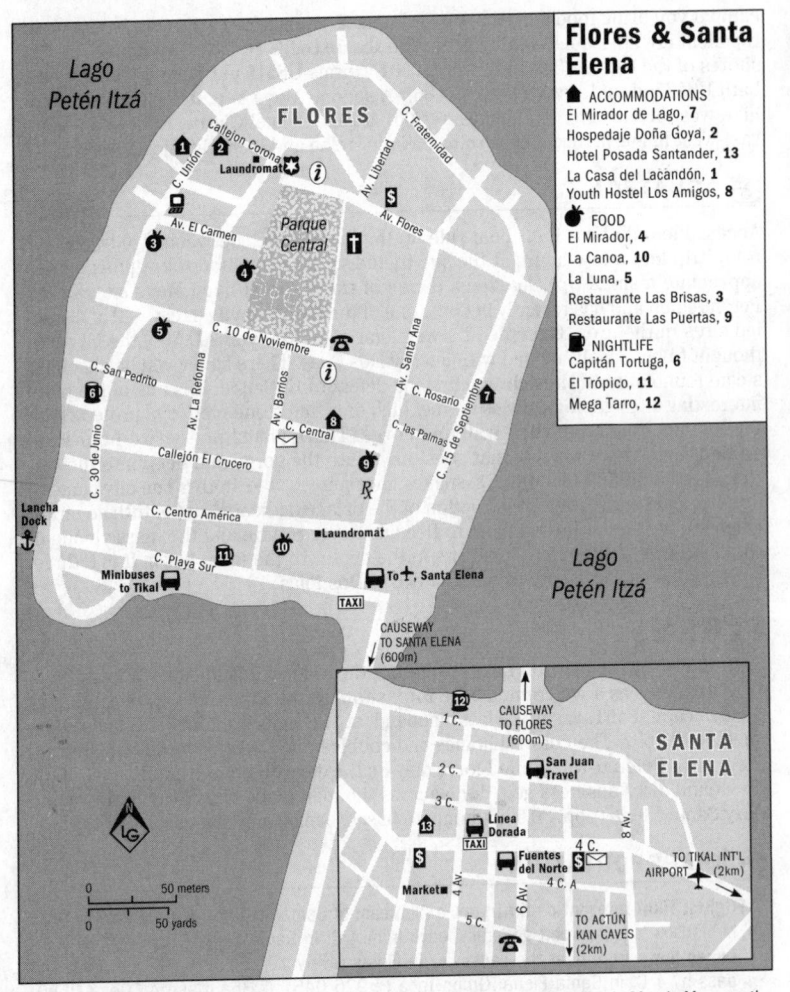

Flores & Santa Elena

⌂ ACCOMMODATIONS
El Mirador de Lago, **7**
Hospedaje Doña Goya, **2**
Hotel Posada Santander, **13**
La Casa del Lacandón, **1**
Youth Hostel Los Amigos, **8**

🍴 FOOD
El Mirador, **4**
La Canoa, **10**
La Luna, **5**
Restaurante Las Brisas, **3**
Restaurante Las Puertas, **9**

🍸 NIGHTLIFE
Capitán Tortuga, **6**
El Trópico, **11**
Mega Tarro, **12**

Guatemala City: Best service on Linea Dorada (☎ 926 0070), with an office in Mundo Maya on the southern Flores shorefront road. Express luxury buses with drink service and movies depart 3 times per day. 8hr.; 8am, 8, 10pm; Q215. Also offers regular Pullman buses (Q120). Fuente del Norte (☎ 926 0517), on 4 C. in Santa Elena, has frequent Pullman departures, bus quality varies. 8-12hr., about every hr. 6:30am-9pm, Q80-Q130.

Poptún: Any daylight Guatemala City-bound bus. (1½hr., Q20.)

Río Dulce: Any daylight Guatemala City-bound bus. (5-6hr., Q50.)

Sayaxché: Pinita bus. (2hr., 6 per day 5am-3pm, Q20.)

Tikal: See **Tourist Minibuses,** below.

Tourist Minibuses: The most popular way of getting to **Tikal** or **El Remate.** Purchase tickets in most hotels or travel agencies for hotel pickup, or catch one on the southern shore road in Flores (about every hr. 5am-noon, more sporadic in afternoon). Also run directly from the airport. **Linea Dorada** runs the best and cheapest service. (☎ 926 0070. Q25 round-trip.) **San Juan Travel** is slightly pricier. (☎926 0041. Q40 round-trip.) The same two companies travel into Belize and Mexico. Linea Dorada/Mundo Maya offers very low rates to **Belize City** (4hr., Q63) and **Chetumal, Mexico** (7½hr., Q120). If and when they raise their rates, they may match those of San Juan travel (Q160 and Q280).

☀🛈 ORIENTATION AND PRACTICAL INFORMATION

Island Flores to the north and Santa Elena to the south are connected by a paved **causeway** across the lake. In Flores, the *parque central* is on top of the hill at the center of town. Santa Elena's main street, **4 Calle,** is 3 blocks south of the end of the causeway. Banks, stores, and buses are all along this street. To get to Flores from the bus drop-off, head east (right as you face the lake) on the main drag until the road signs point you left across the causeway. The **airport** is 2km from Santa Elena along the highway toward Tikal; minibuses and local buses head into town.

Tourist Information: INGUAT (☎926 0894), in Flores' *parque central.* Open M-F 8am-4pm. In the airport as well (☎926 0533). More info at **CINCAP** (☎926 0718), on the north side of the *parque.* Open M-F 9am-1pm and 2-6pm. The **Destination Petén** magazine is also useful.

Travel Agencies and Guided Tours: Recommended agents in Flores are the knowledgeable **Quetzal Travel** (☎926 3337) and **Martsam** (☎926 3225). **Evolution Adventures** (☎926 3206) has tours and community projects.

Banks: Head to Santa Elena for banks—there's an abundant supply along 4 C. Try **Corpobanco,** which has a **Western Union** (open M-F 8:30am-7pm, Sa 9am-1pm). **Banco Industrial** opposite the Hotel Posada Santander cashes Visa and Citicorp traveler's checks and has a 24hr. Visa **ATM** (open M-F 9am-7pm, Sa 10am-2pm). In Flores, the lone **Banrural** on Av. Flores will cash traveler's checks and exchange currency (M-F 8:30am-4pm).

Laundry: Lavandería Peténchel, on C. Centro América. Wash and dry Q25. Open M-Sa 8am-7pm.

Police: ☎110, emergency 120, just north of Flores' *parque.*

Hospital: Hospital Privado, 3 Avenida 4 (☎926 1140), in Santa Elena. Open 24hr.

Pharmacy: Farmacia Nueva, (☎926 1387) a few doors down from Restaurante Las Puertas. Open daily 8am-9pm.

Telephones: Telgua (☎926 1299), 2 blocks south of 4 C. in Santa Elena. Open M-F 8am-6pm, Sa 9am-1pm.

Internet: Internet Tayazal, on C. la Unión down the street from Doña Goya in Flores, has the fastest connection and best rates. Q6 per 30min. Open daily 8am-10pm.

Post Office: In Flores, 1 block south of the *parque.* Open M-F 8am-noon and 2-5pm.

Car Rental: San Juan Travel (☎926 2013), in Santa Elena by the causeway, has rentals for Q450 per day. **Tabarini** (☎926 0272) and others at the airport.

🏠 ACCOMMODATIONS

Accommodations in Santa Elena are closer to the bus station, but Flores is safer and more enjoyable.

■ **Youth Hostel Los Amigos** (☎716 7702), across from Las Puertas restaurant on C. Central. Brand new and winning rave reviews, Matias the Dutchman and his wife have put together the most relaxed place in town. Hammocks surround the courtyard and evening always brings a bonfire. The attached restaurant is clean and cheap. Tidy dorms Q25 per person, private rooms Q30 per person. ❶

FROM THE ROAD

MAN'S BEST FRIEND

Whether working in the fields, managing a guest house, or waiting tables at a bar, the machete is every Guatemalan man's accessory. While the sheer number of machetes is surprising, more shocking still is its versatility.

My first appreciation for its usefulness came at a hostel in Flores. Two young men were standing outside their rental car, peering in. They had locked their keys inside. To my surprise, the hotel clerk quickly resolved the problem with his machete and a long wire: with the machete he pried open the top of the door just a crack, then inserted the wire to fish for the keys. After a few tries he successfully lifted the keys from the seat and out the opening in the top of the door.

Once inside, he used the same machete to serve us fruit; the back end is used for cutting coconuts into two perfect halves. It is the country's most prevalent lawn mower, and the perfect back scratcher for those hard-to-reach places. Millions of fruits, fish, and game have been cleaned or peeled with the trusty machete. Some Guatemalans can't resist brandishing one menacingly after a night at the bars, reminding this traveler that machetes are not all fun and games. So whether he does construction or runs the government, every Guatemalan man will bring along his trusty two-foot-long renaissance-man of an instrument: his machete.

—Ian Campbell

El Mirador de Lago (☎926 1153), on the east side of the island. Bright, comfortable rooms and a great dock for swimming (if you can stand the bath-water-warm lake) make this hotel popular. Rooms have fans and hot-water private baths; lobby has a TV. Singles Q50; doubles Q90; triples Q125. ❸

Hospedaje Doña Goya (☎926 3538), on the north side of the island. Bright, spacious rooms. There's a lake-view rooftop and space to sling hammocks, plus a book exchange. Dorms Q25 per person; doubles Q80, with bath Q100. ❷

La Casa del Lacandón (☎926 4359), on the northwest side of the island. Clean 2nd fl. rooms with views of the lake and a breezy balcony. Singles Q60; doubles Q95, with A/C Q130. ❸

Hotel Posada Santander (☎926 0574), near the bus terminal on 4 C., is the best choice in Santa Elena. Rooms are well-maintained; those in the new wing are nicer and more spacious. Singles Q40, with bath Q60; doubles Q60/Q60. ❷

◻ FOOD

◼ **Restaurante Las Puertas**, on Av. Santa Ana, off C. Centro América. A popular meeting place with just the right amount of hip ambience (read: paint-splattered walls and political posters in an old wooden house). Sandwiches and pasta are tasty and well-priced. Spaghetti al pesto Q30; pizzas and sandwiches Q25-30. Live evening performances 9pm. Cine-bar plays new international films daily at 4:30pm and 7:30pm (Q10). Open M-Sa 8am-midnight. MC/V. ❸

Restaurante Las Brisas, close to Hotel Doña Goya on C. La Unión. One of the few standing comedores. Always full of locals' birthday parties or other celebrations. *Chapín* breakfast Q15. Open daily 7am-9pm. ❷

La Luna, on the west side of the island, by Eco Maya. Excellent food, a warm ambience, and an adjacent patio with tropical plants justify slightly higher prices. Chicken cordon bleu Q61; real burgers Q34. Open daily noon-midnight. MC/V. ❸

El Mirador, on the west side of the *parque*. Serves locals the tastiest budget food in Flores with a nice balcony overlooking the town and lake. Full breakfast Q15. The real bargain is the Q14 buffet served noon-2pm. Open M-Sa 7am-9:30pm. ❷

La Canoa, on C. Centro América. Inexpensive renditions of *comedor* food served in a cozy, family-run cafe. Chicken dinner Q25, tacos Q15. Open M-Sa 8am-3pm, 5-9pm. ❷

NIGHTLIFE

Considering its small size, Flores has myriad options for drinking, eating, and enjoying the waterfront or sunset. Two of the best include **El Trópico**, on the south shore, and **Las Puertas**. Weekend nights are great at **Mega Tarro**, a disco with a hopping lakefront location 100m to the right of the causeway in Santa Elena. Fridays boast *ranchero* music; Saturdays feature hip-hop, Top 40, and reggae. **Capitán Tortuga** on C. 30 de Julio has the best patio in town, way in the back, for watching the sunset. Try armadillo or gibnut (Q105) or a more mundane burger or sandwich for Q25-Q40. (Open daily 10:30am-10pm.)

SIGHTS AND OUTDOOR ACTIVITIES

Local boaters will take visitors out for **tours** of **Lago Petén Itzá**, which may include visits to the lookout point **El Mirador** or the **Peténcito zoo** (M-Su 8am-5pm). Look for boats near the causeway or at the west end of C. Centro América, by Hotel Santana; speak directly with the captain rather than with the agents roaming the streets. (2hr., Q150-200 for small groups.) To go on your own, rent **kayaks** at La Casona de La Isla on the west side of the island (Q20 per hr., starting at 7am, MC/V). Or, alternatively, **rent a bike** from Backabush tour guides on Av. Barrios by the basketball court (Q15 per hr.), and hop a *lancha* to San Andrés (from the *lancha* dock, leave only in the early morning, Q7). The dirt road around the lake is rough and virtually impassable by car so traffic is low. Three minutes outside of San Andrés is the Playita (commonly known as Playa de las Gringas). There are a couple ranchitos offering shade and a small area for swimming. The road goes all the way to El Remate (about 30km) from where you can catch a pickup or bus back to Flores, or flag down a *lancha* in San Andrés or San José to return to Flores.

If the Peténcito zoo doesn't fill your animal needs, check out the **Asociación de Rescate y Conservación de Vida Silvestre (ARCAS)**. An animal rescue station on the mainland featuring macaws, parrots, monkeys, and coatis a 45 min. walk east of San Miguel. A short trail leads through well-marked jungle and past some animals that cannot be re-released into the wild. (Q10, daily 9am-3pm).

The **Aktun Kan Cave**, 2km south of Santa Elena, hosts 300m of well-illuminated paths as well as several unlit kilometers (bring your own flashlight) through standard limestone caves. There is a wide variation of stalactites, though nothing of the magnitude of Candelaría or Lanquín. To get to the cave, follow the causeway south; bear left at the fork and then turn right at the sign. A thorough investigation takes about 30 min. (Open daily 8am-5pm. Q5.)

If interested in learning more about the Petén jungle area, **Eco-Escuela de Español** in San Andrés, a community-run Spanish school has afternoon excursions and volunteer opportunities M-F for anybody interested. (One week with homestay Q1200. Excursions Q40.) Besides teaching Spanish, the school has also taken on some small reforestation projects and the maintenance of Sendero Sacbaquecan, a trail outside of town through secondary forest. The town itself is a wonderful, isolated place to learn Spanish and get a feel for Guatemalan life, as compared to the heavily-touristed Flores. Nobody in town speaks English.

EL REMATE

On the beautiful shores of Lake Petén Itzá, the village of El Remate is known for its woodcarving, though it's the location—halfway between Flores and Tikal and conveniently near the Belizean border—that makes it a popular base for exploring the region. The area has some interesting diversions and nice lake swimming, and is a great change of pace after the bustle of Santa Elena and tourist-centered Flores.

TRANSPORTATION. Tourist minibuses traveling between Flores and Tikal stop in El Remate, and there are also direct **public buses** from Santa Elena (8am, 1, 3, and 4pm). Public *colectivos* are usually cheaper; flag one down anywhere along the highway (Q20 from Melchor or Flores). You can also take a Flores-Belize border bus and get off at **El Cruce/Puente Ixlú,** 2km south of El Remate. From here it's a 30min. walk to town along the main road. Note that en route to **Tikal,** only the 5:30am minibus stops at the hotels; later minibuses must be flagged down. Ticket sellers visit hotels in the evening; you can also buy tickets at **La Casa de Don David** (see below) where a public bus bound for Tikal passes by around 2pm. Catch all buses and minibuses at the shed in front of La Casa de Don David.

ACCOMMODATIONS AND FOOD. Budget accommodations in El Remate are more rustic than those in Flores. The standout is ■**La Casa de Don David ❺,** at the junction of the dirt road veering left along the lake and the highway. It's the most relaxing place between Flores and Tikal with hammocks, local flora, and topiary in the well-trimmed garden. David Kuhn and his staff provide tourist information, good cheer, and delicious food (dinner Q30-Q40). Comfortable rooms have private hot bath; bungalows are great for families. (☎928 8469, cell 306 2190; www.lacasadedondavid.com. Most rooms Q160 per person, nicest rooms Q200 per person. All rooms come with 1 meal.) Popular **John's Lodge ❶,** or the **Casa de Don Juan,** on the highway just before the dirt road near La Casa de Don David, offers basic dorms with mosquito nets and communal bath. (Q20 per person.) **Casa Doña Danita ❶** offers sparse rooms with a key lock and a dock for swimming. (☎701 7114. Dorms Q20; singles Q30, doubles Q35.) The **Biotopo Cerro Cahuí** (see below) has a few free campsites along Lake Petén where campfires are allowed. **Las Orquideas ❹,** half a mile down the gravel road from Don David's, serves great Italian food. (Handmade pizzas Q44, spaghetti Q35, handmade tagliatelle Q40. Open daily 7am-9pm.)

SIGHTS AND OUTDOOR ACTIVITIES. The **Biotopo Cerro Cahuí,** 2km from the highway on the dirt road along the lakeshore, contains 2½ sq. mi. of protected lands, including ponds and tropical forest. Two interconnecting **loop trails**—4km (2hr.) and 6km (3hr.)—traverse the reserve. Just past the first turnaround awaits a *mirador* with a view of the lake. Be careful, though, as violent assaults on tourists have occurred along the road to the Biotopo and in the surrounding areas as recently as 2001. Since then, tourist police have been placed to make things safer, but you should still check with locals before going. Traveling in a group is a good idea. (Open daily 7am-5pm, though visitors may stay later. Q20.) An excellent way to explore beautiful Lake Petén is by renting a **mountain bike.** Don David will lend free bikes to his guests, or can point you to a local to rent one (Q5 per hr.; Q25 per day). Horseback rides are available (Q75 for 2½hr.) through the Biotopo Cerro Cahuí. Guides know some English but knowledge of Spanish makes for a better tour. In the evening, take a boat ride across the lake for Q75. **Lou's Boat Tours** boasts bird watching, swimming in the pristine water, and an excellent view of the sunset. (Q75, 4:30-7pm, inquire at Don David's.) La Casa de Don Juan offers **tours,** including the **Night Crocodile Tour.** (2hr., 1-4 people Q150. Sightings are not guaranteed, but you might get a chance to touch a baby croc on a good night.) In the little village of Puente Ixlú (El Cruce), 2km south of El Remate, stand the ruins of **Ixlú.**

TIKAL

Tikal attracts visitors from every corner of the globe and elicits such a powerful reaction that the site draws nearly as many repeat visitors as first-timers. The ruins, 65km northeast of Flores, encompass more than 3000 Maya stone constructions. The site was featured in *Star Wars*—and no wonder; with five massive tem-

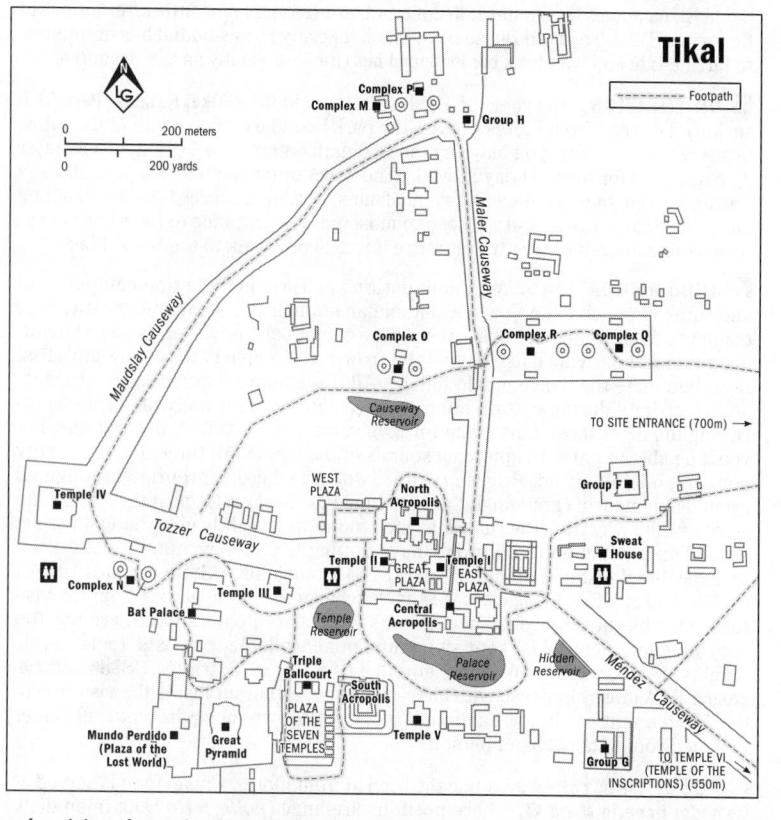

ples rising above the dense jungle, Tikal embodies a magical, mythical quality no modern-day movie set could match. As impressive as the buildings themselves are, it's the surrounding forest that distinguishes Tikal from other great Maya sites. Falling fruit gives away the spider monkeys hiding overhead; remote paths conceal parrots, iguanas, toucans, and wild boars; lucky early risers may spot a sacred jaguar slinking through the undergrowth. Signs at the pond near the lake warn of "cocodrillos peligrosos (dangerous crocodiles)," and one can usually spot at least a small one basking just a few yards from visitors milling around the gift shop.

Many package tours are scheduled so that you can visit Tikal in a single day, and while this is enough time to see the highlights, a longer visit allows for a more leisurely pace and the opportunity to savor the ruins and the jungle as they change with the light. Sunrise and sunset at Tikal are particularly magical.

▐ TRANSPORTATION. From Flores/Santa Elena, El Remate, or the airport, tourist **minibuses** are the easiest way to reach the ruins (see the Flores and El Remate sections for more details). Minibuses arrive in Tikal throughout the morning and return in the afternoon and evening as soon as they accumulate enough passengers. There's also a daily **local bus** from **Santa Elena** (2hr., 1pm, Q10; return 7am). If you're coming from Belize, change buses at **Puente Ixlú/El Cruce** and wait for northbound transport. Frequent minibuses pass by in the morning; the local bus from

Santa Elena comes by around 1:45-2pm, but otherwise there is little afternoon traffic toward Tikal. To get to Belize from Tikal, take any Flores-bound bus or minibus to Puente Ixlú and wait for a **border-bound bus** (the last usually passes around 6pm).

■ **ORIENTATION.** The ruins of Tikal sit in the middle of **Tikal National Park** (550 sq. km). The road from Flores crosses the park boundary 15km south of the ruins; buses will stop so that you may pay the Q50 park entrance fee. (Tickets sold after 3pm are good for the next day as well.) The **visitor center** maintains a post office, a restaurant, and one of the area's two museums. Nearby are three hotels, a camping area, three *comedores*, and the second museum. The entrance to the ruins is near the visitor center, but from the entrance it is a 20min. walk to the Great Plaza.

▛ **ACCOMMODATIONS.** Accommodations at Tikal include one campground and three expensive hotels (by Guatemalan standards). Some budget travelers commute from El Remate or Flores. An overnight stay, however, is an exhilarating treat for those who'd like to beat the crowds to Temple IV to see the sun's first rays illuminate the dense jungle foliage. All three hotels listed have restaurants and electricity during certain hours only (electricity is usually off 11pm-5am). During the night those fans make for lovely, motionless ceiling decorations, but you'll be able to enjoy the piercing sounds of the jungle. All three hotels are very popular so book ahead. Prices are in US dollars where appropriate, though all establishments will (grudgingly) accept Quetzals. **Tikal Inn ❺**, past the Jaguar Inn as you walk away from the ruins, has nice rooms and slightly nicer bungalows set around an inviting pool. All rooms have hot baths in the evenings. (☎926 1913. Includes breakfast and dinner. Singles US$40, bungalow US$50; doubles US$60/US$75. AmEx/MC/V.) **Jungle Lodge ❺** is the cheapest option, across from the visitor center by the ruins entrance. Rooms with shared bath and fan are not too appealing but clean. Well-kept swimming pool available to guests. (☎476 8775. Singles US$26, with bath US$54; doubles US$31/US$72; triples US$86.) **Campground ❶**. A grassy expanse with check-in at the restaurant inside the visitor center. Pitch a tent or sling a hammock (bring your own mosquito netting) under thatched-roof huts (Q25 per person).

◖ **FOOD.** Three *comedores* line the road in from Flores. Cheap food is served at **Comedor Imperio Maya ❸**, where portions are huge (*pollo frito* Q30; open daily 6am-9pm)—but all offer similar fare. For finer dining, head to the restaurant at the **Jungle Lodge** (open 7-9am, noon-2pm, and 7-9pm), which serves tasty food in a more upscale environment (Q30-Q50) and features an outdoor pool.

▨ THE RUINS OF TIKAL

Tickets (Q50) are typically purchased on the bus at the park entrance, but may also be purchased at the entrance to the ruins themselves. The site is open officially from 6am-6pm daily, although tickets can be purchased as early as 4:30am once inside the park. Both museums open M-F 9am-5pm, Sa-Su 9am-4pm; Museo Lítico free with park admission, Museo Cerámica Q10 extra. A few explanatory signs are scattered throughout the ruins, but hiring a tour guide makes for a more informed visit. Guides wait in the visitor center. Ask around if you have a particular interest, since guides have different areas of specialization. Tours in Spanish or English (about 4hr., 1-5 people US$40, US$10 per additional person). William Coe's helpful Tikal Guidebook *includes a detailed map (Q75).*

◗ HISTORY

The Maya settled Tikal around 700 BC; they were likely attracted both by its hilltop location above the Petén lowlands and the abundance of flint useful for weapons and tools. The earliest buildings date from 500 BC, and by AD 250—the dawn of the Classic period—Tikal had been established as a major population center. At this time, the powerful city of **El Mirador** (65km to the north) fell into decline, making **Tikal** and **Uaxactún** the dominant cities of the region. In AD 378, Tikal, aided by an alliance with the mighty highland center of **Kaminaljuyú**, on the modern site of Guatemala City, and the powerful **Teotihuacán** of Central Mexico, handily defeated Uaxactún. From that moment on, Tikal reigned over the Petén and grew in population and splendor. By the 6th century it spanned some 30 sq. km and supported a population of 100,000. The middle of the 6th century, however, saw Tikal's power overshadowed by that of **Caracol** (in Belize's Maya Mountains). In AD 700, the city embarked on a splendid renaissance. Led by the mighty **Ah Cacau (Lord Chocolate)** and his band of chocolateers, Tikal regained its supremacy in the Petén. Ah Cacau and his successors built all five of Tikal's massive temples (unfortunately made of limestone, not chocolate) in the span of a single century.

Around AD 900, the entire lowland Maya civilization suddenly and mysteriously collapsed, and Tikal was largely abandoned. Contemporary theories of the Maya collapse suggest a combination of regional warfare, overpopulation with declining agricultural productivity, popular uprisings, and drought. While post-Classic descendents of the original population continued to live and worship at Tikal, they did little of lasting significance other than pillage the centuries-old tombs. By AD 1000, jungle had completely engulfed the city. Save for a few passing references by Franciscan friars, the modern world did not rediscover Tikal until the Guatemalan government sponsored an expedition led by **Modesto Méndez** and **Ambrosio Tut** in 1848. The first photographs were taken in 1881 by English archaeologist Alfred P. Maudslay. Reprints of some of the photos are on display in the Museo Lítico.

THE MAIN SITE

THE GREAT PLAZA. One kilometer west of the entrance lies Tikal's geographic and commercial heart, the Great Plaza. Towering above the plaza, **Temple I**, built by the son of the great Ah Cacau after his father's death in AD 721, is known as the Temple of the Jaguar. Tikal's most recognized symbol, the 44m high temple is topped by a three-room structure and a roof comb that was originally painted in bright colors. Unfortunately, it's no longer possible to climb Temple I. You can, however, climb **Temple II** (38m), known as the Temple of the Masks and located at the west end of the Plaza. The top affords a wonderful view of the Plaza's architectural design. The complicated **North Acropolis** also stands on the Plaza. It has been rebuilt and now contains the remains of around 100 structures—a few dating back more than 2000 years. The two huge stone masks near the base of the North Acropolis make for another highlight. One is displayed under a thatched roof, and the other can be reached by following an adjacent dark passageway (you'll need a flashlight). To the south of the Great Plaza is the **Central Acropolis**, a complex of buildings probably used as an elite residential area. The configuration of rooms changed over time, perhaps to accommodate different families.

THE WEST PLAZA TO TEMPLE IV. The **West Plaza**, north of Temple II, features a large late-Classic temple. Following the Tozzer Causeway north from here you'll reach **Temple III**, still covered in jungle vegetation. Continuing on, you'll come upon **Complex N**, one of seven identical temples at Tikal, all believed to have commemorated the completion of a Katun (a 20-year cycle in the Maya calendar). At the end of the Tozzer Causeway is **Temple IV**, the tallest structure in Tikal (64m). Built in AD 741, possibly in honor of the ruler Coon Chac, the temple affords a stellar view, especially at sunrise and sunset; steep stairways facilitate the ascent.

FROM MUNDO PERDIDO TO THE TEMPLE OF THE INSCRIPTIONS. The **Mundo Perdido** is signposted between Temples III and IV, includes 38 structures, and is capped by the 32m-high **Great Pyramid.** The Pyramid dates to the pre-Classic era, and during its time was certainly one of the most impressive structures in all of Mesoamerica. If you can handle the steep climb, the top of the Great Pyramid provides one of the park's nicest views: all five towers look down on the jungle. Just east is the **Plaza of the Seven Temples.** The visible structures are late-Classic, but the hidden complex dates back at least 2000 years. The north side of the plaza was once the site of a unique **triple ball-court.** To the east of the Plaza of the Seven Temples are the unexcavated **South Acropolis** and the **Temple V** (58m tall), under restoration until 2005. The contrast between the temple's condition before and after restoration is striking. Also interesting is the fact that the Temple V laborers slaved for years to build a 58m temple, and then put only a few square meters of floorspace on top. A 1.2km (20min.) walk along the Méndez Causeway from the Great Plaza leads to the **Temple of the Inscriptions (Temple VI),** noted for the hieroglyphic text on its 12m roof comb; it is unique to Tikal and dates from AD 766.

OTHER STRUCTURES. Complexes Q and **R,** between the Great Plaza and the entrance, are Late Classic twin pyramids. Complex Q has been well restored; to its left lies a replica of the beautiful **Stela 22,** which portrays Tikal's last known ruler, **Chitam.** The original is now in the visitor center. One kilometer north of the Great Plaza lie **Group H** and **Complex P,** additional examples of twin temples.

OTHER ATTRACTIONS

■ **MUSEO LÍTICO.** A must-see. Located in the visitor center, the museum has an excellent scale model of Tikal, photographs of the restoration process, and a fine collection of Tikal stelae, including intricate #16 of Ah Cacao in brilliant costume. Entrance is free with park admission.

RUINS NORTH OF TIKAL

Hidden in the vast tropical forests north of Tikal await several other Maya sites; the most accessible is the important site of Uaxactún. El Zotz, Río Azul, and the splendid El Mirador are all largely unrestored and uncleared, but it's precisely the isolation and mystique that make a visit memorable. Other attractions in the region include the Maya ruins of Yaxhá, Nakum, and El Pedro—where the jungle and wildlife are the primary attractions.

UAXACTÚN

The cheapest way to visit Uaxactún is to take the Transportes Pinita bus from the market in Santa Elena (3hr., 1pm, Q20) or Tikal (about 3pm, Q20), and then catch the return bus the next morning (6am). Some travel agencies in Flores organize daytrips to Uaxactún. Groups of 4 or more can ask minibuses or hotels at Tikal for transportation (Q78-Q118 per person). The Jungle Lodge at Tikal offers trips (8am, return 1pm; Q120 per person, 4-person min., Q470 total for smaller groups). Uaxactún is always open. The road passes through the Tikal entrance, where visitors heading to Uaxactún must pay the Q15 entrance fee.

The dense forest north of Tikal hides Uaxactún (wah-shak-TOON), a small Petén village built around an airstrip and surrounded by Maya ruins. Uaxactún, the Maya word for 'eight stones,' rivaled Tikal at its prime, but was defeated in battle in AD 378. For the Maya scholar, the site holds some of the best pre-Classical Maya architecture in Mesoamerica. Uaxactún's most astounding beauty, however, is in its way of life as one of the few Guatemalan villages still relatively free of western influence.

Upon entering town you'll hit the disused airstrip; walk to your right for 10min. and you'll notice **Group E**. These buildings are most impressive not for their size or beauty but instead for their astrological significance. There three side-by-side temples served as an observatory. The sun rises behind the south temple on the shortest day of the year and behind the north one on the longest day when viewed from atop a fourth temple. On the equinox, the sun rises and sets in line with the two smaller temples that border the south temple. Beneath these temples is **E-VII-Sub,** the oldest surviving building in Petén, with foundations dating to 2000 BC. On the other side of the old airstrip, a dirt road beginning at the far end of the field passes through unexcavated **Group B** and leads to the grander **Group A,** the second most notable site in Uaxactún. Mainly a series of temples and residential compounds, the area is topped off by **Temple A-18,** whose roof peers over the jungle canopy.

The impressive Uaxactún museum is hidden within a small one-room building next to Hotel Chiclero, on the left side at the end of the retired airstrip. It features pieces of pottery, jade, and human skulls—most dating back 2000 years. Entrance is free; ask at Hotel Chiclero. The hotel offers bare-bones rooms (singles Q42; doubles Q82; meals Q30-Q40), and will arrange Spanish-speaking *niños* as guides for the ruins (see box below, Q20). The village only has electricity from 7 to 9pm.

While the ruins provide an interesting look into the ancient culture of the region, the modern day local scene is equally enlightening and worth an extra day in town. The local economy is dependent on the harvest of the Xate (sha-tay) palm, which is used in Japan and America for flower arrangements. Xate is harvested straight from the jungle; Jaime Nuñez, local Xate farmer, will take you with him for Q50 per day, so ask for him in town. Also, look for the observation tower on the road to Uaxactún, 6km before the village. It's a great place to look out over the surrounding hills and the peaks of ruins at Tikal.

◉ EL MIRADOR

Reaching El Mirador is no easy task; it involves a 4½hr. bus journey and two tough days on foot and horseback. The cheapest option in Flores is Quetzal Travel (see the Flores section), which offers a 5-day trip for US$200 per person for a 2-5-person group and US$150 for a 6-10-person group. Another option is to take the daily bus from Flores to Carmelita, the starting point for the trek to the ruins (4½hr., 1pm, Q25). There, you can arrange for a guide and horse (US$25 per day), but you must supply your own food and equipment.

The most magnificent of these sites and also the most remote, El Mirador was once a tremendous city, certainly greater than Tikal in the Pre-Classic era. Archaeologists believe that the city reached its peak around 2000 years ago, making it the first great Maya city. The 16 sq. km site features a number of pyramids, including on that is 70m high, the tallest structure anywhere in the Maya world, with a base the size of three football fields.

◉ OTHER MAYA SITES AND JUNGLE EXCURSIONS

Yaxhá is about 60km northeast of El Remate and accessible by road, with Nakum about 20km farther north. El Zotz is about a 4½hr. walk from Cruce Dos Aguadas (on the Carmelita bus route from Flores) and 30km west of Uaxactún along a sometimes-drivable dirt road. Río Azul is 95km north of Uaxactún, a journey of 1 day by jeep (if passable) or 4 days by horse. El Perú is about 100km northwest of Flores. The most competitively priced tours in Flores are offered by Quetzal Travel and Martsam.

Situated in thick jungle close to the east shores of Lago Yaxhá are the ruins of **Yaxhá,** meaning "green water," or water the color of sacred jade. The third-largest Maya site in Guatemala, Yaxhá appears to have been built in an unusual grid pattern more typical of sites such as Teotihuacán, and it holds one of the Maya world's most extensive constructions, a twin pyramid complex comprising hundreds of structures. Also interesting are the ruins of **Nakum**, 20km to the north, which are also considered a bird- and animal-watching paradise.

El Zotz is a large ruin noted for its huge bat population. The bats' mass exodus from nearby caves at dusk is a famed spectacle. It is possible to hike the El Zotz-Tikal trail with guides. Río Azul, an unrestored mini-Tikal, is home to a 47m temple and some impressive tombs. The ruins of El Perú are part of the scarlet macaw trail. In addition to the ruins and the macaws, the trip also features a pleasant boat ride, during which crocodiles and turtles are regularly spotted.

■ BORDER WITH BELIZE

The Guatemalan border with Belize, in the town of **Melchor de Mencos**, is 101km from Flores. Border-bound buses from Santa Elena pass by Puente Ixlú/El Cruce, 2km south of El Remate; coming from Tikal or El Remate you can catch a ride here. At the border, the **immigration office** is open daily 6am-8pm. Guatemalan immigration officially charges no fee, but usually does anyway—often Q10 to leave and as much as US$10 to enter. Ask for a receipt and they may let you off the hook. **Exchanging** quetzals and Belizean dollars with the countless money changers on either side. The most convenient place for food or accommodations is **Hotel Palace**, by the immigration post, along the river. The owner is a good source of information, and Internet is available for Q15 per 30min. (☎926 5196. Singles Q75; doubles Q90.) From the border, **buses** head to **Flores** (2hr., every 2hr. 7am-7pm, Q15). Three afternoon buses (3, 5, 6:30pm) travel to **Guatemala City**.

■ BORDER WITH MEXICO

There are two established routes from Flores to **Palenque** in Chiapas, Mexico. The quickest and easiest route is through **Bethel**. Transportes Pinta buses leave from Flores (5hr., 5am and 1pm, Q40). Once there, catch one of the fairly frequent 30min. boats (Q225 per group) to **Frontera Corozal** in Mexico. In Corozal it's possible to arrange a trip to the beautiful ruins at **Yaxchilán**. From Corozal, minibus *colectivos* leave for Palenque until about 2:30pm for the 3hr. trip. The other route begins with a bus from Flores to the Guatemalan border post in **El Naranjo** (5hr., 7 per day 5am-2:30pm, Q25). There are a few basic hotels in El Naranjo, but it's best to set out early and catch the midday boat from El Naranjo to the Mexican border post in **La Palma** (3hr., US$20-25 per person). From there, buses depart for Palenque via **Tenosique**—the last leaves around 5pm; if you miss it, there's camping and a few basic rooms in La Palma. Whichever route you choose, plan on the trip taking at least one day. It might be wise to organize the trip with the help of a Flores travel agency; **San Juan Travel** has a 5am, 6hr. trip to Palenque for US$30.

HONDURAS

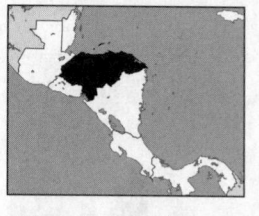

A land of jagged mountains and dense jungle, Honduras has the most rugged geography in the region. Ironically, the indomitable terrain that once kept the country isolated is now a huge draw for tourists. Pristine cloudforests full of wildlife, long stretches of Caribbean beach, pine-covered ridges, and tropical rainforest all beckon adventurers. For the more subdued visitor, western Honduras hosts the magnificent Maya ruins at Copán, attracting professors of archaeology and laymen alike. Non-Maya indigenous groups survive alongside colonial architecture elsewhere in the country, displaying Honduras' wide cultural array. Years of military oppression in the 80s rendered Honduras one of Central America's poorest countries—and, for better or worse, one of the cheapest to visit. Though Honduras isn't known for tourism, the *gringo* trail is well defined. Copán, Tela, and the Bay Islands have well-established tourist industries, but it's the back country's scattered frontier towns, and engaging locals that truly make Honduras worth visiting.

HIGHLIGHTS OF HONDURAS

The Hieroglyphic Stairway describes the divine genealogy of Copán's kings at the Maya ruins of **Copán,** an essential stop on La Ruta Maya (p. 456).

The extraordinary **Bay Islands** boast silky beaches, excellent snorkeling, and the cheapest diving on the planet (p. 494).

Trujillo, the last town of any size heading east along the Caribbean coast, hosts indigenous Garífuna culture, clean beaches, and all-night dancing (p. 490).

For adventure seekers, true wilderness awaits in the rugged cloudforest of **Parque Nacional La Muralla** and the expansive and diverse **Biosfera Río Plátano,** in the isolated Mosquitia (p. 517 and p. 510).

SUGGESTED ITINERARIES

ONE WEEK. Honduras is only a two hour flight from Houston or Miami, and even a short trip can combine culture, coast, and cloudforest. Fly into the capital **Tegucigalpa** (p. 423) and head straight to **Valle de Angeles** (p. 433) with its great views and galleries. Travel northwest through the former capital **Comayagua** (p. 438) on your way to the magnificent Maya ruins of **Copán** (p. 456). Then it's time for some beach, baby. Head to **La Ceiba** (p. 482), the base for exploring paradise at the **Bay Islands** (p. 494). Of the main islands, **Roatán** (p. 499) is the largest and most popular; **Utila** (p. 494) has a distinctive young, party atmosphere. Finish with a trip to Honduras' best national park, **PN Jeanette Kawas** (p. 481) on your way back to **San Pedro Sula** (p. 465) for your departure flight.

TWO WEEKS. An extra week gives you just enough time to work in some really hardcore adventure. Add a trek through **La Mosquitia** (p. 509) to your route and see what real backpacking is all about. From **La Ceiba** (p. 482), fly to **Palacios** (p. 510) or **Puerto Lempira** (p. 514) and be sure to check out the Mosquito Coast and the amazing **Reserva de Biosfera del Río Plátano** (p. 510).

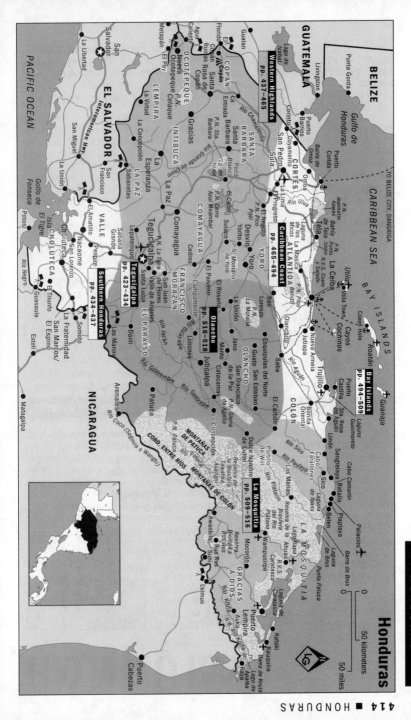

Honduras

Honduras

THREE WEEKS. After a week in the Mosquitia, you deserve some time on the beach. From **Palacios** (p. 510), you can head to **Trujillo** (p. 490) and enjoy some Caribbean tanning. From there head back toward La Ceiba to check out the **Cuero y Salado** wildlife reserve (p. 487) where divers have a good shot at swimming with manatees. Ecotourists can use the remainder of the week to check out **PN Izopo** (p. p. 482), **PN Pico Bonito** (p. 488), or **PN La Muralla** (p. 517). Travelers looking for a real cultural experience can use the last few days to check out **Cayos Cochinos** (p. 508) for a glimpse of Caribbean lifestyle or **Santa Barbara** (p. 444) for more mainland colonial history.

LIFE AND TIMES

LAND, FLORA, FAUNA

Honduras is the second largest country in Central America, after Nicaragua. The **Crystalline Highlands** cover most of the country with peaks reaching 2100m, but unlike most of the isthmus, these mountains are non-volcanic. The ridges are mostly covered by pine forest and transition into cloudforests at higher altitudes.

Deep mountain valleys support Honduras' agriculture and cattle raising; however the mountains tend to push most of the fertile land toward the sea. East of the Caribbean coastal plain is the untainted and untamed **Mosquitia** (p. 509), Central America's largest intact rainforest region which includes the Río Plátano Biosphere—one of the most magnificent rainforests in the world. Off the Caribbean coast, a few lingering fragments of the continental shelf form the **Bay Islands** (p. 494). An extension of Belize's reef system, the water near Roatán and Utila is teeming with colorful fish and impressive coral. Divers of all skill levels come to Roatán to take advantage of some of the cheapest diving training in the world.

Honduras' many ecosystems ensure an abundant wealth of **biodiversity.** With over 2000 animal species and more birds than you can keep track of, any area of Honduras is sure to be a treat for the animal lover. Even if you miss spotting the beautiful but elusive quetzal, there are still over 10,000 vascular plant species to keep you entertained. With 100 protected areas, there are more tree species per square hectare in Honduras than in the Amazon jungle.

HISTORY

Honduras, a Spanish word for "depths," speaks not only to the country's deep coastal waters, but to its rich and far-reaching history as well. From the days of the Maya, through post-independence political turmoil, to its role in the Contra War, Honduras has often been at the mercy of external interests of the US, Spain, Great Britain, and Central American neighbors. As if interfering global powers didn't make life hard enough, Mother Nature has repeatedly pummelled Honduras with devastating natural disasters.

LONG LONG AGO (1000 BC-AD 1500). Before the Spaniards even knew the Western Hemisphere existed, a thriving **Maya** civilization sprawled across Honduras. Archaeologists have found cities dating back to 1000 BC, and the most impressive collection of Maya history in Honduras can be found at **Copán** (p. 456). The Maya of Copán mysteriously disappeared around AD 900, leaving a perplexing puzzle for historians.

The **Lenca** are another Mesoamerican civilization that inhabited central Honduras beginning around 2000 BC. During the Classic period, the Lenca were considered the nucleus of the Mesoamerican jade trade. When the Spaniards arrived, Lenca chieftain Lempira amassed 30,000 Lenca to fight off the invaders. Afraid of being overrun, the Spaniards lured Lempira into fake peace talks where they deceitfully beheaded him.

NOT SO INDEPENDENT (1502-1838). Shortly after Columbus first sighted Honduras in 1502, the *conquistadores* Hernán Cortés and Pedro de Alvarado established modern-day Comayagua and Tegucigalpa in their all-consuming quest for gold. When Central America finally shook off Spanish rule in 1821, Honduras found itself in a more difficult situation than its neighbors. The fledgling nation fought off British attempts to seize control, all the while struggling to raise crops in isolated mountain settlements plagued by floods and droughts.

Honduras briefly joined the **United Provinces of Central America,** sending liberal leader **Francisco Morazán** to head the alliance. However, the federation was short-lived. Increasing Conservativism caused Honduras to break from the United Provinces, declaring independence on November 5, 1838.

A NATION DIVIDED (1840-1876). The Conservative regime in Honduras struggled to establish national unity, but constant British, American, and Central American intervention disrupted all chances of internal stability. After the 1862 assassination of **President José Santos Guardiola,** 20 leaders ruled Honduras in just 10 years, and six different constitutions were drafted between 1865 and 1924. As factions fought for control, the federal capital bounced between liberal Tegucigalpa and conservative Comayagua. In the end, soil erosion and fire in Comayagua, not political forces, cemented Tegus as the seat of government.

In the late 1870s, Liberal president **Marco Aurelio Soto** pacified warring factions and expanded the education system, making some strides toward national reunification. However, the lack of a commercial bourgeoisie class created an economic and political vacuum that US companies rushed to fill.

BANANA REPUBLIC (1880-1954). American company **United Fruit** bought huge tracts of land for banana plantations, set up its own banks and railroads, and created an elaborate political machine. By 1918, United Fruit and two other companies controlled 75% of the nation's banana-growing land, much of it taken from small farmers through threats or violence. For the next 40 years United Fruit held Honduras in its grip, with convenient military support from the US.

Domestic unrest allowed **General Tiburcio Carías Andino** to seize power in 1932 and rule as a dictator until 1948, when he was replaced by **Juan Manuel Gálvez.** In 1954, the famous **Banana Strike** took place. Beginning among dock workers, the strike spread through the foreign-owned banana industry, supported by sympathetic strikes in other industries. The strike initiated Honduras' labor movement and prompted the legal recognition of unions the next year.

MILITARY MAKE-OVER (1963-1988). The military assumed center stage again in 1963, when **Colonel Oswaldo López Arellano** took control of the government with the support of the fruit companies. During his rule, frustrations with neighboring El Salvador increased, and in mid-July 1969 tensions erupted after the two countries confronted each other in a *fútbol* match. While the **"Soccer War"** resulted in a wave of Honduran nationalism, it left 2000 Honduran civilians dead and sent 130,000 Salvadoran refugees fleeing across the border.

Despite a series of corruption scandals, the military ruled until 1981, when a civilian government was elected. However, Honduras was not quite destined for peaceful civilian rule; US President **Ronald Reagan** chose Honduras as the launch pad for attacking the new Sandinista government in Nicaragua. Anti-Sandinista forces set up bases in Honduras with millions of dollars' worth of American weaponry and the help of the CIA. The improved social conditions that the Hondurans hoped their civilian government would deliver were postponed even further as the Honduran military operated from behind the scenes to support the Nicaraguan Contra presence on Honduran soil. Victims of US-supported death squads included peasant leaders and priests who opposed the Contra's efforts. As growing anti-US protests spread through the nation, the Honduran government ordered the Contras out of Honduras in 1988. When US-backed **Violeta Chamorro** was elected president of Nicaragua in 1990, US troops evaporated from Honduras, only to be replaced by 11,000 armed and aimless Contras seeking refuge.

BEYOND THE CONTRAS (1989-PRESENT). Rafael Leonardo Callejas Romero's term as president from 1989 to 1993 was characterized by high inflation and falling wages, all in the name of economic adjustment. The Liberal **Carlos Roberto Reina** was elected in 1993 on a platform of political reform, but the value of the lempira continued to shrink as unemployment grew. The current president, **Ricardo Maduro Joest,** is continuing the work of the previous government, headed by Carlos Flores, to combat poverty. However, elected civilian governments have yet to meet their promises, and the military continues to exercise power behind the scenes.

TODAY

In 1998, Hurricane Mitch swept across Central America, and Honduras bore the brunt of the attack. More than 5000 people died in what is considered one of the worst natural disasters in recent years. Through this hardship and others, the lack of a strong government has become painfully obvious. Perhaps the biggest problem facing the country today is the level of domestic crime associated with drug trafficking. Tegucigalpa, once controlled from afar by foreign puppet masters, is now literally controlled by roaming street gangs known as *maras*.

CULTURE AND ARTS

PEOPLE

Honduras is predominantly *mestizo* (90%) and Roman Catholic (97%). Indigenous people account for 7% of the population. Although western Honduras was a major Maya area, few intact indigenous communities survive. Of the remaining communities, most are concentrated in the west and consist of the **Lenca** and **Chorti**. While these communities frequently interact with the *mestizo* population, the **Miskito, Pech,** and **Tawahka** isolate themselves from mainstream Honduras in the northeastern rainforests. The **Garífuna,** descendants of Carib Indians and African slaves, maintain a strong cultural identity along the north coast and on the Bay Islands.

FOOD AND DRINK. Honduran *típico* fare is a hodgepodge of rice and beans, tortillas, and fresh seafood. Hondurans have their own word for just about every regional specialty. For starters, a *baleada* is sort of like a burrito; most often, it's a tortilla smeared with fried beans and onions. Garífuna food usually includes *casabe* (cassava) drenched in coconut milk. A favorite dish on the Bay Islands is *tapado* (or *machuka*), comprised of fish, potatoes, yuca, and vegetables cooked in diluted coconut milk, served over rice. Vegetarians will want to look for yuca, a long, slender, green vegetable sold in markets. *Guanábana frescos* are a delicious natural beverage. If the *fresco* doesn't have enough kick for you, try some Salva Vida beer, the most popular and tastiest of Honduras' brews.

ARCHITECTURE. Honduras has thus far escaped the extreme earthquakes and fires that ravaged the architecture of other Central American countries. The ancient architecture of the Maya offers a rare glimpse into the calm, religious lifestyle of the past. In many urban areas such as Tegus, style is modern, but with a pervasive, Spanish colonial theme. Many buildings destroyed by Hurricane Mitch in 1998 have benefited from intense reconstruction efforts.

IT'S GREEK TO ME

f you own this book and are traveling through Central America, chances are you've heard the word "gringo." Throughout the Spanish-speaking world, "gringo" s a term frequently applied to foreigners, especially Westerners. With so many backpackers fitting he bill, we figure a little etymology lesson is in order.

The most popular story explaining the word "gringo" dates back o a popular English song from he mid-18th century: "Green Grow the Rushes." Supposedly, Latinos heard foreigners passing through Latin America sing the song and adopted the Spanish pronunciation of the title: gringo. Another claim points to the Mexican-American War, when soldiers would shout "Green Go!" to the advancing, green-clad American troops, in the hopes they would back up and head home.

These stories all sound plausible except for one small problem: he word "gringo" predates both song and war. In reality, gringo's origins stem from an expression as common in English as in Spanish. Dating to Shakespeare's ime, the expression "it's Greek to me," referred to foreign languages. "Griego," Spain's word for "Greek," applied to foreigners who spoke poor Spanish. In the New World, "Griego" transformed nto "gringo" and the name stuck.

While the origins of the word are blurry, one thing's for sure: it beats having people yell "Hey white guy!" all the time.

FINE ARTS. Painting and the fine arts, from Maya artifacts to colorful modern paintings, are a strong testament to Honduran culture. Fine arts first impacted Honduran culture in the 18th century with religious-themed paintings by **José Miguel Gomez,** who inspired a generation of Honduran painters to capture their culture in vibrant color. **José Antonio Velásquez** and his "primitive" paintings of Honduran life are a more modern legacy. A common Honduran theme is the "rain of fish," which is based on a story from a northern village where townspeople woke up one morning after a thunderstorm to find the ground mysteriously covered in fish.

Honduran art is not without its controversial pieces. Three bronze statues recently erected in San Pedro Sula by artist **Regina Aguilar** were intended to honor the writer of the Central American Declaration of Independence—José Cecilio del Valle. Instead, they launched a raging controversy because Valle is depicted in the nude, conspicuously lacking the "appropriate" fig leaf.

LITERATURE. A rich heritage of legends, folklore, and devotion to nature defines Honduran literature, which has developed slowly due to the extreme poverty of the region. There is a limited market for books, and most authors are initially published in newspapers. The modern and prolific author Guillermo Yuscarán writes books in English reflecting Honduran culture.

MUSIC. The Garífuna represent Honduras' most locally grounded music, while the mainstream musical taste is a conglomeration of Mexican, Guatemalan, and Caribbean styles. The National Symphonic Orchestra plays an array of classical music during its spring festivals. Drums, whistles, clay and wooden flutes, and the *marimba* and *caramba* stringed instruments are the core instrument group for Honduran music. On buses or in taxis, you're likely to hear Latin American and US pop from a few years back.

TV AND NEWS. Particularly in the cities, Hondurans stay on top of the news through one of the country's six dailies. *La Prensa* (www.laprensahn.com) is the oldest and most respectable, but all six papers have become increasingly guilty of sensationalism over the last few decades. Few Hondurans have TVs, and crowds gather around electronics shop windows when big stories break or when there's a big soccer game on. The English-language *Honduras This Week* is comprehensive and informative (www.marrder.com/htw).

SPORTS AND RECREATION. *Fútbol* is the name of the game in Honduras. With a national soccer league and international-caliber competition, soccer is more of an obsession than a hobby. Baseball is also a popular sport, and interest in basketball is growing. Although most younger girls pursue dance, national teams for women in soccer and basketball are competitive. For more low-key recreation, chill out with some locals over a game of checkers, chess, cards, or marbles. A game of *cantarito* or "kick the can" with local kids is a great way to reconnect with your inner child. Sport fishing and diving are obvious enjoyments in coastal areas.

ESSENTIALS

PASSPORTS, VISAS, AND CUSTOMS
Passport (p. 19): Required for all visitors.
Visa (p. 421): Citizens of Australia, Canada, Ireland, New Zealand, the US, or the UK can stay up to one month (extendable) without visa. 1 month to issue.
Tourist Stamp: Issued upon arrival. Valid for 30 days but can be extended twice for US$25 each time at immigration offices.
Inoculations and Medications (p. 27): None required.
Work Permit (p. 421): Required for all foreigners planning to work in Honduras.
Driving Permit (p. 37): Foreign driver's license and registration required.
Airport Departure Fee: US$25. Domestic flying tax L20.

EMBASSIES AND CONSULATES

Honduran **embassies** in other countries include: **Canada,** 151 Slater St., Suite 805, Ottawa, Ontario, K1P 5H3 (☎613 233 8900; fax 613 232 0193; emhonca@magma.ca); **UK,** 115 Gloucester Pl., London, WIH 3PJ (☎0171 486 4880); **US,** 3007 Tilden St., NW, Suite 4M, Washington, D.C. 20008 (☎202-966-7702; www.hondurasemb.org). **Honduran consulates** within the **US** include one in **Washington D.C.,** 1528 K St. NW, 2nd fl., Washington, D.C. 20005 (☎202-737-2972 or 202-737-2978; consul.hondurasdcusa@verizon.net), **New York** (☎212-714-9450; www.hondurasny.org), Atlanta, Chicago, Houston, Los Angeles, Miami, New Orleans, Phoenix, and San Francisco. For embassies located within Honduras, see **Tegucigalpa: Practical Information** (p. 426).

MONEY

US$1 = L18.83	L1 = US$0.05
EURO€ = L23.28	L1 = EURO€0.04
CDN$1 = L14.41	L1 = CDN$0.07
UK£1 = L32.77	L1 = UK£0.03
AUS$1 = L12.80	L1 = AUS$0.08
NZ$1 = L11.86	L1 = NZ$0.08

LEMPIRAS

The rates above are accurate as of August 2004. The Honduran currency is the lempira. Bills are divided into 100 centavos and come in denominations of one, two, five, 10, 20, 50, and 100. The 10-centavo coin is sometimes called a daime; you'll occasionally hear a 20-centavo coin called a búfalo and a 50-centavo piece called a tostóne. Large banks, exchange shops, hotels, and international airports will change **traveler's checks,** but prepare for long forms and high charges. **Western Union** can be found in main towns, and banks occasionally have money-wiring systems. Most banks give **cash advances** on credit cards. Banks don't change currencies of other Central American countries, but officials at border crossings will.

PRICE DIVERSITY

Honduras is definitely made for budget travelers. Comfortable lodging exists in many places for a few bucks, and food and beer are just a hair above free. The number icons below describe establishments' prices throughout the chapter.

SYMBOL	❶	❷	❸	❹	❺
ACCOMM.	L0-50	L50-100	L100-150	L150-200	L200+
FOOD	L0-20	L20-70	L70-100	L100-140	L140+

SAFETY

Small Honduran towns are relatively safe, but urban centers are extremely dangerous. Street crime and gang violence are very serious problems in some areas such as San Pedro Sula, rural Olancho, and parts of Tegucigalpa. In Tegus, armed gang members are a more common sight than armed police officers. The Caribbean coast has also suffered from escalated crime. Don't walk the streets at night and don't carry anything valuable. For more safety info, see **Safety and Security**, p. 25.

> **!** Women should never travel alone in Honduras under any circumstances.

HEALTH

The most serious health concerns for travelers are **malaria** and **dengue fever. Chloroquine** is the most effective anti-malarial medicine for travelers to Honduras. Recommended vaccines include: hepatitis, rabies, typhoid, tetanus/diptheria, and varicella. For more information, see **Health,** p. 25 and the CDC website, www.cdc.gov/travel/camerica.htm. Consult your **physician** before traveling. Nearly every Honduran town has a **pharmacy** open from 8am to 6pm. Throughout Honduras, it is best to avoid tap water, uncooked vegetables, and fruit that has already been peeled. When traveling in the Mosquitia region, **bring all emergency supplies.**

BORDER CROSSINGS

GUATEMALA. There are two land crossings: **El Florido** (p. 464) and **Agua Caliente** (p. 456), 16km west of Nueva Ocotepeque and 10km east of Esquipulas (p. 376).

BELIZE. Weekly **boats** link Puerto Cortés (p. 472) and coastal Belize.

EL SALVADOR. There are three land crossings: **El Poy,** south of Nueva Ocotepeque (p. 454), **El Amatillo** (see p. 304) near Choluteca, and **Sabanetas** (p. 304), 165km southeast of Gracias. **Ferries** connect the countries in the Gulf of Fonesca.

NICARAGUA. There are three land crossings: **Guasaule** (p. 434), 50km southeast of Choluteca, **San Marcos/El Espino** (p. 579), 70km east of Choluteca; and **Las Manos** (p. 578), 150km east of Tegucigalpa.

KEEPING IN TOUCH

A letter sent from Honduras takes two to three weeks to reach the US. EMS offers **express mail,** but it is pricier. You can receive mail in Honduras through **general delivery** (*Lista de Correos*); address envelopes as follows:

Corey RENNELL [First Name, LAST NAME]
a/c Lista de Correos
Tegucigalpa [town], Francisco Morazán [department]
República de Honduras

Honduran **telephone** phone numbers are seven digits and require no area code. For info on making international calls from Central America, see **Keeping in Touch** (p. 38.) National phone company **Hondutel** provides efficient service and has an office in most towns. From the phone offices, Sprint calling cards are easiest to use, followed by AT&T. Company access codes are: Sprint (121), AT&T (123), and MCI (122). **Faxes** and **telegrams** are generally available in Hondutel offices.

COUNTRY CODE	504

TRANSPORTATION

Airlines including Taca, Isleña, Sosa, and Rollins Air offer relatively low domestic fares. Each destination in the extensive **bus** system is served by a different company from a large city. Be especially cautious riding buses at night.

ORIENTATION

Landmarks, not street names, are the mainstay of directions. The larger towns have streets in a grid of north-south *avenidas* and east-west *calles*. A building at "3/5 Av. Nte., 2 C. Pte." is on Calle 2 Poniente between Avenidas 3 and 5 Norte.

NATIONAL PARKS

Honduras' national parks are quickly becoming a big ecotourism draw. Some of the best places to see are **La Tigra, Pico Bonito, Celaque, Cusuco,** the **Biosfera Río Plátano,** and the **Cuerro y Salado Wildlife Refuge.** The rules for each site vary considerably; some require guests to submit a written request to an office in the capital, others only allow guided tours. For more information visit: www.nps.gov/centralamerica/honduras and www.honduras.com/travel/parks.

TRAVEL RESOURCES

Honduran Institute of Tourism, 299 Alhambra Circle, Suite 226, Coral Gables, FL 33114 US (☎1-800-410-9608; www.letsgohonduras.com). Open M-F 9am-5pm. In **Tegucigalpa,** Col. San Carlos, Edificio Europa, Tegucigalpa, Honduras, Apdo. Postal N° 3261 (☎/fax 222-2124). Open M-F 8:30am-4:30pm. Will mail brochures and maps.

Garífuna Tours, Tela, Parque Central, Atlántida, Honduras, C.A. P.O. Box 74 (☎504 448 1069; fax 448 0338; www.garifunatours.com). Offers all-inclusive local tours and package tours that are more expensive than doing it on your own.

HOLIDAYS

Public holidays include: **April 14,** Day of the Americas; **May 1,** Labor Day; **September 15,** Central American Independence Day; **October 3,** Francisco Morazán's birthday; **October 12,** Discovery of America/Columbus Day; **October 21,** Armed Forces Day.

ALTERNATIVES TO TOURISM

This section lists some of the organizations in Honduras that offer opportunities outside the typical tourist experience. For more information on Alternatives to Tourism as well as tools for finding programs on your own, see the chapter at the beginning of the book (p. 53).

VISA INFORMATION

All foreigners wishing to study or work in Honduras must first apply for a **resident visa.** The only exceptions are Canadians, who may study for 6 months before needing to apply for residency. To apply for a resident visa, submit a valid passport, 4 passport size pictures, notarized medical certificate, bank letter, income tax references, work contract (if needed), copies of a birth or naturalization certificate, letter of good conduct, and a marriage certificate (if applicable) to the **Honduran Consulate** in your home country (p. 419). Once all documents are processed at the consulate, your passport will be stamped with the appropriate visa.

LANGUAGE SCHOOLS

Escuela de Español Ixbalanque, Copán Ruinas (☎ 898 3432), located 1½ blocks west of the *parque central,* offers one-on-one instruction 4hr. per day, 5 days per week, with homestay and full board. One week of classes costs US$195, with room and board US$270; 4 weeks US$800/US$900. Other available options include additional weeks (US$135/US$210), airport pick up from San Pedro Sula (US$100), and additional homestay nights (US$10). Students can register through Amerispan for US$100 (US ☎ 1-800-879-6640 or 215-751-1100; www.amerispan.com).

Languages Abroad.com, 413 Ontario St., Toronto, Ontario M5A 2V9, Canada (☎ 1-800-219-9924 or 1-416-925-2112, www.languagesabroad.com), offers Spanish programs in Copán ranging from 2-12 weeks. New programs start weekly all year long. Students either stay with locals or in self-serve apartments. Tuition includes classes, meals, and accommodations and is based on a weekly rate with the 2 week program starting at US$530.

Central America Spanish School, P.O. Box 1142, La Ceiba, Atlantida, Honduras (☎ 440 1707, www.ca-spanish.com), has programs in La Ceiba, Copán, and Utila. The school offers a "Mayan & Beach Program" that includes a week of classes at all three locations. The Utila program combines language classes and scuba diving lessons. Programs range US$220-$825 for 1-3 weeks. Students can register through Amerispan for US$100 (US ☎ 1-800-879-6640 US, 215-751-1100; www.amerispan.com).

VOLUNTEERING
BIOLOGY/ECOLOGY PROGRAMS

United Planet, 41 Appleton St., Boston, MA 02116 US (☎ 1-800-292-2316, fax: 617-292-0712, www.unitedplanet.org), has a volunteer program in a number of the national parks along Honduras' northern coast. Activities include planting saplings, maintaining paths, caring for the orchid nursery, and teaching English to local children.

Utila Iguana Conservation Project, (www.utila-iguana.org), is a program based on Utila in the Bay Islands that works to preserve the endangered *Ctenosaura bakeri* (the Utila iguana). Breeding season is March-May, but volunteers are welcome year round.

EDUCATION

Bilingual Education Central America, 118 W118th St. #4, New York, NY 10026, US (☎ 212-932-8138 from the US or 672 1799 from Honduras, www.becaschools.org), looks for teachers to volunteer as English instructors for young Honduran children. Volunteer commitments last the entire school year (mid-August to June), and room and board are provided.

i-to-i, 190 East 9th Ave., Suite 320, Denver, CO 80203 or, US Woodside House, 261 Low Lane, Leeds, LS18 5NY, UK (US ☎ 1-800-985-4864 or UK 870 333 2332; www.i-to-i.com). An established international program that offers orientation, language training, airline pickup, and insurance (room and board an additional US$11 per day). Volunteers will teach English in either Tegucigalpa or La Esperanza. Programs cost US$1500-$2095 for 4-12 weeks.

Nuestros Pequeños Hermanos, Apdo. Postal 3223, Tegucigalpa, Honduras (☎ 224 0203, www.nphhonduras.org), cares for orphaned children, striving to raise them to be productive members of their community. Volunteer opportunities range from doctor to speech pathologist to English teacher. The NPH home is based in Rancho Santa Fé, one hour outside of Tegucigalpa.

HUMANITARIAN

International Cultural Youth Exchange, Große Hamburger St., D -10115, Berlin, Germany (☎49 30 28390550; www.icye.org), hosts an array of youth based programs in Honduras dealing with health, hunger, and education.

Proniño Honduras, Edificio Eco Centario, El Progreso, Yoro, Honduras (☎/fax 647 3424), is a charitable organization that focuses on the street children of El Progreso. These children often suffer from physical or substance abuse and many are homeless. Volunteers usually stay for 2-12 months. Proniño provides housing for US$250.

TEGUCIGALPA

Tegucigalpa (pop. 897,000) and its sister city of Comayagüela (not to be confused with Comayagua) were incorporated into a "central district" constituting the official national capital in 1938. Over the past four hundred years, the city has maintained a more provincial air than that of a capital city. At 3000 ft. above sea level, Tegus (as the city is familiarly called) sprawls out across river-cut valleys and emerald mountains, scattering the rough terrain with a hodgepodge of clay roofs.

While Tegus looks picturesque from afar, a closer look reveals contaminated rivers, homelessness, blaring horns, and intense gang violence. In spite of the gangs *(maras)*, central Tegus is one of the safest parts of Honduras for travelers. But beware, a few blocks can be the difference between tourism zone and war zone. Tegus boasts gourmet restaurants, colorful fruit stands, and flashy malls. The city's Galería Nacional de Arte is a must-see.

✈ INTERCITY TRANSPORTATION

Flights: Toncontín International Airport, 7km from downtown (L40-L80 by taxi). Airline offices cluster here and around the Hotel Honduras Maya on Av. República de Chile.

Domestic: Taca (☎233 9797, 220 7608) flies to: **La Ceiba** (8:30am and 2pm, L760); **Palacios** (8:30am, L600); **Puerto Lempira** (6am) **Roatán** (8:30am and 2pm); **San Pedro Sula** (6am and 10:10am); and **Trujillo** (8:30am). **Atlantic Airlines** (☎220 5231 or 236 8297) flies to **La Ceiba, San Pedro Sula, Roatán, Utila, Guanaja, Puerto Lempira.**

International: Continental (☎220 0994, 220 0999) is located on Av. República de Chile across from Mundirama Travel (open M-F 8am-6pm, Sa 8am-noon). **Copa Airlines,** Hotel Real Clarion, Av. Juan Manuel Gálvez No. 1521, Colonia Alameda (☎233 2672; www.copaair.com) flies to **Panama, San José, and South America. American** (☎232 1720) has an office across from Hotel Honduras Maya (open M-F 8am-4:30pm, Sa 8am-3:30pm). **Taca** (☎239 0148 or 233 9797), on Blvd. Morazán, next to Credomatic, flies to Central American capitals and select cities within the US (open M-F 8:30am-8pm, Sa 8:30am-4pm). **Atlantic Airlines** (☎220 5231) flies to **Belize** and **Guatemala. Sol Air,** Hotel Real Clarion, Av. Juan Manuel Gálvez No. 1521, Colonia Alameda (☎235 3737), flies to **Miami.**

Domestic Buses: Most companies cluster in the 2 blocks surrounding 8 Av., 12 C. in Comayagüela. Buses fill up quickly and leave when they are full. You can be dropped off anywhere along a given route. Buses run from the following terminals:

Aurora: 6/7 Av., 8 C., ☎237 3647. To **Catacamas** (5am-5pm) and **Juticalpa** (3hr., 5am-5pm, L31). Buses go on from Juticalpa to **La Unión.**

Cristina: 8 Av., 12 C., ☎220 0117. To **La Ceiba** via **Tela** (4:30, 6:15, 7:30, 8:30, 9:30, 10:30am, 2, 3pm).

Congolón: 8 Av., 11/12 C., ☎238 0133. To **Agua Caliente** (3:45am).

Cotraipbal: 7 Av., 11/12 C., ☎237 1666. To **Trujillo** (7:15, 10:15am, 12:15pm; L185).

Discovery: 7 Av., 12/13 C., ☎222 4256. To **Juticalpa** (7:30am, 12:45, 3:15, 4:15, 6:45pm) and **Catacamas** with regular stops at **Talango, Guaymaco, Lepaguare, Jutiquile,** and **Campamento** (6:15, 9:15am, 12:15, 1:15, 2:15, 3:30, 4:15pm).

Discua Lenta: ☎230 0470, at Mercado Jacaleapa. To **Danlí** (2hr., 6:30am-7:30pm every hour, L38) and **Las Manos** (2hr., every hr., L38).

El Jungueño: 8 Av., 12/13 C., ☎237 2921. To **Santa Barbara** (M and F 4:30, 7am, 2pm; Tu-Th 7am, 2pm; Sa-Su 8:30am, 2pm).

El Rey: 7/8 Av., 12 C., ☎237 8561 or 237 8584. To **San Pedro Sula** (5:30am-6:30pm every hr., L95) with transfers to **La Ceiba, Utila, Roatán, Copan, Tela,** and **Antigua, Guatemala.**

Empresa Hedman Alas: 11 Av., 13/14 C., ☎237 7143. To: **Copán** (6, 10am); **Guatemala** (6am); **La Ceiba** (6, 10am, 1:30pm); **Tela** (6, 8:15am, 1:30pm); **San Pedro Sula** (6, 8:15am, 1:30, 4:30pm).

Etrusca: 8 Av., 12 C., ☎222 6881. To **La Ceiba** (7, 10am, noon, 4pm).

La Sultana: 8 Av., 12 C., ☎237 6101. To: **Agua Caliente** (6, 7, 8, 11:30am); **Ocotepeque** (9hr.; 6, 7:30, 8:30, 10am; L130); **San Pedro Sula** (7:30, 8:30, 10, 11am, noon); **Santa Rosa de Copán** (6, 8:30, 9:30, 10:30am, 2pm).

Maribel y Flores: 8 Av., 11/12 C., ☎237 3032. To **La Paz** (6am-5pm every 30min.).

Mi Esperanza: 23/24 Av., Blvd. Villa Adela, ☎225 1502. Buses with A/C, TV to **Choluteca** (2hr., 4am-6pm every hr., L25) and to **Comayagua** (1½hr., every hr. 6am-4pm, L19). From Choluteca, buses run to Guasale and San Marcos on the **Nicaraguan border.**

Norteños: 6/7 Av., 12 C., ☎237 0706. To: **San Pedro Sula** (6:30am-4:30pm every 1½hr., L25-L60); **Saenz** (4½hr., every 1½hr. 6:30am-4:30pm); and **Lago de Yojoa** (3hr., L32).

Buses to **Valle de Ángeles** (1hr., every 45min. 5:30am-5:45pm, L8) and **Santa Lucía** (30min., every 45min. 5:30am-5:30pm, L6) leave from the ESSO gas station across from the Hospital General on Av. La Paz.

International Buses: Tica Bus, Av. 5/6, C. 16(☎220 0590 or 225 0579). To: **Managua** (9hr., 9am, L375); **San José** (1 day, 9am, L655); **Panama City** (2 days, 9am, L1120); **Guatemala City** (L430); and **San Salvador** (L280). **King Quality** (☎225 5415) goes to **Guatemala City** (6am, L895); **Managua** (9hr., 6am, L375); and **San Salvador** (7hr., 6am and 1pm, L40).

■ ORIENTATION

The **Río Choluteca** divides Tegucigalpa into two regions: **downtown** Tegus northeast of the river, and **Comayagüela** to the southwest. *Avenidas* in downtown Tegus run east-west and *calles* run north-south, while in Comayagüela *avenidas* run north-south and *calles* run east-west. Most buses arrive in Comayagüela, while most sights, services, and hotels are in Tegus. Tegus' colonial-era streets form a tangled web centered around the *parque central,* also called the **Plaza Morazán.** The *parque* contains the **Cathedral** and is bordered by **Av. Cristobal Colón** to the north and **Av. Miguel de Cervantes** to the south. One block north of the *parque,* **Avenida La Paz** runs west to east and connects the *parque* with the **US Embassy** to the east, before running out of town toward **Valle de Ángeles.** East of downtown, **Colonia Palmira** is home to the tourist office, embassies, restaurants, and nightlife. Most clubs are on **Blvd. Morazán,** which is the main street of the city's more wealthy area. Patrons should stay along the main street at night and take taxis back to hotels.

Across the river, Comayagüela has its own independently numbered grid surrounding **6 Av.** Comayagüela is home to tons of budget hotels and the city's largest market; however, high crime rates make this area ill-suited for anything more than an overnight stay while waiting for a bus. Travelers should never venture near the cemetery between C. 1 and C. 4 west of 6th Av. or anywhere west of 10th Av.

If you are ever lost, turn to Jesus—his plaster statue is always visible to the north on top of **El Picacho** alongside a Hollywood-esque Coca Cola sign. Another good reference point is the forested area just south of downtown known as **Monumento de la Paz** (Monument of Peace). Forested areas in general should never be visited, day or night, unless in very large groups.

Tegucigalpa

⬧ ACCOMMODATIONS
Granada #2, 6
Granada #3, 5
Hotel Iberia, 4
Nan King, 12
Tobacco Road Inn, 10

✴ FOOD
Catracho-Mex, 17
Comedor Vegetariano, 14
La Terraza de Don Pepe, 7
Licuados al Paso, 8
Señor Café, 11

🍴 NIGHTLIFE
Café Paradisio, 16
Gecko, 21
Hipa Hipa, 22
O-Bar, 20
Sayka Bar & Disco, 23

● PUNTOS DE TAXI
Buenos Aires, 2
Cerro Grande Centro, 1
Kennedy, 18
Llanos, 15
Loarque, 3
San Miguel, 9
Torocogua, 13
Villa Olímpica, 19

COMAYAGÜELA

SEE COMAYAGÜELA MAP p. 429

BARRIO ABAJO

BARRIO MORAZÁN

BARRIO SAN RAFAEL

BARRIO LA CABAÑA

BARRIO CASAMATA

TEGUCIGALPA

BARRIO GUADALUPE

COLONIA PALMIRA

With the exception of Colonias Palmira, Las Mintas, and Ruben Darío, all *barrios* and *colonias* outside Tegus should be avoided at all times.

▐ LOCAL TRANSPORTATION

Local buses: Local buses, rarely used by tourists, cut through unsafe barrios and are always jam packed. Robberies occur while in transit. Buses stop regularly at blue bus signs and gas stations on the north side of the *parque central*. They also stop across the bridge from Comayagüela and between the US Embassy and Hospital General on Av. La Paz. Destinations are listed above the windshield. Fares M-F L2.50, Sa-Su L3. **Rapidito** buses to El Picacho, La Cumbre, and El Hatillo leave from Av. Cervantes southwest of the Teatro Nacional and are safer than walking. Rapiditos run from morning until around 9:30pm (L5.50). For return trips, wait beside the road; buses pass every 15-20 min.

Taxis: Yellow cabs outside the airport charge L80 to travel into the city, but white cabs out on the street charge L40-L60. Prices are negotiable; agree on one before departing. Within the city L20-L40; *barrios* and El Picacho L40-L60. Prices increase after dark.

Collective taxis *(taxis colectivos):* Ideal for the budget visitor. *Puntos de taxi* are located throughout the city. Cars run a pre-set loop from the *punto*. Passengers share the taxi and are let out anywhere along the route for a fraction of the cost of a personal taxi. Schedules vary. A typical fare is L7.50 per person.

Taxi Points in Tegus: La Kennedy, behind El Prado Hotel's parking lot, go to the **Discua Litena bus station. La Torocagua,** at the corner across from Banco Credomatic on Blvd. Morazán makes a loop to **La Laguna of Comayagüela,** near the bus stations. **La Villa Olimpica,** left on Av. Molina after walking down the street to the national stadium, heads to **Multiplaza Mall. La San Miguel,** on the same corner as Banco Atlántida, will take you to the **Valle de Ángeles bus station. Loarque,** next to Herrera park, on C. Morelos, makes the rounds through the **Airport, La Granja and Colonia Loarque. Cerro Grande Centro** is located on C. Morelos between Av. Lempira and Av. Paulino Valladares. **Buenos Aires** is on C. Buenos Aires under the overpass next to Iglesia Los Dolores.

Taxi Points in Comayagüela: El Rey is located on 6 Av. between 8 and 9 C. next to Hotel San Pedro, while **Centenario Unah** can be found across from Cinema Centenario on 6 Av. between 9 and 10 C. **Norteños** is on 12 C. between 6 and 7 Av. across from Norteño Bus Terminal.

Car rental: Low-priced agencies rent for L1120-L1310 per day (with insurance); high-end L2245. **Hertz** (☎239 0772), **Avis** (☎233 9548), **Budget** (☎235 9531 or 233 6927) are at the airport and around Hotel Honduras Maya. 25+. AmEx/MC/V accepted.

▐ PRACTICAL INFORMATION

TOURIST AND FINANCIAL SERVICES

Tourist Information: Instituto Hondureño de Turismo (☎800 222 8687 Honduras, 800 460 9608 US and Canada; www.letsgohonduras.com), on the 5th fl. of the Edificio de Turismo, C. República de México, 2 blocks east of the US Embassy. Maps, CD-ROM encyclopedia of tourism, and English-speaking representatives. Be sure to ask for *Honduras This Week* and the *Honduras Tips Book* (www.hondurastips.honduras.com, online information may not be up to date). Open M-F 8:30am-4:30pm.

Travel Agencies and Guided Tours: A wide variety of competing travel agencies cluster around Hotel Honduras Maya. **Mundirama Travel Service,** Edificio CICSA, Av. República de Panama (☎232 3909), a block from Hotel Honduras Maya, doubles as an **AmEx** office. English spoken. Open M-F 8am-5pm, Sa 8am-noon. **Trek Honduras,** Edificio Midence Solo 218 Colonia Olmeda, Av. Julio (☎239 0743), offers tours of Tegus, Copán, and the Bay Islands. **Gray Line Tours** (☎220 1552), between C. Ramon

Rosa and Instituto de Turismo, offers individual city and whole country tour packages. Open M-F 8:30am-5:30pm, Sa 8:30am-12:30pm. **Travel Express** (☎236 6747 or 236 9455; travelex@multivisionhn.net), in three locations: on Av. La Paz across from Mas X Menos; on Blvd. Morazán near Av. Juan Lindo; and on Av. Cervantes east of Hotel Prado. Open M-F 9am-5pm, Sa 8am-noon.

Embassies: Canada: Centro Financiero Banexpo, Blvd. San Juan Bosto, 3rd fl. (☎232 4557). Open M-F 8am-4:30pm. **US:** on Av. La Paz, apartado 3463 (☎238 5114, ext. 4400; www.usmission.hn). It's a large building; anyone you ask will know where it is. Open M-F 8am-5pm (observes American holidays). **UK** has a regional Embassy in Guatemala. For other embassies, call the Ministerio del Exterior (☎234 1922).

Immigration Office: Av. La Paz. Next day visa extension service for L7.50 (3pm pickup, temporary copies available). Open M-F 8:30am-noon and 1-4:30pm.

Banks: Most banks change US dollars and AmEx Traveler's checks. In the Mall Multiplaza there is a *centro financiero* where all the banks have offices and keep convenient hours. Expect very long lines. **BGA,** Av. La Paz, C. Los Dolores (☎232 0909), a block south of Iglesia Los Dolores and across from the Hospital General, cashes traveler's checks and gives V cash advances. Open M-F 9am-4pm, Sa 9am-noon. **Banco Atlántida** (☎232 1050) is in Hotel Honduras Maya (open M-F 9am-3pm, Sa 9am-noon) and Mall Multiplaza (open M-Sa 10am-7pm). **Banco Credomatic** (☎238 7220) on Blvd. Morazán across from Torocagua taxi point, accepts Cirrus cards, gives cash advances for V/MC. Open M-F 9am-5pm, Sa 9am-noon; in Mall Multiplaza open M-Sa noon-7pm.

ATM: ATMs are all over the city, including on the east side of the *parque,* at Texaco gas stations, at Mall Multiplaza, and most supermarkets. AmEx/Cirrus/Plus/MC/V.

LOCAL SERVICES

Bookstores: Metromedia (☎221 0770 or 232 1294), 2 blocks behind the US Embassy in Edificio Casa Real and in Mall Multiplaza, sells a wide selection of new and used books plus CDs in English and Spanish. Movie rentals. Open M-Sa 10am-8pm, Su noon-6pm. **Shakespeare's Books,** inside Tobacco Road Inn, trades books.

Markets: ▓**San Isidro,** along 7 Av., 1 C. in Comayagüela, is Tegus' main outdoor market, spread over several blocks. An impressive market, crowds make it easy to get lost. Proximity to a *mara* nucleus is a safety concern. Don't visit at night. **San Miguel,** next to Hotel Granada #1 on Av.1 Gutemberg, is the main indoor market. The area around **Iglesia Los Dolores** hosts a large market as well.

Supermarket: Mas X Menos, Av. La Paz, 3 blocks from the US embassy. Called "mas por menos." Open daily 7am-9pm. Other supermarkets are in the mall on the corner of Blvd. Morazán and Av. Juan Lindo (open daily 8am-8:30pm), south of C. Peatonal on C. Salvador Mendieta (open M-Sa 6:30am-8:30pm, Su 8am-6pm), and across the street from Hotel Nan King.

Laundry: Below Hotel Granada #3. Offers wash, dry, and fold, usually in under 3hr. Wash and dry L140. Open M-Sa 8am-5:30pm.

EMERGENCY AND COMMUNICATIONS

Emergency: Medical ☎195, **police** 199, **fire** 198, **Red Cross** 237 8654.

Police: Preventiva (☎222 8736, emergency 237 8540; jepaturametropolitana@yahoo.com), behind Iglesia Los Dolores, on C. Buenos Aires. Open 24hr. Lt. Martinez speaks English and has up-to-date safety information (☎237 7928). Unit of female police officers (☎237 2184).

Pharmacy: There are pharmacies on just about every block in central Tegus. One popular chain is **Farmacia Regis** (☎237 0101), open M-Sa 8am-6pm. For a list of pharmacies open until 10pm and on weekends, call ☎192 or check hours in any pharmacy window.

Medical Services: Clínicas Viera (☎237 3160), Av. Colón 1 block away from Hotel La Ronda. Open 24hr. for emergency care. Some English spoken. L300 visit. **Centro Medico San Martin** (☎237 8947) in Comayagüela at the corner of 8 Av. and 13 C. 24hr. emergency care. **Clínicas Médicas AWAD** (☎220 5343), on 12 C. next to El Rey Terminal. General adult and children's care. M-F 9am-5pm, Sa 9am-1pm. **Hospital General** (☎236 7499), Av. La Paz east of the US Embassy. **Clínica Médicas Palmeria** (☎232 2040), Av. República de Chile, west of Hotel Honduras Maya. **Honduras Medical Center,** Av. Juan Lindo en Colonia Ruben Darío. **Hospital Escuela,** Blvd. Suyapa.

Telephones: Hondutel (☎238 3131; fax 237 9715), Av. Cristobal Colón before C. Telégrafo, in a large building called the *palacio.* Open daily 24hr. In Comayagüela (☎238 1448), next to the post office. Open M-F 8am-4pm. L97 for 3min.); calls are cheaper at Internet cafes. Call collect ☎190, 192; foreign calling card ☎800 0122.

Internet: The only thing Tegus has more of than pharmacies is Internet cafes. Rates generally run from L10-L30 per hour. **Express Cyber Café** (☎220 4540), 1 block north of the *parque* on Av. Gutemberg between C. Palace and C. Matute, has a snack bar. L20 per hr. Open M-Sa 8am-8:30pm, Su 1pm-7pm. Across the street is **Antonella's Web Site** (☎237 3916). L15 per hr. M-Sa 8am-9pm, Su 9am-4pm. **Chat Cyber Cafe,** east of the Palacio on Av. Colón, speedy service, A/C, discount for volunteers. L15.

Post Office: Correo Nacional, Av. Paz Barahona, C. Telégrafo. Open M-Sa 7am-6pm. In Comayagüela, 6 Av. by Instituto Abelardo R. Fortín. Open M-F 8am-7pm, Sa 8am-1pm. **PakMail,** between the US Embassy and Instituto de Turismo on C. República de Mexico, offers FedEx, DHL, copying, faxing, and Internet. Open M-F 8am-6pm, Sa 8am-noon. **Postal Code:** Tegucigalpa 11101; Comayagüela 11103.

▐ ACCOMMODATIONS

Hotels in downtown Tegus are the safest. If you need to catch an early morning bus from Comayagüela, stay close to 6 Av. or right around the bus terminals. Make sure the hotels have a locking front door. In all areas, try to get a room facing away from the street to avoid bus fumes and loud traffic. Basic rooms *(sencillos)* don't have private baths, *privados* do.

TEGUS

▨ **Tobacco Road Inn** (☎222 4081, tobaccord@yahoo.com), Av. Juan Gutemberg between C. Corletto and C. Las Damas (look for sign welcoming backpackers). Knowledgeable English-speaking Tom Taylor runs this friendly hostel with a rock-and-roll bar, large book exchange, coffee shop, laundry, bike rentals (L160 per day), a safe for valuables, and hot water. Safest place for travelers according to police. Beds L80. ❷

▨ **Hotel Iberia** (☎237 9267), 2 blocks down C. Los Dolores from C. Peatonal off the *parque.* Though lacking hot water, rooms and communal bath are clean. Upstairs lounge has TV. Singles L100; doubles L150, with bath L200; triples L240. ❸

Hotel Nan King (☎238 0291), Av. Juan Gutemberg, past Hotel Granada from the *parque;* look for the roof-top pagoda. In the heart of Tegus's small Asian community, Nan King has spotless rooms with hot baths. A pricey Chinese restaurant and Internet cafe (L20 per hr.) on site. Singles L140; doubles L250. TV, A/C extra charge. ❹

Hotel Granada #2, Subita Casemata 1326 (☎238 4438), and **Hotel Granada #3** (☎222 0597) across the street (hotelgranadategus@hotmail.com). Two similar hotels near Parque Guanacaste, an area that is pleasant by day but somewhat dangerous at night. Rooms have hot baths. Each fl. has a comfortable lobby with couches and chairs; upper floors have great views. Accessible 24hr. Granada #2: singles L160; doubles L300. Granada #3: singles L185; doubles L232. Cable TV, A/C extra L50. ❹

HONDURAS

COMAYAGÜELA

■ **Hotel Maria Jose,** 7 Av., 12 C. (☎220 1424 or 237 7295). Safe facility with a convenient bus location and in-house cafeteria. Clean rooms with private bath, hot water, A/C, and TVs. Accessible 24 hr. Singles L185; doubles L220-L260. Cable extra L20. ❹

Hotel Condesa, 6/7 Av., 12 C. (☎237 7857), next to Norteño Bus Terminal. Clean, locking rooms with bath. Set in the safest and most convenient area of Comayagüela. Singles L230; doubles L250. Cable TV, A/C, and room phone extra L65. ❺

🖸 FOOD

Tegus' options are somewhat unimpressive. Fast food chains abound and Chinese restaurants are scattered throughout the city. For bargain food, head to the *comedores* set up in the *plaza* of Iglesia Los Dolores. Comayagüela has cheap options.

■ **Comedor Vegetariano,** Av. Cervantes, C. Telégrafo, a block from the post office. The only *comedor* in Honduras specializing in vegetarian food. Filling gourmet portions come at bargain prices. Order a drink, dessert, soup, and the special of the day for L37. Open M-Sa 11am-4pm, though if they're home, they'll probably feed you. ❷

Catracho-Mex, between Kennedy Taxi Point and Mercedes Park, serves complete *típico* breakfasts, lunches, and dinners for L30-L35 including coffee, beans, rice, meat, plantains, eggs, and salad. English-speaking owner serves guacamole well worth the trip. ❷

Licuados al Paso (☎237 9140), on Av. Colón around the corner from the movie theater. Honduran-style smoothie bar with ice or milk blends of fresh fruit for L10-L14. Personal pizzas, ham and cheese sandwiches, or soup L10. Open M-Sa 8:30am-6pm. ❶

La Terraza de Don Pepe, Av. Colón, 3 blocks from the *parque*. Good family restaurant with chicken cordon bleu L53, banana splits L28. Open daily 9am-9:30pm. ❷

Cam Lee (☎237 6016), across from Hotel La Ronda on Av. Jerez. One of many cozy and clean Chinese restaurants offering hearty portions for L48. Open daily 10am-10pm. ❷

Señor Café, 1 block down from the *parque* on the right hand side of C. Peatonal. A relaxing place to get coffee (L7-L9), or tasty sandwiches (L8-L10). Open daily 7am-8pm. ❶

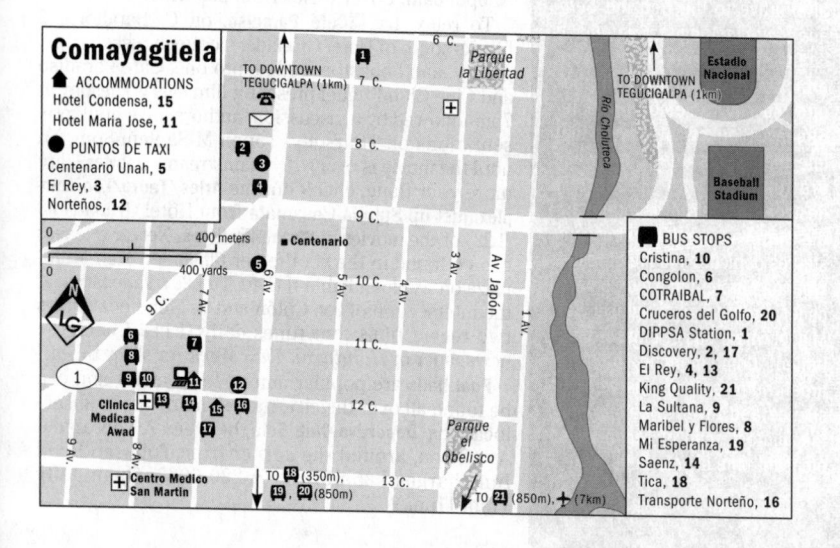

Comayagüela

🔺 ACCOMMODATIONS
Hotel Condensa, **15**
Hotel Maria Jose, **11**

⬤ PUNTOS DE TAXI
Centenario Unah, **5**
El Rey, **3**
Norteños, **12**

TO DOWNTOWN TEGUCIGALPA (1km)
Parque la Libertad
Estadio Nacional
Río Choluteca
Baseball Stadium

TO DOWNTOWN TEGUCIGALPA (1km)

400 meters
400 yards

■ Centenario

Clínica Medicas Awad
Centro Medico San Martin

Parque el Obelisco

TO 18 (350m)
19, 20 (850m)
TO 21 (850m), ✈ (7km)

🚌 BUS STOPS
Cristina, **10**
Congolon, **6**
COTRAIBAL, **7**
Cruceros del Golfo, **20**
DIPPSA Station, **1**
Discovery, **2, 17**
El Rey, **4, 13**
King Quality, **21**
La Sultana, **9**
Maribel y Flores, **8**
Mi Esperanza, **19**
Saenz, **14**
Tica, **18**
Transporte Norteño, **16**

HERE IS EVERYBODY?

Exhaust-filled air, excessive honk-
ng, and incessant hustling drive
most tourists away from Tegucigalpa the moment they get off
he plane. Whether it is noon or 4
am, Tegus never seems to give it
a rest—except for one week at the
end of March, when the city emp-
ies completely, leaving the capi-
al all to its lonesome.

During the week leading up to
Easter, residents vacate the city
en masse to spend the week-long
holiday at the beach. With city-
dwellers gone and the downtown
area closed to traffic, the cobblestone streets are wide open to
tourists looking to peruse the
colonial architecture and market
free of congestion and chaos.
Hotels are generally empty as
well, making Tegus an excellent
alternative to the frenzied *Semana Santa* in Antigua, Guatemala.

The serenity ends in an abrupt
explosion as residents pour back
into the city to celebrate Easter
Sunday. Blankets of flowers that
line the streets during the week
are replaced with elaborately
designed carpets of colorful saw-
dust, over which 100 men carry
statues depicting the life of Jesus.
Wearing purple and white, crowds
cheer the men on to Iglesia San
Miguel where Easter mass is celebrated. Come morning, the usual
urban hum replaces the week of
silence and revelry, leaving only
the faintest echo of Tegus' most
pleasant time of year in its wake.

🎭 🎵 NIGHTLIFE AND ENTERTAINMENT

Fear not, revelers—Tegus nightlife heats up to a
feverish pitch on weekends. Restaurants keep late
hours and college-age partyers line Blvd. Morazán.
There are also clubs on Blvd. Juan Pablo II, but the
street is notorious for gangs and criminal activity.
Taxis (L30-L50) are the safest way to travel to any
destination away from the main street. Women
should always travel in groups. Men in the clubs are
pushy; travelers should especially beware. While
most discos are up and running Thursday to Sunday,
Fridays and Saturdays are the big nights.

Discotecas come and go quickly, so ask around for
the latest rage. **Gecko** (formerly Arenas), about 300m
east of Av. Juan Lindo on Blvd. Morazán, is the hot
spot for students and gringos to grind to hip-hop and
have a beer under the stars. (☎990 2448. Open F-Sa,
9pm-3am. Cover L60.) If city life has got you down,
boogie to a tropical beat at **Sayka Bar & Disco**, reputa-
bly the safest club in Tegus, located a block and a
half west of Av. Juan Lindo on Blvd. Morazán. (☎231
0461. Open Th-Sa 7pm-5am. Cover L70.) **O-Bar,** just
west of Av. Juan Lindo on Blvd. Morazán, has plenty
of rooms to booze in and a dance floor with some of
the best music in town. (☎235 3437. Open Th-Sa 8pm-
3am. Cover L100; open bar Th, no cover F.) Break out
the finer dancewear at **Hipa Hipa,** about 1km east of
Av. Juan Lindo on Blvd. Morazán, for the hardcore
club scene and open bar Fridays. (Open W-Sa
9:30pm-5am. Cover varies from L60-L130.)

To relax, try ◼**Café Paradiso,** on C. Barahona, 2
blocks south of Hotel Granada, a coffeehouse, bar, art
gallery, and bookstore rolled into one. Café Paradiso
and Cine Club Buñuel present a film every Tuesday at
7pm followed by a discussion; authors have book presentations on Thursdays (open M-Sa 9am-8pm, Tu
until the movie is over). If mainstream **movies** are
more your thing, check out the **Aries/Tauro/Leo complex,** just up Subida Casamata from Hotel Granada #3
(L22) or the movies at **Plaza Miraflores.** Newer releases
can be found in the six-theater **Cinemark,** Mall Multiplaza on Av. Juan Pablo II (L40; Tu L20). **Variedades,** at
the intersection of Av. Colón and C. Mendieta, shows
two recent films four times daily (L11). Check the
newspaper or *Honduras This Week* for show times.

Pool halls are popular among local males and can
be found all over the city, though many are in unsafe
locations. **Deportivo Club Bola,** between Av. Jerez and
Av. Colon, around the corner from Tobacco Road
Inn charges L25 per hr. (☎220 6083. Open daily
11am-11pm.)

Theater goers head to the **Teatro Nacional** on C. Peatonal opposite Parque Herrera for nightly choral performances, ballets, jazz shows, or operas. Tickets are sold in the afternoon for L30. (☎222 4366. Open M-F 8:30am-4:30pm.)

🖸 SIGHTS

The city's attractions are all within a short walking distance of the *parque central*, which the Mayor recently renovated as a monument to himself. The whole city seems to converge here at all hours of the day and night to relax and socialize.

◪GALERÍA NACIONAL DE ARTE. One block south of the *parque* on C. Bolívar, statues of past presidents and Honduran heroes guard the National Congress and the National Art Gallery. Constructed in 1654, this convent-turned-university-turned-museum houses Honduras' best art of the past three millennia. The downstairs gallery displays works from prehistoric to colonial periods, including exhibits of petroglyphs from the Mosquitia, artifacts from Copán and well-preserved pre-Columbian ceramics. Paintings such as *Mineros* by Canales and *Melodia en Nuestros Manos* by Zelaya skillfully capture scenes of modern Honduras. A photo project completed by 18 local children depicts the hardships of barrio life. (☎237 9884. Open M-Sa 9am-4pm, Su 9am-1pm. L20, students L10.)

◪PARQUE LA CONCORDIA. Down Av. Las Delicias from C. Morelos, detailed replicas of Honduras' most famous ruins recreate the feeling of the Classic-era Maya beneath a full grown forest canopy. The cool air and songbirds in this magical park make it a favorite place for young lovers, so bring a friend.

IGLESIA LOS DOLORES. One block north and 2½ blocks west of the *parque*, this church retains the flavor of its Afro-Honduran construction, with an exuberantly sequined altar and a neon John the Baptist. Two blocks east of the cathedral is the 16th-century **Iglesia San Francisco,** the oldest church in Tegus. (Mass M 5pm; Tu-Sa 7am, 4:30, 5:30pm; Su 7, 8:30, 10, 11:30am, 4, 5pm. Iglesia San Francisco open Su.)

CATEDRAL SAN MIGUEL. Anchoring the eastern side of the *parque*, Catedral San Miguel, built between 1765 and 1782, is full of the tombs of former Honduran presidents. At the entrance the walls are covered in plaques praising the Virgin, and throughout the church terracotta sculptures chronicle the life of Jesus. At the heart of the cathedral's simple interior stands a gold baroque altar. (Mass M-Sa 6:30, 7am, noon, 4, 5pm; Su 6:30, 8, 9:30, 11am, 4pm. Doors open from first to last mass.)

EL PICACHO. Take the Rapidito bus from Av. Cervantes just southwest of the Teatro Nacional, ask to get off at El Picacho then follow the signs. Stop along the path at the **El Picacho Zoo,** home to rare and exotic Honduran animals like pecari, tapir, and capybara. Amid this high-altitude rain forest at the edge of El Picacho a towering statue of Jesus, invites you to enjoy the panoramic view of Tegus below. While it's tempting to linger as Tegus becomes a city of lights, the park is not safe at night. (Zoo: ☎211 9112; www.sema.gob.hn. Open M-F 8am-3pm, Sa-Su 9:00am-4:30pm)

MUSEO HISTÓRICO DE LA REPÚBLICA. Two blocks north of Parque La Concordia., the *museo* is housed in the former Presidential Palace. Check out the exhibits depicting the volatile history of Honduras' railroad and the banana industry. Be sure to take a close look at the tiled mosaics of the 17 departments. (☎222 1468, ext. 117; ihah2002@yahoo.com. Open M-Sa 8am-4pm. L20. English speaking staff.)

HONDURAS

◤ PARQUE NACIONAL LA TIGRA

Take a bus marked El Hatillo/Los Limones from the DIPPSA gas station on Gutemberg Av., across from Hotel Nan King. (1¼hr., 6:30am-4pm, L9.) Ask to get off at Jutiapa in Parque Nacional La Tigra; walk uphill 1.5km to the Jutiapa visitor center. To reach El Rosario visitor center from Tegus, take a bus marked San Juancito or Cantarranas from the ESSO gas station on Av. La Paz, across from Hospital San Felipe. Once in San Juancito, a steep gravel road across the bridge has signs to El Rosario (4km). Locals will drive you up to the park for L150. Return buses to Tegus leave from the bridge (M-F 5:45, 6:45am; Sa 6:45am, 12:30pm; Su 12:20, 3pm). Buses also stop along the highway, 35min. up the road from the bridge (1½hr.; 7:45, 8:15, 10:30am, 1, 3:15pm). Although Let's Go doesn't recommend it, travelers and locals occasionally hitchhike from the highway to Valle de Ángeles where they catch the bus back to Tegus before its last return at 5:30pm. The park and the Jutiapa visitor center (☎972 1928) are open daily 8am-5pm. For more information, contact the park management organization AMITIGRA. Their offices are located in Tegus on the 6th fl. of Edificio Italia, on Av. República de Panamá 2 blocks west of Av. República de Chile. (☎235 8493; amitigra@mail.cablecolor.hn. Open M-F 9am-5pm.)

Parque Nacional La Tigra is only 21km northeast of Tegucigalpa, but the two settings couldn't be more different. Covering some 240 sq. km, the park's cloud forest boasts 400 plant species, including beautiful orchids, and more than 200 species of birds, ocelots, monkeys, and pumas. While large portions of the forest were cut down by miners in the early 1900s, many grandfather trees still stand. Wildlife is more visible in the morning and the park entrance closes at 2pm, so arrive early. Bring rain gear, water, a sack lunch, and warm clothes if planning to stay at night.

There are two **visitor centers,** one by the western entrance near **Jutiapa** and another by the eastern entrance near **El Rosario.** Jutiapa is easier to reach and has more accessible trails, making it the more desirable starting point. El Rosario on the other hand is a good exit point with accommodations and an easier trek down to **San Juancito.** Both centers have restrooms, drinking water, picnic areas, snack bars, free maps, and charts identifying the park's flora and fauna. El Rosario has a self-guided walking tour of the old mining settlement. Guides offer tours in Spanish from either center (L45-L250 depending on the trail). Visitors must register at the center and pay the trail fee (L190, seniors and persons with disabilities L95) in order to enter and exit the park. Mountain bikers race along the **sendero principal,** the main trail that cuts through the park, connecting the two visitor centers.

All of the trails branch off of the sendero principal. The most popular and hardest of the six trails is **La Cascada** (2.5km), whose steep up-and-down path leads to the park's centerpiece, a 60m waterfall. At the base of the falls, a small trail leads from the picnic areas up to the top. To get to La Cascada from Jutiapa, take **Bosque Nublado** (1.5km) and stop at the *mirador* to spy on the birds along the way. **La Mina** (2.5km), the easiest trail, climbs to the entrance of one of the larger mines passing breathtaking vistas of the valley between La Tigra and Cantarranas. **Jucuara** (1.9km) winds through coniferous and broad leaf forests to a natural spring before joining the park's longest trail, **Los Plancitos** (6.6km), a six hour walk recommended only for people in very good shape. Rancho Quernado, a peak at the end of **La Esperanza** (2km), offers views of the surrounding valley. All trail connections and junctions are marked with large signs. Hiking from Jutiapa to El Rosario takes between two and eight hours depending on the trail.

Camping is permitted anywhere within the park, but be careful to keep an eye out for fire ants when pitching your tent. There is a designated campground on La Esperanza trail marked with a black dot on the map. Entrances to the closed-off mine shafts are the best places to find dry, level ground.

During its mining days, El Rosario used to generate over US$100 million worth of gold, silver, and bronze from the mines per year. Today it exports fresh water to Tegus and 33 surrounding villages. **El Rosario Ecolodge ❸**, located in the Rosario visitor center just beyond the lookout platform at the end of La Mina trail, has dorm-style accommodations and *típico* meals for L40. (☎233 8493 to reserve in advance, L100.) Forty minutes downhill, San Juancito's **Hotelito San Juan ❶**, with mattresses for L20, is convenient for catching an early morning bus, but for safety reasons travelers should avoid walking to San Juancito after dark.

� DAYTRIPS FROM TEGUS

SANTA LUCÍA

Ride the Santa Lucía bus all the way to the last stop or get off the Valle de Ángeles Bus at the "Bienvenidos a Santa Lucía" sign. (30min., every 45min. 5:30am-5:30pm, L5.50.)

Santa Lucía (pop. 2500) is as tranquil as Tegus is frenetic. From a panoramic perch high above you can see gardens overflowing with flowers, bricks laid out to dry, and local pottery shops lining the cobblestone streets of this pleasant village. When Tegus gives you a headache, and it will, Santa Lucía's small-town Honduran living is the perfect antidote.

If you don't want to head back to Tegus, stay at **Posada Doña Estefana ❺**, which offers four large sleeping quarters, a spectacular view, and a pool for hotter days. Look for a yellow house across from the school named José Cecilillo del Baille. (☎779 0441. Accessible 24 hr. Doubles and suites L272-L724.)

VALLE DE ÁNGELES

To get to Valle de Ángeles, take a bus from the ESSO station across the street from the Hospital General on Av. La Paz in Tegus. (1hr., 5:30am-5:45pm every 45min., L8.50.)

A hamlet in the mountains outside Tegus, Valle de Ángeles (pop. 3500), with its cultural and natural richness, is the favorite weekend getaway for Honduras' elite. Though the city began as an overnight stop for miners commuting from Tegus to San Juancito, today Valle de Ángeles is the capital of the country's *artesanía* trade. Galleries and craft stores line every street and sell Honduras' most expertly carved woodwork, radiant woven hammocks, detailed pottery and leather, as well as colorful canvases.

THE HIDDEN DEAL

MONKEY AROUND

In a gas station parking lot, a beat-up sign resting against an even more dilapidated blue pickup reads: "Fun to the Extreme." Normally we'd suggest you avoid investigating such suspect promises of ultimate enjoyment, but this truck is legit. Put thoughts of hookers and hash out of your head—the extreme fun this truck has in mind is all about harnesses and highwires.

Sure, everyone's heard of zip lining; but for a mere US$20 Honduras Canopy Tours will really show you a good time. A short horse ride up the road leads you to a canopy high in the trees strung with cables. Strapped to the wires, you'll start 60 ft. above the ground. Before you know it you'll be hanging upside down whizzing by superman-style, and dodging branches and trees. Then, just when you thought the fun was over, the instructors will have you tuck your feet around the pulley and drop your arms and head beneath you, letting you swing like a jungle monkey as they sway the cable. Back on the ground, horses wait to take you on a steep but pleasurable descent through the valley below.

☎960 8318; www.hondurascanopytours.com. Take a Valle de Angeles bus from the gas station across from Tegus' Hospital San Felipe. Get off at the Valle de Angeles market and walk back down the hill to the gas station. Open Tu-Su 9am-5pm. Call ahead to make arrangements.

Be sure to take an hour for the **Honduras Canopy Tours** (see p. 433), where you can fly through the jungle on a series of ziplines. (☎960 8318. Open Tu-Su 9am-5pm. L350.) If the adrenaline has you yearning for more adventure, sign up for a tour of the overgrown jungle mines at the tourist office. (2hr. tour. Ask to be on horseback.) On the weekend the towns population booms with visitors and you can listen to **mariachis** in the *parque central* as you take a free painting class from the **Casa de Cultura** next to Jalapeños. (☎228 0662. Open M-F 8am-6pm.)

SOUTHERN HONDURAS

A thin part of Honduras runs south to the Golfo de Fonseca, giving the country all-important access to the Pacific Ocean. Travelers here are usually going somewhere else: both El Salvador and Nicaragua are an easy trip down the Carretera Panamericana. From Choluteca, tourists head to Isla El Tigre, the only completely Honduran island in the gulf, with relaxing black-sand beaches.

CHOLUTECA

Honduras' fourth-largest city, Choluteca (pop. 76,300) boasts the best collection of colonial-style buildings in the country. Architecture aficionados share the town with other travelers to El Salvador and Nicaragua who enjoy Choluteca's prime location.

TRANSPORTATION. The main **bus** station, 5Av., 4 C., is in Barrio El Tamarindo. Buses go to: **Amatillo** (2hr., every 25min., 3:30am-5:55pm, L20); **El Triunfo** (45 min., every 30min., 5am-6pm, L18); **San Marcos** (2hr., every 30min., 6:15am-5pm, L15); **Tegucigalpa** (4hr., every 15min., 5:45am-5:45pm, L38). The main station, 1½ blocks down, is Mi Esperanza (☎882 0841), a private bus carrier with rides to **Guasaule** (45 min., 9am, L12); **Tegucigalpa** (3hr., every 2hr., 4am-5:15pm, L120); **San Marcos** (1hr., every 2hr., 7am-7pm, L14). Tica Bus (☎962 9102) is in front of the Puma gas station, about 800m down the Carretera Panamericana from Hotel la Fuente. Buses pass by on the *Carretera* to **Managua** (L280), **Panama** (L940), **San José** (L470), **San Salvador** (L280), **Guatemala City** (L455), and **Tapachula** (L740). **Taxis** from the station to hotels are L10.

ORIENTATION AND PRACTICAL INFORMATION. Choluteca is organized along the standard Honduran grid, except the *parque central* (also called **Parque Valle**) is on 6 C., 6 Av. Nte. instead of in the middle of town. The main commercial strip is **4 Calle,** 2 blocks south of the *parque.* **Parque de la Madre,** in the middle of the main street heading toward the *mercado viejo,* has cheaper hotels.

Banco Atlántida, on the corner of Av. Roosevelt and C. Vicente William, changes money, accepts traveler's checks, and has a Visa **ATM.** (☎882 0121. Open M-F 8:30am-3:30pm, Sa 8:30-11:30am.) The **police** station is on the northwest corner of the *parque* (☎882 0951 or 880 2000, emergency 199. Open 24hr.) There are plenty of **pharmacies** on 4 C.; they take turns staying open until 10pm. The public **Hospital Del Sur** (☎882 0231), between 5 C. and 6 C., and the private clinic **Phillips Centro Médico,** on 4 C. (☎882 0261), are open 24hr. for emergencies. Some doctors speak English. **Hondutel,** on the corner of 4 Av. and 2 C., has phones but no Internet. (☎882 2990. L22 per min. Open M-F 8am-4pm.) Next door, the **post office** (☎882 2513) is open M-F 8am-4pm and Sa 8am-noon, and has **EMS** service. **Internet** is at **CiberNet,** in front of the main bus station (☎882 0276. L20 per min.)

▐ ▐ ACCOMMODATIONS AND FOOD. Hotel Pacifico #1 and **#2 ❸,** both located on 4 C. 3 blocks from the main bus station, have clean rooms, courtyard and very good security. (☎882 3249. Singles L120, with A/C, bath, and TV L200; doubles L180/L250; triples L330.) If you want a treat and are ready to pay for it, **Hotel Internacional ❺,** on Boulevard Enrique Weddle in front of the Texaco gas station, is the place to come and be pampered. Rooms have A/C, bath, phone, and TV. (☎882 3940. Laundry on site. Singles L399; doubles L508; triples L611. AmEx/MC/V.) **Hotel Pierre ❹,** just off Vicente Williams St., has the advantage of being in downtown Choluteca, though the location will cost you. (☎882 0676. Singles with fan, bath, TV L161, with A/C L287; doubles L200/L353; triples L247/L443. AmEx/MC/V.) A more inexpensive downtown option is **Hotel Bonsai ❶** on Av. Valle, 1 block away from the *parque.* Named after a miniature tree, this place has miniature rooms with fan and bath. (Singles with A/C L20; doubles L125, with A/C L210.)

❚Café Espresso Americano ❷, Av. Roosevelt, C. Vicente, is Honduras' version of Starbucks minus the global domination. (Espresso L8, cappuccino L10-L14. Open daily 8am-6pm.) **Tío Rico ❸,** on Vicente Williams, 3 blocks south and 2 blocks west of the *parque central,* is a bit more expensive and serves good seafood (L70-L100) and meats (L65-L100). Friday and Saturday evenings this place turns into a hopping dancing floor (open Su-Th 8am-10pm, F-Sa 8am-2am). **El Burrito ❶,** located 2 blocks from the Hotel Pacifico going away from downtown, offers some of the best Mexican food in Choluteca. The burritos are obviously the specialty (two for L40). The *taco gigante* (L22) is an excellent option (open daily 10am-11pm). **Yi Kim ❹,** behind the police station, offers a rich menu of Honduran-style Chinese dishes. (☎882 2149. Soups L58-L113, seafood L103-L263, rice L83-L98.)

▐ ▐ SIGHTS AND ENTERTAINMENT. The pride of Choluteca is **La Iglesia de Concepción,** at the southern end of the *parque central,* and the colonial **Barrio Corbeta** that surrounds it. The church, dating from the 17th century, was destroyed by an earthquake in the late 19th century and rebuilt in 1918. A white facade, powerful dome, and long nave make this one of the best examples of colonial-style architecture in the country (open daily 8am-noon, 2-4:30pm; mass Su 8am, noon). The only downtown nightlife spot is **Disco Metro,** next to Hotel Pierre, that plays the usual *salsa* and *merengue* (open weekends 10pm-2am).

SAN LORENZO

The Port of Henecan, the country's main Pacific outlet, makes San Lorenzo (pop. 38,000) a bustling commercial center. Some of the best restaurants and nightlife in southern Honduras and a variety of interesting sites attract many travelers.

The **bus** station, behind the Mercado Nuevo, sends buses to **Choluteca** (1 hr., every 45min. 5:40am-9pm, L11), **Coyolito** (45min., every 40min. 6am-5:40pm, L12), and **Tegucigalpa** (3hr., every 45min. 6:20am-9pm, L28). Decorated with crocodile, lobster, and crab sculptures, the flamboyant *parque central* is at the center of town. To get there from the bus station, turn left on the Panamerican Hwy. and continue for 500m up to a small square; turn left again on C. Principal and continue for 6 blocks. The **tourist office** (☎881 2330; turismosanlorenzo@hotmail.com) is located in the Alcaldia in front of the *parque* on C. Principal; talk to knowledgeable Wilson. The **police station** (☎881 2199, emergency 199) is in Barrio San Antonio. **Hospital San Lorenzo** (☎881 2432), 400m down the highway then left 1km from the crossing of Panamerican with C. Principal, is open 24hr. On C. Principal between the crossing with the Panamerican and the *parque* you can find **Farmacia San Lorenzo**. (☎881 2185. Open M-Sa 8am-noon, 2-6pm.) **Banco del Ocidente** changes money and traveler's checks and has an **ATM**. (☎881 2030. Open M-F 8:30am-4:30pm, Sa 8:30-11:30am.) **Mercado Nuevo** is a great mall; from the hospital walk 200m toward the Panamerican then left for 300m.

Hotel Morazán ❺, in front of the hospital, has a swimming pool, games for children, and a restaurant with nice ambience. Rooms are a bit small, but clean and welcoming with A/C, bath, phone, and TV. (☎881 3588. Singles L450; doubles L600; triples L760. AmEx/MC/V.) A cheaper downtown option is **Casita Chou ❺,** on C. Principal 2 blocks past the *parque*. Basic rooms have bath, fan, and TV. (☎881 3389. Rooms L200-L250, with A/C L350.) Casita Chou also runs a **restaurant.** (Rice L53-L85, *sopa China* L60-L135, *carne de res* L60-L105. Open 10:30am-11pm.) All the best restaurants and some nightlife spots are on **Paseo Turistico La Cabaña,** a scenic walkway 300m south of the *parque* toward the coast. **Maravilla's ❹** seafood plates (L120-L250) are famous nation-wide (open daily 11am-10pm). **Bahía Azul ❸** also has amazing seafood soup for L80-L150 (open daily 11am-10pm). For a relaxing cup of coffee, head to **Sun Café ❶** on C. Principal 300m from the intersection with the Panamericana. (☎881 3305. Coffee L7-L22. Open daily 7am-9pm.)

▓ BORDERS WITH NICARAGUA AND EL SALVADOR

From Choluteca, a *colectivo* goes directly to **Guasaule** passing through El Triunfo. The crossing, at the bridge over the Río Guasale, is open 24hr. and Nicaraguan buses continue on the other side of the border. In Guasaule, one option is to hire a bike for 10 córdobas to get to the other side of the border. Border fee US$11 (payable only in US dollars).

Most travelers to Nicaragua use **Las Manos** crossing instead of **El Espino** because it is more accessible and has more convenient hours. The bus to Las Manos leaves from the Discua Litena station in Tegucigalpa and travels for 2½ hr. through breathtaking mountains. A more comfortable, albeit more expensive, option is to take the TICA bus from Choluteca or Tegucigalpa. TICA bus drivers take care of all the crossing details. Exchange rates are not good here. Besides money changing and immigration services, Los Manos has little to offer. Crossing fee is US$11.

El Amatillo is the border crossing into El Salvador. Crucero del Golfo **buses** leave the station on the Blvd. de la Comunidad Europea in Tegus (3hr., L120). Direct buses to El Amatillo leave the main bus station in Choluteca (2½hr., L120). The border is open 7am-10pm. US citizens must get a **visa** in Tegucigalpa at the Salvadoran Embassy or pay US$10 to get one at the border. **Banco Atlántida**, on the Honduran side, changes traveler's checks for colones, lempiras, or US dollars (open M-F 8am-5pm, Sa 9am-noon). **Banco Comercio,** on the Salvadoran side, does the same. **Money changers,** clustered on either side, are usually above-board and offer fair rates to change lempiras directly to colones or vice versa.

ISLA EL TIGRE

A 10min. ride from Coyolito, the beautiful beaches Playa Grande and Playa Negra await on Isla El Tigre. La Cima (783m), the central peak, has great gulf views.

LOCAL TRANSPORTATION. Take a **bus** to **Coyolito** from San Lorenzo (30-45min. every 40min. 6am-5:40pm, L12). The last stop drops you at the docks (10min., last boat 5pm, L20). Hire a car in Apanema to take you anywhere you want on the island (L50-L60 to Playa Negra or Playa Grande).

ORIENTATION AND PRACTICAL INFORMATION. All services are located in **Apanema,** the island's main town. From ferry drop-off, walk about 300m on the dirt road to get to the **Parque Bonilla** and the **church.** The **tourist office,** opposite the church on the ground floor of the Alcaldia, has free maps and organizes tours (☎895 8524 or 895 8664. Open M-F 8am-noon and 2-5pm, Sa 8am-noon.) **Hondutel** is half a block past the tourist office. (☎895 8500. Open M-F 8am-noon, 2-5pm; Sa 8am-noon). **Centro de Salud Sesamo,** 1 block down and 1 block left from Hondutel, is equipped for any medical emergency (☎895 8563. Open M-F 7am-4pm.) The island doesn't have a bank. The **post office** (☎895 8524), temporarily located on the second floor of the Alcaldia, is open M-F 8am-noon and 2-4pm. **Postal Code: 52111.**

ACCOMMODATIONS AND FOOD. If you decide to stay in Apanema, the only option is **Apartamento Victoria ❺.** Head to El Faro Victoria (run by the same person, see below) to get a room. Rooms are clean and come with private bath, fan, and TV. (Singles and doubles L300; triples L375.) **Playa Negra ❺,** on the beach of the same name, is an all-inclusive resort with bar, disco, scuba gear, swimming pool, and every amenity you can imagine. (Luxury rooms with AC, TV, and private bath start at L750. AmEx/MC/V.) The **tourist office ❷** in Apanema has a list of locals who rent rooms. Prices are standardized. (Breakfast L30, lunch L50, dinner L45. Singles L100; doubles L150; L50 per additional person.)

El Faro Victoria ❷, in front of C. La Marina and 200m to the right from lancha drop-off, has a pleasant patio dining area directly over the ocean. Enjoy the seafood and the barside evening entertainment. (☎895 8543. Meals L60-L80. Open daily 10am-11pm.) Playas Negra and Grande have various **food stands** (L20-L40).

OUTDOORS. The island has incredible beaches surrounding its perimeter, but the two best are **Playa Grande** and **Playa Negra.** Playa Grande is the best for tanning and swimming. From here you can also visit the **Cueva de la Sirena,** a beautiful cave that is only accessible during low tide. Playa Negra is named after its black volcanic sand. **Isla el Tigre** has a large mountain for an island of its size. **La Cima** (783m) is a 2-3 hour climb. The path is quite steep but the views of El Salvador, Honduras, and Nicaragua make it worthwhile. US soldiers were stationed here during Central America's years of civil war, and remains of the base are still visible. Views of the Golfo de Fonseca are breathtaking on a clear day. Guided tours can be arranged at the **tourist office.** From Amapala, travel west on C. La Marina and turn left past the Naval Base where the sign says *Caracol:* follow the path the entire way. Bring lots of water.

WESTERN HIGHLANDS

The highland's star attraction is undoubtedly the magnificent Maya site of Copán, but there's so much more: forest-covered mountain ranges call to the outdoor enthusiast and time-warped colonial towns charm romantics. Along the busy high-

Western Highlands

— Paved Road
--- Dirt Road

0 — 20 kilometers
0 — 20 miles

Golfo de Honduras

Puerto Cortés
Omoa
Bahía de Omoa CA13
CORTÉS
El Merendón
P.N. Cusuco San Pedro Sula
El Progreso
Lago de Izabal
GUATEMALA
Río Motagua
CA4
Río Chamelecón
CA5
20
Santa Rita
YORO
P.N. Cerro Azul
El Puente
La Entrada
SANTA BARBARA
Río Ulúa
San Buenaventura
Catarata de Pulhapanzak
Los Naranjos Peña Blanca
Río Jicatuyo
CA11
Parque Sta. Barbara
CA4
Santa Barbara
La Guama
El Florido
Santa Rita
COPÁN
El Níspero
Lago de Yojoa
P.N. Cerro Azul Meambar
Copán
Copán Ruinas
Santa Rosa de Copán
R.V.S. Puca
Río Higuito
Río Otoro
Arada
COMAYAGUA
R.V.S. Erapuca
Gracias
R.V.S. Montaña Verde
Monumento Nacional Cuevas de Taulabe
Siguatepeque
Agua Caliente
P.N. Celaque
Cerro Las Minas
R.B. Opalaca
R.V.S. Mixcure
TO TEGUCIGALPA, COMAYAGUA
OCOTEPEQUE Belén Gualcho
P.N. Trifinio
Nueva Ocotepeque
R.B. Guisayote
San Manuel Colnonhete
San Juan
INTIBUCÁ
El Poy
EL SALVADOR
LEMPIRA
Monumento Nacional Congolón
CA11A
La Esperanza

HONDURAS

way between Tegus and San Pedro Sula, the first noteworthy stop is colonial Comayagua, the country's first capital. Not far north lies the relaxing Lago de Yojoa, the country's largest lake, and the fabulous waterfall, Catarata de Pulhapanzak. The rest of the region's attractions are farther west, most easily accessible from San Pedro Sula or across the border in Guatemala and El Salvador. After exploring the majesty of Parque Nacional Celaque, travelers recoup in the nearby colonial towns of Gracias and Santa Rosa de Copán.

COMAYAGUA

The town of Comayagua (pop. 57,300), 80km northwest of the capital, has recently evolved from a tranquil highway pit-stop into a splendid historical treasure, though the low-altitude heat may limit your visit to a single day. Comayagua, founded in 1537 by Spanish captain Alonso de Caceres, was the nation's capital for over 300 years. A popular rumor claims that in 1880, the unpopular wife of President Marco Aurelio Soto took her revenge on Comayagua's social elite by convincing her husband to move the capital to Tegucigalpa. This ironic twist of fate stripped Comayagua of its capital title, lowering its national prestige, but may have also saved the city's rich culture. Reconstruction efforts have preserved the colonial and Lenca traditions from the city's early days: today, wooden signs hang above establishment doors, a fountain overflows in the park, and the 16th century cathedral shines as white as the day it was built.

▣ TRANSPORTATION. Buses run regularly from both **Tegus** and **San Pedro Sula.** Direct buses arrive 4½ blocks south of the *parque central* at the **Catracho bus station.** Drop-off is on the highway just below the Texaco station, 3 blocks west and 7 blocks south of the *parque* between Av. 1 and Ave. 2 de Julio and Calles 4 and 5. **Transporte Rivera** bus company has a station 6 blocks south of the *parque* which hosts buses to **San Pedro Sula.** (☎772 1208. 1½hr. Daily on the hour 5am-4pm. L19.) Catracho bus terminal sends buses to **Tegus.** (☎772 0260. 1½hr.; Tu-Th every 40min.; M and F-Su every 30min.; 5:20am-5:20pm.)

▰ ▨ ORIENTATION AND PRACTICAL INFORMATION. The San Pedro Sula-Tegus highway runs along the western edge of the town. *Avenidas* run east-west and *calles* run north-south with the *parque central* at the center of the grid pattern. Standing in the center of the *parque*, the cathedral lies directly to the east and the municipal building to the north.

The **Municipal Office of Tourism,** next to the municipal building in the northeast corner of the *parque*, provides bilingual tourist information, free maps of the city, and hotel and restaurant information. Call ahead to schedule a guided tour. (☎772 2028; www.camayagua.hn. Open Tu-Su 8am-noon and 2-5pm.) Banks line the edge of the *parque:* **Banco del País,** on the park's southwest corner, cashes AmEx Traveler's Cheques and gives cash advances on MC/Visa. (☎772 1872. Open M-F 8am-3:30pm, Sa noon-3pm; window teller open M-F 3:30-6pm.) **Banco Ficensa,** on the west side, gives cash advances on MC. (☎772 0016. Open M-F 9am-3pm, Sa 8:30-11:30am.) **Banco Atlantida,** 1 block south of the *parque's* southwest corner on Av. 1 has an **ATM** that accepts Visa. (Open M-F 8:30am-3:30pm and Sa 8:30-11:30am.) All hotels and many stores and restaurants will accept US dollars and credit cards. The **Red Cross** offers emergency service (☎195). For medical assistance, public **Hospital Santa Teresa,** 3 blocks west and 8 blocks south of the park, is open 24hr. for emergency care (☎772 0208). **Farmacia San Martin** is 1 block south of the southeast corner of the *parque.* (☎772 0056. Open daily 8am-noon and 2-6pm.) The 24hr. **police station** is 2 blocks behind the cathedral. (☎772 0080, emergency 772 3040.) **Idal Colonial,** 3 blocks north and 1 block west of the *parque central,* around the corner from the movie theater, **laundry service.** (☎772 0082. Open M-Sa 7am-6pm, Su 7am-noon. L100 per load.) **Supermercado Carol** has a wide selection and is one of several locally owned supermarkets; 2 blocks down from the southwest corner of the *parque.* (☎772 0071. Open M-Sa 8am-noon and 2-6pm, Su 8am-noon.) **MediaNet,** 1 block north of the *parque's* northwest corner, offers Internet access for L12 per hr. (☎772 6944. Open daily 9am-10pm.) The **post office** (open M-F 8am-4pm, Sa 8-11am), 1 block behind the cathedral, is in the same building as **Hondutel,** which have a row of public phones. (Open daily 7am-noon, 12:30-6pm. About L20 per min. to the US.) **UPS** has an office 1 block east and 1½ blocks south of the *parque.* (Open M-F 8am-noon and 2-5pm; Sa 8am-noon.) Comayagua is a very safe city, though *mara* MS-13 is known to be active. As always, nighttime walking should be avoided.

▨ ▢ ACCOMMODATIONS AND FOOD. Comayagua has a wide selection of accommodations ranging from the uberbudget to the ultra-chic. The best value close to the center of town is the **Hotel America Inc. ❷,** 3 blocks south of the southwest corner of the *parque*, with queen-size beds in old but clean rooms, cable TV, fans, and hot water private baths. (☎772 3060. Singles L140; doubles L195.) **Hotel**

HONDURAS

Norimax ❸, 4 blocks south and 3 blocks west of the *parque*, on Av. Manuel Bonilla has similar services to Hotel America with slightly older rooms. (☎772 1210. Singles L170; doubles L200.) **Hotel Norimax Colonial ❸**, 4 blocks south and 1 block east of the *parque*, has newer rooms and is close to the center of town. (☎722 1703. Singles L200; doubles L300, add L50 for A/C. English spoken.)

By far the best dining experience in the city is ⬛**Villa Real ❸**, 1 block east and 1 block south of the *parque central*. Family owned since 1750, this restaurant and museum sits in the 15th century former living quarters of two Honduran presidents, including José Trinidad Cabañas (the guy on the 10 lempira bill). A stone fountain and shady coconut trees create the most elegant dining atmosphere in town. While the chefs are preparing your meal, check out the presidential bedroom, General Morazán's pistol, and the collection of rare Bavarian china. (☎772 0101; turireal@hotmail.com. Open daily 8am-10pm. Corvina in lemon sauce L90, onion soup L45, pasta L65-L75.) For a pleasant taste of home, Westerners often head to **Hannemanns ❸**, 3 blocks west and 1 block south of the *parque*, where Mississippi Shawn serves up hearty portions of nachos (L35), chicken wings (L35), and meat dishes (L100). (☎772 1746. Open M and W-Sa 6-10:30pm, Su 11:30am-2:30pm and 5:30-10pm. English spoken.) Enthusiastic eaters take advantage of the all-you-can-eat buffet at **Comida Rapida Vencia ❶**, a block south of cathedral on C. de Comercio. (☎772 1734. Open M-Sa 7am-7pm, Su 7am-12:30pm. Rice L12, salad L10, meat L16-L30.)

⬛🎶 **SIGHTS AND ENTERTAINMENT.** Comayagua's 17th-century **cathedral**, alongside the *parque central*, is an astounding display of colonial architecture. Originally built by the Moors for the Alhambra palace in Granada, Spain, the 800-year-old clock in the church tower was given to the town by Spain's Philip II, and is the oldest working clock in the Western Hemisphere. Interestingly, the roman numeral four is written as "IIII" because of Moorish influence. Despite ongoing renovations, you can still see the magnificent golden altar and small side chapel. (Open every morning for individual prayer and all day Sunday for mass.)

One block north of the cathedral, across from the Plaza San Francisco, the ⬛**Museo Regional de Arqueología** resides in the 400-year-old former presidential palace. The museum's prized exhibits include leg bones of a *megatherium* (prehistoric gigantic bear), the printing press used to make the first Honduran book, and rooms full of Lenca artifacts. The library once served as Honduras' first court of justice. (☎772 0386. Open daily 8:30am-4pm. L20.)

Three blocks south and 1 block east of the cathedral stands the oldest church in Honduras, **Iglesia San Merced**, which was built in 1536. Inside, the statues are made of balsa wood so that they would float to shore in the event of a shipwreck on the way over from Spain (open daily 5-7pm). The 16th-century **Iglesia de la Caridad**, 3 blocks north and 3 blocks west of the *parque*, integrates Spanish and indigenous cultural influences. **San Sebastián Church**, 11 blocks south and 3 blocks east of the *parque* (15min. walk; taxi L10), is famed for its altar and the tomb of ex-president General José Trinidad Cabañas (open daily 8-10am. Service daily 6pm). Across the street from the cathedral is the **Museo Colonial**, a three-room colonial museum that displays 15th- and 16th-century artifacts culled from churches in and around Comayagua. (Open Tu-Su 9am-noon and 2-5pm. L20.)

Nightlife in Comayagua centers around restaurants. **Villa Real** becomes a hopping karaoke bar. (Open Th-Sa 7pm-midnight, Su 7am-10pm.) **Hannemann's** supplies an extensive bar with two to three special events a month. Cine Valladolid, a block west and 2 blocks north of the park, is the local **movie theater** and shows Hollywood hits. (Spanish subtitles. Shows daily 7pm, Su 1pm. L20, matinee L10.) Travelers can also enjoy the town's two *discotecas*, **Celios** across from the Texaco station, and **Paso Real** down 5 C. beyond the highway.

LAGO DE YOJOA

The centerpiece of a national conservation project, serene Lago de Yojoa nestles in Honduras' fertile mountains. Originally inhabited by the Lenca, this town's horseback riding, boating, and fishing are among the many excursions available for the outdoor traveler. Three large hotels offer the best access to Lago de Yojoa, while nearby Peña Blanca, named for the white rocks that protrude from the cliff face to the north, is a convenient and cheaper base from which to explore the lake.

◰ TRANSPORTATION. Buses run regularly from **San Pedro Sula** and **Tegucigalpa** (via **Comayagua**) and stop at the roadside town of **La Guama**, which lies along the main highway on the southern end of the lake. Buses run regularly between here and **Peña Blanca**, the main town on the northern side of the lake. (25min. Every 30min. 7:00am-5:20pm. L6.) Leaving from the north end of Peña Blanca buses marked "Mochito" head to **San Pedro Sula** or **Catarata Pulhapanzak.** Buses marked "Etimol" travel once daily to **Santa Barbara** from the intersection of the two main streets in Peña Blanca (5:30am) or from anywhere along the road to La Guama before 6am, return at 2pm. (1½hr. L33.)

◪ PRACTICAL INFORMATION. In **Peña Blanca,** a tiny **Hondutel** office is located inside the Cafetería y Repostería Candy (open daily 7am-8pm). There is no local phone service in Peña Blanca, but long distance calls can be made from the office of hotel La Finca (see **Accommodations** below) provided you have a calling card. No banks cash traveler's checks, but you can wire money at **Banco Occidente** (open M-F 8am-3pm, Sa 8am-noon). Mini-supermarkets and fruit stands line up side-by-side on the main street. Hotel Maranata on the northern end of town has a small **pharmacy** (☎898 8106, open daily 5am-10pm) and a larger pharmacy is up the road at **Farmacia Monte Sinai.** (☎898 8132. Open M-Sa 8am-5pm.) **Centro Medico Santa Cecilia,** a half block up Peña Blanca's only side road, offers 24hr. medical assistance. (☎394 5796. Pharmacy open daily 8am-5pm. Visit L80.) The **police station** (open 24hr.), across the street from Hotel Maranata, is 1 block above the **post office.** (☎965 9860. Open daily 8am-5pm. Letters L11.) For faster delivery **Urgente Express** is across from Banco Occidente. (Open daily 8am-5pm. US delivery L28.) **Rena Blanca Net & Cafe,** 1 block up the hill from the Hotel Maranata and around the corner from the *licuados* cafe, has Internet for L20 per hr. and a patchy but cheap Internet phone for L4 per min. to the US. (Open M-Sa 8am-8pm, Su 10am-5pm. English spoken.)

⌂☐ ACCOMMODATIONS AND FOOD. Lempira-pinchers, beware! All three hotels on the road from La Guama to Peña Blanca charge a pretty penny for their lake-view property, outdoor pools, and hot water showers. All resorts accept AmEx/MC/V and have bilingual restaurant menus. **Hotel Auga Azul ❺,** the first resort on the road towards Peña Blanca, has slightly cheaper rates. (☎991 7244. Doubles and triples L377, five to six person cabins L673.) However, **Las Brisas del Lago ❺,** 6km north of Agua Azul, may be the best bet if you are looking to spoil yourself with panoramic views of the lake, spacious balconies, cable TV, A/C, and recreation facilities. (☎992 2937. Singles L586; doubles L733. Reception open 7am-10pm. Recreation facilities open Sa-Su. *Discoteca* open F-Sa 8-11pm.) **Hotel Las Glorias ❺,** down the long pathway beside Las Brisas, has a splendid waterfront setting for similar damage to your wallet. (☎566 0461; www.hotellasglorias.com. Reception open 7am-9pm. Singles L650; doubles L700; triples L800.) For a cheaper option, local guide **Jorge Medrano** (☎396 9767) will open his house to you; he lives a few doors down towards Peña Blanca from the entrance to Agua Azul. **Hotel**

HONDURAS

Maranata ❺, next to the bus stop from La Guama, is a noticeably cheaper option, with shared bathroom *sencillos* and well kept *privados*. (Singles L100, with bath L200; doubles/triples with bath L250. Locked 10pm-5am.)

Scenic restaurants along the lake combine beautiful views and tasty meals. **Hotel Agua Azul ❷** serves a hearty breakfast for L60. (Sandwiches L45-L60, filet mignon L120, margaritas L40.) **Las Brisas del Lago's ❸** gorgeous view goes well with the fish dishes (L90-L120), cordon bleu (L95), and beer (L18). **Hotel las Glorias ❸** (☎396 9767) serves pancakes (L65), *típico* (L95), lobster in wine sauce (L175), and daiquiris (L60). In Peña Blanca many *comedores* dish up cheap fried foods. **Cafeteria la Roca ❷,** a block towards La Guama from the bus stop, is a cool place to sit indoors and enjoy a filling meal. (Open daily 7am-9pm. Hamburgers L30, standard Honduran fare L30-L40.)

◨ ♫ SIGHTS AND OUTDOOR ACTIVITIES. As the dozens of vendors lining the road just before La Guama demonstrate, **fishing** on the lake is the main attraction for Hondurans. Agua Azul rents a limited number of fishing poles, and Las Glorias sells the necessary accessories (hook, line, bait L50).

The resorts have the best equipment for touring the lake. Paddle boats (L200 per hr.), and kayaks (1 person L100, 2 person L150) line the docks at Agua Azul. Las Brisas has a pool (L40 per day), kayaks (L50 per hr.), and guided boat tours for up to eight people (L400 per hr.), while Las Glorias rents paddle boats (L100 per hr.), horses (L100 per hr.), bikes (L100 per hr.), and motorboats (L250 per 30min.) and organizes catamaran rides (L60).

◪ CUEVAS DE TAULABE

Take any bus headed to San Pedro Sula from Tegus, Comayagua, or Siguatepeque and ask to get off at the Cuevas de Taulabe. You can also get off at the regular stop of Taulabe City and then walk back up the highway 20 minutes to the Km104 marker. The cuevas will be on your right (☎898 8705. Open M-Tu 8am-4pm, W-Su 8am-7pm. Cave entrance L35 plus tip for your guide.)

The caverns at Taulabe were discovered by accident in 1969 and have only recently opened to tourists. Still largely unexplored, a paved and lit path leads 300m in from the mouth of the cave, revealing millions of years worth of nature's underground artwork. Stalactites along the path that, with a little creative interpretation from your tour guide, look like a sombrero, a frog, a pig, and a map of Honduras. The caves were originally carved when Honduras was still submerged under the ocean, before the volcanic formation of Central America. Small bats hang from the walls inside the caves and the seeds from their guano have sprouted along the floor of the cave. At the end of the path comes a rare opportunity for adventurers; if you bring your own flashlight and lots of water, you can explore beyond the touristed area. Though a guide must accompany you, you are free to travel for as long and as far back as you like. The truly ambitious spelunker can set her sights on finding the exit to the caves, which has yet to be discovered.

◪ CATARATA DE PULHAPANZAK

Take a Tima company bus labeled "Mochito" toward San Pedro Sula from Hotel Maranata in Peña Blanca and get off in San Buena Ventura. (20min. Every 30min. L6.) A yellow sign points the way to Centro Turístico Pulhapanzak. Follow the main concrete road for about 1km and bear left at the cul-de-sac at the top of the hill. After about 15min., a sign on your right will direct you inside the gated entrance to the Centro Turístico. There are a couple of small stores and comedores in San Buena Ventura that serve drinks, snacks or a cheap meal. With the exception of camping, the nearest lodging is at Peña Blanca. Return buses to San Pedro Sula and Peña Blanca leave from the drop-off about every hr. (☎995 1010. Open daily 6am-6pm. Entrance L25. Camping L25; bring your own gear.)

An easy trip from San Pedro Sula or Lago de Yojoa that could last an afternoon or all day, this 43m waterfall along the **Río Lindo** has carved out a spectacular natural water park beneath its cooling mist. The water at the top of the falls is a refreshing place for a dip and a cement stairway about 100m downstream will take you to the base of the falls. Once at the falls, **swimming holes** abound, many deep enough to dive into from the overhanging rocks. Beneath the blinding spray and torrential pour of the main shoot hides the narrow entrance to a small cave where the non-claustrophobic can find refuge as well as some very unique calcite formations. For a mere L50-L100 tip (depending on how long you stay) **guides** can reveal all of these secret nooks and ensure your safety. If a guide doesn't appear on your way down to the falls, the men working the entrance to the park will find one for you. The area around the falls is a **public park** that allows camping and has a small restaurant (with public bathrooms) just upstream from the falls (meals L45-L55). Next to the restaurant is the **Plaza Ceremonial,** an unexcavated archaeological site believed to have been a center of Lenca religious ceremonies.

◤ LOS NARANJOS ECO-ARCHAEOLOGICAL PARK

Take the small yellow school bus marked El Jaral from Hotel Maranata in Peña Blanca (10 min., every hr. 6:30-11:30am and 1-6pm, L5) or look for the large green "Los Naranjos" sign 3km down the road that begins on the lake side of Las Peñas. Camping is technically not permitted within the park and the nearest lodging is in Peña Blanca. A cafeteria operates within the park serving meals for L40-L50. (☎394 8102. Open daily 8am-4pm. L80. Comprehensive audio guide in Spanish L30 at the gift shop.)

On the west side of the lake, Los Naranjos Eco-Archaeological Park (see p. 443) reveals the area's Lenca past as well as stunning flora and fauna. The yellow-tailed Montezuma Oropendola, the largest oriole in the Americas, is just one of the species in this incredibly diverse bird population. There are four side excursions off one of the main pathways that leads through the park. **El Jaral,** named after the earliest period of Lenca inhabitance, is the principal trail and leads past an enormous grandfather tree into the forest. The first trail to the left, **Sobre Polines,** leads

THE LOCAL STORY

PROFESSOR LENCA

Rosemary Joyce is Professor of Anthropology at the University of California, Berkeley. She has done archaeological fieldwork in Honduras since 1977.

LG: What is special about Los Naranjos Archaeological Park?
A: This is one of the earliest groups of monumental structures in Mesoamerica. Twenty meters high and 100m long, when these terraces were first constructed in 400 BC they were unprecedented projects.

LG: What can travelers hope to come across in Honduras?
A: Only a small portion of Honduras has been systematically surveyed, and every time an archaeologist does a survey they find new sites. Basically, if you watch as you travel throughout Honduras you will eventually notice clusters of earthen mounds in roadside pastures. These are for the most part the remains of the cities and villages of the Classic Period (circa AD 500-1000).

LG: Do you have any crazy archaeologist stories to share?
A: Well, there were a fair number of times I ran to get through barbed wire fences before an angry cow could catch me, but that's about it. Archaeology, contrary to its media image, is not the most exciting thing you can choose to do with a PhD—until you get to the part where you can think about what you discovered.

down a poorly-maintained boardwalk to a picnic area looking out on the lake. Sobre Polines connects to **Gualiqueme,** which tours diverse tropical plants and end at a rickety suspension bridge with a breathtaking view of the canal. The bridge is in serious disrepair. Across the bridge, **Isla Las Ventanas** leads to a smaller archaeological site and panoramic lake vista at the base of Santa Bárbara National Park. Pathways from all of the trails lead to the Los Naranjos **ruins.** Three mounds represent some of the earliest and largest monumental architecture in Mesoamerica, dating from around 800 BC. The site is not fully excavated, but with a little imagination the ancient Lenca village comes to life, showing visitors a basalt column, cutaway steps, and a stone human statue on display at the park's entrance.

◪ PARQUE NACIONAL CERRO AZUL MEAMBAR

Las Pavas trail (11km) is the most scenic route to the Los Pinos visitor center. The trail begins behind Restaurante La Naturaleza, located right before La Guama on the road from Tegus. After 2km, you will come to a sign that directs you through the village of Santa Elena. Follow a second sign that directs you along a 4.5km winding path to the visitor center. The visitor center has maps and drinking water, as well as guides for hire. (☎ 951 3754, panacam@hondutel.hn. Open daily 7am-6pm.) Restaurante la Naturaleza coordinates room and board reservations for the cabins Los Pinos. (☎ 990 6021, lanaturaleza@paghonduras.com.) 4 very clean cabins with private baths and A/C house 5 for L100 per person. There are 2 designated camping areas, one next to the visitor center, and the other at the top of the mountain (L30 per person, tent rentals L30). Breakfast (L50), lunch (L70), and dinner (L60) are served at the restaurant next to the office; meals must be arranged in advance. (☎ 733 0539 Siguatepeque or 239 8311 Tegus.)

Though right up the road from Honduras' main thoroughfare, much of the 304km Parque Nacional Cerro Azul Meambar has yet to be explored. Three well-marked trails radiate from Los Pinos visitor center, revealing cascading waterfalls and stunning vistas within the cloud forest. **El Sinai,** the longest trail, is a steep 8km climb through secondary forest to a 10m waterfall with a swimming hole and a lookout point over the lake (keep an eye out as it's easy to miss). **El Venado** is a shorter 1.2km hike leading through the forest to the parks' most famous waterfall as well as a refuge for white-collared swifts and the park's mascot, the *pisote.* The waterfall can also be reached from the short and well-maintained **Los Vencejos.**

SANTA BÁRBARA

Situated to the west of Lago de Yojoa, Santa Bárbara (pop. 15,000) is a quiet town with a serene and friendly atmosphere. Moss grows on power lines above the *parque central* and fresh spring-water spas are a perfect symbol of the town's relaxed pace. Basket weaving, introduced in 1857 by Governor Marcos García, has come to define Santa Bárbara's culture and brought the town international *artesanía* renown. Just outside the city, the entrance to one of Honduras' most inaccessible parks and numerous unexplored caves make sure adventurous nature lovers and easygoing tourists alike visit this quiet town.

⌨ TRANSPORTATION. Most **buses** stop across the *parque central* from the church. Just down the hill from here, **Terminal Cotisba** runs buses to San Pedro Sula (☎ 643 2308. 2hr. Every 30min. 4am-5pm. L25.) A block down the street in front of the church, **Terminal Junqueños** runs buses to Siguatepeque that continue on to Tegucigalpa. (☎ 643 2689. 1½ hr. to Siguatepeque, 3hr. to Tegus; M-F 5, 7am, 2pm; Sa-Su 8:30am, 2pm. L39/83.) Directly across the park from the church, city buses marked **Urbano** take you to the *balnearios*, **Nispero,** or some of the *junco* villages.

⚐ 🔢 ORIENTATION AND PRACTICAL INFORMATION. Santa Bárbara is a small, easily navigable town. From the middle of the *parque*, the church faces due east and the main street is across the park. Following it to the right for 20min. will lead you past the **hospital**, located near the highway turn off (☎ 646 2721, 24hr. emergency care), and then across the bridge to the **police station** (☎ 643 2120, emergency ☎ 199, open 24hr.). **Banco Atlántida,** 1 block down the main street to the left of the church, cashes traveler's checks and gives advances on V (open M-F 8:30am-3:30pm, Sa 8:30-11:30am). **Hondutel** has an office on the street directly in front of the church, 1 block to the right on the far corner of the intersection. (☎ 643 2422. Open daily 7am-9pm.) The **post office** is next to the Hondutel office. (☎ 643 2121. Open M-F 8am-4pm, Sa 8am-noon. Letters L11.) **Internet** is available at **Andromeda.com,** up the circular stairwell on the street directly in front of the church, one half block to the right. (Open M-Sa 8am-9pm, Su 8am-noon. L25 per hr.) The **Office of Tourism,** 2 blocks down and to the right on the main street, across the park from the church, offers an extensive cultural exhibit, free city maps, and guided tours of the city and its environs. (☎ 381 9659, guide Gabriel Reyes 643 2563; www.santabarbara.gob.hn. Open M-F 8am-noon and 2-5pm. Guides L100-L150 per day.)

🔢 📧 ACCOMMODATIONS AND FOOD. There are a few hotels to choose from in Santa Bárbara. **Hotel Ruth ❸,** about 1½ blocks to the left of the church on your left-hand side, has rooms with hot water and private baths. (☎ 643 2632. Singles L100; doubles L150; triples L250, TV extra L50.) **Hotel Ejecutino ❸,** just to the right of Hotel Ruth, has cleaner rooms with large windows and televisions but no hot water. (☎ 643 2206. Singles L170; doubles L230.) **Boarding House Moderno ❸,** 1 block to the right of the church and 1 block left from there, has hot water. (☎ 643 2829. Singles L150, with A/C L250; doubles L225/360. Reception open 5am-noon.)

Tap your feet to smooth jazz amid Renaissance decor as you gorge on the amazingly good and incredibly cheap lunch buffet at ◼**Casablanca.** (☎ 643 2839. Open M-Sa 7am-8pm. Plate of the day served breakfast and dinner. Vegetarian friendly. Buffet L40-L60.) For a freshly baked treat at the local favorite try **Cafetería y Pastelería Charlies ❷,** down the street to the left of the church on the corner of the *parque central.* (Meals L34-L40, pizza L12, baked goods L3-L6.) Fresh fruit overflows from the *mercado* just behind the church.

🔢 🎬 SIGHTS AND ENTERTAINMENT. Santa Bárbara is a city full of sights, rich in culture, adventure, and relaxation, all crowned by its *junco* **(basket weaving)** trade. Villagers come into the city to sell baskets, purses, dolls, mats, and their famous woven hats. Interested travelers will be rewarded by a trip to nearby towns where the crafts are produced. Some recommended towns are **Santa Rita Oriente, La Zona,** and **Ilama.** Different towns specialize in different *artesanía* products; the tourist office can help you find transportation to each *pueblo.* Outlet stores like **Tersenia Tencoa,** located up the road directly in front of the church half a block to the right, specialize in high quality wood and *junco* crafts. (☎ 643 2188. Open Daily 7:30am-5pm.) **Artesanías Yahamala,** located 2 blocks to the left beyond Tersenia Tencoa (open daily 7:30am-noon and 2-5pm), and 30-year veteran hatmaker **Estrella de Zamora,** located to the right of the park 1½ blocks up the main street (☎ 643 2689, open daily 8am-6pm, hats L40-L250) sell quality crafts.

High above the city, the 180 year old weekend-getaway **castle** of President Luis Bogran has a spectacular vista of the valley below. *El Castillo* (open daily, free) is just a cab ride away from town (L50-L70); remember to arrange for a return trip. **Video Cine Camelot,** 1 block to the right down the main street from the park, shows a newly released movie at 7pm every night.

For the outdoor explorer, there are few areas in all Honduras with more rugged and unscathed wilderness than the 30,000 hectares of **Parque Nacional Santa Bárbara**. The park is home to two giants: Maroncho Mountain (2740m), the second highest peak in Honduras and the largest limestone formation in Central America and the Aguila Arpía, the largest eagle in the Americas. Lack of access keeps the park pristine, but presents a challenge for any hiker. Thirteen kilometers up the road past the castle, **Don Mario Orellana's** is the best source of information for trail and camping advice plus the occasional bed for the weary. Ask any taxi driver to head to his house or ride the Urbano bus that climbs the steep hill at 1:30pm. The area around the edges of the park is a spelunker's paradise, home to a host of unmapped **caves**. The tourist office has information on how to find them.

Water lovers can also entertain themselves among the five natural spas, called balnearios, and thermal springs just down the highway from Santa Bárbara. **Hotel Guacamaya** (☎643 2206), 3km north of the park, offers the only balneario within the city limits. The rest are just outside the city: **Balneario Santa Lucia** (13km past the hospital on the highway), **Balneario Tencoa** (☎643 2561 or 634 2557, 7km towards Tegus), **Balneario Bella Vista** (facing Tencoa) and **Balneario Torre** (☎643 2406) just a little further up the highway. For faster moving water, take an Urbano bus 46km to the southwest to the village of **Nispero** to the area's prize waterfall.

LA ESPERANZA

Placed atop a 1980m peak, cool mountain air gives La Esperanza (pop. 5300) the most pleasant climate in the country. Even though La Esperanza includes the original *pueblo* of Intibuca, the population is less than 10,000, making this town both charming and endearing. Large stone streets lead up to a hill just a few blocks past the *parque central* where prisoners carved La Gruta, a shrine to the Virgin Mary.

▐ TRANSPORTATION. La Esperanza has **two bus stations.** For buses heading outside the department, there is a bus terminal 1 block left of the *parque central* behind the police station with buses running to **San Pedro Sula** (3.5hr., every 2hr. 4:30am-2:30pm, L66) and to **Tegucigalpa** (3.25hr., every hour 4:45am-2:00pm, L66). The Tegus bus also stops in **Siguatepeque** (1½hr., L30). A different station services buses with destinations inside the department. From the *parque central* walk 5 blocks up the main street in the opposite direction from the shrine and then 1½ blocks to the left. Buses run to **San Juan** (2hr.; 10, 11:30am, 1, 2, 3:30pm; L25) and other small towns in the area. The city's **Punto de Taxis** are 2½ blocks away from the shrine on the right hand side of the main street.

◪▐ ORIENTATION AND PRACTICAL INFORMATION. The main street runs right past the *parque central* and the **church** (mass Su 6, 8, 10am, 7pm), continuing straight uphill past the white-framed shrine to the Virgin Mary. **Banco de Occidente**, on the main street, to the left of the *parque central* when facing the church, cashes traveler's checks and has a **Western Union** office (open M-F 8:30am-4pm, Sa 8:30am-noon). A large **city market,** across from the **Punto de Taxis,** is up and running daily and especially busy Sunday. **Mi Lavandería,** 2 blocks down the main road away from the shrine and then 5 blocks to the left, will do your **laundry** so well you'll think your mom is traveling with you. (☎783 2136. Open M-Sa 8am-6pm. Wash and dry L11 per kg.) The **police station** is in the turreted building next to the church. (☎783 1007, emergency ☎199. Open 24hr.) The city **hospital** is 2km down the main street past the right hand side of the church. (☎783 0184. Open 24hr.) While there are many medical clinics around the park, **Clínica Médica San Carlos** is the best bet, 1 block from the *parque* past the right-hand side of the church. (☎783

0290. Open 24hr.) Around the corner from the post office is the local **Hondutel.** (Open daily 7am-9pm. L20 per min. to the US.) There is **Internet** access at **Solef Cafe Internet** next to the intercity bus stop 1 block towards the shrine on the road behind the police station. (☎783 0726. Open daily 8:30am-8:30pm. L30 per min. Photocopying available.) The **post office** is kitty-corner across the park from the church (open M-F 8am-noon and 2-5pm, Sa 8-10am).

⌐⌐ ACCOMMODATIONS AND FOOD. For travelers on a tight budget, **Hotel Mejin Batres ❷** can't be beat, located 1 block along the main road from the park toward the shrine and 1 block to the left, the hotel provides guests with spacious rooms, balconies, and hot showers, which are especially welcome on brisk mountain nights. (☎783 0051. Singles L70, with bath L125; doubles L100/L180.) Another budget option is **Hotel Venecia ❶**, 4½ blocks down the main road from the *parque* in the opposite direction of the shrine, on the left. (Singles L50, with bath L150; doubles L100/L200.) **Hotel Mina ❹**, 4 blocks down the same road from the *parque* and 1 block to the right, boasts elegant, spotless rooms with hot water baths and cable TV. (☎789 1071. Singles L180-L200; doubles 280. Cafeteria meal L35.) For lunch and a cold soda, stop by **Kiosko ❷** in the middle of the *parque* to enjoy your meal from the second-story balcony. (Open daily 6:30am-9pm. Drinks L18, enchiladas L14, pastries L4-L8.)

◙ SIGHTS. The crisp weather makes La Esperanza an ideal place to stop for a few days and soak up small-town Honduran life. The dramatic **shrine** to the Virgin Mary, poised conspicuously at the end of the main street, is the main city landmark. Staircases hewn into the stone on both sides of the shrine lead to the top of the hill, presenting a view of the entire town. Cool **spring baths** wait at the end of the path down the hill and to the left of the shrine. Alternatively, facing the shrine, take a left at the last road and then the next right down a dirt road which leads to the springs. (Open during daylight hours. Free.) On the third sunday in June, elegant floral altars decorate every street corner in honor of *Cuerpo de Cristo*.

SAN JUAN

Though far away from the most frequented tourist routes, San Juan (pop. 3900) has a surprisingly large array of fun and interesting activities for travelers. Within this cozy Honduran farming town, visitors learn to make and fire Spanish roof tiles and bricks under guidance from **clay artisans.** Nearby, bulls squeeze juice from sugar cane and the **coffee plantation** allows you to taste and learn about the region's main crop. For a little adventure, hike to the **Waterfall of the Elves** through the virgin **Opalaca Biological Reserve** and then climb the treeless **El Pelon Peak** for a mountain view of the valley. At sunset, the **Haunted Canyon** and its resident ghost may frighten off the timid, but you can relax your nerves at the **natural hot spring.**

Getting to San Juan can be difficult. Buses are infrequent and the dirt highway is in poor condition. **Buses** run from La Esperanza (2hr.; 10, 11:30am, 1, 2, 3:30pm; L25) and arrive at a group of supermarkets just down the hill from the town. Return buses to La Esperanza circle the town looking for passengers (2hr.; 6, 7:30, 8:20am; L25). Buses from San Juan to Gracias pass by the highway at 6:30 and 7:30am (L25), however no buses run from Gracias to San Juan. To get to Gracias, La Esperanza, or surrounding *aldeas*, most locals flag down passing trucks and pay L25 for a ride—though *Let's Go* does not recommend hitchhiking. The best place to wait is where C. Principal intersects the highway.

San Juan is centered around two main streets: one that leads up from the La Esperanza bus stop on the highway, and the **C. Principal** that leads back to the highway towards Gracias. The **Palacio Municipal** is on the Gracias side of the *parque* *central* and the **police station** is just across the street (open 24hr.). The first stop for any traveler should be the **San Juan visitor center,** located up the C. Principal in the same building as **Docucentro Israel,** 1 block towards Gracias and 1 block to the right of the *parque central.* From this office, **Gladis Nolasco** will arrange home-stays, meal packages, and guided tours for any traveler. (☎662 1131; rachelcleghorn@yahoo.com. Open daily 8am-5pm.) **Clínica Médica Paracelso,** located 2 blocks from the park towards Gracias, is open daily. A **Hondutel** office is available 1 block towards La Esperanza from the park, on the left. (☎783 2022. Open 7:30am-9:30pm. L30 per min. to the US.) The **post office** is the second to last house before the bend on C. Principal heading towards La Esperanza. (Open M-F 8am-noon and 1-4pm. Letter to the US L11.)

The visitor center coordinates housing. Ask for the **Posada de Doña Soledad ❷** across the street from Comedor Patty, which has a large room with hot water (one person L60, two people L100). **Posada de Patty ❶** behind Comedor Patty has a room alongside a garden courtyard. No hot water. (One person L50, two people L65.) **Comedor Yamileth** and **Comedor Patty ❶,** just up C. Principal from the visitor center towards La Esperanza, offer *típico* meals. (Open daily 6am-8pm. L35.)

GRACIAS

Ever since Juan de Chávez, the first settler of the region, exclaimed, "Thank God we've finally found flat land!" Gracias (pop. 7200) has served as a comfortable base camp amidst rugged terrain. Once capital of all of Spanish Central America, Gracias' importance faded when the country's economic center of gravity shifted, but its colonial flair endures. Major cultural attractions include the **festival** celebrating the native Lenca leader Lempira, a longtime enemy of the Spanish (all July, peak days 19th-20th), and the festival held September 24th in honor of San Marcos, the city's patron saint. Visitors to Gracias typically make trips to nearby **hot springs** and the breathtaking **cloud forest** in Parque Nacional Celaque.

▐ **TRANSPORTATION.** Gracias' two **bus companies** conveniently arrive and depart from the same location. From the corner of the *parque* next to the Palacio Municipal, take the road headed west and towards Banco Occidente for 3 blocks; turn right and go 1 block to the bus parking lot. **Lempira** bus company (☎656 1214) runs regular service to Santa Rosa de Copán. (1½ hr., every 30min. 5:30am-3:30pm, L26.) **Gracianos** buses leave irregularly from Gracias to San Pedro Sula (4hr.; 6, 8:30, 9:50am; L60) with a stop in Santa Rosa.

▐▌ **ORIENTATION AND PRACTICAL INFORMATION.** In uncommon fashion, the *parque central* is not quite the center of town. Most action takes place in the several streets parallel to the *parque* toward the west. The turreted **Fuerte de San Cristobal** and the towering peaks of **Parque Nacional Celaque** are off in the same direction. When standing in the middle of the *parque,* Gracias' cathedral, **Church of San Marcos** is to the south and the **Palacio Municipal** is directly north (☎656 1154. Open M-F 8am-4:30pm). Inside the house in the center of the park, the **Tourist Office** assists with hotel reservations, has displays on the history of Gracias, and provides free maps of the city and PN Celaque. (☎656 1154. Open daily 8am-noon and 1-4:30pm.) **Froni** at Guancascos Restaurant (☎/fax 656 1219; see **Food,** below) is a great English-speaking source of information on trips around Gracias. **Banco de Occidente,** 1 block down the road from the Palacio, headed west toward the bus stop, wires money and cashes traveler's checks. (☎656 1024. Open M-F 8:30am-4:30pm, Sa 8:30-11:30am.) The **police station,** between the cathedral and the Palacio in the northeast corner of the *parque*

(☎656 1326 or 656 1327, emergency ☎199), and the **hospital** (☎656 1425), on the outskirts of town 3 blocks past the bus station, across from the Texaco station, are both open 24hr. for emergency service. **Hondutel** is 1 block south of the park. (☎656 1004. Open daily 7am-9pm.) **Internet** access is available at **Millennium Computer School Cyber Café** across the street. (☎656 1140. Open M-F 8am-noon and 2-6pm, Sa 8am-noon. L36 per hr.) The **post office** is located nearby. (Open M-F 8am-noon and 2-5pm, Sa 8-11am.) **Postal code:** 1301.

⌂ ACCOMMODATIONS AND FOOD. Gracias has a good range of options for lodging. **Hotel Erick ❷**, 3 blocks east of the bus terminal, 1 block north of the *parque* past the Palacio, has spacious rooms with private baths and a friendly owner who can arrange rides to PN Celaque and the Aguas Termales. (☎656 1066. Singles L60; doubles L90, with fan and hot water L130. Rides L180 for four people.) **Hotel Guancascos ❹**, 1 block south of the *parque* past the church and 3 blocks west, has airy rooms with hot-water baths, fans, and TV. Some rooms also have dramatic views of the town framed by distant mountains. (☎656 1219. Singles L175; doubles L320; triples L340.) Froni, Guancascos' trilingual owner, has topographical maps of the park and rents two nicely equipped cabins there for hikers (L250 a night for two people). **Hotel San Antonio ❶**, the turquoise and pink building 1 block west towards Banco Occidente and 5½ blocks north of the *parque* on the left, has clean rooms, common TV area, and cafeteria. The entrance is a terrace with unobscured views of the peaks in Celaque. (☎656 1071. Singles L50, with bath L80, with hot water L150; doubles L100/L100/L246.) **Hotel Don Juan ❺**, set inside a courtyard opposite Banco de Occidente, is ideal for group and family stays with its clean, tiled floors, high ceilings, and hot water. (☎656 1020. Singles L210-L240, with A/C L280; doubles L360/L410. Cafeteria meal L34-L37.)

With 100% organically grown products, **▧Rinconcito Graciano ❷**, 2 blocks west of the cathedral and 1½ blocks south, puts a new twist on the word *típico* with home grown herbs and spices. Locally brewed apple wine makes for a refreshing treat as you browse through a diverse selection of fine crafts, traditional fishing nets, clay pots, and drinking gourds. (☎656 1171. Meal L40, wine L20, juice L7, desert L7. Open daily 7am-9pm.) Perched on a balcony high above town, **▧Restaurante Guancascos ❷**, in Hotel Guancascos, is a great place to grab breakfast before heading out to tackle Celaque, lunch on the way to the Fuente, or a beer when the day is over. (☎656 1219. Breakfast L38, *cena típica* L60, beer L17, vegetarian sandwich L38. Open daily 7am-10pm. AmEx/MC/V.) **La Exquisita Repostería y Pizzería ❷**, half a block west of the Palacio Municipal, has delectable pizzas (L40-L110), hamburgers (L25), and cakes (L5). Vegetarian pizza is available (open daily 6am-9pm).

◙ SIGHTS. Like many other Central American towns, Gracias is a great place to walk around and soak in that romantic, colonial feel. Each within a block of the *parque*, **Iglesia San Marcos** is the city's cathedral and **Iglesia La Merced**, built in 1544, housed the Audiencia de los Confines, the Spanish governing body of Central America. Across the street from San Marcos is the former **presidential palace.** Just south is a white arched facade portraying two lions, the only remains of the **Spanish tribunal** that oversaw Central American expansion. A short walk, starting just behind the stairs to Guancascos, leads up to Gracias' main attraction, the **Fuerte San Cristóbal,** with the tomb of former President Juan Lindo and magnificent views of **Parque Nacional Celaque** and the town. (Open daily 8am-noon and 1-5pm, often later. Free.) Honduras' famed Galeano family certainly left its mark on Gracias: **Plaza San Sebastian** is bracketed by the **Casa Galeano** (open M-F 7am-noon and 1-4pm, Sa 7-11am) on its southeast corner and the **studio** of Mito Galeano, Gracias' most famous contemporary painter, on the northwest corner.

PARQUE NACIONAL CELAQUE

Looming to the west of Gracias is the 267 sq. km **Parque Nacional Celaque,** whose main attraction is **Cerro Las Minas** (2850m), the tallest mountain in the country. *Celaque* means "box of water" in the local Lenca dialect, and the name is quite appropriate—the park's heavy rains provide water for more than 16,000 people every year. The journey to the peak is a long and strenuous, a challenge to do in one day. Most travelers spend the night at the visitor center or in one of the camp sites along the trail. Those without the time or inclination to climb will still find plenty to see on the lower reaches of the mountain, where dense forests surround the trail. The park's wildlife includes pumas and white-faced monkeys and, within the cloud forest's higher elevations, quetzals and toucans. Spider webs span across all the trails, so this may not be the best hike for the arachnophobic.

AT A GLANCE	
AREA: 226 sq. km.	**GATEWAYS:** Gracias (p. 448), Belén Gualcho, San Manuel Colnonhete.
CLIMATE: Rainforest, Cloudforest.	**CAMPING:** No permits necessary. Bring your own bedding.
FEATURES: Cerro las Minas, Santa Lucía Waterfall.	
HIGHLIGHTS: Climbing Honduras' tallest peak, roughing-it camping, wildlife.	**FEES AND RESERVATIONS:** L50 entrance fee, call Proyecto Celaque Office in advance to arrange a guide for L200.

⬅ TRANSPORTATION

The best way to reach the park is to arrange for a ride in Gracias, especially for groups that can split the cost. Froni at **Guancascos Restaurant** charges L150 for up to four people, and rides from **Hotel Erick** cost L180. Be sure to arrange a return trip (L150) prior to departure. If you don't know when you will be returning, simply look for a returning car around the village of Villa Verde, right below the park entrance where taxis drop you off (L170). Otherwise, you will have to walk 8km back to town. From Guancascos, walk left until you pass the remains of San Sabastian church. At the intersection turn left, but stay to the right of the DIPPSA gas station. Go to the right around the pink and white church of Santa Lucia, then follow the road with a sign saying "*a pie*" (on foot) for 6.4km. The park is 2hr. straight ahead. The peak can also be tackled from the opposite side. This option takes much longer and requires a guide. To access these routes, you need to hire a truck in Belén Gualcho or San Manuel Colnonhete.

🛈 PRACTICAL INFORMATION

The **Office of the Proyecto Celaque,** has the latest information on the park. (☎656 1362. Open daily 8am-5pm.) **Corporación Hondureña de Desarollo Forestal** (COHDE-FOR), with its main office off the road to Celaque near the junction with the road to La Campa, also provides info and maps. A **visitor center** at the foot of the trails has park info, and a list of regulations. (Open M-Sa 8am-4pm. Entrance L50. Arrivals before or after hours have to pay the fee at a house in Villa Verde.) Be sure to get a trail map from the **Office of Tourism** in Gracias' *parque central*, as the visitor center seldom carries them.

Any excursion into the park will require sturdy hiking boots, a light rain jacket, and warm clothes. A hat and something to gently move spiderwebs aside with are also recommended. Bug repellent might also be useful. Stock up on food and bottled water, as there's none beyond the visitor center. Ample stream water is available at certain points along the trail, but it needs to be purified.

▼ CAMPING

There are three rudimentary shelters along the way, but none have bedding, so bring your own sleeping gear. **Restaurante Guancascos** rents sleeping bags (L25) and two-person tents (L50). The **visitor center** at the beginning of the trails has the most comfortable lodging in the park. Once on the actual hike, the first campsite, **Don Tomás,** is approximately 2½-3hr. along the main trail. The camp is basically a snug tin shack with mattress-less bunks, a latrine, and a firepit. Be sure to get the key if you plan to use the shack. There are also flat areas that accommodate about three tents. At the beginning of the cloudforest, **El Naranjo** campsite, a steep 1½-2½hr. hike from Don Tomás, is not much more than a firepit with a nearby creek and some level spots. Naranjo is about 2hr. from the summit.

▣ HIKING

To conquer Celaque there are a few strategies. If your time is limited to one day, you need to arrive at the visitor center by 5:30am in order to scale the mountain before losing daylight. It takes 7½ hours to reach the peak and 2½ hours to return. If you have more than one day, arrive by 4pm and stay at the visitor center.

In addition to the main trail **Bosque Nublado** (7½hr.), there are two shorter scenic trails. Starting on Bosque Nublado, a sign off to the left will indicate the beginning of **Corto** trail (30min.), a fairly easy 1.5km circle back to the visitor center. **El Mirador** (2½hr.) follows the main trail past the rest area up 1800m where it veers off to the right to a 2000m overgrown lookout of the **Santa Lucía waterfall** (150m). All trails are marked by rocks with white and red paint or ribbons tied to trees. Pay special attention to these markers on the way down and at higher elevations.

On the main trail, the hike to the first camp, **Don Tomás** (2000m) is a moderately strenuous 2-3hr. hike that begins by following the **Río Arcagual** and then a series of switchbacks. At 2560m, the terrain begins to transform into a glorious cloudforest with towering trees covered in dripping moss. Still another 2hr. away from the **summit,** this less-trodden portion of the trail is at times camouflaged by encroaching brush and debris; keep your eyes peeled for the bright ribbons that mark the way. From the top, enjoy a breathtaking view of the valleys below, or just imagine one through the clouds. To avoid cloud cover, the best times to reach the summit are early in the morning from February to April.

In addition to the route described above, the peak can also be climbed from the other side starting from the villages of **Belén Gualcho** or **San Manuel Colnonhete,** accessible by infrequent buses from Santa Rosa de Copán or by hired truck. These routes are very underdeveloped and considerably more difficult. A guide from one of the villages is necessary (L200-L300 per day) and you will need several days to make the full trip. Contact the staff at the Proyecto Celaque Office (see above) to help plan such an adventure.

▨ AGUAS TERMALES

From PN Celaque, your return driver or a taxi in Villa Verde (L150-L200) can drive you the 14.5km to the hot springs. In Gracias, Restaurante Guancascos and Hotel Erick take groups of up to 4 to the hot springs (L80). The other option is a 1½hr. hike (not recom-

mended at night). From the southwest corner of Gracias' parque central, head south toward the police station. The roads merge after 5 blocks; make a left at the next corner, cross the street in front of you, and you'll see the path to the springs. Go through a coffee field, across a stable hammock bridge, and continue until you hit the road again. Turn right, and the springs are just ahead. Open daily 6am-midnight. L20.

The *aguas termales* provide the physical therapy necessary after romping through Celaque. Nestled in a river gulch 6.5km south of Gracias, the beautifully crafted stone pools hold crystal-clear water that reaches 38°C (100°F). The springs are very popular in the evenings with locals who eat *papas fritas* and drink beers at the small spring-side *comedor*.

SANTA ROSA DE COPÁN

Visitors arriving at the unimpressive bus station should not be disappointed—a charming colonial center waits 1km up the hill. A pleasant base for exploring nearby indigenous villages and the Honduran highlands, Santa Rosa (pop. 27,800) is a popular stop for visitors intrigued by the country's cultural history. A former tobacco center, the area still produces first-rate cigars (see p. 453), but the nearby countryside is now devoted to another addiction: caffeine. Coffee beans from Santa Rosa are sold nationwide and are considered among the country's finest. A festival on August 30 honors Santa Rosa, the city's patron saint.

E TRANSPORTATION. A transportation hub, Santa Rosa's terminal, on the northwest outskirts of the city, about 1km from the city center, can be a frenzied place, with bus companies competing for business. **Buses** to **San Pedro Sula** leave every half-hour. (3½hr., 4am-5:15pm, L40. Express 2½hr.; 8, 9:30am, and 2pm; L65.) To get to **Tegucigalpa,** take any bus to San Pedro and transfer there, or look for the less frequent "Sultana." (7½hr. 6, 8, 9, 10, 11am. L145.) If you are headed to **Copan Ruins,** catch a bus to **La Entrada** (45min., every 30min. 5am-5pm, L20), and connect there to the ruins (2hr., every 40 min. 6am-6pm, L35). Buses also run to: **Nueva Ocotepeque** (1½hr., every hr. 6am-5:30pm, L45); **Gracias** (1½hr., roughly every hr. 6:30am-6:30pm, L20); **Agua Caliente** (2hr., 9:30am-3:30pm every hr. and at 5pm, L60); and **San Salvador** (daily 8am, L200).

⯑⯑ ORIENTATION AND PRACTICAL INFORMATION. Once you get to **El Centro,** the city is easy to navigate and most activity clusters within a short distance of the *parque*. The main drag, **C. Centenario,** runs east-west along the *parque*'s south side in front of Banco Atlántida and Banco Occidente. The yellow **Cathedral of Santa Rosa** marks the *parque*'s northeast corner.

An awesome ⯑**Office of Tourism** recently opened in the kiosk in the middle of the park with four computers, maps, walking tours of the city, English-speaking representatives, and an upper patio with food and drinks. **Lenca Land Tours** (see **Day Trips from Santa Rosa,** below) can also be scheduled from here. (www.santarosacopan.org. Open M-Sa 8am-8pm, Su 8am-2pm.) **Warren Post,** the American expatriate owner of **Pizza Pizza** (see below), is another great source of information. Both of the towns' **banks** cash traveler's checks and give advances on Visa. **Banco de Occidente** in the southeast corner of the *parque* can wire money and has a second branch next to the terminal (open M-F 8:30am-noon and 2-4:30pm, Sa 8:30-11:30am). **Banco Atlántida,** on the *parque*'s south side next door to Banco Occidente, has a 24hr. **ATM** is Plus network and Visa friendly. (☎662 0138. Open M-F 8:30am-3:30pm, Sa 8:30-11:30am.) A 24hr. **UNIBANC** ATM around the corner from Banco Atlántida, across from Flamingo's, accepts AmEx/Cirrus/Plus/Visa. Take laundry to either **Super Lavandería Florencia,** 4½ blocks west of the southwest corner of the *parque* on C. Centenario towards the soccer fields (☎662 1419, open M-Sa 8am-noon and 1:30-5pm, L78 per load) or **Lavandería Wash and Dry,** 2½ blocks east of the northeast corner of the *parque* past the cathedral (☎662 1653, open daily 6am-9pm, L70 per load). The **police station** is the yellow building on the north end of the *parque*. (☎662 0091, 662 0840, emergency ☎199. Open 24hr.) To get to **Hospital de Occidente**, take C. Centenario 8 blocks west of the *parque*, turn left just before the soccer field, and head up the hill 1 block. (☎662 0112. Open 24hr. for emergencies.) **Hondutel**, on the west side of the park, permits collect calls but no foreign phone cards (open daily 7am-10pm). **Mayanet.com,** in Casa Areas mall 1½ blocks west of the *parque*, across from the cigar outlet, offers the best price in town for fast Internet service. (☎662 1159. Open 8am-noon and 1-10pm. L15 per hr.) If all of the computers are full, another Internet cafe is in the next building over towards the park (L20 per hr.). **Farmacia Central** is one of many pharmacies on the southeast corner of the *parque*, across the street from Banco Atlantida. (☎662 0465. Open M-Sa 8am-6pm.) For basic food shopping, **Manzanitas Supermarket** is 1 block down C. Centenario to the west of the *parque* (☎662 0029. Open daily 8am-6:30pm. AmEx/MC/V.) The **post office** is next to the Hondutel office on the west side of the *parque*. (☎662 1226. Open M-F 8am-noon and 2-5pm, Sa 8am-noon.) **Postal code:** 040101.

⌂⌂ ACCOMMODATIONS AND FOOD. Hotel Maya Central ❷ provides clean, spacious rooms with private baths. The hotel can be found 3 blocks west of the northwest corner of the *parque*. (☎662 0073. Singles L80, with cable TV and hot water L140; doubles L140/L250.) For more style, **Hotel VIP Copán ❸,** 2 blocks east of the northeast corner of the *parque*, has an exquisite lobby, dark wooden ceilings, great rooms, and nice baths. (☎662 0265. Singles L140, with TV L195; doubles L280/L370. Cafeteria open 7-10am and 5-9pm.) **Hotel Blanca Nieves ❷,** 2 blocks east and 2 blocks north of the *parque*'s northeast corner, has cheap uninspiring rooms. (☎662 3012. Singles L70, with hot bath L150; doubles L120/L150 per person.)

⌂Pizza Pizza ❶, 4 blocks east of the southeast corner of the *parque*, bakes brick oven pizza; plenty of topping choices and a cheap L30 lunch special. Owner Warren Post runs a book exchange. (☎662 1104; www.pizzapizza.vze.com. Open M, Tu, Th-Su, 11:30am-9pm. Personal pizza L22.) For a romping good time, **El Rodeo ❸,** 2 blocks south of the *parque*'s southeast corner, is a western style restaurant known for its steak and a decor that includes

mounted cow heads and a stuffed snake. (☎662 0697. Open M-Th 10am-11pm, F-Sa 10am-1am. Rodeo Chicken L83. Steak L103. Tequila Sunrise L30. AmEx/MC/V.) **Restaurante Las Haciendas,** 1 block south and 2 blocks east of the *parque*, serves wood-grilled international specialties with black and white photos of Santa Rosa de Copan's history lining the courtyard walls. (☎662 3518. Open M-Sa 11am-9pm. Meat dishes L65-L80. *Típico* L55. Cordon Bleu L85. AmEx/MC/V.) **Comedor Villa Los Llanos,** 1 block east and a half block north of the *parque*'s southeast corner, is so popular you may have trouble finding enough elbow room to eat your meal. (Open M-Sa 7:30am-7pm. *Típico* L20.) **Flamingo's ❷,** half a block south of the southeast corner of the *parque*, around the corner from Banco Atlántida, serves up fancy food with superb service in a very pink setting. (☎662 0654. *Spaghetti flamingos al horno* L60; seafood and meat dishes starting at L84. Open M, W-Su 10am-10pm. AmEx/MC/V.)

◪ SIGHTS AND ACTIVITIES. Santa Rosa is yet another pleasant spot for a romantic colonial stroll. Take a peek in the yellow and white **Catedral de Santa Rosa,** on the *parque*'s east side, where wooden side altars display devotional items particular to the saints. (Open M-Sa 8am-7pm, Su 5:45am-9:30pm; mass Th 5pm, Su 6am.) The ◪**Flor de Copán** cigar factory, 3 blocks toward the city to the right of the bus terminal, hand-rolls Honduran *puros*, said to rival those of Cuba. Watch the grueling and meticulous process while overwhelmed by the rich aroma. (L35 for Spanish guided tours M-F 10am, 2pm. No cameras allowed.) The **Factory Outlet,** 1½ blocks west of the *parque* on C. Centenario through an inconspicuous gate, sells Flor de Copán's excellent cigars. (☎662 1419. Cigars L80. Box of Corona Santa Rosa L670. Open M-F 8am-noon and 2-4:30pm, Sa 8am-1pm.) At the western end of C. Centenario, past the soccer fields, climb the steps to the top of **El Cerrito** to see the sculpture of an AD 753 Mayan king complete with a beaded necklace and an extravagant headdress. Demonstrating more modern iconography, the "18" graffitied on the statue's chest is the mark of the local gang.

The **Balneario Ecoturístico Las Tres Jotas (JJJ)** is a swimming spot featuring mountain spring water. The pools and cafeteria are on the site of an old fish and tobacco farm, a 10min. ride on the bus headed to Gracias (L12). Be sure to remind the driver when you get close. (Admission and swimming L20. Lunch L45. Open daily 7am-6:30pm.) A pleasant picnic spot with swimming on weekends is **La Montañita,** a 5min. ride on the same bus away from the city (L10).

Hot and sweaty *jovenes* rock out at the popular new-age *discoteca* **Luna Jaguar** 2 blocks east and 1 block south of the *parque*'s southeast corner. The club has a full bar and occasional live bands. (☎662 0910. Open W-Sa 9pm-5am. Entrance varies from L20-L70. Domestic beer L20, imported L30.)

◪ DAYTRIPS FROM SANTA ROSA. For more in-depth exploration of the countryside, **Max Elvir** of **Lenca Land Trails** (at Hotel Elvir in town) can arrange a variety of custom tours starting at around L375 per day. Possibilities include visits to small **Lenca villages, horseback tours,** and **hikes** in Celaque National Park. Contact Max (☎662 1374; lenca@hondutel.hn) to set up a trip or ask questions. Ask about details on how to get to **Quetzal Hill,** a nature preserve just outside the city in San Augustine known for its bird watching.

NUEVA OCOTEPEQUE AND THE BORDER

Wiped out by a flash-flood years ago, the town of Nueva Ocotepeque (what's left of Antigua Ocotepeque) has rebuilt itself into one gigantic bus depot, taking advantage of its close proximity to the borders of both El Salvador and Guatemala.

TRANSPORTATION. The **San José bus** company, 2 blocks north of the park on 1 C., shuttles people to the Salvadoran border at El Poy (15min., every 30min. 7am-7pm, L8); the Guatemalan Border at Agua Caliente (30min., every 30min. 5am-6pm, L15); San Pedro Sula (5hr.; 6, 8, 10, 11am, 1pm; L90); and express to Santa Rosa de Copán (3pm). **Torito/Copanecos,** a half block towards the park on the same side of 1 C., runs to San Pedro Sula with stops at Santa Rosa de Copán and La Entrada (5hr., every hour 4am-6pm, L95); express to Tegus (8hr.; every hour 4am-10am, L175); and shuttles to Agua Caliente (30min., every 30min. 5am-7pm, L15). Across from the southwest corner of the *parque* beneath the large chief logo, **Congolón,** leaves daily for San Pedro Sula stopping at the major cities along the way (5hr.; 2, 6, 6:40, 9:30, 11:30am, 12:30, 1:10, 3:45, 5:30pm; L95); Guatemala City (7½hr., 9:45am, L124); and San Salvador (1½hr., 10:30am, L90). More frequent buses to cities in Guatemala and El Salvador can be found just after crossing the border. The local **Punto de Taxis** is across the street from the San José bus terminal.

ORIENTATION AND PRACTICAL INFORMATION. Calle 1 is the main drag, and runs north-south through the town center along the west side of the *parque central.* Across the *parque,* the **church** faces due east and two smaller streets run parallel to the main street, one directly in front of the church, and the other bisecting the *parque.* The **Municipal Office** anchors the south side of the *parque* across 1 C. **Banco Atlántida,** 1 block north from the northwest corner of the *parque* towards the San José terminal, gives cash advances on Visa (open M-F 8:30am-3:30pm, Sa 8:30-11:30am). Across the street, **Banco de Occidente** wires money and exchanges traveler's checks for US dollars or lempiras, but not colones or quetzals. (☎653 3469. Open M-F 8am-4pm, Sa 8-11am.) The **police station** is 1 block south and 5 blocks west of the southwest corner of the park. (☎653 3199. Open 24hr.) The **Periferica** (☎653 2221), a 10min. ride north of town towards Agua Caliente, provides 24hr. **medical service.** Turn left down the dirt road at the sign indicating medical care. **Hondutel** has an office half a block down the street that bisects the park. (☎653 3001. Open daily 7am-9pm.) Fast and cheap **Internet** access is available at **Skynet,** 1 block west of the southwest corner of the park on the street just before the Congolón terminal. (☎653 3975; juanjmolina@yahoo.com. Open M-Sa 8am-10pm. L15 per hr.) The **post office** is kitty-corner to the church (open M-F 8am-noon and 2-5pm, Sa 8am-noon).

ACCOMMODATIONS AND FOOD. Nueva Ocotepeque is a transit town, but there are some options if you get stranded. Finding clean, affordable accommodations can be tough if you arrive at night, as hotels fill up in the early evening. For a clean room with a private bath the best deal is at **Hotel Internacional ❹,** opposite the northwest corner of the park to the right of the municipal building. Hot water, fan, and a complementary breakfast come with most rooms. Balconies let you spot your bus coming before it arrives (☎653 2357. Reception open 24hr. Singles L169, with A/C L235; doubles L260/L345.) To be close to the bus stops, **Hotel Congolón ❶,** right next to terminal Congolón on 1 C., is new and clean. (☎653 3092. Reception open 5am-noon. Singles L50, with private hot bath, cable, and A/C L150; doubles L120/L250.) **Hotel Ocotepeque ❸,** right next to Torito/Copanecos terminal on 1 C., shows more wear. (☎653 3310. Reception open 24hr. Singles L115, with hot water L130; doubles L180/L200.) Another budget option is **Hotel Turista ❷,** two blocks north on the street that bisects the park, with rooms of varying size. (☎653 3639. L50 per person, with bath L80, with TV L120.)

Comedor San Antonio ❶, on 1 C., provides good budget food in one of the nicest *comedores* you'll see. There's no menu, but a typical plate is L30. (☎653 3041. Open M-Sa 8am-6pm, Su 8am-3pm. Drinks L8.) On the corner, 1 block north on the street that bisects the *parque* is the clean, well-lit **Restaurante Sandoval ❸**. (Breakfasts L30-L40; dinners L60-L100; beers L20. Open daily 6am-9pm. MC/V.) **Restaurante Don Chepe ❸** is in the Maya Chortis hotel. (Chicken entrees L50-L80; salads L30-L80; beers L16. Open daily 7am-10pm. AmEx/MC/V.)

⚑ EL POY: BORDER WITH EL SALVADOR

To get to the border, take a bus from the San José terminal in Nueva Ocotepeque, 2 blocks north of the park on 1 C., marked El Poy. Buses leave approximately every 30 min. (15min., 7am-7pm, L8). Border open 24hr. While there is no fee to leave Honduras, citizens of Canada, US, Malaysia, Mexico, China, Portugal, and Singapore must purchase a tourist card for US$10 to enter Guatemala. To the left of the immigration booths, a tourist office provides bus information and free country maps. In El Salvador, Route 119 buses leave from a parking lot down the street from the gate, running regularly to La Palma (30min., every 30min. 4am-4pm, US$0.60), continuing on to San Salvador (3hr., US$1.70). King Quality buses also go to San Salvador (2hr., 10:30am and 5pm, US$8).

The border at El Poy is about 10km south of Nueva Ocotepeque. **Banco Occidente,** just before the border crossing has **Western Union** service but does not change currency, accept traveler's checks or credit cards. (☎653 3400. Open M-F 8:30am-noon and 1-4:30pm, Sa 8:30-11:30am.) Money changers usually offer good exchange rates for lempiras, quetzals or US dollars.

⚑ AGUA CALIENTE: BORDER WITH GUATEMALA

The San José terminal 2 blocks north of the park on 1 C. and the Torito/Copanecos is a half block towards the park on the same side of 1 C. Both terminals run buses from Nueva Ocotepeque (30min., every 30min. 5am-6pm, L15). Border open 24hr. Honduras exit fee L20. Enter Guatemala free of charge for 90 days. Shuttle runs up the hill to the border whenever it's full (3:30am-8pm, Q5). In Guatemala minibuses run to Esquipulas, where you can connect to destinations throughout the country.

The crossing into Guatemala is 22km from Nueva Ocotepeque. Money changers trade US dollars, quetzals, lempiras, and pesos. If you're stuck here, **Hospedaje Hermanos Ramírez ❷,** across the street from the immigration booths, is your best bet. (☎652 3828. Rooms L100, with bath L250. Cafeteria meal L30. Reception open 3am-9pm.) **Sona Lopez ❹** also offers a few rooms behind the red comedor next door (☎502 422 0123. Rooms with bath L200.) The **border police** are around the corner from the immigration booths. (☎652 3839. Open 24hr.)

COPÁN RUINAS

One kilometer from the ruins, the town of Copán Ruinas (pop. 6300), a pleasant place in its own right, has all of the area's accommodations and restaurants. Hidden in a deep mountain valley, the otherworldly ruins of Copán are a special link in the chain of ancient Maya cities that sweep south from the Yucatán. While some Maya ruins such as Guatemala's Tikal may have taller structures, no site can match the magnitude of Copán's detailed hieroglyphic inscriptions. With an eclectic mix of archaeologists, backpackers, and expats, Copán Ruinas maintains a traveler-friendly atmosphere without losing its tranquility.

▐▀ TRANSPORTATION

Buses: Hedman Alas provides luxury bus service (with A/C, bathroom, and videos) to **San Pedro Sula** (daily 5:30, 10:30am, F-Su 2:30pm; L166), with connections to **Tegus** or **La Ceiba** (L330). Bus departs from the Information Office of Hacienda San Lucas (☎651 4037), 2 blocks north of the park's northeast corner. Office open daily 5am-6pm. The **Casasola** (☎651 4078, office open daily 7am-8pm), next to Hotel Posada, also provides direct shuttle service to **San Pedro Sula** (daily 5:35, 7am, 2pm; L77) which stops at **La Entrada** (L38). **Monarcas Travel**, 1½ blocks north of the *parque's* northeast corner, has a shuttle to **Antigua** (6½hr., daily 2pm, US$15) via **Guatemala City** (5½hr., US$15). **Etumi** bus company (☎651 4021), in the lobby of Hotel Patty 1 block north of the park's northeast corner, runs direct buses to **San Pedro Sula** (3hr.; 6, 8am, 1pm; L80) that stop in **La Entrada** (1hr., L25) and **Santa Rosa de Copan**. Office open daily 6am-9pm. Buses for Casasola, Monarcas, and Etumi companies stop just beyond the bridge from the city, 2 blocks east of the park's northeast corner.

Shuttles: Yaragua Tours leaves 1:30pm daily **Antigua** (6hr., L270); **Guatemala City** (5hr., L360); **Río Dulce** (5hr., L540); **Copán** (6hr., L270); **Flores** (9hr., L1080); **Quirigua** (6hr., L540); **Río Hondo** (2hr., L270); **Tikal** (10hr.); **Panajachel** (9hr.); and **Cichicastenango** (9hr.). **Copán Tours** leaves daily at 2pm to: **Antigua** (L270); **Guatemala City** (L270); **Río Dulce** (L540); and **Panajachel** (L450).

Pickups: Run regularly by Etumi bus service, leave from the bridge 1 block west of the park's northwest corner, to the **Guatemalan Border at El Florido**, 10km away (30min.; leave when full 6am-5:30pm; L10).

Taxis: A few small, red, three-wheeled vehicles transport passengers around town as well as to Macaw Mountain, Enchanted Wings, and the ruins (L5-L50).

▟◿ ORIENTATION AND PRACTICAL INFORMATION

Most buses stop at the bottom of a hill on the eastern edge of Copán Ruinas 2 blocks east of the park's northeast corner, along the path leading from town to the ruins. To get to the *parque central*, head straight uphill and take your second left; you'll be at the *parque's* northeast corner, marked by **Banco de Occidente**. The **church** sits on the east side of the park and the town hall lies along the west side. The entrance to the **ruins** is 1km from Copán Ruinas on the road east of the northeast corner of the park; all of the services and hotels are in town.

Tourist Office and Tours:

Tourist Information Office (☎651 4495; www.copanhonduras.com.), ½ a block north of the park's northeast corner, has city maps and can help with hotel and restaurant reservations. Open daily 2-6pm.

Yaragua Tours (☎651 4147; www.yaragua.com), next to the Yaragua Hotel, has free maps and tour packages to a number of local attractions. Office open daily 7am-9pm. Call beforehand to arrange tour. Traveler's checks accepted. AmEx/MC/V.

Via Via Tours, at the Via Via Cafe (see below), is run by former world-traveling backpackers who share their wealth of travel information. Tours include horseback riding (3-4hr., L180), Finca Marisol (4-5hr., L270), bushwhacking (3-6hr., leave at 7:30am daily, L90), Hacienda San Lucas (entrance fee L30), Aguas Termales (3-4hr., shuttles at 8am and 2pm, L90 plus entrance fee), and Finca El Cisne (L180-L1080, camping L90).

Go Native Tours, in Tunkul Restaurant (☎975 2974, 651 4410) plans tours and rents mountain bikes (L15 per day). Ask about the "cowboy for a day" package.

Copán Tours, across from the Tourist Information Office, has similar tour deals to Yaragua.

MC Tours (☎651 4453; www.mctours-honduras.com), across the street from the Hotel Marina Copán, 1 block north of the park's northwest corner, offers fairly expensive packages.

Banks: All banks cash traveler's checks. **Banco Atlántida** (☎651 4505), on the *parque's* south side, gives Visa advances. 24hr. ATM. Open M-F 8:30am-3:30pm, Sa 8:30-11:30am. **Banco Credomatic** (☎651 4686), next door to Atlántida, has a 24hr. ATM that accepts AmEx/Cirrus/MC/Plus/V. Open daily 9am-5pm. **Banco de Occidente** (☎651 4084), on the *parque's* northeast corner, wires money. Open M-F 8:30am-4:30pm, Sa 8:30am-noon.

Police: FUSEP (☎651 4060), 4½ blocks west of the southwest corner of the *parque.* A 2nd outpost is on the road to the ruins. Both open 24hr.

Pharmacy: Farmacia Ángel (☎651 4603). ½ a block south of the *parque's* southeast corner. Open M-Sa 8am-8pm and Su 8:30am-7pm. AmEx/MC/V.

Medical Services: Dr. Luis Castro (☎651 4504), west from the northwest corner of the *parque,* across the street from the cemetery toward the Guatemalan border, speaks English. Open M-Sa 8am-5pm. Two **medical clinics** are in town, one located 1 block south of the park's southwest corner and ½ a block to the west, the other 1 block east of the park's northeast corner and ½ a block north.

Telephones: Hondutel (☎651 4004), ½ block south of the *parque's* southwest corner on the right. Open daily 7am-9pm.

Internet: Cop0225n Net (☎651 4460), 1 block south and 1 block west of the southwest corner of the park, offers service for L20 per hr. with a 30min. minimum. Open daily 9am-9pm. **Maya Connections** (☎651 4315 or 651 4469) has one location in Casa de Todo, 1 block east of the park's northeast corner, and another 1 block south of the *parque's* southwest corner. L20 per hr. with a 15min. minimum. Open daily 7am-9pm. AmEx/MC/V. Both locations have **laundry service.** L8 per lb. for a same day wash, dry, and fold. Open daily 7am-9pm.

Post Office: Honducor is ½ block west of the southwest corner of the *parque.* Open M-F 8am-noon, 2-5pm; Sa 8am-noon. Postal code: 41209.

▌ ACCOMMODATIONS

Local kids on the street or at the border may try to steer you away from your desired hotel to a friend's guest house by claiming the hotel does not exist or is more expensive than it really is. Usually, these kids are trying to rob you.

▨ **En la Manzana Verde** (☎980 0355; www.enlamanzanaverde.com), 1½ blocks north of the *parque's* northeast corner on the left, may be Central America's best hostel. Dorm-style rooms with a sense of humor have individually named beds, fans, and hot water showers. Full kitchen, TV lounge, sink for washing clothes, and luggage storage. If you're in town for a while, help run the place and stay for free. L70 per night. ❶

▨ **Via Via Copán** (☎651 4652; www.viaviacafe.com), 1½ blocks west of the park's southwest corner, has an environment worth the price tag. Run by four world travelers, Via Via Copán has become a Mecca for all who pass though Copán. Spotless rooms all have hot baths, fans, and free iced lemonade and unlimited purified water. Eclectic cafe. Reception open 24hr. Check-out 10am. Singles L180; doubles L220. Discounts if you stay longer than a week. ❹

Hostel Iguana Azul (☎651 4620; casacafe@hondutel.hn). From the *parque's* southwest corner go 1 block south, right 5 blocks, then turn left again toward the blue building. Clean dorm-style hostel with friendly management, communal showers, hot water, and comfy beds. Bunks L75 per person; singles L150; doubles L200. ❷

Los Gemelos (☎651 4077), just up the street from the bus stop, 1 block east of the park and ½ a block north on the right. A traveler favorite for its friendly service, low prices, central location, and clean, simple rooms with shared hot showers. The courtyard is a great place to meet other travelers. Reception open 7am-11pm, check-out 10am. Free luggage storage. Singles L80; doubles L120; triples L180. ❷

Posada Honduras (☎651 4082), just north of Gemelos on the same block. Standard issue, with clean rooms and baths. Large, open courtyard with tropical plants. Desk open 5am-11pm. Singles L70, with hot water and fan L100; doubles L80/L120. ❷

FOOD AND NIGHTLIFE

▨ **Via Via Café** (☎651 4652; www.viaviacafe.com), in the hotel of the same name (see **Accommodations,** above) is a traveler's heaven. With a delectable health food menu including two dozen daily vegetarian entrees and freshly baked bread (loafs for L30), every meal will bowl you over with savory flavor. At night, candle-lit tables set the scene while international music keeps the atmosphere hopping. Granola L10, *chili sin carne* L65, sweet and sour chicken L80, shakes L25. Open daily 7am-10pm. ❷

▨ **Vamos a Ver** (☎651 4627; www.vamosaver.com), ½ block south of the southwest corner of the parque on the right. Friendly Dutch couple serves fresh baked bread (L30) in a fun multi-lingual environment. Patrons entertain each other on the guitar borrowed from the owners. Vegetarian dishes. Muesli and fruit L45; vegetarian quiche L85; lasagna L80. Happy hour 5-7pm with 2-for-1 cocktails. Open daily 7am-10pm. ❸

Jim's Pizza Copan (☎651 4381), ½ block south of the southwest corner of the park, on the left. An American sailor cooks up 12″ handmade pizza using only the freshest local cheese and vegetables. Come for nightly movies at 7pm. Pizza with the works ("Captain Pat") L150. Veggie L100. Open daily 11am-9pm. ❷

Casa de Todo (☎651 4495), 1 block east of the park's northeast corner, offers delicious fresh smoothies (L25) and sandwiches (L45) on a charming patio. Surf the Internet while you wait for your laundry or pick out a book from the large book exchange. Knowledgeable owner Sandra is a good local travel resource. Open daily 7am-9pm. ❷

Licuados Express (☎651 4152; justoatiempo@yahoo.com), 1 block east of the park's northeast corner across the street from the Tourist Office. Run by a warm-hearted Texan who hand rolls sourdough bagels and tantalizes travelers with secret hummus and cinnamon rolls recipes. Open daily 6:30am-5pm. Smoothies L20-L30, cappucino L25, Belgian waffles L35, sandwiches L35. Fresh bag meals for takeout. ❷

Carnitas Nia Lola (☎651 4196; nialola@yahoo.com), 2 blocks south of the southwest corner of the *parque*, at the end of the street on the right. Fun bungalow atmosphere with a book exchange, open hearth cooking, and waitresses who bring your drinks balanced on their head. Free nachos with meal. *Pinchos* L100, chicken tacos L32. Happy hour 6:30-8pm with 2-for-1 margaritas. Open 7am-10pm. AmEx/MC/V. ❷

Twisted Tanya (☎651 4182), 1 block south of the park then 1 block to the right toward the west. Tanya is known among the locals for having the best drinks in town. Enjoy the fine dining on the 2nd fl. seating and 2-for-1 cocktails during happy hour (4-6pm). Salmon in lemon sauce L180. Tequila L40. Open M-Sa 11am-10pm. ❺

Tunkul Restaurante and Bar (☎651 4410), 1½ blocks west of the *parque*'s southwest corner, next to Via Via. The place to see and be seen in Copán, whether you're gringo, expat, or local. Friendly owners play host to the town's nightlife during happy hour (7-8pm and 10-11pm with 2-for-1 cocktails). Delicious rum punch L30 all night. Kitchen serves a good variety, including a vegetarian plate (L65), chicken fajitas (L90), and chef salad (L65). Open daily until midnight. AmEx/MC/V. ❸

 SIGHTS

IN TOWN

Though originally designed for children, the ▨**Casa K'Inich Museum,** just behind a series of stores on the northern edge of the *parque*, has interactive displays that now teach visitors of all ages how to read the symbols in Maya hieroglyphics, how stelae are dressed, and the rules of the ancient ball games. (www.casakinich.com. Open daily 8am-noon and 1-5pm. Free.) On the *parque*'s east side, across from the church, **The Copán Museum of Archaeology** contains very detailed information on countless aspects of Maya civilizations and stunning displays of well-preserved ceramics, stone carvings, and human fossils. (Open daily 9am-5pm. L35. English-speaking guides of the ruins L70.) **The Galería de Arte,** 1 block south of the park's southeast corner, displays and sells magnificent pieces, demonstrating more contemporary Honduran artwork. (Open daily 7am-7pm. AmEx/MC/V.)

OUTSIDE OF TOWN

From the northwest corner of the park, walk west down the road to Guatemala, past the cemetery, to the highway intersection where you will find the **Enchanted Wings Butterfly House.** More than 15 butterfly species flutter around the 3200 sq. ft. terraced enclosure, floating above 200 species of native orchids. (☎651 4133; www.hondurasecotours.com. Open daily 8am-5pm. L100. Bilingual tour guides L50. Best time to see orchids is Apr.-May.) In the opposite direction, **Macaw Mountain** is a park dedicated to Central America's tropical birds. Two kilometers north of town, this sanctuary began as an adoption agency for pet birds left behind by temporary residents of Roatán. Today, Macaw Mountain houses more than 95 flamboyantly colored birds in a thick forest with many native species of its own. Guides bring them out of their cages for tourists to admire. (☎651 4245; www.macawmountain.com. Open daily 9am-5pm. L180.)

THE RUINS OF COPÁN

Dubbed the "Athens of the New World" by archaeologist Sylvanus Morley, the Classic Maya civilization of Copán contains over 4500 ruins and more stelae and altars than any other Maya site in Central America. Visitors see first hand the extensive hieroglyphics of Mesoamerica's most developed ancient written language along with the longest inscribed text in the New World. Although Copán has given archaeologists one of the most complete pictures of Maya culture, a sense of mystery and wonderment still lives in these walls.

◑ HISTORY

Called *Xukpi* by the Maya, Copán's impressive history is inscribed on the surface of Altar Q, dedicated to the founder of the Copán dynasty: Yax K'uk' Mo'. The inscription explains that in AD 426, Yax K'uk' Mo' rose to power in a city far from Copán. On September 8th of that year, he left his kingdom, setting out for Copán. When he arrived in Copán, he displaced the ruler and erected a new palace of his own. Part of Yax K'uk Mo's success was that his arrival coincided with the end of a *Baktun*, a symbolically important 400-year-long period on the Maya calendar. This event, similar to the modern day millennium, made Yax K'uk' Mo's arrival seem both powerful and miraculous.

Yax K'uk' Mo' solidified his god-like image by transforming Copán into a majestic city. Building on the people's religious beliefs, he commissioned four new structures (the ball court and structures 7, 11, and 26) reflecting the four corners of the cosmos and commemorating the 400-year-long period that ended with his arrival. By inscribing the name of his son into the floor of one of the structures, Yax K'uk' Mo' gave supernatural legitimacy to his dynasty and also created an intense belief in numerology that eventually lead to Copán's desertion.

In AD 763 a new king, Yax Pasah, rose to the throne without any blood relation to Yax K'uk' Mo. With the end of another 400-year period on the horizon and the original bloodline no longer on the throne, Yax Pasah foresaw the end of the

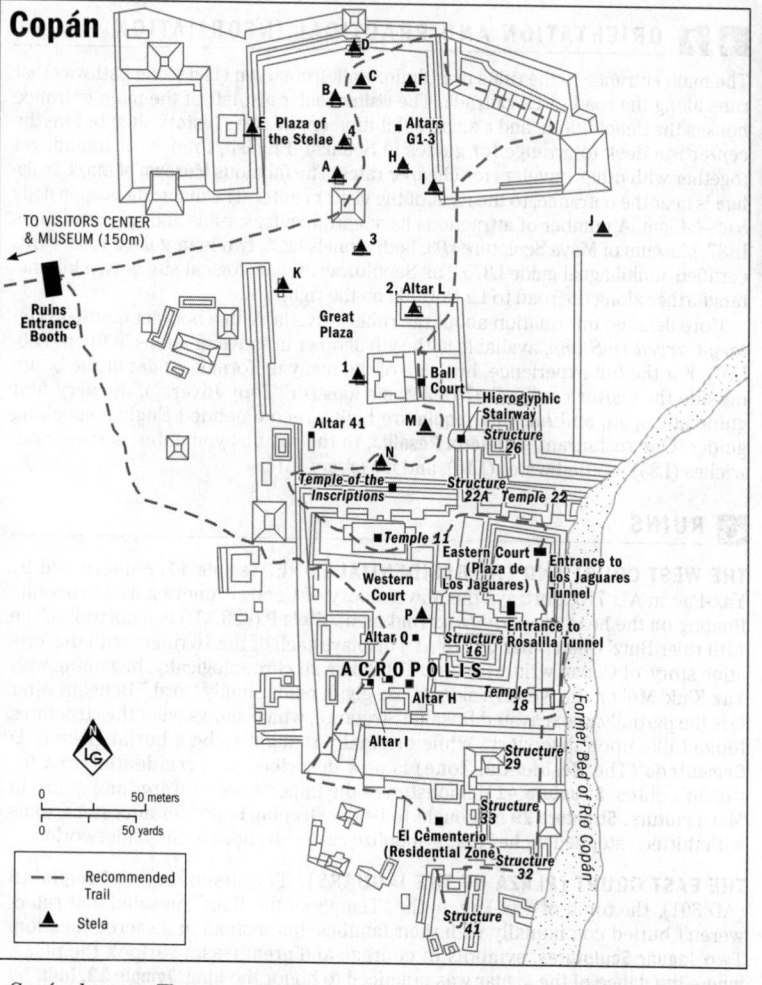

Copán dynasty. The city had been ruled by 16 kings, four sets of four over a 400 year period: a perfectly calculated end to a great civilization. He dedicated his rule to finishing the projects started by his predecessors. When all of the structures were completed, Yax Pasah ordered the construction of Altar Q, which depicts the end of the dynasty. When Yax Pasah died in AD 820, the people accepted the dynasty's end and burned his funerary temple. Before the city was abandoned, one last stela was erected depicting Yax Pasah passing the dynasty's emblem to "a king who never rules, on an altar that is never completed."

In 1834, Spaniard Juan Galindo drew the first map of the ruins, sparking the interest of Americans John L. Stephens and Frederick Catherwood, whose 1841 book *Incidents of Travel in Central America, Chiapas, and the Yucatán* introduced Copán to the world. In 1891, the first archaeological study was made and today this UNESCO site is the most studied Maya site in the world.

 **ORIENTATION AND PRACTICAL INFORMATION**

The main entrance to the ruins is a 15min. walk from town via a stone pathway that runs along the road to La Entrada. The **visitor center** just left of the main entrance houses the ticket booth, and a small exhibition on the site's history. Just before the center is a desk to arrange for guides in Spanish, English, French, or Italian; get together with other travelers for cheaper rates. The fabulous **Museum of Maya Sculpture** is near the entrance, to the right of the visitor center. The main site is open daily 8am-4:45pm. A number of attractions have entrance fees: ruins and Las Sepulturas L187, Museum of Maya Sculpture L93, both tunnels L225, two-hour guided tour with a certified, multilingual guide L375. Las Sepulturas archaeological site is two kilometers farther along the road to La Entrada on the right.

More detailed information about the ruins is available in a booklet entitled *History Carved in Stone*, available in the gift shop or in souvenir shops in town (L60-L70). For the full experience, hire one of the many uniformed **guides** at the booth outside the visitor center (L375). **Antonio Ríos** (or "Tony Rivers"), the very first guide at Copán, and **Juan Marroquín** are highly recommended English-speaking guides. One restaurant, **Cafetería Rosalila,** to the right as you enter, serves sandwiches (L35), bottled water (L10), and ice cream (L18).

⊙ RUINS

THE WEST COURT AND THE RESIDENTIAL ZONE. Temple 11, constructed by Yax-Pac in AD 773, portrays the Maya theory of Central America as a crocodile floating on the head of *pauahtuns* (old men). **Stela P** (623 AD) is a portrait of the 11th ruler Butz' Chan. **Altar Q** (775 AD) displays each of the 16 rulers with the 'creation story' of Copan written on top. The rulers sit chronologically, beginning with Yax K'uk' Mo' on the western side whose glyph reads simply "lord." Beneath Altar Q is the partially unexcavated Rosalila Structure, which shows what the structures looked like upon discovery. While originally thought to be a burial ground, **El Cementerio** (The Residential Zone) is now described as a residential area for Copán's elites. **Structure 41** demonstrates the importance of water and maize in Maya culture. **Structure 29** is thought to be the sleeping house for ancestors' souls with thirteen stepped niches that symbolize cave entrances to the underworld.

THE EAST COURT (PLAZA OF THE JAGUARS). The discovery of **Temple 18** (AD 801), the tomb of Yax-Pac, in the "Temple of the Rain" revealed that rulers weren't buried communally with their families, but instead in a sacred location. Two **Jaguar Sculptures,** symbols of courage and greatness, overlook the plaza, where the dance of the jaguar was practiced to honor the king. **Temple 22,** built by 18 Rabbit, has some of Copán's most intricate carvings and elaborate symbolism. Used as the king's seat for ceremonies, the plateau represents the mouth of a cave or earth monster. Atop **Structure 22A** sat the throne of Smoke Monkey and the Council House, or *Popol Nah*. The nine figures that once stood here pointed towards the divisions they controlled, all wearing loincloths to show their rank, but each with different headdresses from their regions. White flowers indicate that the soul of the community resides in this place.

TUNNELS. Many travelers find the **Rosalila Tunnel** and **Los Jaguares Tunnel** overpriced (L225) and overrated. Without an expert's eye it's hard to appreciate the architecture, but they are an interesting experience just the same. Excavations within **Structure 16** found the beautifully preserved stucco Rosalila Structure AD 571, which honors the sun god. This building was so sacred the Maya did not destroy and rebuild it as they did with most other structures. For this reason, Rosalila is one of the most well-preserved underground temples on earth. The Los Jaguares tunnel displays evidence of an advanced draining system and the only private bath in all Maya civilization.

THE GREAT PLAZA. The **Hieroglyphic Stairway** is the longest known piece of hieroglyphic writing in the Americas. The intricate carvings and inscriptions on the 63 steps depict the genealogy of Copán's rulers and the city's history from its mythical beginnings through the reign of its 15th ruler, Smoke Shell, the last of Yax K'uk' Mo's line. **Stela M** (AD 756) recounts a solar eclipse, which along with an accurate depiction of Venus' orbit in the **Temple of Inscriptions**, demonstrates the Maya's advanced understanding of astronomy. The **Ballcourt** (AD 738), is where teams would try hitting one of the three macaw heads on either side of the court with a solid rubber ball using only their hips. The game was viewed as a religious conquest over evil and the winning players were sacrificed to the sun god. **Stela 2** (AD 652) overlooking the Ballcourt is the portrait of Smoke Jaguar. Behind it, **Altar L** (AD 882) is the last sculpture constructed in Copán by U Kit Tok in an attempt to revive the ruling authority. One side depicts Yax Pasah passing the torch of authority and the other side was never finished. The **Great Plaza** is surrounded by the ruins of a massive stadium and the well-preserved **Structure 4** anchors the middle. Stelae in this area depict 18 Rabbit. **Stela C** shows him as a young, unbearded man on one side, and as an old man on the reverse, symbolizing the life cycle.

🏛 MUSEUM OF MAYA SCULPTURE

The large building by the site entrance is a splendid museum that will give you an informed perspective on the ruins; you may want to come here before entering the site. Unique in the Americas, the massive complex was built to house and protect the park's most precious sculptures from the area's moisture and temperature fluctuations. Several important stelae and altars have already been relocated inside the museum and replicas left in their place in the ruins. Of these, highlights are the famed **Altar Q, Stela A,** and **Old Man Head.** Be sure not to miss the **Hijole Structure,** the highest relief sculpture found at Copán, that originally adorned an earlier version of Temple 22. The centerpiece of the museum, however, is the full-sized, brightly painted replica of **Rosalila,** the temple found buried beneath Structure 16, with all of its original paint and carvings intact. The replica suggests how flamboyant and colorful Copán was in its heyday.

🔁 DAYTRIPS FROM COPÁN

LAS SEPULTURAS

Las Sepulturas is 2km beyond the main site headed east on the road towards La Entrada from Copán Ruinas. Admission to Las Sepulturas is included with admission to the ruins. Open daily 7am-4pm. Guides are available in Spanish for an appropriate tip.

A nearby site that is getting an invigorating reexamination, Las Sepulturas (the tombs) are not too aptly named. These structures were actually residential appendages to Copán for Maya elite. The platforms are not as awe-inspiring as the ruins at Copán, but they've sparked a small frenzy among archaeologists intrigued with the social stratification of the Copán dynasty. When approaching the site on foot, take the small trail off to the right rather than continuing on the dirt road. The trail winds through pleasant green foliage before opening up to the first series of residential dwellings. As you continue, buildings get taller and culminate with the residences of the rich and powerful and the impressive scribe's palace with scribes on either side holding ink pots and styluses and the central figure above the doorway portraying the owner.

LOS SAPOS

To walk to the Hacienda from Copán Ruinas, head south from the parque's southeast corner on the street in front of the church. Stay to the right as the dirt road begins, passing the carwash. Continue to the bridge, cross the river, and turn left. Up the hill, Hacienda San Lucas on the right has great trail maps included with an L30 entrance. The trail to Los Sapos, marked by white painted rocks, is off to the left just past the farmhouse. To reserve rooms at the farm house or schedule a guide for your trip, turn left facing the church and walk straight from the northeast corner of the park about 2 blocks up the hill to the Hacienda's information center in the same building as the Hedman Alas terminal (☎651 4106; open daily 9am-5pm). Lunch L180, shuttle to San Lucas (L300). Entrance fee is included in the package trips run by the information center.

One small piece of the Copán story, Los Sapos (The Toads) sits on the town's outlying hills, about a 30min. walk from Copán Ruinas. A group of rock outcroppings carved around AD 300 features two very amphibian looking beings, leading some archaeologists to believe the site was a birthing site for Maya women. Toads are the Maya symbol of fertility and one stone appears to resemble a pregnant woman. Some archaeologists have declared that the pregnant woman is not a woman at all, but an abnormally well-endowed man holding a perforator for self-sacrifice.

The stones sit on the grounds of the **Hacienda San Lucas ❺**, a beautifully restored *hacienda* with views overlooking the entire valley. The property also includes a network of birdwatching trails and a small waterfall. Meals and lodging with hot private baths are available. Horseback rides around the *hacienda* (L187) are a fun way to spend the afternoon. (☎651 4495; sanlucas@copanruinas.com. Singles L900; doubles L1080; triples L1260. Breakfast included.)

POOLS AND CAVES

The hot springs are open daily 8am-8pm, L20. Both Vamos a Ver and Yaragua Tours organize trips daily 2pm (L180 per person). Via Via Tours also has daily departures at 8:30am and 2pm (3-person minimum, L90 per person) or can arrange for a private truck to take a group (L700 round-trip for up to eight people.) Cave trips are led by Go Native Tours (L655 per person, 3-person minimum.) and Yaragua Tours (L540). Ruby Waterfall (3-4hr., L270) and tubing (2-3hr., L180) excursions are run by Yaragua Tours.

A respite from civilizations past and present, the **hot springs** 23km north of town are a welcome sight for the weary. Lounge in the two large stone pools or stroll down to where the springs meet the river to find your favorite water temperature. A short hike above the pools, watch the spring water bubbling up from its volcanic roots, but be cautious as the water here is extremely hot. There are several caves near town, but you must hire a guide to access them. A good option is to explore the extensive cave system and underground river of **Cueva de Boqueron,** 23km from town. While a November 2001 machete attack made **Ruby Waterfall** a less frequented destination, Yaragua Tours now organizes trips lead by two armed guides to this watering hole's smooth rock banks and deep water. Yaragua also offers one of the most popular activities for people with extra time: **tubing** down the river, where visitors enjoy a tour of much of the countryside in the slow, relaxing flow.

⚞ EL FLORIDO: BORDER WITH GUATEMALA

Border open daily 6am-7pm (☎651 4442). Pickups run back and forth 6am-5:30pm (L10-L20). Transportes Vilma (open 6am-6pm) on the Guatemalan side, runs buses to Chiquimula (1½hr.; M-Sa every hour, Su every 30 min. 5:30am-4:30pm; Q8-12); Guatemala City (4½hr.; M-Sa 4:15am, Su noon; Q30); and Petén (daily at 6am, Q35). Taxis also run to nearby Jocotan at any hour.

A commonly attempted scam is for border officials to charge travelers for a US$20 passport extension instead of the required US$3 pass. For those just entering Honduras to see Copán, request a longer stamp than the 72hr. permit to avoid having to pay the US$20 fee on the way back. A 24hr. Guatemalan **police office** is just beyond the border on the left. **Banrural** which does not accept traveler's checks or credit cards but does wire money (open M-F 8am-5pm, Sa 8am-1pm). **Money changers** offer good rates on lempira, quetzal, or US dollar exchange. If you get stuck, **Las Rosas,** above the red *comedor*, offers adequate rooms with shared bath, but no hot water. (☎502 979 7543. Reception open 5am-8pm. Q25 per person.).

CARIBBEAN COAST

Honduras' long, hot Caribbean coastline is lined by great beaches, beautiful national parks, wildlife reserves, old Spanish forts, and tiny Garífuna villages. La Ceiba, the region's urban center is the country's main party town. Other cities include backpacker favorite, Tela; Caribbean hub Puerto Cortés; and the gateway to La Mosquitia, Trujillo. The region has a gregarious Caribbean atmosphere where English or Creole are as common as Spanish.

The 17th century saw this region marred by the African slave trade. As slaves escaped or were emancipated, they intermarried with South American indigenous people. Their descendants built fishing communities along the northern shores, with a distinctive culture and language. Today, the **Garífuna,** (as they came to be called) are one of the fastest-growing ethnic groups in Central America. Their thatched-roof villages, dugout canoes, and colorful *punta* music are among the most captivating highlights of the Caribbean coast.

SAN PEDRO SULA

Once a sleepy provincial town, modern San Pedro Sula (pop. 415,000) is Honduras' major industrial city. *Maquiladoras,* foreign-owned factories, pop up all along the city's well-maintained highway system, profiting off of minimal-wage labor. Despite its recent industrial awakening, San Pedro has a relaxed air that makes it an ideal gateway to either the ancient Maya ruins at Copán or the pristine beaches of the Caribbean. A recent crackdown has reduced crime; however, the southeast quadrant still remains dangerous and travelers should use taxis at night.

▐▀ TRANSPORTATION

Flights: Villeda Morales International Airport is 15km out of town. It is best to take a taxi to and from the airport (L150). **Continental** (☎557 4141; fax 552 9766) and **American** (☎558 0518) fly to the US. **Isleña Airlines** (☎552 8335; fax 552 8322) flies to **La Ceiba** (20min.; 8:30am and 2pm; L380, round-trip L646), from where you will need to connect to go to **Roatán** (1¼hr.; take La Ceiba and change; L667; round-trip L1220). **Taca** (☎550 2640) heads to **Tegucigalpa** (25min.; 6:55, 10:45am, 4:15pm; L476, round-trip L953).

Buses: Located in the southwest (SO) sector, most bus stations are little more than parking lots with temporary wooden shacks. Any station can direct you to the bus you need. **Chicken buses** run from 4 stations: one on 1 Av. and 2/3 C. on the slightly sketchier side of the tracks; the 2nd from a parking lot on 2 Av. and 7/8 C. SO; the 3d from the corner of 8 C. and 8 Av. SO; and the 4th from the south side of 9 C. between 4-6 Av. SO. Buses run to destinations within and just outside the city such as **Chalmeca, Naco Cortez,** and **San Marcos.** It is best to travel during the day. If you

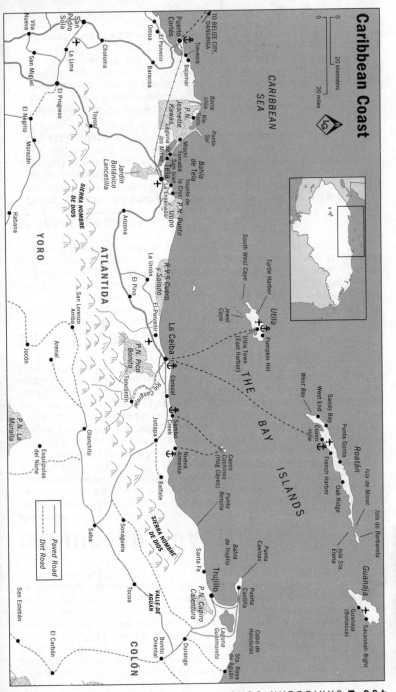

Caribbean Coast

HONDURAS

CARIBBEAN SEA

THE BAY ISLANDS

Paved Road
Dirt Road

TO BELIZE CITY,
DANGRIGA

20 kilometers
20 miles

San Pedro
Sula

Villa
Nueva

Omoa

El Porvenir

Choloma

La Lima

San Miguel

El Progreso

El Negrito

Morazán

Habana

YORO

SIERRA NOMBRE
DE DIOS

Jardin
Botánico
Lancetilla

Puerto
Cortés

Travesía

Bajamar

Baracoa

Toyos

Barra
Río
Ulúa

Punta
Sal

P.N.
Jeanette
Kawas
Laguna de
los Micos

Miami
Tornabé
San Juan
La Cruz

Bahía
de Tela

Triunfo de
la Cruz

Tela

La Ensenada

Arizona

La Unión

El Pino

R.V.S Cuero
y Salado

El Porvenir

ATLANTIDA

P.N. Pico
Bonito

Toncontín

Río Cangrejal

La Ceiba

Corozal

Sambo
Creek

Nueva
Armenia

Olanchito

Jutiapa

Balfate

Sonaguera

Saba

Tocoa

Arenal

San Lorenzo
Arriba

Jocón

P.N. La
Muralla

Esquipulas
del Norte

San Esteban

El Carbón

COLÓN

Durango

Bonito
Oriental

Laguna
Guaimoreto

Sta. Rosa
de Aguán

Cabo de
Honduras

Puerto
Castilla

Trujillo

P.N. Capiro
Calentura

VALLE DE
AGUÁN

SIERRA NOMBRE
DE DIOS

Santa Fe

Bahía
de Trujillo

Punta
Caxinas

Cayos
Cochinos
(Hog Cayes)

Punta
Betulia

South West Caye

Turtle Harbor

Jewel
Caye

Utila

Pumpkin Hill

Utila Town
(East Harbor)

West Bay

West End
Sandy Bay
Half
Moon

Coxen
Hole

Flowers
Bay

French Harbor

Oak Ridge

Punta Gorda

Roatán

Isla de Morat

Isla Sta.
Elena

Isla de Barbareta

Guanaja
(Bonacca)

Guanaja

Savannah Bight

must make a connection between terminals at night, cabs are strongly advised even for a few short blocks; otherwise, you could arrive with less luggage than you began with. La Ceiba's bus companies are:

Casasola: Av. 6/7, C. 6 SO. Buses to: **Copán Ruinas** (3hr.; 8, 10:30, 11:30am, 1, 2pm; L77).

Catista-Tupsa: ☎552 1042 or 553 1023, Av. 2, C. 5/6 SO. Buses to: **La Ceiba** (3hr., 6am-6pm, L65); **Progreso** (every 8min. 5am-8:30pm, L11, direct L13.65); and **Tela** (every hr. 5am-8:30pm.).

CITUL: ☎553 0070 or 558 1594, Av. 6, C. 7/8, SE. Minibuses to **Puerto Cortés** (1½hr., every 15min. 4:30am-9pm; direct buses 1hr., every 30min., L16.50/L20).

Congolón: Av. 8, C. 9/10 SO. Buses to: **Agua Caliente** (4½hr.; 6, 7:30, 9, 11am, 1:30pm, midnight; day buses L110 and midnight bus L145); **Guatemala City** (8½hr.; 5:45am; L445); and **San Salvador** (5hr.; 6:15am; L265).

Copanecos: ☎553 1954, Av. 6, C. 8/9 SO. Buses to **Santa Rosa de Copán** (3hr., every 30min. 4am-5:15pm, L40; 1½hr. direct L66).

COTRAIPBAL: ☎557 8470, Av. 1, C. 6/7SE. Runs to **Trujillo** (5½hr., every 45min. 5:15am-4pm, L110).

El Rey: ☎553 4264, Av. 7, 6 C. SO. Buses to: **La Ceiba** (3hr.; every hr. 6am-5:30pm; L66) and **Tegucigalpa** (5hr.; 3:30am, every 1½hr. 6am-6pm; L65).

El Rey Express: ☎ 225 1112 or 550 8355; mercado@reyexpress.net, Av. 9, C. 9 SO. Buses to: **Copán Ruinas** (2½hr., 8, 11am, 2pm; L77); **La Ceiba** (3hr.; 6, 7:30, 8:30, 10:30am, 12:30, 1:30, 2:30, 4:30, 5:30pm; L66); and **Tegucigalpa** (4hr.; every hr. 5:30-9:30am, 11:30am, 1pm, every hr. 2:30-6:30pm; L94).

Etica: Av. 5, C. 10/11 SO. Buses to **Cofradia** (1hr., every 20min. 5:45-10:10pm, L9).

Hedman Alas: ☎553 1361; www.hedmanalas.com, Av. 9, C. 3 NO. Buses to: **Antigua** (9hr., 9:50am, L941); **Copán Ruinas** (3hr.; 10:40am and 2:50pm; L132); **Guatemala City** (8hr., 9:50am, L830); **La Ceiba** (3hr.; 6, 10:20am, 2:20, 6pm; L132); **San Salvador** (7hr., 9:35am, L612); **Tegucigalpa** (4hr.; 5:45, 6:30, 8:30, 9, 10:30am, noon, 1:45, 3, 4, 5:30pm; L118-L165); and **Tela** (2hr.; 10:10am, 2:15, 6:10pm; L148).

Impala: ☎553 3111, Av. 2, C. 4/5SE. Buses to **Puerto Cortés** (1½hr., every 20min. 4am-6pm, L47).

King Quality: ☎534 4547, Av. 9, C. 2, SO. Buses with A/C to **San Salvador** (6hr.; 6:30am, 2:30pm; L46).

Norteños: ☎552 2145, Av. 6/7, C. 6, SO. Buses to **Tegucigalpa** (4½hr., every 1½hr. 6am-4pm, L60).

San José: Av. 6, C. 7, SO. Buses to **Ocotepeque** (5hr.; 5, 7:30, 9, 10:30am, 1pm; L100).

San Ramón: ☎977 0757, Av. 1/2, 9 C., SE. Buses to **Siguatepeque** (2½hr.; 6am, 4pm; L35).

Sultana: Av. 6, C. 8/9 SO. Buses to: **Agua Caliente** (5hr.; 11:30am, 12:30, 2:30, 3pm, midnight; L110) and **Ocotepeque** (4½hr.; 11:30am, 12:30, 2:30, 3pm, midnight; L95).

Torito: ☎553 4930, Av. 6, C. 8/9 SO. Buses every hr. to: **Agua Caliente** (4½hr.; 7, 8am, 10:30am-3:30pm; L110); **Ocotepeque** (4½hr.; 10:30am-3:30pm, additional buses 7, 8am; L95); **Santa Rosa de Copán** (2hr., 10:30am-3:30pm, additional buses 7, 8am; L65); **San Salvador** (5hr., 6:15am, L264); and **Tegucigalpa** (4½hr., 7, 11:30am, 1pm, 2, L65).

Transporte de Gama: ☎552 2861, Av. 6/7, C. 6, SO. Buses to **Copán Ruinas** (3hr.; 7, 11am, 1:30, 3pm; L77).

Local Transportation: Taxi rides within the city are L30-L40, after dark L40-L60. Establish a price beforehand. Taxis are generally safe and should be used around the city at night, even for short distances.

✳❼ ORIENTATION AND PRACTICAL INFORMATION

San Pedro Sula is organized along the standard grid, with *avenidas* running north and south and *calles* running east and west. The city is divided into quadrants: NO (northwest), NE (northeast), SO (southwest), and SE (southeast), with the *parque central* in the center. The **Circunvalación,** a fast-food infused commercial strip, forms a beltway around the city, with highways to other cities radiating from it. Bus stations and most budget hotels are southwest of the *parque*. The railroad

San Pedro Sula

🏠 ACCOMMODATIONS
Hotel Bolivar, **5**
Hotel El Centro, **11**
Hotel Real, **21**
Hotel San José, **16**
Hotel Terraza, **10**

🍎 FOOD
Café Skandia, **36**
Espresso Americano, **8**
La Fuente de Salud, **12**
Mister Pan, **7**
Pizzería Italia, **4**
Restaurant Fumg Kim, **9**

🍷 NIGHTLIFE
Confetti's, **2**
Keop's, **1**
Shauki's Place, **17**

🚌 BUS STOPS
CATISA-TUPSA, **19**
CITUL, **22**
Congolon, **31**
COTRAIBAL, **23**
El Rey, **14**
El Rey Express, **29**
Etica, **35**
Expresos del Caribe, **27**
Hedman Alas, **3**
Impala, **13**
King Quality, **6**
Norteños Casasola, **18**
San Jose, **20**
San Ramon, **34**
Torritos y Companecos,
    Sultana, **28**
Trans Gama, **15**

⬤ CHICKEN BUS STOPS
to Chalmeca, **32**
to Choloma, **24**
to Cofradía, **25**
to Naco Cortez, **30**
to Potrerillos, **26**
to San Marcos, **33**

tracks running alongside Av. 1 mark a boundary into the southeast quadrant that travelers should never cross, even during the day. The neighborhoods north of the *parque*, near the museums, tend to be more affluent.

Tourist Information: Municipal Tourist Office (☎ 550 6040; suyapaml177@hotmail.com), 1 block east of the stadium towards the movie theatre on 1 C. SO behind the Museo de la Naturaleza. Free city maps, schedules of Feria Juniana events, and English-speaking representatives. Open M-Sa 8am-5pm. Info on Honduras' national parks available next door at the **Fundación Ecologista H.R. Pastor Fasquelle.**

Travel Agencies: Agencies are scattered throughout the city and especially near the *parque*. **Maya Tropic Tours,** 1 C., Av. 2-3 (☎ 552 2405), in the lobby of the Gran Hotel Sula by the *parque*, specializes in pricey domestic tours. English spoken. Open M-F 7:30-11:30am and 1:30-5:30pm, Sa 7:30-11:30am. Tickets and flight info available at **Astro Tour,** Av. 4, 2/3 C. (☎ 557 2550; astrocook@123.hn). Open M-F 8am-12:30pm and 2-5:30pm, Sa 8am-12:30pm. Try also **Mundirama,** 2 C., Av. 2/3 (☎ 550 0490; mundirama@mundiramatravel.com). Open M-F 8am-5pm, Sa 8am-noon. **Cano Grand Tour** (☎ 557 5763; cano@sulanet.net) has large offices and a wide range of resources. Open M-F 8am-noon and 2-6pm, Sa 8am-noon. **Vito Tour** (☎ 557 3808; vtour@sulanet.net), on 2/3 Av. NO., 2 C., is another option. Open M-F 8:30am-5:30pm, Sa 8am-12:30pm.

Banks: Most major banks in Honduras have their main office surrounding the *parque;* you will have no trouble cashing traveler's checks or using **ATM** cards at any of them. **Banco Atlantida,** on the northeast corner cashes traveler's checks and gives Visa cash advances. Connecting **ATM** accepts AmEx/MC/V. Ask if you need to have your check endorsed at a separate desk before going to the teller. Open M-F 9am-3pm, Sa 9am-noon. **Creditlan,** just across the street on 3 Av., 1/2 C. NO, also gives cash advances on Visa cards. Open M-F 8:30am-5pm, Sa 8:30am-noon. To the west, **Banco Credomática,** 5 Av., 2 C. NO, has a UNIBANC ATM for AmEx/Cirrus/Plus/V. **Western Union** service is in the connecting **Banco Ficensa.**

Bookstore: Coello Bookstore, 9 Av., 4 C. SO. Stocks a handful of used English paperbacks and an eclectic Spanish collection that is well worth a browse. Open M-F 8am-noon and 1:30-5:30pm, Sa 8am-noon. MC/V.

Laundromat: Lavandería Almich, 9/10 Av., SO, 5 C. Wash and dry L5 per lb. Open M-F 7:30-11:30am and 1-5pm, Sa 8am-2pm. **Lavandería Lavamatic,** 9 Av., 2/3 C. NO (☎ 550 9226). Wash and dry L8 per lb. Open M-F 8am-6pm, Sa 8am-noon.

Emergency Numbers: ☎ 199. **Fire** ☎ 198.

Police: Southwest corner of 1 Av., 9 C. SE (☎ 552 3171). Open 24hr.

Tourist Police: ☎ 550 3452, corner of 1 C. and 12 Av. NO east of Morazán Stadium. Open 24hr.

Pharmacies: To find out which pharmacy is open late or on weekends, call the operator (☎ 192). **Clínica Ferraro** (☎ 557 6438) in Barrio Medina on 12/13 C. has a 24hr. pharmacy. The massive **Superfarmacia Simón** (☎ 553 0321), at 6 Av. So, 5 C., is comprehensive. Open M-Sa 8am-5:30pm, Su 8am-noon.

Hospitals: Centro Médico de Emergencias, 11 Av., 5/6 C. (☎ 553 1214). **Hospital Leonardo Martinez** (☎ 550 3411 or 550 8410), 10 Av. 10, 7/8 C. Open 24hr. **Clínica Bedana** (☎ 553 1618 or 553 1614; hospitalbedana@globalnet.hn), on Circunvalación just south of the intersection with 8 C. SO. Open 24hr.

Telephones: Hondutel, 4 Av., 4 C. SO. AT&T and Sprint calling card booths. **Fax** available. Open 24hr. Phone booths around town and clustered at 5 Av., 5 C. SO at the other Hondutel office, use 20- and 50-cent coins. 3min. local calls cost 50 cents.

Internet: Internet y Más, 8 Av., 5 C. SO (☎ 550 5736), provides Internet for L15 per hr. and phone calls to the US from L3 per min. Open daily 8am-8pm. **Chatspace Internet,** 3/4 Av., 2 C., just off the *parque*'s southwest side. Internet L10 per hr., phone calls to the US L3 per min. Open M-Sa 7am-8pm, Su 10am-8pm. **Telinter** (☎ 557 9121), on the northwest corner of the intersection of 4 Av. and 2 C. NO. Internet L15 per hr. Sprint phone card service. Open daily 8am-9pm.

Post Office: 3 Av., 9/10 C. SO, around the corner from the police station. Open daily 7:30am-6pm. **Express mail** from the same building at **E.M.S. Honduras** office. Open M-F 8am-7pm, Sa 8am-noon.

ACCOMMODATIONS

In the sticky, sweltering heat of San Pedro, fans are a must and the lack of hot water isn't a problem. The SO quadrant, site of most of San Pedro's bus terminals, contains a number of "bargain" *hospedajes* convenient for catching an early morning bus. Be sure to inspect your room before committing to these understandably cheap deals.

Hotel El Centro, 6 Av., 4/5 C. SO (☎ 553 0196). While the faded sign outside may send an unwelcoming message, clean rooms, large beds, cold baths, and a breezy shared balcony make this the best deal around. Reception open 6am-10pm. Singles L100; doubles L150. ❸

HONDURAS

Hotel San José, 6 Av., 5/6 C. SO (☎557 1208). Attentive proprietors maintain the relatively spacious rooms exceptionally well. Front door locked 11:30pm-5am; call to arrange check-in during these times. Married couples pay single rate, giving you all the incentive you need to pop the question. Singles L140; doubles L196; triples L252. ❸

Hotel Real, 6 Av., 6/7 C. SO (☎550 7929). Family run and very professional. Clean rooms with cable TV, cold baths, fans and ice water surround a welcoming courtyard complete with comfy couches. Singles and doubles L240, with A/C L350. ❺

Hotel Terraza, 6 Av., 4/5 C. SO (☎550 3108). Clean rooms vary in size so make sure to check yours out first. Fans and TV included. Singles and doubles L190, with hot water and breakfast L295, with A/C L380. ❸

Hotel Bolivar, 2 Av., 2 C. NO (☎552 7129; hbolivar@emu.hn). A block from the central park, this pricey but elegant stay is ideal for families. Complimentary breakfast. Wet bar off the patio overlooks the pool. A/C, cable TV, hot water. English spoken. Singles and doubles L525; triples L625. Pasta L50, filet mignon L110. AmEx. ❺

◖ FOOD

After *fútbol*, San Pedro's favorite pastime seems to be eating. Although many places are surprisingly expensive, careful backpackers can squeeze by on cheap local food. For a fast-food fix, head to the cluster of US chains from Av. 4 and C. 3, SO. to the *parque*. Fresh fruit of varying quality can be found just about anywhere in the *centro;* the best selection is at the **Mercado Guamilito,** C. 6, Av. 8/9 NO, on the southwestern stretch of the Circunvalación. Aptly named **Restaurant Row,** it has both casual and elegant sit-down places.

Café Skandia, Av. 4, C. 1 NO (☎552 9999), in the lobby of the Best Western Gran Hotel Sula on the northwest corner of the *parque*. 1950s Americana with a Honduran twist. Palm-shaded outdoor tables. Take a dip in the pool while waiting for your meal. Club sandwich L55, waffles L42, apple pie L24. Some veggie dishes. Open 24hr. ❷

Pizzería Italia, Av. 7, C. 1 NO (☎550 7094), serves a wide variety of flavors on a crispy thin crust pizza that's arguably the best in town. A much-welcomed frigid A/C and freshsqueezed juices refresh the weary traveler. Ham or sausage pizza L72, veggie L95, lasagna L60. Open daily 10am-10pm. ❶

La Fuente de Salud, Av. 8, C.s 5/6, SO (☎550 0951). Natural-remedies clinic and a vegetarian paradise all just a short walk from most hotels. Serves vegan *típico* (L15), soup (L12), and tofu sandwiches (L5). Bakery has freshly baked loaves (L30), just-add-water soy milk (L28), and soy cheese (L10). Open M-F and Su at 11:30am. Bakery and clinic open daily 7am-5pm. ❶

Restaurante Fumg Kim, Av. 6, C. 4/5 (☎550 9562), across from Hotel El Centro, is conveniently close to bus terminals and budget hotels, with hearty portions at good prices. Soups L50-L70, vegetarian chop suey L50, chicken dishes L55-L75. Open daily 10am-9pm. ❷

Mister Pan, on the southwest corner of Av. 6 and C. 3, is a haven of icing-doused sweets and baked goods shipped in fresh from all over town. Giant cake L15, cookies L4, baguettes L9, *licuados* L11-L17. Open M-F 7am-6:30pm, Sa 7am-6pm. ❶

Espresso Americano (☎552 4793), at the southwest corner of the *parque* on C. 2, Av. 4. A packed local hangout with a variety of hot and cold caffeinated beverages like cappuccinos (L10) and chai lattes (L12). Big cookies L7. Open daily 7am-8pm. ❶

◖ SIGHTS

From Maya pottery to pickled snakes and honey-covered women, San Pedro Sula is quirky enough to intrigue you. For a respite from the museums, get lost in the crowd at the *parque central* or catch a local soccer game at the stadium.

▓MUSEO DE LA NATURALEZA. Newly renovated, this unique museum has its very own bat cave, manatee, and one of the biggest collections of pickled reptiles in Honduras. Ecotourists will enjoy phyla-divided exhibits on local flora and fauna. For those headed to PN Cusuco, study the large display on the park's wildlife and then stop into the foundation's library next door for trail maps. (☎557 6598 or 550 1832. Open M-Sa 8am-noon and 1-4pm. L20. Tours in Spanish and English.)

▓MUSEO DE ANTROPOLOGÍA E HISTORIA. Permanent and temporary exhibit spaces, a library, and a massive theater feature displays from Maya times through colonial life. The museum's top floor boasts an impressive collection of pre-Columbian pottery and artifacts. Most exhibits are translated into English. Allow 1-2hr. for a visit, and be sure to ask the receptionist about any cultural events taking place in the theater. (Av. 3, C. 3/4, NO. ☎557 1496. Open M and W-Sa 9am-4pm, Su 9am-3pm. L36, students with ISIC L20, children L10; group discount 1st Su of month. Gift shop open Tu-Su 10am-4pm. Cafeteria meal L30, tacos L15.)

ASOCIACIÓN NACIONAL DE ARTESANOS DE HONDURAS. Besides being a good source of traditional food, the Mercado Guamilito houses the best Honduran artisan's market. Wander through the maze of handmade carvings and ceramics. For better quality goods at slightly higher prices, cross the road to **Casa del Sol.** (☎557 1371; casadesol@sigmanet.hn). Be ready to bargain. (Av. 8/9, C. 6, NO. Asociación open M-Sa 7am-5pm, Su 7am-noon. Casa del Sol open M-Sa 8:30am-6:30pm, Su 8am-noon.)

CENTRO CULTURAL SAMPEDRANO. The center has both permanent and rotating gallery spaces which display traditional San Pedro handicrafts as well as contemporary paintings. (C. 3, Av. 3/4. ☎553 3911. Open M-F 8am-6:30pm, Sa 8am-5pm.)

GETTING COVERED WITH HONEY. For females with a food fetish, a 1hr. massage is given by the all-female Seventh Day Adventists at the La Fuente de Salud (p. 470). The massages include a rubdown with lotion or honey, which supposedly soften the skin. Sorry, guys, this one's for women only. (Massages begin at 8am. Come early. Showers available. L50.)

▓▐ NIGHTLIFE AND ENTERTAINMENT

In the evening, San Pedro's chic-est residents head out to the **discotecas** on the western half of the Circunvalación. All have a minimal dress code (no shorts, t-shirts, or sandals), and it's standard to be frisked upon entry. Bars and restaurants are legally required to close at 10:30pm, making *discotecas* the only form of late night entertainment. Women should be warned that city bars ooze with *machismo*, and everyone should be aware that San Pedro Sula can still be dangerous at night. Taxis are strongly recommended. Stay with a group you trust.

The place to go for the young and restless is **Confetti's**, on Circunvalación near the Puerto Cortés exit, where modern Latin and North American disco hits are pumping. (Beer L25. W ladies' night. Cover L60. Open Tu-Su 7pm-dawn.) **Keop's** (formerly Henry's), a few blocks west on the Circunvalación, attracts a slightly older crowd. **Shauki's Place,** an upscale restaurant, has a bar under the stars in a lush courtyard. With a more laid-back atmosphere, this is a good option for women who would like to avoid being badgered (open M-Sa 4pm).

For a more sophisticated evening, the **Francisco Saybe Theatre** on Avenida Circunvalación, across from the San Pedro Sula University, has nightly performances. **Gemini Cinemas,** C. 1, Av. 11/12, shows newly released movies. (☎550 9060. Show times 3, 5, 7, 9pm; L36).

FERIA JUNIANA

San Pedro Sula is nationally famous for its **Feria Juniana** (June Festival), which begins with a bang in the early morning on June 1 and culminates in the last week of the month. The festival features Garífuna dancers, a drum corps, and pre-teen beauty queens parading down the street. During the last two weekends, vendors and booths stay open late and a bevy of musical groups keeps the streets throbbing into the wee hours. The last night is traditionally *carnaval*, so grab a cardboard mask and join in, but keep your belongings somewhere safe. Some locals warn tourists against hanging out too late during the fair, especially in areas outside the main drag.

PARQUE NACIONAL CUSUCO

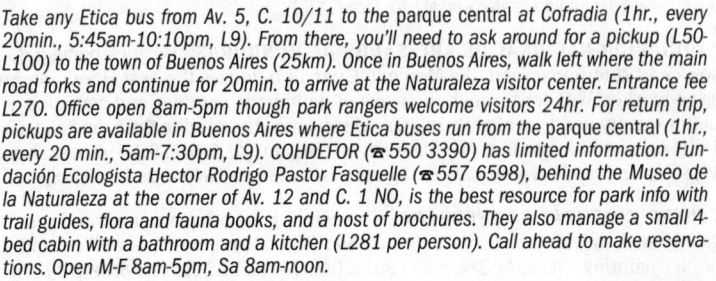

Take any Etica bus from Av. 5, C. 10/11 to the parque central at Cofradia (1hr., every 20min., 5:45am-10:10pm, L9). From there, you'll need to ask around for a pickup (L50-L100) to the town of Buenos Aires (25km). Once in Buenos Aires, walk left where the main road forks and continue for 20min. to arrive at the Naturaleza visitor center. Entrance fee L270. Office open 8am-5pm though park rangers welcome visitors 24hr. For return trip, pickups are available in Buenos Aires where Etica buses run from the parque central (1hr., every 20 min., 5am-7:30pm, L9). COHDEFOR (☎550 3390) has limited information. Fundación Ecologista Hector Rodrigo Pastor Fasquelle (☎557 6598), behind the Museo de la Naturaleza at the corner of Av. 12 and C. 1 NO, is the best resource for park info with trail guides, flora and fauna books, and a host of brochures. They also manage a small 4-bed cabin with a bathroom and a kitchen (L281 per person). Call ahead to make reservations. Open M-F 8am-5pm, Sa 8am-noon.

The rich cloud forest of Parque Nacional Cusuco is centered in the Merendon mountain range. With 2000 to 3000mm of rainfall each year, the park is an essential resource for the 150,000 people in the San Pedro valley. This wet habitat is home to the park's mascot, the pizote, as well as many tropical birds such as elusive quetzals, coas, gilgeros, as well as plant species such as bamboo, ferns, and sirin. Its highest peak, **Cerro Jilinco** (2242m), has no established trails, daring you to set out on a bushwhacking adventure.

There are six hikes within the park. **La Cascada el Quetzal** (1-2hr., 760m) begins 1km towards Buenos Aires from the visitor center and descends down a ravine along the Río Cusuco to the waterfall. Guides are necessary and swimming in the pool below at the base of the waterfall is prohibited as this is a source of drinking water for villagers down-stream. **El Colorado** (3-4hr.) begins 300m along Las Minas, left down the fork in the trail, and offers awesome vistas and birdwatching before finishing at the small village of Ladrillo. **Las Minas** (1.5-2hr., 2215m) begins 10m before the "Welcome to the Park" sign on the left and runs along a gorge carved by a tributary of the Río Cusuco. **El Quetzal** (1-2hr., 809m) begins across the parking lot from the visitor center and winds 1700m past pines, palms, broad-leaf trees, ferns, and orchids as well as the remains of the Río Cusuco timber company. **El Pizote** (1-1½hr., 671m) begins a ways up the El Jardín road from the visitor center on the right. It's a fairly easy trail through mixed and secondary forest. **El Danto** (1-2hr., 2000m) is a loop that begins 100m past the "Welcome to the Park" sign and features a self-guided tour accessible for people of all fitness levels.

PUERTO CORTÉS

Puerto Cortés (pop. 47,100), Honduras' largest port, is situated on a deep, natural harbor 64km north of San Pedro Sula. Although Puerto Cortés is mostly frequented by travelers planning boat trips to Belize or the Garífuna communities, the *parque central* and new waterfront park are pleasant perches for watching the constant commerce of the free trade port. Puerto Cortés is also an easy jump to the fort at Omoa or to the Guatemalan border crossing at Corinto.

▐▔ TRANSPORTATION. Buses cluster in the area off the northwest corner of the *parque central* on Av. 3/4 and C. 3/4. Impala Av. 4, C. 3/4, 1 block north and half a block west of the *parque*, runs to **San Pedro Sula**. (☎553 3111. 1hr., every 15min. 4:30am-8pm, L20.) Direct buses to the beach of **Omoa** leave from the same parking lot (45min., every 30min. 6am-7pm, L9). Citul, 4 Av., 4 C., also runs to **San Pedro Sula** (☎665 0466. 50min., every 15min. 4:30am-7pm, L20). CITRAL/Costeños, 3 C. 4/ 5, has buses marked "Frontera de Guatemala" that head to the border crossing at **Corinto** from just around the corner (☎665 0888. 3hr., every hr. 6am-4pm, L29). Tela-bound travelers should take a bus to San Pedro Sula, switch to a Progreso-bound bus, and grab a bus to **Tela** from there. Alternatively, the charming but rusty old train that cuts through banana plantations also heads to **Tela** (4hr., F and Su 8am, L15). To get to **Baracoa**, take a Transporte Unidos bus from 4 Av., 4/5 C. across 4 C. from Citus headed to Puente Alto and get off at Baracoa (45min., every 10min. 5:10am-7:30pm, L7).

Departing from the *laguna* are two regularly scheduled **boats** to **Belize**. Boats depart irregularly to ports all over the Americas from here, so ask at the docks for upcoming trips. One boat, Gulfa Cruza (☎665 5556 or 984 3938), leaves for **Belize** (M 10am), stopping at **Big Creek** (2hr.), **Placencia** (3hr.), and **Belize City** (3½hr.), with prices starting at L670. The other boat, Nesyumein Neydy (☎984 9544), heads to **Dangriga** (3hr., Tu 9am, returns Sa). To get to the *laguna*, either take a taxi or catch the local bus (L3) headed east from the northwest corner of the *parque* next to Pizza Hut. Get off at the main bridge and walk underneath to the fish market. For both boats, you must be at the port by 8am the day of departure. It is a good idea to stop by the *laguna* the day before and talk to someone at the *comedores* on the far side of the bridge to make sure the boat is making the trip.

▐▋ ORIENTATION. Puerto Cortés occupies a peninsula surrounded by the Caribbean to the north and west, the **Bahía de Cortés** to the south, and the inland **Laguna de Alvarado** to the southeast. The docks, recognizable by the loading cranes, line the south side of downtown. *Avenidas* run east-west, parallel to the docks, starting with Av. 1 and increasing numerically as you head north into the city. *Calles* run perpendicular to the *avenidas*. The large *parque central* sits on Av. 2/3, Calles 4/5. Buses generally arrive on Av. 4, leaving passengers 1 block north of the *parque*. Choppy open ocean water at the northern beaches **Marejada** and **Vacacional** send most beach-goers south across the bay and to the sheltered **Coca-Cola** and **Cieneguita,** which tend to be empty on weekdays.

> **❗** While Puerto Cortés is a fairly safe city, beaches on the west side of the peninsula (particularly **El Faro** and **Costa Azul**) and **Barrio Faro** should be avoided at all times, while **Barrio San Ramon** should not be visited at night.

▐ PRACTICAL INFORMATION. Ocean Travel, Av. 1/2, C. 3, arranges flights and tours. (☎665 2445. Open M-F 8am-4pm, Su noon-11pm. V.) The **immigration office** is 2 blocks north and half a block west of the northwest corner of the *parque* on 5 Av., 3/4 C. (☎665 0582. Open M-Sa 7am-noon and 2-6pm.) Foreign currency and traveler's checks can both be exchanged at **Banco de Occidente,** Av. 3 and C. 4 off the northwest corner of the *parque*, which also has a **Western Union.** (☎665 0660. Open M-F 8:30am-4:30pm, Sa 8am-noon.) **Banco Ficensa,** 1 block west of the southwest corner of the *parque*, on the corner of 2 Av. and 3 C., has a 24hr. AmEx/Cirrus/Plus **ATM** and also serves as a **Western Union.** (☎665 0323. Open M-F 9am-4pm, Sa 9-11:30am.) **Banco Atlántida,** half a block toward the *parque* from Ficensa at 2 Av., 3/4 C., cashes traveler's checks and has a 24hr. Plus/V ATM. (☎665 1286. Open M-F 9am-4pm, Sa 9am-noon.) For provisions, head to **Supermercado Rigo** (☎665 0117) on the southwest corner of the *parque* at the corner of 2 Av. and 4 C. (open M-Sa 7am-7pm, Su 8am-noon). The 24hr. **police** station (☎665 0420 or 665 1023) is at the corner of Av. 1 and C. 9 in the southeast part of town. **Hospital Cemeco,** Av 4/ 5, C. 8 (☎665 0460 or 665 0057), 3 blocks east and 2 blocks north of the *parque,* has an English-speaking doctor on call 24hr. **Centro Médico Litoral Atlántico** (☎665 0787 or 665 0558), 1 block south at the corner of 3 Av. and 8 C., also provides 24hr. emergency medical service. An **ambulance** is also available (☎665 2439 or 997 9267). Both charge L150 for consultation. Across the bay, **Hospital Area #2** (☎665 0562) is a 24hr. public hospital just off Coca-Cola beach. Different **pharmacies** take turns staying open until 10pm; check the list posted at any pharmacy. **Hondutel** (☎665 0005) is open M-F 8am-noon and 1-4pm and shares an office with the post office (see below). **Internet** access is available at **Rudon's Cyber Net,** Av. 1/2, C. 3, which also has phone service to the US (☎665 5822. Internet L20 per hr. Calls L3 per min.) Next door, **Deven Cafe Internet** offers Honduras' cheapest Internet service (☎665 2829; cappy052002@yahoo.es. L8 per hr. Phone calls to the US L2 per min. Open daily 7:30am-10:30pm.) **Cortés Net** on C. 2, Av. 2/3 is a third option. (☎665 4574. L16 per hr. Calls to the US L4 per min. Open M-Sa 8:30am-9pm.) The **post office** (☎ 665 0454) and **EMS express mail** (☎665 0455) share a building with Hondutel on C. 1 between Av. 1 and 2 (open M-F 8am-4:30pm).

⌂⌂ ACCOMMODATIONS AND FOOD. Stick to the more reputable hotels near the center of town for a full-night stay, avoiding sketchy establishments with hourly rates. Many visitors skip town to spend the night in either San Pedro or Omoa, just 45min. away. The **Formosa Hotel ❷,** Av. 3, C. 1/2, 2½ blocks west of the *parque,* has adequate rooms down long hallways. Try for a breezier upstairs room farther down the hall to get away from the noise and traffic of downtown. (☎665 0853. Singles with fan L139, with TV L174, with TV and A/C L225; doubles L232, with A/C L278; triples with A/C and TV L348.)

Restaurants in Puerto Cortés are sprinkled around the *parque;* some of the best line Av. 2. For *típico* portions to satisfy your appetite, **Repostería and Pastelería Plata ❷,** on the corner of 2 C., 3 Av. across from Hotel Formosa, serves buffet-style breakfast, lunch, and dinner. (☎665 2383. Meals L40-L60, desserts L3-L15. Open daily 6am-6pm. AmEx/MC/V.) **Golosinas Alex ❶,** hidden down a green, tunnel-like hallway from Av. 3 between C. 3/4, offers some of Honduras's most varied and best-tasting *típico* treats. (☎665 4447. Meals L15-L20. Open daily 7am-9pm.)

⚐ TRAVESÍA. While only a few kilometers from the busy, industrial Puerto Cortés, the small Garífuna fishing community of Travesía has escaped modernization. Wooden and grass covered huts look out over the ocean along the one main road that runs along the beach, while smooth Caribbean music and savory scents waft out from family-run *comedores.* To get to Travesía, take a **bus** marked Etumesca or Urbano from 4 Av., 5/6 C. in Puerto Cortés (20min.; 7, 9, 10am, noon, 3, 5:30pm; L6). You can also take a **taxi** (5-10min., L50-L60), but a round-trip gets expensive. To catch a return bus, wait 1 block west of the Hotel Frontera del Caribe (20min.; L6). There is only place to stay in town: **Hotel Fronteras del Caribe ❷,** 1km in the opposite direction from the *parque* before the fork in the road. Delightful second-story beachfront rooms have fans and purified water. Ask for a corner room. (☎665 5001. Reception open 24hr. Restaurant open 8am-6:30pm. *Sopa marinara* L120, fried chicken L75, beer L18. Triples L250.)

Miles of empty beaches stretch in either direction from the *parque central.* Every year the **Feria de Travesía** is held the middle two weekends in June featuring Garífuna dances, horseback riding, traditional food, *bailes de punta,* fishing, and dancing in the *parque central.* A couple of weeks later, the **Festival Garífuna de Bajamar** kicks off on the last weekend in July in the connecting village of Bajamar. Nightly dancing takes place at **Glorieta la 3a Edad** on the eastern edge of the park.

OMOA

The idyllic fishing village of Omoa (pop. 2500) feels like one big sedative. The massive Fortaleza de San Fernando de Omoa, an 18th-century Spanish fort, is the best-known attraction, but the town is quickly becoming a popular tourist stopover for a variety of other reasons. Though lacking the traditional Caribbean flavor, palm-shaded empty beaches and clean waters are a great place to kick back and go for a swim. Two spectacular waterfalls are just a short hike from the beach. A two-day stopover in Omoa can easily extend to two weeks of hiking and catching rays, so leave yourself extra time.

TRANSPORTATION. Get to Omoa by **bus** from Puerto Cortés. Buses marked "Omoa" will go all the way to the beach; others (often marked "Frontera") drop you off 1km away on the main highway from where you can easily walk. (45min., every hr. 5:45am-5pm, L9.) On Sunday, buses only pass on the main road. If you're heading back to **San Pedro Sula,** hop a bus back to Cortés and get off at the Texaco station just outside of town, where **express vans** to San Pedro stop every 10min. (1hr., 5:30am-7pm, L20).

ORIENTATION AND PRACTICAL INFORMATION. It takes a special kind of traveler to get lost in this one-road town. The street connects the highway from Puerto Cortés to the beach, snaking by the *fortaleza* along the way. At the beach, a road lined with restaurants and hotels follows the curve of the bay. The town center sits at the intersection of the highway and the road to the beach.

For **tourist information,** stop by **Roli's Place** (see **Accommodations,** below) in the evening and talk to Roli. You can exchange traveler's checks and quetzals at **Banco de Occidente,** located at the junction with the main road 1km from the beach, though the exchange rate for quetzals is better at the border. (☎658 9283. Open M-F 8:30am-4pm, Sa 8:30am-11:30am.) **Laundry** services are available at Roli's (L5 per lb.), at Pia's Place or Hotel Bahía de Omoa (L18 per load), or Hotel Playa Resort (L30 per load). The **Red Cross,** across the beach at the main junction with the pharmacy, can help with minor surgical emergencies. (☎658 9022. Open M-Sa 1-5pm, 24hr. for emergency. L50). **Farmacia San Antonio** is across the main junction from the bank. (☎658 9198. Open M-Sa 8am-6pm, Su 8am-noon.) The **Hondutel** office is in the municipal building up the road towards Puerto Cortés. (☎658 9004. Calls to the US L22 per min.) There's a pay phone along the beach in front of the Hotel Bahía de Omoa. **Rooster Net** offers international calls(L5 per min.) and **Internet** access for L20 per hr. (open daily 9am-10pm).

ACCOMMODATIONS. ⊠**Roli's Place ❶,** on the dirt road just before the beach, is owned by veteran backpacker and sits on lush, shady grounds. Guests get a cheap, comfortable place to stay complete with a common kitchen and free bike and kayak rental. Roli will charter direct transport to anywhere in town for more than six people for US$20 per person. (☎658 9082; roli@yaxpactours.com. Reception open until 9pm. Hammocks L50; camping L30 per person; dorms L60; doubles L150.) **Pía's Place ❶,** around the corner from Roli's to the left across the street from the beach, is another splendid hostel with charming wooden cabins and ocean views from porch-side hammocks. (☎658 9076; piaton@hondutel.hn. Laundry L18 per load. Dorms L50; doubles L140.) To escape the traveler scene, head to the quiet beachside lodging at **Sunset Playa Resort ❹**, to the right up the road along the bay down the left fork on the right. Large rooms come with cold baths, fans, and TVs. (☎658 9166. Laundry L30 per load. Rooms L180.) For more expensive beachside lodging, **Flamingo's Hotel ❺** serves complimentary breakfast on an exclusive ocean-view balcony. Rooms have A/C, cable TV, and hot bath. (☎658 9199; flamingosomoa@yahoo.com.ar. English spoken. Singles L580; doubles L650. Discounts for longer stays. AmEx/MC/V.) **Hotel Tatiana ❹**, with a well-maintained lawn and spotless rooms, is a more private option. (☎658 9186. Reception open 24hr. Singles with fan L150, with TV L250, with A/C L400; doubles L200/L300/L500.)

📭 **FOOD.** A number of good restaurants have recently sprung up along the beach. With excellent seafood and panoramic views of the bay, these are ideal places to spend a relaxing evening. 🏠**Jardín Romántico ❸**, along the beach to the left of the road that connects with the highway, is a cozy bungalow with a diverse menu, all to the beat of oldies love songs. (Vegetarian soup L70, ginger red snapper L90, kingfish steak L90, piña colada L35.Open daily 8am-10pm.) The **Sunset Playa Resort ❷** is a *gringo* favorite on the quiet side of town with cheap food and beachside seating. Take a right when you hit the beach and follow the left fork where the pavement ends. (☎658 9166. *Pescado* L50, Omoa Iced Tea L45, cordon blue L85. Open F-Sa 2pm-1am. AmEx/MC/V.) For a splurge, **Flamingo's ❹**, to the left when you hit the beach, is a well-decorated restaurant overlooking the bay with delicious platters. (☎658 9199. Chicken L90, famous Flamingo's rice with lobster, shrimp, and fish L150. Open M-F 7am-9pm, Sa-Su 7am-midnight.) Budget prices and a great view come together at **Tropical Breeze ❸**, next door to Flamingo's. (☎658 9191. Pancake breakfast L34, soups L60-L100, meat dishes L60-L75. Open daily 8am-7:30pm.) Off the beach, you'll find the cheapest meals at **Los Amigos de Huicho ❶**, down the road towards the highway and past the fort on the left. (Plate of the day L30, chicken soup L20. Open daily 7am-11pm.)

🎦 🔣 **SIGHTS AND OUTDOOR ACTIVITIES.** Although the **Fortaleza de San Fernando de Omoa** no longer sits directly on the water, its imposing presence is still captivating. The best-preserved Spanish fort in Honduras, this national monument was built between 1759 and 1775 to protect gold and silver shipments from buccaneers and the British navy, a job it wasn't too successful at. The feisty Brits seized the fort for five months in 1779, and, some 40 years later, famed pirate Luis Aury controlled it for a brief but glorious period. Once the foreign threat dissipated, the damp, dark cellars were used to hold political prisoners of the Honduran government during the first half of the 20th century. In the nearby museum, exhibits display swords and rifles from the fort's former pirate aggressors. (☎658 9167. Open M-F 8am-4pm, Sa-Su 9am-5pm; L20. Guide books in Spanish L20.)

While the local beaches are a relaxing place to spend the day, those wanting a little more adventure can take a short hike up to either of the two nearby **waterfalls.** Both have refreshing swimming holes and are located up the dirt road, south of the intersection on the highway past Baneo de Occidente and the cemetery. Climbing up to the waterfall provides an exhilarating, if dangerous, experience, but successful attempts reward climbers with a constantly cascading natural masseuse. The closer of the two falls is a 45min. hike (4km) from the beach; the second one is about 15min. longer (6km). Both hikes involve walking up the river a bit, so wear shoes that can get wet. When you reach the river, walk alongside until the trail ends, then trek upstream to the right for the farther waterfall and to the left for the closer one.

✖ CORINTO BORDER WITH GUATEMALA

Direct buses marked "Frontera Guatemala" head to Corinto from Omoa's main road (every 2hr. 6:50am-3pm, L29). From there, you'll have to grab a pickup for the last 3km to the border (L20), where buses head to Puerto Barrios, Guatemala (L20) and stop at the immigration office along the way. It will take about 4hr. to get from Omoa to Puerto Barrios. Guatemala entrance fee L20.

In Corinto, money changers stand next to the immigration center and change lempiras, dollars, and quetzals. There are no money changers on the Guatemalan side. If you get stuck in Corinto, lodging is available next to **Pulperia Arnold** (L50). Note that the "jungle trail" and boat crossings to Guatemala are not widely used. For up-to-date information on crossing, check with **Roli** (p. 475) at Roli's Place in Omoa.

TELA

Halfway between San Pedro Sula and La Ceiba on the Caribbean coast, Tela (pop. 30,100) is a former banana plantation tucked between two nature preserves and a mountain range. The United Fruit Company has left behind some pleasant reminders of its short reign: its big-wig execs used to live in what is now the impressive Hotel Villas Telamar and it established the Lancetilla Botanical Gardens, a major tourist attraction. Nearby outdoor opportunities and very traditional Garífuna villages give Tela ever-increasing tourism potential. Due to unemployment street crime has been somewhat of a problem, but as businesses have been rebuilding and rehiring, crime has settled down.

▐ TRANSPORTATION

Bus: Long distance buses leave from **Empresa de Transportes LTDA,** Av. 9, C. 9, (☎448 2235) for **La Ceiba** (2hr., every 25min. 4:10am-6pm, L25) and **El Progreso** (1¾hr., every 25min. 4:30am-6pm, L20) from where they continue to **San Pedro** (last bus 6pm). Direct buses run to **San Pedro Sola** from **Terminal Trasul/Tela Express** on the corner of 2 Av., 6 C. (1½hr.; M-F 6, 7, 8, 10am, 12:30, 2, 3:30, 5pm; Su 7, 8, 10:30am, 1, 2:30, 3:30, 4:30, 5:30pm; L53). Local buses at Av. 8, C. 10, 2½ blocks east of the *parque*'s northern corner, go to **Triunfo** via **La Enseñada** (1hr., every 30min. 6am-6pm, L8) and **Tornabé** via **San Juan** (1hr., every 30min. 6am-6pm, L7).

Train: A loud, rusty train, one of the last in Central America, chugs to **Puerto Cortés** from the outdated and rundown station 3 blocks south of the *parque*'s southeast corner (4hr., F and Su 1:45pm, L50).

▐ ⁊ ORIENTATION AND PRACTICAL INFORMATION

Remember that the sea is always to the north. The city is divided in two by the Río Tela; east of the river is **Tela Vieja** and west of the river is **Tela Nueva.** *Calles* run east and west and *Avenidas* run north and south. **Calle 11** runs east to the beach, and **Av. 1** begins just east of the Río Tela. The main drag, **Calle 9,** forms the southern edge of the *parque central* and is between Av. 5 and 6.

Tourist Information: While an **Office of Tourism** has recently opened inside the Municipal Building on the southeast corner of the *parque,* it only has basic info in Spanish. Open M-F 8am-4pm, Sa 8am-noon. A more comprehensive source is **Garífuna Tours,** Av. 5, C. 9 (☎448 2904; www.garifunatours.com.), located opposite the southwest corner of the *parque.* Open daily 7:30am-6:30pm. **PROLANSATE** (☎448 1686), across the street and 2½ blocks west, is the organization that oversees the national parks near Tela. It sells maps and pamphlets of nearby nature preserves (L3). Open M-F 7am-noon and 2-5pm, Sa 7-11am.

Banks: BGA, Av. 3, C. 9, cashes traveler's checks and has a 24hr. V/Plus **ATM**. Open M-F 8:30am-3:30pm, Sa 8:30-11:30am. **Banco Atlántida,** Av. 4, C. 9, 1 block west of the park, accepts Visa and has a 24hr. ATM. **Banco Occidente,** Av. 6, C. 10, in the northwest corner of the park, serves as a **Western Union**. Open M-F 8:30am-3:30pm, Sa 8:30-11:30am.

Bike Rental: Garífuna Tours rents **mountain bikes** (L90 per day) from M@ngo Café (p. 479). **Villas Telamar** also rents bikes for L20 per hr.

Police: The **Tourist Police** (☎448 0150 or 448 0253), on the corner of Av. 4, C. 11 in the *parque municipal,* are the most central and reliable. Free Tela and Honduras maps. Bilingual. Open 24hr. The **Policía Preventiva** (☎448 2909), along C. 7 on your right, are farther away and unsafe to walk to at night. Open 24hr. **FUSEP** (☎448 2079) is at the east end of Av. 7; follow the street uphill to the 1st left.

Medical Services: Centro Médico Cristiano, Av. 8, C. 7/8 (☎448 2456; eliseo@hondotel.hn). Open 24hr. Some doctors speak English. **Red Cross** ☎448 2121.

Telephones: Hondutel, Av. 4, 7 C. (☎448 2002; fax 448 2942). **Fax** available. Open daily 7am-8pm. **Garífuna Tours** call to the US (L3 per min.).

Internet: Available at **Garífuna Tours** (L20 per hr.). **Tela Computers** (☎448 1654), Av. 2/3, C. 9, has cheaper rates (L11 per hr.). Open M-Sa 8:30am-9pm. **Mundinet** (☎448 2849), Av. 6., C. 9, opposite the southeast corner of the *parque,* offers service (L24 per hr.). and phone calls to the US for L4 per min. Open daily 7am-8:30pm.

Post Office: White building on Av. 4 C. 7/8 next to Hondutel. Open M-F 8am-4pm, Sa 8am-11am. **Postal Code:** 31301.

■ ACCOMMODATIONS

Tela has many beautiful beachside hotels while wallet-friendly cozy cabins fill the surrounding Garífuna villages.

■ **Hotel Marazul,** Av. 4, C. 11 (☎448 2313), is a backpacker favorite with large rooms, a cozy courtyard, the tourist police across the street, and the beach just a block away. Reception open 24hr. Singles with fan L80; doubles L100; triples L150. ❷

■ **Boarding House Sara,** Av. 8, C. 11 (☎448 1477), evokes memories of a childhood tree house. Ask for a front room with a balcony view of the sea. Nightclub across the street is noisy on weekends. Kitchen facilities available. Free long term bag storage. The attached *comedor* serves cheap *típico* (L30). Reception open 24hr., *comedor* 7:30am-9pm. L60 per person, group and longer stay rates available. ❶

Hotel Sinai, Av. 6, C. 6NE/5NE (☎448 1486), 6 blocks from the beach in front of the train station, is cozy and tranquil. Singles L80, with bath L150, and A/C L200; doubles L120/L200/L260. ❷

Hotel Mi Porvenir, C. 9, Av. 8. With a little bargaining, these small rooms and communal bath are the best deal. Singles L50; doubles L100. ❶

M@ngo Hotel, C. 8, Av 5. A bed and breakfast providing large, clean rooms with hot baths and a choice of American or *típico* breakfast at M@ngo Cafe. Singles L170, with TV L260; doubles L250/L350. ❹

Hotel Tela (☎448 2150), next to the PROLANSATE office on C. 9, Av. 2/3, offers large, clean rooms with fans and hot water baths as well as large balconies facing away from the beach. Singles L200; doubles L250. AmEx/MC/V. ❺

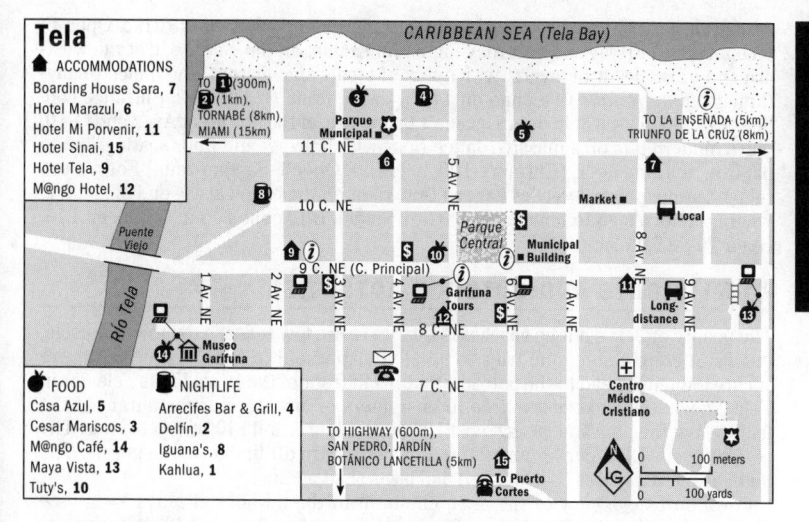

Tela

♠ ACCOMMODATIONS

Boarding House Sara, **7**
Hotel Marazul, **6**
Hotel Mi Porvenir, **11**
Hotel Sinai, **15**
Hotel Tela, **9**
M@ngo Hotel, **12**

🍴 FOOD
Casa Azul, **5**
Cesar Mariscos, **3**
M@ngo Café, **14**
Maya Vista, **13**
Tuty's, **10**

🍸 NIGHTLIFE
Arrecifes Bar & Grill, **4**
Delfín, **2**
Iguana's, **8**
Kahlua, **1**

🏠 FOOD

M@ngo Café, on the ground fl. of the Museo Garífuna at the west end of C. 8. Aura, the chef, serves mouth-watering, 3-course gourmet meals, ranging from traditional Garífuna to Italian. Peaceful riverside patio seating. The lasagna is outstanding. Pancakes L60, vegetable soup L50, pasta L100, pizza L100. Open daily 6:30am-10pm. ❷

Maya Vista (☎448 1497; www.mayavista.com). Take C. 8 east and take the 1st left after Av. 9 at the crest of the hill; continue to the top. The view alone is reason enough to come here, but the entrees don't hurt either. Amazing architecture and well-placed hammocks round out the perfection. Book exchange on site. Baked chicken L90, vegetarian pasta L90, lobster L210, delicious cake of the day L18, beer L19. Open Tu-Su 9am-9pm. ❷

Cesar Mariscos (☎448 2083), at the northern end of Av. 3 on the beach with palm shaded coastline seating, is popular with traveling families and provides a communal guitar, kayak (L50 per hr.), and swimming to pass the time. Ecological breakfast L35, grilled conch L140, beefsteak L140, Bloody Mary L40. Open daily 7am-10pm. ❷

Casa Azul, 6 Av., 11 C. (☎448 1443), 1 block north of the *parque's* northeast corner. The Garífuna art gallery (L300-L500) and 450-title book exchange (L20) welcome locals and visitors to generous portions of Italian food with particularly good garlic bread. Personal pizzas L45, vegetarian pasta L80. Open M W-Su 4pm-midnight. ❷

Tuty's, Av. 4/5, C. 9, (☎448 0013), across from Garífuna Tours. Huge breakfasts (L36) delicious mango *licuados* (L10-L18), and baked treats (L5-L10) make this a local favorite. *Tacos de pollo* (L20) are a tasty, inexpensive lunch. Open daily 7am-8pm. ❶

🎭 ENTERTAINMENT

Though slow during the week, Tela transforms itself on the weekends from sleepy beach town to party central. While the clubs directly alongside the beach may look like a good time, their clientele are often armed and aggressive; it's best to steer clear, or at least ask around first. For more security, try ■**Delfín** at the Hotel Villas Telamar, where you can boogie barefoot to modern Latin pop right on the beach in a huge gazebo. Entry is free, but beer costs an arm and a leg. (☎448 2196. Open F-Sa 9pm-3am.) Friday and Saturday nights fill **Kahlua,** on the cul-de-sac at the western end of Boulevard Playero, with a mix of locals and visitors who dance to anything from *merengue* to techno on a cozy dance floor. (☎448 2592. Entrance L50, beer L15. Open F-Sa 8pm-4am.) **Iguana's Sports Bar,** at the corner of Av. 2 and C. 10, plays modern hits on a massive dance floor with balcony and floor seating; safety pat-downs at the door. (Entrance L30, beer L14. Open F-Sa 8pm-3am.) For a more relaxed atmosphere, **Arrecifes Bar and Grill,** right on the beach at the end of Av. 4, is where the locals go to have a beer. (Garlic steak L70, conch soup L65, beer L16. Open Tu-Su 8am-3am.)

◎ ♌ SIGHTS AND OUTDOOR ACTIVITIES

The beauty of Tela's public **beaches** is that there are few reasons to move a muscle, unless of course someone tries to steal your purse. For less relaxed but more secure lounging, head to the patrolled shores in front of the Hotel Villas Telemar in Tela Nueva. Beach access is free to customers of any store or restaurant in the facility, but the pool and jacuzzi cost L50 on weekdays and L100 on weekends. The golf course is L150 per hr. and the tennis courts are off-limits to non-guests. The hotel also rents **horses** (L50 per hr.) and **bikes** (L20 per hr.).

For a bird's eye view of the area, climb up to the mirador at Maya Vista (see **Food,** p. 479). Garífuna Tours also offers package trips to **Roatán** (L4000 per person, minimum 2 people) that include the flight and four days at Hotel Pura Vida. Dive packages are available and an extra night can be arranged for L675. Garífuna Tours also administers the **Garífuna Museum** upstairs from the M@ngo Cafe, at the western end of C. 8. The museum has self-guided Spanish tours of Garífuna history, music, and culture. (Open daily 8am-5pm. Free.)

⌕ DAYTRIPS FROM TELA

Tela is a springboard for some great adventures. A trip to one of several Garífuna villages offers a peek at a traditional culture and some quiet beach time. Nearby outdoor activities include the Lancetilla Botanical Gardens, the spectacular Parque Nacional Jeanette Kawas and the untamed Punta Izopo Reserve.

GARÍFUNA VILLAGES

The Garífuna's story starts on the island of St. Vincent in 1635, the year the Kalipuna tribe from South America attacked St. Vincent's native Arawaks. Kalipuna warriors killed all the Arawak men and took the women as wives. The Garífuna are the descendents of this bloody union. Today, the Garífuna are an intriguing culture, different from the *Mestizo* population in Central America.

WEST OF TELA. About 8km from Tela, **Tornabé** is accessible by bus or bike along the coastal dirt road and has a few rooms rented by families for around L100. **The Last Resort ❸,** on the left just as you cross the river into the village, has beautiful beach cabins with an in-house restaurant and bar. (☎970 6521 or 958 5632. Singles with fan and hot bath L200; doubles L250, with A/C L400. Reception open 24hr. Restaurant open 7:30am-11pm. Beer L15.) Much more beautiful and rustic, though harder to get to, the tiny village of ◪**Miami** (pop. 250) is located another 7km west of Tornabé, on a spit of land no wider than 50m. Blue Caribbean waves crash on the bright white shore to one side and a small lake laps gently on the other. Miami looks the way most Garífuna villages looked 50 years ago, with thatched huts and cooking fires. Delicious traditional foods (L40-L50) are cooked by the **Narcisco family** who also rent rooms (L50) and has places to sling your hammock for free. The new **PROLANSATE** office next door gives out maps and tourist info on the area's national parks and also houses a Garífuna museum and extensive wildlife information. From here **Alejandro** leads guided birdwatching boat tours for L400 per hr. *(Tornabé is a 1hr. bus ride from Tela. Bus leaves every 30min. 6am-6pm, L8. From there it's 7km to Miami. Alternatively pickup L50-L100. Garífuna Tours has info on shuttles to Miami.)*

EAST OF TELA. The smaller of the two villages to the east, **La Ensenada** is easy to reach and has calm waters and a cozy family feel. A multitude of locals flock here on weekends and there are eateries and a couple of small hotels. To get to **Hotel Mirtha ●** take a right at the entrance to the village. Guests stay in wooden huts with communal outdoor cold baths. (☎984 6551. Huts L80; doubles with private baths L150; triples with garage L200.) **Hotel Budari ❸,** down the left fork from the city entrance on the left, offers nice doubles with fans and hot baths. Prices are negotiable. (☎381 0234; perlaandrea2001@yahoo.com. Doubles L300, with A/C L500.) The **food huts ❸** by the beach are mainly open on weekends and serve delicious fresh grilled fish and conch soup for around L70. Dozens of them line the fluffy-white beaches, inviting visitors to stay a little longer.

Farther from Tela, **Triunfo de la Cruz** (pop. 10,000) is the second largest Garífuna village in the country. The introduction of urban influences has already begun to take its toll. Several hotels and rooms are available in town for around L100 a night, and restaurants are easy to find. Though some huts are being replaced by concrete boxes and a ritzy luxury resort is currently under construction, thatched roofs still populate the beach. The **Playas Miramar Restaurant ❷,** in the west end of town right next to the cemetery, serves delicious and authentic Garífuna seafood in grass-hut seating on the beach. (☎981 3533. Entrees start at L50. Open daily 8am-11pm.) Just east of the *parque central*, **Arenas** serves drinks (L15) and plays *punta* music for a large Garífuna crowd. *(Walk along the beach from Tela to La Ensenada for about 2hr. If alone, it's safer to take a taxi from Tela L50. Buses run to Triunfo via La Ensenada every 30min. 6am-6pm from C. 10, Av. 8. Any La Ceiba bus can drop you off.)*

LANCETILLA BOTANICAL GARDENS

The gardens are 6km from Tela. Rent a bike or take a taxi to get there (L40-L70). The entrance is on the left side of the main road toward El Progreso and San Pedro Sula. Take Av. 2 out of town to the highway, turn right, and look for the signs. Alternatively, hop on any bus headed for El Progreso or San Pedro and get off at the gate. A taxi from Tela to the gate L10, to the park L50. From the gate, the park is 3.5km away along a dirt road. Once you see buildings, head for the small house on the right—it's the visitor center, with maps and info in Spanish and English. Refreshment stands are inside. The Administrative Center (beyond the bamboo tunnel) has info, tours, and camping permits. For more info, contact COHDEFOR (☎448 2165) or ESNACIFOR (☎448 1740). Open daily 8am-3pm. L110. Tours free M-Th and F-Su L50 per guide. Self-guided tour L5.

Easily accessible from Tela, the Lancetilla Botanical Gardens were developed by the United Fruit Company in 1925 to determine which fruits would grow well in Honduras and to preserve the region's diverse flora and fauna. Visitors can see 200 species of soaring and singing birds and a staggering variety of plants. The reserve is divided into two sections: the **Wilson Popenoe Arboretum**, where experimental trees are grown, and the **Biological Reserve of Virgin Forest.**

PARQUE NACIONAL JEANETTE KAWAS

The easiest way to visit the park is with a guided tour. Garífuna Tours leads guided expeditions to the Punta Sal Peninsula (8am-3pm, L329 including snorkeling gear, 6 person minimum). The company also offers full-day bird-watching trips to Laguna de los Micos with lunch in Miami (L369, minimum 5 people). If traveling alone, arrange ahead of time in Tela: you'll need a tent, food, water, and a few free days. Arrange a drop-off and pickup by boat in Cocalito from Garífuna Tours or a local fisherman (L150 is reasonable). Garífuna Tours or PROLASANTE can help plan a trip.

To the west of Tela, Parque Nacional Jeanette Kawas (formerly called Parque Nacional Punta Sal) supports rare species and diverse ecosystems, from jungle to coral reefs. **Laguna de los Micos** boasts mangrove waterways, an abundance of birds, and, farther west, the white sand beaches of the **Punta Sal Peninsula**. On the west side of the peninsula, **Puerto Escondido**, a sheltered cove, provides great snorkeling in a pristine coral reef that is home to many manatees. In the 18th century the famed pirate Captain Morgan used this port, and supposedly his treasure still remains buried somewhere on the sandy shores. For home-cooked meals (L60), on the east side by the beach, head to the tiny, two-family Garífuna village of **Cocalito**. From Cocalito, you can take a steep 0.6km trail to the left to the top of a cliff for panoramic views from the Punta Sal **lighthouse**. A trail to the right of the village leads up to another lookout point and then down a steep wooden stairway to a beach popular with monkeys and Montezuma's Oriole (1-1½hr.). The park's namesake, naturalist Jeanette Kawas, was a strong defender of the preserve until she was murdered in her Tela home in 1995. Many think she was killed by profiteers interested in developing the land.

PUNTA IZOPO RESERVE

Garífuna Tours leads excellent kayaking trips (L300). Local guides can be found in Triunfo de la Cruz; ask a day in advance at the Pulpería Soraya. Be sure to bring long pants and bug repellent and plan to get wet. If you are headed to the park on your own, PROLANSATE has maps (L261-L2000).

One of Honduras' 77 wildlife preserves, this 1100-hectare reserve is home to a host of plant and animal species. The bird-watching in particular is great—parrots, toucans, blue herons, tiger herons, and kingfishers all nest here. Within the park's mangrove forest lies a vast network of canals accessible only by kayak or canoe. Paddle quietly to increase the chances of spotting the extremely shy creatures. Though tempting, it's unwise to come here alone. The local Garífunas often say *"entra si quieres, sal si puedes"* (enter if you want, leave if you can); it's easy to get very lost very quickly.

LA CEIBA

A popular Honduran saying goes, "Tegucigalpa thinks, San Pedro Sula works, and La Ceiba parties." La Ceiba (pop. 122,800) is the largest city on the north coast and the country's third-largest overall. Although the town's namesake, the giant, umbrella-shaped *ceiba* tree, died out long ago and its beaches aren't the greatest, tourists still visit to catch a plane to the Bay Islands or to enjoy the city's famous *carnaval*. Because of its location and its airport, La Ceiba is quickly becoming a hub for ecotourists making trips to hike PN Pico Bonito, raft the Río Cangrejal, and kayak in search of manatees in RVS Cuero y Salado.

⌐ TRANSPORTATION

Flights: Aeropuerto Goloson, 6km west of town on the road to Tela. Snag any Tela-bound bus (L1) and ask to be let off by the airport, or take a taxi (L50) from the *punto de taxis* at the corner of the *parque*. **Isleña, Taca,** and **SOSA** airlines have offices opposite the eastern side of the *parque*. It's best to call ahead to make a reservation, but during the low season you can usually catch a flight without calling. Pay at the airport.

Isleña: (☎440 0827, *parque* office 443 0179) flies to: **Grand Cayman** (2hr., M and F 9:30am, L8268); **Guanaja** (25min.; M-Sa 10am, 4pm; Su 4pm; L618); **Roatán** (15min.; 7:20, 10am, noon, 2:30, 4, 5:30pm; L582); **San Pedro Sula** (25min.; 7:40, 10am, 1, 4pm; L790); **Tegucigalpa** (40min., M-Sa 7:30am, 2pm; Su 2pm; L1035). Airport office open daily 6am-7pm; *parque* office open M-F 7am-5pm, Sa 7am-11am.

HONDURAS

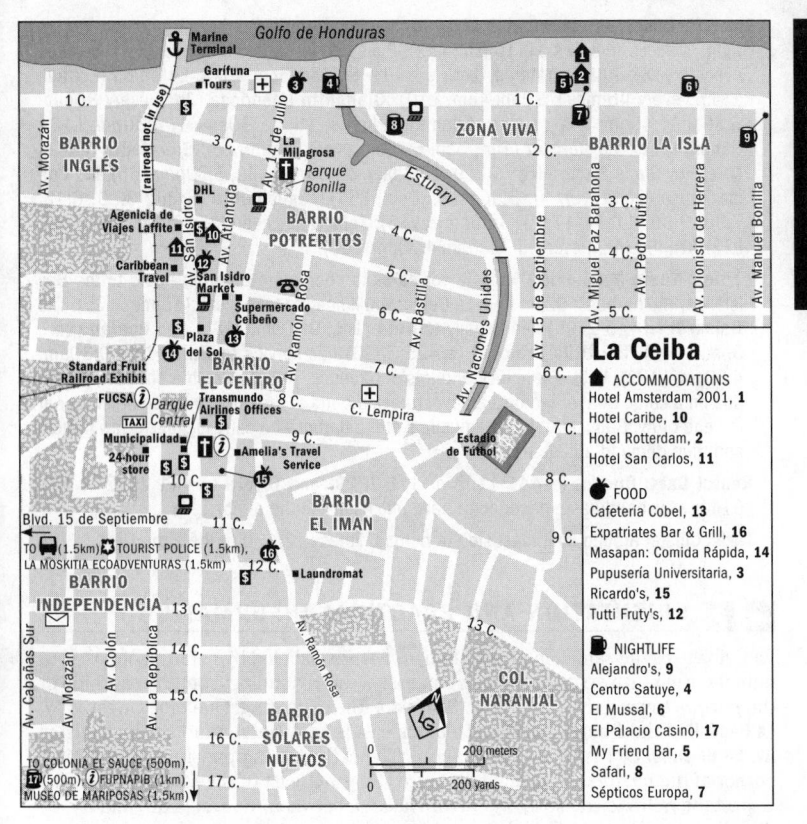

La Ceiba

🔺 ACCOMMODATIONS
Hotel Amsterdam 2001, **1**
Hotel Caribe, **10**
Hotel Rotterdam, **2**
Hotel San Carlos, **11**

🍴 FOOD
Cafetería Cobel, **13**
Expatriates Bar & Grill, **16**
Masapan: Comida Rápida, **14**
Pupusería Universitaria, **3**
Ricardo's, **15**
Tutti Fruty's, **12**

🍸 NIGHTLIFE
Alejandro's, **9**
Centro Satuye, **4**
El Mussal, **6**
El Palacio Casino, **17**
My Friend Bar, **5**
Safari, **8**
Sépticos Europa, **7**

SOSA: ☎440 0692 or 441 2513, *parque* office 443 1399; www.aerolineassosa.com, flies to: **Ahuas** (1hr.; M, W, F 6am; L1204); **Bros Laguna** (55min.; M, W, F 6am; L1208); **Guanaja** (26min.; M-Sa 10am, daily 4pm; L618); **Kauquira** (1½hr.; Tu, Sa 6am; L1384); **Palacios** (45min., M-Sa 6am, L1045); **Puerto Lempira** (1¼hr., M-Sa 6am, L1321); **Roatán** (16min.; M-Sa 6:15, 8:45, 9:45am, 12:15, 2:15, 3:15pm; Su 8:45am, 12:15, 2:15, 3:15pm; L556); **San Pedro Sula** (26min.; M-Sa 7:30, 9:45am, 1:30pm, Su 9:45am; L762); **Utila** (10min.; M-Sa 6:30am, 3:15pm, Su 3:15pm; L556); **Wampusirpe** (1hr., Th 6am, L1510). Airport office open M-Sa 5am-5:30pm, Su 6:30am-4:30pm; park office open M-F 7:30am-5pm, Sa 7:30am-noon.

Rollins Air: (☎441 2560) flies to: **Guanaja** (2 daily, L390) and **Tegucigalpa** (2 daily, L513).

Taca ☎441 2519, *parque* office 443 0173, has flights to: all central American capitals including **Belize City** (daily, L2950) and **San José** (daily, L3382); **San Pedro Sula** (daily 7:45am, 1:40pm, L1400); **Tegucigalpa** (daily 1:40pm, L2200); and worldwide connections. Airport office open daily 5:30am-6pm; *parque* office open M-F 8am-5pm, Sa 8am-noon.

Atlantic Airlines: (☎440 1220, 440 0863, or 440 2343; atlanticairlines.com.ni). An office is on Av. La República and at the airport. Flies to: **Ahuas** (1¼hr., M-Sa 6am, L1258); **Belize City** (2hr.; M, W, F 7am; L2743); **Grand Cayman** (2hr.; M, F 9am; L5168); **Guanaja** (35min.; 7am, 3:45pm; L617); **Managua** (1¾hr.; M, W, F 7:15am; L3157); **Puerto Lempira** (1¼hr.; M-Sa 6am, M and Th 3pm; L1321); **Roatán** (15min.; 7:15, 9:45am, noon, 3:15, 5pm; L540); **San Pedro Sula** (26min.; daily 8:30am, additional 7am flight M, W, F; L761.25); **Tegucigalpa** (45min.; 7:15am, 1pm; L1009); **Utila** (10min.; 7:15am, 3:15pm; L540). Airport office open daily 5am-5:30pm; Av. La República office open M-F 8am-5pm, Sa 8am-1pm.

Intercity Buses: The **terminal,** halfway to the airport on Blvd. 15 de Septiembre on the right, is accessible by **taxi** (10min., L12). Buses go to: **El Porvenir** (30min., 6am-5pm every hr., L8); **Jutiapa** (Meren, 1hr., every hr. 8:45am-5pm, L14); **La Union** (Ectraul, 1¼hr., every 45min. 6:30am-4pm, L10); **Olanchito** (Mendosa, 2hr., every 30min. 6:30am-4:45pm, L42); **Nueva Armenia** (2hr.; 8, 10, 11:30am, 1, 4:30pm; L16); **Sambo Creek** via **Corozal** (1hr., 5am-6:10pm every 35min., L8); **San Pedro Sula** is served by Diana Express (6, 7:30, 9, 10:30am, 12:30, 2, 4:30, 5:30pm; L66) and Catisa/Tupsa (3hr., every hr. 5:30am-5:30pm, L55); **Tegucigalpa** (6½hr.; 3:30, 6:15, 7:30, 9:30, 11am, 12:30, 3:30pm; L145); **Tela** (2hr., every 25min. 4:20am-6pm, L22); **Trujillo** (4hr., every hr. 5:30am-4:30pm, L60).

Ferries: Nuevo Muelle de Cabotaje serves as the departure point for boats to the Bay Islands. The harbor is 22km from La Ceiba; you'll need to take a cab (15min., L25). The **Galaxy II** (☎445 1795) heads daily to **Utila** (1hr., 9:30am, L185) and **Roatán** (2hr., 3pm, L140). The **Utila Princess** (☎425 3390) has service to **Utila** (1hr.; 9:30am, 4:30pm; L185). With a little luck and lots of patience, you can catch a cheaper, longer ride on a cargo boat or motorized *cayuco*—ask around at the dock or at the other pier at the end of Av. San Isidro. Beware hustlers at the harbor who carry luggage a few meters and then demand a huge tip.

Rental Cars: Budget (☎441 1105 or 441 2929) and **Toyota** (☎441 2532 or 441 0140; www.hondurasrentacar.com) have offices inside the airport.

Taxis: Cluster around southeast side of *parque.* Fares L12, L50 to the airport.

✴🛈 ORIENTATION AND PRACTICAL INFORMATION

La Ceiba uses the same old grid system; *avenidas,* labeled by name as opposed to number, run north-south and *calles* run east-west. Extending from the east side of the *parque* toward the water is **Av. San Isidro,** the main drag. One block west is **Av. La República** and 1 block north and a block east is **Av. Atlanta.** Another block east is **Av. 14 de Julio.** C. 1 runs along the shore. The cathedral is opposite the southeast corner of the *parque.* Most nightclubs are along 1 C. east of the **Estuary.** West on 1 C. past the railroad tracks is *el centro.* The area between Av. San Isidro and Av. 14 de Julio from 1 C. to 11 C. is the safest part of town.

Tourist Information: Consejo Municipal de Turismo, C. 1, (☎440 3045), a block east from the *parque*'s southeast corner next to the cathedral, has *carnaval* information. Open M-F 8:30am-5pm, Sa 8am-noon. **FUCSA** (☎443 0329; www.cueroysalado.cjb.net), opposite the northwest corner of the *parque* on C. 8 across from the Standard Fruit Railroad Exhibit, is the organization that administers the Cuero y Salado Wildlife Refuge and has extensive info on transportation, trails, guides, and lodging within the park. Open M-F 8am-5pm. **FUPNAPIB,** 1 Etapa, 2 C. (☎440 0966; fupnapib@hondutel.hu or fupnapib@iaceiba.com), is the organization that oversees PN Pico Bonito and has information about volunteering, guides, tours, and how to get to the numerous public access points of the park. **Garífuna Tours** (☎440 3252) on the corner of C. 1 and Av. San Isidro, is a highly respected tour operator. Open daily 7:30am-noon and 2-6pm. **Jungle River** (☎440 1268; www.hondurasjungetours.net), 1 block south of Hotel Potleidam on Av. Miguel Paz Barahona, C. 1/2, and **Omega Tours** (☎440 0334; www.omegatours.hn), at the Río Cangrejal, are also great sources of information on local adventures.

Travel Agencies: Transmundo (☎443 2840), Av. San Isidro, C. 9/10 across from Banpais. English spoken. Open M-F 8-11:30am and 1:30-5pm, Sa 8-11:30am. **Caribbean Travel** (☎443 1360; ctravel@caribe.hn), Av. San Isidro, C. 5/6, located next to Hotel

San Carlos. Open M-F 7:30-11:30am and 1:30-4:30pm, Sa 7:30-11am. **Agencia de Viajes Laffite**, Av. San Isidro, C. 5/6, (☎443 0115), opposite Hotel San Carlos. English spoken. Open M-F 7:30-11:30am and 1:30-4:30pm, Sa 7:30-11am.

Banks: BGA, on C. 9 Av. San Isidro/14 de Julio ½ block east of the southeast corner of the park, cashes traveler's checks and has a 24hr. Plus/Visa **ATM**. Open M-F 9am-4pm, Sa 9-11:30am. **Banco Credomatic**, Av. San Isidro, C. 5, across from Hotel Iberia, gives cash advances on AmEx/MC/V. Open M-F 9am-5pm, Sa 9am-noon.

Markets: San Isidro, C. 6, 1 block east of Av. San Isidro. Spilling onto the street is one of the biggest indoor markets in Central America, selling everything from food to puppies. Open approximately M-Sa 7am-7pm, Su 7am-noon. **Supermarket Super Ceibeño** has 2 locations: one next to San Isidro market, the other 1 block north of the *parque* on Av. La República and C. 7. Open M-Sa 7am-7pm, Su 7am-noon.

Police: Preventiva (☎441 0995 or 441 1899, **Tourist Police** ☎441 6288 or 441 1885), off Blvd. 15 de Septiembre, next to the bus terminal. Open 24hr.

Hospital: C. 8 (☎442 2195), 4 blocks east of the *parque*. 24hr. emergency service.

Telephones: Hondutel, C. 5/6, Av. Ramon Rosa (☎443 0024; fax 443 0700), 3 blocks east of Av. San Isidro, under the red and white radio tower. 24hr. Sprint and AT&T services. **Fax** available M-F 8am-noon and 1-3:30pm.

Internet: Cafe@Cafe, (☎440 2441; benedettocafe@hotmail.com) Av. San Isidro, C. 6/7, in Plaza del Sol, is centrally located with A/C, gourmet pastries, a *licuado* stand, and cafeteria. Internet L22 per hr. Calls to US L2 per min. Open M-F 7:30am-8pm, Su 7:30am-noon. **Cybercafe La Ceiba** (☎443 0460) on C. 1 just across the Estuary in the mall on the right offers Internet for L20 per hr. and calls to the US for L3 per min. Free coffee for Internet users. Open M-Sa 7am-9pm, Su 8am-6pm.

Post Office: Av. Morazán, C. 13, in Barrio Independencia in the southwest part of town. **EMS Express Mail** in the same building. Both open M-F 8am-3pm, Sa 8am-noon.

▐ ACCOMMODATIONS

The cheapest spots in town are on Av. San Isidro and Av. 14 de Julio; be careful at night. Some hotels have deceptively attractive lobbies; if in doubt, ask to see a room first. Electricity in town is not very reliable—blackouts are frequent.

Hotel San Carlos, Av. San Isidro, C. 5/6 (☎443 0330), is hidden behind a restaurant and bread factory next to Hotel Iberia. Rooms are basic and well kept with helicopter-sized ceiling fans, baths, and great hospitality. Singles L90; doubles L120. ❷

Hotel Rotterdam (☎440 0321), 7 blocks east of Av. San Isidro on C. 1 and Av. Miguel Paz Barahoa. A newer offshoot of the older Amsterdam 2001 (see below). ½ block from the beach, freshly painted rooms, all with baths, open out onto a grassy courtyard. Singles L180; doubles L180; triples L250. ❷

Hotel Amsterdam 2001 (☎443 2311), next door to Hotel Rotterdam, has a large dorm room above owner Jan's woodworking shop. Close to the beach. Haggle with him for group discounts. Singles L75; dark doubles with bath L180; triples L200. ❷

Hotel Caribe, C. 5, Av. San Isidro/Atlántida (☎443 1857). Spacious rooms off a poorly-lit hallway. Singles and doubles with bath L100, with cable TV L150, with A/C L220. ❷

▐ FOOD

La Ceiba boasts enough mid-priced *comedores* and buffets to keep budget travelers healthy and wealthy. **Barrio La Barra,** an entertainment district on the east end of C. 1 along the beach, is home to a good number of traditional places. Vendors sell *platos típicos* and fruit in the *mercado* on C. 6.

Expatriates Bar and Grill, C. 12, at the eastern end at the corner of Av. Ramon Rosa. Sit under Expats' thatched roof for some buffalo wings (L80) and a beer (L16) while listening to Bob Dylan and catching the latest baseball game. Meals from the grill L50-L120. Many vegetarian options; veggie platter L29. An excellent cigar emporium is housed here along with free Internet access and Pacman. Happy hour 4-6pm. Open M-Sa 4pm-midnight, Su 11am-midnight during American football season (Sept.-Jan.). ❷

Pupusería Universitaria (☎440 1070), at the intersection of Av. 14 de Julio and C. 1. High quality meals for some of the cheapest prices in town. Elegant, relaxed atmosphere. *Pupusas* L11-L45, tacos L27; beer L14. Open daily 10am-11pm. ❶

Tutti Fruty's, on 6 C., Av. Isidro/Atlantida across from Multinet, serves up delicious fresh fruit smoothies (L16-L30), tropical fruit salads drenched in honey (L30), and sandwiches (L27) on wooden stump chairs in a rich Caribbean atmosphere. ❷

Ricardo's (☎443 0468), Av. 14 de Julio, C. 10, around the corner from Banpais. The perfect place to get a dash of unpretentious elegance. The steaks, seafood, and pasta are considered some of the best in Central America, and the chef has the awards to back it up. Dressy casual attire required (i.e., no jeans or sandals). Bilingual menu. Meals L145-L400. Open M-Sa 11:30am-1:30pm and 5:30-10pm. AmEx/MC/V. ❺

Cafetería Cobel (☎442 2192), on C. 7 between Av. Atlántida and Av. 14 de Julio. Cheap Honduran fare in a dining room that's become a *ceibaño* institution. Breakfast and lunch L34-L44. Open M-Sa 6:30am-6pm. ❷

Masapan: Comida Rápida (☎443 3458), 1 block north of the northwest corner of the *parque* on 7 C., Av. Isidro/República. A cafeteria with stations for sandwiches, meats, and fruits. Great for large groups of people with different tastes. Meals L60-L80. Open daily 6am-10pm. ❷

👁 🌸 SIGHTS AND FESTIVALS

La Ceiba might be the third largest city in Honduras, but there's surprisingly little to see when it's not *carnaval* time. Not even the beaches are a big asset; for clean, swimmable shores, head to the Garífuna villages of **Corozal** or **Sambo Creek.** Buses go back and forth every 35min. 5am-6:10pm (1hr., L8). Garífuna meals (L40-L60) and simple rooms (L50-L100) are available in both towns.

One block northwest of the *parque central* between 8/7 C., the influential United Fruit Company has maintained a modest but beautiful **botanical garden** curiously combined with a **railroad museum.** A free stroll around the lush grounds will reveal a dozen engines, cabooses, and handcars. You can also ride the passenger train next to the park. (Round-trip 30min., L4. Open daily 6am-6pm.) In Colonia Sauce Etapal, C. 5, 2 blocks east and 3 blocks south of FUPNAPIB, the jam packed **Butterfly and Insect Museum** is a jaw-dropper, featuring 12,000 insects from 110 countries. Be sure to check out the moth with the world's largest mouth and the moth with the world's largest wingspan—and you know what they say about moths with large wingspans. Robert Lehman, primary provider of local specimens, is frequently in the office and available to chat. (☎442 2874; www.hondurasbutterfly.com. Open M-Sa 8am-5pm. Subtitles in English and Spanish. Free tours in English or Spanish. L25, children L15.) Also consider taking in some *fútbol* at the local **stadium;** cheap seats are only L30. (Info available at the tourist office.)

During *carnaval*, in the second and third weeks of May, La Ceiba fills with over 100,000 visitors who come to enjoy the wild tangle of parades, costumes, and tributes to local patron saint San Isidro. The great *ceibaño* pride fills neighborhood parties as residents cheer on contestants in the numerous youth beauty pageants.

◙ NIGHTLIFE

If you're looking for a good time, Honduras's biggest party town will not let you down. Large crowds keep the sidewalk safe and buzzing all night in the **Zona Viva**, the heart of La Ceiba's action. In addition, most clubs hire private security to keep an eye on things on weekends. Still, use common sense: stay alert, take taxis, and leave valuables behind. Thanks to a La Ceiba ordinance, minors (17 and under) aren't allowed in nightspots, so have your ID ready. Clubs rarely have dress codes, but few people wear sandals or shorts. The popular **Arenas** pumps out a mix of Latin and US Top 40. (Cover L20. Open Th-Su 8pm-4am.) For *punta* music, the Garífuna crowd packs into ◙**Centro Satuye**, next to the bridge behind Queen Burger on C. 1, with a live band. (Cover L30. Open 9pm-4am.) Pricey drinks at **El Mussal**, a popular beach dance club, pay for extra security and air-conditioning. (Beer L20. Cover Th-Sa L40-L170. Women free except F-Sa after 11pm.) The mix of an express restaurant, sports bar, and disco have made **Crash** another hip spot, especially on weekends. **Safari** is probably the only club between here and Texas that plays country-western music. (Pop music on Sa. Open daily 6pm-6am.) Another popular but pricey disco is **Alejandro's**. (6 beers L50. Cover F-Sa L40-L50. Open Tu-Sa from 8pm.)

A collection of bars dots the city. **Expatriates Bar and Grill** (see **Food**, above) is a fun place to mix with other foreigners. **My Friend Bar** is a beachside locale perfect for a nightcap accompanied by the sound of crashing waves and Latin music. Next door, the well-decorated **Sépticos Europa** bar plays an eclectic selection of local, European, and American music (open W-Sa 8pm-5am). Try your luck on the one-armed bandits at **El Palacio Casino**, in La Quinta Hotel at the southern end of Av. San Isidro; take a cab (open daily 7pm-4am).

⚠ ◙ OUTDOOR ACTIVITIES AND GUIDED TOURS

La Ceiba makes a great base for expeditions into the wilderness, and there are many tour operators in the city. Ask around about reputations and remember that what may seem like a super-cheap deal may mean lousy service. **La Mosquitia Ecoaventuras**, (☎442 0104; www.honduras.com/moskitia) runs trips to nearby **Pico Bonito**, (3-day/2-night trekking L2894, day hiking 8am-3pm L657), **Cuero y Salado** (day tour by motor board or kayak beginning at 7am, L1315), and rafting in the **Río Cangrejal** which has some of the best rapids in all of Central America, reaching Class III in the dry season and Class IV in the rainy season (half-day beginning at 8am or 1:30pm, L650.) La Mosquitia runs some of the best-planned trips around to the **Mosquito Coast**, ranging from two-day jaunts to 500km expeditions through the entire region. Though these tours are a bit pricey, they feature jungle hiking, Garífuna dancing, and petroglyph-viewing; La Mosquitia can airlift sick or injured adventurers to safety (4-day/3-night, with bilingual guide, food, and airport taxes L6050. 5-day all-inclusive L21,800). **Garífuna Tours** runs trips to **Pico Bonito** (minimum 3 people, 8am-2pm, L357), **Río Cangrejal** rafting (minimum 2 people, 8:30am-2pm, L488), **Cuero y Salado** (minimum 5 people, 7:30am-3pm, L490), and to **Cayos Cochinos**, where you can snorkel and enjoy Garífuna culture (minimum 6 people, 7am-3pm, L545). **Omega Tours** runs highly acclaimed two-week rafting adventures in the **Moskita; Jungle River,** has **canopy ziplines,** Río Cangrejal rafting, and **horseback riding** in Pico Bonito.

◙ DAYTRIP FROM LA CEIBA: CUERO Y SALADO RESERVE

Take the direct bus to La Unión (every hr. starting at 6:20am, L9.50). Get off at the train tracks where you will find a small building labeled "Tren Turistico" and a hand-operated railcar that you can pump all the way to the visitor center (1hr., L40). Alternatively, the

Ferrocarril Nacional (M-F ☎ 443 3525, Sa-Su 443 4395) runs a normal train on the same tracks (30min., every hr. 7am-3pm or on-call from FUCSA. L180 per trip.) Keep in mind that the last bus for La Unión leaves at 3pm. The visitor center has trail maps and a cafeteria to your right at the end of the tracks in Saldo Burra. (Entrance fee L180, children L90, and students L90. Naturalist guides for up to 7 people L100. Boat use L200-L350 for up to 7 people.) The FUCSA office is down the path that runs in front of the visitor center to the left. Only 30 people may enter the refuge per day, so call early to reserve a spot.

The Cuero y Salado Wildlife Refuge, 33km west of La Ceiba, is one of the most biologically diverse regions of Honduras. Spilling out into the Caribbean Sea, the 13,225 hectares of freshwater wetlands, saltwater marshes, and coastline protect 350 different species of animals, including jaguars, ocelots, sloths, and boa constrictors. Two hundred species of birds—more than a quarter of all those in Honduras—can also be found here. Topping it off, 10% of all the manatees in the world live in the reserve, which explains why they are the park's mascot.

There are four designated trails through the park; three are aquatic and one is terrestrial. Of the aquatic trails, **El Espejo** is the most easily accessible and mainly serves as an entryway to the other two aquatic trails. It follows the Estero de Garcia river that runs along the visitor center, south to Ríos Termita, Bujaja, and Monos and north to the bay and Campo Salada Barro (2hr.). **El Olingo** breaks off from El Espejo and heads up the Río Salado to the Río Limon and into Río Cocodrillo (famous for its crocodile sightings) and Marínero (2hr.). From the coast, **Boca Cerrada**, the longest trail, follows the Río Cuero through the entire length of the park, starting near the visitor center and going past Barra Río Cuero to the westernmost point of the park in Lago Boca Cerrada where the majority of the park's manatees reside (3½hr.). **El Coco** (9km), the park's only land trail, heads east from the visitor center along the coast (2½hr.). For those staying overnight, FUSCA rents four-person tents (L150 per night) and also has newly built cabins; bring your own sheets. Camping on the beach is allowed (L25 per night), but bring your own food, water, and bug repellent.

PARQUE NACIONAL PICO BONITO

Fluttering butterflies and prowling jaguars are among the few creatures who have witnessed the mostly undisturbed splendors of PN Pico Bonito. Sheer cliffs, deep canyons, and mist-enshrouded peaks are absolutely jaw-dropping. Trails through the park can be explored with or without a guide.

AT A GLANCE	
AREA: 560 sq. km.	**GATEWAYS:** La Ceiba (p. 482).
CLIMATE: Rainforest.	**CAMPING:** Near Campamento de CURLA or on El Mirador trail.
FEATURES: Zacate Waterfall, Río Cangrejal, El Pico.	
HIGHLIGHTS: Amaras wildlife center, Butterfly farm, Serpentarium.	**FEES AND RESERVATIONS:** L18 entrance fee.

▐ TRANSPORTATION

To get to the **Campamento de CURLA,** take any bus marked "1 de Mayo" or "Armenia Bonito" from either the *parque central* or the Parque Bonilla in La Ceiba to the last stop in Armenia Bonito. (15min., every 30min. 6am-6pm, L3.50.) From the bus stop in Armenia Bonito, head east towards the mountains and take the first right at the fork. Follow the road for 45min. and continue across the river bed to the park;

the *campamento* is on the right. Any **taxi** can get to the **Zacate Waterfall**. Alternatively, take any westbound bus toward Tela from the San Jose Terminal and ask the driver to let you off at the Zacate trailhead, 2km past El Pino on the left side of the road (L50; most drivers know where it is).

To get to **AMARAS,** take any westbound bus toward Tela to the entrance sign for El Pino village, 13km from La Ceiba. Walk back 50m toward La Ceiba on the highway and take a right at the AMARAS sign just before Km 177. Proceed down the drive for 1km, go right at the fork and the complex will be directly on your left.

To get to the **Tropical Butterfly Farm and Serpentarium,** head the opposite direction from the El Pino town sign for 100m. Turn left at the sign for The Lodge at Pico Bonito and after 45min. it will be on your left. To get to the **Río Cangrejal visitor center** take the Yaruca-Urraco bus that stops before Naranjo village. Ask to get off at Sendero Behuco where there is a small cabin that operates the chairlift over the river and has information on how to get to the visitor center.

🛈 PRACTICAL INFORMATION

The two main sources of information are FUPNAPIB in La Ceiba and the Campamento de CURLA in the park. **FUPNAPIB**, Colonia El Sauce Etapa 1 C. 2 (☎ 440 0966), has maps and extensive information on getting to the park, the different areas to be explored, and ongoing volunteer projects. **Campamento de CURLA** is home to park ranger **Fernando Martínez** who can also serve as your Spanish-speaking guide for L200 per day. An entrance fee of L18 is due at the Campamento de CURLA. **La Mosquitia Ecoaventuras, Omega Tours, Jungle River,** or **Garífuna Tours** can all arrange guides for L300 per day (see **Tourist Information**, p. 484).

🏠 ACCOMMODATIONS

The park ranger's house at **Campamento del CURLA** is a cabin used by researchers with an accompanying campground for travelers. If you get the key from the ranger and bring your own food, you can stay here overnight and use the bare mattresses and grill. Otherwise, camp near the house or up El Mirador trail.

🥾 HIKING

The park ranger's house serves as a base for several of the trails that wind through the foothills of El Pico. From the Campamento, the road soon becomes **El Mirador** trail (3km). If the water isn't too high, it's possible to walk upstream along the river on huge, slippery boulders. If you can't follow the river, take the trail along the bank until you reach the Campamento del CURLA. From here, **El Behuco** trail (1km) leads a little way up the mountain and then arches back down; **Guatvza** trail (1km) heads down to a swimming area. Any farther into the park, trails disappear and it is recommended that you have a guide.

🗻 SIGHTS

ZACATE WATERFALL. Probably the most popular sight in the park, the 40m cascade is easily accessible. Visitors enjoy the view from up top and the swim down below. Ask the guard to point out the trail when you pay the entrance fee. From the beginning of the trailhead, walk down the road until you reach the guardhouse for the Dole Pineapple plantation. After about 250m, you'll see a small waterfall called **Cascada Ruidosa** ("noisy cascade"). Another 1km along the trail will bring you up to the Zacate falls.

AMARAS WILDLIFE REHABILITATION CENTER. Founded in 1993 to house animals rescued from the black market, AMARAS lets visitors see animals up close before they are released back into the wild. Caretaker Guillermo Benson can often be found helping with white-faced monkeys, macaws, sloths, or even baby jaguars. Nearby Zacate Waterfall makes for a nice joint-daytrip with AMARAS. Although there is no fee, gifts of food (carrots, bananas, meat) are greatly appreciated to help support the center. The center is open whenever you'd like to stop by, but the road is dangerous to travel at night or alone. Check with FUPNAPIB beforehand to see which animals are being treated. (☎443 3824; amaras@honduras.com.)

TROPICAL BUTTERFLY FARM AND SERPENTARIUM. Located at the base of the Pico Bonito National Park at the Lodge at Pico Bonito, 20-30 species of butterfly inhabit a 190 sq. m enclosure. Nearby, 12-15 species of reptiles wow visitors with colors rivaling the butterflies. (☎440 0388. Butterfly farm L35, children L20. Serpentarium L40/L25. Open W-Su 8am-4pm. English-speaking staff.)

RÍO CANGREJAL. The site of the park's recently opened **visitor center,** this whitewater rafting, hiking, kayaking, and canopy-zip-lining paradise is quickly becoming the park's recreation nucleus. Many tour operators run daily activities; Jungle River and Omega Tours have cabins on the river. (Visitor center open daily 8am-5pm.)

THE PEAK. Climbing the park's primary peak is extremely difficult and requires technical skill. It takes 6-10 days to reach the summit and 3-4 days to return. Experienced climbers interested in attempting the feat should contact **Germán Martínez** (☎440 0388) at the Lodge at Pico Bonito before going to Honduras. A slightly less exhausting option is **Sendero Quetzal,** a trail winding up 1745m past four levels of vegetation to a nearby lower peak. (To get to Sendero Quetzal take a bus from La Ceiba to Olanchito and then connect to Santa Barbara.)

TRUJILLO

With El Olancho to the south and La Mosquitia to the east, Trujillo (pop. 9200) is a popular launch pad for adventurous expeditions. After the city's founding in 1525, attacks by British pirates made the Spanish work to keep enough inhabitants to defend it. The pirates are long gone, but near abandonment has worked to preserve a quiet, small-town feel despite miles of Caribbean beaches.

▐ TRANSPORTATION

Flights: The **airstrip,** 1.5km from the town's center down C. Río Negro, is more or less abandoned. **Atlantic** (☎440 1220 or 440 0863) and **SOSA** (☎440 0692 or 441 2513) planes arrive 1 to 2 times per week to drop off passengers. Planes only pick up passengers if there are more than 3 and a call is made to La Ceiba ahead of time.

Buses: Buses leave from the bus terminal next to the Texaco gas station, a 10min. walk or L13 taxi ride from 1km west of the parque on C. Río Negro. To get to **La Unión,** take a bus to **Saba.** Buses to **Santa Fé** leave in front of the old cemetery on C. de Mercado (1hr.; 9, 10:45am, noon, and 3pm, returns 6:30 and 11am; L12). **Puerto Castilla** buses depart from the unmarked gas station on C. Río Negro at the bottom of the hill, headed away from the park (30min., every 2hr. 7:30am-6pm, L11).

Cotraipbal: (☎434 4932) to: **La Ceiba** (3hr., every 45min. 1:15am-2:15pm, L66); **San Pedro Sula** (6hr., every 45min. 1:15am-2:15pm, L110); and **Tegus** (9hr., 1am and 4:45am, L188).

Cotuc: (☎444 2181) buses to: **La Ceiba** (2¾ hr., every hour 1am-2:15pm, L66); **Progreso** (5½hr., every hour 1am-2:15pm, L110); **Saba** (1¼hr., every hour 1am-2:15pm, L40); **San Pedro Sula** (6hr., every hour 1am-2:15pm, L110); **Tela** (4½hr., every hour 1am-2:15pm, L100); and **Tocoa** (45min., every 30 min. 1am-2:15pm, L26).

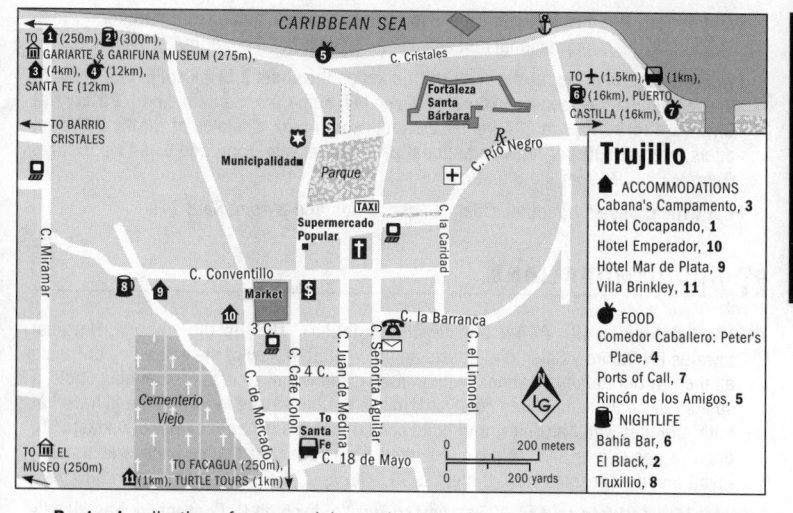

CARIBBEAN SEA

TO **1**(250m), **2**(300m), **GARIARTE & GARIFUNA MUSEUM** (275m), **3**(4km), **4**(12km), SANTA FE (12km)

← TO BARRIO CRISTALES

C. Cristales

Fortaleza Santa Bárbara

TO **+**(1.5km), **□**(1km), **6**(16km), PUERTO CASTILLA (16km), **7**

Municipalidad

Parque

R. Río Negro

TAXI

Supermercado Popular

C. la Caridad

C. Conventillo

Market

C. la Barranca

C. Miramar

C. el Limonel

C. de Mercado

C. Juan de Medina

C. Señorita Aguilar

C. Cafe Colon

Cementerio Viejo

TO **™** EL MUSEO (250m)

TO FACAGUA (250m), **⑪**(1km), TURTLE TOURS (1km)

To Santa Fe

C. 18 de Mayo

0   200 meters
0   200 yards

Trujillo

🛏 ACCOMMODATIONS
Cabana's Campamento, 3
Hotel Cocapando, 1
Hotel Emperador, 10
Hotel Mar de Plata, 9
Villa Brinkley, 11

🍴 FOOD
Comedor Caballero: Peter's Place, 4
Ports of Call, 7
Rincón de los Amigos, 5

🍸 NIGHTLIFE
Bahía Bar, 6
El Black, 2
Truxillio, 8

HONDURAS

Boats: A collection of commercial vessels leaves from Trujillo to the **Bay Islands,** and from there to **Jamaica.** Ask at the docks for information. **FUCAGUA** (☎434 4294) sends boats to **Cayo Blanco** (L470) for day trips. Boats also travel to **Palacios, Everta Lempira,** and other places in La Mosquitia at irregular times.

Taxis: Taxis queue at the southeast corner of the *parque* and cost L13 to any point with in the city, including the bus station and airport. At night, prices jump to L20-L40. Taxis are recommended for anyone going to or from the bus stop at night, or those not taking the bus to Sante Fe. Arrange for a taxi to pick you up in advance for L70-L100.

▦ ▐ ORIENTATION AND PRACTICAL INFORMATION

Trujillo's main street, **Calle Conventillo,** parallels the beach one block south of the *parque central.* All streets in Trujillo are *"calles"* and are marked by wooden signs at major intersections. The beaches in Barrio Cristales are excellent, but best avoided at night.

Tourist Information: Turtle Tours (☎/fax 434 4431; info@turtletours.de), at the Villa Brinkley Hotel. Info on attractions in and around Trujillo, as well as bike rentals. English, German, and Spanish spoken. Open M-F 8-11am and 2-5pm, Sa 3-11am. AmEx/MC/V.

Bank: Both banks cash traveler's checks. **Banco de Occidente,** C. Conventillo, C. Cafe Colon (☎434 4990). Open M-F 8:30am-4:30pm, Sa 8:30am-noon. Has **Western Union. Banco Atlántida** (☎434 4830), on park's northwest corner, gives V cash advances and has a 24hr. Visa **ATM.** Open M-F 9am-4pm, Sa 8:30-11:30am.

Supermarkets: Supermercado Popular (☎434 4438) has the largest grocery selection in town and accepts traveler's checks. Open M-Sa 7:30am-7pm, Su 8am-noon.

Laundry: Lavandería Colón (☎988 4433), west on C. Conventillo heading toward Barrio Cristales, 1½ blocks from Banco Occidente. L50 per load. Open M-Sa 8am-5pm.

Police: Preventiva (☎434 4038), in the northwest corner of the *parque.* Open 24hr.

Medical Services: Clinica de Especialistas Farmacias (☎434 4414), on C. Río Negro 1½ blocks east of the *parque.* Open M-F 7:30am-noon and 2-5pm, Sa 7:30am-noon. Hospital (☎434 4093), 1 block east of the *parque* on C. Río Negro. Little English spoken. Open 24hr.

Telephones: Hondutel, beside the post office, 1 block behind the cathedral on C. Señorita Aguilar. International and collect calls. Open M-F 7am-8pm, Sa 7am-noon.

Internet: TechniFuturo, across from the market on the street 1 block south parallel to C. Conventillo. Internet service L20 per hr. Open M-F 8am-6pm, Sa 8am–noon. **Galaxy Net Cafe** (☎434 3090), on C. Miramar 2 streets south of C. Cristales at the "7 UP" sign, offers Internet L30 per hr., international calls L5 per min., and copies L43 per page. Open M-Sa 8am-9pm, Su 9am-9pm.

Post Office: Beside Hondutel. Open M-F 8am-noon and 2-4pm, Sa 8-11am.

ACCOMMODATIONS

▨ **Villa Brinkley** (☎434 4444; brinkley@hondutel.hn), 1km up the steep C. Naranjal towards PN Capiro y Calentura, boasts an unforgettable view of the entire Bay of Trujillo all the way out to Punta Caxinas. With a disco-gymnasium, jacuzzi, 2 swimming pools, a sauna, and a turtle-inhabited courtyard, this is the best place in town. Rooms have hot bath, doubles with balconies, and hand-carved mahogany headboards. Breakfast L50, open to non-guests and includes unlimited fresh-squeezed orange juice, watermelon, toast, and an awesome view. Budget L299, with A/C L480, with marble tub L600. ❺

Hotel Mar de Plata (☎434 4051), next to Truxillo disco on C. Conventillo, has friendly management and nice rooms with bath, city view, free purified water, fan, and TV. Loud on weekends, good for the party-goer. Singles L100, Doubles L150. ❷

Hotel Emperador (☎434 446), on C. Mercado next to the market, is a well-kept and colorful hotel offering clean rooms with bath, fan, and TV. The owner, a professor, has useful info about the area. Open 24hr. Singles and doubles L120. ❷

Hotel Cocapando (☎434 4748), 2 blocks from C. Miramar on C. Cristales, down the hill next to the water. Rooms have bath, fan, and a good breeze. Ask for a room facing the water to avoid the noise of the weekend disco next door. Make sure toilets have seats. Singles L100; doubles L150, with A/C and TV L250. ❷

Cabana's Campamento (☎991 3391), 4km west of town on C. Cristales. Take a taxi (L60) or the Santa Fé bus and get off at the welcome sign. These peach-colored *"casitas"* on miles of private beach are ideal for a group of 4 or 5 wanting a rural location and quiet, pristine coastline. Cabins have A/C, hot bath, and TV in a fruit tree garden with access to a basketball court, pool, Spanish school, and in-house restaurant. Breakfast L35-L70, soup L90-L150, fried rice L80-L90. Quads L450; 5-person room L650. ❺

FOOD

In-town eateries are unexciting, but a plethora of bars and restaurants with seafood and Gantuna specials line the beach all along Barrio Cristales.

Comedor Caballero: Peter's Place, tucked away in the Gantuna community of Santa Fé, has the best seafood dishes around. All meals prepared by an excellent ex-cruise ship chef who whips up huge, savory platters that easily feed 2. Fish cakes L75; garlic shrimp L150; mixed veggie plate L60. Open daily. ❸

Rincón de los Amigos (☎988 7084), on C. Cristales north of the *parque*, right on the beach. This Italian restaurant serves wonderful brick-oven pizza on a breezy patio. The nearby dock offers great sunset views. Pizza L70-L110, spaghetti L60-L90, *licuados* L12-L15. Open M-Sa 11am-10pm. ❷

Ports of Call is a charming beachside bar near the airport. Beer L15. Opens at 9am. ❶

👁 SIGHTS

LA FORTALEZA DE SANTA BÁRBARA. Just east of the *parque*, this fort was built in 1575 to repel pirate attacks, a duty it fulfilled with only modest success. The fort's faded ramparts are one of the most poetic spots in Honduras, looking out upon the glistening bay. *(L55, students L10 with ID. Open daily 9am-noon and 1-5pm.)*

CEMENTERIO VIEJO. Here lies **William Walker,** the would-be enslaver of Central America. After unsuccessfully trying to impose plantation slavery on the isthmus, Walker was executed in 1860. The gate is usually locked, though many locals climb the walls in order to pay their respects to loved ones. *(Located near El Museo Riveras del Peregal. Walk down the main street with the sea to your right and turn left at Hotel Mar de Plata.)*

GARÍFUNA MUSEUM. The main attractions at the museum, located in Barrio Cristales across from Hotel Cocopando, are the beautiful, authentic Garífuna works of art for sale downstairs in **GariArte.** *(☎ 444 4365. Open daily 8am-noon and 2:30-6pm.)*

PUNTA DANCING. For the real Garífuna cultural experience, the owner of Hotel Cocopando teaches exhausting **punta** dance classes. *(☎ 434 4748. Call ahead to reserve space. Offered F and Sa 9am-3pm.)*

🎭 🌺 NIGHTLIFE AND FESTIVALS

If there's one thing the Garífuna know how to do, it's party. This is especially true the last full week of June, when Trujillo has its annual festival and each *barrio* holds a block party with huge speakers, contests, beer, and dancing. The last night culminates in a huge party with the biggest bands in Honduras coming to play. **Barrio Cristales** throbs until dawn, with beachfront bar patrons spilling out onto the sand—usually face-first. Beers are an unbelievably cheap L10-L15, and bars often host authentic and spontaneous *punta* displays, the trademark Garífuna dance.

El Truxillo, up C. Conventillo past Hotel Mar de Plata; look for the giant beer bottle. Currently the hottest disco around, with televisions, black lights, good security, and a large dance fl. Cover L35. Beer L15. Open 8pm-5am Su, Th-Sa.

Bahía Bar (☎434 4770 or 981 8045; jguzmanv@yahoo.com), behind the airstrip right on the beach. Owners tailor activities to the clientele and are always up for requests. Beer L15. Long Island Ice Tea L110. Open daily 8am-midnight, later on weekends.

El Black (a.k.a. "Disco Black and White"), in front of the Hotel Cocopando. Almost never has a cover. The party usually shuffles up to the 2nd fl. terrace for a breeze when the dancing gets hot. Beer L12-L14. Open Su, F-Sa 9pm-4am.

⚠ OUTDOOR ACTIVITIES

For info on the nearby parks and lagoons, stop by the **FUCAGUA** office 250m up C. Naranjal towards Villa Brinkley. Visitors to the two national parks are expected to stop by the office to pay a fee. (☎434 4294. L50 per person. Open M-F 7:30am-noon and 1:30-5pm.) Although guides are not necessary, FUCAGUA can arrange for one (L100) with a day's notice. **Turtle Tours** (see **Practical Information,** above) sells trips to the top of **Cerro Calentura** in a 4WD vehicle (1¼hr., L375 per person). It also offers guided hikes (L280 per person) and **canoe** trips in the Guaimoreto Lagoon (L375 per person). Though pricey by backpacker standards, guided tours are a worthwhile way to visit the **Crocodile Reserve** at the **Hacienda El Tumbador** (L375 per person plus L95 entrance fee).

PARQUE NACIONAL CAPIRO Y CALENTURA. Named for towering peaks Cerro Capiro (eastern) and Cerro Calentura (western), this park covers the forested slopes behind Trujillo. The best time to go is around 4am, when animals are most likely to appear; if you go in the afternoon, the creatures won't show, but the view from the top is still worth the effort. On clear days you can see Roatán. *(To reach the summit, walk or take a 4WD taxi up the hill past Villa Brinkley Hotel. It's a 9km hike to the top.)*

PARQUE NACIONAL LAGUNA GUAIMORETO. A park centered around a lagoon northeast of Trujillo, PN Laguna Guaimoreto is an excellent place to birdwatch and spot the occasional crocodile. It is best seen very early in the morning or late afternoon via a guided boat tour. Make arrangements a day in advance through the FUCAGUA office or Turtle Tours. *(L400 for a boat, L100 for a guide for up to 5 people.)*

CAY FOR A DAY. Talk to FUCAGUA or Raul in Santa Fé about visiting of **Cayo Blanco,** a 5km sinking caye. Bring food and water. *(L400 boat and L100 guide.)*

◗ DAYTRIP FROM TRUJILLO: SANTA FÉ

A 9km trek west along the beach or a 1hr. bus ride through the *campo*, ends at the beautiful and friendly Garífuna community of **Santa Fé,** with picture-perfect beaches, excellent food and great hotels. **Hotel Orquídeas ❷,** a two-story white building at the end of town, is a great find, with well-maintained, spacious rooms that have private bath and fan. (L100 for 1 bed, L150 for 2.) Santa Fé celebrates the **Virgen del Carmen** with three weeks of festivities. Sports tournaments and a range of dramatic and celebratory dances begin the first weekend of July. **Cabo de Honduras,** accessible by the Puerto Castilla bus (see **Transportation,** above), has excellent beaches. To explore the area, rent a motorcycle from Turtle Tours (L670 per day).

BAY ISLANDS

Though the silky white-sand beaches and world-class diving off the Bay Islands are Honduras' biggest tourist attraction, the islands feel less commercialized than many other Caribbean destinations. Dive prices and certifications are among the cheapest in the world and jungle coastline still outnumbers beachfront estates. Bay Island reef diversity is unmatched, so if you don't want to bother with scuba certification, snorkeling in the crystal clear water is almost as fun. Utila, just 32km by boat from La Ceiba, is the most budget-friendly island and is famous for sightings of the rare whale shark, the biggest fish in the sea. Roatán is the most developed of the islands with gorgeous beaches and phenomenal snorkeling. Once ravaged by Hurrican Mitch, Guanaja is now a sparsely populated island, perfect for private romantic getaways. Cayos Cochinos, with their beautiful tropical vegetation, are a miniature version of the main islands.

UTILA

Legend has it that if you drink the water in Utila (pop. 1700), you'll stay forever. The legend probably dates back to Robinson Crusoe who spent a lot of time here in 1659 when he shipwrecked on the island. Today, travelers have an easier time finding boats to the mainland, but still find it hard to leave behind the excellent seafood, nightly beach parties, and the best budget diving on the planet. Locals joke about how the most frequent lie heard on Utila is "I'm leaving tomorrow."

▐ TRANSPORTATION

Flights: Morgan's Travel (☎425 3161), at the foot of the main dock, is the best place to buy plane tickets. Open M-Sa 8am-noon, 2:30-5:30pm. **Atlantic Airlines** (☎425 3241) has an office across from Banco Atlantida three houses east of the dock. Open M-F 8am-4pm. Flies to **La Ceiba** (15min., daily 7:30am and 10am, L541). **Isleña** (☎425 3364) has an office across from the fire station west of the dock. Open M-F 8:30am-4pm. **SOSA** (☎425 3166) flies to **La Ceiba** (15min., M-Sa 6am and 3:30pm, Su 3:30pm, L556).

Ferries: Ferries leave from the main docks. **Galaxy II** runs to La Ceiba (1½hr., 9:45 am, L195 from Morgan's Travel). **Utila Princess** (☎425 3390; open 8am-4:30pm), across from Morgan's Travel, also runs to **La Ceiba** (1½hr., 6:30am and 2:30pm, L195). **Easy Going** yacht makes a weekly trip to **Livingston, Guatemala** from the dock at Gunter's Dive Shop arriving in Utila on Tuesday and leaving 4pm on Thursday (10hr., US$95).

Taxi: ☎425 3311 or 425 3187.

▄▐ ORIENTATION AND PRACTICAL INFORMATION

Utila clings to the **East Harbour** on the southeast side of the island. **Main Street** runs from the decommissioned airstrip on the eastern lip of the harbor and hugs the bay until it reaches Crepes Beach and the Blue Bayou Restaurant on the western tip. Ferries land at the **Municipal Dock** directly in the middle of main street. **Cola de Mico Road** leads inland from the dock to **Pumpkin Hill** and the airport. Most services on the island are listed in US dollars but lempiras are also accepted.

Tourist Information: For info, go to **www.utilainfo.com.** Also, stop by the **Bundu Café** (see **Food,** below), always packed with hungry divers eager to share a tip or two. Most dive shops offer free maps of the island; the one at **Alton's** is particularly good. **Utila Tours** (blaquecommando@yahoo.com; www.allthingsutila.com), behind Munchie's, offers tours to water caye (L250) and the freshwater caves (L150). Open M-Sa 6:30am-9:30pm, Su 6:30am-1:30pm. **Bay Islands Conservation Association** runs a unique historical tour of the life of Robinson Crusoe. Open M-F 9am-noon and 2-4pm.

Banks: BGA (☎425 3257), the first building up from the dock on the eastern side of the main road, exchanges travelers' Visa checks and cash advances. Open M-F 8:30am-3:30pm, Sa 8:30-11:30am. **Banco Atlántida** (☎425 3374 or 425 3375), diagonally across the street from BGA, also accepts Visa. Open M-F 9am-4pm, Sa 8:30-11:30am. **Bundu Café** (see **Food,** below) and **Bush's Supermarket** (☎425 3147), three buildings east of Banco Atlántida, also exchange traveler's checks and currency. **Reef Cinema,** next to Bush's, gives cash advances on AmEx/MC/V (6% commission).

Police: ☎425 3255, upstairs from the post office by the Municipal Dock in the municipal office. Open M-F 9am-noon and 2-5pm. For off-hour emergencies, call **Preventiva** (☎425 3145), next to the football field up Moummy Lane. Open 24hr.

Medical Services: Centro de Salud (☎425 3277), on top of the fire station 5min. west of the dock. 24hr. emergency care, for consultation daily 8am-noon. Across the street, **Community Methodist Medical Clinic** (☎425 3137; utilaclinic@yahoo.com), gives medical consultations and has a **pharmacy.** Open M-F 8am-noon. **Medical Store Utila** (☎425 3154), next to Banco Atlántidas open M-Sa 8am-7pm.

Telephones and Internet: Hideout Internet (☎425 3248), hidden between Alton's diver shop and Utila Dive Center. Internet L30 per hr., international calls L35 per min. Open M-Sa 8am-8pm, Su 2-5pm. **Caye Caulker,** across from Reef Cinema, has the best Internet and international calling rates on the island during its happy hour (7-10pm). Internet L22 per hr., L34 per hr. regularly. Phones L7 per min. to the US. Open daily 8am-10pm.

Laundry: Caye Caulker (see above) charges L2-L5 per item. Open 7am-4pm. The **Mango Inn,** up Colade Mico Road on the corner of the 2nd intersection, charges L2-L12 per item. Open 7am-3pm. The **Tropical Hotel** office, a few houses west of the Mango Tree Gelatería, charges L75 per load. Open 8am-9pm.

Market: Bush's Supermarket (☎425 3147), a few houses east of Banco Atlantida, has everything you'll need. Open M-Sa 6:30am-7pm, Su 6:30am-noon.

Post Office: Beneath the municipal building on the dock marked by a yellow headboard. Open M-F 9am-noon and 2-5pm, Sa 9-11:30am. **Postal code:** 34201.

ACCOMMODATIONS

Hotels are being built at warp speed to satiate growing legions of travelers. Reservations are necessary in high season (July to Sept. and Dec. to Apr.). Some dive centers include lodging as part of the package.

Freddy's Place (☎425 3142), on the right just after the bridge almost all the way to airport beach, is run by a British islander family. Suites with 2 doubles, full kitchen, hot water bath, refrigerator, and a big porch with hammocks. Reservations recommended. US$15 per room, with A/C US$25. Discounts for longer stays. ❺

Rubi's (☎425 3240), east of the main dock, next to Reef Cinema. Brand new rooms with hot baths. Large coral courtyard. Singles US$13; doubles US$18, with A/C US$25. ❸

Mango Hotel, (☎425 3305 or 425 3335), up Cola de Mico Rd. at the 2nd intersection, has beautiful resort-style rooms with wooden floors. Amenities include cable TV, hot baths, and phones. Pool and sauna on site. Real steal is the 3 or 4 person room. Doubles US$30, with A/C US$35; shared rooms US$7. Office open daily 6am-8pm. ❺

Hotel Celena (☎425 3228), a few houses east of Cooper's. Great rooms with fans, hot baths, TV lounge, and kitchen. Singles and doubles L250, with A/C L300, with shared bath L125. Reception open 8am-noon and 2-7pm. Accepts traveler's checks, MC/V. ❷

Backpacker's Lodge (☎425 3350; ecomar@hondutel.hn), across from Gunter's Dive Shop west of the dock past the fire station, has clean private rooms with a double bed and shared bath just minutes from Chepe's beach. Dorms US$2; private rooms US$6. Check in at Gunter's Dive shop. ❶

Cooper's Inn (☎425 3184), east of the dock just past Zanzibar Cafe, is a friendly spot with good sized rooms with fans, a common room and communal kitchen, and shared bath. Singles L100; doubles L120; doubles in the new building L150. ❷

Margaritaville (☎425 3366; margaritavillehotel@yahoo.com), just past Gunter's Dive Shop headed west. Rooms with 2 double beds, hot baths, and charming porch seating overlook the beach. Doubles L290, with A/C L565; cabins L945. ❶

FOOD

Heaping fruit salads and vegetarian entrees are refreshingly common among an assortment of local, European, and North American menu choices.

Bundu Café, east of the dock across from Banco Atlántida. Popular for comfy couches and a youthful atmosphere. Great sandwiches (L30-L35). Beat the heat with fruit salads (L30-L42). Friendly Canadians Jen and Jackie stock Chilean wines and rolling papers (we didn't ask). Large book exchange. Open M-Sa 8am-4pm. Tu curry night with free tango lessons, W bbq, F live local music, and Sa Mexican night. ❷

Dave's, down the boardwalk towards Cross Creek Dive Center across from 7 Seas with neon "Open" sign, is the most popular locale among dive shop staff. Home cooked specials (L60-L140) always include at least one vegetarian entree. Fish is as fresh as it can get without being sushi. Open Tu-Su 10am-9:30pm. ❸

Munchiés (www.allthingsutila.com), a few houses down to the left of the dock across from Deep Blue Divers, serves up delicious lobster quesadillas (L60) and thick fruit smoothies (L25). Open M-Sa 6:30am-9:30pm, Su 6:30am-1:30pm. ❷

RJ's BBQ and Grill, east on the main road before Alton's. The island's most popular bbq. Come early to avoid crowds drawn by grilled wahoo fish (L70), barracuda (L70), hamburgers (L40), and heaping portions of vegetables and rice. Open W, F, Su 5:30pm. ❷

Mango Cafe, (☎425 3305), attached to the Mango Inn up Cola de Mico road at the 2nd intersection, serves mouth watering Italian wonders from a picture menu specially made for any language. Pizza L85-L148. Nightly specials. Open daily 6am-8pm. ❸

Seven Seas (☎425 3377), before Utila Dive Center east of the dock. Just about every diver's bag lunch has banana bread (L10) and a famous *baleada* (L20) from here. Peanut butter shakes L23. Open Tu-Su 7am-10pm. ❶

Mango Tree Gelatería, next to Munchie's west of the dock. 10 types of gelato and 2 all-fruit sorbets (L30-L50). Open M-Sa 9am-10:30pm, Su noon-10:30pm. ❶

Tropical Sunset (☎425 3190), across the bridge almost to the old airport strip, is the island's classiest restaurant. Grilled conch L140, king crab L175, jalapeño chicken L110, veggie pasta L60. Open Tu-Su 10am-9:30pm. ❸

🎵 🎭 ENTERTAINMENT AND NIGHTLIFE

Utila can always find an excuse to party; locals literally celebrate the rising of the sun and moon. The annual Sun Jam (www.sunjamutila.com), typically held the first Saturday in August, draws a crowd second only to La Ceiba's *carnaval.* For nightlife, Utilans head to **Coco Loco's,** a thatched-roof bar on its own pier, to start out the evening. Dip your feet in the ocean through the jacuzzi-like hole in the pier, laze in a hammock overlooking all the action, or dance to an eclectic mix of music, but don't bring anything you don't want to get stolen. (Beer L20. Open daily 4pm-midnight and later on weekends. Happy hour 4-7pm.) The **Tranquila Bar** on the pier just next to Coco Loco's has a more relaxed scene. (Beer L19. Open daily 3pm-midnight.) **Bar in the Bush,** on the left at the third intersection up Cola de Mico Rd., is popular for cheap drinks and late-night volleyball. (Beer L19. Open W, F 9pm-3am.) **Tropical Sunset Bar,** (☎425 3190) almost on the airport beach, has a great location. (Beer L20. Open daily 4-9pm. Happy Hour daily 4-7pm.) Party hard, but whatever you do, don't forget your **bug repellent.** Locals go to the **casino,** across from the bank (open F, Sa 8-11:30pm). Non-gamblers head to **Reef Cinema** (☎425 3254. Movies M-Tu, Th, Su 7:30pm; Sa 6:30, 8:30pm; L45. Video rental open M-F 11:30am-6pm, Sa 4:30-5:30pm. L30).

🏃 OUTDOOR ACTIVITIES

A trail from the old strip along the coast heads east to the beaches and tidal pools of **Big Bight,** on the eastern shore. It's also possible to canoe through the mangrove-lined canal that runs from the lagoon near Blue Bayou all the way past Cross Creek into the eastern bay. Rent **bikes** from **Delco Bikes** (☎425 3158), west of the dock just after Deep Blue Divers (L50 for 24hr., open Su-F 8am-6pm), or **Utila Bike Rental** (☎425 3317), east on the main road, behind Howell's Internet (bikes L80 per day, open Su-F 7am-6pm). Kayaks can be rented from **Alton's Dive Shop** or **Captain Morgan's Dive Center** (half-day single L95; double L150; full day L150/L280). **Bando,** at Airport Beach, lends free kayaks, catamarans, paddle boats, and jet skis with the purchase of a dive package. **Bodden Rentals** (☎425 3245), up Cola de Mico road next to Thompson's Bakery rents 4-wheelers (L1130), scooters (L945), bicycles (L80), golf carts, and dirt bikes.

HONDURAS

Guided **horseback rides** to nearby caves and Pumpkin Hill are offered by **Jo Jo.** Ask at Bundo Café for directions. To check out the unique Utila iguana, known commonly as "swamper," head for **Iguana Station;** walk up Mammy Lane and turn left at the first intersection just before Stuart's Hill. Guided tours around the visitor center are included in admission and are especially exciting during egg-laying season (Apr.-May). Tours are also led to local **bat caves.** (Tour L40, kids L20, bat cave L120. Open M, W, F 2-5pm.) **Gunter's Dive Shop** runs sunset cruises, including beer and punch for up to six people (US$60 for the boat).

 SCUBA AND SNORKELING

Lots of people come to Utila to get their open-water certification or to train to be instructors. If you want to try out scuba diving, do a one hour "Discover Scuba" session (US$99). The session counts toward the open-water certification, and it's easy—all you have to do is breathe and a dive master will do the rest. Open-water classes typically take between three and five days; advanced classes are two to three days.

> ↙ **GETTING CERTIFIED.** Utila has recently standardized prices for certification courses, and though this eliminates the real cheapies, the set price is still low—Open-water (or advanced) certification is US$179, including insurance and reef tax. Certification courses typically include classroom instructions, five or six instructional dives, and sometimes free dives after the course for fun. During low season some dive shops provide free or discounted hotel rooms. Dive shops conduct training in many languages, from Hebrew to Maori.

Dive Shops:

Utila Dive Centre (better known around town as UDC), halfway to airport beach east of the dock next to Seven Seas. The most frequented dive shop on the island. Experienced divemasters teach in nine languages. Shop has a fun social atmosphere and a bar.

Cross Creek Dive Centre (☎ 425 3326, info@utiladivecentre.com), across the street from UDC, has canal-side rooms with private shower included with dive packages. Office open daily 7am-5:30pm. Fun dives US$15 per tank or US$125 per 10-pack. Divemaster US$500, includes free diving for the rest of your life. Rooms US$6.

Deep Blue Divers (☎ 425 3211; www.deepblueutila.com), west from the dock across from Munchies, has the newest and best-kept equipment with 3 on-site shower included with dive packages. The only dive center that goes to the north side every day, guaranteed, Deep Blue dives are the most likely to see a whale shark. They have private rooms next door as well as the all inclusive Deep Blue Resort. Office open 6:30am-6:30pm. Divemaster US$550. Rooms US$4. Resort US$850-$1200 per week includes 3 meals per day, 3 dives per day, and unlimited shore dives.

Gunter's Dive Shop (☎ 425 3350; www.riconet.de/ecomarine), all the way west from the dock near Crepe's beach, is the oldest shop on the island, and claims to have the cleanest off-the-dock diving. With a maximum class size 4, Gunter's focuses on quality and personal attention. Daily north side trips weather permitting. Complimentary waterskiing and kayaking. Gunter's hosts divers in the Backpacker Lodge (US$2 dorm, private US$6) across the street and the elegant Colibri Hill Resort (US$25 private, US$35 with A/C). Divemaster US$550. AmEx/MC/V.

Alton's Dive Shop (☎ 425 3108; www.divealtons.com), near airport beach, is the hippest shop in town with a young crowd and nightly new-age dance beats. Fast boats make daily trips to the north side weather permitting. Underwater camera rentals, a water polo net, and waterfront accommodation included with open water or advanced courses. Office open 7am-7pm. Fun dives US$15 or US$125 per 10 pack. Divemaster US$600. Singles US$6. AmEx/MC/V.

Dive Sites: For those already certified, the standard prices are US$30 for a "fun dive" or US$125 for a package of 10 dives. Divers swim in from around the world for a chance to spot the not-so-elusive biggest fish in the sea: the bespeckled **whale shark,**

which are frequently seen on Utila's **north side** during morning trips. Whale shark high season lasts from the end of February to the end of June. The **south side** has fewer big fish but compensates with greater coral diversity and unbelievable wall drops. Some of the best diving can in fact be found right outside the harbor on the east side, where eagle rays flap by in huge numbers. Divers also enjoy the open hull and pilot house of the submerged Haliburton ship (40m down). A little farther east, Utila's most popular dive site, Black Hills, is an underwater mountain that houses turtles, big schools of fish, and barracuda.

Snorkeling: Snorkeling is free for those taking a scuba course, and rentals are available at **Alton's** for L95 per day or L190 for snorkeling boat tours. The **Snorkeling Center,** up the main road just before Airport Beach, is known as the best snorkeling site on the island because of its east side proximity. Half a day of snorkeling and transportation to any of dozens of marvelous sites around the island (L190). Those who want to strike out on their own can rent gear (L45 per day), get snorkeling sight orientation and fish identification, and safely leave belongings at the Snorkeling Center. **Blue Bayou Hotel,** a 30min. walk past Gunter's, also has snorkeling (rentals L40 per hr.) The inlet just after Margaritaville Hotel is another nice spot to check out.

▶ DAYTRIPS FROM UTILA

For relaxation and snorkeling on an even more deserted island, you can arrange to spend the night on one of several nearby cayes. **Water Caye** is popular for beach bbqs and star-gazing. Before heading out, ask your guide to stop at the crowded fishing town of **Pigeon Caye** to buy dinner, then sway the night away in bug-free bliss on rented hammocks. There is a L25 entrance fee for the island. Trips to Water Caye with **Utila Tours,** inside Munchies, include a full bbq meal, snorkeling, and volleyball (L250). Utila Tours also offers half-day trips to explore the island's **freshwater caves** (L150). **Sandy Caye** is an island up for grabs; for about US$85 per night you can have the whole thing to yourself. Talk to **sailing** instructor Captain Erick about paying to sail to the **Cayos Cochinos** (lessons US$150), though it's cheaper to get there from La Ceiba.

ROATÁN ISLAND

Roatán is paradise. The largest and most populous of the Bay Islands, Roatán is blessed with powder-soft beaches, world-famous diving and snorkeling, and a well-manicured beachfront town. While this gem was once a well-kept secret, it's clear to see the word has gotten out: the all-inclusive resort, L30 Coke, 16% sales tax, and superb but pricey international menus all point to the recent tourist influx. Budget travelers can still find a home in West End, smack in the middle of some of the world's cheapest diving (a close second to Utila) and just a water taxi away from stunning beaches like West Bay. Coxen Hole is the Islands' crowded and unpleasant capital. Sandy Bay, Roatán's third major town, is home to ecological foundations, parks, and the world renowned Anthony's Key Resort.

▣ TRANSPORTATION

Roatán International Airport, 1.5km east of Coxen Hole, is accessible by taxi and microbus. **Isleña** (☎ 445 1387, open daily 5:30am-6pm) flies to: **La Ceiba** (15min.; 6:50, 9am, 1, 3pm; L557); **Guanaja** (10min., 10:30am, L888); **San Pedro Sula** (40min.; 6:50, 9am, 1pm; L1321); and **Tegucigalpa** (55min.; 6:50am, 1pm; L1569). **Taca** (☎ 445 1918) partners with Isleña to provide international service to: **Houston** (Sa

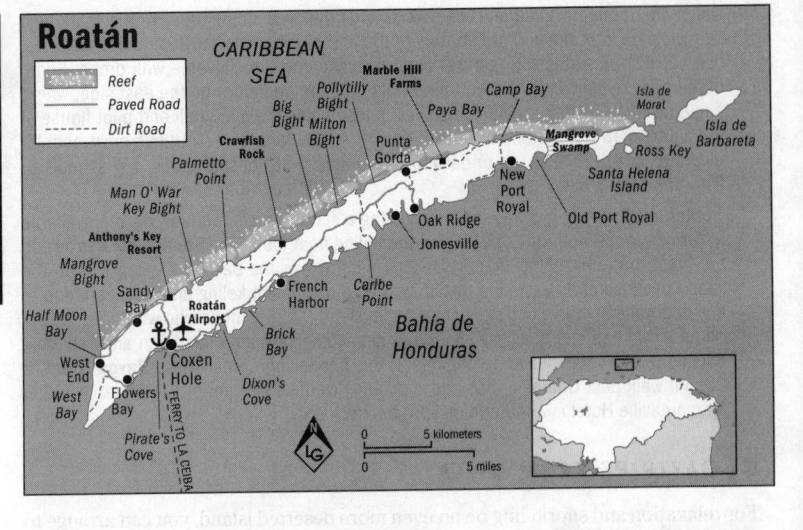

10:30am); Miami (Su 9:30am); and **San Salvador** (Su 4:20pm). **SOSA** (☎445 1658, open daily 5:30am-5pm) flies to: **La Ceiba** (15min.; 7, 9am, noon, 2:30, 4pm; L557); **San Pedro** (35min.; 7, 9am, noon; L1321); and **Tegucigalpa** (45min.; 7am, noon; L1569). **Atlantic Airlines** (☎445 1179 or 445-0055) flies to: **La Ceiba** (20min.; daily 6, 8, 10:30am, 12:30, 3:50pm; L516); **San Pedro Sula** (50min.; 8am, additional flight M, W, F at 6am; L1280); **Tegucigalpa** (50min.; 12:30pm, additional flights M, Sa at 6am; L1532); **Utila** (10min. direct, 30min. via La Ceiba; direct 6am, via La Ceiba 12:30 and 3:15pm; L1033); **Managua** (M, W, F, 6am, US$173); **Belize City** (4hr.; M, W, F 6am; US$156); and **Grand Cayman** via La Ceiba (2hr., M, F 8am, US$304). **Guanaja** flights leave from La Ceiba (40min., 7am, 4pm; L888).

The **Galaxy II Ferry** (☎445 1795), across the street from the dock in Coxen Hole, leaves daily for La Ceiba (2hr., 7am, L195). **Paradise Tours,** next door to H.B. Warren's in Coxen Hole, sells tickets or you can buy them at the airport. (☎445 0392; aifoag@hondutel.hn. Open M-F 9am-5pm, Sa 9am-noon.) **MC Tours,** in the airport, sells local and regional packages (☎445 1930. Open M-Sa 9am-noon, and 2-4pm).

Toyota (☎445 166), **Avis** (☎445 0122 or 445 1658), **Caribbean** (☎445 1430, www.caribbeanRoatán.com), and **Best** (☎445 1494) rental car operators all have offices inside the airport. **Microbuses** traverse the island, ferrying passengers between West End, Coxen Hole, and Sandy Bay. You have to take a **taxi** from the airport to Coxen Hole in order to catch the bus to West End or Sandy Bay. Taxis will take you anywhere on the island from the airport. If you want to go directly, tell the driver to go *directo* (L190) or to cut down costs and meet new friends, tell him to go *colectivo* (L25 per person).

■ ORIENTATION

Coxen Hole, the departmental capital and site of the international airport, is on the southeast side of the Island in Pirate's Cove. From here the main highway heads north passing **Sandy Bay** (6km) and then west to **West End** (11km) where you'll find the best housing and dive shops. Roatán's best beach, **West Bay** (15km), is just southwest with more expensive beachfront housing.

COXEN HOLE

Coxen Hole (also known simply as Roatán) is the capital of the Bay Islands, but it's hard to tell by its looks: the charmless, bustling town is perhaps the single blemish on Roatán's picture-perfect coastline. Almost all travelers will need to pass through here, but most will move on to greener pastures and bluer waters. Make sure that you have enough cash before leaving; only Coxen Hole has banks.

Coxen Hole's layout is straightforward: **Front Street** runs along the beach while **Back Street** runs parallel to and behind it. From the dock, Front Street runs to the airport to the right and past the *parque central* to the left. **Thicket Road,** a few blocks to the west of H.B. Warren's, cuts through both streets and connects to the highway headed to West End. For environmental education and tourist information, go to the **Bay Islands Conservation Association** (☎445 1424, open M-F 8am-noon and 1:30-5pm), on the second floor of the green Cooper Building next to the also-green Municipal Building. **Banco Credomatic,** on the first floor, gives cash advances on AmEx/MC/V and has a 24hr. UNIBANC **ATM** (open M-F 9am-5pm, Sa 9am-noon). **Banco Atlantida,** two buildings west of H.B. Warren's, on the left, also has a 24hr. ATM (open M-F 9am-4pm, Sa 8:30-11:30am). **H.B. Warren's,** next to the *parque* and across from BGA, is a large grocery store that also cashes traveler's checks. (☎445 1208. Open M-Sa 7am-6pm. AmEx/MC/V.) The **Preventiva police** office is up Thicket Rd. on the left next to the hospital. **Hospital Roatán,** on Thicket Rd. 2 blocks up from Front St. on the left, has 24hr. emergency medical assistance (☎445 1499, English spoken) as does **Wood Medical Center,** right before the Cooper Building west of the dock (☎445 1080; English spoken; consultation L300). **Farmacia Roatán** is 1 block up Thicket Road from Front St. (open M-F 8am-4pm, Sa 8am-noon). **Hondusoft Internet Cafe,** around back in the building next to H.B. Warren's, has **Internet service** for L60 per hr. and international phone calls for L8 per min. (☎445 1415. Open M-Sa 8am-6pm.) **Traveler's Internet Cafe,** on the corner of Front Street and Thicket Road offers also offers Internet service for L50 per min. and international calls for L8 per min. (☎445 1816. Open M-Sa 8am-9pm.) There is a **Hondutel** phone outside the Cooper Building. The **post office,** across from BGA, receives but does not send packages (open M-F 8am-noon and 2-5pm, Sa 8am-noon).

For travelers staying in Coxen Hole, **Hotel Sarita ❶,** sitting partly over water next to the dock on Front St., has rooms with bath, fans, and TV. (☎445 1541. Singles L230; doubles L280.) **Hotel Coral ❶,** on the 2nd floor of the green building across from the schoolhouse west of H.B. Warren's, has small and simple rooms, with common bath and fans. (Singles L150, with TV L180; doubles L200/L250.) The supermarket **H.B. Warren ❷** has an attached diner with rotisserie (daily special L60). **Tirza's Snacks ❶,** on Front St. across from H.B. Warren's, sells at reasonable prices. (Breakfast L20-L35; quesadillas L40; dinner L30. Open daily 7am-10pm.)

SANDY BAY

A small community (pop. 1100) 6km west of Coxen Hole and halfway to West End, Sandy Bay holds a few interesting diversions, among them outstanding snorkeling in the well-protected **Sandy Bay Marine Reserve.** You can also visit the **Carambola Botanical Gardens,** across the highway from Anthony's Key Resort, where just about every kind of plant and lizard native to the tropics thrives. One of the best trails ascends about 20min. to the summit of Carambola mountain, from which you can see Roatán's reefs and Utila in the distance. (☎445 1117. Ask for Bill or Irma Brady. US$4, with **tour** US$6. Open daily 7am-5pm.)

Make sure to check out the **Tropical Bird Park,** between Anthony's Key Resort and Coxen Hole. Tell the bus driver that you want to go there and he'll drop you off. The large collection of tropical birds includes some which have been rehabilitated and saved from hunters. (☎445 1314. Open Tu-Sa 10am-5pm.) **Roatán Butterfly Gar-**

HONDURAS

den is the newest attraction, displaying butterflies native to Honduras and the Bay Islands. Hop on a bus to Coxen Hole and get off after about 2min. (Open M-Sa 9am-5pm, US$5.) Anthony's Key Resort houses the **Roatán Museum** and the **Roatán Institute of Marine Sciences**. The museum has a small display on the archaeology and history of the island, with exhibits in English. (US$5. Open Th-Tu 8am-5pm.) The Institute features a dolphin enclosure with dolphin shows. (US$3. Open M-F 10:30am and 4:30pm; Sa and Su 11:30am and 1:30pm.) Sandy Bay is a 2hr. walk from Coxen Hole; buses depart regularly from the front of the park (every 5min. 6am-7pm, L5).

WEST END

Near the island's west tip, Roatán's *"gringo"* central" is home to dive shops, waterfront and budget lodging, some of Honduras' best international restaurants, and *gringo*-fied prices. You can't blame people for coming—nearby beaches are phenomenal, especially West Bay, and there is no shortage of diving, snorkeling, and relaxing Caribbean style.

■✈🛈 ORIENTATION AND PRACTICAL INFORMATION

Almost all of West End surrounds one main drag running along the shore. The main intersection is with the highway, a little north of the center of town where *colectivos* and buses wait to pick up passengers. The intersection faces Half Moon Bay to the west, home to great snorkeling and a popular public beach. Most hotels and services are south, to the left of the intersection along West Bay and towards West Bay beach. While the island lists prices in US dollars, items can be paid for with lempiras.

Tourist information: For up-to-date hotel, dive shop, resort, restaurant, and attraction info, visit www.roatanet.com. At the airport, the **Island Information and Hotel Reservation Center** sells island maps (L5) and can help you get organized before you arrive in West End. Open daily 8am-6pm. Speak to island veterans Susan and Henrik Jensen at the **Beach House Information Center** (☎445 1548; jensens@hondutel.hn), located at the corner of the main intersection. Head to **Barefoot Charlie's** (☎445 1008; monomail2003@yahoo.com), across from Foster's and Papagayo's Restaurant, for info on attractions and lodging, a comprehensive guidebook collection, and the island's biggest **book exchange.** Open daily 9am-9pm.

Bike and Motorcycle Rental: Captain Van's (elcaptvan@yahoo.com), south of the main intersection just before Cannibal Cafe on the main road toward West Bay. Bikes US$9 per day, US$36 per week; scooters US$35/US$175; motorcycles US$39/US$175. All come with free treasure map and 10-point safety orientation. Open daily 9am-4pm.

Car Rental: Roatán Rentals (☎445 1171; www.Roatansalesandrentals.com), across the street from Cannibal Cafe south of the intersection on the main drag. Vehicles US$58-$98 per day. Open M-Sa 7:30am-6pm. AmEx/MC/V. **Best/Brito's Car Rental** (☎445 0339), on the corner of the main intersection in the Beach House Information Office has various vehicles for US$50-$65 per day.

Banks: While the only banks on the island are in Coxen Hole, **Woody's Grocery Store,** across the side street from the Argentinian Grill a block north of the main intersection, cashes traveler's checks up to US$100. Open Su-Th 7am-6pm, F 7am-5pm.

Market: Woody's Grocery Store (☎445 1428) has all your island needs. Open Su-Th 7am-6pm, F 7am-5pm. AmEx/MC/V.

Laundry: Bamboo Hut Laundry, next to the Mango Hotel south of the main intersection behind Tony's Pizza, charges L15 per lb. for wash and dry. Open M-Sa 8am-4pm. Laundry service also available at **Valerie's** (see **Accommodations,** below) for L50 per load.

Police: (☎445 1199 or 445 1138). Open 24hr.

Medical Assistance: Cornerstone Emergency Medical Service (☎/fax 445 1049 or 445 1003; radio CH26), at Anthony's Key Resort, up the highway towards Coxen Hole on the left. Hyperbaric chamber, 2 doctors who speak English. **Fantasy Island Resort** on the south side of the island has a hyperbaric chamber.

Pharmacy: West End Farmacia (☎445 1173), just before West End Divers south of the intersection on the main drag towards West Bay Beach. Open M-Sa 8:30am-7:30pm.

Telephone and Internet Access: Barefoot Charlie's, (☎445 1008) across from Fosters south of the main intersection, satellite Internet service (L4 per min.), international phone calls (L18 per min.), and fax. **King's Cafe Internet,** right before Dian's Garden of Eaten' next to Coconut Tree Diving south of the main intersection, offers high speed satellite Internet L4 per min. and international phone calls L18 per min. Open M-Sa 9am-6pm. **Paradise Computers** (mark@paradise-computers.com), in the same building as West End Divers south of the main intersection charges the same prices as King's Cafe. Open daily 8am-9pm.

ACCOMMODATIONS

⚅ **Chillie's** (☎445 1214; www.nativesonsRoatan.com), north of the main junction behind Native Sons Diving. Rooms accommodate up to 3 people. "Dorms" are in fact bedrooms. Communal bath, a nice porch, and a backyard sweeten the deal. Phone service and free kitchen use. Office open 8am-1pm and 4-7pm. Beds L160; doubles L320; Cabin with kitchen L400; camping L90 per person. ❹

Seagrape Plantation (☎445 1428), up the main drag to the north veering off to the right. Sitting on volcanic rock, this spacious hotel has a large communal kitchen with fridge and shared bath; also has a dock, picnic tables, and hammocks. Cabins have A/C. Budget singles L170; doubles L320; cabins L330. 16% surcharge on MC/V. ❹

Valerie's Youth Hostel (www.Roatanonline.com/valeries), uphill from Tyll's Dive Shop about 20m from the wooden boardwalk. Sweet-natured Valerie has a wide variety of cheap beds, from dorms to apartments. Laundry service available. Communal bathrooms and kitchen. Free snorkel equipment for guests; mosquito nets available. Beware of theft. Dorms L90; private rooms with 1 large or 2 small beds L200-L240; apartments with 7 beds A/C, balcony, bath, cable TV, and kitchen L600. Tents for 2 L145. ❸

THE BIG SPLURGE

DIVING FOR JULES

Some people can't take the pressure—others can't get enough o it. If the 130 ft. recreationa scuba limit isn't as exciting as you'd hoped, explore the depths Jules Verne-style with **Stanley Submersibles.**

Legacy submarine builder Kar Stanley operates two custom sub marines from Half Moon Bay Roatán. He built the first sub in 1997 and named it C-BUG (Con trolled by Buoancy Underwate Glider). Karl liked C-BUG, but he wanted more, so along came Isa bel. Not just "bigger and better, Isabel is the only sub ever made specifically for Roatán.

With the world's deepest tou ist submarine, and the only glid ing sub in the world, Karl run dives as deep as 1500 ft. Though life and light are scarce, the depths are home to some of the strangest creatures on earth including coral that glows with neon pink spots, prehistoric sea lilies, and the oldest form of livin mollusk in the world, which onl survives below 300ft. Gliding through fossilized reefs and underwater caves in search o sharks will provide all the excite ment you could ask for. Jules Verne, eat your heart out.

Visit: www.stanleysubmarines.com Located on the northern side of Hal Moon Bay in West End, on the dock just in front of Half Moon Bay Cab ins. 2hr. 1000ft. trip US$500. 3hr 1500ft. trip US$800. Sub weigh limit is 500lbs.

Mango Hotel (☎445 1033; remishaki@yahoo.com), across the street from Sueño del Mar south of the main intersection. Bar out front. Dorms L90 per person with fans and communal bath; doubles to quads with private bath L470, with A/C US$40. ❺

Pinnochio's (www.Roatanet.com/pinocchios), 50m from the intersection, after Pura Vida Divers. Swiss Family Robinson feel. Restaurant downstairs serves international cuisine, with several vegetarian specialties (chicken with ginger sauce L150, veggie stir fry L120). One person L565, 2 L620, 3 L850, 4 L1130. AmEx/MC/V. ❺

Posada Arco Iris (☎445 1264; www.Roatanposada.com), on the main street north of the intersection behind the Argentinian Grill. Gorgeous, new, large wooden rooms with A/C, porches, refrigerators, and tiled hot baths in the midst of a lush tropical garden with monkeys and parrots. Free Internet and kayak use for guests plus a book exchange. English spoken. High-season rooms L565, with full kitchen L620, with 2 rooms L850; add L90 per person over 2. Discount for week-long stays. ❺

Mariposa (www.mariposa-lodge.com), up the dirt road just to the left of West End Divers on the left. A hill estate offers clean and spacious rooms with full kitchen, hot private bath, and TV. Good for families. No-noise policy. Rooms L825 per night. ❺

🚩 FOOD

It seems every restaurant in town has a gourmet cook in the back kitchen, putting together a gourmet menu accompanied by—you guessed it—gourmet prices.

🍴 Cannibal Cafe (☎445 0020), south of the main intersection just after Captain Van's. This mainly Mexican restaurant serves rich feasts, crowned by the Big Kahuna Burrito (L104-L169); if you can eat 3 they're all free. *Grande quesadillas* (L65), banana smoothies with a hint of chocolate (L39), and the unique guacamole (L34) are all excellent. Vegetarian options. Open daily 10am-10pm. ❷

🍴 Dian's Garden of Eaten' (diansdelights@yahoo.com), just beyond the King's Cafe south of the main intersection on the main drag. Dian dishes up extravagant meals in her own garden. Menu includes Caribbean cooking with an Asian spice; tofu and grilled fish are staples here. If your favorite sauce isn't on the menu, don't be surprised if Dian whips it up on the spot from fresh garden ingredients. Entrees with saffron rice, veggies, and soup L160-L240, French and Chilean wines L60 per glass, key lime pie (L40). Reservations recommended for large parties. ❹

Lighthouse Restaurant (☎445 1209), south of the main intersection, across the street from Captain Van's. Popular among locals for its excellent coconut sauce, fish tacos (L90), chocolate fudge cake (L40), and fun oceanside dining atmosphere. Fish *a la coco* L70, conch soup L100, shrimp pasta L160, veggie stir fry L100, homemade sorbet L40, fresh squeezed lemonade L25. Open daily 8am-10pm. ❸

Brick Oven Pizza (☎991 2690), following signs from Pinocchios, take a right at the intersection and follow the road through the field on your right. The most worthwhile 10min. walk you'll take on the island. Enjoy nightly movies at 5 and 7pm. Mouth-watering 10" pizza (L140-L195), focaccia (L175), eggplant parmesan (L130), and rich homemade lemonade (L25). Open M, W-Su 5-10pm. ❹

Argentinian Grill (☎445 1264; www.Roatanposada.com), connected to the hotel Posada Arco Iris just north of the main intersection on the main drag. Elegant and delicious dining overlooking Half Moon Bay. Conch soup L45, vegetarian plate L120, catch of the day L165, king crab L300, entrees L135-L300. Open M, W-Su 3-10pm. ❹

Rudy's Coffee Stop (☎445 7394; georphi@yahoo.com), just before Barefoot Charlie's south of the main intersection on the left, serves delicious fruit pancakes (US$2.50), bulging omelettes (L45), dripping french toast (L35), and thick whole fruit smoothies (L40). Open Su-F 6am-5pm. Accepts traveler's checks. ❷

HONDURAS

Mango Verde (mangoverde@hotmail.com), next to Reef Gliders dive shop south of the main intersection on the main drag, is a popular stop for healthy meals at great prices. Veggie pitas L55 and chicken sandwich L65. Open daily 8am-midnight. ❸

SNORKELING AND OUTDOOR ACTIVITIES

You don't have to blow a lot of cash to enjoy the remarkable reefs, since two of the best dive spots are even easier to reach by snorkeling. All dive shops have snorkeling equipment (free for divers). **On the Top of the Water Sports,** above the Cannibal Cafe south of the main intersection, rents snorkeling gear, kayaks, wake board, inner tubes, knee boards and water skis. (☎445 0020; seabreeze@hondusoft.com. Snorkeling US$10 per day, US$5 for half day; double kayaks US$7 per hr., US$8 for half day, full day US$21; single kayaks US$5/$14/$18; wake boarding, waterskiing, kneeboarding, or inner tubing US$60 per hr. or US$40 per 30min.) The **Lighthouse Restaurant** also rents out equipment for reasonable prices, including an underwater camera for US$25 per day; film not included. (☎445 1209. Snorkel gear US$5 for 24hr. Single kayaks US$16 and double kayaks US$22 for a half day, US$3/US$5 per hr. Free snorkel gear with kayak rental. Open daily 7:30am-10pm.)

Half Moon Bay, at the north end of town, is sinfully easy to jump into and delightfully impossible to avoid—roll out of bed anytime you want and wade into its refreshing waters for a swim around the coral megalopolis at its mouth. Some of the best snorkeling on the island is in nearby West Bay (see below). Go deeper than any diver around with **Stanley Submersibles** (see p. 503) in the **world's deepest tourist submarine,** located just off the dock next to the Half Moon Bay Cabins. See prehistoric animals, underwater canyons, sharks, and the oldest living mollusk form in the world (karl@stanleysubmarines.com, 2hr. trip to 300m US$500, 3hr. trip to 460 m US$800). Off the same dock, try dry snorkeling in the **Glass Bottom Boat.** (45min., US$20 per person.) **Catamaran Fun Sailing** out of Eagle Rays Restaurant at Sueño del Mar dive shop south of the main intersection in the house out on the water offers day sailing trips, sunset sails, and island sails to Cayos Cochinos. **Eddie and Danny Fishing Charters,** south of the main intersection just before the Reggae Bar on the right as the road winds back to the beach, offers half day fishing adventures where they will cook what you catch for a delicious meal you can be proud of. (☎445 0332 or 445 1087. US$120-$250.)

◢ SCUBA DIVING

With reefs no farther than swimming distance from the coast, Roatán is a diver's paradise. Most shops offer high quality products and services, work within the same area, and run about the same prices. Dive prices have not been standardized as they have on Utila; prices for Open Water and Advanced Certification (Adv.) vary between US$150-$200; for Divemaster (DM) between US$400-$500; and fun dives US$15-$30 per tank. All shops run night and wreck dives on request.

Pura Vida Dive Center (☎445 1141; www.puravidaresort.com) has earned Gold Palm Resort distinction for its equipment, fast boats, and experienced instructors. Ritzy singles have A/C, fans, and cold baths, and TV US$50; doubles US$60. Open US$175, Adv. US$160, DM US$400, shark dives US$75. Underwater cameras US$10, dive computers US$10. Daily boats at 9, 11:30am, and 2pm. Office open daily 8am-6pm.

Native Sons Diving (☎445 1214, www.nativesonsRoatan.com), north of the main intersection next to Chilie's specializes in individual attention. Accommodations through Chilie's. Open water US$200, Adv. US$180, DM US$500, fun dives US$15-$25. Boats daily at 9am and 2pm. Office open daily 8am-5pm.

THE BIG SPLURGE

WE ARE THE HISTORY

f Goldilocks went to the Bay slands, she'd sound something like his: "Roatán is too touristy; Utila needs more beaches, but Chachahuate is juuuust right." When t comes to balancing culture and beaches, Chachahuate is the Bay slands' perfect bowl of porridge.

Until recently, poor transportaion kept the island paradise off nost itineraries, but now one sland resident, Julian Solis, has begun to offer a four day cultural mmersion that makes this Caribbean jewel an awesome destination. Though pricey for most budget ravelers, the tour doesn't cost much more than finding your own ransportation to the cayes. Named "Waguia Uragabei," which in Garíuna means "We are the History," he tour's goal is not to have you visit the island, but to have you become part of the community."

The experience begins in La Ceiba at the Hammock Hotel with a brief oral history of the Garifuna. The next morning a bus will take you to Nueva Armenia where the nainland relatives of the Chachahuatans perform nightly ounta, maripol, and mascaro dances. A motorized lancha departs for the cayes in the morning where a hike through Cayo Mayor shows the Garifuna in their natural suroundings. The final night is spent in a hut eating tradiional meals with the islanders.

₅ 441 0291. US$150 per person. Reservations required. Bring your own snorkeling gear.

West End Divers (www.westendivers.com), past the First Baptist Church next to Pura Vida hotel, is the most frequented shop in town with a friendly and experienced staff, social atmosphere for all ages, and cushy covered boat. Open US$180; Adv. US$170; DM US$500; fun dives US$25 per tank. Special Saturday two-tank trips US$55 including lunch. Boats daily at 9, 11:30am, 2:30pm. Office open daily 7:30am-6pm.

DIVE SITES. Half Moon Bay Wall, just a short swim out from the main intersection, remains one of the best in Roatán with spectacular wall drops and colorful marine life. **Mary's Place,** the island's premier dive site, maintains its high diversity because it covers an impressive span of reef along the south shore from West End. More frequented are **Peter's Place,** at the end of Marine Park, with tons of big fish, deep canyons, and vertical walls, and **Pablo's Place,** with the island's highest and healthiest coral diversity. **West End Wall,** another wall densely packed with marine life, features terrific drift-diving. Nearby, **Overheat** and **Ulysess** reefs are great shallow dives. **Las Palmas** is an exhilarating dive while the famous **Hole in the Wall,** a sand-chute that swimmers can wriggle through, is suited for advanced and very cautious divers. **Bear's Den,** with enclosed canyons ready for exploration, is also an exciting experience for highly skilled divers. A popular tune-up for rusty divers, **Blue Channel** is a shallow dive (35ft.) through a natural channel packed with bright fish and the occasional octopus. The most popular wreck dive is massive **El Águila,** near Sandy Bay, while experienced divers find thrills at the deep and dark **Texas.** Recently sunk for recreational purposes, the **Odyssey** is drawing large crowds as the 3rd largest wreck this side of the Caribbean.

◨ NIGHTLIFE

Famous for its well-stocked bar and Daniella, the wild dancing bartender, the **Twisted Toucan** rocks every night. Just past Barefoot Charlies, the Toucan is hard to miss; patrons inevitably spill out into the streets when stools run out. Grab a "Jamaican-me-crazy" (L60) or a chocolate-banana daiquiri (L40). Thursday is ladies' night (L30 cocktails) and men in drag are welcome. (Twistedtoucan@yahoo.com. Open M-Th 11am-midnight, F-Sa 11am-2am, Su 2-10pm. Happy hour two-for-one cocktails daily 4-7pm and all day Sunday.) The **Cardiac Kitchen,** part of the Toucan, serves wings, mozzarella sticks, and cheeseburgers. (L50-L100. Sa L50 bbq. Open daily 4pm-closing.) **Sundowners** is a favorite sunset bar among locals and *gringos* with Sunday quiz night. Light grill food (L40-L80) includes your first drink. (Open daily 3-

9pm, happy hour 5-7pm. Beer L20.) **Reggae Bar,** on the beach just beyond Eddie & Danny Fishing Charter, has solid beers (L10), rasta punch (L40) and *cuba libres.* (Open M-Th 1-10pm, F and Sa noon-2am. Happy hour 5-9pm.) Head to **Loafer's,** on the beach a bit beyond Reggae Bar, for beer and billiards (Open M-Sa). Look for the Papagayo's sign to find **Foster's,** a good place to kick back and ponder the stars above. Beer and philosophy are standard weeknight pastimes, while Fridays feature a more lively atmosphere. (Beer L25; mixed drinks L60-L80. Cover F-Sa after 9pm L40, includes one free drink.) **Luna Beach,** the latest Roatán hotspot, features several bars including buffet dinner (starting at 7pm, L110-L340), great music, and a pier stretching out into the water. (Mixed drinks L40-L80, beer L25. Open Sa. Cover L50.) English movies show 8pm M-Sa at the **Blue Channel Restaurant,** south of the main intersection before Tyll's Dive Center, and 5 and 7pm M, W-Su at **Brick Oven Pizza,** up the road past Pinocchios.

WEST BAY

Can one beach possibly be this good? Yes, yes it can. Powder-white sand, swaying palms, and crystal-clear water with phenomenal snorkeling—West Bay has it all. The **snorkeling** is particularly good on the west part of the beach, where the reef is just 10 or 20m off the shore and a volcanic wall is nearby. However, as West Bay is becoming more and more developed, crowds and prices are increasing, so those traveling on the cheap might want to bring their own food and drink.

From West End, West Bay is a 45min. walk along the beach. Leave valuables at home, go in groups, and avoid walking after dark. You can also wave down a **water taxi** from any dock along the shore or the ones that regularly stop on the dock opposite West End Divers (5min., L30). Bring repellent to ward off sandflies.

EAST OF COXEN HOLE

French Harbour, the island's biggest fishing port, lies 10km east along a curvy paved road that traverses rolling green hills with great ocean views. Yachts stop here, but there is no beach. For those who find the place alluring there are some inexpensive hotels: try **Britos** or **Dixon's Plaza.** From French Harbour, the main road runs across the mountain ridge at the center of the island. Along the way, a side road branches out to **Oak Ridge,** a charming fishing village. From here, boat tours hit the beautiful **Jonesville mangroves** and go through a mangrove tunnel. Stop and get a snack at the **Hole in the Wall** restaurant. A 1½hr. boat ride will cost around L375-L400. A good place to spend the night in Oak Ridge is the comfortable **San José Hotel ❺.** (☎435 2328. L220, with fan and bath L250.) Buses run to Oak Ridge from Coxen Hole (about 1hr., L15). Once in Oak Ridge all transport is by water taxi (L20). The rustic, small **Reef House Resort ❺** may be too expensive for budget travelers, but its attached restaurant is a great place to grab a drink and watch the dolphins pass by. (All-inclusive package L1880.) Around 5km from Oak Ridge, the paved road ends at **Punta Gorda,** the oldest town on the island and the oldest Garífuna community in Honduras. The village celebrates its founding every year from April 8 to 12, and Garífuna from all over come to join the celebration. **Ben's Restaurant,** along the coast south of the village, rents moderately-priced **cabins.** Beyond Punta Gorda a dirt road continues past new resorts to **Camp Bay,** a beach now partially closed. It ends at **Port Royal,** site of the remains of a British fort surrounded by the rather inaccessible **Port Royal Park and Wildlife Refuge.**

GUANAJA

In November 1998, Hurricane Mitch unleashed its fury on Guanaja (pop. 1900), by far the hardest hit of the Bay Islands. 30 straight hours of 180 mph sustained winds turned the island into the epitome of mass destruction. Though determined to reconstruct the town, the hard-working community is still reeling in the aftermath of the hurricane "made especially for Guanaja." Resorts remain the only option for visiting; the most popular being **Posada del Sol.** The few available lower-priced accommodations can be found with most of the local services in **Bonacca**, or **Guanaja town,** a small caye 1km off the southern coast of the big island. Farthest from the mainland, Guanaja waters are the most pristine, keeping its reefs the most unscathed. White-sand beaches and cascades like **Big Gully Falls** make it a true island paradise.

CAYOS COCHINOS

Those looking for an isolated alternative to the Bay Islands need look no further than Cayos Cochinos. Sixty kilometers offshore from La Ceiba, a cluster of 16 mostly uninhabited islands wait for travelers who want time to themselves. All but two of the islands are actually composed of coral; 66 species directly off-shore make up this **National Marine Monument.** The Smithsonian Institute has been conducting marine research here since 1994. (For more information about research projects email fundcayos@caribe.hn or the director at acubas@caribe.hn.)

Getting to the islands requires a bit of patience and an extra day for travel. You must arrive in one of the villages opposite the cayes a day early and head over to the Cochinos the next morning; early-morning departures are necessary to avoid the wind that kicks up later. **Sambo Creek** is easier to reach from La Ceiba (1hr., 5am-6:10pm every 35min., L8), but is not the best base for reaching the cayes, since the direction of the waves can make transport difficult. In Sambo Creek, it's possible to stay at **Hotel Avila** (L100-L120). **Nueva Armenia,** the village across from the cayes, takes longer to get to from La Ceiba (2hr.; 8, 10, 11:30am, 1, 4:30pm; stops in Jutiapa; L21), but has regular daily transportation to the cayes.

Cayo Menor, the smaller of the two big islands, hosts the headquarters of the Cayos Cochinos Foundation: the **Turtle and Coral Marine Research Center.** You can arrange for an island tour guide. (☎442 2670 or 443 4075; fundcayos@caribe.hn. La Ceiba office located in Colonial Naranjal, Opuesta St. in the Standard Fruit Company laboratory. Open daily 8am-5pm.)

Cayo Mayor, the larger of the two big islands, is occupied on the western side by the only resort in Cayos Cochinos, the all-inclusive **Plantation Beach Resort.** Diving packages include seaside accommodation with private hot baths and fans, three dives per day, unlimited shore dives, kayaking, snorkeling, and fishing and hiking tours of the islands. For those not staying at the resort, 12 complementary moorings are available for sea vessels and dive gear can be rented. For US$10 visitors can use all of the resort facilities. A transport service is available to the Lagoon Marina (1hr., min. 2 people., US$30).

The eastern side of the Cayo Mayor is home to **East End,** the small fishing village where recreational trails to the lighthouse begin. **Francisco Velásquez** coordinates most tourist activities and has recently completed cabins with shared cold baths for L80-L100 per night (☎382 1159; jofravehn@yahoo.com. Spanish only. Advance reservations preferred). Ask around in the village for beds that usually run L50 per

Beware of weather and scammers. If the severe winds pick up around the islands, it's no longer safe for small crafts to make the trip. You could wind up stuck on an island for up to several days, so plan accordingly. Also, some canoe operators have a nasty tendency to charge visitors inflated prices for the ride back to the mainland once alternatives are no longer possible. Get recommendations on reputable operators before leaving, and hold your ground for as long as possible, but be prepared to pay a "fee" (US$10-$15) to get back.

night. Women in the community cook solely traditional food (L70). In the middle of the village their is a small *pulpería* with drinks, snacks, and beer. Francisco and others offer tours of Cayo Grande on foot or in a motorboat around the cayes (L200), as well as the opportunity for travelers to try their luck fishing in a *cayuco* of the eastern coast (L80-L100).

THE MOSQUITIA

The vast Mosquitia holds magnificent tropical forest, coastal marshlands, and flat savannah in an endless stretch of uninhabited terrain, creating an area like nothing else in the country. Getting to the northeast coast of Honduras is half the adventure; the few towns are frontier settlements and travel requires patience and good Spanish skills. A growing tourist industry has made trips possible, but they're not cheap. The **Biosfera Río Plátano,** known as "the little Amazon," is the largest tract of virgin tropical rainforest north of the equator. Travelers to the Biosfera will find themselves in virtually unexplored territory. Most travelers come on **guided tours** that reach otherwise inaccessible regions. Though expensive, the extra service is well worth the added cost. Two good companies are **Mesoamerica Travel** in San Pedro Sula (☎557 0332; www.mesoamerica-travel.com) and **Omega Tours** (☎440 0334) in La Ceiba.

There are a number of details to bear in mind while in the Mosquitia. Travelers should bring all necessary **cash** in the smallest denominations possible as bills above L150 are hard to change. The only **bank** in the region is in Puerto Lempira. Don't forget to take into consideration the boat ride to Las Marías (L2000), and plane tickets out of Palacios (L1045) or Puerto Lempira (LL1326). The only **public phone** service is in Puerto Lempira. Belén and Palacios have communal phone service, but other than that everyone communicates by **radio** (long wave channel 68, shortwave channel 6222.2). Beyond Puerto Lempira there is **no bottled water** and filtered water is hard to come by; bring your own filtration system or only drink boiled or chlorine-treated water (4 drops per gallon). Refrigeration is uncommon, so check all meat before eating it. Most of the Biosfera, including Las Marías, is dry: **no alcohol** is sold and bringing your own is a no-no. Where there are cantinas, they tend to attract unsavory criminal-types. When walking along trails without a guide, beware of the **Fer-de-Lance viper** that lies camouflaged in forest leaves awaiting prey; its bite can be fatal. If bitten, go directly to a clinic for antivenom. Local **women never travel alone** and female travelers should adhere to the same practice. Some indigenous residents are sensitive about being photographed, so ask first.

BUGS! **Mosquitoes** and other insects are prevalent, especially at night, and can carry dangerous diseases like **malaria** and **dengue fever** (p. 420). Never go barefoot or use open-toed shoes or you may encounter **niguas,** small insects that lay egg sacs in your cuticles. If you see what appears to be a blister, open it with a needle and squeeze the eggs out. **"Kissing bugs"** carry the incurable Chagas disease and commonly bite around the lips of sleeping hikers, so be sure to tuck mosquito netting into your mattress. **Chiggers,** similar to ticks, are common in Las Marias; tuck your pants into your socks and use a rubber band for added protection. Also make sure to shake clothing and shoes before getting dressed as **scorpions** are common in the area. Because of the humidity and frequent rains in the Biosfera, bug bites or small cuts can lead to **impetigo** or **tropical ulcers** if untreated. If you see any strange marks on your body or your **skin turns purple,** and **yellow polka-dots** begin to appear, consult the nearest doctor. We know this all sounds like a joke, but trust us, it's not.

PALACIOS

Palacios is the first and last stop on the way into the jungle. The city has the area's main airport, provisions, guides, and the only hospital in the Biosfera.

◪ TRANSPORTATION. Most travelers fly into Palacios from La Ceiba. **SOSA** (☎ 968 8397. Radio frequency 6222.2) has an office next to Hotel Moskitia on the north side of the airstrip and flies to **La Ceiba** (45min., 7am daily, L1059). The office is open daily 5:30-11am and 2-4pm. **SAMI** (☎ 966 6465), located in the last doorway of the white strip mall two buildings down the main drag from the northwest side of the airstrip, has flights to **Ahuas** (L1544), **Brus** (L504), **Patuca** (L695), **Puerto Lempira** (1hr., L790), and **Wampusirpe** (L902). Planes leave when full; arrive at 7am to and expect long waits. Only chartered planes go to **Trujillo** (L2800, up to 5 people).

Colectivo **boats** leave sometime after SOSA flights arrive and travel to the **Río Plátano** (1-3hr., 7-9am departure, L50-L100). Boats also pass throughout the day and can be flagged down by yelling your destination and waving from anywhere along the shore. Crossing the river costs L25 and a trip anywhere along the coast should not exceed L100. Express boats head to **Cocobila** (L800), **Belén** (L1000), or **Las Manas** (L3000). For coastal destinations, talk to the owner of Hotel Samira.

◪ PRACTICAL INFORMATION. On the south side of the airstrip, **Hospital Bayan** is open 24hr. for emergencies and has an extensive **pharmacy**. (Open for consultation M-F 8am-noon and 2-4pm. L20.) Across the runway, the **police station** is open M-Sa 8am-4pm and can be called by radio. Several **pulperías** coexist with a few small grocery stores. **Ana Argelia Marmol,** owner of the Río Tinto Lodge (see **Accommodations,** below) and the *pulpería* near the runway, can help you set up transportation. Make **phone calls** from the SAMI office (L45 per min. to US or Europe).

◪ ACCOMMODATIONS. Hotel Soby ❸, down the main path on the right, has it all: large rooms with multiple cold baths, fans, queen beds, and TVs. Relaxing views compliment the restaurant's over-the-water seating. (☎ 979 2015. Singles L150; doubles and triples L200.) The **Rio Tinto Lodge ❸** is down the main path east of the airstrip, on the right past the SAMI office. Rooms have clean cold bath, electricity from 4-9pm, and a balcony overlooking the river (doubles L150; triples L200). **Hotel Samira ❶,** a Christmas-colored building just beyond Hotel Soby on the left, has clean and simple private rooms with cold shared baths. The owner is extremely nice, knowledgeable, and may offer to show you around Palacios on his boat (singles L80; doubles L100).

◪ FOOD. Food prices are slightly higher than in the cities because of the town's remote location. Connected to the Hotel Soby, classy **Comedor Soby ❷** pairs white table cloths with riverside seating. Excellent seafood includes *sopa de pescado* for L50 and *baleadas* for L5 (open daily 7am-8pm). Connected to the SOSA office on the airstrip, **Comedor Palacios ❷** serves large *típico* plates (L40) on a breezy riverside patio next to a tropical-looking bar that rocks to smooth Spanish tunes. Step out onto the runway to catch the sunset (open daily 5:30am-8pm).

BIOSFERA RÍO PLÁTANO

Most visitors to La Mosquitia spend their time in Biosfera Río Plátano, a massive swath of jungle that covers over 8100 sq. km of lowland forest, pine savanna, coastal wetland, and farmland. Designated a World Heritage Site by UNESCO in 1980, Río Plátano is now the focus of major environmental preservation efforts by the World Wildlife Federation, Nature Conservancy, and USAID. The Biosfera hosts over 400 bird species, thousands of plants, and the coastal nesting grounds of four species of endangered sea turtle, including the famed Leatherback.

⌐ TRANSPORTATION: FROM PALACIOS TO BELÉN

To explore deeper into the Mosquitia, you'll need to get to the Miskito villages on near Laguna de Ibans. A *colectivo* (public **tuk-tuk**) leaves Palacios M-Sa sometime after the SOSA and Atlantic **flights** come in (7:30am), usually 8-10am. It reaches the first village, **Plaplaya** (45min., L40), then continues to **Ibans** (1hr., L70), **Cocobila** (1.5hr., L80), and **Raistá** (2hr., L100). Ride the *colectivo* all the way to Raistá or hop off in Plaplaya and head there on foot. The easy walk makes for a leisurely afternoon exploring coastal Garífuna and Miskito life. *Expresos* can be hired from Palacios to **Belén** (2hr., L600). Belén is right next to Raistá and is a good place to arrange guides and transport farther into the reserve to **Las Marías.**

PLAPLAYA. Garífuna Plaplaya abounds with *punta* dancing and beautiful beaches. The town is famous for the **Sea Turtle Conservation Project,** almost exclusively coordinated by local residents. Since 1996, the community has worked to preserve the endangered Loggerhead and Leatherback turtle populations that nest in the coastal sands, successfully protecting over 21,000 eggs in nine years. The turtles nest from April to July, and visitors can partake in an egg collection from 8pm-midnight or 1-5am (free). To sign up, speak to Doña Dora, the project coordinator, in the white house behind Hospedaje Bacilia y Porfillio. Between June and September, visitors can witness the release of the hatchlings. May and September host festivals exclusively devoted to the town's patron animal.

Farthest west on the lagoon side, **Hospedaje Bacilia y Porfillio ❶** houses guests in traditional Garífuna huts with mosquito netting and serves home-cooked meals in **Comedor Doña Neti ❷** just across the strip from the sea turtle nesting grounds (beds L60, meals L40). **Doña Cedi ❷** serves meals in a giant, open-air *comedor* overlooking the river and sells cold *refrescos* (1.5 liters, L30) and beer (L20). She rents rooms for L70 per person.

IBANS, COCOBILA, AND RAISTÁ. Follow any of the footpaths to the beach, turn right, and walk for 1-1½hr. until you see a scattering of dugout canoes. The paths over the dunes will lead into this picturesque Miskito village, nestled along the lagoon of the same name. You may come to a smaller neighboring village first, but just turn left on the path until Ibans. **Hospedaje Miss Vanesa ❷** has doubles with mosquito netting, large windows, tables, and personal lights by electric generator, as well as a small *pulpería* next door. Room 3 is the nicest. (Beds L80; breakfast L35, lunch and dinner L40. Radio access.)

From Ibans, continue east along the truck path to **Cocobila,** a slightly more developed Miskito village dotted with unappealing trash piles. The **police** station for the Lake Ibans strip is located down the street from Hospedaje El Nopal (open daily 8am-4pm; radio access Channel 68). Next to Hospedaje Mynerto Castillo in the green and yellow cement building, **Commercial Villares** sells SOSA tickets and has a relatively large *pulpería*. (Open daily 6am-8pm. Radio access, Islena 2 call sign.) On the east side of the village, **Hospedaje Mynerto Castillo ❷** maintains tight singles and doubles with *mosquiteros* and a cozy indoor lounge with couches, fans, and a CD player. Prices are negotiable. (Beds L70, meals L30). Mynerto also takes passengers to **Las Marias** (3 days L2500) and **Brus Laguna** for L1000. Farther west, **Hospedaje y Comedor Ethelina ❷** offers singles and doubles with a porch. (Beds L70, meals L40.)

From Cocobila, a short walk along the same path will lead to **Raistá. Eddie Boden,** the first person born here, is your go-to man for just about anything you need. He runs a transportation service to **Las Marias** (2 people L2200, up to 5 people L2500) for a two-night stay, and leads an unforgettable hiking excursion from there (3-4 people L500 per day). **Hospedaje Ecocentro Raistá ❷**, in the grass hut by the dock in the center of town, is Eddie's venture into real estate, complete with electricity, mosquito netting, towels, and toilet paper (beds L70). Eddie and his brother Sergio run **lagoon tours to** hidden secrets like **Bonacca**, with its white-faced monkeys, waterfalls, and cabins on the lagoon. (L150 per day, L100 per day additional fee for boat operators.) **Elma's Kitchen ❷** next door serves solid meals accompanied by *pan de coco* (meals L40). **Cecilia Boden** and her family run an excellent *hospedaje* on the white and yellow path just back from Ecocentro; there's no electricity or running water, but the porch is inviting (beds L70). Hang around in Raistá long enough and you'll meet 101-year-old legendary patriarch Willy Boden, who founded the village and is known as "Abraham of la Mosquitia."

RÍO PLÁTANO. Located on a point of land stretching out into the ocean is the last community in the string of villages. From Ibans to Río Plátano, the divisions between towns is unclear. Río Plátano is not the most developed place on earth, but it does have six local radios for communication. To cross the river to Río Plátano, take a small wooden canoe; it is very unsafe to ford. Just ask around for locations and distances. **Morgan Devis,** the best source of information in town, offers nearby crocodile tours (L30-L40 per person), transportation to **Las Marías** by **motor** (6hr., L2400 for up to 3 days) and by **wooden canoe** (1½ days, L1500 for up to 4 days), and **express boats** to Brus Laguna or Palacios (big boat, 1hr., L1500; 15hp motor, 2½hr., L1000). **Colectivo boats** also run to **Brus Laguna** (L150) on a completely random schedule once or twice per month. **Hospedaje Doña Ardinia Mollina ❸,** in the southwest corner of the soccer field, has singles with mosquito netting and electricity (L100, mats L30). **Hospedaje Saira ❸,** next to Doña Ardinia and closer to the ocean, has dorm-style beds with mosquito netting for L100. Just off the landing point, **Restaurante Mari ❷,** in the *pulpería*, has seafood meals for L40-L50 (open M-Sa 5am-10pm).

LAS MARÍAS

Las Marías, 25km up the Río Plátano from Belén, is a jungle outpost at the heart of the Biosfera. A trip to Las Marías and the interior of the Biosfera is unforgettable, but be prepared to part with a large wad of cash: gas and guides are expensive.

☐ TRANSPORTATION. Motorized **pipantes** or **tuk-tuks** make the trip to **Las Marías** 4-6hr.; **cayucos** make it in 3-4hr. Unmotorized *pipantes* take up to 12hr. All methods of transportation cost a painful L2000-L2500 round-trip, hold 4-6 people depending on the boat, and leave from either Raistá, Belén, Palacios, Plaplaya, Cocobila, Kuri, or Plátano. This fare assumes a three-day stay in Las Marías—those wanting longer stays will need to negotiate the price. Try to make arrangements the night before, as river guides will not leave after 1pm. Trips can be arranged by **Mandarino, Marvin,** or **Tinglas** in Palacios; **Eddy Boden** in Raistá; **Mynerto Castillo** or **Humberto Marmol** in Cocobila; **Morgan Debbins** in Río Plátano; **Hildo Ramos** in Belén; and **Rollins George** in Kuri. Mandarino is well connected all along the river and will arrange friendly, professional service. Mynerto is said to provide the cheapest rates. The journey is long and you need to come prepared; bring a raincoat and sun protection, and make sure your gear is waterproof. Transportation farther up the river can only be completed in an unmotorized *pipante* from Las Marías (L100 per day for the boat and L200 per day for two operators).

A scenic way to reach Las Marías is to **hike** in. The breathtaking 7-8hr. walk winds through dense jungle on the far side of the lagoon, passing through several indigenous farming communities. During the rainy season, hikers often have to wade through waist deep water and mud. Eddy Boden in Raistá can arrange the trip (L500 per day for the hike, up to 4 people; L200 for the canoe across the laguna; L100 per day in Las Marías, 2 days minimum).

To get back out of the region, float or hike back. The *colectivo* back to **Palacios** leaves Raistá and Belén between 4:30 and 5am, in time to catch a **flight** out of Palacios. The SOSA office in Cocobila, Eddy Boden in Raistá, or any local with a radio can call ahead to reserve a spot on the plane and make sure the *colectivo* stops to pick you up. Flights can also be chartered on **SAMI** from La Ceiba, holding up to five people for L3575. **Don Luis** of Hospedaje Los Angeles (see **Accommodations,** below), runs trips back to the **north coast.** (*Colectivo* 2 times per week, L500 per person one-way; express L2000 round-trip to Raistá.)

⁊ PRACTICAL INFO. The **Centro de Salud,** on the edge of the soccer field, provides medical service. (Open M-F 8am-noon and 2-4pm. Consultation L3.) The closest **hospital** is in Palacios, for which the town has an emergency transport vehicle. Halfway between Hospedajes Tinglas and Justa, **Pulpería Yehiny** has toothpaste and snacks (open M-Sa 5am-6pm, Su 8am-noon). At the western edge of the soccer field, **Pulpería Nuñez** offers the same (open daily 6am-6pm).

⋔ ACCOMMODATIONS. All *hospedajes* are of excellent quality, with meals of beans, rice, and a stack of super-thick tortillas (L40). None have electricity; mosquito netting is a must. **Hospedaje Doña Diana ❷,** the second *hospedaje* along the river, provides doubles and quads with mosquito netting in a charming riverside setting with hammocks and a porch. (Cocoa desserts L30 and hot chocolate L5. Beds L70 per person.) Next door, **Hospedaje Tinglas ❸** offers doubles with tables, mosquito netting, hammocks, and porches overlooking the river. (L140. Radio access.) Up the road towards Las Marías, **Hospedaje Doña Justa ❶** has dorm-style beds with mosquito netting, patio seating, and purified water (beds with 1 thin mattress L50, 2 thin mattresses L70). Across the soccer field, **Hospedaje El Centro ❷,** run by Olvidio Martinez, has doubles and triples with mosquito netting (L70 per person). Down and up the hill continuing west on the path through Las Marías, **Hospedaje Los Angeles ❷,** run by Don Luis, lays beds with mosquito netting (L60 per person). For those headed upstream to the petroglyphs, **Hospedaje Bernardo ❶,** halfway to the first set of petroglyphs, has rooms with mosquito netting (L50 per person) and meals (L30).

⬙ EXCURSIONS. Though Las Marías is fascinating in and of itself, the wilderness areas that surround it are stunning beyond description. Guided adventures are planned and coordinated by the **Ecotourism Committee of Las Marías.** Guides cater each trip to the

THE LOCAL STORY

HUNTING WITH THE TAHUACA

Mark-Andre Dunn, a doctoral candidate in the Department of Geography at Carlton University, US, lived in a Tahuaca village in La Mosquitia studying the spatial patterns of subsistence hunting.

On lifestyle: Subsistence is hard because the Tahuaca have to buy the bullets and guns which has integrated the market economy into their lifestyle. Life is very hard for them; they work a hell of a lot and don't really get any days off. They make very little money though it costs a lot of money to send their children to school or to get treated for illness.

On hunting: It was very hard keeping up with them through the mud and walking for hours and hours. They seem to have a mental compass. They pray every time before they go into the forest as they say that there are many enemies like snakes. There is an aura of respect around the hunters in the community.

On animals: On a three day expedition with some Mosquito men, I heard this steamroller running through the forest. They told me it must be a Tapir that got startled. Apparently when the Tapir gets startled it sticks its head down and barrels through the forest knocking down everything in its path. You actually see the paths when you walk and it looks like something about waist high blasted through everything.

group size and experience level of travelers. **Prudencio,** the *saca-guía* (guide coordinator), is the best resource for setting up tours; the owner of your *hospedaje* will put you in contact with him. **Primary guides** who lead hikes and explain surroundings along the river cost L150 per day; **secondary guides** who are usually just as knowledgeable but operate *pipantes* charge L100 per day. Seven trips are offered around Las Marías. To conduct your own expedition or follow your own itinerary, notify the committee president, **Martin,** who lives in the last house on the road through Las Marías away from the river.

Two **river tours** are offered. The first is a one-day *pipante* ride to the **petroglyphs** of **Walpaulban Sirpi,** 4km upriver, including a moderate 1-2hr. hike through a jungle trail, wildlife sightings, and a chance to swim in the river (9hr.; bring lunch, mosquito repellent, rain gear, and a swimsuit; L550). The second is a two-day extension of the previous trip to visit the second set of petroglyphs at **Walpaulban Tara,** including riverside camping and additional hikes upon request (2 days, L1000).

Through **jungle trails,** hikers can make a difficult two-day trek across the lowlands to the northwest of Las Marías and ascend **Cerro Baltimore,** the highest peak in the region (1083m). From this viewpoint, you can enjoy sweeping views of the Laguna de Ibans and the sea beyond. The true peak can be ascended by special arrangement, but requires much more physical stamina (2 days, L600). The most grueling of the regularly arranged trips is a three-day guided trek to **Pico Dama** (863m). After a 1-2hr. canoe ride upriver, the trail leads through farmland and forests, before turning steep and muddy as it heads into the mountains. The top, reached on the second day, affords spectacular views of the entire region (3 days, L1250). For a less rigorous trip within the same area, a two-day hike to the peak of **Cerro Mico** begins along the same trail and then makes a loop through less frequented jungle known as "Monkey Hill" (2 days, L800).

A good compromise hike for those with limited time is **Cerro de Zapote,** which goes halfway up the trail to Cerro Baltimore and has large tracts of primary forest and great early-morning birdwatching. In heavy rains, water levels may be too high to cross; wear your fording outfit either way (1 day, L150). Lastly, the **Village Trail** is an easy hike that begins along the river, winds up through the forest and comes down to the village. (2-3hr., L150 with guide or free to follow on your own.) Customized trips to more remote destinations can be arranged by sitting down with the *saca-guía* and a map.

PUERTO LEMPIRA

Located 250km southeast of Palacios, Puerto Lempira (pop. 4300) is the administrative capital of the Mosquito Coast, and is surrounded by Miskito and Pech indigenous villages. The settlement fascinates visitors with its rustic frontier-trading-town character and a culture that exists almost completely out of contact with the rest of the world. Just beyond the city limits, thousands of square kilometers of untouched wilderness in Caratasca reserve and excellent snook and tarpin fishing beckon the outdoor enthusiast. Travel here is no piece of cake: visitors should plan ahead and arrive in Puerto Lempira well-informed, and well-supplied.

⌐ TRANSPORTATION. Almost all visitors travel to and from Puerto Lempira by **plane;** airlines are cash only and small bills are preferred. There are no flights in or out of Puerto Lempira on Sundays and heavy rain often delays or cancels flights Oct.-Dec. At**lantic Airlines** flies directly from Tegucigalpa to Puerto Lempira (Tu and F 7:30am). **Atlantic** (☎440 1220) and **SOSA** (☎440 0692) operate from the small office on the airstrip (☎898 7500) fly to La Ceiba (M-Sa 8am, L1326) and Tegucigalpa (Tu, F, 7am, L1668). **SAMI/Honduras Air** flies to destinations within Gracias a Dios: **Ahuas** (L465), **belén** (L728), **Brus Laguna** (L555), **Palacios** (L790), **Patuca** (L566), **Wampusirpe** (L606). A backwards and aggravating system mandates that all passengers arrive at 7am, however the flight schedule is determined by how many passengers want to go to a certain destination, resulting in a several hour wait. SAMI also charters flights for L2800 for up to five people anywhere in Gracias a Dios. To purchase Atlantic tickets or schedule SAMI express flights in town visit the white building 1½ blocks northeast of the park on C. Muelle (☎898 7663. Open M-Sa 8am-noon and 2pm-8.) There are no roads that connect Puerto Lempira with the rest of the country, but roads do lead to the surrounding areas. Regular **pickups** leave from the intersection on C. Muelle just before the dock to **Leimus** (border crossing with Nicaragua, 7am, L80), Mistruk beach (45min., L400 round trip), and **Rus Rus** (5-6hr., 6am and noon, L100). Gray and red taxis go anywhere in La Mosquitia (L2000). **Boats** leave from the main dock charging L1000 for an express daily transport anywhere or L60 for *colectivos* to Krata, Kaukira, and Katski (M-Sa 9am). **Ralston Haylock** is an excellent and trustworthy English/Spanish speaking Mosquito boat operator charging L600 (plus gas) to Krata or Kaukira. The dock office can help coordinate your travel (open M-Sa 6:30am-4pm).

■ **?** **ORIENTATION AND PRACTICAL INFORMATION.** Puerto Lempira follows a confusing grid system centered around the *parque central* with the corners of the park facing the cardinal directions instead of the streets. **Calle Muelle,** runs along the southeast side of the park. From the airstrip, head north towards the billboards and take a right at the intersection; after 1 block take the first left and go straight for 2 blocks to hit C. Muelle.

Electricity in Puerto Lempira is only available from approximately 8am-4pm and from 5:30pm-3am. The **Palacio Municipal,** 1 block towards the water on C. Muelle from the eastern corner of the *parque* and 1 block right headed southeast is open M-F 8am-4pm. **Banco Atlántida,** next to Gran Hotel Flores on the corner across from the parque central, is the only bank in La Moskitia. Cash traveler's checks and get cash advances on Visa M-F. (☎898 7580. Open M-F 8am-3pm, Sa 8:30-11:30am.) The **police station** is located alongside the airstrip. (☎898 7500. Open 24hr.) **Clinica Medica Renacer,** 2 blocks northwest of the park's western corner and 2 blocks left headed southwest past the local prison, provides 24hr. emergency medical service and has an attached pharmacy. (☎898 7646. Pharmacy open daily 3-9pm.) **Hospital Puerto Lempira,** provides 24hr. public emergency medical service 15min. south of town. (☎898 7439 or 898 7562. Taxi recommended.) **Cybercalderon.com,** beneath Hotel Gran Flores two doors down from the hotel office, has a monopoly on Internet service in town, allowing it to get away with attachment-wary and occasionally slow service for L1 per min. and well as staticky international calls for L10 per min. (open M-Sa 8am-4pm and 6-10pm).

■ **♥** **ACCOMMODATIONS AND FOOD.** **Gran Hotel Flores ❸** (☎898 7421), across from the southeast side of the *parque central* and three blocks up from the dock, has snug rooms with A/C, private cold bath, and TV. Rooms at the end of the hall leak during rainy season. (☎898 7421 or 898 7609. Singles L150, with A/C L200; doubles L300; triples L350.) **Hotel El Gran Samaritano ❷,** 1 block northeast from the eastern corner of the *parque* towards the water and 1 block left, has very clean rooms with private cold water baths, fans, and complementary condoms. (☎898 7582. Singles L250; doubles L300.)

All of the streets fanning off from C. Muelle between the dock and the park are packed with modest *comedores* offering local staples like chicken or beans for L20-L40. Head to **Calderon ❷,** on the eastern corner of the *parque*, on Sundays to celebrate with the winning team from the *fútbol* match and eat particularly good *típico*. (☎898 7530. Open daily 6am-10pm). **Lagún View ❷,** to the right of the dock,

HONDURAS

is Puerto Lempira's classiest restaurant serving up *típico* breakfasts (L45) as well as a selection of fast food (tacos L40, sandwiches L45). Lunch and dinner options depend on what the supply boat has brought in lately, but usually includes fried chicken, steak, and shrimp. (Meals L95-L120. Open daily 8:30am-11pm.)

FISHING. To the southwest of Puerto Lempira, locals claim **Mistruk Beach**, on Laguna de Tansin, as the nicest in the region. The famed **tarpin** or **snook** that have come out of this series of lagoons are reportedly bigger than the people that caught them. **Warunta Lake Lodge**, on Garunta Island in the sparsely populated northwest sector of Caratasca Reserve knows where to find the now elusive brutes. *(800-654-9915, trek@treksafaris.com, www.treksafaris.com. Reservations required. US$250/night. Transportation included. Open Jan-Sept.)*

DAYTRIPS. Most travelers to Puerto Lempira use it as a "launch pad" to some exotic destination. Miskito communities like **Krata** and **Katski** are relatively easy to reach from Puerto Lempira and offer beach camping and an opportunity to see an indigenous ocean-fishing community at work (45min.). **Raya,** near the Nicaraguan border, is an even more remote coastal experience. From Puerto Lempira, take a boat across the lake to Kaukira (L60) and ask around the dock for the next boat is leaving for Raya. **Rus Rus,** over 160km inland in a savannah-like landscape, is a village few visitors ever see. To get there, talk to the owner of Hotel Flores to hire a car (3-4hr., L1000). Bring a tent and all supplies. Ingri runs a *comedor* in the south part of the village (L30). Ask for Tomás Manzanares, who leads hikes into the surrounding area (L100 per day) such as to the **Savannah del Pino,** a unique locale inhabited by spot parrots and hawks. The trip into the broad leaf forest requires two to five days, but you'll probably see lots of animals. The best time to visit is the dry season (Feb.-Apr.) There is an **Amigos de las Americas** (Friends of the Americas) **clinic** in Rus Rus that treats snake bites and has radio communication.

OLANCHO

In what might be called the "wild wild east" of Honduras, imposing mountain ranges rise between far-flung cattle ranches, coffee plantations, and vast swathes of dense pine forest that give parts of Olancho a strangely un-Central American appearance. Comprising more than 20% of the country and inhabited by fiercely loyal *Olancheños*, the region has been nicknamed "the Independent Republic of Olancho." The friendly mountain towns belie the area's war-torn history, though travelers ought to stick to day-buses as private transportation is often unsafe.

LA UNIÓN

La Unión (pop. 3800) is a small village halfway between Tegus and Trujillo in the heart of Olancho. Though its rolling hills are starting to recover from exhaustive coffee growing, farming remains the central industry and there are often more cattle than *rancheros* enjoying the shade of the *parque central*. The dense **Parque Nacional la Muralla** 14km up in the mountains is the area's main tourist draw.

TRANSPORTATION. From La Unión there are daily buses to **Tegucigalpa** (4-5hr.; 5, 7:30, 11am; L70) and **Juticalpa** (2-3hr.; 5:30, 6:30, 11am; L45); it's possible to take Juticalpa buses to **Limones** and catch Tegus buses there. The bus to **Trujillo** passes through town at 11am, stopping in **Mame** (2hr., L50) and **Saba** (3hr., L65). To get to **La Ceiba,** catch a bus to Mame and transfer.

⚡ 🔟 ORIENTATION AND PRACTICAL INFORMATION. La Unión operates on the standard grid system centered around the *parque central*. **COHDEFOR,** 4½ blocks south of the *parque's* southeast corner, has info on Parque Nacional La Muralla and helpful brochures (open M-F 8am-4pm). The municipal building is on the south side of the *parque central* and **Calle Principal** runs north-south along the *parque's* western side. C. Principal heads south to Tegus and north to Parque Nacional La Muralla. **Banh Café,** the only local **bank,** does not change money and does not accept credit cards or traveler's checks (open M-F 8:30am-3:30pm, Sa 8am-11:30pm). The **police station** is 5 blocks south of the park's southwest corner on C. Principal. (Radio channel 7. Office open 5am-2am daily; knock hard for after-hours emergencies.) The **Centro de Salud,** 4 blocks south and half a block west of the park's southwest corner, has consultations for L5 (open M-F 8am-3pm). **Hondutel** (☎885 0032 or 885 3021) has installed communal phone lines and calls can be connected to most businesses. Around the corner, 1 block east and 1½ blocks north of the southeast corner of the park, **Ecocafe Internet** offers Internet service and international calls. (Internet L30 per hr., calls L4 per min. Open M-F 9am-8:30pm, Sa-Su 10am-8pm.) As a rural village, La Unión has running water on a rotating schedule, either only in the day or only at night. The **post office** is 1½ blocks east of the *parque's* southeast corner (open M-Sa 7am-5pm).

📁 🔳 ACCOMMODATIONS AND FOOD. The best deal in town can be found at the small **Hotelito La Posada ❶,** across the street from the COHDEFOR office, 4 blocks south of the *parque's* southwest corner and half a block left headed east. It has big rooms. (Singles L60; doubles L100; L800 per month.) **Hotel Los Arcos ❷,** 2 blocks south of the *parque's* southwest corner on C. Principal and 1 block left headed east, has spacious, simple rooms with fans, tables, and TVs. (Singles L50, with bath L110; doubles with bath L150.) **Hotel La Muralla ❺,** 2½ blocks south of the *parque's* southwest corner, on the left side of the C. Principal has giant, sparkling tiled rooms with fans, hot bath, TV, and a shared *pila*. Ask to use the Internet. (Singles L200; doubles L250.)

Across the street from Hotel La Muralla is the **Restaurant y Repostería Ruth ❶,** where you will find delicious *pastelitos de piña* (L6) and other sweet breads. (Fried chicken *típico* meal L25. Open daily 6am-9pm.) **Restaurante Bola de Oro ❸,** on the right 2 blocks south of the *parque's* southeast corner and 1 block left headed east, serves large Chinese platters. (Entrees L30-L60. Open daily 5-10pm.)

PARQUE NACIONAL LA MURALLA

Pickups run from the COHDEFOR office. Alternatively, the 14km (5-6hr.) hike to the park entrance is rigorous but pleasant. Follow C. Principal north out of town; take a right at the main intersection. At the visitor center welcome sign take a right. Schedule a pickup in advance for the return trip. Info is available at the COHDEFOR office in Tegus (☎885 2252). Guides can be hired at the COHDEFOR office in La Union for L150-L200 per day; ask for Eduardo Ferrera (☎889 0196). The park's caretaker, Milton Urbina, can be found in the visitor center and also works as a guide (L100 per trail). The visitors center has bilingual info on park plants, insects, and topography; the center also has bathrooms and a trail register. The park has 2 campgrounds (with latrines) on the trails; there is also a camping spot and 3 dorm-style beds at the visitor center (L40 per bed with private bath). Bring your own food and water. Admission and camping are free, though donations are appreciated.

High in the hills behind La Unión, Parque Nacional La Muralla is best known for its birds: toucans, peacocks, parrots, eagles, and, of course, the elusive quetzal all inhabit Muralla's cloudforest canopy. While the toucan is the official park mascot, this may be the only place in Central America where quetzals actually flock right

HONDURAS

by the visitor center (Feb.-June). Monkeys, white-tailed deer, jaguars, and pumas are among the 58 species of mammals that share the park along with 822 species of plants, 179 species of birds, 51 species of reptiles, and 294 species of insects.

There are five well-marked trails in the park. The shortest trail is **El Liquidambar**, a 1km loop through the primary forest south of the visitor center. **El Pizote**, the most popular hike, makes a 3.78km (2-3hr.) loop up the south side of the mountain range and is great for quetzal-watching. A shoot off of the eastern side of this trail, **Las 4 Pavas**, has a campsite with a latrine. **El Jaguar** (4km) is a 3hr. hike north through the heart of the park. The challenging 10km **Monte Escondido** is a 5-6hr. climb through several different levels of primary forest. Along the way there is a campsite with a latrine.

JUTICALPA

Deep in Honduras's central mountains, Juticalpa (pop. 19,600) is the capital of Olancho and the largest city in eastern Honduras. A bustling city seems out of place in the midst of endless miles of rural farmland, but travelers appreciate the chance to pamper themselves with luxuries not found in the rest of the department. Flanked by the untamed Parque Nacional Sierra de Agalta, the mysterious glowing skulls of Cuevas de Talgua, and the 10 cascading waterfalls at the Streams of Babylon, Juticalpa is a great launchpad for the adventure traveler.

TRANSPORTATION. There are two bus stations, the **Regional Transport Center** (known commonly as the main bus station) and the shared **Discovery** and **Aurora Bus terminals,** both located across the street from each other at the intersection of 5 Av. and 12 C. From the main bus station, buses leave for **Catacamas** (1hr., every 30min. 6am-6pm, L16); **Gualaeo** (1½hr.; 5, 8, 9, 10, 11am, 1, 2:30pm, L35); **San Esteban** (3hr., 6am and 2pm, L47); and **La Unión** (3hr., 1am and noon, L45). One half block across the street headed away from the park, **Discovery** (☎885 2237) and **Aurora** (☎885 2237; offices both open daily 4:30am-6pm) send buses to **Tegucigalpa** on the same schedule (3hr., express 2½hr.; 17 per day 5am-6pm; L57/40.50), passing through **Campamento** (L26.50) and **Limones** (L18.50).

ORIENTATION AND PRACTICAL INFORMATION. Juticalpa could possibly be the only city in Honduras that has taken the time to label all of its streets. Numbered *avenidas* run north-south, while *calles* run east-west. Ascending south and west of the park, the main drag is **5 Avenida,** usually referred to as the **Boulevard,** which runs north-south in front of the **cathedral** along the *parque*'s east side and passes the bus station (8 blocks south of the *parque*). **Calle 3,** the main east-west drag, runs along the *parque*'s south side passing in front of the *Casa de Cultura* and the Shell station leading to the hospital.

COHDEFOR, 7 Av., 13/12 C., administers Parque Nacional Sierra Agulta but has limited tourist info. From the main bus station, cross 5 Av. on 12 C. and walk 2 blocks; turn left onto 7 Av. and find the office 50m down on your right. (☎885 2252. Open M-F 8am-4pm.) **Greko Tours,** 3 C., 7/8 Av., inside the strip mall across from the Shell gas station and 2 blocks west of the *parque*, has travel information and pre-planned tours to Roatán, Montelimar, or La Ceiba. (☎885 2775 or 885 3407; yansyet@hondutel.hn. Open M-F 8am-noon and 1:30-5pm.)

Banco Atlántida, 2 C., 5 Av., on the northeast corner of the *parque*, changes traveler's checks, gives cash advances on Visa and has a 24hr. Visa **ATM.** (☎885 2020 or 885 2719. Open M-F 8am-3:30pm, Sa 8:30-11:30am.) **Banpais,** 5 Av., 4 C., serves as a **Western Union.** (☎885 2431. Open M-F 9am-3:30pm, Sa 8am-noon.) On the corner of 4 Av. and 2 C., 1 block east of the northeast corner of the *parque*, a 24hr. ATM accepts AmEx/Plus.

Clínica Médica PMQ, 7 Av., 1/2 C. (☎885 2413 or 885 1408), accepts Visa. Attached, **Pharmacy Suyapa** is open M-F 8:30am-1pm and 2:30-6pm, Sa 8:30am-1pm. Both have 24hr. emergency medical care. Public **Hospital San Francisco**, Barrio Campo, has several dozen doctors on staff. Look for the tall cylindrical tower. (☎885 2675 or 885 2655. Open 24hr. Consultation L3.) **Farmacia Santa Teresita**, 3 C. 5/6 Av., is on the south side of the *parque* next to the Centro de Cultura. (☎885 2181. Open M-F 8am-12:30pm and 2-5:30pm, Sa 8am-1pm.) The **police station**, Barrio Belén, 9 Av. 4 C., can be accessed from 8 Av. next to the Centro Penal. (☎885 2110 or 885 2111. Open 24hr.)

Both the police station and the **municipalidad** have **Hondutel** phones outside that accept foreign calling cards (L97 for 3min. to the US). Hondutel has an office on 4 Av., 4/5 C. (☎885 2486. Open M-F 7am-12:30pm and 1-4pm, Sa 7am-noon.) The **post office** is currently relocating the office at the corner of 4 Av., 4 C. Look for a posting on the door or ask around for the new location. **Sico's**, C. 5, Av. 7/8 has faster phone service. (☎885 2542. L20 per hr., L3 per min. for calls to US, L4 to Europe. Open M-F 8am-7pm, Sa 8am-5pm.) The cheapest **Internet** in town is at **Serviciber**, 3 C., 7 Av., but the connection speed tends to be slow. (Open 7:30am-9pm daily. Internet L16 per hr. International calls L4 per min. Copies L1.)

For shopping needs, **Supermercado Santa Gerna**, 2 C., 9 Av., has a large selection. (☎885 2523. Open M-Sa 7am-7pm. Accepts Visa.) On 5 Av., C. 4/5, **Bodega de Frutas y Verduras La Sureana** sells the best-looking produce in town. (Open daily 6am-8pm.) **Cinemaya**, 2 C., 8/9 Av., has daily showings of recent Hollywood hits. (Daily showings 7:30pm, Su 9am. Entrance L20.)

☗ ACCOMMODATIONS. Most of Juticalpa's hotels are west of the *parque* behind the *municipalidad*. ▓**Hotel Reyes ❷**, 7 Av., 3/4 C., 1 block west and half a block south of the *parque*, has big, well-kept rooms with bath and fan. The common room has a TV. (☎885 2232. L60 per person, with private bath L80. Front door closes at 10pm.) **Hotel Colonial ❶**, on 3 C. 2½ blocks west past the Shell gas station and headed away from the park, is the best deal in Honduras, with comfortable doubles that have A/C, cold bath, fan, and TV. (L30. Reception open 24hr.) In a more central location, **Hotel Honduras ❹**, 7 Av., 2/3 C., across 3 C. from Hotel Reyes, offers spotless rooms with cable TV, hot bath, and telephone. (☎885 1331. Singles L180, with A/C L314; doubles L215/L464.) **Hotel Juticalpa ❷**, 7 Av., 1 C., is a good backpacker establishment with shared baths and fans, soap, and towels in well-kept rooms. (☎885 1260. Free purified water. L55 per person.)

▟ FOOD. Over 100 years old, **El Nuevo Rancho ❷**, Av. 4, C. 2/3, 1 block east and half a block south of the *parque*'s northeast corner, serves up a mean bbq on a patio oasis. (☎885 1202. Entrees L35-L90. Open M-Sa 11am-10:30pm.) **Antonioni's Pizza ❷**, 7 Av., 3/4 C., next to Hotel Reyes, has fast thick pizza, complimented by friendly service and free delivery. (☎885 2621 or 885 3568. Personal pizzas L40-L46, vegetarian L43. Open daily 8am-9pm.) **Fast Burger ❶**, 7 Av., 1 C., has a chill environment, good American burgers, and cheap beer. (Hamburger L25; beer L13. Open daily 10am-8pm.) **Comedor Los Arcos ❶**, 4 blocks from the park, serves large *platos típicos* and drinks (L22-L35). Patrons get the bonus of great views of the surrounding towns and hills through the arches. **Casablanca ❶**, C. 4, Av. 4/5, serves cheap buffet-style breakfast, lunch, and dinner within intriguing white architecture. (☎885 1026. Rice L4, beans L4, tortilla L1. Open M-Sa 7am-4pm.) After nightfall, several cheap food stands pop up along the perimeter of the park. For dessert, **Helados Santa ❶**, 5 Av., 6 C., prepares inexpensive and amazing mango sorbet. (Waffle cone L17. Open daily 9:30am-8pm.)

■ MONUMENTO NATURAL EL BOQUERÓN. Halfway between Juticalpa and Catacamas, El Boquerón captures a broad cross-section of Olancho's ecological diversity in a relatively small area. Both dry and wet tropical forests, in addition to cloudforests, are nestled around the **Agua Buena** mountain (1433m) and bisected by the Río Olancho. **Las Cuevas de Tepescuintle** line the **Laguna de Agua Buena,** which provides water for many Olancheños. An abandoned little cement house at the entrance can be used as shelter from the rain, though it is best to bring a tent. There are three marked trails as well as innumerable hikes once you reach the mountains. The most popular and accessible hike is **Sendero Río Arriba** (6km, 3½hr.), which is great to spot birds and Blue Morph butterflies. This hike follows the river up the mountain to caves. There are crystal-clear swimming holes and 2-3 ft. waterfalls all along the trail. Bring a flashlight if you want to crawl into the caves for a fun but dirty adventure. **Sendero Tempiscapa,** the shortest and most accessible of the hikes (4km, 2hr.), is a nature trail with frequent toucan-sightings amidst the medicinal plants. José organizes two-day trips to the summit (L200) and other extended excursions. *(El Boquerón is easily accessible from Juticalpa—hop on one of the frequent Catacamas buses and ask to be let off at El Boquerón at the base of the mountain. The ranger and guide, José Mendosa, prefers a couple days notice to arrange a hike; contact him through the COHDEFOR office in Juticalpa or ask around in El Boquerón to find his residence.)*

■ PARQUE NACIONAL SIERRA DE AGALTA. Dwarfed only by the nearby Mosquitia, PN Sierra de Agalta consumes 69,500 hectares of Olancho and houses the department's tallest peak, **La Picucha** (2354m). With five types of forest, 470 species of birds, 230 species of butterfly, and an astounding 61 species of mammals including two-toed sloths and jaguars, this park is ideal for any ecotourist. Cultural enthusiasts might be interested to know that the largest Pech tribe in Honduras also resides here. Trails into the park range between 1hr. and 5 days and depart from surrounding villages; Gualaco has the best access. **Hotelito ❶,** by the *parque central,* is clean and has communal bathrooms (L25 per person). There are *comedores* throughout town but **Comedor Sharon ❶** is known for being friendly and helpful to travelers. *Pulperías* are scattered throughout town, but it is best to stock up on food in Juticalpa for more variety and better prices. There are no phone lines in town, though the COHDEFOR office has a radio. Find Francisco Urbina to help you plan your route through the park or to serve as a guide (L80-L100 per day). The most rewarding hike is the challenging, lengthy (3-5 days), quetzal-laden trail to the peak of **Cerro La Picucha** (2354m), which passes through five different ecosystems including cloud and dwarf forest. The trail also leads past swimming holes beneath **La Chorrera** waterfall and to two campsites. **Las Cuevas de Susmay** are an exciting daytrip from Gualaco, where a subterranean river runs between stalagmites and stalactites, and dry and wet tunnels beckon adventurers. Just north of Gualaco, **Los Chorros de Babilonia,** a series of 10 waterfalls, can be accessed on the road to San Esteban from the small village of El Ocotal. A few trails dart between the falls, though they aren't easy to navigate. The thundering water adds some fun and adventure to the trip. Swimming holes abound and an unforgettable night can be spent camping above the falls in **Los Planes de Babilonia.** *(Access the park via Gualaco by catching a bus from the main station in Juticalpa and going to either Gualaco or San Esteban. 2hr.; every hr. 5am-2pm, additional bus at 2:30pm; L35.)*

CATACAMAS

Sandwiched between Monumento El Boquerón, Parque Nacional Sierra de Agalta, and the western stretches of the Río Platano Biosfera, Catacamas sprawls across rugged wilderness as Olancho's second-biggest city (pop. 75,000).

TRANSPORTATION. Buses to **Juticalpa** leave from the **Cotical bus** station, 5 blocks south of the *parque's* southeast corner down Av. La Independencia and 1 block to the left (1hr., approx. every 45min. 5:50am-4:45pm, L16). **Discovery** and **Aurora** buses headed to **Tegucigalpa** pass through town 1hr. before their scheduled departure time from Juticalpa (p. 518). **Sur-Rubano** buses leave from Barrio Juan Pablo II on the Boulevard to **Cuevas de Talgua** (45min., every hr. 6am-5pm, L10).

ORIENTATION. Catacamas is organized on the standard grid system around the *parque central*, with most activity in the eastern part of town. The main drag, **Avenida La Independencia,** runs north-south along the eastern side of the *parque*. One block south, **2 Calle,** commonly referred to as the **Boulevard,** runs east-west and is the town's largest street. The city **market** is 4 blocks east on the Boulevard. Parallel to the Boulevard and 8 blocks south of the park; the main **highway** heads south to Tegus and north to Dulce Nombre de Culmi. The cathedral and *municipalidad* are 3 blocks north of the *parque* on what is known as the *parque arriba*.

PRACTICAL INFORMATION. The best source of tourist and park info as well as city maps (L35) is the ticket office for the Cuevas de Talgua 8km out of town. **Travel Express,** 6½ blocks south of the southwest corner of the *parque*, is the local travel agency. (☎899 4323. Open M-F 8am-noon and 2-4pm.) **BGA,** 1 block east and 2 blocks north of the *parque's* northeast corner accepts Visa cards and has a 24hr. Plus/V ATM. (☎899 4422. Open M-F 8:30am-3:30pm, Sa 8:30-11:30am.) **Banpaís** (☎899 5098; open M-F 8am-3:30pm, Sa 8am-noon), 1 block east of the *parque's* northeast corner, and **Banco de Occidente** (☎899 4458; open M-F 8am-4pm, Sa 8am-1:30pm), on the northwest corner of the market along the Boulevard, have **Western Union** service. The **preventiva police,** 3 blocks east and 5 blocks south of the southeast corner of the *parque*, recommend that travelers not wander the streets after 9pm. (☎899 4367. Open 24hr.) **Medicentro,** 1 block south of the *parque's* southwest corner and 2 blocks east on the Boulevard, is open **24hr. for emergency medical care.** (☎899 5554. Consultation L150.) **Farmacia Catacamas** has two locations with resident doctors: one on the corner of Av. Independencia and the Boulevard (☎899 5106; open M-Sa 8am-9pm, Su 8am-noon) and another block south of the market (☎899 5261; open daily 8am-6pm). **Servicenter Internet** on the southeast corner of the *parque* offers Internet service and international phone calls. (☎899 4282 or 899 4288. Internet L20 per hr.; calls to US L4 per min. Open daily 8am-9pm.) **Internet Serviciber,** 1 block east of the *parque's* southeast corner, has Internet service for L25 per hr. and international calls for L4 per min. (☎899 2122. Open 8am-8pm daily.) **Su Hogar Supermercado** is across from the northwest corner of the market on the Boulevard. (☎899 4430. Open daily 6:30am-9pm.) The **post office** is 1 block north of the *parque's* northeast corner. (☎899 4091. M-F 8am-4pm, Sa 8-11am.)

ACCOMMODATIONS. Most accommodations in Catacamas are either within several blocks of the west side of the parque or along the highway just before Av. La Independencia. **Hotel Oriental ❶,** 1 block south of the *parque's* southwest corner, has *sencillos* with fan, and a shared bath. *Privados* come with cold bath, fan, and TV. (☎899 4032 or 980 0864. Singles L50; doubles L85, with bath L130.) Next door, **Hotel La Colonia ❹** has large clean rooms with big TV, fan, and hot bath. (☎899 4153 or 899 4488. Singles L170; doubles L180.) **Hotel Rapalo ❹,** 1 block south of the *parque's* southeast corner on Av. La Independencia and 1 block east, gives you your pick of simple rooms with bed and clean shared bath. (☎899 4348. Singles L70, with bath and TV L180; doubles L80, with A/C L250; triples with A/C L300.) **Hospedaje San Jose ❶,** on the northern edge of the *parque*, has shared baths and clean rooms for a great price. (☎899 3222. Rooms L30, with fan L60.)

❏ FOOD. ⬛TakiMex, 3 blocks east of the northwest corner of the *parque*, serves excellent Mexican delicacies. Don't miss the mountainous *chilaquiles* (L17) and plump burritos wrapped in thick tortillas. (☎899 4463. *Baleadas* L5, burritos L5. Open daily 10am-9:30pm.) **Cafe de Tilapia's Centro ❸**, 1 block east and 2½ blocks north of the northeast corner of the *parque*, looks like a standard *comedor* from the street, but opens up into grassy courtyard seating in the back. (☎899 4544. Entrees L35-L60. Open Tu-Su 9am-9pm.) **Deli Hamburguesas ❷**, half a block south and 2 blocks east of the *parque*'s southeast corner, has speedy and cheap American fast food; delivery optional. (☎899 5372. Double cheeseburger, fries, and salad L35. Open daily 8am-9pm.) **Tropical Goloisinas ❶**, 2½ blocks north of the *parque*'s northeast corner, serves a fast and cheap lunch menu. (☎984 6647. *Enchiladas* L6, tacos L15. Open daily 9am-10pm. Lunch served approximately 11am-1pm.)

◙ CUEVAS DE TALGUA. The famous **Cuevas de Talgua Archaeological Park,** on the edge of PN Sierra de Agalta, is a series of million-year-old caves filled with huge caverns and massive calcite formations. Aside from its natural splendor, the caves once served as the ceremonial burial site for an enigmatic ancient people whose chronology and customs don't fit in with any other known Mesoamerican civilization. Over 250 fossilized individuals have been discovered in the cave walls or beneath subterranean river sediment. The remains are made even more mysterious by the calcite coating that lends the skulls an eerie sheen. Dedicated **Desiderio Reyes** (☎999 8092 or 980 8264) discovered the park and has remained on site as the caretaker. He continues to excavate and search for the still unknown entrance to the caves. Farther up the trail, a small museum documents the park's discovery and has several well-preserved artifacts including copies of unearthed skulls.

Two caves are currently open to visitors. **Cueva Principal,** whose entrance is just below the ticket office, has a path over the subterranean river to the entrance of the ceremonial burial site. If you're lucky, your guide will spot one of the cave's residents, the longest-legged scorpion in the world (don't worry, it's not poisonous). Thirty minutes up the trail, **Cueva Grande** beckons adventurers into its three tremendous caverns. While the river that formed it has dried up, parts of the cave are still flooded with knee-high water; bring your own flashlight. Just beyond the museum is a designated camping area. Desiderio can help you plan three-day trips to **La Picucha.** (*L95 entrance fee must be paid at the security office. Mandatory tour guides wait at the ticket office and cost an additional L10 per person. The cafeteria below the ticket office is open 8:30am-4pm and serves vegetarian típico for L20, with meat and drink for L40. Public restrooms are across the path.*)

NICARAGUA

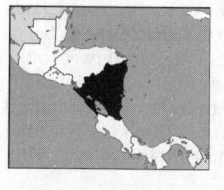

Nicaragua, known as the "land of lakes and volcanoes," is a dream come true for many travelers: a tropical paradise largely undiscovered by tourists, complete with picturesque colonial towns, spectacular natural phenomena, and a vibrant, welcoming population. At peace for more than a decade, Nicaragua is shedding its reputation from the Contra War of the 1980s, and you'll find that outside the messy urban jungle of Managua, the country clearly deserves recognition as one of the most beautiful and fascinating places on the continent.

Though Nicaragua is the most populous country in Central America (5.5 million people), its land mass (also largest in the region) makes it one of the least densely populated. More than 90% of citizens live in the Pacific lowlands and less than 15% of its territory. Unfortunately, it also remains the poorest country in the region, in part due to political unrest over the past few decades, and also because of the devastation unleashed by Hurricane Mitch in November 1998. As the tourism industry is practically nonexistent in many parts of the country, exploration requires initiative and courage. Volcanoes on the Pacific coast, beaches on the Caribbean, and tracts of rainforest dwarf even Costa Rica's park system, and yet remain largely untouched. Those willing to leave the tourist trail and tolerate fewer amenities will find Nicaraguan destinations extremely rewarding—are you up to the challenge?

HIGHLIGHTS OF NICARAGUA

On **Isla de Ometepe,** ancient petroglyphs adorn the rocky landscape amidst perfectly conical twin volcanoes beckoning hikers. For untouched nature and a unique artisan colony head to the **Archipiélago de Solentiname** (p. 563).

Two beautiful, well-situated colonial cites with strikingly different politics, liberal **León** has a vibrant student culture (p. 544), and conservative **Granada**'s wealth (p. 552) lights up the shores of **Lago de Nicaragua** (p. 563).

Home to the country's most famous handicrafts market, **Masaya** (p. 552) also hosts a striking volcano.

Pochomil and and **Casares**, on the Pacific coast, are calm beaches in quaint fishing villages near Managua and Masaya (p. 543 and p. 559).

Both natural park and coffee plantation, **Selva Negra** allows you to hike through the cloudforest and learn about environmentally sound farming techniques (p. 581).

SUGGESTED ITINERARIES

ONE WEEK. After flying into **Managua** (p. 535), spend only a day here before moving on. Eat some quality Nicaraguan fare, check out the night scene, and ask around to see if there's a baseball game. Keep partying right on through the next day or two with the young, studious crowd in **León** (p. 544). Continue on to picturesque **Granada** (p. 552), whose colonial charm will tempt you to stay forever. An easy day trip from Managua or Granada is **Masaya** (p. 556), where the famed markets and handicrafts are a shopper's paradise. If nature is more your thing, climb the **Masaya Volcano** (p. 558) and check out the national park. You should plan to spend your final days along the shores of **Lago de Nicaragua** (p. 563). Take a boat to **Isla de Ometepe** (p. 564) for more volcanoes and the beach for the ultimate relaxation before heading back to Managua for the flight home.

TWO WEEKS. Building on the one-week itinerary, extend your trip from **Isla de Ometepe** (p. 564) on Lake Nicaragua farther down the lake to **Archipiélago de Solentiname** (p. 569): you'll be amazed by the distinctive artist colony. Head over to the Pacific and hang out at beach towns **Pochomil** and **Casares** (p. 543 and p. 559) before starting a journey into the **Central Highlands,** where fresh air and natural beauty combine for an impressive area. City hop starting in **Estelí** (p. 574), the region's largest, then head to refreshing **Matagalpa** for your caffeine kick (p. 579). Don't forget to check out nearby **Selva Negra** (p. 581).

LIFE AND TIMES

LAND, FLORA, AND FAUNA

Nicaragua is divided into three distinct regions: rugged **Highlands** of the heavily agricultural northern and central parts of the country, from Matagalpa to the Honduran border; volcanic **Pacific Lowlands,** complete with the Lago de Nicaragua and most of the country's arable land, low altitude forests, and lakes; and the immense **Caribbean Lowlands** of the east, known as the **Mosquitia,** with rainforests and coral reefs hosting extreme biodiversity. Variously set among volcanic mountains and island chains, pristine freshwater lakes and ocean towns, central highlands and forest river jungles, Nicaragua is a veritable paradise of biodiversity. Most visibly, though certainly only the tip of Nicaragua's natural diversity, northeastern Nicaragua is home to the **Bosawas Biosphere Reserve** (p. 593), the largest rainforest in Central America. With 12,000 classified species of plant life and 5000 more identified but not classified, hanging with monkeys, jaguars, toucans, parrots, macaw, poison-dart frogs, eyelash vipers, and green iguanas should be easy. Sticking to the trail will be difficult for the adventurous who want to meet the Nicaraguan challenge.

HISTORY

Ask any Nicaraguan about the nation's history and you're sure to launch a complex political debate. Nicaragua has always been a political battleground for power, often involving a foreign presence. Spanish conquest brought Europeans; then came American William Walker's imperial attempts. During the last century, tangles between Somoza dictators and Sandinista socialists were only complicated and escalated by U.S. interests. This contentious political spirit and passion continues into the present, apparent in street arguments you're sure to overhear, if not participate in. Despite corrupt governments, coups, and earthquakes, the people's enduring kindness and vitality, along with breathtaking natural beauty, remain constants in the colorful, vibrant Nicaraguan life.

THE FIRST FOREIGNERS (PRE-COLUMBIAN-1820). When the Spanish arrived in Central America in the 16th century, they found three major cultural groups in Nicaragua: the **Niquirano,** the **Chorotegano,** and the **Chontal.** These groups vied for dominance in their shared territory and were frequently involved in violent skirmishes. With the arrival of Europeans, foreign disease crept into the country's western highland areas and effectively wiped out indigenous populations. In areas where Europeans didn't settle, the indigenous population remained relatively unharmed.

Nicaragua

Paved Road
Dirt Road

0 50 kilometers
0 50 miles

HONDURAS

Tegucigalpa ☆

EL
SALVADOR

San
Miguel

Golfo de
Fonseca

Choluteca

Volcán
Cosigüina

Potosí

Guasaule

PACIFIC
OCEAN

Corinto

Poneloya
Las Peñitas

Puerto Sandino

El Tránsito

Montelimar
Masachapa
Pochomil
La Boquita
Casares
Huehuete

Las Salinas

San Juan
del Sur

Danlí

Las
Manos

Ocotal

San Marcos/
El Espino

Somoto

Condega

Estelí

Volcán
Chinandega
Volcán San Cristóbal
Volcán Momotombo
León
Viejo
Izapa
Xiloá

Managua
pp. 535–543

Jinotepe

La Boquita

Moyogalpa

Rivas

Sapoa

CORD.
LOS MARIBOS

Pacific Lowlands
pp. 543–563

Laguna de
Apanás

Jinotega

Matagalpa

Sebaco

Esquipulas

Boaco

San Benito

Masaya
Granada

Isla de
Ometepe

Altagracia

Peñas
Blancas

CORDILLERA ENTRE RIOS

Río Pauca

Río Coco (Segovia o Wangki)

Río Bocay

CORD. ISABELLA

Río Tuma

Río Grande de Matagalpa

Río Kurinwas

Central Highlands
pp. 573–584

Bosawas
Reserve

North Atlantic
Autonomous Region
(RAAN)

Rosita

Siuna

Río Bambana

South Atlantic
Autonomous Region
(RAAS)

Caribbean Coast
pp. 584–591

Prinzapolka

Makantaka

Waspán

Río Wawa

Puerto
Cabezas

Lg.
Bismuna

Lg.
Páhara

Lg.
Karatá

Lg.
Woonta

Northeast Nicaragua
pp. 591–594

Laguna de
Perlas

Laguna
de Perlas

Rama

El Bluff
Bluefields
Bahía de
Bluefields
Ramaqui

Corn
Islands
(Islas de
Maíz)

Lago de
Managua

Lago de
Nicaragua

Lago de Nicaragua
pp. 563–573

Juigalpa

Santo
Tomás

Río Escondido

Archipiélago
de Solentiname

San Carlos
de Nicaragua

Los
Chiles

Río Maíz

Castillo Viejo

Río San Juan

San Juan
del Norte

Bahía
Punta Gorda

CARIBBEAN
SEA

COSTA RICA

Liberia

Lago de
Arenal

M O S Q U I T O   C O A S T

NICARAGUA

In 1524, the first permanent Spanish settlement was established, and the country was named after the powerful indigenous chief **King Nicarao.** León and Granada were founded shortly thereafter and quickly became territorial population centers, sharing a rivalry that has continued for three centuries. Spain retained control of the colony into the early 1800s, instituting colonial rule and establishing permanent settlements. By 1820, Spanish rule over Central America was threatened by nationalist independence movements; within the year, Nicaragua was brokering its autonomy from European control.

INDEPENDENCE DAY (1821-1857). Nicaragua gained independence from Spain in 1821 as part of the Mexican empire and joined the short-lived **United Provinces of Central America** before attaining full independence in 1838. Without Spanish presence, British and North American influence grew as Britain re-established control over the Mosquito Coast. American Cornelius Vanderbilt started the Accessory Transit Company, which carried thousands of forty-niners from New York City and New Orleans by boat and stage coach to California via Nicaragua during the 1849 California Gold Rush. With the support of León, **William Walker,** a renegade American, attacked Granada in 1855 with 56 men; he captured the city and declared himself president. After drawing Vanderbilt's ire by seizing the transit company, Walker was expelled from Nicaragua by the US Navy, the transit company, and five other Central American republics in 1857, only to unsuccessfully attempt to regain power twice. In 1860 he was taken captive, tried by Honduran court martial, and sentenced to death.

AUTOCRATS AND ASSASSINATIONS (1857-1934). In 1857, **Managua** was chosen as the fledgling nation's capital city, a geographic compromise between rival cities León and Granada. Following Walker's overthrow, conservatives gained power and held it until 1893, when left-leaning **José Santos Zelaya** overthrew the government and proclaimed himself dictator. An autocrat with leftist ideas, Zelaya became Nicaragua's first nationalist leader, and his overthrow would mark the beginning of a succession of US military interventions. In this situation, the US State Department was alarmed by rumors of Zelaya's plans to grant land to Japan.

In 1909, resorting to a rather sneaky brand of imperialism, the US government encouraged Zelaya's conservative opponents to supplant him while also sending in the Marine Corps to eventually force his resignation. Although the White House refused to recognize Zelaya's successor, José Madriz, the US supported the subsequent three conservative regimes. The Americans retained a military presence with a 100-person Marine guard at the US Embassy, and in 1916 they signed a treaty granting the US exclusive canal-building rights in Nicaragua.

During most of this period of de facto US occupation, three liberal leaders maintained steady resistance. In 1927, **Juan Bautista Sacasa, José María Moncada,** and **Augusto César Sandino** led their troops into fiery rebellion in response to the new conservative president and an additional infusion of US Marines. Six months of fighting was enough for Sacasa and Moncada, who both settled peacefully with the US-backed government in exchange for a pre-packaged presidency for each (1928-1933 and 1933-1936, respectively). Sandino, on the other hand, continued to fight against the US and the later US-sponsored dictatorship until his assassination.

SOMOZAS (1934-1972). The Marines left their replacements, the brutal **Guardia Nacional,** under the command of **Anastasio Somoza García** (a.k.a. "Tacho"), who used it to support the Somoza family dictatorship for the following 50 years. In 1934, Somoza had Sandino assassinated, and the Somozas and their associates began amassing huge fortunes and land holdings while the rest of Nicaragua wallowed in poverty. To remain in power, Somoza implemented vicious repression in the form of torture, murder, and "disappearances." The Somoza monopoly became so extensive that even Somoza's counterparts among the elite grew resentful. Nonetheless, US support for the regime was unfaltering—US President Franklin D. Roosevelt once said of Somoza, "He may be a son of a bitch, but he's our son of a bitch." Opposition grew as the Somoza dynasty continued. In 1961, **Carlos Fonseca Amador,** a radical student leader and prominent Somoza opponent, formed the socialist **Frente Sandinista de Liberación Nacional (FSLN)** in honor of Sandino. Faced with growing opposition and ineligible to succeed himself, Somoza agreed in 1972 to cede his power to a ruling triumvirate, of which he was a key member. However, this reduced power structure would not last long.

FROM RUBBLE TO REVOLUTION (1972-1979). In 1972, a massive earthquake virtually leveled Managua, killing 6000 Nicaraguans and leaving over 300,000 others without food or shelter. Somoza exploited the opportunity to marshal the Guardia Nacional into a "National Emergency Committee" and declared martial law. Before the rubble from the quake had settled, he had altered the constitution and re-installed himself as president in 1974. As the Somozas embezzled most of the international relief money, opposition to his regime solidified. Both the **Unión Democrática de Liberación (UDEL)** and the FSLN were gaining ground. In response, the government waged a counter-insurgency campaign which cost the lives of thousands of uninvolved peasants. In January 1978, the Guardia Nacional assassinated **Pedro Joaquín Chamorro,** leader of the UDEL and publisher of the popular and respected newspaper *La Prensa.* The cold-blooded murder of such a popular figure galvanized the population, and the revolution began in earnest.

The Sandinistas seized the national palace in August, successfully winning many of their demands in return for the release of 1000 hostages. For over a year, strikes and armed standoffs plagued the nation. Several thousand innocent Nicaraguans were killed, mostly by government troops. In some cases, Somoza's troops conducted summary executions of hundreds of teenage boys. Such abuses became untenable even for an ally as durable as the US. Finally, on July 17, 1979, Somoza fled the country as the Sandinistas again advanced upon the capital with the support of the Nicaraguan people. Two days later, on July 19, the Sandinistas marched victorious into Managua. Towns all over Nicaragua are still named "17 Julio" and "19 Julio" in remembrance. Somoza was assassinated a year later in Paraguay.

THE CONTRAS AND THE SANDINISTA REGIME (1979-1990). After the euphoria of victory subsided, the victors set about resuscitating a country in sorry shape: over 40,000 people had been killed, 100,000 were wounded, and 500,000 homeless. During their first few years of control, the Sandinistas expropriated and redistributed land held by members of the Somoza government, nationalized banks and natural resources, and brought food trade under government control. Throughout the 1980s, the FSLN improved agriculture, health care, and literacy rates. For more information on peacekeeping and restabilization, see *Peacekeeping in Central America* (p. 52).

Repairing the nation was the first formidable challenge facing the Sandinistas; the second was the US. In 1981, the US government, embroiled in a Cold War hysteria, was angered to discover that Nicaragua had formed ties with Cuba and other communist countries. Newly elected president **Ronald Reagan** decided to bring an end to the leftist Sandinista government. To accomplish this, he resorted to well-worn US interventionist tactics, setting in motion covert CIA operations and pouring US tax dollars and supplies into the counter-revolutionary group who came to be called the **Contras.** The Contras were ex-Guardia Nacional members, mercenaries, scared teenagers pressed into service, and civilians ideologically opposed to the Sandinistas. Trained by the Argentine army and supported by US funds, the Contras set up camps in border towns of Honduras and Costa Rica, which they used as bases for their sporadic attacks on the country.

During the 1980s, the Contra-Sandinista war ravaged Nicaragua, making it virtually impossible for the Sandinistas to focus on repairing the battered country. In 1984, **Daniel Ortega** of the FSLN won a neutrally-monitored popular presidential election which was generally accepted as honest. The US, in response, mined Nicaraguan harbors and spearheaded an economic embargo. Food and supplies ran short and inflation spiraled to a staggering 30,000%. Revolutionary idealism began to wane, and the war became one of attrition. With the acquisition of expanded military equipment, forces, and tactical info, however, the Sandinista government was able to contain the insurrection. In 1987, Costa Rican president **Oscar Arias Sánchez** negotiated an end to the civil war.

A NEW ERA (1990-1998). As the 1990 elections approached, US President George Bush made it clear to Nicaraguan voters that if a new party were to take office, the US would consider lifting the embargo and provide badly needed aid. Sure enough, Nicaraguans replaced the Sandinistas by voting in **Violeta Chamorro** of the Unión Nacional Opposición (UNO), a coalition of 14 smaller parties. Chamorro, the widow of Pedro Joaquín Chamorro, carried 55% of the vote. When she assumed office, the majority of the Contras disarmed, but the Nicaraguan government has continued its struggle to disarm the last remaining groups, termed *recontras*, ever since. When Chamorro took the reins, Nicaragua was still a very poor, if peaceful, country where just a few families controlled the nation's little wealth, and unemployment reached as high as 70%. No longer burdened with an economic embargo, however, the UNO government attempted to promote market-driven capitalism, a trend opposed by the socialist Sandinistas.

TODAY. In March 1998 the International Monetary Fund and the Nicaraguan government agreed on a loan package totaling almost US$150 million to finance the restructuring of the Nicaraguan economy. This loan package took place during the presidential administration of Arnoldo Alemán of the rightist **Partido Liberal Constitutionalista (PLC) party** and was a hopeful precursor to further foreign investment. Unfortunately, in November of that same year Hurricane Mitch wreaked havoc on Central America; 10,000 were killed in Nicaragua alone, and the physical terrain was overturned. Though many countries were generous enough to cancel Nicaragua's financial debt, it continues to be one of the poorest countries in the West.

Former president and newly-admitted "centrist," Daniel Ortega remains at the healm of the still-powerful Sandinista movement despite accusations of sexual abuse by his stepdaughter in 1998. In the most recent elections in 2001, **Enrique Bolaños** of the **PLC** narrowly defeated Ortega in free, democratic elections. The election was a bitter struggle, and largely influenced by promises of economic reform, especially in the tourism sector. Alemán, as stipulated by Nicaraguan law, as ex-president is now the leading figure in the Nicaraguan legislature. Bolaños was vice president during the administration of Alemán, but their current relationship is not entirely harmonious as Bolaños has spearheaded corruption allegations against Alemán. Despite recent peace, occasional Sandinista-motivated violence does erupt in the Atlantic coastal, rural region. The balance of power between the different political parties and headstrong leaders in the next few years will determine Nicaragua's potential or plight for the future. The next national elections will take place in November 2006.

CULTURE AND ARTS

PEOPLE. The **Nicarao** people who resisted Spanish forays into Nicaragua in the 16th century have essentially disappeared in the last 400 years, as have most western Nicaraguan indigenous peoples. As a result, the western half of the country is almost exclusively populated by **mestizos,** who live in and around the urban cores and compose almost 70% of the country's population. The next largest population groups are descendants of Europeans, about 17% of the population, and then black descendants of slaves imported to the Caribbean coast by the British, constituting almost 9%. Nicaragua's indigenous people, 5% of the country's population, are concentrated in the eastern half of the country. The most prevalent denomination within this group is the **Miskito,** who enjoy a degree of self-rule in the **North Atlantic Autonomous Region,** created by the Autonomy Statute of 1987. Other indigenous groups in the east include the **Rama** and the **Sumu.** No religion has been officially declared, though Nicaragua is predominantly **Catholic** with a Protestant minority. The official language is **Spanish,** though English is common due to lingering British influences along the Caribbean coast and American commercialization.

FOOD AND DRINK. Chicken, fruit, and tortillas, standard fare throughout Central America, are Nicaraguan staples. However, regional specialties abound: *gallo pinto* is rice and beans, usually fried, which most Nicaraguans eat two to three times a day; *plátanos* (plantains) are served up fried as **maduros** (greasy and sweet) or **tostones** (crispy, like potato chips); *carne asada* is barbecued, marinated meat; and *mondongo* is tripe (stomach) cooked with beef knuckles. Most restaurants offer a lot of meats. For vegetarians, *ensaladas* usually consist of cabbage with tomatoes, beets, and vinegar dressing. Mealtimes are 7-10am breakfast, noon-3pm lunch, and 6-9pm dinner. Scrumptious rums are produced and drunk locally in huge quantities. *Flor de Caña*, produced in Chinandega, is the most popular brand. Luckily, it's also very cheap and makes a great gift for friends at home. Victoria and Toña are the national beers. *Refrescos naturales* are fruit juices mixed with water and sugar.

FINE ARTS AND CRAFTS. Nicaraguan art mirrors the country's natural beauty and political strife. Sculpture, pottery, and paintings all have a distinctive tropical island flair on the east. Particularly in the cities, political murals and advertising adorn the side of almost every building. The bright colors and detailed charm of Nicaraguan art tell its complicated but optimistic history—the artist colony on Isla de Ometepe is internationally recognized for its progressive ideology. Nicaraguan hammocks are also of renowned quality.

LITERATURE. Probably the greatest known Central American literary figure is Nicaragua's own **Rubén Darío** (1867-1916), an inventor of the modernist style (see **National Hero, Wandering Soul,** p. 582). His definitive works include *Blue* (1888) and *Songs of Life and Hope* (1905). Darío had a turbulent and emotional relationship with Nicaragua: he spent much of his life outside the country and at times feared estrangement. His poetry is therefore a unique blend of Nicaraguan and foreign influences. Subsequent Nicaraguan writers have been concerned with the urgency of their country's sociopolitical condition. Vanguardist **Pablo Antonio Cuadra,** born in 1912, and poet **Ernesto Cardenal,** born in 1925, are both eminent examples. Check out **Cosmic Canticle:** written over a 30 year period, this is considered the crowning achievement of the world-renowned poet.

ARCHITECTURE. Much architecture was destroyed by the huge earthquake in 1972, subsequent mudslides and floods, and Hurricane Mitch in 1998. The effects are particularly notable in Managua, where there really is no downtown area. The largest buildings are usually international businesses or hotel chains. For a glimpse of the beauty of historic Nicaraguan architecture, visit **Granada** (p. 552) or **León** (p. 544) where the quaint streets, colonial charm, and religious atmosphere will leave a lasting impression. Individual residences in other areas range from impressive, gated compounds to heart-breaking, poverty-stricken shanty towns.

MUSIC. Native musicians jam on a variety of instruments, including the *chirimía*, a primitive clarinet, and the fearsome, thunderous *juco*, played by pulling a string through a drum head. Nicaragua is the southern terminus of "marimba country" (an instrument related to the xylophone, though lower in pitch). Young Nicaraguans groove to the sounds of a variety of Latin pop artists, including the ever-present Shakira and Elvis Crespo. Clubs and bars often feature a mix of *salsa*, *merengue*, and Latin house. US pop music and techno are also common. Lucky travelers may see **El Güegünse,** a farcical musical street drama about an old man who repeatedly outwits authorities.

TV AND NEWS. Nicaraguans stay abreast of news through TV programming from the US. **Telenovelas,** the heartwrenching soap operas broadcast throughout Latin America, are popular. For local news (and the latest baseball standings and statistics), the most popular newspapers are right-leaning *La Prensa* (www.laprensa.com.ni), left-leaning *La Barricada* (www.labarricada.com.ni), and centrist *El Nuevo Diario* (www.elnuevodiario.com.ni).

SPORTS AND RECREATION. While soccer is an obsession in most of Latin America, **baseball** reigns supreme in Nicaragua. Managua is home to a huge stadium and "world series" in May. Tickets are cheap—great seats sell for under US$20. **Water sports** (diving, surfing, snorkeling, fishing, etc.) are also very popular on Lake Nicaragua and along both coasts.

HOLIDAYS

Holidays in Nicaragua are often accompanied by spirited folk dancing, particularly during celebrations for towns' patron saints. Easter is traditionally spent at the beach; shops and businesses close for most of Holy Week, or Semana Santa. The anniversary of the revolution is celebrated by Sandinistas with fireworks, revelry, marches, and a huge rally in downtown Managua. Holidays include: **January 1,** New Year's Day; **March/April,** Semana Santa (Holy Week). **May 1,** Labor Day; **July 19,** Anniversary of the Revolution; **September 14,** Battle of San Jacinto; **September 15,** Independence Day; **November 2,** All Souls Day (Día de los Muertos); **December 7 and 8,** Immaculate Conception; **December 25,** Christmas.

ESSENTIALS

PASSPORTS, VISAS, AND CUSTOMS
Passport: (p. 19) Required for citizens of all countries.
Visa: Not required for citizens of Australia, Canada, Ireland, New Zealand, South Africa, the UK, and the US.
Inoculations and Medications: None required.
Work Permit: (p. 533) Required for all foreigners planning to work in Nicaragua.
Driving Permit: No special permit is needed—just a valid driver's license, registration, and title to the car. **Entrance Fee:** US$5 airport tax/tourist card; US$20 immigration fee.
Airport departure fee: US$30 by air; US$5 by land.

EMBASSIES AND CONSULATES

Embassies of Nicaragua: UK, Vicarage House, 58-60 Kensington Church St., London W8 4DB (☎44 207 938 2373; fax 937 0952). **US,** 1627 New Hampshire Ave., NW, Washington, D.C. 20009 (☎202-939-6570; fax 939-6545).

Consulates of Nicaragua: Honorary Consul in Canada, 87 Beausoleil Dr., Ottawa, Ontario K1N 8W3 (☎613-241-0682). **US,** 1627 New Hampshire Ave. NW, Washington, D.C. 20009 (☎202-939-6531; fax 939-6574). Consulates also in Los Angeles, Miami, and New York.

MONEY

AUS$1 = 11.14C	1C = AUS$0.09
CDN$1= 12.11C	1C = CDN$0.08
EUR€ = 19.15C	1C = EUR€0.05
NZ$1 = 10.37 C	1C = NZ$0.10
UK£1 = 28.50C	1C = UK£0.04
US$1 = 16C	1C = US$0.06

The above rates were accurate as of August 2004. The Nicaraguan unit of currency is the **córdoba** (C). There are 100 **centavos** to one córdoba. Colloquially, córdobas are sometimes referred to as *pesos* and 10 *centavos* are referred to as one *real*. Coins come in 1 and 5 córdoba pieces. Large bills are hard to break. US dollars are usually accepted and welcome at larger banks, hotels, stores, and even street vendors or markets. Changing dollars to córdobas is never a problem, and most banks will exchange at the official rate. Nicaragua's **coyotes**, guys on streetcorners with a calculator in one hand and a wad of bills in the other, will also change dollars at comparable rates. While technically illegal, this black market is usually not dangerous; avoid changing currency at night, and make sure the bills are genuine.

Many Nicaraguan cities have at least one bank that changes traveler's checks. Watch out for long lines, forms, and service charges. Most hotels and restaurants do not accept traveler's checks, though some take credit cards. *Coyotes* are less willing to change traveler's checks than cash. Most cities have **Western Union** offices, but some still route their orders by phone to Managua, sometimes with a one-day delay. **ATMs** are found in Managua and most other larger cities. ATMs are linked to Visa, Master Card, American Express, and Cirrus. There's no withdrawal charge, but there is a 2000C maximum per day. Tipping policies vary—use discretion. For more info on **Tipping and Bargaining** customs, see the like-named section at the start of the book, p. 23.

PRICE DIVERSITY

PRICE RANGES AND RANKINGS. The most significant costs for travelers in Panama will be accommodations, notably more expensive than those in other parts of Central America. While basic rooms and dorms can certainly be found for under 100C, more safe and comfortable lodgings are 150C-200C. Food is cheap, with *típico* usually 15C-30C. While the assiduous traveler may be able to scrape by on 200C-300C per day, a safer bet would be 400C-500C, excluding transportation.

SYMBOL	❶	❷	❸	❹	❺
ACCOMM.	0-79C	80-160C	160-200C	200-400C	400C+
FOOD	0-20C	20-70C	70-100C	100-200C	200C+

SAFETY

As always, the smart traveler will stay alert and check the latest US State Department warnings before departing. Managua, like any large city, demands a certain degree of caution and common sense, especially to avoid pickpockets. Touristed areas are often hot spots for petty crime; poorer neighborhoods and political demonstrations are best avoided entirely. Buses are notorious for their deft-fingered thieves. Avoid traveling alone in rural areas. Sporadic armed violence is reported throughout the country, and bandits have been known to operate on the roads, especially in the rural northeast, where the US State Department warns against travel. See **Safety and Health,** p. 25, for more tips.

HEALTH

Nicaragua carries the same health risks as neighboring countries. For descriptions of disease prevention, see **Health**, p. 25. **Malaria** and **dengue** fever are present.

BORDER CROSSINGS

HONDURAS. There are three land crossings. **Guasaule** is 77km north of Chinandega, near Choluteca, Honduras (p. 434). **San Marcos/El Espino** is 25km west of Somoto, near Choluteca, Honduras. **Las Manos** is 25km north of Ocotal, and 150km east of Tegus, Honduras (p. 578). It's also possible to cross by boat via the Caribbean port town of **Puerto Cabezas** (p. 593).

COSTA RICA. There is one land crossing: **Peñas Blancas/Sapoá**, 36km southeast of Rivas, near Liberia, Costa Rica (p. 173 and p. 563). There is also a river crossing at **Los Chiles**, south of San Carlos (p. 570).

KEEPING IN TOUCH

Nicaraguan **mail** is comparable to other Central American postal systems. Allow a good 15 days for addresses within the US and 20 days for Europe. **Correos de Nicaragua,** the national mail system, uses the private company EMS. You can receive general delivery *(Lista de Correos)* mail at any Correos de Nicaragua office. In most cases, mail will be held for one month, though sometimes for only two weeks. Mail should be addressed as follows:

> Emily MATCHAR [first name, LAST NAME]
>
> Lista de Correos
>
> San Carlos [town name], Río San Juan [department name]
>
> Nicaragua

Nicaraguan **phone numbers** use seven digits and require no area codes. For US phone company access codes, see this book's inside back cover. Many hotels and shops let patrons use their **telephones** for local calls (about 5C per call). Generally, your link with the rest of the world will be through **ENITEL**, the national communications service often still known by its old name, **TELCOR**. Most every city and town in Nicaragua has an ENITEL/TELCOR office, usually identifiable by a tall radio tower; generally open daily from 7am-9pm. Important phone numbers are: ☎112 for info, ☎114 for international info, ☎110 for a national long-distance operator. To make long-distance national calls (for example, to call Bluefields from Managua), dial 0, then the seven-digit phone number. The general country code is 505, but several cities also have individual codes which are included with town coverage.

COUNTRY CODE	505

TRANSPORTATION

Buses are the primary mode of transport in Nicaragua. Most of Nicaragua's bus fleet is composed of yellow school buses retired from North America. Buses usually leave from one main terminal in town (except Managua, where there are five terminals), and each terminal has a small office with info on schedules. Nearly every town and certainly every city has a local bus system. The roads, if paved, are usually in decent condition. Don't drive at night unless necessary. La Costeña (☎263-1228; http://centralamerica.com/nicaragua/tran/costena.htm) offers **flights** to several destinations in Nicaragua, including Bluefields, the Corn Islands, Puerto Cabezas, and San Carlos. The main office is in Managua, but most travel agencies sell tickets. Within cities, taxis are the easiest mode of transport.

ORIENTATION

Street directions inevitably revolve around landmarks rather than names. A town's *parque central* is the most common marker; it's also usually the focal point of the grid system by which the *avenidas* (avenues) and *calles* (streets) are laid out. Generally, *avenidas* run north-south, while *calles* run east-west. Often *calles* above and below a focal point have the same number, but are distinguished by *norte* (north) and *sur* (south), as in 3 C. Nte. and 3 C. Sur. Often, as in the case of Managua, words like *arriba* (up) and *abajo* (down) are understood to refer to certain compass directions; in other towns, they refer to elevation. In Managua, north becomes *al lago*, and some of the cardinal landmarks haven't existed for years. Another directional device is *al salida* or *al entrada*, as in *"al salida a Juigalpa"*—look for this address where the road for Juigalpa leaves town.

TRAVEL RESOURCES

Guía Interamericana de Turismo, a comprehensive website covering all of Central America. In Spanish. http://www.guiainteramericana.com.

Ministerio de Turismo (☎222 6652; fax 222 6618), a block south and a block west of the Intercontinental in Managua. Friendly, helpful staff speaks English.

Nicaragua's Best Guide, http://www.guideofnicaragua.com.

ALTERNATIVES TO TOURISM

Nicaragua continues to struggle with fallout from civil war, dictatorship, and years of economic inequality in a near-oligarchic governmental system. Widespread poverty is exacerbated by frequent natural disasters; the most recent was Hurricane Mitch in 1998. Promised land redistribution after the civil war is still to be completed, and Nicaragua's heavy reliance on agriculture (particularly coffee) has been hurt as a result of falling international crop prices and high rates of inflation. Illiteracy and education are major issues, as nearly 40% of school-aged children are unable to attend classes since their parents cannot afford education fees.

This section lists some of the organizations in Nicaragua that offer opportunities outside the typical tourist experience. Approach the Nicaraguan Embassy; they will be able to refer you to the National Federation of Voluntary Organizations, which matches volunteers with relevant vacancies. For more info on Alternatives to Tourism as well as tools for finding programs on your own, see the chapter at the beginning of the book (p. 53).

VISA INFORMATION

For those wishing to work or study in Nicaragua, a **resident visa** is required. To apply for residency, travelers may enter with a passport and obtain a letter from the school or place of employment. This, plus a medical certificate, birth certificate, and police record should be submitted to the Immigration Office in Managua.

LANGUAGE SCHOOLS

Academia Europea, ALKE Carretera Masaya, 1c. abajo, ½c. al sur (☎278 0829), Managua and León. An international language school that offers classes at every level in private (US$15 per hr.), semi-private (US$19 per hr.), and full immersion (US$222).

Casa Xalteva, (☎/fax 552 2436; www.ibw.com.ni/~casaxal), 5 blocks west of the *parque* on C. Real, next to la Iglesia Xalteva, Granada. Approximately US$125 per week, US$425 per month, plus a $25 registration fee. Homestays US$60 per week. Internships available. This non-profit Spanish language school offers classes of 1-4 students, as well as activities and volunteer opportunities.

Centro Nicaraguense de Aprendizaje Cultural (CENEC), P.O. Box #10, Estelí (☎/fax 713 2025; cenac@tmx.com.ni; www.tmx.com.ni/~cenac), on C. 9 S., 300m east of the Carretera Interamericana. CENAC participants choose between language classes, homestays, service projects, or any combination of the 3 (weekly costs about US$120).

Escuela de Español Leonesa (☎311 2116; nssmga@ibw.com.ni), in the *casa de cultura*, León. Customized Spanish classes start any day of the week. Part of Nicaragua Spanish Schools in Managua (☎244 1699).

Escuela Horizonte, Estelí (☎713-4117; http://www.ibw.com.ni/~horizont/escuela.htm; horizout@ibw.com.ni). Focused on raising awareness of community development and is a great resource for volunteering in the area. 20hr. of morning or afternoon instruction and 7 day homestay with meals US$150; without homestay US$100.

Los Pipitos (☎713 5511; sacuanjoche@ibw.com.ni), a large language school just south of town in Estelí, Nicaragua. Started by parents of disabled children to raise money for the attached school for the handicapped. 2 outside activities per week. 20hr. of instruction with 7-day homestay and meals included, US$170; US$120 without. US$150 for 3 weeks or more.

Proyecto Ecológico Escuela de Español, (☎882 3992 or 265 7225; www.guegue.com.ni/eco-nic; eco-nic@guegue.com.ni), Laguna de Apoyo, Nicaragua. Language classes in this beautiful dry forest and protected region. One-on-one classes start weekly on Sundays. Also offers concurrent dive instruction with prior arrangement. Bike, scuba, swim, and kayak after class. One week US$190 with lodging and meals; two weeks US$365; 3 weeks US$535; 4 weeks US$690.

VOLUNTEERING

BIOLOGY/ECOLOGY PROGRAMS

Centro Ecológico de Los Guatuzos (☎283 0139; www.geocities.com/guatuzos/guatuzos.html), in front of the Nazareno church in San Carlos. El Refugio de Vida Silvestre Los Guatuzos is one of the most diverse concentrations of ecosystems, flora, and fauna in Central America. Possible volunteer options include scientific experiments and social development programs in the center and surrounding communities.

EDUCATION

Travel Quest, 40 Magdalen Ave., Bath BA2 4QB, UK (www.travel-quest.co.uk), provides an opportunity for volunteers to live in local communities in the Central Highlands, primarily in the Miraflor Nature Reserve. Teach English for guides and ecotourism to small agricultural cooperatives.

HUMANITARIAN

Global Exchange, 2017 Mission St., Suite 303, San Francisco, CA 94110, USA (☎800 497 1994, www.globalexchange.org), accepts volunteers from the world over to get involved with sustainable coffee farming and fair trade initiatives, first on-site and then back in home communities.

Nuestros Pequeños Hermanos, Apdo. Postal 27, Rivas, Nicaragua (☎505 453 3051, www.nphnicaragua.org). An organization that cares for orphaned and abused children, striving to raise them as productive community members. Volunteer opportunities range from doctor to speech pathologist to English teacher.

MANAGUA

With a series of massive, disorganized *barrios* in place of tall buildings, the city feels more like an overgrown suburb than the capital of Central America's largest country. Downtown Managua was leveled by an earthquake in 1972, and what remained was then left to the mercy of the revolution. Today, empty dirt lots surround shopping centers and bustling markets border gutted buildings. Nonetheless, Managua remains the entertainment, commercial, and transportation hub of Nicaragua and vitality continues to pump through the public art—revolutionary murals and graffiti—that saturates the city. Although it may be less safe than other parts of Nicaragua and its cultural life is suffering—many museums and galleries have closed due to inadequate funds—Managua does have bright spots: the famous Teatro Rubén Darío, the impressive Palacio Nacional, and, during season, emotional baseball games.

Pickpocketing and robbery occur frequently and are the main crimes that travelers in Managua have to worry about. Watch your pockets on city buses. The **Mercado Oriental** and the surrounding *barrio* **Ciudad Jardín** are dangerous and best avoided day or night. Although **Barrio Martha Quezada** seems peaceful, there have been a significant number of assaults in front of *hospedajes* at night. Always walk in groups, don't carry lots of cash, and take taxis after dark.

✈ INTERCITY TRANSPORTATION

FLIGHTS

Domestic Flights: **César Augusto Sandino International Airport** is 12km east of the city. **La Costeña** (☎263 1228 or 263 2142) flies to **Bluefields** (1hr.; M-Sa 6, 6:30, 10am, 2pm; 6 and 10am not serviced Su; one-way 750C, round-trip 1280C); the **Corn Islands** (1½hr.; 6:30am and 2pm; one-way 945C, round-trip 1670C); **Puerto Cabezas** (1¼hr.; M-Sa 6:30, 10:30am, 3pm;Su 6:30am, 3pm; one-way 895C, round-trip 1410C); **San Carlos** (50min.; M-Th and Sa 9am, F and Su 12:30pm; 750C, round-trip 1210C) and **Siuna** (1¼hr.; 9am; 675C, round-trip 1210C). **Atlantic Airlines** (☎233 2791 or 233 3103) has same flight prices to **Bluefields** (1hr.; 6:45, 10:30am, 2pm) and the **Corn Islands** (1½hr., 6:45am and 2pm).

International Flights: International carriers departing from the same airport include: **American** (☎266 3900; open M-F 8am-6pm and Sa 8am-1pm); **Continental** (☎278 2834), on Carretera Masaya (open M-F 8am-6pm and Sa 8am-noon); **Copa** (☎267 0045), on Carretera Masaya, (open M-F 8am-12:30pm and 2-5:30pm); **Grupo Taca** (☎266 3136); and **Iberia** (☎266 3136).

BUSES

Domestic Buses: Buses depart from 4 widely scattered markets (see map): **Mercado Roberto Huembes** and **Mercado Israel Lewites,** both in the southwest part of the city; and **Mercado de Ivan Montenegro** and **Mercado Mayoreo,** both in the eastern part of the city. Next to the **UCA,** a small lot on the highway also has a few minibuses leaving for points south. It's best to take a taxi or a local bus from one station to another.

Israel Lewites: Chinandega (2½hr., every 30min. 4am-6:30pm, 25C) or **minibuses: Lewites** (2¼hr.; every 15-30min. or when full 5am-6pm; 30C); **Jinotepe** (1¾hr., every 15min. 5:25am-7:30pm, 7C), minibuses (UCA, 50min., every 15-20min. 5:30am-9:30pm, 10C); **León** (2¼hr., every 20min. 5am-7:30pm, 13C), by minibus (2hr., every 15min. 4am-8pm); and **Pochomil** (1½hr., every 30min. 6:30am-4pm, 10C).

Ivan Montenegro: Costa Atlántica (☎ 817 0073 in Rama) runs a bus and boat combo to **Bluefields** (12hr., 9pm, 200C).

Mayoreo: Boaco (2hr., every 30min. 6am-6pm, 30C); **Estelí** (3hr., every 30min. 4am-5:45pm, 22C; express 2½hr., 30C); **Juigalpa** (3hr., every 30min. 4am-5:45pm, 25C; express 2hr., 30C); **Matagalpa** (2¾hr., every 30min. 4:15am-6:15pm, 22C); **Ocotal** (4hr., about every hr. 5:10am-5:15pm, 42C); **Rama** (8hr., every hr. 4am-10pm, 80C); **Puerto Cabezas** (24hr., 2pm and 5pm, 200C); **Siuna** (10hr.; 4am, 5, 8pm; 100C), reserve a seat a day in advance; and **Somoto** (3½hr.; 7:15, 9:45am, 1:45, 3:45pm; 37C).

Roberto Huembes: Granada (1¼hr., every 15min. 5:30am-9pm, 9C), or in minibuses (UCA, 50min., every 15min. 5:30am-8pm, 10C); **Masaya** (40min., every 15min. 4:30am-5:30pm, 6C; indirect 1hr., every 10min. 5C) or by minibus: UCA, (30min., every 20min. 5:50am-7:30pm, 10C); **Rivas** (2½hr., every 30min. 8:30am-5pm, 13C; express 1½hr., 4pm, 30C); and **San Jorge** (2½hr., every 30min. 8:30am-5:30pm, 30C).

International Buses: Catch **Tica** buses (☎ 222 6094), 2 blocks east of the Casino in Barrio Martha Quezada, to: **Guatemala City** (18hr., 5am, 525C); **Panama City** (48hr., stopover in San Salvador; 6am, 7am; 620C); **San José, Costa Rica** (9hr.; 6, 7am, noon; 160C); **San Pedro Sula, Guatemala** (12hr., 5am, 450C); **San Salvador** (12hr., 5am, 400C); **Tapachula, Mexico** (48hr.; stopover in San Salvador; 4:45am; 765C); and **Tegucigalpa** (7hr., 5am, 320C).

⊟ LOCAL TRANSPORTATION

Local Buses cost 2.50C, and once you get the hang of it, they are invaluable. Routes are tricky and there's no published schedule; ask locals for assistance. While the city recently got US$2.5 million to modernize the bus system, the current equipment is aging; crowding, pickpocketing, and violence are frequent problems. The **#119** stops at the Mercado Roberto Huembes, Carreterra Masaya, Universidad Centroamericana, Plaza España, and Iglesia Lezcano. The **#118** can be caught on Av. Williams Roberto and serves Mercado Ivan Montenegro, Mercado Israel Lewites, and the Red Cross. The **#109** runs from Barrio Martha Quezada and the Hotel Intercontinental to the attractions of the Plaza de la Democrácia. The **MR4**, passing along C. 27 de Mayo, is the quickest way to Mercado Huembes from Martha Quezada. The **#110** lumbers among 3 markets: Israel Lewites, Roberto Huembes, and Ivan Montenegro.

Taxis: An abundance of taxis honk at pedestrians to show availability. Arrange prices in advance and beware of "*gringo* fares." A crosstown ride should never be more than 25C. A trip to the airport is about 40C. Bargaining is often easier if you offer the initial price rather than ask for it. A typical fare is 10C-20C during the day and 15C-40C at night, depending on distance.

Car Rental: Budget (☎ 222 2336), **Dollar** (☎ 222 2275), **Hertz** (☎ 222 2320), all in the Hotel Intercontinental lobby, rent super-compacts 320C per day plus tax and insurance; 4WDs start at 880C-1120C. Open daily 7am-7pm. 25+. All have airport branches.

◼ ORIENTATION

UPON ARRIVAL. Arriving by air, you'll land at **César Augusto Sandino International Airport,** 12km east of the city on the Carretera Norte. **Taxis** from the airport to hotel-rich *barrio* Martha Quezada cost 240C-320C; walk 100m right or left after exiting the terminal to the highway and the price suddenly drops to 80C-110C. **Arriving by international bus** from another Central American capital, you'll most likely be at the well-situated **Ticabus** terminal in Martha Quezada, 2 blocks east of the Casino Royale and near numerous hotels. **Sirca** buses from San José arrive in the south part of the city on Av. Eduardo Delgado. **Arriving by domestic bus,** you'll find yourself at one of four markets scattered about the city. Crowded **local buses** go between the markets and the hotel areas; **taxis** are usually easier to find (20C-25C).

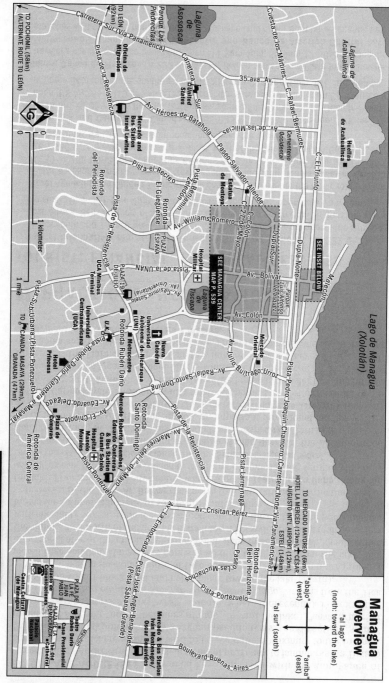

Managua Overview

"al lago" (west)

(north: toward the lake)

"arriba" (east)

"al sur" (south)

NICARAGUA

Map Labels

Laguna de Acahualinca

Laguna de Asososca

Parque Las Piedrecitas

Cuesta-de-los-Mártires

Carretera Sur (Vía Panamericana)

TO LEÓN (92km)

TO POCHOMIL (58km) (ALTERNATE ROUTE TO LEÓN)

Pista-de-la-Resistencia

Oficina de Migración

Mercado and Bus Station Israel Levites

Rotonda del Periodista

Pista-el-Recreo

Rotonda El Güegüense

Pista-de-la-Resistencia

Av.-Héroes-de-Batahola

Oficina de United States

Carretera-Sur

Av.-de-las-Milicias

Paseo-Salvador-Allende

Cementerio Occidental

C.-Rafael-Bermúdez

35-ava.-Av.

C.-E.-Triunfo

Huellas de Acahualinca

Laguna de Acahualinca

Estatua de Montoya

Pista-Belén

Av.-Williams-Romero

PLAZA ESPAÑA

Pista-de-la-UNAN

PLAZA 19 DE JULIO

Hospital Militar

C.-Colón

C.-27-de-Mayo

Dupla-Sur

Dupla-Norte

SEE INSET BELOW

Parque Luis Alfonso Velásquez

Av.-Bolívar

SEE MANAGUA CENTER MAP P. 539

Laguna de Tiscapa

Av.-Colón

Av.-Casimir-Sotelo (Av.-Universitaria)

UCA Minibus Terminal

Universidad Centroamericana (UCA)

U.K.

Rotonda Rubén Darío

Pista-Rubén-Darío

Hotel Princess

Pista-Sub-Urbana (Pista-Portezuelo)

TO CANADA, MASAYA (29km), GRANADA (47km)

Universidad Autónoma de Nicaragua (UNI)

Nueva Catedral

Metrocentro

Av.-Julio-Buitrago-Urroz

Mercado Oriental

Pista-Pedro-Joaquín-Chamorro (Carretera-Norte-Vía-Panamericana)

TO MERCADO MAYOREO (6km), HOTEL LA MERCED (12km), AUGUSTO INTL AIRPORT (12km), CESAR, ESTELÍ (148km)

Lago de Managua (Xolotlán)

Av.-Radial-Santo-Domingo

Rotonda Santo Domingo

Mercado Roberto Huembes & Bus Station Eduardo Contreras

Av.-Eduardo-Delgado

Av.-El-Chipote

Hospital Manolo Morales

Plaza de Compras

Rotonda de América Central

Av.-Mártires-del-4-de-Mayo

Hospital Cesani Sotelo

Av.-Martín-de-la-Resistencia

Pista-de-la-Resistencia

Pista-Larreynaga

Rotonda Bello Horizonte

Pista-Portezuelo

Av.-El-Ensoscada

Av.-Cristian-Pérez

Pista-Las-Muchachos

Pista-Portezuelo

Pista-José-Ángel-Benavides (Pista-Sábana-Grande)

Paseo

Mercado & Bus Station Iván Montenegro y Oscar Benavides

Boulevard-Buenas-Aires

Inset (Plaza de la Fé / Plaza de la Democracia)

PLAZA DE LA FÉ JUAN PABLO

Palacio de Comunicaciones

PLAZA DE LA DEMOCRACIA

Teatro Rubén Darío

Casa Presidencial

Palacio Nacional

Centro Cultural (de Managua)

The Old (cathedral)

Scale / Compass

1 kilometer

1 mile

LG

0 0

LAYOUT AND ADDRESSES. Managua has dispensed with the annoyance of street names. "Addresses" are given in terms of proximity to landmarks—a Texaco station, a statue, where a cinema used to be—and their proximity to the rotunda. Even the cardinal points have Managuan pseudonyms: the direction "south" remains *al sur*, but "north" becomes *al lago* (toward the lake), "east" is *arriba* (i.e. where the sun rises), and "west" is *abajo* (where it descends). For example, *"De Tica Bus una cuadra abajo y media cuadra al lago,"* means from the Tica Bus Station walk 1 block west and half a block toward the lake (north).

Managua lies on the south shore of **Lago de Managua**, locally and more properly called **Lago Xolotlán**. Managua expands in all directions away from the lake. The effective center of the city is the pyramid-like **Hotel Intercontinental**, locally called the "Inter." Just north of the hotel is **Plaza Inter**, a US-style shopping mall complete with speciality stores, a cinema, and a food court. To the east, on the same hillside, looms the somber silhouette of *sombrero*-clad Sandino.

Just west of the Inter, **Av. Bolívar** runs north to south 1km north from the hotel to the lakeshore and the old city center, where it meets **Teatro Rubén Darío**. Along the way, it passes the **Asemblea Nacional,** the Bank of America skyscraper (the only one in the city), the **Palacio Nacional,** and the **Santo Domingo Cathedral.**

Across Av. Bolívar from the Inter is **Barrio Martha Quezada,** the neighborhood that houses most of Managua's budget hotels and *hospedajes*. Situated in the center of the *barrio* is the **Tica** bus station, an important directional landmark. The western border of the *barrio* Martha Quezada is **Av. Williams Romero,** with the now-defunct **Casino Royale,** another popular reference point. The northern border of the *barrio* is **C. 27 de Mayo.** Both of these streets are larger and busier than the bumpy byways of Martha Quezada. Eight blocks south of C. 27 de Mayo, on Av. Williams Roberto, is the **Plaza de España,** home to a number of banks, several travel agencies, and a supermarket. Most of the discos, chain restaurants, and the Metrocentro Mall are located on the **Carretera a Masaya.**

■ PRACTICAL INFORMATION

TOURIST, FINANCIAL, AND LOCAL SERVICES

Tourist Information: Ministerio de Turismo (INTUR; ☎222 6652, fax 222 6618), 1 block south and 1 block west of the Inter. Staff speaks English, but offers little substantive advice. Sells a variety of maps and guides and gives out free INTUR literature when in stock. Open M-F 8am-2pm. **Airport office** (☎263 3176), open daily 7am-7pm.

Travel Agencies and Guided Tours: The big complex southeast of the traffic rotary in the Plaza de España houses several travel agencies, including **Viajes America** (☎266 1130 or 266 0968. Open M-F 8am-6:30pm, Sa 8am-1pm). **Tours Nicaragua** (☎/fax 266 6663), 2 blocks south and a ½ block west of the Inter in Edificio Bolívar, is not cheap, but is well-informed about tours throughout the country.

Embassies and Consulates: Canada (☎268 0433). Open M-F 8am-noon. **UK** (☎278 0014 or 278 0887), on Reparto Los Robles, south of Av. Rubén Darío. Open M-F 9am-noon. **US** (☎266 6010 or 268 0123 for consular services), 4.5km down Carreterra Sur in Barrio Botahola Norte, southwest of Barrio Martha Quezada. Open M-F 8am-noon.

Banks: Banco de Finanzas (☎222 2444), Av. Bolívar across from Plaza Inter, changes traveler's checks at 3% commission. Open M-F 8am-4pm, Sa 9am-12:30pm. Inside the Metrocentro's financial center, **Bancentro** and **Banco de America Central** have branches with extended hours, including Su service until noon. Both banks change trav-

Managua Center

🏠 ACCOMMODATIONS
Casa Vanegas, **8**
Hospedaje Quintana, **4**
Hotel El Conquistador, **5**

🍴 FOOD
Ananda, **1**
Café Mirna, **9**
Comedor Sara, **3**
Doña Pilar, **6**

🍸 NIGHTLIFE
Amatl Café, **11**
KTV Discotheque, **7**
El Quetzal, **12**
La Ruta Maya, **2**
Shannon's Irish Pub, **10**

eler's checks and offer credit card cash advances. Most other national banks also have branches here. AmEx/MC/V **ATMs** are at all **Texaco Star Marts** and **ESSO on the Run** stores. The nearest to Martha Quezada are in the parking complex on the ground fl. of Plaza Inter, and at the ESSO station just west of Plaza Inter.

Western Union: (☎266 8126), south from the Inter on Av. Bolívar; turn right at the fork. 400m down the hill, on the right. Open M-Sa 8am-8pm, Su 8am-3pm.

Supermarket: La Colonia, in the Plaza España, above the roundabout. US-style supermarket with 15 aisles. Open M-Sa 8am-8pm, Su 9am-7pm.

EMERGENCY AND COMMUNICATIONS

Police: (☎249 8342, emergency 118 or 126), at the Mercado Oriental.

Red Cross: (☎265 2081, emergency 128), in Belmonte at Km 7 of Carretera Sur. 24hr. ambulance service.

Hospitals: Hospital Bautista (☎249 7070 or 249 7277). **Hospital Militar** (☎222 2763). For nearby help in an emergency, **Farmacia del Buen Pastor** (see below) has a small clinic open daily for consultations (10am-noon, 100C). Emergency visits available 24 hr. (emergency cell ☎8843481, emergency visit 150C). Doctors can make home visits (300C).

Pharmacies: Farmacia del Buen Pastor (☎222 6462), 1 block north and 1½ blocks east of the Casino, has the best hours. Open M-Sa 8am-8pm, Su 7am-noon.

Telephones: At the Palacio de Comunicaciones, **Correos de Nicaragua** offers all phone services. Open M-Sa 7am-9pm and Su 7am-6pm. There are phones with a direct connection to **Sprint** around the city, including on the 2nd fl. of Plaza Inter. Pick up public phones and dial access codes (ATT ☎174, MCI 166, Sprint 161) to connect to a bilingual operator. Info: ☎112. Public phones work with coins or phone cards that can be bought at gas stations. **FonoCenter** (☎222 2611), on the bottom fl. of Plaza Inter, has local, national, and international phone service (calls to the US 30C per min., to Europe 130C per min). You can also use the **Internet** (20C per hr.), or send **faxes,** and there is a **Western Union** (open M-Sa 10am-10pm, Su 10am-8pm).

Internet: Banisa Cyber@Center (☎222-5383) 1 block north of the casino, 40C per hr., 32C with ISIC card. M-Su 8:30am-10pm, Su 8:30am-5pm. **Kafe@Internet** (☎264 0252), 2½ blocks north of the casino. (Open M-Sa 8am-8pm, Su 9am-6pm. 10C per 30min. Internet calls 3C-10C per min. to most countries.)

Post Office: In Palacio de Comunicaciones west of the Old Cathedral, Palacio Nacional. **Fax, Internet, phone service,** express mail. Open M-F 8am-5pm, Sa 8am-noon for mail.

ACCOMMODATIONS

All hotels and *hospedajes* listed below are in **Barrio Martha Quezada,** a neighborhood 8 blocks north of Plaza España, between Hotel Intercontinental to the east and the northwestern stadium. Though the comfortable homes, bohemian lodgings, and occasional wandering pig seem peaceful, it's quite dangerous. As soon as you hop out of your taxi or bus, you'll be swamped by young children. Nothing but the most forceful telling-off will disperse them; it's probably easier to go with it and tip the standard 1C. As a general rule, the farther west of Inter, the cheaper.

Casa Vanegas (☎222 4443), formerly known as Hotel Bambú, on the southwest corner of the intersection a block east of the Tica bus station in a peach-colored house. Feel right at home in this clean hostel. All rooms with private bath. 95C per person. ❷

Hospedaje Quintana (☎228 6090). A backpacker favorite. Clean, basic rooms in a secure family house. Rooms with shared bath 80C. ❶

Hospedaje El Dorado (☎222 6012), ½ a block east of the Casino Royale. The homey, fanned rooms clustered around an indoor patio are stuffy yet comfortable. Communal baths are kept clean, and the friendly owners are security-conscious. Singles 70C, 140C with bath; doubles with bath 180C. ❶

Hotel El Conquistador (☎222 4789; www.hotelelconquistador.com), 1½ blocks north of the tourism office. A/C, bright yellow walls, carved wooden doors, hot water, refrigerators, tile floors; free breakfast and airport shuttle. Single 640C; double 880C; 80C-160C discount with ISIC card. ❺

La Merced, directly across from the highway coming from the airport. Best Western hotel popular with business travelers; plush rooms with all the amenities. Singles 640C. ❺

FOOD

Managua has an abundance of *fritangas*—sidewalk *comedores* that offer traditional, deep-fried buffets; you point at something and they throw it into a pan of boiling oil. The stews and *platos típicos* dished up at the city's markets are another cheap, authentic option, while the food courts at Plaza Inter and Metrocentro will satisfy those homesick for Happy Meals and Subway. The streets around the Inter are home to more upscale spots.

Comedor Sara, right across the street from Guest House Santos. A very friendly woman and her four daughters serve up hot and tasty spaghetti or curry to a packed crowd of travelers (25C-35C). Open daily for dinner. ❷

Café Mirna, 1 block east and 1 south of the Casino Royale. Every morning, the city's expat crowd packs in for Managua's best pancakes (25C). *Gallo pinto* with eggs and toast 25C; *batidos* 14C. Open M-F 6:30am-3pm, Sa-Su 6:30am-1pm. ❷

Ananda, across from the Montoya statue. A popular vegetarian restaurant with garden seating, known especially for its tropical fruit drink blends. Delicious *ensaladas* (25C-50C), *jugos* (12C), and *plato del día* (30C). Open M-Sa 7am-8:30pm. ❷

Doña Pilar, ½ block west and south of Hotel Quintana. This restaurant bustles in the evenings with its cheap, fast, and good *típico*. Open daily 5-10pm. ❶

⊙ SIGHTS

The sights in Managua surround the **Plaza de la Democracia** (formerly Plaza de la Revolución), on the northern end of Av. Bolívar, near the lake. A restored monument to Rubén Darío sits on the *plaza's* north side. From Martha Quezada to the *plaza*, walk 12 blocks north or take bus #109 from the corner of Av. Bolívar and C. Julio Buitrago. Head to the *plaza* for the colorful light show choreographed to classical music in the central fountain at 6 and 9pm nightly.

■ **TEATRO RUBÉN DARÍO.** About 200m north of the Plaza de la Democracia along the lakeshore, **Teatro Rubén Darío** is a 1200-seat concert hall considered one of the best venues in Central America. It regularly welcomes groups from around the world and is permanently home to the National Symphony Orchestra. The **Experimental Theater** has 200 seats in the building and hosts dance performances, plays, and great children's shows. The **Sala de Cristales,** a chandeliered hall on the second floor, rotates international art exhibits, usually free. (☎ 222 3630. *National groups and symphony 80C-160C; international performances 160C-640C. Experimental Theater 20C-50C. Check with box office or papers for schedules, prices.)*

■ **FERIA EXPLICA.** One of the biggest annual events in Managua and in all of Central America, the Feria Explica is held for 11 days at the end of July on fairgrounds west of the city center, near the Huellas de Acuahalinca, an archaeological excavation about 10 blocks west of the Teatro Rubén Darío. Thousands of farmers and ranchers from all Central American countries come to show off prize livestock and horses, and to buy the latest equipment and supplies. The event features daily rodeos, food stands, nightclubs, live music, and an array of artisan booths from all over the isthmus. (*Admission to fair 10C, 20C after 4pm.)*

EL CATEDRAL VIEJO. On the eastern side of the Plaza de la Democracia, the cathedral was nearly destroyed by the 1972 earthquake. It has been partially restored with a new fiberglass roof but plans for re-opening are still up in the air. The shadowy crypt, located underneath the altar, is an eerie sight. (*Closed to the public at publication. Check to see if open.)*

CATEDRAL DE LA INMACULADA CONCEPCIÓN.
Located at the Rotonda Rubén Darío across from the Metrocentro Mall, it's sometimes called *Nueva Catedral.* The earthquake-proof church maintains a mystical air, perhaps because it looks more like a moon base camp. (*Services M-F 6pm; Su 8am, noon, 4, 7pm.)*

THE LOCAL STORY

¡JÓN-RÓN!

Nicaragua is one of the few Latin American countries where soccer doesn't reign supreme. Rather, baseball (in Nicaragua, *base*) is the overwhelming favorite. As proof of the sport's popularity, Managua's stadium holds 40,000 spectators. And as proof of its standards, Nicaragua's national baseball team came fourth in the 1996 Olympic games in Atlanta, US.

As in the Dominican Republic, the sport is a legacy from US Marine occupation in the 1920s, when soldiers passed on this pastime. Now, most towns have a baseball field, and children, no matter what social or economic class, learn to play, sometimes even with make-shift bats and balls. Multiple national professional teams keep the country riveted on regional competitions.

Pitcher Dennis (Denny) Martínez is one *nica* who has had some success in the US major leagues and at home; he was recently offered a government position heading the domestic athletics department. The country has glorified another Latin American baseball player, Roberto Clemente, whose name lives on in Masaya's stadium. The famed outfielder died in a plane crash on his way to deliver aid to Nicaraguan earthquake victims in 1972.

PALACIO NACIONAL. Due to budget cuts, Managua's museums have been consolidated into the Palacio Nacional, on the south side of the *plaza*. The **Hall of Natural History,** on the first floor, has displays about national parks and Nicaragua's natural history. A small **art gallery** exhibits the work of current local artists and collections of pre-Columbian pottery. The second floor boasts the **National Library** and **National Archives;** much of Rubén Darío's work is exhibited here. The museum tour (in Spanish and English) includes a guide. (☎ 222 2905. *Open M-F 8am-5pm. 30C.*)

🗋 SHOPPING

The city comes to life in Managua's excellent *mercados*. 🎦**Mercado Roberto Huembes,** also called Mercado Central, east of the universities, is an enormous market where you can find just about anything you're looking for and a whole lot more, from a Masayan hammock to a skinned pig's head. **Mercado Israel Lewites,** commonly called "Israel," in the southwest of town, has a notable array of sizzling *comedores*, as well as a pharmacy and a wide selection of apparel from such "fine" manufacturers as "Rebok" and "Adibas." **Mercado Ivan Montenegro** and **Mercado Mayoreo,** visited mainly for bus departures, don't have anything that Roberto Huembes doesn't. **Mercado Oriental,** a sprawling labyrinth of shops closer to downtown, is one of the city's most dangerous areas and **should be avoided.**

MOVIES AND BASEBALL

For the latest Hollywood flick, head to the multiplexes at the Plaza Inter or Metrocentro. (40C; 35C for students, 35C before 4pm and all day Tu.) The Centro Cultural shows movies during the day. Unlike its *fútbol*-crazed neighbors, Nicaragua's national sport is **béisbol** (see **Jón-Rón,** p. 541). You can join the fun by going to the stadium in Martha Quezada to watch a game. Pro teams play from October to June and college teams duke it out from June to September.

🗐 🖸 NIGHTLIFE AND ENTERTAINMENT

> ❓ Due to safety concerns, the nightlife listings in Managua were not updated for this edition of *Let's Go Central America*. All listings are based on research conducted in August 2002.

Managua has something to satisfy all tastes, from classic large discos to international music venues. You'll need a cab to get to places for safety and convenience. Women should never, under any circumstances, go out alone at night.

BARS AND CLUBS

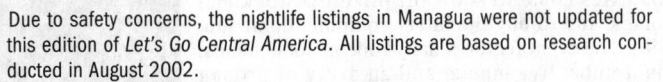
Hippa-Hippa, a beach bar in the city, the hottest at the moment, attracts Managua's young elite; slick attire suggested. Cover 40C-120C depending on DJ; drink specials, special events. Open W-Sa 8pm.

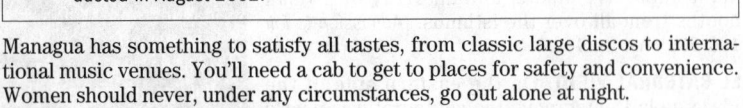
Shannon's Irish Pub, 1 block east and ½ block south of Tica Bus. An authentic Irish pub with cold cider, Guinness, darts, tasty snacks (excellent homemade chili 37C), and a friendly mix of locals and foreigners. Open M-Th 5pm-midnight, F-Sa 5pm-3am.

Amatl Café, 1 block south of the Hotel Intercontinental. A cozier atmosphere; hip bands play this trendy spot. Students, older folks, and a fair number of *gringos* all mix here on weekends. Live music every Th-Sa 6pm-midnight. Cover 30C-50C.

El Quetzal, on Carretera Masaya across from La Colonia Supermarket, draws an all-ages local crowd that dances the night away to live *salsa* music. Come early if you want a table. Full-service kitchen (chicken tacos 35C). No cover. Open Th-Su 6pm-3am.

La Ruta Maya, just east of the Montoya statue behind the *parque*. An open-air bar and dance club with classic rock and *salsa*. Sa night stand-up political comedy (in Spanish). Occasional cultural performances. Open Tu-Sa 5pm-2am. Cover 40C-80C.

KTV Discotheque, a classy disco in the bottom fl. of the Plaza Inter. Private karaoke rooms with large-screen TV. There is also a casino in the hotel. 60C cover and 60C minimum drink order. Foreigners get in free. Open Th-Sa 7pm-4am.

♫ DAYTRIPS FROM MANAGUA

 Information, including prices and hours, on beaches near Managua is based on research conducted in August 2002.

BEACHES. About 60km southwest of Managua, the adjacent Pacific beaches of Pochomil, Masachapa, and Montelimar make a great daytrip for travelers and residents overfrenzied by the capital. On weekdays you'll have the beach to yourself. The view of the city is spectacular. ☀**Pochomil,** managed by INTUR (the Nicaraguan tourist board), is the southernmost beach: wide, clean, with a boardwalk full of seemingly identical restaurants. Restaurant owners bombard you to eat and laze in their rancho (a palm-covering on the beach. Fish 50C; shrimp 70C; lobster 80C.). Hammocks (30C per day) are usually free with food. Restaurants tend to be cheaper south of the estuary (left as you face the sea). There is an unmarked *corriente* that should be avoided; waves get huge. If unsure, ask any local "*corriente?*" and point to the sea. **Masachapa** and **Montelimar** are less clean and touristy, but have a pleasant fishing village atmosphere. *(Buses to Pochomil leave from Mercado Israel Lewites in Managua: 2hr., every 30min., 8C. You can also walk between the 2 beaches 30min. To get to Montelimar from Masachapa walk 3km north up the road or take a bicycle taxi 10C. The last sure ride home is 4:30pm. Hotel Altamar, on the hill south of the estuary, has basic, well-kept rooms. ☎269 9204. 1-3 people 100C-150C, with bath 150C-200C. Many restaurant owners have a few rooms behind their kitchens, varying in quality.)*

XILOA. Ten kilometers west of Managua, Xiloa (heel-WA or eel-WA) is a **volcanic lake** set on a lush mountain backdrop. Lined by picnic tables and *refresco* stands and cool and inviting waters; unfortunately on weekends it fills with intoxicated Managuans. *(Catch one of the buses from Israel Lewites headed for Mateare, Nagorote, or León, and ask to be let out at the entrada principal a Xiloa 2C. Alternatively, take city bus #113 2.5C from the road in front of Israel Lewites or the Metrocentro to Sandino, 5km shy of Xiloa. A taxi to the laguna should run 40-80C. Use of the lake's facilities 2C.)*

PACIFIC LOWLANDS

The Pacific lowlands, stretching from Chinandega in the north to Rivas in the south, is Nicaragua's population center. A long string of volcanoes along the coast has made the lowlands the most fertile farmland in the country. Shielded from the Caribbean rains by the mountains, the lowlands are hot and dry. For a breeze, migrate to any body of water—Lago de Nicaragua or the Pacific. León, where student radicals keep things lively, and Granada, a tourist favorite for its architectural wonders, are both steeped in history. Artsy Masaya is a gold mine of local crafts, while San Juan del Sur offers visitors a taste of beach bum life.

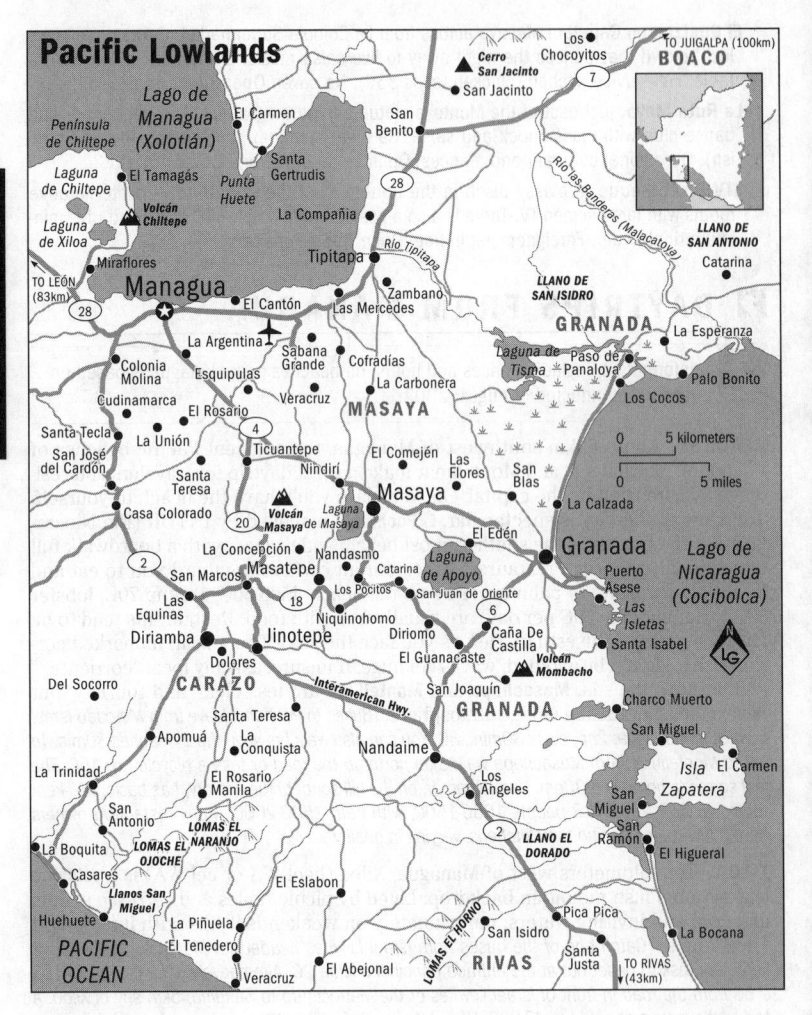

Pacific Lowlands

LEÓN

The streets of Leon (pop. 130,000) blend colonial with modern at every step. Horse-drawn carriages and liberal students fill the streets, while bells from the 19 churches compete with taxi horns and *camionetas*. Prayer to saints is never far from town parties where spirituality is easily forgotten. Despite the constant mixing of eras, echoes of the town's Spanish founders ring loud and clear.

León Viejo was founded on the shore of Lake Xolotlán in 1524. Destroyed by an earthquake in 1610, León (full name: León Santiago de los Caballeros) was rebuilt 30km to the west. Once a poor center, the new León soon became a cultural and intellectual stronghold, and the capital of Nicaragua, for more than 300 years. The heady atmosphere fueled the imagination of its favorite son, Rubén Darío, whose poetry launched the Modernist movement in Latin America. As bumper stickers on many cars proclaim, León is *orgullosamente liberal* (proudly liberal). The Universidad Nacional Autónoma de Nicaragua (UNAN), the country's first university, sharpens León's politics to a keen radical edge.

▐ TRANSPORTATION

The **main terminal,** 6 blocks north and 7 blocks east of the *parque central,* has **buses** to: **Chinandega** (bus 1hr., every 30min. 4am-6pm, 8C; minibus 30min., every 15min., 5:30am-6pm, 18C); **Estelí** (3hr., 3pm, 30C); **La Paz Centro** (1hr., every 30min. 8am-11am, returning at 2pm, 6C); **Managua** (2hr., every 30min. 4am-6pm, 12C; express 1½hr., every hr. 5am-6pm, 15C; minibus 1½hr., every 20min. 4:30am-6pm, 20C); **Matagalpa** (3hr., take bus to San Isidro, 16C, then transfer to Matagalpa-bound bus, 20C); and **San Isidro** (2½hr., every 30min. 4am-5:30pm, 16C).

For **local** transportation, the **#101** bus and *camionetas* (15min., every few minutes, 2.5C) run between the **Central Terminal** on the East side of town and West side **El Mercadito,** where buses depart for the beach. The bus travels along C. Central and passes through the *parque central.* **Taxis** to the center from the station, 8C.

▐▐ ORIENTATION AND PRACTICAL INFORMATION

One of the few cities in Nicaragua where street names are used in directions, León is surprisingly easy to get around. León's center is the *parque central,* **Parque Jerez.** If you're standing in the *parque* with the fountain of lions, the massive **cathedral** is to the east, and the imposing **ENITEL** antenna is to the west. León's *calles* run east and west and its *avenidas* run north and south. **Calle Central Rubén Darío** fronts the north side of the *parque.* **Av. Central** would run right between the *parque* and the cathedral, except that the *avenida* is discontinued for a block at this point. León's 19 churches dot the landscape every few blocks and are frequently used as reference points in directions farther away from the *parque* or cathedral. **La Iglesia de La Merced,** a block north of the *parque's* northwest corner, and **La Iglesia de La Recolección,** 1 block east and 2 north of the *parque's* northeast corner, are useful landmarks. The **bus terminal** sits on the edge of town, 6 blocks north and 7 blocks east of the *parque central.* To get to town from the bus station, take a right onto the main street that you came in on, walk past the market, and continue for several blocks before taking a left on 1 Av. Noreste. The walk to the center of town can be a hot and dusty 20min. trek, but it's manageable. Take advantage of the shade provided by overhangs.

Tourist Office: Instituto de Turismo (☎311 3682), 1 block west and 2½ blocks north of the *parque.* Open M-F 8am-12:30pm and 2-5pm.

Travel Agent: Viajes Mundiales (☎311 5920 or 311 6920), 3 blocks north and ½ block west of the *parque's* northeast corner. Good for international flights and travel within Nicaragua. Open M-F 8am-6pm, Sa 8am-12:30pm.

Banks: BanCentro, ¾ of a block north of the *parque's* northwest corner. Open M-F 8am-4:30pm, Sa 8am-noon. **Banco de America Central,** 1 block north and 20m east of the cathedral's northeast corner. Open M-F 8:30am-5pm, Sa 8:30am-12:30pm. Both cash traveler's checks and give cash advances on AmEx/MC/V. Plus/Visa ATMs located inside La Unión Supermarket and Plaza Siglo Nuevo, both 1 block north and ½ block east of the *parque's* northeast corner.

Western Union: (☎311 2426), 1 block north and 1 block east of the cathedral's northeast corner. Open M-F 8am-12:30pm and 2-5pm, Sa 8am-12:30pm.

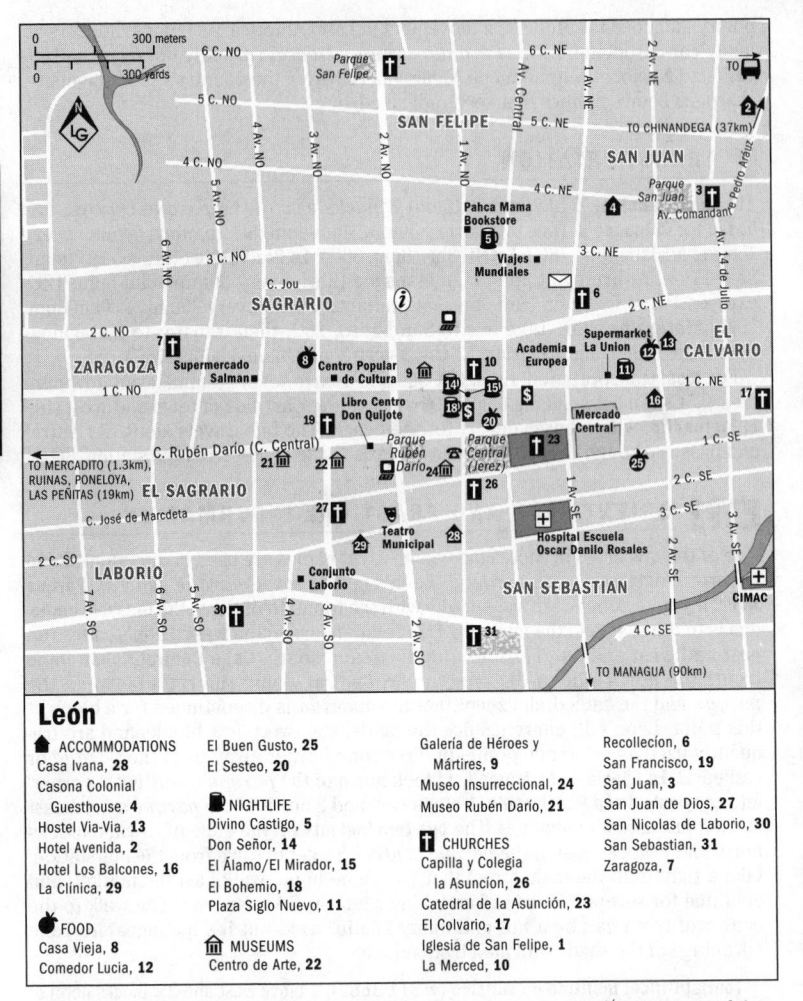

León

ACCOMMODATIONS	
Casa Ivana, **28**	
Casona Colonial	
Guesthouse, **4**	
Hostel Via-Via, **13**	
Hotel Avenida, **2**	
Hotel Los Balcones, **16**	
La Clínica, **29**	

🍴 FOOD
Casa Vieja, **8**
Comedor Lucia, **12**

El Buen Gusto, **25**
El Sesteo, **20**

🍸 NIGHTLIFE
Divino Castigo, **5**
Don Señor, **14**
El Álamo/El Mirador, **15**
El Bohemio, **18**
Plaza Siglo Nuevo, **11**

🏛 MUSEUMS
Centro de Arte, **22**

Galería de Héroes y
    Mártires, **9**
Museo Insurreccional, **24**
Museo Rubén Darío, **21**

🕇 CHURCHES
Capilla y Colegia
    la Asuncion, **26**
Catedral de la Asunción, **23**
El Colvario, **17**
Iglesia de San Felipe, **1**
La Merced, **10**

Recollecíon, **6**
San Francisco, **19**
San Juan, **3**
San Juan de Dios, **27**
San Nicolas de Laborio, **30**
San Sebastian, **31**
Zaragoza, **7**

Supermarket: La Unión, in Plaza Metropolitana, 1 block north and ½ block east of the cathedral's northeast corner. Open M-Sa 7:30am-8pm, Su 8am-6pm. Supermercado Salman, 1 block north and 3 blocks west of the *parque*'s northwest corner. Open daily 7am-8:30pm.

Police: (☎311 3137, emergency 115), 2km from Central León, on Carretera Chinandega (taxi 10C).

Hospital: Hospital Escuela Oscar Danilo Rosales (☎311 6934), 1 block south of the cathedral, in a big grayish, yellow building.

Telephones: ENITEL, on the west side of the *parque central*. Open daily 7am-8:45pm.

Internet: Puerto Café Ben Linder, 2 blocks north of the northwest corner of the *parque*, on the left-hand corner. 10C per hr. Open daily 8:30am-11pm. Leonet, 1 block west of the *parque* on 2 Av 50. 15C per hr. Open daily 8am-9pm.

Post Office: Correos de Nicaragua, 2½ blocks north of the cathedral's northwest corner. Fax and telegram service available. Open M-F 8am-noon and 2-5pm, Sa 8am-noon. *Lista de correos* open M-F 8am-11am and 2-5pm.

▌ ACCOMMODATIONS

Hotels in León vary from elegant colonial hotels to friendly, bare-bones *posadas*. A luxury lodging won't break the bank, and a super cheap room doesn't necessarily mean you'll be sharing your bed with the chickens. Avoid staying near the bus station for safety reasons.

Hostel Via-Via (☎311 6142), 75m south of the Servicio Agrícola Guardián gas station. This spacious, Belgian-run hostel is a relaxed hangout spot and cultural center for locals and tourists alike. Presently offering 3 private rooms, Via-Via has plans to expand. A street-front cafe opens into a large patio with hammocks and a lush garden lined with funky murals. Clean but minimalist shared bathroom in the back. Laundry, book exchange. Cafe/bar open and packed 8am-midnight. Dorm beds 47C; singles 126C; doubles 158C. ❶

La Clínica (☎311 2031), almost 2 blocks south of the southwest corner of the *parque*. An annex to the home and dental clinic of the very friendly Dra. María Mercedes Galo. Rooms and bathrooms are sparse but clean, and the Doctora tries to accommodate all budgets by allowing camping on the back patio. Self-service lunch. 50C in high season, 45C in low. ❶

Casa Ivana (☎311 4423), 1 block south and 1½ blocks west of the southwest corner of the *parque*, across from Teatro Municipal. HIdden behind the steel gate and a small sign, Casa Ivana is a great value, rooms tend to go quickly. Cable TV, laundry, towels. Singles 70C; doubles 100-120C; triples 180C. ❶

Hotel Avenida (☎311 2068), 4 blocks west and ½ block south of the bus station (across from the ESSO gas station), is a popular resting spot for locals and foreigners. Cable TV, fans, self-service laundry, private baths in all rooms larger than singles, and a *cafetín* that serves basic breakfast (14C). Singles 50C, with bath 70C; doubles 100C; triples 150C; quads 180C. ❶

Hotel Los Balcones, Esquina de los Bancos, 1 C. al Este (☎311 0233; www.hotelbalcones.com). Upscale option with simple rooms, tiled courtyards, balconies, and elegant detail. Pleasant cafe on the ground fl. is always crowded with travelers enjoying inexpensive *platos* (79C for entree with meat, rice, plantains) and stocked bar. All rooms have A/C, cable TV, and private bath. Singles 620C; doubles 820C; triples 980C. ❺

Casona Colonial Guesthouse (☎311 3178), 4 blocks north and ½ block west of the cathedral's northwest corner. Rooms are luxurious, with hand-sewn quilts and sparkling private baths. Large sitting area with color TV and a pleasant garden. Guests get a key to the front door when they check in. Singles and doubles 158C; triples 237C. ❷

▐ FOOD

Like any college town, León has plenty of pizza joints. However, since most restaurants provide an equally enjoyable atmosphere and food, you can do better. The market is a great option for hot grilled and fried snacks (0.5C-20C).

Casa Vieja, across from the west side of Casa de Cultura, 2½ blocks west and 2 blocks north of the *parque central*. Dishes piled high with colorful vegetables and other *nica* food that shows off all the country has to offer. Soft music and relaxed atmosphere draw local couples from the posh set. Entrees 35-70C. Open daily 4-10:30pm. ❷

El Sesteo, on the northeast corner of the park, with a pretty view, good for people-watching. Though upscale and tourist-oriented, the English/Spanish menu offers some moderately-priced goodies, like *sandwich de pollo* (38C) or *Ceviche* (42C). Wide variety of desserts and *licuados,* and a huge, icy *cacao* (22C). Open daily 8am-10:30pm. ❷

Comedor Lucia, 1½ blocks north and 2 blocks east of the *parque central* on 2 Av. Sureste, across the street from the Via-Via hostel. Traditional Nicaraguan lunch buffet at great prices in a simple, no-nonsense environment. Platos with meat, *gallo pinto,* plantain and tortilla 20C. Open daily 10am-2pm. ❶

El Buen Gusto, 1½ blocks east of the southeast corner of the *parque.* Apron-clad women cook up hearty meat stews over an open flame. *Platos* 15C, *nacatamales* 12C, *cacao* or *jugo de tamarindo* 5C. Open daily 10am-10pm. ❶

NIGHTLIFE AND ENTERTAINMENT

Nighttime is when León really comes alive. University students spend weekend nights dancing until dawn—or at least until authorities shut clubs down (1-2am), after which the party moves to bars. Popular areas are well lit and patrolled by *vigilantes* (local watchmen hired by the town). The local tourist board sponsors **Tertulias Leonesas** in the *parque* every few Saturdays. The events—part concert, part culture, part fiesta—are free to the public and draw huge crowds. Artisans and street vendors set up mid-afternoon, and a music show starts around 6:30pm.

Don Señor, 1 block north of the northwest corner of the *parque,* is a popular university dance spot. 2 dance floors provide slightly different atmospheres: *Arriba* (upstairs) is larger, darker, plays more Latin music, and has A/C, while *Abajo* (downstairs) is a cabana bar with a small but packed dance floor in the corner, playing a mix of Latin, US pop, and rap. Open W-Su 8pm-2am. Cover W-Th 15C, F 20C, Sa 25C.

El Alámo/El Mirador. This split-level bar with lots of local traffic is perfect for those who would rather converse than bump-n-grind. El Alámo, downstairs, has A/C with a classic dive-bar feel; El Mirador (the lookout) is a relaxing rooftop patio with great views. Beer 15C. Open M-W 11am-10pm, Th-Sa 11am-1am.

Divino Castigo, 3 blocks north of the northwest corner of the *parque.* Hardly the whips-n-chains place its name (Divine Punishment) might invoke, a pretty, blue-painted bar and restaurant with live music streaming out open windows Tu and Sa. *Antojitos* from french fries to nachos (15C-30C), bottles of *flor de Caña* (80C). Open M-Sa 11am-1am.

El Bohemio, 1 block north of the northwest corner of the *parque.* This popular college hangout features psychedelically-painted walls and what must be the world's tiniest dance floor, always packed. Cheap beer and even cheaper rum. Open daily 7pm-1am.

Plaza Siglo Nuevo, 1 block north, ½ block east of the northeast corner of the cathedral. A modern movie theater and coffee shop tucked into a beautiful colonial building. Catch an almost-new flick, then relax with a cappuccino in the courtyard. Movies 40C, 32C with ISIC card.

 SIGHTS

CENTRO POPULAR DE CULTURA. This lively cultural center is a great place to get info, engage in political debates, look at artwork, or relax with a beer. Situated in a large colonial house, El Centro was at one point a Sandinista headquarters, and the radical feeling remains—check out the painting of Ronald Reagan sitting on the shoulders of a bleeding indigenous woman while holding a rifle and grinning.

Swing by to check out times for various lessons and workshops—Spanish and Salsa classes offered. Cafe, small library, and back patio increase its allure. *(1 block north and 2 blocks west of the northwest corner of* parque.*)*

MUSEO DE INSURRECCIONAL LUIS TORUÑO CHARATA. A tiny gem, this shrine to the Sandinista Revolution is hard to forget. The museum's owner, Marvin Benito, participated in the insurrection of 1979. He'll take you through photos and faces of Sandinista leaders and martyrs, but only in Spanish. *(10m west of the southwest corner of the parque central. Open daily noon-2pm. Suggested donation 10C.)*

CENTRO DE ARTE. In a large colonial building, the impressive exhibit covers the walls of three beautiful courtyards—complete with roses and fountains—and those of almost a dozen rooms. The collection spans numerous genres, including pre-Columbian ceramics, European religious paintings, and Latin American works. Relaxing atmosphere, especially at sunset. *(2 blocks east and 15m south of the northeast corner of the parque. Open Tu-Sa 10:30am-6:30pm, Su 11am-7pm. 12C Tu-Sa includes written Spanish guide, Su free.)*

CATEDRAL DE LA ASUNCIÓN. The huge restored **Catedral de la Asunción** is the largest cathedral in Central America, a reputation the imposing facade won't let you forget. Rubén Darío rests here, on the right side of the altar, his tomb guarded by one of the cathedral's many giant lion statues. The cathedral is also famous for *Stations of the Cross*, a series of paintings by Antonio Sarria. There are over a dozen other churches around town to check out. *(On the* parque's *east side.)*

MUSEO ARCHIVO RUBÉN DARÍO. Three blocks west of the *parque* is the museum and former home of the country's favorite poet, Rubén Darío. Collected are some of his clothes, paintings of his family, his death mask, and many manuscripts and first editions. It is an impressive representation of this well-respected literary figure. With permission, you can read the books in the archive. *(☎311 2388. Open Tu-Sa 9am-noon and 2-5pm, Su 9am-noon. Free.)*

MUSEO DE TRADICIONES Y LEYENDAS. Don't let the pleasant garden in front fool you: the building was a prison for Somoza's political enemies 1921-1979. Converted in 2000, it's a mixture of the happy, the superstitious, and León's violent past. *(3 blocks south and ½ block east of the cathedral's southwest corner, across from San Sebastián Church. Open Tu-Sa 8:30am-noon and 2-5:30pm, Su 8:30am-3pm. 7C.)*

GALERIA DE HÉROES Y MÁRTIRES. The gallery contains a sobering collection of black-and-white photos of León residents who died during the Sandinista revolution, respectfully reminiscent of a shocking era. The caretaker, Concepción Coruño, lost her husband, a son, and a daughter in the war and gives a moving account of the stories behind the pictures. *(1 block north and 1½ blocks west of the northwest corner of the parque, under a sign that says "La Galería Bazar de Artesanía." Open M-Sa 8am-5pm. Donations appreciated.)*

EL CENTRO DE INICIATIVAS MEDIOAMBIENTES (CIMAC). This riverside botanical garden includes specimens from all of Nicaragua's bio-zones. Borrow a pair of binoculars and if you're lucky, you'll catch a glimpse of the colorful *guardabarranco*, Nicaragua's national bird. A variety of interesting plants and trees with all sorts of fruits, pods, and spikes growing off them populate the garden. *(3 blocks east and 2 blocks south of the southeast corner of the cathedral, after a small bridge. Open M-F 8-11am and 2-5pm, Sa 8-11am. 20C per person.)*

LEÓN VIEJO. "Old León" lies 30km southeast of León, on the shores of Lago de Managua. Founded in 1524 by Francisco Hernández de Córdoba, it was the colonial capital of Nicaragua until early 1610, when **Volcán Momotombo,** standing at the edge of town, caused an earthquake that destroyed the city. Hurricanes have since taken their toll on the partially-excavated ruins. To prevent further damage, UNESCO have covered the remaining brick foundations so all that can be seen are footprints of buildings. A Spanish-speaking guide will tell you the story of their past splendor. Tours take 45min. and start at the foundations of the cathedral, a 5min. walk past the museum, where a statue marks the spot of Hernández de Córdoba's beheading. Córdoba's remains were exhumed from the Iglesia de La Merced here in May 2000 and are now entombed below the statue. (*From León, take a bus to La Pax Centro (1hr., every 35-40min. 5:50am-6:40pm, 8C). Then, catch a bus for the town of Momotombo and ask to be let off at "Las Ruinas." 30min., 9 buses per day 6:30am-5pm, 6C. From Managua, take a bus from Mercado Israel Lewites to La Paz Centro. 1¼hr., every 20min. 4am-6pm, 10C. Buses return to La Paz Centro every 1-2hr. 8 buses 8am-5pm, 5C. Once in Momotombo, follow the blue-and-white signs to Las Ruinas de León Viejo for about 10min. The road veers to the left. Site open daily 8am-5pm. 10C, with ISIC 5C.*)*

⚑ OUTDOOR ACTIVITIES

SAN CRISTÓBAL VOLCANO. The highest volcano (1786m) in Nicaragua, San Cristóbal affords amazing views, but you don't get them for free. Once you get to Chinandega (see **Chinandega,** below), the climb is hard, and it's likely that on the way you will have little time to look around if you want to get up and back before nightfall. Getting a guide is a must, since following a random trail will likely take you nowhere. The 8-10hr. round-trip is steep and mostly above the tree line.

There are two routes to the top, the first via **El Ranchería.** From the bus stop in Chinandega, walk along the highway toward Guasaule for 1 block. Turn right where you see the few houses in the area and ask locals to show you where the *guardabosque* (responsible for this green area) lives. He should be able to find a guide as well as horses. Come early, or the guide will probably refuse to take you to the top since hiking past nightfall isn't advisable. (Guide plus horses 110C-140C plus tip). The other route to the volcano is via **Las Bolsas.** From Las Bolsas, it's 11km up the road to **Hacienda Rosas,** at the foot of the volcano. No buses pass this way, so if you don't have a car you'll either have to walk or borrow a horse from Socorro Pérez Alvarado (☎883 9354) who lives at the Las Bolsas stop. It's best to go with a guide to the summit (tip 40C-50C). Vincente Pérez Alvarado (Socorro's brother) is knowledgeable and can arrange to meet you. (5hr. round trip climb from the base of the volcano; 9hr. walk from Las Bolsas.) There is no water on either route, so bring plenty. (*From Mercado Bisne in Chinandega, take the bus headed toward Guasaule on the Honduran border. Ask to be let off at the Campusano stop in El Ranchería (40min.; every 30min. 4am-7:30pm, return every 30min.; 8C). Buses leave for El Bolsa from El Mercadito in Chinandega (30min., 5am-6pm; approx. every hr; 6C).*)

VOLCANOES. León is situated close to several breathtaking volcanoes, all of which can be scaled in guided treks, ranging from half-day walking tours to three-night camping excursions. Your best bet is to go with the **Quetzaltrekkers,** a group of friendly, young international volunteers who donate all the trek money to a local charity for street children. Try a relatively untaxing half-day and overnight trip to **Cerro Negro.** A pleasant hike up **Telica** includes swims in volcanic pools. More hard core camping/trekking tours up Cosiguina and Momotombo for those in decent shape. Any local tourism office or hostel can hook you up with other guides and treks to your liking as well. (☎507 843 7647; www.quetzaltrekkers.com. *Trip to Cerro Negro 250C, overnight 600C; Telica 2-day hike 500C; 3-day Cosiguina trip 900C; to Momotombo over 2 days, 700C.*)

BOILING MUD PITS. For an untouristed geo-thermal outing, head to **Los Hervideros (The Boiling Springs) de San Jacinto,** located 25km west of León on the road to San Isidro, to see a small and hot field full of vigorously boiling pits of muddy water and holes spewing sulfuric steam. For a small tip, eager local kids will show you where to step to avoid breaking through the crusted earth and being boiled alive—beware the white clay. If you ask, your guide will show you a nearby hot spring where you can bathe with the locals; watch your belongings here. *(Take the bus bound for San Isidro from León and ask to be let off at Los Hervideros in San Jacinto (35min., every 30min. 7C). The driver will let you off on the road just above the arch marking the entrance.)*

PONELOYA AND LAS PEÑITAS

Peaceful and deserted twin beach communities, 21km southwest of León, they can be distinguished by their position relative to a rocky outcropping known as La Peña del Tigre, and in terms of differing degrees of wealth. Poneloya is less upscale and touristy; facing the water, Poneloya is to the right, Las Peñitas, left. Killer waves and currents make swimming risky; the best spots are the south and north ends of Las Peñitas and Poneloya respectively.

Take the **#101 bus** or a **camioneta** (10min., every 10min., 2.5C) from the main **bus station** in León to **El Mercadito,** on the outskirts of town, or walk 15min. west down C. Rubén Darío. Buses run from El Mercadito to Poneloya and Las Peñitas (40min., every 55min. 4:45am-6pm, 8C). The bus first stops in Poneloya, farther west, and then retreats east to Las Peñitas. The main road splits right before Poneloya, the left leads to Las Peñitas. Walk between the two beaches either on sand or road 35m inland (25min.). Buses heading back to **León** leave every hr. 6:15am-6:40pm.

There are two hotels in Poneloya. **Hotel Lacayo ❶,** on the beach 1 block north to the right of La Peña, has creaky floors and old cots, but a spacious covered patio and great ocean views. (☎886 7369. 60C.) **La Posada ❷,** a block inland and currently under renovation, promises large bathrooms and thick mattresses, as well as a pool and back patio for Saturday night parties. (☎031 7378. Breakfast included. 3 or 4 beds with A/C 395C.)

In Las Peñitas, **Hotel Barca de Oro ❷** has rooms with sturdy locks and mosquito netting. One of the owners is a turtle activist and can organize trips to the nearby **Isla Tuan Uenado Reserve.** (☎317 275; tortuga@bw.com.ni. 2 rooms 95C-158C; all-inclusive packages available.) **La Montaña ❶** offers rooms for every price range and a pleasant tiled patio with restaurant and bar, breakfast 35C. (☎317 264; mirthamer@hotmail.com. Basic rooms 50C per person; doubles and triples with A/C, hot water, and TV 316C; with bath 395C.) **Mi Casita ❷** has a few clean, brightly painted rooms. (☎862 9792. Doubles and triples 330C.) **Supaya Beach Hotel ❹** is the most luxe option in Las Peñitas, catering to wealthy Nicaraguan vacationers who lounge on the deck or around the pool sipping *cerveza*. Rooms are spacious. (☎885 8345. Doubles 460C, with A/C 550C.) Ask hotels about body board rentals.

Restaurante Pariente Salidas ❷, 1 block to the right of Hotel Lacayo, is the only restaurant in town. (Entrees 50C. Open daily 7am-9pm.) Las Peñitas offers a few more options within a short walk of the bus stop. The restaurant and bar of **Hotel Barca de Oro ❷** share the *torre* that overlooks the sea (French and local food 40C-70C). The **Supaya Beach Hotel ❹** restaurant overlooking the water is delicious. (*Camarones al ajillo* 200C. Restaurant open daily 7-10am and 11:30am-8pm.)

CHINANDEGA

Chinandega (pop. 120,000), 36km northwest of León, is one of Nicaragua's hottest, driest, and flattest. A bustling commercial center, it has little to offer the tourist unless they enjoy chaotic *mercados* or want to see thousands of bottles of *flor de caña*, the famous rum, arriving from the ports of Corinto, León, and Chichigalpa. The only reason to stop is to climb San Cristóbal, the country's tallest volcano.

Buses leave from Mercado Bisne to: **Chichigalpa** by **minibus** (20min., every 10-15min. 6am-6pm, 7C); **Corinto** (45min., every 15min. 6:40am-6:40pm, 6C); the border at **Guasaule** via **Somotillo** (2½hr., every 30min. 5am-7:30pm, 15C); **León** by bus (1¼hr., every 11min. 5am-6pm, 9C) and minibus (45min., every 15min. 5am-9pm, 12C); and **Managua** (2hr., every hr. 4:15am-6pm, 30C). Buses drop you off literally in the middle of **El Mercado Bisne**. To get to the *parque central* walk approx. 600m continuing in the direction the bus was traveling, until you arrive at an intersection with a **Western Union**. (☎341 2455. Open M-F 8am-5pm, Sa 8am-noon.) Turn left and walk 1km to get to the *parque;* halfway there you'll pass through the *mercado central.* **Supermarket Palí** is directly in front of the *parque* (open M-Sa 7:30am-8pm, Su 8am-6pm). Exchange currency, traveler's checks, and advance money at **Bancentro**, on the corner of 2 C. Ote. and 1 Av. Sur (open M-F 8am-4:30pm, Sa 8am-noon; AmEx/MC/V). The **Red Cross** (☎341 3867, emergencies 341 3132), on 5 C. between 4 and 5 Av. Sur, provides 24hr. ambulance service. **Police** (☎341 3456, emergency ☎118) and **Hospital Mauricio Abdalab** (☎341 4902) are both in front of the *parque;* **Cyber World** has **Internet,** 1 block behind the police (open M-Sa 8am-6pm, Su 9am-1pm; 15C per hr.); the **post office,** is on Av. Manuel Fernández 2 blocks from the *mercado* (open M-F 8am-noon and 2-5pm, Sa 8am-noon; fax).

This is not a tourist town, so you have to take whatever resources are available for local commuters. Pricier **Hotel Glomar** ❷, close to Hotel Chinandega, is clean and relatively welcoming. All rooms have fans. (☎341 2562. Singles 140C, with A/C 200C, with bath 260C; doubles 210C/270C/330C; triples 280C/340C/400C.) **Hotel Chinandega** ❶, on Av. Martin 1 block away from the *mercado central,* offers simple rooms with communal baths (50C per person). **Comedor Reyes** ❷, close to Hotel California, is the town's most popular dining option, understandable given the generous portions. (*Comida corriente* 25C; chicken 30C. Open daily 6:30am-9pm.) Another nearby option is **Doña Leo** ❷, where they grill fast, filling, cheap food out front. (20C-30C. Open daily 7am-10pm.)

GRANADA

Granada's (pop. 90,500) prime location has determined its history from the start. Francisco Hernández de Córdoba founded the city in 1524 for its gold, and though the Spanish soon exhausted the region's supply, Granada continued to prosper as a trading center, thanks to its central location. Granada soon emerged as the country's politically and socially conservative stronghold, rival to liberal León. Then, in 1855, American adventurer William Walker traveled up the Río San Juan and captured the city. After a 51-day rule, he was forced out and upon retreat ordered his officers to burn the city to the ground, leaving a sign reading "Here was Granada."

Fortunately, most of the city survived, and today Granada is hands-down the most touristed city in Nicaragua. Worlds away from the chaos and grime of neighboring Managua, Granada is a peaceful city of astonishing beauty. Palm trees shade wide boulevards of colorful colonial houses, ribboned horse-drawn taxis rattle by, and vendors hawk random wares in the *parque central.* Located on the north shore of Lake Nicaragua, Granada is a good place to begin a journey to Ometepe or beyond; though if you decide to stay you won't be disappointed.

▐ TRANSPORTATION

Buses: Buses (☎552 4069) to and from Managua use a terminal 700m west of the *parque,* near the old hospital, while most others leave from 1 block south of the market and the *parque.* Buses to: **Managua** (1½hr., ever 20min. 4am-7pm, 14C); **Masaya** (30min., ever 20min. 5am-6:15pm, 6C); **Rivas** via **Nandaime** (1½hr., every hr.

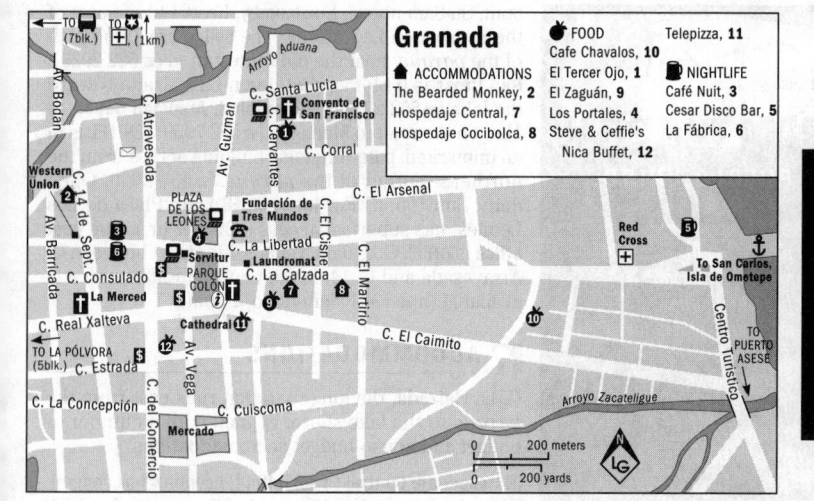

Granada

♦ FOOD
Cafe Chavalos, **10**

Telepizza, **11**

▲ ACCOMMODATIONS
The Bearded Monkey, **2**
Hospedaje Central, **7**
Hospedaje Cocibolca, **8**

El Tercer Ojo, **1**
El Zaguán, **9**
Los Portales, **4**
Steve & Ceffie's
Nica Buffet, **12**

▮ NIGHTLIFE
Café Nuit, **3**
Cesar Disco Bar, **5**
La Fábrica, **6**

5:05am-3:10pm, 15C). Fast **minibuses** to **Managua** depart from a lot just south of the southwest corner of the *parque*, near Banco Central (1hr.; M-Sa 5:45am-8pm, Su 5:45am-7pm; 14C).

Ferries: Boats (☎522 8764) leave from the dock at the foot of **La Calzada**, 1km from the center. To: **Morillo** (9hr., 30C 2nd class, 60C 1st class); **San Carlos** (15½hr.; M, Th 3pm; 50C, 1st class 100C) via **Ometepe** (4hr.; 20C, 1st class 50C); and **San Miguelito** (13½hr.; 40C, 1st class 80C). Be at the dock by 2pm to buy tickets. First class cabins, complete with A/C, are worth the extra expense in order to avoid the sweltering seat wedged between sacks of green peppers you'll inevitably find in 2nd class. There is a small *cafetín* on board that serves plates of *típico* for about 20C.

🔳🈂 ORIENTATION AND PRACTICAL INFORMATION

The centerpiece of Granada is the spacious and verdant *parque central*, or Parque Colón. To find the *parque*, look for the looming white dome of the cathedral on its eastern edge. Granada's main north-south street, C. Atravesada, runs 1 block west of the *parque central*. C. La Calzada, the main east-west street of mostly *hospedajes*, heads toward the lake off the *parque*'s eastern side. Volcán Mombacho is south of town and to the west of Lago de Nicaragua.

When the staff decides to come in, **Oficina de Delegación del Turismo (INTUR),** on the southeast corner of the *parque*, has info about cultural events. (☎/fax 552 6858. Open M-F 8am-noon and 2-5pm, Sa 8am-noon.) For guided tours, **Servitur** (☎/fax 552 2955), on the northwest corner of the *parque* next to Hotel Alhambra, leads visits to: *Isletas* (160C-240C per person); Volcán Mombacho (872C per 2 people); or the main sights of Granada (400C per hr.). English spoken (open M-F 8am-noon and 2-5pm, Sa 8am-noon). For a view of the city from horseback, take a tour with **Coches de Caballo** (30min., 70C). There are numerous banks around town. **Banco de América Central,** at the *parque*'s southwest corner, changes traveler's checks (open M-Sa 8am-5pm); **Bancamerica,** in the yellow building across from the Gon-Per bookstore, has an **ATM** (open M-F 8am-5pm, Sa 8am-noon). The **Western Union** is 2 blocks west and ½ block north of the *parque*. (☎552 2654. Open M-F 8am-1pm and 2-5pm, Sa 8am-1pm.) **Supermercado Lacayo** is 2 blocks west on C. Real (open M-Sa 8am-

It was July 19th, 2004, and I was standing in the Plaza de la República in Managua, listening to thousands of red-and-black-clad people shouting pro-Sandinista slogans. The rally was held in honor of the 25th anniversary of the FSLN revolution, during which leftist rebels overthrew the right-wing dictatorship of Anastasio Somoza. For the occasion, towns across Nicaragua had decorated local buses with red and black flags and turned them into "revolutionary vehicles," free transport for anyone who wanted to go.

. Some friends and I took the bus from Granada. I was nervous, not knowing what to expect from a socialist rally in Nicaragua and anticipating something angry, perhaps violent. The "revolutionary vehicle" occupants were mostly young men, faces painted with the letters FSLN and red and black bandanas in their hair; many of them rode on top of the bus in the luggage racks. It was a merry atmosphere, with frequent stops as more buses joined the parade. The passengers sang,

8pm, Su 8am-noon). For **laundry,** head 1 block east of the *parque* on La Calzada. The **police** are 1km north of the *parque,* near the old train station (☎522 2929). **Red Cross** is 6 blocks east down La Calzada toward the lake (☎552 2711). The **hospital, Armistad Sapon,** is 1km on the road to Managua (☎552 7050). **ENITEL** is in an unmarked, pale-turquoise building across from the northeast corner of the *parque.* (☎552 2090. Open daily 7am-10pm.) For **Internet, HDL,** on Plaza de Los Leones, has superfast access (30C per hr.). The **post office** is off C. Corral on a small side street between C. Atravesada and C. 14 de Septiembre; EMS service is available (open M-F 8am-noon, 1-5pm).

■ ACCOMMODATIONS

C. La Calzada, the long road that runs east from the *parque* to the lake shore, is lined with a number of budget and not-so-budget accommodations.

■ **Hospedaje Central** (☎522 4044; hcentral@tmx.com.ni), on La Calzada 1½ blocks east of the *parque.* This labyrinthine, mural-covered hostel has the cheapest dorm beds and beers in town, as well as a variety of rooms that attract a diverse mix of travelers. Good restaurant open 7am-11pm. Laundry 65C, Internet 20C per hr. Free coffee and tea and movies. Dorms 40C; singles with shared bath 80C; doubles with private bath 190C; triples with kitchenette 270C. ❶

The Bearded Monkey (☎552 4028; www.thebearded-monkey.com), on Bamba del Mono, 2 blocks west and 2 blocks north of the *parque.* Party-atmosphere hostel with every amenity a backpacker could dream of (bar, Internet, movies, restaurant, and TV). Bills run on the "tab" system; keep track of your expenses as you go to avoid any nasty surprises. The owner runs a nice day-trip to his "Monkey Hut" property on Laguna de Apoyo. Don't expect to sleep before the bar closes at 11pm. Dorms 50C; singles 135C; doubles 142C; triples 200C; suite 255C. ❷

Hospedaje Cocibolca (☎552 1237), 3 blocks from the cathedral toward the lake: a homey living room with Internet, TV, kitchen, and rooms with bath. Helpful owner ensures comfy stay. Breakfast 35C. Singles 185C; doubles 222C; triples 285C. ❸

◗ FOOD

Comedores abound at the corner of the market (3 blocks south of the *parque*); a few are 1 block west of the southwest corner of the *parque* in a courtyard with a fountain. Granada boasts some of the most diverse eating options in Nicaragua, so take advantage and eat up while in town.

▨ **Cafe Chavalos** (cafechavalos@yahoo.com), a block down from Hotel Granada on the left. The brainchild of an American expatriate, Chavalos takes street boys and turns them into restaurateurs. Under the tutelage of a professional chef from Mexico, the boys run every aspect of the cafe, from waiting tables, to cooking, to doing the books, while attending school during the day. International prix-fixe menu (100C) changes nightly, and includes soup, salad, entree, dessert, and coffee, all served with a gourmet touch. Founder Donna Tabor is a good source of volunteer info. Open Tu-F 6:30-whenever. ❸

▨ **El Zaguán,** behind the cathedral. What could only be described as Nouvelle Nicaraguan cuisine served in an elegant interior courtyard. Charbroiled top sirloin (120C) and fresh pasta with fish (75C). Onion soup (30C), delicious honey-soaked coconut flan (15C). Open daily 11:30am-3pm and 6-11pm. ❷

Los Portales, Plaza de Los Leones northeast of the *parque,* across from ENITEL. View of the *parque* and cathedral. Good for a quiet dinner while people-watching. Meals mostly Mexican (30C-90C); try the salsa-covered chicken (90C). Open daily 7am-10pm. ❸

El Tercer Ojo, Across from the Convento de San Francisco. Spanish-influenced "fusion cuisine" with plenty of good vegetarian options. Tapas 30C-65C, crepes ranging from classic lemon-sugar (45C) to poached salmon (75C). Open Tu-Th 10am-11pm, F and Sa 10am-midnight. ❷

Telepizza, ½ block east of the cathedral on C. El Caimito. Advertises as "The Best Pizza in Granada," and actually is pretty tasty. Small slices 5C, large 10C. Enormous calzones with as many filling as you want (30C) are particularly popular with the hoards of hungry backpackers who keep the place packed morning to night. Open daily 7am-10pm. ❷

Steve and Ceffie's Nica Buffet, 1 block south and 1 block west of the southwest corner of the *parque.* Serves American-style breakfasts (bagel and cream cheese 25C; pancakes and juice 35C-40C; omelette and coffee 35C-45C). Open M-Sa 6:30-11am. ❷

⚙ SIGHTS

LA CASA DE LOS LEONES. This beautiful colonial house with two lions on its facade was spared when the city burned in 1857. It presently houses the **Fundación de Tres Mundos,** which offers art exhibits, performances, and classes. Pick up a weekly program of events at the office. Some weekends, more large-scale cultural events take place on the walkway out front. *(East from the southeast corner of the parque. Fundación ☎ 522 4176. Open daily 6am-6pm. Free.)*

smoked cigarettes, drank guaro (moonshine rum), jumped off the bus to pee in the bushes, or grab mangos from the trees.

After three and a half hours, the bus parade wound its way into downtown Managua, and we spilled into the streets, joining the streams of people walking towards the old city center. In the arena-sized Plaza across the street, a podium with speakers had been set up, and crowds were dancing to pro-FSLN tunes. The Sandinistas have not been in power since 1990, when free elections were allowed and they were voted out, but their presence is still strongly felt, especially on the local level. Current president Enrique Bolaños says that the FSLN has nothing to celebrate, as they "did much damage to the country." But the thousands of celebrants in the Plaza, dancing, eating fried chicken, forming human pyramids, would disagree.

The party went on till after dark. The president of Venezuela spoke, then Catholic Church officials pardoned the FSLN, which Daniel Ortega, former party leader, accepted. Everyone was stuffed with greasy street food and high on Flor de Caña as we climbed into the buses for the long ride back.

Politics aside, the fact that the people of Nicaragua are now able to spend the day drinking and dancing, after so many years of war are repression, strikes me as the best indication of freedom.

-Emily Matchar

NICARAGUA

CONVENT OF SAN FRANCISCO. Next door to the shockingly bright-blue facade of the **Iglesia de San Francisco**, which is the first church founded by Córdoba and one of the oldest in the Americas, the yellow Convent holds a museum with great displays on indigenous life and a collection of well-preserved statues of humans and their animal alter egos. Also exhibited are early religious images, a photo history of Granada, and excellent "primitive" art. *(1 block north and 2 blocks east of the* parque. ☎ *522 4237. Open daily 9am-6pm. 30C includes guided tour.)*

LA PÓLVORA. This white fortress, built in 1749 and later used by Somoza forces as a military base and a prison, has been partially restored and affords impressive city views. *(8 blocks west of the* parque. *Free.)*

THE LAKE. Head down the wide La Calzada for about 1km to reach the town pier on the lake. A block west of the pier is a tourist plaza, the *complejo turístico*, lined with restaurants and discos. About 30min. south of the pier lies **Puerto Asese**, for a *lancha* to see **Las Isletas**, lake islands teeming with birds. *(Lanchas hold up to 10 people, 243C per hr. Hire a cab to Puerto Asese, 10C. Horse-drawn carriage, 50C.)*

■ NIGHTLIFE

The bar at the **Bearded Monkey** (see **Accommodations,** above) bustles with a tourist crowd every evening until around 11pm. Happy hour 4-7pm.

La Fábrica, 1½ blocks west of the northwestern corner of the *parque,* has a large outdoor patio, where a young crowd and older regulars blast North American rock or listen to live bands. Th features a wildly popular ladies night, with shockingly-colored cocktails *gratis* for the girlies. Open Su, Tu-Sa 6:30pm-2am.

Café Nuit, across from La Fábrica physically and the ambience is likewise of an opposite style. An elegant affair, with candlelit tables, Spanish music, and crowds of *salsa*-dancing locals. F and Sa cover 30C. Open Su, Tu-Sa 7pm-2am.

Cesar Disco Bar, on the lakeshore—take a left at the docks and walk a few blocks. A local hangout with a large dance floor, always open late. Always take a taxi after dark (10C). Su, Tu-Sa 8pm-4am. F and Sa cover 30C.

■ ENTERTAINMENT AND FESTIVALS

Each Friday night (6pm-midnight) near La Casa de Los Leones is **Noche de Serenada de Granada.** Local restaurants set up stands and sell traditional food and beer, while wandering musical trios serenade diners. Granada also hosts an annual **Folklore and Food Fair** (the third weekend in March) and celebrates its patron saint, la Virgen de la Asunción, on August 15. They also have a **running of the bulls** the second week of August. During the first nine days of December, Granada celebrates **Concepción,** the patron saint of Nicaragua.

MASAYA

Any Nicaraguan souvenir you're seeking can be found in one of hundreds of crowded stalls within the two overflowing markets in Masaya (pop.119,900). With more than 65% of Nicaragua's handicrafts collected here, making decisions will be a challenge and your bargaining prowess will be put to the test. T-shirts, festive blouses, polished woodwork, ceramics, leather, and the famous Nicaraguan handwoven hammocks are some of the goodies awaiting in Masaya's markets.

Outside the market's bustle and a few popular festivals, Masaya is a simple town, with long *siestas* when the streets empty and parks full of loungers. Given its proximity to **Granada** and **Managua**, Masaya can be a perfect daytrip from either. Even if you don't plan to scale the nearby **Volcán Masaya, Malecón** on the western edge of town provides a beautiful, relaxing view.

⊟ TRANSPORTATION. Departure times will definitely vary, despite what the schedule says. The prices listed here are for school buses; faster **minibuses** called *luaus* double the price. **Buses** leave from east of the Mercado Nuevo to: **Managua** (indirect 1hr., 7C; direct 40min., every 15min. 3:30am-8pm; 8C); **Granada** (40min., every 20min. 4:40am-6pm, 6C); **Carazo** (1¼hr., every 20min., 12C) via **Catarina** (20min., 6C); **Laguna de Apoyo** (40min.; 3 per day 5:30, 10:30am, 3:30pm; 8C); **Niquinohomo** (25min., every 20 min. 6am-6:45pm, 12C); and **San Marcos** (45min., every 20min. 5am-6:30pm, 7C).

⊞⊞ ORIENTATION AND PRACTICAL INFORMATION. All of Masaya's main thoroughfares run into the geographic and directional center of town, the **Parque 17 de Octubre**. The *parque's* eastern border is **Av. Sergio Delgadillo**, which runs north and south. **Buses** arrive and depart from the lot just east of the Mercado Nuevo. To get to the *parque*, exit the bus lot at the northwest corner and hang a left on C. Ernesto Fernández. Walk 6 blocks west, past the **Mercado Viejo** on your right, until you reach the *parque*. You can also catch a town bus (2.50C), a horse-drawn carriage (5C), or a cab (5C).

For **tourist info**, the **Tourist Office**, on the northern edge of the Mercado Viejo, is very helpful and has info about festivals and regional attractions. (☎552 7615. Open M-F 8am-12:30pm and 2-5pm.) The friendly proprietor of **Hotel Regis** (see below) has a wealth of knowledge on the city; he speaks slow, clear Spanish. For **banks, BanCentro,** on the west side of the *parque*, changes traveler's checks and gives cash advances on AmEx/MC/V. (☎522 4337. Open M-F 8am-4:30pm, Sa 8am-noon.) **Banco de América Central,** 1 block east of the *parque's* northeast corner, changes traveler's checks and gives cash advances on MC/V. (Open M-F 8:30am-2:30pm.) There is an **ATM** available in the *mercado viejo*. **Western Union** is inside the **Palí supermarket** (☎522 6410; open M-Sa 8am-6pm, Su 8am-noon), which is on the west side of the *parque*. (Open M-Sa 7:30am-8pm, Su 8:30am-5pm.) The **police** are half a block east of the *parque's* northeast corner, in a blue complex on the south side of the street (☎522 4222, emergency ☎118). Head to the **Red Cross,** 1 block south on the street that bisects the *parque's* southern edge, for medical attention. Look for the flag on the left corner (☎522 2131 or 522 2499). **Farmacia Masaya** is half a block east of the *parque's* southeast corner (☎522 2780. Open M-Sa 8am-6:30pm.) and **Hospital Hilario Sánchez** is a distant 9 blocks east of the *parque* (☎ 522 2778). **ENITEL,** on the west side of the *parque*, has telephone services. (☎522 2599 or 522 2499. Open daily 7am-9pm.) Phone cards and public phones available on the northeast corner of the *parque* at **Farmacia Emilia Arrieda**. (☎522 2501. Open M-F 8am-8pm, Sa 8am-7pm.) **Internet** services are available at **Servicios Computarizados,** 3½ blocks north of the *parque*, next to Hotel Regis (Open M-F 8am-8pm, Sa 8am-noon.), and at **Cyber-1,** 1½ blocks east of the *parque's* northeast corner. (☎522 3022. 15C per hr. Open M-Sa 8am-10pm, Su 9am-10pm.) The **post office** is next door; **fax** service available (open M-F 8am-noon and 1-4pm).

⊟⊡ ACCOMMODATIONS AND FOOD. Since many visit Masaya as a daytrip, the city has relatively few accommodations. **█Hotel Regis ❶**, 3½ blocks north of the *parque* on Av. Sergio Delgadillo, has friendly Francisco Castillo, a source of regional info. Shared baths, fan, and storage included. (☎522 2300. Huge breakfast

25C. Rooms 50C per person up to 4.) On Av. Sergio Delgadillo, **Hotel Maderas Inn** ❷, 4½ blocks north of the *parque*, boasts an enterprising management that speaks English and is happy to provide info (and a free ride) to tourist sites in the surrounding area. (☎522 5825. Breakfast 25C. Laundry 30C for up to 12 pieces. Checkout 11am. Communal baths. Single 90C; double 160C. AmEx/MC/V.)

Masaya has an abundance of street vendors; most restaurants cluster in the first few blocks north of the *parque*. **Restaurante Che-Gris** ❸, 3 blocks north of the *parque* on Av. Sergio Degadillo, then half a block east, has an outside patio and well-done cuisine. The waitstaff is attentive. (Che-Gris chicken 85C. Open daily 10am-10pm. AmEx/MC/V.) If you're longing for American food during your stay, popular **Pizza Hot,** 3 blocks north of the *parque* on Av. Sergio Degadillo, has spaghetti, fried chicken, and of course, pizza. (Open Su-M, W-Sa 11am-11pm. 30C-95C for a large pie.) For giant smoothies (15C) and lots of veggie-friendly salads (15C-35C), head to **Fruta Smoothie** ❷, near Pizza Hot (open daily 9am-7pm).

🎊 **FESTIVALS.** With the right timing, you can see some of Masaya's worthwhile cultural events; pick up a schedule at the tourist office or ask around. Nicaraguans flood in from Managua (p. 529) and Granada (p. 6) for these events, and the city really comes alive. Every Thursday night, Masayans young and old turn out for the fiesta **Verbena,** held in the Mercado Viejo. Local musicians play lively Latin music while masked dancers court one another on the stage. Food stands sell exotic delicacies and local favorites. Every Sunday from late September through November, Masaya commemorates **San Jerónimo,** its patron saint, with festivals, parades, and street dances. The third Sunday of September and the last Sunday of October are marked by **bull runs** and on the last Friday of October, locals disguised in handmade papier maché masks parade around town in the **Procesión de Ajüezote.** In the **Bailes de Negras** on the fourth Sunday of November, only men can perform dances, meaning that half the performers are dressed in drag and wear wigs. (Food begins at 5pm, traditional dancers and musicians 7-9:30pm, disco 9-11pm. Entrance 3C.)

🔲 **SIGHTS.** The main place to browse for Masaya's renowned arts and crafts—especially Nicaragua's famed hammocks—is **Mercado Nuevo,** at the east end of town, 6 blocks east of the *parque* on C. Ernesto Fernández (open M-Sa 5am-4pm, Su 5am-noon). The hammocks are complemented by shoes, bicycles, fruit, and even haircuts. Though the market is potentially intimidating at first, signs outside will direct you; wander around a bit to begin, as much of the merchandise is similar but quality varies. Don't accept the first price offered—bargaining is expected. The tourism department has poured untold funds into restoring the castle-like edifice of **Mercado Viejo,** 1 block east of the *parque,* which resembles more an open-air mall than a *mercado.* (Open daily 9am-6pm. AmEx/MC/V accepted by most.) Artisans who display their wares here are carefully chosen and so quality is unbeatable. The atmosphere here is easier on the nerves than the chaos of Mercado Nuevo, but you pay for sophistication and bargaining isn't taken well. Hammock prices range from 90C for a chair to over 700C for elaborate, wood-barred hammocks. Local children are glad to translate and help for a small tip.

Parque Nacional Volcán Masaya, Nicaragua's first national park (declared in 1979), boasts a pair of spectacular twin volcanoes, **Volcán Masaya** and **Volcán Nindirí,** along with five craters. The parque offers bedazzling views of the Lago de Managua. The 16th-century Spaniards thought the volcano was the mouth of Hell and put a cross there to keep the devil in his place. The entrance to the park is 7km northwest of Masaya on the highway to Managua; any of the frequent buses between the two will drop you off. Two kilometers past the entrance are an impressive museum and a visitor center. There's no public transportation, but catching a ride with one of the passing tourists is easy, especially on weekends, though *Let's Go* doesn't recommend this tactic. Also, park rangers often give rides to visitors who arrive just before the park opens at 9am. Taxis from Masaya will take you to the top of the volcano and back for 80C-100C, plus the entrance fee for you and your driver. Walking up and back to the highway is 3-5hr. (Ranger station ☎ 522 5415. Open daily 9am-4:45pm. Foreigners 50C, children under 4 free. Guides 5C per person.)

From the museum (1.5km past the entrance), it's 5km along a shadeless paved road to the rim of the Santiago crater. Once at the top, the best view of the crater is from the replica of the Cruz de Bobadilla (the cross placed by those devil-fearing Spanish). A 40min. hike around the Volcán Masaya to the left leads to a mirador with a marvelous vista including Volcán Mombacho, La Laguna de Masaya, and El Lago de Nicaragua. Check with rangers before entering, as some of the paths are closed for maintenance. The Coyote Trail and Bat Cave and Tzinaconostoc Cave, and the path to El Comalito (a small volcanic cone emitting vapors) are open to visitors with a guide arranged at the visitor center

A protected lagoon with a view of Volcán Mombacho and teeming in tropical birds and howler monkeys, **Laguna de Apoyo** is the largest crater lagoon in Nicaragua. The turn-off for Laguna de Apoyo is just south of Masaya at Km 37.5 on the highway to Granada (it is the first triangle as you exit Masaya to the south). It is a hair-raising 2km descent through thick jungle to a small triangle symbol in the road on the north edge of the Laguna. Turning left at the triangle symbol, the main restaurant and public beach area are 2km away.To spend the night, check out the ⬛**Proyecto Ecológico Escuela de Español ❷**. Clean rooms, hot water, a large open house, and a garden are supplemented by bike rentals (80C-160C) and scuba gear (masks 80C). Breakfast is included. (☎ 882 3992; econic@guegue.com.ni. 200C per night. AmEx/MC/V.) **The Monkey Hut,** with the same owner as the Bearded Monkey in Granada, offers a lovely wooden house located lakeside with comfortable rooms, kitchen, and modern toilets. (Rooms 143C per person. Non-overnight guests can use the facilities 63C per day.)

At the breathtaking **Malecón,** a 10min. walk west from the *parque* next to the baseball fields, the city ends and the land drops off a ledge into the Laguna de Masaya, with Volcán Masaya in the background. The view is spectacular. Catch a baseball game along the way, as there is almost always at least one in progress. The ancient **Fortaleza Coyotepe** outside Masaya requires a 1.5km climb up a steep asphalt road, but it's worth it: the view is great, and you can explore the spooky, labyrinthine depths of this former military prison fort.

🄲 BEACHES NEAR MASAYA

The beaches of **La Boquita, Casares,** and **Huehuete** offer three very different atmospheres. They are relatively easy to get to and bus schedules are compatible with day trips. Take any bus to Diriamba; from Masaya and Granada you'll go via Catarina. Once in Diriamba, buses and minibuses leave to Casares via La Boquita and occasionally continue on to Huehuete. (From Diriamba to Casares: 30min.-1hr., every 20min., 6-9C. From Diriamba to Huehuete: 50min.-1½hr., 10am and 4pm. Minibus 7:40am and 1:40pm, 9-12C.)

LA BOQUITA. The farthest north and first stop on the bus route, this beach is the most touristy of the bunch. It is run by the national tourist board INTUR and is relatively well maintained. When it rains, the ocean near the beach takes a dark brown color from all the run-off. Public bathrooms cost 2C. Expect to pay double high season prices if you go during *semana santa*. **Hotel Puertas del Cielo ❶** has small, well maintained rooms. (☎ 552 8717. Mid-May to Nov. 1-3 people, 150C; Dec-mid-May 200C; AmEx/MC/V.) **Hotel and Club Las Palmas del Mar ❺** is more expensive, but compensated by amenities such as a big screen TV, pool, private baths, and A/C. (☎ 522 8715 or 522 8716; palmasdelmar.com.ni. Mid-May-Nov. 600C per night; Dec.-Apr. 400C-550C.) A number of similar restaurants line the edge of the beach. In the low season, most give a group rate. (*Comida corriente* 30C; beef or chicken 60C-70C; seafood 100C-150C; AmEx/MC/V.)

CASARES AND HUEHUETE. Casares is a small fishing village just south of La Boquita, with a fish market just off the beach. (Open 8am-noon.) North of the fishing boats, the beach gets considerably cleaner. **Huehuete** is the farthest south of the three beaches and least frequented, 7km past Casares. Mid-way between Huehuete and Casares lies ◪**Costa del Mar Hotel/Restaurant ❷**. Attractive grounds, clean rooms with private baths, and a laid back atmosphere on the beach are ideal. Surfboard rentals are available—ask in advance. (Breakfast 25C, lunch and dinner 50C. ☎ 278 3235 or 522 2003; hoteleco@interlink.com. May-Sept. doubles or 2 bunk beds 200C, Nov.-May 400C). **Restaurante Don Sergio Cruz ❷** is the only place to eat in town. (*Carne asado* 30C, fish 40C, lobster 120-150C.)

RIVAS

Rivas (pop. 25,500) is known as "the city of mangos." It's also recognized as the infamous launching point of William Walker and his troops in the early 19th century, lending it the same historical and cultural aura as Granada, with fewer tourists. Rivas was once a stop along the fortune-seeking route during the California gold rush; today, with its culture and proximity to Costa Rica, San Juan del Sur, and Lago de Nicaragua, the town is convenient for a quick stop and look-around.

Buses to Rivas drop off passengers in the market at the north end of town. Buses continuing on to Managua or the border drop off near the Shell station on the highway, 7 blocks east of the market. Buses head to the border at **Granada** (1¾hr., every 1¼hr. 6:15am-4:25pm, 15C); **Managua** (2hr., every 25min. 3:30am-6:15pm, 22C); **San Juan del Sur** (45min., every 45min. 6am-5:40pm, 10C); and **Sapoá** (45min., every 30min. 5am-4:30pm, 12C). To get to **Isla de Ometepe,** take a bus to **San Jorge** (30min., every 30min. 6:30am-6:30pm, 4C) and then a *lancha* (1hr., 6 per day, 9:30am- 4:30pm, 15C) or **ferry,** with *cafeterías* and a smoother ride (1hr.; 10:30am, 2:30, 5:30pm; 20C). Either buy your ticket at the port office or pay on the boat. Around Rivas, **horse cart rides** are 20C, **tricycle** rentals 5C, and **taxis** 50C. **Colectivo Taxis** to **San Juan del Sur** or to **San Jorge,** 15C.

If you arrive in the market, cardinal directions can be a bit flustering. Go straight ahead to the exit (in the direction of the yellow Western Union sign), from which right is south and straight is east. **Parque Arriba,** (the *parque central*) is 3 blocks south and 3 blocks east of that point. **Iglesia San Francisco** is on the east side of the *parque.* If you get off at the Shell station on the highway, south is toward the Texaco gas station and east is toward San Jorge, 5km away. The **tourist office** is 2 blocks south and 4½ blocks east of the market. (☎ 453 4914. Open M-F 8am-noon and 2-5pm.) The **MARENA** headquarters, on the west side of Colegio Berto Méndez, is a good source of ecotourism info. (☎ 453 4264; delrivas@ibw.com.ni.) Head to **BanCentro,** 300m west of ENITEL on the southwest side of the *parque,* to change traveler's checks or US dollars, or for the 24hr. **ATM** (open M-F 8am-6pm, Sa 8am-noon). To buy or sell Costa Rican colones, go to *coyotes* who hang around the market. Follow signs to **Western Union,** 1½ blocks south of the market in the mini Arco Iris mall (open M-F 8am-5pm, Sa 8am-noon). The **police station** (emergency ☎ 118) is 3½ blocks south of the market. Other services: **Red Cross,** 2 blocks south and 5 blocks east of the bus stop (☎ 453 3415. 24hr. emergency); **Farmacia Auxiliadora,** in the market (open daily 7am-5:30pm) and **ENITEL,** on the *parque*'s west corner. (☎453 3499. Open M-F 8am-8pm, Sa 8am-7pm, Su 8am-6pm.) **Internet** at **Internet Princess Diana** by the ice-cream store northeast of the *parque* (☎453 3345; 15C per hr. Open M-F 8am-9pm, Sa-Su 8am-5pm); the **post office** is half a block west of Humberto Méndez gym (open M-F 8am-noon and 1-5pm, Sa 8am-1pm).

Hospedaje Primavera ❶, on the south side of the Shell gas station on the highway, is clean and spacious. The low price indicates the long walk out here. (☎453 3982. Singles 40C, with private bath 50C; matrimonial 70C/80C. Breakfast 15C-20C.) Similarly distant, **Hospedaje Internacional ❶**, on the highway 1½ blocks south of the Shell station, provides a homey ambience. (☎453 3652. *Típico* meals 20C-30C. Singles 50C; doubles 80C; triples 120C.) For chicken, beef, or pork any style, head to **Pollo Dorado ❷**, half a block west of the northwest of the *parque*. (Half roast chicken 40C. Open daily 10am-10pm.) **Restaurante Chop Suey ❷**, on the *parque*'s southwest side, serves chop suey, beefsteak, and seafood, each 60C (open daily 10am-9pm). **Pizza Hot ❷**, on the north side of the San Francisco church in the main plaza, serves reliable pizza. (Single slice 35C; medium pizza 65C; family size 95C. Open Tu-Su 10am-midnight.) **Soda Rayuela ❶**, north of the national police, and **Antojitos Rayuela ❶**, next to the Pellas house, serve fast food (10C-25C.)

The imposing **Iglesia San Francisco** is on the east side of the *parque*. Rivas's history is on display at the **Museo de Antropología e Historia de Rivas,** 2 blocks west of the market, complete with ceramics and mounted animal heads. (Open M-F 8am-noon and 2-5pm, Sa 8am-noon. 15C.) **Nicarao Canopy Tour** offers a beautiful 2hr. flight crossing creeks and forest 20m above ground on seven safe steel cables. (☎886 7548; www.nicaraolake.com.ni. 400C.)

SAN JUAN DEL SUR

In the days of the gold rush before the Panama Canal, Nicaragua was the quickest route between the Atlantic and Pacific. Money-hungry prospectors would sail from the eastern US coast, proceed up the Río San Juan, and disembark at Granada to San Juan del Sur (pop. 6700) for the northbound ride. No longer only a transportation hub, most of the year this port and fishing town is packed with local tourists, backpackers, and surfers (apparently 161 residents are *gringos*). In May 2002, it hosted Nicaragua's first international surf competition on Playa Madera.

⊏ TRANSPORTATION. Buses leave from the *mercado* 2 blocks east of the beach. Coming to town from the Costa Rican border at Peñas Blancas, take the Rivas bus via **La Vírgen** (30min., 6C), and catch an inbound San Juan bus from there. Buses head to **Rivas** (45min., every hr. 5am-5pm, 10C); **Managua** (3hr., every hr. 5am-8pm, 25C; express 2hr.; 5, 5:45, 7:15am, 3:30pm; 40C); and the **northern beaches** (40min.; 9, 11am, 1pm) and the **southern beaches** (1½hr.; 1, 4, 5pm). **Taxi** *colectivos* to **Rivas** cost 15C per person (20 min). A **water taxi** leaves from the town's main intersection, across from Hotel Estrella, and goes to **Majagual** and **Madera** (30min., 50C). **Transporte Jorge**, in the first house on the dirt road, left of Texaco on the town's northwest, runs **express car** and **minibus** rides. (☎450 2116; baloy28@hotmail.com. To Madera and other destinations 200C, **La Flor** 300C; 5 person maximum.)

▆▐ ORIENTATION AND PRACTICAL INFORMATION. Entering San Juan del Sur, the school, Indian stone, and Finca Holman are to your right (north). Continue on this road to the beaches of **Marsella** (5km), **Madera** (12km), and **Majagual** (14km). The road to the left (south) coming in from Rivas after the bridge leads to the southern beaches: **Remanso** (6km); **Tamarindo, Hermosa, Yankee** (12km); **Coco** (18km); **Braselito** (24km); and **Refugio de Vida Silvestre La Flor.** The town's "main intersection" is where the main street hits the beach.

For **tourist info,** check out the town's website (www.sanjuandelsur.org.ni). Info is also available at **Ricardo's Bar,** 3 blocks north of the main intersection (☎458 2502), and **Marie's Bar,** 1 long block north of the main intersection (☎458 2555). There are no banks; few places accept traveler's checks, so change money in Rivas. The **police** are 4 blocks south of the main intersection (☎458 2382). For **medical attention, Servicios Médicos** is 2½ blocks east of Marie's in the Clínica Farmacia Comunal. There are private **doctors** and even a **pharmacy** (open M-Sa 7am-7pm, Su 8am-noon). **ENITEL** telephones, 2 blocks south of the main intersection, are available for collect and international calls; alternatively, use the red Sprint phone in the corner: wait for the operator to help you; no dialing is necessary. (☎458 2261. Open daily 7am-5pm.) Access **Internet** in **Hotel Costa Azul,** 1 block east of main intersection, on the left, or at **Leo's Internet,** 1 block east and half a block north of intersection (both places 30C per hr.). The **post office** is next to the ENITEL building, and offers **fax** service (open M-F 8am-5pm, Sa 8am-1pm).

⌐ ACCOMMODATIONS. Accommodations here are geared toward the beach-loving backpacking crowd. **Casa el Oro ❶,** 1 block south of General Store Sánchez, in particular is tailored toward this type of traveler. The communal kitchen is complemented by the bag deposit, book exchange, hammocks, laundry, tourist info, and transportation (80C to beach). The friendly owners speak English, French, and Spanish. (☎458 2415; www.casaeloro.com. Dorms 75C; doubles 180C, with bath 275C.) **Guest House Elizabeth ❶,** with its popular bar, is across the street from the bus stop and has basic, cozy rooms with tables, thin beds, a TV downstairs, and sunset views from the hammock on the upstairs patio. Additional amenities include bike rental (80C per day), breakfast (25C) and a photogenic pet monkey named Tuty. (☎458 2270. 60C per person.) One block north of the main intersection, **Hotel Casablanca ❺** sits in front of the sea on the *paseo marítimo.* Indulge in the A/C, cable, hot water, and pool. (☎450 2135; www.sanjuandelsur.org.ni/casablanca. Singles 640C; doubles 730C; triples 870C.) For a breezy and pleasant house, head to **Hotel Estrella ❶,** on the corner of the main intersection right on the beach. It's the oldest hotel in town. Bright and airy rooms, some with balconies and great views, justify the hotel's heavenly name. (☎458 2210. 70C per person.) **La Fogata ❶,** across from the bus station, is the cheapest dig in town and has basic rooms with fans clustered around a concrete courtyard. (50C per person.)

⌐⌐ FOOD AND NIGHTLIFE. Comedor Ixtel ❶, the *comedor* with yellow walls, inside the market, is the cheapest and best of the town's *típico* food. The breakfast is outstanding and the accompanying *café con leche* (18C) is particularly good (lunch and dinner 22C-35C). **Doña Elena ❶,** in a red Coke stand 2 blocks south of the bus station, serves great chicken and beef grilled in front of you, accompanied by thick tortillas and savory side dishes. (Meals 15C-30C. Open daily for lunch and dinner.) **Ricardo's Bar,** 3 blocks north of the main intersection, is the evening social center. Locals and tourists alike often spend all evening sitting among the license plates and stuffed fish hanging on the walls while listening to music and sipping cold beers. (Beer 17C. Open M, W-Su noon-midnight.) Head to **Otangani Beach Bar, Restaurant, and Disco ❷** to dance to the most modern music. (Cover 20C, 100C on special nights with open bar. Open F-Sa 8pm-dawn.) Two blocks north of the main intersection on the corner, **Marie's Bar ❷** has outstanding food and a friendly atmosphere. The knowledgeable staff speaks some English. Try the curry chicken (70C) and sweet crepes (38C), foods you probably haven't been able to enjoy in a while (open Tu-Sa 5:30pm-midnight).

◪ BEACHES AND WATERSPORTS. The further north you walk along the beach, the less driftwood and coconut shells you'll have to sidestep before staking your claim in the sand. **Arena Caliente**, 1½ blocks north of the bus stop, rents surfboards (100C per day; open daily 7am-5:30pm), though San Juan itself does not have good surfing—you've got to go to beaches north or south to catch the waves. **Ricardo's Bar** arranges fishing trips (6 hr., 5155C for up to 6 people, includes lunch), as do local fishermen **Clemente** (☎0458 2557; pacifico@ibw.com.ni) and **Sergio** (☎0874 0940; sergionica@hotmail.com) for comparable prices. **Fidel** runs diving trips (790C for 2 tanks; ask at Arena Caliente). **Pelican Eyes**, 4 blocks east and 1 block south of main intersection, organizes **sailing** daytrips with fishing and bbq. (☎458 2511; pelican@ibw.com.ni. 870C, children under 10, 470C.)

◪ REFUGIO DE VIDA SILVESTRE LA FLOR. The reserve contains mangroves, tropical dry forest, and a beach where up to 3000 sea turtles come to lay their eggs during an *arribada* (arrival) every quarter moon in high season (admission 60C). Two **buses** run from **San Juan del Sur** via **La Flor** (1¼hr; 1 and 4pm, return 5:30pm; 10C). You can also hire a **taxi. Casa el Oro** owners offer trips to the reserve (320C).

◪ PEÑAS BLANCAS: BORDER WITH COSTA RICA

In Nicaragua, buses leave Peñas Blancas from behind the pink hostel walls for Rivas (45min., every 30min. 7:30am-6pm, 12C). Buses from Peñas Blancas go to Costa Rica via Liberia (1½hr., 5 per day 6:30am-5pm, ¢500) and San José (5½hr. to San José, 9 per day 5am-5pm, ¢1500) and charge in colones. Costa Rican Immigration is open for regular services M-F 8am-5pm. Also open M-F 6-8am and 5-8pm, Sa 6-8am and noon-8pm, Su 6am-8pm; US$2 extra during these times. If entering Nicaragua from Costa Rica, try to arrive before 3pm and expect long lines. US dollars only, typical fee US$7, though "tipping" might be expected.

Sapoá was the crossing prior to 1999. Note that to enter Costa Rica you may be asked to show an onward ticket, which can be purchased at the **Tica Bus** counter nearby. There are **money changers** on both sides of the border (double-check what they give you), a **bank** on the Nicaraguan side exchanging US dollars, three small **hospedajes** (all 100C), and on the Costa Rican side a helpful **tourist office.** Check out the **Dirección General de Servicios Aduaneros** (DGA) for the most recent frontier policy info (☎454 0041; www.dga.gob.ni).

LAGO DE NICARAGUA

Fed by more than 40 rivers, streams, and brooks from Nicaragua and Costa Rica, Lago de Nicaragua is the largest lake in Central America and the tenth-largest freshwater body in the world. Hundreds of islands—430 to be exact—dot the lake's surface, notable as much for the water's wildlife as for the myths of the pre-Columbian petroglyphs. The lake is home to the **bullshark,** the only freshwater shark in the world. Many years ago these animals migrated up **Río San Juan** from the Caribbean Sea and slowly adapted to the freshwater environment.

Farther south, the **Archipiélago de Solentiname** is renowned for both its natural beauty and the minimalist paintings it has inspired. On the southeastern side of the lake sits **San Carlos,** where the Río San Juan begins its lazy trek toward the Caribbean. Four hours from Granada, some of Nicaragua's most treasured spots—two enormous volcanoes and the paradise of the **Isla de Ometepe**—sit in waiting.

ISLA DE OMETEPE

In **Náhuatl**, the ancient language of the Aztecs, *ome* means "two" and *tepetl* means "hills" or "volcanoes." On Ometepe, the freshwater island with the highest altitude in the world, the twin volcanoes are **Volcán Concepción** (1610m), still active with a perfect cone, and **Volcán Maderas** (1394m), extinct with an exquisite crater lake. Ometepe is one of Nicaragua's jewels, with pre-Columbian petroglyphs, friendly inhabitants, fresh fish dinners, and above all, natural beauty. With the exception of the two main towns of Moyogalpa and Altagracia, the island is glorious primary forest with upper elevations and small coastal villages and farms.

▐ TRANSPORTATION

Ometepe can be reached by **ferry** from Granada (p. 549) to **Altagracia. (☎552 4313. 4hr.; M and Th 3pm, arrive at 2pm to buy tickets; below-deck 20C, upper deck with A/C 50C.)** You can also take a **bus** to **Rivas San Jorge** (30min., every 30min., 3C.) or a **taxi** *colectivo* (10min., 15C), and then a small ferry to **Moyogalpa** (1hr. every 30min. M-Sa 9am-4:30pm, 20C). Strong winds and currents can mean delays or cancellations. Boats also leave for **San Carlos** from Altagracia (4hr.; W and F 11am; 2nd class 20C, 1st class 50C).

On the island, a bus circles **Volcán Concepción,** going between Altagracia and Moyogalpa on both the 1½hr. long (southern) and 1 hr. short (northern) routes (usually one per hr., 4:40am-5:20pm). From Altagracia there are three daily buses to **Balgüe** (4:45, 9:30am, 1:40pm) and one daily bus to **San Ramón** (10:30am). On Sundays, service is minimal. For reliable taxi service call **Marvin Arcia** (☎459 4114) or **Romel Gómez** (☎459 4112). Many hotels and individuals will rent **bikes** (105C per day) or boats (45C per hr.).

Buses head to **Altagracia** from **Moyogalpa** via the north road stopping in **El Flor** (40min., 6C) and passing by the south road stopping in **Charco Verde** (30min., 4C) and **Santo Domingo** (50min., 6C). Buses leave Altagracia to all sites on the eastern side of Ometepe: **Moyogalpa south** (1½hr., every hr. M-Sa 4:30am-5:30pm, 10C), through **Santo Domingo** (45min., 4C); **El Quino** (50min., 5C); **Charco Verde** (1hr., 8C); **Moyogalpa north** (1¼hr., M-Sa every 3¼hr., 8:30am-4:30pm, 10C), via **San Marcos** (25min., 2C); **El Flor** (40min., 4C).

▐▐ ORIENTATION AND PRACTICAL INFORMATION

A decent road circles the Concepción Volcano (northwest), while a poorer one to Balgüe in the north and Mérida in the south makes it halfway around the Madera Volcano. The island's two largest towns, **Moyogalpa** and **Altagracia,** both lie on the Concepción side. Although these towns contain several *hospedajes*, many travelers skip them for the hotels on the beaches of Santo Domingo or San Ramón.

MOYOGALPA

Despite being the second largest town on Isla de Ometepe, located on the western coast near the entry point from San Jorge, Moyogalpa remains a peaceful port town for most of the year. The quiet is broken, however, on July 23rd with the Fiesta Patronal de Santa Ana, celebrating the domestication day of bulls with eating, dancing, and revelry. Those who like to groove might be lucky enough to participate in weekend dances, *cochamambas*. Moyogalpa is an ideal base for climbing Concepción.

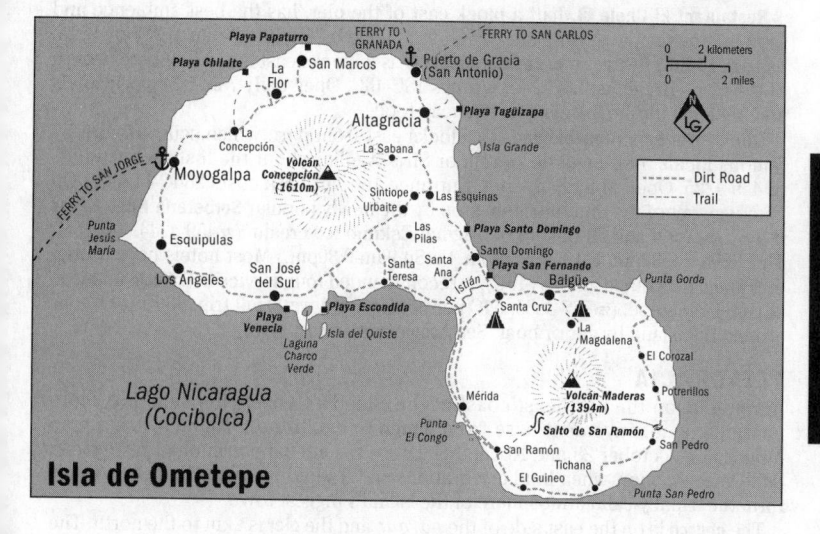

Isla de Ometepe

As you step off the dock, east is straight ahead and to your right is a large, three-dimensional fountained model of Ometepe. Back up the **central street** there are hotels and *hospedajes* for 2 blocks; a right turn leads to the newly constructed Hospedaje Central. The elegant white Catholic **church** stands at the end of the main street behind the colorful park, 5 blocks from the **bus station**. The **tourist office** (Oficina de Información Turística or CANTUR), left of the dock, is the only tour operator and office on the island; talk with the informative **Hugo Navas** (☎ 045 4218). **Comercial Hugo Navas**, 1½ blocks up main street on the left, changes dollars and traveler's checks. (☎ 459 4244. Open M-Sa 7am-7pm, Su 8am-noon.) **Hotel Ometepe** (see below) is the only other option for exchange; however, traveler's checks are exchanged at poor rates here. The **police** are 1½ blocks south and 3 blocks east of the pier. (☎ 459 4231. Open 24hr.) The **hospital**, 5 blocks east and 3 blocks south of the pier behind a fence, is available 24hr. for emergencies (☎ 459 4247), while **Doctor Pedro Bejaranom**, on the south side of the park, can also help with medical needs (☎ 459 4137; open M-Sa 4am-7pm). **ENITEL phone service** is next to the police. (☎ 459 4277. Open M-F 8am-noon and 2-5pm, Sa 8am-noon.) Access the **Internet** at **La Curaco Isla Area Comercial**, 2 blocks east from the center of the main street. (☎ 459 4137. 40C per hr. Open M-Sa 8am-7pm.) Hotelito Aly houses the **post office** (open M-F 8am-noon and 1-4:30pm).

⬛**Hospedaje Central ❶**, 2 blocks east and south of the corner, has a branch in Granada and carries the same charm, though this one is quieter and less funky. Ask Valeria Petrone about pitching tents in the backyard. (☎ 095 4262. Dorms are 30C per person, singles 70C-100C.) **Hotelito Aly ❶**, 1½ blocks uphill from the pier on the left, has 10 pleasant family-style rooms set around a shaded patio restaurant. (☎ 459 4196. Restaurant open 6am-10pm. Internet 40C per min. Rooms 50C per person, with bath and TV 80C.) **Hotel Ometepe ❺**, right ahead from the dock, is your standard hotel; nice big beds. Restaurant with breakfast, 40C and lunch, 45C-100C. (☎ 459 4276. Singles 400C; doubles 640C.) **Hotel Bahía ❶**, next to the Shell gas station 1½ blocks east. The pre-fab hotel offers a 5% discount for *Let's Go* readers. (☎ 459 4273. Restaurant 15C-50C, boat trips 60C; cheap rooms 30C, with bath 40C.)

NICARAGUA

Restaurant El Chele ❷, half a block east of the pier, has the best ambience and food in Moyogalpa. (Fish dishes 25C-50C; chicken 35C-40C. Open M-F 9am-9pm, Sa 9am-10pm.) **Restaurante Los Ranchitos ❷** is 2 blocks east and a half block south of the pier. (Breakfast 20C-25C, entrees 18C-40C. Open daily 7am-9:30pm.) Hotels and the local *pulperías* also serve cheap food.

Don't miss **Sala Arqueológica**, 3½ blocks east from port, which sells artwork by famous locals. Ask Ligia de García or Siria Aguilar about the historic artifacts. (☎459 4225. Open M-Sa 8am-5pm. Entrance 16C, artwork costs 280C-1120C.) On your way out of the mini-museum stop by the newly popular **Sorbetería Hugo Navos ❶** for fast food and 20 flavors of original Eskimo ice cream. (☎459 4244. Open M-Th 11:30am-9:30pm, F 10am-9:30pm, Sa-Su 9am-9:30pm.) Most hotels have tourist info and can arrange guides (40C). A recommended tour service is **Ecflorin Ometepe** at Hotel Ometepe. (☎777 3835. 64C per person for a waterfall trip; 400C for a tour around the island by car or boat. See **Accommodations** above.)

ALTAGRACIA

Altagracia, on the northeast coast of the island's Concepción side, is a more charming and convenient base from which to explore the island's sights than Moyogalpa. October 28 and November 18 are the annual patrimonial festivals in San Diego's honor, when loud celebrations and traditional folkloric dances transform the usually calm atmosphere of the island's biggest town.

The **church** is on the east side of the *parque* and the **pier** is 2km to the north. The best source for **tours** and guides is **Hotel Castillo**, half a block west of the *carretera* and 1 block south of the *parque*. Many of the beaches, including **Paso Real** (1km north) and **Playa Taguizapa** (2km northeast), are within walking distance.

The **Castillo brothers**—Manuel, Carlos, and Julio—are authorities on the island's petroglyphs. (Julio7464@hotmail.com. Guided tours to Maderas 50C per person, to Concepción 60C per person.) Next door to Hotel Castillo in **Tienda Fashion**, Gustavo Condega (gustavoc@tmx.com.ni) can give valuable tourism info (as well as info on the gay scene in Ometepe). The **Centro de Salud** is 1 block north of the mayor's office. (Open 8am-noon and 1-5pm for appointments. Open 24hr. for emergencies.) **Farmacia María Auxiliadora** is half a block south of the *parque*'s southeast corner. (☎552 8758. Open M-Sa 8am-8pm, Su 8am-noon.) **Farmacia Jany**, in front of the south side of the *parque*, sells medicine, repellent, etc. (open M-Sa 8am-9pm). Exchange traveler's checks in the **post office** building 1 block south of the *parque* (open M-F 8am-5pm, Sa 8am-noon). **Post office** and **telephone** services are in the **Enitel** building, next to the Alcaldía. (Open M-F 8am-5pm, Sa 8am-noon.) Two computers in Altagracia connect to the **Internet,** one in Hotel Castillo (40C per hr.) and one in Tienda Fashion (45C per hr.). The **Ometepe Museum** is located in Altagracia next to the *alcaldía* on the south side of the *parque* and west of the Centro de Salud. (☎552 8745. Open M-Sa 9am-5pm. 10C.) **Mauricio,** across the street from Hotel Central, will rent his **pickup truck** for 500C per day. Señor Carlos Guillén rents **horses** (next to the Hotel Don Kencho, 35C per hr.), as do most hotels. **Soda Paraíso,** 2 blocks north of the park, rents **mountain bikes.** (☎552 8758. 120C per day. Open M-Sa 6am-6pm.)

Hotel Castillo ❶, 1 block south of the park and half a block to the west, offers hammocks, spacious and clean rooms, and a spotless, tasty restaurant. (☎552 8744; hotcatll@hotmail.com. Meals 20-70C. Rooms 50C per person, with private bath 75C.) **Hotel and Bar Restaurante Central ❶**, 2 blocks south of the *parque*'s southeast corner, has a beautiful garden, comfortable rooms, and restaurant. (☎552 8770. Rooms 40C per person, with bath 80C; private cabins 120C.) **Hospedaje Ran Luna ❶**, 1 block east of Hotel Castillo and run by Gustavo from the Tienda Fashion in a warm, familial style (see **Orientation,** above), offers six cheap rooms

(35C) in addition to a kitchen and TV. **Hospedaje Kencho ❶**, 1 block south of the *parque*'s southeast corner, has a balcony and hammocks. (☎552 8772. Rooms 35C per person, with bath 50C.)

Buen Gusto ❷ is Hospedaje Kencho's nice outdoor restaurant, serving *comida corriente* (15C-20C); entrees (25C-50C); and *sopa de pescado* (35C), an entire *guapote* lying in a bowl of broth. Buen Gusto turns into a hot spot at night. (Restaurant open daily 6:30am-9:30pm, bar until midnight.) There are six *comedores* set around the *parque*. **Soda Bar Johanna ❸**, in front of the basketball court in the *parque*, serves reliable breakfasts and lunches (Meals 15C-38C, pizza 30C. Open M-Sa 7am-10pm.) The **kiosk** in the park is also good for a snack. (15C plate comes with *maduros*, meat, rice, and salad. Open daily 8am-10pm.)

SIGHTS AROUND THE ISLAND

To access much of the island, it is best to hire a guide—see **Practical Information** under Moyogalpa and Altagracia for suggestions. Everyone on the island is a guide for something, and prices are generally reasonable. Renting a truck is another alternative to spotty public transport, but the roads are terrible, and all cars are manual transmission.

SANTO DOMINGO. Along the isthmus between the two islands, Santo Domingo is the island's most popular and biggest beach. It's a pleasant place to relax for a day or two, and a number of hotels can help you hang out in style on the gray sand beaches. ◪**Hotel Villa Paraíso ❷**, near the south end of the beach, is the most luxurious place on the island: a gorgeous stone hotel with lush gardens and an excellent outdoor restaurant directly on the beach. (☎453 4675. Restaurant open daily 7am-9pm.) The owners will arrange for horse rental and guided tours. (Doubles or triples with bath 285C; quads 320C; *cabañas* 640C.) **Hotel Finca Santo Domingo ❷**, just next door on the right, has a volleyball net on the beach and a young crowd of vacationers. Dark rooms have portals that let in light and sea air. (☎881 6603. Restaurant open daily 7am-8:45pm. Rooms 160C per person, with bath for 2-5 people US$25.) **Hotel Istiam** (☎045 942 67), 1 km south of Playa Santo Domingo. Though a bit further away, it offers pleasant rooms surrounding a garden with fan and shared bath. An added perk: the resident monkey loves to be held (80C per person; private *cabañas* with bath and A/C, 320C). The newly constructed **Hospedaje el Bosque Tropical ❶**, across the street from Villa Paraíso, was once a disco and is now eight well-sized, sparse rooms with shared bath (50C per person).

For cheap food and good company, walk north along the main street from the Playa Santo Domingo entrance to **Comedor Carta al Mundo ❶**, where Mama Ana Julia cooks *típico*. (15C-25C. Open daily 7am-9pm.) A 30min. (1.5km) walk north of the Playa Santo Domingo will bring you to beautiful **Presa Ojo de Agua**, on the left before crossing the bridge. For 15C you can bathe in the crystalline water.

VOLCÁN MADERAS. Reaching Maderas' summit requires an early start; it's 5-8hr. of fairly steep hiking to the top and back, not including stops. The hike passes through tropical dry forest, then dense tropical rainforest, and finally cloud forest. On the way to the lagoon in the crater you'll likely cross paths with deer, howler monkeys, white-faced monkeys, and many wildflowers. Be prepared: the trails can be muddy and chilly near the summit. It is possible to continue down into the crater with a rope to assist you, though this is better attempted with a guide. Unless you're staying overnight, you'll want to be on the first bus to Balgüe. (5am from Altagracia. Climbing the volcano is 23C solo and 240C for guided groups of two or three.) Begin your climb either at Finca Magdalena on the east side or at the biological station in San Ramón on the west side. Ask the bus driver to drop you off at the entrance to Magdalena, from which a 15min. walk up the path leads to **La Finca**

Magdalena ❶, an organic coffee farm with spectacular views, selling quality cups of joe and 100% pure bee honey. Workers live off the ecologically friendly solar energy system. It is popular for tourists to stay overnight here, often in exchange for work, during November and December. The restaurant serves delicious, typical food (12C-25C), but is only open until 8pm. (Hammock 20C; dorm 25C; single 50C; double 70C; camping 30C.)

VOLCÁN CONCEPCIÓN. The taller of the two volcanoes (1610m), Concepción is said to have the most perfect conical shape of all the volcanoes in Central America. Concepción is still active and the terrain near the top consists primarily of loose rocks and sand, so it is less popular than Maderas. Low visibility, especially during the rainy season, often makes reaching the crater challenging (and pointless). The lower half of the volcano is covered with tropical dry forest. **Floreana** (about 2hr. to the top) is a good destination and offers the first clear, breathtaking *vista* from the volcano. Most hikes begin at **La Flor,** 6km northeast of Moyogalpa and reachable by bus (6:30, 10am, 1:30pm; returns every hr. 12:10-5:10pm.) Trails also start at: **La Concha,** 4km from Moyogalpa on the road to La Flor; **La Sabana,** a 1km walk from Altagracia; **Cuatro Cuadras,** 2km from Altagracia; and **San Ramón.** A guide is essential; paths on Concepción are unmarked and hard to find.

PETROGLYPHS. Most of the petroglyphs lie between **Balgüe** and **Magdalena,** on the Maderas side of the island. Another group is located near **El Porvenir,** a 30min. walk from Santo Domingo and 10min. from Santa Cruz and La Palma. Carved between the 11th and 13th centuries, these simple etchings contain spirals and circles of unknown significance—take advantage of this glimpse into the pre-Columbian world. Find them yourself by renting a bike or car and asking around (most children will be willing to show you the way for a few córdobas), or hire a guide.

SAN RAMÓN. On the south side of the Madera cascades is the **Salto de San Ramón,** a waterfall accessible from the village of San Ramón. The pleasant hike to the falls through tropical dry forest takes about 2hr., and the return about half that. There are two possible trails; the old one is to the right of the Enitel bus stop, and the renewed one, which one can be climbed by car or bike, is to the left. There is only one bus to San Ramón. (M-Sa leaves Moyogalpa 8:15am, Altagracia 10:45am. The infrequent bus schedule means you might have to stay overnight.) 🔲**Biological Station of Ometepe ❺,** 300m north of the chapel across from the only dock with coconut trees, is a luxurious place to stay and is often crowded with biologists. The stay includes three delicious buffet-style meals, kayaks, guides to Volcán Madera, and snoozing rights to a hammock on the dock. (☎/fax 453 0875. Meals 80C-95C. New dorms 80C, with A/C 115C.) About 20 min. north of San Ramón in the tiny hamlet of **Mérida** awaits brand-new **Hospedaje Hacienda Mérida ❷,** on the lake and with enough amenities to entrap any backpacker for days. The guest perks are endless: rental of high quality mountain bikes (130C) and kayaks for trips to nearby Monkey Island (80C) for the length of your stay; horse rental (40C per hr.); Internet (45C for entire visit); a restaurant with veggie options and delicious homemade oatmeal bread. They'll organize volunteer opportunities with local schools through a program called "*Si a la Vida*." (☎868 8973; www.lasuerte.org/merida. Dorms 45C; singles 95C; doubles 160C; quads 240C; camping or hammock-hanging 24C with your own gear.)

CHARCO VERDE LAGOON. On the south side of Volcán Concepción, near the town of San José close to the beach, hide the marshy pond and hidden myths of Charco Verde lagoon. According to legend, every Friday night at midnight, *Chico Largo,* a devil-like ghost of a former Rivas shaman, comes out of the lagoon to give money to those who pray to him and to take the souls of those who don't. Ask local legend José del Carmen García Aquire, who always hangs out at the lagoon (except Fridays) to tell you more. Charco Verde offers excellent **birdwatching** and occasional freshwater **turtle spotting.** A path leads around the lagoon (1hr.), passing the very private **Playa Escondida** or **Playa Balcón** with beautiful views of Isla Quiste up at the *mirador.* Entrance is free but donations are appreciated.

Look for the Charco Verde sign on the main Moyogalpa-Altagracia road (ask the bus driver to let you off at Charco Verde). Another option is to get free transportation from Moyogalpa to Charco verde by *camioneta* (bus) with Conny and Ramiro, who bring you directly to their **Posada de Chico Largo ❶.** The three private rooms in a house next door on the lake have gorgeous views and croaking Betsy bullfrogs (rooms 70C per person). Next to the Posada is charming **Playa Venecia Hotel ❷** (single or double rooms 160C). Five minutes left along the beach from the end of the signed road is **Hospedaje Charco Verde ❶,** probably the nicest hotel around, with a large outdoor restaurant (entrees 35C-50C) and picturesque *cabañas.* (Doubles 160C. Horseback rides or bike rental 30C per hr.)

PUNTA DE JESÚS MARÍA. On the west side of Volcán Concepción sits simple Punta de Jesús María, a pebble spit extending into the lake near Esquipulas town, an hour's walk (3km) from Moyogalpa. In addition to breathtaking views it sports a small bar that serves lots of rum. (Half-bottle 50C. Open Sa-Su 8am-8pm.) Swim on both sides of the point, but beware strong currents at the point itself. The most popular time to come for both locals and tourists is during Semana Santa. The *punta* is accessible via the Moyogalpa-Altagracia bus; though the turn-off on the right side of the road is unmarked, if you see the green and white sign for Esquipulas, you're too far. It's 15min. walking to the point from the road (1.5km).

ARCHIPIÉLAGO DE SOLENTINAME

The archipelago, comprised of 36 small, sparsely populated islands, and 20km northwest of San Carlos, is one of Nicaragua's best hidden treasures. The name Solentiname, in *Nahuatl,* means "site of/for many guests." But with Nicaragua's slowly increasing tourism and few local residents, the only true guests to return annually are the 10 species of migratory birds. **Padre Ernesto Cardenal** arrived in 1966 and changed Solentiname forever. Poet, sculptor and evangelical priest, he taught his first 12 farmer "disciples" the unique art of primitivist painting and balsa carving (which soon became infamous both nationally and internationally). The artisans live on the main islands of **San Fernando** (also known as **Elvis Chavarría**) and **Isla Mancarrón.** Mancarrón has the best tourist accommodations, and is a great base for an extended stay. Other islands include: **Mancarroncito** with its impressive primary forest; **El Venado** with its well-known petroglyphs and caves; **Isla del Padre,** which hosts the majority of the mammalian species of the whole archipelago; and **Isla el Zapote,** also known as "Bird Island."

Public *lanchas* **(boats)** leave San Carlos for Solentiname on Tu and F at 12:30pm, return around 4am, and stop at Mancarrón and San Fernando. (2½-3hr., 25C one way.) If you miss them, hire private transportation, although it is much more expensive (usually 50C; ask around for Silvio). Plans for public service on Th and Su are underway. **Hotel APDS** on Mancarrón can provide transportation from San Carlos. (see below. 1460C round-trip.) **Solentiname Tours,** in Managua, Km 8 Carretera Sur (☎265 2716; zerger@ibw.com.ni), runs from Granada to Solentiname, passing through Moyogalpa, Ometepe (10½ hr. F from Granada 7am) and back again (Su from Solentiname 8am). The main islands have Italian-built *senderos,* especially useful with the sporadic *lancha* schedule. The art colonies of **San Fernando** and **La Venada** are a 10min. boat ride from Mancarrón (720C round-trip). **Tours Nicaragua** (☎228 7063; www.toursnicaragua.com; nicotour@nic.gbm.net) and **Careli Tours** (☎278 2572; www.carelitours.com; info@carelitours.com) are two reliable **tour operators** that offer complete packages to Solentiname. There is only one **health center** on the Isla de Mancarrón, a grey cement house 20km to the left of the hospedaje and *pulpería* **La Lidia Castillo.** (Open M-F 8am-noon and 1:30pm-5pm.) In an emergency, hotel APDS has a cell **phone.** Wait until San Carlos to send **letters.**

On Mancarrón, **Hotel APDS ❾,** (☎283 0083; ramses@ibw.com.ni) is a good place to stay and offers daytrip packages to the museum in San Fernando (400C) and tours of **Los Guatuzos Wildlife Refuge** near Río Papachure, 4km south of Isla Zapote (800C). **Hotel Mancarrón ❺** has rooms with private baths and good meals. (☎/fax 265 2716 in Managua; 453 0294 in Solentiname. Singles 1200C; doubles 1600C.)

Museo Archipiélago de Solentiname, a five-minute walk along the path from Julio Cesar's cabinas, after the *taller*, up the stairs. Constructed in 2000 by the Italian **Asociación de Cooperación Rural en Africa y America Latina (ARCA)** and the local artisans, the Museo introduces guests to Solentiname's flora, fauna, art, history and geology in three colorful rooms. (In San Carlos ☎/fax 283 0095; www.una.edu.ni/soleiname. Open M mornings, T-Su 7am-noon and 2pm-5pm. Admission 15C.)

SAN CARLOS DE NICARAGUA

San Carlos (pop. 12,500) sits at the head of the Río San Juan on the southwestern shore of Lago de Nicaragua. There's not much in town itself; what previously was a touristed Spanish fort on the north side of the *parque* is now a few moss-covered walls. San Carlos often smells like rotten fish, with lots of bugs and seldom running water; most travelers use the town as a launching point for adventures to the artistic culture and abundant wildlife of the Archipiélago, or go down the Río to the rainforest of the Reserva Biológica Indio-Maíz and the Spanish outpost of Castillo Viejo. It's also possible to cross into Costa Rica through nearby Río Frío and Los Chiles.

La Costeña planes take off from an **airstrip** 10min. from town by **taxi** (10C) to **Managua** (M-Th and Sa 9:30am, F and Su 1pm; round-trip 1190C). The **ticket office** (☎283 0271) is 2 blocks northwest of the main ENAP port. **Buses** stop in a lot 30m northeast (right) of the main port across from the new market, about 5 blocks east of the *parque*. Buses from San Carlos leave for **Managua** (8hr., 5 per day 2am-9pm, 90C) via **Juigalpa** (5hr.; 10, 10:30, 11am, 12:40pm; 70C); and **Granada** via Managua (9½hr., Tu and F 4pm, 100C). **Boats** leave from the main ENAP dock behind the gate just west of the new market, and head to **Castillo Viejo** (via *lancha* 2¾-4hr.; M-Sa 8am, noon, 1:30, 3pm, Su 1pm; 48C); and **San Juan del Norte** (10hr.; Tu and F 6am, return Th and Su leaving San Juan 5am; 160C). Buy tickets at the pink booth (open daily 8am-4pm). Boats to the **Archipiélago de Solentiname** leave from the floating dock in front of the tourist kiosk on the *malecón* boardwalk (3hr., Tu and F 2pm, 30C) and stop at **Isla San Fernando** and **Isla Mancarrón.** Private *pangas* are available at the floating dock (1110C). Talk to Armando Ortiz (see below). Boats for **Los Chiles, Costa Rica** leave from the immigration office 30m west of the main ENAP dock (1hr.; 10:30am, 1:30, 3:30pm; 90C).

The **church** tower is on the west side of the *parque;* the fort to the north. The *malecón* is south, and the new market to the east. **Viajes Turísticos Armando Ortiz** (☎283 0039), 2 blocks south of the *parque*'s southwest corner, runs tours throughout the area. You cannot change traveler's checks, but for US dollars, try **Banco de Finanzas,** 1 block southeast of the *parque*'s east side. (☎283 0144. Open M-F 8:30am-4pm, Sa 8:30am-noon.) Three **Western Union** offices are in San Carlos; the main one is opposite Kaoma restaurant. (☎283 0250. Open daily 7am-8pm.) The main **police** station (☎283 0365) is a 15min. bus ride on the *carretera* out of town; the downtown office (☎283 0092) is in the Antiguo Telcor building. The **Red Cross** (☎283 0234) is 3½ blocks north of the *parque*'s northwest corner; a **hospital** (☎283

0362) is a block beyond. **ENITEL** is 1½ blocks north of the *parque*'s northwest corner on the *carretera* heading out of town (☎283 0001, open daily 7am-8pm); **Farmacia Fabiola** is about 200m south of ENITEL (☎283 0025; open daily 10am-9pm. 24hr. emergency medical assistance.); and the **post office**, 2 blocks south of the *parque*'s southeast corner (open M-F 8am-noon and 1-5pm, Sa 8am-1pm).

Hotel San Carlos ❶, on the *malecón*, 50m south of the immigration office, is next to Clínica San Lucas. The sweltering rooms have fans and bathrooms are tight. (☎283 0265. Singles 60C; doubles 100C.) Most other hostels in town are similarly inexpensive—for good reason. *Comedores* and *sodas* line so-called C. Comercial from the new market to the *malecón's* end, also facing the lake. Going out at night in San Carlos is not recommended, especially for solo travelers and women.

RÍO SAN JUAN

The gorgeous Río San Juan runs over 200km connecting Lake Nicaragua and other tributaries to the Caribbean Sea. It also marks the border between Nicaragua and Costa Rica and is one of the biggest ecotourism attractions in Nicaragua. Swirling, expanding, and churning from San Carlos to San Juan del Norte, the waters have washed away history and legends from since the 16th century and the San Juan counts many admirers, including the American author Mark Twain. The lucky visitor is sure to find a mini-Amazon full of untouched flora and fauna, including the *sábalo real* (giant fish) and endless tropical flora like the *lechuga*, a type of lettuce that grows on floating vegetation.Apart from the sited main attractions, there are many hidden places along the river—farms, mountains, *pueblos*, and *comarcas* like **Boca de Sábalos** and **Raudal del Toro**. Boca, **El Castillo Viejo**, and **San Juan del Norte** all make their homes along the San Juan.

BOCA DE SÁBALOS

The first stop from San Carlos or San Juan del Sur down the Río San Juan, this small, muddy town has a bit of natural charm and a splash of adventure. Build your own boat out of wood (1586C) or fiberglass (15,860C), fish with the locals (100C in wood boat; 200C in motorboat), and enjoy this new-found treasure.

Public **boats** leave San Carlos from the main dock to **Castillo Viejo**, stopping first in **Sábalos**. (1½hr.; M-Sa 8am, noon, 1, 3pm; Su 1pm; 35C). Private *lanchas* are more expensive but convenient; all leave before 4pm.

Past the pharmacy and Nintendo game room **Hotel Central ❶**, run by Lillia Martínez, has a restaurant which serves meals in the breezy shade. (Restaurant open daily 8am-midnight, 20C. Rooms 30C per person, 50C with fan; 80C for fan and matrimonial bed.) **Sabalos Lodge (La Casa de Yaro) ❸**, an ecotourism lodge of picturesque palm-thatched huts on a calm stretch of river, with great hikes right out the back door, is located about 6km past Bocas de Sábalo; just ask the *lancha* driver to let you off at Yaro's place. Yaro is a local legend and a huge source of regional info; he offers a nice tour of nearby Castillo and Refugio Bartola (160C-190C per person, depending on group size) and can arrange for private transport to and from **San Carlos** and **Solentiname**. (☎278 1405; sabaloslodge@ibw.com.ni. Horse rental 40C per hr., kayak rental 80C per day. Good restaurant has breakfast, 45C-65C, and dinners, 80C-160C. "Backpacker" rooms with shared bath 95C; double *cabañas* with bath 320C; triples 400C.) **Hotel Sábalo ❶**, on the edge of the Río San Juan and the Boca de Sábalos estuary, has clean, modern rooms with porches overlooking the river (room 60C per person with shared bath). At the entrance of Sábalos, past the fish fountain and town general store (stocked with basic necessities, complete with a phone), **Parates' Miscelanea Mi Favorita**, the **Comedor Koma Rica ❶**, serves cheap *típico*. For nightlife, you can dance every other Saturday away at disco parties in the hills of Sábalos (10C).

EL CASTILLO VIEJO

Some 60km down the Río San Juan lies the small, clean, and picturesque river town of El Castillo, home to various points of interest for foreigners and locals. In addition to projects focusing on surrounding natural wonders, the town is home to **Fortaleza de la Inmaculada Concepción,** a Spanish fort built in 1675 to prevent pirates from coming upriver and sacking Granada. Perched on a hill next to an especially shallow and dangerous stretch of river, its defensive location was well suited. In 1993 it was renovated, and now visitors are free to wander its stony walkways.

E TRANSPORTATION. The best option is to travel via public **lancha,** which leaves from the main dock across from the bus station, next to the new market in **San Carlos** (2¾hr.; M-Sa 8am, noon, 1, 3pm; Su 1pm; 48C). A private *panga* from San Carlos to El Castillo (with a stop in Bartola) is a three-day trip. (4000C, 8 person maximum.) You can also try to catch any cargo boat; they leave at various times from the main dock until 4pm. Buy your ticket at the pink office in the corner of the *fortuaria* (open M-Su 8am-4pm). Once in El Castillo, you can rent a horse for a day and ride to nearby **Costa Rica** through mountains and small *comarcas.* (Ask Danny at Hotel Richardson. 160C per person, five person maximum.) Numerous attractions are accessible by short daytrips.

■ ⁊ ORIENTATION AND PRACTICAL INFORMATION. As you get out onto the dock, a faded red-and-gray Sandinista flag greets you at the bottom of a steep stairwell leading straight up to **Hotel-Albergue El Castillo,** which dominates the primary view of the city's entrance. You can catch a glimpse of the impressive *fortaleza* to the left above the mountain, but the clearest open view of the fort is when coming downstream toward San Carlos, looking up from the rapids known as **Diablo Rapids.** One main street runs parallel to the river and uphill. The well-organized and informed **tourist office** in front of the dock offers tour packets and two English-speaking guides, Gilbert Haragón and Efraín Gonzales. (Open Tu-Sa 8am-noon and 2pm-5pm, Su 8am-11:30pm and 2pm-4pm. 4hr., 400C.) **Police** are 75m south of the Catholic church on the left. There is one **health center** (1 block from the *fortaleza* on the right) and one *pulpería,* **Variedades Ruiz,** across from El Cofalito, for **pharmacy** needs (open M-Su 6:30am-8:30pm). The **ENITEL** phone company, 50m up right from the dock, has sporadically functioning phones (☎283 0200). The only other public phone is at Hotel Albergue El Castillo (16C per minute for local calls, 95C for international calls). There is neither Internet nor an official post office.

⁊⍾ ACCOMMODATIONS, FOOD, AND NIGHTLIFE. El Castillo ❸ is by far the poshest option in town, though the fanned rooms are nothing special aside from the amazing view from their sprawling decks. Clean communal bathrooms are located downstairs; breakfast included. (☎892 0174. 400C per room.) Supposedly decorated by the famous Nicaraguan painter Ricardo Peña, clean and well-lit **Hotel Richardson ❸.** To get there turn left at the dock and then right after the Catholic church. Amenities include a bar, restaurant, and TV lounge. (Rooms 160C per person.) A cheaper option is **Hotel Aurora ❶,** right on the water 50m from the dock, with a well-positioned upper deck (40C per person).

The best and cheapest meal in town is served by ⍾**Doña Luisa Jerez ❶** in her house; turn left from the dock and follow the road to its end: the house is on the left. She rents three rooms. (Heaping *comida corriente* 15C; shrimp 75C; chicken 50C. Rooms 30C per person.) A bit more expensive but worth it, **Restaurante El Cofalito ❸** is right of the dock. (*Comida corriente* and beverage 45C; *camarones* 100C; *pescado* 70C. Open daily 7am-10pm, later Sa-Su.) For late-night food and drink, try reasonably-priced **Bar y Restaurante La Brisa del San Juan ❶,** 150m after the bridge, geared toward a local clientele (open M-Su 10am-1pm, 6pm-midnight).

◙ SIGHTS. The **Fortaleza de la Inmaculada Concepción** gives the town both its namesake and principal sight. Tours are given by Eddy in Spanish. (Open M-Su 8am-noon and 2-5pm.) One of the chambers is now a first-rate **museum** on the fort's history and the importance of the Río San Juan in European exploration (10C). For education about the Río San Juan regional environment, check out **Centro de Interpretación de la Naturaleza del Río San Juan.** Turn right after the health center and listen to Doña Teresa impart her wisdom (in Spanish) on water cycles, deforestation, and dangerous monkeys. If butterflies are more your thing, a dozen steps out the back of the Centro de Interpretación is the beautiful **Mariposario,** preserving five local species. (15C. Open M-Su 8-11am and 1-4pm.)

GÜISES DE MONTAÑA AND REFUGIO BARTOLA

Six kilometers away from El Castillo is the protected **Reserva Indio Maíz.** For nature enthusiasts, at the entrance of the **Río Bartola,** on the left side, is the **Güises de Montaña** and **Refugio Bartola,** where there are more species of trees, insects, and birds than in all of Europe. This mountain **hospedaje** functions on solar energy and is the last "civilized" spot before the 7hr. ride to **San Juan del Norte** (see below). It is an ideal spot for pure relaxation in the jungle and a huge center of interest for researchers and biologists the world over. University students come every year to study the infinite critters; fear not, layman tourist, there are guides to bring you for a cool dip or bird watch on the Río Bartola; to see the small indigenous village of **Buena Vista Comarcas ❹;** and to protect you from a chance encounter with the *chancho de montes,* wild boar. (☎ 088 213 31; www.refugiobartola.com. Rooms 320C per person. 10% discount for large groups.)

SAN JUAN DEL NORTE (NEW GREYTOWN)

 The information on San Juan del Norte, including all prices and hours, is based on research conducted in August 2002.

This town (pop. 2000) is most noteworthy for its strategic position at the mouth of the Río Indio, between the Río San Juan and the Caribbean Sea. The town has burnt down three times and Contra warfare once forced evacuation; today, the area is poor and underdeveloped, but it is a beautiful region of both coast and nature preserve. An airport and US$60 million road are currently underway in San Juan del Norte, but until they are finished the only mode of transport is *panga*. The public *lanchas* come and leave town only twice a week from **San Carlos** (9-12hr.; Tu and F 6am, return Th and Su 5am; 160C.), as well as from **El Castillo** (Tu and F 10am, return Th and Su 2pm). There are no passages to **Costa Rica.** If you find yourself stuck here at night, **Tío Poon's Place ❶,** on C. Primera across from Disco Fantasía, has rooms with shared bathrooms. (Rooms 60C.) **Bar y Restaurante los Delicias del Indio ❶,** on C. Primera, serves cheap *corriente* (20C) under a gazebo along the Río Indio. Two disco-bars entertain locals: **Discoteca Tropical,** a cabin-hut across from the Casa de Compaña on C. Central, and **Disco Fantasia,** in front of Tío Poon's on C. Primera. (Open M-Su 6pm-11:30pm. No cover.)

CENTRAL HIGHLANDS

The central highlands are a region of rugged mountains accessible by steep, curving, scenic roads. They were the political stronghold of the *Contras* during the late 1980s, and fighting continued here long after it had died out in the lowlands.

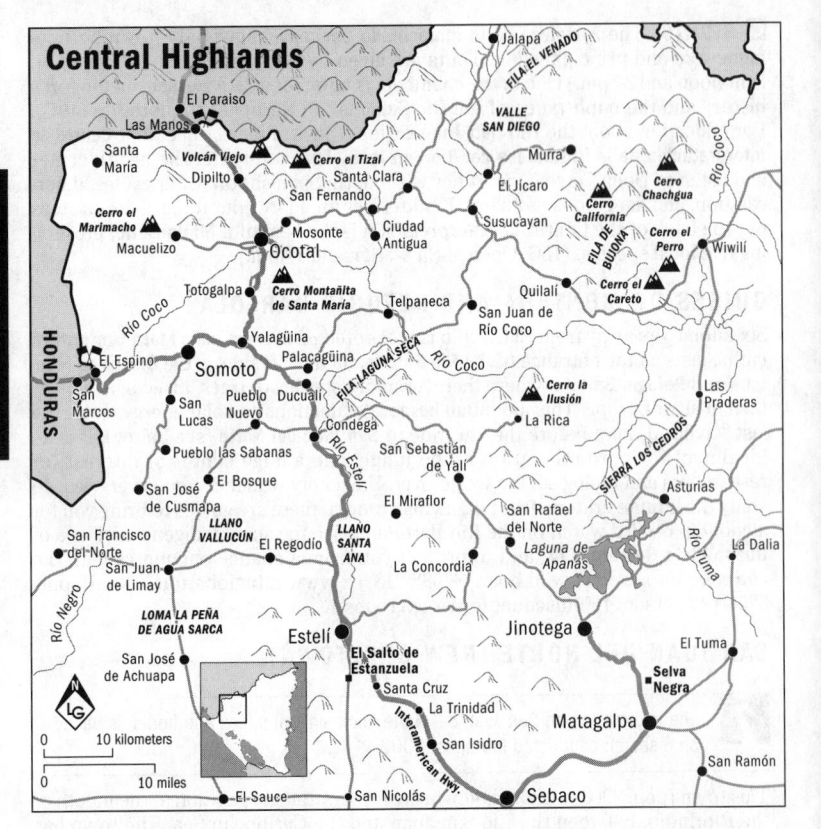

Nearly every individual over age 25 has a story to tell about the war's impact. The fiercely free-thinking highlanders have always been difficult for the government to control, with passionate viewpoints spanning the political spectrum.

Estelí, the largest city in the north, has some compelling reminders of the war and is easily visited en route from Managua to the Honduran border along the Interamerican Hwy. South of Estelí is a turnoff for the beautifully situated town of Matagalpa—gateway to Selva Negra, one of Nicaragua's most accessible forest preserves. A separate highway running east from Managua toward the Caribbean coast passes near Boaco, a mountainous cowboy town, before reaching Juigalpa, a good place to stop if you're making the trip all the way to the coast.

ESTELÍ

The amicable agricultural town of Estelí (pop. 201,000), about halfway between Managua and the Honduran border, is a welcome escape from the pounding heat of lowland cities. While it is the largest town in northern Nicaragua, its cobbled streets turn to dirt roads just a few blocks from the *avenida central,* and the verdant nearby countryside remains fairly unsettled. The colonial-style **Catedral Nuestra Señora del Rosario** towers over the surrounding cobblestone streets, providing an excellent example of the past this town is zealously trying to preserve.

Estelí is the principle tobacco center of Nicaragua, producing volumes of hand rolled cigars which rival the quality of those made in Cuba. The town also has a lively coffee industry. Many foreigners can be found in Estelí, volunteering or sharpening their Spanish skills at the town's many language schools (see **Alternatives to Tourism**, p. 53). As is the case for much of Nicaragua, the recent past still resurfaces: in July of 1993, violence erupted here between former Sandinistas and rebellious *Contras* frustrated with the government.

▣ TRANSPORTATION. There are two **bus terminals** in Estelí, both on the *carretera* and 3 blocks away from each other. Destinations from **Terminal Norte** include: **Condega** (1hr., take any bus that goes to Ocotal, 7C); **Ducuale Grande** (1¼hr.; any bus to Ocotal 7C from Estelí, 2C from Condega); **León** (2hr., 3:10pm, 35C); **Matagalpa** (2hr. 5:35pm, 14C); **Ocotal** (2hr.; every hr. 4:10am-5:35pm, 14C); and **Somoto** (2hr., every hr.; 5:30am-5:20pm; 14C). Buses to the **Las Manos Honduran border** can be caught from Ocotal, and for the **El Espino Honduran border** from Somoto (see p. 579). Buses going south leave from **Terminal Sur** to: **León** (6:45am, 2hr., 35C), or take a Managua or Matagalpa bus to San Isidro (45min., 9C) and change there to a León bus (2hr., every hr., 20C). For **Managua,** there's both an indirect bus (3hr., every 30min. 3:30am-6pm, 25C) and the Managua Express (3:30am-6pm, 30 min., 2h, 35C). Buses also head to **Matagalpa** (2hr., every 30min. 5:20am-4:50pm, 14C). A **Tica Bus** office (☎835 3134), sits on Av. Central between 3 and C. 4. Buses depart 6:30am to **Guatemala City** (525C), **San Salvador** (400C), **Tegucigalpa** (320C), **San Pedro Sula** (400C), and **Tapachula** (760C).

Local buses run north-south, 1 block west of Av. Central, from Barrio Rosario to the new hospital, including a stop at the bus terminal. The same buses, usually marked "Rosario-Hospital," run south to north along Av. Central (2C).

Taxis are regulated by the mayor's office and should charge a mandated price. Watch out for cabbies trying to up the price, especially by charging 10C before 5pm. They will pick up other passengers and drive *colectivo*, so don't be surprised when you find yourself sharing a ride (5am-5pm, 5C; 10pm-5am, 10C; slightly more for leaving the city.)

▣ ▨ ORIENTATION AND PRACTICAL INFORMATION. *Avenidas* (running north-south) and *calles* (running east to west) are numbered in the usual way, increasing the farther away from **Avenida Central,** which spans the length of the city, and **Calle Transversal,** running near the center of town 1 block south of the *parque*. The **Interamerican Highway** runs along the eastern edge of town, 6 blocks east of Av. Central. The **Esquina de los Bancos** (financial district) sits at the intersection of Av. 1 SO and C. Transversal. The town is divided into quadrants (NO, NE, SO, SE) that start from the four corners of the *parque central*. The **Terminal Norte** is at the south end of town; 3 blocks up **Terminal Sur** is located on the same *carretera*. People will refer to the entrances to Estelí as the *carretera al norte y al sur* when giving directions.

INTUR Tourist Office, 1 block north and 2 blocks east of the northeast corner of the *parque*, has info on tours and the city's history. (☎713 6799. Spanish only.) The **Casa de la Cultura,** half a block west of ENITEL, has info on local arts, dancing, and changing painting exhibits. (☎713 3021. Open M-F 8am-noon, 2-5pm.) The adjacent museum has reports from the prehistorical sight of Las Pintadas (open M, W 8am-noon; Tu, Th, F 1-5pm).

The **Banco de América Central,** on the Esquina de los Bancos on C. Transversal, serves as a Credomatic, changes traveler's checks, and advances cash on AmEx/MC/V. (☎713 7101. Open M-F 8:30-5pm, Sa 8:30am-12:30pm.) **Western Union** is 2 blocks north and about 25m west of the *bus terminal sur*. (☎713 6756. Open M-F 8:30am-5pm, Sa-Su 8:30am-4pm.) The **Super Económico** supermarket, on Av. Central, is 4 blocks south of the *parque central* (open daily 7:30am-9pm). For a **library** go to the **Biblioteca Pública Dr. Samuel Meza Brones**, 1 block south of the Esquina de los Bancos (open M-F 8am-noon and 2-5pm). The **police** are available 24hr. (☎713 2615, emergency 118), half a block north of the intersection of the Panamericana with Av. Gustavo Norte. **Farmacia Medina** is on the Plaza Ubau on the corner of Av. Central and 9 C. (☎803 06260. Open daily 8am-9pm.) For emergency medical attention, go to the **hospital** at Km 144 on Carretera Sur at the entry of town from Managua. (☎713 6203, 713 6200. Open 24hr.)

For **Internet Access, Cyber Pl@ce** (☎713 6762), 1½ blocks north of the northwest corner of the *parque*, charges C12 per 30min., C20 per hr. (open M-Sa 8am-8pm and 10am-3pm). **Cafe@net** (☎713 4056), on the north side of the park, has rates of 10C per 30min., 20C per 1½hr. (open daily 8am-9pm). The **post office** (☎713 5632; fax 713 2240), half a block west of Av. Central on C. Transversal (open daily 7am-4pm; 240C express mail to the US).

⌗ **ACCOMMODATIONS. Hotel Nicarao ❷**, on Av. Central 1 block down the *parque*, is the first choice for all backpackers: the bright colors of the open courtyard decorated with local *artesanías* make it the ideal place to chill and meet fellow travelers. Reservations are highly recommended. (☎713 2490. Large breakfast 25C. Ten basic rooms with fan and TV. For 1 or 2 people, 150C; with private bath 400C.) Friendly and knowledgeable management, open colorful spaces, and sparkling new facilities at **Hotel Los Arcos ❺**, on the corner opposite Hotel Mesón, make the cost worth it. Fan, private bath, and TV are in 18 rooms. Profits go to the social project in the Estelí urban area, ask for further info. (☎713 3830; hotelosarcos@hotmail.com. Singles 480C; doubles 640C, with A/C 580C; suite 960C. Check out the terrace with a beautiful view of the *parque*. European breakfast included. Visa.) **Hotel Mesón ❸**, 1 block north of the northeast corner of the *parque*, also has a courtyard, this one with a gazebo surrounded by plants to welcome the weary traveler. Eight very clean and relatively large rooms surround the courtyard with fan, private bath, and TV. (☎713 2655; barlan@ibw.com.ni. Singles 173C, with A/C 316C; doubles 253C/442C. AmEx/MC/V.) Finally, **Hospedaje San Francisco ❶**, on Av. Central, C. 7/8 S, is rather dark and unwelcoming, but it's one of the cheapest beds in town. Houses nine small, basic rooms with fans. (☎713 3787. Singles 40C; doubles 60C; triples 90C. Front door locks at 11pm. Cash only.)

⌗ **FOOD. Bar Café Vuela Vuela ❸**, on the corner opposite Hotel Mesón and associated with Hotel Los Arcos, is the ideal spot for a relaxing meal accompanied by music. Try one of the *paellas* (80C-100C) or the *marisco* plates (*frito con salsa* 90C, *camarones* 140C). Like its host hostel, this is a non-profit. (☎713 3830. Breakfast 26C-30C. Open daily 7am-11pm. Visa.) On C. Trasversal **El Rincón Pinareño ❷**, half a block east of Av. Central serves authentic, inexpensive Cuban cuisine served in a well-decorated ambience. Upstairs seating available. The specialties are *cerdo* (55C) and *pollo asado* (45C). Try the *cubano* sandwich (25C-35C) for a quick meal. Take-out available. (☎713 4369. Open W-M 8am-10pm. AmEx/MC/V.) One block east of the southeast corner of the *parque*, **Taquería Beverly ❶** specializes in Mexican food and grills everything before your eyes in a friendly and relaxed environment. Portions are modest. (Tacos 24C, burritos 15C, quesadillas 12C. Open Tu-Su 5pm-11pm.) For the closest thing to a local McDonald's, head to **Hamburloca ❶**, 1 block down the southeast corner of the *parque* and 1 block left. The clean A/C interior is a nice treat. (☎713 4822. Combos 30C-45C. Open daily 9am-10pm.) Though at first dark and foreboding, inexpensive **Comedor Popular la Soya ❶**, south on Av. Central, C. 1/2, is perfect if you're experiencing a veggie dishes fix. Soy specialties include *torta de soya* and *chorizo de soya* (15C; open daily 7am-7pm).

ENTERTAINMENT. Cinema Estelí, close to Terminal Sur, plays long-outdated Hollywood flicks and random "foreign" films, on a four-day rotation (20C; 8pm). **Rancho de Pancho,** 2 blocks down from Terminal Sur, is the traditional hang-out for locals. Two big dance floors, full restaurant menu (90C-150C), *salsa, merengue,* reggae, and pop hits keep things bumping. (Open daily 11-2am. No cover.) **Studio 54,** on the *carretera* 2 blocks up Terminal Norte, is your typical disco on weekends with a nice, albeit small, dance floor. The bar and casino next door are under the same management. (☎713 7177. Open Su, Th-Sa 7pm-3am.) For a stereotypical discotheque, try **Traksig.** Thursday, ladies night, includes two free beers. (Beer 10C; rum and coke 10C. Cover 20C.)

SIGHTS. Catedral Nuestra Señora del Rosario, with the imposing white facade in neoclassical style, looms over the *parque central.* Surprisingly, the interior is quite new. The wooden altar is worth a quick visit (open during daylight). Half a block south of the southeast corner of the *parque,* the memorial of the **Galería de Héroes y Mártires,** operated by the Madres de los Héroes y Mártires, has exhibits that trace the lives and writings of some key revolutionary figures. There's also a display of weapons and a stunning abstract mural. If you have the time, ask to see the poignant testimonies of the mothers translated into English and the photos of the young men and women. Contact Gloria Castillo for more info. (☎713 3753; emmayorga70@yahoo.com. Open M-Sa 8am-4pm. Donations appreciated.) At **Estelí Cigar,** 5 blocks east of the southeast corner of the *parque* and just across from the highway, watch the workers hand roll cigars at one of Estelí's many cigar companies. The manager on duty will usually explain the process if you ask. They also sell single cigars or blocks of 25. (400C-480C. Open M-F 7am-5pm.)

OUTDOOR ACTIVITIES. Seven kilometers south of Estelí, **El Salto de Estanzuela,** a beautiful 35-40m **waterfall,** spills into a deep pool excellent for swimming. It's definitely worth a visit, especially during the rainy season (May-Nov.). Catch a bus at Terminal Nte. (6:30am, 13.30pm, 1hr.; 12C), ask the driver to stop at the wooden gate and from there walk 200m (1½hr.) to the falls for great views of Estelí. Bring lots of water, not much money or baggage, and never leave your belongings unattended, as the unscrupulous have been known to lighten the loads of distracted swimmers. **Reserva Miraflor** is a beautiful nature reserve perfect for appreciating the fauna and flora of this region. Watch for birds: the variety of species present here is impressive and you might be able to catch sight of some endangered ones. To reach Ucamiraflor (☎713 2971), the company in charge of *reserva* preservation, walk 3 blocks away from the *parque* then 3½ blocks right. Catch a bus at Terminal Nte. (1½hr., 6am, noon; C12). Guides 160C per day, inquire at Ucamiraflor.

NORTH TO HONDURAS

There are two options to get to Honduras from Nicaragua: **Las Manos** and **El Espino.** The former is preferable if planning to stay in Honduras for a while because it's closer to Tegucigalpa, the most convenient transportation hub in Honduras. The latter is preferable if planning to go directly to **El Salvador** or further north, as it gets you to **Choluteca** where all buses to El Salvador pass through. The towns of **Condega, Ducuale Grande** and **Ocotal** are low-key and small, ideal if you need to rest before continuing to another country.

CONDEGA

All buses from Estelí to Ocotal stop here (30min. north of Estelí, every hr. from Terminal Norte 4:10am-5:35pm, 7C).

The main attraction in Condega is at **Casa de la Cultura,** home to the government-sponsored **Museo Arqueológico Julio César Salgado** and its fine collection of pre-His-panic ceramics. The prized possessions of the museum are the **Incensarios Indíge-nas**—large spike-covered ceramic incense burners. Donations to the museum go to the education of local children in traditional arts such as leather working, instrument making, and ceramics moulding.

Spending the night here isn't a great option since there are no places for travelers, just motels that rent by the hour. **Hospedaje Framar ❶,** on the south side of the *parque,* has basic, well-kept rooms with fans and private baths. The owner speaks some English. (☎ 752 2393. 10pm curfew. 30C per person.) **Bar y Restaurante Linda Vista ❶** on the highway serves *típico* (chicken or beef with *frijoles* 25C-30C).

⚑ DUCUALE GRANDE

The turn-off to Ducuale Grande is a 20min. walk north of Condega along the highway; look for the Taller Communal de Cerámica sign. Buses from Estelí to Ocotal pass here every hr. from Terminal Norte, 1¼hr., 4:10am-5:35pm, 7C.

The *pueblito* of Ducuale Grande is famous for its ceramics. From the bus drop-off on the highway, one option is to hitch a 5min. ride to town, though *Let's Go* doesn't recommend it. Otherwise, follow the gravel road for 20min., past tobacco sheds and across a small river into town. Continue straight and soon you'll see two signs by a latrine. Take the road to the left and after 200m, you'll reach the cooperative factory. Here they'll gladly show you the ceramic process beginning with raw clay and resulting in jewelry (variously shaped earrings 12C-20C, rings 10C-15C, small statues 8C-50C, pots 25C-30C). Visitors are welcome to look through final products in a tarp-covered lean-to. Bring a variety of bills to help with change.

⚑ OCOTAL AND THE BORDER AT LAS MANOS

Buses from Ocotal run to: Managua (3hr., eight daily 6:30am-3:15pm, 50C); Estelí (2½hr., every hr. 4:45am-6pm, 14C); Somoto (45min., every 30min 5:15am-5:30pm, 7C); and the border (45min., every 35min. 5am-4:20pm, 7C). Nicaraguan immigration and customs open daily 7am-7pm. US$11, or 175C, to cross the border. Customs will inspect luggage. Money-changers convert US dollars and lempiras at fair rates. Meals are available at the comedores on either side. Buses continue from Honduras.

Ocotal has perhaps the best *parque central* in Nicaragua, which makes it an attractive and notably clean first or last stop in the country. To get to the *parque* from the bus station, walk 1km north along the highway (to the Texaco station) and then right 5 blocks, or take a taxi (5C). **Banco Mercantil,** 1 block west of the *parque*'s northwest corner, changes US dollars (open M-F 8:30am-4:30pm, Sa 8:30am-noon). Emergency services include **police** (☎732 2333), 1 block west of the *parque,* and a **hospital** (☎732 2491) along the highway 500m past the Texaco station. **INTUR** has a satellite office here which is 1 block west of the northwest corner of the park. (☎782 3429. Open M-F 8:30am-5pm, Sa 8:30am-noon.) **Western Union** is 1 block north of INTUR. (☎732 2918. Open M-F 8am-12:30pm and 2-5pm, Sa 8am-noon.) **Enitel** is 1 block north and half a block east of the northwest corner of the *parque* (open M-F 8am-5pm, Sat 8am-12:30pm).

Most accommodations are motels which charge by the hour. The least motel-like option is **Hotel El Mirador ❷,** across the highway from the bus station. Spacious rooms have private baths and some have TVs. (☎732 2040. Breakfast 20C. Singles 120C; doubles 140C; triples 180C.) **Hospedaje Viajero ❶,** about 500m north and half a block east of the bus station, is an average budget accommodation. (☎732 2040. 70C per person; doubles with bath, fan, and TV 170C. AmEx/MC/V.)

The most popular eatery is **Restaurante La Merienda ❷**, 6½ blocks north and 2 blocks east of the bus station. Look for the sign north on the *carretera*. (Most meals 50C-70C; *comida corriente* 20C. Open Tu-Su 10am-11pm.) For a cheap, fast meal try **Cafetín Llamarada del Bosque ❶**, on the *parque's* south side. A coffee with *pastel* is 15C-20C (open M-Sa 6:30am-8pm).

✗ SOMOTO AND THE BORDER AT EL ESPINO

Buses from Somoto run to: Estelí (2hr., every 40min. 4am-5:20pm, 13C); Managua (indirectly, 4½hr.; 4, 4:45, 7:20am; 40C; or express 3½hr., 5 per day. 5am-3:10pm, 50C); and Ocotal (1hr., every 30min. 5:45am-4:30pm, 9C). The El Espino Honduran border is 20km from Somoto (45min., every hr. 5:40am-5pm, 8C). You'll need to take a taxi (L10) into the village of San Marcos, Honduras to catch a continuing bus. Nicaraguan Immigration is 200m from the Honduran border (open daily 8am-noon and 1-5pm). It costs 175C to enter or exit Nicaragua, so come prepared. Money changers and comedores pack the Honduran side of the line.

Somoto is the classic small town border crossing and transport hub. The *parque central* is 1 block west down the carretera and then 4 blocks south. **Banco de la Frontera,** 1 block south of the *parque's* southwest corner, changes traveler's checks and converts US dollars to *córdobas* (open M-F 8:30am-4pm, Sa 9am-noon). **Western Union** is half a block south of the southeast corner of the *parque*. (☎722-2038. Open M-Sa 7am-7pm, Su 8am-noon.) From the *parque*, the **police** (☎722 2252) are on the southwest corner and a **hospital** (☎722 2247) is 3 blocks west and 1 block south. **ENITEL** is 1 block east and 1 block south from the *parque* (open M-Sa 7am-8:30pm, Su 10am-8pm).

If you're stuck here for the night, **Panamericano ❷**, in front of the *parque*, offers more than you would expect for these prices with a big common areas and well-kept rooms. Rooms with fan and private bath. (☎722 2100. Singles 90C, with A/C and refrigerator 170C; doubles 140C/220C). The spotless **Hospedaje Solentiname ❶**, 1½ blocks east of the bus station on the *carretera*, is cheaper. Rooms are a bit tight, with very thin beds. (☎722 2100. 50C per person, with bath 140C.) For good food in a relaxed atmosphere, try **El Almendro ❷**, 1½ blocks south of the southeast corner of the *parque*. (*Comida corriente* 30C-40C. Open Tu-Su 10am-10pm.)

MATAGALPA

In the heart of coffee country 25km east of the Interamerican Hwy., Matagalpa (pop. 77,000) is a somewhat unexceptional town elevated in status by an extraordinary location. Situated in a small valley ringed by lush mountains, clouds graze the town's rooftops, resulting in a thin mist. Those arriving from hotter climates will be refreshed by the pleasantly cool days and downright chilly nights. Originally settled in the 19th century by European immigrants, Matagalpa was an FSLN (Sandinista) stronghold during the revolution, and was one of two towns (the other being León) that voted FSLN in recent elections. Like the rest of Nicaragua, locals take their politics very seriously. The majority of visitors come to Matagalpa for the spectacular Selva Negra National Park, a short bus ride from the city.

☎ TRANSPORTATION. Departing from a well-developed bus station (with a written schedule no less), located 2 blocks south and 5 blocks west of Parque Rubén Darío, **buses** run to: **Estelí** (1¾hr., every 30min. 5:15am-6:15pm, 17C); **Jinotega** (1½hr., every 30min. 5am-7pm, 14C); **León** (2¼hr., 6am and 3pm, 35C). You can also get to León by taking an Estelí bus and getting off at **San Isidro** (8C), from where buses to León leave every 30min. (3hr., 23C). Finally, buses to **Managua** (3hr., every 30min. 3:30am-6pm, 33C; express 2hr., every hr. 5:20am-4:50pm, 38C). For **Boaco,** take a Managua bus to **San Benito** (2hr., 18C) and change there. **Taxis** within town cost about 8C.

ORIENTATION AND PRACTICAL INFORMATION. Unlike many Central American towns, Matagalpa has not one *parque central*, but two: **Parque Rubén Darío** in the south, and **Parque Catedral** in the north (across from a cathedral and sometimes called **Parque Morazán**). The bulk of "downtown" lies between them: the main street, **Calle de los Comercios,** begins at the northwest corner of Rubén Darío and continues north for 7 blocks before ending in the middle of Parque Catedral. One block east, **Avenida de los Bancos** (Av. Central) also connects the two parks, and contains most banks and some *artesanías*. The **bus terminal** is 5 blocks west and 2 blocks south of Parque Darío, along the river.

INTUR tourist office (☎ 612 7060). 3 blocks west and 3½ blocks north of northwest corner of Parque Darío, on the other side of the river. Open M-F 8am-12:30pm and 2-5pm.

Viajes America (☎ 612 7060). 1 block south and ½ a block west of Parque Darío's southwest corner, is one of the prominent travel agencies. Open M-F 8am-noon and 2-5pm, Sa 8am-noon.

Banks:

Banco de América Central, 2½ blocks south of the *catedral* on Av. de Los Bancos, is lord of the credit cards. Open M-F 8am-6pm, Sa 8am-1pm.

Credomatic, 1 block east of the southeast corner of Parque Catedral. Open M-F 8am-5:30pm, Sa 8am-1pm.

Western Union (☎ 612 4984). 1 block south and ½ a block west of the southwest corner of Parque Darío in Comercio Calero Mendieta. Open M-F 8am-12:30pm and 2-5:30pm, Sa 8am-1pm.

Palí, 1½ blocks north of the NE corner of Parque Catedral. Open daily 8am-8pm.

Police (☎ 612 3511 or 612 3870, emergency 118). Waits on the south side of the Parque Catedral. Open 24hr.

Red Cross (☎ 612 2059 or 612 3786, in an emergency 119). Just over the river, 2 blocks west of the southwest corner of the Parque Catedral by the hospital.

Farmacia Alvarado (☎ 612 2830). Pharmacies spot the town, though this one opposite Parque Darío's northwest corner, is easy to find. Open M-Sa 8am-1pm and 2-9pm, Su 8am-1pm.

Hospital (☎ 612 2081). On the north edge of town, 5C away from the *parque* by taxi.

ENITEL (☎ 612 3656). Near its antenna 1 block east of the Parque Catedral's northeast corner. Open M-Sa 7:30am-9pm.

Cibernet sits across from the Parque Catedral. 25C per hr. Open M-F 8am-8pm, Sa 8am-10pm, Su 10am-5pm.

Post office (☎ 612 2004). Correos de Nicaragua is 1 block south on the C. de los Comercios and ½ block east. Fax service. Open M-F 8am-6pm, Sa 8am-1pm.

ACCOMMODATIONS. There is no shortage of accommodations in Matagalpa—expect clean, basic, family-run hotels and a mostly Nicaraguan clientele.

Hotel Fuente Azul (☎ 612 2733), 4 blocks north and 2½ blocks west of the northwest corner of Parque Catedral, located across the river over the yellow and green bridge. Undoubtedly the cleanest and nicest hotel in town. White tiled floors and lush gardens give a bright feel. 24hr. hot water, laundry and 7-9am breakfast. Doubles 150C, with private bath 250C; triples 350C; quad 500C; 6-person 750C. AmEx/MC/V. ❷

Hotel Matagalpa (☎ 612 3834). Located 1½ blocks east of the northeast corner of Parque Rubén Darío and down one very long passageway. Friendly and immaculate best describes Matagalpa, though the mattresses are thin. Upstairs rooms have pleasant views, and downstairs there are common areas with cable TV. Singles 60C; doubles 100C. ❷

Hotel Plaza (☎612 2380), on the south side of Parque Rubén Darío; basic, well-kept rooms right in the center of town. Nice common area with cable TV. Singles 60C, with bath 80C; doubles 110C/140C. ❷

Hotel El Centro's, 2 blocks north of the northwest corner of Parque Darío. Couched cable TV area overlooks the C. Comercial. Comfy beds in box-like rooms. No phone. Rooms 70C. ❷

◘ **FOOD.** In addition to normal *típico* places, Matagalpa has a few nice restaurants, though a bit pricey.

▨ **La Casona,** on C. de Comercios 2½ blocks south of the Parque Catedral, is all *carne*, all the time, in a brightly-painted interior. Any way you want it, with all the fixin's, 25C-55C. Open daily 8am-midnight. ❷

Delicias, 1 block west and 3½ blocks north of the NW corner of Parque Rubén Darío. For food, service and intimate, riverside ambience, head to Delicias; try the garlic or jalapeño steak (90C). Soup on M 35C. Open daily 7am-9pm. ❸

La Posada, ½ a block west of the northwest corner of Parque Darío, provides elegant, dimly-lit dining in an old house. If you're feeling brave, try the *huevos de toro* (bull's testicles; 60C). *Comida corriente* 40C. Open M-Th 10am-10pm, F-Su 10am-midnight. ❷

▓ **NIGHTLIFE.** In terms of nightlife, Matagalpa really hops on the weekends. **La Posada** restaurant turns into the most popular local disco from Friday to Sunday night. On Fridays, head to **Noche Cultural en la Casena** for live music. **Rancho Escondido,** 2 blocks west of the southwest Rubén Darío, has a spacious dance floor which sometimes hosts nationally famous groups. (30C cover when live bands play.) The last weekend of every month, the local restaurants set up shop at one of the *parques* for **Noches Matagalpinas,** full of traditional dance and music (Sa-Su 5-11pm). The new **Cinema Margot,** on Av. de los Bancos, 2 blocks south of Parque Catedral, gets Hollywood flicks a few weeks after their Managua openings (40C). Local festivals include the **Fiesta Patronales de la Merced** on September 24, and the **Festival de Polkas, Mazurcas y Jamaquellos** on the last weekend of September.

◙ **SIGHTS AND CRAFTS.** The **Casa de Cultura,** 2½ blocks south of the southwest corner of the Parque Catedral, houses the usual assortment of local artwork and workshops. (☎612 3158. Open M-F 7am-12:30pm and 2-5pm.) **Museo de Café** is 3½ blocks north of the northwest corner of Parque Darío on the right-hand side. This small museum celebrates the bean that sustains the region with displays explaining the progress from seedling to cup-of-Joe. (Open M-F 9am-noon and 2-5pm.) Fine examples of Nicaragua's **cerámica negra** can be found in Matagalpa. One workshop, **Tradicional Cerámica Negra,** is located 4 blocks south and 4 steep blocks uphill east of the cathedral. (Open M-F 8am-6pm, Sa 8am-noon.)

▚ ▨ **SELVA NEGRA.** "Black Forest", 12km north of Matagalpa, is a coffee plantation, hotel, and private forest reserve. Nearly 80% of the 2000-acre estate is protected, with a marvelous network of labeled hiking paths. Vibrant toucans, howler monkeys, and even the elusive quetzal inhabit 150m dense canopy foliage.

From Matagalpa, any Jinotega-bound bus will drop you off at the Selva Negra turnoff (marked by a rainbow-painted army tank; 25min., every 30min., 7C), from where it is a 2km hike to the restaurant, hotel, and visitors area. You can take a taxi (140C) from town to the **restaurant** ❹. (Entrance fee to park 25C. Breakfast 40C-70C, entrees 90C-130C, cakes 25C, coffee 10C. Open daily 7:30am-8pm.) Reservations are recommended for the **hotel.** (☎612 3883. Horse rentals 25C per

NATIONAL HERO, WANDERING SOUL

According to official reports, he died in 1916, but in Nicaragua, Rubén Darío still lives-parks, streets, schools, and landmarks everywhere bear his name. Born in 1867 in Metapa (now Ciudad Darío), he gained almost instant fame in Spain and Latin America for his inventive, modern style. In fact, Darío is thought to have initiated Latin American Modernism, perhaps single-handedly, with his poem "Azul." The resulting poetic movement was dubbed "ruben-darismo."

Darío reveled in the aesthetic and believed in art for art's sake. Some of his most poignant poetry including "Sonatina" and "A Roosevelt") expresses the con-licting emotions he felt toward his homeland. Though a self-iden-ified as a Nicaraguan, and as a Central American, he spent most of his life abroad. On the one hand, he loved it and felt a deep tie to the region; on the other, he resented its perceived inferior position in world affairs.

After serving as Nicaraguan ambassador to Spain and France, and living in Panama and Chile, he died penniless in León. Despite his reputation as Latin America's greatest poet, later poets have tried to distance them-selves from the man who urged Latin America to "learn con-tancy, vigor, and character from the Yankee."

30min. 480C-800C per night.) Regular rooms, albeit expensive, called *apartamentos*, are available at the charming **◙Hotel and Restaurant Selva Negra ❺**. With hot-water baths, soft sheets, and fluffy towels, you'll enjoy this needed respite from the trails. A **youth hostel ❸** opens up for groups starting at 6 (160C per person). From November to February you might see the attached plantation in action. On Sunday, horses can be rented. The coffee and local history museum is worthwhile.

Try the **Peter and Helen** trail (1¾hr.) ascending the reserve's highest point. For those interested in more independent hikes, there are maps available at **Centro Girasol**, 2 blocks south and 1 block west of the Terminal Sur. Created by Dutch hiking enthusiast Emile, hikes range 4-8hr. Maps 25¢, all proceeds go to the **Centro Girasol** for handicapped children. However, *Let's Go* warns against hiking alone, women especially. Signs are in English; a free map is available at the hotel desk.

BOACO

A *pueblo* amidst the clouds, Boaco (pop. 22,000) is a beauty with a vibrant cowboy culture, which it shows off every 7th of July with the *Hípica*, a horse parade where almost everyone in town either rides or shows up to watch. Residents are proud of the place and they show it off during the annual *fiesta patronal* for the apostle Santiago during July 21-25. Soak up the scenery and talk to the locals.

Buses head to **Managua** (2hr., every 30min. 4am-5pm, 20C) and **Río Blanco** (3hr., every 30min. 5:15am-4:30pm, 35C). To **Estelí, San Isidro, Matagalpa,** or the **Honduran border,** take a Managua bus as far as **San Benito.** For **Juigalpa** or **Rama,** take a Managua bus 20min. to the *enpalme de Boaco* intersection.

Boaco is known as the *ciudad de dos pisos* (city of two floors) because of the economic and physical gap between the wealthier *ciudad alta* (high city) atop a hill to the north and the poorer *ciudad baja* (low city) to the south. The **highway,** home to the **bus station,** runs along the southern edge of town. Boaco's main street, 1 block west of the bus station, runs directly into *ciudad alta* and the main *parque*, **Parque Niebrowsky** (5 blocks from the bus station). Cash travelers checks at **BanCentro** on the main street. (Open M-F 8am-4pm, Sa 9am-noon). The **police station** (☎ 842 2574) is across from the *parque*'s northwest. The **Red Cross** (☎ 842 2200) is 1 block west of the main street. **Healthcare** facilities include **Clínica El Socorro** (☎ 842 2543) on the main street, and **Hospital Niebrowsky** (☎ 842 2301 or 842 2302), following signs from the bus station. **ENITEL** is 1 block east of the southeast the *parque* (☎842 2490; open M-Sa 8am-5pm), and the **post office** is a block and a half north of the *parque's* church (open M-F 8am-noon and 1-5pm, Sa 8am-1pm).

Most hotels are surprisingly rustic and have running water only in the mornings. **⊠Hospedaje Alma ❶** has some of the best rooms in the city. (☎842 2620. Breakfast 20C. Singles with fan, TV, and shared bath 50C; with private bath, new beds, and cable TV 150C. AmEx/MC/V.) **⊠Hotel Sobalvarro ❶**, on the *parque's* south side, is the best place for gorgeous views and prime location in the center of town. Anticipate very basic rooms, communal baths, and a cable TV lounge. (☎842 2515. Breakfast 25C. Singles 50C; doubles 80C; triples 100C.) Spring-green **Hospedaje Boaco ❶**, just north of the bus station, has fairly bright rooms with thin beds and dark private baths. (60C per person.)

The best restaurants are in the *ciudad alta*, while the best street cuisine is in the market near the bus station. **El Alpino ❷**, 1 block east and 1½ blocks north of the *parque's* northeast corner, is a popular, laid-back place. (Breakfast 30C; sandwich 12C; chicken and beef 65-90C. Open Tu-Su 8am-10pm.) The **Sorbetería Sobalvarro ❶**, an ice cream parlor in Hotel Sobalvarro, is a local "hot" spot serving huge hamburgers (15C), sandwiches, and coffee. **La Cueva ❸**, east of the south side of the *parque central*, has good *ranchero* provisions. The place becomes a full scale **disco** on weekend nights, with the latest music and a large dance floor. Its location is ideal, as most nights crowds of people gather in the park just to be social, especially on weekends and holidays. (Beef dishes 75-120C. Beer 12C. Restaurant open Tu-Su 11am-10pm. Cover 15C. Disco open Th-Su 8pm-midnight. AmEx/MC/V.)

The *ciudad alta* has many *paseos* that provide great views of *ciudad baja* and surrounding mountains. **Parque el Cerrito,** 1 block west and 2 north of the northwest corner of the main *parque*, is a well-maintained park in the highest part of the *ciudad alta*, with a tower offering 360° views. **Paseo los Poetas,** 1 block north and 1 east of northeast corner of *parque*, and **Paseo del Balaute,** 1 block east of the southeast corner of *parque*, are also worth a visit. The **Termales Aguas Claras** (☎244 2916), 4km west of the *Enpalme de Boaco*, is a sprawling complex of brightly painted cement swimming pools and thatched *ranchos*. Take any Managua-bound bus and ask to be dropped off. (40 min., 8C.)

JUIGALPA

A tranquil place between Managua and the Caribbean, Juigalpa (pop. 48,000) makes for a manageable stopover, should your bus break down, to enjoy the surrounding mountains and fresh air. The city's impressive views of surrounding peaks, archaeology museum, and zoo are options to while away the time.

Buses drop passengers off at the **bus station/mercado**, 2 blocks east of the *parque central*, which is recognized by the two tall steeples of the cathedral on its eastern edge. Everything of interest lies within a few blocks of the *parque*. Buses head to: **Managua** (3hr., every 15min. 4am-5pm, 25C; express 2¼hr., 5:45am and 2:40pm, 35C); **San Carlos** (7hr., 9 per day 4am-2:30pm, 50C); and **Rama** (4½hr., every 30min. 4:30am-2:30pm, 55C). For **Estelí** and **Matagalpa,** take the Managua bus as far as **San Benito** (2½hr., 25C). To **Boaco,** take the Managua bus as far as the Enpalme de Boaco intersection (1½hr., 15C) and hop a bus into town (30min., 8C).

INTUR is inside the *alcaldía*, 2 blocks north of the northeast corner of the *parque*. (☎812 3066. Open M-F 8am-noon and 1-5pm.) The **Viajes Universe** travel agency is 3½ blocks east of the *parque's* southeast corner, under the Nica Airlines sign. **BanCentro,** a block north of the *parque's* northwest corner, changes traveler's checks. (☎812 1504. Open M-F 8am-4:30pm, Sa 8am-noon.) **Western Union** is inside the Ferretería Reinaldo Hernández, 2 blocks east of the northeast corner of the *parque*. (☎812 2621. Open M-F 7:45am-6pm, Sa 7:45am-5pm.) Other services include: **police** (☎812 2945 or 812 2727), **Red Cross** (☎812 2233; open daily 8am-

5pm), and **Hospital Real Asunción** (☎812 2332), all on the highway at the exit to Rama. **ENITEL** is 3 blocks north of the *parque*'s northwest corner (☎812 7777; open M-Sa 8am-noon and 2-6pm) and the **post office** is a block east of the southeast corner of the *parque*. (Open M-F 8am-6:30pm, Sa 8am-1pm.)

▧**Hospedaje el Nuevo Milenio ❶**, 2 blocks east of the *parque*'s northeast corner, has bright, clean rooms, strong ceiling fans, and sparkling, modern common baths. Downstairs has cable TV. (☎812 0646. 60C per person.) **Hospedaje Angelita ❶**, just west of the *parque*'s northwest corner, is a friendly, family-run place. Relaxing public areas make up for cramped, rooms with thin beds. All beds have mosquito netting. (☎812 2408. Reception open 24hr. Singles 40C; doubles 80C.) **Hotel Casa Country ❸**, 4 blocks east of northeast *parque*, has quality mattresses; private baths make the price worth it. (☎812 2546. Doubles 200C, with A/C 250C. AmEx/MC/V.)

▧**Palo-Solo ❸**, 5 blocks east of the northeast corner of the *parque*, inside Parque Palo-Solo, is the classiest place in town for food, drinks, and breathtaking views—and the prices reflect it. (Beef and chicken 80-100C; fajitas and other *bocas* 35C; beer 15C. Open daily 10am-10pm. AmEx/MC/V.) A block and a half east of the *parque*'s northeast corner resides **Restaurante 24/7 ❶**, a 24hr. bar/restaurant with a huge menu and decor reminiscent of a fast-food joint. (Burgers 15C, lo-mein 35C, chicken 40C. Open 24hr.) **Cafetín Arco-Iris ❶**, on the northwest corner of the *parque*, serves good food quickly in the *típico* tradition. (Breakfast 20-25C, sandwiches 20-25C, comida corriente 20-40C. Open daily 8am-8pm.)

At the far east end of town, the ▧**Parque Palo-Solo** allows unparalleled views of the Cordillera de Amerrisque, the southernmost extension of the central highlands. The *parque*'s bubbling fountain, shady trees, and promenade are a great place to relax. ▧**Jardín Zoológico Thomas Belt,** 8 blocks south of the southeast corner of the *parque*, is a large, well-maintained zoo. Some 95% of the 60 species represented are from Nicaragua and include primates, cats, reptiles, rodents, and birds. Founded in 1958 and run by the city, they just added a *cafetería* with reasonable prices. Avoid walking under the corners of the monkey cage, as they've been known to use visitors for target practice. (Entrance 5C, 5C to take pictures, 10C for video permission. Open daily 8am-5:30pm.) The **Museo Arqueológico Gregorio Aguilar Barea**, 2½ blocks east of the *parque*'s northeast corner, has Nicaragua's largest collection of pre-Columbian statues, though the cluttered, faded displays inside aren't great. Don't miss the sideshow of "interesting" stuffed animals, like the two-headed cow. (Open M-F 8am-noon and 2-5pm, Sa 8am-noon. 4C.)

CARIBBEAN COAST

Nicaragua's Caribbean coast is unlike the rest of the country, and the fact that it is only reachable by boat or plane only broadens this gap. The region is part of a geographical area known as the Mosquitia (Mosquito Coast), a sparsely populated expanse of rainforest, plains, and coastland extending the length of Nicaragua's east coast and north into Honduras. The Mosquitia is home to the country's largest group of *indígenas*, the Miskitos, who maintain their own language and have a semi-autonomous government system. Other indigenous groups, including the Sumos, Garífunas, and Ramas, also reside here. Most Caribbean-coast residents identify more strongly with their West Indian heritage or indigenous community than with a Nicaraguan identity.

Travel here is tricky, as there are almost no roads. Unless you're flying, getting from one place to another involves a great deal of puttering around in small boats. The extra effort is rewarded by relaxing beaches and colorful villages. Be aware that the remote nature of the Atlantic coast means little policing in some areas, so exercise extra caution.

RAMA

Rama's *fama* (pop. 24,600) comes not from its position as the land gateway to the Caribbean coast, but because the highway heading east from Managua ends, and boats leaving for Bluefields, Nicaragua's most important Caribbean port, pushes off from here. There's just about nothing to do in Rama, and if you get in after 10am you'll probably have to stay the night in order to catch a boat down the river to the coast.

Buses stop at Rama's *mercado*, 2 blocks north of the *parque central*, Parque Parrochial. The tall hill with communications towers indicates north. Buses depart for Managua (8-9hr., about every hr. 3-9am, 90C) via Juigalpa (4½hr., 55C). **Boats** leave from the dock 1 block west of the market to Bluefields (slow boats 5hr., Su, T, Sa noon; 63C; express *panga* 1½hr., daily 5:30am-4pm, leave when full, 140C; sometimes extra luggage 30C). An office in a green house near the dock sells tickets (opens 5:30am). There is **no bank**, but there is a **Bancentro** in the yellow building across the corner from Hotel Jahanna that changes traveler's checks and gives cash advances (open M-F 8am-noon and 2-5pm). The **police** (☎817 0026) are 1 block north and 5 blocks east of the *mercado;* **Red Cross** (☎817 0181), 1 block north and 2 blocks east of the *mercado.* The **hospital** (☎817 0019) is 6km north of town on the highway while **ENITEL** is 1 block east of the bus stop (☎817 0100; open M-Sa 7am-9pm). The **post office** is across the street from ENITEL (open M-F 8am-noon and 2-5pm, Sa 8-11am).

While you're waiting for your ship to come in, you might as well grab a *cama* in Rama. All the options listed are 40C-45C per person. **Hospedaje Jiménez ❶**, on the northwest corner of the town's main intersection along the same street as the dock, is a clean building surrounded by a tall grid-iron fence. The mid-*mercado* location ensures a sunrise wake-up call as the town bustle starts. **Hotel Johanna ❶**, 1 block east and half a block south of the *parque*, has clean rooms with fans, and the showers and baths here are the best of Rama's lot. There's a cheap *cafetín* across the street, and a decent, reasonably priced restaurant on the bottom floor (fried fish 80C, hamburgers 40C).

There are good *comedores* near the *mercado.* **El Expreso ❷**, 3 blocks east of the *mercado*, serves steak and shrimp dishes. (50C-60C; open daily 11am-10pm). Locals come to **Los Vindes ❷**, half a block south of the market, for the jukebox and beer. (Shrimp dishes 90C; enormous steak 60C. Open daily noon-midnight.) In the evening, the bars in **Hotel Johanna** and **Hotel Manantial**, 1 block south and 1 block west of the market, tend to keep the neighbors awake.

BLUEFIELDS

 TIP Don't walk alone at night and use caution during the day—robberies have been reported. It's a good idea to take a cab when going out after dark in Bluefields, even for short distances, for safety assurance.

Chaotic Bluefields (pop. 48,000) is Nicaragua's most important Caribbean port, though the port itself is actually across the bay in Bluff. The city is a fascinating urban jungle: on the streets you'll hear English with a sonorous West Indian lilt as Spanish, Miskito, and other indigenous languages pipe in. Come nightfall, you'll hear and see some of the most vibrant nightlife around as reggae rhythms and Caribbean sounds provide relief from the usual Top 40 grind. On a more negative note, safety is highly questionable; people can get in your face and harassment of women is common, especially at night. Bluefields lacks swimming beaches and big tourist attractions, and is often used as a launch pad to the Corn Islands or other more remote points on the Caribbean coast. The only real way to get to Bluefields is by boat or plane.

⌨ TRANSPORTATION. Flights from the **airstrip** 3km south of town. La Costeña goes to: **Managua** (1hr.; 8:30am and 3:30pm; one-way 800C, round-trip 1400C); the **Corn Islands** (30min.; 8am and 3pm; one-way 600C, round-trip 1200C); and **Puerto Cabezas** (1hr.; 12:10pm; one-way 850C, round-trip 1600C). Atlantic Airlines flies slightly larger and more modern planes to **Managua** (8:45am and 3:45pm; one-way 800C, round-trip 1400C) and the **Corn Islands** (8:30am and 3pm; one-way 600C, round-trip 1200C). Buy tickets at the **airline office** at Av. Cabezas and C. Central or arrive at the airport 1hr. early.

Boats to **Rama** leave from the main pier. Choose between slow, covered *expreso* boats (4hr.; 5am Su, Tu, Th, Sa; 60C) and speedier **pangas** (1½hr., 120C). A *panga* run by Vargas y Peña leaves M, W, and F at 5:30am, other days at 6am; boats leave throughout the morning as they fill up, but past mid-morning the chances of catching a Rama-bound *panga* are virtually non-existent. Arrive at least 30min. early to buy a ticket and be prepared to endure some jostling for a seat. Be sure to bring rain gear. Buy a *panga* ticket to Rama and then catch a **bus** to Managua or to other cities from Rama; or, a **panga/bus combo** ticket to Managua (230C) gets you a guaranteed seat on the bus. To El Bluff (15min., 15C), take a *panga* from the dock 3 blocks south of the main pier. The *pangas* leave intermittently but more frequently early in the morning (starting at 6am, every 20min.). It's also possible to hitch a ride on a passing **supply boat.** There are two boats a week to Big Corn Island: one departs Wednesday and returns Friday, the other departs Friday and comes back Sunday. All departures occur at 9am (6½hr., 175C). Boats will not leave in inclement weather and don't expect on-time departures (sometimes hours-long delays). Remember, these are freight boats and not conventional passenger boats; be prepared to claim your grain sack seat on deck for the trip. Above and below deck berths are available for an additional fee. Purchase tickets in the office on the corner of Av. Reyes and C. Commercial, up the green staircase.

⛶ 🛈 ORIENTATION AND PRACTICAL INFORMATION. The murky Caribbean borders Bluefields on the east. The central artery, **C. Central,** curves along the coast north to south; at the top of this road, north of the tall, red-roofed **Moravian church,** is the town's **main pier.** Three main streets run east to west; **Av. Reyes** is northernmost, next **Av. Cabezas,** and **Av. Aberdeen** to the south. The **market** and the **pier** for boats to El Bluff are on Av. Aberdeen, the only *avenida* that extends east past C. Central. The **airstrip** is 3km south of the town center (**taxis** 10C-20C).

It is recommended that you take advantage of the services here if planning on heading out to the islands, where services are limited. The **police** (☎822 2448) are on C. Central, 4 blocks south of the Moravian church. Health services are the **Red Cross** (☎822 2582), south of town on C. Patterson; a **hospital** (☎822 2391 or 822 2621), about 2km southwest of town, past the airport; and pharmacies, such as **Pharmacy Godoy Farmacia** (☎822 2471), on C. Cabezas, 1 block west of C. Central (open M-Sa 8am-9pm, Su 9am-5pm). There are numerous banks: **Banco Caley Dagnall** is across from the Moravian church (open M-F 8:30am-4pm, Sa 8:30am-noon); and **BanCentro,** across from Mini-Hotel on C. Cabezas, cashes traveler's checks and is the only place on the Caribbean coast where you can get a credit card cash advance (open M-F 8:30am-4pm, Sa 9am-12:30pm). Telephone services are at **ENITEL** (☎822 2222), 3 blocks west of C. Central in the municipal building on Av. Reyes. (Telephones open M-Sa 8am-8:45pm, Su 8am-6pm.) Internet services at the creatively-titled **Internet Cafe,** 2 blocks west of C. Central on Av. Aberdeen, then half a block north. (Free coffee. 15C per hr. Open M-F 8am-8pm, Sa 8am-6pm, Su 10am-6pm.) The **post office** is found 1½ blocks west of C. Central on Av. Aberdeen. EMS and **fax** services available (open M-F 8am-noon and 1-5pm, Sa 8am-noon).

ACCOMMODATIONS. During high season (Jan.-May), the nicer hotels in Bluefields become considerably crowded, prices rise, and reservations are recommended. **Caribbean Dream ❸**, on C. Central half a block south of Av. Aberdeen, has extremely helpful staff. Light-green walls lend a bright, clean feeling to the large rooms and the pleasant social area in front. All rooms have private bath, and there is a direct telephone line to Sprint on the patio. (☎822 0107. Double bed 230C; 2 double beds 315C. Prices increase for A/C.) For something a bit cheaper and family-run, head to **Hotel Marda Maus ❸**, half a block east of C. Central on Av. Aberdeen. The breeze from the upstairs balcony in this sparkling-clean place continues into the rooms, all of which have fans. (☎822 2429. Double bed 200C; 2 double beds 275C, with A/C 300C.) The cheapest option is **Hotel Hollywood ❷**, in an unmarked house with a large porch across from Caribbean Dream on C. Central, half a block south of Av. Aberdeen. The rooms range from dark and closet-like singles with a fan, to spacious "suites" with bath and TV. Cracks in the floor may admit lizards. (☎822 2067. Singles 85C; doubles 140C, with private bath 250C.)

FOOD AND NIGHTLIFE. Mini-Hotel Cafetín Central ❷ (see **Accommodations,** above) is one of the most popular eateries, thanks to frosty beer mugs, wide-screen cable TV, and constant table-wiping. (Fish, chicken, and beef dishes 40C-60C, *batidos* 20C. Open daily 8am-10pm.) **Cafetín "Pesca-Frita" ❷**, in an unmarked building on the southwest corner of the intersection of C. Central and Av. Aberdeen, has a funky Caribbean decor along with an army of fans fighting to keep you cool. The fish (60C) is succulent and worth every *córdoba*, though if you want cheap *comida corriente*, ask for the *super-económico* full meal (35C). Lobster 100C. (Open daily 8am-1am.)

At night, Bluefields turns up the juice, in terms of both fun and danger. The best place for real Caribbean reggae is ◪**Cuatro Hermanos,** a famous open-air joint right on the water and popular with foreign volunteers. To get there, walk 2 blocks west of C. Central, then south to the water. **Bella Vista,** inside Bella Vista restaurant (see above), is the fanciest of the clubs. Its intimate dance floor overlooks the water south of town, at the end of C. Central.

DAYTRIPS FROM BLUEFIELDS. Laguna de Perlas (Pearl Lagoon) is a small community on the southern edge of a large lagoon of the same name 80km north of Bluefields. The 1-2hr. trip is an excellent way to get a look at Caribbean coastal culture and wildlife. The pearl cayes—18 small, uninhabited, white-sand tropical islands with coral off the coast—are ideal for snorkeling. *Pangas* leave Bluefields' main pier each morning for Laguna de Perlas, 1hr., up to 3 **boats** per day leave when full, first at 6am, last at 10am, 70C. *Pangas* return to Bluefields 6am, noon, and occasionally 10am, 70C. **Green Lodge Guesthouse ❷**, has basic, clean rooms with fans and outside baths, 85C, and excellent food, such as shrimp, 30C. Electricity is limited. Bring your own snorkeling equipment, food, and drinks. In the village, local boats can take you to these even smaller communities around the lagoon (1600C-1920C for the *panga*). About one hour south from Bluefields by boat, **Ramaqui** is a small island community home to descendants of the Rama. Corrugated metal buildings stand next to traditional bamboo huts, and dugout canoes pull up next to more modern fishing vessels. Though the island sees few visitors, local families are usually willing to host guests for a negotiable price. An ecotourism ranch is in the works. (You'll have to hire your own boat; recruit a group to split the cost, 600C-700C.)

NICARAGUA

THE CORN ISLANDS

> ! Unfortunately, safety is as much of a concern on the Corn Islands as in Blue-fields; violence and robbery are both common. Take as little as possible with you, and be constantly aware of your surroundings. Paying more for increased security is a good idea.

The Corn Islands, 70km off the coast from Bluefields, offer white sand beaches, warm turquoise water, and a uniquely untouristed Caribbean atmosphere. Most visitors stay on Big Corn Island (pop. 10,000), with a small but reasonable selection of hotels and restaurants. With no resorts and no cars or roads, splendid Little Corn Island (pop. 700), 18km away, feels even more untouched. The islands, populated by English speakers of British West Indian descent, have excellent fishing and colorful coral reefs, but most of all they simply offer the chance to curl your toes in pure Caribbean sands and do absolutely nothing.

BIG CORN ISLAND

The Corn Islands are not frequented as much as other Caribbean hotspots in Central America due to lacking infrastructure and widespread drug traffic. However, with increasing development of the island's natural beauty, Big Corn might be the next big thing in Nicaragua.

TRANSPORTATION. La Costeña and **Atlantic Airlines** (offices on airstrip open daily 7am-4:30pm) have daily flights to **Managua** (8:30am and 3:30pm) that stop in **Bluefields** along the way. (One-way 780C, round-trip 1400C.) From Managua, planes leave at 6:30am and 1:15pm, stopping in Bluefields at 7:30am and 3pm for the same prices. Make reservations and get tickets in advance. Arrive one hour early. Unlike other businesses on the islands, airlines accept credit cards. **Boats** depart from the main pier in Briggs Bay, 5 blocks from the airstrip, to: **Bluefields** (4-6hr.; Tu 11am, M, W-Sa 8am, Su 9am; 175C) and **Little Corn Island** (10am and 4pm, return 7am and 2pm; 90C). The *pangas* are synchronized with arriving aircraft and tend to wait if a plane is late. The airlines, however, are not as nice, and will leave without you. **Buses** circle the island all day (every 40min. 6am-6pm, 5C).

ORIENTATION AND PRACTICAL INFORMATION. Big Corn Island is approximately 6 sq. km. The island's main road runs all the way around its coast, and a few dead-end drives branch off either inland or out to the ocean. The **airstrip** runs southwest to northeast, marking off **Briggs Bay** and the western quarter of the island, where most of the businesses and hotels are located. In the eastern part of the island are the beach communities of **North End** and **South End,** with **Sally Peachie** in between. Pick up **maps** of the island at **Nautilus Ecotours** about 5 blocks north of Fisher's Cave Restaurant. **Banco Caley Dagnall** is at the south end of the airstrip just up from the pier. Credit cards are generally not accepted on the island, so bring cash. (☎285 5107. Open M-F 8am-4:30pm, Sa 8am-noon.) Other services include: the **police station** (☎285 5201), 2 blocks north of the road from Fisher's Cave Restaurant; a **pharmacy** on the road south from the airport to Briggs Bay (open daily 6am-9pm); and another available 24hr. for emergencies in the **hospital** (☎285 5233), 1km down the road leading east across the airstrip; and **ENITEL,** 3 blocks north of the Fisher's Cave restaurant (open M-Sa 8am-noon and 1-5pm). **Internet** is available at Hotel Paraiso. 100C per hr. for slow connection. The **post office** is in the pharmacy south of the airline offices.

ACCOMMODATIONS. Expect to spend a bit more on Big Corn than on the mainland; nice budget digs are available starting at around 160C per night. **Casa Blanca ❶,** on the southeast side of Briggs Bay (the unpaved road is right next to Reggae Palace), offers the best deal for budget travelers. Large porches overlook the water amidst a cool breeze. Mosquito netting and laundry (self-service) are offset by thin beds and toilets in the ground. (Singles 160C; doubles 190C.) On the northwest corner of the island, in Sally Peach and near some great snorkeling, **Hospedaje Sunrise ❷** is known locally as Marcus Gómez, the owner's name. It has basic rooms in a very yellow house with an open kitchen; a few private *cabañas* next-door. (☎285 5187. Singles 160C; doubles 210C. 75C per extra person.) Perhaps the nicest hotel on the island, **Hotel Paraiso ❺,** on the southern edge of Briggs Bay, is the only one that accepts credit cards. Well-tended, family-oriented *cabañas* surround manicured gardens that are home to a lively monkey named Irma. (☎285 5111. Slow Internet 100C per hr. Singles 640C; quads 960C. 160C extra for A/C.) The **Nautilus** dive shop rents several clean, colorful rooms on its property. The restaurant is the best vegetarian option on the island. (Singles with hard beds, 160C; doubles with nicer beds 240C.)

FOOD AND NIGHTLIFE. Impatient personalities beware: Big Corn's "relax, take it easy" attitude definitely applies to its very leisurely restaurant service. **Fisher's Cave Restaurant ❸,** a 10-sided concrete building, sits at the foot of the pier, overlooking Briggs Bay. The outdoor seating area affords fabulous sunset views. Try the lobster *al vapor* for 100C. (Fish 70C-90C; meats 75C-100C; shrimp 100C; lobster 100C. Beer 15C. Open daily 7:30am-9:30pm.) **Hotel Paraíso Club ❹** (see above) has one of the nicest restaurants in town set on a thatched-hut patio with soft background music. (Pasta dishes 60C; fish 85-120C; meat dishes 140-220C. Open daily 7am-10pm.) **Restaurante Seva ❸,** on the northeast side of the island, overlooking the sea, has cozy dining rooms and a balcony with a nice view. The food is no slouch either. (Fish 50C-70C; lobster or shrimp 100C; beer 15C. Open daily 10am-10pm.)Two small discos come alive with local fishermen and visitors grooving to reggae music. **Island Style** is on Long Beach, on the southeast side of the island. This open-air disco spills right onto the beach and is especially popular on Sundays at sunset; **Morgan's Reggae Palace** is in a large concrete building.

TALK LIKE A NICA

Learn to speak like a *nica*, in only five minutes! Your mother will wash your mouth out with soap.

Alright then (Corn Islands Creole English): Ubiquitous greeting when passing anyone on the street, even strangers.

Ex: "Alright then." (Nod).
    "Alright then." (Nod).

Bolo: Drunk.

Ex: "Miguel was so bolo he fell asleep in the *parque* with his pants down!"

Bush (Corn Islands Creole English): Salad.

Ex: (Waitress). "You like to eat bush with that? We have cabbage bush and regular bush."

Chavalo/Chavala: Kid.

Ex: (A street child handing out slips of paper on a bus). "I'm a *chavalo* with very few resources, and prefer to ask rather than steal."

Chele/Chela: Literally, white boy/girl. The frequency with which this is shouted at you on the street will decrease exponentially with deepening of tan. Blonds/Redheads are out of luck.

Ex: (A man sitting on a stoop as a foreign women walks by). "Hola, chela! Chelita! Adios."

En el once: By foot. Literally means, "on the eleven," ironically referring to a non-existent bus line.

Goma: Hangover.

Ex: "I must have had a whole bottle of Flor de Cana last night, and now I've got the worst goma ever."
    -Emily Matchar

BEACHES AND OUTDOOR ACTIVITIES. A walk around most of the island is worthwhile and takes about 4½hr., though Bluff Point on the south side of the island has a crack problem and is unsafe to walk through. The **Picnic Center** should also be avoided. **Long Bay,** just south of South End, is a sweeping crescent of white sand, turquoise water, and coconut palms, perfect for sunbathing and relaxing. Water currents, however, make the swimming less than ideal. The best **snorkeling site** is **Sally Peachie Beach,** on the east side of the island. Here you can swim among schools of iridescent fish and drift over reefs teeming with marine life. On the west side are many sunken ships ripe for exploration. A number of places rent snorkel equipment: Marcus Gómez at **Hospedaje Sunrise** (see **Accommodations,** above) rents new gear (60C per day, 160C deposit.); **Yellow Tail House,** in Sally Peachie, also rents gear (80C per day, 160C with a 2hr. tour.); **Nautilus Ecotours** (☎ 285 5077), 5 blocks north of Fisher's Cave Restaurant, offers a menagerie of activities for experienced divers. (2 tank dive 720C). They also rent snorkel gear (half day 64C, full day 110C), new bikes (95C-60C), and horses (half day 190C). Remember to check equipment for quality. A guided hike around the island runs 64C for a half day, and boat excursions, 1040C-2000C.

LITTLE CORN ISLAND

> **!** Remember, this paradise has a dark side—there is a crack and crime problem and no police on the island. It is not safe to walk alone at night, especially as a woman. Violence is rampant and personal security should be a focus.

Little Corn Island can be an unexpected hidden delight, if you are especially careful about your safety. On *La Islita*, footpaths wind through lush palm forests and reach uninhabited beaches where splendid coral reefs sit just offshore. The swimming and snorkeling are great. On the far side of the island a shipwrecked fishing boat, just visible above the surface of the reef, awaits exploration. The 50ft. lighthouse on the island's highest point yields a gorgeous *vista.* Sportfishing is excellent; snag some giant barracuda and get a free dinner. Ask around, and you may be able to tag along on a local fishing boat for free or for a gas contribution.

Four daily **pangas** run from Big Corn Island (9am and 4pm; return 6:30am and 2pm; 70C), 18km away. There are no cars or bikes.

Don't be fooled by the signs; it's a 40min. (not 20min.) walk to **Hotel Derrek's Place** from the *panga* stop. Derrek's is worth the walk: it may be the most beautiful location on the island, so reservations are recommended. Breakfast and dinner are 48C-80C. Tents 60C per person; basic *cabañas* 110C per person; raised rooms 240C. **Casa Iguana ❺,** up a 1km trail from the *panga* drop-off, is popular with an older crowd of vacationers. The American owners of the eco-tourism lodge grow or catch most of their own food and collect rainwater to drink and use. The hotel also arranges fishing trips (720C for one person, 825C for two). Non-guests can partake of the nightly communal dinners by booking before 1pm (135C-165C) or walk in for breakfast (70C). The connected "William Walker" Internet Cafe is 40C per 15min. 9am-noon. (casaiguana@mindspring.net. Singles 400C; doubles with fan 560C, with A/C 720C.) **Bridgette ❷,** in the small village at the Comedor First Stop, offers worn rooms with fans and outdoor bathroom facilities (160C). Following the path toward Casa Iguana, then turning right and walking along the beach, will take you to **Miss Gracie's ❷,** a beachfront bar and restaurant that rents five basic rooms with mosquito netting and shared bath. The reef in front offers amazing snorkeling, though the bar attracts people who hang around the hostel late at night. (Rooms 160C per night.) **Lobster Inn ❸** is the two-story pink building in the village offering clean, comfortable rooms with fans and private baths for 320C per night. The ground floor restaurant has standard island food.

Habana Libre ❸, known locally as "The Cuban," is located in the village in a white building with a large patio. The Cuban owner and his islander wife serve up delicious Cuban specialties such as *ropa vieja* and snapper *al ajillo*, accompanied by wonderful *mojitos* when mint is in season. (Entrees 60C-100C. Open daily 11am-10pm.) **Delfina's ❷**, in the hotel, is popular with locals and tourists alike. Relax on the breezy upper porch overlooking the ocean. Notable breakfasts 30C-55C, sandwiches 25C-35C, dinners 70C-150C. At **Farm Peace and Love,** on the far side of the island, the owner will cook a sumptuous Italian feast; great for special occasions. Arrange a day in advance in the dive shop.

There are a handful of *tiendas* in the village which stock basic provisions along with plenty of rum and soda. **Oliver's,** on the right side of the main path after turning right out of the dive shop and walking 5min., has the greatest variety. **Miss Gracie's** bar hosts popular full moon parties, and **Happy Hut** bar and disco is the island's social magnet, playing reggae, pop, and *salsa.* (Beer 15C.)

Diving is why many come to Little Corn, with its very own healthy barrier reef and a quality, fully-equipped dive shop. **Dive Little Corn** (www.divelittlecorn.com) is staffed by friendly and professional PADI-certified instructors who speak English and Spanish, with new equipment available for rent with scheduled dives. They offer morning, afternoon, and night dives as well as PADI certifications from one-day resort courses to divemaster. (One tank dive 640C; 580C for each tank thereafter; discover scuba and resort course 960C; open-water certification 5000C. Snorkel gear 80C per day, guides additional 80C. AmEx/MC/V with 4% surcharge.)

NORTHEAST NICARAGUA

Due to safety concerns, coverage of Northeast Nicaragua was not updated for the 2005 edition. All information, including prices and numbers, is based on research conducted in August 2002.

Northeast Nicaragua, largely encompassed by the Northern Atlantic Autonomous Region (RAAN), is one of the least developed areas in Central America. It is a difficult region in which to travel, and few make the effort. The large Miskito village of Puerto Cabezas is the capital and second largest Caribbean port in Nicaragua, but offers little of interest to the average traveler. The town of Siuna is part of RAAN but actually lies significantly inland. This former gold-mining settlement is notable for the flawless rainforest of the nearby Bosawas Reserve. This area has a legacy of Sandinista instability, but has become more safe in recent years. The adventurous traveler looking for untouched, natural perfection and seclusion will find it in the Bosawas Reserve and northeast Nicaragua.

SIUNA

The Siuna area is still plagued by armed and active bands of Sandinistas and Contras. Most recently, in June 2004, after shots were fired, police took prisoner a gang of kidnappers who possessed various arms including automatic weapons. Efforts to curb rogue groups seem to be working, but the danger of unpredictable and unprovoked attacks still exists. Travel in the region is currently not advisable. Check the latest situation before considering a visit.

The frontier outpost of Siuna sprang up almost overnight as a gold rush town back in the day. The mine shut down in 1979, causing an economic slump. Locals continue to mine gold by hand, denting the once lush hillside. The large pit was excavated by the company and the smaller pit right next to it has been dug completely by hand. The real reason to come all the way here is for the untouched rainforest that begins near town. The environmentally conscious locals proudly call their forest—the largest swath of unbroken rainforest north of the Amazon—the "lungs of Central America." A serious visit will take "roughing it" to a whole new level, but the plants and animals that await are astounding.

La Costeña has daily **flights** to **Siuna** from: **Managua** (☎263 1228; 1hr.; 9am, returning at 10:30 am and 2:15pm; one-way 595C, round-trip 1070C) and **Puerto Cabezas** (1 hr.; 1:15pm, returns at 10:30am; 510/900C). Flights to and from Puerto Cabezas stop in **Bonanza** and **Rosita** (from Siuna 355C/500C, from Puerto Cabezas 510/900C). Siuna, Rosita, and Bonanza are often referred to collectively as **Las Minas.** Flights operate subject to demand; always have a reservation or show up a few hours early. There is a small ticket office on the runway. A Siuna bound **bus** leaves Managua's Mayoreo market daily and makes a bumpy trip through the forest. Reserve a seat earlier that day. (10hr., 5pm, 80C; 8hr., 8pm, 100C.) **Buses** leave the market daily for: **Managua** (9hr., 8pm; 10½hr., 5:30pm, 70C; 12hr., 4pm, 100C.); **Puerto Cabezas** (12hr., 4am, 100C); **Rosa Grande** (2hr.; 6, 11am, 1pm, 30C); **Hormiguero** (1¼hr., 6:30am and noon, 15C). Road conditions and transit schedules in northeast Nicaragua are poor and constantly changing. **Taxis** are 5C. Transit is never guaranteed and often cancelled due to weather, road conditions, broken equipment, or lack of passengers. Always check in the market for the latest info and budget extra time and money for travel in the region.

It's hard to describe Siuna's tangled web of roads, but luckily, the town is small. The north side of the runway contains large portrait **murals.** The main cement road runs parallel to and then north from the runway. It winds around and up the hill, past the mine ruins, and turns to dirt after the market. There is then a small *parque* and the road winds around the opposite side of the hill, passing the mayor's office and eventually intersecting itself just north of the airport. Just south of La Costeña another dirt road runs east for a block then turns north. The **Bosawas Reserve Office** is 1 block after it turns north. (☎273 2036 in Siuna, 233 1594 in Managua. Open M-F 8am-noon and 1:30-5pm.) The **Caruna Bank,** just next to the mayor's office, doesn't offer traveler's check or credit card advances, but does have **Western Union** services. (☎273 2016. Open M-F 8:30am-noon and 1-4:30pm, Sa 9-11am.) The **police station** is south of the mayor's office (☎273 2000). **Hospital Carlos Centeno,** west of the *parque*, has a 24hr. emergency pharmacy (☎273 2003); other pharmacies are available in the market. **ENITEL** is on the west side of the *parque*. (☎273 2005; fax 273 2101. Open M-F 8am-noon and 1:30-5pm.) The **post office** is just beyond the reserve office (open M-Sa 8am-8pm).

The town lacks running water, but all places listed compensate with cleanliness. The only place with 24hr. running water is **Hospedaje Siu ❷,** a few blocks west of the mayor's office (singles 75C; doubles 120C). **Hotel Cauta Gallo ❷,** east of the park on top of the hill, was the club and bunkhouse for mine executives. Cherrywood floors and walls and the best beds in town tell of its former glory. It can be difficult to get a room. (☎273 2019. Reception open 7am-4:30pm only, best to call a day or more ahead. 135C per person.) **El Desnuque ❶,** along the airstrip, has large basic rooms with bucket-flush private baths. Attached restaurant has the town's largest portions and best food, 40C-80C. (☎273 2049. Singles 60C; doubles 80C.)

BOSAWAS RESERVE

To gain access to the Bosawas Reserve you must have a guide and permission from the reserve office in Siuna. The Bosawas Reserve Office (see Practical Information, above) has a very friendly and helpful staff who can assist you in planning a route and will organize a knowledgeable guide. They will also assist in figuring out the sporadic transportation to Rosa Grande or El Hormiguero, the entrances to the park. You should call 1 week in advance so that the office has time to organize a guide. A strenuous 1-day hike into the park is feasible from either entrance if you take the early van; but to truly experience Bosawas you'll need three to 5 days. Guides 80C per day. Cooking about 75C per person. Horseback excursions 80C per person.

Five-hundred-year old trees, monkeys, mountains, waterfalls, parrots, rivers, natural medicinal flowers, and even a few elusive quetzals await in the isolated Bosawas Reserve, where diehards come for the deep, dark primary rain forests. Two ecotourism camps, covered shelters with latrines and garbage cans, are used as launching points for those wishing to delve deeper into the wilderness. From Rosa Grande, the camp at **Salto Labú** is 4km, right next to a waterfall (a 10 foot cliff is perfect for jumping into the deep pool of emerald green water at Labú's base). From El Hormiguero, the camp at **El Magague** is 6km and is rich in monkeys, parrots, and wildlife. While guides will prepare meals if you've made prior arrangements, visitors should come stocked with a water filter or purification tablets, first aid kit, lots of bug spray, rain gear, and sturdy waterproof hiking boots (suffer with the thin plastic boots you can buy at the market, 80C.) Visits here are amazing at any time of year, but best in the dry season.

PUERTO CABEZAS

Far from Managua, in the country's northeastern corner, Puerto Cabezas (locally called Bilwi) is visited more often by volunteers and business people than tourists. It takes some effort to get to, and there's not too much to see once here. Even though the town is right on the ocean, its Caribbean beaches are seldom visited, and it lacks the natural beauty of the rest of northeastern Nicaragua. Still, one might stay here for practical reasons—it is the largest town in all of Mosquitia.

La Costeña and Atlantic Airlines **fly** into the **airport** a few kilometers north of town. Flights to: **Managua** (1¼hr.; LC Su-F 6:30, 8:20am, 12:20pm; M-Sa 4:10pm; AA M-Sa 8am, 12:10pm. One-way 850C, round-trip 1570C); **Bluefields** (1hr.; LC daily 11am; one-way 770C, round-trip 1420C); **Siuna/Las Minas** (30min.; LC daily 1:10pm; one-way 510C, round-trip 900C). **Buses** leave for **Managua** (24hr., daily noon, 200C). Fishing and cargo **boats** sometimes run to and from Bluefields and Trujillo, Honduras. A **taxi** to either spot shouldn't be more than 15C. It's possible to hire a boat at the dock to go to one of the dozens of tiny, uninhabited **Cayos Miskitos.** *Pangas* (small boats) can fit 12-14. (4hr. one way, 150C-400C; express 3hr. one way, 3000C) Inquire a day or two in advance at the dock south of town.

The nearest **beach, La Bocana,** is a few kilometers north along the coast, near the airport. The town has a **bank** that changes traveler's checks. (☎282 2272. Open M-F 8am-4:30pm.) Other services include: **police** (☎282 2257), **hospital** (☎282 2259), **ENITEL** (☎282 2300; Open M-Sa 8am-9pm, Su 8am-5:30pm), and **post office.** The best bet for lodging is **Hospedaje El Viajante ❶,** on the main street, with friendly, English-speaking owners. (☎282 2237. Rooms with fan and shared bath 60C; with private bath, cable TV, fridge, and A/C 175C.) **Hotel Pérez ❷,** is north on the main street. (Singles with shared bath and TV 150C, with private

NICARAGUA

bath, A/C, and TV 375C). If you're by the beach stop in at **Kabu Payaska/Aires del Mar/Seabreezes ❷** (tri-named in Miskito, Spanish, and English) for verdant grounds right on the ocean with, of course, a breeze. (*Bocas* 30-35C, beer 13C, entrees 85C.) Closer to town is **Disco Bar Miramar ❸,** a four story building above the ocean affording un-matched views of the Caribbean. The restaurant turns into a bar and disco at night. If you decide to go dancing, be careful. Puerto Cabezas is not known for the character of its nightowls. (Entrees 70-85C; beer 13C; rum and coke 10-15C. Restaurant open 10am-3am. Disco open 7pm-3am.)

PANAMA

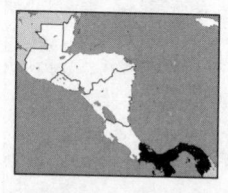

True, the Panama Canal might be one of the greatest human-made wonders of the world. Put that aside for the moment and consider Panama's other wonders: lush mountain forests, Caribbean beaches surrounded by coral reefs, a thriving and skyscraping metropolis, vast ranches of highland villages. Panama's 2.5 million people create a diverse culture, including vibrant indigenous groups and recent international immigrants. However, the canal's influence cannot be understated: the money it has pumped into the economy has led to well-maintained roads, efficient buses, reliable electric power, and almost universal indoor plumbing. The capital's cosmopolitan influence extends throughout the country, dwindling only in the far east in San Blas and Darién, where dugout canoes provide access to hidden remote villages and images of Western pop culture's fashions are replaced by Kuna *molas*, traditional patched cloth panels. Pristine Caribbean shores and untouched forests are within a few hours' drive of Panama City, Central America's most modern city. With both the traditional and modern to tempt, it's a wonder so few budget travelers come to Panama. Prices, though higher than in other parts of Central America, are still affordable; the political situation is stable; and the tourist and national park infrastructure is unmatched.

HIGHLIGHTS OF PANAMA

The beautiful beaches, clear water, and Caribbean atmosphere make **Bocas del Toro** one of the most popular sites for Panamanians and foreigners alike (p. 670).

Known for stunning cloud forest, resplendent quetzals, and Panama's highest peak, (p. 663), **Parque Nacional Volcán Barú.**

Panama City, the definition of cosmopolitan in Central America, where discos and museums compete for attention and international restaurants adjoin bohemian cafes (p. 605).

San Blas Archipelago, home of the semi-autonomous Kuna Indians, whose tiny villages provide an authentic and peaceful Caribbean island getaway (p. 678).

Often called the heartland of Panama, **Azuero Peninsula** is where Spanish influence is still strong and the traditional festivals are raucous (p. 643).

SUGGESTED ITINERARIES

ONE WEEK: PANAMA CITY ENVIRONS. Explore **Panama City**—don't miss **Panamá Viejo** (p. 617), well-preserved **Casco Viejo** (p. 611), or **Parque Natural Metropolitano** (p. 620). Party the night away in bohemian **Bella Vista** (p. 615) and the increasingly popular **Amador** (p. 628). See the **Panama Canal** at **Miraflores** (p. 623), and visit nearby **Parque Nacional Soberanía** (p. 625). Relax in **Portobelo** (p. 632) and enjoy the Caribbean flair of **Isla Grande** (p. 635) to the north. Back in Panama City with some time left, spend a few days and a lot of money treating yourself to the beach luxuries of **Isla Contadora** (p. 627) in the **Archipiélago de las Perlas** (p. 627).

2-3 WEEKS: EAST-WEST. From Panama City head out west to hike in nearby enchanted **El Valle** (p. 636) for a day, perhaps stopping at the Sunday market, **Mercado El Valle** (p. 636). Buy a world-famous Panama hat in **Penonomé** (p. 639), and

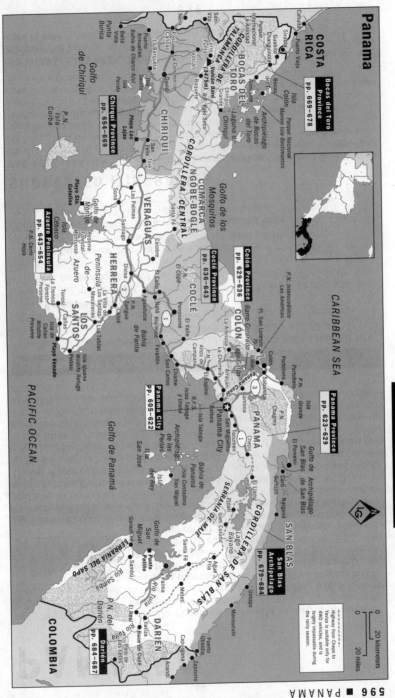

Panama

Bocas del Toro Province
pp. 669–678

Chiriquí Province
pp. 654–669

Azuero Peninsula
pp. 643–654

Coclé Province
pp. 636–643

Colón Province
pp. 629–636

Panama Province
pp. 623–629

Panama City
pp. 605–622

San Blas Archipelago
pp. 679–684

Darién
pp. 684–687

COSTA RICA

BOCAS DEL TORO

CHIRIQUÍ

VERAGUAS

COMARCA NGÖBE-BUGLÉ

HERRERA

LOS SANTOS

COCLÉ

COLÓN

PANAMÁ

SAN BLAS

DARIÉN

COLOMBIA

CARIBBEAN SEA

PACIFIC OCEAN

Golfo de Chiriquí

Golfo de Montijo

Golfo de Panamá

Golfo de San Miguel

CORDILLERA DE TALAMANCA

CORDILLERA CENTRAL

SERRANÍA DE MAJE

CORDILLERA DE SAN BLAS

SERRANÍA DEL SAPO

Highway from Chepo to Yaviza is suitable only for 4WD vehicles, and is largely impassable during the rainy season.

0   20 kilometers
0   20 miles

pay pristine **Parque Nacional Omar Torrijos** (p. 641) and its many wild animals a deserved visit. Explore Panama's traditional heartland, the **Azuero Peninsula** (p. 643), and don't miss **Las Tablas** and the peninsula's many *fiestas.* Continue west to **Volcán** (p. 665) or **Boquete** (p. 660) via **David,** to climb Panama's highest peak, **Volcán Barú** (p. 663) and hope to catch a glimpse of one of the rare **quetzals** in surrounding rain and cloud forest **national parks.** After the arduous hikes in thin air, hop on a bus along the scenic drive from David to Almirante, and embark on a water taxi to **Bocas del Toro** (p. 669). Explore the marine life around **Isla Bastimentos** (p. 674) or simply relax on empty picture-perfect Caribbean beaches. If by now you haven't decided to burn your return ticket, hop on a plane or bus back to Panama City. For more sun and san, fly to one of many islands in the **San Blas Archipelago** (p. 679) and stay with the **Kuna,** the indigenous people who govern the region, to experience a slower lifestyle in a paradisiac tropical setting. Alternatively, if you feel adventurous and active, fly into **Darién** (p. 684), where Panama's untamed wilderness awaits at **Río Sambú** (p. 686) and **Parque Nacional Darién** (p. 687).

LIFE AND TIMES

LAND, FLORA, AND FAUNA

Panama is shaped like a sideways S running west to east, with the Caribbean Sea to the north and the Pacific Ocean to the south. The western half is split in half by the southern end of a volcanic chain—the **Cordillera Central** (or Tabasará Mountains)—while the non-volcanic **Cordillera de San Blás** divides the eastern lowlands. Nestled between the mountain ranges is the **Panama Canal,** bounded by Colón in the north and Panama City in the south. The **Azuero Peninsula** juts out and elongates the Pacific coast in central Panama. Island constellations, including the **Pearl Islands** and the **Bocas del Toro Archipelago,** can be found on both coasts. Panama's unique geographic location has contributed to both its economic and natural wealth. Harboring literally thousands of plant and animal species, ecotourism in Panama is a fascinating option for the environmentally-conscious traveler.

HISTORY

Panama's fate has always been tied to other nations' interest in its strategic position as a double bridge connecting the Americas and two oceans. Panama declared its independence from Spain in 1821, after which it shared closer ties with South America than Central America. While the other Central American nations became independent by the 1840s, during the next century Panama was controlled briefly by France, then by Colombia, and eventually the US. From 1850 to 1900, Panama had 40 different governments and 13 major US interventions.

EARLY HISTORY (15TH CENTURY-1840). In 1502, Columbus set foot on the shores of Central America in present-day Portobelo, Panama. Vasco Nuñez de Balboa established the first colony, became governor, and "discovered" the Pacific Ocean in 1513—and thus Panama's distinctive place in the world. The isthmus soon became the route through which Inca riches were shipped back to Spain. Once the Spanish empire declined, attempts by other European nations (particularly the Scottish) toward colonization failed to obtain the same level of domination in Panama, and trade continued to fall. In 1821, Panama became part of the **United Nations of Gran Colombia.** The construction of a US-owned transcontinental railroad through Panama in 1855 brought greater US intervention and whispers of a future canal, and planted the seeds of an independent Republic of Panama, attained in 1903.

A MAN, A PLAN, A CANAL: PANAMA—READ IT BACKWARDS (1840-1910).

The railroad prompted global interest in the construction of a canal. The first attempt by the French in 1848 ultimately failed, opening the door to a US-led plan. Because Colombia opposed a deal between the US and France that would allow the former to build the canal, the US stoked Panamanians' resentment of Colombia, which initiated the revolutionary junta that declared the **Republic of Panama**. Within two weeks the rights to the Canal Zone were traded away to the US, and work began promptly in 1904. The canal was completed 10 years later.

US-PANAMA RELATIONS (1915-1981).

Along with control to the waterway, Panama's new constitution granted the US political intervention rights. These were exercised several times throughout the century, despite Panama's increasing interest in total canal control. In 1936, five years after an insurrection and coup against the Panamanian oligarchy's political elite, the US agreed to abandon intervention rights and increased the fees paid to them in the Canal Zone. In order to strengthen their claims against the US, Panama responded by building a fortress (located near the city jail) and militarizing the police. As World War II approached, the US tried to arrange for the use of various Panamanian locales outside the Canal Zone, which the new Panamanian executives eventually allowed—largely out of sympathy for the Pearl Harbor attack—but ousted US military forces soon after the war. In 1964, US presence provoked student riots against both the Panamanian and US governments, leaving many Panamanians dead. For the first time, the Panamanian government cut ties with the US, however briefly.

After the 1968 presidential election, the Guardia Nacional supplanted the president-elect with their **General Omar Torrijos Herrera** as dictator of Panama. Splurging on the country's public works, despite a steadily growing debt, he developed housing for the poor, raised wages, sponsored a nationalistic program, and established the banking secrecy regulations that enabled Panama to become a money-laundering paradise. To encourage jingoist sentiment, he signed a treaty with US President Carter ensuring total Panamanian control of the canal by the year 2000. A mysterious 1981 plane crash ended Torrijos' life, opening the door to a new political crisis: the leadership of **General Manuel Noriega**, Torrijos's head of intelligence.

NORIEGA AND OPERATION JUST CAUSE (1982-1999).

Previously hired by the US as a spy in Perú and a CIA operative in contact with Nicaraguan Contras, Noriega eventually became head of Panamanian intelligence. Upon seizing control of the Guardia in 1983, the Panamanian General granted himself dictatorial powers: he controlled the press, created military goon squads, and managed Panama's drug traffic. In 1984, Noriega permitted a national election; popular **Arnulfo Arias** seemed a clear winner, but **Ardito Barletta,** Noriega's candidate, emerged victorious to become a puppet president. In 1988, Noriega was indicted in the US for drug trafficking. As US President Ronald Reagan tightened sanctions on Panama, Noriega closed his grip, nullifying another election his candidate had lost.

No sooner did Noriega declare himself maximum authority (with yet another puppet president in place) than word spread that Panama was at war with the US. After a confrontation between Panamanian soldiers and four unarmed US Marine officers, **President George Bush** ordered 24,000 troops to Panama to remove Noriega. Noriega fled into the Papal Nuncio, where American soldiers assailed him with a bizarre form of psychological torture: they blared "Voodoo Child" and other rock tunes to flush him out (we're not making this up). A few days later, Noriega (who claims not to have heard the music) surrendered and was flown to Florida to await trial. In 1992, he was found guilty on eight charges of "conspiracy to manufacture and distribute cocaine" and sentenced to 40 years in prison.

Despite its stated goals of liberating Panama from tyranny, protecting American lives, and bringing Noriega to justice, **Operation Just Cause** (known in some circles as Operation "Just Cuz") was criticized internationally as bullying, self-interested foreign policy. Panamanians are divided on what they call "the invasion"; they are thankful to the US for ridding Panama of Noriega, but resentful of the bombings and overbearing, imperialistic presence. And while demilitarization became possible as a result, the newly installed government of **Guillermo Endara** faced high post-invasion poverty, crime, and unemployment rates.

Endara successfully engaged Panama in Central American affairs, establishing the country's membership in the **Central American Parliament** in 1993 and committing Panama to economic integration in the **Central American Common Market (ALCA). Ernesto Pérez Balladares** replaced Endara in 1994. Balladares's administration increased privatization and improved health care, education, and the country's overall infrastructure.

In May 1999, **Mireya Moscoso** was elected, the first female president. The victory was particularly sweet for Moscoso and the Arnulfista party: she defeated Martín Torrijos, whose father Omar had deposed Moscoso's husband Arias from the presidency in the 1968 military coup. The election also marked the second peaceful transition of the 1990s. Despite the stable democracy, the country remains a center for drug trafficking due to inadequate border and airport security. Moscoso's cabinet has been the butt of corruption and economic complaints.

TODAY. After almost a century under US jurisdiction, the **canal** was officially handed over to Panama on December 31, 1999. Symbolically handing over the canal to Panama on December 14th, former US president Jimmy Carter provided closure to the treaties he signed in 1978, which described the gradual and systematic removal of US presence. The patriotic ceremony, celebrating the inception of a new era of complete Panamanian self-sovereignty, was accompanied by nationwide celebration. Huge renovation and development programs are currently underway for the canal equipment and the land left by the US. These include new locomotives, tugboats, and even a flashy golf and casino resort. The two most ambitious projects, however, are a conservation effort for the canal's watershed (to keep it from drying up), and a widening of the Gaillard Cut. The latter project is to be completed next year to allow large vessels to traverse the canal simultaneously in both directions.

The most pressing concern for Panama's leaders has been the administration and patrolling of the canal. With the US gone, illegal drug trafficking, money laundering, and airport security problems have increased. Contamination remains from the US presence, with toxic waste buried beneath the zone's military bases and explosives in the rain forest. Moscoso's government has complained about the slow efforts of the US in the clean-up process. Both countries are currently investigating the severity of the damage to determine a plan of action.

President Moscoso worked to strengthen social programs, particularly in education. She successfully presided over the transfer and administration of the canal, and she has helped pass counter-narcotics, counter-money laundering, and intellectual property rights legislation. Panama supports the "Free Trade for the Americas" proposal and was host of official negotiations until 2003; the country is currently negotiating free trade with Mexico and its Central American neighbors. May 2004 found Panama voting for a new president: **Martin Torrijos,** an illegitimate son of former military leader Omar Torrijos, defeated ex-president Guillermo Endara and took power on September 1, 2004.

CULTURE AND ARTS

PEOPLE

Survivors from Pre-Colombian days—most notably, the **Ngöbe Buglé** (also called Guaymí), **Kuna,** and **Chocó Indians**—are the most prominent of the few but widespread indigenous groups composing 6% of the Panamanian population. Generally, these indigenous descendants, who still speak their traditional languages, live by subsistence agriculture. Nearly 70% of Panamanians are *mestizos*, and concentrate in the lowlands on either side of the canal. The canal attracted and brought other groups into the country, including Africans, East Indians, Chinese, and Jews, contributing to the country's international flavor. Spanish, Panama's official language, is spoken by over 90% of the population. The clearest exception to this rule is in the San Blas Archipelago, where Kuna is the predominant language and Spanish won't get you very far. As in other Latin American countries, Roman Catholicism is the dominant religion; however, Protestants have a foothold in the country, especially among the indigenous and African descendants. Santería, a mixture of Catholic and West Indian rites, is still practiced by some minority groups.

FOOD AND DRINK. The typical Panamanian meal, known simply as *comida*, consists of rice, beans, beef or chicken, and plantains prepared in one of numerous ways, and is usually available at *típico* (typical Panamanian) restaurants. *Sancocho*, a spicy chicken and vegetable stew cooked in a big pot, is the national dish. On the coast, seafood, like *corvina* (sea bass) is popular and delicious. Panama City boasts some of the most diverse fare in Central America, offering plenty of alternatives to standard rice and beans. At kiosks throughout the country you will find *frituras*, bits of deep-fried dough and meat, and *empanadas*, fried dough shells stuffed with chicken, beef, or cheese. Vegetarian, and also kosher, options are easy to come by in Panama City. Panama produces a number of fine beers—a great dark is Balboa; for a lighter option, try Atlas. Soberana, Panama, and Cristal are also popular. The national liquor is *seco*, potent stuff rated on an increasing potency scale two to eight. The most popular type, Herrerano, is nicknamed *nueve letras*, for the nine letters in its name.

FINE ARTS AND CRAFTS. Panamanian art is graphic, colorful, and reflective of the indigenous and Central and South American mix. Nearly every town has a *mercado artesanal*, where you can purchase and admire local art. Pottery with geometric patterns fills markets in western and central Panama, much of it replicating the folk art of Guaymí Indians. Predominant in the east are *tagua* nut carvings, and intricately patterned and hand-stitched Kuna cloths, called *molas*. Check out the Museum of Contemporary Art in Panama City for more modern national work (p. 617).

LITERATURE. Panama's distance from the cultural centers of Guatemala and Colombia resulted in a weak literary scene until the 20th century. Prior to then, poetry like that of **José María Alemán** (1830-1887) and **Darío Herrera** (1870-1914) was mainly an outlet for Romantic and Modernist thought. Since the canal's building, foreign nations' roles in Panamanian affairs have become the dominant themes of authors like **Renato Ozores** and **Carlos Francisco Changmarín.**

ARCHITECTURE. Panamanian architecture combines the best aspects of Spanish, French, Caribbean, and indigenous architecture into a new distinct form. Look for Spanish colonialism and tiled roofs, French balconies, and the rustic, traditional Panamanian *quincha*—made of mud and clay-covered wooden cane used in indigenous house construction. However, the most impressive example of Panamanian architecture certainly isn't any of the skyscrapers or attempted sophistication of Panama City, but rather 82km of water connecting two oceans.

MUSIC AND DANCE. The most popular types of music in Panama are by far *merengue* and *salsa*. If that doesn't keep you moving, shake your groove thing to reggae (or rather, *regetón*, a Latin interpretation of reggae), or relax to jazz and the symphony. The national Panamanian dance, the *tamborito*, mixes colonial Spanish movements with African-inspired rhythms and is accented by claps and drums. Other characteristic forms are the *mejorana*, with two guitars and a square dance; and the quicker *punta*.

ESSENTIALS

FACTS FOR THE TRAVELER

ENTRANCE REQUIREMENTS

Passport: (p. 19) Required for citizens of all countries.

Visa: Not required for citizens of Australia, Canada, Ireland, New Zealand, UK, or US.

Tourist Card: Required for citizens of Australia, Canada, Ireland, New Zealand, UK, or US. Available upon arrival and issued for 30 days; may be extended for up to 90 days (US$5). Visitors must have an onward/return ticket.

Inoculations and Medications: (p. 27) None required.

Work Permit: Required of all foreigners planning to work in Panama.

Driving permit: (p. 37) An international drivers' license is recommended.

Airport Departure Fee: US$20.

EMBASSIES AND CONSULATES

Embassies of Panama: Canada, 130 Albert St. #300, Ottawa, Ontario K1P 5G4 (☎613-236-7177; fax 236-5775). **US,** 2862 McGill Terr. NW, Washington, D.C. 20008 (☎202-483-1407; fax 483-8413). Open M-F 9am-5pm; consulate closed noon-2pm.

Consulates of Panama: UK, 40 Hertford Street, London W1J 7SH (☎44 20 7409 2255; fax 7495 0412). **US,** 1212 Av. of the Americas, 47/48 St., 6th fl., New York, NY 10036 (☎212-840-2450; fax 840-2469). Open M-F 9am-2pm. Other consulates in Atlanta, Chicago, Houston, Los Angeles, Miami, New Orleans, New York, Philadelphia, Tampa.

MONEY

US DOLLARS		
AUS$1 = US$0.55		US$1 = AUS$1.82
CDN$1 = US$0.64		US$1 = CDN$1.56
EUR€1 = US$0.98		US$1 = EUR€1.02
NZ$1 = US$0.47		US$1 = NZ$2.14
US$1 = US$1		US$1 = US$1
UK£1 = US$1.55		US$1 = UK£0.65

The rates below were accurate as of August 2004. All prices in this book are quoted in US dollars, as the Panamanian currency, the **balboa**, is directly linked to the dollar—effectively, the balboa *is* the US dollar. Panama uses actual US bills but mints its own coins. A huge 50¢ piece, known as a **peso**, is used regularly, and a nickel is often called a **real**. **ATMs** (marked by red *Sistema Clave* signs) are everywhere in Panama City and throughout David, and though uncommon in rural areas are found in a number of towns west of Panama City. The machines don't always accept foreign cards. There are several **Western Union** offices around the country. Some more pricey hotels and department stores accept **traveler's checks,** but few budget establishments or businesses will honor them. Many banks are willing to exchange American Express checks and sometimes other types. Bring proper ID and be prepared to pay a fee unless you are exchanging at the AmEx office. Outside Panama City, national banks satisfy money needs, but at border crossings, money is exchanged at bad rates—in other words, bring US dollars. **Visa** and **Mastercard** are easier to use than other cards, but many hotels and restaurants demand cash regardless. Visitors can often obtain AmEx/MC/V **cash advances**, and there are a number of US banks (Citibank, Fleet, HCSB) where charges may be less substantial. All international cards work, but PINs should be in numbers to accommodate letter-less keypads. **Tipping,** 10% at least in the big cities, is generally expected except at self-service restaurants. "Free" guides usually expect a tip. For more info, see **Tipping and Bargaining,** p. 23.

PRICE RANGES AND RANKINGS. The most significant costs for travelers in Panama will be accommodations, notably more expensive than those in other parts of Central America. While basic rooms or dorm beds can usually be found for under US$7, more elaborate lodgings are US$10-$15, and a private single with some amenities is at least US$20. Food is cheap, with easily-found *típico* US$1-$3. While the assiduous traveler may be able to scrape by on US$15-$20 per day, a safer bet would be US$25-$30, without transportation.

SYMBOL	❶	❷	❸	❹	❺
ACCOMM.	US$1-7	US$7-15	US$15-25	US$25-50	US$50-100
FOOD	US$1-3	US$3-6	US$6-9	US$9-12	US$12-15

SAFETY

The regions west of Panama City are politically stable and safe. In Panama City, standard big-city rules apply; some neighborhoods are best avoided at night, and a few are best avoided altogether (see **Panama City: Orientation,** p. 607). Outside the free trade zone, Colón is generally unsafe—take taxis from the bus station and don't walk (see **Colón,** p. 629). Guerrillas and paramilitaries are active in the Darién area along the Colombian border, especially since the US military left in 1999. Both US and Panamanian governments warn travelers not to enter the region (p. 684). **Women travelers** will find the same *machismo*, catcalls, and stares as in the rest of Central America, though Panama is no worse than other countries (see **Women Travelers,** p. 48). While public displays of homosexuality are not accepted anywhere in Panama, **gay and lesbian travelers** shouldn't have major problems as long as they keep a low profile. There is a large but disorganized gay population, especially in Panama City, where there is some gay nightlife.

HEALTH

For details on diseases, see **Health** (p. 25). **Malaria** is of special concern in Panama, as there are strains of mosquitoes that are **chloroquine-resistant;** if traveling east of Panama City, take an alternative anti-malarial. Malaria risk is greatest in rural areas in Bocas del Toro, San Blas, and Darién provinces. **Yellow fever** vaccination is recommended. Contact the US Centers for Disease Control for updated info (see **Health,** p. 25). Water is generally safe to drink, except in Bocas del Toro. Almost no travelers have problems with Panama City tap water; it's among the best urban water supplies in the world.

BORDER CROSSINGS

COSTA RICA. There are three land crossings. **Paso Canoas** (p. 659) is 50km west of David, Panama, and near Ciudad Neily, Costa Rica. To get there, catch a bus from David. **Sixaola/Guabito** (p. 678) are on the Caribbean coast 15 minutes from Changuinola, Panama, and near Puerto Viejo de Talamanca, Costa Rica. **Río Sereno,** at the end of the Concepción-Volcán road, is rarely used.

COLOMBIA. The Darién Gap, in the far east of Panama bordering Colombia, is the only break in the Interamerican Hwy. as it makes its way from Argentina to Alaska. Transport to and from Colombia, short of flying, is difficult at best. The **ferry** service between Colón and Cartagena has been discontinued, but occasional passage can be found on **cargo ships** from Panama. There are currently two land/sea routes into Colombia. One involves island-hopping through the San Blas Archipelago via **Puerto Obaldía** (see p. 684). The other involves a trek through Panama's Darién. As of August 2004, both routes were considered prohibitively unsafe due to local guerrilla and paramilitary activity.

KEEPING IN TOUCH

Mail from Panama takes about two weeks to get to the US, although occasionally a letter slips through and makes it in a few days. Postage is cheap (US$0.10-$1). To receive mail in Panama, *Lista de Correos* is *not* the phrase of choice; instead, use *Entrega General*. Also, be sure to write *República de Panamá* and not just *Panamá*, since Panama City is referred to as *Panamá*. Domestic mail travels pretty quickly (usually by bus or plane), though postal codes are not used. Address letters as follows:

> Maria Luisa ROMERO [first name, LAST NAME]
> Entrega General
> David [City], Chiriquí [Province]
> República de Panamá

Phone numbers in Panama have seven digits, no area codes. Generally reliable public phones are everywhere and the majority take calling cards. Panama's only phone provider, Cable & Wireless, sells pre-paid phone cards, but doesn't have public phones in its offices. International calls are pretty expensive (US$0.30-0.40 per min.), though cheaper with a calling card (US$0.25). Phones as a rule don't give change. **Internet** is widespread (about US$1 per hr.).

COUNTRY CODE	507

TRANSPORTATION

The major domestic airline is **Aeroperlas** (☎315 7500; www.aeroperlas.com). There are a few smaller airlines connecting Panama City to San Blas and Darién. **Buses** are the major means of budget transport and the only means of reaching remote interior locations. Bus quality is generally good, and long trips tend to be served by luxury coaches. Other intercity routes are run by mini-buses, while in remote areas, vans provide service. A bus's destination is almost always written on the front. If there's no terminal, many buses linger around the *parque central*. Pay when getting off, but confirm the fare before embarking. Consider taking warm clothes on board to protect yourself from the chilling air conditioning or the constant breeze from open windows. Travelers say **hitchhiking** becomes easier the farther one gets from the Interamerican Hwy., but *Let's Go* does not recommend it. Truck drivers have been known to offer *"un lif"* from gas stations.

PANAMA

ORIENTATION

As in all of Central America, directions favor landmarks over addresses which really are rarely used. Nevertheless, most Panamanian cities label streets in a grid of numbered north-south *avenidas* (avenues) and east-west *calles* (streets), organized the *parque central*. Generally, *avenidas* increase in number to the west, and *calles* increase to the south. Other major landmarks tend to be churches.

HOLIDAYS AND FESTIVALS

Regardless of the official date, most holidays are celebrated on Monday to create a long weekend. The largest festival is Carnaval, the Panamanian equivalent of Mardi Gras, celebrated during the four days prior to Ash Wednesday. Holidays include: **January 1,** New Year's Day; **January 9,** Martyr's Day; **March/April,** Good Friday, Easter Sunday; **May 1,** Labor Day; **August 15,** Founding of Old Panama (Panama City only); **November 1,** National Anthem Day; **November 2,** All Souls' Day; **November 3,** Independence Day (independence from Colombia); **November 4,** Flag Day; **November 10,** First Cry of Independence; **November 28,** Emancipation Day (from Spain); . **December 8,** Mother's Day; **December 25,** Christmas; **December 31,** New Year's Eve.

ALTERNATIVES TO TOURISM

Panama is the wealthiest Central American nation besides Costa Rica, thanks in large part to the consistent commerce provided by the Canal. However, drug trafficking, and poverty are issues. The indigenous groups have attained a high level of political and cultural autonomy and do not face rights issues as severe as in other parts of the region. This section lists some of the organizations in Panama that offer opportunities beyond the typical tourist experience. For more info on Alternatives to Tourism as well as tools for finding programs on your own, see the chapter at the beginning of the book (p. 53).

VISA INFORMATION

If you are working for a foreign company in Panama, you do not need a **work permit.** If you are hired by a Panamanian company, you will need a permit from the Ministry of Labor; they are good for 1 year, and renewable. You must also have a passport, a police record notarized by the nearest Panamanian Consulate, an original birth certificate, 6 passport-sized photos, and a negative HIV test. If married, you must show a certificate. Alternately, if you live in Panama legally for 5 years, you can become a resident alien with working rights. You may need a lawyer.

LANGUAGE SCHOOLS

Panama, like the other Central American countries, has a great variety of language schools scattered throughout the country. It is possible to search through the Internet for most of these options; check out the section on language schools in **Alternatives to Tourism** (p. 53).

Spanish Learning Center, Panama City, 6 blocks past Trapiche's restaurant, off Via Argentina (☎213 3121; spanishlearning@hotmail.com). One-on-one Spanish instruction tailored to your needs, learning style, and schedule (block of 10 hours distributed as you choose, US$100). Also offers intensive homestay and instruction (classes 4hr. per day 4 days per week, US$950 a month). Daytrips and Latin dance classes optional.

Spanish4Students, (www.spanish4students.com) lists various schools, including Spanish by the Sea, behind the Hotel Bahía in Bocas del Toro (☎507 757 9518; www.spanishbythesea.com). Accommodations, Internet, volunteer programs, nature outings and dive training available in addition to college credit. Prices vary by season.

VOLUNTEERING

BIOLOGY/ECOLOGY PROGRAMS

Forest Restoration Program, (kellykeefel@yahoo.com), Bocas del Toro near Bocas del Drago. Run by the Institute for Tropical Ecology and Conservation (ITEC), volunteers are welcome. US$15 per day includes food and facilities.

Sea Turtle Conservation Program, (contact Aideen ☎ 757 9244; acomerford18@hotmail.com), Bocas del Toro and Isla Colón. Volunteers live on the archipelago and help out scientists and biologists. 1 week minimum stay.

PANAMA CITY

Few cities in the world have a history, fortune, and character so intimately and singularly related to their geography. Permanently marked by the canal and the commerce it brings, not to mention a century of partial US occupation, Panama City (pop. 500,000) is unlike anything else you'll find in the country or the rest of Central America. It's a surprising and welcoming combination of the historic and ultra-modern, where Spanish and indigenous traditions coexist with immigrant cultures from the world over. The result is a metropolis that defines "cosmopolitan."

Panama City's location, a calm harbor on the narrow bridge between two continents, has made it a transit point for both people and currency for over 300 years. Originally the gateway for all the gold from Spain's Pacific colonies, the first Panama City, known as Panamá Viejo (Old Panama), was founded by the Spanish in 1519 on the site of an Indian village on the Pacific. In the late 17th century, pirate invasions, infertile swamps, and numerous fires forced residents to move 8km west to a more defensible site, what is today San Felipe. There the city flourished under Spanish, French, and American occupations. During the California Gold Rush, hordes of prospectors flowed in from North America, fattening the pockets of steam-ship barons and resulting in the construction of the trans-isthmic railway joining the Pacific and Atlantic Oceans for the first time. This fostered dreams for the French of a more ambitious inter-oceanic connection until their attempt to build a Canal failed at the end of the 19th century. By the early 20th century, US plans for a water passage were complete, and during the Canal's construction the city began to expand and spread eastward, moving to its current site. The first ship passed through the canal's Miraflores Locks in 1914. Since then, Panama has gained control over the canal, and its favorable tax regulations have made Panama City an international banking and commercial center.

With its first-world infrastructure, a diverse population and continuing international influence, an extremely varied cuisine and shopping scene, and a lively nightlife that continues until the sun rises, Panama City boasts all the advantages of a large, modern city. However, should you want to escape and explore Panama's other amenities, rainforest, Indian villages, and beautiful beaches are all located within an hour from the center.

■ INTERCITY TRANSPORTATION

Domestic Buses: Most buses to the rest of the country leave from the brand-new **Gran Terminal Nacional de Transporte** near Marcos Gelabert Airport (☎ 232 5803). Services include 24hr. ATMs, Internet, and luggage storage. Despite the following schedules, buses may depend on demand and sometimes wait to fill up. Buses head to: **Almirante** (9hr., 8pm, US$23); **Chitré** (4hr., every hr. 6am-10pm, US$6); **Colón** (2hr., every 30min. 4:45am-10pm, US$1.25; express US$2) via Sabanitas (1-2hr., US$1); **David** (6hr., US$10.60; express 5hr., US$15); **El Valle** (2hr., every 30min. 7am-7pm,

US$3.50); **Metetí** (7-8hr., 6 per day 4:15am-3:45pm, US$9); **Paso Canoas** (10hr., every 1½-2hr. 7am-8pm, US$12; express 8½hr., 11pm and midnight, US$17); **Penonomé** (2½hr., every 20min. 4:45am-10:45pm, US$3.70); **Santiago** (3½hr.; every 1½ hr. 1am-11pm, and midnight; US$6); and **Yaviza** (10-13hr., US$14). Buses to Metetí continue to Yaviza when the road is dry enough. If the road is muddy, there are 4WD *chivitas* in Metetí, US$5.

International Buses: Tica Buses (☎314 6385) go to **San José, Costa Rica** (18hr., 1 per day 11am, US$25).

Domestic Flights: Marcos Gelabert Airport (☎315 9000) handles all domestic flights and is a US$2 taxi ride from the Santa Ana neighborhood. Airlines and their destinations are:

Aeroperlas (☎315 7500; www.aeroperlas.com) has flights to **Bocas del Toro** and **Changuinola** (1 hour, M-F 8:30am and 1pm; Sa 7am and 3pm; Su 8am and 3pm; US$58 to Bocas, US$59 to Changuinola); **Chitré** (20 min., M-F 6:15am and 4pm, US$37); **Contadora** (20 min., M-F 8am, 5 and 5:30pm; Sa 8:50am and 5pm; Su 8:50am, 3:50 and 4:40pm; US$29); **David** (1 hour, M-F 6:30am, 4:30pm; Sa 7, and 3:30pm; Su 8am and 3:30pm; US$59); **El Real** (45 min., M, W, F 9:05am; US$48.30) and **La Palma** (50 min., US$40). Low-season student discounts usually 25%. Low-season standby 50%.

Turismo Aéreo (☎315 0279) runs the following schedule with the same prices as Aeroperlas: **Chitré** (M-F 6:45am, Sa 8am, Su 3:45pm); **Contadora** (M-Th 9am, Sa-Su 9am and 4:30pm); **El**

Real and **La Palma** (M, Th and Sa 9am). It also flies to **San Blas**—including **El Porvenir** (6am, US$30) and **Puerto Obaldía** (M, W, and F 6am; US$59). Starting in September of 2004, they will also offer flights to **Bocas del Toro.**

Aerotaxi (☎315 7520), a subsidiary of Aeroperlas, flies to **El Porvenir** (40 min., daily 6am, US$32) and other **San Blas** islands.

Mapiex Aero (☎315 0888, www.mapiexaero.com) flies west to: **Bocas del Toro** and **Changuinola** (M-F 6:45am and 2pm, Sa 6:30am and 1pm, Su 1pm; US$58 to Bocas, US$59 to Changuinola); and **David** (M-F 6:25, 10:45am, and 4pm; Sa 7, 10:45am, and 4pm; Su 8am and 4pm; US$59).

International Flights: Tocumen International Airport (☎238 2700) lies 30min. east of the city and can be reached by cab (US$15) or any bus marked "Tocumen" (US$0.20-$0.30). Buses depart from C. 12, Av. Perú, Vía España, Av. Balboa, or C. 50 to the airport parking lot. Airlines and local numbers include: **American** (☎269 6022); **Continental** (☎265 4400); **Copa** (☎217 2672); **Delta** (☎214 8118); **Taca** (☎260 8222); and **United** (☎225 3087).

Boat: The Panama Canal is a major transit point for cargo ships and yachts, and with plenty of time and even more luck, travelers may be able to hitch a ride, though *Let's Go* does not recommend hitchhiking. To get to the **Yacht Club,** take a bus marked Balboa (US$0.25) from Plaza 5 de Mayo in Santa Ana. Open M-Sa 8:30am-5pm. From Balboa, commercial boats travel to **Isla Taboga** on Expreso del Pacífico (☎261 0350. 20min.; M-F 8:30am and 3pm, Sa-Su 8:30, 10:15am, and 4pm; round-trip US$10) or Calypso Queen (☎264 6096; ½hr.; Tu 8:30am, Sa-Su 8 and 10:30am; round-trip US$8), and to **Isla Contadora** on National Tours (☎269 8749; 2 hr.; leaves daily at 9am, returns at 2pm except for W when it returns at 12:30pm; one- way US$20).

▚ ORIENTATION

ARRIVAL. After arriving at Tocumen International Airport, head to the parking lot for a bus (45min. to Santa Ana, US$0.35) or a taxi (30min.; US$25 for 1 or 2 people, US$30 for 3, US$15 per person for a shared van). The domestic airport is a US$2 taxi from the center. Most buses arrive at the new Gran Terminal.

LAYOUT. The **Canal** occupies the far southwestern border of the city, running inland to the northwest. The city's main sprawl runs west to east along the **Bahía de Panamá** (Panama Bay) east of the canal's mouth. The peninsula of **San Felipe** (also known as Casco Viejo) on the west side of the bay is home to a few budget hotels and numerous sights, and is centered on Plaza de la Independencia. The city's largest street, **Avenida Central,** runs from the tip of San Felipe northeast into the neighborhood of **Santa Ana** (often pronounced "Santana"). Between Parque Santa Ana, just north of San Felipe, and **Plaza 5 de Mayo,** in the heart of Santa Ana, Av. Central becomes a pedestrian mall. Beyond the plaza, cars return as the road runs east through Calidonia before becoming Vía España and entering the quieter residential neighborhood of **Bella Vista.** The bay-side skyscrapers of downtown stand south of Calidonia, and Bella Vista merges into the swanky "banking district" on its southeastern side.

SAFETY. While Panama City is welcoming to visitors, it is a big city and certainly has its share of dangers, including crime. Problems have been reported in San Felipe, Santa Ana, Panamá Viejo, and Calidonia, especially at night. This is no reason to avoid these parts of the city, but use your common sense and take extra care at night—avoid walking long distances and don't flaunt your wallet, watch, or any item that marks you a tourist. Women traveling alone will probably feel most comfortable staying in Bella Vista, the safest bet for travelers. The city's poorest and most dangerous section, El Chorrillo, borders San Felipe and Santa

PANAMA

Ana to the west. Panamá Viejo basically shuts down at night. If traveling long distances in San Felipe, take a taxi and be careful. *Gringos* in particular are advised not to venture here, since US troops burned many area residences to the ground during the 1989 invasion, leaving Panamanians embittered. Curundu, San Miguel, and Santa Cruz, north of Santa Ana and Calidonia, are also best avoided (though Calidonia has recently become safer).

▐ LOCAL TRANSPORTATION

Local Buses: Stops are generally unmarked, and you won't find maps of routes. Instead, find a bus that has your destination painted on the front windshield and wave it down. Most buses run through **Plaza 5 de Mayo**, or along **Av. Perú, Calle 50, or Vía España.** The cost within the city is always US$0.25 (Tocumen Airport, US$0.35); pay the driver or the bus-jockey as you get off. Luxury buses, which have "Corredor" marked on the front in addition to the destination, are more expensive because they have A/C and use the expressway (US$0.75). If the bus doesn't seem to stop where you want, yell ¡*parada!*. Buses run 24hr., but from 11pm-4am they are less frequent.

Taxis: Taxis can be found everywhere. Fares are based on a 6-zone system spanning from **Balboa** to just beyond **Río Abajo.** Rides within a zone for one person cost US$1; every zone boundary crossed adds US$0.25. Each additional person costs US$0.25, and there is a US$0.15 surcharge 11pm-5am and on Su. A US$0.40 surcharge applies for called cabs (**Radio Cabs** ☎223 7694 or 220 8510). Certain "sites" (Marcos Gelabert Airport and Puerto Balboa) are supposed to be US$1.25 more, though it's often overlooked. One person rides from San Felipe to Vía España for US$1.50; to Panamá Viejo US$2. Settle on a price before getting in: tourists are prime targets for price hikes.

Car Rentals: Prices range from US$50 to US$100 per day, depending on car size and insurance options. At major chains, drivers must be 25 or older. Companies include: **Avis** (☎264 0722, www.avis.com.pa); **Barriga** (☎269 0221); **Budget** (☎263 8777; www.budget.panama.com); **Dollar** (☎270 0355; www.dollarpanama.com); **Hertz** (☎264 1111; www.hertz.com.pa); **National** (☎265 2222; www.nationalpanama.com); **Thrifty** (☎264 2613; www.thrifty-pa.com). Website reservations are often easier.

▐ PRACTICAL INFORMATION

TOURIST AND FINANCIAL SERVICES

Tourist Information: Instituto Panameño de Turismo (IPAT). National office at the Atlapa Convention Center, Zona 5 (☎226 7000 ext. 112, 113, or 278), on Vía Israel just off C. 77 and the Hotel Caesar Park. Extremely helpful, basic English spoken. Open M-F 8:30am-4:30pm. Other **branches** at both airports, the kiosk across from Hotel Continental on Vía España, and at Panamá Viejo. Open daily 8:30am-4:30pm. The *Autoridad Nacional del Ambiente* (National Environmental Authority), known commonly as **ANAM** (☎315 0855) has an office housing its *Areas Protegidas* (Protected Areas) division in Albrook airport facilities. Info on the parks is available, though there's more at regional offices and park headquarters. Open M-F 8am-4pm.

Travel Agencies and Tour Companies: Ancon Expeditions, C. Elvira Méndez at C. 49 A Este (☎269 9414; www.anconexpeditions.com), in Edificio El Dorado, offers a wide range of options for ecological trips to Bocas del Toro, San Blas, Chiriquí, and Darién, and daytrips in Panama City. Open M-F 8am-5pm, Sa 9am-1pm. **Aventuras 2000** (☎227 2000), on C. 50 and 59 Obarrio, leads many excursions, including tours to Colón and El Valle. Open M-F 8am-5pm, Sa 8am-noon. **Aventuras Panama** (☎260

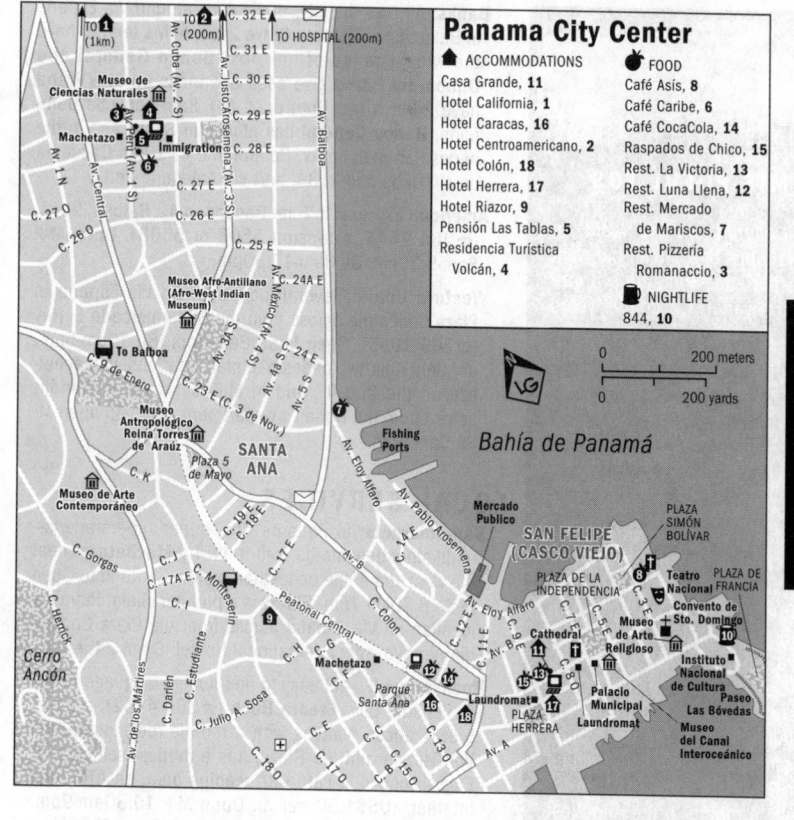

Panama City Center

🏠 ACCOMMODATIONS
Casa Grande, **11**
Hotel California, **1**
Hotel Caracas, **16**
Hotel Centroamericano, **2**
Hotel Colón, **18**
Hotel Herrera, **17**
Hotel Riazor, **9**
Pensión Las Tablas, **5**
Residencia Turística
  Volcán, **4**

🍎 FOOD
Café Asís, **8**
Café Caribe, **6**
Café CocaCola, **14**
Raspados de Chico, **15**
Rest. La Victoria, **13**
Rest. Luna Llena, **12**
Rest. Mercado
  de Mariscos, **7**
Rest. Pizzería
  Romanaccio, **3**

🍺 NIGHTLIFE
844, **10**

PANAMA

0044, www.aventuraspanama.com), on Av. El Paical in Transístmica, offers white-water rafting trips on the Chagres River. Open M-F 8am-5pm, Sa 8am-noon. **Canal and Bay Tours** (☎314 1349), in Balboa, has half- and full-canal cruises some Sa. Call in advance as full cruises are only offered once a month. Other companies include: **Agencia de Viajes Continental** (☎263 6162), on Vía Veneto, Condominio del Caribe; **Viajes Panamá S.A.,** C. 52, Av. Federico Boyd, Edificio Costa del Sol (☎223 0630); and **Viajes Riande** (☎269 4569), in the Hotel Continental on Vía España.

Embassies and Consulates: Canada (☎264 9731; www.dfait-maeci.gc.ca/panama), Marbella, C. 53 Este near C. 50, Edificio World Trade Center, 1st fl. Open to the public M-F 8:30am-1pm; hours of operation continue M-Th until 4:30pm. **Colombia** (☎223 3535; fax 223 2811), C. 53, Edificio World Trade Center, 18th fl. Open M-F 8am-1pm. **Costa Rica** (☎264 2937; fax 264 6348), Av. Samuel Lewis, Edificio Plaza Omega, 3rd fl. Open M-F 9am-3pm. **UK** (☎269 0866; fax 223 0730), C. 53, Edificio Swissbank, 4th fl. Open M-F 8am-noon. **US** (☎207 7000; http://usembassy.state.gov/panama), Av. Balboa, C. 39, Apartado Postal 6959 Zona 5. Open M-F 8am-noon.

Immigration: Av. 2 Sur (Av. Cuba), C. 29, in Calidonia, 1 block south of Machetazo on Av. Central (☎207 1800). Visa extensions and exit stamps. Show up early and prepare to wait. Open M-F 8am-3pm. For **passport photos,** go across the street to a supermarket or to one of the big Farmacias Arrocha on C. 50 or Av. Balboa.

THE HIDDEN DEAL

MIS PUEBLITOS

Can't afford room and board, let alone a bus or a plane, but want to experience Panama's broad cultural variety? A couple years ago, Panama City's mayor addressed this problem and decided to recreate the country's most distinctive towns and main ethnic groups within a 500 sq. meter park. Hence **Mis Pueblitos:** a whirlwind Disney-style cross-section of Panamanian culture.

"Mi Pueblito Interiorano" is a replica of an interior town; you can see the expected Spanish influence, especially in the church, the houses around the plaza, and the *pollera* museum. Visit also "Pueblito Indígena," where the lifestyles of different Panamanian indigenous groups are mimicked. Particularly unique, "Mi Pueblito Afroantillano," mostly a tribute to the Afro-West Indian population that worked on the Canal, provides a glimpse of the colorful wooden mansions built by France and the US to house workers in Colón, few of which still survive today.

Part Disney attraction, part shopping mall, this is your one-stop-shop for Panamanian culture.

Open Tu-Th 9am-7pm, F-Sa until 9pm. Entrance US$1. Take a bus every hr. 5:45am-6pm, (US$0.25) from the SACA terminal at Plaza 5 de Mayo toward Howard; ask to be dropped off.

Banks: All over the city, particularly around Vía España in Bella Vista. **Sistema Clave** 24hr. **ATMs** tend to have the widest range of link-ups. **Banco General** and **Banco del Istmo** give cash advances on MC/V and have 24hr. ATMs. Both open M-F 8am-3pm, Sa 9am-noon. **Banco General** has offices in Santa Ana in the pedestrian mall on Av. Central and C. 10; in Calidonia on Av. Cuba and C. 34, and Vía Argentina and C. D.

American Express: In Torre Banco, on Av. Balboa, 9th fl. (☎264 2444, extension 5503 or 5506). Open M-F 8am-5:30pm, Sa 8am-12:30pm.

Western Union: Several locations. On Vía España in Plaza Concordia across from the Supermercado El Rey (☎269 1055). Open M-Sa 8am-8pm, Su 10am-5pm. In Santa Ana, two pedestrian mall locations: in Machetazo on the 2nd fl., and in Multicentro San Ramón, across from the Dorian's department store. All open M-Sa 9am-6pm.

LOCAL SERVICES

Supermarkets: In Panama City, super-supermarkets—multi-story behemoths—sell it all. Try **Machetazo,** near the west end of the pedestrian mall in Santa Ana. Open M-Sa 8:30am-7pm. **El Rey** is a popular chain; there's a location on Vía España across from the Plaza Concordia near Voyager International Hostel. Open 24hr.

Bookstores: It's not easy to find foreign-language books in Panama City. **Exedra Book** (☎264 4252), a large, brown stucco building with a red-tile roof, located on Vía España and Vía Brazil, has a modest selection of English books, a cafe with reading area, an ATM, and Internet. (US$1.50 per hr. Open M-F 10:30am-9pm, Sa 10:30am-8pm, Su noon-7pm.) **Gran Morrison** (☎223 3286), is at Vía España across from Plaza Concordia. (Open M-Sa 9am-6:30pm, Su 9:30am-6pm.)

Markets: A large open-air market, **El Mercado Público** hosts vendors selling all types of fresh food. Centered on Av. Alfaro and C. 12 in Santa Ana. Beware of pickpockets and carry purses in front, clutched close to the body. Open daily 5am to 3pm. **Seafood market** on the coast, at Av. Balboa and C. 24E. Open daily early morning to early afternoon.

Laundromats: Machine laundromats (many provide drop-off, pick-up service) are called *lavamáticos*; dry-cleaning services are *lavanderías*. Both are everywhere. *Lavamáticos* charge per load and *lavanderías* charge per item. In San Felipe, try **Lavandería Plaza Herrera**, off Plaza Herrera on C. 9, or **Lavamático Luchín**, on Av. Central, C. 87, across from the cathedral. Both charge US$1 per load and sell detergent for US$0.25-0.40.

EMERGENCY AND COMMUNICATIONS

Police: Emergencies (☎104). **Calidonia, San Felipe, Santa Ana** (☎262 4539); **San Francisco** (☎226 5692); **Bella Vista** (☎223 4411); **Balboa** (☎228 0481); **Tocumen** (☎295 1020).

Firefighters: ☎103.

Red Cross: (☎228 3014) ambulance service.

Pharmacy: Farmacia Arrocha is everywhere; the Bella Vista branch (☎223 4505), just off Via España on C. 49 across from the Hotel Panamá, is open 24hr.

Hospital: Hospital Nacional, Av. Cuba and C. 38/39 (☎207 8100), 3 blocks from the US embassy. Offers extensive services and modern facilities.

Telephones: Public phones are everywhere, though they may not always work. **Phone cards,** for sale at supermarkets, pharmacies, and airports, are a good option since public phones rarely give change. Info and Directory Assistance ☎102.

Internet access: Web cafes are now almost as common as pay phones in many parts of the city, especially in Calidonia and Bella Vista. Rates hover around US$1 per hr. In Santa Ana, try the Internet Panama Cafe, on Plaza Santa Ana (US$0.50 per hr), which also offers extremely cheap rates for international calls (US$0.06 per min. to the US). Open daily 8am-11:30pm.

Post Office: (☎225 0748.) On Av. Balboa. Open M-F 7am-5:45pm, Sa 7am-4:45pm.

⚐ ACCOMMODATIONS

SAN FELIPE (CASCO VIEJO)

Casco Viejo, at the western end of Av. Central, is a lively colonial neighborhood with a few budget options clustered between Plaza de la Independencia and Plaza Herrera. Renovation projects seek to revitalize the bohemian neighborhood, but for the foreseeable future, lodgings here are uniform: cheap, locked-gate, gritty places retaining few traces of colonial grandeur. During the day, when Tourist Police abound, the streets are relatively safe, but avoid walking long distances at night, especially if alone. Unless you're looking to save those extra bucks, developed Calidonia and Bella Vista have better deals and more options.

Hotel Herrera, Av. Central and C. 9 (☎228 8994), 2 blocks west and 1 block south of Plaza de la Independencia, in an old yellow-and-white aristocratic home on Plaza Herrera. Probably the best budget deal in the area thanks to its quiet location and friendly English-speaking manager, Gerardo, who keeps backpackers' needs in mind. Spacious common room with dining tables and TV. Singles US$6; doubles US$7 (with 1 bed) and US$11 (with 2 beds), with bath US$9, with A/C, fridge, and TV US$16.❶

Casa Grande, Av. Central C. 8/9 (☎211 3316), in another old yellow and white building; good location. Get used to the locked gates. Basic rooms have high ceilings that keep it cool. Common baths, tiny showers. Rooms with fan US$7, A/C US$9. ❶

SANTA ANA

Noisy, bustling Santa Ana is closer to the city center and has hotels a step above those in San Felipe, though not nearly as bohemian and charming. It's slightly safer, though don't stray far from Av. Central, especially at night, and always watch your belongings. It's a popular shopping area and pickpocketers are not uncommon. Women traveling alone may attract unwanted attention.

Hotel Colón (☎228 8506), on C. B and C. 12, a short block away from the gate of the pedestrian mall at Plaza Santa Ana. On the far side of the Plaza from the pedestrian mall, face San Felipe, follow the trolley track 1 block, and turn right; it is the blue building with white trim. Colón has been offering basic, cheap, and dependable accommodations since 1915. Includes bar and multiple common areas with TV. Roof access offers a great harbor view. Singles with fan US$9, with fan and bath US$11, with A/C, private bath, and TV US$13.20; doubles US$9-$11/US$13/US$14. ❷

Hotel Caracas (☎228 7232). With your back to the gate of the pedestrian mall at Plaza Santa Ana, facing San Felipe, the hotel is on the right, 100m up the street. Three fl. of big, clean rooms with baths, phones, and TVs. Doubles US$10, with A/C US$12; triples US$21/US$24. ❶

Hotel Riazor, C. 16 and Av. I (☎228 0777; fax 228 0986), around the corner from the Banco Nacional building in the pedestrian mall. A good deal in a central, though noisy, location. Offers 46 comfortable, spotless rooms, all with fans, hot baths, and TVs, as well as a bar and restaurant on the ground fl. Singles US$10, with A/C US$18; doubles US$14/$18; triples US$21/$24. ❷

CALIDONIA

Calidonia, running east from Plaza 5 de Mayo along Av. Central, has many full-service hotels in the US$15 to US$25 range, particularly along C. 29 and 34 near Av. Perú. It's easy and worthwhile to shop around here, and despite chaos and noise, is relatively safe. Prices rise in high season.

Hotel Centroamericano, C. 34 (☎227 4555). Just north of Av. Justo Arosemana. More expensive than the neighbors, but a step above and a great value. Fountain, elevator, and large rooms with baths so sparkling white you need sunglasses. All with A/C, hot water, phone, and TV. Singles US$20; doubles US$22; triples US$30. MC/V. ❸

Residencia Turística Volcán, C. 29 (☎225 5263), between Av. Perú and Cuba. Hard mattresses in comfortable rooms, popular with backpackers. All have baths and sporadic cable TV. Singles US$12, with A/C US$14; doubles with A/C US$16; triples US$18. ❷

Pensión Las Tablas, Av. Perú, between C. 28 and 29, across from Machetazo, marked by a tiny sign. Small, clean rooms have baths, fans, and TVs. Rooms facing Av. Perú can be noisy. Singles US$8, with bath and TV US$10; doubles US$12. ❷

BELLA VISTA

Bella Vista is as close as you can get to the action around Vía Argentina and C. 50 without spending a fortune. Attractive, well-priced hotels sit along Vía España as it enters Bella Vista, with a broad accommodation market. This area is safer than the neighborhoods with only budget hostels.

Voyager International Hostel, C. Manuel María Icaza, Edificio Di-Lido, Apt. 8 (☎260 5913; www.geocities.com/voyagerIH), 100m from Hotel Continental. The only place in Panama City following a backpacker-hostel formula. Common room with TV, kitchen facilities, laundry (US$4 wash and dry), and a multilingual book exchange complement clean, simple rooms with A/C, bunkbeds, and common baths. Airport pickup US$12. Breakfast and 30min. of Internet access (US$0.50 per extra hr.) included. 3- or 6-person dorms US$9, US$8 with ISIC card; double US$17. ❶

Hostal La Casa de Carmen, C. 1 in El Carmen, house #32; off Vía Brazil, it's the street parallel to Vía España behind Exedra Books. (☎/fax 263 4366; www.lacasadecarmen.com.) This new and welcoming B&B is one of the city's best finds: safe; near to Vía España with homey rooms decorated in charming style with local furniture. Airport pickup (US$10 per person for at least 2 people), continental breakfast, free Internet,

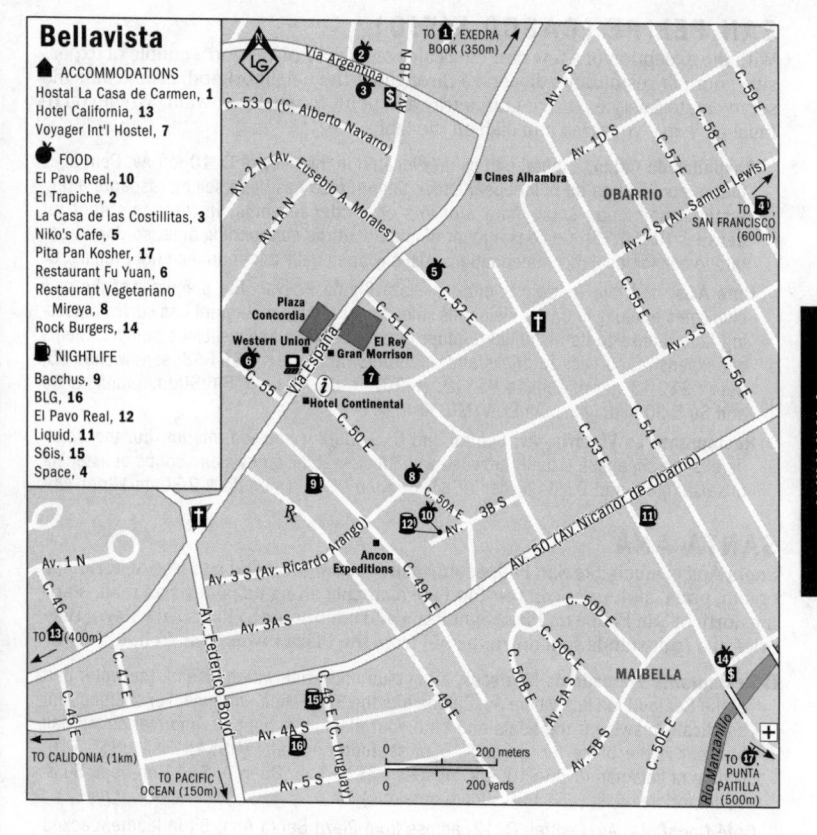

Bellavista

↑ ACCOMMODATIONS
Hostal La Casa de Carmen, **1**
Hotel California, **13**
Voyager Int'l Hostel, **7**

🍴 FOOD
El Pavo Real, **10**
El Trapiche, **2**
La Casa de las Costillitas, **3**
Niko's Cafe, **5**
Pita Pan Kosher, **17**
Restaurant Fu Yuan, **6**
Restaurant Vegetariano
Mireya, **8**
Rock Burgers, **14**

🍸 NIGHTLIFE
Bacchus, **9**
BLG, **16**
El Pavo Real, **12**
Liquid, **11**
S6is, **15**
Space, **4**

PANAMA

kitchen, library, and self-service laundry (US$0.25 wash, US$0.75 dry) on premises. 6-person room (A/C and shared bathroom) US$11 per person; 3-person room US$13.50. 10% discount with ISIC card. AmEx/MC/V. ①

Hotel California (☎263 7736, www.hotel-califonia.ws), on Vía España at C. 43, 300m east of Av. Perú, beside the old Teatro Bella Vista. Quality location, much-deserved pampering at a fair price. A/C, cable TV, firm beds, hot baths, phone, and a restaurant and bar. Some views of the bay. Singles US$20 with a 2 night minimum stay, US$25 for one night only; doubles US$33; triples US$40. AmEx/MC/V. ③

🍴 FOOD

Given the variety of cultures that have passed through this country, it isn't surprising that Panama City is the heart of international cuisine in Central America. Prices are diverse, from the cheap *típico* food of San Felipe and Santa Ana to the international flavors of Bella Vista and Marbella. Throughout the city, street vendors sell hot dogs, *fritura*, fresh fruit, and *chichas* (a sweet fruit juice concoction). You can find vendors around C. 13, the pedestrian mall, Plaza 5 de Mayo, in the *mercadito* at Av. Perú and C. 34, or the giant **market** on Av. Alfaro.

SAN FELIPE (CASCO VIEJO)

With the exception of a few new chic cafes on Plaza Bolívar and a couple of expensive gourmet restaurants dispersed throughout the neighborhood, establishments serve cafeteria-style *típico;* grab a tray and point to what you want. When you're finished, leave your tray and dish on the table.

Raspados de Chico, a metal cart usually located in the alley of C. 10, off Av. Central, 2 blocks above Plaza de la Independencia. Señor Chico has been selling *raspado,* a fantastic Panamanian snow cone with lots of condensed milk, in the same spot for decades (US$0.25). Chico is a fount of info about the surrounding area, so don't hesitate to ask for local recommendations. Usually open daily mid-morning until evening. ❶

Café Asís, near the Teatro Nacional on Plaza Simón Bolívar. The precursor of the new chic cafes opening in Casco Viejo, this small but charming restaurant has survived passing fads thanks to its historical outdoor plaza ambience and delicious sangria. Meals get expensive, so stick to drinks and appetizers. Appetizers US$4-$8, sandwiches $5; beer US$2-$3, jar of sangria US$19. (☎262 9304. Open M-F 6:30pm-midnight, Sa and Su 5:30-midnight.). AmEx/V/MC. ❸

Restaurante La Victoria, Av. Central and C. 9. Dark windowed interior, but the *típico* here is the cheapest. Usually crowded with locals watching news and soaps or listening to *salsa.* Meat and 2 side dishes US$1. *Ceviche* US$1. Open daily 9:30am-10pm. ❶

SANTA ANA

Santa Ana is much like San Felipe, only a little more crowded and less historic. Ice cream, pizza, and American fast food are available along its pedestrian mall, starting north of San Felipe on Plaza Santa Ana and continuing to Plaza 5 de Mayo. Bakeries and fruit stands spill down the hill from the Plaza toward San Felipe.

🌑 **Restaurante Mercado de Mariscos,** a big blue and white warehouse on the water part of the Seafood Market, where Av. Balboa hits the San Felipe entrance. For seafood that practically crawls off the boats and onto your plate, this popular, informal dining hall and bar is the place for the city's best seafood cocktails (US$4). Fish US$5-$10; shrimp or calamari US$6-$10; and lobsters US$10-$15. Open Tu-Sa 11am-8pm, Su 8-10am for breakfast (US$3.50 shrimp omelette). ❸

Café CocaCola, Av. Central, C. 12, across from Plaza Santa Ana. Sit in leather-backed chairs and enjoy the A/C. Supposedly the oldest cafe in Panama, this is a gathering spot for old men wearing typical Panamanian caps and *guayaberas,* the traditional four-pocket shirts, who come to surround themselves with old photos of Casco Viejo and discuss the cafe's heyday during the 1920s and 30s. Sandwiches US$1.50-$2.75, breakfast US$1-$1.75, meat dishes US$2.50-$4.50, pasta US$1.80-$2.75, seafood US$3-$7. Open daily 7:30am-11:15pm. ❶

Restaurante Luna Llena, on the *Peatonal* Central at Plaza Santa Ana. Varied menu, cheap prices, and a billiards bar in the back. Sandwiches US$0.55-$2.25, full meals US$2.25, breakfast combo US$1.10. Open daily 6:30am-8pm. ❶

CALIDONIA

Calidonia's establishments serve the same fare as other areas for slightly higher prices (*típico* US$1.50-2.75), and many close at 4pm when area workers go home. Eateries cluster on C. 29-32, between Central and Arosemena.

Café Caribe, Av. Central between C. 28 and 29, across from Machetazo. Caribe has a local crowd and a large variety of *típico* and international meals. Near many Calidonia accommodations. Clean, with A/C. Breakfast specials US$3.50, chicken with rice US$2. Open daily 7am-11pm. AmEx/MC/V. ❶

Restaurante Pizzería Romanaccio, on C. 29 and Perú. A bit overpriced, this quality Italian eatery, frequented by many workers in the area, is a nice break from the crowded streets. Pasta, calzones and pizzas (US$4.50-10). Open M-Sa 9am-10pm. MC/V. ❷

BELLA VISTA

From Vía España near Vía Argentina, down past C. 50 to the bay, international upscale cuisine flourishes. Be prepared to shell out extra cash for anything but fast food—it will be worth it.

Niko's Cafe, on C. 51 B between Av. Samuel Lewis and Vía España and many other locations throughout the city. A local favorite for its variety of reliable and cheap meals served cafeteria style. Late night you'll find many Panamanians on their way home from clubs and bars. Try *sancocho* (US$1.50), the national recipe for a hangover. Gyro US$2.25, with french fries and soda US$3.40. Open 24 hr. ❶

Rock Burgers, on Plaza Florida, C. 53E. This informal restaurant serves the best burgers in town, cheap and fast. Specialty or veggie burger US$3.50, kosher hot dog US$4.50, sandwiches US$3-$4.50. Open M-Sa 8am-10pm, Su 10am-10pm. ❷

La Casa de las Costillitas, on Vía Argentina, 1½ blocks from Vía España. Huge portions of good seafood and bbq. The 15-page bilingual menu includes witticisms on literature and philosophy. Seafood US$5-9, ½ chicken US$4, ribs US$5-$9. Beer US$1. Open M-Sa noon-11pm, Su noon-10pm. MC/V. ❸

El Trapiche, on Vía Argentina, 1½ blocks off Vía España. Real *típico*: serves a variety of dishes from across Panama. Excellent and popular *criollo* breakfast (US$1.25-3.25), deep-fried specialties (US$0.60-$2), entrees US$3.25-$8. Cheaper but equally filling *hojaldra* sandwich US$2.25-$4. *Sancocho* US$3. Beer US$2. Open Su-Th 7am-11pm, F-Sa 7am-midnight. AmEx/MC/V. ❷

Restaurante Fu Yuan (☎223 8002), in a little storefront on C. 55, just off Vía España and across from the side entrance to Hotel Panama in Bella Vista. Classic Chinatown style, from the chintzy decor to the authentic menu—parts of it are not even translated. #51-54 are delicious hot-pot concoctions; #77-90 desserts; #53 is eggplant in ginger; #77 is coconut tapioca. Cheap (US$2-$5) and huge. Open daily 11:30am-11pm. ❷

El Pavo Real, at the end of Av. 3 Sur, 2 curvy blocks from Voyager International Hostel, is a convincing English pub with hearty hamburgers and fish n' chips (US$5-7). Open M-Sa 4:30pm until the bar empties. AmEx/MC/V. ❷

Pita Pan Kosher (☎264 2786), on Bal Harbour, Paitilla, in a shopping center off Av. Balboa. Located in a neighborhood populated mainly by Panama's Jewish community, this extremely clean bakery turned cafeteria offers a great value for good Kosher meals. A varied menu with everything from sushi to pizza (US$2.50-$7.50). Open M-Th 7am-9pm, F 7am-5pm, Su 9am-9pm. ❷

Restaurante Vegetariano Mireya (☎269 1876), at the base of C. Ricardo Arias. Of the few vegetarian restaurants in the city, this is one of the oldest. Simple cafeteria-style selection of ultra-cheap veggie versions of Panamanian *típico* and other concoctions (US$1.25 per portion). Delicious veggie *empanadas* (US$0.50). Open daily 6am-9:30pm. ❶

◎ SIGHTS

SAN FELIPE (CASCO VIEJO)

The second "Panama City" was founded on January 21, 1673, after pirate avarice and a fire destroyed the original city. Known today as Casco Viejo, it is a striking blend of lively community and grand, crumbling history. Old Spanish colonial churches blend in among houses with iron balconies, inspired by the French when they undertook the initial Canal-construction effort. In 1997, UNESCO declared the area a World Heritage Site for its rich architectural diversity. Though the whole neighborhood seems to be under renovation, it is loaded with striking memorials to politicians and heroes. Begin at **Plaza de la Independencia**, on Av. Central and C. 7, which honors Panama's founders, among them the first President of the Republic, Manuel Amador Guerrero.

CATHEDRAL. Facing the Plaza de la Independencia is the huge Cathedral, which features a chiseled stone facade and whitewashed, mother-of-pearl towers and domes. Be sure to check out the intricate sacrament inside. The cathedral has been around since 1798 and was one of the few buildings in the city to survive the 1882 earthquake. If the front is closed, try the side door.

MUSEO DEL CANAL INTEROCEÁNICO. This excellent museum is housed in what used to be the headquarters of the French company that first worked on the Canal. It offers tons of info about the canal's construction, history, and operations, as well as colonial weapons from the *Camino de Cruces* (see **Portobelo: Sights**, p. 634). Displays are in the standardized government collage format. Even if you can't read Spanish, the museum is worth seeing for the pictures of the canal's construction. (*With your back to the cathedral, the museum is on your right.* ☎211 1649; www.museodelcanal.com. Open Tu-Su 9:30am-5:30pm. US$2, students US$0.75. English, French audio tours available, US$5.)

PALACIO MUNICIPAL. Formerly the legislature of the country, it now houses the city government on the second floor and the **Museo de Historia de Panamá** on the first. The museum covers everything from Columbus's landing in Panama through recent times. An attendant can give you a tour. (*The Palacio is right next door to the Museo del Canal, on the Plaza de la Independencia.* ☎228 6231. Open M-F 8:30am-3:30pm. Museum US$1, students US$0.25.)

PASEO LAS BÓVEDAS. This walkway, with great views of the Pacific, was once used as a buffer against pirates and prisoners. Now the arbor-covered footpath offers breathtaking views of the skyline, as well as cool shade. At the end of the Paseo lie the *bóvedas*, vaults which once held prisoners but now house a restaurant and a small but impressive art collection. The gallery faces **Plaza Francia**, engineered by Leonardo de Villanueva and built in honor of the Frenchmen who died during the 19th-century attempt to build a canal. Walk around the semicircle starting at your left to learn more about the important men and ideas surrounding the Canal's history. Chamber orchestras sometimes play in the small park's plaza. (*From Plaza de la Independencia, walk south away from the Cathedral along Av. Central until the street winds past the Pacific. The Paseo begins just after the big ruined house by the water. Gallery open M-F 8am-5pm. Paseo always open. Both are free.*)

CHURCH AND CONVENT OF SANTO DOMINGO. Dating to 1678, the church's **Arco Chato** was famous for its mortar construction and lack of internal supports—right up until it collapsed in 2003. Panamanian leaders used the arch's long survival to prove the country was earthquake-proof, important in the fight for the transisthmian canal. Connected to the old church ruins, the **Museo de Arte Religioso Colonial** is a modest hall that contains a gigantic altar, sculptures, and religious paintings. (*Av. A, C. 3. 1 block south and 2 blocks east of the Plaza de la Independencia.* ☎228 2897. Museum US$0.75, children US$0.25.)

TEATRO NACIONAL. The Neoclassical theater was built at the turn of the century by an Italian architect and then reconstructed after part of the ceiling caved in. Stunning frescoes on the ceiling were painted by Panamanian Roberto Lewis.

Speak with administrators for permission to sink into the heavenly red velvet balcony chairs overlooking the grand theater. Performances in the theater range from classical to folk. (☎ 262 3525. *Av. B, C. 3. From the Plaza, stand with your back to the Cathedral and walk east 2 blocks down Av. Central and turn left. Open M-F 8am-4pm. Call for a schedule of concerts and shows. Tickets US$5-$30.)*

OTHER SIGHTS. Parque Simón Bolívar features a monument honoring the namesake liberator with friezes depicting his feats (1 block east and 1 block north of Plaza de la Independencia). There are a number of cafes here (see **Food**, p. 614). The Moorish-style **Palacio Presidencial**, also known as the "Palace of the Herons," is home to Panama's President; security is extremely tight. (On Av. Alfaro, 2 blocks north of the Plaza de la Independencia.) The **Iglesia de San José** houses the **Altar de Oro**. According to legend, a priest covered the magnificent golden altar in mud to disguise its worth from pirate Henry Morgan, who sacked Panamá Viejo in 1671. (Av. A and C. 8, 1 block south and 1 block west of the Plaza.) San Felipe's biggest collection of fresh food kiosks crowds Av. Alfaro, northwest of the Plaza de la Independencia in the **Mercado Público**. A great area to find souvenirs is **Sal Si Puedes** (literally "Get out if you can"), which runs from the Mercado Público to the pedestrian mall. Note the name and take precautions against pickpockets and thieves.

SANTA ANA

Santa Ana's busy pedestrian mall runs north from San Felipe to Plaza 5 de Mayo. The mall was erected in honor of the firemen who battled the flames of an exploded gunpowder warehouse in 1914.

MUSEO ANTROPOLÓGICO REINA TORRES DE ARAÚZ. Overlooking Plaza 5 de Mayo, the museum documents Panamanian ethnography from pre-Columbian times and is home to 15,000 pieces of artwork in gold, ceramic, and stone. An exhibit also shows how the Indians in Panama live today compared to pre-Hispanic times. Free English-speaking guides are available; tours last around 45 min. and are absolutely worth it. (☎ 262 8338. *Open M-F 9am-4pm. US$2, children US$0.25.)*

MUSEO DE ARTE CONTEMPORÁNEO. Houses a small and underdeveloped collection of modern Panamanian and other Latin American artwork. *(West of the Plaza 5 de Mayo on Av. de los Mártires.* ☎ 262 8012. *Open T-Su 9am-5pm. US$1.)*

CALIDONIA

MUSEO AFRO-ANTILLANO. Housed in a tiny gray church, this one-room museum used to be the chapel of the Christian mission, around which Panama's Afro-West Indian population first organized. The museum expertly recounts their history with photos, antiques, and parts of the old Panamanian railroad that brought immigrants looking for work; it also pays tribute to important cultural, religious, and economic contributions. *(From Plaza 5 de Mayo, continue east 1-2 blocks along Av. Justo Arosemena.* ☎ 262 5348. *Open Tu-Sa 8:30am-3:30pm. US$1. English translations.)*

MUSEO DE CIENCIAS NATURALES. The museum's small displays hold stuffed regional birds, mammals, and insects. Most interesting to a biology or taxidermy buff. *(Av. Cuba, C. 30 Este.* ☎ 225 0645. *Open F 9am-3:30pm. US$1, children US$0.25.)*

PANAMÁ VIEJO

Founded in 1519 Panamá Viejo, the original Panama City, was the first European city on the Pacific Coast of the New World. As the starting point for Spanish expeditions to the rest of the continent, the city quickly became linked to international transport and trade. It flourished as the Pacific terminus of Spain's Camino Real, the transisthmian pipeline for the gold of all of Spain's Pacific Colonies. This importance was short-lived, however, and after a near-raze by Pirate Henry Morgan in 1671 and the fire that followed it, Panamá Viejo was abandoned. Today, it offers an intriguing peek into a 16th century city. The newly built museum has two floors with materials on the city's history and archaeology; a lot of the info is translated into English. An impressive scale model depicts the city prior to 1671.

Panamá Viejo includes ruins, a fort, several convents, a hospital, and other structures, the most impressive of which are the 15m-high **cathedral tower** and the **Bridge of Kings,** one of the oldest bridges in the Americas. Inside the gate at the bend in the road is the **Mercado Nacional de Artesanías,** which houses several touristy mini-shops that sell souvenirs from different regions of the country. There's a pricey restaurant in the same building (*típico* US$3-$5), though some better and cheaper *típico* places lie near the gas station. Wear bug spray, as the ruins border swampland. (*Getting to Panamá Viejo is easy—take any city bus with "Panamá Viejo" on the front window; a good place to wait is Plaza 5 de Mayo. 45min., 7am-11pm, US$0.25. Get off at the visitor center (before the Parque Morelos), with the museum and the IPAT info center inside.* ☎226 4419. *Open daily 8am-4pm. Walk 10 min. to the ruins. Open Tu-Sa 9am-5pm. Ruins open daily 9am-5pm. Entrance to museum and ruins US$2. Student US$0.50. Market open daily 9am-6pm.*)

🎭 ENTERTAINMENT

Theater: Teatro Nacional (☎262 3525), in San Felipe, is the city's biggest theater, showing plays, concerts, and ballet. Call for a schedule. Tickets US$5-$30. Also try **Teatro en Círculo** (☎261 5375), near Vía Brazil and Transísmica, which features mostly plays and musicals. A cheaper option for live music and dancing is **Mi Pueblito** (☎228 9785), where you can see performances of the national dances by children in flowing *polleras* (traditional Panamanian costume) F and Sa nights US$1. Call for other showings. Park open Tu-Th 9am-7pm, F and Sa 9am-9pm.

Cinema: Movie theaters abound; most show American hits with subtitles soon after their US release. The newest and most modern, **Extreme Planet** (☎214 7022) is located on Av. Balboa. Other major screens are located on Vía España or near the pedestrian mall. Try **Cine Alhambra** (☎223 2016), on Vía España at Via Argentina, or **Cine Universitario** (☎264 2737), which shows artsier fare, on the campus of Universidad Nacional de Panamá, behind Iglesia del Carmen (US$2, students US$1).

🛍 SHOPPING

For upscale shopping, try **Vía España** near Via Argentina or C. 53E from C. 50 towards Punta Paitilla. Albrook and Multicentro are two new malls that offer a little bit of everything, but are definitely on the expensive side. For the best values, go to the pedestrian mall, better known to locals as "La Central," or to the Centro Comercial Los Pueblos. Some popular stores where you're guaranteed to find pretty much everything for under US$10 are Modas Saks and El Costo.

The best prices city-wide for typical crafts are in the *artesanía* markets of Balboa and at **Casa de la Pollera** in Santa Ana, the corner of Av. Central and Salsipuedes (open M-Sa 9am-5:30pm). Bargain in Panamá Viejo for sweet deals. **Flory Saltzman's Artesanía,** across Hotel El Panamá on C. 49B Oeste, sells *molas*, individual pieces and sewn into quilts. (☎223 6963. Open M-Sa 8:30am-6pm.)

NIGHTLIFE

Whether you're looking to strut your stuff on the dance floor or just sit to back and watch the locals network, this metropolis has it all—from quiet back rooms to full-tilt fashion raves. Panamanians dress well most of the time, especially so for night-life: men wear long pants and collared shirts, and women aren't afraid to show some skin. Jeans and short-sleeve shirts are acceptable for bars and discos, but shorts and sandals are not. You must be 18 or over to enter; expect to show ID. San Felipe can be a blast, but take extra care at night—if you're alone, stick to taxis and avoid walking anywhere. Bella Vista is considerably safer.

The action in clubs usually picks up around 11pm, but clubs will stay open as long as there are people—and there usually are, as Panamanians don't consider it a night without some serious dancing. For an early start, grab drinks at a bar. On average, beer costs US$2, cocktails US$4, and a bottle of national alcohol US$30.

For **live music,** good bets for jazz include **Restaurante Las Bóvedas** on Plaza de Francia (☎298 8068; F-Sa 10pm, no cover) and **Take Five Restaurant and Bar** on C. Primera Oeste in Casco Viejo (☎211 3199; F-Sa 10:30pm with a minimum of US$10 in drinks). For *salsa,* try **Guaguanco** on C. 42 Bella Vista (☎225 3348); and for traditional *típico* music, **Las Tinajas** on Av. 3 Sur near Av. Federico Boyd (☎263 7890). You can also have a typical Panamanian dinner and enjoy an excellent show of the country's folkloric dance (M, Tu, F, and Sa at 9pm). Many of the luxury **hotels** have shows (with a cover) in their bars and cafes. Bars and discos sometimes have live music and shows.

844, on C. 1 Oeste, just off Plaza Francia in trendy Casco Viejo. Classy bar/lounge/club in a restored section of the old city. 4 different rooms let you find your preferred ambience. Young, hip, local crowd. Music ranges from *salsa* and *merengue* to heavier dance grooves. Beer US$2.50, cocktails US$5, cover US$8-$10. Open Th-Sa at 9pm.

S6is, on C. Uruguay between Av. 4 Sur and C. 50. Owned by 6 young friends, this luxurious modern bar with great service is it if you want a taste of Panama's exclusive social scene. Music is varied, but don't expect to dance *salsa* or *merengue.* F brings a mid-20s crowd. Cover usually US$5. Open Tu-Sa at 5pm. AmEx/MC/V.

Bacchus (☎263 9005), on C. 49 E between Vía España and Av. 3 Sur. Tried and true, it's a big, busy, fully-loaded club with a karaoke bar and Greek disco. VIP 2nd-fl. M is electronic night, with open bar until midnight (cover US$5). Other nights music varies. Th and Sa women enter free until 11pm, men US$10.50; F free. Beer US$1-$2. Karaoke opens M-Sa 9:30pm, disco M and Th-Sa 9:30pm. AmEx/MC/V.

Liquid, in the big shopping center on Marbella, at the corner of C. 50 and C. 53E, has passed its peak, but the good-size dance floor still attracts the golden children of the city's elite. World-class DJs spin stripped-down drum-and-bass while cool steel-and-blue lighting completes the scene. Don't bother showing up until 11pm (Tu-Sa). Tu is ladies night, open bar for everyone. Cover US$10. AmEx/MC/V.

El Pavo Real (see **Food,** p. 615) has free pool-tables and pitch-perfect live classic rock on F nights during happy hour. Popular among tourists. US$6 cover. AmEx/MC/V.

GAY AND LESBIAN NIGHTLIFE

The gay community is much better organized than the lesbian community in terms of nightlife, so clubs are frequented mostly by males and some heterosexual couples. Although gay bars and clubs tend to have great parties, they are still rarely advertised and can be hard to find if you don't know what to look for. Check the following websites for info: www.chemibel.com; www.rumbanight.com.

BLG (☎ 265 1624), on Av. 4 Sur off C. Uruguay next to Nobu club. A white modern building with no name houses one of Panama's most frequented gay-friendly clubs, thanks to its excellent music and dancing. Heterosexuals also love BLG. Popular W comedy show and Sa special show. The club will be moving in Jan. 2005 1 block behind its current location, on C. 48, and the new name will be ARENA. W open bar, cover US$3 before 11pm. Cover usually US$5. Open W-Sa at 10pm-4am, Su 10pm-midnight.

Space, on C. 70, Obarrio. Behind a dark facade and tiny door hides a great gay ambience and a lot of dancing. Music is varied and includes pop, rock, techno, trance, *salsa,* and *merengue.* All are welcome any night, though there are theme nights: Th and Sa are special show nights, sometimes with cover. W is girls night, cover US$3; otherwise, geared toward male homosexuals. Beer US$1.50. Open Tu-Sa 9pm-5am.

⚠ OUTDOOR ACTIVITIES

PARQUE NATURAL METROPOLITANO

The easiest way to Metropolitano is by taxi (US$1.25-$2), or take a direct bus to Albrook from Vía España (US$0.25) and get off at the Universidad de Panamá at Curundu. From there, with the university to your back, walk left and then go right at the fork. The park entrance will be on the left. Park trails open daily 6am-6pm; dusk and dawn are the best times to see wildlife. Ranger station open daily 6am-6pm. Trails US$2, students US$0.50; map US$1.50. Call at least a week ahead to reserve a guided tour (English spoken). US$4 per person if less than 5 people, US$5 if more (☎ 232 5552). Bring bug repellent.

Panamanians boast "the most accessible rain forest in the world," which just might be true. It's certainly the only natural park in Central America within metropolitan city limits. Though occupying 265 hectares of forest—75% of which is fragile Pacific dry forest, an ecosystem almost extinct in the region—the park is just minutes northwest of the city's downtown areas and somehow still home to hundreds of plant and animal species such as the Two- and Three-toed sloth, Trogon, Toucan, Egret, and Geoffrey's tamarin.

There are five **trails** in the park, four named after a particular plant or animal often seen on the trail. In order of increasing difficulty, trails include: **Los Momótides** (900m, 30-45 min.), named after the motmot bird; **El Roble** (700m, 25-30min.), named for an oak tree; **Los Caobos** (900m, 45min.-1hr.), named after the *caoba* (mahogany) tree; **Mono Tití** (1.1km, 1hr.), named for the *tití* monkey; and **La Cienaguita** (1.1km, 1hr.), named for its oft-swampy nature. This last trail also contains a lookout point 150m above sea level featuring spectacular views (best in dry season) of the city, canal, and bay.

🔀 DAYTRIPS FROM PANAMA CITY

LA ARENOSA

Getting to isolated Arenosa by bus involves transfers and patience. From Panama City take a bus to Parque Feulliet in the city of La Chorrera. Buses leave for La Arenosa from the greenish-yellow building of the Corregiduria de Barrio Colon 1 block west of the parque (45min., every hr., 7am-7pm, US$1). Boats and guides can be hired at the docks in Arenosa, 1 block from the church.

Heads up fishing aficionados: the name "Panama" is thought to mean "abundance of fish" in an indigenous language. The country is famous for expensive deep-sea fishing tours, but a more budget option is La Arenosa, a small fishing spot on Lake Gatún. Even if the fish aren't biting, the view is ample compensation. Boat tours with a local guide are also possible (at the dock they charge US$30 per half day,

US$40 per full day; four people fit). Tree trunks and other obstacles stand as reminders of the land that was flooded during the canal's construction—a guide will know how to avoid them and find good fishing areas. The most common catches are a type of bass referred to as *sargento*.

Since services are limited in the tiny town, La Arenosa is best as a daytrip. Bring poles, bait, and food, though a few food stands hover around the church plaza and near the docks. The restaurant at the dock serves fish and *patacones* for US$1.75-$2.50. Fishing equipment is rented for US$3 and enough bait to fish for days costs US$5. You can also rent *ranchitos* (US$2 a day; baths US$0.25). If you decide to stay overnight, head to **Campestre La Arenosa** for rooms and guided fish tours. Take the first right after the green sign marked La Arenosa, which signals the town's entrance. (☎671 3247. Rooms for four with A/C and hot bath US$25. Fishing tour with a maximum of five people including equipment and bait, US$50.)

ISLA TABOGA

From Balboa (in Panama City), Expreso del Pacífico boats (☎261 0350) head to Taboga (20min.; M-F 8:30am, 3pm, Sa-Su 8:30, 10:15am, 4pm; US$5), and back (M-F 9:30am, 3:45pm; Sa-Su 9:15am, 3, 5pm; US$5, children US$3). Calypso Queen (☎264 6096) runs to Taboga (1hr.; Tu 8:30am, Sa-Su 8 and 10:30am; US$4) and back (Tu-F 4:30pm, Sa 4:30pm, Su 5pm; US$4, children and seniors US$3).

Clear blue waters, sandy beaches, lush greenery, and a small picturesque town: Isla Taboga (20km offshore from Panama City) legitimately earns its name, "Island of the Flowers." Discovered by Balboa in 1513 before Panama City was founded, officially founded in 1524 by a Spanish priest, and the base for Pizarro's journeys to South America, obviously Taboga is rich in history. The church in the town center, founded in 1550, is considered the second oldest in the Americas. Taboga's proximity to the capital results in overcrowding, especially on weekends.

The town clusters around the dock near the island's north end. There are no roads, but the main walkway passes the dock. From the dock, most of town is to the left with **Cerro de la Cruz** at the end, opposite the **main beach** and Hotel Taboga.

With few accommodation options, Taboga is best visited as a daytrip. **Hotel Taboga ❸**, a block to the right off the dock, offers amenities and comfort for high prices: dimly lit rooms with A/C, baths, pool access, basketball courts (US$1 per hr.), ping-pong table (US$1 per hr.), and kayaks (US$7.35 per hr.). (☎250 2122; in Panama City 264 6096;

FROM THE ROAD

PUSHIN' ALL THE BUTTONS

Hourly rates and "button"-pushing acquire new meanings in Panama, with sex hotels called *empuja botones*, or "push buttons." And no, this doesn't refer to what happens inside the motel, or even between people. Shame on you.

The name actually comes from the original "push" hotels, located on the outskirts of Panama City (mostly along the Transístmica Hwy.), where people go for some lovin'. They provide individual parking garages for your room; in order to close the garage door you must push a button. Once inside, you walk into a room and pay an hourly fee at a small window where only the person's hands are visible. This way, no one sees you walk in, and no one can see your car parked outside.

These hotels can initially be identified by suggestive lights and names. Another immediate indication is the price, given in hourly and not daily rates. While they generally attract a sketchier clientele, they shouldn't be rejected if they seem the safest option and are clean. More and more inexpensive hotels in Panama City, including *pensiones*, are starting to act as push buttons in order to make money—just without a garage.

However, *empuja botón* continues to be an apt expression for what happens inside.

– *Maria Luisa Romero*

htaboga@sinfo.net. Doubles US$55-$66, depending on season; triples US$60-$70.) The hotel houses a rather expensive restaurant (sandwiches US$2.40-$4, dinners US$8-$10). **Cool Hostel ❷**, following the only path to this big house from the dock, is perfect for backpackers. Fan and hot water in all rooms; breakfast included. (☎596 7836, luisveron@hotmail.com. Rooms US$10, with A/C US$12.50. Bike rental US$5 per day; tours to Vigia and Cruces, US$3. Snorkel and fishing equipment, each US$3.) About 10 minutes to the left of the dock, **Donde Pope sí Hay ❷**provides a calm atmosphere in a small restaurant with a varied menu including *comida típica* and fish. (☎261 1101; US$1-$5. Open daily 8am-10pm). Meals are cheap at **El Mirador de Taboga ❶**, to the right of the dock just before the entrance to Hotel Taboga. (Burger US$1, *empanada* US$0.35, chow mein US$3.50. Open daily 7am-11pm.)

◪ BEACHES AND WATERSPORTS. Playa Honda is to the left of the dock, while **Playa La Restinga** is to the right. Don't be fooled by Hotel Taboga's near-monopoly on beachgoers—La Restinga is a public beach. To get there without entering hotel property, turn toward the beach at the sign just before the grounds. Go through a narrow alley between the *batido* stand and El Mirador restaurant. Bathrooms (US$0.50) and changing rooms (US$0.25) are on the right as you exit the passage. Hotel Taboga has *ranchitos*, showers, changing rooms, lockers, and bathrooms by the beach, but day visitors must pay to enter (US$7). At the gate you receive a plastic bracelet and five "Taboga Dollars" to spend anywhere on the grounds.

Right in front of La Restinga, connected to the main island at low tide, is **Isla El Morro,** the 19th-century headquarters of the Pacific Steam Navigation Company. Don't get stranded by the tide; while it's not far from shore, strong currents make swimming dangerous. For **snorkelers, Playa Piedra Llana** and **Playa El Jobo** are more secluded rocky beaches with good coral reefs; walk 45min. down the road behind Hotel Taboga to the right of the dock (turn left before the hotel). Beyond the white apartments next to Hotel Taboga, bear left at the fork and then left again. Follow the wheel tracks in the road to reach beaches. During the rainy season, this walk is muddy and unkempt, so go by boat (get one at La Restinga; the price will vary depending on number of people and time). Schools of fish congregate in front of **Playa La Restinga** near a sunken ship whose mussel-encrusted frame is visible at low tide. You can usually find **Señor Perea** cruising the beaches renting equipment, especially during high season and weekends; if not, call or ask the guard at the hotel entrance. (☎620 8805. Mask, snorkel, and fins US$2 per hr.; US$5 per day.)

◪ OUTDOOR ACTIVITIES. There's a lookout point at a former US army bunker, **La Vigia,** with a view of the surrounding hills. While Hotel Taboga offers transport to the vista, the best way up is an hour-long trail through the forest. At the church, facing the phone booth from the basketball court, take the path to the left and follow ANAM's black-and-yellow signs to the trailhead. The climb is tough. Along the way up, you'll pass **Cerro Tres Cruces** (the three crosses in the ground); either head left to La Vigia, or go straight and follow the trail down the other side of the island. This entire side is forested, protected by the **Refugio de Vida Silvestre Islas Taboga y Uraba.** It's a major nesting area for migratory seabirds, especially from December to March, when the island is mobbed by pelicans visiting from California. ANAM recommends a guide call ahead and ask for Christian Pérez. Before you go, visit the office of the Marine Authority to the dock's right to pick up **trail maps** or ask how to get to the ANAM office. (☎250 2082. Usually open daily 7am-4:30pm.) The trail from Cerro Tres Cruces goes to **San Pedro Playa** as well. Another way to see the island is to hire a **boat** at Playa Honda or Hotel Taboga (US$25 for four).

PANAMA PROVINCE

With 1.4 million people, Panama Province is the country's most populous province. Its borders encompass a wide range of both natural and engineered wonders, all within easy reach of Panama City. The most famous of the area's attractions, the Panama Canal, neighbors tropical islands and superb national parks. Most visitors head north along the road to Gamboa toward the canal locks at Miraflores and amazing bird-watching at Soberanía. To the west are sweeping views of Parque Nacional Altos de Campana and numerous nearby beaches, while offshore in the Golfo de Panamá, the Archipiélago de las Perlas glitters.

PANAMA CANAL

The Panama Canal, extending 80km of water connecting the Atlantic and Pacific Oceans, is one of the greatest engineering feats. It is a lock-type canal, with three sets of locks that elevate ships 26m above sea level, to the altitude of the Gatun Lake, and then lower them back down on the other side of the isthmus. Boats use their own propulsion, but when passing through the locks electric locomotives align and keep them in position. Commercial ships pay an average US$460,000 each to pass, and over 30 vessels do so daily. More than a technological marvel, the Canal is both the defining feature and the economic foundation of modern Panama. For Canal history, see **Daytrips from Colón**, (p. 631).

🔄 VISITING THE CANAL

Take a bus from Plaza 5 de Mayo in Panama City toward Gamboa (every 30min. 5am-11pm, US$0.35; with A/C US$0.50) or Paraíso (every 30min., 4:30am-10:30pm) at the SACA terminal and ask the driver stop at Miraflores. Buses are less frequent on weekends so check schedules (☎212 3420). Cross the bridge and up the road 10min. to the new visitor center. (☎276 8617. Open daily 9am-5pm. Entrance US$10, children US$5.) MC/V. Partial boat tours of the canal through Canal and Bay Tours leave Sa at 7:30am from Muelle 1 in Balboa. (☎314 1349. US$100 per person. Full tours one Sa per month. US$150 per person.)

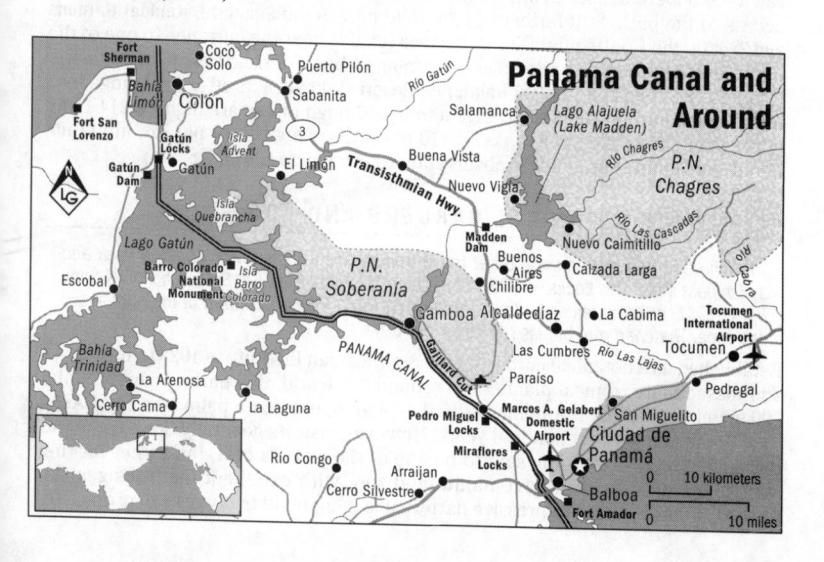

Panama Canal and Around

To see the canal in action, the best dry-land spot is the visitor center at **Miraflores Locks,** the largest on the canal and closest to Panama City. The center includes a recently inaugurated four-story museum, a film about the canal, a viewing deck with commentary in Spanish and English, and an expensive restaurant and souvenir shop. The museum is divided into four modern exhibits: Canal History; Water: Source of Life; Canal in Action; and The Canal in the World. When boats pass, presentations on the viewing deck explain how it works. The largest ships tend to pass between 9-10:30am and 2-5pm; call ahead for details. When boats aren't passing, a 10min. film alternates between English and Spanish to recount canal history.

Contractors Hill, on the western side of the canal, is the most accessible place from which to see **Gaillard Cut** wind through 8 miles of highland region, but even this can only be reached by private vehicle. On the Atlantic side, you can view **Gatún Locks** (see p. 629), the highest and busiest of the three locks. The best way to experience the canal is **by boat**—see the locks in action in gorgeous scenery. Panama City travel agents book the tour, but the main operator is **Canal and Bay Tours.**

THE ROAD TO GAMBOA

Traveling north out of Panama City you'll eventually come to Gamboa, where the Río Chagres enters Lago Gatún. Combining a visit to Miraflores Locks with a stop at Summit Gardens and a short hike in Soberanía makes a great daytrip from Panama City. Overnight trips are more difficult because Gamboa has no budget rooms; a good alternative is to camp at the Gardens.

To access the area, take a Gamboa-bound **bus** from the SACA terminal (☎212 3420) at Plaza 5 de Mayo in Panama City (40min., every 30min. during the week, M-F 5am-11:15pm, Sa 5:30am-11pm, Su 6am-10:30pm; US$0.65, with A/C US$0.80). If your first stop is **Miraflores,** you can take a bus headed to **Paraíso** as well—these also leave from 5 de Mayo (see above). Nine kilometers from the city is the turnoff to the Miraflores Locks (see above). The harder-to-see **Pedro Miguel Locks** are 2.5km farther along, beyond which the road continues past the town of Paraíso before reaching the headquarters of the densely forested and wildlife-rich Parque Nacional Soberanía (see below). Various trailheads farther down the road provide access to the park. Still farther on, the road passes the **Summit Botanical Gardens and Zoo,** on the Continental Divide. **Gamboa** itself is near the entrance to one of the park's best hikes and is a good place to arrange a boat for Lago Gatún or up the Río Chagres. The **Gamboa Tropical Rainforest Resort** (take a right after the bridge into town) is the easiest place to arrange a tour, although prices are high. (☎214 1690; www.gamboaresort.com. Kayaks US$10 per hr., rowing US$15 per hr., mini tour US$10 for 30min., 3hr. wildlife observation tour on Lago Gatún US$35.)

⚜ SUMMIT BOTANICAL GARDENS AND ZOO

Take the Gamboa bus and hop off at the entrance, about 9km shy of Gamboa itself and 10km past Miraflores Locks. ☎232 4854. Open M-F 8am-4pm; Sa, Su and holidays 8am-5pm. US$1, children under 12 free. Camping US$5. Ask for a trail map of the park at the entrance. Thatched roof bohíos (US$5-$8 per day).

Established as a botanical garden by the Smithsonian Institute in 1923 to introduce and disseminate tropical plants from around the world, this park occupies about 300 spacious hectares. Among the 15,000 plant species is a palm tree from Asia that blooms once every hundred years. However, visitors generally don't come for the unique palm collection, said to be one of the world's best, but rather for the sporting and expansive, well-maintained zoo, with excellent facilities geared toward children and an impressive harpy eagle compound that works to propagate endangered populations throughout the country. You will be able to enjoy up-close views of many endangered animals from the Panamanian rain forest, including Geoffrey's tamarin, Night and Spider monkeys, tapirs, jaguars, alligators, and Macaws. The Summit is an ideal base from which to explore nearby Parque Soberanía and Gamboa. Call in advance to make reservations so the security guard will let you in after closing. Bring your own tent, food, and insect repellent.

◪ PARQUE NACIONAL SOBERANÍA

The road forks at the ranger station (☎ 232 4192), with Chilibre to the right and Gamboa to the left. To reach trails, hop on a bus or passenger van. Admission US$3, camping US$5 per night (only permitted near the ranger station, not in the park itself). Station open daily 8am-4pm, but rangers work weekends for emergencies. Guides can be arranged in advance through the ranger station or with naturalist companies in Panama City—usually US$40 an afternoon, and worth it. Ranger Melesio Sánchez, highly recommended, leads weekend tours. (☎ 692 9778. Usually US$25 per person.)

Spanning 19,540 hectares on the canal's east bank and encompassing the Río Chagres, part of Lago Gatún, and even rich tropical forest, Soberanía is the most accessible national park in Panama, just 25km (40min.) from Panama City. In addition to several good trails, it protects the canal's watershed and harbors an abundance of wildlife and birds (more than 500 species, among them Panama's national bird, the endangered harpy eagle, which is the most powerful bird of prey and one of the world's largest eagles). The park also hosts 105 species of mammals, 79 of reptiles, 55 of amphibians, and 36 freshwater fish species.

Stop by the **ranger station** to pay the admission fee and pick up helpful maps. About 10min. toward Gamboa from the station and past Summit Gardens, **Sendero El Charco**, the shortest and easiest trail, is a well-maintained loop (less than 1km) through the forest. It follows a creek and ultimately leads to a waterfall and pond suitable for swimming and picnicking. The walk takes an hour and gets crowded on weekends. Fifteen minutes farther along the main road, turn right down a side road onto **Plantation Loop;** follow the blacktop, then the dirt road, for a mosquito-ridden trail weaving through secondary forest. The park's longest trail, **Pipeline Road** (Camino de Oleoducto), has the best bird-watching around. The Panama Audobon Society has reported a record 525 bird species sighted in one day. To reach the trail, follow the main road to Gamboa (15min. by bus). Stop for the awe-inspiring canal view from the bridge into town. After walking straight 10min. through town, bear left at the fork and continue 5min. up a dirt road until the trail sign. Strikingly colorful butterflies, howler monkeys, and phenomenal bird life inhabit the hilly, challenging 17km hike. If you don't know a tanger from a tangerine, it might behoove you to get a guide who knows the region's birds.

◪ PARQUE NACIONAL CHAGRES

To visit the indigenous villages take a boat from Nuevo Vigía or Corotú, both in Colón Province, but easily accessible from Panama City. To Nuevo Vigía take a Panamá-Colón bus (not autopista) at the Albrook bus terminal and get off at the Cooperativa de Transporte La Victoria (45min., every 30min. 4:45am-10pm, US$0.65). From there you can take a taxi to Nuevo Vigía (US$1) or take the Colón-Buena Vista bus (every 15 min., 4am-10pm, US$0.20). To Corotú it's the same Panamá-Colón bus, but get off at La Cabima (30min., US$0.40). Then take a bus to Nuevo Caimitillo (30min., every hr. 7am-6pm, US$0.65). The communities of Tusi Pono (☎ 648 1588) and Parará Purú (☎ 509 8069) pick you up at Nuevo Vigía or Corotú; call in advance. Daytrip includes transport to the village, lunch, traditional dances, an explanation of the culture, a waterfall visit, and possible hikes (US$15-$25; US$20-$30 overnight). A more expensive option allows you to visit more vil-

lages and the park. At Nuevo Vigía, contact Sr. Toto (☎ 434 0713) and in Corotú, Sr. Cholo (☎ 598 5609). The ANAM office is a bit before the Corotú port. Try to get the bus to wait for you while you pay and get a map; if not, it's a 20 min. walk down. Entrance US$3 (office open 8am-4pm). For white water rafting tours on the Río Chagres, contact Aventuras Panamá (☎ 260 0044; www.aventuraspanama.com).

Located between the provinces of Colón and Panama and covering 135,000 hectares on the east bank of the canal, this park is unlike any other national park in Panama. It was created in the early 1980s to protect the canal watershed, guaranteeing the functioning of the waterway. The park encompasses Río Chagres and several other rivers, in addition to the Lago Alajuela. Four different forest zones and diverse wildlife make Chagres an ecological gem among Panama's national parks, but the opportunity it provides to experience indigenous culture is unparalleled. The Emberá Indians migrated from Darién and live on islands created when Lago Gatún was formed. One of the three major indigenous groups in Panama are the Emberá, who have preserved their traditions—the huts on stilts in which they live, and their costumes—for centuries, although they've been influenced by modernization. Visiting indigenous villages is a chance to learn about native food, life, traditions, and beliefs. If feeling experimental, they'll paint you in the traditional way with black ink that looks like ash but comes from a fruit called *jagua* (US$1).

PARQUE NACIONAL ALTOS DE CAMPANA

AT A GLANCE	
AREA: 48 sq. km.	**GATEWAYS:** Panama City (see p. 605).
CLIMATE: A bit cooler than Panama City, increasingly so in the higher altitudes; also wetter than the city.	**CAMPING:** Campsites, numerous *refugios*, and 2 cabins. Call ahead to reserve.
FEATURES: Cerro La Cruz, Cerro Campana.	**FEES AND RESERVATIONS:** Park admission US$3 per person. Reservations recommended for the house.
HIGHLIGHTS: Extensive Pacific views, camping, hiking, escape from the city.	

Created in 1966, Panama's oldest national park extends over the Cordillera Central mountain chain. Altos de Campana's location—1½hr. from Panama City—makes it a quick getaway. Although deforestation has threatened many of the park's animals, the biodiversity remains stunning, and the resulting rolling grasslands mix with cloud forest to create a relaxing and refreshingly cool environment. An elevation of 600-1000m presents brilliant views of the Pacific as far as Isla Taboga or the Azuero Peninsula. Numerous hikes, of varying difficulties and altitudes, will reward visitors with Pacific views and a glimpse into the wildlife that once covered Panama. On the Atlantic side colorful birds such as trogons, woodpeckers, toucans, and hummingbirds abound. The park is also home to a variety of mammals including the leopard, wild hog, forest rabbit, and two-toed sloth. Begonias and orchids are common throughout.

⌨ TRANSPORTATION

Buses heading west on the Interamerican Hwy. from Panama City can drop you off at the turnoff for the park (US$1). The main **entrance** and **ranger station** are 6km up a steep dirt road (Carretera Chicá) from the Interamerican Hwy. Take a bus going to **Chicá** and ask to be dropped off at the ranger station (US$0.25), or wait for a 4WD **taxi** (US$3), but be advised, they don't pass frequently. The entrances to the park's trails are a 1½hr. hike past the station.

⁇ PRACTICAL INFORMATION

In case of **emergency**, ANAM (☎/fax 254 2848) has a regional office in La Chorrera; rangers are on service 24hr. Ask for Jose Antonio Chen, in charge of the park. The **climate** is moderate, certainly cooler than in Panama City; expect higher precipitation than in the city. **Ranger stations** have rangers stationed 24hr. Whether you plan to camp or hike, check in for updates on weather and guided walks. (Station open daily 8am-4pm; tipping is appreciated.) There is a US$3 park entrance fee.

⁇ ACCOMMODATIONS AND CAMPING

The park has six **refugios** and two **camping** areas; ANAM has two cabins (US$5 per night). The kitchen is available but bring food and kitchen utensils; the beds are bare, so bring sheets as well. To get to the first refugio, continue 10min. down the hill and to the right where concrete wheel tracks head. There are no beds, but it will keep you dry; latrine and untreated water nearby. Let the rangers know if planning to stay so they can open it. For a little more comfort and a lot more company, American expat Richard "de Campana" rents a funky old **house** on the park boundaries and provides meals (bring your own food and they'll cook). Calling in advance is recommended, but the white house is big and you're likely to get a spot. It's fifteen minutes past the sign for trails on the main road. (☎ 601 2882. 10 beds US$120 per night; individual suites US$5-$10 per person; camping US$5 per night.)

⁇ HIKING TRAILS

The park's most popular trail, **Sendero La Cruz** (1.5km), winds uphill for 1hr. to **Cerro La Cruz**, which has the best views in the park. Climb another 30min. to forest-covered **Cerro Campana**; at 1007 meters it's the park's highest point. From there you can continue another hour, this time downhill, to get back to the road—you'll end up about 15min. uphill from the ranger station. La Cruz is the park's most difficult trail, but the refreshing temperatures, views, and bird variety make it worthwhile. **Sendero Panamá** (1hr., 1.4km) and **Sendero Podocarpus** (30min., 1km) are both considered easy. A ranger truck or 4WD taxi can take you part of the way if you don't want to hike. The entrances to all the trails are a 1½hr. hike past the station, which is marked by a sign that says *No estoy*.

ARCHIPIÉLAGO DE LAS PERLAS: ISLA CONTADORA

About 90km southeast of Panama City, this archipelago—of 2003 *Survivor Pearl Island* fame—consists of over 200 islands, about 10 of which are inhabited. Most visitors to the islands go to Isla Contadora, the only public island with tourist facilities that aren't strictly for the super-rich—though you wouldn't know it given its beauty. The history of the islands is chock-full of pirates and pearls, including the gigantic 31-carat "Peregrina" pearl, currently owned by Elizabeth Taylor, discovered in 1515 and once presented to the Spanish Queen.

Contadora, the primary tourist destination in the Archipiélago de las Perlas, may just be paradise on earth. Beneath an intense sun await soft beaches, crystal-clear waters full of rainbow-colored fish, and the most easygoing people assembled in one locale. Like many of Panama's islands, Contadora is home to increasing tourist developments (witness the "Contadora Mall").

TRANSPORTATION. Aeroperlas (☎315 7500) has **flights** from Panama City (**Marcos A. Gelabert Airport**) to **Contadora,** some via San Miguel, on Isla del Rey: (M-F 20min., 8am, 5, 5:30pm; Sa 8:50am, 5pm; Su 8u 8:50am, 3:50, 4:40 pm; US$29). The planes turn right around and fly back. Turismo Aéreo (☎315 0279) has daily flights to and from Contadora for the same price (M-Th, Sa-Su 9am, Sa-Su 4:30pm). **National Tours** runs a **boat** service from **Balboa** to the island. Call in advance as schedules change depending on demand. (☎269 8749. 2 hr.; leaves daily at 9am, returns at 2pm except for W when it returns at 12:30pm; one-way US$20.)

ORIENTATION AND PRACTICAL INFORMATION. The airstrip cuts across the entire island on the eastern side. Most tourist facilities cluster around the north end of the airstrip (where the planes stop) and on the eastern side of the island. Follow the road around the end of the strip and into **Hotel Contadora,** along the brown-and-white fence, to get a free map. Heading up the road on the airstrip's western side leads to a small circle with the **police station,** and, to the right of the radio tower, the new blue-and-white **health center** (open M-F 7am-noon and 2-5pm, weekends for emergencies only). The main **market** is downhill to the left of the police station (open daily 8am-8pm). **Public phones** are in front of the radio tower, beside the airstrip, and next to the health center.

ACCOMMODATIONS AND FOOD. Lodging on the island is not cheap unless you camp. Building fires is prohibited. ◪**Hotel Villa Romántica ❷**, on Playa Cacique, has expensive rates, but offers a student room for two with fan (US$30). The beautiful beach right in front of the hotel, great service, and excellent food make for an unforgettable stay. The friendly owner will pick you up at the airport for no extra charge. (☎250 4067; www.contadora-villa-romantica.com.) The cheapest lodging, **Cabañas de Contadora ❸**, offers four small suites about a 5min. walk from the beach, each with two rooms and a small kitchen. From the end of the airstrip, bear left at the police station, and continue 1km. It's on your left, just as the road takes a sharp dip toward the sea. (☎250 4214; www.cabanascontadora.tripod.com.)

The two cheapest restaurants are near the airline offices and the police station, in the town on the western side of the airstrip. On the hill-top is Restaurante Sagitario ❶, with *comida típica* and pleasant outdoor seating. (US$2-$3.50; open daily 6:30am-8:30pm.) A few yards farther toward the airstrip Mi Kioskito ❶ serves ice cream (US$1), beer (US$1), and good US$2-$5 fish and pork dishes (open daily 9am-9pm, sometimes later). **Multicomidas ❶** is a new restaurant uphill right across from the airport that serves good fast food for relatively cheap prices (sandwiches US$1.80-$4. Open daily 3-11pm). Especially during low season, there's basically no nightlife, and many places won't open unless you advise them. If open, try Julio's Beach Bar, the only bar and disco; from the airport, walk uphill, it's to the right.

BEACHES. The island's ultimate beach, if not the Pacific's, is a 10min. walk from town. Heading uphill from the airstrip, fork right at the police station and continue to the right along the road; take a right at the soccer field and the first right past the lake. At the bottom of the hill lies ◪**Playa Ejecutiva**, nestled among the cliffs of a turquoise cove: the perfect place to laze through an afternoon.

With 13 different beaches, it's hard to choose. All beaches are consistently clean, with clear water (except after heavy rain) and gentle currents. At the northern tip of the airstrip is **Playa Galeón**, with coral formations perfect for snorkeling, but often crowded due to the looming presence of nearby Hotel Punta Galeón. In front of the Hotel Contadora, **Playa Larga** is the longest and most crowded. Many of the rental shops and bars along the beach are closed in low season. If you follow Playa Larga south to the end past Hotel Contadora, a small path leads to **Playa de las Suecas,** which has more rocks, and less clothes—it's the only official nude beach in Panama. A road branching off the path between Larga and Suecas leads around the southern end of the airstrip past the dilapidated former pier to **Playa Cacique,** also known as Playa Hawaii. This gorgeous expanse of sugar-white sand is framed by rocky cliffs and dark blue waters.

◪ **WATERSPORTS AND GUIDED TOURS.** Glass-bottom boat tours are offered around the island (US$20 per person per hr.). Eight glass panels on the floor allow you to see all kinds of fish, turtles, dolphins, and even sharks. Ask at Playa Larga for time info. There aren't many other facilities on the island that offer tours or watersports for low prices. The Hotel Contadora rents snorkeling equipment (US$5 per hr.). The Hotel Galeón rents jetskis for exorbitant rates (US$65 per hr).

COLÓN PROVINCE

Historically, Colón Province has lured people for one reason: the bling. In the 16th and 17th centuries, the Spanish used the region to transport gold and silver across the Atlantic. Three centuries later, in 1948, Panamanian entrepreneurs established what has become the world's second-largest free-trade zone in the city of Colón (after Hong Kong). What is more noteworthy to the traveler is the legacy of Spanish bullion—some of the region's highlights include well-preserved colonial fort ruins, used to protect riches. At Sabanitas, 10km shy of Colón, the road from Panama City forks—one side continues to Colón, the other heads to the Caribbean *costa arriba* and seaside Portobelo, home to several fort ruins. Off the coast near Portobelo, the diving and snorkeling of Isla Grande is popular with weekenders. West of the city of Colón, the Gatún Locks are the largest of the Panama Canal.

COLÓN

> Much of daily life in Colón is lived on the street—from balcony musicians to domino games to dumpster-pickers. The city is vibrant and active, but also quite dangerous for visitors. Colón, like any city, has good and bad areas; yet most of the good ones are behind **Zona Libre** walls, with its own post office and police force. If forced to walk in the city, avoid C. 8, 3, and 4, as these are the worst. Extreme caution should be used at all times. In general, it is not advisable to walk on the street, even just a few blocks. Take taxis whenever possible.

When most Panamanians are asked about Colón, they simply reply, "Don't go there." Poverty, desperation, and danger mark the city, which suffers the highest rate of violent crime in the country. Colón's former elegance has faded throughout the century, as has the hope of its citizens. Aside from the fact that muggings do occur in broad daylight, however, Colón is simply of little interest to the traveler because there's not much to see or do in the city itself. Other than shopping in Colón 2000, the new cruise port, or the **Zona Libre** (Free Zone), the only reason to pass through is to reach Gatún Locks or San Lorenzo. At the city's **yacht club**, where smaller boats wait to pass through the canal, it is often possible to get a crew job on boats heading south.

TRANSPORTATION. All **buses** in Colón come and go from the terminal on C. 13 and Av. Bolívar. Buses leave to: **Coco Solo** (40min., every 15min. 6:15am-10pm, US$0.30); **La Guayra** (2hr., every 2hr. M-Sa 9:30am-5:30pm, Su 9:30am and 3:30pm, US$2); **Panama City** (2hr., every 15min. 3:50am 1am, US$1.20; express service 1½hr., every 30min. 5am-midnight, US$2); and **Portobelo** (1½hr., every 30min. 6:15am-9:45pm, Sa-Su 7am-9pm, US$1.30) via **Sabanitas** (30min., US$0.30).

The **airport** hasn't functioned since Aeroperlas cancelled all flights to Colón. However, **boats** are another, albeit adventurous, transport option. Boats eastward to San Blas or Colombia are at **Puerto Coco Solo**, reachable by bus from the terminal. These trips are negotiated with vessel captains, but be careful: it is inadvisable to journey to Colombia by boat. Drug busts occur on such boats, and *Let's Go* doesn't recommend this method. Smaller private boats north into San Blas can occasionally be negotiated in Colón or on the Costa Arriba. Check at the Cristóbal Colón Yacht Club, a few blocks behind the bus terminal.

Train service between Panama City and Colón resumed in August 2002 and it has been met with complete success as most of the workers in the Colón Free Trade Zone choose this as the preferred mode of transport. The Panama Railway was built in 1855 and was the first intercontinental railway. Once a major passageway for young men seeking gold in California, this historical route across the isthmus, which passes through jungle, with water on both sides, allows you to see the transatlantic ships passing trough the Canal. It is now a scenic option to Colón. (Daily trips between the cities cost US$20 one-way or US$35 round-trip, children US$10/$17.50. Train leaves from Estación de Corozal in Albrook at 7:15 am and returns from Colón at 5:15pm; 1hr. ride. From the Colón train station, a cab ride to the center is US$2 (☎317 6070; www.panarail.com).

ORIENTATION AND PRACTICAL INFORMATION. Colón is laid out in a north-south grid pattern on a roughly square piece of land that was once an island, with a bulge in the southeast corner occupied by the **Zona Libre** and a bulge in the southwest, the Port of Cristóbal. The city is connected to the mainland by a bridge from the Zona Libre to the airport, and by a strip of land in the southwest corner. The southwest strip has two main roads running parallel to each other: **Av. Bolívar**, and 5 blocks east, **Paseo del Centenario**, or **Av. Central**. In general, *avenidas* and *paseos* run north-south, and numbered *calles* run east-west, from C. 1 in the north to C. 16 in the south. **Av. Amador Guerrero**, between Bolívar and Central, has some budget eating and lodging in a relatively better neighborhood, from C. 9 to C. 12. The massive **Colón 2000** shopping center is on the east side of town at the end of C. 9-11. The **yacht club** is in the southwest, near the bus station.

For **tourist info**, head to **IPAT** (☎441 9644), on Av. Central and C. Domingo Díaz. The regional director, Raúl, is helpful and speaks English. Open M-F 8:30am-4:30pm. **Banks** are all over the Zona Libre and dispersed throughout the city. **Banco General** (☎431 5011), at Av. del Frente (all the way west) and C. 10, has an **ATM;** it might be a good idea to have a taxi waiting right outside as a safety precaution. Open M-F 8am-3pm, Sa 9am-noon. **Banistmo**, on Port Cristóbal, requires you to take a right before the port entrance; it also has an ATM and changes traveler checks (Open M-F 8am-3:30pm, Sa 9am-noon.) There are various **Western Union** locations, including one on C. 13 and Av. Central and another on C. 2 and Av. Bolívar. Open M-F 8am-5:30pm, Sa only until 5pm. Also in Zona Libre. Several **supermarkets**, including **Super 99**, are located in Colón 2000; open M-Sa 8am-11pm, Su 9am-7pm. For **laundry**, many, including **Lavamático/Lavandería Luis N-2, are** on Av.

Guerrero near C. 11, next to several hotels and restaurants. (US$0.75 wash and dry each load. Open M-Sa 7am-8pm, Su 7am-6pm.) It's safest to use hotel laundry services (around US$5 for a load), not here. The **police** main station (☎441 2015, emergencies 104), is on Av. Meléndez, 4 blocks east of Av. Central, on C. 11; also in Zona Libre (☎445 0458). **Hospital Manuel A. Guerrero** (hospital and ambulances ☎441 5077), on Paseo Gorgas (all the way east) and C. 10, is pretty run-down, but works for emergencies. The intersection of Av. Guerrero and C. 11 has **Farmacia Galénica** (☎441 4683. Open M-Sa 8am-11pm, Su 9am-7pm.) For mail, the **post office** is on C. 9 and Av. Bolívar (open M-F 7am-6pm, Sa 7am-5pm).

⌐⌐ ACCOMMODATIONS AND FOOD. Lodgings ranging from budget to classy cluster around Av. Guerrero and C. 10 and 11, near restaurants, the pharmacy, and the laundromat. The town's only budget hostel is more removed, but the following options have relative advantages in security. *Let's Go* recommends you make Colón and the Locks daytrips from Panama City. If you stay overnight, **Hotel Carlton ❹**, on Av. Meléndez and C. 10, is one of two good hotels. Extra cash means great location near Zona Libre, peace of mind, and amenities: laundry (US$1.50 per item), pharmacy (open 8am-10pm), and in-house restaurant. Singles easily sleep two; doubles, four. (☎447 0349. Singles US$30-$35; doubles US$40; triples US$45; suite US$55.) One of the cheapest, **Pensión Acrópolis ❶**, on the corner of Guerrero and C. 11, has rooms with a sink, fan, desk, and solid bed. The gate is locked at night. Across the street from 2 budget restaurants and beside a bakery. Small communal bath lacks water pressure. (☎441 1456. US$6.50.)

Eat at or near your hotel if possible. The following are near or inside the listed accommodations. **Cafetería Nacional ❶**, on the corner of Guerrero and 11, catty-corner from Acrópolis, has a cool interior and English-language menu with a large selection. (☎445 2403. Breakfast US$1.50-$3.50, chicken soup US$1.50, sandwiches US$1.75-3.25, full meals US$3-$6. Open M-Sa 7am-10pm, Su 8am-3pm.)

➋ DAYTRIPS FROM COLÓN

GATÚN LOCKS AND GATÚN DAM

From the main bus terminal in Colón, catch a bus to Cuipo or Costa Abajo (both 20min., every hr. 5am-10pm, US$0.75) and get off either right before crossing the locks or 5min. down the road at the dam. From the locks' bus stop, head up the hill alongside the locks to the visitor center, the white building with the Panamanian flag. (☎443 8878. Open daily 8am-4pm. Free.) To reach the dam, wait for the next bus (US$0.25) or walk 20min. For an impressive walk, cross the locks and go left after the gate. When the road forks to the right, follow it to the dam. Frequent buses return to Colón 5am-11pm.

Just 10km south of Colón, Gatún Locks and Dam make a good half-day trip. The **Gatún Locks,** on the northern end of the Panama Canal and the longest of the three, raise and lower ships a total of 26m between the Caribbean and Lago Gatún. There are three pairs of locks allowing simultaneous passage of two ships in opposing directions (although for logistical purposes ships usually go in the same direction depending on the time). Unique to Gatún Locks is the small bridge that allows cars and buses to pass across the canal, bringing visitors within meters of the enormous locks as vehicles travel along the bottom of the great metal gates. The **visitor center,** a tower above the middle lock, has a great view of boats passing through the entire length of the locks (almost 2km) as well as Lago Gatún. Presentations in both English and Spanish are given as boats go by; foreign language brochures available. Only by seeing the chambers without water can you appreciate their monstrous size. By the entrance a retired *mula*, an electric locomotives that aligns and helps tow each ship through the locks. Ships pass 24hr. a day.

Gatún Dam, 2km away, was the largest earth dam in the world when it was built in 1906. Over 800m wide and 2km in length, the dam formed the largest artificial body of water in the world, Lago Gatún. The dam's construction caused Río Chagres to flood, covering villages, the Panama Railroad, and 262 hectares of forest. Today the dam generates a major part of the electricity needed for canal operation. Lago Gatún provides a total 52 million gallons of fresh water per transit.

FORT SAN LORENZO

30 kilometers from Colón, Fort San Lorenzo isn't accessible by public transportation. It's possible to take a (begrudging) taxi from Colón, but there are no emergency facilities, and the road isn't in good condition (1hr.). Expect to pay US$40 or more (round-trip fare includes exploring time); agree on the price beforehand. Open daily 8am-4pm.

The faster of the two original trans-isthmian routes for Spanish colonial gold was overland from Panama City to Las Cruces and then by water down the Río Chagres to the Caribbean. North of the river, on a high point overlooking the river and the sea, the Spanish built Fort San Lorenzo to protect their gold and silver against pirates. Apparently their efforts were to no avail: the fort was sacked three times, most notably in 1671 by the Welsh pirate Henry Morgan, who then sailed up the Chagres and routed Panamá Viejo. In 1686, the fort was burned by English seafaring bandits. The beautiful, haunting ruins encompass moats, walls, and a row of cannons. Fort Sherman, a former US base now in Panamanian hands, stands between Gatún Locks and San Lorenzo and is closed while its future is debated (it may become the base for a national park; for info visit www.sanlorenzo.gob.pa). Since San Lorenzo is difficult to access, the Portobelo ruins are a better option.

PORTOBELO

Verdant hills gently bend through Spanish colonial ruins to meet azure Caribbean waters, creating the quiet allure of this *puerto bello*. For 200 years after its 1597 founding, Portobelo (pop. 8500) was the commercial center of the Spanish colonies. It hosted famous fairs merging the old and new worlds, during which ships from Spain came to collect gold and silver from the south in exchange for European goods, to be redistributed throughout the Americas. Until 1738, for several weeks the streets of Portobelo would become the backdrop for these huge exchange markets whose spirit of commerce and vigorous enterprise is today echoed in the Colón Free Trade Zone (p. 629). Forts were built to protect outgoing gold supplies against pirates and the English Navy, who in the end caused this port's demise. Today the fort's ruins, one of the area's premier tourist attractions, are the only reminders of this small and modest town's glorious past. In addition to the fish and coconut trades, tourism's golden mixture of diving, snorkeling, ruins, patron saint celebrations, and Panamanian-Caribbean cultures draw crowds, especially during the weekend. Attendance swells during dry season, but mid-year Portobelo enters a lull, and establishments are shuttered.

⌂ TRANSPORTATION. To **Portobelo,** take a *ruta* **bus** from Panama City toward **Colón** (1-2hr., US$1); for a faster, more upscale (read: A/C and movies) option, take any Colón bus from the main bus terminal (1½ hr.; every 20-40 min. M-F 4:45am-10pm, Sa 5:40am-10pm, Su 6:40am-9pm; US$2). In either case, ask your driver to stop at **Sabanitas** (look for shops with "Sabanitas" signboards, or for the new McDonald's on the left side of the road and the pedestrian bridge overhead). From the turn-off in front of El Rey supermarket, catch a Portobelo or **Costa Arriba**-bound bus (1hr., every 15-30min. 6:30am-9pm, US$1). In Colón, buses to Portobelo leave from the bus terminal on C. 13 and Av. Bolívar (1½hr.; every 30min. M-F

6:15am-9:45pm, Sa-Su 7am-9pm; US$1.30). Returning from Portobelo, buses travel down the main road toward Colón (1-2hr., every 30min. 4:30am-6pm, US$1) via Sabanitas, where you can catch buses heading to **Panama City.**

⚡🛈 ORIENTATION AND PRACTICAL INFORMATION. Portobelo itself lies 34km east of Sabanitas, but dive shops and higher-class establishments gather a few kilometers before town on the main road. To go directly to one of these places, get off the bus when you see the "Scuba Portobelo," "Portobelo Bay Center," or "Coco Plum" signs on your left. From **Scuba Portobelo,** the tiny town is a 30min. walk east along the main road past the **Santiago de la Gloria** ruins.

There are few services beyond the friendly **IPAT** office (☎448 2200) 20m to the left of the **aduana,** the large tan building on the *parque central* in the town center. (Open daily 8:30am-4:30pm.) There are several **mercaditos**—two near the *parque central* and two between the dive shops. The **medical clinic** (☎448 2033) is near the town center toward the church, and the **police** (☎448 2082) are next to the Diver's Haven entrance, 2km west on the main road.

🛏🍴 ACCOMMODATIONS AND FOOD. There are four options for overnighters in Portobelo, only one of which is actually in town. Above **La Aduana ❷** bar on the *parque,* a local family rents four cheap, tidy rooms with double beds. (☎448 2925. Rooms US$10, with bath US$12, with A/C US$15.) Along the road west of town are a hotel and two dive shops that provide co-ed dorm rooms. A 25min. walk from town is **Coco Plum Ecolodge Resort ❸,** boasting a pretty beach accompanied by dock and restaurant, both with awesome views. Rooms are big and decorated with bright colors and sea themes. (☎448 2102; www.cocoplumpanama.com. Doubles with A/C and bath US$45, special rates for backpackers in a room with fan and shared bathroom for up to 10 people, US$10 per person.)

The cheap eats are in town, while more specialized menus and ambiences, along with higher prices, are on the road west. Seafood is the regional specialty, but most restaurants also serve non-seafood options. When business is slow, mainly on weekdays during low season, restaurants tend to close earlier than posted. For conch and other Caribbean delights, try **Restaurante Los Cañones ❸,** two minutes west of Scuba Portobelo. Named after the rusting cannons that dot the Portobelo region, the restaurant has a great bay view. (☎448 2980. Fish *ceviche* US$4, seafood with salad and rice US$6-$8, beer US$1.50. Open M-F 8am-10pm, Sa-Su 8am-10pm. MC/V.) In town, there are several cheap restaurants within 1 block of the *parque.* Next to Portobelo Bay Center, bar and disco **Don Luiso** is a good option for nightlife entertainment in a town that is otherwise usually quiet.

🎭 FESTIVALS. The El Nazareno statue first arrived in Portobelo in 1646 en route to Cartagena, Colombia. During a furious storm, the ship captain tossed everything overboard, including a statue of christ. Miraculously, the cholera epidemic that had been ravaging Portobelo disappeared at the same time that fishermen recovered the statue and brought it to town. On October 21, upon healing, the last 40 men carried the statue around town on a heavy platform. This same procession, with the steps now ritualized, occurs throughout the year, notably for **Cristo Negro** on October 21, when thousands of purple-robed, black-faced believers descend on Portobelo to celebrate what is one of Panama's most important religious traditions. Another lively celebration is the performance of the **congo,** an upbeat Afro-Caribbean dance performed during *carnaval* (February). Women wear long dresses and men decorate themselves with odds and ends: bottles, old radios, and just about anything else. Then they take turns dancing with the *rey* and *reina* (king and queen). As part of the ritual, participants walk and talk backwards.

⊙ SIGHTS. Gold from Spanish South American colonies was carried by mule from Panama City to Portobelo through the Camino de Cruces and then the Río Chagres. In order to protect the city from constant pirate assaults, the Spanish built four main fortresses and seven minor batteries, all constructed with a coral base. Portobelo boasts at least nine major **fort** ruins, along with others interspersed among houses. Built in the early 1600s, **Santiago de la Gloria,** on both sides of the road before entering town, contains a number of evocative ruins and is an excellent spot to wander or just lounge about. Its tremendous walls, cannons, moats, and dark hallways beckon intrigued travelers. **San Gerónimo,** with cannons, vultures, and a harbor view, rests behind the *aduana* near the ocean. **San Fernando,** across the bay, was built around 1753 and has a great view and intact colonial bathroom (catch a boat at the dock behind Fort Santiago for a 5 min. ride, round-trip US$2). Be sure to arrange for a pickup time to return, allowing yourself 30min. to an hour for exploration. The **Iron Castle** (a.k.a. **San Felipe** or **Todo Fierro**) once guarded the entrance to the harbor, but was dismantled earlier this century to provide stones for the Gatún Locks of the Panama Canal and the breakwater at Colón. Other less complete fortresses in the area,—including **Punta Farnese, La Matrinchera,** and **La Batería de Buenaventura**—crowd along the ocean. History tells that in a famous surprise attack by land in 1668, the English pirate Henry Morgan got to Buenaventura, crossed the mountains, and attacked Santiago de la Gloria, where he took priests and nuns hostage in exchange for the San Gerónimo castle.

El Nazareno, the sacred statue of Christ carrying the crucifix, rests in the large, white church of San Felipe, 1 block east of the *parque* (see **Festivals,** below). The **aduana** (royal customs house), built in 1630 out of the same coral reef blocks used for the forts, was used to store gold before shipping it to Spain. The building recently underwent a joint Panamanian-Spanish restoration effort. It now houses a modest **museum** on the second floor; one room has replicated colonial weapons, the other displays scores of purple cloaks worn by El Nazareno. The statue is dressed in a new, luxuriously-decorated cloak each year. There is a Cristo Negro Museum behind the church. (Free. Both open M-F 8am-4pm, Sa-Su 8am-5pm.)

⊿ WATERSPORTS. Portobelo's diving isn't stellar, but it is cheap and offers some great wreck dives. **Scuba Portobelo,** the oldest and best-known dive shop and a branch of Scuba Panama, offers rides to nearby beaches (US$4-$10), 2-dive days (with divemaster and equipment US$55), and a PADI-certification class including full equipment and lodging (4-5 days US$130). Basic equipment costs US$25. They also rent snorkel equipment for US$10 per day. (Scuba Panama ☎261 3841; www.scubapanama.com.) **Portobelo Bay Center** and **Coco Plum** also offer dive tours, classes, and full equipment at similar prices. Coco Plum has a half-day sailing tour that allows you to explore the historic sites around Portobelo (www.twinoceans.com. US$25). A popular diving spot is **Salmedina Reef,** a 3m-deep reef featuring a shipwreck, complete with cannons and anchors. The region's coral reefs are full of the **wrecks** from the many naval battles fought above. For example, Sir Francis Drake was buried at sea near Drake's Island, a small island with good coral formations and tons of lobsters and crabs. His lead coffin is somewhere on the bottom, still undiscovered. Farther from the bay is Farallones, a rocky island with one of the best reefs in the area and visibility up to 25m. Other diving spots include Bubble Rock, Iron Castle, Buenaventura, and El Avión.

ISLA GRANDE

Isla Grande, 20km east of Portobelo and just 100m off the coast, is busy compared to most Panamanian islands in the Caribbean—active villagers and vacationing mainland families splash around and relax until late night. The island has lovely beaches and good surfing, but most of all a chance to kick back and have a cocktail on the beach with locals and *capitalianos* (people from Panama City).

During daylight hours, **boats** travel frequently between **Isla Grande** and **La Guayra,** the closest mainland town (5min.; US$1, US$1.50 to Hotel Sister Moon). If you don't see a boat ask a local. **Buses** to La Guayra leave **Colón** (M-Sa every 2.5hr. 9:30am-5:30pm, Su 9am and 3:30pm; US$2), passing through **Sabanitas** (connect here to and from Panama City) and **Portobelo** (1hr., US$1 to La Guayra); returns from La Guayra (M-F 5:30, 6:30, 7:30, 9am, 1pm; Sa-Su 6, 10am, 1pm, and Su 4pm).

Directly in front of the main dock sits a green building called **Bodega Jackson.** The store has a large selection of liquor and a few groceries. Facing inland, walk 100m to the right to find a **medical clinic, Sub-Centro de Salud** (open M-F 8am-4pm, 24hr. for emergency), next to a **public phone.** From the Bodega walk left to get to Cabañas Cholita and Villa Ensueño. Next to the Villa Ensueño restaurant there's a store with practical things such as insect repellent, drinks, t-shirts, and postcards.

Most places to stay are either modest, bland buildings in the village, or busy vacation complexes on the outskirts—both raise prices during high season (Nov.-Apr.) and during Panamanian school vacations (mid July-early Aug.). The sprawl of concrete hotels at the island's western end is crowded and overpriced, but the sheer number of rooms may let you negotiate a deal. **Cabañas Cholita ❸** caters mostly to mainland vacationers and their kids, with a common patio, mini-boardwalk, bar, and restaurant. All rooms have A/C and bath, and a few have a balcony and harbor view. (☎448 2962. Singles US$20-$25; doubles US$40. MC/V.) **Sister Moon ❹,** a complex of beautiful *cabañas* spread along the hill a short kilometer east of town (follow the path around the rocky point), overlooks the main set of surfing breaks on the island. The beach here is rocky, but the surf is decent and the bar is well-stocked. (☎448 2182; www.hotel-sistermoon.com. *Cabañas* US$50, with ocean view US$60.) **Hotel Isla Grande** charges US$3 per day to use the beach and facilities. Residents of the island sometimes rent out rooms (around US$15-$25); ask around or look for the occasional sign. Facilities and privacy are often limited, and security can be less than ideal. For the cheapest option, **camp** on the beach. (Free; bring mosquito net.)

Pleasant open-air restaurants line the center of the island and serve average coastal *típico*. The best value is **Restaurante Teletón ❶**, two buildings east of Sub-Centro de Salud, serving seafood with *patacones* or coconut rice (US$2-$3.50). A new restaurant with great view and ambience is **Restaurante-Bar El Congo ❸**, right on the water with its own boardwalk and Caribbean music. (Seafood meals US$6-$10. Open 11am-8pm M-F, Sa-Su 11am-11pm. Bar is open as long as people are there.) All of the hotels also have their own restaurant. There's usually a good crowd at **Villa Ensueño ❷**, 5min. east of the dock (meals US$2.50-$6).

Nightlife on Isla Grande consists of sitting and splashing and talking—with a constant flow of cocktails facilitating both. **Ensueño** and **Cholita** (see above) both run bars popular with vacationers and play loud Panamanian Top 40 Hits. At Ensueño try the house specialty drink, Easy Touch, a secret and delicious mixture of various liquors and coconut juice served in a coconut (US$3.50). For a few more locals, enormous range of drinks, and an unbroken stream of dub and reggae, stop by **Punta Proa** (aka Pupy's), an inviting thatch structure east of the medical clinic.

In terms of **island activities,** and for an ocean and island view, climb to the lighthouse on top of the island. Walk 15min. east from the main dock until the path splits at the surfers' beach; turn left and continue up the path another 15min. You can't enter the lighthouse itself, but past it is a small **lookout.** Wear adequate shoes; it can be slippery during the rainy season. Another option is a boat tour of the mangroves nearby. **Hotel Isla Grande** charges US$45 for 8-person tours, but cheaper rates can be found in town (☎503 7088; ask for Enrique).

Other than **surfing, snorkeling** is the activity of choice, especially on the reef in front of Villa Ensueño where schools of fish gather around a striking black crucifix in the water. The crucifix stands near a breach in the reef where the current is strong, so be careful. For better, though less accessible, reefs, follow the path west until you reach the beach point. Then swim 200m across the inlet toward the pink house on the hill. Beware: this can be a hard swim. In front of the house are the best reefs on the island. **Villa Ensueño** (☎448 2964) rents snorkeling equipment (US$2.50 per hr.). **Isla Grande Diving Center** (☎232 5943 or 656 6095), a blue and yellow house 100m west of the dock, has snorkeling and scuba gear and offers scuba courses. Call in advance to make sure someone will be there, especially if going during the week; ask for professional Andrés. (Snorkeling tour US$35, scuba tour US$45-$65, full 5-day scuba course US$200, mini course US$55. Snorkeling equipment US$8 per day. English spoken.)

COCLÉ PROVINCE

The intense rain forest in the highlands and friendly rural atmosphere along the coast make this region an important part of Panama's breadbasket. Grains and sugar dominate the fertile lowland plain, while coffee and fruit reign the mountain slopes. The country's main producer of sugar cane, this province is also known for being the birthplace of the largest number of Panamanian presidents relative to population size. Weekend visitors escape the city to flood El Valle's Sunday market, birdwatch in Parque Nacional Omar Torrijos, or peek into the Iglesia de Natá.

EL VALLE

El Valle is a pleasant village (pop. 6200) set in a well-groomed nature paradise rising 600m above sea level, in the second-largest inhabited crater in the world (a result of an extinct volcano). Nearby day hikes lead to powerful waterfalls and the distant mountains forming the giant silhouette of the India Dormida, both of which are attractions. Situated 28km north of San Carlos and the Interamerican Hwy., El

Valle is also a weekend and summer home for well-off *panameños* escaping the hustle and heat of Panama City. With beautiful sites and fresh climate, this picturesque mountain town is a popular destination for a weekend trip. It may be the only opportunity to wear a sweater (at night) while in Panama. Go during the week for better prices and availability.

TRANSPORTATION. Buses fill up quickly in El Valle; it's best to catch them at the **market.** TUVASA (☎983 6446) runs down the main road to **Panama City** (2½hr., every 20-25min. 3:45am-3:40pm, US$3.50). For travel later in the day, take any bus heading to **San Carlos** (45min., every 30min. 5am-7pm, US$1) on the Interamerican Hwy. From there you can catch buses going just about anywhere. La Mesa bus runs west past the **Macho waterfalls** from El Valle (5min., every 30min. 7am-7pm, US$0.25). **Local buses,** marked "La Compañía El Hato," loop through the town's few streets (US$0.25). **Taxis** are easy to find and should never cost more than US$2.

ORIENTATION AND PRACTICAL INFORMATION. The main road enters town from the east and runs west. The open *mercado* is in the middle of town. Generally, sights are to the west and lodgings to the east. Unlike much of Panama, most places are open Sunday for lunch. The **tourist office, IPAT** (☎983 6474), has plenty of helpful maps (open Tu-Su 8am-4pm). There are **no banks**, though an **ATM** on the corner of Av. Principal and the street to El Níspero accepts Cirrus/MC/Plus/V. Across the street from the *mercado is* the **supermarket, Supercentro Yin** (open daily 7am-noon and 1-7pm). **Lavamático La Libertad,** is ½km east of *mercado*, does laundry (open M-Sa 8am-4pm). Hotel Don Pepe (see **Accommodations,** below) lets you use its bathrooms (US$0.25, shower US$0.50). **Police** (☎983 6222; emergency 104) are down the road to El Níspero; the **health clinic,** Centro de Salud (☎983 6112), down the street behind the church, has assistance 24hr. The **pharmacy, Farmacia Cano,** is next to the church (open daily 5:30am-6pm). **Internet access** at FSR Technology Systems (☎983 6688), next to Lavamático La Libertad, is US$1 per hr. (Open M-Sa 8am-noon and 1:30-6pm, Su 10:30am-2pm.) The **post office** is behind the *mercado* (open M-F 9am-2:45pm; 7-11:45pm).

ACCOMMODATIONS AND FOOD. In response to weekend crowds from Panama City, *cabañas* and hotels are opening up all over town, though most are not budget. Some camp unofficially in the woods to the west of town, but there are no facilities. Restaurants cluster all along the main road.

Hotel Don Pepe ❸, on Av. Central across from Supercentro Yin, caters to families. Huge, gorgeous rooms sleep up to five, and include clean hot baths, fan, and TV. The super-friendly owner will arrange tours. (☎983 6835. Internet US$1.50 per hr. Laundry wash US$1.50, dry US$1.50. Singles US$20; doubles and triples US$30; quads US$40. Discounts for long stays. MC/V.) Down the block and across the street from the Lavamático, **Hotel y Restaurante La Niña Delia ❷** has fairly clean rooms. The *comedor* in the back serves *típico* for US$2. (☎983 6110. Singles US$12; doubles US$15; triples US$18; quads US$25.) To get to **Aparthotel El Valle ❷,** hang a left past the *mercado*, up the road before C. los Millonarios. Clean and spacious apartment-style rooms have A/C, cable TV, hot water, and living room; there are jacuzzis, natural thermal pools, and a big garden in the back. Some rooms have kitchens. The largest apartments sleep up to 12. The best deal is to get regular rooms without A/C, given El Valle's cool temperatures. (☎264 2272. Doubles US$24, with A/C US$29; quads with kitchen US$69; US$5 for each additional person. On weekends and during high season add US$10. AmEx/MC/V.)

The restaurant at **Hotel Don Pepe ❶** serves *típico* and a variety of excellent meals, mostly seafood and pasta (US$2.50-$10). **Santa Librada ❸** (☎513 3944) is a hostel with a restaurant in front serving desserts, seafood, and meat (US$2-$7.50).

SIGHTS. Follow the blue signs that lead from the main road toward the west. The **Sunday Crafts Fair,** one of the most popular in Panama, takes place in the **Mercado El Valle.** Artisans, mainly Indians, gather from surrounding farms to sell sculpted pots, carved soapstone figurines, wooden trays called *bateas,* intricately woven basketwork, and more. Panama's national flower, an orchid known as the Flor del Espíritu Santo (Holy Spirit flower) can usually be found for sale. The rest of the week fresh produce and flowers is mostly sold, with a few handicrafts. Prices are usually negotiable. (Open daily 7am-5pm.)

El Níspero, 1km north down the road by the ATM, and the first right after the fire station, is the local botanical gardens and zoo. Housing capybaras, *titi* monkeys, iguanas, scarlet macaws, giant sleeping tapirs, and leopards, it entertains your inner child. The beautiful and well-groomed gardens are a great place to enjoy a pleasant stroll. (☎983 6142. Open daily 7am-5pm. US$2, children US$1.) After a long day hiking, relax in the hot springs, natural pools, and mudbaths of **Pozos Termales,** which locals believe are therapeutic. You can picnic at the tables nearby. Turn south at the sign at the west end of town and walk 10min. past houses to the entrance. (Open daily 8am-5pm. US$1, children US$0.50.)

OUTDOOR ACTIVITIES: HIKING.

EL MACHO. To view **El Macho,** the famous 85m rainforest waterfall, guides lead a great 5min. hike via suspended log walkways overlooking the Río Guayago (El Valle's water source) and lush primary forest. From a platform 20m away, the many cascades formed by the black volcanic rock make for an impressive view. A 3hr. hike through the surrounding **Refugio Ecológico Chorro El Macho** brings you to the top of the falls. The *refugio* also runs **Canopy Adventures,** which enables fearless tourists to see the falls and surrounding forests while speeding along a zipline. Petroglyphs cover the giant rock **Piedra Pintada.** Nearby is a splendid **waterfall,** less famous but more accessible than El Macho. (*It's a walkable 30min. to El Macho, just follow the signs from the western end of the main road. The La Mesa bus will take you from the market for US$0.25. Admission US$2.50, children US$1.25; natural bathing pool costs US$2.50. Admission with guided hike US$10.50; guided hike for wildlife observation US$25 per person. Open daily 8am-5pm. Canopy Adventures is recommended. (☎983 6547. US$42 per person. Short canopy tour US$10.50.) There's a refugio for campers; call for details (☎983 6547). Hop on the La Pintada bus (US$0.15) at the mercado or walk 20min. to the western end of the main road: take a right after you pass a bridge and get to a fork. When the paved road ends near some kiosks, take the path to the left but don't cross the 1st bridge. Instead, follow the river 200m and cross there; the 10m rock is 5min. farther up the path. For the waterfall, continue along the path past the petroglyphs, sticking to the river. After about 10min., you'll see it on the right. Almost without exception, you'll find local school boys as soon as the paved road ends eager to guide you US$0.50-$1 tip recommended.*)

LA INDIA DORMIDA. Legend has it that when the *indígena* maiden daughter of legendary Indian Chief Urracá, Flor del Aire, fell in love with a conquering Spaniard, her previous lover, *Yaraví,* killed himself. The girl, tormented and disgraced, wandered into the hills to die, lying down to stare forever at the skies. With a little imagination, her silhouette can be deciphered by visitors in the hills to the west. (*The more difficult of 2 trails takes you to her head; explore small caves full of bats. Follow the signs to Piedra Pintada at the western end of town. From the rock, continue on the trail for 1hr., staying on the south side of the river until you get to the top. The hike is steep but cuts through incredible forest and has amazing views. The other way up is less steep and exciting; head to the western end of the main road and bear left after the small bridge. At the first street, turn right, then left when you see a brightly painted school. The walk continues an hr. up La India's arm.*)

PENONOMÉ

Founded in 1581, this provincial capital (pop. 15, 840) was important enough to be the country's capital after the sacking of Panamá Viejo in 1671. Now it's known as the best place to buy the famous Panama hats. Though fashion historians agree that the hat hails from Ecuador, these ones are unique to Panama. Aside from a good selection of hats, Penonomé is a rather unappealing transportation and service hub for the rest of the province; El Valle or La Iguana are alternatives.

Buses leave from the **terminal** on the Interamerican Hwy. across from the ESSO station to **Panama City** (2½hr., every 20min. 4:20am-7pm, US$3.70). Buses coming from Panama City and heading to **Chitré, David,** and **Santiago** stop if you wave them down (every hr. to Chitre and Santiago; more frequently to David). Sometimes these buses stop at Restaurante Universal, 300m east of the ESSO gas station on the Interamerican Hwy.; check there for lower fares.

Minibuses head to local destinations: **Aguadulce** (45min., every 10 min. 5:30am-7pm, US$2) via **El Caño** (25min., US$1) and **Natá** (35min., US$1.50); **El Copé** (1hr., every 25min. 6:30am-6:30pm, US$1.50); **El Valle** (1½ hr.; 6:30, 11am, 12:45, 3:15pm; US$2.50); and **La Pintada** (20min., every 20min. 6:20am-8:30pm; US$0.70). They leave from behind the **Mercado Público,** 2 blocks southeast of the *parque* on Av. Guerrero. Buses to **Playa Farallón** and **Santa Clara** leave from **Supercentro El Fuerte** on Av. Principal (15-20min., every hr. 9am-7pm, US$1).

Central Penonomé lies 1km north of the Interamerican Hwy. The town is connected to the highway by **Avenida Juan Demostenes Arosemena,** known as **Av. Principal,** which runs northwest from an ESSO station on the highway and ends at the church. On the opposite side of the *parque*, **Avenida Amador Guerrero** runs parallel to Av. Principal, merging with it halfway to the highway at the Delta gas station. The **IPAT** provincial office for Coclé is in Playa Farallón, a couple minutes' walk from where the bus leaves you. If coming to Coclé from Panama City stop here first to get info. Otherwise, the ride from Penonomé is 15min. (☎ 993 3241. Open M-F 8:30am-4:30pm.) Four **banks** with **ATMs** crowd the Interamerican Hwy., but **Banco Nacional de Panamá,** at the merger of Av. Guerrero and Av. Principal, is the only one that changes MC/V traveler's checks (open M-F 8am-3pm, Sa 9am-noon). **Western Union** is located on Av. Principal in the Casa Peter building. (☎997 7117. Open M-Sa 8am-noon and 1-5:30pm, Su 8am-12:30pm.) The top of Av. Guerrero is packed with **grocery stores. SuperCentro Coclé,** at the highway next to the Hotel Dos Continentes, has a **pharmacy** (open M-Sa 8am-7:30pm). **Lavamático Central** is just past CITA on the same side on Av. Central. (☎997 8333. Wash US$0.50, dry US$0.75. Open M-Sa 8am-7pm, Su 8am-noon.) Primarily a jail, the **police** station (☎997 8438 or 104) is on the *parque*'s northwest. The new **Hospital Aquilano Tejeira** (☎997 8455) is on the Interamerican Hwy., east of the bus station. **Internet access** is available at **CITA,** about a block up Av. Principal on the right. (☎996 1846. US$1 per hr. Open M-F 8:30am-6:30pm, Sa 8:30am-3pm.) **Junto a Ti,** at the terminal on the Interamerican Hwy., offers **Internet** access and facilities to make **international calls.** (Internet US$1 per hr., calls to the US, US$0.23 per min. Open M-Sa 7am-7pm, Su 9am-7pm.) The **post office** is behind the fire station on street Damián Carles near the *parque* (open M-F 7am-6pm, Sa 7am-5pm).

New hotels are popping up around the town center and along the Interamerican Hwy. **Hotel Dos Continentes** ❸, across from the bus terminal, is near restaurants, a bank, and hat vendors. Rooms come with A/C, hot water, phone, private balcony, and TV. (☎997 9326. Singles US$20-22; doubles US$22-25; triples US$31; quads US$43.) **Pensión Estrella Roja** ❶, the cheapest place to stay in town, is 4½ blocks south of the *parque*, opposite the church. Bare rooms with double bed, fan, and outdoor bath, US$8 per room. The **Albergue Ecológico La Iguana,** 20min. by bus from Penonomé, is great for people who want to camp (see below).

THE HISTORY BEHIND THE HAT

Despite its name, the famous lightweight, straw-colored Panama hat, encircled by the characteristic black band, is not Panamanian, at least not in origin. Panama hat was actually first made in Montecristi, Ecuador, and can be traced as far back as the 16th century, when the Inca first used the Toquilla plant to craft headware. Panama hats got their name from the place they were first sold internationally: starting in the 1800s, it was through Panamanian ports that these hats were re-exported to the rest of the world. The hats became increasingly associated with Panama when, during the construction of the Canal, workers used them to guard against the intense sun. Today, their origins are recognized in the updated, specific name: Montescristi Panama hat.

Another type of hat typical to Panama is the well-known *sombrero pintado*, or *pintao*, as it is pronounced in Panama, and sold in Penonomé and in other parts of Coclé Province. The *pintao* is used as part of the *Montuno*, the country's national attire for men. Once again, the name does not reveal its bearer's origin: it is called *pintao* not because a great majority of them is produced in the town of La Pintada, as might be imagined, but because the hat has a combination of white and black "paints" decorating it.

Many locals recommend **Gallo Pinto ❶** for cheap *típico*, with several locations throughout town and the Interamerican Hwy.; one is on Av. Principal behind the ESSO station. Meals vary from *arroz con pollo* to chow mein and *corvina*. (Open daily 6am-9pm, the one on the Interamerican Hwy. stays open until 11:30pm. US$1.65-$4.50.) For *típico* in an a-*típico* upscale atmosphere, try **Restaurante Las Tinajas ❶**, located across the Interamerican Hwy., just west of the bus terminal in a thatched tiki lounge. (Meals US$2-$3. Open daily 7am-10pm.)

To commune with nature at the **Albergue Ecológico La Iguana ❷**, a haven for regional wildlife, take a bus to Churruquita Grande from the **Mercado Público.** Located 14km from Penonomé, this eco-lodge boasts a restaurant, small zoo, birdwatching observatory, trails through dense vegetation and waterfalls, and eight rooms for five each. Reservation is required. (☎983 8056. Rooms US$30; camping US$5, free with meals. English spoken.) Alternatively, grab a bus to Panama City or El Valle and stop in **Playa Farallón** or **Playa Santa Clara** to soak up sun. Farallón is the former site of one of Noriega's Panama Defense Force bases. The first combat target of then-new US F-117A stealth fighters—the runway can still be seen from the Interamerican Hwy.—it is now home to Panama's largest tourist resort.

NATÁ

Founded in 1522, the small town of Natá (pop. 5900) is home to the **Basílica Menor Santiago Apóstol de Natá,** thought to be the oldest church still in use in the Americas. The church's regal white facade was renovated in 1998. Pre-conquest Natá was a huge *indígena* town, first discovered by **Gaspar de Espinosa** in 1517. Now, Natá is known for the **Fiesta de Santiago el Apóstol,** celebrated July 25 with parties and processions. **Buses** along the Interamerican will stop in front of the cheap **Supermercado Vega** (from **Penonomé** 45min., US$1.50; from **Chitré** 1¼hr., US$2.50). **Hotel Rey David ❷** (☎993 5149), the town's only hotel, is on the main road just behind the **Supermercado.** Clean rooms with A/C, private bath, and TV are in an outdoor garage complex (US$13). **Restaurante y Refresquería Vega ❶**, next door, serves cheap *típico*. (*Arroz con pollo* US$2. Open daily 7am-10pm.)

Parque Arqueológico del Caño, the most notable pre-Columbian site in Panama, pales in comparison to those elsewhere in Central America, but is an interesting break from a long Interamerican trip. A sacred burial ground is part of the remnants of the Natá nation, named after their *cacique* Nató. There are both primary and secondary burials; the former indicate the body was buried surrounded by possessions, while the latter indicates their absence. Primary burials were reserved for *caciques*, while secondary were for people of lesser but still important status, such as warriors. Hundreds more burials in the surrounding area are estimated. Near the burials stand the ruins of what is thought to have been a solar calendar and of columns thought to have been part of a field to play a game similar to soccer. A small **museum** has stone and ceramic artwork dating AD800-1500. See the mural and captions inside for a glimpse of Natá life and first European contact.

Any **bus** on the Interamerican will drop you off at **El Caño village**, 3km (30min.) from the entrance to **Parque Nacional Omar Torrijos Herrera** (see below). A US$1 taxi from the Interamerican Hwy. takes you; taxis are scarce in Natá (see p. 640, US$3), so ask one of the buses on the Aguadulce-Penonomé route to leave you closer. Open Tu-Sa 9am-4pm, Su 9am-1pm. Adults US$1, students and children US$0.25. Bring bug repellent.

PARQUE NACIONAL OMAR TORRIJOS HERRERA

Straddling the continental divide in northern Coclé, Parque Nacional Omar Torrijos Herrera, known to locals for its nearby village **El Copé**, is so named because of the 1981 plane crash of General Torrijos on Cerro Marta. Covering four different forest zones, the incredible biodiversity attracts researchers the world over: scientists often stay in one of the *refugios* while collecting samples. Despite its beauty and proximity to Panama City, the park remains mostly unknown to tourists, allowing visitors to experience pristine nature. Homestays in nearby villages allow you to experience rural Panamanian lifestyle in remote communities.

AT A GLANCE

AREA: 253 sq. km.

CLIMATE: Hot and humid at low altitude, a bit colder and much wetter higher up. Can get chilly at night.

FEATURES: Cerro Peña Blanca, Cerro Marta.

HIGHLIGHTS: Simultaneously observe the Pacific Ocean and the Caribbean Sea from El Calvario, learn about Panamanian culture with a homestay in La Rica.

GATEWAYS: El Copé (see p. 642), Penonomé (see p. 639), La Rica (see p. 642).

CAMPING: Camping platform for sleeping bags with a nearby *refugio* which includes bath and hot water. A newly built *cabaña* has bunk beds and kitchen.

FEES AND RESERVATIONS: Park admission US$3; camping US$5, *refugio* US$5; *cabañas* US$5. For all lodging notify the rangers at least 5 days in advance.

 ORIENTATION

The park boasts large tracts of primary forest and watersheds, home to 350 species of birds and frogs found nowhere else in Panama: the sicklebill white-tipped hummingbird heavily populates these mountains (and thus is the park's symbol), as does the golden frog, unique to Panama and an endangered species. Other animals include the Baird's tapir, Puma, Jaguar, and Ocelot.

ANAM has been involved in sustainable development work, educating communities living in the park. As part of a cultural exchange, nearby La Rica invites visitors for homestays, which include room and board, to view some of this work.

⌐ TRANSPORTATION

To **El Copé**, take a **bus** from the *mercado público* in **Penonomé** (1hr., every 25min. 6:30am-6:30pm, US$1.50). Alternatively, take any bus along the Interamerican Hwy., get off at the turnoff for **El Copé**, and wait for the next northbound bus into town (45min., every 25min. 6am-6pm, US$1). In El Copé, get off at the last stop, in front of the mini supermarket, and go to **park headquarters** at the uphill end of the main road for info and possibly a ride to the park. (☎983 9089. Open M-F 8am-4pm, but call ahead because rangers are often in the park.) Barring a ride from friendly rangers, look for a *chivita* bound for **Barrigón**, the last community before the park entrance (20min., every 45min. 5am-7:30pm, US$0.30). Call the night before for a **4WD taxi** from Barrigón to the park. (☎983 9077. US$5.) Otherwise, from the van's last stop, **El Potroso** (same bus to Barrigón, $0.40), it's a steep 45min. hike to the park's main entrance, ranger station, *refugio*, and *cabañas*.

Accessible from **El Copé** (just west of Penonomé), the park entrance is near **Cerro El Calvario** (a.k.a. El Aserradero), on the continental divide, which is 950m above sea level and on clear days is a perfect place to observe simultaneously the Pacific Ocean and the Caribbean Sea.

⁊ PRACTICAL INFORMATION

For **emergencies**, call the ANAM central phone line (☎997 9089). To check on the weather and **climate**, the regional ANAM office in Coclé has an info line; call for weather updates (☎997 7538). Just beyond, a small office run by the community of El Copé is the **ranger station**. Stop here to arrange guided **tours** of the park (US$10).

⌐ ACCOMMODATIONS AND CAMPING

Near the ranger station is a camping platform and a *refugio* with bath and running water (bring a warm sleeping bag and your own food and water). The camping platform affords gorgeous views of the valleys below, as do two short trails. The newly constructed *cabaña* has two bunk beds, solar-powered energy, hot-water bath, full kitchen with gas stove, living room, and attic space for sleeping. Much of the furniture is made by local artisans, creating an elegantly rustic setting.

To get to La Rica and the Navas family residence ❷ for a typical Panamanian homestay, rendezvous with a member of the family at their home in Barrigón. (☎983 9130. US$22 per day includes lodging, 3 meals, and guided hikes of your choice.) Ask the driver of the van from El Copé to let you off at "la casa de Navas."

⌑ HIKING TRAILS

Wide, easy **Sendero Los Helechos** is a 30min. loop. Wooden hand rails, stairs, and path demarcations make it accessible for hikers of all levels. For more of a challenge, take **Sendero La Rana**, which winds down to a mountain creek (30min.). Ask the rangers about more ambitious undertakings, like the trail that US Peace Corps are currently working on, or a day-long hike to **Cerro Marta**, the park's highest accessible point. Ask about the park's interesting background; they're working on a community effort in sustainable development; the much-needed US$1 charge goes to support the project. A short trail leading to a refreshing dip at Chorro Las Yayas is an easy hike.

A 2hr. hike beyond the entrance leads to **La Rica** (p. 642) a village of 40 or so families who farm and raise cattle in the middle of the park under ANAM's watchful eye. The community offers the opportunity to stay with a local family and experience rural Panamanian life and traditions that are characteristic of most of the interior of Panama, while also exploring the park's dense inner reaches. The **Navas** families are great hosts and provide lodging, meals, and guided hikes.

AZUERO PENINSULA

The Azuero Peninsula is Panama's heartland: center and origin of *típico* music and the *pollera* (traditional Panamanian dress), it's also the location of Panama's grandest *fiestas*, involving bullfighting, drinking, traditional music, drinking, religious processions, and drinking. *Campesinos* continue to wear *guayaberas* (the traditional men's shirt) and classic straw hats, and the horse is the preferred mode of transport. The peninsula's flatlands and rolling hills have been inhabited for thousands of years; as a result, little of the area remains forested. However, natural attractions still lure: snorkeling and diving on Isla Iguana, world-class surfing at Playa Venado, and thousands of sea turtles on Isla de Cañas. The towns of interest—Chitré, Las Tablas, and Pedasí—all lie on the eastern side of the peninsula and are linked by the Carretera Nacional, which branches off the Interamerican Hwy. at Divisa. Santiago is farther west along the Interamerican Hwy., inland from the peninsula, heading toward David and Costa Rica.

CHITRÉ

The largest town on the Azuero Peninsula (pop. 42,467), Chitré itself does not offer much, but serves as a gateway to the rest of the Peninsula: head out to nearby Los Santos or Guararé to get a taste of Panama's most traditional fiestas. Go farther south to surf, snorkel, or simply relax on some of the most beautiful, unexplored beaches on Panama's Pacific coast. Chitré itself gets going on June 24th for the Fiesta Patronal, celebrating the life of John the Baptist.

F TRANSPORTATION. The **airport** is north of town up Av. Central. Aeroperlas has daily **flights** to **Panama City** (☎996 4021. 35 min.; M-Sa 7am and 4:45pm, Su 4:45pm; US$36.75). The **bus terminal** is south of town (15min. walk; taxi US$1; local bus from behind the terminal US$0.15). **Buses** leave the terminal for: **Aguadulce** (1hr., every 15-20min. 5:55am-5:40pm, US$2) via **Divisa** (40min., US$1); **Las Tablas** (40min., every 10min. 6am-9pm, US$1) via **Guararé** (30min., US$0.80); **Monagre** (30min., every 35min. 7am-6pm, US$1); **Ocú** (1hr., every 25min. 6:30am-7pm, US$2); **Panama City** (4hr., every hr. 1:30am-6pm, US$6) via **Penonomé** (1.5hr., US$3.30); **Parita** (12min., every 20min. 8:50am-6:30pm, US$0.50) via **La Arena** (5min., US$0.25); **Santiago** (1¼hr., every 30min. 3:30am-6:30pm, US$2); and **Tonosí** (2½hr., every hr. 8am-4pm, US$4). All schedules are subject to change on Sundays, when fewer buses make trips, so check in advance. South-bound buses stop in **Los Santos** (5min., US$0.25). **Local buses** (not *chivitas*) stop at Panadería Chiquito, 2 blocks north of the cathedral. Buses going to Monagrillo that stop here pass by **Los Santos**. **Taxis** are common. (☎996 7996. Available 24hr.)

◪ ⛴ ORIENTATION AND PRACTICAL INFORMATION. Just about everything in Chitré can be found on the two main roads. Hwy. 2, the **Carretera Nacional**, enters from the west, where it becomes **Calle Manuel Correa**. Near the center of town, C. Manuel Correa intersects **Avenida Herrera** (or **Av. Central**) which runs north-south. Two blocks south is the **cathedral**, next to the *parque;* 3 blocks farther, Av. Central bends east, becoming the Carretera Nacional, on to **Los Santos** and **Las Tablas**. To reach the *parque* from the bus terminal, turn left out the front parking lot and continue 500m. Turn left on the Carretera Nacional at the hospital and follow it until the fork, then right on Av. Central. The cathedral is 3 blocks up.

The **IPAT** regional office of Azuero is in Los Santos, 5km down Av. Nacional from Chitré. To get there, take a bus heading to Los Santos and get off at the *parque central;* the office is next to the church. (☎966 8013; fax 966 8040. Open M-F 8:30am-4:30pm.) IPAT also has an office in La Arena, 5min. by bus from Chitré, with an informative exhibit about the Herrera province. (☎974 4532. Open daily 8:30am-4:30pm.) **ANAM** also has an office in Los Santos, but it is 2km past the turn-off for the center on Av. Nacional. To get there, take a bus going toward Las Tablas; get off when you see the sign on the right. (☎966 9352. Open M-F 8am-3pm.) The **immigration office** is 1 block south and 3 blocks east of the cathedral; look for the Panamanian flag. (☎996 3092. Open M-F 8am-3:30pm.) **Banistmo,** 3 blocks west of Av. Central on C. Correa, changes traveler's checks, gives MC/V cash advances, and has a 24hr. **ATM** (open M-F 8am-3:30pm, Sa 9am-noon). Four blocks north of the cathedral is **Lavamático Panchan** for **laundry.** (Wash US$0.50. Open daily 7am-7pm.) Other services include: **police** (☎996 4333 or 104), in the western part of town; **Hospital Cecilio Castillero** (☎996 4444), 4 blocks southeast of town on the Carretera Nacional; **Internet** at **Sanchi Computer,** half a block north of the cathedral on Av. Central, on the left (US$0.50 per hr. ☎996 2134; open daily 8:30am-midnight), and the **post office,** 4 blocks west and 1 block north of Av. Central on C. Correa, tucked under a Cable and Wireless building, across from a gas station (open M-F 7am-6pm, Sa 7am-5pm).

⚑⬚ ACCOMMODATIONS AND FOOD. The best of the many budget hotels is ▨**Pensión Central ❷,** a half block north of the cathedral. Large, clean rooms have cable TV, baths, and those puffy toilet seats everyone loves. Service is great. (☎996 0059. Optional breakfast US$2. Singles or doubles US$8.50, with A/C US$10; triples US$15, with A/C and TV US$20; add US$2 on weekends.) These are special prices for tourists so you'll be asked to show a passport. **Hotel Hawaii ❸,** around the corner from Machetazo, is a full-service hotel at those low self-service prices. (☎996 3524. Singles US$20.25; doubles US$29.)

Restaurante y Panadería Chiquita ❷, 2 blocks north of the cathedral, sells pizza (US$2-$5), delicious *chichas* (US$0.25), and baked goods. (Open daily 5am-10:30pm.) For good *típico,* head to **La Estrella #2 ❶,** right in front of the cathedral, where *comida* is US$1.50 and a giant mound of *arroz con pollo* costs US$2; you'll be charged only a few coins for breakfast (open daily 6am-11pm). Get American food at **Tastee-freez ❶,** down from Manolo. (Chili dog US$1.10. Open daily 24hr.)

◪ SIGHTS. Check out the town's **cathedral,** the Iglesia San Juan Bautista, featuring a beautiful mahogany and gilded altar. Any of the pleasant *parques* that dot the city are also worth a stroll. **Museo de Herrera,** on Av. Manuel Correa 2 blocks west of Av. Central, has exhibits on the archaeology, history, and traditions of the Herrera province. (☎996 0077. Open Tu-Sa 9am-4pm, Su 8am-11am. US$1.)

⬚ DAYTRIPS FROM CHITRÉ: VILLAGES AND BEACHES

LA VILLA DE LOS SANTOS

To get to Los Santos, take any south-bound bus from the terminal and ask the driver to drop you off (5 min., US$0.25).

In addition to the *carnaval* shenanigans the week before Ash Wednesday, and the celebration of Semana Santa the week before Easter, the small town of **La Villa de Los Santos,** 5km south of Chitré, really goes crazy for Corpus Christi (see p. 604) and the Day of Panama's First Cry for Independence from Spain (November 10, 18 days before the rest of the country). All four occasions call for gargantuan no-holds-barred parties with assorted revelry and debauchery. The center of attention during the *fiestas*, the ▨**Iglesia de San Atanasio**, is worth a peek. Beautiful, white-washed woodwork frames a life-size, wooden statue of San Pedro (Saint Peter). Of interest to those in Los Santos is the small **Museo de la Nacionalidad** (☎/fax 966 8192) in the *parque central*, across from the church, which honors the fact that La Villa was the first place in the country where the call for independence erupted. The museum has Panamanian artifacts and items from the struggle for independence. (US$1, children US$0.25. Open Tu-Sa 9am-4pm, Su 9am-1pm.)

GUARARÉ

To get to Guararé from Los Santos, take a bus to Las Tablas (30min., US$0.80) and ask to be dropped off.

If Los Santos's *fiestas* aren't enough, check out **Guararé**, 18km south of Chitré. The **Festival de la Mejorana**, every September 24th, celebrates the region's traditional music, played on accordions, tambourines, and the *mejorana* (a small guitar-like instrument made from mango wood). Guararé's Semana Santa festivities are more intricate than most. Dancing and singing form the backdrop for an Easter Story reenactment, culminating in a bonfire where an effigy of Judas is burned amid great celebration. If you happen to be there when Guararé returns to its usual state of tranquility, visit the **Casa-Museo Manuel F. Zárate**, home to famous folklorist and full of *polleras*, masks, and costumes (open Tu-Sa 8am-4pm, Su 8:30am-midnight).

LA ARENA

La Arena is north; go by car or bus to Parita (US$0.25).

Artisans in the small village of **La Arena** produce some of the finest ceramics in Panama. Stores line the highway from Chitré, only 5min. away by car or bus. Prices are low and most vendors won't bargain unless you're buying more than a couple of pieces. For a glimpse into the age-old process and the ceramics tradition, follow the street to the right of the church about 2 blocks. You'll find *talleres de cerámica* (ceramics workshops) where the pieces are made. Custom work is welcome, so bring your ideas and designs. La Arena is also famous for its tender bread, bringing people from all over the country to any of the *panaderías* that line the Carretera Nacional. (Panadería La Arena has fresh bread right out of the oven at around 7am and 3pm. Loaf US$0.25. Open 5am-9pm.)

DIRTY DANCING DEVILS

At 4am on the Thursday six weeks after Easter, most of the Republic of Panama is fast asleep. In Los Santos, however, people are busy running and dancing through the streets, chasing a giant papier-maché bull's head. The celebration of Corpus Christi is one of the most raucous festivals in the country, though the day's Catholic significance (commemorating the institution of the Eucharist) is barely visible through the chaos of nine different traditional dances. La Danza del Torito Santeño (Dance of the Little Los Santos Bull) kicks it off, but the 10am mass is where things get interesting. Dances begin in the church, then spill out into the square and streets. Among these performances is La Danza de Los Diablicos Sucios (the Dance of the Dirty Little Devils). Historically, the Dirty Devils wore clothing striped red (with mud) and black (with charred corn), as well as intricate masks. In those days, the violent, leaping devil dance caused the dancers to sweat profusely, which mixed mud and corn soot to make the name choice pretty clear. Nowadays, the Dirty Devils' masks and striped silk outfits are easier to clean up.

Every one of the 10 dances comes with a unique accompanying story; to get the lowdown on the hoedown, buy a wise local a beer and enjoy the narration while you observe the festivities.

OCÚ

Ocú is 1hr. by bus east of Los Santos.

The village of **Ocú** is where most of the hats sold in Penonomé (p. 639) are actually made. Ocú's **Festival de Manito** (August 9) honors the folklore and traditions of the region's farmers, complete with traditional wedding celebrations.

BEACHES

The closest beach to Chitré is Monagre, near Los Santos, or El Rompío next door. Monagre bus leaves from Chitré to either beach (30 min., every 35min. 7am-6pm, US$1).

The black sands are home to many crabs, so look out for the little holes when you put your towel down. Enjoy freshly caught fried fish and plantains (US$2.50) at the **Complejo Turístico Monagre** close by Monagre (tell the bus to drop you off there), which has *ranchitos* with hammocks, bathrooms, showers, a full bar (beer US$0.45), pool, billiard tables, and good music all day long. (Use of facilities is free if you consume; if not, cost is US$0.25. Open daily starting 6am.)

LAS TABLAS

Las Tablas (pop. 8600) is often considered the symbolic center of Panama. The country's national dress, the *pollera*, originated here, and is celebrated annually in the joint *Fiesta de la Pollera/Fiesta de Santa Librada* (July 19-22), the most famous festival in the country. It begins with a procession from the church through town on the 19th, continues on the 20th and 21st with 10am mass, and ends with an all-day street party on the 22nd where the *reinas* (queens) are chosen for the parade. In addition to the *reina* competition there is a *pollera* contest, and violin and *sombrero* contests for men. *Carnaval* comes once a year, and starts the Friday before Ash Wednesday. Much like Río and New Orleans, Las Tablas is a nonstop festival with beautifully ornate costumes and competitions. It is known as the most popular *carnaval* celebration in the country. When the town isn't partying, it is crowded with vendors and sidewalk markets until sundown, as older folks chat in the park and younger people cruise around town bumping the newest *salsa* or *cumbia* from their stereo systems. *Tableños* know how to mix religious tradition with fun, as evidenced by frequent religious processions followed by fireworks.

TRANSPORTATION. Buses leave from various spots in town. Four blocks north of the *parque* the big green gas station serves as the terminal for buses to **Panama City** (5hr., every hr. 2am-4:30pm, US$6.50). Schedules change on weekends (☎994 6247 for more info). Two blocks south, **Chitré**-bound buses leave from the Supermercado Las Tablas (45min., every 10min. 6am-7pm, US$1). Those going to **Pedasí** and other points south on the peninsula leave from the Restaurante Praga on the main road 3 blocks east of the *parque* (45min., every hr. 6am-7pm, US$2). Note that not every bus from Las Tablas to Cañas passes through Pedasí. To **Santiago** or farther west, either take a bus to Chitré and transfer or take a Panama City-bound bus as far as the Interamerican Hwy., then look for a westward bus.

ORIENTATION AND PRACTICAL INFORMATION. The main road comes in from the north (from the Villa de los Santos and Chitré) and turns left at the southeast corner of the *parque central* (across from the church) on **Calle Belisario Porras**. It travels east through town before heading out to Pedasí. With the church in front of you, north is to your right. An **ANAM** office is about 2km out of town on the road to Pedasí in a large government compound. (☎994-7313; fax 994 6676. Open M-F 8am-4pm.) Take a taxi (US$0.75) or a bus heading to Pedasí and get off when you see the sign on your right, or walk 25min. past Restaurante Praga. **Banks**

are plentiful; **Banco Nacional de Panamá** is 3 blocks north of the *parque* on the right and has a 24hr. **ATM** (open M-F 8am-3pm, Sa 9am-noon). Other services include: **Western Union,** next to Hotel Manolo (☎994 6279; open M-F 8:30am-4pm, Sa 9am-2pm); **Lavandéria y Lavamático El Éxito,** 2 blocks east of the northern end of the *parque* (☎994 6765; wash and dry US$1.50; open M-Sa 7:30am-5:30pm); **police station** (☎994 7000 or 104), across from the big green gas station; **hospital** (☎994 7997; open 24hr.), at the end of Av. Central, on Via Santo Domingo; **Zona Inter.net,** facing the church take a left at the park's southeast corner; and the **post office,** half a block west of Supermercado Las Tablas (open M-F 7am-5:30pm, Sa 7am-4:30pm).

▐▐ ACCOMMODATIONS AND FOOD. It's a good idea either to make reservations in advance during *fiestas* or to stay in Chitré. **Hotel Manolo ❸**, about a block farther east than Zafiro, has nine brand new rooms with A/C, cable, hot water, and a restaurant serving notable tacos, US$0.90. (☎994 6372. Singles US$17; doubles US$20; triples US$30.) **Hospedaje Zafiro ❷**, on the southeastern corner of the *parque central*, if not still under construction, offers a balcony overlooking the *parque*, and spacious, clean rooms with A/C and private baths. (☎994 8200. Singles US$14.30; doubles US$19; triples US$21.)

Restaurante El Caserón ❷ is a distinguished environment in comparison to most in Las Tablas, and offers an extensive menu including pasta, burgers, pizza, and sundaes. (US$2-$8. ☎994 6066. Open daily 7am-11pm.) **Pizzeria Portofino ❶**, on the southern corner of the *parque*, provides a break from *típico* and is an excellent location for watching the town's activities. (☎994 7605; call for delivery. Small cheese pizza US$1.50; family-size vegetarian US$7.25; hamburgers US$1.50. Open M-Sa 8am-11pm, Su 5-10pm.) Among Las Tablas' indistinguishable eateries, **Restaurante Praga ❶** (open daily 7am-11pm) and **Salón Popular ❶** next door, both 3 blocks east of the *parque* (open 8am-midnight), serve *comida corriente* (US$2.)

◙ SIGHTS. Built in 1679, the recently renovated **Iglesia de Santa Librada,** with its gold-leaf altar, massive wooden doors, and a statue of the crucified saint, is the focal point of the town's cultural and religious energy. A short biography of "La Moñona" (the saint's nickname, derived from her long locks) is posted by the altar. The one-room **Museo de Belisario Porras,** facing the *parque* to the south, stands as a monument to the visionary three-term president of Panama, born and raised in Las Tablas. (☎994 6326. Open Tu-Sa 8am-4pm, Su 8am-noon. US$0.50.)

PEDASÍ

Populated by fishermen and sprinkled with tourists looking for excellent angling, Pedasí (pop. 2000) is a quiet town 41km southeast of Las Tablas. The birthplace of Panama's first female president, Mireya Moscoso, has yet to spawn an honorary museum, though a monument at the town entrance greets all visitors. Most come to fish, visit nearby Isla Iguana, or surf Playa Venado.

▐ TRANSPORTATION. Buses to Las Tablas head up the main street (45min., every hr. 6am-6pm, US$2) from the municipal building. Note that not every bus from Las Tablas to Cañas passes through Pedasí. The most feasible way of getting from Pedasí to **Playa Venado** or **Isla Cañas** is to take a **taxi** (US$12); they leave 3 blocks south of the municipal building on the main road.

▐▐ ORIENTATION AND PRACTICAL INFORMATION. Avenida Central is a continuation of the Carretera Nacional that hugs the east coast of the peninsula, and Av. Central enters running north-south. The municipal building marks the rough midpoint of the main road. The *parque central* is 2 blocks south and 1 block east of the municipal building.

The **ANAM** office in charge of Isla Iguana is 3 blocks south from the southeast corner of the *parque.* Open M-F 8am-4pm.) **Buzos de Azuero,** a snorkel and dive shop, is next to the gas station and has maps of Isla Iguana; Jeff, a Californian expat, will gladly dish out the inside scoop on Pedasí. (☎995 2405; bdazuero@hotmail.com. Snorkeling gear rental US$10 per day, scuba US$30 per day.) Right next to Buzos de Azuero an **IPAT** office provides useful info about the region. (☎995 2339. Open daily 8am-4pm.) You can also contact Eduardo Moscoso, a knowledgeable tour guide of the area (eduardomoscoso@hotmail.com). **Banco Nacional de Panamá** is directly across the street from the Hotel Residencial Pedasí, near the town's entrance (open M-F 8:30am-3:30pm, Sa 8:30am-12pm). Other services include **Internet** at **Info Plaza Pedasí,** right next to the IPAT office (US$0.50 for the first hr;. open Tu-F 9:30am-8pm, M and Sa 10am-6pm.); the **police station** (☎995 2122, emergency 104), at the town's entrance, before the Banco Nacional; *and* the **health clinic** (☎995 2127) east of the park. The **post office** is behind the municipal building (open M-F 7am-6pm, Sa 7am-5pm).

⌂⌂ ACCOMMODATIONS AND FOOD. All three budget hotels in Pedasí are clean and well-kept, with friendly staff. The best one, a real catch for budget travelers, is ▨**Dim's Hostel ❷,** on Av. Central before the Palacio Municipal on the right. This cozy B&B is set in a charming family home. Friendly owner Mirna will go out of her way to make sure your stay in Pedasí is a pleasant one. All rooms have A/C and bath. Great buffet-style breakfast is included and served in a communal outdoor living space beneath the branches of a mango tree. Calling ahead is recommended. (☎995 2303; mirely@iname.com. Singles US$15; doubles US$20, extra US$5 for third person.) **Residencial Moscoso ❷,** on the main road about 3 blocks south of the municipal building, rents impeccable rooms with private bath. The owners know Pedasí well. (☎995 2203. Call ahead to reserve a room. Singles US$14, with TV and A/C US$16.50; quads with TV and A/C US$22.) Three blocks farther north along Av. Central is **Hotel Residencial Pedasí ❷,** offering a common area and clean rooms with A/C and private bath. (☎695-3892. Singles US$15, with TV $18; doubles US$22; triples US$25-$30.)

Most restaurants are open only around mealtimes. Get good food quick and cheap at the popular **Restaurante Angela ❶,** across the street from the municipal building. (Open M-Sa 6am-8pm, Su 6am-6pm. *Comida corriente* US$1.50.) If you are in the mood for homemade dessert, you won't want to miss a stop by **Refresquería y Dulcería Yely** (take the first right after Residencial Moscoso). A delicious glass of the *típico chicheme* and a piece of freshly baked cake cost US$0.50. (☎995 2205. Open daily 9am-9pm.)

◪ BEACHES. Though most beachgoers make tracks for Isla Iguana or Playa Venado, **Playa El Toro** and **La Garita** both lie 3km east of town, providing isolation and good swimming. They are reachable by taxi (US$2.50) or foot. Follow the road east from signs at Residencial Moscoso. Every October or November, **Playa El Arenal** hosts a huge fishing tournament. Call **IPAT** (☎966 8013) in Los Santos for info.

▸ DAYTRIPS FROM PEDASÍ

▥ ISLA IGUANA

Pedasí's big draw is nearby **Refugio de Vida Silvestre Isla Iguana,** a diving, snorkeling, and fishing hotspot 7km from Pedasí's closest beach. Its beauty alone attracts visitors. The island has the largest coral mass on Panama's Pacific Coast, covering some 16 hectares on the front part of the island to a depth of 8m. Snorkelers and divers, bring your own equipment or rent at **Buzos de Azuero** in Pedasí. Isla Iguana has two fantastic white-sand **beaches** with clear water, bordered by dark rocks that look like baked mud castles. The boat drops you off at Playa El Cirial; Playita El Faro is a more secluded beach 200m from there. The island is also a great place for birdwatchers, with at least 16 different species of birds.

The owners of all 3 hotels in Pedasí are happy to find you transportation to the island and can do it at a moment's notice. Expect to pay a **local fisherman** US$30 plus US$10 for gasoline. Find a group of up to seven to share the cost. Another option is to arrange a tour with **Buzos de Azuero,** which is slightly more expensive, but you'll enjoy the comfort and facilities of a nicer boat as well as a knowledgeable staff. To rent life jackets for the fishermen's boats, check with Buzos. **Boats** leave from Playa El Arenal (also called El Bajadero), a 5min. ride from the gas station at the northern edge of Pedasí, from which you can take a **taxi** (US$2; arrange a ride back). From the beach, it's a 20min. boat ride to Isla Iguana, where you will probably be dropped off in front of one of the best coral reefs. Entrance fee US$3.

An ANAM **visitor center** is scheduled to open before the end of 2004, where visitors will be asked to register and will be able to learn more about what the island offers. You will also be able to arrange birdwatching, snorkeling, or hiking tours. The island boasts a small **refugio** for spending the night, with an outhouse and some hammock posts under a roof. **Camping** is possible if you bring everything you need, including food and drinking water. There are some very rough **trails** leading from the *refugio;* one leads to the lighthouse; another to Playita El Faro. Be sure not to stray off the trails: though unexploded **landmines** left over from when the US Navy occupied the island no longer seem to be a threat, African bees have been spotted deeper into the forest.

◪ PLAYA VENADO

Getting to **Playa Venado** requires a **taxi** (US$12) or hitchhiking, which *Let's Go* does not recommend. Since July 2004 there has been no reliable bus service to Playa Venado. Check with Pedasí's ANAM office for up-to-date transport info (☎ 995 2134; open M-F 8am-4pm). To Playa Venado by **bus** take one from **Pedasí** to **Cañas,** and ask to be dropped off at the entrance of the beach. There's one bus daily, 3pm.

Thirty minutes southeast of Pedasí by bus, "Playa Venao," as it is often pronounced, is one of the greatest surfing breaks in Panama. Even on a bad day, constant sets of three and four waves are good for bodysurfing. Venado's waves are big enough (2-3m, breaking both ways) to host the annual Billabong Pro Panama International Surfing Contest in late May. The 1.5km crescent of black sand is flanked by two land points, backed by verdant hills. The best break (and worst trash) is the end of the road. Constant waves make casual swimming impossible.

In the center of the beach, where the road ends, there is a **restaurant** and **bar,** and the four **spare rooms ❸** are the only option for staying on the island other than camping. The rooms have two beds and a private bath and stand barely 20m from the water. Plans for remodeling might hike the price up a bit. (US$16 per person, US$14 in low season.) The relaxed owner doesn't mind if you camp on the beach or hang a hammock. It's free, but you must wait for the locals to clear out at night (usually by 9pm), and you must clean up by 10am the next morning. Its **restaurant ❶** serves *típico*, often with fresh fish, and has some limited snack food (beef, rice, beans, and salad or fish with plantains US$2).

◪ ISLA DE CAÑAS

Combining a trip to Isla de Cañas and Playa Venado is wise, as you'll cut your transportation costs considerably. You can take the same bus in the direction of Cañas that passes by Playa Venado. **Taxis** from Pedasí run US$15 each way and will leave you at the boat pickup. At the end of the dirt road, bang the wrench against the wheel rim hanging from the tree to let someone know you're there, and then wait for a boat to show up. If the creek at the end of the road doesn't look big enough to allow a boat to travel up it, it's low tide. Remove your shoes, think happy thoughts free of snakes and crocodiles (which aren't a threat—during low tide), and trudge left down the creek and then left again about 50m to a small bank on the right side; wait here for the boat. The ride itself (5min., US$0.50) is spectacular and goes past thousands of crabs congregating among the mangrove roots. Bug repellent is recommended. Island admission is US$3 when ANAM is open.

West of Pedasí and Playa Venado lies Isla de Cañas, a large island off the southern coast of the Azuero Peninsula. The southern edge of the island boasts 14km of beautiful beaches, the chosen nesting ground of five of the world's eight species of sea turtle. The reproductive antics climax in *arribadas*, when more than 10,000 turtles hit the beach in just two or three nights to lay eggs. Apart from *arribadas*, there are many nights in the egg-laying season when 100 or more turtles spawn on the beach. The island is managed cooperatively by ANAM and the local community, which subsists mainly on turtle egg sales. The community has a nursery program: 1.5km of protected land on the beach means that about 15,000 nests are left untouched. The rest of the eggs are given to those who work with the program so they can profit from eggs. The egg-laying season is May-Dec. (Leatherbacks are primarily Dec.-Mar.), though *arribadas* are usually October or November.

There are many tour guides on the island who will take you to see the turtles and give you background (Spanish only) on the different species. Tours of the island's mangrove forests are also available (half day US$10). A good idea is to call ahead and ask for Nando, the owner of the only restaurant on the island, who can arrange everything from transportation and tours to lodging. The island's public phone (☎995 8002) on the island, just outside the ANAM office, is always answered by someone knowledgeable, but you might have to call twice as it could take a while to find Nando. Staying overnight is necessary if you want see the *tortugas*, although if you have your own transportation a better option is to stay only for a couple of hours as accommodation facilities on the island are not great. There are two rustic **cabañas ❶** for rent, with private bath and optional A/C (fit four people, US$5 per person plus $10 per room for A/C). Cleaner, more comfortable rooms for two with fans and an outhouse are rented in private houses for $10.

Nando's restaurant, **Mi Ranchito ❶** (which you'll see as soon as you get off the boat), serves a tasty meal of rice with black clams (a Los Santos favorite), fresh fish, and plantains for US$2.50. There you'll find transportation to the beach for US$1 both ways, consisting of a pleasant ride in a rustic horse-drawn carriage.

SANTIAGO

Halfway between Panama City and David along the Interamerican Hwy., Santiago (pop. 34, 800) is a convenient base for forays to waterfalls, wilderness areas, beaches, and small traditional villages. Aside from the *Fiesta Patronal de Santiago Apóstol* (July 22-25), Santiago itself doesn't offer visitors much.

▐ TRANSPORTATION. Transportes David-Panamá (☎998 4006) goes to **David** (3½hr., every hr. 9:45am-2am, US$6; after midnight US$7.50) and **Panama City** (5hr., every ½ hr. 9am-2am, US$6; express 10:45pm US$7.50). The terminal is near Hotel Piramidal on the Interamerican Hwy. east of the fork. **Buses** leave from the main terminal on Calle 10 halfway between Av. Central and the Interamerican Hwy. to: **Arenas Flores** (3hr., 2pm, US$7); **Atalaya** (30min., every 10-15min. 5:15am-8:30pm, US$0.45); **Las Palmas** (1¼hr.; every hour 5:20am-6pm; US$2.50); **San Francisco** (30min., every 30min. 6:30am-6pm, US$0.65); **Santa Fé** (1½hr., every 20-30min. 5am-7pm, US$2); and **Soná** (1hr., every 20min. 6:30am-6pm, US$1.50). In Santiago, air-conditioned **taxis** provide a cheap and convenient means of transportation (fare around US$0.75). Slightly **cheaper buses** are also available.

▣ 🛈 ORIENTATION AND PRACTICAL INFORMATION.

The main road, **Avenida Central,** branches off from the Interamerican Hwy. and runs west about 2km to the **cathedral** and the town's *parque central. Calles* run north-south between Avenida Central and the Interamerican Hwy., with Calle 2 next to the *parque* and Calle 10 about halfway between the *parque* and the fork. To get to the *parque* from the main bus terminal, turn right on C. 10 out of the front of the terminal and continue for 5 blocks. Turn right at Av. Central and continue straight to the cathedral.

Santiago has an **IPAT office** in the white Plaza Palermo shopping complex on Av. Central just east of Calle 10. (☎ 998 3929; fax 998 0929. Open M-F 8:30am-4:30pm. No English is spoken.) On the Interamerican Hwy. fork, in the Galería shopping center, is **Mary's Tours,** a **travel agency.** It is mostly useful for booking or confirming domestic flights (US$5 fee) or for extending your visa (US$10 fee). It also offers a few one-night trips. (☎ 998 0072. Open M-Sa 8am-5:30pm.) The most comprehensive and convenient supermarket in town is **Los Compadres,** under the huge pink sign, 4 blocks east of the *parque*. (☎998-4579. Open daily 8am-8pm). The Santiago **immigration office** is across from the Escuela Normal, on C. 7, 4 blocks north of Av. Central. (☎ 998 7447. Open M-F 8am-4pm.) **Banco General,** 3 blocks east of the *parque* on Av. Central, cashes traveler's checks and gives Visa cash advances (open M-F 8am-3pm, Sa 9am-noon). Sistema Clave **ATMs** are on Av. Central between C. 2 and 10 and at the bus station. **Western Union** is on C. 8 across from the Escuela Normal. (☎998-5431. Open M-F 8am-5:30pm, Sa 8:30am-2pm.) There's a **Budget car rental** (☎ 998 1731) at the fork. **Lavamático El Carmen #3** is next to Super 99, on C. 8 just north of Av. Central. (Wash US$0.50, dry US$1. Open M-Sa 7:30am-7:30pm, Su 7:30am-6pm.) **Police station** is east of town past the fork and at the corner of Av. Central and C. 4. (☎ 998 2119 or 104. Open 24hr.) The local **Farmacia Elysin** chain has branches all over, the largest at Av. Central with C. 7 (☎998 3411. Open daily 8am-9pm). For emergencies, the **Hospital Regional de Veraguas** (☎ 999 3146) is past the eastern fork. For less dire medical problems, **Clínica Médica Coopeve,** near the fork on Av. Central across from the Plaza Palermo shopping complex, does consultations. (☎998 6421. Open M-F 7am-5pm, Sa 7am-1pm. US$4) **Hal's Internet** runs a small but fully up-to-date web cafe on C. 10, 10min. from Avenida Central (☎/

THE HIDDEN DEAL

MINE...ALL MINE

Isla Cébaco, off the southern coast of Veraguas on the Pacific Ocean, is an island paradise only recently discovered Panamanians. Covered by pristine tropical vegetation, lined by soft white sand, and framed by enormous rock formations, it's no surprise that it normally costs hundreds of dollars to stay on the island.

A cheaper option is to stay on the mainland at night and then find cheap water transport to the island during the day. **Cabañas Torio** is a hidden deal south of Mariato in Veraguas, from which you can easily organize daytrips to the island. Friendly Spanish hostel owners Yolanda and Fernando will arrange budget boat rides to the *Isla* with local fishermen. And their six spotless and comfortable *cabañas,* with concrete floors, double beds, private bath, and thatched roof, are a steal at a mere US$16 per night.

From Santiago to Mariato (2.5 hr. 6am and 4pm, ask in advance for specific schedule, US$3.50), which is next to Torio. The trip to Isla Cébaco takes 1hr. from Torio. Ask to go to the farthest tip of the island. Stay away from overpriced private tours (US$120-$200) and instead pay US$45-$60; or, find a group and get a fisherman in Hicaco or Puerto Mutis (US$90-$100 for three). Call in advance 620 3677; yolandaf16@hotmail.com to make sure the owners will be there.

fax 998 2663. Open M-F 8am-11pm, Sa 8am-10pm. US$1 per 1½hr.). There's a **DHL** inside Mary's Tours (see above). The **post office** is on C. 8, 5 blocks north of Av. Central (open M-F 7am-5:30pm, Sa 7am-4:30pm).

ACCOMMODATIONS AND FOOD. Accommodations range from luxurious (along the highway) to basic and a little dodgy (in the middle of town). **Hotel Gran David ❸**, west of the fork on the Interamerican Hwy., is one of Santiago's best hotels and a great value. Comfortable rooms have A/C, phone, private bath, and TV. The 24hr. restaurant serves excellent meals at affordable prices (*corvina* with plantains US$5). Internet US$1 per hr. (☎998 4510; hgrandavid@hotmail.com. Singles US$17.50; doubles US$22; triples US$30.) **Hotel Santiago ❷**, 1 block south of the southwestern end of the cathedral, in a classic house with an interior garden, offers quiet, bare-bones rooms with private baths. None of the rooms have fans but there are some with A/C. (☎998 4824. Singles US$8; doubles US$11, with A/C US$13; triples US$13.)

Típico restaurants huddle around the center of town between Av. Central and C. 10. All stick rigidly to the standard cafeteria formula: chicken (roasted or fried) with white rice and plantains. **Mi Pueblito ❶**, on the Interamerican Hwy. across from Hotel Gran David, is a cafeteria-style diner that's open 24hr. (☎998 7280. *Sancocho* US$1.25; *comida corriente* US$3.)

SIGHTS. There isn't much to explore in Santiago, but the **◪Escuela Normal Juan Demóstenes Arosemana** is an excellent diversion. Built between 1936 and 1938, it's a fully functioning school for teachers that boasts dazzling architecture, sculpture, and painting. The facade is a gorgeous hodgepodge of stone carvings hiding miniature figures of *pollera*-clad girls amid columns and faces. Head through the archway of the entry hall, framed by the Allegory of Time and Philosophy (that's Plato and Aristotle leaning on the clock) and through the doors to the Aula Máxima. This huge room was painted by Roberto Lewis, the famous painter responsible for the Palacio Presidencial in Panama City. The school is in the middle of C. 7, 4 blocks north of Av. Central. (Open M-F 8am-7pm. Free.)

DAYTRIPS: SANTA FÉ AND OTHER VILLAGES.

Buses run between Santiago's main bus terminal and Santa Fé's center (1½hr., every 30min. 5am-6pm, US$2).

To the north of Santiago, the mountain village of **Santa Fé** is an ecotourist's dream. With waterfalls, mountains, plantations, and wildlife, not to mention the enchanting Orchid Fair in August, Santa Fé has a little of everything, though not many tourist facilities exist. The town is laid out in a rough V-shape along the top of a ridge, with **Cerro Tute** looming on the western side and a deep, lush valley to the east. The Santiago-Santa Fé road enters along the ridge from the southeast and splits into 3 roads at the *Bienvenidos a Santa Fé* sign. The left branch heads off toward the forested area of **Alto de Piedra** and the Hotel Jardín Santafereño (see below). The central branch leads uphill 500m to the town's modest church and the cluster of **Santa Fé-Santiago buses.** The right branch takes you toward the Orquideario (see below). No amount of directions is likely to save you having to ask—luckily, the local residents are extraordinarily friendly.

Hotel Santa Fé ❷ occupies a lovely piece of land 1km south of town on the Santiago-Santa Fé road (*comidas* US$2-$3). **Guides** into the verdant forests of **Cerro Tute** and **Alto de Piedra,** and to the many nearby waterfalls, can be hired here (US$20-$25 per day) but make sure to call several days in advance so that the owner can arrange the tour. The hotel also runs tours of **El Salto,** a nearby organic farm packed with waterfalls, and to a local **coffee processing** business for US$3 per group. (☎954 0941. Singles US$13; doubles US$15; triple with DirecTV US$25.) More removed and rustic **Hotel Jardín Santafereño ❶**, at the northwest corner of town, rents well-worn *cabañas* for two with bath US$11. The restaurant and *cantina* right next to the *cabañas* might make it somewhat noisy during the weekend (☎954 0866; ask for directions).

Santa Fé's chief assets are its tranquility and its virgin forests, but there are a few eclectic human enterprises worth checking out. Just downhill from where the buses cluster is a modest **Artisan's Market**, where a lonely scattering of handicrafts from Veraguas and Chiriquí are for sale at lower prices than in their places of origin (open daily 7am-6pm). Further up, take the second right (100m past the bus station) to find the **Santa Fé Cooperativa** (don't be fooled by the big, concrete store of the same name—you want the little thatched building that you'll see on your right). This tiny collective sells staples like beans and plantains, but most visitors will be more interested in taking home a souvenir bag of the locally-grown strong and bitter coffee (US$0.95 per ½ lb.) or a classic Panama hat (US$7-$20). It's a good opportunity to support the community that's supporting your peace of mind.

Santa Fé's original attraction is the mesmerizing and obsessed **Orquideario** (☎954 0916; zaguiji15@cwpanama.net), an intricate private garden containing hundreds of orchids of all shapes, sizes, and species that have won numerous awards (walk south of the bus stop, take the first left and ask for the house of the Zapata family).

San Francisco and **Atalaya**, nearby villages, have gorgeous churches. The church of the first, not surprisingly dedicated to San Francisco de Asís, is closed for remodeling. The intricate baroque interior contrasts with the exterior's simplicity. The ceiling of the second town's church is covered in biblical frescoes. Southwest of Santiago, otherwise unexciting **Soná** comes alive during La Feria de Veraguas in February or March, and La Fiesta de San Isidro Labrador on May 15.

SANTA CATALINA

Santa Catalina, recognized as one of the best year-round surfing spots in the Americas, is a small town of fishermen located in the Soná district 110km south of Santiago. People from all over the world come to Panama and hop on a bus for six to seven hours to get straight to Catalina. Although surfers are the majority here, this beach supports great nearby fishing, diving, snorkeling; it's also a good leap-off point to Pacific islands such as Coiba and Cébaco.

From Santiago, **buses** leave for **Soná** every 20 min. (1hr. M-F 5:40am-9:30pm, Sa-Su 6am-8pm; US$1.50.) There are only three buses a day from Soná to **Santa Catalina** (2 hr., 5am, noon, and 4pm, US$3). **Taxis** charge US$25 for the trip (up to 5 people). From Santa Catalina to Soná buses leave at 7, 8am, and 2pm. Brace yourself for the last kilometers of the unpaved and bumpy road toward Santa Catalina.

There are only two main roads, one from Soná and to the main beach, the other that takes you to Playa El Estero (turn left before the first restaurant). Little to no services in town and very few equipment rental options mean that surfers should come well-prepared. The town is usually short on change, so bring small bills and lots of coins. The only way to communicate with the outside world is through pay phones (no phone lines or Internet). The closest **bank** is in Soná.

Most hostels in the area have dorm-style rooms. The majority of surf camps branch off from the road that goes to El Estero except for **Cabañas Rolo ❶**, which is at the end of the road from Soná and is easiest to get to (though not from the beach). Friendly Rolo is a surfer himself. Seven cabins, shared outside bath, kitchen, international crowd, hammocks and a common eating area (US$7). **Kenny's Surf Camp ❷**, the third right off of the road to El Estero, has rooms with bunk beds and a balcony that overlooks the center point break. (With fan US$10, with A/C US$15, or rent a tent for US$3.50.)

There are few eating options in Santa Catalina. **La Fonda Café Bistro ❶**, right before getting to Rolo's, serves coffee and light meals. (Sandwiches and salads US$0.35-$2.50. Open daily 7am-7pm.) **Pizzeria Jamming ❷** is on the road to Playa El Estero—take the first right and follow the signs—has a good ambience with its hammocks, wooden tables, and *ranchitos*. It's a popular night hangout. (Pizza US$3.50-6, beer US$0.80. Closed M.) It's possible to get cheap *comida* throughout town, about US$2. The town is also eagerly awaiting an Argentine Parrillada, **Los Pibes,** set to open August 2004 (take the second right off the road to El Estero).

Santa Catalina waves are rarely under 4 ft. and can be as big as 15-20ft.; although the **surf** breaks both ways, it's best known for the right break. Punta Brava, after Estero Beach, also has a good wave that breaks both ways. Surf booties are recommended because of the volcanic rock bottom. For non-surfers, **Scuba Coiba,** the only **dive** shop in Catalina (www.scubacoiba.com), offers some good alternatives: dive tours to Coiba and Cébaco, PADI certification tours, and snorkeling trips. Located next to La Fonda Bistro Cafe, credit cards are not accepted unless prepaid in Panama City and they won't take checks unless contacted in advance.

CHIRIQUÍ PROVINCE

Located on the southwest extreme of Panama, Chiriquí exhibits the Central American traveler's dream: enticing rain forests, endless beaches, and sky-scraping volcanoes. Playa Las Lajas draws the beach crowd to stretches of Pacific pleasure; the northern highlands entices visitors to volcanoes. The indigenous Ngöbe named it "Valley of the Moon," and the cloud-enshrined hills above the valley cloak hot springs, lakes, and the elusive quetzal. A few hours north from the provincial capital David, refreshing villages, at moderate temperatures, sit at the base of gorgeous mountain trails. For years there has been talk of forming an independent República de Chiriquí: *Chiricanos* are proud of their origin and that they live in the most productive province, both in terms of agriculture and cattle. The expression "Soy Chiricano, meto!" is the phrase through which habitants of this province show their pride to distinguish themselves from the rest of the Panamanians.

DAVID

David (pop. 78,000) is the capital and center of the rich commercial and manufacturing Chiriquí Province. Hot and humid year-round, with few tourist attractions, David functions for most as a pit stop to Bocas del Toro, the Chiriquí highlands, or San José, Costa Rica. Fitness gyms, low-rider trucks, and a Top-40 radio station hint at the town's cosmopolitan aspirations. Although the party scene is only just beginning—very enthusiastically, it must be said—David steps out of its lethargic routine for 10 days around March 19, for its rowdy patron saint festival, La Feria de San José. Visitors from other provinces and Costa Rica join to celebrate.

◪ TRANSPORTATION

Flights: Aeropuerto Enrique Malek is 4km south of the city. **Aeroperlas** (☎775 7779; open M-F 8am-5pm) has flights to **Bocas Isla** and **Changuinola** (M-F 8am, US$31.50); **Panama City** (M-F 7, 11:30am, 5pm; Sa 8:30am, noon, 5pm; Su 9:30am, 5pm; US$58.50). **Mapiex Aero,** on the corner of C. D Nte. and Av. 2E (☎775 0812, at airport 721 0842. Open M-Sa 8am-10:30am, 1:30-5pm) has daily flights to **Panama City** (M-F 7:35am, noon, 5:10pm; Sa 8:15, 11:45am, 5:10pm; Su 9:15am, 5:10pm; US$60).

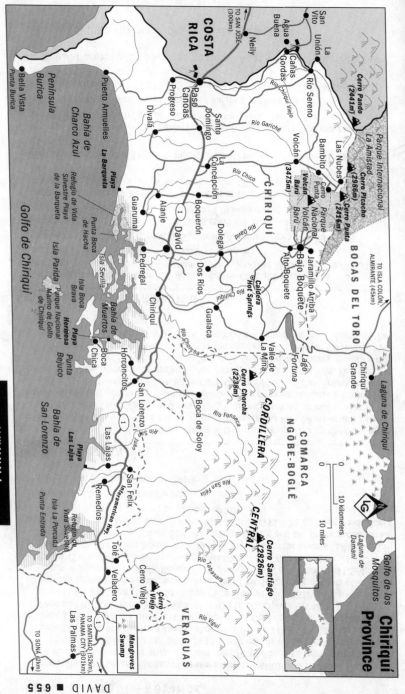

Buses: There are several options to **Panama City**. PADAFRONT has a terminal on Av. 1E (9 de Enero), just south of Av. Obaldía. (☎774 9205. 7hr., every 1½hr. 7:15am-8:15pm. US$10.60. Express 5½hr., 11pm and midnight, US$15.) **Expreso Cinco Estrellas** is 1 block south on Av. 1E, shows movies. (☎774 8017. 6hr.; 3, 10:45am, 4pm; US$9.) From the main terminal, north of Av. Obaldía on Av. 2E, buses head to **Panama City** (7hr., every hr. 6:45am-8pm, US$10.60; express 10:45pm and midnight, US$15) via **Santiago** (3hr., US$6) and **Penonomé** (4½hr., US$8). Other departures from the terminal: **Almirante**, where ferries leave for Bocas until 6:30pm (4hr., every 30min. 4:30am-7pm, US$7); **Boquete** (1hr., every 20min. 5am-7pm, US$1.20); **Cerro Punta** (2hr., every 15min. 5am-8pm, US$2.65) via **Volcán** (1½hr., US$2.30); **Changuinola** (4hr., every 30min. 4am-7pm, US$8) via **Chiriquí Grande** (1½hr., US$5); **San Félix** (1½hr., every 30min. 5:30am-7:30pm, US$2); and the **Costa Rican border at Paso Canoas** (1½hr., every 10min. 4am-10pm, US$1.50); and **San José, Costa Rica** (7hr., 1 per day 8:30am, US$12.50) on TRACOPA.

Local Buses: US$0.25 within the city.

Taxis: Easy to flag down. Most destinations US$0.50-1.50.

■ ORIENTATION

David is laid out in a grid, cut off northeast of the *parque central* by the busy diagonal **Av. Obaldía** and to the northwest by the **Interamerican Hwy.** North-south *avenidas* are numbered with *Oeste* and *Este* designations, starting on either side of **Av. Central**. East-west *calles* have similar *Norte* and *Sur* designations with letters, increasing to the north and south from **Calle Central**. Many of the streets are now labeled by names instead of numbers—for example, Av 3E is now Av. Bolivar, Av 1 E is 9 de Enero, and C. A Sur is called Ruben D. Samudio, but locals usually stick to the old number/letter combinations. The *parque central*, **Parque Cervantes**, lies between Av. 3/4 Este and C. A/B Norte. The major shopping zone is north of the *parque*, between C. 3/5 Este.

■ PRACTICAL INFORMATION

Tourist Information: IPAT (☎775 4120), on Av. Central between *C.* A and B norte, inside the parking lot. Open M-F 8:30am-4:30pm. Regional **ANAM** office (☎775 3163), on the road to the airport, then turn south onto Av. 8E.

Immigration: (☎775 4515), on C. C Sur, near Av. Central. Open M-F 8am-2pm.

Consulates: Costa Rica (☎774 1923), just off the Interamerican Hwy., on the way toward, that's right, Costa Rica. Open M, W, F 9am-noon and 1-4pm; T, Th 9am-noon.

Banks: Of many, **Banco General**, at the corner of C. C Norte and Av. 3E (Av. Bolivar), cashes traveler's checks. MC/V advances. 24hr. **ATM.** Open M-F 8am-3pm, Sa 9am-noon.

Western Union: (☎7749910), 3½ blocks south of the *parque* on Av. 4E. Open M-Sa 9am-6:30pm.

Supermarket: Supermercado Romero, behind Romero's clothing store east of the *parque*. Open M-Sa 8am-9pm, Su 8am-1pm. 24hr. branch on C. F Sur.

Market: Mercado Público, 3 blocks north of the *parque* on Av. 4E.

Lavandería Panamá Real (☎775 2053), around the corner on Av. 3E between C. Central/A Sur, dry-clean only.

Car Rental: Budget (☎721 0845), at the airport. Open M-F 6am-6:30pm., Sa 7am-6pm, Su 8am-5pm.

Police: (☎775 2121, emergency 104), on C. F Sur and Av. 4 Este.

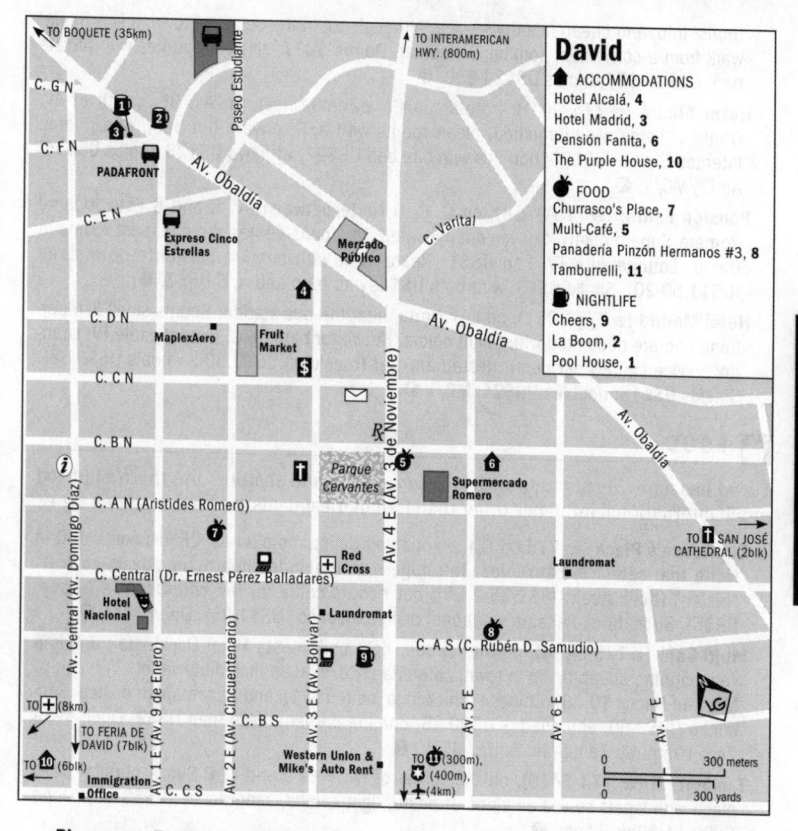

David

🏠 ACCOMMODATIONS
Hotel Alcalá, 4
Hotel Madrid, 3
Pensión Fanita, 6
The Purple House, 10

🍴 FOOD
Churrasco's Place, 7
Multi-Café, 5
Panadería Pinzón Hermanos #3, 8
Tamburrelli, 11

🍺 NIGHTLIFE
Cheers, 9
La Boom, 2
Pool House, 1

PANAMA

Pharmacy: Farmacia Revilla (☎ 775 3711), has a branch across from the *parque*'s northeast corner. Open 7am-11pm. MC/V.

Hospitals: Hospital Regional Chiriquí (☎ 775 2161), about 3km from the *parque* on the Interamerican Hwy. Take a bus to Hospital Regional-Centro (15-20 min., US$0.25).

Internet: Speedlán Ciber Café (☎ 774 2572), 2 blocks south of the park on Av. 3E. Fast new computers and A/C. US$1 for 3hr. Open 24hr. **Speed Explorer** (☎ 774 3142), on C. Central between Av. 2 and 3 Este. US$0.50 per hr.

Post Office: A block north of the park on C. C Norte. Open M-F 7am-5:45pm, Sa 7am-4:45pm.

🏠 ACCOMMODATIONS

Sleeping options in David are numerous, especially around the *Parque Central*, but the majority are expensive hotels. Although the *centro* is a convenient area to stay, safety is a concern; consider staying a bit further from the center. Make reservations in advance if visiting during March, when the city's festival takes place.

The Purple House (☎ 774 4059; www.purplehousehostel.com), on C. C Sur and Av. 6 Oeste. A popular hostel with many amenities, this is the only place in David designed with backpackers in mind. Free Internet, kitchen, cable TV and movies, book exchange, tourist info, and cheap laundry service. Although not in the center of town, it is a 5 min. walk from a convenient commercial center. Dorms $US7; singles, doubles with private bath US$19-$21; triples US$24-$30. ❷

Hotel Alcalá (☎774 9018; hotelalcala@cwpanama.net), on Av. 3E, south of Av. Obaldía. Large, well-furnished, clean rooms with A/C, private hot bath, and phone; Internet. Singles US$20; doubles with one bed US$22, with two US$26; triples US$35. AmEx/MC/V. ❸

Pensión Fanita (☎775-3718), on C. C. B Norte between Av. 5 and 6 Este (behind Romero Supermarket). Conveniently located, this *pensión* has the cheapest rooms in David. Lounge with TV. Fan US$1. Restaurant with *comida corriente* downstairs (US$1.50-20). Single US$3, with bath US$4, with bath and A/C US$7. ❶

Hotel Madrid (☎775 2051), on C. F Norte, near the bus station. Rooms smell like perfume and are decorated with bright colors. Hot-water bath, A/C, phone, cable TV. Laundry service ($0.80 per item). Restaurant/bar (breakfast US$0.50-2, meals US$3-$8). Singles US$18; doubles US$24. MC/V. ❸

🍴 FOOD

David has many restaurants with *comida típica* and seafood, but there's not too much international influence other than Italian. Best deals are around the *parque*.

Churrasco's Place (☎774 0412), an open-air dining room on Av. 2E just south of C. A Norte that caters to carnivores. The huge menu includes hearty breakfasts such as "bistec" (beef steak US$1.25-2.50), but people come for the *churrasco* (a T-bone; US$6). Su features Panama's national dish, *sancocho* (US$1.25). Open 24hr. ❷

Multi-Café (☎775 5194), on the *parque*, right underneath Hotel Occidental; this is a very popular, cheap *típico* in town, cafeteria style, with an incredible variety. A blend of Mexican (tacos $0.75), Chinese (chicken lo mein US$1), and Panamanian dishes. *Sancocho* US$0.60, *empanadas* US$0.25, *comida corriente* less than US$2. Open M-Sa 7am-10pm, Su 7am-3pm. AmEx/MC/V. ❶

Tamburrelli (☎774 6410), on the corner of Av. 4 Este and C. E Sur. A popular pizza place with locals serves all kinds of pasta, light salads, sandwiches (US$3.50). Open Tu-Su 11:30am-11pm. ❷

Panadería Pinzón Hermanos #3, on Av. 5E across from Pensión Costa Rica. By day, a mild-mannered bakery (pastries US$0.20-0.35); when darkness falls, a happening sandwich and burger joint (US$0.35-2.50). Open M-Sa 7am-9:30pm, Su 4-9pm. ❶

🎭 ENTERTAINMENT AND NIGHTLIFE

Multi-screen **Cinema Alhambra**, on Av. 1E, C. A Sur, 2 blocks west and 2 blocks south of the *parque*, shows recent US films with subtitles. (☎775 7889. US$1.80-2.50, M-W half-price). **Pool House**, near the bus terminal and next to Hotel Madrid, has pool and ping-pong tables (US$1.50 per hour) and pitchers of beer for US$2.10. (☎775 0002. Open daily 3pm.) Blow the cash you saved on cheap beer at the **casino** in the Hotel Nacional. (Open daily noon-4am.) There are a couple of places to choose from at night; you can probably check out the scene in all of them before settling (especially girls, who enter for free in most places). **Cheers**, on C. A Sur between Av. 3 and 4 Este, is a small sports bar and a good starting place. Karaoke on Th; local band on F with three beers for the price of two. (Beer US$0.50. Open Tu-Sa at 5pm.) **La Boom** (www.laboomdavid.com), across from Pool House on Av. Obaldía, is the most modern and popular dancing place in David. (Lady's night W, girls enter and drink for free until 11:30pm, guys US$5. Open W, F, Sa 9pm-4am.)

🗘 DAYTRIP FROM DAVID

PLAYA LAS LAJAS

Any bus trawling the Interamerican Hwy. will drop you off or pick you up at the road to Las Lajas, a 13km taxi ride south to a small cluster of buildings on the beach. With few accommodations or eateries, Las Lajas is probably best as a daytrip from David. Buses from David to the highway intersection US$2 (any bus going towards Panama will work). From the drop-off, taxis run to the beach (US$5); agree on prices beforehand.

Almost halfway along the Interamerican, between David and Santiago, awaits Las Lajas, an unremarkable town north of a remarkable beach. Though only about 15m wide, the smooth, palm-lined strip of sand stretches straight along the Pacific as far as the eye can see, disappearing into the mist on either end. Waves are good for bodysurfing but not big enough to prevent swimming. During the week, especially between April and November, the beach is nearly empty. Though Las Lajas has few facilities for the visitor, basic services await 1km north of the highway entrance in San Félix. This long town follows the one main road north, becoming a Ngöbe village. There is a **police station** (☎ 727 0531), and a **Banco Nacional** across (☎ 727 0541. Open M-F 8am-3pm, Sa 9am-noon) with an **ATM**. The **Hospital,** as well as some assorted **supermarkets** (**SuperCentro San Félix** is right next to the hospital) function. For daytrippers from David, the **El Carrizal complex** (at the left at the end of the paved road) rents palm-covered *ranchitos* (US$5, low season US$3), bathrooms (US$0.25) and showers (US$0.50) to the public.

To reach the only accommodation at the beach, turn right at the end of the paved road and follow a dirt road 1km along the beach (you can also walk on the beach). **Las Lajas Beach Cabins ❶** rents out a row of bamboo *cabañas*, with lights, picnic tables, and paper-thin mats in the loft above (US$7). A couple rustic cabins made of concrete and with private baths are available (double US$35). Breakfast US$2.50, lunch or dinner US$3.50. The town, stretched out south of the highway, hides a few *típico* kiosks and restaurants, most notably s **Mayra's ❶** at the southern end of town (*comida corriente* US$1-$2). During the low season, accommodations and restaurants are even less prepared to welcome travelers than usual, as there are few visitors. For less proximity but a little more formality, **Restaurante Hotel El Cruce ❷** (☎ 592 8964) stands at the entrance to Las Lajas on the Interamerican, where most buses drop off for the beach. Upstairs, well-worn rooms have fans and private baths (US$10); downstairs cheap *típico* is served (US$2).

🗘 PASO CANOAS: BORDER WITH COSTA RICA

Unappealing Paso Canoas, on the Interamerican Hwy., is the principal crossing between Panama and Costa Rica. To get to the border, take a bus from **David**, 50km east of Paso Canoas. You may have to buy a rather expensive round-trip bus ticket as proof of exit; a plane ticket out of Costa Rica is the only other accepted proof.

Entering Costa Rica, travelers need a passport, a tourist card (available at the border checkpoint; US$5, lasts 30 days), and a return ticket; Panama has the same requirements. Tourist cards are sold at the Costa Rican **General de Migración,** 175m west of the main intersection (☎ 732 2150; open daily 7am-10pm), and at the **Instituto Panameño de Turismo** (☎ 727 6524) on both sides of the border (open 6-11am and 1-5pm, but schedule varies). Note that Costa Rica is an hour behind Panama. **Money changers** abound. *Bolsijeros* on the Panamanian side, identifiable by the fanny packs slung across their chests, give the best exchanges, but check the rate before approaching them to avoid hustling. The **police** are 50m from either border. (Costa Rica ☎ 732 2402 or 911 for emergencies; Panama ☎ 727 6521.) The **Banco Nacional de Panamá** is 25m from the crossing and has a 24hr. **ATM** that spits out US dollars. (☎ 727 6522. Open M-F 8am-3pm, Sa 9am-noon. MC/V.) Buses drop off in front of the **post office** in Costa Rica. (☎ 732 2029. Open M-F 8am-noon and 1-5:30pm.) There's another one in Panama (open M-F 8-11am and 2-5pm, Sa 8am-2). For accommodations and food, see **Paso Canoas: Border with Panama**, p. 659.

BOQUETE

Thirty-eight kilometers north of David, mountain scenery and fresh air envelop Boquete (pop. 15,500), Panama's main producer of coffee. Boquete is the land of *"bajareque,"* a light drizzle accompanied by a cool breeze that fools anyone into thinking it's getting chilly—in reality it will last only a couple minutes. Referred to affectionately by Panamanians as the "Valley of the Flowers and the Eternal Spring," Boquete has quickly become a popular destination for international travelers and daytrippers from David, all eager to hike, horseback ride, bird watch, or escape the heat. As tourist numbers increase, prices rise. Despite this recent change, Boquete remains a backpacker's heaven and usually keeps them longer than they planned. The rainy season presents some difficulties in ascending the volcano, and roaring rivers tend to overflow, causing landslides and blocking nearby trails. In these situations, it is still possible to explore the nearby countryside through many pebbled roads that loop out of and back into town. Indigenous areas, coffee farms, and creative gardens make this alternative equally attractive.

⎚ TRANSPORTATION

Buses leave from the western side of the *parque central* for **David** (1hr.; M-Sa every 20min. 4:30am-7pm, Su every 25min. 5am-7pm, US$1.20). **Local Buses:** Zona Urbana and Zona Rural buses serving the local area (Palmiro, Alto Quiel, Bajo Mono) leave 1 block up the main street in front of Super Mercadito Bruña. The mini-buses have destinations painted on their front. (US$0.35-2.) Many **taxis** are 4WD; hail in front of the park. Fares vary but short trips are usually US$0.25.

✴🛈 ORIENTATION AND PRACTICAL INFORMATION

Boquete is laid out in a near-grid, with the main north-south *avenida* running along the western side of the *Parque Central*. The main *avenida* comes in from David and continues north, where it splits through the surrounding countryside. Numbered *calles* run east-west. The **Quebrada Grande** cuts through town. The **Avenida Central** runs parallel to **Avenida Cincuentenario**, and the road west is labeled **Hacia Valle Escondido** (across the bridge).

Tourist Information: Before getting to Boquete town, you should plan to stop at the official tourist center, **Cefati** (☎ 720 4060), about 1.5km south of town on the main road, where you can get maps, brochures, and kind assistance, while enjoying an awesome view of the town. It also has a small exhibit on Boquete history, although it has only a few English translations. As usual, the classy building and staff don't have much info for backpackers. Open daily 8am-4pm. For the best info in town, talk with multilingual Frank at **Pensión Marilós** (see **Accommodations,** below). However, all hostel owners are full of suggestions, phone numbers, and self-drawn maps.

Banks: Banco Nacional (☎ 720 1328 or 720 2776), 1½ blocks south of the *parque* on the main *avenida*, across from the Delta gas station, cashes AmEx traveler's checks and has free coffee. They have a 24hr. MC/V **ATM**. Open M-F 8am-3pm, Sa 9am-noon. **Global Bank,** across the street, also has a 24hr. ATM and will change MC/V and traveler's checks. Open M-F 8am-3pm, Sa 9am-noon.

Supermarkets: Supercentro El Mandarín (☎720 1815), across the main street just north of the *parque*. Open Su-F 8:30am-9pm, Sa 8:30am-10pm.

Laundry: Lavamático Las Burbujas, across from the church at the town's northern end. Wash and dry US$2.25. Soap US$0.30. Iron US$0.60 per item. Open M-Su 8am-6pm.

Pharmacy: Farmacia Any (☎720 1296), 3 blocks north of the *parque.* Open daily 8am-9pm.

Police: (☎104 or 720 1222), 1 block east and 1 block south of the *parque.*

Emergency: Ambulance ☎720 1356.

Medical Services: Centro Médico San Juan Bautista (☎720 1881), on the Av. Central going towards Los Naranjos. Open M-F 8am-6pm, Sa 9am-1pm. Doctor on call 24hr. For a bilingual doctor ask for Dr. Pretel.

Internet: Professional Center (☎720 2047), next to the laundromat, across from the church. US$1 per hr. Open daily 8am-10pm. **Kelnix** (☎720 2803; kevilgo@hotmail.com), across the street from the southwest corner of the *parque.* Fewer computers and slower connections. US$1 per hr. Open M-Sa 8am-8pm, Su 8am-6pm. **Kalima Suites** (☎ 720-2884), 2 blocks south and 1 block east of the *parque* across from Pensión Marilós. US$1 per hr. Cheap rates for international calls to the US, Canada, and Europe (US$0.20 per min.)

Post Office: (☎720 1265) Large green building across from the east side of the *parque.* Faxes to within Panama, US$1 per page. Open M-F 7am-5:45pm, Sa 7am-4:45pm.

ACCOMMODATIONS

Boquete has the best backpacker hostels in Panama: rooms are often shared and cheap. Hostel owners are often eager to help and make connections between travelers and tour guides. Boquete locals are especially helpful people, but beware: advice cannot be relied upon blindly. Be prepared for overbearing treatment at all accommodations. If you're going to Boquete in January, make reservations in advance as all the hotels fill up early because of the fair.

Pensión Marilós (☎720 1380; marilos66@hotmail.com), 2 blocks south and 1 block east of the *parque.* Comfort and cleanliness for next to nothing make it the best hostel in town. Hot water, beautiful common area, kitchen, book exchange, and a multilingual owner (Frank) with encyclopedic knowledge of the area. Free use of laundry machine with two-day stay. Reservations recommended year-round. Singles US$7, with bath US$10; doubles US$10/$15.40. ❶

Pensión Topás (☎720 1005; schoeb@cwpanama.net), 3½ blocks south of the southeastern corner of the *parque.* Large, bright and clean rooms surround a garden with pool and original murals. Knowledgeable owners speak English and German. Massive breakfasts US$4. Singles US$8, with bath US$15; doubles with bath US$18-$20; triples US$27; quads US$33. Dec.-May prices 20% higher. ❷

Hostal Palacio (☎720 1653, cell 628 6679), off the northwest corner of the *parque.* Shared rooms tightly packed with beds. Common kitchen, common baths, garden, hammocks, and an uncommonly helpful owner, Pancho, who will probably solicit your stay as you get off the bus. US$5-$6 per person depending on season and other factors. ❶

Hospedaje Sueños del Río (☎720 2736), east of the *parque,* take left right before getting to the bridge. A family house now turned hostel, this place is a great value. For US$7 per person, you get to use all the facilities of the house, including the living room with TV, the kitchen, and laundry. Right by the river. Triples and quads only. ❶

Hotel Rebequet (☎720 1365, rebequet@hotmail.com), right across from Pensión Marilós. Attractive and upscale, this hotel offers a good location and great comfort for US$20. Hidden deal: in addition to use of hotel facilities, there are 3 separate, simple, clean rooms right next to the hotel US$10, US$15 per couple. ❷

◘ FOOD

As Boquete rapidly expands, restaurants multiply, prices rise, and menus become increasingly varied. A variety is guaranteed: from cheap *típica* to gourmet-style meals; places located around the park or farther away in the mountains. *Duros*, kind of like a fresh frozen fruit drink, are very popular in the Chiriquí highlands.

Punto de Encuentro (☎ 720 2123), 1 block south and 1 block east of the *parque*. Follow the blue sign for Hotel Rebequet, then right down a small driveway. Superb breakfasts in a relaxing garden setting. Open-air dining area. Omelettes US$3.25; french toast with fruit US$3; coffee US$0.50; and yogurt US$1. Open daily 7-11:30am. ❶

Taquería Antojitos Mexicanos, north of the park, at the end of C. 1 A Sur; take a left right after passing Bistro Boquete on the Av. Central. A small and authentic Mexican restaurant with colorful decorations that is still undiscovered but probably won't remain that way much longer. Try the delicious fajitas for only US$3.50 and the fresh strawberry *chicha* for US$0.40; nothing exceeds US$4.50. Open Tu-Su noon-10pm. ❷

El Sabrosón on Av. Central near the northern end of town is as cheap and as popular as they come for *comida típica*. (US$1-$2. Open Su-F 6am-11pm, Sa 6am-midnight.) ❶

La Volcánica Pizzería (☎ 720 1063), a block south of the *parque* on the main road. Not authentic Italian recipes, but fun favorite locale among tourists. Good thin crust pizza. Small US$3.50-$4.50, medium US$4.50$6.50, large US$7.50-$8.50. Milkshakes US$1.25. Open M-Th 3pm-10pm, F-Su 10am-10pm, Sa until 11pm. ❷

Java Juice (☎ 720 2502), across from Casona Mexicana and next to an Internet cafe, serves healthy vegetarian options including salads, sandwiches, and soy milkshakes (US$1-$30). Open daily 10am-10pm. ❶

◪ OUTDOOR ACTIVITIES

HIKING. Plenty of trails head into Parque Nacional Volcán Barú (p. 663), but there is much to see without even entering the park. North of town are *fincas*, worked mostly by indigenous **Ngöbe** people, recognizable by women's long, colorful dresses, called *naguas*. One of the best circuits is **Bajo Mono;** follow the signs to the left at the fork north of town. This 4-5hr. hike skirts the Río Caldera past Los Ladrillos rock formation, San Ramón waterfall, a castle, and numerous bridges. If you don't have time to hike the whole route, take a bus through part of the loop to see the views. Almost all roads starting in Boquete loop back into the town center, so it's hard to get lost. Locals proudly mention that recent ex-president, **Mireya Moscoso,** has a farm along this road.

GARDENS. Mi Jardín es Su Jardín, 1km north of town, is a private garden with hundreds of varieties of flowers, ponds, and fountains. As the name implies, the family generously opens their grounds for free. It's a must especially if you'll miss the Flower Fair in January The garden has clearly marked paths and views of all of Boquete. It is essentially the fantasy land of its creator. With profound quotes, silly faces on recycled junk, and beautiful flower beds, it's perfect for anybody's inner child *(Follow the road to Palo Alto, turn right at the Jaramillo Arriba school, and then a right at the Explorador sign. The entrance is a decorated fence on your left across from the radio tower. ☎ 627 6908; ammsa7@cwp.net.pa. Open Tu-Su 9am-6pm. US$2.)*

CALDERA HOT SPRINGS. Locals and tourists alike adore these seven natural springs. Most visit the swimming holes at night. However, the intricate hikes through the surrounding area, which pass five hidden springs, are best attempted during the day. Take a bus south toward David and ask to be let off at the turnoff for Caldera. It's easiest to hitchhike the remaining 14km to Caldera, since buses are irregular and infrequent along this road; however, *Let's Go* does not recommend hitchhiking. *(A bus directly to Caldera also leaves from the mercado público at 7:30, 10:30am, and 3:30 pm. During the day, Caldera has plenty of 4WD taxis (follow the signs). These travel up an extremely rocky road and drop you off at a bridge that is a 15min. hike to the first set of holes 45min.-1hr.; most locals provide the service, more like a taxi service than a tour. US$15 per car, though you can walk this stretch about as fast as a car. The best option: find a few other interested folks and hire a guide. The path to the first spring passes a small farm with horses and an abandoned house; turn right to the holes. US$0.50, rarely charged.)*

COFFEE PLANTATIONS. Cafe Ruiz is a local coffee factory that you can reach after a 15-20min. walk along the left fork of the road north of town. They offer a tour demonstrating the coffee-making process, with samples at the end; for true coffee lovers, they have a full tour through the farms and the factory. **Café Sitton** in Alto Quiel, out the left fork of the Bajo Mono loop, offers more in-depth but less organized tours that include picking beans in the field. *(Open M-Sa 7am-4pm. Partial tour 25min., US$4. Full tour 3hr. M-Sa at 9am and 1pm; US$14. Tours in Dutch, English, German, and Spanish. Cafe Sitton ☎720 1353. Go in advance to arrange a tour, prices negotiated at the site.)*

GUIDED TOURS

Boquete offers many excellent tour guides, though few have offices.

Feliciano's Tours (☎624 9940, ask for Feliciano González). Local guide is well regarded in town—rightfully so given his extensive knowledge of the area—and leads several hiking tours. His 4WD truck will also get you to the hot springs (around 3 hrs.). Special trips across the Cordillera into Bocas del Toro (2-3 days one way, US$50) can be arranged with advanced notice. Most tours are US$10. Tours aren't limited to predetermined ones; Feliciano will take you almost anywhere. Negotiable student discounts.

Chiriquí River Rafting (☎720 1505; www.panama-rafting.com), has an office across the street from the southwest corner of the *parque*. White-water rafting trips depart form Boquete at 7am sharp and return around 5:30pm. US$60-$105 per person; negotiable student discounts. Open M-Sa 8:30am-5:30pm. AmEx/MC/V.

Panama Rafters (☎720 2172, evening 633 4313; rafting@panamarafters.com), across the street and next to Java Juice. Class II-V white-water rafting. Trips leave at 7:30am. The beginning level (US$75) returns at 3pm, the advanced (US$90) at 5pm. Discounts for groups. Open daily 9:30am-5:30pm. MC/V.

Horse Tours (☎720 1750, or 629 0814) Señor Eduardo Cano offers tours for US$8 per person per hr., US$5 for every additional hr.

AJ Tours (☎624 0350; anaj07@hotmail.com), with Ana Julia Serracín, specializes in nature hikes (Volcán Barú, Sendero los Quetzales, and others). US$20-$40 for 2-3 people. Negotiable student discounts.

Boquete Mountain Cruisers (☎720 4697 or 624 0350), also run by Panamanian Ana Julia Serracín and an American named Patsy, offers trips to the hot springs and around the Boquete mountains in a picturesque 1978 classic Toyota land cruiser that has been restored to fit passengers in back. US$15-$20.

🏔 PARQUE NACIONAL VOLCÁN BARU

Protecting the slopes of Volcán Barú, Panama's highest point (3475m), Parque Nacional Volcán Barú has panoramic views and the nation's highest concentration of elusive quetzals. During dry season (Dec.-Mar.), you can see both oceans at once from the Volcano's peak. The ascent of Barú is best done from Boquete, though a guided hike is possible from Cerro Punta. Keep careful note of weather conditions; you could face hours of cold rain. On the other hand, captivating Sendero Los Quetzales, a hike through cloud forest, is easiest from Cerro Punta. Many other hikes are possible with guides, available in both Cerro Punta and Boquete.

🔰 **CLIMBING THE VOLCANO.** The easiest, most popular way to climb Volcán Barú starts in Boquete, from which a rough dirt road (barely passable even in a 4WD) climbs 2500m vertically in about 14km. Ask about road conditions during the rainy season (Apr.-Nov.), lest a river suddenly materialize beneath. If you've got $100 or so to spend, you can hire a car to take you up there; contact the tour guides in Boquete. Locals will try to dissuade you from making the ascent during the rainy season because they have seen plenty of miserable, cold, wet travelers come back down to Boquete. However, if you leave early and dress properly, you can have an excellent experience year-round. Camping up top is possible but very cold. Various people head up the mountain, mostly to work on the antennae up top. If you hit the road by 6am, you have a decent shot of scoring a ride all the way (some trucks leave as late as 10 or 11am), although hitchhiking is not recommended by *Let's Go*. The entrance to the park, with an occasionally-staffed ranger station, is 8km from Boquete on a paved road—turn left on C. 2 Nte., 1½ blocks past the church. A taxi will take you as far as the ranger station for US$5 (ask to go *al fin del pavimento*), but most locals will do it for free if you start walking.

Another option is to climb the other side from a village called **Paso Ancho,** a few kilometers from the Volcán on the road to Cerro Punta. However, you should be in good shape; the trail can be hard to find, especially when parts have been washed away by landslides, so ask a guide in Volcán. It's a full-day hike up this side (wear sunblock), and if you decide to camp, be sure to bring warm clothes.

🔰 **SENDERO LOS QUETZALES FROM CERRO PUNTA.** This trail connects Cerro Punta and Boquete, but it's easier to start in Cerro Punta. Either take a 4WD taxi from the town's center to Respingo (US$10), or catch a Ruta Urbana bus and explain where you're going, then walk to Respingo, a steep 45min. hike on the rocky road. **Respingo,** a ranger station, has beds, kitchen, and bathroom facilities (bring food and sheets). Rangers are friendly and will do everything possible to get you shelter for the night, including letting you crash on the couch. Grounds are beautifully kept and bunk beds clean. (US$5 per tent, US$5 per bed; park entrance US$2). From Respingo, the trail becomes decreasingly well-marked, resulting in about a half-day's hike to **Bajo Mono** in Boquete (8km). Along the way, a 90m detour takes you to the **Mirador,** a well-marked elevated wooden porch with views spanning most of the park. You will also pass a possible camping area with picnic tables, **Respinguito,** 3km from the ranger station. Once you reach **Bajo Mono,** a bus usually passes every hour to **Cerro Punta,** where you can arrange guides through Hotel Los Quetzales (☎771 2182). The trail is extremely popular during all seasons, though recent rains create deep mud along the path.

🔰 **SENDERO LOS QUETZALES FROM BOQUETE.** From Boquete, the trail is harder and longer. It begins at the top of the Bajo Mono road 3km north of town. Take a taxi (US$5) or a *Zona Urbana* bus (US$0.50) to the entrance, and stay on the main path to the right across the creek. Follow the red pipeline alongside the rough road for 30min. until a smaller gravel trail veers left uphill. There are four fixtures in a row on top of the pipe at that fork; take the left up the hill to the beginning of the park at **Alto Chiquero** (12km from Cerro Punta, 3km from Boquete), where there is an unstaffed ranger station (unless you call ANAM in advance). You'll find beds, bathrooms, and kitchen facilities, but bring a sleeping bag; temperatures can drop as low as 4°C. The road continues for 45min. until you reach a barbed wire fence, where an easy-to-miss sign points out the path to the left.

The difficult but extremely rewarding hike truly begins at this point. The path reaches a clearing and an empty house, then continues to the right. Twenty minutes later, you must fork off the main path to the left at a patch of bamboo and some tree stumps. Take this path directly to the creek, and then continue, crossing often to **La Victoria** for an awesome view of the valley. This is two-thirds of the way through the hike. From here, two paths diverge, one through the valley and one climbing farther uphill. Both are 5km paths ending in Respingo. From **Respingo,** it's about a 45min. walk downhill to the paved road, where it's possible to get a ride from a taxi, a bus, or any car that stops. Keep in mind that during rainy season, the creek becomes harder to cross and the mud becomes harder to trudge through.

VOLCÁN

An hour north of David, the town of Volcán (pop. 10,188), lies on the eastern slopes of its namesake, Volcán Barú, and can be reached only by bus from David or through the Sendero los Quetzales from Boquete. With similar access to countless natural attractions, but fewer travelers, Volcán is the perfect alternative to touristy Boquete. Not as many guides are available and night stays can be pricey, but Volcán is certainly worth the extra trouble, offering a tight-knit, kind community where the helpful locals are eager to share outdoor adventures with visitors.

PANAMA

⫛ TRANSPORTATION. From the kiosk at the main intersection, **buses** go to **Cerro Punta** (30min., every 15min. 5am-7pm, US$0.90) and the **Costa Rican border** at **Río Sereno** (45min., every hr. 5am-6pm, US$2.85). The bus to **David** comes from Cerro Punta and stops at the Shell station, but will also stop wherever it is flagged on the southbound road. (1½hr., every 15min. 5:30am-7pm, US$2.30.) **4WD taxis** (☎771 4288) patrol the main road and hang out at the intersection.

◼◪ ORIENTATION AND PRACTICAL INFORMATION. The main road comes in from Concepción (a little west of David on the Interamerican Hwy.) in the south, heads northwest through town, and then heads out toward Río Sereno, on the Costa Rican border. At the main intersection, a road branches right to Cerro Punta, 20km north. Most of the town's services cluster around this intersection. The town itself is divided into two districts: **El Hoto** to the southeast and **Nuevo California** past the intersection. Locals often refer to these districts to point you in the right direction, and street names are never used.

The local **ANAM** office, the main office for Volcán Barú and La Amistad, is on the left side of the road to Cerro Punta, 300m north of the main intersection. (☎771 5383. Open M-F 8am-4pm.) They offer some info, but not nearly as much as private offices in town, and do not offer guided tours. One well-respected guide in town, **Arturo Rivera,** will take you to **Las Lagunas** or **Los Pozos** (US$60 for a group of three) and other attractions, such as **La Amistad** or **Sendero los Quetzales** (US$20-$80). His house is 200m past the ANAM office on the road to Cerro Punta; look for the "Guía" sign. (☎771 5917; coraliagonzales@hotmail.com.) A pricier option for guided tours is **Highlands Adventure,** just across the street from the intersection on the main road, offers 43 organized tours. (☎685 1682, or 771 4413; ecoaizpurúa@hotmail.com. Open daily 7am-7pm.) On the way to David, **Finca Guardia** rents fairly expensive horses. Ask the bus (US$0.25) to stop there (☎616 2521. US$15 per hr., US$40 per day.)

Other services include: **Banistmo,** a block south of the main intersection, changes traveler's checks and cash advances on Visa. (☎771 4711; open M-F 8am-3:30pm, Sa 9am-noon.) **Laundry** at **Lavamatico Volcán,** 500m south of the intersection. (Wash US$1.25, dry US$1.50; open M-Sa 7:30am-8pm; the owner lives in the house next door and will open shop for travelers desperate for Sunday cleaning.)

Helpful **police** are at the fork in the road (☎771 4231; emergency ☎104) and **Farmacia Celina** is next to the gas station at the main intersection (☎771 5075; open M-F 7:30am-11pm, Sa 9am-11pm.) Get **medical attention** at the **Centro de Salud**, left at the church on the Cerro Punta fork. (☎771 4283. Open M-F 7am-3pm.) Access the **Internet** at **Volc@netPlace**, on the main road 800m west of the intersection (☎771 5482; US$0.75 per hr.; open daily 8am-10pm), and 200m farther west at **Internet Rural**. (☎771 5144; US$0.75 per hr.; open 24hr.) The **post office** is on the main road. (☎771 4222. Open M-F 7-11am and 1-4:30pm, Sa 8am-noon.)

⌂ ACCOMMODATIONS. Most lodgings in Volcán are well-furnished but pricey *cabañas*. Reservations are recommended during the high season (Jan.-May); many families rent rooms so ask around. South of town, **⬛Talamanca Ecolodge and Restaurante Cerro Brujo ❷**, a mother-daughter business, offers a small, luxurious *cabaña* with kitchenette, and a gourmet new-world cuisine restaurant on site. Gorgeous grounds invite campers, though its isolated nature makes it a bit hard to get to. English and French are spoken. (☎669 9196; cerrobrujo@hotmail.com. Restaurant open daily 11am-10pm. Meals US$10-$12. Four people US$55; camping US$8.) Probably the best deal in Volcán is the **Hostal El Cubano ❷** (take a left after Farmacia Don Bosco on the road towards David, near the fire station), an inviting house and host with comfortable and clean rooms, private bath with hot water, and a lounge with TV. (☎771 4731. Optional meals US$1-2, laundry service US$1. Singles US$9; doubles US$17.) **Hotel Oasis ❷**, on the first left after the intersection along the westbound road, has space for up to 300 people, making it ideal for large groups. Internet US$1 per hr. (☎771 4644. Singles with hot bath US$12; doubles US$15; triples US$20; discount for large groups and long stays.)

Since the firemen cannot charge you, **camping** behind the fire station on an uncovered cement platform is free; take the first right on the road to Cerro Punta and bear left at the *parque*. The station has a toilet and sink, but no shower. If you ask nicely, especially if it's cold and rainy, the fireman on duty may let you crash on the couch. (For camping equipment rental see **Practical Information**, above.)

◖ FOOD. **Panadería-Dulcería Cafetería Mole ❶**, right at the bus stop at the main intersection in town, serves ice cream pastries (US$0.15-0.45) and luscious baked loaves. (Open daily 7:30am-10pm.) Pleasant wooden benches draw many local families. There are several kiosks with *comida típica* around the Panadería-Dulcería (US$0.50-2). **Restaurante Don Tavo ❶**, next to **Internet Rural**, offers good *típico* (*comida del día* US$2.50) and more exotic options such as tacos (US$1.50. ☎771 4258. Open Tu-Su 8am-9pm.) **Hotel Oasis** has a restaurant serving medium-priced meals, and the disco is a local hangout, especially during the rainy season.

▦ SITIO ARQUEOLÓGICO BARRILES. 5.5km west of Volcán, this is one of Panama's famed archaeological sites. The location of the civilization of Barriles was named after the rounded stone barrels first found on the site. At the same moment that the volcano destroyed the civilization, it also ironically helped to preserve its memory. Although some of the artifacts were removed from the site during the 1950s and sold to museums in the United States and Europe, in recent excavations more has been found hidden in the surrounding gardens. Figures include representations of sacrificial tables, maps of the area (with symbolic notations of the volcano and other peaks), whistles, urns, and outdoor statues. *(The owners of the farm on which the site sits, José and Edna Landaou, are very knowledgeable and lead 1½hr. tours. Accommodations in the area are geared toward agrotourism. To get to the site, take a bus marked Caizah. 10-15min., US$0.35. Get off when you see the black and white sign. (☎592 5397. Open daily 7am-8:30pm. Free. Donations accepted.)*

LAS LAGUNAS. Two placid lagoons popular with migrating birds, are only 5km southwest of town. Many families frequent the lagoons to relax, picnic, or hike the lakeside trails. Suitable swimming holes are hard to find, but the river that cuts through the area, Río Colorado, passes by a couple. *(Continue on the main road a few blocks west of the main intersection (the road after the turnoff for Motel California), and turn left at the road where a sign points to the airport. Follow signs all the way down this road until you see the lakes. You can also take a taxi (US$2 each way). Hikers can soak their bunions in the medicinal hot springs of Los Pozos, 19km from Volcán. To get to Los Pozos, take the Río Sereno bus and ask the driver when to get off. Right after Silla de Pando, a large hill, you'll make a sharp right off the main road; continue on this road until the end, keeping left at three forks. 3.5km, about a 2hr. walk. It's easier to take a 4WD taxi US$35, which will wait to bring you back; or, hire a guide. No signs mark the way and generally nobody's around to point you in the right direction.)*

ARTE CRUZ. This is the studio of local artist José Cruz, who specializes in wood carving, sculpture, and crystal etching. *(South of town 3km on the main road, accessible by taxi US$2 or any bus heading toward David. Open W-Su 8am-noon and 1:30-6pm.)*

MACHO DE MONTE. An amazing gorge where orchids and birds abound, it has yet to be discovered by tourists, but many locals consider it their favorite natural getaway. The nearby *mirador* is private property, but you can descend into the gorge for the views of the rapids rushing through it. Some picnic and swim in the basin, but since the gorge is isolated, exercise extreme caution. Some wooden planks and fences have been put in place to keep visitors from danger. *(From Volcán, hop on a David-bound bus and ask to get off in Cuesta de Piedra. US$0.65, 15min. Then grab a taxi to Macho de Monte US$1.50-2 or ask locals about the bus that passes about every 2hr. on its way to Concepción US$0.50, 20min. If you take the bus, make sure to ask the driver to let you off at the right time. Both the bus and the taxi will drop you off at a bridge 50m above the river. From here, various hikes encircle the gorge and lead to its basin.)*

CERRO PUNTA

Twenty kilometers north of Volcán, tiny Cerro Punta (pop. 6860), is tucked in a valley between Volcán Barú and the Cordillera de Talamanca. The village is surrounded by beautiful mountains dotted with plantations; a bit farther off is a pristine cloud forest. It was originally settled by Swiss immigrants, as the architecture attests. At almost 2000m, Cerro Punta's cool climate and picturesque scenery provide an ideal base for exploring the nearby national parks of Volcán Barú and La Amistad. The nearby farming villages of Guadalupe (2km north), Las Nubes (3km west), and Nueva Suiza (1km south) are equally charming.

The main road comes in from Volcán and continues to **Guadalupe** a few kilometers north (also to **Respingo** and **Parque Nacional Volcán Barú**). At the main intersection, just north of the police station, a road turns left into the countryside, heading west to the village of **Las Nubes** at the entrance to **Parque Internacional La Amistad** (see below). Little yellow Ruta Urbana **buses** stop at the main intersection (US$0.25) and provide the best transportation around, taking you almost anywhere. Schedules vary, but buses pass by in either direction every 15min. Buses head to **David** (2hr., every 15min. 5am-8pm, US$2.65) via **Volcán** (30min., US$1).

All vital services are within a block of the main intersection, except the closest **bank**, in Volcán. Guides are hard to come by—it's better to arrange one in Volcán. **Supercentro Cerro Punta** is south of the intersection on the main road (open Su-F 8am-10pm, Sa 8am-midnight). The **police** station (☎771 2013; emergency ☎104) is at the intersection, and **Farmacia Zarina** is on the left a block west of the intersection on the road to Las Nubes. (☎771 2012. Open M-Sa 8am-8pm, Su 11am-7pm.) **Medical attention** can be received at the **Centro de Salud,** across the street from

Zarina. (☎771 2159. Open M-F 7am-3pm.) For phone calls, **public telephones** are in front of the police station and in front of the Centro de Salud. The **post office** is two doors to the left of the police. (☎771 2052. Open M-F 7am-6pm, Sa 8am-5pm.)

The best housing might be in nearby parks, which have beds, showers, and cooking facilities. For info, head to the ranger stations, the closest of which are at Respingo and at the entrance to Parque La Amistad. Locals recognize the area's lack of budget accommodations and often open their homes to lone travelers. A few kilometers to the north in Guadalupe (ask the driver when to get off the bus) is the ⬛**Hotel Los Quetzales** ❷, with luxurious rooms that have phones, hot water, queen-sized beds, small sofas, and some bathtubs. Newly-built dormitories in a separate building across the playground have the feel of the rest of the hotel, only without making a dent in your wallet. Inquire about transportation to their **Cloud Forest Retreat** ❺, phenomenal cabins actually located in the cloud forest 20min. away. Quetzals are no longer elusive here, as they appear almost daily late November to April, and frequently the rest of the year. Guides lead tours into the Parque Nacional Barú, and hiking equipment is available to rent. (☎771 2182; www.losquetzales.com. Continental breakfast included at the hotel. Dorms divided by gender, US$12 per person. Hotel US$50, with bathtub US$60. Cabins for 6-8 people US$125-$150. AmEx/MC/V.) The cheapest accommodation in Cerro Punta proper is the comfortable **Pensión Eterna Primavera** ❶, a few minutes west of the intersection on the road to Las Nubes, on the right in the blue and white house. Marked only by a small sign that reads "La Primavera," the house has four rooms and a well-kept garden. (Double with hot communal bath US$12.50; triple with private bath US$15.50; quad US$20.)

🄲 **FOOD.** There are a couple of *típico* restaurants around the intersection in Cerro Punta. **Restaurante Anthony** ❶, 100m west of the intersection on the road to Las Nubes, serves heaping plates of *comida corriente* for US$1.75—a cheap and reliable, though not outstanding, option. (Open M-Sa 6:30am-7pm.) For a taste of the sweet strawberries grown all over Cerro Punta, visit **Fresas "El Pariente"** ❶ and order the strawberries with cream (US$1.25). For US$1, you can also go see the strawberry plantations behind the store and go up the mirador for a great view of all the various mountain plantations. (☎771 1034. Open daily 9am-6pm.)

🔼 PARQUE INTERNACIONAL LA AMISTAD

To reach the ranger station, take a Ruta Urbana bus from Cerro Punta to Las Nubes (15min., US$0.50), then walk 30min. uphill. During the rainy season, buses don't run often, in which case a taxi is US$1-$3. Park admission US$3.

Parque Internacional La Amistad, together with its adjoining Costa Rican sister park, form **La Amistad Biosphere Reserve**, the largest protected area in Central America. The reserve is mostly undeveloped—the facilities on the Panamanian side consist of a small ranger station and a few trails near Cerro Punta and Wetzo, in Bocas del Toro province (p. 669). In addition to the famed elusive quetzal, visitors may lay eyes on jaguars, pumas, tapirs, snakes, frogs, and butterflies. Most of the park is in Bocas del Toro province, but Chiriquí houses the park offices and the easiest access to the park on the Panamanian side, with clean trails supported by wooden stairs, bridges, and stepping blocks.

The **trails** at the ranger station near Cerro Punta are representative of what can be found further inside the park. The best way to enjoy La Amistad is on an expedition to the beautifully untouched forest of the park's interior; talk to rangers for arrangements. You can also enter the park from the Costa Rican side. The four main trails on the Panamanian side, which are extremely well maintained, leave from right next to the ranger station. **Sendero El Retoño**, an easy trail with primary-forest views, cuts a circular path through secondary forest (2km, 1hr.). If you take a right onto a small trail 500m after the start of this *sendero*, you will hit a series of abandoned barracks built by Noriega's military. **Sendero La Cascada**, a difficult but more rewarding trail, climbs along an old cattle path through forest to the Mirador La Nevera (2500m) and gorgeous views of the nearby mountains, including the very imposing Volcán Barú. Fifteen minutes later, you will reach the views of Mirador El Barranco (2488m). From here you can see the mountain ranges 360 degrees around the park, including the Cerro Cordillera, Cerro Picacho, Cerro Derrumbe, and Cerro Respingo. Finally, you will reach a serene waterfall (2.7km, 2hr. round-trip). The third and fourth trails are short easy loops (20 and 45min. respectively), the larger of which is ideal for birdwatching. Talk to rangers about longer hikes—you'll need a guide and machete. **Guides** are available through the **Hotel Los Quetzales** (☎771 2182), the Grupo Ecoturístico La Amistad in Las Nubes, Amigos del PILA in Guadalupe, or FUNDICEP (☎771 2171). Rangers are reluctant to guide tourists, but have maps at the station and will give clear directions to hikers.

The **ranger station** has sheetless beds, a kitchen, bathrooms with cold water, and a toasty fireplace. You can **camp** outside the station or anywhere in the park. (Lodging per person or camping per tent US$5.) It gets chilly at night; bring a sleeping bag. For more info, contact ANAM in David (☎775 3163) or FUNDICEP in Cerro Punta (☎771 2171). **Los Quetzales Cloud Forest Retreat**, mentioned above under Cerro Punta (p. 667), is a fantastic camp-out at the border of the park.

BOCAS DEL TORO PROVINCE

North of Chiriquí Province, Bocas del Toro, (pop. 89, 260), is the shared name of the province, archipelago, and provincial capital. Drawing travelers with an entirely different siren song than its southern neighbor, Bocas del Toro doesn't promise rugged high-altitude thrills or posh high-priced resorts of neighboring islands, but rather a Caribbean allure. If you're arriving from the interior or from the Pacific coast, you'll hear Spanish give way to a dense mix of English creole and indigenous languages (known as *guari-guari*), and see rugged forests and ranch-lands ease into beaches, mangroves, and sea-warm docks that frame island life.

Once a port of entrance for immigrants and money due to the prosperous 19th century banana industry, the archipelago, though still home to the Ngöbe (NO-beh), Bribrí, and Naso tribes, now attracts foreigners with its natural wonders: deserted, white sand islands, coral-rich underwater views (with over 58 species), hikes through dense untouched vegetation, and great surfing spots are all boat rides away. In addition to native peoples, inhabitants include a mix of Latino, and Afro-Caribbean peoples. Many islands, reflecting the local multi-lingual stew and Columbus' overzealous naming practices, have more than one name.

The archipelago is made up of six large islands (Colón, Bastimentos, Cristóbal, Popa, Cayo Nancy and Cayo Carenero) and many smaller ones. Called "Bocas Isla," by the *bocatoreños*, charming Isla Colón is the main base for visiting the archipelago. Besides the town of Bocas itself, **Isla Colón** has a few other tiny towns (notably Boca del Drago on the opposite side) and plenty of natural attractions. The mainland, including half of Parque Internacional La Amistad, teems with wild-life and spooky swamps, and is perfect for hardcore exploration. Weather here changes quickly and dramatically. It's drier mid-August through mid-November and mid-January through mid-March, but expect rain at least once a week during the rest of the year. However, fear not: after a quick tropical rain, the sky will clear up to a hot—albeit humid—sunny day.

BOCAS DEL TORO AND ISLA COLÓN

Bocas (pop. 4300) is the essence of small-town Caribbean life, seamlessly melding a welcoming atmosphere of easy aimlessness with the energy and drive of a tightly knit community. The warm and welcoming people, along with the Caribbean-influenced wooden architecture and fresh seafood straight from the water all make for the perfect vacationers' backdrop. Isla Colón is full of activity, but before getting on a boat to another island, throw your watch off the ferry and get ready for real relaxation—breathe deeply, slice open a mango, and let the sea and the palms calm you. Ambitious visitors can work a few side trips during their stay, including Isla Bastimentos, Boca del Drago, and other nearby islands.

⌐ TRANSPORTATION

Flights: The airport is on Av. F, C. 6. From the park, walk a block north and a couple of blocks west. Aeroperlas (☎757 9341; open M-Sa 7am-5pm, Su 7:30am-5pm) has daily flights to **Panama City** (M-F 9am, 2:30pm; Sa 8:10am, 4:50pm; Su 9:30am, 4:50pm; US$57.75) and **David** (M-F 9:40am, US$31.50) via **Changuinola** only if the demand is high enough (US$13.65). Mapiex Aero (☎757 9841. Open M-Sa 6am-6pm, Su 9am-6pm) runs daily to **Panama City** via **Changuinola** for the same prices. If you're a student, ask about discounts, as it's possible to receive as much as 50% off.

Water Taxis: Bocas Marine Tours (☎757 9033), on C. 3 between Av. B and C, and Taxi 25 (☎757 9028), next to the police station on C. 1, have water taxis almost every hr. to **Almirante** (30min., 6am-6pm, US$3 one-way). Bocas Marine Tours also has boats to **Changuinola** that pass through **Boca de Drago** (1 hr., 8 boats 7am-5:30pm, US$5). Because of the new road between Almirante and Chiriquí Grande, there are no boats from Chiriquí Grande.

Ferry: The ferry (☎615 6674 or 261 0350) leaves from the dock at the southern end of C. 3 for **Almirante** (W 5pm, Th-Su 4pm, US$1.50).

Local Boats: Locals with *botes* hang out at the **public docks** south of the police station or at the Bocas Marine Tours **pier** on C. 3 (especially in the morning). Fares are negotiable, though the price to Old Bank on Isla Bastimentos is set (US$2).

◼◼ 🛈 ORIENTATION AND PRACTICAL INFORMATION

Tiny Bocas is laid out in an L-shaped grid; numbered *calles* run north-south and lettered *avenidas* run east-west. With the docks at your back, north is to the right and south to the left. Just about everything is on **Calle 3**, the main street, or on **Calle 1**, further east. The water cuts across the grid from C. 3 at the south end of town to C. 1 at the east end. A small park lies between C. 2 and 3 and Av. D and F. **Av. G**, at the northern end of town, is the only route out to the rest of the island. Billboard maps are posted around town.

Immigration: (☎757 9263), in the government building north of the *parque*. Open M-F 9am-noon and 12:30-3pm.

Tourist Information: IPAT (☎757 9642), near the police station, in a large yellow house on C. 1, has a small but very educational exhibit about the history and ecology of Bocas. Cheap Internet access (US$1.50 per hr., students US$0.75; available 10am-4:30pm). Open M-F 8:30am-4:30pm.

Banks: Banco Nacional, Av. F, C. 1/2, a block north and 1½ blocks east of the park. Cashes traveler's checks. Open M-F 8am-2pm, Sa 9am-noon. 24hr. **ATM** right next to the bank.

Laundry: Don Chicho's restaurant on C. 3, across from the *parque* (Wash and dry US$3.30). **Lavamatico** on Av. G. (US$3).

Supermarkets: Mini Super Isla Colón, on C. 3 to the south of the *parque* (Open M-Sa 7:30am-11pm, Su 8am-10pm). Scattered fruit and vegetable markets on C. 3, just south of the *parque*.

Police: (☎757 9217, emergency 104), on C. 1 by the water, next to the IPAT.

Hospital: (☎757 9201), on Av. H, a few blocks west of town. 24hr. emergency.

Internet Access: Boc@s Internet Cafe (☎757 9390), next to the Mini Super Isla Colón on C. 3 has fast connections and many computers (US$2 per hr., open daily 8am-10pm). **Don Chicho's** (☎757 9838), across from the *parque* on C. 3, is a little slow. (US$2 per hr., open M-F 8am-9pm, Sa-Su 9am-7pm). Access also at the **IPAT** office (see above).

Post Office: in the government building just north of the *parque*.

▐ ACCOMMODATIONS

PANAMA

Bocas is strewn with tons of excellent, inexpensive hotels (US$5-$10), but they fill up in high season as prices increase (Nov.-Apr.; make reservations in advance). There are a number of resorts that offer breezy rooms; another option for the independent is to ask around for a house or small family establishment that rents rooms; try C. 3 or around the northern corner along Avenidas G and H.

▨ **Casa Max** (☎757 9120), on Av. G 50m west of C. 3, has perfected the high-end model of the classic backpacker hostel. Live the sweet life in the multi-colored hammocks and dreamy rooms of this "old Caribbean house dressed in a new coat." Book exchange and common stereo; private baths; fruit and coffee in the morning. Singles US$22; doubles US$25-$27.50; triples US$33. ❸

▨ **Mondo Taitú** (☎757 9425), across from Casa Max on Av. G. If Casa Max perfects the fancy side of backpacker lodging, friendly and communal Modo Taitú does the same for the budget set. Kitchen facilities available. Dorm US$7 per person; private doubles US$16. ❶

Hospedaje Heike (☎757 9708), centrally located on C. 3 across from the *parque*. A great option with comfortable, attractive rooms on the 2nd fl., a communal veranda, and a kitchen. Two shared bathrooms. Singles US$7, doubles US$12.❶

Hotel Las Brisas (☎757 9248; bendi69@yahoo.com), on the northern end of C. 3 is a "botel" (a hotel by the water) with spacious rooms, A/C, cable, and private hot bath. Boats will pick you up and drop you off right at the deck of the hotel, making it an excellent place for your own low-key party at night. Doubles US$22-$35. ❸

Hostal Bocas Caribe (☎757 9154; hotelbocascaribe@hotmail.com), on C. 3 across from Bocas Marine Tours, offers simple rooms for the cheapest rates in Bocas. Surfers and backpackers hang out on the veranda looking at the great view of the water. Dorms US$5-$6 (depending on the season); singles with private bath US$7-$9. ❶

◖▨ FOOD

Restaurants, almost all on C. 3 or just off of it, range from *típico* to classy Italian, though they tend toward more expensive than most in the interior of Panama. Lots of *Bocatareño* food, including seafood with spicy coconut-lime juice flavoring and plantains that is said to have some Thai influence, is served. Bocas doesn't have clean tap water, but some places have filters. To paraphrase the advice of the Peace Corps: peel it, wash it, cook it, or vom-it.

■ **The Reef** (☎ 757 9021), at the far southern end of C. 3, serves tasty *bocatareño* food right by the sea. Excellent seafood meals accompanied by rice, potatoes, or *patacones* are quickly consumed for US$5-$7. After 8pm or so, the restaurant shifts into bar mode. Open daily 7am-midnight. ❷

Restaurante Gourmet Criollo Desuze, across from Bocas Marine Tours. According to locals, Desuze serves the best creole food on the island. The chef works mostly alone, so service is somewhat slow, but the wait is worth it. Meals include lobster, shrimp, or octopus US$5-$10. Open daily for dinner only. ❸

La Ballena (☎ 757 9089), on Av. F, just off C. 3, serves the best authentic Italian food known on the island with an outstanding collection of wines, matched with affordable prices. La Ballena imports the food, the cooks, and the owners directly from Italy. Dinners, from butterfly pastas to lobster risotto US$15-$20. Reservations necessary during high season. Open daily 8-11:30am, noon-2:30pm, and 7-10pm. ❺

Buena Vista Deli & Bar (takeout ☎ 757 9638), next to Starfleet. A foreigner favorite, with great sandwiches (US$4.50-5), veggie treats, filtered water and ice, DirecTV athletics, mellow music, and mean margaritas (US$3.50). Open M, W-Su noon-10pm. ❷

◪ NIGHTLIFE

The bar scene, like everything else in Bocas town, swells in the winter months (especially around Christmas). But even the rainy summer nights bring an amiable mix of locals, tourists, and expats out to the dockside *cabañas* and comfortable pool halls. Things generally pick up (if they pick up at all) around 9 or 10pm and run until 1 or 2am. Sunday nights are often quiet. On C. 3, across from Hospedaje EYL, **Bar El Encanto** attracts more locals than foreigners with its reliable out-pouring of thunderous dance hall and *cumbia*. On C. 1, near Taxi 25, ◪**Barco Hundido** (aka Wreck Deck) keeps the night alive; it has been the hippest hang-out in town for a long time. The boardwalk surrounds a sea-water pool, around which people dance all night. If lucky, you might catch the **Beach Boys de Bastimentos**, a local calypso band rumored to have once played for 15 hr. straight.

◉ SIGHTS AROUND THE ISLAND

From Bocas town, Av. H leads west across a small isthmus to the main body of the island. From here, the road forks; the left side leads 15km through the middle of the island past La Gruta to Boca del Drago and the right fork follows the eastern coast, passing Big Creek, Punta Puss Head, Playa Paunch, and Playa Bluff along the way. Playa Paunch and Playa Bluff are good surfing spots. Many of these beaches are infested with *chitras* (tiny sandflies with an irritating bite), especially in the late afternoon. Walking and biking are the cheapest transportation options around the island, but roads are alternately bumpy and muddy—bring sturdy shoes or a well-maintained bike, especially after rain.

EASTERN BEACHES. The best of these beaches is relatively *chitra*-free **Playa Bluff**. The sand beach stretches almost 2km, with good surfing and casual swimming on smaller-wave days. Between March and September (especially June-July), the beach attracts **sea turtles** laying their eggs. To arrange a trip to see nesting turtles on the island's eastern coast, go to the CARIBARO office, 2 blocks north of the park on C. 3, across from the church in an unmarked green-and-yellow building. *(Trips depart 8pm or midnight; stop by earlier in the day. Office is sporadically closed June-Aug. Playa Bluff is about 8km north of Bocas town; biking takes about 45min.)*

BOCA DEL DRAGO. On the western side of the island, 8km past La Gruta on a hilly road, the little town of Boca del Drago maintains a slow pace. Here you'll find beautiful beaches and a coral reef walkable at low tide. The town has lodging and food, but no services. (*Look left near the end of the road for Cabañas Estefany 2, where most cabins have their own kitchen, bath, and mosquito nets. From May 15 to August 15, they are generally rented out to a school program, but you may be able to scrounge an extra room or camp on the property. ☎618-3155 or 604-5623. Ask for Chino or Fátima. Double with shared bath US$15; quad US$25; 2-person cabaña US$28; 8-person room US$55. Reservations recommended. Next door is the gringo-tour favorite Restaurante Yarisnori 2, which also rents snorkel gear and a paddle boat. ☎615-5580. Típico ceviche US$3 and other seafood US$7-$10. Open M, W-Su 7:30-9:30am and noon-7:30pm.*)

ISLA DE PÁJAROS OR SWAN CAYE, WRECK ROCK AND SAIL ROCK. About 15min. by *bote* from Boca del Drago, **Isla de Pájaros**, or **Swan Caye**, attracts hundreds of seabirds which circle a huge rock and a few hardy trees. There's a coral reef with excellent deep-water snorkeling right off Isla de Pájaros, although the water isn't always clear, particularly after rain. Tour operators in Bocas all offer trips here. Just past Swan Caye are two smaller rocky islands: **Wreck Rock**, which looks like the wreck of a ship, and **Sail Rock**, a phallic rock sticking straight out of the water. (*By water, the best way to get to Boca del Drago is to take a water taxi that goes to Changuinola at Bocas Marine Tours; tell the driver you're going to Boca del Drago. 20 min., US$3. A pricier option is to hire a boat for the day—a trip to Boca del Drago and Isla de Pájaros costs US$25. A taxi between Boca del Drago and Bocas del Toro runs round-trip US$25. There's also a bus that leaves Drago at 7:30am, waits in front of the mercado in Bocas, and returns to Drago at about 2pm. 1 hr., US$2 each way. If there are a few people who want to go, you might be able to convince the driver to make another run.*)

LA GRUTA CAVE. A small cave with plenty of bats and bat guano, **La Gruta** is considered a religious shrine and is the site of an annual pilgrimage celebrating Nuestra Señora de la Gruta, the Virgen del Carmen. A torchlight parade down C. 3 takes place every July 16th in celebration of the Virgin; the pilgrimage to her cave happens the following Sunday. (*La Colonia Santeña, where a trail leads to the cave, is about a 45min. bike ride from town. Bring a flashlight and good boots.*)

🔲 🐟 WATERSPORTS AND GUIDED TOURS

DIVING AND SNORKELING AROUND THE ISLAND. In a local economy almost entirely dependent on tourism, nearly every hotel, restaurant, dock, shack, and patch of grass offers some form of tour or rental. These listings are an overview of what's available, focusing on a few unique or especially dependable businesses.

The **Playground** is an open-water dive just 5min. from Bocas town with tons of standard reef fish (angels, damsels, butterflyfish, hamlets, and triggerfish) as well as the occasional giant moray eel. **Big Bank** is for advanced divers, with coral formations as deep as 40m that eagle rays, jewfish, and standard reef fish call home. **Hospital Point,** on Cayo Nancy, is a shallow wall dive home to scorpionfish, toadfish, octopi and Giant Brain coral. **Dolphin Rock,** another open-water dive, has some of the largest, brightest schools of fish around, including parrotfish and barracuda. Also ask about **Bahía Bocatorito,** south of Isla Cristóbal, directly south of Bocas town, to see **bottle-nose dolphins** year-round.

For **diving,** the best rental/tour operator is PADI-certified **Starfleet Eco-Adventures** (☎/fax 757 9630), on C. 1 where it curves east at the southern end of town. A 2-tank dive costs US$450, including boat and all equipment. A PADI open water certification course is also offered. (3-4 days including lunch about US$205, half/full-day crash course US$65-$85.) Dives also vary depending on the time of year, time of day, and weather—though operators try to arrange your choice. For **snorkeling,** most dive shops rent gear (US$5-$8 per day) and run tours (US$15-$20, equipment included). Some options are: **J & J and Transparente Boat Tours** (☎757 9915; transparentetours@hotmail.com), Bocas Water Sports (☎/fax 757 9541; www.bocaswatersports.com), and a particularly knowledgeable guide, Christian, at **Captain Christian's Boat Tours** (☎620 5130; www.ccboattours.com). Local boat owners who hang out by the docks of Bocas Marine Tours on C. 3 are often cheaper than tour companies—try to bargain a little.

BIKE, MOTORCYCLE, AND BOAT RENTALS. Consider exploring via alternative modes of transportation. If opting for a bike or motorcycle, be sure to check bikes for quality. You can rent **bikes** at **Spanish by the Sea Language School,** behind the Hotel Bahía at the southern end of C. 4 (US$5 per day, if you're not staying there you will have to leave a deposit and an ID) or at the stand near Modo Taitú on Av. G. Rent **kayaks** at **Bocas Water Sports,** across from the Hotel Bahía, (US$10 for single kayak per half day, US$12 for double kayak.) A few beat-up **motorcycles,** dirt bikes, and surf boards can be rented on a patch of grass next to the handicrafts stands across from the *parque* on C. 3. (Bikes US$8 per day, motorcycles US$8 per hr., surfboards US$2 per hr.)

OTHER TOURS. Many of the snorkeling tour shops offer half- and full-day **jungle tours** on the mainland. **Ancon Expeditions** (☎757 9600; www.anconexpeditions.com), at the northern end of C. 3, offers more scientific tours of the snorkel and **wildlife sites;** many are guided by botanists and biologists. (Bastimentos National Park tour, 1 day, US$12-$72 depending on group size.) Ancon can also connect you with **Eliseo Vargas** (☎620 0192; turismonaso_odesem@hotmail.com), who leads day trips up an inland river to a **Teribe Indian village** ($70 per person).

ISLA BASTIMENTOS

For a little less of the touristy, gringo-esque flavor of Bocas, and more Caribbean authenticity, head to Bastimentos (pop. 1344) a mere 10min. from Bocas. Here you'll find the small village **Old Bank** (where most boats arrive); kilometers of beautiful, deserted beaches; a Ngöbe village; and **Parque Nacional Marino Isla Bastimentos,** the region's largest and most valued protected natural area. In fair weather, Bastimentos hosts a party at the **Cantina La Feria**—famous "Blue Monday," which attracts Bocas locals and foreigners alike—ask in Bocas town for the latest.

OLD BANK

The village of Old Bank (also known as **Bastimentos**) has no roads, only a semi-paved 1km footpath running along the water. With your back to the water, east is to your right and west to your left. The little park is toward the western end, as are most of the docks, where you can catch a *bote* to Bocas del Toro.

Getting to Isla Bastimentos from **Bocas del Toro** is easy. Local boats leave from the pier of Bocas Marine Tours in C. 3 and head to Old Bank (more frequent in the morning, 6am-6pm, US$2). To reach **Cayos Zapatillas** or the other side of the island your best bet is one of the tour operators. An equally dependable option is to ask around near the docks for a boat—willing independent operators are everywhere. Agree on a fare beforehand. All the accommodations in town are fairly wallet-friendly, though facilities vary widely. **Pensión "Tío Tom" Bastimentos ❷,** near the park in a green building with a red roof, has pleasant wooden rooms on stilts over the water. "Tío Tom" usually cooks family dinners (often veggie-friendly) that everybody loves. (☎/fax 757 9831; tomina@hotmail.com. Singles US$10; doubles US$10, in high season US$12, with private bath US$20; each additional person $7.)

Pelícano Cabinas ❷, a particularly private accommodation at the far eastern end of the path, has the nicest rooms and a restaurant with excellent pizza for US$4-$6. (☎757 9830. Singles US$12; doubles US$16; triple with bunk beds US$18.)

The island's beautiful beaches lie in a string on the northern and eastern coasts and are connected by trails. To get to **Playa Primera**, take the path (marked with a sign for "1st Beach") that branches inland near the eastern end of Old Bank's main cement path, and proceed for 20min. The next beach to the east is **Playa Segunda**, also known as Red Frog Beach for the little red frogs found hopping only here (harder to spot on sunny days). This is a favorite tour destination from Bocas, and a good surfing spot during the dry season (30-40min. walking from Playa Primera), though after rain take a boat to avoid the long walk through the mud (US$2). Boats leave from the "muelle principal" which is close to "Tío Tom" and connected to the Mini Super Adonis. Two beaches farther is **Playa Cuarto**, one of the best beaches in the entire archipelago. Also known as Ola Chica or Don Polo, the eastern end of the beach is sheltered by **Wild Cane Key**, a small offshore island. For more specific directions to get here, talk to Don Polo, a Bocas fixture who cooks delicious seafood meals right by the water in a small spot he owns. Beware: extremely **strong currents** make swimming dangerous in all of these beaches.

At the opposite end of the island from the town of Old Bank lies **Punta Vieja**, a secluded beach with astonishingly clear water and awesome snorkeling. In addition to the breath-taking reef right out front and the nearby Ngöbe village of **Salt Creek**, many turtles nest here during the night. Tour operators in Bocas generally run tours to both the reef and Salt Creek (US$15-$25).

PARQUE NACIONAL MARINO ISLA BASTIMENTOS

After a 3hr. hike along the beach and trails from Old Bank, you'll reach the spectacular 14km **Playa Larga**, an important **turtle nesting** site. The beach holds a ranger station and an entrance to **Parque Nacional Marino Isla**, the interior of Isla Bastimentos, the extensive mangrove swamps on the island's western side, and the two **Cayos Zapatillas** farther out in the ocean to the southeast. The inland forest on Isla Bastimentos is home to fantastic wildlife, and the southern of the two Cayos Zapatillas has a forest trail that leads to golden beaches and underwater cave formations. The crowded ranger stations on the island and on the southern Cayo Zapatillas both have simple **refugios** and allow **camping.** There are no facilities: bring everything you need, including mosquito nets (or heavy-duty repellent), and something to purify water. You no longer need to get a permit from ANAM. Park rangers guide for no fee, although a tip is expected. Talk to the Ancon office at the Bocas Inn (see **Watersports and Guided Tours,** above) for info on turtle-watching. (Camping US$5 per person. Park admission US$10.)

BEACHES NEAR OLD BANK

ISLA CARENERO. Isla Carenero is just a few hundred meters east of the docks on C. 3 in Bocas. You can stop at Carenero on the way back from a tour around the islands to enjoy a calm meal or you can get a boat ride there from a local in Isla Colón, which should be US$0.50-1. There are two good seafood **restaurants** are found on the island along the beach, **Restaurante Pargo Rojo** (☎757 9649; meals US$4-$12 with a different special every night; open daily starting at 5 or 6pm), and Buccaneer Bar and Grill (☎757 9137; meals US$4-$10; open daily 8am-9pm). Pargo Rojo will get you at the public dock in Bocas if you call. To get back, ask at the restaurants or stand on the dock and wave to attract passing boats. For groups, Pargo Rojo also offers good deals on *cabañas* for three people (US$30) and for up to six people (US$50), although prices vary depending on the season. The eastern end of Carenero has a small point with decent snorkeling and a few good surf breaks.

CAYO NANCY. Cayo Nancy (population 4020) is famous for **Hospital Point,** named after the United Fruit Company hospital located there when the company had its headquarters in Bocas del Toro island. One of the best, most accessible snorkeling spots, here you'll find a variety of corals, some barely submerged, others 100 ft. deep, and enough bright fish to keep you ooh-ing and aah-ing all day. Any *bote* can transport you, but bring your own snorkeling gear. There are a few good places to snorkel in the protected waters between Bocas, Isla Carenero, Isla Bastimentos, and Cayo Nancy. If you go by private boat, ask the driver to wait rather than return, as these are open-water sites.

ALMIRANTE

People visit small, run-down Almirante either to hop a boat out to the Bocas del Toro archipelago, or to take a bus to Changuinola or David. Life here revolves around bananas; trains bring fruit from Changuinola to be transported into banana ships. There's not much to do in town, so if you have time to kill before your next ride, get away from the center and go enjoy the view at the Muelle de Almirante.

From the terminal, which has a few unsavory characters lingering around, **buses** leave for **Changuinola** (30min., every 20min. 6am-9pm, US$1) and **David** (4hr., every 45min. 4:30am-7pm, US$8). A more colorful, though less luxurious, route to Changuinola is to jump on the **Banana Train.** This rattling machine leaves from the tracks between the terminal and the water-taxi docks; it is a great way to get to know all the locals. (2hr.; 6:30 and 10am, but likely to vary; US$0.40.) Two **water taxi** companies compete to take passengers to Bocas del Toro: Taxi 25 (☎758 3498; 30min., running every 30min. 6am-6pm, US$3) and Bocas Marine Tours (☎758 4085; every hr. or when boats are full 6am-6:30pm; US$3). For those with more time than money, a **ferry** leaves from the opposite side of town (☎615 6674 or 261 0350; 1½hr; W-Su 9am; US$1.50). For the ferry, turn right at the T across the tracks and take the first left. Follow that road along the tracks and turn right just before the road crosses back over the tracks. **Taxis** charge US$0.50 to run from the bus station to the water-taxi docks; walking takes about 10-15min.

From the **bus terminal,** head left down the main road and then bear left on a dirt track over the railroad at the sign "Taxis Marítimos." To get to the main street from the **dock,** face away from the water and go left along the gravel road until the dirt path veers right: the bus terminal is to the right. To get to **Banco Nacional de Panamá,** bear right at the streets that form a T behind the bus terminal, cross the train tracks, turn left at the first street, and continue 1 block. (☎758 3718. Open M-F 9am-3pm, Sa 9am-noon.) The **hospital** (☎758 3745) is in front of the bank. **Farmacia San Vicente** is 2 blocks down after you bear right at the T coming from the terminal. (☎758 3535. Open M-Sa 8am-8pm, Su 9am-5pm). To reach the **police station** (☎ 758 3721 or 104 for emergency), start off toward the ferry but cross the tracks instead of turning off. The **immigration office** is next door. **Phones** are on the road near the bus terminal, at the post office, and in front of immigration. The **post office** is a block past the bank. (Open M-F 9am-4pm.)

Almirante has few accommodations and eating options. The cheapest place to stay is **Hostal Cristóbal Colón ❶,** one of the oldest hotels in Bocas, whose clean rooms and a wonderful host family only add to its coziness. To get here, take a right when facing the bus terminal and then the second left. (Singles US$6; doubles US$8.50; shared bath outside.) A number of *típico* restaurants line the road between the terminal and the water taxis and snacks are also available at the taxi docks. A restaurant worth your extra time when in Almirante is **Bocas Marina ❷,** right next to the ferry, with arguably the best view of the Almirante Bay. Watch the banana ships pass by as you enjoy your deliciously inexpensive meal. (☎697 0175; meals US$3-$9, beer US$0.75. Open daily 9am-midnight.)

CHANGUINOLA

Changuinola (pop. 71,922), is hot and dirty, but since it houses the bureaucracy for the nearby Costa Rican border crossing it is a good place to run errands and complete any pending paperwork pre-border. The city survives off of merchants and banana plantations, many open for visits and tours, including a Chiquita plant.

⊡ TRANSPORTATION. The airport is at the north end of town, bearing right past the gas station and crossing the railroad tracks. Mapiex Aero (☎758 9841, open M-Sa 6am-6pm, Su 9am-6pm) and Aeroperlas (☎758 7521, www.aeroperlas.com; open M-Su 7am-5pm) have offices at the **airport** where they sell tickets. Both have flights to **Bocas del Toro** (7min., US$13.65) and to **Panama City** (1hr., 2 per day, US$58.80), and Aeroperlas flies to **David** (25min., M-F 10am, US$31.50). Changuinola has two **bus terminals**, located within 300m of each other on opposite sides of the street. **Terminal La Piquera**, next to the Shell station in the center of town, handles short-distance travel. There is no office and though the schedules vary significantly and erratically, buses are in constant supply—you shouldn't have to wait more than 30min. **Collective taxis** are parked under specific destination signs. Those to **Guabito** take 20min. and cost $1. Buses leave from the terminal to the **Costa Rican border** at Guabito (35min., every 30min. 7am-7:45pm, US$0.70); **El Silencio** (40min., every 15min. 6am-7pm, US$0.50); **Finca 44** (25min., every 30min. 5am-9pm, US$0.65) via **Almirante** (45min., US$1). **Finca 60** (referred to simply as "la sesenta"), is the newest way to get to **Isla Colon:** instead of passing through Almirante, it takes a stunning route through mangroves and canals. (15min., 5 runs between 8am and 5:30pm, US$5) **Terminal Urraca** (☎758 8127), north of Terminal La Piquera, is less chaotic though not as modern. Buses head to David (4hr., every 30min. 4am-7pm, US$8) and Panama City (10hr., 7am, US$18).

▉⃗ ORIENTATION AND PRACTICAL INFORMATION. Changuinola is strung along the road from the Guabito border in the northwest and to Almirante in the southeast. The road to Almirante curves along a traffic circle around a large white statue. The center of the town is marked by the Shell gas station, right next to the Terminal La Piquera. If you are facing the gas station from Avenida 17 de Abril, the town's main street with most hotels and restaurants, north is to your left and south to your right. The northern end of town is full of enormous inexpensive stores, while the southern end hosts expensive hotels. Outside of town, unpaved roads cut through many *fincas*, banana plantations which are referred to by number.

The **ANAM** office runs the San-San wetlands and the Wetzo entrance to **Parque Internacional La Amistad**—the out-of-the-way office provides very little info to tourists, but provides permits and entrance tickets to the park. To reach the office, head 3 blocks north of the terminal, turn left at Hotel Hong Kong, bear left, and take the first right at the mosque. (☎758 6603. Open M-F 8am-3pm.) If you've been in Panama for almost 90 days and would like to either extend your visit or cross the border, it is necessary to go to **Migración** (☎758 8651; open M-F 8am-noon and 1-3pm), at the southern end of town past Hotel Carol. If you have been in Panama for fewer than 90 days, get your passport stamped in Guabito. The Migración office is likely to move within the next year—watch for a possible new address.

Banks in Changuinola don't change Costa Rican *colones*—do that at the **Almacén Zona Libre**, a block south of bus terminal La Piquera on Avenida 17 de Abril. The rates aren't great, but Sixaola doesn't offer anything better. (☎758 8493. Open M-Sa 8am-8:30pm, Su 8am-5pm.) Across the street from the Almacén is **Banco Nacional de Panamá**, with a 24hr. Cirrus/MC/Visa **ATM**. (☎758 8445. Open M-F 8am-3pm, Sa 9am-noon.) Cash traveler's checks or get a MC/Visa cash advance at **Banistmo**, a block north of the bus terminal La Piquera. (☎758 7477. Open M-F 8am-3:30pm, Sa 9am-noon.) There's a **Western Union** at Deportes del Cid, across from Banistmo on Avenida 17. (☎758-8644; open M-Sa 8:30am-12:30pm, 1:30-5pm.) The **police** (☎758 7585, emergency 104) and **hospital** (☎758 8232) are down the paved side road in front of Almacén Zona Libre, south of La Piquera terminal. **Public phones** are scattered around the bus terminal and airport. **Foto Centro Arco Iris,** right across from the Terminal La Piquera, has fast **Internet** access in an A/C setting (☎758-8457; US$1 per hr.; open M-Sa 8am-7pm). Get passport pictures here (6 pictures, US$6). The **post office** is on the north end of town in the governmental building.

ⱤⱤ ACCOMMODATIONS AND FOOD. There are few hotels in Changuinola, and all are moderate to high priced. For this reason, unless passport paperwork must be completed, it may make more sense to skip town and continue to other spots. In any case, **Hotel Carol ❶,** 2 blocks south of the terminal La Piquera, has a common room with TV and simple rooms off a dark hallway with A/C and bath. (☎758 8731. Double US$11, with TV US$18; triple US$21/$24; quad US$28/$30.) **Hotel Changuinola ❷,** just north of the airport, is comfortable but farther out of town. (☎758 8678. Singles with fan US$12.50, with A/C US$15; doubles US$13.50, with A/C and TV US$16.50; king-size bed US$19.80.)

A few small kiosks on the main drag serve standard Panamanian fare for slightly inflated prices. If you like bakeries, **El Buen Sabor ❶,** just past Banco del Istmo in the storefront covered by foliage, sells assorted flaky, fresh-from-the-oven treats (US$0.30) clearly labeled with English translations. (☎758 8422, fax 758-7467. Open M-Sa 8am-10pm, Su 10am-9pm.) The **Refresquería ❶,** at Super La Huaca, 1 block north of the terminal La Piquera on the opposite side of the street (there are two of these supermarkets on Avenida 17; this is the one closer to the terminal), has some of the cheapest *comida corriente* in town (US$2) and delicious ice-cold chichas for US$0.30. (☎758 8461. Open M-Sa 8am-10pm, Su 8am-6pm.)

🗙 GUABITO: BORDER WITH COSTA RICA

Guabito is 16km from Changuinola (35min. by bus and 20min. by taxi); Sixaola is across the border in Costa Rica, where you'll get an entry stamp after showing your passport and an onward ticket. The Panamanian side of the border is open daily from 8am-6pm, while the Costa Rican side is open daily from 7am-5pm: the time zone difference assures that the office hours of the two coincide. Both close for lunch in their appropriate time zones (noon-12:30pm).

When you enter Costa Rica, **Sixaola** provides basic necessities and a few clothing stores sell Panama souvenirs; otherwise, most people don't waste time here before catching a bus north. Buy bus tickets with *colones* or US dollars. Buses run to **San José** (6hr.; 5, 7:30, 9:30am, 2:30pm; ¢3145) and **Limón** (3hr., 8 per day 5am-5pm, ¢1070). Some buses enter **Puerto Viejo de Talamanca** (2hr., ¢500), while the others will drop you at the intersection 5km from the town; to be certain, ask before getting on. Frequent buses cover the remaining distance (15min., ¢200). Passengers leaving Sixaola must show their papers, so don't tuck your passport away. There is no money exchange here. The nearest bank is in Bribrí (1½hr. away). For those entering Panama, frequent buses run to **Changuinola** (30min., US$0.70) until about 7pm. El Caiman Internacional and Mini Super El Poderoso, both on the left side of the border crossing, change money. A single phone sits in front of the **Aduanas** (customs), next to the migration office. The **immigration offices** (☎759 7019) are across the street from national **police** posts (☎759 7940, emergency 104), which are connected by a decrepit bridge. Guabito has no accommodations and almost no restaurants; Sixaola, just across the border, has better options.

SAN BLAS ARCHIPELAGO

The *Comarca Kuna Yala* ("Land of the Kuna", pop. 47,000), on the Caribbean coast between Colón and Colombia, is one of two distinct autonomous political regions in Panama, owned and run entirely by the region's indigenous inhabitants, the Kuna. Although they use the mainland for agriculture, most Kuna are concentrated on the islands as the near-absence of mosquitoes and wild animals makes for a healthy, safe environment. There are 50 autonomous Kuna communities, with 45 of them crowded onto only about 40 tiny islands of the 365 that make up the archipelago. With white sand beaches, coconut palms, and coral reefs, the archipelago's mostly uninhabited islands radiate calm, tropical splendor. Transportation here can be difficult and expensive, but tourism is growing in rapid but controlled bursts. Being able to experience the culture of one of Central America's most independent indigenous peoples is in and of itself worth the trip.

HISTORY

By the 1500s the Kuna had migrated into Darién from Colombia, and by the 19th century, war with the Spanish and the rival Emberá tribe had forced them onto the San Blas Islands. Here, the Spanish left them in comparative peace, but in the early 20th century, a newly independent Panama launched attempts to "civilize" the Kuna. Fed up with mistreatment, on February 25th of 1925 the Kuna revolted against the Panamanian police force in the Nele Kantule Revolution (in honor of their contemporaneous leader), and with the help of a US battleship offshore successfully gained a degree of autonomy by committing to a cessation of hostilities, and allegiance to Panama. In 1938, the security of lands for the Kuna was increased by the organization of the *comarca*, or district, and in 1952 San Blas was officially recognized by Panamanian law as self-governing. The Kuna are outside of Panamanian taxation, own the entire region, and send two representatives to the National Assembly. Even so, the older generation is fighting once again (this time without violence) to preserve traditions in the face of growing westernization. On many Kuna town congress halls a banner proclaims, "People who lose their tradition lose their soul;" but modernization is creeping in nonetheless. While the Kuna once survived by trading coconuts with Colombian ships, today the *balboa* (a.k.a. US dollar) reigns supreme, with tourists the new trading partners. As a result, the number of amenities and establishments is constantly on the rise and prices continue to increase. Despite these obvious changes, the Kuna have for the most part succeeded in preserving their culture and unique way of life.

CULTURE AND CUSTOMS

The *comarca* is governed by three *Caciques*, who are the equivalent of provincial governors and act as the elected intermediary between the Kuna and the Panamanian government. Every village has its own smaller Congress, the "*Casa de Congreso*" or gathering house that is the heart of the Kuna community. It is in this enlarged version of a Kuna house where the community celebrates religious ceremonies, resolves disputes, and makes important decisions.

The Kuna have their own language, but most speak at least some Spanish. Men typically wear western clothes, while women wear a distinctive clothing style with golden earrings, nose piercings, bright colored bracelets, and skirts with blouses featuring the famous *mola*. The *mola* is a piece of colorful cloth stitched by hand with cotton textiles featuring all kinds of designs, including animals and scenes from daily life, and even western pop culture icons. One of the most sophisticated and sought-after handicrafts in Latin America, the *mola* is sold to tourists everywhere in Kuna Yala (a small patch is US$5-$10).

With few exceptions, the Kuna live on the beach. Despite the presence of Christian missionaries, most of the Kuna maintain traditional religion. Kuna theology revolves around a divine human, Ibeorgun, sent to teach them how to live based on the principle of sharing within the community. More recent events, such as battles fought against the Emberá, the Spanish, and the Panamanian army, have become part of semi-mythic Kuna cosmology. Kuna Yala culture includes customary puberty rituals, marriage ceremonies, funeral rites, and traditional medicine. If you hang around long enough, you could run into a **chicha fuerte** feast. *Chicha fuerte* is an alcoholic drink made from sugarcane juice and maize and flavored with cacao; like the name suggests, it's not recommended for the meek. The biggest parties of the year are in February, and on the 25th, the anniversary of the 1925 Kuna revolution.

Travelers, particularly if visiting the more isolated islands, should learn about the Kuna before coming. Those arriving on an island that has no hotel first need to see the *sáhila* to ask permission to stay (an entrance fee of US$1-$3 is typically charged). Meeting the *sáhila* also provides an opportunity to ask about meals or accommodation options on the island.

■ VISITING SAN BLAS

San Blas might be too costly for the average budget traveler. Although expensive, it is one of the most remarkable places in Central America, and well worth the cost (about US$60 to fly round-trip from Panama City, and about US$35 per night). Note that tourism is developing rapidly here, so prices and facilities are subject to change. There are a number of hotels in the more populated and touristed Kuna islands (see **The Islands**, below). Since boat travel between islands is so expensive, these places—whose prices typically include meals and daily trips with some degree of flexibility—are the cheapest and best ways to see Kuna Yala. They provide a representative slice of Kuna life while incorporating some sinfully perfect beaches and snorkeling. There isn't much value in doing a highlights tour of the islands; the attractions of each are fairly similar, and picking one or two will give you a good sense of what Kuna Yala is about.

Guided tours of the archipelago are only worth the expense if you're looking for a specific bonus, such as sailing or fishing. All visitors should keep in mind that most Kuna islands (except the one your hotel is on) require visitors to pay a US$1-$5 **fee**; this may be paid at governmental offices or with the local *sáhila*. Even uninhabited islands are privately owned, and a fee may be required. There's also a rule in every inhabited island that people can't walk around with only their bathing suits on. In addition, photographers who want to take pictures of the Kuna will normally be charged US$1 per shot.

⊟ TRANSPORTATION

FLIGHTS
The simplest and cheapest way to San Blas is by plane. Many islands have airports, and one-way flights to or from Panama City range between US$31.50 (El Porvenir) and US$52.50 (Puerto Obaldía). Service is offered by **Aerotaxi** (☎ 315 7520), a subsidiary of **Aeroperlas** and **Turismo Aéreo** (☎ 315 0279), with flights typically departing at 6 or 7am in either direction. For more info, see **Panama City: Transportation**, p. 605. Since planes make multiple stops in the islands, they may be used to island-hops improvised on demand. However, you may have to wait until close to your

flight date to see what's available. Note that airports are often not on the destination island itself; you'll need to arrange for a **boat** in advance. If you make a hotel reservation, the accommodation can help with this.

BOATS

Boats that island-hop along the coast and around the islands are not considered safe, in terms of both water and crime. For these reasons, information on water transport was not updated this year. In past years a few foreigners traveling on Colombian boats have been killed or kidnapped—many boats are involved in smuggling—so avoid these in particular.

You may have to wait on an island up to a week, as there is no schedule. Negotiate with the captain and take a good look at the boat before getting on. Deposit your pack and keep valuables on your body. Food is generally included, though a place to sleep isn't; bring a hammock or inflatable pad. Catch boats to the islands from Puerto Coco Solo in **Colón**. Otherwise ask for ships leaving to San Blas at the *sarpe* (ship documents) office and negotiate with captains at the docks. An overnight ride to **El Porvenir** should cost US$10, while a ride to **Puerto Obaldía** runs US$30-$50 and takes two to seven days, depending on the number of stops. Try to haggle, but if the boat isn't going already, you won't get very far.

🏝 THE ISLANDS

The San Blas Archipelago consist of hundreds of small, tropical isles dispersed throughout the blue Caribbean waters. Often surrounded by scuba and snorkel-ideal reefs, and almost entirely isolated save a few culturally distinguished Kuna, these sandy gems make ideal getaways. In many cases, it is possible to rent an entire island; make reservations far in advance.

Heading the list of popular islands, **El Porvenir** is the farthest west in the archipelago, right next to the well-touristed **Wichub Wala** and **Nalunega**. All three are densely inhabited and quite traditional. Twenty minutes south of Nalunega, **Cartí-Sugtupu** is a slightly more developed Kuna village just across the bay from San Blas. Two hours east by speedboat are **Narganá** and **Corazón de Jesús**, the most westernized of the islands. Fifteen minutes beyond lies **Isla Tigre**, a traditional village quickly becoming a tourist hotspot. Near El Porvenir, 🏝**Achutupu** (Dog Island)—not to be confused with the other Achutupu halfway to Colombia—boasts an offshore shipwreck. Tiny and perfect **Coco Blanco**, between Achutupu and El Porvenir, is host to a new set of lodgings. **Río Sidra** and **Nusatupu** are good halfway points between Cartí and Narganá. **Tikontikí**, another traditional island, lies 45min. east of Isla Tigre by boat. **Mauki** is a group of 40 uninhabited islands farther away. **Islas Aligandi, Achutupu, Ustupo Ogobsucum, Ustupo,** and **Mulatupu,** in order from west to east, are more traditional Kuna villages, and 🏝**Kuanidup** might be the closest you'll ever get to owning your own island.

EL PORVENIR

2 morning flights to Panama City (US$31.50) leave 6-8am. Flights coming in from Panama City arrive daily around 6:30 or 7:30am. Make reservations a day in advance to fly to other islands. Go to the government building a day before your flight and put your name on the list of people leaving, especially if you haven't bought a ticket. Hotels take care of this for guests. Boats to Wichub Huala and Nalunega are arranged at the dock (usually US$1-$2, maximum US$5), though it's easier to arrange for hotel pickup. When arriving by plane, sign in with the immigration or police official who meets each flight.

El Porvenir, which consists of little more than an airstrip and a few administrative huts, is not the place to see a Kuna village. It does, however, have air service and easy access to decent hotels on Wichub Wala and Nalunega. Directly in front of the docks there's a government building with **police station, immigration office** (open daily 8am-4pm), and public **phones.** The airport serves as a **post office;** give letters to the pilot heading out on the morning flight (he'll buy stamps, if necessary) to Panama City. Electricity is available a few hours per night. The only hotel on the island is **Hotel Porvenir ❷,** practically on the airstrip, where someone from the hotel will meet you with reservations. Nightly rates include bamboo rooms with bath, three meals and daytrips for snorkeling, hiking, or sunbathing. (☎221 1397 Panama City office, ask for Mrs. Bibi. US$15 per person, US$30 with food.) The only place to eat on the island is at the hotel. (Seafood begins at US$4). To get in contact with any of the offices at the island or the hotel call the public phone and whoever answers will try to find who you need (☎299 9056).

WICHUB WALA

That there are two hotel options here demonstrates how much San Blas is finally developing a tourist infrastructure. Still beautiful, isolated, and culturally independent, Wichub is one of the more developed islands in the region. On a separate island on the way to Nalunega, waits one of the area's best hotels, the ◙**Hotel Ukuptupu ❹.** This accommodating hotel has clean, breezy bamboo rooms constructed over water, with hammocks outside, a small library of English-language books, and a small walled-in aquarium on the reef where you can pick the lobster you want for dinner. The common, natural-water baths are located outdoors. The hotel has a spacious bar with a pool table that opens whenever people stay at the hotel (Beer US$1, game of pool US$0.25). Rates include three meals and a daily tour of the islands. (☎293 8709; ukuptupu@hotmail.com. Rooms US$35-$40 per person. US$30 with ISIC. Snorkeling equipment rental, US$5 per day.) Five minutes from the public docks on the path heading east into town, **Kuna Niskua Lodge ❹** (☎259 3471), a bamboo-thatched building, offers nice rooms with all-night electricity and hammocks. The all-inclusive rate is US$35 per person, US$45 with private bath. Snorkeling equipment is US$5 per day. The island has a **health center** (open M-F 7:30am-noon, 1-3:30pm) and a community **general store** next to the public docks (open daily 6:30am-noon, 1-5pm, and 6-9pm).

NALUNEGA

Nalunega is home to the relaxing **Hotel San Blas ❹,** the oldest hotel on the archipelago, offering 28 spacious rooms in Kuna-style cabins with sand floors; a more modern building is an option. The owner, Luis Burgos, speaks English and Spanish and can provide info on the Kuna or the surrounding islands. There are plenty of hammocks and the clean, communal baths have running water. Outhouses directly over the water make the beach in front of the hotel less clean than it looks. Prices include three meals and two tours daily. (☎257 3311 in Panama City; hotelsanblas@hotmail.com. Rooms US$35 per person, US$10 without food or tours.) Even if you're not staying at Hotel San Blas, you can still go on their **tours.** (Daily 8am and 2pm. US$25 per person.) The hotel's great **food** costs as little as US$3 for lunch or dinner (lobster US$10) and US$1.50 for breakfast (coffee, bread, and eggs). The hotel also rents **snorkel equipment** (mask and flippers US$3 each per day). Another option with a local feel is **Archimedes Iglesias,** who rents a hut near his house; look for the "Pub Bar" sign off the basketball court behind Hotel San Blas. Prices start at US$7 for lodging and US$15-$20 for lodging, seafood meals, and tours; but negotiating for the final price is half the fun.

CARTÍ-SUGTUPU

Daily flights from Panama City to El Porvenir often stop at Cartí airport, which is currently closed (scheduled to open shortly). It's a 3min. boat ride away (usually arriving M-Sa around 6:30am, Su around 7:30am; US$31.50). This airport is the northern terminus of the El Llano-Cartí road, which is only barely passable even by 4WD. To reach someone on the island, call one of the public phones (☎ 299 9088, 299 9074, or 299 9002) or San Blas Adventures (see below).

Near the southern shore of the gulf that forms western San Blas, Cartí-Sugtupu (pop. 2,000) is the largest, most thickly settled and developed island in Cartí Bay. It's flanked by several smaller islands, including Cartí Tupile and Cartí Yantupu. Cartí-Sugtupu's accessibility and services make tourist visits relatively easy, yet the community remains true to traditional Kuna life. The island is crossed by two **east-west footpaths.** The **public docks** are on the north side, near the middle of the island; walk straight 10m until you come to the first main path. A minute west of the dock on this path you can find two men who give tours around San Blas. First on your right is **Ernie's Paradise Pub** (☎ 299 9088), where you can find English speaking **Ernesto,** leading daily tours for US$25; he can arrange for you to stay with a local family on the island (US$5 per night). When there are a lot of tourists on the island, Ernie opens up his house for beer (US$1), which is a good way to interact with locals. Two minutes west of the dock on this same path is the marked house of Eulogio Pérez of **San Blas Adventures** (☎ 299 9074, Panama City ☎ 262 2031; san-blasadventures@hotmail.com); he runs beach, snorkeling, and rain forest daytrips and arranges for lodging at Achutupu, perhaps the best deal available (US$25 per person per day). He speaks English and Spanish and is a good source of info on Kuna. If he's absent, his brothers or father can direct you. The town's **health center** is at the eastern end of the southern path (open M-F 7:30am-noon and 1-3:30pm, Sa-Su 9am-noon). There are **public phones** by the dock, next to the cafeteria.

Cartí-Sugtupu boasts a friendly community-run **dormitorio ❷** on the east end of town, past the hospital. The colorful building has four simple rooms centered around a sitting room; the communal bathroom is built over the ocean in the Kuna style: a toilet seat over a hole in the floor on top of the water. Reserve in advance. (☎ 299 9088; ask for Antonio Reuter or Tomás Morris. US$8 per person.) The town's **cafeteria ❶** (also owned by the community), directly next to the public dock, serves flavorless *comida* for US$1.75 and sells basic groceries (open daily 7am-10pm). Also in town is the **Kuna Museum,** 5min. east of the public dock on the northern main road; the one room is cluttered and dusty, but offers a bizarre blend of Kuna culture and eccentric personal vision in an attempt to preserve and educate about Kuna life. Owner, curator, and guide José Davies leads visitors on a 1½hr. progression through Kuna artifacts and his own illustrations of Kuna myths and rituals. Tours are in Spanish and, if necessary, broken English. (Open daily 8am-5pm, but room stays open until 9pm. US$2.)

ISLA TIGRE

Less westernized than Narganá and Corazón de Jesús, Isla Tigre approximates traditional Kuna life. The main dock is on the southern side of the island, near a cement **general store.** The two main **east-west footpaths** are straight ahead. Some 20m to the east on the first path is a **public phone** (☎ 299 9092). About 100m east on the second path is a more complete **general store.** The **airstrip** is to the west, and **Cafeteria and Cabañas Digir ❸,** serving locally famous lobster (US$6.50; open 5-11pm, earlier upon request), sits next to it. The *cabañas,* tightly wedged between the airstrip and the beach, have Western bathrooms and hammocks for sleeping (US$20). Isla Tigre is known for its dances, which erupt during *fiestas.* The biggest is the late October celebration of a former *sáhila,* with practices occurring most Friday nights for months in advance. Most nights bring festivities.

PANAMA

■ KUANIDUP

Much like gorgeous and isolated Coco Blanco, though smaller and even more private, Kuanidup is potentially a romantic paradisiacal remove—basically, it'll be your private island. To get here you can take a plane to El Porvenir or Rió Sidra and catch a connecting flight. The **hotel** will pick you up at the airstrip. It's absolutely worth the cost. (☎635 6737 or 299 9058, kuanidup@yahool.com.mx.) The only thing on the island is the hotel's basic but attractive *cabañas* built in the traditional Kuna style: they are surrounded by hammocks, tons of palm trees and beautiful beaches. No electricity is available, though the moonlight is sufficient. The clean, communal bathrooms are outside.

▼ TO COLOMBIA BY SEA

> Due to the degree of criminal activity on the waters of the Panamanian-Columbian border region, this route to Colombia is **not recommended.** For this reason, the information in this section was not updated for this edition. If you must undertake the journey, check with the Panamanian, Colombian, and your home country's government for the latest security information.

Travelers **heading to Colombia** must first get to Puerto Obaldía, either by plane or boat. Aviatur (☎315 0311) has flights from Panama City and Aerotaxi (☎315 7500) flies for the same price—call for schedules and prices. Kuna boats can occasionally be found in San Blas for high rates, though more common and potentially more dangerous are Colombian boats, most of which can be found in Colón's **Puerto Coco Solo** for around US$30. You'll have to haggle with the captain of the boat there and bring a hammock to sleep. In Puerto Obaldía, clear Panamanian and Colombian border formalities before finding a boat heading to **Zapzurro,** the first town in Colombia (US$5-$15). From Zapzurro you continue to the Colombian resort town of **Capurganá,** and from there, if possible, to **Cartagena,** a major tourist destination safely away from unrest.

DARIÉN

> Paramilitary groups, drug smugglers, and bandits, most from across the Colombian border, have a large presence in areas of Darién, and have become bolder since US patrols left in 1999. Travel is prohibitively dangerous in the regions east and southeast of Yaviza and El Real. Travelers have recently been **abducted** in the area; the last recorded murder occurred in 1994. Before traveling in Darién it is imperative to obtain current security information. In Panama City, ANAM, Ancon Expeditions, IPAT, and police are all good places to check. When you get to Darién, first **check in with the police,** who will take your passport information and advise you on how to proceed. Keep all your documents with you at all times.

The Interamerican Hwy., otherwise stretching unbroken from Alaska to Tierra del Fuego, meets its undoing in Darién, Panama's largest but least populated and poorest province. Many who come here are lured by the mystique and risk associated with crossing the dangerous Darién Gap into Colombia. *Let's Go* strongly discourages any attempt to cross the Darién Gap. **Parque Nacional Darién,** running along the entire border with Colombia, is one of the most biologically rich regions

PANAMA

in the world. Amidst the jungle on the shores of rivers such as the Sambú, Jaqué, and Tuira, live the indigenous **Emberá** and **Wounaan** peoples, who follow similar customs but differ in language. Still holding to traditional lifestyles, they wear colorful loincloths, stain their bodies bluish-black with the fruit of the *jagua* tree, and only recently have put down their poisonous blowdarts in favor of more mainstream hunting weapons. Exceptional wood carvers, the Emberá Wounaan are known for delicate handicrafts they carve out of "tagua," an ivory-colored hard nut that comes from a tree of the same name, on which they portray all kinds of animals and human beings. They are also famous for making *piraguas* (wood dugout canoes) that are considered the best in the country, even used by the Panama Canal Authority to get to hard-to-reach areas in the Canal watershed.

From **Metetí** a side road and river route lead to **La Palma**, a relatively safe gateway to the wilderness around the **Golfo de San Miguel** and the **Río Sambú**. In **Yaviza** the 400km roadless Darién Gap begins. Nearby **El Real** is the best gateway to Parque Nacional Darién. The safest, most effective, and most expensive way to visit Darién is a guided tour. **Ancon Expeditions** and **Eco-Tours de Panamá** are recommended (see **Panama City: Practical Information**, p. 608). Even without a guided tour, it is worth the money to fly into Darién. If you do fly, head straight to El Real or Sambú—Darién's towns offer nothing of interest in and of themselves.

METETÍ

Fifty kilometers shy of Yaviza along the highway from Panama City, Metetí is little more than a bump on the already bumpy road. Buses heading to **Panama City** and **Yaviza** usually stop in town every hour but they can be less frequent so some patience is required. From here, a side road leads 10km west to **Puerto Quimba** (30min., every 30min. 5:15am-6:30pm, US$1.25), where there is boat access to **La Palma**. During the rainy season, bus routes from Panama City end here; only **4WD chivitas** can continue to **Yaviza** (4hr., US$6.50). Though there isn't much to do, trails and a small cabin are under development in the **Reserva Filo del Tallo**, 248 lush hectares surrounding the road to Puerto Quimba. For reserve info, talk to Nobel Castro at the **ANAM** office (☎299 6530), just north of the junction on the highway.

You should go to the **police station** (☎299 0612) south of the junction to show your passport. At the junction, there's a **transportation center** with bus schedules. There's a **Banco Nacional** with an **ATM** across from the police station (open M-F 8am-3pm, Sa 9am-noon). The best of the three decent lodging options is **Hospedaje Las Nashiras ❶**20m down the road to Puerto Quimba, with big, airy rooms, A/C, bath, and fans. (☎299 6393. Doubles with fan US$11, with A/C US$16.) North of the highway junction, **Hotel Restaurante Felicidad ❷** has enormous, if spartan, rooms with clean baths and a restaurant below. (☎299 65544. Singles with fan US$10, with A/C US$15; doubles US$12/$17; triples US$18/23; quads with fan US$24. Breakfast US$1.25, *comida corriente* US$1.75.) There are numerous **restaurants** and **kiosks** in town. Pensión Tres Hermanos' restaurant with decent *comidas*.

LA PALMA

La Palma is not much more than a launch pad for boat trips farther south into the Gulf or down the Río Sambú. Even this is little reason to stop here though, as Sambú has its own airstrip. Aeroperlas (☎299 6651 or 315 7500 in Panama City) and Turismo Aéreo (☎315 0279), in the blue-and-white building next to the airstrip, have morning **flights** between **Panama City** and **La Palma** for US$40 (open M-Sa 8-9am and 1-4pm). Aeroperlas has flights M,.W, and F; Aeroturismo flies M, Th, and Sa. La Palma is also accessible by land. From **Metetí**, on the highway between Panama City and **Yaviza**, grab a *chivita* to **Puerto Quimba** (30min., every 30min.

5:15am-6:30pm, US$1.25), where **water taxis** jaunt across the **Río Tuira** to La Palma (40min., every 1½hr. 7:30am-6:30pm, US$2.50). Return trips from La Palma to Puerto Quimba, 5:30am-5pm. **Cargo boats** travel Panama City-La Palma irregularly.

RÍO

Farther south along the coast from Punta Patiño is the mouth of the Río Sambú. The Emberá community of Puerto Indio is the first of a string of villages along the winding, jungle-crowded river that forms the backbone of the Comarca Emberá Sambú. The voyage downriver is like entering another world. Interestingly, in the past, residents were hired by the US Army as consultants for jungle survival skills.

For a trip down the Río Sambú, arrange for a guide and a *piragua* in Sambú; Juan Murillo is highly recommended. The journey is hot and tiring, and toilets, mattresses, and potable water are almost nonexistent. The 2hr. boat ride from La Palma to Sambú runs around US$200. Turismo Aéreo flights from Panama City (departures M, W, and F at 9am; US$42) are a better option. Aeroperlas is scheduled to resume flights in mid-August 2004, call for schedules. For both airlines it's a good idea to call in advance as schedules vary depending on demand. A trip from Sambú to Pavarandó, the farthest village from Sambú, should run US$80-$90, plus food and lodging for yourself and your guide ❷ (around US$15 per person per day, unless you've brought camping supplies). Your guide will be able to set you up with some form of lodging in the villages; nonetheless, camping equipment can be a huge help. You may need to bring gasoline from Sambú to fuel your *piragua*.

◪ DAYTRIP FROM RÍO SAMBÚ: GARACHINÉ AND CASA VIEJA. A relatively inexpensive way to get a taste of the jungle is to visit Garachiné, a small town 15km southeast of the mouth of the Río Sambú. Boats make the trip from La Palma to Garachiné (1½hr., US$150). The same flights that go to Sambú go to Garachiné (US$39.90). If lucky, you might find a boat in La Palma taking passengers to Garachiné and you'll only pay around US$6. It might be hard to find a boat in Garachiné to bring you back without arranging one in advance. ANAM owns cabins near Garachiné for US$10 per night, plus a US$3 entrance fee, payable at the office in Garachiné. Make reservations in advance at ANAM offices in Panama City, Metití, or La Palma. Casa Vieja, complete with kitchen and bath, sits by the muddy beach near a web of jungle paths. It's used primarily by scientists studying the local environment. Hire an ANAM guide for the 3hr. hike to the cabin (US$10).

YAVIZA

The Interamerican Hwy. comes to an unceremonious end in Yaviza, the beginning of the infamous 400km long Darién Gap. Yaviza remains the best starting point for intrepid souls looking to cross the gap, although the trek is dangerous and currently not advisable due to civil and political unrest. It is next to impossible to find a guide willing to go. There are interesting Emberá villages near Yaviza, but they, too, are in very dangerous areas. **Buses** arrive from **Panama City** almost hourly during the dry season. During the rainy season, *chivitas* make the final leg from **Metetí** (3-4hr., usually 3 per day, US$6.50). Sometimes buses only get to Canglón (1½ hours from Metetí); from there you'll need to change to Yaviza. Between Yaviza and **El Real,** you can catch a **boat** ride, US$5; head to the dock around 7:30am (45min.) or talk to any boatmen around to arrange a trip. A special trip can cost up to US$30, but passenger boats are frequent during the day. Register with the **police** (turn left before the Palacio del Pueblo) upon arrival in Yaviza. Local services include: a **pharmacy** (behind the post office, open 8am-noon and 2-6pm), a **hospital** (across the river, open 8am-4pm), public **telephones,** and a **post office.**

There are only two places to stay, the better option being the **Pensión 3 Américas** ❷, across from the basketball court (from the dock walk right and then turn left at the end of the road). Ten large rooms and two shared bathrooms with feeble water pressure perch above a decent restaurant and a loud bar. (☎299 7495, a public phone located right beside the hotel; ask for the pensión when someone answers. Singles or doubles US$11, with A/C US$20; triples with private bath US$15; five-person room with private bath US$25.) It takes *piragua* trips north up Río Chico, a relatively safe area, to visit **El Común** village (trips around US$60 for 4 to 5 people). Check on security with ANAM and the police before embarking on any trip.

EL REAL

El Real (pop. 1300) is the gateway to Parque Nacional Darién. The town is divided into two parts: one a rough grid, the other a path that snakes away from the grid. Boats can arrive at two different places depending on size and tide. Mercadeo is for big boats and can be used at any time, while Gallital is only for small *piraguas* and can only be used during high tide. There are no street names; ask around for directions. **Aeroperlas** has **flights** to **El Real** (1hr.; M, W, and F 9:05am; US$48.30) from Panama City. **Turismo Aéreo** also has flights that leave at 9am, but they depend on demand, so it's a good idea to call ahead and check (☎315 0279). Between El Real and **Yaviza**, **boatmen** take passengers for around US$5 (30min., best to go in the morning). Along the path are services, including the **ANAM office; police station** (☎299 6137), where you should check in and show your passport; **Centro de Salud;** and **post office**. Within the grid section you'll find a **general store, Aeroperlas office,** and the only hotel in town, the scruffy **Hotel El Nazareno** ❶, with a nice entrance, common area, and fans in the rooms (US$5). There are no restaurants in town, although people prepare meals in their homes and sell them. Señora Dolores is recommended by locals; ask at Hotel Nazareno for directions. Water is lacking in El Real (there's usually none post-3pm) and the little there is isn't for drinking. Try to bring your own or buy bottled.

⚠ PARQUE NACIONAL DARIÉN

The Rancho Frío ranger station is a 3hr. walk from El Real in dry season; during the rainy season, take a boat trip (1hr., around US$50) upriver to the Emberá town of Pijibasal and then hike 1hr. Scarce guides are a must (US$10 per day, plus food). There's very basic lodging at the park (US$10 per night), but bring food, a flashlight, and a sleeping bag. Camping US$5. Entrance fee US$3. Wear hiking boots at all times (there are snakes).

With 576,000 hectares of primary tropical forest, Parque Nacional Darién boasts the second-richest neotropical biodiversity in the world after the Amazon. Thousands of plant and animal species are found here, including 64 species native to the area, and some 450 species of bird, including the Harpy Eagle and the extremely elusive and only recently discovered golden head quetzal. The park stretches along most of the border between Panama and Colombia and is most accessible from El Real. Rancho Frío, the closest ranger station to El Real, offers good animal- and bird-watching paths that lead to nearby waterfalls.

APPENDIX

SPANISH QUICK REFERENCE

PRONUNCIATION

ENGLISH	SPANISH
A	"ah" in father
E	"eh" in pet
I	"ee" in eat
O	"oh" in oat
U	"oo" in boot

ENGLISH	SPANISH
H	silent
J	"h" in hello
LL	"y" in yes
Ñ	"ni" in onion
Mayan CH	"sh" like shoe

ENGLISH	SPANISH
GÜ	"goo" in gooey
G before E or I	"h" in hen
GU before E	"g" in gate
RR	trilled
X	Be creative

In the absence of an accent mark, words that end in vowels, "n," or "s" receive stress on the second to last syllable. For words ending in all other consonants, stress falls on the last syllable. Masculine words generally end with an "o": *él es un tonto* (he is a fool). Feminine words generally end with an "a": *ella es bella* (she is beautiful). Pay close attention—slight changes in word ending can have drastic changes in meaning. For instance, when receiving directions, mind the distinction between derecho (straight) and derecha (right).

SPANISH PHRASEBOOK

ESSENTIAL PHRASES

ENGLISH	SPANISH
Hello	Hola/Buenas
Yes/No	Sí/No
I don't know	No sé
I don't speak Spanish	No hablo español
Thank you	Gracias
Excuse me	Perdón

ENGLISH	SPANISH
Goodbye	Adiós
Please	Por favor
Can you repeat that?	¿Puede repetirlo?
Do you speak English?	¿Habla inglés?
You're welcome	De nada
I'm sorry/forgive me	Lo siento

SURVIVAL SPANISH

ENGLISH	SPANISH
Again, please.	Otra vez, por favor.
What was that?	¿Cómo?/¿Qué?
I don't understand.	No entiendo.
What is your name?	¿Cómo se llama?
How do you say (dodge-ball) in Spanish?	¿Cómo se dice (dodge-ball) en español?
Good morning.	Buenos días.
How much does it cost?	¿Cuánto cuesta?
That is cheap/expensive.	Es muy caro/barato.
What's up?	¿Qué pasa?
Who?	¿Quién?
When?	¿Cuándo?
Why?	¿Por qué?

ENGLISH	SPANISH
Are you open/closed?	¿Está abierta/cerrada?
I want/would like...	Quiero/Me gustaría...
How are you?	¿Qué tal?/¿Comó está?
Where is (the center of town)?	¿Dónde está (el centro)?
Could you speak more slowly?	¿Podría hablar más despacio?
I am hungry/thirsty.	Tengo hambre/sed.
I am hot/cold.	Tengo calor/frío.
Let's go!	¡Vámanos!
Stop/that's enough.	Basta.
What?	¿Qué?
Where?	¿Dónde?
Because	Porque

YOUR ARRIVAL

ENGLISH	SPANISH
I am from (the US/Europe).	Soy de (los Estados Unidos/Europa).
Here is my passport.	Aquí está mi pasaporte.
I will be here for less than six months.	Estaré aquí por menos de seis meses.
I don't know where that came from.	No sé de dónde vino eso.

ENGLISH	SPANISH
What's the problem, sir/madam?	¿Cuál es el problema, señor/señora?
I lost my passport.	Me perdió mi pasaporte.
I have nothing to declare.	No tengo nada para declarar.
Please do not detain me.	Por favor no me detenga.

GETTING AROUND

ENGLISH	SPANISH
How can you get to...?	¿Cómo se puede llegar a...?
Does this bus go to (Tierra del Fuego)?	¿Va este autobús a (Tierra del Fuego)?
Where is (Mackenna) street?	¿Dónde está la calle (Mackenna)?
When/from where does the bus leave?	¿Cuándo/de dónde sale el bús?
I'm getting off at...	Bajo en...
Can I buy a ticket?	¿Podría comprar un boleto?
How long does the trip take?	¿Cuántas horas dura el viaje?
I am going to the airport.	Voy al aeropuerto.
Where is the bathroom?	¿Dónde está el baño?
I lost my baggage.	Perdí mi equipaje.
I would like to rent (a car).	Quisiera alquilar (un coche).
How much does it cost per day/week?	¿Cuánto cuesta por día/semana?
Where can I buy a cell-phone/phonecard?	¿Dónde puedo comprar un teléfono celular/una tarjeta telefónica?
Could you tell me what time it is?	¿Podría decirme que hora es?

ENGLISH	SPANISH
Is there anything cheaper?	¿Hay algo más barato/económico?
On foot.	A píe.
What bus line goes to..?	¿Qué línea de buses tiene servicio a...?
Stop here/I want to get off.	Pare aquí/quiero bajar.
I have to go now.	Tengo que ir ahora.
How far is...?	¿Qué tan lejos está...?
Continue forward.	Siga derecho.
The flight is delayed/cancelled.	El vuelo está atrasado/cancelado.
Is it safe to hitchhike?	¿Es seguro pedir aventón?
I'm lost.	Estoy perdido(a)/me perdí.
Please let me off at the (zoo).	Por favor, déjeme en el (zoológico).
Does it have (heating/air-conditioning)?	¿Tiene (calefacción/aire acondicionado)?
Where can I check e-mail?	¿Dónde se puede chequear el email?
Are there student discounts available?	¿Hay descuentos para estudiantes?

DIRECTIONS

ENGLISH	SPANISH
(to the) right	(a la) derecha
next to	al lado de/junto a
straight ahead	todo derecho
near (to/from)	cerca (a/de)
above	arriba/encima de
traffic light	semáforo
street	calle/avenida

ENGLISH	SPANISH
(to the) left	(a la) izquierda
across from	en frente de/a
turn (command form)	doble
far (to/from)	lejos (a/de)
below	abajo/bajo de
corner	esquina
block	cuadra

ACCOMMODATIONS

ENGLISH	SPANISH
Is there a cheap hotel around here?	¿Hay un hotel económico por aquí?
Do you have rooms available?	¿Tiene habitaciones libres?
I would like to reserve a room.	Quisiera reservar una habitación.
Can I see a room?	¿Podría ver una habitación?
Do you have any singles/doubles?	¿Tiene habitaciones sencillas/dobles?
I need another key/towel/pillow.	Necesito otra llave/toalla/almohada.
The shower/sink/toilet is broken.	La ducha/La pila/El servicio no funciona.
There are cockroaches in my room.	Hay cucarachas en mi habitación.

ENGLISH	SPANISH
Are there rooms with windows?	¿Hay habitaciones con ventanas?
I am going to stay for (four) days.	Me voy a quedar (cuatro) días.
Are there cheaper rooms?	¿Hay habitaciones más baratas?
Do they come with private baths?	¿Vienen con baño privado?
Can I borrow a plunger?	¿Me puede prestar una bomba?
My bedsheets are dirty.	Mis sabanas están sucias.
I'll take it.	Lo tomo.
They are biting me.	Me están mordiendo.

EMERGENCY

ENGLISH	SPANISH
Help!	¡Socorro!/¡Ayúdeme!
I am hurt.	Estoy herido(a).
Fire!	¡Fuego!/¡Incendio!
They robbed me!	¡Me han robado!
Call a clinic/ambulance/doctor/priest!	¡Llame a una clínica/una ambulancia/un médico/un sacerdote!
I need to contact my embassy.	Necesito contactar mi embajada.

ENGLISH	SPANISH
Call the police!	¡Llame a la policía!
Leave me alone!	¡Déjame en paz!
It's an emergency!	¡Es una emergencia!
They went that way!	¡Fueron en esa dirección!
I will only speak in the presence of a lawyer.	Sólo hablaré en la presencia de un abogado(a).
Don't touch me!/Let go of me!	¡No me toque!/¡Suélteme!

MEDICAL

ENGLISH	SPANISH
I feel bad/better/worse.	Me siento mal/mejor/peor.
I have a headache.	Tengo un dolor de cabeza.
I'm sick/ill.	Estoy enfermo(a).
I feel fine.	Me siento bien.
I'm allergic to...	Soy alérgico(a) a...
I haven't been able to go to the bathroom in (four) days.	No he podido ir al baño en (cuatro) días.
Where is the nearest hospital/doctor?	¿Dónde está el hospital/médico más cercano?
What is this medicine for?	¿Para qué es esta medicina?

ENGLISH	SPANISH
I have a stomachache.	Mi estómago me duele.
It hurts here.	Me duele aquí.
Here is my prescription.	Aquí está la receta médica.
I am pregnant.	Estoy embarazada.
I think I'm going to vomit.	Pienso que voy a vomitar.
I haven't been able to stop going to the bathroom in (four) days.	No he podido salir del baño en (cuatro) días.
I have a cold/a fever/diarrhea/nausea.	Tengo gripe/una calentura/diarrea/náusea.
I am diabetic/epileptic/anemic/psychotic.	Soy diabético(a)/epiléptico(a)/anémico(a)/psicopático(a).

INTERPERSONAL INTERACTIONS

ENGLISH	SPANISH
What is your name?	¿Cómo se llama?
Where are you from?	¿De dónde es?
This is my first time in Honduras.	Esta es mi primera vez en Honduras.
Do you come here often?	¿Viene aquí a menudo?
Pleased to meet you.	Encantado(a)/Mucho gusto.

ENGLISH	SPANISH
Do you have a light?	¿Tiene fuego?
I'm (twenty) years old.	Tengo (veinte) años.
I have a boyfriend/girl-friend/spouse.	Tengo novio/novia/esposo(a).
I love you.	Te quiero.
What a shame: you bought Lonely Planet!	¡Qué lástima: compraste Lonely Planet!

NUMBERS, DAYS, AND MONTHS

ENGLISH	SPANISH
0	cero
1	uno
2	dos
3	tres
4	cuatro
5	cinco
6	seis
7	siete
8	ocho
9	nueve
10	diez
11	once
12	doce
13	trece
14	catorce
15	quince
16	dieciseis
17	diecisiete
18	dieciocho
19	diecinueve

ENGLISH	SPANISH
20	veinte
21	veintiuno
22	veintidos
30	treinta
40	cuarenta
50	cincuenta
100	cien
1000	un mil
1 million	un millón
Sunday	domingo
Monday	lunes
Tuesday	martes
Wednesday	miércoles
Thursday	jueves
Friday	viernes
Saturday	sábado
today	hoy
tomorrow	mañana
day after tomorrow	pasado mañana
yesterday	ayer

ENGLISH	SPANISH
day before	anteayer
weekend	fin de semana
morning	mañana
afternoon	tarde
night	noche
month	mes
year	año
early/late	temprano/tarde
January	enero
February	febrero
March	marzo
April	abril
May	mayo
June	junio
July	julio
August	agosto
September	septiembre
October	octubre
November	noviembre
December	diciembre

EATING OUT

ENGLISH	SPANISH
breakfast	desayuno
dinner	comida/cena
dessert	postre
fork	tenedor
napkin	servilleta
spoon	cuchara
Where is a good restaurant?	¿Dónde está un restaurante bueno?
Can I see the menu?	¿Podría ver la carta/el menú?
This is too spicy.	Es demasiado pica.
Check, please.	¡La cuenta, por favor!
Do you have anything vegetarian?	¿Hay algún plato vegetariano/sin carne?

ENGLISH	SPANISH
lunch	almuerzo
drink (alcoholic)	bebida/trago
bon appétit	buen provecho
knife	cuchillo
cup	copa/taza
Do you have hot sauce?	¿Tiene salsa picante?
Table for (one), please.	Mesa para (uno), por favor.
Do you take credit cards?	¿Acepta tarjetas de crédito?
Disgusting!	¡Guácala!/¡Que asco!
Delicious!	¡Qué rico!
I would like to order (the eel).	Quisiera el (congrio).

MENU READER

SPANISH	ENGLISH
a la plancha	grilled
al vapor	steamed
aceite	oil
aceituna	olive
agua (purificada)	water (purified)
ajo	garlic
almeja	clam
arroz	rice
bistec	beefsteak
café	coffee
caliente	hot
camarones	shrimp
carne	meat
cebolla	onion
cerveza	beer
chorizo	spicy sausage
coco	coconut
congrio	eel
cordero	lamb
dulces	sweets
dulce de leche	caramelized milk
empanada	stuffed dumpling
ensalada	salad
entrada	appetizer
gaseosa	soda
kuchen	pastry with fruit
leche	milk

SPANISH	ENGLISH
legumbres	vegetables/legumes
lima	lime
limón	lemon
limonada	lemonade
locos	abalone (white fish)
lomo	steak or chop
macedonia	syrupy dessert
maíz	corn
mariscos	seafood
miel	honey
naranja	orange
nata	cream
pan	bread
papas	potatoes
papas fritas	french fries
parrillas	various grilled meats
pasteles	desserts/pies
pescado	fish
pimienta	pepper
plato	plate
pollo	chicken
puerco	pork
pupusa	Salvadoran patty
queso	cheese
sal	salt
tragos	mixed drinks/liquor
vino tinto/blanco	red/white wine

SPANISH GLOSSARY

aduana: customs
aeropuerto: airport
agencia de viaje: travel agency
aguardiente: strong liquor
agua pura/purificada: purified water
aguas calientes/termales: hot springs
ahora: now
ahorita: now / in a little bit
aire acondicionado: A/C
a la plancha: grilled
al gusto: as you wish
alcaldía: mayoral district
aldea: village
almacén: (grocery) store
almuerzo: lunch
altiplano: highland

amigo/a: friend (male/female)
andén: platform
anexo: neighborhood
arena: sand
arribadas: arrivals (sea turtle births)
arroz: rice
arroz chaufa: Chinese-style fried rice
artesanía: arts and crafts
asado: roast
autobús: bus
avenida: avenue
avión: airplane
aviso: warning, advisory
bahía: bay
baleada: soft taco-like food
balneario: bathing area

bandido: bandit
baño: bathroom or natural spa
barato/a: cheap
barranca: canyon
barrio: neighborhood
batido: milkshake
bebida: drink
biblioteca: library
bistec/bistek: beefsteak
bocaditos: bar appetizers
bodega: convenience store
boletería: ticket counter
bonito/a: pretty/beautiful
borracho/a: drunk
bosque: forest
bote: boat
bueno/a: good
buena suerte: good luck

buen provecho: bon appétit
burro: donkey
caballero: gentleman
caballo: horse
cabañas: cabins
cabina: cabin (C)
cafetín: cafeteria
cajeros: cashiers
cajeros automáticos: ATM
calcetines: socks
caldo: soup, broth, or stew
caliente: hot
calle: street
cama: bed
camarones: shrimp
cambio: change
caminata: hike
camino: path, track, road
camión: truck
camioneta: pickup truck
camiseta: shirt
campamento: campground
campesino/a: peasant
campo: countryside
candado: padlock
candela: candle
canotaje: rafting
cantina: macho bar
carne asada: roast meat
capilla: chapel
carne: meat
caro/a: expensive
carretera: highway
carro: car
casa: house
casa de cambio: currency exchange establishment
casado/a: married
casado: rice and beans (C)
cascadas: waterfalls
casona: mansion
catedral: cathedral
catarata: waterfall
cayuco: dugout canoe
cena: dinner
centro: city center
centro de salud: health center
centro financiero: financial center
cerca: near/nearby
cerro: hill
cerveza: beer
ceviche: raw fish marinated in lemon juice
champa: a thatched-roof hut with no walls
cheques viajeros: traveler's checks
chico/a: boy/girl, little
chicharrón: bite-sized pieces of fried meat, usually pork
chichas: sandflies
chicle: chewing gum
chófer: driver
chuleta de chancho: pork chop
churrasco: steak

cigarillo: cigarette
cine: cinema
ciudad: city
ciudadela: neighborhood in a large city
coche: car
colectivo: shared taxi
coliseo: coliseum/stadium
colonia: suburb
combi: collective taxi
comedor: dining room
comida típica: typical/traditional dishes
conductor: driver
consulado: consulate
correo: post office
cordillera: mountain range
corriente: current (as in, underwater; river)
corte: skirt
corvina: sea bass
coyotes: money changers
crucero: crossroads
Cruz Roja: Red Cross
cuadra: street block
cuarto: a room
cuenta: bill/check
cuento: story/account
cueva: cave
cuidado: careful
curandero: healer
damas: ladies
desayuno: breakfast
descompuesto: broken, out of order; spoiled/rotten
desierto: desert
despacio: slow
día: day
dinero: money
discoteca: dance club
dorado: fried
dueño/a: owner
dulces: sweets
edificio: building
email: email
embajada: embassy
embarasada: pregnant
embarcadero: dock
emergencia: emergency
encomiendas: estates granted to Spanish settlers in Latin America
entrada: entrance
estadio: stadium
este: east
estrella: star
extranjero: foreign/foreigner
farmacia: pharmacy
farmacia en turno: 24hr. pharmacy
faro: lighthouse
feliz: happy
ferrocarril: railroad
fiesta: party, holiday
finca: a plantation-like agricultural enterprise, or a ranch
friajes: sudden cold winds

frijoles: beans
frito: fried
frontera: border
fumar: to smoke
fumaroles: hole emitting hot volcanic vapors
fundo: large estate or tract of land
fútbol: soccer
gallo pinto: fried rice and beans
ganga: bargain
Garífuna: Caribbean ethnic group
general: shared (bath)
gobierno: government
gordo/a: fat
gorra: cap
gratis: free
gringo/a: white person; Westerner
grutas: caves
guanaco: animal in the camelid family
habitación: a room
hacer una caminata: take a hike
hacienda: ranch
helado: ice cream
hermano/a: brother/sister
hervido/a: boiled
hielo: ice
hijo/a: son/daughter
hombre: man
hospedaje: inn
hospital: hospital
huipil: an embroidered garment
iglesia: church
impuestos: taxes
impuesto valor añadido IVA: value added tax (VAT)
indígena: indigenous, refers to the native population
Internet: Internet
inundación: flood
invierno: winter
isla: island
jarra: 1L pitcher of beer
jirón: street
jugo: juice
ladrón: thief
lago/laguna: lake
lancha: launch, small boat
langosta: lobster
langostino: jumbo shrimp
larga distancia: long distance
lavandería: laundromat
legumbres: vegetables
lejos: far
lente: slow
librería: bookstore
licuado: fruity shake
linterna: flashlight
lista de correos: mail holding system in Latin America; Poste Restante
loma: hill

lomo: chop, steak
llamada por cobrar: collect call
llave: key
madre: mother
malo/a: bad
malecón: pier or seaside thoroughfare
maletas: luggage, suitcases
máneje despacio: drive slowly
manjar blanco: a whole milk spread
mar: sea
marijuana: marijuana
mariscos: seafood
matas: shrubs, jungle brush
matrimonial: bed for two
menestras: lentils/beans
menú del día/menú: fixed daily meal, bargain meal
mercado: market
merendero: snack bar
merienda: snack
mestizaje: crossing of races
mestizo/a: a person of mixed European and indigenous descent
microbus: small, local bus
mirador: an observatory or look-out point
Miskito: indigenous group in Honduras and Nicaragua
molas: patched cloth panels (P)
montaña: mountain
monte: mountain
moto: motorcycle
muelle: wharf
muerte: death
mujer: woman, wife
museo: museum
música folklórica: folk music
nada: nothing
niño/a: child
norte: north
novio/a: fiancé/fiancée
nublado: cloudy
obra: work of art, a play
obraje: textile workshop
oeste: west
oficina de turismo: tourist office
ola: wave
oriente: eastern
padre: father
palapa: palm-thatched hut
pampa: a treeless grassland area
pan: bread
panadería: bakery
panga: motorboat
pantalones: pants
papel higienico: toilet paper

parada: a stop (on a bus or train)
páramo: barren plain
parilla: various cuts of grilled meat
parillada: bbq or restaurant serving these cuts of meat
paro: labor strike
parque: park
parroquia: parish
pasaporte: passport
paseo turístico: tour covering a series of sites
payaso: clown
pelea de gallos: cockfighting
peligroso/a: dangerous
peninsulares: Spanish-born colonists
peña: folkloric music club
pensión: hostel
pez: fish (alive)
pescado: cooked fish
picante: spicy
picop: pickup truck
piedra: stone, rock
pincho: meat shish kebab
pipa: seed; pipe
pisa de uvas: grape-stomping
pista: airfield
plátano: plantain
playa: beach
población: population, settlement
policía: police
pollera: a traditional woman's garment (P)
pollo a la brasa: roasted chicken
poniente: western
pueblo/ito: town/village
puente: bridge
puerta: door
puerto: port
pulpería: grocery store
puntos de taxi: collective taxi stops (H)
pupseria: *pupusa* vendor
privado: private (bath)
queso: cheese
rana: frog
rebaja: bargain; sale
recreo: place of amusement, restaurant/bar on the outskirts of a city
refrescos: soft drinks
refugio: shelter
reloj: watch, clock
resaca: hangover
restaurante: restaurant
río: river
ropa: clothes
sabanas: bedsheets
sabor: flavor
sala: living room
salida: exit

salto: waterfall
salsa: sauce (can be of many varieties)
santo: saint
seguro/a: lock, insurance; adj.: safe
semáforo: traffic light
semana: week
Semana Santa: Holy Week
sencillo: single
sendero: path
sexo: sex
shaman/chaman: spiritual healer
SIDA: the Spanish acronym for AIDS
siesta: mid-afternoon nap
sillar: white, volcanic rock used in construction
sol: sun/Peruvian currency
solito/a: alone
solo carril: one-lane road or bridge
soltero/a: single (unmarried)
supermercado: supermarket
sur: south
stela: stele, stone monument
tapas: bite-size appetizers served in bars
tarjeta (de crédito): card (credit card)
tarifa: fee
taquería: taco stand
telenovela: soap opera
termas: hot mineral springs
terminal terrestre: bus station
tico: slang referring to a Costa Rican citizen
tienda: store
típico: traditional (food)
tipo de cambio: exchange rate
torre: tower
tortuga: turtle
trago: mixed drink/shot of alcohol
trekking: trekking
triste: sad
trucha: trout
turismo: tourism
turista: tourist
valle: valley
vegetales: vegetables
verano: summer
verde: green
vicuña: a llama-like animal
vino: wine
volcán: volcano
vuelo: flight
zapatos: shoes
zona rosa: red light district; prostitution zone

INDEX

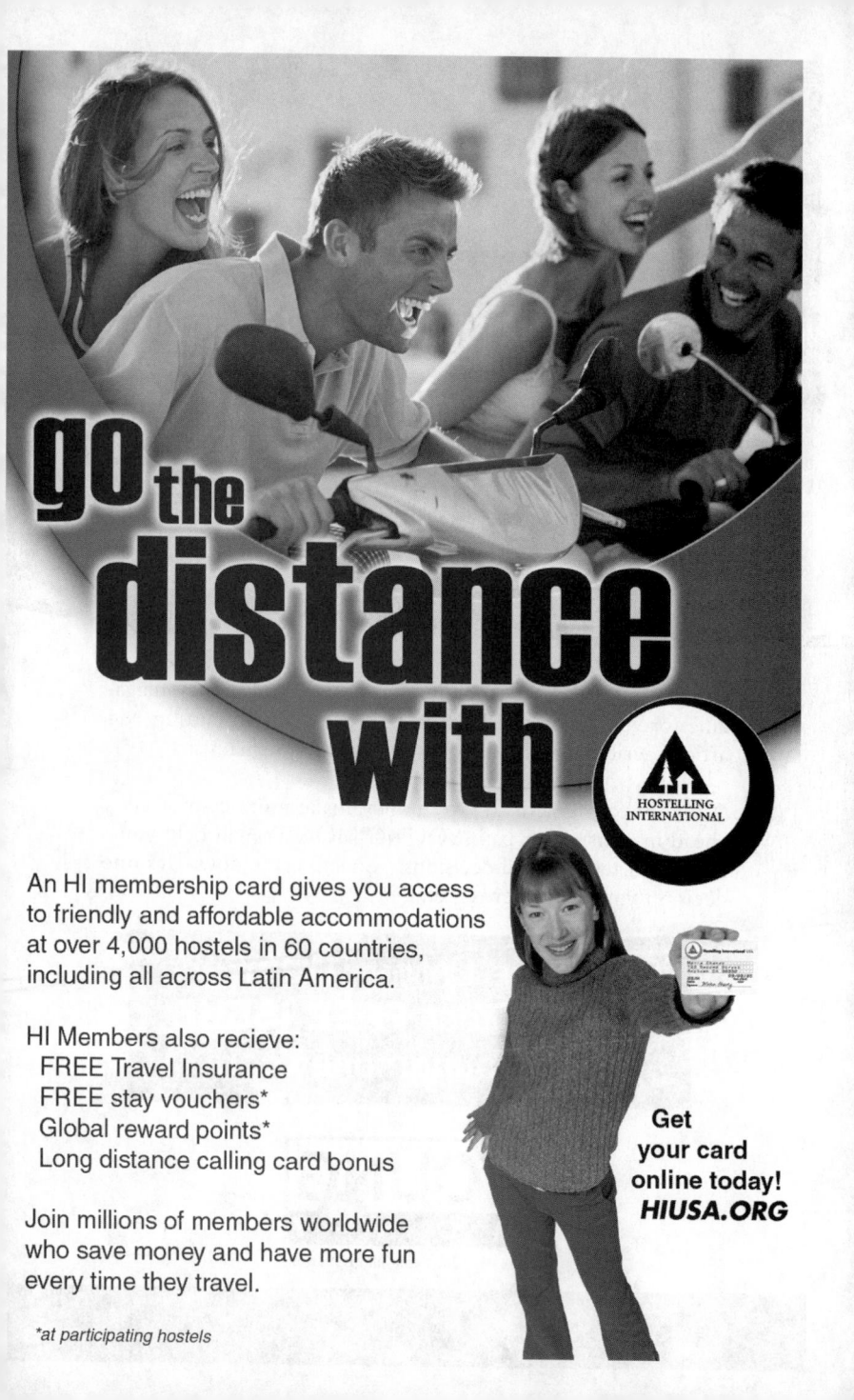

MAP INDEX

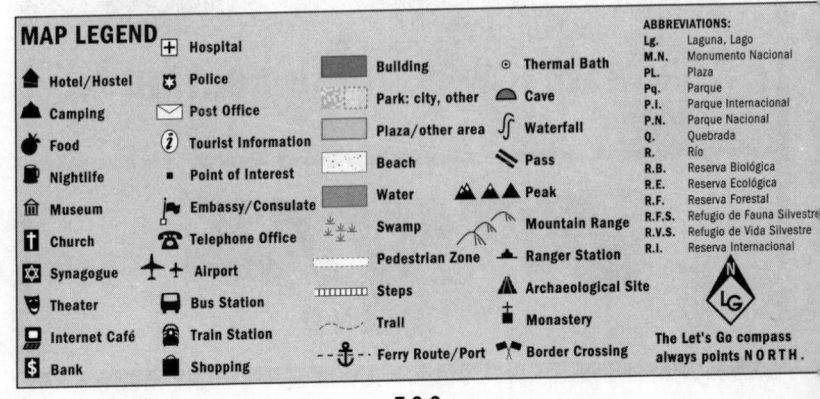

MAP LEGEND

Hospital
Hotel/Hostel
Police
Camping
Post Office
Food
Tourist Information
Nightlife
Point of Interest
Museum
Embassy/Consulate
Church
Telephone Office
Synagogue
Airport
Theater
Bus Station
Internet Café
Train Station
Bank
Shopping

Building
Park: city, other
Plaza/other area
Beach
Water
Swamp
Pedestrian Zone
Steps
Trail
Ferry Route/Port

Thermal Bath
Cave
Waterfall
Pass
Peak
Mountain Range
Ranger Station
Archaeological Site
Monastery
Border Crossing

ABBREVIATIONS:
Lg.   Laguna, Lago
M.N.   Monumento Nacional
PL.   Plaza
Pq.   Parque
P.I.   Parque Internacional
P.N.   Parque Nacional
Q.   Quebrada
R.   Río
R.B.   Reserva Biológica
R.E.   Reserva Ecológica
R.F.   Reserva Forestal
R.F.S. Refugio de Fauna Silvestre
R.V.S. Refugio de Vida Silvestre
R.I.   Reserva Internacional

The Let's Go compass
always points NORTH.